FREEDOM
A DOCUMENTARY HISTORY OF EMANCIPATION
1861 – 1867

SERIES I
VOLUME II
THE WARTIME GENESIS OF FREE LABOR:
THE UPPER SOUTH

Black laborers building stockade at Alexandria, Virginia, 1861
Source: National Archives of the United States

FREEDOM

A DOCUMENTARY HISTORY OF EMANCIPATION
1861–1867

SELECTED FROM THE HOLDINGS OF THE
NATIONAL ARCHIVES OF THE UNITED STATES

SERIES I
VOLUME II
THE WARTIME GENESIS OF FREE LABOR:
THE UPPER SOUTH

Edited by
IRA BERLIN
STEVEN F. MILLER
JOSEPH P. REIDY
LESLIE S. ROWLAND

CAMBRIDGE
UNIVERSITY PRESS

Published by the Press Syndicate of the University of Cambridge
The Pitt Building, Trumpington Street, Cambridge CB2 1RP
40 West 20th Street, New York, NY 10011-4211, USA
10 Stamford Road, Oakleigh, Victoria 3166, Australia

First published 1993

Printed in the United States of America

Library of Congress Cataloging-in-Publication Data
The Wartime genesis of free labor : the upper South / edited by Ira
Berlin . . . [et al.].
p.   cm. – (Freedom, a documentary history of emancipation,
1861–1867 ; ser. 1, v. 2)
"Selected from the National Archives of the United States."
Includes index.
ISBN 0-521-41742-2
1. United States – History – Civil War, 1861–1865 – Afro-Americans –
Sources.   2. Freedmen – Southern States – History – Sources.
3. Working class – Southern States – History – 19th century – Sources.
4. Confederate States of America – History – Sources.   5. Slaves –
Southern States – Emancipation – Sources.   6. Afro-Americans –
Southern States – History – 19th century – Sources.   I. Berlin, Ira,
1941– .   II. Series.
E185.2F88   ser. 1, vol. 2
[E540.N3]
973.7 s–dc20
[973.7'415]   92-30974
                                       CIP

A catalog record for this book is available from the British Library

ISBN 0-521-41742-2 hardback

TO

SARA DUNLAP JACKSON

MENTOR

Contents

Contents

Acknowledgments

A SCHOLARLY ENTERPRISE the magnitude of the Freedmen and Southern Society project is the product of many minds and many hands. In *The Black Military Experience* (1982), *The Destruction of Slavery* (1985), and *The Wartime Genesis of Free Labor: The Lower South* (1990), we thanked the men and women who helped found and sustain the project during its first decade. Publication of *The Wartime Genesis of Free Labor: The Upper South* reminds us how our debt continues to grow.

The Freedmen and Southern Society Project rests, first and foremost, upon the records in the National Archives of the United States. Our admiration for the archivists who, despite successive reorganizations and budgetary shortfalls, have preserved those records and ensured their accessibility knows no bounds. We have especially benefited from the labor and numerous courtesies of Timothy Connelly, Richard Cox, Robert Gruber, Michael Meir, Michael Musick, William Sherman, Aloha South, and Reginald Washington. Their work is essential to ours.

The Freedmen and Southern Society Project could not exist without the financial support of governmental agencies and private foundations. The National Historical Publications and Records Commission (NHPRC), the project's original benefactor, has been consistent in its generosity, a quality greatly prized in times when many worthy scholarly enterprises have fallen to the budgetary ax. For this ongoing vote of confidence, we are grateful to the commission itself; to Roger Bruns, Mary Giunta, and Nancy Sahli, successively head of its publications program; and to Gerald George, the executive director. The National Endowment for the Humanities has also been an important and continuing source of financial assistance. The appreciation of our work exhibited by Kathy Fuller, Gordon McKinney, Douglas Arnold, and Margot Backas of the Division of Research Programs has gone beyond the formal concerns of their office. The project has no better friend than Sheila Biddle of the Ford Foundation. Her willingness to extend additional support in time of need helped when help was most needed. During the last two years, the H. W. Wilson Foundation and Philip Morris Companies, Inc., have joined the list of the project's sponsors. We would like to thank H. W. Wilson and George Powell for their interest in our work.

xi

ACKNOWLEDGMENTS

The University of Maryland, for sixteen years the project's home, has been ever willing to lend its material and moral support. Nothing gives us greater pride than to be seen as an exemplar of the excellence to which the university aspires. For this honor, we are especially grateful to William E. Kirwan, president of the College Park campus, J. Robert Dorfman, provost and vice-president for academic affairs, and Robert Griffith, dean of the College of Arts and Humanities. Of course, our work proceeds less in the spacious theater of the university's aspirations than in the crowded corridors of the history department. Richard Price, the department's chairman, has never gotten the project's ungainly name quite right, but his commitment to our work has been deep and unwavering. It is much appreciated. We also gratefully acknowledge an award from the university's Office of Graduate Studies and Research to help defray publication costs.

A number of young scholars assisted in completing *The Wartime Genesis of Free Labor: The Upper South*. Wayne Durrill and Leslie Schwalm, now on the faculties of, respectively, the University of Cincinnati and the University of Iowa, brought fresh perspective to the volume's content and bore with good humor the tedium of proofreading. Wayne Durrill also critiqued the introductory essay and the chapter on tidewater Virginia and North Carolina and prepared the index, a monumental job with minuscule rewards. John Rodrigue joined the project just in time to be dragooned into final production work.

The Wartime Genesis of Free Labor: The Lower South, like previous volumes of *Freedom*, has benefited from the work of graduate student assistants who culled documents from the National Archives, tracked down obscure references, helped check footnotes, and performed any number of other necessary but largely thankless tasks. We express our gratitude to Mary Beth Corrigan, Margaret Dorrier, Kevin Hardwick, Yong Ook Jo, Cynthia Kennedy-Haflett, Joseph Mannard, Robert Pickstone, Walter Schaefer, Marie Jenkins Schwartz, Richard Soderlund, Brian Sowers, and Peter Way. Gregory LaMotta, for nearly a decade the project's jack-of-all-trades at the National Archives, deserves special thanks. We are privileged to have had access to the talents of these men and women.

Oversight of the project's sizable force, along with innumerable other duties, fell to the project's administrative assistant and general handywoman, Terrie Hruzd. Her inexhaustible energy, knowledge of the university's bureaucracy, and steadfast determination to get the job done right has made our work both better and easier. We also relied upon Claire Dimsdale, who dispatched an array of assignments with an admirable combination of precision and cheerfulness.

Fellow scholars took time out from their own work to review parts of the manuscript. Eric Foner read the introductory essay. Robert F. Engs and Edna Greene Medford – herself an alumna of the project – offered

Acknowledgments

valuable comments on the chapter on tidewater Virginia and North Carolina. We thank them for sharing their special expertise.

Transforming a large manuscript into a big book is a complex, seemingly never-ending task. But the men and women of Cambridge University Press make an inherently complicated process more direct, even if not simple. We wish especially to thank Frank Smith, social science editor, and Edith Feinstein, production editor for both volumes of *The Wartime Genesis of Free Labor*. We have come to expect sharp-eyed and sensible copyediting from Vicky Macintyre, and her work this time around met her usual high standards.

The appearance of this volume marks an important milestone in the Freedmen and Southern Society Project's own history. With its publication, the project has reached its halfway point. Having completed the volumes on the Civil War years, the editors will now address the important question of postwar reconstruction. This shift in intellectual focus comes hard on the heels of another transition. After fifteen years at the helm, Ira Berlin left the project in the fall of 1991 to resume full-time teaching duties at the University of Maryland, and Leslie Rowland succeeded him as director.

The anticipation with which we look to the project's future is tinged with sadness, for we – and the scholarly world generally – suffered a great loss with the death of Sara Dunlap Jackson in April 1991. As our mentor and foremost booster, Sara Jackson never let us forget our privileged place as interpreters of the unique collections at the National Archives – records she mastered as one of the nation's most accomplished archivists. The dedication of this volume is just one indication that we have not forgotten her message.

I.B.
S.F.M.
J.P.R.
College Park, Maryland   L.S.R.

Introduction

NO EVENT in American history matches the drama of emancipation. More than a century later, it continues to stir the deepest emotions. And properly so. In the United States emancipation accompanied the military defeat of the world's most powerful slaveholding class. It freed a larger number of slaves than did the end of slavery in all other New World societies combined. Clothed in the rhetoric of biblical prophecy and national destiny and born of a bloody civil war, it accomplished a profound social revolution. That revolution destroyed forever a way of life based upon the ownership of human beings, restoring to the former slaves proprietorship of their own persons, liquidating without compensation private property valued at billions of dollars, and forcibly substituting the relations of free labor for those of slavery. In designating the former slaves as citizens, emancipation placed citizenship upon new ground, defined in the federal Constitution and removed beyond the jurisdiction of the states. By obliterating the sovereignty of master over slave, it handed a monopoly of sovereignty to the newly consolidated nation-state. The freeing of the slaves simultaneously overturned the old regime of the South and set the entire nation upon a new course.

The death of slavery led to an intense period of social reconstruction, closely supervised by the victorious North, that lasted over a decade in many places. During this period, former slaves challenged the domination of the old masters, demanding land and the right to control their own labor. Former masters, abetted by a complaisant President, defeated the freedpeople's bid for economic independence and imposed on them new legal and extralegal constraints. But whatever the outcome, the struggle itself confirmed the magnitude of the change. Freedpeople confronted their former masters as free laborers in a system predicated upon contractual equality between employers and employees. They gained, if only temporarily, full citizenship rights, including the right to vote and hold public office.

With emancipation in the South, the United States enacted its part in a world-wide drama. Throughout the western world and beyond, the forces unleashed by the American and French revolutions and by the industrial revolution worked to undermine political regimes based upon hereditary privilege and economic systems based upon bound labor. Slavery had already succumbed in the Northern states and in the French and British Caribbean before the American Civil War, and it would shortly do so in its remaining strongholds in Spanish and Portuguese America. Almost simultaneously with the great struggle in the United States, the vestiges of serfdom in central and eastern Europe yielded to the pressure of the age. Only small pockets in Africa and Asia remained immune, and their immunity was temporary. The fateful lightning announced by the victorious Union army was soon to strike, if it had not already struck, wherever men and women remained in bonds of personal servitude.

For all systems of bondage, emancipation represented the acid test, the moment of truth. The upheaval of conventional expectations stripped away the patina of routine, exposing the cross purposes and warring intentions that had simmered – often unnoticed – beneath the surface of the old order. In throwing off habitual restraints, freedpeople redesigned their lives in ways that spoke eloquently of their hidden life in bondage, revealing clandestine institutions, long-cherished beliefs, and deeply held values. In confronting new restraints, they abandoned their usual caution in favor of direct speech and yet more direct action. Lords and serfs, masters and slaves had to survey the new social boundaries without the old etiquette of dominance and subordination as a guide. Their efforts to do so led to confrontations that could be awkward, painful, and frequently violent. The continued force of these encounters awakened men and women caught up in the drama to the realization that their actions no longer ratified old, established ways, but set radically new precedents for themselves and for future generations.

Moments of revolutionary transformation expose as do few human events the foundation upon which societies rest. Although those who enjoy political power and social authority speak their minds and indulge their inclinations freely and often, their subordinates generally cannot. Only in the upheaval of accustomed routine can the lower orders give voice to the assumptions that guide their world as it is and as they wish it to be. Some of them quickly grasp the essence of the new circumstance. Under the tutelage of unprecedented events, ordinary men and women become extraordinarily perceptive and articulate, seizing the moment to challenge the assumptions of the old regime and proclaim a new social order. Even then, few take the initiative. Some – perhaps most – simply try to maintain their balance, to reconstitute a routine, to maximize gains and minimize losses as events swirl around them. But inevitably they too become swept up in the revolutionary process. Barely conscious acts and unacknowledged motives carried over from the past take on a changed significance. Attempts to stand still or turn back only hasten the process forward. At revolutionary moments all actions – those of the timid and reluctant as much as those of the bold and eager – expose to view the inner workings of society.

Introduction

Because they thrust common folk into prominence, moments of revolutionary transformation have long occupied historians seeking to solve the mysteries of human society. Knowledge of the subordinate groups who have formed the majority throughout history has proved essential to an understanding of how the world works. Historians have therefore developed special methods for penetrating the often opaque histories of ordinary people, including peasants, slaves, and wage-workers. Some have viewed them over the *longue durée*, translating glacial demographic and economic changes into an understanding of times past. Others have sought such understanding by focusing on particular events, decoding the fury of *carnaval*, the ritual of a bread riot, the terror of the "theater of death," or the tense confrontation of an industrial strike. Almost all have learned from periods of revolutionary transformation. Whatever the historians' approach, direct testimony by the people involved has usually been a luxury. For this reason, the study of emancipation in the United States promises rich rewards not just to those specifically interested in the question, but to all who seek a fuller view of the human past. Encompassing in full measure the revolutionary implications of all transitions from bondage to freedom, emancipation in the American South has left behind an unparalleled wealth of documentation permitting direct access to the thoughts and actions of the freedpeople themselves. Indeed, it provides the richest known record of any subordinate class at its moment of liberation.

THE RECORDS

As the war for union became a war for liberty, the lives of slaves and freedpeople became increasingly intertwined with the activities of both the Union and Confederate governments. Following the war, federal agencies continued to figure prominently in the reconstruction of the South's economy and society. The records created and collected by these governments and now housed in the National Archives of the United States provide an unrivaled manuscript source for understanding the passage of black people from slavery to freedom. Such governmental units as the Colored Troops Division of the Adjutant General's Office; the American Freedmen's Inquiry Commission; the U.S. army at every level of command, from the headquarters in Washington to local army posts; army support organizations, including the Judge Advocate General's Office, the Provost Marshal General's Office, and the Quartermaster General's Office, and their subordinates in the field; the Civil War Special Agencies of the Treasury Department; individual regiments of U.S. Colored Troops; various branches of the Confederate government (whose records fell into Union hands at the conclusion of the war); the Southern Claims Commission; the Freedman's Bank; and, most important, the Bureau of Refugees, Freedmen, and Abandoned Lands all played a role in the coming of freedom. (See pp. xxxiii–xxxiv for a list of record groups drawn upon.)

The missions of these agencies placed them in close contact with a wide variety of ordinary people, and their bureaucratic structure provided a mechanism for the preservation of many records of people generally dismissed as historically mute. The Bureau of Refugees, Freedmen, and Abandoned Lands (Freedmen's Bureau) illustrates the point. Although the bureau often lacked resources to do more than make written note of the abuses of freedpeople brought to its attention, bureau agents scattered across the South conducted censuses, undertook investigations, recorded depositions, filed reports, and accumulated letters authored by ex-slaves and interested whites. Other agencies whose duties focused less directly upon the concerns of former slaves created thousands of similar, though more dispersed, records.

Alongside the official reports in these archival files, hundreds of letters and statements by former slaves give voice to people whose aspirations, beliefs, and behavior have gone largely unrecorded. Not only did extraordinary numbers of ex-slaves, many of them newly literate, put pen to paper in the early years of freedom, but hundreds of others, entirely illiterate, gave depositions to government officials, placed their marks on resolutions passed at mass meetings, testified before courts-martial and Freedmen's Bureau courts, and dictated letters to more literate blacks and to white officials and teachers. The written record thus created constitutes an unparalleled outpouring from people caught up in the emancipation process. Predictably, many of these documents requested official action to redress wrongs committed by powerful former slaveholders who only reluctantly recognized ex-slaves as free, rarely as equal. Others, however, originated in relationships entirely outside the purview of either federal officials or former masters and employers. They include, for example, correspondence between black soldiers and their families and between kinfolk who had been separated during slavery. That such letters fell for various reasons into the bureaucratic net of government agencies (and thus were preserved along with official records) should not obscure their deeply personal origins.

Selected out of the mass of purely administrative records, these documents convey, perhaps as no historian can, the experiences of the liberated: the quiet personal satisfaction of meeting an old master on equal terms, as well as the outrage of ejection from a segregated streetcar; the elation of a fugitive enlisting in the Union army, and the humiliation of a laborer cheated out of hard-earned wages; the joy of a family reunion after years of forced separation, and the distress of having a child involuntarily apprenticed to a former owner; the hope that freedom would bring a new world, and the fear that, in so many ways, life would be much as before. Similar records offer insight into the equally diverse reactions of planters, Union officers, and Southern yeomen – men and women who faced emancipation with different interests and expectations. Taken together, these records provide the fullest documentation of the destruction of a dependent social relationship, the release of a people from their dependent status, and the simultaneous transformation of an entire society. As far as is known, no comparable record exists for the liberation of any group of serfs or slaves or for the transformation of any people into wage-workers.

However valuable, the archival records also have their problems. They are massive, repetitive, and often blandly bureaucratic. Their size alone makes research by individual scholars inevitably incomplete and often haphazard. The Freedmen's Bureau records, for example, extend to more than 700 cubic feet, and they constitute a relatively small record group. The records of U.S. army continental commands for the period spanning the Civil War era fill more than 10,000 cubic feet. In addition to the daunting volume of the archival records, their bureaucratic structure creates obstacles for studies that go beyond the institutional history of particular agencies or the documentation of policy formation to examine underlying social processes. Governmental practice provided the mechanism for preserving these records, but it also fragmented them in ways that can hinder historical reconstruction. Assume, for example, that a group of freedmen petitioned the Secretary of the Treasury complaining of a Confederate raid on a plantation supervised by his department. Their petition might be forwarded to the Secretary of War, since the army protected such plantations. He in turn would pass it on to a military field commander, who would send it down the chain of command. If black soldiers provided the plantation guard, the petition might be forwarded to the adjutant general, who directed the Bureau of Colored Troops, who would then send it to the commander of a black regiment. On the other hand, if the Secretary of the Treasury wished to act himself, he could forward it to a Treasury agent in the field. Augmented by additional information in the form of reports, depositions, or endorsements on the original complaint, the petition might be passed along to still other federal agencies. In the meantime, the Confederate raiders might have made a report to their commander, perhaps noting the effect of their foray on black morale. Rebel planters, anxious to regain their property, could now have their say, addressing the Confederate Secretary of War, his adjutant and inspector general, or a local Confederate commander. At any or all points, additional documents might be added and portions of the original documentation might come to rest. Only a search of the records of all these agencies can make the full story available. In part because of the scope of such an undertaking, individual scholars have been unable to avail themselves of the fullness of the resources of the National Archives. Research has necessarily been piecemeal and limited to one or two record groups or portions of various record groups. Only a large-scale collaborative effort can make these resources available to the public.

In the fall of 1976, with a grant from the National Historical Publications and Records Commission, and under the sponsorship of the University of Maryland, the Freedmen and Southern Society Project launched a systematic search of those records at the National Archives that promised to yield material for a documentary history of emancipation. Over the course of the next three years, the editors selected more than 40,000 items, which represented perhaps 2 percent of the documents they examined. Indexed and cross-referenced topically, chronologically, and geographically, this preliminary selection constitutes the universe from which the documents published as *Freedom: A Documentary History of Emancipation* are selected and annotated, and from which the editors' introductory essays are written.

The editors found it imperative from the outset to be selective. They have focused their attention upon the wartime and postwar experiences of slaves and ex-slaves, but have also sought to illuminate the social, economic, and political setting of the emancipation process. The formation of federal policy, for example, is not central to the project's concerns, except insofar as the preconceptions and actions of policy makers influenced the shape that freedom assumed. Therefore, the volumes published by the Freedmen and Southern Society Project will not undertake a history of the Freedmen's Bureau, the U.S. Army, the Bureau of Colored Troops, or any other governmental agency; nonetheless, documents about the operations of these agencies will be prominent when they describe activities of freedpeople and shed light upon the context in which former slaves struggled to construct their own lives. Throughout the selection process, the editors have labored to reconstruct the history of the freedpeople rather than the institutions that surrounded them.

Above all, the editors have sought to delineate the central elements of the process by which men and women moved from the utter dependence slaveholders demanded but never fully received, to the independence freedpeople desired but seldom attained. This process began with the slow breakdown of slavery on the periphery of the South and extended to the establishment of the social, economic, and political institutions black people hoped would secure their independence. The editors have also sought to recognize the diversity of black life and the emancipation process, by selecting documents that illustrate the varied experiences of former slaves in different parts of the South who labored at diverse tasks and who differed from one another in gender, in age, and in social or economic status. Although former slaves, like other men and women caught in the transition from slavery to freedom, wanted to enlarge their liberty and ensure their independence from their former masters, how they desired to do so and what they meant by freedom were tempered by their previous experiences as well as by the circumstances in which they were enmeshed. At the same time, the editors have been alert to the shared ideas and aspirations that American slaves carried into freedom and to those features of emancipation that were common throughout the South—and more generally still, common to all people escaping bondage. These common characteristics and the regularities of the process of emancipation connect the lives of former slaves across time and space and link them to other dependent people struggling for autonomy.

Reflecting editorial interest in a *social* history of emancipation, *Freedom* is organized thematically, following the process of emancipation. At each step the editors have selected documents that illustrate processes they believe are central to the transition from slavery to freedom. The first two series concentrate primarily on the years of the Civil War. Series 1 documents the destruction of slavery, the diverse circumstances under which slaves claimed their freedom, and the wartime labor arrangements developed as slavery collapsed. Series 2 examines the recruitment of black men into the Union army and the experiences of black soldiers under arms. The remaining series, while drawing in part upon evidence from the war years, explore most fully the transformation of black life that followed the conclusion of armed conflict. They document the struggle for land, the evolution of new labor arrangements, relations with former masters and other whites, law and justice, violence and other extralegal repression, geographical mobility, family relationships, education, religion, the structure and activities of the black community, and black politics in the early years of Reconstruction. The series are organized as follows:

Series 1 The Destruction of Slavery and the Wartime Genesis of Free Labor
Series 2 The Black Military Experience
Series 3 Land, Capital, and Labor
Series 4 Race Relations, Violence, Law, and Justice
Series 5 The Black Community: Family, Church, School, and Society

Each series comprises one or more volumes, and topical arrangement continues within the volumes. Each chapter is introduced by an essay that provides background information, outlines government policy, and elaborates the larger themes. The chapters are further subdivided, when relevant, to reflect distinctive historical, economic, and demographic circumstances.

Also in accordance with the editors' predominant concern with social process, the annotation (both the notes to particular documents and the introductory essays) is designed to provide a context for the documents rather than to identify persons or places. The official character of most of the records means that vast quantities of biographical data are available for many of the army officers, Freedmen's Bureau agents, and others who cross the pages of these volumes. The editors have nonetheless decided against the time-consuming extraction of details about individuals, because to do so would divert energy from research into the larger social themes and reduce the number of documents that could be published, while adding little of substance to the business at hand.

In its aim, approach, and editorial universe, the Freedmen and Southern Society Project therefore differs fundamentally from most historical editing enterprises. Rather than searching out the complete manuscript record of an individual man or woman, the project examines the process of social transformation, and rather than seeking all the documentary evidence relevant to that transformation, it confines itself to the resources of the National Archives. *Freedom* endeavors to combine the strengths of the traditional interpretive monograph with the rich diversity of the documentary edition while addressing in one historical setting a central question of the human experience: how men and women strive to enlarge their freedom and secure their independence from those who would dominate their lives.

SERIES I

Series I of *Freedom* comprises three volumes. Volume 1, *The Destruction of Slavery*, explicates the process by which slavery collapsed under the pressure of federal arms and the slaves' persistence in placing their own liberty on the wartime agenda. In documenting the transformation of the war for the Union into a war against slavery, it shifts the focus from Washington and Richmond to the plantations, farms, and battlefields of the South, and demonstrates how slaves became the agents of their own emancipation.

Volume 2, *The Wartime Genesis of Free Labor: The Upper South*, and volume 3, *The Wartime Genesis of Free Labor: The Lower South*, concern the evolution of freedom in those portions of the slave states that were held by Union forces for a substantial part of the Civil War (including the border slave states that did not join the Confederacy). Among the subjects they address are the employment of former slaves and free blacks as military laborers; the wartime experiences of former slaves in contraband camps, on government-supervised plantations, and in cities, towns, and military posts; and various kinds of private employment, from evolving labor arrangements with former owners to new forms of independent labor in town and country. In so doing, the two volumes also document federal free-labor policies and practices, and the struggle among former slaves, free blacks, Union army officers, Southern planters, Northern teachers and clergymen, Northern businessmen, and federal officials over the meaning of freedom.

In order to give due consideration to differences in society and economy, patterns of military occupation, and political considerations, national and local, that influenced the evolution of free-labor arrangements, the two volumes of *The Wartime Genesis of Free Labor* are divided geographically. Volume 2 describes developments in Union-occupied portions of the Upper South — tidewater Virginia and North Carolina; the District of Columbia; middle and east Tennessee and northern Alabama; and the border states of Maryland, Missouri, and Kentucky — where small slaveholding units, mixed agriculture, and urban life had characterized the slave regime. Volume 3 documents the evolution of freedom in the plantation regions of the Lower South that were captured and occupied by Union forces — small enclaves in lowcountry South Carolina, Georgia, and Florida, notably the South Carolina Sea Islands; the sugar parishes of southern Louisiana; and the Mississippi Valley, from Memphis to just north of Baton Rouge. In order to compare developments in the various regions and to identify common underlying themes, the same interpretive essay introduces each of the two volumes.

Together with *The Black Military Experience*, the single volume that makes up series 2, the three volumes of series 1 document the death of the old order and the birth of a new one in the crucible of civil war.

Editorial Method

THE RENDITION of nineteenth-century manuscripts into print proceeds at best along a tortuous path. Transcribing handwritten documents into a standardized, more accessible form inevitably sacrifices some of their evocative power. The scrawl penciled by a hard-pressed army commander, the letters painstakingly formed by an ex-slave new to the alphabet, and the practiced script of a professional clerk all reduce to the same uncompromising print. At the same time, simply reading, much less transcribing, idiosyncratic handwriting poses enormous difficulties. The records left by barely literate writers offer special problems, although these are often no more serious than the obstacles created by better-educated but careless clerks, slovenly and hurried military officers, or even the ravages of time upon fragile paper.

The editors have approached the question of transcription with the conviction that readability need not require extensive editorial intervention and, indeed, that modernization (beyond that already imposed by conversion into type) can compromise the historical value of a document. The practical dilemmas of setting precise limits to editorial intervention, once initiated, also suggest the wisdom of restraint. In short, the editors believe that even when documents were written by near illiterates, the desiderata of preserving immediacy and conveying the struggle of ordinary men and women to communicate intensely felt emotions outweigh any inconveniences inflicted by allowing the documents to stand as they were written. Fortunately for the modern reader, a mere passing acquaintance with the primer usually led uneducated writers to spell as they spoke; the resulting documents may appear impenetrable to the eye but are perfectly understandable when read phonetically. In fact, reproduced verbatim, such documents offer intriguing evidence about the spoken language. Other writers, presumably better educated, frequently demonstrated such haphazard adherence to rules of grammar, spelling, and punctuation that their productions rival those of the semiliterate. And careless copyists or telegraph operators further garbled many documents. Both equity and convenience demand, nonetheless, that all writings by the schooled — however incoherent — be transcribed according to the same principles as those applied to the documents of the unschooled. Indeed, a verbatim rendition permits interesting observations about American literacy in the mid-nineteenth century, as well as about the talents or personalities of particular individuals.

Therefore, the textual body of each document in this volume is reproduced – to the extent permitted by modern typography – *exactly* as it appears in the original manuscript. (The few exceptions to this general principle will be noted hereafter.) The editorial *sic* is never employed: All peculiarities of syntax, spelling, capitalization, and punctuation appear in the original manuscript. The same is true of paragraph breaks, missing or incomplete words, words run together, quotation marks or parentheses that are not closed, characters raised above the line, contractions, and abbreviations. When the correct reading of a character is ambiguous (as, for example, a letter "C" written halfway between upper- and lowercase, or a nondescript blotch of punctuation that could be either a comma or a period), modern practice is followed. Illegible or obscured words that can be inferred with confidence from textual evidence are printed in ordinary roman type, enclosed in brackets. If the editors' reading is conjectural or doubtful, a question mark is added. When the editors cannot decipher a word by either inference or conjecture, it is represented by a three-dot ellipsis enclosed in brackets. An undecipherable passage of more than one word is represented in the same way, but a footnote reports the extent of the illegible material. (See p. xxxii for a summary of editorial symbols.)

Handwritten letters display many characteristics that cannot be exactly reproduced on the printed page or can be printed only at considerable expense. Some adaptations are, therefore, conventional. Words underlined once in the manuscript appear in italics. Words underlined more than once are printed in small capitals. Internally quoted documents that are set off in the manuscript by such devices as extra space or quotation marks on every line are indented and printed in smaller type. Interlineations are simply incorporated into the text at the point marked by the author, without special notation by the editors unless the interlineation represents a substantial alteration. Finally, the beginning of a new paragraph is indicated by indentation, regardless of how the author set apart paragraphs.

The editors deviate from the standard of faithful reproduction of the textual body of the document in only two significant ways. The many documents entirely bereft of punctuation require some editorial intervention for the sake of readability. However, the editors wish to avoid "silent" addition of any material, and supplying punctuation in brackets would be extremely cumbersome, if not pedantic. Therefore, the editors employ the less intrusive device of adding extra spaces at what they take to be unpunctuated sentence breaks. Although most such judgments are unambiguous, there are instances in which the placement of sentence breaks requires an interpretive decision. To prevent the ambiguity that could result if an unpunctuated or unconventionally punctuated sentence concluded at the end of a line of type, the last word of any such sentence appears at the beginning of the next line.

The second substantial deviation from verbatim reproduction of the text is the occasional publication of excerpted portions of documents. Most documents are printed in their entirety, but excerpts are taken from certain manuscripts, especially long bureaucratic reports, extensive legal proceedings, and other kinds of testimony. Editorial omission of a substantial body of material is indicated by a four-dot ellipsis centered on a separate line. An omission of only one or two sentences is marked by a four-dot ellipsis between the sentences that precede and follow the omission. The endnote identifies each excerpt as such and briefly characterizes the portion of the document not printed. (See the sample document that follows this essay for a guide to the elements of a printed document, including headnote, endnote, and footnote.)

The editors intervene without notation in the text of manuscripts in two minor ways. When the author of a manuscript inadvertently repeated a word, the duplicate is omitted. Similarly, most material canceled by the author is omitted, since it usually represents false starts or ordinary slips of the pen. When, however, the editors judge that the crossed-out material reflects an important alteration of meaning, it is printed as ~~canceled type~~. Apart from these cases, no "silent" additions, corrections, or deletions are made in the textual body of documents. Instead, all editorial insertions are clearly identified by being placed in italics and in brackets. Insertions by the editors may be descriptive interpolations such as [*In the margin*] or [*Endorsement*], the addition of words or letters omitted by the author, or the correction of misspelled words and erroneous dates. Great restraint is exercised, however, in making such editorial additions: The editors intervene only when the document cannot be understood or is seriously misleading as it stands. In particular, no effort is made to correct misspelled personal and place names. When material added by the editors is conjectural, a question mark is placed within the brackets. For printed documents only (of which there are few), "silent" correction is made for jumbled letters, errant punctuation, and transpositions that appear to be typesetting errors.

Although they faithfully reproduce the text of documents with minimal editorial intervention, the editors are less scrupulous with the peripheral parts of manuscripts. To print in full, exactly as in the original document, such elements as the complete return address, the full inside address, and a multiline complimentary closing would drastically reduce the number of documents that could be published. Considerations of space have therefore impelled the editors to adopt the following procedures. The place and date follow original spelling and punctuation, but they are printed on a single line at the beginning of the document regardless of where they appear in the manuscript. The salutation and complimentary closing, although spelled and punctuated as in the manuscript, are run into the text regardless of their positions in the original. Multiple signatures are printed only when there are twelve or fewer names. For documents with more than twelve signatures, including the many petitions bearing dozens or even hundreds of names, the editors indicate only the number of signatures on the signature line, for example, [86 *signatures*], although some information about the signers is always provided in the headnote and sometimes in the endnote as well. The formal legal apparatus accompanying sworn affidavits, including the name and position of the official who administered the oath and the names of witnesses, is omitted; the endnote, however, indicates whether an affidavit was sworn before a military officer, a Freedmen's Bureau agent, or a civil official. Similarly, the names of witnesses are omitted from contracts and other legal documents, but the endnote indicates that the signatures were witnessed.

The inside and return addresses create special complications. The documents in *Freedom* come from bureaucratic, mostly military, records. Therefore both inside and return addresses often include a military rank or other title and a statement of military command and location that may run to three or more lines. Similar details usually accompany the signature as well. Considerations of space alone preclude printing such material verbatim. Furthermore, even if published in full, the addresses would not always provide the reader with enough information to identify fully the sender and recipient. Military etiquette required that a subordinate officer address his superior not directly, but through the latter's adjutant. Thus, a letter destined for a general is ordinarily addressed to a captain or lieutenant, often only by the name of that lesser officer. To bring order out of the chaos that would remain even if all addresses were printed in full, and at the same time to convey all necessary information to the reader, the editors employ a twofold procedure. First, the headnote of each document identifies both sender and recipient—not by name, but by position, command, or other categorical label. For example, a letter from a staff assistant of the Union general in command of the military Department of the Gulf is labeled as originating not from "Lieutenant So-and-So" but from the "Headquarters of the Department of the Gulf." Confederate officials and military units are indicated as such by the addition of the word "Confederate" before their title or command, while those of the Union stand without modification. Most of the time this information for the headnote is apparent in the document itself, but when necessary the editors resort to other documents, published military registers, and service records to supply the proper designations. Second, the citation of each document (in the endnote) reproduces the military rank or other title as well as the name of both sender and recipient exactly as provided in the original document (except that punctuation is added to abbreviations, nonstandard punctuation is modernized, and superscripts are lowered to the line). Thus, the headnote and endnote together communicate the information from the return and inside addresses without printing those addresses in full.

Bureaucratic, and especially military procedures often created document files containing letters with numerous enclosures and endorsements. Although many routine endorsements served merely to transmit letters through proper bureaucratic channels, others reported the results of investigations, stated policy decisions, and issued orders. Indeed, enclosures or endorsements themselves are often valuable documents deserving publication. The editors therefore treat the material accompanying a document in one of three ways. First, some or all of such material may be printed in full along with the cover document. Second, accompanying items not published may be summarized in the endnote. Third, any accompanying material neither published nor summarized is noted in the endnote by the words "endorsements," "enclosures," "other enclosures," or "other endorsements." The editors do not, however, attempt to describe the contents or even note the existence of other documents that appear in the same file with the document being published but are not enclosed in it or attached to it. Clerks sometimes consolidated files of related – or even unrelated – correspondence, and many such files are voluminous. The editors draw upon other documents in the same file when necessary for annotation, just as they do upon documents filed elsewhere, but the endnote is normally a guide only to the material actually enclosed in, attached to, or endorsed upon the published document.

A technical description symbol follows each document at the left, usually on the same line as the signature. The symbol describes the physical form of the manuscript, the handwriting, and the signature. (See p. xxxiii for the symbols employed.)

An endnote for each document or group of related documents begins with a full citation that should allow the reader to locate the original among the holdings of the National Archives.[1] The citation refers solely to the document from which the printed transcription is made; the editors have searched out neither other copies in the National Archives nor any previously published versions. Because all the documents published in *Freedom* come from the National Archives, no repository name is included in the citation. Record groups are cited only by the abbreviation RG and a number. (See pp. xxxiii–xxxiv for a list of record group abbreviations.) For the convenience of researchers, the editors usually

---

[1] Scholars have cited documents from the National Archives in a bewildering variety of forms, many of them entirely inadequate. The editors of *Freedom* have tried to include all the information required to locate a document in the Archives' holdings. They urge similar completeness, if not necessarily their particular form of citation, upon other researchers and publishers.

provide both series title and series number for each document, but readers should note that series numbers are assigned by the National Archives staff for purposes of control and retrieval, and they are subject to revision. Each citation concludes with the Freedmen and Southern Society Project's own file number for that document, enclosed in brackets. In future the editors plan to microfilm all the documents accumulated during the project's search at the National Archives, along with the various geographical and topical indexes created by the staff. The project's file number for each document will thus serve as a guide both to the microfilm copy of the manuscript document and to other related documents in the project's files.

For ease of reference, the documents published in *Freedom* are numbered in sequence. On occasion, the editors have selected for publication several documents that taken together constitute a single episode. These documentary "clusters" are demarked at their beginning and at their conclusion by the project's logo—a broken shackle. The documents within each cluster bear alphabetical designations next to the number of the cluster.

Because *Freedom* focuses upon a subject or a series of questions, the editors consider the function of annotation different from that required in editing the papers of an individual. The editors seek, in the essays that introduce each section, to provide background information and interpretive context that will assist the reader in understanding the documents that follow, but the documents themselves are selected and arranged to tell their own story with relatively little annotation. When the editors judge annotation to be necessary or helpful, it usually appears in the form of further information about the content of a document or about the historical events under consideration, rather than biographical identification of individuals mentioned in the document. Thus, there are relatively few editorial notes to specific items within a document, but the endnote often describes the outcome of the case or discusses other events related to the episode portrayed in the document. Such annotation, as well as the chapter essays, is based primarily on other documents from the National Archives; those documents are cited in full, and their citations provide a guide to related records that could not be published. Quotations that appear without footnotes in a chapter essay, as well as undocumented descriptions of specific incidents, are taken from the documents published in that chapter. When portions of documents are quoted in endnotes and footnotes, they are transcribed by the same procedures as those employed for documents printed in full, except that, for technical reasons, terminal sentence punctuation is modernized. Annotation is also drawn from published primary sources, and, with few exceptions, the editors rely upon primary material rather than the secondary literature.

THE ELEMENTS OF A DOCUMENT

347: Discharged Maryland Black Soldier to a Freedmen's Bureau Claim Agent

Headnote*

Date and place line (reproduced as in manuscript, except printed on a single line at the top of document regardless of location in manuscript)

Salutation (reproduced as in manuscript, except run into text regardless of location in manuscript)

Body of document (reproduced as in manuscript, except extra space added at unpunctuated sentence breaks)

Complimentary closing (reproduced as in manuscript, except run into text regardless of location in manuscript)

Signature (reproduced as in manuscript, except titles and identification omitted)

Williamsport Washington Co MD oct the 8 /66

Sir   it is With Much Pleser That I seat my self Tu Rit you a few lines Tu Now if you can Git The Bounty That is Cuming Tu us & We hear That The ar Mor for us   if The ar Pleas Tu let us Now & if you Can git it With or Discharges   if you Can I shod lik for you Tu Du so   sum of The Boys ar Giting on Esey A Bout Thear Papars & The Monney Tu   The ar so Menney After Them Tu let Them git it for Them & The Tel Them That The Can git it suner   Nomor But I still Reman you abdiant survent

Charles. P. Taylor

ALS

Technical description of the document* (see list of symbols, p. xxxiii)

Charles P. Taylor to Mr. Wm. Fowler, 8 Oct. 1866, Unregistered Letters Received, ser. 1963, MD & DE Asst. Comr., RG 105[a] [A-9641].[b] Endorsement.[c] Taylor identified himself as a former sergeant in the 4th USCI.[d]

Endnote*
a. Full citation of the document: titles and names of sender and recipient exactly as spelled in manuscript; date; and National Archives citation (see list of record group abbreviations, pp. xxxiii–xxxiv)
b. Freedmen and Southern Society Project file number
c. Notation of enclosures and/or endorsements that are neither published with the document nor summarized in the endnote text
d. Text of endnote

Footnotes, * if any, follow the endnote
* Elements marked with an asterisk are supplied by the editors.

Symbols and Abbreviations

EDITORIAL SYMBOLS

[roman]   Words or letters in roman type within brackets represent editorial inference or conjecture of parts of manuscripts that are illegible, obscured, or mutilated. A question mark indicates doubt about the conjecture.

[. . .]   A three-dot ellipsis within brackets represents illegible or obscured words that the editors cannot decipher. If there is more than one undecipherable word, a footnote reports the extent of the passage.

. . . [5]   A three-dot ellipsis and a footnote represent words or passages entirely lost because the manuscript is torn or a portion is missing. The footnote reports the approximate amount of material missing.

~~canceled~~   Canceled type represents material written and then crossed out by the author of a manuscript. This device is used only when the editors judge that the crossed-out material reflects an important alteration of meaning. Ordinarily, canceled words are omitted without notation.

[*italic*]   Words or letters in italic type within brackets represent material that has been inserted by the editors and is not part of the original manuscript. A question mark indicates that the insertion is a conjecture.

. . . .   A four-dot ellipsis centered on a separate line represents editorial omission of a substantial body of material. A shorter omission, of only one or two sentences, is indicated by a four-dot ellipsis between two sentences.

Symbols and Abbreviations

SYMBOLS USED TO DESCRIBE MANUSCRIPTS

Symbols used to describe the handwriting, form, and signature of each document appear at the end of each document.

The first capital letter describes the handwriting of the document:
A autograph (written in the author's hand)
H handwritten by other than the author (for example, by a clerk)
P printed
T typed

The second capital letter, with lower-case modifier when appropriate, describes the form of the document:

L	letter	c	copy
D	document	p	press copy
E	endorsement	d	draft
W	wire (telegram)	f	fragment

The third capital letter describes the signature:
S signed by the author
Sr signed with a representation of the author's name
I initialed by the author
   no signature or representation

For example, among the more common symbols are: ALS (autograph letter, signed by author), HLS (handwritten letter, signed by author), HLSr (handwritten letter, signed with a representation), HLcSr (handwritten copy of a letter, signed with a representation), HD (handwritten document, no signature).

ABBREVIATIONS FOR RECORD GROUPS IN THE NATIONAL ARCHIVES OF THE UNITED STATES

RG 11 General Records of the United States Government
RG 15 Records of the Veterans Administration
RG 21 Records of District Courts of the United States
RG 45 Naval Records Collection of the Office of Naval Records and Library
RG 46 Records of the United States Senate
RG 56 General Records of the Department of the Treasury

RG 58   Records of the Internal Revenue Service
RG 59   General Records of the Department of State
RG 60   General Records of the Department of Justice
RG 77   Records of the Office of the Chief of Engineers
RG 92   Records of the Office of the Quartermaster General
RG 94   Records of the Adjutant General's Office, 1780s–1917
RG 99   Records of the Office of the Paymaster General
RG 101 Records of the Office of the Comptroller of the Currency
RG 105 Records of the Bureau of Refugees, Freedmen, and Aban-
        doned Lands
RG 107 Records of the Office of the Secretary of War
RG 108 Records of the Headquarters of the Army
RG 109 War Department Collection of Confederate Records
RG 110 Records of the Provost Marshal General's Bureau (Civil War)
RG 153 Records of the Office of the Judge Advocate General (Army)
RG 159 Records of the Office of the Inspector General
RG 217 Records of the United States General Accounting Office
RG 233 Records of the United States House of Representatives
RG 366 Records of Civil War Special Agencies of the Treasury Depart-
        ment
RG 393 Records of United States Army Continental Commands,
        1821–1920

SHORT TITLES

Freedom   *Freedom: A Documentary History of Emancipation,
                 1861–1867.*

                 Series 1, volume 1, *The Destruction of Slavery*, ed. Ira
                 Berlin, Barbara J. Fields, Thavolia Glymph, Joseph
                 P. Reidy, and Leslie S. Rowland (Cambridge, 1985).

                 Series 1, volume 2, *The Wartime Genesis of Free Labor:
                 The Upper South*, ed. Ira Berlin, Steven F. Miller,
                 Joseph P. Reidy, and Leslie S. Rowland (Cambridge,
                 1993).

                 Series 1, volume 3, *The Wartime Genesis of Free Labor:
                 The Lower South*, ed. Ira Berlin, Thavolia Glymph,
                 Steven F. Miller, Joseph P. Reidy, Leslie S. Rowland,
                 and Julie Saville (Cambridge, 1990).

Symbols and Abbreviations

Series 2, *The Black Military Experience*, ed. Ira Berlin, Joseph P. Reidy, and Leslie S. Rowland (Cambridge, 1982).

Official Records U.S. War Department, *The War of the Rebellion: A Compilation of the Official Records of the Union and Confederate Armies*, 128 vols. (Washington, 1880–1901).

Statutes at Large U.S., *Statutes at Large, Treaties, and Proclamations of the United States of America*, 17 vols. (Boston, 1850–73).

MILITARY AND OTHER ABBREVIATIONS THAT APPEAR FREQUENTLY IN THE DOCUMENTS

A.A.A.G.	Acting Assistant Adjutant General
A.A.G.	Assistant Adjutant General
A.C.	Army Corps
A.C.	Assistant Commissioner (Freedmen's Bureau)
Act., Actg.	Acting
A.D.	African Descent
A.D.C.	Aide-de-Camp
Adjt.	Adjutant
A.G.O.	Adjutant General's Office
Agt.	Agent
A.Q.M.	Assistant Quartermaster
A.S.A.C.	Assistant Subassistant Commissioner (Freedmen's Bureau)
Asst.	Assistant
A.S.W.	Assistant Secretary of War
BBG	Brevet Brigadier General
BG	Brigadier General
BGC	Brigadier General Commanding
BGV	Brigadier General of Volunteers
BMG	Brevet Major General
BRFAL	Bureau of Refugees, Freedmen, and Abandoned Lands
Brig.	Brigadier
Bvt.	Brevet
Capt.	Captain
Cav.	Cavalry

C. d'A.	Corps d'Afrique
C.H.	Court House
Co.	Company
Col.	Colonel
col^d, cold., col.	colored
com., comms^y	commissary
comdg., cmdg.	commanding
Comdr., Commr.	Commander
Comr.	Commissioner (Freedmen's Bureau)
C.S.	Commissary of Subsistence
C.S.	Commissioned Staff
C.S.	Confederate States
c.s.	current series
C.S.A.	Confederate States of America
Dept.	Department
Dist.	District
do	ditto
D.P.M.	Deputy Provost Marshal
E.M.M.	Enrolled Missouri Militia
f.m.c.	free man of color
Freedmen's Bureau	Bureau of Refugees, Freedmen, and Abandoned Lands
f.w.c.	free woman of color
G.C.M.	General Court-Martial
Gen., Gen'l	General
G.O.	General Order(s)
HQ, Hd. Qrs., Hdqrs.	Headquarters
Inf.	Infantry
Insp.	Inspector
inst.	*instant* (the current month of the year)
J.A.	Judge Advocate
Lt., Lieut.	Lieutenant
Maj.	Major
MG	Major General
MGC	Major General Commanding
MGV	Major General of Volunteers
M.O.	Mustering Officer
M.S.M.	Missouri State Militia
N.C.O.	Noncommissioned Officer(s)
NCS	Noncommissioned Staff
NG	Native Guard
Obt. Servt.	Obedient Servant
P.M.	Provost Marshal
P.M.	Paymaster
P.M.G.	Provost Marshal General

Priv., Pri.	Private
Pro. Mar., Provo. Mar.	Provost Marshal
prox.	*proximo* (the next month of the year)
Q.M., Qr. M.	Quartermaster
Q.M.G.O.	Quartermaster General's Office
Regt.	Regiment, regimental
RG	Record Group
R.Q.M.	Regimental Quartermaster
S.A.C	Subassistant Commissioner (Freedmen's Bureau)
Sec. War	Secretary of War
ser.	series
Sergt., Sgt.	Sergeant
S.O.	Special Order(s)
Subasst. Comr.	Subassistant Commissioner (Freedmen's Bureau)
Supt.	Superintendent
ult., ult°	*ultimo* (the preceding month of the year)
U.S.A.	U.S. Army
USCA Lt	U.S. Colored Artillery (Light)
USCA Hvy	U.S. Colored Artillery (Heavy)
USCC	U.S. Colored Cavalry
USCHA	U.S. Colored Heavy Artillery
USCI	U.S. Colored Infantry
USCLtA	U.S. Colored Light Artillery
USCT	U.S. Colored Troops
U.S.S.	U.S. Ship
U.S.V.	U.S. Volunteers
V., Vols.	Volunteers (usually preceded by a state abbreviation)
V.M.	Volunteer Militia (preceded by a state abbreviation)
V.R.C.	Veteran Reserve Corps

The Wartime Genesis of
Free Labor,
1861–1865

AS SLAVERY DETERIORATED during the American Civil War, fundamental questions arose about the social order that would take its place.[1]
Amid the tumult and danger of war, former slaves – usually designated
"contrabands" or "freedmen" – struggled to secure their liberty, reconstitute their families, and create institutions befitting a free people. But
no problem loomed larger than finding a means of support. Having
relinquished the guarantee of subsistence that accompanied slavery,
freedpeople faced numerous obstacles to gaining a livelihood. Many had
fled their homes with little more than the clothes on their backs.
Others had been abandoned by their owners. Nearly all began life in
freedom without tools or land, with no certain source of food, clothing,
or shelter, and with no means to provide for the old, the young, the
sick, or the disabled. For generations the slaves' labor had enriched
their owners. Now, in freedom, would they or others benefit from their
toil?

Military operations in the slave states compelled Northern officials to
confront the same questions. Fugitive slaves poured into federal lines,
searching for protection and freedom. Other slaves came under Union
control as Northern forces occupied parts of the Confederacy. From the

[1] This essay is based primarily upon the documents included in this volume, documents pub-
lished in other volumes of *Freedom*, and unpublished documents in the files of the Freedmen and
Southern Society Project. In addition, numerous secondary works have served as guides to the
development of wartime labor arrangements: Louis S. Gerteis, *From Contraband to Freedman:
Federal Policy toward Southern Blacks, 1861–1865* (Westport, Conn., 1973); W. E. B. Du Bois,
*Black Reconstruction in America: An Essay toward a History of the Part Which Black Folk Played in the
Attempt to Reconstruct Democracy in America, 1860–1880* (New York, 1935), chaps. 1–5; Eric
Foner, *Reconstruction: America's Unfinished Revolution, 1863–1877* (New York, 1988), chaps. 1–
3; Leon F. Litwack, *Been in the Storm So Long: The Aftermath of Slavery* (New York, 1979), chaps.
1–4; James M. McPherson, *The Struggle for Equality: Abolitionists and the Negro in the Civil War
and Reconstruction* (Princeton, N.J., 1964), chaps. 3–13; Edward Magdol, *A Right to the Land:
Essays on the Freedmen's Community* (Westport, Conn., 1977), chap. 4; Benjamin Quarles, *The
Negro in the Civil War* (Boston, 1953), especially chap. 13; Lawrence N. Powell, *New Masters:
Northern Planters during the Civil War and Reconstruction* (New Haven, Conn., 1980); James L.
Roark, *Masters without Slaves: Southern Planters in the Civil War and Reconstruction* (New York,
1977), chaps. 1–3; Armstead L. Robinson, " 'Worser dan Jeff Davis': The Coming of Free
Labor during the Civil War, 1861–1865," in *Essays on the Postbellum Southern Economy*, ed.
Thavolia Glymph and John J. Kushma (College Station, Tex., 1985), pp. 11–47; Bell Irvin
Wiley, *Southern Negroes, 1861–1865* (New Haven, Conn., 1938), pt. 2.

first, military considerations encouraged officers in the field and officials in Washington to mobilize former slaves on behalf of the Union war effort. Provision also had to be made for those who could not be usefully employed by the army or navy. Once emancipation became official federal policy, attention turned as well to the task of constructing free labor upon the ruins of slavery. Throughout the Union-occupied South, intertwined questions of labor and welfare forced themselves upon officials concerned chiefly with waging the war.

Federal military authorities were not alone in claiming the labor of the former slaves. Antislavery Northerners hoped to demonstrate the superior productivity of free labor, and Yankee entrepreneurs saw profits to be made in the bargain. Slave owners insisted that the former slaves were still theirs by right, and owners-turned-employers demanded preferential access to the labor of people they had lost as property. White Southerners who had never owned slaves saw an opportunity to break the slaveholders' monopoly of black workers. As the confiscation acts, the Emancipation Proclamation, and the success of federal arms extended freedom, the questions of how former slaves would work and for whose benefit assumed ever-greater importance.

In the course of a complex struggle among many contestants, free labor slowly took root throughout the Union-occupied South. Owing more to wartime necessities than to carefully considered plans, the new arrangements were ad hoc responses, not systematic designs for the future. They were restricted, moreover, to the narrow bounds of Union-held territory, themselves subject to the overriding requirements of the war. Provisional by their very nature, wartime labor programs were certain to be revamped or even jettisoned upon the return of peace. Nevertheless, measures adopted as temporary expedients had far-reaching implications. As the victorious North evaluated wartime developments, precedents solidified that opened certain possibilities and foreclosed others. Meanwhile, thousands of former slaves and former slaveholders entered the postwar world already experienced in the ways of free labor. Reconstruction of the defeated South would begin where wartime measures left off.

Four related circumstances influenced the wartime evolution of free labor: the notions of freedom espoused by Northerners, the beliefs and material resources of former slaves and free blacks, the extent and character of federal occupation, and the policies of federal authorities. If no one circumstance operated independently of the others, each was of special significance at particular moments and in particular places.

Free labor emerged in the Union-occupied South as freedom was being redefined in the North. During the first half of the nineteenth century, Northern merchants and manufacturers had reorganized work arrangements and, in the process, gained unprecedented control over production. They thereby elevated themselves to new positions of social and economic preeminence and set in motion changes that ousted artisans from their crafts and farmers from their land. On the eve of the Civil War, most small towns and farming communities had not yet been touched by these revolutionary changes. But in all the major cities of the Northeast and Midwest, as well as in many small towns, workshops employing dozens of workers and factories employing hundreds had become common. In these places, wage-workers may have outnumbered landed farmers, propertied artisans, and self-employed shopkeepers.

Changing patterns of ownership and production created overlapping and, often, contradictory conceptions of freedom. From one perspective, freedom derived from a man's ownership of productive property, real and personal, which guaranteed a competency and the ability to establish an independent household. Ownership of productive property ensured respectability within a community and membership in its polity. The ideal citizen was a male proprietor whose control over his own labor and its products underlay both economic and political independence. Since men of independent means could not be bought or bribed, they alone—at least until the 1820s, in most states—could vote, hold office, serve on juries, and enjoy the other manifestations of full citizenship. As heads of households, such men could extend some of the benefits of freedom to others under their jurisdiction—wives, children, servants, apprentices, and journeymen—whom they represented in the polity. Depending on their age, sex, and color, these dependents might travel without restriction, assemble at will, bear arms, testify in court, and enjoy other rights, but they were not and could not be citizens in the fullest sense.

The social and economic changes that eroded property-based independence created a different understanding of freedom. From the new perspective, freedom derived not from the ownership of productive property, but from the unfettered sale of one's labor power—itself a commodity—in a competitive market. "Political freedom rightly defined," proclaimed a Union general, "is liberty to work, and to be protected in the full enjoyment of the fruits of labor."[2] Voluntary rather than obligatory labor, represented by contracts based on mutual consent, became the hallmark of the new order. Ideal citizens thus included not only independent farmers, artisans, and shopkeepers, but also upwardly mobile wage-workers who by dint of ambition, industry, and luck improved themselves. Indeed, to the apostles of the emerging order, the process of self-improvement itself made for better workers, better citizens, and better men, thereby affirming the natural—if not providential—origins of the new ideal.

Individual men, able to rise and fall according to their own ability

2 See below, doc. 26. The general was Benjamin F. Butler.

and energy, began breaking away from traditional household structures. By the early nineteenth century, indentured servitude had all but disappeared, apprenticeship was falling into disuse, and the master-journeyman system—increasingly unable to regulate prices, training, or the quality of workmanship—was crumbling. Changes that undermined personal subordination in the workplace also altered domestic relationships. Although fathers retained much of their traditional power and full political rights were not extended to women, the departure of production from the household allowed some women a new authority over domestic life.[3]

As Northerners came to advocate internally generated initiative, rather than personal obligation and external force, as the proper stimulus to industry, they assaulted those social relations that smacked of direct coercion. Southern slaveholders represented everything that advocates of the new freedom despised. By denying the two great incentives to self-improvement—the stick of hunger and the carrot of property accumulation—slaveholders debased both their slaves and themselves and created a social order that was tyrannical, exploitative, and corrupt. Only free labor could make for a society of free and independent men.[4]

[3]   On the transformation of economy and society in the free states, see David Montgomery, *Beyond Equality: Labor and the Radical Republicans, 1862–1872* (New York, 1967), especially chap. 1 and appendix A; Alfred D. Chandler, *The Visible Hand: The Managerial Revolution in American Business* (Cambridge, Mass., 1977), chaps. 1–3; Alan Dawley, *Class and Community: The Industrial Revolution in Lynn* (Cambridge, Mass., 1976); David M. Gordon, Richard Edwards, and Michael Reich, *Segmented Work, Divided Workers: The Historical Transformation of Labor in the United States* (Cambridge, U.K., 1982), chap. 3; Steven Hahn and Jonathan Prude, eds., *The Countryside in the Age of Capitalist Transformation: Essays in the Social History of Rural America* (Chapel Hill, N.C., 1985), chaps. 1–4, 8–11; Peter Dobkin Hall, *The Organization of American Culture, 1700–1900: Private Institutions, Elites, and the Origins of American Nationality* (New York, 1982); Mary P. Ryan, *Cradle of the Middle Class: The Family in Oneida County, New York, 1790–1865* (Cambridge, U.K., 1981); Anthony F. C. Wallace, *Rockdale: The Growth of an American Village in the Early Industrial Revolution* (New York, 1978); Sean Wilentz, *Chants Democratic: New York City and the Rise of the American Working Class, 1788–1850* (New York, 1984). The decline of the master-apprentice system is traced in W. J. Rorabaugh, *The Craft Apprentice: From Franklin to the Machine Age in America* (New York, 1986). For the ideological changes that accompanied and articulated the social transformation, see Eric Foner, *Free Soil, Free Labor, Free Men: The Ideology of the Republican Party before the Civil War* (New York, 1970), chaps. 1–2, and *Politics and Ideology in the Age of the Civil War* (New York, 1980), chaps. 3–4, 6–7; Jonathan A. Glickstein, *Concepts of Free Labor in Antebellum America* (New Haven, Conn., 1991); Robert J. Steinfeld, *The Invention of Free Labor: The Employment Relation in English and American Law and Culture, 1350–1870* (Chapel Hill, N.C., 1991); Barbara J. Fields and Leslie S. Rowland, "Free Labor Ideology and Its Exponents in the South during the Civil War and Reconstruction," *Labor History* (in press). The changing role of women is analyzed in Nancy F. Cott, *The Bonds of Womanhood: "Woman's Sphere" in New England, 1780–1835* (New Haven, Conn., 1977); Ryan, *Cradle of the Middle Class*; Kathryn Kish Sklar, *Catharine Beecher: A Study in American Domesticity* (New Haven, Conn., 1973); Christine Stansell, *City of Women: Sex and Class in New York, 1789–1860* (New York, 1986).

[4]   David Brion Davis, *The Problem of Slavery in the Age of Revolution, 1770–1823* (Ithaca, N.Y., 1975), especially chaps. 8–10; Jonathan A. Glickstein, " 'Poverty Is Not Slavery': American Abolitionists and the Competitive Labor Market," in *Antislavery Reconsidered: New Perspectives on*

The new conception of freedom existed side by side with the old, and rather than see them as mutually exclusive, most Northerners embraced elements of both. Indeed, for many of them, the opportunities of the market offered a way to achieve the old ideal of freehold independence. The promise of social mobility bridged the gap between propertyless proletarian and independent proprietor, suggesting that any industrious individual could attain independent standing. "There is [no] such thing," declared Abraham Lincoln, "as the free hired laborer being fixed to that condition for life. . . . The prudent, penniless beginner in the world labors for wages awhile, saves a surplus with which to buy tools or land for himself, then labors on his own account another while, and at length hires another new beginner to help him."[5] With similar optimism, Northerners also argued that there was no inherent conflict between the propertied and the propertyless. To the contrary, a "harmony of interests" united capital and labor. Governed by the universal "laws" of political economy, that harmony was embodied in the voluntary contractual relations that joined employer and employee.

A growing number of wage-workers discerned conflict, not harmony, between labor and capital. While struggling to improve themselves, they began to articulate new ideas that denied the preeminence of the market and the right of employers to determine their employees' place in society. Those who subsisted by selling their labor power demanded and received title to privileges previously reserved for property-owning freemen. The suffrage and other political rights became prerogatives of dependent proletarians as well as independent proprietors.[6]

The older ideas about independence corresponded to particular notions of dependence. In a community of independent freeholders, households were responsible for the support of their own dependents, be they children, elderly parents, servants, journeymen, or apprentices. Through networks of family and community, households also succored orphans, the physically and mentally ill, and other unfortunates. When such men, women, and children held no claim upon a

---

the Abolitionists, ed. Lewis Perry and Michael Fellman (Baton Rouge, La., 1979), pp. 195–218; Foner, *Free Soil, Free Labor, Free Men*; Louis S. Gerteis, *Morality and Utility in American Antislavery Reform* (Chapel Hill, N.C., 1987).

[5] Lincoln's statement appears in his annual message to Congress of December 1861. (Abraham Lincoln, *Collected Works*, ed. Roy P. Basler, Marion D. Pratt, and Lloyd A. Dunlap, 9 vols. [New Brunswick, N.J., 1953–55], vol. 5, pp. 35–53.)

[6] On the development of the American working class during the antebellum years, see Herbert G. Gutman, *Work, Culture, and Society in Industrializing America: Essays in American Working-Class and Social History* (New York, 1976), especially chap. 1; Dawley, *Class and Community*, chaps. 1–3, 5; Gordon et al., *Segmented Work, Divided Workers*, chap. 3; Wallace, *Rockdale*, chap. 4; Wilentz, *Chants Democratic*. Changes in the requirements for suffrage and officeholding are outlined in Richard P. McCormick, *The Second American Party System: Party Formation in the Jacksonian Era* (Chapel Hill, N.C., 1966).

particular household, local authorities assigned them to one and provided a subsidy from public funds. Respectable men and women who had fallen on hard times were often supported in their own homes – so-called outdoor relief – both to meet their immediate needs and to maintain the integrity of the community. The care of dependents thus lent support to the social order in communities in which face-to-face relations were the standard. Strangers and those deemed not respectable were either "warned out" of town or given short shrift, no matter how desperate.

The new notions of independence altered ideas about dependence. Relief assumed a new form as mobile, unattached individuals began to outnumber settled householders. In the seaboard metropolises of the Northeast, the arrival of thousands of newcomers from the countryside and from foreign lands transformed neighbors into strangers. In response, associations of benevolent individuals, in alliance with public officials, assumed responsibilities once borne by households. Sponsoring an array of new institutions – schools, poorhouses, penitentiaries, and asylums – these reformers offered a new discipline that would guard against permanent impoverishment in the absence of the traditional rewards and restraints. Reformers wanted to ensure that the freedom of propertyless men and women did not lead to license. They sought to demonstrate that even without a foundation in property ownership, civic responsibility and social discipline could rest upon industry, frugality, and sobriety, the personal virtues taught in common schools and Protestant churches and enforced by the market.[7]

On the eve of the Civil War, the conflicting notions about freedom and independence, work and welfare, were far from reconciled. Fighting a war for national reunification heightened the contradictions. Mobilization under the banner of "Union and Liberty" brought together diverse Northern constituencies with different understandings of both terms: New Englanders and midwesterners, factory workers and yeoman farmers, Protestant reformers and Catholic immigrants, antislavery Republicans and proslavery Union Democrats. Contention over the meaning of freedom divided Northerners even as opposition to secession united them.

Southern slaves had their own conceptions of freedom, derived from their experience as slaves within the American republic. Themselves

---

[7] Intertwined ideas of public charity, private philanthropy, reform, and welfare are discussed in Paul Boyer, *Urban Masses and Moral Order in America, 1820–1920* (Cambridge, Mass., 1978), chaps. 1–7; Michael B. Katz, *In the Shadow of the Poorhouse: A Social History of Welfare in America* (New York, 1986), chaps. 1–4; Benjamin Joseph Klebaner, *Public Poor Relief in America, 1790–1860* (New York, 1976); David J. Rothman, *The Discovery of the Asylum: Social Order and Disorder in the New Republic* (Boston, 1971). Robert H. Bremner, *The Public Good: Philanthropy and Welfare in the Civil War Era* (New York, 1980), chaps. 1–5, is especially helpful on the war years.

property, they were denied control over their labor and its product. Without independent standing in the eyes of the law, they were subject to the personal will of their owners. Slaves could be sold, disciplined, and moved without recourse, and they had no right to marry, educate their children, or provide for their parents. They could bear arms, assemble, hold property, and travel only with their owners' consent.

Slaves expected the destruction of their owners' sovereignty to open a world of new possibilities. If slavery denied them the right to control their persons and progeny, freedom would confer that right. If slavery required that they suffer arbitrary and often violent treatment, freedom would enable them to protect themselves against such abuse. If slavery allowed their owners to expropriate the fruits of their labor, freedom would at least guarantee compensation if not the entire product of their labor. As free people, former slaves expected to be able to organize their lives in accordance with their own sense of propriety, establish their families as independent units, and control productive property as the foundation of their new status.

But freedom was not merely slavery's negative. Even before the war, slaves established families, created churches, selected community leaders, and carved out a small realm of independent economic activity. An elaborate network of kinship – with its own patterns of courtship, rites of marriage, parental responsibilities, and kin obligations – linked slaves together. Throughout the South, slaves organized churches – formal congregations in cities and on some large plantations, informal gatherings on small farmsteads. Black ministers articulated a different interpretation of Christianity from that heard in the churches of slave owners. In addition to preachers, slaves chose other leaders from their own ranks. Often these were drivers or artisans, but sometimes men and women of no special status in the owners' view.

While subject to their owners' overwhelming power, slaves struggled to increase the possibilities of independent action in all areas of their lives. They pressed for nothing more relentlessly than control over their own labor, denial of which constituted the very essence of chattel slavery. Conceding what they could not alter, slaves worked without direct compensation but claimed the right to a predictable portion of what they produced. They expected their owners to feed, clothe, and house them in accordance with customary usage and irrespective of age, infirmity, or productivity.

Through a continuous process of contest and negotiation with individual owners, many slaves also established a right to some time of their own in which to cultivate gardens, hunt, fish, raise poultry and hogs, make baskets and practice other handicrafts, hire themselves to neighboring farmers and artisans, or receive payment for overwork. Some slaves were permitted to sell the products of such independent activities, often to their own masters and sometimes to others. Al-

7

though their property usually had no standing at law, it gained recognition in practice, enabling them to accumulate small and generally perishable resources by which they improved their own lives and gave the next generation "a start." The slaves' self-directed economic activities, like their families and religious congregations, fostered a vision of an independent life and shaped their expectations of the postemancipation world.[8]

While the slaves' ideas about freedom everywhere derived from slavery, slavery was not everywhere the same. Regional and local differences affected the character of emancipation. Many of the four million slaves in the South in 1860 lived and worked alongside their owners, sharing intimately, if never equally, in the daily routine. Others hardly knew their owners and instead stood at the end of a chain of command that extended from a black driver or foreman through a white overseer before it reached an absentee master. Some slaves had roots in the land they worked that reached back for generations; others were newcomers, recently torn from old homes and transplanted to a strange and distant place. Some slaves spent their entire lives on one great estate, rarely venturing beyond its boundaries. Others lived on small farms or in cities, interacted regularly with nonslaveholding whites and free blacks, traveled widely, and were sometimes rented out by their owners to different hirers. A few privileged slaves hired themselves out, paying their owners a monthly "wage" and retaining for themselves whatever remained.

Slaves also worked in different ways. Most were agricultural workers, chiefly field hands. Although they shared the experience of tilling the soil, the regimen of different crops and particular forms of labor organization fostered divergent patterns of work. Some slave men and women were assigned daily tasks, after the completion of which they could engage in self-directed activities that supplemented their diets and sometimes generated a small surplus. The majority of plantation slaves, however, worked from sunup to sundown in closely supervised gangs and had relatively little time to cultivate garden plots or accumulate property of any sort. Still other agricultural slaves, especially those in mixed-farming regions, labored at a variety of seasonally defined tasks that required flexible schedules and considerable freedom of movement. Work outside the field – in artisan shops, in urban warehouses and factories, and in the big house – created other distinctive patterns.

[8] The best general studies of Southern slavery in the nineteenth century are Eugene D. Genovese, *Roll, Jordan, Roll: The World the Slaves Made* (New York, 1974), and Kenneth M. Stampp, *The Peculiar Institution: Slavery in the Ante-Bellum South* (New York, 1956). On the family life of slaves, see Herbert G. Gutman, *The Black Family in Slavery and Freedom, 1750–1925* (New York, 1976); on religion, Albert J. Raboteau, *Slave Religion: The "Invisible Institution" in the Antebellum South* (New York, 1978); on the slaves' independent economic activity, Ira Berlin and Philip D. Morgan, eds., "The Slaves' Economy: Independent Production by Slaves in Plantation Societies," special issue of *Slavery and Abolition* 12 (May 1991), especially the introduction and the essays by John Campbell, Roderick A. McDonald, and John T. Schlotterbeck.

The slaves' various work routines influenced both their lives in slavery and their ideas about freedom.[9]

Black people with prior experience in freedom, approximately a quarter-million on the eve of the Civil War, also contributed to the emergence of free-labor relations. Most free blacks resided in the Upper South, where they were so mixed and intermarried with slaves as to have become socially inseparable. Others, particularly those in the port cities of the Lower South, styled themselves "free people of color" and held themselves apart from the mass of rural, black slaves. But no matter how they tried to distinguish themselves, free blacks lived within the close confines of a society that presumed people of African descent to be slaves. Southern lawmakers denied them many liberties enjoyed by white people, forbidding them to travel freely, to testify in court or sit on juries, to bear arms, or (in some states) to hold property in their own names. Yet free blacks were not slaves. They enjoyed the right to marry, establish independent households, control their own labor, and accumulate property. Drawing on their skills and their personal connections with white patrons, a few ambitious free blacks managed to amass considerable wealth and attain a degree of respectability even in the eyes of slaveholders. Their experience engendered a special social outlook and an understanding of freedom that could be as different from that of the liberated as it was from that of the liberators.[10]

No matter what expectations black people brought to freedom, their intentions—like those of everyone else—collided with the realities of war. In some regions of the South, notably the South Carolina Sea Islands and certain areas of the Mississippi Valley, the arrival of federal troops caused slaveholders to abandon both their estates and their slaves. Transformed into de facto freedpeople by their owners' exodus, such former slaves pursued an independent livelihood on their home plantations, surrounded by a familiar landscape, kinfolk, and friends. In much of the seceded South, however, and in the border states that remained in the Union, slaves gained freedom only by flight. Since solitary fugitives stood a better chance of success—especially early in the war—runaways often had to leave family and friends behind. Many fugitive slaves followed familiar paths to hideaways in forests and swamps, while others occupied abandoned farms and plantations. But the vast majority of fugitives sought safety in or near federal encampments, trusting their future to perfect strangers.

Still other slaves secured freedom with their owners in residence. Most notably in southern Louisiana, Tennessee, and the border states,

---

[9] The spatial diversity and temporal development of slavery in the United States are captured in Willie Lee Rose, ed., *A Documentary History of Slavery in North America* (New York, 1976), and Ira Berlin, "Time, Space, and the Evolution of Afro-American Society on British Mainland North America," *American Historical Review* 85 (Feb. 1980): 44–78.

[10] Ira Berlin, *Slaves without Masters: The Free Negro in the Antebellum South* (New York, 1974).

slaves confronted owners who were determined to maintain their old dominance in fact if not at law. Many such slaveholders, professing loyalty to the Union, called upon federal authorities to sustain their claims to black laborers; the officials, hesitant to alienate much-needed allies, frequently complied. Occasionally, even disloyal masters brazenly demanded military backing.[11]

Above all, the march of contending armies determined the possibilities available to former slaves. Where federal lines were secure, freedpeople could sink roots, reconstitute their families, organize churches and schools, and earn a livelihood. Such places were few in number. Enormous though it became, the federal army was never large enough simultaneously to protect the loyal states, defend the occupied regions of the Confederacy, and mount offensives against the rebels. Confederate troops held Union armies at bay during the first two years of the war and enjoyed the ability to counterattack in force well into 1864. Federal lines shifted in the ebb and flow of military campaigns, sometimes incorporating slaves from Confederate territory, sometimes uprooting freedpeople and sending them in search of another safe haven. Certain districts nominally under Union control became the site of guerrilla activity that widened into a war of all against all. If many slaves gained freedom on the run, subsequent events often kept them in motion. Few black men and women passed from slavery to freedom untouched by the uncertainty of military events.[12]

Vagaries of federal policy likewise affected the wartime experience of former slaves. The Union war effort entailed thousands of official decisions, great and small, made by an array of politicians, bureaucrats, and military officers. Although their policies aimed first to secure victory, other considerations also weighed heavily. In the field, soldiers and officers acted to safeguard their lives. In Washington, elected officials and civil servants protected their careers, scrutinizing possible courses of action against their prospects of reelection and advancement. Officials, elected and appointed, kept an eye on the interests of their friends, constituents, and political parties. Only incidentally, if at all, did they consider the effect of their decisions upon the freedpeople. Nevertheless, programs implemented to recruit soldiers, to execute a particular military strategy, to bolster the national treasury, or to determine the ownership of captured property had important implications for the lives of former slaves.[13]

---

[11] The uneven evolution of legal freedom in different parts of the South is described in *Freedom*, ser. 1, vol. 1.

[12] Patterns of federal occupation and their implications for the destruction of slavery are discussed in *Freedom*, ser. 1, vol. 1.

[13] Studies of federal policy include Robert P. Sharkey, *Money, Class, and Party: An Economic Study of Civil War and Reconstruction* (Baltimore, 1959); Leonard P. Curry, *Blueprint for Modern America: Nonmilitary Legislation of the First Civil War Congress* (Nashville, 1968); Fred A.

Nothing had prepared federal officials for the mobilization that followed the outbreak of war. The army and navy needed tons of food and uniforms, herds of horses and mules, miles of wagons and railroad cars, and thousands of rifles, cannons, and caissons – a veritable mountain of materiel – all of which would have to be purchased by a government that had no national tax save a tariff. It would have been difficult enough to amass and pay for the necessities of war under normal conditions, and these were not normal times. Secession had shaken established patterns of commerce and industry and disrupted financial markets throughout the Union, requiring wholesale reordering of agricultural and industrial production.

The demands of making war exceeded the resources of the peacetime nation and strained the Northern labor force. While the leaders of the Confederacy assumed that slave labor would undergird their war effort,[14] Union officials at first evinced little interest in black laborers, either free or slave. Few in number, generally assumed to be unskilled and untutored, free blacks cut a poor figure in the eyes of most white Northerners, who viewed them as the refuse of slave society. Slave laborers seemed no more desirable or – if desired – attainable. Although slaves constituted a large portion of the laboring population in the loyal border states of Kentucky, Maryland, and Missouri, their services could be secured only with the consent of politically powerful slaveholders. Fearful that such a request might push the border states over the brink of secession, Union officials dared not ask.[15]

Border-state slaves, by contrast, were not deterred by the loyal standing of their owners. As soon as Union soldiers appeared in the border states, so did runaway slaves. But federal commanders went out of their way to safeguard the property rights of slaveholders. Fugitive slaves who offered their services to the Union army met a stern and sometimes violent rebuke. The heavy work associated with armies on the move therefore fell chiefly upon Northern soldiers themselves, with an occasional assist from private citizens laboring for wages.[16]

The federal government's respect for slavery extended to the seceded states as well. By reiterating a commitment to honor and protect slavery wherever it existed, President Abraham Lincoln and the Republican-

Shannon, *The Organization and Administration of the Union Army, 1861–1865*, 2 vols. (Cleveland, 1928).

[14] Confederate mobilization of slave and free-black laborers is discussed in *Freedom*, ser. 1, vol. 1: chap. 9.

[15] On Northern free blacks, see Leon F. Litwack, *North of Slavery: The Negro in the Free States, 1790–1860* (Chicago, 1961). On federal policy regarding slavery in the border slave states, see below, chaps. 4–6; *Freedom*, ser. 1, vol. 1: chaps. 6–8; *Freedom*, ser. 2: chap. 4. On early military employment of black laborers in the border states, see below, doc. 131; *Freedom*, ser. 1, vol. 1: doc. 197.

[16] *Freedom*, ser. 1, vol. 1: pp. 332, 397–99, 495–98, and docs. 127–29, 153–54, 157, 160A–C, 197, 199–201.

controlled Congress hoped to win over not only border-state slaveholders and Northern Democrats but also lukewarm Confederates. Accordingly, when Union armies entered areas in rebellion, commanders disavowed any intention to unsettle relations between master and slave. Judicious policy, a War Department official explained, would "avoid all interference with the Social systems or local institutions" of the seceded states.[17]

While Lincoln and his subordinates courted slaveholders, slaves demonstrated their readiness to risk all for freedom and to do whatever they could to aid their owners' enemy. At every turn, federal soldiers met fugitive slaves bearing information, providing food and drink, and volunteering their labor. Determined to make the most of the presence of the Union army, slaves did whatever they could to ingratiate themselves to the invaders. It did not take long for Northern soldiers to see the wisdom of receiving and protecting them, if only to ease the burdens of military life and prevent the rebels from doing the same. Although officially denied entry to Union army lines, frequently manhandled, and sometimes returned to their owners, slaves continued to offer their services. In time, some found shelter in federal encampments, and many more gained residence in their shadow. Before long, the wisdom of common soldiers began to ascend the chain of command. A glimmer of this dynamic appeared in the border states, where most military operations transpired during 1861 and early 1862; it emerged in full brilliance when Union forces advanced into the seceded South.[18]

Events unleashed by the invasion and occupation of Confederate territory transformed federal policy regarding fugitive slaves and their labor. In May 1861, Union troops reinforced Fortress Monroe, a federal installation in tidewater Virginia. The following November, a joint army and navy expedition invaded Port Royal Sound, in the South Carolina Sea Islands, to establish a coaling station for the blockading squadron. The presence of federal troops disrupted slavery in both tidewater Virginia and the Sea Islands. At Fortress Monroe, fugitive slaves from the nearby countryside arrived in search of freedom and military protection. At Port Royal, most of the white residents and virtually all the slaveholders fled when Union gunboats drew near, leaving the slaves in possession of the islands' great estates, including their crops of long-staple cotton. In both regions, federal commanders were confronted by large numbers of slaves whose owners were avowed enemies, not wavering friends.[19]

---

[17] *Freedom*, ser. 1, vol. 1: doc. 18.

[18] See, for example, *Freedom*, ser. 1, vol. 1: docs. 1A, 6, 19, 41, 61, 81, 131A, 160B, 163, 197. The commander of a Union army division in northern Alabama echoed the sentiment of many of his men when he observed that, among local residents, the slaves "are our only friends." (*Freedom*, ser. 1, vol. 1: doc. 86n.)

[19] On the Union occupation of tidewater Virginia and the South Carolina Sea Islands, see *Freedom*, ser. 1, vol. 1: chaps. 1–2.

Far from their base of supply, army and navy officers found themselves badly in need of laborers. White Southerners, even those who professed loyalty to the federal government, displayed little inclination to work on its behalf. Northern laborers, whose wages had increased rapidly with the onset of war, proved difficult to lure south. With few alternatives, Union officials followed the traditional army practice of assigning soldiers to various fatigue duties, offering them "extra-duty pay" for work performed on their own time.[20] But the employment of soldiers had its limits, especially with Confederate troops menacing isolated Union outposts.

Military commanders therefore put able-bodied slaves to work. At Fortress Monroe and at Port Royal, runaway slaves soon composed the bulk of the labor force in the army's quartermaster, engineer, and subsistence departments. Navy officers employed fugitive slaves aboard ship and on shore. For those slaves who were able to work, military employment offered food, protection, and freedom in return for their labor. Women, children, and old or disabled people – who, in the eyes of the generals, could contribute nothing substantial to the war effort – posed a problem for Union officers, as no provision had been made for their support. At Fortress Monroe, General Benjamin F. Butler and his successor, General John E. Wool, applied the earnings of those contrabands employed as military laborers toward the support of those not so employed. At Port Royal, General Thomas W. Sherman paid military laborers a small wage and issued rations to those unable to work.[21]

Ad hoc employment of fugitive-slave men and meager relief for their dependents failed to satisfy those Northerners who were determined to use every available means to punish treason and reunite the nation. Seeing slavery as the root of the rebellion, practical-minded Republicans had no qualms about accepting fugitive slaves into federal lines, if only to punish the rebels. It was foolhardy not to do so, they argued, for the Confederates had already mobilized slaves in behalf of their own war effort. Abolitionists, black and white, turned that utilitarian argument to their own purposes. Seizing the opportunity to realize the egalitarian promise of the American Revolution, they denounced the narrow ground upon which Lincoln and the Congress were fighting the war. They called for outright abolition of slavery and the employment of former slaves as both soldiers and laborers.

Rather than rely upon the half-hearted efforts of federal commanders, abolitionists mobilized on behalf of the former slaves accumulating

---

[20] On the military use of Northern laborers in the occupied South, see, for example, below, docs. 16, 27; testimony of Gen. Dix before the American Freedmen's Inquiry Commission, 9 May 1863, filed with O-328 1863, Letters Received, ser. 12, RG 94 [K-68]; Capt. R. Saxton to Capt. L. H. Pelouse, 12 Mar. 1862, Letters Received, ser. 2254, SC Expeditionary Corps, RG 393 Pt. 2 No. 130 [C-1642]. On the employment of "extra duty soldiers," see below, doc. 6.

[21] See below, doc. 2; *Freedom*, ser. 1, vol. 1: doc. 1A; *Freedom*, ser. 1, vol. 3: docs. 1, 4.

within Union lines. During the fall and winter of 1861–1862, antislavery men and women – often in league with other "educated and philanthropic" Northerners – organized contraband relief societies (subsequently known as freedmen's aid societies). These groups gathered clothing, bibles, schoolbooks, and medical supplies for the destitute ex-slaves at Fortress Monroe, Port Royal, and the District of Columbia. Convinced of their ability "to provide for all [the freedpeople's] proper wants," they assured the Lincoln administration that "there is no necessity for any Governmental charity."[22] But the abolitionists and their allies had no intention of confining themselves to rolling bandages and collecting old clothes. They would guide the passage of the former slaves to freedom.

Before long, philanthropic gentlemen and ladies were taking up stations in the Union-occupied South. Most of them were young men and women of high social standing, who had been raised in the abolitionist tradition and saw their service as a culmination of the long struggle against slavery. As teachers, ministers, and physicians, they brought useful skills and a heightened respect for the former slaves' humanity into federal camps. While these Yankees shared many of the racial preconceptions common among white Northerners, they were sure of both the iniquity of slavery and the superiority of free labor. They assumed that, once freed of the vices of slavery and tutored in the virtues of free labor, evangelical Christianity, and republican citizenship, former slaves would take their place as productive and responsible members of the body politic.[23]

Although united in their determination to free the slaves and transform the South, antislavery Northerners did not share a vision of the social order that would replace the slaveholders' regime. They agreed that abolishing property rights in man and substituting the discipline of voluntary contracts for that of the lash were necessary conditions for a free South. But they disagreed about whether those steps were sufficient. A sizable contingent believed that self-ownership without possession of productive property did not constitute true freedom, but thereafter they too divided among themselves. Some of them recommended that

[22] See below, doc. 4.
[23] On Northern reformers in the wartime South, see Bremner, *The Public Good*, chap. 5; Robert F. Engs, *Freedom's First Generation: Black Hampton, Virginia, 1861–1890* (Philadelphia, 1979), chap. 3; McPherson, *Struggle for Equality*, especially chaps. 7, 11; Frederick Law Olmsted, *The Papers of Frederick Law Olmsted*, ed. Charles Capen McLaughlin and Charles E. Beveridge, 5 vols. to date (Baltimore, 1977–), vol. 4, *Defending the Union: The Civil War and the U.S. Sanitary Commission, 1861–1863*, ed. Jane Turner Censer, pp. 3–4, 20–26, and chap. 4; Joe M. Richardson, *Christian Reconstruction: The American Missionary Association and Southern Blacks, 1861–1890* (Athens, Ga., 1986), chaps. 1–2; Willie Lee Rose, *Rehearsal for Reconstruction: The Port Royal Experiment* (Indianapolis, Ind., 1964), especially chaps. 2–3; Henry L. Swint, *The Northern Teacher in the South, 1862–1870* (Nashville, 1941).

freedpeople be required to purchase such property with wages earned after their liberation; the others maintained that years of uncompensated toil entitled the ex-slaves outright to the land they had "watered . . . with their tears and blood." Charles B. Wilder, a Massachusetts abolitionist assigned to Fortress Monroe by the American Missionary Association, regarded wage labor not as an end in itself, but an opportunity for former slaves to "buy a spot of land" where they could "have a little hut to live in with their families like any body else." Mansfield French, a Methodist clergyman sent to the Sea Islands by the same association, urged the government to endow freedpeople with land as indemnification for past injustice. "[T]he negroes had made [the land] what it was and . . . it belonged to them, and them only," he declared.[24]

The freedpeople's Northern friends drew upon their own notions of dependence as well as their ideas of independence. Antislavery men and women were alert to the development of new modes of poor relief. Many of them had ministered to the downtrodden and preached the gospel of industry, frugality, and sobriety in the North's growing cities. To them, destitute former slaves resembled other impoverished people. The imperative to work or starve would bear upon freedpeople no more lightly than it did upon newly arrived foreigners or rural migrants. The need to support themselves and their families and the opportunity to improve themselves and accumulate property would spur former slaves to diligent and faithful labor just as they did other people. "The negro is actuated by the same motives as other men," asserted one opponent of slavery, "& we must appeal to the *human nature* & make it appear for his interest to work & then he *will* work." To be sure, the freedpeople would require temporary assistance. But only temporary. Opponents of slavery feared replacing one form of dependency with another and believed that charity would create permanent dependency. "Irish souphouses" and other "socialistic institutions" would not make former slaves industrious workers and exemplary citizens.[25]

Agents of Northern aid societies generally received a welcome from federal commanders, who shared many of their ideas about the relationship between private philanthropy and public charity and also saw "the contraband problem" as one of destitution and its relief. This shared perspective propelled some agents of Northern benevolence into positions of authority, with responsibility for distributing government rations and funneling donations from the North to needy freedpeople. At Fortress Monroe, General Wool appointed Wilder to supervise the

---

[24] See below, docs. 16, 28, 43; statement of William B. Lucas, 30 Jan. [1864], enclosed in Wm. Henry Brisbane to Hon. Joseph J. Lewis, 15 Feb. 1864, General Correspondence, ser. 99, SC, Records of or Relating to Direct Tax Commissions in the Southern States, RG 58 [Z-3]. See also *Freedom*, ser. 1, vol. 3: docs. 44–45.

[25] See below, doc. 4; *Freedom*, ser. 1, vol. 3: doc. 40.

"Vagrants or Contrabands." In the District of Columbia, where federal officers had initially lodged fugitive slaves in a jail, it seemed fitting to select Danforth B. Nichols, who had once directed a Chicago reformatory, as superintendent of contrabands.[26] Nowhere, however, did Northern reformers play a more prominent role than in the South Carolina Sea Islands.

During the first weeks after the arrival of Union troops, Sea Island slaves supported themselves from the corn and potatoes they had recently harvested and from the larders abandoned by their fugitive owners.[27] But soon, looking to the future, they also began to prepare the fields for a new year's cultivation. Placing their highest premium upon subsistence, they showed no interest in picking the cotton still in the fields or ginning what had already been harvested. Neither had they any intention of planting anew the crop that had "enriched [their] masters but had not fed them."[28]

Although the freedpeople ignored cotton, cotton would not be ignored. War-induced shortage of the staple had driven its price to record levels, and the long-staple cotton of the Sea Islands fetched the highest price of all. The partly harvested crop of 1861 immediately drew the notice of Treasury Department agents, who espied a source of revenue for the Union war effort. While the agents urged the freedpeople to gather the cotton still in the fields, offering to pay them for the work, Northern entrepreneurs clamored for an opportunity to operate the plantations the following year.[29]

To abolitionists, far more was at stake than public revenue and private profit. Inspired by the opportunity to institute free labor on the plantations of some of the South's most notorious rebels, they mobilized under the direction of Edward L. Pierce, a Boston attorney who had briefly supervised former slaves near Fortress Monroe. In February 1862, Secretary of the Treasury Salmon P. Chase – who construed his authority over trade in the occupied South to include operation of the Sea Island estates – appointed Pierce a special agent to oversee cultivation of the 1862 crop and guide the transformation of slaves into free workers. Assisted by freedmen's aid societies in Boston, New York, and Philadelphia, Pierce selected some fifty men to supervise the plantations. A contingent of ministers, teachers, and physicians also joined the enterprise. By March 1862, the flower of Northern abolitionism – young men

---

[26] See below, docs. 4n., 60. In coastal North Carolina, Vincent Colyer, who in 1862 had charge of both fugitive slaves and white refugees, was given the title "Superintendent of the Poor." (See below, doc. 7.)

[27] On the Sea Islands under Union occupation, see Rose, *Rehearsal for Reconstruction*; Julie Saville, "A Measure of Freedom: From Slave to Wage Laborer in South Carolina, 1860–1868" (Ph.D. diss., Yale University, 1986), chap. 2; *Freedom*, ser. 1, vol. 3: chap. 1.

[28] *Freedom*, ser. 1, vol. 3: docs. 4, 8, 19, 21.

[29] *Freedom*, ser. 1, vol. 3: docs. 3, 5–7.

and women whose mission earned them the sobriquet "Gideonites" – had taken up stations in the Sea Islands.[30]

Prepared to introduce former slaves to the rigors of free labor, the plantation superintendents discovered that their charges had already initiated a new order of their own. To be sure, Sea Island freedpeople generally welcomed the interlopers. They eagerly attended the Gideonites' schools and churches and accepted their gifts of clothing, medicine, and other supplies. But the former slaves contested the newcomers' belief that freedom could be validated only through the cultivation of cotton for wages. Although some plantation superintendents discerned a laudable "republican spirit" in the old slave quarters, they feared that the former slaves would retreat into mere self-sufficiency. Eager to demonstrate the efficiency of free labor in growing cotton and dependent upon revenue from the staple to fund their "experiment," the Northerners insisted that the former slaves take their accustomed place in the cotton fields. When the freedpeople were slow to comply, the superintendents did not hesitate to deny them rations.[31]

The exigencies of war rapidly eroded the sources of subsistence that had enabled the freedpeople to decline work in the cotton fields. Confederate troops raided outlying islands with alarming frequency. Even when they failed to capture and reenslave the inhabitants, the rebels succeeded in ravaging the plantations, burning houses, and carrying off food and livestock. In the wake of such raids, federal commanders relocated former slaves from endangered localities to the more secure islands around Port Royal Sound. There they were forced to rely upon the government for food and shelter. Northern soldiers and sailors also laid claim to the property and people on Sea Island plantations. On numerous islands, uniformed Yankees both with and without authorization stripped the estates of useful items. Military employers and Treasury Department cotton agents detailed hands to suit their own needs and convenience, leaving many plantations to be worked largely by women, children, and old people. When fugitive slaves arrived from the mainland, officials quickly siphoned off able-bodied men for military labor and remanded all others to the plantations. The destitute new arrivals added to the burdens of the resident plantation population. Having begun the year with high hopes of subsisting themselves through their own self-directed labor, freedpeople found their goal increasingly difficult to achieve.[32]

Former slaves elsewhere in the South faced many of the same difficul-

---

[30] *Freedom,* ser. 1, vol. 3: docs. 8, 10, 36; Edward L. Pierce, "Persons recommended by the 'Educational Commission' of Boston . . ." and "Persons approved by the 'National Freedman's Relief Association' of New York . . . ," [Mar. 1862], vol. 19, #80, Port Royal Correspondence, 5th Agency, RG 366 [Q-9]; Rose, *Rehearsal for Reconstruction,* chap. 2.

[31] *Freedom,* ser. 1, vol. 3: docs. 10–11, 13, 21.

[32] *Freedom,* ser. 1, vol. 3: docs. 2, 8, 11–13, 21.

ties, and their numbers grew rapidly when the federal army launched its spring campaign. Invasion of coastal North Carolina in March 1862 resulted in the establishment of Union posts at Roanoke Island, New Berne, and other points on the perimeter of Pamlico and Albemarle sounds. By April, army and navy operations had brought additional South Carolina Sea Islands into the Union fold, along with a few Georgia islands and small coastal enclaves at Fernandina and St. Augustine, in northern Florida. Events moved more quickly, and with more momentous implications, in the western theater. By early spring, forces of the Department of the Gulf commanded by General Butler had captured New Orleans and the southern Louisiana parishes between the city and the Gulf of Mexico. At about the same time, federal armies farther north embarked from winter quarters in Kentucky and Missouri for a three-pronged offensive into Arkansas and Tennessee. By midsummer 1862, the Union army had established major posts at Nashville and Memphis, Tennessee; Helena, Arkansas; Huntsville, Alabama; and Corinth, Mississippi; as well as lesser points along strategic waterways and railroads. These operations in the western theater left Union forces well situated for further strikes into the Confederate interior.

As federal troops advanced, slaves gained their freedom under circumstances as different from each other as they were from those in the Sea Islands. In southern Louisiana, many slaveholders fled their estates, but a substantial proportion remained, proclaiming loyalty to the United States government and demanding that it sustain the slave regime. Eager to reassure slaveholding unionists, General Butler acceded to their entreaties during the first months of occupation. But before long, slaves had successfully challenged their owners and undermined Butler's policy. By the fall of 1862, slave insubordination and flight had disrupted the old order in the sugar parishes and forced Butler to reorganize plantation labor, requiring planters to pay wages and employing federal troops to enforce labor discipline. Taking the pragmatic stand that such intervention was necessary to save the region's crop, control unruly black workers, and restore peace in the countryside, Butler pushed legal slavery to the edge but stopped short of outright emancipation.[33]

As was true in southern Louisiana, the agricultural year was well under way when federal forces secured footholds in middle and west Tennessee, eastern Arkansas, northern Mississippi, and northern Alabama. Many slaveholders remained in residence, although few possessed the unionist credentials of their counterparts in the sugar parishes. In the vicinity of Union posts, slavery retreated and free labor slowly began to emerge. Federal installations became magnets for fugitive slaves. Most of

[33] On Union occupation and the undermining of slavery in southern Louisiana, see *Freedom*, ser. 1, vol. 1: chap. 4. On wartime labor arrangements, see *Freedom*, ser. 1, vol. 3: chap. 2.

them were young men who had left their families behind. Although they arrived tired and hungry, they were ready to do whatever was necessary to gain freedom and protection.[34]

Federal commanders had plenty for them to do. With the expansion of Union-held territory during the spring and summer of 1862, the army and navy experienced persistent shortages of laborers. Setting aside reservations about the employment of former slaves, quartermaster, commissary, and engineer officers hired freedmen as artisans, teamsters, and common laborers. Medical officers put freedwomen to work as nurses and laundresses and freedmen as hospital attendants. Individual officers and common soldiers found countless jobs for both men and women, from policing camps to washing clothes and preparing food.

The employment of black laborers received growing support from Washington. As hopes of quick victory and easy reunification dwindled, Lincoln and his advisers became convinced that defeating the rebellion demanded more than the mobilization of Southern white unionists and the conversion of deluded secessionists. It required the destruction of Southern armies, occupation of substantial territory in the Confederate states, and demoralization of those who supported the rebellion. To achieve these goals, the Union needed all the help it could get. "It is a military necessity to have men and money," the President observed in July 1862, "and we can get neither in sufficient numbers or amounts if we keep from or drive from our lines slaves coming to them."[35]

That same month, the Congress and the President ratified the practice of accepting fugitive slaves into Union lines and putting them to work. The Second Confiscation Act and the Militia Act, both enacted on July 17, 1862, declared free the slaves of disloyal owners, authorized the President to mobilize "persons of African descent" against the rebellion, and granted freedom to any slave so employed. Within days, Lincoln ordered his commanders in the seceded states to "employ as laborers" as many black people "as can be advantageously used for military and naval purposes, giving them reasonable wages for their labor."[36] By the fall of 1862, the Union war effort rested in large measure upon the labor of former slaves. That dependence enabled federal commanders at last to comprehend abolitionist arithmetic: Every slave employed by the army or navy represented a double gain, one subtracted from the Confederacy and one added to the Union. Some

---

[34] On military developments and the destruction of slavery in the Mississippi Valley (including middle and east Tennessee and northern Alabama), see *Freedom*, ser. 1, vol. 1: chap. 5. Wartime labor arrangements in Union-occupied territory along the Mississippi River are considered in *Freedom*, ser. 1, vol. 3: chap. 3; those in middle and east Tennessee and northern Alabama are treated separately below, in chap. 3.

[35] *Official Records*, ser. 1, vol. 53, pp. 529–30.

[36] *Statutes at Large*, vol. 12, pp. 589–92, 597–600; *Official Records*, ser. 3, vol. 2, p. 397.

officers learned the lesson too well, adopting dragnet methods of labor recruitment. Slave men who had once begged to enter federal camps found themselves dragooned into service by *"forcible persuasion."*[37]

Most former slaves needed no coaxing. Understanding the connection between Union victory and their own liberty, large numbers volunteered for military labor. Freedpeople in coastal North Carolina, reported one military superintendent, "consider it a duty to work for the U.S. government" and "tabooed" any of their fellows who refused to do so. Accustomed to long workdays under hard taskmasters and eager to secure their freedom, former slaves tolerated conditions that other workers would not. Irish laborers brought to Fortress Monroe, noted Charles Wilder, "are crabbed and will work only so many hours a day." Freedmen, by contrast, "if they are decently paid . . . will work nights or any time and do any thing you want done."[38]

That commitment convinced numerous military employers of the superiority of black workers over Northern and immigrant laborers, and especially over soldiers. Among such employers in the Mississippi Valley, reported a superintendent of contrabands, "the lowest estimate is . . . that one negro is worth three soldiers." Union officers commonly rationalized their preference for black laborers with stereotypes of African docility or the putative ability of black people to withstand the subtropical sun and lowland diseases. While these notions obscured both the commitment of the former slaves to the Union cause and their desperate circumstances, they also reflected the centrality of black workers to the federal war effort.[39]

Military labor assumed different forms, each with its own implications for the ex-slave employees. Thousands of fugitive slaves found work as personal servants to Union officers or soldiers, or hired on as company cooks or regimental laundresses. So prevalent was the employment of black servants at Helena, Arkansas, in the summer of 1862 that it seemed as if "[e]very other soldier" had one. Living in close quarters and sharing the rigors and camaraderie of camp life, servants often developed strong personal relationships with their employers. Yankee soldiers who hired black men and women simply because "we can get no others" frequently found that they had come to "like them as servants . . . and to feel an interest in their welfare." Such connections offered fugitive slaves a measure of protection from pursuing owners, as well as from hostile Northern soldiers. That same personal dependency also rendered black servants liable to exploitation by their employers, some of whom demanded the performance of degrading duties, refused to pay agreed-upon compensation, or inflicted physical abuse. Women were especially vulnerable to sexual assault. Yet the promise of protec-

---

[37] On the impressment of black laborers, see, for example, below, docs. 19–20, 25.
[38] See below, docs. 7, 16.
[39] See below, docs. 27, 62, 206; *Freedom*, ser. 1, vol. 3: doc. 159.

tion counterbalanced such risks, especially during the first year of the war when the status of fugitive slaves remained largely undefined.[40]

While thousands of former slaves worked as servants, tens of thousands toiled as common laborers. They performed the army's most taxing, tedious, and dangerous tasks: building fortifications, felling trees, constructing roads, laying railroad track, repairing levees, and digging canals. Laborious even under the best of circumstances, such work was often done double-time, in unhealthy surroundings, and under hostile fire. Supervisors drove the workers hard and frequently afforded them insufficient rest and food. Such usage took its toll, as debilitated workers fell prey to disease. At one post in southern Louisiana, where federal officers had assumed authority over the maintenance of levees, military laborers toiled for three long months without a single day's rest. Shoeless, clad in rags, living in filthy quarters, and given meager rations of rice and sugar, the laborers endured conditions that moved one Northern officer to declare, "*My cattle at home are better cared for than these unfortunate persons.*"[41]

Unlike personal servants, who usually worked for individual employers, laborers stood at the bottom of a vast hierarchy. Most worked in large groups, sometimes encompassing several hundred men (and, occasionally, a smattering of women). In their sheer size, such units exceeded all but the largest field forces in the slave South and rivaled the huge labor gangs on the great antebellum canal and railroad projects. Working under the immediate supervision of white overseers or foremen – usually civilians or junior officers – black gang workers seldom knew the higher-ranking officers who employed them. They were subject to an impersonal regimentation and discipline resembling that of unskilled factory operatives. Engineer employees at Fort Clinch, Florida, wore numbers on their hats to simplify monitoring the work completed by each hand.[42] Such impersonality distanced workers from their bosses. It also encouraged a solidarity with their fellow workers that, among other things, facilitated collective protest against unacceptable conditions.

Many black military workers endured neither the suffocating closeness experienced by personal servants nor the regimentation of gang laborers. Instead, they worked singly or in small groups, driving teams, caring for sick and wounded soldiers, and performing a host of other duties. Like other military laborers, these freedpeople found themselves assigned to tasks shunned by others. Army medical authorities in Washington, for example, put black men to work "cleansing cesspools,

---

[40] See below, doc. 119B; *Freedom*, ser. 1, vol. 1: docs. 158, 160B; *Freedom*, ser. 1, vol. 3: docs. 150, 157, 160.

[41] See below, docs. 4, 52, 90, 102; *Freedom*, ser. 1, vol. 3: doc. 80.

[42] On the scale and organization of military labor gangs, see below, docs. 52, 90, 102–3; *Freedom*, ser. 1, vol. 3: doc. 24.

scrubbing privies and policing the grounds"—work white civilians spurned and soldiers performed only "under the fear of punishment."[43] The hours were as long as the labor was arduous, especially when "military necessity" demanded prompt completion of a job.

Whether they toiled indoors or out, individually or in gangs, black men and women often found that their work for military employers failed to fulfill the most elemental promise of free labor—compensation. Unlike most Northern wage-labor arrangements, in which workers were responsible for purchasing their own and their families' necessities, military labor was generally accompanied by a guarantee of subsistence in the form of rations and sometimes clothing and shelter. Many military employers made similar provision for the immediate families of their employees, usually deducting the cost from the laborers' wages. Former-slave and free-black military laborers, who had few other resources with which to provide for their families, relied heavily on such allowances. Some federal officers therefore reckoned that the boon of freedom, plus nonmonetary remuneration, was compensation enough. Rejecting the appeal of one group of black military laborers for wages, Quartermaster General Montgomery C. Meigs contended that "[s]ustenance & freedom given at great cost by the United States has fully compensated" the claimants.[44]

For many ex-slaves fresh from bondage, sustenance and freedom were compensation enough, at least at first. But even on Meigs's terms, freedpeople found reason to complain. The quality of rations and clothing issued by military employers often fell below what their owners had provided. Even if rations and clothing were furnished to black workers' families, they still required money to meet other expenses, and whenever military laborers had to purchase their families' subsistence, they depended on regular wages.

Few federal officials recognized the depth of this dependence. Confusion within various government bureaus, as well as simple negligence, kept many laborers from receiving compensation. Because of faulty record keeping, hundreds of black men who worked at Fortress Monroe during the first months of the war were still awaiting their wages at war's end. Negligence was compounded by corruption, as the freed-people's illiteracy and incomplete documentation of their employment made them easy targets for dishonest employers and paymasters. Often, however, the problem stemmed from the enormous wartime strain on the national treasury. At times, the army simply could not meet its payroll.[45]

The complexity of federal policy also contributed to difficulties in

[43] See below, docs. 65A–B; *Freedom*, ser. 1, vol. 3: doc. 20.
[44] For examples of the monetary and nonmonetary compensation of black military laborers, see below, docs. 2–3, 54–55, 87n.; *Freedom*, ser. 1, vol. 3: docs. 8, 15, 24, 64–65, 148, 160.
[45] See below, docs. 1, 12, 14, 17, 20, 59A, 87; *Freedom*, ser. 1, vol. 3: docs. 157–58, 160, 226.

paying military laborers. The Militia Act stipulated that black military laborers were entitled to rations and wages of $10 per month (minus $3 for clothing), and Lincoln's executive order called for payment of "reasonable wages." But the law also stipulated that "in proper cases," compensation might be made to loyal slaveholders.[46] Pending official determination of which cases were "proper," many military employers hesitated to pay laborers whose owners might yet enter a claim. In some places, especially in the border states, paymasters issued vouchers or wages to putative owners rather than to the workers themselves. Such procedures made one military employer "ashamed to look a negro in the face." Indefinite and sometimes contradictory instructions from Washington and from field commanders put military employers in an awkward position, because army and navy regulations made them personally liable for improper expenditures. Even officers who wished to pay their workers fully and fairly could not do so without the authorization of superiors and, when proper records were lacking, could not do so at all.[47]

Newly arrived fugitives might endure such shabby treatment for a time, out of gratitude for freedom and the protection of federal arms. But before long, the hard work, the abuse, and the inability to support themselves and their families drove many of them away. Much to the disgust of military employers, black workers "deserted" in large numbers to find employers who would treat them decently and pay them regularly.[48]

While affording large numbers of former slaves employment with the Northern army or navy, Union occupation also created opportunities for free labor on different terms. A federal presence over the ridge or around the bend enabled slaves to negotiate new conditions of labor with their masters and mistresses. The slaves pressed for working arrangements that accorded them a measure of self-direction, increased their access to the resources of farms and plantations, or provided compensation. A good many slaveholders met such demands, knowing that if they refused, their slaves would leave them to work for the Yankees. Other farmers and planters, who despaired of making a crop under wartime conditions, abandoned their estates. Often they left their property in the custody of their slaves, who were promised that they could keep a portion – sometimes the entirety – of what they produced. Desperate to salvage some financial return, a few slaveholders

---

[46] *Statutes at Large*, vol. 12, pp. 597–600; *Official Records*, ser. 3, vol. 2, p. 397; *Freedom*, ser. 2: doc. 64.

[47] On complications involving payment of wages to the owners of military laborers who were legally still slaves, see below, docs. 92, 99, 103, 132, 217; *Freedom*, ser. 1, vol. 1: doc. 26B; *Freedom*, ser. 1, vol. 3: doc. 148.

[48] On turnover among military laborers, see, for example, below, docs. 3, 16, 56, 92; *Freedom*, ser. 1, vol. 3: docs. 157, 182.

renounced slavery altogether and rented land to their former slaves. Other intrepid ex-slaves did not depend upon negotiation to attain independent occupation of land. They simply squatted on abandoned tracts.[49]

Wherever and by whatever means freedpeople secured a chance to farm independently, they demonstrated a preference for food production similar to that exhibited by former slaves in the Sea Islands. They cultivated fields of corn or other grains, planted gardens, raised poultry, and hunted, fished, and foraged in the wild. At times they availed themselves of the smokehouses, corncribs, and poultry yards of the estates, or appropriated hogs ranging in the forests and swamps. As their crops matured, many of them sold or bartered their surplus with Yankee soldiers, neighboring farmers, or the residents of nearby towns. Independent occupation of land could entail a rugged and dangerous existence, especially in disputed territory, but those ex-slaves who managed to gain a foothold clung to their hard-won independence.

In some places, military officials supported the freedpeople's attempts to farm on their own. Charles B. Wilder legitimated the self-organized settlements just inside federal lines in tidewater Virginia, and he permitted other fugitives to "cultivate the Ground and use the property of Rebels in Arms against the Government." At Helena, Arkansas, General Samuel R. Curtis, commander of the Army of the Southwest, went a step further. Deeming the former slaves who had remained on nearby plantations to be the rightful owners of the cotton they had grown as slaves, he and other officers paid them for whatever they brought in. Curtis's policy permitted former slaves to support themselves on the old estates and gave them a small endowment of capital with which to begin their lives in freedom. But Wilder and Curtis had few imitators among federal officials in the occupied South. A military court of inquiry chastised Curtis for his actions.[50]

The war made it difficult and dangerous for freedpeople to farm on their own. Independent black farmers drew the ire of neighboring slaveholders, who attacked them personally or enlisted Confederate raiders to do so. Union troops foraged in the freedpeople's fields, gardens, and stockpens, and sometimes dismantled buildings in which they had taken refuge. Even under agreements with former owners and with guarantees of federal protection, independent black farmers stood on precarious ground, as new terms of employment could revert to the old when lines of military occupation shifted. Nonetheless, a handful of black men and women braved the danger to gain the independence they

---

[49] See below, docs. 112–13, 116–17, 127; *Freedom*, ser. 1, vol. 1: doc. 123; *Freedom*, ser. 1, vol. 3: docs. 104–5, 156.

[50] On Wilder, see below, doc. 5. On Curtis, see *Freedom*, ser. 1, vol. 3: doc. 151.

had long desired. Believing themselves entitled to the land, they some-times took up arms against those who contested their right to it.[51]

Former slaves in the Union-occupied zones who could not or dared not farm independently sought other ways to earn a living. For all its attendant hardships, the war allowed many freedpeople new latitude to pursue self-directed activities. Army camps and garrisons housed cus-tomers aplenty for anyone with cordwood, meat, fish, produce, milk, eggs, or baked goods to sell. Similarly, Union occupation created an unprecedented demand for wood to fuel the engines of steamers and locomotives. Black men and women who as slaves had occasionally sold food or wood now did so routinely, and some managed to support themselves entirely by huckstering or wood chopping. At military posts, where men generally outnumbered women several times over, freedwomen took in laundry or cooked for soldiers; some turned to prostitution to support themselves and their families.[52]

Pursuit of such opportunities often drew former slaves from the countryside. Cities in the Union-occupied South expanded rapidly, particularly those like Washington and Nashville that served as bases for Northern military operations. Their warehouses, arsenals, repair shops, stables, and naval yards employed tens of thousands. Freed-people in these and other cities and towns also found work catering to enlarged civilian and military populations as barbers, stable keepers, draymen, laundresses, cooks, and domestic servants. The wartime boom allowed some of them to establish businesses of their own. Car-penters became contractors, draymen established their own stables, and cooks opened small restaurants or saloons. Former slaves who lacked marketable skills frequently tried to earn an independent livelihood as peddlers. Some of this entrepreneurship stood outside the law. Cook-shops and groceries could serve as fronts for illicit trade, in which contraband or proscribed articles were exchanged for other goods or for cash.[53]

Union-occupied cities and towns emerged as centers of black institu-tional life. Long-established black churches gained new standing, and Northern missionaries – black and white – founded new congregations.

---

[51] See below, docs. 12, 112, 116, 127; *Freedom*, ser. 1, vol. 1: docs. 20, 25A–B; *Freedom*, ser. 1, vol. 3: docs. 23, 91, 97, 104, 114, 156.

[52] See, for example, below, docs. 7–8, 17, 58; *Freedom*, ser. 1, vol. 3: doc. 212.

[53] On black petty proprietors, see below, docs. 10, 20, 97–98, 118. Useful studies of Southern cities under Union occupation include Peter Maslowski, *Treason Must Be Made Odious: Military Occupation and Wartime Reconstruction in Nashville, Tennessee, 1862–65* (Millwood, N.Y., 1978), chap. 6; James T. Currie, *Enclave: Vicksburg and Her Plantations 1863–1870* (Jackson, Miss., 1980), especially chaps. 1–2; Gerald M. Capers, *Occupied City: New Orleans under the Federals, 1862–1865* (Lexington, Ky., 1965), especially chap. 10; Constance McLaughlin Green, *Washington: Village and Capital, 1800–1878* (Princeton, N.J., 1962), chaps. 10–11, and *The Secret City: A History of Race Relations in the Nation's Capital* (Princeton, N.J., 1967), chaps. 4–5.

Churches both old and new sponsored schools where former slaves could gain the rudiments of literacy. Mutual-aid societies and other associations took shape to address the particular concerns of members and the general concerns of former slaves at large. In these organized settings, and less formally wherever freedpeople congregated, they discussed old times and new possibilities. By such exchanges, they apprised each other of the going wages, the reputations of various employers, and the opportunities for self-employment.[54]

Yet life in the cities and towns was no easier than in the countryside. Although wages were high, wartime inflation drove prices higher. Even in Washington, where most black military laborers were paid $25 per month, more than twice the rate specified by the Militia Act, former slaves and free blacks had a difficult time making ends meet. Heavy migration swelled urban populations so that the number of workers outpaced expanding employment, creating pitiless competition. Women found their opportunities especially limited and their pay inadequate to support themselves, much less children and other dependents. Former slaves—like other rural migrants—discovered urban housing to be scarce and expensive. The shortage of housing forced black people to reside in alleys, outbuildings, or shanties on the edge of town. Crowded and lacking clean water or sanitary facilities, such quarters bred disease, fueling frightful mortality and driving many black city-dwellers back to the countryside.[55]

In city and countryside alike, the changing composition of the fugitive-slave population added to the freedpeople's woes. Beginning in the fall of 1862, the government's guarantee of freedom for all who reached Union lines encouraged slaves to flee not individually or in small groups, but en masse. The arrival of families, and sometimes entire plantation units, increased the number of women, children, and old people under federal jurisdiction. The approach of winter added to the rush, as tens of thousands of fugitive slaves made for Union lines in hopes of obtaining food, shelter, and protection during the cold months.[56]

Many Northern officers welcomed the families of black men and women who labored for the government. They offered them shelter and rations not only as a matter of justice, but also because the able-bodied freedpeople would not work if their families were neglected or abused. But other officers saw their employees' dependents as impediments to

---

[54] On urban schools and churches, see below, docs. 30–31, 102, 170–72. On benevolent societies, see below, docs. 30, 84.

[55] On urban living conditions, see below, docs. 17, 30, 53, 55–57, 59A–B, 64, 66, 76, 179n.; *Freedom*, ser. 1, vol. 1: doc. 107.

[56] On the changing character of the fugitive-slave population in late 1862, see *Freedom*, ser. 1, vol. 1: pp. 32–34. See also *Freedom*, ser. 1, vol. 3: docs. 71, 152–54.

efficient military operations. Such officials made no provision for their support and did much to discourage them—damning the women as whores and the parents and children as so many "useless mouths."[57] Despite the abuse, the women, children, and old people remained, erecting makeshift villages and scratching out a living as best they could. Their stolid persistence forced federal officials in the field and in Washington to reconsider the "contraband question."

As they had before the war, numerous white Northerners proposed removing former slaves from the United States. From the founding of the Republic, some white Americans had advocated the "repatriation" of black people—particularly free blacks—to Africa or their removal to another nation in the Americas. During the antebellum years, proponents of "colonization" had promoted Liberia as a home for free blacks and manumitted slaves. Despite the vehement opposition of the vast majority of black people, colonizationist sentiment continued to find considerable support among antislavery politicians and their constituents.[58]

Among the proponents of removal was Abraham Lincoln. During the first year of the war, the President entertained various proposals from foreign nations and private individuals concerning colonization, and in December 1861 he recommended that the government acquire territory outside the United States in which to resettle slaves freed by the First Confiscation Act. Prodded by Lincoln, Congress enacted several measures in support of colonization during the spring and summer of 1862. In April, the law emancipating slaves in the District of Columbia set aside $100,000 to defray the cost of relocating any black people in the District who might "desire to emigrate to the Republics of Hayti or Liberia, or such other country . . . as the President may determine." Subsequent legislation appropriated additional funds for colonization, and the President frequently pledged federal assistance in removing emancipated slaves and free blacks.[59]

Although most black people spurned colonization, a few held so dim a view of their prospects in the United States that it seemed an attractive possibility. During the 1850s, support for emigration had grown among free blacks, who faced harsh discriminatory legislation throughout the nation, mob violence in the North, and threats of deportation and enslavement in the South. While suspicious of the colonizationists' mo-

[57] *Official Records*, ser. 1, vol. 6, pp. 201–3.
[58] On the colonization movement during the late antebellum and wartime years, see P. J. Staudenraus, *The African Colonization Movement, 1816–1865* (New York, 1961); Floyd J. Miller, *The Search for a Black Nationality: Black Emigration and Colonization, 1787–1863* (Urbana, Ill., 1975); Willis D. Boyd, "Negro Colonization in the National Crisis, 1860–1870" (Ph.D. diss., University of California, Los Angeles, 1953).
[59] Jason H. Silverman, " 'In the Isles beyond the Main': Abraham Lincoln's Philosophy on Black Colonization," *Lincoln Herald* 80 (Fall 1978): 115–21; Lincoln, *Collected Works*, vol. 5, pp. 35–53; *Statutes at Large*, vol. 12, pp. 376–78, 422–26, 589–92.

tives, a number of black men and women tried to turn the wartime legislation and the President's proposals to their own purposes. In April 1862, just days after slavery was abolished in the District of Columbia, at least sixty free blacks petitioned Congress to provide a homeland in Central America where they could "secure, by their own industry, that mental and physical development which will allow them an honorable position in the families of God's great world." But the growing Northern commitment to emancipation, embodied in the Second Confiscation Act and in Lincoln's preliminary Emancipation Proclamation, rapidly deflated such sentiment.[60] By the end of 1862, virtually all black Americans had rejected emigration.

While colonization foundered, the transfer of "surplus" contrabands to the North seemed more practical. In the absence of instructions from Washington, some military commanders saw the relocation of former slaves as a convenient way to rid themselves of people who clogged their lines, devoured their supplies, and demoralized their soldiers. Besides, "help" was increasingly hard to find in the free states, as the military enlistment of white men shrank the civilian labor force. Accordingly, in September 1862, General Ulysses S. Grant, commander of the Department of the Tennessee, proposed to transport former slaves from Union encampments in the Mississippi Valley to Cairo, Illinois, where arrangements had been made to hire them to civilian employers. About the same time, General John A. Dix, commander of the Department of Virginia, asked the governors of several northeastern states to receive some of the contrabands who had accumulated at Fortress Monroe.[61]

Initially Grant's proposal received approval from the War Department. But the merest whisper that former slaves were to be shipped North evoked impassioned protest in the free states, some of which had erected legal barriers against the immigration of black people. Hostility to such migration crested during the latter half of 1862, as Democrats exploited the "Negro Influx Question" in state and congressional elections. Fearful that federal sponsorship of migration would undermine support for the war, Republican politicians made their objections known to the Lincoln administration. Even abolitionists like John A. Andrew, governor of Massachusetts, opposed the relocation of black people from the slave states. Andrew objected on the grounds that black men should remain in the South and be armed as soldiers, but

---

[60] For the petition from free blacks in the District of Columbia, see below, doc. 51. On opposition by black people to wartime colonization, see William Seraile, "Afro-American Emigration to Haiti during the American Civil War," *The Americas* 35 (Oct. 1978): 185–200; Ira Berlin, Wayne K. Durrill, Steven F. Miller, Leslie S. Rowland, and Leslie Schwalm, " 'To Canvass the Nation': The War for Union Becomes a War for Freedom," *Prologue* 20 (Winter 1988): 241–42.

[61] *Official Records*, ser. 3, vol. 2, p. 569; see below, doc. 11; *Freedom*, ser. 1, vol. 3: doc. 154; *Freedom*, ser. 2: doc. 41n.

other Republican leaders cared only that freedpeople stay out of the North.[62]

Determined not to be outflanked by racist Democrats, the Lincoln administration squelched proposals to settle former slaves in the free states. Secretary of War Edwin M. Stanton, who had approved Grant's plan, abruptly reversed himself. After Governor Andrew exposed Dix's scheme to public view, Dix let the matter drop. In his annual report of December 1862, Stanton assured the Northern public that "no colored man will leave his home in the South if protected in that home"; putting freedpeople to work in the South would ensure that they had "neither occasion nor temptation . . . to emigrate to a northern and less congenial climate."[63] By the end of 1862, the Lincoln administration had decided that whatever the fate of the former slaves, it would be in the South.

Unable or unwilling to ship former slaves to Africa, to Central America, or to the North, Union military commanders sought means to support them within the occupied South. From the outset, the war had created unprecedented relief problems, and the number of displaced and destitute people – black and white – increased exponentially as continued fighting suspended agricultural production, disrupted local economies, and sent refugees in search of a safe haven. As Union forces occupied Confederate territory, army rations constituted the principal form of aid to impoverished civilians. Whatever the justice of providing relief from federal coffers, other demands upon the treasury encouraged both niggardly assistance and a determination to find alternative sources of support. Northern churches and aid societies assumed part of the burden, but private charity could not begin to meet the need. In some places, Union commanders levied special assessments upon prominent secessionists, on the theory that those who had caused the rebellion should help alleviate the consequent suffering. Such assessments, however, were both locally unpopular and difficult to enforce. More important, they, too, were inadequate to the task. With respect to relief for former slaves, federal officials turned increasingly to the idea that able-bodied freedpeople who succeeded in finding employment should be required to support those who remained dependent and unemployed.[64]

---

[62] See below, doc. 13; *Freedom*, ser. 2: doc. 41. On Northern opposition to immigration by former slaves, see V. Jacque Voegeli, *Free But Not Equal: The Midwest and the Negro during the Civil War* (Chicago, 1967), chap. 4; *Freedom*, ser. 2: docs. 30, 194. One Northerner proposed to keep former slaves out of the free states by hiring them to " 'poor white' Southrons," who would be allowed to purchase forty-acre plots from confiscated plantations. Such a solution, he argued, would retain the former slaves' "trained labor on cotton & tobacco." (Robert A. Maxwell, "To Save Fall elections on Negro Influx Question," 25 July 1862, Miscellaneous Letters Received: K Series, ser. 103, RG 56 [X-243].)

[63] *Official Records*, ser. 3, vol. 2, pp. 663, 897–912.

[64] Bremner, *The Public Good*, pp. 91–92. For examples of assessments upon secessionists, see *Official Records*, ser. 1, vol. 15, pp. 538–39, and ser. 3, vol. 2, pp. 720–25, 731–32; Andrew

Generalizing from longstanding Northern welfare policies, some Union officers insisted first that individual families must care for their own. But in the midst of war, it was difficult for former slaves to fulfill these expectations, however much they struggled to do so. Even when families had fled bondage together or were reunited behind Union lines, they were often separated when military authorities redeployed black laborers or relocated their dependents. In such circumstances, federal officials sought to extend the principle of familial obligation. The idea, in the words of one army chaplain, was to "[keep] families together in responsibility if not in fact."[65]

On the assumption that all Southern black people were members of a single community, federal authorities in some jurisdictions charged relief expenses against the earnings of black military laborers. In September 1862, when a quartermaster in west Tennessee requested instructions regarding provision for black women and children, Quartermaster General Meigs urged that a portion of the wages owed to black military laborers be set aside to assist the needy. "The labor of the men & those women able to work," Meigs reasoned, "should support the whole community of negros at any station." Secretary of War Stanton approved. By the same logic, the War Department authorized a $5 monthly deduction from the wages of black military laborers in the District of Columbia and nearby Alexandria, Virginia. Similar assessments were later made upon black wage-earners in other jurisdictions.[66]

Former slaves expected to support their families and frequently went out of their way to assist the needy, even those to whom they bore no kinship obligations. However, black military laborers objected to taxes that took a large portion of their wages. In the District of Columbia, black freemen – many of whom had never been slaves – thought it unfair that the federal government tax them for the benefit of destitute ex-slaves, especially since white workers were not similarly assessed. Authorities brushed aside such protests and continued to take deductions for the "contraband fund."[67]

Revenue realized through these levies defrayed some of the expense of supporting former slaves. However, it went but a small way toward ameliorating the problems of health, sanitation, and housing created by the presence of large numbers of ex-slaves within federal lines. With winter fast upon them, necessity – as well as humanity – impelled field commanders to establish makeshift bivouacs or "contraband camps" for

Johnson, *The Papers of Andrew Johnson*, ed. Leroy P. Graf, Ralph W. Haskins, and Paul H. Bergeron, 8 vols. to date (Knoxville, Tenn., 1967–), vol. 5, pp. 623–25. For an order issued late in the war that proposed to assess "avowed rebel sympathizers" for the care of "sick, helpless, and needy" former slaves, see below, doc. 142.

[65] *Freedom*, ser. 1, vol. 3: doc. 158n.
[66] See below, docs. 54–55; *Freedom*, ser. 1, vol. 3: doc. 153, 166n.
[67] See below, docs. 56, 66, 69–70, 82.

the reception, relief, and employment of black refugees. In doing so, they placed all freedpeople under direct military oversight and simplified the distribution of rations, clothing, and medical supplies. By the end of 1862, large camps had been established at LaGrange, Bolivar, and Memphis in west Tennessee and at Corinth in northern Mississippi. "Contraband colonies" on the outskirts of New Orleans housed several thousand residents. In the eastern theater, Craney Island, near Norfolk, Virginia, was set aside for unemployed contrabands, as was Camp Barker in the District of Columbia, only blocks from the President's mansion.[68]

As they established separate settlements for former slaves, federal commanders assigned subordinate officers to supervise their labor and welfare. Many of the new superintendents of contrabands came from the ranks of army chaplains, including John Eaton, Jr., and most of his subordinates in the Department of the Tennessee. Some, such as Lieutenant George H. Hanks in the Department of the Gulf, were quartermasters whose duties had involved mobilizing black laborers. Nearly all had connections to Northern aid societies, and a few were themselves agents of those societies. The appointment of the superintendents thus conferred official recognition upon some abolitionists and the organizations they represented. Although their formal incorporation into the Union chain of command gave them new authority, it also signified that private philanthropy would play a subaltern role. The superintendents operated within the framework of military bureaucracy and were subject to the dictates of superior officers.[69]

The new superintendents organized residents of the contraband camps into working parties according to age and physical condition. Healthy men and some women were assigned to the quartermaster, commissary, medical, and engineer departments of the army. The remaining women, children, and old and disabled men did what work they could. Virtually every camp required such freedpeople to police grounds, construct and repair buildings, and generally maintain the premises. Beyond that, the character of their labor depended upon the location of the camp and the timing and circumstances of its establishment. Residents of contraband camps in northern Mississippi and west Tennessee harvested cotton under the direction of government overseers, sometimes from abandoned fields, other times from the fields of resident owners who paid the government for the labor. At Camp Barker, in Washington, the superintendents hired hundreds of former slaves to civilian employers, including slaveholders. Some camps were

---

[68] See below, docs. 13n., 17–18, 42, 60; *Freedom*, ser. 1, vol. 3: docs. 64–65, 71, 154–55, 160; Registers of Freedmen at Camp Barker, June 1862–Dec. 1863, ser. 570, Camp Barker DC, RG 105 [A-10092]. See also Cam Walker, "Corinth: The Story of a Contraband Camp," *Civil War History* 20 (Mar. 1974): 5–22.

[69] See below, docs. 4n., 22, 64, 72; *Freedom*, ser. 1, vol. 3: docs. 110, 155, 157n.

poorly situated to provide employment. On desolate Craney Island, there was little but make-work; despite the freedpeople's desire to be "of some account," their superintendent had nothing to offer but unpaid labor refurbishing grain sacks and sewing Union uniforms.[70]

Even in the most favorable circumstances, residents of the contraband camps had to rely upon the government for at least a portion of their livelihood. Not only did the army regularly remove those men and women best able to support themselves and their dependents, but it also made no provision to distribute the earnings of laborers to their relatives and friends. Attempts at self-support were overwhelmed by the continued influx of fugitive slaves. And because most camps were not established until the fall of 1862, their inhabitants could not plant food for immediate consumption. At best, they could forage from nearby woods and abandoned fields.

For all its privations, life in the contraband camps permitted former slaves some latitude in shaping their own lives. Although most residents received only subsistence, some earned modest wages outside the camp, with which they purchased additional food, clothing, and amenities like bibles and schoolbooks or tobacco and liquor. In the camps, many freedpeople reconstituted families separated during slavery or in the travail of war. They eagerly attended schools taught by the agents of Northern aid societies, sympathetic officers and soldiers, or the literate within their own ranks. They organized both informal prayer meetings and formal congregations of the faithful, celebrated weddings, and – all too often – mourned the dead. Freedpeople shouldered much of the responsibility for their own medical care – a considerable burden because disease flourished among the crowded, ill-housed, and malnourished inhabitants of the camps. With army physicians and nurses in short supply, black "aunties" and "grannies" ministered to the sick, applying the healing skills they had learned as slaves. Although rude, the contraband camps were the first home in freedom for many former slaves.[71]

The contraband camps and large-scale employment of black military laborers epitomized the transformation of Union policy toward former slaves. By the end of 1862, the necessity of mobilizing former slaves had become apparent to all but the most intransigent federal officials. In defending the Union, declared Quartermaster General Meigs, "it is impossible to cast aside the millions of recruits who will offer themselves for the work, accustomed to the climate, inured to labor, acquainted with the country, and animated by the strong desire not merely for political but for personal liberty." Secretary of War Stanton urged that the Union "turn against the rebels the productive power that

---

[70] See below, docs. 17–18, 60–61; *Freedom*, ser. 1, vol. 3: doc. 160.
[71] On everyday life in the contraband camps see, for example, below, docs. 17–18, 60–61, 72–74; *Freedom*, ser. 1, vol. 3: docs. 160, 164, 170.

upholds the insurrection." "By striking down this system of compulsory labor, which enables the leaders of the rebellion to control the resources of the people," Stanton intoned, "the rebellion would die of itself."[72]

The Emancipation Proclamation, issued by President Lincoln on New Year's Day, 1863, at once ratified developments of the previous year and set new terms for the subsequent evolution of free labor. The proclamation declared free all slaves in the Confederacy, except those in Tennessee and in the Union-occupied parts of southern Louisiana and tidewater Virginia. Congress had already abolished slavery in the District of Columbia and the western territories. The Militia Act had liberated slaves who worked for the Union army or navy. The Second Confiscation Act had extended freedom to those slaves coming under Union control whose owners were disloyal. Now Lincoln's proclamation made emancipation an official aim of the war. Thenceforward, as federal troops advanced into the Confederate heartland, they marched as agents of freedom.[73]

The Emancipation Proclamation closed some doors as it opened others. Whereas the preliminary proclamation of September 1862 had included the customary pledge to support the removal of freed slaves from the United States, the final edict was silent on the subject. The folly of exiling the very men and women whom Union commanders were trying to mobilize – and who showed no interest in emigrating – seemed increasingly manifest. No less important, the heads of several Central American states had bluntly refused to accept black immigrants. Although Lincoln later gave occasional lip service to colonization, it had become a lost cause. In early 1864 the widely publicized debacle of a government-sanctioned venture in Ile à Vache, Haiti, where unscrupulous Northern promoters abandoned several hundred black emigrants to sicken and die, ended the administration's involvement in such schemes.[74]

While it silently rejected colonization, the Emancipation Proclamation explicitly authorized a larger role for former slaves in the Union war effort. The President enjoined persons freed by the proclamation, "in all cases when allowed, [to] labor faithfully for reasonable wages." More important, he invited black men to support the Union cause as soldiers. Northern free blacks and their abolitionist allies had long viewed military service as a lever for racial equality, as well as a weapon against slavery, and they rushed to accept the President's invitation. In mid-January 1863, Massachusetts Governor Andrew secured permis-

---

[72] *Official Records*, ser. 3, vol. 2, pp. 786–809, 897–912.
[73] For the Emancipation Proclamation, see *Statutes at Large*, vol. 12, pp. 1268–69. For the earlier emancipation measures, see *Statutes at Large*, vol. 12, pp. 376–78, 432, 597–600. For an example of federal officers arming former slaves and sending them back to their home plantations as "*missionaries*" of freedom, see *Freedom*, ser. 1, vol. 1: doc. 101.
[74] Boyd, "Negro Colonization in the National Crisis," chaps. 5, 7, 13.

sion from Secretary of War Stanton to organize a black regiment, and within weeks volunteers from all over the North were enlisting in the 54th Massachusetts Infantry.[75]

As winter turned to spring, events in the North reemphasized the connection between emancipation and the success of federal arms. In March, Congress authorized the enrollment and conscription of Northern white men. The draft created a firestorm of opposition to the Lincoln administration and to the war itself. In part to shift the burden from Northern whites, the War Department moved quickly to enlist black men, expanding recruitment first to free blacks throughout the North and then to Southern slaves liberated by Lincoln's proclamation and congressional emancipation measures. By the end of April, Secretary of War Stanton had dispatched specially commissioned officers to virtually every part of the Union-occupied Confederacy to organize black regiments. Only the border states and middle Tennessee remained off-limits, and they not for long.[76]

With the nation committed to emancipation and black men marching under the American flag, Northerners contemplated a future in which all black people would be free. To plan for that day, Stanton impaneled the American Freedmen's Inquiry Commission in March 1863, instructing its members to recommend "practical measures for placing [the former slaves] in a state of self-support and self-defense, with the least possible disturbance to the great industrial interest of the country," and asking them to suggest how the government might "[render] their services efficient in the present war." In the year that followed, the three commissioners traveled throughout the Union-occupied Confederacy and the border slave states, interviewing military officers, white civilians, free blacks, and former slaves about slavery and freedom, work and property, God and family. In May 1864, the commission submitted its blueprint for reconstructing the South and the nation.[77]

In the meantime, with the beginning of both the spring military campaign and the agricultural season of 1863, the freedpeople's desperate condition required more immediate measures. President Lincoln concluded that it was time for former slaves to start "digging their subsistence out of the ground."[78] His terse formulation struck a sympathetic chord with many Northerners who agreed that the interests of

---

[75] *Statutes at Large*, vol. 12, pp. 1268–69. On the recruitment of black soldiers in the North, see *Freedom*, ser. 2: chap. 2.

[76] On the expansion of recruitment in the North and its extension to the Union-occupied South, see *Freedom*, ser. 2: chaps. 2–3.

[77] *Official Records*, ser. 3, vol. 3, pp. 73–74. For the commission's preliminary and final reports, dated June 30, 1863, and May 15, 1864, see *Official Records*, ser. 3, vol. 3, pp. 430–54, and ser. 3, vol. 4, pp. 289–382. An excerpt from a supplement to the final report is printed in *Freedom*, ser. 1, vol. 3: doc. 115.

[78] *Freedom*, ser. 1, vol. 1: doc. 107.

the Union and of the freedpeople themselves would be best served by putting them to work on land abandoned by their erstwhile owners. In the view of Secretary of War Stanton, the loyalty of former slaves and the treason of their former owners made it both right and necessary to give black people "protection and employment upon the soil which they have thus far cultivated, and the right to which has been vacated by the original proprietors."[79]

Putting the freedpeople to work on abandoned plantations promised to solve many of the problems created by fighting a war for both national unity and universal liberty. By providing former slaves with a way to earn their own food, clothing, and shelter, it would reduce federal expenditures for relief. The resumption of cotton production would stoke the Northern economy and return revenue to the national treasury via wartime taxes on the staple and on commerce in the occupied zones. Furthermore, it would speed the transformation of slaves into free workers. Liberated by the President's proclamation, former slaves would learn to labor for wages in the Union-occupied South.

Its many advantages notwithstanding, the decision to establish freedpeople on abandoned plantations and farms raised numerous practical questions. One of the most important involved ownership of the land. Beyond the customary practices of war, which sanctioned the use of captured property for military purposes, Congress had given President Lincoln the legal means to effect lasting changes in Southern landholding. The Second Confiscation Act, which permitted the government to seize real and personal property belonging to disloyal citizens and sell it to loyal ones, provided one tool, but an unwieldy one. Confiscation required formal proceedings in federal courts, which had ceased to function in the seceded states. Moreover, the President had the power to pardon individual rebels, and, at his insistence, Congress had adopted an "explanatory resolution" prohibiting forfeiture of land beyond the life of the offender. Like most Northerners, Lincoln had no taste for wholesale expropriation and, even in wartime, remained wary of any seizure of property by the state.[80]

The Direct Tax Act of June 1862 offered a more straightforward way to transform property holding. In order to collect in the seceded states a federal tax that had been levied upon each state in 1861, the act provided for assessments on individual parcels of land, which would be forfeited to the government if the owner failed to pay. Tax commissioners, appointed by the President for each insurrectionary state, would then assume control, with authority to rent out the property or to

---

[79] *Official Records*, ser. 3, vol. 2, pp. 897–912.
[80] *Statutes at Large*, vol. 12, pp. 589–92. On the framing and enforcement of the act, see James Garfield Randall, *The Confiscation of Property during the Civil War* (Indianapolis, Ind., 1913), chaps. 1–6, and John Syrett, "The Confiscation Acts: Efforts at Reconstruction during the Civil War" (Ph.D. diss., University of Wisconsin, 1971).

subdivide and sell it at auction. In contrast to transactions under the Confiscation Act, the sale of land under the Direct Tax Act would convey fee-simple title, with no restrictions whatsoever. Indeed, as its authors readily admitted, the purpose of the act was less to raise revenue than to "[divest] . . . by law, the titles of rebels to their lands." By the end of 1862, Lincoln had appointed direct-tax commissioners for South Carolina and for Florida, and the South Carolina commission was taking the steps required to put a substantial number of Sea Island plantations on the block. Commissioners were not yet appointed for the other Union-occupied states, however, and the President showed no inclination to speed proceedings.[81]

Only a tiny amount of land within Union-occupied territory had been formally alienated from its owners by the confiscation or direct-tax acts, but the army controlled large tracts by military occupation. Although they lacked authority to determine final disposition of captured or abandoned land, military authorities did not hesitate to use it temporarily for the benefit of the Union war effort, the former slaves under their jurisdiction, and the nation in general. In doing so, they did not lack for offers of assistance.

Ambitious men with an eye on the soaring price of cotton urged federal authorities to open the South—particularly the rich plantation lands of the Mississippi Valley and the South Carolina Sea Islands—to the invigorating influence of Northern capital. Tough-minded capitalists, they argued, could transform Southern society more effectively than abolitionist dreamers or government bureaucrats. None was more impatient to bring the plantations "within the reach of private Enterprise" than Edward S. Philbrick, who had spent 1862 as a plantation superintendent in the Sea Islands. Other Northern newcomers to the occupied Confederacy sounded similar themes. For George B. Field, a New York attorney who toured the Mississippi Valley in the early months of 1863 on behalf of Secretary of War Stanton, nothing would ensure public support for emancipation better than a demonstration that "free negro labor under good management can be made a *source* of *profit* to the *employer*." Seeing no contradiction between private gain and public good, would-be planters pledged their lives and their fortunes to recast the plantation South in the image of the North.[82]

Not all Northerners shared this confidence that the interests of private investors would benefit either former slaves or the public at large.

---

[81] For the Direct Tax Act, see *Statutes at Large*, vol. 12, pp. 422–26; for a summary of its provisions, see *Freedom*, ser. 1, vol. 3: doc. 27n. On its authors' intent, see *Freedom*, ser. 1, vol. 3: doc. 30. On the appointment of direct-tax commissioners, see U.S., Senate, "Letter of the Secretary of the Treasury . . . [on] the collection of direct taxes in insurrectionary districts . . . ," *Senate Executive Documents*, 38th Cong., 1st sess., No. 35.

[82] *Freedom*, ser. 1, vol. 3: docs. 34, 76, 159, 206. On the outlook of Northern planters and would-be planters, see Powell, *New Masters*, especially chaps. 1–2.

From his perspective as superintendent of contrabands in the Department of the Tennessee, Chaplain John Eaton feared the consequences of placing the freedpeople in the hands of speculators. Eaton advocated a system of plantation labor similar to that earlier instituted on the Sea Islands, in which government-appointed superintendents, not private employers, would control agricultural operations and all other aspects of the former slaves' transition to freedom. Meanwhile, on the Sea Islands, the machinations of Philbrick and a "horde" of other Yankees who wished to purchase direct-tax land alarmed the Gideonites, their military allies, and the former slaves. General Rufus Saxton, military governor of the islands, feared that the engrossment of land by private purchasers would put the freedpeople "at the mercy of men devoid of principle," to the detriment of "their future well being." Saxton wanted the national government to "give the negroes a right in that soil to whose wealth they are destined in the future to contribute so largely."[83]

In the end, such misgivings yielded before the promise of Northern entrepreneurs to diminish the government's expenses and increase its revenue. In the South Carolina Sea Islands, the Mississippi Valley, and southern Louisiana, Yankee capitalists gained access to some of the most productive land in the United States. Nowhere, however, did they enjoy as clear a field as they desired. In the Sea Islands, President Lincoln instructed the direct-tax commissioners to reserve a substantial portion of the forfeited land from sale. He also empowered them to bid on behalf of the government for what land was to be offered at auction. In March 1863, when the first direct-tax sales came off, Northern entrepreneurs acquired half the available land. By far the largest purchaser was a syndicate of investors organized by Philbrick.[84]

In southern Louisiana, resident planters obstructed the path of Northern businessmen. Sugar planters claiming loyalty to the federal government retained control over many of the great estates. Heartened by the region's exemption from the Emancipation Proclamation, they pressed General Nathaniel P. Banks, Butler's successor in the Department of the Gulf, to respect their right to manage their plantations and command slave labor. Banks responded by instituting a "voluntary system of labor" that, like Butler's expedient of the previous fall, required small wage payments and promised military enforcement of plantation discipline. Abandoned estates, along with those owned by planters who refused Banks's terms, fell to the department quartermaster, who was authorized to lease them out or operate them under direct government supervision. But because most loyal planters accepted the new regime, however reluctantly, relatively few estates came into government hands. Yankee entrepreneurs leased some of them, but the

---

[83] *Freedom,* ser. 1, vol. 3: docs. 27, 30, 158n.
[84] *Freedom,* ser. 1, vol. 3: docs. 27n., 30, 31.

others were so ravaged by the war or so vulnerable to Confederate attack as to dissuade prospective investors from risking their capital.[85]

Farther north in the Mississippi Valley, Northern planters had a freer hand. In March 1863, Secretary of War Stanton sent Adjutant General Lorenzo Thomas to the valley to inaugurate the recruitment of black soldiers. Traveling in the company of George Field, Thomas soon saw a connection between mobilizing black men, providing for their families, fostering loyalty to the Union, and reestablishing plantation agriculture. Within days of his arrival, he had appointed a commission, headed by Field, to lease plantations to Northerners. Assuming that "the employment and subsistance of negroes [was] a matter to be left to private enterprise," Thomas expected the lessees to hire the families of black soldiers and provide for at least some dependent freedpeople. The leased plantations, protected by newly organized black troops, would unite staple production and many of the relief functions previously borne by the contraband camps.[86]

In most of the Union-occupied Mississippi Valley, however, Thomas's plan could not yet be implemented. At Helena, Arkansas, for instance, where the reach of the small garrison extended barely beyond the town, thousands of former slaves languished in an overcrowded and unhealthy contraband camp for want of securely held plantations. In early 1863, the local commander began transporting them to Cairo, Illinois, and St. Louis, Missouri. Before long, a St. Louis-based network had been established to hire former slaves to midwestern farmers. By the fall of 1863, more than 1,000 had been relocated from Helena to the free states.[87] Midwesterners generally welcomed these migrants. A year earlier, proposals to move black Southerners to the North had sparked Negrophobic hysteria, but circumstances had changed. Even as the conscription of white men created a labor shortage in the North, emancipation and the enlistment of black soldiers engendered a new respect and sympathy for former slaves. Self-interest and sentiment jointly refuted Democratic predictions of race war.

The removal of several hundred former slaves from the Mississippi Valley to the Midwest hardly alleviated the plight of most fugitive slaves or solved the problems of military commanders. Resumption of agricultural production in the South offered the best hope of providing for the increasing number of freedpeople entering Union lines. In 1863, however, secure territory was extremely limited. Adjutant General Thomas found only one promising setting for his plantation-leasing scheme, a small area in northeastern Louisiana that was held by

---

[85] For the orders establishing Banks's system, see *Freedom*, ser. 1, vol. 3: docs. 81, 84. On the estates leased out or operated by the government, see *Freedom*, ser. 1, vol. 3: doc. 93.

[86] *Official Records*, ser. 3, vol. 3, pp. 100–101; *Freedom*, ser. 1, vol. 3: doc. 162; *Freedom*, ser. 2: doc. 194.

[87] On the relocation, see below, docs. 162–63, 165, 171; *Freedom*, ser. 1, vol. 3: docs. 161, 167.

Northern troops operating against Vicksburg. There Thomas's commission rented at least forty plantations to Northern entrepreneurs and a few Southern loyalists. By the fall of 1863, between 3,500 and 5,300 former slaves were living on the leased plantations. Despite the small territory embraced, Thomas believed his plan would eventually "line the [Mississippi] river with a loyal population" of Yankees, emancipated slaves, and native white unionists.[88]

Lured by the prospect of bonanza profits from cotton, Northern lessees bypassed the regions of mixed farming that had also fallen under Union control. No eager capitalists challenged Charles Wilder for land and labor in tidewater Virginia. During the spring of 1863, after receiving Stanton's authorization, Wilder and his fellow superintendent of contrabands, Orlando Brown, settled freedpeople on land abandoned by disloyal owners. Residents of "government farms" literally worked for the government, which supplied rations, livestock, and farm implements and, at the end of the year, paid the laborers with a portion of the crop. Some months later, Colonel Elias M. Greene, chief quartermaster of the Department of Washington, instituted a similar system on several abandoned estates in northern Virginia, just across the Potomac River from the District of Columbia. However, the number of freedpeople working government-controlled land remained small. As of August 1863, only 1,600 former slaves resided on government farms in tidewater Virginia – about 6 percent of the region's black population. Fewer than 200 worked the abandoned estates near Washington.[89]

While the expansion of Union-held territory made it possible for some former slaves to return to the land, it also changed the character of military labor. The surrender of Vicksburg and Port Hudson in July 1863 gave federal forces control of the Mississippi River and set the stage for offensive operations elsewhere, notably Arkansas and middle and east Tennessee. Union armies on the move had little use for laborers to erect stationary fortifications. Instead, they needed teamsters to drive wagons, hostlers to tend the teams, drovers to herd livestock to the front lines, wood choppers to supply fuel for steamboats and locomotives, and laborers to construct and repair roads, bridges, and railbeds. Naval vessels that patrolled the Mississippi and its tributaries also

[88] On the extent of territory and number of plantations leased in 1863 under Thomas's system, see *Freedom*, ser. 1, vol. 3: docs. 180 (which estimates the number of leased plantations at sixty) and 189 (which puts the number at forty). The total number of residents on the leased estates has been estimated by first calculating the average number on twenty-one plantations whose residents were enumerated in October 1863 (*Freedom*, ser. 1, vol. 3: doc. 177) and then multiplying that average (eighty-eight per plantation) by each of the two figures for the total number of leased plantations.

[89] On the tidewater farms, see below, docs. 16–17, 28; *Freedom*, ser. 1, vol. 1: doc. 13. On those near Washington, see below, docs. 63, 77. In the summer of 1864, with farm operations considerably larger than they had been the previous year, only 241 laborers were employed on the northern Virginia farms. (See below, doc. 77n.)

required a large number of hands. Both the army and the navy needed thousands of workers to operate supply depots and maintain lines of communication. In the most active theaters, Union officers mobilized every black man within their reach. By August, the army was employing 11,000 black laborers in middle Tennessee alone.[90]

During the summer and fall of 1863, black men also enlisted in the federal army in large numbers. The opportunity to don Union blue and strike a blow at slavery drew thousands of ex-slaves and free blacks to recruiting stations in the Union-occupied South. Recruitment officers promptly sent the new volunteers into the field to enlist friends and relatives. Black soldiers also participated in raids and foraging expeditions that brought still more ex-slaves into Union ranks. By war's end, 179,000 black men – the vast majority former slaves – had served in the federal army. More than half of them originated in the Confederate states, from some of which they constituted a substantial proportion of the black men of military age. More than a fifth of such men in Arkansas and Mississippi served in the Union army, as did nearly a third of those in Louisiana and almost two-fifths in Tennessee.[91]

Black soldiers often found themselves assigned to menial labor instead of combat duties. Laborers for the quartermaster or other military departments formed the nucleus of several black regiments, which, once mustered into service, continued to work much as before. From the standpoint of their military employers, black soldiers had two advantages over civilians. First, they were subject to army regulations and could not leave their duties at will. Second, in areas where civilian workers commanded high wages, black soldiers performed the same work for lower pay. The combination was too much to resist. Although all Union soldiers performed fatigue duty, black soldiers did more than their share.[92]

Black men struggled to realize their own expectations of martial life. Upon learning that black soldiers earned less than white soldiers, less than white military laborers, and also less than many black military laborers, they often refused to enlist. In Nashville, where black quarter-

---

[90] See below, doc. 95. The 11,000 laborers represented more than one-fifth of the 51,000 black men between the ages of eighteen and forty-five who lived in the entire state of Tennessee in 1860. (*Freedom*, ser. 2: p. 12.)

[91] On the extension of recruitment to the Union-occupied Confederacy, see *Freedom*, ser. 2: chap. 3. For the number of black soldiers credited to each state, see *Freedom*, ser. 2: p. 12.

[92] See below, doc. 100; *Freedom*, ser. 2: chap. 10, and docs. 42, 68, 130A, 243, 265. If black soldiers often worked as laborers, black laborers sometimes served as quasi soldiers. Even before Adjutant General Thomas inaugurated the enlistment of black men in the Mississippi Valley, armed ex-slaves were guarding contraband camps. Black civilians in the valley and elsewhere were often provided with weapons and organized to defend work parties and leased plantations, and black military laborers were liable to duty in local militias. (See, for example, below, docs. 28, 138; *Freedom*, ser. 1, vol. 3: docs. 23, 160; *Official Records*, ser. 3, vol. 4, pp. 874–902.)

master employees received $25 per month, more than double the $10 allotted to a black private, "no laborer with his eyes open" would join the army. When they did enlist, even the greenest recruits insisted upon being treated as soldiers rather than uniformed drudges. Before long, some of them had the opportunity to meet their old masters on the field of battle. At Port Hudson, Fort Wagner, Milliken's Bend, and dozens of lesser encounters, black men did a soldier's work.[93]

Large-scale employment of black men as soldiers and military laborers affected plans both to reorganize plantation agriculture on free-labor principles and to provide for destitute former slaves. The mobilization of adult men restricted the pool of laborers available to private planters and government superintendents. Work gangs had to be constructed around able-bodied women, assisted to varying degree by the old and the young of both sexes. Throughout the Union-occupied South, black women constituted the backbone of the agricultural labor force.[94] Although the planters would rather have had nothing to do with aged, sick, or disabled freedpeople and preferred not to hire women with numerous small children, they usually had no choice but to accept some of the dependent relatives of their workers. Former slaves spurned employment that entailed separation from their families, and military authorities forbade hiring practices that worsened the government's burden of relief. There remained, however, some dependent freedpeople who had no one to provide for them. To accommodate such unfortunates, federal officials in southern Louisiana and the Mississippi Valley reserved several plantations as "infirm farms," where unemployable former slaves received rations while contributing whatever they could to their own support.[95] The officials also abandoned all illusion that the contraband camps could function merely as receiving depots, from which fugitive-slave men would be inducted into the army and virtually all others hired to plantation owners or lessees.

However genuine their acceptance of the government's responsibility for relief, military officials were overwhelmed by the thousands of slaves liberated by Union victories in 1863. Refugees who sought shelter at contraband camps faced recurrent shortages of food, clothing, housing, and medical supplies. Skyrocketing mortality – the result of wartime privation and of diseases fostered by overcrowding and unsanitary facilities – horrified sympathetic observers. In November 1863, officials of the Western Sanitary Commission ventured the

---

[93] *Freedom*, ser. 2: doc. 68. In accordance with the provisions of the Militia Act of July 1862, black soldiers earned $10 per month, $7 in cash and $3 in clothing. On the combat role of black soldiers, see *Freedom*, ser. 2: chap. 11.

[94] On the character of the wartime agricultural labor force, see, for example, below, docs. 28, 42; *Freedom*, ser. 1, vol. 3: docs. 36, 163, 165.

[95] *Freedom*, ser. 1, vol. 3: doc. 177; Geo. B. Field et al. to the Hon. E. M. Stanton, 16 May 1863, filed with #1315 1886, Letters Received, ser. 12, RG 94 [K-574].

bleak prediction that half the black people in the Mississippi Valley were "doomed to die in the process of freeing the rest." Much to the discomfiture of the Lincoln administration, opponents of emancipation seized upon such reports to support their contention that black people would be worse off in freedom than in slavery. General James S. Wadsworth, who investigated conditions in the Mississippi Valley, deliberately understated the extent of suffering, for fear of putting "ammunition in the hands of the copperheads."[96]

Whereas the contraband camps of the Union-occupied Lower South operated as adjuncts to the plantations, those in the Upper South played a more independent role, chiefly because federal authorities controlled so little abandoned land. In the tiny Union-held enclaves of tidewater North Carolina, where nearly all able-bodied black men had enlisted in the army, contraband camps were established at New Berne and Roanoke Island to house their families, who had no other means of support. Drawing upon government funds and private donations, Horace James, "superintendent of blacks" in North Carolina, strove to make Roanoke Island a model of life in freedom, with right-angled streets, gardens, and a hospital. Officials in the District of Columbia had similar goals in establishing "Freedman's Village" on the estate of Confederate General Robert E. Lee, across the Potomac River from Washington. Freedman's Village became a showplace to which government officials directed foreign visitors and other dignitaries eager to witness the progress of the former slaves.[97]

In the loyal border states, where slavery remained legal and the recruitment of black soldiers had barely begun, only a few contraband camps came into existence in 1863. Because federal policy in the border states required deference to civil authority and noninterference with slavery, these camps evolved as sanctuaries not for border-state fugitive slaves but for those who had escaped from the Confederacy. Point Lookout, a military installation at the southernmost extension of Maryland's western shore, attracted black refugees from Virginia, among whom mingled a number of Maryland slaves. The post quartermaster employed many of the men and eventually inaugurated an informal contraband camp by issuing rations and tents to the women and children. In Missouri, military authorities established a sizable camp at St. Louis, but not to provide for local fugitive slaves. Instead, it was the arrival of hundreds of freedpeople from Helena, Arkansas, that forced the army to issue rations and set up quarters, first in an abandoned hotel and then at Benton Barracks, on the outskirts of the city. Simi-

---

[96] *Freedom*, ser. 1, vol. 3: doc. 107; James E. Yeatman et al. to His Excellency, A. Lincoln, 6 Nov. 1863, vol. R–S 1863, #342, Miscellaneous Letters Received: K Series, ser. 103, RG 56 [X-12]. See also *Freedom*, ser. 1, vol. 1: doc. 110.

[97] See below, docs. 22, 70–71; Horace James, *Annual Report of the Superintendent of Negro Affairs in North Carolina, 1864* (Boston, 1865), pp. 6–7, 21–26.

larly, the contraband camp at Columbus, on the western border of Kentucky, signaled no offer of protection to slaves from that state. Established in conjunction with the recruitment of black soldiers, the camp, like the new regiments, consisted almost entirely of fugitive slaves from Tennessee. To reduce their unsettling effect upon Kentucky slaves, military officers steadily transferred residents of the camp to nearby Island 10, Tennessee, in the middle of the Mississippi River.[98]

Throughout the Union-occupied South, the desperate poverty of most inhabitants of the contraband camps proclaimed the hollow legacy of chattel bondage. However, not all fugitive slaves traversed the ground between slavery and freedom empty-handed. A good many brought personal possessions – clothing, bedding, and cooking utensils – to ease the transit. Some managed to carry away tools and other productive property. A former slave with an axe, a hoe, a wagon, or the implements of a trade stood a better chance of gaining an independent livelihood than one without such tools. Possession of a horse or mule also improved the possibilities for self-employment. Procured by various means – purchased during slavery, "borrowed" from a former master, picked up as strays, or acquired with the proceeds of wartime labor – draft animals enabled some ex-slaves to set up for themselves. Former slaves with a horse or mule worked as self-employed draymen and wagoners in such cities as Nashville, Memphis, and Washington, whose wartime economies depended heavily upon the transportation of goods. In some rural areas, freedpeople who were similarly endowed bargained with landowners for rental or crop-sharing arrangements. Freedpeople who left slavery in possession of productive property had a wider range of choices than those who owned only their ability to labor.[99]

A handful of former slaves gained legal control over land in 1863. At the South Carolina direct-tax sales, freedpeople who had pooled their resources purchased as many as eight plantations in competitive bidding. In the Mississippi Valley, about fifteen black men leased land from Thomas's plantation commissioners, and an indeterminable number struck subleasing bargains with Northern planters. Although military authorities in southern Louisiana made no effort to rent land to black lessees, a few elderly and disabled former slaves who had remained on abandoned estates won informal approval to work the land for their own benefit.[100]

If only a minuscule number of former slaves enjoyed either formal or informal possession of land, their control over other productive prop-

---

[98] See below, docs. 133, 162–63, 165, 171–72, 205, 209.

[99] For examples of former slaves' ownership and use of productive property, including draft animals, see below, docs. 10, 96–97, 112, 116–17; *Freedom*, ser. 1, vol. 3: docs. 51, 104, 174–75, 184.

[100] *Freedom*, ser. 1, vol. 3: docs. 31, 91, 97, 180.

erty was not much more extensive, in part because almost everything fugitive slaves brought into Union lines was subject to expropriation. Military regulations permitted freedpeople to retain their possessions only if they could prove ownership, making it difficult for them to hold any property that was of use to the army. Even when assured that the expropriated livestock, tools, and other goods would be used in the contraband camps or on government-controlled plantations, former slaves could not help but feel a twinge of bitterness as their belongings were pressed into government service. Only rarely did their complaints receive a hearing.[101]

Former slaves were not alone in their protests. Observing that many freedpeople "use their property to make a living," General John Hawkins argued that "[t]he immediate gain to Gov,ment by the seizure is very small compared with the great loss to them." "By letting the property remain in their possession," he asserted, "they will be enabled next year to cultivate a few acres of ground and the Gov,ment be relieved of their support. By taking it away they or their families are made paupers for perhaps all time to come." But Hawkins's views were rare within Union officialdom, and his superiors rejected his appeal. Draft animals and other items brought into federal lines by former slaves remained subject to confiscation.[102]

Owning little or no productive property, former slaves were perforce dependent upon whatever compensation they could obtain by laboring for an employer. Black military laborers, soldiers, and urban and agricultural workers shared a reliance upon wage work. Accordingly, the amount and kind of compensation and the regularity of payment became important issues, at times critical ones. But in the various settings in which freedpeople became wage laborers, questions of compensation merged with other matters pertaining to control over production, especially the nature and extent of supervision and the length of the workday and workweek. The ex-slaves' experience in bondage had produced sensibilities and expectations opposed to those of former slaveholders and, in many respects, equally foreign to those of Northern planters and military officers. Struggles brought forward from slavery intertwined with those characteristic of free labor. Whereas some matters of contention – including the provision of subsistence, corporal punishment, freedom of movement, and compensation – were common to military laborers, soldiers and sailors, and agricultural and urban workers, others depended upon the particular character of each type of work.

Of all former slaves, black military laborers were perhaps the most fully attuned to the wage relation. Unlike soldiers and plantation laborers, whose work was accompanied by the promise of subsistence for

---

[101] On military policy respecting personal property claimed by former slaves, see *Freedom*, ser. 1, vol. 3: docs. 35, 160, 175A–B.

[102] *Freedom*, ser. 1, vol. 3: docs. 175A–B.

nonworking family members, military laborers usually had to feed and house their dependents from their earnings alone. The amount and frequency of pay therefore weighed heavily in their lives. Although the wages of military employees arrived with greater regularity during 1863, as the federal government's fiscal crisis receded and its bureaucracy gained experience, a substantial number of black laborers found themselves short-changed on account of irregularities or fraud. Nonpayment ranked high among the causes leading black military laborers to "desert," but it was not the only reason. Long hours of work, abusive superintendents, and substandard food, clothing, and shelter all prompted disgruntled workers to search for more attractive employment. To the consternation of military employers, black laborers learned only too well that their new status allowed them to sell their labor power wherever they wished. With the freedom to change employers, however, came the "freedom" to be discharged. Many military laborers experienced periods of unemployment or irregular employment, with the accompanying uncertainty of support for themselves and their families.[103]

Black soldiers surrendered the right to change employers, but they gained other rewards, including the respect of their comrades-in-arms and the gratitude of the nation for which they fought. Former slaves expected military service to mean, at the very least, that they would be treated the same as other soldiers, but black soldiers found themselves barred from promotion, assigned to labor gangs instead of combat, issued inferior rations and equipment, and subjected to punishments that, at times, bore uncomfortable resemblance to those meted out by slaveholders. Despite the fact that military discipline rested upon impersonal law rather than personal sovereignty, corporal punishment of any form infuriated men who had known the master's lash.[104]

These burdens aside, black soldiers were guaranteed rations, clothing, and a wage. To be sure, the quantity and quality of rations and clothing frequently fell short of their expectations, and black soldiers complained of the deficiency. But nothing angered them more than the government's failure to pay them at the same rate as their white comrades. Connected as it was with both their ability to support their families and their conviction that equal service merited equal recompense, their demand for equality had special resonance in the wider black community. Their families and friends – along with many Northern abolitionists – joined the soldiers in demanding justice. "We have done a Soldiers Duty," protested a black corporal to Lincoln in June 1863. "Why cant we have a Soldiers pay?"[105]

---

[103] See below, docs. 16–17, 20, 22, 25, 27, 55–56, 60, 62, 70, 82, 92, 99, 102–3; *Freedom*, ser. 1, vol. 3: docs. 31, 182; *Freedom*, ser. 2: doc. 45.

[104] For the experience of black soldiers, see *Freedom*, ser. 2, especially chaps. 6–11.

[105] *Freedom*, ser. 2: doc. 157A. The struggle for equal pay is discussed more fully in *Freedom*, ser. 2: chap. 7.

Farm and plantation workers also wished to enjoy the rights and privileges of free laborers. They especially wanted to erase the hallmarks of personal sovereignty that characterized slavery. At first, some asked little more than the prohibition of corporal punishment and a guarantee of family security. A group of former slaves in southern Louisiana assured an emissary of General Banks that they were "willing to go to work immediately . . . even without remuneration," provided that "they would not be whipped and separated from their families." Objections to the lash extended to the men who had historically wielded it. Steadfastly opposed to working under "Secesh overseers," freedpeople sometimes nominated a replacement of their own, either a fellow freedman or a Northerner who respected their determination not to be commanded by force.[106]

With plantation laborers united in opposition, planters courted rebellion if they refused to accede. The consequence of trying to maintain the old order, according to one army provost marshal, was "trouble, immediately – and the negroes band together, and lay down their own rules, as to when, and how long they will work &c &c. and the Overseer loses all control over them." Occasionally, former slaves took matters into their own hands. Armed with sticks, laborers on one plantation drove the overseer away, declaring that "they would make Laws for themselves."[107]

Union military authorities generally sympathized with the freedpeople's efforts to obliterate vestiges of the slave regime. Although they stopped short of removing overseers, army officers prohibited corporal punishment and established procedures for adjudicating disputes between employers and employees. They also required that freed laborers be paid. In their view, prohibiting physical coercion and guaranteeing compensation were fundamental to free labor. To some officers, the principle of compensation mattered far more than its character or amount. "It is free labor if but one cent a year be paid," declared the head of General Banks's "Bureau of Negro Labor," to the ready assent of the general himself.[108]

To the former slaves, Banks's penny represented not the certainty of their liberation but the narrow confines of their freedom. Without exception, military regulations prescribed low wages for plantation hands, substantially lower than the earnings of black soldiers or military laborers. In 1863, monthly wages for the highest-rated field hands ranged from $2 in southern Louisiana to about $6.50 in the Sea Islands and $7 in the Mississippi Valley. The great majority of plantation workers – women, children, and old people, all of whom were rated

---

[106] *Freedom*, ser. 1, vol. 3: doc. 87. On the rejection of overseers, see below, doc. 43; *Freedom*, ser. 1, vol. 3: docs. 34, 86, 94, 106C, 116–17, 121.

[107] *Freedom*, ser. 1, vol. 3: docs. 90Cn., 94.

[108] *Freedom*, ser. 1, vol. 3: doc. 110.

below first-class hands – earned even less. Like black soldiers and military laborers, plantation laborers received rations in addition to wages but, except in southern Louisiana, had to pay for their own clothing. Unlike black soldiers and most military laborers, plantation laborers also received rations for dependent family members, the value of which, for some large families, may have offset the lower wage rates. Nevertheless, their cash income barely sufficed to purchase blankets, supplemental foodstuffs, medical care, and tobacco. Little or nothing remained to buy items like schoolbooks and Sunday clothes, much less to save toward future independence.[109]

Differences in the organization of work and relief gave free labor a somewhat distinctive cast in each region of the Union-occupied South. These differences derived from antebellum practices, particular military circumstances, and the policies of individual commanders. In the Sea Islands, for instance, the antebellum organization of labor by "tasks" left its mark on wartime arrangements. At least initially, military officials and civilian plantation superintendents saw task work as readily adaptable to the requirements of free wage labor, because it assigned responsibility for particular work to particular workers, facilitating both the measurement of each individual's labor and payment in proportion to work accomplished. General Saxton issued plantation regulations that organized all steps of cotton production (except harvesting) into daily tasks, each with a precise monetary payment. In effect, federal authorities transmuted antebellum task labor into piecework, expecting that some laborers would redouble their efforts and complete more than one task per day. Piecework also prevailed during harvest, with each worker paid on the basis of the amount of cotton picked. To encourage former slaves to remain at work to the end of the year, wages for planting and cultivation were set at a low level, with picking pegged at higher rates. At the heart of the new regime lay cash payment for work in cotton. With the money they earned, plantation hands were expected to purchase their clothing, whatever food they did not raise, and "luxuries" like tobacco, which in the past had often been provided by the owner. Obligatory labor on provision crops earned no wages at all.[110]

The reorganization of plantation labor was accompanied by new provisions for nonworkers. Except where the estates had been stripped by Union soldiers, Saxton and the plantation superintendents refused to dispense rations, on the grounds that such issues encouraged depen-

---

[109] *Freedom*, ser. 1, vol. 3: docs. 28, 84, 162. The rate for the Sea Islands, where wages were set by the day rather than the month, is calculated on the basis of twenty-six days of work per month, at $.25 per day.

[110] For the order establishing the labor system on government plantations in the Sea Islands, see *Freedom*, ser. 1, vol. 3: doc. 28. For elucidations of its provisions, see *Freedom*, ser. 1, vol. 3: docs. 31–32, 36.

dency and resembled the old system of "allowances" from the master. Instead, the laborers on each government plantation collectively produced food for the entire plantation population, workers and dependents alike, on land designated for that purpose. Each family also received a garden plot. Alone among the federally supervised plantation systems, that of the Sea Islands permitted the laborers some voice in decisions about what crops they would cultivate, and in what proportion. The freedpeople clearly preferred food crops. On plantations controlled by private entrepreneurs in 1863, cotton accounted for 40 percent of the cultivated acreage; on those operated under the direction of government superintendents, only 25 percent was in the staple.[111]

In most other respects, however, Saxton's regulations for the government plantations set the standard for those in private hands. In particular, the freedpeople employed by Northern planters expected prompt remuneration. One planter complained that he could induce them to cultivate cotton only "by going among them and paying on the spot." Northern entrepreneurs had little choice but to provide garden plots, because the laborers demanded them. To the extent that the planters were therefore able to reduce capital outlays in the form of rations, they found the system acceptable, though they rued the tendency of the laborers to devote their energies to food production instead of additional tasks in the cotton fields. Some laborers failed to complete even a single daily task, leaving the field at midday to work in their gardens.[112]

In another concession to the freedpeople, some Northern planters divided the fields into separate tracts, each worked collectively by the members of one or more households. Edward Philbrick, for one, favored such allocation of land because it gave the laborers "a proprietary interest in the crop." By this arrangement, households or other self-organized work groups in effect supplanted individual task hands. These collective work units allowed the former slaves a greater measure of control over the disposition of their own labor, permitting some family members, for example, to leave the field early to perform domestic tasks, or allowing more experienced workers to assist the weaker and less experienced.[113]

In southern Louisiana and the Mississippi Valley, Union military officials devised a substantially different plan for organizing labor and relief. Both General Banks and Adjutant General Thomas retained certain formal features of the old regime. Plantation laborers continued to be organized into gangs whose composition was determined by the operator of the estate, not the workers. Despite the opposition of the freedpeople, the vast majority of planters – whether former slaveholders or Northern lessees – employed overseers. Hours and condi-

---

[111] Calculated from figures in *Freedom*, ser. 1, vol. 3: doc. 36.

[112] *Freedom*, ser. 1, vol. 3: docs. 32, 34, 40.

[113] *Freedom*, ser. 1, vol. 3: docs. 31, 34; see also Saville, "A Measure of Freedom," pp. 75–82.

tions of labor were left to the discretion of planters and overseers, subject only to the restraints of custom, the army's ban on corporal punishment, and a vaguely worded insistence that workers receive "proper" and "humane" treatment. The subsistence of plantation residents also remained largely the responsibility of planters, who were required to feed, clothe, and house nonworkers as well as workers. In the view of military authorities, the planters' assumption of that responsibility, together with the risks of planting in a war zone, justified low wages. For their part, former slaves were expected to devote their energy to raising staple crops, not food. Government officials, resident plantation owners, and Northern lessees were of one mind: Cotton and sugar, not corn and potatoes, promised profits for the planters and taxes for the treasury.[114]

Whatever the particular stipulations, military regulation of labor delivered a crippling blow to the master's sovereignty and limited the employer's power. No longer was the planter the court of first and last resort. Freedpeople recognized even the most rudimentary recourse to higher authority as a radical departure from slavery. When an employer trampled on their rights, they protested to the nearest superintendent of contrabands or provost marshal. Throughout the Union-occupied South, employers complained that their laborers appealed even "the least thing," undercutting all discipline. No matter what the decision in any given instance, intervention by federal officials signified the demise of the slaveholder's omnipotence.[115]

Union soldiers, black and white, often interposed their authority on behalf of agricultural laborers. Just as they had disseminated news of freedom, soldiers expounded the rights of free men and women, informing one group of ex-slaves, for example, that "they need never mind a driver any more, that each of them was good as a driver." Some soldiers attempted to redress forcibly the wrongs suffered by plantation workers. From the planters' perspective, black soldiers wielded especially subversive influence. Armed, mobile, and politicized, their very presence demonstrated the freedpeople's new power. Because most black soldiers had themselves toiled in the fields and often had families and friends on the plantations, they identified with those who worked the land and were determined to prevent their abuse.[116]

Plantations that had once been virtual fiefdoms, whose proprietors jealously guarded their boundaries and screened all visitors, became subject to all manner of intrusion. The separation of able-bodied men – most of whom were serving as soldiers or military laborers – from the women, children, and old people who made up the bulk of the

[114] For the military regulations governing plantation labor in southern Louisiana and the Mississippi Valley, see *Freedom*, ser. 1, vol. 3: docs. 81, 84, 162.
[115] See, for example, *Freedom*, ser. 1, vol. 3: doc. 32.
[116] See, for example, *Freedom*, ser. 1, vol. 3: docs. 19, 74, 77, 199; *Freedom*, ser. 2: doc. 55.

plantation work force necessitated frequent visits, because former slaves viewed a secure family life as fundamental to freedom. Planters protested the visits as violations of their private domain, but their complaints availed little. Although military regulations generally forbade plantation laborers to leave an estate without permission, such rules were often honored only in the breach. "[W]e cannot keep our people at home," complained a Sea Island planter, who lamented the effect upon labor discipline.[117] The new permeability of plantation boundaries broke down the isolation of plantation life, permitting rural laborers to gain broader knowledge of the world and to develop solidarity with their counterparts on other estates and with black townspeople.

Within the narrow geographical bounds of Union occupation, the circumstances of plantation life forced all but the most intransigent slaveholders to accommodate the changes wrought by emancipation. Slowly and reluctantly, former masters began to come to terms with the reality of free labor. Few retired the lash voluntarily, and none welcomed the necessity of paying wages, but most planters were compelled to accept at least the rudiments of free labor in order to continue operations. Before long, they even discerned certain advantages in the new order.

Whereas former slaveholders were loath to assume the responsibilities of free labor, they eagerly jettisoned the burdens of mastership. Under the slave regime, they had been obliged to support sick, young, and elderly slaves; under free labor, they derived no benefits from doing so. Employers in the North, they pointedly insisted, bore no such responsibility. Accordingly, many erstwhile slaveholders evicted elderly and unproductive laborers with no consideration for years of service or putative bonds of affection. The wives, parents, and children of black soldiers became special targets of the planters' zeal to "sift out" unproductive former slaves, but anyone unable to contribute labor was liable to be ousted. Masters-turned-employers also refused to provide medical care, declaring that such expenses were no longer their responsibility. "When I owned niggers," announced a Louisiana planter in characteristic fashion, "I used to pay medical bills and take care of them; I do not think I shall trouble myself much now."[118]

The entry of Northerners into the plantation business and the acquiescence of former slaveholders in the requirements of free labor placed relations between planters and laborers on new ground. Even as corporal punishment and the employment of overseers remained live issues, the reorganization of agricultural labor inaugurated new contests over the length of the workday and the workweek. Planters struggled to exact as much labor as possible from freedpeople determined to work

[117] See below, doc. 21; *Freedom*, ser. 1, vol. 3: docs. 32, 74, 79, 90B.
[118] See below, docs. 102, 129; *Freedom*, ser. 1, vol. 3: docs. 100–101, 106A, 108, 110, 200.

less than they had as slaves. In the Mississippi Valley and southern Louisiana, where gang labor predominated, planters tried to hold former slaves to the antebellum standard: dawn to dusk, six days a week, and, during harvest, additional labor at night and on Sunday. Freedpeople resisted such extensive claims on their time, often shortening both the workday and workweek, much to the disgust of former masters, Northern lessees, and federal officials. A government superintendent was chagrined to discover that the hands on one sugar estate "only work five days in the week and then very little." In the Sea Islands, where the task had defined a day's work, the contest centered on Saturday labor, with plantation superintendents and Northern planters insisting that the day belonged to the workweek and freedpeople claiming it as their own.[119]

Like employers elsewhere, planters in the Union-occupied South also wanted to pay their workers as little as possible, and at the last possible moment. Federal regulation of wages averted much potential conflict. But even the low rates set by military orders were too high for most planters, who would have preferred to compensate their workers with "a great present" at year's end – maintaining the fiction of their paternal rule and leaving to their own discretion the amount and form of payment. Meanwhile, the former slaves, confined to federally mandated wages, wanted more.

Within the possibilities permitted by military regulations, both planters and workers looked for ways to gain advantage. At times, each found reason to prefer that compensation take the form of a share of the crop rather than cash. Where planters lacked the resources with which to pay cash wages, they gladly acquiesced in laborers' demands for a share. In a good year, a postharvest share wage might return more to the laborers than monthly cash payments, although a short crop would result in smaller compensation. From the standpoint of the planters, share wages offered the important benefit of holding laborers through the entire year, lest they forfeit their portion by leaving before the harvest. Federal officials also encouraged year-long commitments. In southern Louisiana, General Banks offered the option of a postharvest payment instead of monthly cash wages, setting the rate at one-twentieth of the crop, to be divided among the workers. Even when there was no explicit sanction of share wages, freedpeople and planters occasionally negotiated such arrangements on their own.[120]

Gradually former slaveholders and former slaves navigated the terrain of free labor more comfortably. Former slaveholders discovered that wage-earners expected to be paid, and paid promptly. They also came to see advantage in allowing their employees access to the resources of

---

[119] See, for example, *Freedom*, ser. 1, vol. 3: docs. 19, 21, 100n., 106B.
[120] See below, doc. 129; *Freedom*, ser. 1, vol. 3: docs. 84, 86.

the plantation: the right to cultivate garden plots, to hunt or cut wood in forests and fish in streams, to keep swine and poultry. Such concessions were prized by former slaves, who saw them as a means to labor for their own benefit and to expand control over their own lives. Acceding to their wishes helped employers attract and retain a work force and, at times, permitted reductions in the amount or frequency of monetary compensation.[121] Employers learned not only to cater to the "wants" of the freedpeople, but also to turn them to their own ends. Yankee planters, familiar with the operation of a wage system, pioneered in establishing plantation stores where laborers could purchase items previously beyond their reach. Before long, Southern planters also realized that such stores could help keep their workers on the plantation and provide another source of profit.[122]

While they continued to condemn military regulation as a poor substitute for physical compulsion, planters learned to benefit from the authority of local superintendents or provost marshals. Denouncing anarchy in the quarters and presenting themselves as friends of good order, planters cultivated the goodwill of nearby army officers, who often welcomed the attention and granted them a sympathetic hearing. General James Bowen, provost marshal general of the Department of the Gulf, went so far as to instruct his subordinates that "planters must be regarded as conservators of the peace" on their estates. Planters found the army particularly useful in curbing the former slaves' freedom of movement. Military restrictions against unauthorized travel dovetailed conveniently with the planters' insistence that black workers, once committed to a particular estate, not be allowed to leave except by permission.[123]

Free-labor arrangements, however circumscribed, endangered the old regime, a truth rebel leaders clearly understood. In the summer of 1863, the Confederate high command unleashed a series of raids on the plantations operated by Yankee lessees and reconstructed Southerners. The results were devastating. In the Mississippi Valley, rebel soldiers killed several lessees and hundreds of freedpeople, hundreds more of whom were captured and reenslaved. The attacks thoroughly disrupted the plantation-leasing system, sending panicked laborers and lessees to nearby army posts. Some lessees returned to their homes in the North, and many freedpeople refused to accept work in the countryside. Freedpeople in more secure areas, including the South

---

[121] See, for example, *Freedom*, ser. 1, vol. 3: docs. 141, 171.

[122] *Freedom*, ser. 1, vol. 3: docs. 40, 100, 108; Powell, *New Masters*, pp. 87–93.

[123] Bg. Genl. James Bowen to Captain Fitch, 27 Apr. [1863], vol. 296 DG, pp. 594–95, Press Copies of Letters Sent, ser. 1839, Provost Marshal, Dept. of the Gulf, RG 393 Pt. 1 [C-1099]. For examples of military restrictions upon the mobility of rural laborers, see below, doc. 21; *Freedom*, ser. 1, vol. 3: docs. 15, 54, 109, 198.

Carolina Sea Islands and tidewater Virginia, escaped such wholesale terror, but they, too, suffered harassment by Confederate soldiers and guerrilla marauders.[124]

The Confederate raids failed to shake the federal commitment to reconstructing Southern agriculture on the basis of free labor. By the fall of 1863, many erstwhile secessionists were suing for peace. Disloyal planters, reports claimed, were "discouraged and hopeless of the rebellion, and ready to do almost anything that will keep their negroes in the fields." Such accounts were not long in reaching President Lincoln, who liked what he heard. Eager to revive Southern unionism, Lincoln directed his generals, particularly those in the Mississippi Valley, to encourage slaveholders to accept free labor. Adjutant General Thomas endorsed unionist associations in such former hotbeds of secession as Vicksburg and Natchez. Other federal officers courted both long-time loyalists and repentant rebels, promising them protection from Confederate raiders and assistance in marketing crops and acquiring supplies, if they agreed to compensate their laborers and abjure corporal punishment. Military commanders in Arkansas aided in the formation of a provisional unionist government, while the brightening fortunes of war invigorated antislavery unionists in Louisiana and Tennessee. Sensing the change, Lincoln urged General Banks in southern Louisiana and Military Governor Andrew Johnson in Tennessee to mobilize opponents of slavery in support of loyal state governments.[125]

As the new order spread to areas exempt from the Emancipation Proclamation, federal officials evaluated the success of the labor and welfare arrangements established during 1863. Secretary of War Stanton solicited suggestions from knowledgeable observers, and he dispatched a special emissary, General James S. Wadsworth, to the Mississippi Valley. Equally interested was Secretary of the Treasury Chase, to whose department the President had assigned control over all abandoned and captured "houses, tenements, lands, and plantations" that were not needed for military purposes. Preparing to devise new regulations for leasing plantations and organizing agricultural labor, he, too, sought suggestions from military and civilian authorities. Still other

---

[124] *Freedom,* ser. 1, vol. 3: docs. 96, 168, 177, 196.
[125] *Official Records,* ser. 1, vol. 24, pt. 3, pp. 549–50. On unionist politics in the Mississippi Valley, see *Freedom,* ser. 1, vol. 1: doc. 110; *Freedom,* ser. 1, vol. 3: doc. 182; *Official Records,* ser. 1, vol. 24, pt. 3, pp. 549–50, 570, 578, 582–88; Lawrence N. Powell and Michael S. Wayne, "Self-Interest and the Decline of Confederate Nationalism," in *The Old South in the Crucible of War,* ed. Harry P. Owens and James J. Cooke (Jackson, Miss., 1983), pp. 29–46. On Louisiana, see LaWanda Cox, *Lincoln and Black Freedom: A Study in Presidential Leadership* (Columbia, S.C., 1981), chaps. 2–4; Peyton McCrary, *Abraham Lincoln and Reconstruction: The Louisiana Experiment* (Princeton, N.J., 1978), chaps. 5–8. On Tennessee, see below, doc. 101; *Freedom,* ser. 2: docs. 64–65, 67; John Cimprich, *Slavery's End in Tennessee, 1861–1865* (University, Ala., 1985), chaps. 7–8.

Northerners, stirred by the possibility of remaking the South, needed no invitation to volunteer their views.[126]

Nearly all such commentators agreed that the experience of 1863 had demonstrated the superior productivity of free over slave labor. "Every body admits that the cash System works better than the lash system," declared a treasury agent. Freed black laborers had given the lie to the proslavery dogma "that negroes are very valuable as slaves, but when free, worthless, and unable to take care of themselves." "[I]t is now generally conceded," observed Charles Wilder, "that the labor of one freeman, is worth that of two slaves." From the Sea Islands, General Saxton reported with satisfaction that the 1863 crop had proven beyond doubt "that the cotton fields of South Carolina can be successfully cultivated by free labor, that the negroes will work cheerfully and willingly with a reasonable prospect of reward." Evidence from the Mississippi Valley seemed to bear out Adjutant General Thomas's earlier prediction "that the freed negro may be profitably employed by enterprising men."[127]

And so it did. Despite unfavorable weather and Confederate raids, lessees in the Mississippi Valley had made money, some of them a good deal of it. Northern planters in the South Carolina Sea Islands had also reaped handsome profits. Even under wartime conditions, the new labor system had fulfilled the prophecy of a New England textile magnate who touted "Cheap Cotton by Free Labor." To judge from the hundreds of Northerners who sought permission to operate plantations in the occupied South for the coming year, the profitability of free labor – at least in cotton-growing regions – had been established beyond cavil. For some Northerners, that was quite enough. In granting the former slaves ownership of their own persons and transforming them into wage-workers, the government had done all it should to secure freedom.[128]

Others disagreed. As long as the war continued, military and political constraints precluded any thoroughgoing overhaul of Southern society, but many Northerners worried that steps taken during the conflict might foreclose options available in peacetime. They therefore viewed wartime labor arrangements with one eye on what was immediately possible and the other on what was ultimately desirable. Because acceptance of the possible did not necessarily imply concurrence on the desirable, observers divided among themselves in complex ways. Their

---

[126] *Official Records*, ser. 3, vol. 3, pp. 872–73; *Freedom*, ser. 1, vol. 3: docs. 185–86.

[127] Tho. Heaton to Hon. Wm. P. Mellen, 10 May 1864, Letters Received from Assistant Special Agents, Records of the General Agent, RG 366 [Q-169]; see below, doc. 43; *Freedom*, ser. 1, vol. 3: docs. 36, 162, 180.

[128] For arguments that cotton and other staples could be produced more profitably with free labor than with slave labor, see *Freedom*, ser. 1, vol. 3: docs. 7, 36, 70, 93; [Edward Atkinson], *Cheap Cotton by Free Labor: By a Cotton Manufacturer* (Boston, 1861).

debates focused on four related questions: the condition of black wage-workers in the Union-occupied South as compared with their Northern counterparts; the proper disposition of land controlled by the government; the ultimate political status of the former slaves; and the political status of former Confederates, particularly large property owners.

While acknowledging the productivity of black wage laborers amid the uncertainty of war, many Northerners denounced the limited prospects afforded former slaves under the new regime. Pointing to the meager pay, regimentation of labor, restriction of physical movement, and absence of written contracts and lien laws, they emphasized the extent to which freedpeople were denied rights that Northern wage-earners took for granted. General John Hawkins, whose command included almost all the Mississippi Valley plantations leased out in 1863, attacked the leasing system as a travesty of free labor. Although he expected most former slaves to remain wage laborers, at least for the immediate future, he condemned the terms under which they were working. By renting immense tracts of land to unscrupulous "adventurers" and setting low wages for laborers, the government had ceded control to "a monopoly." Hawkins urged federal authorities to subdivide the great estates into small farms and lease them to Northerners and ex-slaves, multiplying the number of agricultural units and, accordingly, the demand for hired labor. Wage rates, he argued, should be established by the market instead of the government, workers should be permitted to change employers at any time, and employers should have the right to discharge workers for any cause. Only then, Hawkins emphasized, would the labor of the former slaves become "as free as the labor of the northern white man."[129] In two influential reports prepared in late 1863, James E. Yeatman, president of the Western Sanitary Commission, disseminated Hawkins's antimonopoly views to a wider audience, adding his own unflattering judgments about the leasing system and suggestions for its reform. Yeatman thereby established himself as the leading critic of existing policy and gained the attention of Secretary of the Treasury Chase.[130]

Many Northerners concurred with Hawkins and Yeatman in their harsh assessment of free labor in the Union-occupied South. General Wadsworth, Stanton's emissary, was particularly critical of Banks's regulations because they denied what he believed to be the essential right of wage laborers: the freedom to rise to the limits of their own ability. Low wages, inadequate legal protection, and restrictions upon

[129] *Freedom*, ser. 1, vol. 3: docs. 177, 181.
[130] Yeatman, *A Report on the Condition of the Freedmen of the Mississippi, Presented to the Western Sanitary Commission, December 17th, 1863* (St. Louis, 1864), and *Suggestions of a Plan of Organization for Freed Labor, and the Leasing of Plantations along the Mississippi River . . .* (St. Louis, 1864). For a summary of the latter, see *Freedom*, ser. 1, vol. 3: doc. 189n. For Yeatman's influence on Chase, see *Freedom*, ser. 1, vol. 3: doc. 186.

freedom of movement, he feared, would immobilize former slaves at the bottom of the social order, "not as freedmen, but as serfs." James McKaye, a member of the American Freedmen's Inquiry Commission, shared Wadsworth's reservations. "If the only object to be accomplished [were] simply 'to compel the negro to labor' in a condition of perpetual subordination and subjection," he argued, Banks's system would suffice. But it was unacceptable "if the object [were] to make the colored man a self-supporting and self-defending member of [the] community." The freedpeople, maintained McKaye, Wadsworth, and many others, deserved more at the hands of the government.[131]

Among the things they deserved was land to cultivate on their own account. Widespread acquisition by purchase seemed impossible, given the poverty of most former slaves, the insecurity of wartime land tenure, and the absence – except in the Sea Islands – of legal procedures for conveying forfeited property. But renting was another matter. The government had leased abandoned and confiscated land to poorly capitalized Yankees; surely those ex-slaves who had the experience and resources to work a farm might be similarly favored. The success of those few black farmers who had rented land in 1863 reinforced such reasoning. In the course of debates about the government's leasing policy for the coming year, some Northerners, including James Yeatman, advocated preferential treatment for black lessees. Influenced by their arguments, Secretary of the Treasury Chase directed his subordinates to give special consideration to former slaves who wished to rent land from the government.[132]

A handful of Northerners continued to see the war as an opportunity to endow former slaves with an independent competency. General Saxton maintained that restricting freedpeople to the status of wage laborers would lock them "in the condition of a peasantry only a little higher than chattelism . . . when so many of them had proved their fitness to be owners of the soil." McKaye argued that the interests of both former slaves and the nation would be best served by permitting them to own the land they occupied, for "you can never have in any country a democratic society, or a society substantially, practically free, where the land all belongs to a few people."[133] Asserting the connection between productive property and freedom against those who viewed self-ownership as the ultimate goal, men like Saxton and McKaye revealed the ongoing conflict within Northern society over the sources and meaning of liberty – a conflict that was fast being transferred to the former slave states.

[131] *Freedom*, ser. 1, vol. 3: doc. 107; J. McKaye, "The Emancipated Slave face to face with his old Master: Valley of the Lower Mississippi," [Apr.? 1864], filed with O-328 1863, Letters Received, ser. 12, RG 94 [K-66].

[132] See below, doc. 28; *Freedom*, ser. 1, vol. 3: docs. 107, 186.

[133] *Freedom*, ser. 1, vol. 3: docs. 57, 187.

Advocates of redistributing land gained support from the growing number of Northerners who believed that loyal ex-slaves had a better claim to the land than traitorous rebels. The freedpeople's uncompensated labor during slavery and their loyalty during the war, declared one treasury agent, gave them "an equitable lien upon the lands of their masters." Arguing upon similar grounds, General Saxton declared that the freedpeople deserved their former owners' land as a matter of "simple justice." Such Northerners thought it morally wrong as well as politically naive to restore land to former slaveholders while dispossessing former slaves. Fully aware that ultimate settlement of the question would await the end of the war, proponents of a property-based freedom wished to avert wartime policies that might prejudice the outcome. Actions taken during the conflict, they feared, could leave former slaves economically dependent and politically subordinate when peace finally came.[134]

If the constraints of war limited the possibilities for transforming Southern society, those possibilities became narrower still with President Lincoln's Proclamation of Amnesty and Reconstruction, issued in December 1863. The edict offered to pardon most participants in the rebellion (excepting, most notably, high-ranking Confederate military and civil officials), on condition that they forsake the Confederacy, swear allegiance to the United States, and agree to abide by wartime laws and proclamations concerning emancipation. That done, they could again enjoy all rights of property, "except as to slaves." Moreover, the amnesty proclamation proposed a method by which the loyal people of a seceded state could form a government and seek readmission to the Union. The new state governments, Lincoln suggested, might then assume legal control over the former slaves. Although he acknowledged that he lacked constitutional power to dictate terms of reunification, the President hinted that he would welcome state legislation confirming emancipation and providing for the education of former slaves, "which may yet be consistent as a temporary arrangement with their present condition as a laboring, landless, and homeless class." In proposing his own model for reconstructing the South, Lincoln fueled the ongoing debate about the character of the war, the terms of national reunification, and the future of the former slaves.[135]

Widely praised in the North as a magnanimous yet politically shrewd measure, the amnesty proclamation also received high marks from most federal officials in the South. George Field, chief plantation commissioner in the Mississippi Valley, regarded the edict as the foundation for "an enduring and mutually advantageous reconstruction of the Union." Within a month of its issue, two-thirds of the Mississippi

---

[134] *Freedom*, ser. 1, vol. 3: docs. 47B, 57.
[135] *Statutes at Large*, vol. 13, pp. 737–39.

Valley plantations leased out during 1863 were restored to their antebellum owners. Field lauded the "amicable connections" that were forming between *"loyal Northern men"* and Southern *"owners* of the soil."[136] Others took a more skeptical view. Many Northerners feared the consequences of remanding homeless, landless freedpeople to the tender mercies of "loyal" state governments. Under such a reconstruction policy, predicted Wendell Phillips, a noted abolitionist, the restored states would render "the freedom of the negro a sham," leaving the South "with its labor and capital at war." Some Union field commanders, drawing upon firsthand experience with former slaveholders, expressed similar doubts. Disputing the notion that the occupied Confederate states were ripe for readmission, General Napoleon B. Buford, commander of the District of Eastern Arkansas, avowed that he had "not yet seen a man of fortune or standing in the South who was to be relied on as a Union man." Far from accepting the demise of slavery, "every slaveholder sticks to the institution as his only hope for fortune[,] respectability and means of liveing." Northerners in the army and out worried that the Lincoln administration was conceding too much too soon in allowing such "unionists" to reclaim both their political rights and their land.[137]

To the extent that the President's amnesty policy promised to reinstate Southern planters, it also threatened the prospects of former slaves, who expected still more radical changes to follow wartime emancipation. Like Northern critics of federal labor policies, freedpeople objected to the low levels of compensation, restrictions upon freedom of movement, and inadequate protection against fraud or abuse. But their criticism extended beyond the details of wage labor. Freedom from a master, they believed, should mean more than the right to change masters. It implied access to those productive resources, especially land, without which freedom would be compromised.

Not even those Yankees most sympathetic with the aspirations of the former slaves viewed landownership precisely as they did. Land, ex-slaves and Northerners concurred, could provide subsistence and foster independence from former owners. But there agreement usually ended. Former slaves, like many of their contemporaries throughout the world, generally did not view land as property in the abstract or as a commodity whose worth was determined by the market. Instead, they valued it in proportion to labor expended and suffering endured. Given a choice, they preferred to own or occupy not just any plot of ground,

[136]   *Freedom*, ser. 1, vol. 3: doc. 189.
[137]   Edward McPherson, *The Political History of the United States of America, during the Great Rebellion* (Washington, 1865), p. 412; Brig. Genl. [Napoleon B. Buford] to Hon. Secy. of War, 11 Dec. 1863, vol. 37 DArk, pp. 240–42, Letters Sent, ser. 4664, Dist. of Eastern AR, RG 393 Pt. 2 No. 299 [C-7539]. See also Berlin et al., " 'To Canvass the Nation,' " pp. 243–44.

but the land where they had been born and reared and in which they and their forebears had invested so much blood and sweat. Land was a link to generations past and future and a foundation for family and community among the living. Nor did former slaves fully subscribe to Northern concepts of absolute property. Instead, rights to particular tracts might bear little resemblance to the specifications of a deed. When left to their own devices, freedpeople often allowed for overlapping rights in any one property; conversely, an individual's use rights might encompass several parcels, not necessarily contiguous. Nonetheless, under the terms of the Yankee occupation, freedpeople desiring to obtain control over land had to comply with the incongruous conventions of the Northerners.[138]

The most favorable wartime opportunities to acquire land were those afforded freedpeople in the Sea Islands, where absent proprietors had been dispossessed under the Direct Tax Act. Developments in the latter months of 1863 held special promise. Under instructions from President Lincoln, the direct-tax commissioners reserved certain of the forfeited estates for "charitable" purposes, to be sold in twenty-acre tracts exclusively to heads of black households. That policy, which won the favor of two of the three commissioners and several prominent military officials, spared former slaves from having to bid against Northern speculators in order to obtain any land at all. But the freedpeople and many of their advocates – including General Saxton, Mansfield French, and Abram D. Smith, the dissenting tax commissioner – felt that Lincoln's instructions did not go far enough. The total reserved acreage, they pointed out, was far too small to provide a homestead for all black residents of the Sea Islands. They wanted former slaves to enjoy preferred access to any of the forfeited land on the islands, not solely to that on the reserved estates. Hoping to circumvent the instructions, Saxton, French, and Smith encouraged would-be black landowners to settle wherever they wished and lobbied the Lincoln administration to permit the freedpeople to enter preemption claims.[139]

For a time, the strategy worked. On the last day of December 1863, Lincoln instructed the direct-tax commissioners to permit loyal residents of the Sea Islands to preempt forty-acre tracts on any government-controlled land before it was put up for auction.[140] The news seemed a vindication for the freedpeople of the Sea Islands, many of whom had already staked out a claim "on the old homestead, where they had been

[138]   *Freedom*, ser. 1, vol. 3: docs. 47A, 58; Saville, "A Measure of Freedom," pp. 59–64. See also Ira Berlin, Steven Hahn, Steven F. Miller, Joseph P. Reidy, and Leslie S. Rowland, "The Terrain of Freedom: The Struggle over the Meaning of Free Labor in the U.S. South," *History Workshop* 22 (Autumn 1986): 127–29. On Northern concepts of absolute property, see Morton J. Horwitz, *The Transformation of American Law, 1780–1860* (Cambridge, Mass., 1977).
[139]   *Freedom*, ser. 1, vol. 3: docs. 39, 45.
[140]   *Freedom*, ser. 1, vol. 3: doc. 41.

born, & had laborered & suffered." Former slaves on some plantations made applications "in mass . . . without the names of the negroes & without designating the particular tracts for each." But preemption evoked strong opposition from Smith's colleagues on the direct-tax commission, whose objections led in February 1864 to a reinstatement of Lincoln's initial instructions. The disappointment of the freedpeople was "almost unbearable." Although a number of them eventually acquired plots on the estates earmarked for "charitable" purposes (110 families by March 1864), the undoing of preemption marked the passing of the former slaves' best wartime hope for landownership.[141]

However disappointing, the opportunities of Sea Island freedpeople to acquire land far exceeded those afforded their counterparts elsewhere in the Union-occupied South. Although the President possessed authority to appoint direct-tax commissioners for every seceded state, by the beginning of 1864 he had done so only for South Carolina, Florida, Virginia, and Tennessee.[142] Lincoln's inaction, coupled with the Proclamation of Amnesty and Reconstruction, signaled his intention to use expropriation chiefly to induce Confederates to return to their "proper allegiance," and not as a means to recast Southern society. Although his policy did not foreclose entirely the possibility of providing former slaves with homesteads from the land of disloyal owners, it established a precedent that had momentous consequences in the postwar struggle over land.

The waning possibility of acquiring land was only one source of concern to the freedpeople and their Northern allies in the spring of 1864, as Union armies once more took to the field and the new agricultural season commenced. As earlier, military considerations shaped the evolution of free labor. With the territory under federal control substantially enlarged, especially in the western theater, the army needed every black soldier it could get. Like veterans, the new recruits spent most of their time at noncombat duties, garrisoning towns, guarding railroad bridges, protecting leased plantations and contraband camps, and performing heavy fatigue labor. But increasingly large numbers of black troops traded shovels for rifles. Experienced black soldiers, some of whom had served for over a year, demanded more from military service than did raw recruits, and greater familiarity with official regulations and procedures aided their struggle against the inequities of military service. A handful of black men attained the status of commissioned officers. Of far greater significance for the common soldier, Congress abolished the difference in the pay of black and white soldiers, and Adjutant General Thomas ordered that black regiments perform no

---

[141] *Freedom*, ser. 1, vol. 3: docs. 39, 42, 45, 49, 62; see also Rose, *Rehearsal for Reconstruction*, chap. 10.

[142] U.S., Senate, "Letter of the Secretary of the Treasury . . . [on] the collection of direct taxes in insurrectionary districts . . . ," *Senate Executive Documents*, 38th Cong., 1st sess., No. 35.

more than "their fair share of fatigue duty." Eventually Congress also guaranteed the freedom of all black soldiers' families, whatever the loyalty of their owners and even where slavery remained legal.[143]

The expansion of Union-held territory and the extension of federal supply lines also increased the need for military laborers. In the two major offensives of 1864 – the drive from Chattanooga to Atlanta in the western theater, and the campaign against Richmond and Petersburg in the east – the labor shortage was exacerbated by the scarcity of suitable black men in the contested territory. As a result, laborers and teamsters from previously occupied areas worked endlessly moving supplies and materiel from distribution points in the rear to armies in the field. Black "pioneers," many of them from Tennessee, built miles of corduroy road during the Atlanta campaign. Black men from the contraband camps and towns of tidewater Virginia and North Carolina were dispatched to the James River to dig a canal at Dutch Gap and to construct field works for the troops operating against Richmond.

At times, this heightened demand for military laborers worked to the advantage of black men. Some short-handed quartermasters, commissary officers, and engineers offered premium wages, favorable working conditions, and refuge and support for the families of their laborers. Black women benefited from the construction of general hospitals at Washington, Nashville, Louisville, and St. Louis, which provided employment for hundreds of nurses and laundresses. At the great supply depots, notably Washington and Nashville, black laborers received pay increases along with their white counterparts, and both were paid with greater regularity, as their employers sought to minimize discontent. The War Department eliminated another longstanding grievance when it decided to pay wages directly to black laborers whose loyal owners still claimed them as slaves.[144]

Union military authorities did not always meet their labor needs by increasing the rewards of service. Often they resorted to subterfuge and force, seizing black men without so much as first soliciting volunteers. Sometimes the superintendents of contrabands found themselves forced to do the army's dirty work. Operations against Richmond and Peters-

---

[143] For the experience of black soldiers, see *Freedom*, ser. 2, especially chap. 6 on black commissioned officers, chap. 7 on the struggle for equal pay, and chap. 10 on disproportionate assignment to fatigue duty (including Adjutant General Thomas's order, doc. 201). The families of black soldiers were freed in March 1865 by joint resolution. (*Statutes at Large*, vol. 13, p. 571.)

[144] For examples of wage increases for military laborers, see below, doc. 70; *Freedom*, ser. 1, vol. 3: doc. 122; Ass't. Qr. Mtr. General Chs. Thomas to Brig. Gen'l. M. C. Meigs, 22 Jan. 1864, vol. 74, pp. 158–60, Letters Sent, ser. 9, Central Records, RG 92 [Y-681]; unsigned note, [Nov. 1864], enclosed in A.A. Genl. Wm. Fowler to Bvt. Brig. Genl. G. V. Rutherford, 8 Nov. 1866, Letters Received from the Freedmen's Bureau, ser. 34, Central Records, RG 92 [Y-664]. For the policy respecting direct payment of wages to black laborers who, their owners claimed, were legally still slaves, see below, doc. 99.

burg in mid-1864 led to the impressment of hundreds of men from contraband camps and government farms throughout tidewater Virginia and coastal North Carolina. Elsewhere, too, the opening of a new front or an impending Confederate raid occasioned mass levies that wrenched black men from their homes and sent them to distant places to labor for the army.[145]

The entry of black men into federal service, whether by their own volition or at gunpoint, placed at risk other freedpeople whose livelihood depended upon their labor. To reduce this vulnerability, some military commanders promised to provide "suitable subsistence" to the families of black soldiers. Others, particularly at garrison towns in the Mississippi Valley, tolerated (and sometimes sanctioned) the creation of "regimental villages" near the camps of black troops. In these settlements, the soldiers' kin could share the men's rations and wages and contribute to their own support by cultivating garden patches or working for military or private employers. Such possibilities continued to attract former slaves to federal posts, despite the determined efforts of government officials to assign them to plantation labor. In the Vicksburg area, 3,700 former slaves left contraband camps for leased plantations during a single week in March 1864, yet at week's end the population of the camps had not diminished appreciably.[146]

When the recruitment of black soldiers was extended to the Upper South, contraband camps assumed an importance in both federal policy and the lives of fugitive slaves that had formerly characterized only the Lower South. Given the opportunity to gain freedom through military service, slaves left their owners and enlisted by the tens of thousands. Eventually, 57 percent of Kentucky's black men of military age served in the army, as did 39 percent of those in Missouri and in Tennessee and 28 percent of those in Maryland.[147] Slave men fled to recruiting stations in large numbers, often accompanied by their families. Black women and children also made their way to army posts when their owners, having lost the labor of the men, heaped overwork and abuse upon the remaining slaves or simply refused to support them any longer. The influx of fugitive slaves re-created in Tennessee and the border states the problems of relief that federal officials had earlier confronted in other parts of the Union-occupied Confederacy, but with the added complication that slavery was still legal.[148]

[145] See below, docs. 36, 40, 47A, 104, 113, 129, 165. In December 1864, an urgent need to repair the levees along the Mississippi River had similar effects; military authorities impressed hundreds of ex-slaves and free blacks. (*Freedom*, ser. 1, vol. 3: docs. 131–32.)

[146] See below, docs. 26, 33; *Freedom*, ser. 1, vol. 3: docs. 204n., 212; *Freedom*, ser. 2: docs. 47A–C, 313. On the Vicksburg camps, see *Freedom*, ser. 1, vol. 3: doc. 200.

[147] *Freedom*, ser. 2: p. 12.

[148] See below, docs. 177, 181, 225A–C, 226, 229; *Freedom*, ser. 1, vol. 1: docs. 191–92, 237; *Freedom*, ser. 2: docs. 90B, 91, 106–7, 111, 294, 298, 302.

The soldiers' families and other black refugees overwhelmed the resources of established camps such as Freedman's Village and Roanoke Island. Freedman's Village became so crowded that military authorities shunted new arrivals to an employment depot on Mason's Island, in the Potomac River, which itself quickly became overcrowded and disease-ridden.[149] In middle and east Tennessee and northern Alabama, where enlistment of black men did not begin in earnest until late 1863, contraband camps sprang up at major recruiting posts. By June 1864, some 5,500 former slaves were living at seven camps, the largest at Clarksville, Nashville, and Gallatin, in middle Tennessee, and at Decatur Junction and Huntsville, in northern Alabama.[150]

In the border states, by contrast, the recruitment of black soldiers crippled slavery without impelling the federal government to sponsor either contraband camps or free labor. Despite the pleas of soldiers' relatives and other runaway and castaway slaves, military authorities refused to provide rations or housing: Since they were legally still slaves, their owners, not the government, were responsible for their care. Orders called upon local commanders to enlist the able-bodied men but turn away all other black refugees.[151]

Border-state black soldiers protested vehemently against such treatment of their families, and they found numerous allies among sympathetic army officers. General William A. Pile, superintendent of black recruitment in Missouri, repeatedly sought permission to transfer fugitive slaves to the contraband camp at Benton Barracks, there to be furnished both protection and rations. Loath to assume responsibility for the fugitives, Pile's superiors instead authorized another officer to remove them to the Kansas border. In central Kentucky, hundreds of black women and children gathered in and near Camp Nelson, which in mid-1864 became the state's largest center of black recruitment. But Union military authorities, from the post commander to Adjutant General Lorenzo Thomas, refused to care for the soldiers' families. Throughout the summer and fall, in a drama that became more somber with each enactment, the women and children were driven from the post, often into the clutches of owners who had received advance notice of the expulsion. A final wholesale eviction, undertaken on a freezing November day, caused such suffering that the ensuing publicity forced military authorities to reverse their policy. At the end of the war, the "Colored Refugee Home" at Camp Nelson sheltered about 1,000 black women and children.[152]

---

[149] See below, docs. 47A, 77, 80.
[150] On the Tennessee and Alabama camps, see below, docs. 108, 110, 114, 123, 129.
[151] See below, docs. 167, 169, 177, 219; *Freedom*, ser. 1, vol. 1: doc. 233; *Freedom*, ser. 2: docs. 93, 102A−C, 105.
[152] See below, docs. 176−77, 182, 187, 190, 219, 225−27, 230; *Freedom*, ser. 1, vol. 1: doc. 191; *Freedom*, ser. 2: docs. 94, 107, 312A−B.

In addition to spawning contraband camps, military enlistment sped the disintegration of slavery, encouraged legal emancipation, and, especially in Tennessee, advanced the development of free labor. Without the direct sanction of military or treasury officials, many slaves negotiated new terms of work, either with their owners or with nonslaveholders who welcomed an opportunity to employ black laborers. Such informal accommodations, usually involving one-to-one bargaining, had appeared with increasing regularity in late 1863 as recruitment diminished the pool of young black men. Private free-labor arrangements proliferated during early 1864, as landowners rushed to secure workers for the coming year. In the Nashville basin and in parts of the border states, farmers and planters made numerous concessions in order to retain "the services of there slaves – or in other words to conciliate & prevent them from running away." Some promised cash wages; others, to match the terms offered by government employers or to pay "as much as was given to other colored persons"; still others permitted former slaves to cultivate land as renters.[153]

Based on verbal agreement, private free-labor bargains left broad latitude for conflicting interpretation, renegotiation, or abandonment by either party. Employers generally held the balance of power and seldom hesitated to use it. Many of them simply refused to pay what they had promised. Eviction might take place at any moment and for any reason. Families of black soldiers were especially liable to be driven off or denied food and clothing, as was any former slave who showed "a disposition to send his children to school or to favor the *Yankees*." Employers who had lured workers into the field with promises of a postharvest payment often reneged and, instead, drove them away "to save taking care of them during the winter."[154]

The disruptions of war and the continued legality of slavery also hindered the spread of private free-labor agreements – sometimes fatally. In many places, guerrilla bands took direct action against planters and farmers who countenanced any breach of slavery or who introduced black laborers into previously all-white communities. The guerrillas reserved especially deadly venom for the black laborers themselves. Such attacks were widespread in much of Missouri, but by no means confined there. In their struggle to contain free labor, defenders of slavery also deployed

---

[153] See below, docs. 102, 105, 107, 113, 125, 128, 139, 188, 222; *Freedom*, ser. 1, vol. 3: docs. 231A–B; *Freedom*, ser. 2: docs. 95–96. In Kentucky, where slavery remained legal until the ratification of the Thirteenth Amendment in December 1865, such informal, unsanctioned, and unstable free-labor arrangements also characterized the summer and fall following the end of the war. (See below, docs. 231–32, 234–36, 238–42; *Freedom*, ser. 1, vol. 1: docs. 240–41, 245–51, 253–54.)

[154] See below, docs. 114, 125, 127, 130, 139, 177n., 181, 193, 222, 226; *Freedom*, ser. 1, vol. 1: docs. 150A–B, 152, 191–92, 231, 233; *Freedom*, ser. 2: doc. 298. On similar developments in the Lower South, see *Freedom*, ser. 1, vol. 1: docs. 122–23; *Freedom*, ser. 1, vol. 3: docs. 211, 231A–B.

the law. Threats of prosecution under statutes that prohibited hiring a slave without the owner's consent deterred many would-be employers from dealing with "slaves" – even when the "slaves" were beyond reclamation by their "owners." Although they eventually capitulated to the new regime, slaveholders and their allies retained many weapons to obstruct its progress. Their bitter resistance prevented free labor from taking root in some areas and stunted its development in others.[155]

Free labor stood on firmer ground in those parts of the Upper South that were under the jurisdiction of federal superintendents – tidewater Virginia, coastal North Carolina, the District of Columbia, and the immediate vicinity of Union posts in middle and east Tennessee and in northern Alabama. During 1864, only a small proportion of the freedpeople in these areas lived and worked on government-controlled land. A far greater number labored under contracts with local farmers or other private employers. In Union-occupied tidewater Virginia, which had a total black population of approximately 35,000 at the end of 1863, only a few thousand ex-slaves and free blacks cultivated "government farms" as either wage laborers or renters. A similar pattern appeared in middle and east Tennessee and northern Alabama, where probably no more than 1,000 former slaves resided on estates leased out by treasury agents. The impact of federally sponsored labor arrangements extended, however, well beyond their direct participants. Private employers in the vicinity generally had to meet the same standards in order to retain their laborers, and military officials sometimes supervised free-labor contracts between masters-turned-employers and slaves-turned-employees.[156]

Union officers exerted much greater control over labor and relief in the Lower South, where they continued to view the plantations as the proper place to employ and subsist most former slaves. In the cotton-growing regions along the Mississippi River, the government-supervised plantations stretched from Helena, Arkansas, to Natchez, Mississippi, in 1864. They included not only estates leased to Northern entrepreneurs, but also those operated by Southern planters pardoned under Lincoln's amnesty proclamation. In mid-March, an estimated 60,000 freedpeople resided on the leased plantations alone, and the number on owner-operated places probably approached the same dimensions. In southern Louisiana, where the northern boundary of federal occupation reached beyond Baton Rouge, free labor under federal auspices also became more widespread. As of the summer of 1864, 35,000 former slaves were working under formal contracts supervised by the army; about 15,000 more labored under terms similar to those mandated by military regula-

[155] On guerrilla attacks, see below, docs. 141, 178, 186, 193, 195–96, 197n., 199; *Freedom*, ser. 1, vol. 1: doc. 196; *Freedom*, ser. 2: doc. 85. On prosecution under antebellum statutes, see below, docs. 184, 189, 238–39, 241; *Freedom*, ser. 1, vol. 1: docs. 239, 242, 246, 248–49, 252, 255; *Freedom*, ser. 2: doc. 112.

[156] See below, chap. 3, and docs. 42–43, 105–6c, 109.

tions, but without written agreements. Meanwhile, in lowcountry South Carolina, Georgia, and Florida, the extent of Union-held territory remained largely unchanged. Approximately 15,000 freedpeople lived within federal lines, most of them on the South Carolina Sea Islands; roughly half were employed on plantations.[157]

In all parts of the Union-occupied South, the struggle between former slaves and former slaveholders involved more people and a broader range of issues than it had during the previous two years. Many of the freedpeople were fresh from bondage, having lately escaped to Union lines or fallen under the control of advancing federal armies; others had one or more years' experience in freedom. While recently liberated slaves prepared to fight the old battles, the veterans undertook new ones. More experienced freedpeople not only tutored neophytes in their rights as free men and women, but also led the way. Those who had acquired tools, agricultural implements, and work animals served as exemplars; occasionally, they even employed other ex-slaves.[158]

The interchange between veterans and neophytes proceeded among the employers as well. Planters were an even more diverse lot than plantation laborers, including among their number both newly arrived lessees and old-time proprietors, Northerners conversant with free-labor practices and Southerners entirely unfamiliar with them. Northern entrepreneurs expounded upon the rights of employers and the myriad ways to encourage productivity without resorting to force, while Southern planters shared their technical knowledge of plantation routine and their notions about the peculiar characteristics of black workers. In many instances, exchanges between Northern and Southern planters took place within formal partnerships, in which the latter supplied the land and the former the capital and good offices necessary to resume staple production in a war zone. Like their laborers, planters entered the new crop year with more definite ideas about what they wanted, what they would accept, and what they would not tolerate.[159]

Federal policy makers had also learned from experience, and they, too, acquired new responsibilities. In the Sea Islands, where the government-operated plantations passed into private hands at direct-tax sales in March 1864, General Saxton and his subordinates were reduced to the role of arbiter between private employers and contract laborers. Elsewhere in the Union-occupied Lower South, federal officials continued to supervise plantation labor on both the estates leased

---

[157] *Freedom*, ser. 1, vol. 3: docs. 57, 197; Chaplain Thomas W. Conway to Major General N. P. Banks, 9 Sept. 1864, C-228 1864, Letters Received, ser. 1920, Civil Affairs, Dept. of the Gulf, RG 393 Pt. 1 [C-732].

[158] For examples of freedpeople employing other ex-slaves, see below, doc. 58; *Freedom*, ser. 1, vol. 3: docs. 177, 208–9, 216n.

[159] On relations between Southern planters and Northern planters, see Powell, *New Masters*, especially chaps. 3–5. See also *Freedom*, ser. 1, vol. 3: docs. 182, 189, 209.

out by the government and those operated by antebellum owners. Early in 1864, they revised the regulations governing agricultural labor. Designed chiefly to resolve conflicts that had arisen the previous year, the new guidelines also endeavored to placate Northern critics by requiring terms of agricultural labor more like those in the free states. In the sugar- and cotton-growing regions along the Mississippi River, where labor regulations had been sketchy outlines in 1863, federal officers elaborated more fully the rights and duties of both employers and laborers. The new regulations were particularly specific about the amount and form of compensation, the days and hours of work, and the use of garden plots and work animals. They addressed, moreover, vexatious questions concerning which plantation residents were obligated to work, whether laborers or employers should pay for food, clothing, and medical care, and who should provide for nonworkers.

Both plantation laborers and planters gained from the new labor codes. For the laborers, improvements were substantial. The regulations increased minimum wages, limited daily hours of labor to ten in summer and nine in winter, and required extra pay for work on Sunday. They gave workers a lien on the crops they produced and codified their right to garden plots. In addition, military authorities urged planters to offer such incentives as compensation for extra work and "appropriation of land for share cultivation." By such means, General Banks believed, former slaves and former slaveholders could prepare themselves "for the time when [the laborer] can render so much labor for so much money, which is the great end to be attained." At the same time, Union officials recognized that wartime conditions prohibited a shift to full monetary compensation. Military orders reinforced the claim of all plantation residents — workers and nonworkers, healthy or sick — to a subsistence, by requiring the plantation owner or lessee to provide food and clothing for all former slaves on the estate.

The new regulations also strengthened the employer's hand. In the interest of maintaining plantation discipline, federal officials barred soldiers from visiting without authorization and prohibited workers from leaving the estates without permission. To secure the fidelity of laborers to year-long contracts, the regulations required monthly payment of only half wages, with the remainder withheld until after the harvest. Once a laborer had "exercised the highest right in the choice and place of employment, he must be held to the fulfillment of his engagements."[160]

Rather than resolving all differences, the new rules became objects of contention, as both planters and laborers tried to turn them to their own advantage. Workers exercised "the power to be idle" until desperate planters were willing to meet their terms. Many former slaves

[160] *Freedom*, ser. 1, vol. 3: docs. 109, 198.

67

declined to sign contracts until early spring. In February, after Confederate raiders again terrorized leased plantations along the Mississippi River, laborers increased their demands, refusing to return to work without suitable protection and greater pay. The raids were occasional events, but the regular seasonal rhythm of agricultural production also operated both for and against the former slaves. Once workers had "laid by" the crop in the summer, they became expendable until harvest time, when the demand for hands again strengthened their bargaining position. During slack periods, they found themselves liable to dismissal, despite regulations that required planters to support their workers for the duration of the contract.[161]

Sensitive to the dynamics of the new relationship, both plantation hands and planters took care to specify their terms of agreement. Contracting time became an occasion to ventilate grievances from the past and maneuver for future advantage. Laborers took special pains to guarantee their families' subsistence by securing access to gardens, woodlots, and forage, and to insist upon assurances of protection from Confederate raiders. Many workers – a majority in some areas – demanded compensation in a share of the crop instead of a monthly wage. For their part, employers enumerated workers' responsibilities in greater detail, including standards of acceptable deportment. The increased length and specificity of contracts attested to the breadth of the contest.[162]

Both at contracting time and throughout the year, freedpeople sought to allocate the labor of family members at their own and not their employers' discretion. Planters – eager to compensate for the shortage of men by claiming the labor of most women and children – distinguished only between workers and nonworkers, insisting that all of the former should be in the field. The freedpeople, on the other hand, believed that their new status implied greater opportunity for wives and mothers to devote time to child care and to productive labor in house and garden. Moreover, wage scales that accorded female field hands substantially less than their male counterparts offered women scant inducement to labor for the planters. Those whose husbands were at work on the same estate were especially likely to spurn such employment. On one Louisiana plantation, the women would work only "on the patches of ground given to their husbands by the overseer"; on another, "[s]ome of the women peremptoraly refuse[d] to work in the field stating that they are ladies and as good as any white trash." The labor of children also became a

[161] *Freedom*, ser. 1, vol. 3: doc. 130. On the effects of Confederate raids in 1864, see below, doc. 39; *Freedom*, ser. 1, vol. 3: docs. 196–97, 209.

[162] For examples of crop-sharing arrangements, see *Freedom*, ser. 1, vol. 3: docs. 192, 214n. On the prevalence of such arrangements in one Louisiana parish, see *Freedom*, ser. 1, vol. 3: doc. 129. For examples of nonmonetary compensation for plantation work, see *Freedom*, ser. 1, vol. 3: docs. 125–26. On plantation laborers' insistence upon physical security, see *Freedom*, ser. 1, vol. 3: docs. 201, 209.

matter of contest. The planters' insistence upon putting them into field gangs conflicted with the freedpeople's desire that they attend school or perform domestic chores.[163]

As the range of free-labor relations increased, the struggle between planters and laborers moved beyond matters of production to matters of consumption. During 1864, a growing number of planters established plantation stores that sold a variety of merchandise. The availability of consumer goods, they argued, would "multiply [the workers'] simple wants & stimulate industry." One plantation manager confessed that exhortations about the virtues of honest toil failed to motivate his workers as much as did their desire "to procure a coveted calico dress or straw Hat." For some Northern planters, well-developed purchasing habits and a wide array of merchandise were veritable hallmarks of civilization.[164]

Whatever their boon to civilization, plantation stores also served more immediately useful ends. The ready availability of consumer goods helped keep workers at home, and if their purchases drew them into debt, so much the better. Clever planters learned to manipulate accounts to keep their laborers in arrears. Those who thought they could get away with it set retail prices at levels above the mark-up permitted by government regulations. Some planters-turned-merchants flouted the regulations altogether and required their workers to purchase clothing or rations that were supposed to be furnished free of charge.[165]

Freedpeople appreciated the availability of goods but resented attempts to gouge them. Wherever possible, they patronized stores operated by merchants more friendly to their interests. Former slaves in the Vicksburg area took their business to a special "freedmen's store," whose proprietors were prohibited by military order from overcharging. Elsewhere in Union-occupied territory, establishments operated by Northern freedmen's aid societies gave former slaves an alternative to the plantation stores.[166]

While most former slaves struggled to earn a living wage during 1864, some managed to rise above the status of wage laborer. Several hundred Sea Island freedpeople entered the ranks of small landowners by purchasing plantations cooperatively or by acquiring plots earmarked for "charitable" purposes. In the Mississippi Valley, chiefly around Vicksburg and Helena, a similar number leased land from the

[163] *Freedom*, ser. 1, vol. 3: docs. 100n., 116, 199. For examples of former slaves' desire to send their children to school, see below, doc. 42; *Freedom*, ser. 1, vol. 3: docs. 21, 110, 217. On postwar struggles over family labor, which exhibit many of the same themes, see Ira Berlin, Steven F. Miller, and Leslie S. Rowland, "Afro-American Families in the Transition from Slavery to Freedom," *Radical History Review* 42 (Fall 1988): 89–121.

[164] *Freedom*, ser. 1, vol. 3: docs. 40, 216. See also Powell, *New Masters*, pp. 87–90.

[165] *Freedom*, ser. 1, vol. 3: docs. 108, 120A–C, 227. See also Powell, *New Masters*, pp. 90–92.

[166] See below, docs. 32, 42; *Freedom*, ser. 1, vol. 3: docs. 47A, 225, 227.

government. Possessed of little capital, nearly all the black lessees rented small farms, not large plantations, and they generally worked the land with only the labor of their families, occasionally augmented by hired workers. On a still smaller scale and in more informal fashion, former slaves tended plots on "home farms" administered variously by the Treasury Department, military officials, and representatives of Northern benevolent associations. Such cultivators – whose ranks included some black soldiers and their families – worked tracts ranging from a few acres to a small homestead.[167]

Some black families in the Upper South also gained access to land through official channels. Superintendents of "Negro Affairs" in tidewater Virginia made about 200 parcels available to black tenants, charging them cash or a share of the crop as rent and otherwise allowing them to control their own farming operations. Similarly, treasury agents in coastal North Carolina leased small farms to former slaves, as well as rights to collect turpentine from the pine forests.[168]

In both the Upper and the Lower South, black landowners, lessees, and residents of the home farms placed greater emphasis upon subsistence than upon commercial agriculture. Seeking first of all to provide food for their own households, ex-slave farmers generally put most of their land in corn and vegetables. Any surplus could readily be sold to the residents of nearby towns and army posts. When their resources permitted, they added other marketable crops. The chief limit upon such additional production was often the number of workers in the household, a problem that some black farmers solved by hiring additional laborers.[169]

In regions where cotton had been the predominant crop, some black landowners and lessees planted none at all, and those who did grow the staple generally cultivated modest amounts. Nevertheless, at stratospheric wartime prices, the proceeds of small cotton patches permitted black farmers not only to improve their families' living conditions, but also to purchase livestock, tools, and other productive property. Late in 1864, the superintendent of freedmen at Helena reported that "[a]ll of the colored lessees have made more than a living, and will be ready to begin another year with capital that will enable them to work to better advantage than in the past."[170]

In general, black lessees in tidewater Virginia and North Carolina reaped fewer material rewards than those in the Mississippi Valley. The land they farmed was depleted from years of tillage, and military superintendents lacked both the means and the will to invest in improvements and fertilizer. The only available draft animals were worn-

[167] *Freedom*, ser. 1, vol. 3: docs. 49, 207–9, 217.
[168] See below, docs. 38, 42–43.
[169] See below, doc. 28; *Freedom*, ser. 1, vol. 3: docs. 144, 171, 208.
[170] *Freedom*, ser. 1, vol. 3: docs. 217, 222A.

out beasts "condemned" by the quartermaster's department. Many of the leaseholds were too small and unproductive to support the renters and their families. Often the lessees earned a subsistence by working for white farmers in the neighborhood; their share of the crop on their leaseholds thus became "profit for their seasons work." Such arrangements usually involved a division of labor whereby the father hired out for wages while the mother and children worked the rented plot. But, depending upon the number of people in the household and their age and sex, the division sometimes differed, reflecting each family's assessment of how best to preserve an independent standing. Although their choices were dictated in part by the local demand for agricultural labor, access to land, however limited, reduced their dependence upon wage employment and often permitted them to engage in such labor for only part of the year.[171]

A large number of freedpeople who had neither the means nor the opportunity to rent land found other ways of earning a living without entering into year-long contracts for agricultural labor. Fishing, oystering, and crabbing provided a means of self-support for former slaves near the water who could afford a modest investment in nets, lines, and perhaps a small boat.[172] Wood yards that supplied fuel for steamers and locomotives offered another alternative, though seldom a means of self-sufficiency. Operated variously by government superintendents, individual landowners, and private contractors, wood yards employed thousands of freedpeople, especially along the Mississippi River and other waterways and in the vicinity of military railroads. Both men and women labored in the wood yards, the men cutting wood and the women cording it. They were paid at piecework rates that probably permitted vigorous workers to surpass the earnings of agricultural laborers. Although taxing, work in the wood yards also allowed considerable control over the hours and pace of work. That measure of self-direction made wood-yard workers reluctant to hire out for agricultural wage labor.[173]

Short-handed planters and farmers complained when former slaves were able to make a living on their own, and they begged military authorities to curtail independent employment. Their appeals met a favorable reception from those officials who viewed year-long contracts for wage labor—not subsistence cultivation or independent jobbing—as the key to social stability. A superintendent of contrabands in the Sea Islands deplored the practice of "getting a precarious livelihood by doing a little at this thing, & a little at that." To encourage "*honest steady* labor" and control "the floating Negro population," military authorities restricted physical movement and confis-

---

[171] See below, docs. 42–43.
[172] See below, doc. 42; *Freedom*, ser. 1, vol. 3: docs. 53, 55.
[173] See below, docs. 17, 115; *Freedom*, ser. 1, vol. 3: docs. 171, 177–79, 193, 200, 210.

cated boats. In the Mississippi Valley, superintendents reduced the issue of rations to wood-yard workers as a means of inducing them to hire to planters.[174]

In Union-occupied cities and towns, too, federal regulations often undermined the ability of former slaves to support themselves. Many military officials saw unemployed or irregularly employed black people as a threat to good order. Accordingly, they adopted pass systems and vagrancy regulations to "clean out" former slaves who lacked "steady" employment or independent means, thereby treating as criminals those who were self-employed or who earned a living by "chance work." In Natchez, Mississippi, orders ostensibly issued to prevent the spread of "pestilential diseases" virtually forbade any "contraband" to live or work independently of a white employer. The regulations resulted in the expulsion of numerous self-supporting freedpeople, including relatives of soldiers. Their outraged protests were seconded by agents of Northern benevolent societies, provoking a controversy that eventually reached Congress and contributed to the resignation of the general who had approved the "health" orders.[175]

In the border states, the legality of slavery obstructed the development of free labor. Consequently, border-state slaves and former slaves generally had to leave their homes in order to obtain freedom and free-labor employment. The District of Columbia remained an attractive destination for fugitive slaves from Maryland, as did nearby Northern states. Kansas, Illinois, and Iowa received refugees from Missouri, where the continued strength of slavery, guerrilla warfare in the countryside, and the refusal of military authorities to provide contraband camps or free-labor employment made it difficult for fugitive slaves to find work or protection. Meanwhile, Kentucky slaves who could successfully evade civil authorities and military pickets crossed the Ohio River into freedom, especially at Cairo, Illinois; Jeffersonville, Indiana; and Cincinnati, Ohio. Beginning in late 1863, when black recruitment opened in neighboring Tennessee, slave men from southern Kentucky fled to the Tennessee camps, often with their families in tow.[176]

On occasion, federal officials supported the efforts of freedpeople to migrate north; indeed, they attempted to remove freedpeople from "overpopulated" parts of tidewater Virginia, the District of Columbia, and Missouri. Midwestern army chaplains in St. Louis relied on connections in their home states to find employment for hundreds of former slaves. Elsewhere in Missouri, the army sought less to help freedpeople find work than simply to expel them. During the spring and summer of

[174] *Freedom*, ser. 1, vol. 3: docs. 53–55, 210n.
[175] *Freedom*, ser. 1, vol. 3: docs. 15, 89, 166, 169, 202A–B, 212.
[176] See below, docs. 132, 158B, 173, 177, 179n., 194, 224; *Freedom*, ser. 1, vol. 1: docs. 41, 44, 46, 51, 135–37, 144–45A, 190, 194–96, 213A, 219A–B, 224, 227, 228A–B, 232; *Freedom*, ser. 2: docs. 72, 85, 97–98, 303.

1864, General Egbert B. Brown ordered the removal of former slaves – chiefly women and children – from military posts in central Missouri to the Kansas border. Although they eschewed the harsh methods of General Brown, officials in tidewater Virginia and Washington also sought to reduce the number of black people under their charge. As new arrivals swelled the ranks of dependent freedpeople, superintendents of "Negro Affairs" in tidewater Virginia worked with Northern benevolent societies and "intelligence offices" (the employment agencies of the day) to transport several hundred black women and children to northeastern cities, where they were hired out as domestic servants. Military officials in Washington used similar tactics to reduce the population of former slaves dependent on the government. Yet, no matter how desperate their condition, most freedpeople refused offers to live and work among strangers in the North. As the end of the war neared, and with it the prospect of freedom on their home ground, they gave even shorter shrift to northward migration.[177]

The deterioration of slavery hastened the progress of legal emancipation. By the end of 1864, unionist governments in Arkansas and Louisiana had ended slavery, as had the new state of West Virginia and the border state of Maryland. During the early months of 1865, Missouri and Tennessee also wrote slavery out of their fundamental law. Meanwhile, congressional passage of a constitutional amendment abolishing slavery and its ratification by a number of Northern states placed further pressure on those Union-held regions of the South in which slavery remained legal. Of the areas exempted from the Emancipation Proclamation, only tidewater Virginia failed to enact emancipation before the end of the war, and citizens in those few Union-controlled counties were scarcely in a position to take such action had they so desired. The loyal slave states of Kentucky and Delaware also refused to act, holding fast to the remnants of chattel bondage until the incorporation of the Thirteenth Amendment into the Constitution. Even in those places, however, slavery's supporters were on the defensive well before the end of the war.[178]

The advent of legal freedom insinuated free labor into the lives of previously unaffected Southerners. The process whereby slaves became employees and slaveholders employers repeated itself on new terrain, with many of the same false starts and dead ends that had characterized

---

[177] See below, docs. 34–35, 41–42, 176–77, 179n., 182, 187, 190, 194; Capt. J. M. Brown to Jos. M. Truman, Jr., 31 Dec. 1864, vol. 60, p. 39, Press Copies of Letters Sent, ser. 527, Asst. Quartermaster & Disbursing Officer, DC Asst. Comr., RG 105 [A-10639].

[178] For the legal changes enacting emancipation, see Francis Newton Thorpe, comp., *The Federal and State Constitutions*, 7 vols. (Washington, 1909), vol. 1, pp. 288–306, vol. 3, pp. 1429–48, 1741–79, vol. 4, pp. 2191–2229, vol. 6, p. 3445; Richard O. Curry, *A House Divided: A Study of Statehood Politics and the Copperhead Movement in West Virginia* (Pittsburgh, Pa., 1964), pp. 100–130; Henry Wilson, *History of the Antislavery Measures of the Thirty-Seventh and Thirty-Eighth United-States Congresses, 1861–64* (Boston, 1864), chap. 13.

such developments earlier in the war. At the same time, increasing numbers of nonslaveholders began bidding for the labor of men and women previously beyond their reach. Eager to hire black workers, they augmented the ranks of Southern supporters of free labor.[179]

Even in the wake of formal emancipation, not everyone accepted the new order. Many erstwhile slaveholders resorted to naked force to sustain their accustomed power over black people. Others, more far-sighted, fashioned new modes of exacting labor. Often they made use of the same state authority that had recently legislated emancipation. In Maryland, former slaveholders drew upon antebellum apprenticeship statutes. Within a month of emancipation, local courts had apprenticed more than 2,500 black children and young adults, generally to their former owners. Reluctant to intervene in the affairs of a loyal state that had voluntarily abolished slavery, federal authorities in Washington overruled orders by the local military commander to "break up the practice now prevalent of apprenticing young negroes without the consent of their parents." Newly freed black people found themselves with little protection.[180]

If some former owners tried to maintain control over their erstwhile slaves, others used emancipation as an excuse to eliminate costly and unwanted responsibilities. Often they simply terminated customary issues of food and clothing. In many places, freedpeople were driven from their homes. In an increasingly familiar scenario, Missouri slaveholders took "unprofitable, and expensive" black women and children "within a convenient distance of some military post, and set them out with orders to never return home – telling them they are free." Freed from the former owner's support as well as his control, such slaves had little choice but to take refuge in cities, contraband camps, or garrison towns. The collapse of the old order heaved up new hardships as well as opportunities.[181]

The steady advance of Union armies accelerated that collapse. Cutting a broad swath of destruction across Georgia, General William T. Sherman and his troops arrived at Savannah in December 1864. Accompanying them were thousands of hungry, footsore slaves who, despite discouragement, had joined their fortunes to those of the Yankee invaders. Their hostile reception by Sherman's army extended in one widely reported instance to removing a pontoon bridge upon which the soldiers had crossed a swift stream; the black refugees who followed were

---

[179] See, for example, below, docs. 154, 159A, 196–97.
[180] On the forcible maintenance of slavery after emancipation, see, for example, below, docs. 122, 141, 144–45; *Freedom*, ser. 1, vol. 3: docs. 145, 211. On apprenticeship in Maryland immediately following emancipation, see below, docs. 140–43, 146–49, 151–54, 158–60; *Freedom*, ser. 1, vol. 1: doc. 151; Richard Paul Fuke, "A Reform Mentality: Federal Policy toward Black Marylanders, 1864–1868," *Civil War History* 22 (Sept. 1976): 222–24.
[181] See below, docs. 150, 153, 155A, 192–93, 221; *Freedom*, ser. 1, vol. 1: docs. 152, 196.

thereby abandoned to the mercy of pursuing Confederates. Many of them drowned when they attempted to swim to safety.[182] Concerned both about such accounts and about Sherman's long-standing opposition to the enlistment of black soldiers, Secretary of War Stanton journeyed to Savannah in early January. He found Sherman preparing to advance into South Carolina and searching for a way to disencumber his army of its black followers. On January 12, 1865, at Stanton's instance, he and Sherman met with local black religious leaders to ascertain their views about how former slaves could best defend and support themselves. Freedom, declared Garrison Frazier, a spokesman selected by the twenty churchmen, "is taking us from under the yoke of bondage, and placing us where we could reap the fruit of our own labor, take care of ourselves and assist the Government in maintaining our freedom." "The way we can best take care of ourselves," he advised, "is to have land, and turn it and till it by our own labor. . . . until we are able to buy it and make it our own."[183]

Within days, General Sherman responded in a way that addressed both his own pragmatic military problems and the former slaves' fondest hopes. His Special Field Order 15 "set apart" the coastal islands and mainland rice plantations between Charleston and the St. Johns River of Florida "for the settlement of the negroes now made free by the acts of war and the proclamation of the President." The order authorized families of former slaves to occupy as much as forty acres each in the reserved district, for which they would receive "possessory title." Aside from military officials, "no white person whatever" was to reside in the area. "[S]ole and exclusive management of affairs will be left to the freed people themselves, subject only to the United States military authority and the acts of Congress." As the black people who had followed his army through Georgia took up land in the Sherman reserve, thousands of other slaves and ex-slaves set out for the coast, including many lowcountry natives who had been "refugeed" inland by their owners. Their numbers further increased as Sherman's army marched northward through the Carolinas. By the time of the Confederate surrender, about 20,000 former slaves had settled on 100,000 acres in the reserved district. Understanding Sherman's grant as official recognition of their rightful claim to the land, they began to put in crops. Tens of thousands more would join them in the months to come.[184]

---

[182] Joseph T. Glatthaar, *The March to the Sea and Beyond: Sherman's Troops in the Savannah and Carolinas Campaigns* (New York, 1985), chap. 3.

[183] Benjamin P. Thomas and Harold M. Hyman, *Stanton: The Life and Times of Lincoln's Secretary of War* (New York, 1962), pp. 343–45. For the meeting with black churchmen, see *Freedom*, ser. 1, vol. 3: doc. 58.

[184] For Sherman's special field order, see *Freedom*, ser. 1, vol. 3: doc. 59. On the earliest settlement of freedpeople under its provisions, see Bvt. Maj. Genl. R. Saxton to Maj. Genl. M. C. Meigs, 6 Apr. 1865, "Negroes," Consolidated Correspondence File, ser. 225, Central Records, RG 92 [Y-211].

As former slaves in lowcountry Georgia and South Carolina took possession of land under Sherman's order, acreage in tidewater Virginia was offered for sale under the Direct Tax Act and the confiscation acts. Hoping to secure "a spot of land" for at least some of the freedpeople under his jurisdiction, Charles Wilder, the local superintendent of "Negro Affairs," joined with representatives of Northern aid societies to buy six estates. He and his partners hoped thereby not only to prevent eviction of the black people occupying the land, but also to subdivide and resell the property to them.[185] The possibility of additional purchases for the same purpose ran aground, however, when the Lincoln administration suspended further sales until deliberations about a bureau of emancipation were concluded. In March 1865, Congress established the Bureau of Refugees, Freedmen, and Abandoned Lands (Freedmen's Bureau), with a mandate to supervise the transition from slavery to freedom in the former slave states, provide for destitute freedpeople and white refugees, and administer the land that had fallen into the hands of the government by confiscation, abandonment, or military occupation.[186]

An expectation that fundamental changes would accompany the return of peace and the organization of the Freedmen's Bureau tempered plans for the new crop year. Unwilling to take steps that might only be undone, federal authorities for the most part continued extant labor arrangements. A proposal to revise labor and welfare policies in southern Louisiana and the Mississippi Valley provoked considerable debate, for it would have sharply increased the wages of plantation workers and made them responsible for their own food and clothing. But, in the end, superiors of the treasury agent who drafted the new rules, including President Lincoln himself, refused to sanction them. Agricultural operations in 1865 therefore commenced under regulations little different from those of the previous year. Throughout the Union-occupied South, nearly everyone – Northerners and Southerners, black people and white – expected the end of the war to bring a full reconsideration of the terms of free labor.[187]

By the spring of 1865, at least 474,000 former slaves and free blacks had taken part in some form of federally sponsored free labor in the Union-occupied South – as soldiers, military laborers, residents of contraband camps, urban workers, or agricultural laborers on government-

---

[185] Proceedings of general court-martial in the case of Captain Charles B. Wilder, 1–16 May 1865, MM-2065, Court-Martial Case Files, ser. 15, RG 153 [H-54]; Adjutant General L. Thomas to Hon. Edwin M. Stanton, 5 June 1865, filed as A-1411 1865, Letters Received, ser. 12, RG 94 [K-223].

[186] *Statutes at Large*, vol. 13, pp. 507–9.

[187] *Freedom*, ser. 1, vol. 3: docs. 119, 135, 137, 222A–B. An attempt to revamp the system of relief in the District of Columbia was squelched by Quartermaster General Meigs. (See below, doc. 77.)

supervised plantations and farms.[188] In addition, an indeterminable number had negotiated private free-labor bargains with their former owners or other employers.[189] Still other former slaves, whose numbers are also impossible to estimate, had left the South to become free workers in the North, some of them under the auspices of official relocation and employment programs, others on their own or with the assistance of individual army officers.

Of the black people who worked under officially sanctioned free-labor arrangements, about 271,000 lived in the plantation regions of the Lower South that came under Union control. Some 125,000 were in the Mississippi Valley.[190] Those in southern Louisiana numbered about 98,000.[191] Another 48,000 experienced wartime free labor in the South Carolina Sea Islands or elsewhere along the south Atlantic coast; two-fifths of these were latecomers who took up land in the Sherman reserve.[192]

---

[188] The number of black people who experienced some form of federally sponsored free labor can be estimated only roughly. Because many slaves were "refugeed" away from areas that came under Union control and others fled to Union lines from Confederate-held territory, the wartime black population of Union-occupied counties cannot be derived from the slave and free-black populations of 1860. Official estimates – ranging from systematic censuses to barely educated guesses – exist for some regions. When such figures seem reliable, the editors have used them; when contemporary evidence is lacking or seems unreliable, they have tried to arrive at an estimate by other means.

Louis S. Gerteis has estimated that 237,800 black people were "organized by freedmen superintendents during the war," a category that overlaps, but is not identical to, the one used here. For example, the regional figures that make up his total do not consistently incorporate black soldiers. His geographical focus is also different. While his estimate accounts for most Union-occupied parts of the Confederacy, it does not include such territory in Alabama, Florida, Georgia, and middle and east Tennessee; in addition, it omits the District of Columbia and the border states. (*From Contraband to Freedman*, pp. 193–94.)

[189] To the private free-labor arrangements that were individually negotiated throughout the Union-occupied South might be added the more generalized labor systems that began to take shape in Maryland, Missouri, and Tennessee during the final months of the war, following the abolition of slavery by state action.

[190] The figure is derived from a report in July 1864 by Colonel John Eaton, which noted that 113,650 former slaves (including soldiers) were engaged in free labor under his jurisdiction. Assuming that new arrivals from Confederate territory increased that number by 10 percent before the end of the war, the total becomes 125,015. (Eaton, *Grant, Lincoln and the Freedmen: Reminiscences of the Civil War* [1907; reprint ed., New York, 1969], pp. 133–34.)

[191] According to an official estimate, 80,000 black people (apparently not including soldiers) were living under free-labor arrangements in southern Louisiana in September 1864: 50,000 in the countryside and 30,000 in New Orleans. There is no reason to assume any significant change during the remaining months of the war. Adding to that number the black soldiers recruited in the region (perhaps three-fourths of those credited to Louisiana, or 18,039 men), the total reaches 98,039. (Chaplain Thomas W. Conway to Major General N. P. Banks, 9 Sept. 1864, C-228 1864, Letters Received, ser. 1920, Civil Affairs, Dept. of the Gulf, RG 393 Pt. 1 [C-732]; *Freedom*, ser. 2: p. 12.)

[192] Estimates of the number of former slaves who lived and worked under federal supervision in the South Carolina Sea Islands include 16,000 in 1862 (before the opening of black recruitment) and 15,000, exclusive of soldiers, in 1863. The latter number probably did not increase by more than 10 percent (to about 16,500) during 1864; many of the new arrivals

In the Upper South, some 203,000 former slaves and free blacks lived and worked under federal auspices. About 74,000 could be found in tidewater North Carolina and Virginia.[193] Perhaps 37,000 were in middle and east Tennessee or northern Alabama.[194] Another 40,000 lived in the District of Columbia, in Alexandria, Virginia, and in the contraband camps on the Virginia side of the Potomac River.[195] In all

were refugees from points in Florida and Georgia that were held for a time by Northern troops but subsequently abandoned. Perhaps 1,200 additional freedpeople could be found at Fernandina, Florida, and the handful of other coastal outposts that remained continuously in federal hands. Nearly 10,000 black soldiers were credited to South Carolina (5,462), Georgia (3,486), and Florida (1,044); they bring the total to 27,692. Finally, some 20,000 former slaves had been settled in the Sherman reserve by mid-April 1865, making a grand total of 47,692. (*Freedom*, ser. 1, vol. 3: docs. 29n., 36; *Official Records*, ser. 3, vol. 4, pp. 118–19; *Freedom*, ser. 2: p. 12; Bvt. Maj. Genl. R. Saxton to Maj. Genl. M. C. Meigs, 6 Apr. 1865, "Negroes," Consolidated Correspondence File, ser. 225, Central Records, RG 92 [Y-211].)

[193] The figure for tidewater North Carolina is derived from a census conducted in January 1865, which counted 17,307 black people (evidently excluding soldiers) in the territory under Union control. Adding the 5,035 black soldiers credited to the state brings the total to 22,342. (James, *Annual Report*, p. 4; *Freedom*, ser. 2: p. 12.) The total for tidewater Virginia (52,004) has been reached by adding figures from censuses taken in late 1864, which enumerated 24,850 black people south of the James River (including more than 4,000 soldiers) and 13,305 north of the James (excluding soldiers), plus an estimated 1,000 soldiers in the latter district, plus 12,849 former slaves and free blacks on the eastern shore (the black population of Accomac and Northampton counties in 1860). (See below, docs. 42–43; U.S., Census Office, 8th Census, *Population of the United States in 1860* [Washington, 1864], pp. 504–13.)

[194] Rough estimates can be obtained by beginning with the number of black soldiers recruited in the three regions and assuming a relationship between that figure and the number of other former slaves and free blacks who lived in contraband camps, performed military labor, or worked as agricultural laborers under military supervision. About 18,400 black soldiers enlisted from these areas (assuming that middle and east Tennessee contributed two-thirds of Tennessee's total, and northern Alabama all the soldiers from that state). (*Freedom*, ser. 2: p. 12.) If it is assumed that an equal number of black people participated in other free-labor arrangements, the total becomes 36,800. (The ratio of only one civilian to each soldier is employed because middle and east Tennessee and northern Alabama had relatively few contraband camps – all established late in the war – and very limited government-sponsored agricultural operations; the number of black civilians in federally supervised labor settings was therefore much smaller in proportion to black soldiers than was the case in tidewater Virginia and North Carolina or the occupied regions of the Lower South, where, for every one soldier, between two and nine civilians participated in Union-sponsored free labor.)

[195] Estimates for the District of Columbia, Alexandria, and the contraband camps across the Potomac from Washington, D.C., involve consideration of several different sets of figures, as well as an element of conjecture. According to the 1860 census, 3,185 slaves and 11,131 free blacks lived in the District, virtually all of whom presumably had free-labor experience during the war, as did untold thousands of fugitive slaves from Virginia and Maryland. A military census of March 1865, which was almost certainly marred by undercounting, enumerated 16,092 black refugees (excluding quartermaster employees living in government housing, and house servants) in the District, Alexandria, Freedman's Village, and Mason's Island; other estimates of the number of wartime black migrants to Washington and its vicinity run as high as 40,000. Probably the most useful figures come from a census taken in 1867, which placed the black population of the District alone at 31,937, of whom 22,747 had been resident since at least 1864. Beginning with the latter figure, and then assuming that 17,000 other black people experienced free labor in Alexandria and the northern Virginia

the border states combined, probably no more than 52,000 black people took part in Union-sponsored free labor.[196] Former slaves in the Union-occupied South worked in a wide variety of free-labor settings. Most of the men – about 101,000 in the seceded states and 47,000 in the border states and the District of Columbia – served as soldiers or sailors.[197] Many of them had previously worked as military laborers, along with tens of thousands of men who never entered the armed service. A few thousand women also worked for military employers. Most ex-slave women in Union-held territory, and a sizable proportion of the men, toiled as agricultural laborers on plantations and farms supervised by federal officials. A similar number – mainly women, children, and elderly people – lived in contraband camps, infirm farms, or "regimental villages," where they received rations and occasionally performed remunerative labor. Significant numbers of black men and women found free-labor employment that was not directly sponsored by Union authorities. Most civilian workers in towns and cities did so, and an indeterminable number of rural ex-slaves negotiated new terms of labor on their own. The experiences of soldiers, military laborers, residents of contraband camps, and agricultural and urban workers provided somewhat different perspectives on freedom. These variations were compounded by differences in antebellum status, the character of federal occupation, and the policies of particular Union commanders.

Yet a common thread ran through the diverse experiences. Only a tiny minority of black people in Union-held territory attained the status of independent proprietor or tenant; the overwhelming majority provided for themselves through some form of wage labor. In escaping slavery they had relinquished any claim upon their owners for subsistence, protection, or provision for old age, youth, and illness. Their survival now depended, not upon their place in a system of hierarchical personal relations, but upon the sale of their labor power in an impersonal market. Granted self-ownership but no productive property, former slaves were simultaneously permitted and compelled to work for wages.

Although wartime wage labor did not satisfy the aspirations of

camps during the war or else had lived and worked in the District during the war but were gone by 1867, results in a total of 39,747 for the nation's capital and nearby northern Virginia. (*Population of the United States in 1860*, p. 588; see below, doc. 86; Green, *Secret City*, p. 62; Allan John Johnston, "Surviving Freedom: The Black Community of Washington, D.C., 1860–1880" [Ph.D. diss., Duke University, 1980], pp. 162–66.)

[196] Estimates of the extent of federally sponsored free labor in the border states, excepting that for soldiers, are highly conjectural. Although a sizable proportion of border-state black men served in the Union army, few other forms of free-labor employment were available: Military labor was limited in scope, contraband camps few in number, and government-sponsored agricultural operations almost nonexistent. More than 42,000 black soldiers and sailors were credited to the states of Missouri, Kentucky, and Maryland (*Freedom*, ser. 2: pp. 12, 14n.); perhaps an additional 10,000 black people worked in other federally sponsored free-labor settings.

[197] *Freedom*, ser. 2: pp. 12 (soldiers), 14n. (sailors).

former slaves to become freeholders, it broke decisively and irrevocably with slavery. Freedpeople gained proprietorship over their own persons. The new conditions of labor generally prohibited physical punishment, encouraged independent family, religious, and social life, and required compensation. Ex-slave laborers gained rudimentary legal protection, backed by the force of federal arms. They made the most of whatever opportunities the war created. Except for the youngest, oldest, and most infirm, nearly all black people within the Union-occupied Confederacy were self-supporting at the time of Appomattox.[198]

Even in territory still controlled by Confederate forces, particularly those areas adjacent to Union lines, the proximity of free labor and the prospect of universal freedom eroded slave discipline. With freedom within reach, some slaves demanded new terms of labor – an end to corporal punishment, the elimination of overseers, more time to work garden plots, payment in cash or in kind. To slaveholders, such notions smacked of rebellion, to be answered by the lash, sale, or removal to the interior. But as Confederate military hopes dimmed, slaveholders found themselves increasingly unable to wield the old authority. Free labor in the Union-occupied South helped subvert slavery far beyond federal lines.[199]

The advance of free labor within Union-occupied territory and the disintegration of slavery within the Confederacy seemed to vindicate Northerners' faith in the superiority of free over slave labor. Having planted the seeds of free labor in the South, however, federal officials disagreed about how they should be nurtured. Some, like Colonel Samuel Thomas, superintendent of freedmen in the District of Vicksburg, believed the government had done enough. Its job was simply to put the former slave's "labor on an equal footing with white labor . . . [g]uard him against imposition, give him his just dues at the end of each month, . . . and let him work his way up." "Capital does now, and will for some time to come carry on great enterprises," Thomas affirmed, "and a large portion of the human family, both white and black, must labor for this capital at regulated wages, without any direct interest in the result of the enterprise." Arguing that "[o]ur country has enough to bear without undertaking the enormous task of starting out each freedman with a competency," he considered the opportunity for individual self-improvement to be the true boon of freedom.[200]

Others believed that meddling Northerners had already done too much. Colonel Frank J. White, superintendent of "Negro Affairs" on Virginia's eastern shore, condemned benevolent associations and "enthusiasts" in the army for having made the former slave "dependent upon a bounty that can not last [and] would enevitably render him

[198] For assessments of the extent of self-support in one region, see below, docs. 42–43.

[199] *Freedom*, ser. 1, vol. 1: pp. 40–43, and chap. 9, especially docs. 327–31.

[200] *Freedom*, ser. 1, vol. 3: doc. 209.

helpless in the future." White also rejected "communistic" plans to settle freedpeople on abandoned or captured land, on the grounds that they would "[divide], instead of [unite] the interests of the two classes" — former slaves and their former owners — whose futures were necessarily intertwined.[201]

Still others were convinced that not enough had been done to aid the emancipated slaves. Reporting upon conditions in Tennessee shortly after the war, Captain Richard J. Hinton, an officer of a black regiment from Kansas, urged the government to allot land to the freedpeople. "Nothing," he argued, "not even the bestowal of suffrage, will so materially aid [in] destroying the effects of Slavery [as] the creation of a self-reliant independent yeomanry out of the former slaves." Hinton feared that black people would be subject to "the serfdom of capital" if the nation were merely to grant "personal freedom, secure no political or civil rights, and leave the freed class to struggle out of the slough the best way they can with the narrow plank of free labor."[202]

No one knew better than the freedpeople just how deep the slough and narrow the plank. Resolutely determined never again to be slaves, they were nevertheless ambivalent about their wartime encounter with free labor. If the "freedom" of wage work marked their long-awaited liberation from the personal dependency of the past, it also fell far short of the independence to which they aspired. The imminence of Northern victory and the final destruction of slavery therefore encouraged them to become increasingly active in pursuit of their own interests. In so doing, they confounded those federal officials who viewed them as mere objects of policies or a "problem" to be solved. Pointing to their vital contribution to the Union cause, as soldiers and as civilians, former slaves established their claims upon the government that had granted them liberty and in many instances was also their employer. Although frequently couched in the language of supplication, their communications to federal authorities — from local commanders to the President himself — asserted their rights as free citizens and the nation's obligations to them. A group of black men in coastal North Carolina took such ground in a protest against impressment, declaring it inconsistent with "there cause as Freemen and the Rights of their families."[203]

As black people began to assert the prerogatives of citizenship, they assumed a more visible place in public affairs. Throughout the Union-occupied South, former slaves and free blacks formed political and quasi-political associations. Such organizations were particularly active in New Orleans, Nashville, and Washington, where federal control dated from early in the war and large antebellum free-black communi-

---

[201] See below, doc. 46.
[202] Captain Richard J. Hinton to Captain T. W. Clarke, 31 July 1865, H-47 1865, Registered Letters Received, ser. 3379, TN Asst. Comr., RG 105 [A-6135].
[203] See below, doc. 25.

ties were ready to take the lead; but they also appeared elsewhere, especially in localities where black soldiers were stationed. These associations became vehicles by which black people sought to elevate their political status, demanding the right to testify in court, to sit on juries, and to vote. As the movement to reconstruct the South gained momentum, they became an active, though not yet fully sanctioned, force in local politics.[204]

The divisions among federal officials and the burgeoning political presence of black people revealed that if the Civil War had destroyed slavery, the meaning of freedom was no more certain than before the first shots at Fort Sumter. Wartime labor and welfare policies had necessarily rested more upon military exigencies than upon considered decisions about the future of the former slaves. Restricted to the narrow confines of securely held territory and subordinate at all times to the demands of waging war, they bore little resemblance to the requirements of ordinary times. Almost everyone – North and South, black and white – saw peace as an opportunity to begin afresh.

Yet wartime experience did not count for nothing. As the victorious North set about reconstructing Southern society, the labor and relief programs established within Union lines became points of reference for postwar plans. In the course of the debate, both those who equated freedom with independent proprietorship and those who understood it as the unfettered right to sell one's labor power cited wartime developments to bolster their positions. For their part, the former slaves and free blacks who had lived and worked in Union-occupied territory entered the contest with a confidence born of the pivotal role they had played in the Union's triumph and their wartime initiation into the practices of free labor. As freedom burst the bounds of its wartime limitations and advanced into the entire South, more than three and a half million newly liberated slaves joined the half-million who had experienced free labor amid civil war. Their abrupt passage into the American working class as propertyless, unenfranchised free laborers raised fundamental questions about the nation's "new birth of freedom."[205] The answers would affect all Americans.

[204] See, for example, below, docs. 84–85; *Freedom*, ser. 1, vol. 3: doc. 139; *Freedom*, ser. 2: doc. 362.
[205] The phrase appears in the Gettysburg Address. (Lincoln, *Collected Works*, vol. 7, pp. 22–23.)

CHAPTER I
Tidewater Virginia and North Carolina

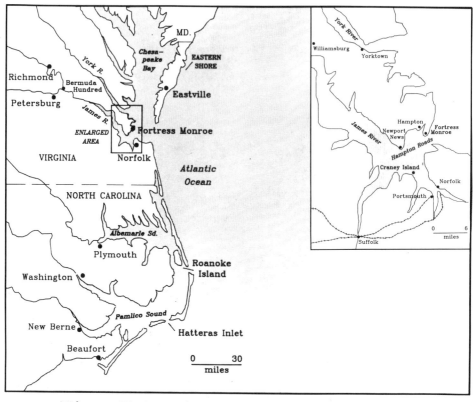

Tidewater Virginia and North Carolina. Inset shows the York–James Peninsula and its vicinity.

I

Tidewater Virginia and North Carolina

IN MID-MAY 1861, with the war only a month old, the first fugitive slaves arrived at Fortress Monroe, Virginia, an isolated federal outpost at the tip of the peninsula formed by the York and James rivers. Union General Benjamin F. Butler, commander of the Department of Virginia, denominated the runaways "contrabands," offered them protection from recapture, and put them to work for the army. During the next four years, military occupation undermined slavery and ushered in free labor in tidewater Virginia and parts of coastal North Carolina. By the end of the war, the federal government was employing thousands of former slaves and free blacks as military laborers, as soldiers, and as workers on "government farms." It had also assumed responsibility for the welfare of black people unable to find employment, whether temporarily or permanently.[1]

Former slaves in tidewater Virginia and North Carolina fashioned new lives in freedom, but they did so in circumstances not of their own choosing and often entirely beyond their control. The same wartime events that enabled them to escape bondage often undermined their efforts to support themselves. The same Union army that safeguarded their freedom made claims on their labor. The freedpeople's wartime struggle for economic independence brought them into contact not only with federal soldiers and officers, but also with Northern clergymen and teachers and Southern slaveholders loyal to the Union – all of whom had plans of their own for the former slaves and different visions

---

[1] In this essay, quotations and statements of fact that appear without footnotes are drawn from the documents included in the chapter. Published accounts of wartime free labor in tidewater Virginia and North Carolina include Louis S. Gerteis, *From Contraband to Freedman: Federal Policy toward Southern Blacks, 1861–1865* (Westport, Conn., 1973), chaps. 1–2; and Robert Francis Engs, *Freedom's First Generation: Black Hampton, Virginia, 1861–1890* (Philadelphia, 1979), chaps. 2–3. Also pertinent are Joe A. Mobley, *James City: A Black Community in North Carolina, 1863–1900* (Raleigh, N.C., 1981), chaps. 1–3; Stephen Edward Reilly, "Reconstruction through Regeneration: Horace James' Work with the Blacks for Social Reform in North Carolina, 1862–1867" (Ph.D. diss., Duke University, 1983), chaps. 2–3; Edna Greene Medford, "The Transition from Slavery to Freedom in a Diversified Economy: Virginia's Lower Peninsula, 1860–1900" (Ph.D. diss., University of Maryland, 1987), chap. 2; Wayne K. Durrill, *War of Another Kind: A Southern Community in the Great Rebellion* (New York, 1990); and David Cecelski, "A Thousand Aspirations," *Southern Exposure* 18 (Spring 1990): 22–25.

of their future after the war. A many-sided conflict shaped the meaning of freedom along the coasts of Virginia and North Carolina.

An economic and social transformation several generations in the making preceded the Union occupation of tidewater Virginia and North Carolina. In Virginia, on both shores of Chesapeake Bay, extensive tobacco cultivation had by the early nineteenth century given way to a mixed agriculture featuring wheat as the chief staple. Landowners, great and small, increasingly met the seasonal labor demands of the new agriculture by the short-term hire of slaves and free-black workers. Many planters left the region for fresh tobacco lands to the west or joined the migration to the cotton frontier. Those who remained often sold off part of their landholdings or subdivided them for cultivation by tenant farmers. Owing to the forced migration of slaves with their owners and to extensive sales in the interstate slave trade, the region's slave population stagnated. On the eve of the Civil War, slaves accounted for about one-third of the population of tidewater Virginia. Black people who were free made up another 12 percent of the inhabitants. Although plantations with twenty or more slaves could be found here and there, especially on the peninsula between the York and James rivers, most slaves lived in smaller units. In no county of tidewater Virginia did the median slaveholding exceed seven; on the eastern shore and in the vicinity of Norfolk it dropped as low as two or three. Small slaveholdings, a population in which free people outnumbered slaves, and widespread use of hired labor also characterized the area of coastal North Carolina that came under Union control, although there cotton was a more important crop than tobacco and free-black people composed only 6 percent of the population. In both regions, large numbers of hired slaves and free blacks worked at nonagricultural pursuits, including fishing, oystering, lumbering, and – in North Carolina – the extraction of turpentine.[2]

For slaves near Fortress Monroe, Union occupation opened the way to freedom and free labor early in the war. With much work to be done and none but soldiers to do it, General Butler could employ able-bodied fugitive slaves "very profitably." He therefore accepted all who came to the post, putting the men to work as common laborers and officers' servants. Butler issued rations to the laborers and their families, as he did to other fugitive slaves, but he made no provision to pay wages. Instead, he ordered accounts kept of the labor performed by the runaways and the rations issued to both workers and

---

[2] On slave and free-black life in tidewater Virginia, see Luther Porter Jackson, *Free Negro Labor and Property Holding in Virginia, 1830–1860* (Washington, D.C., 1942); Ira Berlin, *Slaves without Masters: The Free Negro in the Antebellum South* (New York, 1974), especially chap. 1; Willard B. Gatewood, Jr., ed., *Free Man of Color: The Autobiography of Willis Augustus Hodges* (Knoxville, Tenn., 1982); Medford, "Transition from Slavery to Freedom," chap. 1.

nonworkers, pending a decision by his superiors concerning their legal status. By this bookkeeping arrangement, Butler sought to charge the "care and sustenance of the non-laborers" against the services of the laborers. At the end of May 1861, Secretary of War Simon Cameron approved Butler's course, directing him to employ the contrabands as he saw fit and await instructions about "their final disposition." In August, he advised Butler to continue receiving all fugitive slaves — even though the recently approved Confiscation Act liberated only those who had been employed in the Confederate war effort — but to maintain careful records so that, "[u]pon the return of peace," Congress could "provide . . . just compensation to loyal masters."[3]

While Butler and Cameron wrestled with legal niceties, many of the former slaves who had fled to Fortress Monroe supported themselves without federal assistance. Most of them lived within the narrow expanse of Union-held territory between Fortress Monroe and the post of Newport News, including the town of Hampton. In this area, which had been abandoned by nearly all its white residents, many ex-slaves earned a living by selling goods or services to Union soldiers. Black women washed, cooked, and sewed for both officers and enlisted men. Some black men plied the traditional trades of fishing and oystering, while others did odd jobs for cash to supplement rations earned by stints of military labor. Both men and women hawked baked goods and produce — and sometimes whiskey and other proscribed articles — to the troops. A few former slaves squatted on abandoned farms and plantations and worked them as their own.[4]

The success of such endeavors depended upon military protection, which was by no means guaranteed. Union forces controlled only a few square miles of territory, and former slaves stood at risk of rebel raids. In late July 1861, a redeployment of troops to the defenses of Washington, D.C., forced Butler to abandon Hampton. A subsequent Confederate attack left the town in ashes, dispossessing its black residents and dislodging the squatters on nearby plantations. Hundreds of former slaves sought safety at Fortress Monroe.

The evacuation of Hampton increased both the number of slaves at the fort and federal expenses for relief. Some 900 contrabands crowded around Fortress Monroe, about a third of them men between the ages of eighteen and forty-five.[5] General John E. Wool, a septuagenarian officer who succeeded Butler in mid-August, confronted a problem that threat-

---

3 *Freedom*, ser. 1, vol. 1: docs. 1A–C; Benjamin F. Butler, *Private and Official Correspondence of Gen. Benjamin F. Butler during the Period of the Civil War*, 5 vols. (Norwood, Mass., 1917), vol. 1, pp. 114, 120. See also [Edward L. Pierce], "The Contrabands at Fortress Monroe," *Atlantic Monthly* 8 (Nov. 1861): 626–40.
4 In addition to the relevant documents in this chapter, see Butler, *Private and Official Correspondence*, pp. 185–88; [Pierce], "Contrabands at Fortress Monroe."
5 Butler, *Private and Official Correspondence*, pp. 185–88.

ened to worsen as the approach of winter induced other fugitive slaves –
"vagrants," in Wool's eyes – to seek shelter and protection within Union
lines. "[W]hat I am to do with the negro slaves that are almost daily
arriving at this post[?]" he asked Cameron. Cameron's suggestion that he
send "all negro men capable of performing labor" to Washington, along
with their families, was no solution at all, for those same men were
needed locally for military labor.[6]

Like Butler, Wool presumed that the earnings of contrabands who
were employed should support the unemployed. In October 1861, he
ordered army officers and private employers who hired black people as
servants to furnish them with subsistence and pay them at least $8 per
month for men and $4 for women. Wages earned by free men and
women were paid directly to them, but wages owed to escaped slaves
were deposited in a fund for the support of unemployed and dependent
contrabands. Wool soon extended the withholding system to black men
employed by the army itself. Setting nominal pay at $10 per month for
able-bodied adult men and $5 for teenaged boys and "sickly and in-
firm" men, he permitted the laborers to receive as much as $2 "as an
incentive to good behaviour." The remainder – the bulk of their
wages – went to the relief fund rather than the workers.

Neither the compensation nor the conditions of military labor satisfied the laborers. An army sergeant entrusted with supervising employees of the quartermaster countenanced and sometimes participated in
their physical punishment. Moreover, although the contraband fund
had accumulated $7,000 by January 1862, officers reduced the amount
of rations issued to the laborers' families. When several of the men
refused to work because their wives and children were hungry, military
officials had the protestors jailed and whipped. Deterred by reports of
such treatment by army employers, some black men worked instead for
the navy, which paid $10 per month and allowed them "absolute
control of their wages." Others hired themselves to individual officers
as servants or to companies of soldiers as cooks. And "quite a number"
simply "disappeared."

General Wool's policy regarding the contrabands, and his subordinates' callous implementation of it, angered Northern abolitionists as
well as the former slaves. A handful of antislavery Yankees had come to
Fortress Monroe to teach and preach among the contrabands, and
Union military ranks also included some staunch opponents of slavery.
These abolitionists regularly reported to their counterparts back home,
many of whom were active in newly formed freedmen's aid societies.
Certain of the superiority of Northern civilization and confident that
the free market played no favorites, they believed that black people –
once delivered from bondage, given a common-school education, and

---

[6] *Official Records*, ser. 2, vol. 1, pp. 770–71.

tutored in the fundamentals of Christianity – would profit from their freedom. Throughout the war, they provided the contrabands with a link to public opinion in the North and policy makers in Washington.[7]

Led by Lewis C. Lockwood, a minister at Fortress Monroe, Northern abolitionists protested the army's mistreatment of the former slaves. By compelling black men to work "for a miserable pittance," Lockwood charged, the Union was engaging in "government slavery." That "practical oppression" was as immoral as chattel bondage and perhaps less humane, because military masters had no interest in the workers beyond their labor. In letters to antislavery legislators, Lockwood publicized the "enormities, committed in the name of Union, freedom and justice under the Stars and Stripes."

The complaints brought results. In late January 1862, Wool appointed a commission, consisting of three officers from his personal staff, to investigate the treatment of former slaves at Fortress Monroe. Their report, issued in March, confirmed charges of abuse and disclosed widespread peculation in the quartermaster's department. The commissioners cast doubt on the army's legal authority to force the contrabands to work or to "compel them to be the recipients of its charity." They judged the existing policies not only "highly objectionable," but also "wholy illegal and now entirely unneccessary."

The commissioners especially objected to Wool's labor and relief measures, which they likened to "Irish souphouses" and "socialistic institutions." There was no need for "Governmental charity," they declared; "educated and philanthropic gentlemen" assured them that Northern aid societies would provide for the contrabands' "proper wants, in connection with their moral and intelectual culture." Private benevolence, not the public dole, could best assure the welfare of the freedpeople. Moreover, Wool's labor policy provided "no incentive to ambition." Former slaves would never be fit for freedom unless allowed to earn their own keep, perfect their skills, and improve themselves. If a few failed in the attempt, then so be it. "[B]etter by far to let one here and there fall by the wayside," concluded the commissioners, "than to encourage the people, that the Herculanian arm of the Nation is to be weilded in clearing their path."

Chastened by the commission's criticism, and aware that its report had been requested by Congress, Wool immediately revised his policy. He ordered that wages thereafter be paid directly to ex-slave laborers, at rates "determined by individual skill[,] industry and ability." Mandatory contributions to the contraband fund ceased. Wool also appointed

---

7 For examples of antislavery sentiment among the Union soldiers, see [Pierce], "Contrabands at Fortress Monroe." On the activities of Northern missionaries in tidewater Virginia, see, in addition to the relevant documents in this chapter, Engs, *Freedom's First Generation*, chap. 3; Henry L. Swint, ed., *Dear Ones at Home: Letters From Contraband Camps* (Nashville, Tenn., 1966); Reilly, "Reconstruction through Regeneration," chap. 3.

Charles B. Wilder, a "gentleman of wealth . . . and high social posi-tion" who was working at Fortress Monroe under the auspices of the American Missionary Association, to supervise the contrabands.

Wilder attacked the abuses documented by the commission. He implemented Wool's pledge of regular pay and persuaded him to allow black artisans a premium wage. Wilder had greater difficulty securing back pay for laborers who had been employed by the government before his appointment. The quartermaster balked at transmitting his employ-ment rolls and, when he finally did so, the records were in total disarray. Because it was impossible to substantiate their claims of ser-vice to the Union, many of the black workers employed at Fortress Monroe in the first months of the war were still trying to collect their pay at its end.

Wilder worked not only to remedy past injustices, but also to lay the groundwork for the freedpeople's future independence. Noting that some black men and women were already working farms abandoned by rebel owners, he urged the government to permit others to do the same. Such a policy, he argued, would reduce outlays for relief and enable the settlers to become self-sufficient. In April 1862, he gained Wool's permission to allow former slaves to settle on the periphery of federally controlled territory, "cultivate the Ground and use the prop-erty of Rebels in Arms." Wilder thereby legitimated the presence of black squatters and encouraged others to join them. Bearing "colored passes" issued by Wilder, black men and women left the fort and took up homesteads.

Unfortunately for the settlers, the spring of 1862 brought a major Union military offensive. Having transported his Army of the Potomac from northern Virginia to Fortress Monroe, General George B. Mc-Clellan began inching up the James-York peninsula toward Richmond, eventually coming within six miles of the Confederate capital. Many of the tramping soldiers abused the former slaves they encountered, and foraging parties, heedless of distinctions between the property of rebels and of contrabands, stripped their farms of livestock and supplies. By midsummer, when the campaign ground to a halt, federal control extended as far up the peninsula as Williamsburg and the Confederates had evacuated Norfolk and Portsmouth, on the south side of Hampton Roads. These modest gains in Union-held territory had been purchased at great cost to black squatters as well as McClellan's army.

While freedpeople in tidewater Virginia struggled to support them-selves and resist the impositions of Yankee troops, Union victories in coastal North Carolina enabled many slaves to emancipate themselves. Capturing Roanoke Island in February 1862, a joint army and navy expedition gained control of Albemarle and Pamlico sounds. Within three months, forces under General Ambrose E. Burnside, commander of the Department of North Carolina, had occupied the coastal towns of New Berne, Washington, Beaufort, and Plymouth. After that initial flurry of activity, however, tidewater North Carolina became a military backwater. Union control never extended far beyond the towns, while rebel forces roamed the intervening countryside.

However limited in extent, federal occupation disrupted slavery in North Carolina just as it had in tidewater Virginia. Disregarding his initial pledge to safeguard the property of loyal slaveholders, Burnside welcomed all fugitive slaves into his lines and assigned the able-bodied to a variety of military chores. At the end of March 1862, he placed both former slaves and white refugees under the supervision of Vincent Colyer, an agent of the Christian Commission, whom he designated "superintendent of the Poor." Quartermaster General Montgomery C. Meigs approved the employment of ex-slave men for "necessary work," but also instructed local quartermasters to issue no rations without requiring "some equivalent in occasional labor." Military appropriations, he insisted, were "not for charity." By midsummer, more than 10,000 black people were living in Union-occupied North Carolina, including 7,500 at New Berne, 1,000 at Roanoke Island, and a total of 1,500 at Washington, Beaufort, and Hatteras Inlet. Only 2,500 of them were able-bodied men.[8]

The freedpeople quickly made themselves indispensable to the Northern war effort. Military employers, Colyer later declared, "never could get enough of them." Black men constructed fortifications at New Berne, Roanoke Island, and Washington; loaded and unloaded cargo ships; joined the crews of Union steamers; drove teams; built bridges; and repaired wharves and docks. They served as scouts and spies, volunteering for dangerous missions into Confederate territory. Black women, who had fewer opportunities for military labor, worked in army hospitals. The former slaves labored willingly, even enthusiastically, for the Yankees. Though many of them could have earned more money at other employment, Colyer reported, they "consider[ed] it a duty to work for the U.S. government" and "tabooed" anyone who refused to do so.

Most of the former slaves not employed by Burnside's army managed to eke out a living on their own. Freedwomen supported themselves by washing and cooking for Union soldiers, selling baked goods and produce, and doing odd jobs. Only a few ex-slaves – those too young, too old, or too sick to work, and who had no friends or relatives to support them – required more than temporary relief. Even though the black

---

[8] In addition to the relevant document in this chapter, see *Freedom*, ser. 1, vol. 1: doc. 6; General Order No. 2, Head Quarters, Roanoke Island, N.C., 12 Mar. 1862, A. E. Burnside Papers, Generals' Papers & Books, ser. 159, RG 94 [V-118]; Vincent Colyer, *Brief Report of the Services Rendered by the Freed People to the United States Army in North Carolina, in the Spring of 1862, after the Battle of Newbern* (New York, 1864).

people under Colyer's charge outnumbered white refugees more than four to one, they received only one-sixteenth as much in government rations.

By midsummer 1862, the Union war effort had come to depend upon the labor of former slaves. Congress and the President recognized as much. The Second Confiscation Act of July 17 declared free the slaves of all disloyal owners and forbade Northern officers to return fugitive slaves to their claimants. The Militia Act, adopted the same day, and an executive order based upon its provisions instructed federal commanders to employ as many black laborers "as can be advantageously used for military and naval purposes," paying them "reasonable wages."[9]

In tidewater Virginia, the new guarantee of freedom to all slaves who came under federal military control encouraged large numbers to flee to the Union-occupied zone. Black men and women uprooted during McClellan's campaign made their way to Fortress Monroe and its vicinity. New arrivals also hailed from the region south of the James River, including the northernmost counties of North Carolina. Before long, successful escapees returned home to lead relatives and friends out of bondage, further swelling the number of slaves within Union lines. In November 1862, General John A. Dix – who had succeeded Wool in June – reported more than 3,100 black people in the federally controlled section of the York-James peninsula. About 500 of them were at Newport News, where Dix appointed an army surgeon, Orlando Brown, to serve as superintendent of contrabands. Hundreds more gathered in the vicinity of Norfolk and Portsmouth, on the south side of the James.[10]

Some military employers took advantage of events in the field and the policy changes in Washington to add unprecedented numbers of freedmen to their rolls. Major C. Seaforth Stewart, an engineer at Fortress Monroe, used black laborers to break a strike by Irish and German workingmen who had been imported from the North. The new hands received substantially lower wages than their predecessors, enough "to enable an industrious person to support himself & family" only if he indulged in no "wasteful expenditure" or "intervals of idleness." With his reconstituted work force, Stewart boasted, construction progressed "far more satisfactorily to all concerned and with less cost to Government."

Not all federal officers were so enthusiastic about employing black workers. Although General Dix deemed ex-slave men to be "of great importance in a military point of view," he feared that their dependents would tax the resources of his command. A free-soil Democrat who had

[9] *Statutes at Large*, vol. 12, pp. 589–92, 597–600; *Official Records*, ser. 3, vol. 2, p. 397.
[10] In addition to the relevant documents in this chapter, see *Freedom*, ser. 1, vol. 1: doc. 12.

held a cabinet post under President James Buchanan, Dix also worried that federal support for emancipation was alienating unionist slaveholders. If Dix was ambivalent, many of his subordinates were disdainful. Quartermasters in the Department of Virginia hired hundreds of white laborers from the North while black men willing to accept one-third the wages were "begging for work." When they did employ black laborers, Dix's subordinates took a casual approach toward paying them. They also refused to pay black mechanics the higher wages mandated in early 1862.[11]

Underpayment, nonpayment, and irregular payment meant hardship for the workers and their dependents. Unable to support their families, many military laborers moved on in search of other employment. By May 1863, according to Wilder's estimate, 2,000 black people had left Union camps on account of unpaid wages. Some returned to their former owners. The Union army's failure to pay wages on time, if at all, undercut the freedpeople's confidence in free labor.

In both North Carolina and Virginia, unionist slaveholders and their Northern allies strove to counter the effects of Union occupation upon slavery. Edward Stanly, a native North Carolinian whom President Lincoln appointed military governor, opposed the army's acceptance and employment of fugitive slaves and attacked Colyer's work among the contrabands.[12] In tidewater Virginia, General Dix championed the rights of loyal slaveholders. After Lincoln's announcement of the preliminary Emancipation Proclamation in September 1862, Dix abetted the efforts of local unionists to avoid the "penalties of disloyalty." His advocacy helped them win a temporary reprieve: The final Emancipation Proclamation exempted four Union-occupied counties bordering Hampton Roads and the two counties of Virginia's eastern shore.[13]

Intent upon tightening military discipline and protecting the property of loyal slave owners, Dix circumscribed Wilder's authority to issue passes, restricting the ability of former slaves to move about. With a complaisant general in command, slaveholding unionists stiffened their resolve. They refused to allow freedpeople to visit relatives who remained in slavery and called upon the army to enforce slave

11 In addition to the relevant documents in this chapter, see testimony of Gen. Dix before the American Freedmen's Inquiry Commission, 9 May 1863, filed with O-328 1863, Letters Received, ser. 12, RG 94 [K-68]; *Freedom*, ser. 1, vol. 1: doc. 12.

12 *Freedom*, ser. 1, vol. 1: docs. 8, 11; Vincent Colyer to Major General Burnside, 31 May 1862, A. E. Burnside Papers, Generals' Papers & Books, ser. 159, RG 94 [V-127].

13 Maj. Genl. John A. Dix to His Excellency A. Lincoln, 17 Nov. 1862, vol. -/3 VaNc, p. 418, Letters Sent, ser. 5046, Dept. of VA & 7th Army Corps, RG 393 Pt. 1 [C-3293]; Abraham Lincoln, *Collected Works*, ed. Roy P. Basler, Marion D. Pratt, and Lloyd A. Dunlap, 9 vols. (New Brunswick, N.J., 1953–55), vol. 6, p. 26. For the preliminary and final emancipation proclamations, see *Statutes at Large*, vol. 12, pp. 1267–69. The exempted counties were Elizabeth City, York, Norfolk, Princess Anne, Accomac, and Northampton.

discipline. In a few instances, they bribed Union soldiers to serve as slave catchers, in defiance of federal law.[14]

To escape the logistical and political difficulties posed by the growing number of contrabands within his lines, Dix proposed to transport them elsewhere. Asked to forward black laborers to the defenses of Washington in October 1862, Dix promptly sent some 200 men, accompanied by 100 women and children.[15] The following month, he contemplated destinations further afield. With the approval of the War Department, he asked the governors of several northeastern states to accept some of the former slaves until peace was restored or "a permanent Colony" established for them. But his proposal met immediate and vehement opposition. Convinced that mobilizing liberated slaves on behalf of the Union would advance the cause of emancipation, Governor John A. Andrew of Massachusetts flatly refused to cooperate. Instead of being removed from the South, he insisted, the black men at Fortress Monroe should be armed to fight for the defense of their families, their freedom, and the Union. Andrew's determined opposition helped scuttle the emigration scheme.[16]

With removal to the North impracticable, Dix began transferring black women, children, and old people from Newport News to Craney Island, a small tract at the mouth of the Elizabeth River, about five miles from Norfolk.[17] By January 1863, about 1,800 freedpeople were crowded onto the desolate island. Separated from their menfolk, who were working for the army, they lived in desperate poverty. Without a local source of food or firewood, with medical supplies scarce, and with a cutting wind blowing from Chesapeake Bay, hundreds sickened and died. "Every woman will say she lost three or more children," observed Lucy Chase, a Northern teacher.

The grave-digging squad had plenty to do, but there was little else to occupy the residents of Craney Island. Orlando Brown, their superintendent, introduced various schemes, among them a sewing circle whose members refurbished tattered uniforms and grain sacks. But most of the freedpeople on the island languished in enforced isolation. Unhappy in their exile, they begged Brown to resettle them where they could be "of some account." Chase found the women eager to work and particularly noted their "ravenous fondness for washing," though she was unsure "whether it is natural or because they have nothing else to do."

14 In addition to the relevant documents in this chapter, see *Freedom*, ser. 1, vol. 1: doc. 12.
15 Qr. Mr. Genl. M. C. Meigs to Col. D. H. Rucker, 18 Oct. 1862, vol. 63, p. 363, Letters Sent, ser. 9, Central Records, RG 92 [Y-640]; Major Genl. John A. Dix to Genl. Meigs, 20 Oct. 1862, and Maj. Genl. John A. Dix to Gen. Meigs, 22 Oct. 1862, D-149 (Book 50) 1862 and D-153 (Book 50) 1862, Letters Received, ser. 20, Central Records, RG 92 [Y-640].
16 In addition to the relevant documents in this chapter, see *Freedom*, ser. 2: doc. 41.
17 On Craney Island, see, in addition to the relevant documents in this chapter, Swint, *Dear Ones at Home*, especially pp. 19–73.

The manifest limitations of the "Government poor house" on Craney Island prompted the superintendents of contrabands and General Dix to devise more systematic arrangements for the ensuing year. So did the certainty that the expansion of federal occupation south of the James River would bring thousands more fugitive slaves under Union jurisdiction. Attention focused on farms and plantations abandoned by their owners. In January 1863, Charles Wilder visited Washington to meet with Secretary of War Stanton, urging him to make government-controlled land available to the freedpeople. Doing so would hasten the day when (as Wilder later put it) "every black man [could] have a little homestead of his own where he can live and go out to work." Such freeholds constituted "one of the conditions of freedom."

Interested in measures that would make the freedpeople self-supporting and reduce federal expenditures for relief, Stanton empowered Wilder to take control of "all the vacant lands and plantations . . . and put them in possession" of freedpeople for one year. General Dix approved, insisting only that the rights of loyal tenants already on the estates be respected.[18] He placed Orlando Brown in charge of abandoned land south of the James River, leaving Wilder to supervise that on the peninsula north of the James. Both superintendents received commissions as captains and quartermasters, giving them a rank commensurate with their new responsibilities and the authority to issue government supplies.

During the early months of 1863, Wilder and Brown resettled freedpeople from army posts and contraband camps onto the abandoned estates. With a relatively small acreage at their disposal and inadequate supplies of draft animals, tools, and seed, the superintendents expected to do little more than house, feed, and employ the former slaves. They assigned the neediest people to the estates that were most easily protected and least devastated by the war. By May, about fifty properties had been transformed into "government farms," including the plantations of former President John Tyler and Confederate General Henry A. Wise, a former governor of Virginia. By August, more than 1,600 black people were living on the government farms. They accounted for about 10 percent of the black population of the York-James peninsula and about 5 percent of that in the Union-occupied zone south of the James.[19]

Most of the former slaves on the government farms worked under share-wage arrangements. In return for their labor, they received a portion of the crop (usually one-half, sometimes one-third), which was divided among them in accordance with the amount of labor each had

---

[18] *Official Records*, ser. 1, vol. 18, pp. 570–71, 591; Major General John A. Dix to Dr. O. Brown, 22 May 1863, vol. 56/67 VaNc, pp. 8–9, Letters Sent, ser. 5046, Dept. of VA & 7th Army Corps, RG 393 Pt. 1 [C-3257].

[19] For the figures from which the percentages are derived, see *Freedom*, ser. 1, vol. 1: doc. 13.

performed. The government, aided by Northern freedmen's aid societies, furnished rations, draft animals, implements, and seed. The livestock and tools were generally army property that had been "condemned" – that is, judged unserviceable for further military use. Government-appointed overseers directed operations. Most of them were local white men whose agricultural experience derived from slavery, for the superintendents generally failed to find Northerners qualified to supervise the farms. The laborers grew corn for food and forage and tobacco and cotton for the market. Each family also tended a garden. All the government estates in Brown's district were evidently worked under such terms. On the land in Wilder's jurisdiction, most black people also worked under overseers for share-wages, but a few families rented small tracts – chiefly on the farms farthest from federal military protection and in the most dilapidated condition – and worked them without direct supervision.

As the government farms began operation in tidewater Virginia, black men in tidewater North Carolina entered the Union army. In April 1863, General Edward A. Wild received the War Department's permission to enlist black soldiers in Union-occupied North Carolina. Drawing from the contraband camps and military labor gangs, Wild quickly brought his "African Brigade" to full strength. By the end of the war, about 5,000 black men from North Carolina had served in the Union army, nearly all of them from the coastal counties. Until the fall of 1863, enlistments in tidewater Virginia lagged behind those in North Carolina, in part because of tepid support from General Dix. Thereafter, however, recruiting proceeded briskly, and the tidewater region provided most of the 5,900 black soldiers ultimately credited to the state.[20]

The establishment of the government farms and the recruitment of black soldiers dealt heavy blows to what remained of slavery in the Virginia counties exempted from the Emancipation Proclamation. The old discipline crumbled, and slaves pressed their owners for the rights of free people. Many slaveholders reluctantly conceded some of freedom's attributes, fearing that refusal would spur flight. They ended corporal punishment, allowed greater freedom of movement, and gave their slaves more time to themselves. Some masters provided plots of land for independent cultivation or agreed to pay wages in cash or a share of the crop. Planters and farmers in tidewater Virginia, Wilder reported, were so dependent upon black laborers that "if they can't have them as slaves they must have them as freemen." Although at least 5,000 black people in tidewater Virginia remained slaves as late as

<hr>

[20] On the recruitment of black soldiers in tidewater Virginia and North Carolina, see *Freedom*, ser. 2: pp. 113–16, and docs. 41–49. For the number of soldiers credited to each of the two states, see *Freedom*, ser. 2: p. 12.

August 1863, a significant proportion of them were working on terms similar to those of juridically free men and women.[21]

Many former slaves chose to remain at home under privately negotiated free-labor arrangements rather than risk the hardships of life in a Union camp or on a government farm. In all likelihood, more black people in tidewater Virginia worked for resident landowners than for the federal government. But such employment had its drawbacks. Reverting to old habits, the new employers sometimes subjected freedpeople to slave-style punishments and reneged on promises of compensation. Scattered among the barely reconstructed former slaveholders were die-hard rebels determined to prevent former slaves from engaging in any sort of free labor. Military and private employment coexisted in dynamic tension, and a good many black people did both sorts of work.

The recruitment of black men into the Union army, and raids into Confederate-held territory by newly organized black troops, brought thousands of additional slaves into federal lines. Of the 26,000 freedpeople residing in the Union-occupied part of tidewater Virginia in the summer of 1863, nearly 8,500 had arrived since the beginning of the war. Most of the newcomers lived south of the James River, where two out of five black people were "Transient Residents." On the peninsula north of the James, the proportion was about one in six. In coastal North Carolina, too, a significant number of freedpeople were recent immigrants. The new arrivals had generally escaped slavery with little more than their lives, and those who brought property with them often saw it confiscated, either by quartermasters under orders to appropriate useful goods or by freebooting soldiers.[22]

Once within Union lines, former slaves fell under the purview of military superintendents, who established depots for their reception and relief. On Virginia's York-James peninsula, Wilder housed most incoming fugitives either at a camp near Williamsburg or on the Downey plantation, near Hampton. South of the James River, Brown lodged newcomers at Craney Island or a converted ropewalk in Norfolk. From these depots, most able-bodied men were taken up by recruiters or military employers, while all but the most helpless of the remainder awaited resettlement on the government farms.

Within the narrow confines of Union-occupied North Carolina, where no government farms had been established, receiving depots became

---

[21] For the number of titular slaves in tidewater Virginia, see *Freedom*, ser. 1, vol. 1: doc. 13.
[22] On the number of newly arrived refugees, see *Freedom*, ser. 1, vol. 1: doc. 13; Horace James, *Annual Report of the Superintendent of Negro Affairs in North Carolina, 1864* (Boston, 1865), p. 6. On the seizure of newcomers' property, see, in addition to the relevant documents in this chapter, testimony of Corporal Sykes before the American Freedmen's Inquiry Commission, [11 May 1863], filed with O-328 1863, Letters Received, ser. 12, RG 94 [K-68].

permanent settlements. Chaplain Horace James, who was appointed "superintendent of blacks" by General John G. Foster, Burnside's successor, dispatched incoming fugitives to camps at Roanoke Island or New Berne. In the fall of 1863, with black recruitment in full swing, James put the Roanoke Island refuge on more formal footing. He surveyed and assigned tracts of land "to the families of colored soldiers, to invalids, and other blacks in the employ of the Government." Patterning the settlement after an idealized New England village, James prescribed right-angle streets and cabins adjoined by garden plots, all constructed by the former slaves. In September, the population of the "African colony" on Roanoke Island approached 1,200; by the following January, 2,700.[23]

Throughout tidewater Virginia and North Carolina, military employers and army recruiters vied for the services of the healthy young men among the fugitive slaves. The competition occasionally redounded to the freedmen's benefit. Faced with the prospect of losing their laborers to the recruiters, quartermasters and engineers offered wages exceeding the $10 per month paid to black soldiers. Despite such inducements, many freedmen eschewed government service of any sort, preferring to work independently or to hire themselves to civilians. Both recruiters and military employers obtained men by force when other measures failed.[24]

In addition to local employers, officials from other jurisdictions periodically entered a claim to the labor of black men. In June 1863, short-handed quartermasters from Washington set out for tidewater Virginia and North Carolina in search of black laborers. To their dismay, most suitable men in both regions eschewed employment that would take them far from home and leave their families without secure means of support. Returning to Washington nearly empty-handed, the frustrated quartermasters called for the use of *"forcible persuasion"* to obtain the necessary labor, and Quartermaster General Meigs and Secretary of War Stanton soon sanctioned such means. Military authorities swept through tidewater Virginia in July, seizing every black man they could grab. Press gangs dragooned elderly and infirm men along with healthy ones, property-owning freemen along with destitute ex-slaves. At Norfolk, soldiers surrounded a black church and ushered men from their pews straight to the docks. Impressment agents at Craney Island enacted a cynical ruse in which freedmen were lured aboard ships with promises that they would finally be paid long-overdue wages for military labor, only to receive passage to Washington instead.

The threat of impressment cast a shadow over the lives of all black people in tidewater Virginia and North Carolina. A month after the dragnet by the quartermasters from Washington, Captain Wilder re-

---

[23] On the establishment of the Roanoke Island colony, see, in addition to the relevant documents in this chapter, James, *Annual Report*, pp. 3, 21–26.

[24] In addition to the relevant documents in this chapter, see *Freedom*, ser. 2: doc. 45.

ported that the freedpeople remained fearful and skeptical of the government's intentions, and "it would require some time to dispel their fears."[25] To avoid impressment, many men took to the woods. Opposition to forced military labor spurred collective as well as individual protest. In December 1863, impressed freedmen at Beaufort, North Carolina, avowed that "in Consequence of this System of fource labor, they Have no means of paying Rents and otherwise Providing for ther families." Declaring their "[e]ntire Willingness to Contribute to the Cause of the union," they insisted that such service be "consistant with there cause as Freemen and the Rights of their families." Other black men elsewhere in the tidewater region protested impressment as a blatant violation of their newly won freedom. Personal liberty, including the right to travel without fear of detention, ranked among the most fundamental boons of emancipation.

These views struck a responsive chord among friends of the former slaves. Captain Wilder believed that freedpeople should enjoy an unimpeded right to travel; any infringement was tantamount to "Government slaveholding." Accordingly, he protested attempts by his superiors to limit his authority to issue passes. But Wilder's complaints failed to persuade his superiors. General Foster, who assumed command of the newly merged Department of Virginia and North Carolina in July 1863, insisted that military occupation necessitated restrictions upon the mobility of all civilians, of whatever color or condition. Black men were "wanted either to enlist or work, & not to be allowed to be running about in idleness." Ex-slave and free-black men remained vulnerable to impressment for the duration of the war.

Whether black military laborers and soldiers entered Union service voluntarily or under duress, their families faced an uncertain future. Although some women and teenaged children found work with the army or civilian employers, most households relied largely if not entirely upon the wages of their menfolk. Not only were soldiers and military laborers often paid tardily or irregularly, but their duties often took them away from their families. The army provided no formal means of allotting the men's wages to their dependents. Impoverished families of black soldiers and laborers therefore augmented the ranks of former slaves requiring federal assistance, if only temporarily or occasionally.[26]

In providing relief, the superintendents cultivated connections with freedmen's aid societies in the North, which donated clothing, books, garden seed, and other items. The Northern societies also sponsored ministers, teachers, and doctors, who helped the former slaves create institutions befitting a free community. Churches, schools, and mutual-aid associations appeared throughout tidewater Virginia and North Caro-

---

[25] *Freedom*, ser. 2: doc. 35.
[26] For a general discussion of the significance of black soldiers' wages for the livelihood of their families, see *Freedom*, ser. 2: chap. 16, especially docs. 290–94.

lina, some established by Northern missionaries in conjunction with the former slaves, others organized independently by black people themselves. In response to the skyrocketing cost of food and clothing and the profiteering of merchants, a few freedmen's aid societies established stores to sell goods to the former slaves at more modest prices. Yet neither private charity nor government relief kept pace with the needs of the refugees.[27]

For those freedpeople who worked on the government farms, the vicissitudes of farming in a war zone and the caprice of nature hampered efforts to support themselves. Union soldiers afforded scant protection from rebel guerrillas and often added to the freedpeople's woes by raiding their gardens and henhouses. To make matters worse, a severe springtime drought made for short crops throughout the tidewater region.

Nevertheless, many former slaves achieved a measure of independence. According to Francis W. Bird, a Massachusetts abolitionist who toured several government farms in tidewater Virginia in late 1863, the residents had succeeded in producing enough to support themselves until the next harvest. Indeed, the program established by Wilder and Brown had laid "the foundation of an industrious and self supporting peasantry," whose members would cultivate their own small tracts and also "work for the owner of the central farm." Bird cited still greater achievements among black farmers working land outside government control. Gibberty Davis, a former slave who with his wife and two hired hands cultivated the plantation abandoned by his former owner, produced a large surplus above their subsistence. Such examples convinced Bird that "all that is needed to establish . . . a truly loyal and prosperous community is that the men and women who have watered the soil with their tears and blood, should be allowed to own it when they have earned it by their own labor." Working for wages had only intensified the freedpeople's longing for "the right to own the soil," something "they crave above all other boons." With at least a year of freedom under their belts and some hard-earned cash in their pockets, many former slaves on government-controlled land looked to the new year with high hopes.

General Benjamin Butler, who replaced Foster as commander of the Department of Virginia and North Carolina in November 1863, also looked ahead to the new year. In a broadly framed order issued shortly after his return to Fortress Monroe, Butler placed his imprimatur upon the labor, relief, and recruitment measures that had evolved during his

[27] In addition to the relevant documents in this chapter, see Horace James to the Public, 27 June 1863, enclosed in Horace James to Major Gen. J. G. Foster, 1 July 1863, J-83 1863, Letters Received, ser. 3238, Dept. of NC & 18th Army Corps, RG 393 Pt. 1 [C-3317]; George Whipple to Hon. Sec. of War, 4 Apr. 1863, filed as S-280 (Book 52) 1863, Letters Received, ser. 20, Central Records, RG 92 [Y-618].

absence. To encourage further enlistment of black soldiers, he directed, the government would provide "suitable subsistence" for the dependents of recruits, who enjoyed neither the large bounties paid to white soldiers nor "the machinery of 'State aid' for the support of their families." Decrying the fact that the army was "competing against itself" for the labor of black men, Butler forbade military employers to hire men who were fit for armed service or to pay unskilled workers more than the wages allotted black privates. He also urged prompt payment of military laborers – whose families, unlike those of soldiers, had to be "supported from the proceeds of their labor."

"Political freedom rightly defined is liberty to work, and to be protected in the full enjoyment of the fruits of labor," thundered Butler. To protect that "liberty to work," he forbade the impressment of black laborers except in cases of military necessity. Even then, impressment required a departmental order, and "white and colored citizens" would be equally liable. Butler also promised black people protection from military abuse, and he ordered that disputes between them and white people be adjudicated by military courts.

To administer his system, Butler consolidated the responsibilities of the various superintendents of contrabands into a "Department of Negro Affairs." He appointed his aide-de-camp, Colonel J. Burnham Kinsman, general superintendent; Wilder, Brown, and James remained in their previous jurisdictions, which became, respectively, the first, second, and third districts of the Department of Negro Affairs.[28]

Scarcely had the superintendents begun to pursue their new duties when their control over abandoned land came into question. President Lincoln's Proclamation of Amnesty and Reconstruction, issued in December 1863, offered most repentant rebels the opportunity to reclaim their property – except slaves – upon taking an oath of allegiance to the Union and swearing to abide by wartime emancipation measures.[29] Landowners whose Confederate sympathies had cooled, or who feared that their land would be confiscated and sold unless they accepted Lincoln's terms, returned to recover abandoned estates. Several of the Virginia properties restored to their owners had been cultivated in 1863 as government farms.

Wilder and Brown nevertheless pressed ahead in settling former slaves on other government-controlled land. General Butler afforded timely assistance, ordering the seizure of additional Virginia farms and plantations. As a result, the two superintendents began the 1864 crop

---

[28] In January 1864, after the eastern shore of Virginia was added to the Department of Virginia and North Carolina, Caleb S. Henry, a Northern physician, was designated superintendent of Negro affairs for that region (the 4th district). (Special Orders No. 9, Head Quarters Dept. of Va. & N.C., 9 Jan. 1864, vol. 54 VaNc, pp. 14–16, Special Orders Issued, ser. 5084, Dept. of VA & NC & 18th Army Corps, RG 393 Pt. 1 [C-3387].)

[29] *Statutes at Large*, vol. 13, pp. 737–39.

season in charge of considerably more acreage than they had the previous year, notwithstanding the amnesty proclamation.[30] Both Wilder and Brown expanded agricultural operations, but they instituted different policies regarding labor and land tenure. As he had in 1863, Brown worked a large majority of the land in his district with wage laborers supervised by overseers, although cash wages of $10 per month for men and $5 for women replaced a share of the crop as the standard compensation. Brown also permitted rental arrangements, but on a much smaller scale. He leased plots of eight to ten acres to approximately 100 black people, for one-third of the crop. Many times that number worked as wage laborers.[31]

Wilder, by contrast, favored renting over wage labor. He made eighty-five properties available to black tenants, about half of whom paid rent in cash and the remainder in shares of the crop ranging from one-fifth to one-half. Respectful of the "dread" they harbored toward "[a]nything resembling 'overseeing,'" Wilder allowed the renters to make most everyday decisions about farm operations. Instead of appointing a supervisor for each plantation, he and his subordinates made periodic visits to the tenants, offering them both "encouraging words" and "firm correction of all abuses." By permitting ex-slaves to rent land rather than work for hire, Wilder hoped to instill "a self reliant knowledge that they can take care of themselves." Only one government farm in his district, the "asylum" on the Downey Plantation, was cultivated by wage hands. There, the workers received amounts "corresponding to the services respectively rendered," in order to teach them "that even with infirmities, it was more honorable to work, than 'to eat the bread of idleness.'"[32]

Still another pattern of labor and tenure arrangements emerged in tidewater North Carolina. In accordance with a War Department order

[30] In addition to the relevant documents in this chapter, see Circular Order, Head-Quarters 18th Army Corps, Department of Virginia & North Carolina, 2 Feb. 1864, Letters, Orders, & Telegrams Received by Lt. Col. J. B. Kinsman, ser. 4108, Ft. Monroe VA Dept. of Negro Affairs, RG 105 [A-8306]; General Orders, No. 20, Head Quarters 18th Army Corps, Department of Virginia and North Carolina, 12 Feb. 1864, Orders & Circulars, ser. 44, RG 94 [DD-45].

[31] In addition to the relevant documents in this chapter, see "Abandoned Farms or Plantations in the Second District of Negro affairs Dept. Va. and South of the James River," 15 May 1864, enclosed in Lt. Col. J. B. Kinsman to Sir, 16 May 1864, #21678, Case Files of Claims for Cotton & Captured & Abandoned Property, ser. 370, Miscellaneous Division, RG 56 [X-522]; Lt. Col. Horace Porter to Brevet Major Gen. John W. Turner, 24 Mar. 1865, filed with V-87 1865, Letters Received, ser. 12, RG 94 [K-118].

[32] In addition to the relevant documents in this chapter, see Register of Land Rented on Shares, 1863–1865, vols. 220–21/531–33 VaNc, ser. 5192, Dept. of VA & NC & 18th Army Corps, RG 393 Pt. 1 [C-8863, C-8864]; "Abandoned Farms and Plantation in First District Department Va.," 9 May 1864, enclosed in Lt. Col. J. B. Kinsman to Sir, 16 May 1864, #21678, Case Files of Claims for Cotton & Captured & Abandoned Property, ser. 370, Miscellaneous Division, RG 56 [X-522].

of October 1863 giving the Treasury Department jurisdiction over abandoned property not required for military purposes, David Heaton, supervising agent of the treasury's 3rd Special Agency, assumed control over numerous cotton plantations and turpentine forests in the vicinity of New Berne.[33] By the spring of 1864, he had permitted more than 100 lessees – most of them black – to work properties ranging "from a single acre to 'a one horse farm' . . . or an entire plantation." Black renters worked most of the turpentine land, while all but a few cotton-growing estates were leased to local white unionists or Northern entrepreneurs, on condition that they employ freedpeople as wage laborers. Heaton also permitted former slaves to remain on estates abandoned by their owners, without paying any rent. The tenants and squatters received draft animals, implements, and supplies from the Department of Negro Affairs. More than 1,200 black people, Heaton reported in May, were working as renters or wage hands under "the free and compensated labor policy." During 1864, he later estimated, their earnings supported at least 6,000 people.[34]

For all the regional variations, freedpeople on government land in tidewater Virginia and North Carolina shared certain experiences. First, farm work became largely the province of women, children, and old or disabled men. Of those young men who were not employed by the army as soldiers or laborers, a substantial proportion earned a livelihood by means other than agriculture. Some fished; others worked in the forest cutting firewood, sawing lumber, or hewing staves and shingles. Meanwhile, their families tended crops on the government-controlled land. Second, because the former slaves' demand for land outpaced the amount available, most households cultivated very small tracts. As a result, a large majority of the freedpeople who rented government land had to perform occasional wage-work to make ends meet. Even the best-situated black farmers could seldom do more than support themselves and their families; a profitable surplus was practically out of the question. Most of the land had been depleted by years of hard usage, and the government lacked both the resources and the will to improve it. The condemned horses and implements provided by the army frequently broke down, making field work more toilsome and less productive. Finally, many of the plantations and farms operated by the

---

[33] Treasury agents in tidewater Virginia never controlled as much abandoned land as their counterparts in North Carolina, evidently because General Butler invoked military necessity to retain the property under army jurisdiction. (See Maj. Genl. Benj. F. Butler to Lieut. Col. H. Biggs, 29 Dec. 1863, Correspondence Received by the Supervising Special Agent, 7th Agency, RG 366 [Q-300].)

[34] On labor under treasury auspices in North Carolina, see, in addition to the relevant document in this chapter, *Treasury Department, Economic and Pecuniary results of Leasing Abandoned Lands, Employment of Freedmen and the Disposition of Captured and Abandoned Property in North Carolina*, 11 Feb. 1865, Records of the Supervising Special Agent, 6th Agency, RG 366 [Q-181]; James, *Annual Report*, pp. 4–12.

freedpeople lay on the fringe of Union territory, subject to attack by Confederate troops or hostile civilians.

Events in North Carolina during early 1864 demonstrated the danger of proximity to Confederate forces. After a rebel attack on New Berne in February caused federal commanders to withdraw troops from outlying posts, freedpeople working in the no man's land between Union and Confederate lines had to abandon their crops and take refuge in town. The refugees eventually crowded into a camp along the Trent River, which grew into a sizable village of more than 5,000 people. In April, when the rebels overran Plymouth and forced the evacuation of Washington, hundreds of freedpeople were murdered or reenslaved. Northern military authorities relocated the survivors to New Berne and Roanoke Island, where the refugees had to rebuild their lives. A large proportion eventually succeeded in supporting themselves without federal assistance. But the Confederate raids dramatized the fragility of wartime labor arrangements.[35]

Union military operations also disrupted the lives of freedpeople in tidewater Virginia and North Carolina. In early May 1864, General Butler moved his Army of the James upriver from Fortress Monroe to join the campaign against Richmond and Petersburg. Making his headquarters at Bermuda Hundred, at the confluence of the James and Appomattox rivers, he began to build a line of fortifications and ordered construction of a canal bypassing Confederate works at Dutch Gap, on the James. These ambitious operations required hundreds of laborers, and there was little doubt about who would do the digging.

Butler's pledge to protect black men from impressment yielded to "military necessity," as superintendents of Negro affairs and other Union officers seized laborers wherever and by whatever means they could obtain them. Established contraband camps and military posts were the most popular hunting grounds. On Roanoke Island, impressment agents used force and chicanery "to take up every man that could be found indiscriminately young and old sick and well." Throughout tidewater Virginia and North Carolina, impressment separated hundreds of black men from their families and sent them to the battlefront. Most of the workers did not return for months and many not until the end of the war. Some never returned at all, for hard labor and exposure to enemy fire exacted a heavy toll.

Freedmen objected both to the means used to obtain their labor and to the problems created for their families. Residents of Roanoke Island protested that the impressed men had been treated like "dum beast" and given no opportunity to provide for those they left behind. As a result,

---

[35] In addition to the relevant documents in this chapter, see James, *Annual Report*, pp. 3, 7–10, 34–38; Mobley, *James City*, chap. 3.

their wives and children had to subsist on meager government rations. Although the military laborers sent to Virginia from Roanoke Island deemed it their "duty to help the goverment all we can," they demanded that the Union acknowledge their contribution by supporting – not subverting – their quest for independence. "[A]ll we wants is a Chance and we can Get a living like White men," declared a group of men who had escaped the labor dragnet. They wanted to take care of their own rather than be "beholding to the Government for Something to Eat."

The families of black soldiers found themselves in equally precarious circumstances. Even after June 1864, when Congress legislated parity in the wages of black and white troops, late pay complicated black soldiers' efforts to support their families. Promised subsistence when their menfolk enlisted, the soldiers' kin discovered that the terms might be revised without warning. Beginning in the spring of 1864, Captain Brown withheld rations from soldiers' relatives who refused to live on a government farm reserved for their occupancy. Later the same year, the superintendent of Negro affairs on Roanoke Island reduced the rations issued to the families of black soldiers. Absent at the front, the soldiers protested angrily but unavailingly.[36]

The military operations that mobilized legions of soldiers and laborers also brought thousands of destitute black refugees under Union control, especially in Virginia. Owing chiefly to the influx of newcomers, the number of black people in Captain Wilder's district grew from 10,500 in January 1864 to 13,300 in December. Brown estimated that 3,600 of the 25,000 freedpeople in his district at the end of the year had arrived during the same period. Recruiters and military employers claimed the healthy men, leaving the women, children, and old and sick men to the superintendents of Negro affairs. The continual accession of refugees burdened the contraband camps and government farms, especially those south of the James River, where, by midsummer, all the abandoned land under federal control was already occupied by needy former slaves.[37]

Despite the efforts of the superintendents and Northern aid societies, the neediest freedpeople often lived in desperate conditions. Some of the government farms came to resemble sprawling villages, where a dozen or more people might share a one- or two-room dwelling. At the Downey Plantation, scores of dependent freedpeople resided in a dilapidated tobacco house that an army inspector deemed "wholly unfit for human beings to occupy." Such accommodations, he declared, were "a disgrace to the 'peculiar institution' in its better days, and a reproach to

---

[36] On the struggle of the families of black soldiers to receive the promised support, see, in addition to the relevant documents in this chapter, *Freedom*, ser. 2: docs. 314A–E.

[37] In addition to the relevant documents in this chapter, see Capt. O. Brown to Lieut. Col. Kinsman, 22 June 1864, Letters, Orders, & Telegrams Received by Lt. Col. J. B. Kinsman, ser. 4108, Ft. Monroe VA Dept. of Negro Affairs, RG 105 [A-7848].

the age, and country in which we live."[38] Conditions in the towns and cities were little, if any, better. Scarce housing and high rents fostered overcrowding in Norfolk, Portsmouth, Suffolk, and New Berne. Food and clothing were expensive in both town and country, and prices rose faster than wages. Crowding created sanitation problems and bred disease. Smallpox, yellow fever, and other illnesses took a frightful toll.

Attempts to alleviate destitution ran afoul of efforts to conserve scarce resources and reduce expenditures. At Portsmouth, for instance, the superintendent of Negro affairs refused to issue rations to black schoolchildren deemed capable of working for a living. His policy forced many children to leave school, but only a few of them could find employment in the overcrowded town. Instead, they congregated around army camps, neither earning nor learning.

Unable to provide adequately for all the freedpeople under their supervision, federal officials showed renewed interest in proposals to transport some of them to the North. General Butler suggested that a Massachusetts textile factory hire black women and children as operatives, comparing them favorably to "green Irish" millhands. Benevolent associations in northeastern cities, responding to local demand for domestic servants, solicited the aid of military authorities in sending black women and working-age children north for employment with "humane and Christian families." Emigration, they suggested, would benefit both those who left and those who stayed behind. In Virginia, Captain Wilder praised domestic service in the North as an opportunity for black women to save money before returning to buy land and "become permanent citizens upon the soil that gave them birth." Brown and James were equally eager to relocate some of their charges.[39]

For all their privations, the freedpeople demonstrated no desire to leave family and friends to work among strangers in a distant place. Reports that earlier emigrants had suffered abusive treatment further cooled their enthusiasm. Despite Brown's suggestion that emigration be made compulsory rather than voluntary, probably only a few hundred former slaves made the journey—an insignificant number compared with the thousands of black refugees who entered Union lines.

At the end of 1864, the superintendents of Negro affairs reported that most black people in their districts had supported themselves by their own efforts. North of the James River, nearly four-fifths of the adults were "independent of assistance." South of the James, half had earned their own living, asking nothing from the government but "impartial execution of Military law." Most of them labored for wages,

[38] A.A. Surgeon L. D. Seymour to Col. J. B. Kinsman, 18 May 1864, Letters, Orders, & Telegrams Received by Lt. Col. J. B. Kinsman, ser. 4108, Ft. Monroe VA Dept. of Negro Affairs, RG 105 [A-7845].
[39] In addition to the relevant documents in this chapter, see James, *Annual Report*, p. 10.

but some worked independently as farmers, tradesmen, or fishermen. Soldiers and their families made up an additional one-third of the black population south of the James; military authorities guaranteed their subsistence as a condition of enlistment. Only the remainder—fewer than one-fifth of the total—relied upon the government's charity, and their dependence was generally temporary. Throughout the tidewater region, long-term recipients of assistance were few indeed; Wilder counted only seventy-six in his district. In both Virginia and North Carolina, a larger proportion of the white population than the black received rations from federal authorities. The freedpeople's achievements, Wilder boasted, had "exploded" the slaveholders' claim "that negroes are very valuable as slaves, but when free, worthless and unable to take care of themselves." "[I]t is now generally conceded," he added, "that the labor of one freeman, is worth that of two slaves."

While Wilder lauded the success of the regimen he had instituted, a different labor system took shape on Virginia's eastern shore. In October 1864, Colonel Frank J. White, commander of U.S. forces in the region, became superintendent of Negro affairs. To provide for destitute former slaves, White's predecessor had established two "House[s] of Refuge" on government-controlled estates.[40] White had a different agenda. He dismissed government farms as "communistic" and condemned the other superintendents as impractical "enthusiasts" whose policies demoralized the former slaves and antagonized their former owners. White initiated a new program of employment and relief designed to introduce all parties to the discipline of the marketplace, so that "the planter might learn the value of free labor, the freedman the value of a market for that labor, and both, to respect their mutual rights."

White's goal would be attained by means of compulsory labor contracts, rigidly enforced. In November 1864, he ordered all black people on the eastern shore to find "steady employment" or be forced into contracts by military authorities. To promote regular employment, he urged black workers to contract by the month or year and discouraged employers from hiring casual laborers. Wages were to be set by the market, not by military regulations; although White asserted his "right to require industry," he would not "force any man to labor for a less sum, than the highest he could procure." Convinced that black Virginians could not obtain justice in civil courts, he directed his subordinates to supervise contracts and adjudicate labor disputes. Characterizing his regulations as "milder . . . than any Vagrant Act of a Northern state," White blasted critics for believing that "labor Can only signify *bondage,*

---

40 C. S. Henry to Lt. Col. Kinsman, 7 June 1864, Letters, Orders, & Telegrams Received by Lt. Col. J. B. Kinsman, ser. 4108, Ft. Monroe VA Dept. of Negro Affairs, RG 105 [A-8309].

and the Common industrial restraints imposed in every Civilized Community — *oppression*."

The "industrial restraints" imposed by White provoked sharp opposition. Free people, who composed one-third of the eastern shore's antebellum black population, regarded the new regime as a threat to longstanding rights. Former slaves who earned a living as casual laborers, oystermen, and crabbers bristled at obligatory long-term contracts. Moreover, White's superintendents — largely chosen from the ranks of local white civilians — forced some black workers to accept wages far below market rates and others to labor for nothing more than food and clothing.[41] They even required independent black farmers to contract formally to hire their own wives and children, paying a fee to the superintendents. In January 1865, White's attempt to compel one such farmer to contract for the labor of his own sons prompted protests that reached the new commander of the Department of Virginia, General Edward O. C. Ord, and the Secretary of War. But Ord defended White, arguing that any "individual hardship" was outweighed by the importance of teaching employers and employees that they were "laboring in a Common Cause for their mutual benefit."

Developments in the early months of 1865 gave former slaves throughout tidewater Virginia and North Carolina reason to doubt that any "Common Cause" united their interests with those of former slave owners. As the war wound down and the planting season approached, a contest opened over the farms and plantations controlled by the government. Availing themselves of Lincoln's amnesty program, rebel landowners returned to reclaim their property. Some rushed home as federal officials advertised the forthcoming auction of land that had passed into government hands under the confiscation acts and the Direct Tax Act of June 1862. Slated for February 1865, the impending sales threatened the livelihood and future prospects of former slaves who were renting tracts or working for wages on the estates.

Although the freedpeople seldom possessed enough resources to bid against other would-be purchasers, some of their friends did. Captain Wilder saw the sales as an opportunity to provide former slaves with the freeholds they so fervently desired. In concert with prominent members of Northern freedmen's aid societies, Wilder purchased six estates near Hampton that were sold under the confiscation act. He planned to subdivide at least three of them into small plots for sale or rental to freedpeople, while retaining one plantation for his own use. If the

---

41 See the contracts from the eastern shore filed in Labor Contracts, ser. 4111, Ft. Monroe VA Dept. of Negro Affairs, RG 105 [A-8399]. After the war, Freedmen's Bureau agents annulled such "unjust and unconscionable" agreements, insisting that wages accord with antebellum slave-hire rates. (Clipping from the New York *Herald*, [mid-Aug. 1865], enclosed in Capt. A. S. Flagg to Col. O. Brown, 29 Aug. 1865, Unregistered Letters & Telegrams Received, ser. 3799, VA Asst. Comr., RG 105 [A-7493].)

government would not provide the freedpeople with "a spot of land," perhaps benevolent men and women could.[42] General Ord saw Wilder's transaction as a criminal abuse of office. He demanded that Wilder relinquish the property. When Wilder refused, Ord relieved him from duty, ordered an investigation into his conduct as superintendent of Negro affairs, and brought him before a court-martial. In the end, the officers composing the court not only exonerated Wilder but also praised his long service to the country and the freedpeople.[43] Meanwhile, however, Ord removed Wilder's subordinates, installed his own aide-de-camp as general superintendent of Negro affairs, and instituted labor policies that resembled White's more than Wilder's.

Certain that the measures adopted to meet wartime exigencies would be unnecessary, if not counterproductive, after the return of peace, General Ord rescinded or revised them. His subordinates drastically reduced issues of rations to the families of black soldiers, insisting that the availability of work for able-bodied women and the increase in soldiers' pay made such provisions unnecessary. Ord suggested that black women who failed to find employment be assigned to "a grand *general* washing establishment," where "[a] little hard work and confinement [would] soon induce them" to do so.[44] Although the superintendents of Negro affairs retained jurisdiction over abandoned farms, they worked assiduously to reduce the number of people living on them. Moreover, the rapid return of amnestied landowners discouraged federal officials from making arrangements that might soon be undone. So did the Lincoln administration's decision that spring to suspend further sales under the confiscation and direct-tax acts, pending organization of the newly created Freedmen's Bureau.[45]

The new direction of federal labor and relief policy suited Captain Brown, who continued to have charge of the district south of the James River. Brown, reported a military official approvingly, thought it best

---

[42] Adjutant General L. Thomas to Hon. Edwin M. Stanton, 5 June 1865, filed as A-1411 1865, Letters Received, ser. 12, RG 94 [K-223]; proceedings of general court-martial in the case of Captain Charles B. Wilder, 1–16 May 1865, MM-2065, Court-Martial Case Files, ser. 15, RG 153 [H-54].

[43] A.A. Gen'l Edw. Smith to Brig. Gen'l. George H. Gordon, 25 Apr. 1865, vol. 13 VaNc, p. 211, Letters Sent, ser. 5046, Dept. of VA & Army of the James, RG 393 Pt. 1 [C-3278]; Bvt. Major General Charles K. Graham et al. to Major General O. O. Howard, [June? 1865], enclosed in Maj. Gen'l O. O. Howard to Bvt. Maj. Gen'l M. C. Meigs, 13 July 1865, filed as F-9, Letters Received from the Freedmen's Bureau, ser. 34, Central Records, RG 92 [Y-662].

[44] *Official Records*, ser. 1, vol. 46, pt. 2, pp. 647–48; *Freedom*, ser. 2: doc. 314B.

[45] On the suspension of land sales, see Edwin M. Stanton to John Underwood, Esquire, 10 Mar. 1865, filed with U-24 1865, Letters Received, RG 107 [L-326]; *Official Records*, ser. 1, vol. 46, pt. 2, pp. 975–76, and ser. 1, vol. 46, pt. 3, p. 799; Hugh M'Culloch to Collector of Customs, Norfolk, 14 Mar. 1865, and Edwin M. Stanton to Major General Ord, 14 Mar. 1865, Telegrams Sent by the Secretary of War, Telegrams Collected by the Office of the Secretary of War (Bound), RG 107 [L-257].

that freedpeople work for wages until they learned "the true reward of industry and economy." By April 1865, his headquarters was functioning largely as an "intelligence office" where would-be employers applied for workers. To encourage the freedpeople to enter into labor contracts, Brown terminated the issue of rations to anyone who refused to accept "a good place."[46]

Long-absent rebels were not the only antebellum residents of tidewater Virginia and North Carolina who returned to their homes at the end of the war. Large numbers of former slaves who had been removed to the Confederate interior also journeyed back to reunite with family and friends and reconstruct their lives. These newly liberated men and women, largely untutored in the ways of free labor, found their old home transformed by four years of warfare and military occupation. They came in contact with freedpeople – some of them lifelong residents, others recent arrivals – who had worked for the Union army, cultivated government-controlled land, negotiated new working arrangements with former slaveholders and other private employers, and, in a few cases, established themselves as independent farmers and tradesmen. Together they would build new lives as free men and women in a region emerging from war into a tumultuous peace.

[46] Lt. Col. Horace Porter to Brevet Major Gen. John W. Turner, 24 Mar. 1865, filed with V-87 1865, Letters Received, ser. 12, RG 94 [K-118].

1: Affidavit of a Virginia Freedman

State of Virginia   Eastern District   2nd day of September 1865
No. 18.

Suthey Parker (calored) of the town of Hampton   Elizabeth City County being duly sworn doth depose and say, That about the first day of June 1861 deponent was employed by Sergeant Smith of the Regular Military service of the United States to work in the Q.M. Department at Fort Monroe   Said Smith told deponent that he would recive ten dollars and one ration per month,   deponent says, that he worked under Said Smith as laborer about two Months,   Said Smith then at the expiration of Said two Months employed deponent as cook for the teamsters under Capt Porter   deponent served as cook under Said Capt Porter for the period of ten Months or untill the 3rd day of June 1862.   Deponent says about the Month of March 1862 Said Smith was removed and was succeeded by Mr Marsh who remained untill about the first of May 1862, at which time Said Marsh was succeeded by Captain C. B. Wilder.   Deponent says, that he received from Capt Wilder the Sum of Fifteen Dollars pay for his work for the Month of May 1862   Deponent Says, that Capt Wilder told him that he would receive pay for the former time previous to the Month of May but that he has not received any pay from the Government or from any persons for the time he worked previous to the Month of May 1862.

HDS   Suthey Parker

Affidavit of Suthey Parker, 2 Sept. 1865, "Negroes: Employment," Consolidated Correspondence File, ser. 225, Central Records, RG 92 [Y-719]. Sworn before a notary public. In the same file are more than fifty other affidavits, most of which claimed pay for military labor at Fortress Monroe, Camp Hamilton, or Hampton, Virginia, during 1861 and 1862. Notations indicate that Calvin Pepper, a white Northerner based in Norfolk, was acting as attorney for the claimants.

2: Order by the Commander of the Department of Virginia

Fort Monroe {*Va.*}. November 1st 1861

General Orders N° 34   The following pay and allowances will constitute the valuation of the labor of the Contrabands at work in the Engineer, Ordnance, Quartermaster, Commissary, and Medical Departments at this post to be paid as hereinafter mentioned,

Class 1st Negro men over 18 years of age and able-bodied ten dollars per month, one Ration and the necessary amount of Clothing,

Class 2nd. Negro boys from 12 to 18 years of age and sickly and infirm negro men, five (5) per month, one ration and the necessary amount of Clothing,

The Quartermaster will furnish all the Clothing. The departments employing these men, will furnish the subsistence specified above, and as an incentive to good behaviour, (to be witheld at the discretion, of the Chiefs of the departments, respectively) each individual of the 1^{s} Class, will receive, two (2) dollars per month; and each individual of the 2nd Class one (1) dollar per month for their own use. The remainder of the money valuation of their labor, will be turned over to the Quartermaster, who will deduct from it the cost of the Clothing issued to them, the balance will constitute a fund to be expended by the Quartermaster under the direction of the Commanding Officer of the department for the support of the women and children, and those that are unable to work,

For any unusal amount of labor performed they may recieve extra pay, varying in amount from (50) fifty cents to one (1) dollar, this to be paid by the departments, employing them, to the men themselves, and to be for their own use.

Should any man be prevented from working on account of sickness for six consecutive days, or ten days in any one month, one half of the money valuation will be paid, For being prevented from laboring for a longer period than ten days in any one month all pay and allowances cease, By command of Maj Genl Wool

HD

General Orders No. 34, Head Quarters Dept. of Va. &c, 1 Nov. 1861, vol. -/4 VaNc, pp. 69–70, General Orders Issued, ser. 5078, Dept. of VA & 7th Army Corps, RG 393 Pt. 1 [C-3064]. Two weeks earlier, General Wool had issued a similar order with respect to former slaves employed as personal servants. Special Order 72, issued on October 14, had provided that "[a]ll colored persons called contrabands employed as servants by officers and others" at Fortress Monroe, Camp Hamilton, and Camp Butler would receive subsistence, plus wages of at least $8 per month for men and $4 per month for women; however, rather than being paid to the laborers themselves, the wages, minus the cost of clothing, were to be turned over to the chief quartermaster of the department "to create a fund for the support of those contrabands who are unable to work for their own support." (*Official Records*, ser. 2, vol. 1, p. 774.)

3: Northern Minister to a U.S. Senator from Massachusetts

Seminary near Fortress Monroe Va Jan 29 /62
Respected Sir, I wrote you, as you remember, by Mr Coan, a few weeks ago concerning the desirableness of a Committee of Investigation to search into the affairs of the Colored Refugees at Fortress Monroe. I was told that it was seen reported in a paper that you had moved the appointment of such a Committee. Will you please inform me soon whether one has been appointed. With this request I will respectfully present other urgent reasons for such appointment

Contrabandism at Fortress Monroe is but another name for one of the worst forms of practical oppression — government slavery. Old Pharaoh slavery was government slavery, and Uncle Sam's slavery is a Counterpart — the subordinate officials of the latter vieing with the taskmasters of the former in bad preeminence. And Genl Wool, through fear, acts the Gallio,[1] ignoring as far as possible all responsibility in reference to the delicate matter. Masters who are owners or who have been brought up with their slaves; but what do government officers generally care how they treat these poor waifs, who have been cast upon their heartless protection.

But by what constitutional right does government treat these persons as slaves? Certainly not on the basis of the Fugitive Slave law, whose provisions are of a specific character, and give sanction to no such treatment. And by what military right does government become a great practical slaveholder? Was it not enough to throw the shield over state slavery? Must general government adopt the accursed system and reduce it to practical working to carry on the war or pay its expenses? Yet such is the repulsive unconstitutional fact. If a man was a slave by the laws of Virginia, his slave status is recognized by government; if free, his free status. The free colored man is allowed to work for himself; or if he work for government, he is paid fair wages, – some, a dollar a day. A few of the slaves are allowed to work for themselves, and they are making a good livelihood for themselves and families; & if all were allowed to do so – or were employed by government as freemen – there would be no want Among them. But most of the slaves are compelled to work for government for a miserable pittance. Up to two months ago they had worked for nothing but quarters and rations. Since that time they have been partially supplied with clothing – costing on an average $4 per man. And in many instances they have received one or two dollars a month cash for the past two months. Some – an engineer Corps, at work on the rail-road, who were promised the pay of freemen by Genl Wool, and whose labor, according to the estimate of the Assistant Engineer, Mr Goddard, was valued at from one to two dollars a day, have recieved but one dollar cash for five & six months' work & but little clothing. Genl Wool told me that from the earnings of these slaves a surplus fund of $7000. has been accumulated. Yet, under the direction of Quarter Master Tallmadge, Sergeant Smith has lately reduced the rations, given out, in Camp Hamilton, to the families of these laborers and to the disabled, from 500 to 60. And some of the men, not willing to see their families Suffer, have withdrawn from government service. And the Sergeant has been putting them in the Guard-house, whipping and forcing them back into the government gang. In some instances these slaves have been knocked down senseless with shovels and clubs –

But I have just begun to trace the long catalogue of enormities, committed in the name of Union, freedom and justice under the Stars and Stripes. Yours with great respect

Lewis. C. Lockwood

P.S. I have sent duplicates of this to Senators Sumner, Hale, Fessenden & Wade; And Representatives Lovejoy and Van Wyck. –

L. C. L.

Addenda– About 70 of the slaves are worked on the Sabbath and on an average three nights in the week, sometimes till 10 & 2 o'clock, and sometimes till morning, and then compelled to work on through the day. For this extra work they get 50 cts for Sabbath & 50 cts for 3 nights' work; but in that case they do not receive the one or two dollars a month given to others. –

P.S. I understand that Genl Wool is to appoint a commission to which our mission will be accountable– I hope it will not be another "High Commission".

ALS   L. C. L

Lewis C. Lockwood to Hon. Senator Wilson, 29 Jan. 1862, L-130 1862, Letters Received, RG 107 [L-9]. Lockwood signed as "Missionary to the Colored Refugees at Fortress Monroe."

1 Gallio was a Roman governor in Corinth during the apostle Paul's sojourn there. When a group of Jews complained that Paul's proselytizing in their synagogue was "contrary to the law," Gallio refused to rule on the charges, insisting that because they involved religious and not civil law he would "be no judge of such matters." (Acts 18:12–17.)

4: Report of an Investigating Commission to the Commander of the Department of Virginia

Fort Monroe [*Va.*],   March   1862.

The Commission appointed under General Orders N° 5 & 6[1] have the honor respectfully to report:

As the object of the orders related more especially to persons in this Military Department known as "vagrants" or "contrabands," embracing their relations to the Military Power as an economy and a duty, and also how far their condition might be improved in connection with these relations. The Commission started with the general proposition, that the Military Power has not only a right, but it is its highest duty to avail itself of any and all means within its control, to perfect its discipline – render its position secure – or make it effective for an advance against an enemy, to compel service or use from anything, animate or inanimate, which a Military necessity may demand. At the same [*time*] they consider that

114

necessity is the only measure of the extent to which such power could be exercised.

They proceeded upon this basis, to require of the several subordinate departments of your Command, and also of all other persons who had had official intercourse, in any way, reports of the number of vagrants or contrabands employed, and such other information as your order contemplated. Full reports and tabular statements have in most instances been promptly furnished together with a mass of information, all of which has been carefully examined. These reports and statements are respectfully submitted and accompany this report in the order in which they will be found numbered.

The General Orders call for special information under the following heads — 1$^{st.}$ clothing, 2$^{nd.}$ subsistence, 3$^{rd.}$ shelter, 4$^{th.}$ medical attendance, 5$^{th.}$ pay, and 6$^{th.}$ treatment, moral and physical, 7$^{th.}$ also the economy of this kind of labor to the Government, 8$^{th.}$ and such suggestions as the Commission may deem proper for the improvement and management of these people.

. . . .

Suggestions — Your Commission after a carefull review of the Reports and the personal examination of the several heads of the investigation, and also an examination of the laws of Congress embracing the question of Military neccessity, are forced to the conclusion that the practical working is highly objectionable, the system wholy illegal and now entirely unneccessary —

1st Want of Power. — Without discussing the laws of Congress bearing on this subject, the question of state rights, or anything covering the question of title which are entirely matters to be determined by civil power; all of which however might with propriety be considered if neccessary in this examination even by a Military Commission — The Commission beleive there is a want of authority in the Government to hold these people and compel them to be the recipients of its charity —

Military Neccessity — We suppose it cannot be urged as a Military neccessity to retain them, for the same voluntary labor can be obtained at as cheap or a less rate: It will hardly be denied that more is not performed by a person who has a voice in the wages of his labor, than one who has not; beside the Military neccessity could not extend to the women and children and those who are sick and infirm — Their position would be one of quasi slavery, without being compelled to do their full work: — But admitting the military [*necessity*] of using those whose labor it requires, where is the authority for fixing a price by which others may employ them, and using the wages of such labor to support those who do not or cannot support themselves

The plan of giving the same pay to all alike is discouraging to the skillful, honest industrious labourer who fully earns his wages, while it only confirms the lazy and shiftless in their laziness; there is no motive for the industrious in their regular appointed tasks, no matter how great their industry or perfect their skill, they can gain no more than the lazy or unskillfull, and if they are not absolute drones, they get as much as if they gave their best exertions to the task; there is no incentive to ambition to approve themselves good workmen — Is it just; to make the industrious and single work for a fund to support the lazy mans family. It is no argument against these people's ability to provide for themselves that under these discouragments they do not show an activity as great as the white man under the incentive of proportionate remuneration, for if white men were placed in the same situation who can prove that the result would not be the same —

It is destructive to the energies of an individual, or people, to assure them of charity whenever they apprehend difficultys. Witness the effect of Irish souphouses and all socialistic institutions; better by far to let one here and there fall by the wayside than to encourage the people, that the Herculanian arm of the Nation is to be weilded in clearing their path.

The demand of Government labor at this post is limited: but the Government would have as its arms advanced, almost no limit to the demand on it for charity — The system is therefore incapable of expansion and cannot from its very expensiveness to Government be carried on with a much larger number — Is it well to establish a precedent for the benefit of an inferior race, which has always been refused to a superior one; establishing a system which will be quoted against the Government by all parties; by its foes for its failures, by its friends for its expenses, by the recipients of its charity because it was not continued and taught them to rely on a hope which could not be realized —

As in evidence of the verification of our argument, reference is made to a tabular statement under the head of "Economy of Labor,"[2] by which it will be found that for the months of November and December the number of rations issued to women, children and the infirm brought the cost of subsistance to those who labourerd to 33 cts. pr. *capita* a day, and in the months of Jany and February, when, it will be reccollected these issues to women and children were very largely suspended, the cost of subsistance on those who laboured was 22 1/2 cts per capita per day the decreased cost of labor is owing entirely to a curtailment of this charity, which compels these people to rely upon their own exertions, and yet the Commission, cannot accertain that any amount of suffering ensued

Your Commission are assured by educated and philanthropic

gentlemen that there is no neccessity for any Governmental charity
to these people; that societies at the North will undertake to provide
for all their proper wants, in connection with their moral and
intelectual culture – We earnestly recommend that it be left as
Government, leaves all simalar demands; to the intelligence and
generosity of the people They also recommend that the use of the
quarters near the Fort, be granted. under the direction of the person
who may be appointed as Agent. for day schools for Children and in
the evening for adults and on Sundays for divine service provided the
hours devoted to this purpose do not interfere with messings of the
men and labourers subject to the military authorities; they also
recommend that a site be granted for the purpose of erecting a
school house and chapel, provided that all structures erected for
them be built and sustained without any expense to the
Government, and removed whenever the Military Authorities require
without any claims on the government for said removal; that all
Blacks or "Contraband" not in the employ of the Government or
with officers or others stationed at the Fort be removed, if they
remain in this vicinity, beyond Mill Creek.; that no more buildings
be erected at the Goverment expense except for the shelter of those
who are in Government service; that wages be paid to these people
for their own use and enjoyment, prices to be determined by
individual skill, industry and ability, and regulated as all labor
values are regulated, by supply and demand, or by any other
standard system which governs the departments of the army – as a
part of the compensation labourer to receive one ration a day, and
quarters in all respects similar to what has been used heretofore
white or black free labor.

They eminently recomend the appointment by Government or by
the Commanding General of a person, always subordinate to the
Military Authorities, not connected with the Military service; a man
of high social position and intelligence, who would consent to serve
from motives of philanthropy – such a person would be most
fit – that the Military Authority protect him in all proper efforts to
improve them physically, Moraly, and religiously – to vindicate the
virtues indispensible to the above, such as honesty industry,
temperance Econemy patience, and obedience to all rightful
Authority, leaving out of these questions their social and political
rights beleiving these questions belong more properly to the
Government

In any event, your Commission reccommend the appointment of a
Provost Judge who clothed with Civil Powers and Military
Authority, will protect these ignorant people from abuse to their
Persons & in recovering from all who may employ them their just
wages. This officer is especially neccessary here in the absense of all

civil law to protect loyal citizens in this Department from continued marauding by the soldiers and negroes; that all officers, soldiers and attaches of the Army who have had the services of these people shall be compelled to pay them the wages of their labor by virtue of Special Order No 72[3]

Your Commission are aware that their suggested reforms. conflict with the present system, which was doubtless the plan of a benevolent and patriotic heart, and perhaps the best which could be desired for the time being – It was a new thing to all, beset with difficulties and antagonisms on all sides, but like all systems requiring practical results to develop its weak points, and time to remedy its errors

Your Commission are concious of having taken much time in the examination of this delicate and interesting question but feel a conciousness that they have founded their opinions entirely upon facts presented and relying upon this they have the honor to be Very Respectfully Your Ob[t] Servants

T J. Cram –
LeG B Cannon
William P. Jones

The Commission submit a census of the "vagrants or contrabands" in this Department though it was not required in your order; yet in considering the questions embraced it is deemed important – The census submitted is not supposed to be entirely accurate, as quite a number are in private service, with Officers, Sutlers and Traders; it is estimated that one hundred are thus employed

Latterly very few have come into our lines and not as heretofore in large parties – A considerable number have taken service in the Navy, some have gone off as servants to officers in Regiments, for the south and quite a number have disappeared –

There seems to be little or no inclination among them to leave here to go North – Service in the Navy is decidedly popular with them: The Navy rate them as boys, they get ten dollars a month and are entitled to all the privileges of ships crews and have absolute control of their wages –

Place	Adults		Children		Total		Aggregate
	Male	Female	Male	Female	Male	Female	
Fort Monroe	387	117	93	94	480	211	691
Camp Hamilton	191	224	161	167	352	391	743
Camp Butler	74		74[4]		74		74
Total	652	341	254	261	906	602	1508

HDS

Excerpts from report of Col. T. J. Cram et al., Mar. 1862, filed as V-222 1862, Letters Received, ser. 12, RG 94 [K-751]. Endorsement. About thirteen pages of a thirty-seven-page document. The blank space in the date line appears in the manuscript, but it is known that the report was completed on or before March 12. Colonel Thomas J. Cram signed as aide-de-camp and inspector general, and Colonel LeGrand B. Cannon and Major William P. Jones as aides-de-camp, all on the staff of General John E. Wool, commander of the Department of Virginia. The omitted portion surveyed the clothing, "Subsistence," shelter, medical care, pay, and "Physical & Moral" treatment of the former slaves at and near Fortress Monroe. On February 10, about a week after the commission began its work, General Wool had sent Colonel Cannon to Washington to inform Secretary of War Edwin M. Stanton that he had ordered an investigation "in relation to Contrabands or Blacks" at Fortress Monroe. "As far as [Cannon] and those associated with him have progressed in the investigation," Wool had noted, "it is not by any means, favorable to those who have the Blacks in charge." (Major Generl John E. Wool to the Hon. Edwin M. Stanton, 10 Feb. 1862, filed as V-240 1862, Letters Received, ser. 12, RG 94 [K-751].) On March 12, Wool sent Cannon to Washington again, this time bearing the commission's report and a letter indicating that, if Stanton approved of the report, Wool would "issue orders accordingly." (Major General John E. Wool to Hon. Edwin M. Stanton, 12 Mar. 1862, filed as V-224 1862, Letters Received, ser. 12, RG 94 [K-751].) Meanwhile, on March 7, the House of Representatives adopted a motion calling upon Stanton to report "the number, age and condition of the Africans who have been under the supervision of Major-General Wool, commanding at Fortress Monroe, . . . together with the amount of work or service performed by them, the pay if any which they have received and the cost to the Government for their maintenance and support." On March 22, Wool responded to the congressional inquiry by transmitting a copy of the commission's report and an order he had issued on March 18 revising labor policies at Fortress Monroe—both of which the House ordered to be printed. (*Official Records*, ser. 2, vol. 1, pp. 809, 812; U.S., House of Representatives, "Africans in Fort Monroe Military District," *House Executive Documents*, 37th Cong., 2nd sess., No. 85.) Wool's action upon the commission's recommendations had begun on March 15, when he appointed Charles B. Wilder "superintendant of the Vagrants or Contrabands" in the Department of Virginia, informing Stanton on the following day that Wilder, who was from Boston, Massachusetts, would fill the office "vacated by the removal and arrest of Sergeant Smith, for fraudulent conduct, and other abuses." "Mr. Wilder," General Wool assured the Secretary of War, "is a gentleman of wealth—elevated moral character, intelligence and high social position, and consents to serve without any compensation, except his Quarters, fuel and forage." As superintendent, Wilder would control no government property or funds; "[h]is chief duty will be to organize [the contrabands'] labor, supervise their conduct, and . . . protect these people from abuse and imposition, both of which . . . have been too common." In his order of March 18, Wool overturned previous policies respecting employment and compensation, including those he had established himself. Thenceforward, he declared, "all wages earned by persons of African Blood in this department will be paid to them for their own use, and support under such regulations as may be devised by [Wilder], prices to be determined by individual skill industry and ability, and regulated by the

Standard usual" in the various departments of the army. Each laborer was to receive rations and quarters "[a]s a part of the compensation." Wool also ordered officers and civilians who had employed black laborers under his earlier orders of October and November 1861, or before their issue, to furnish Wilder with accounts of labor performed by, items issued to, and wages owed to each laborer. Finally, he gave Wilder "discretionary powers" over the fund already accumulated "for the support of the poor & needy of the so called contrabands," subject, however, to Wool's approval. (General Orders No. 21, Headquarters, Dept. of Va. &c, 15 Mar. 1862, and General Orders No. 22, Headquarters, Dept. of Va., 18 Mar. 1862, vol. -/4 VaNc, pp. 205–7, General Orders Issued, ser. 5078, Dept. of VA & 7th Army Corps, RG 393 Pt. 1 [C-3297, C-3064]; Major General John E. Wool to Hon. Edwin M. Stanton, 16 Mar. 1862, filed as V-242 1862, Letters Received, ser. 12, RG 94 [K-751].) For Wool's orders of October and November 1861, see above, doc. 2.

1 General Orders 5 and 6, issued by General John E. Wool, commander of the Department of Virginia, on January 30 and February 4, 1862, respectively, had appointed a commission to make "a critical examination of the condition of the persons known as Vagrants or 'contrabands' who are employed in this Department." (General Orders No. 5, Headquarters, Dept. of Va. &c., 30 Jan. 1862, and General Orders No. 6, Headquarters, Dept. of Va. &c., 4 Feb. 1862, vol. -/4 VaNc, pp. 154–55, General Orders Issued, ser. 5078, Dept. of VA & 7th Army Corps, RG 393 Pt. 1 [C-3326].)
2 The table summarized the number of black laborers in the army's quartermaster, engineer, subsistence, ordnance, and medical departments; the amount and cost of rations issued to all black people, workers and nonworkers; and the average monthly expenditure.
3 For Special Order 72, see above, doc. 2n.
4 An error; the space should be blank.

5: Superintendent of Contrabands in the Department of Virginia to the Commander of the Department

Fort Monroe [*Va.*], Apr. 15 /62
Sir, I have the honour to report that in obedience to your orders, I have vacated all buildings at or near the Seminary of all Coloured people except such as Dr. McKay wishes to retain to work for him.[1]

I have received 80 to 100 more Contrabands, & these, with those turned out at Camp Hamilton, many of them, at least, being women & children will need Considerable support. one of them is blind.

I submit whether it would not be better to induce as many as possible, of all who do not work for government, to go over beyond

Hampton Bridge, & there take care of themselves, with what aid we can give them.

In that event, if you approve of it, will you authorise some one to arrange for them, & use some discretion in regard to places, & decide what old tools, carts or beasts, they may use, that are left, belonging only to Rebels, as would be of little or no use to any others & see that they are protected as far as possible in the use of those things & such lands as may be assigned them for the season—

I think it all can be done without much, if any cost to the government, except a little lumber to those who the government owes for past labor & a team to carry it over for them—

As yet I have been unable to get any thing more from Capts. Sawtelle or Talmage in the way of funds for the support of the Contrabands, nor the books & effects removed from the Quarters, as you requested or Ordered

We have some men unable to work in gangs, but could do something. I think if you would order a Cart or team for our use, we could employ all such men in work on the roads & filling up the impure lands back of the Quarters &c. &c. to very good advantage   All of which is respectfully submitted

ALS   C. B. Wilder

C. B. Wilder to Maj. Gen. Wool, 15 Apr. 1862, W-98 1862, Letters Received, ser. 5063, Dept. of VA & 7th Army Corps, RG 393 Pt. 1 [C-3199]. Captain Charles G. Sawtelle was, and Captain Grier Tallmadge had been, chief quarter-master of the Department of Virginia. (General Orders No. 30, Headquarters Dept. of Va., 4 Apr. 1862, vol. -/4 VaNc, p. 214, General Orders Issued, ser. 5078, Dept. of VA & 7th Army Corps, RG 393 Pt. 1 [C-3327].) General John E. Wool, the department commander, had already, on April 13, "empower'd" Charles B. Wilder "to grant passes to Colored persons to go to Hampton, Fox Hill, or within the lines, and to cultivate the Ground and use the property of Rebels in Arms against the Government, or who have abandoned their homes," but no letter or order has been found in the records of the department to indicate whether, in response to Wilder's letter of April 15, Wool authorized further encouragement of such settlement or the use of tools, carts, and work animals left behind by rebels. (General Orders No. 36, Headquarters Dept. of Va. &c., 13 Apr. 1862, vol. -/4 VaNc, pp. 213–14, General Orders Issued, ser. 5078, Dept. of VA & 7th Army Corps, RG 393 Pt. 1 [C-3327].)

1 Orders to remove "the contrabands . . . from the brick building adjoining the Seminary, into a Camp" had been issued by the department commander on March 31, "[i]n order to make room for sick soldiers." (Special Orders No. 84, Headquarters Dept. of Va. &c, 31 Mar. 1862, vol. -/5 VaNc, p. 79, Special Orders Issued, ser. 5084, Dept. of VA & 7th Army Corps, RG 393 Pt. 1 [C-3064].)

6: Chief Quartermaster of the Department of North Carolina
to the Quartermaster General, and the Latter's Reply

New Bern [*N.C.*] April 29. 1862
General, I have the honor to report that there are already about six
hundred "Contrabands" in this Department, dependent upon the
Army for a support. General Burnside directed me, after the battle
of New Bern, to take all that applied for work upon my rolls at
$8 oo/100 per month and a ration and clothing. They are
continually coming in and I respectfully request that I may be
instructed by you concerning them. I do not know what the custom
is at other Posts in regard to them, nor what regulations for their
Government may have been established by the authorities at
Washington. The number will soon be very large and I hope that a
Superintendent may be appointed over them. I am General Very
respectfully Your ob'dt Svt.

HLS   Herman Biggs

[*Washington, D.C.*] May 6ᵗʰ 1862.
Captain; Your letter of the 29ᵗʰ ult, relating to the employment of
colored persons, has been received.
   While much of the work in the Quarter Master's Department,
should properly be done by extra duty soldiers, who are entitled to
the opportunity to earn the extra duty pay, there is no objection,
but, an advantage, in the employment at fair rates, of such able
bodied colored men, as can be profitably employed in doing
necessary work. Beyond this, the Department has no right to go; —
no right to originate or carry on, unnecessary work, for the purpose
of employing either white or black men.
   The appropriations, are for the public service, and the public
work, not for charity.
   It is probably necessary in some cases, in order to prevent
starvation, to issue rations to persons, who may not be really needed
for necessary work. From such persons, I think some equivalent in
occasional labor — should be required.
   They might be set to policing a city, or the Camps, or be
engaged in other such employment, which will prevent their
becoming, entirely useless charges upon the public.
   Black men, make very good teamsters and hostlers for the general
train. The Regimental train is driven by the enlisted wagoners of
the companies.

HLcSr   (Sgd) M. C. Meigs.

122

Chief Qr. Mr. Herman Biggs to Brig. Genl. M. C. Meigs, 29 Apr. 1862, "New Berne, N.C.," Consolidated Correspondence File, ser. 225, Central Records, RG 92 [Y-154]; M. C. Meigs to Captain Herman Biggs, 6 May 1862, vol. 59, pp. 478–79, Letters Sent, ser. 9, Central Records, RG 92 [Y-154].

7: Former Superintendent of the Poor in the Department of North Carolina to the Chairman of the American Freedmen's Inquiry Commission

New-York May 25th 1863.
Hon Rob Dale Owen   Agreeably to your request, I give you a brief report of the freed blacks in the department of North Carolina during the time they were under my charge.

I received my appointment a few days after the taking of Newbern, & on March 30th the following commission was sent to me the office being honorary without pay except one ration.

> Head Quarters Department of North Carolina
> Newbern Mach 30th 1832 [*1862*].
> Mr Vincent Polyed [*Colyer*] is hereby appointed Superintendent of the Poor and will be obayed respected accordingly,
> By command of Major General Burnside
> Lewis Richmond Asst Adjt General

My first order from Genl Burnside under this appointment, was to employ as many negro men as I could get up to the number of five thousand to offer them eight dollers a month. one ration of clothes. They were to work on the building of forts. This order remained standing on my book,s up to the day I left the Departement with General, July 6th without our ever being able to fill it   Up to the time I left there were not over twenty five hundred able bodied men within our lines, so that it will be readily understood why the negroes were mover [*never*] a burden on our hands.

The truth was we never could get enough of them, and although for a little while there were a few more at Roanoke Island then were wanted there—after the cost [*fort?*] was completed.

They were brough to Newbern as it was known.

There were all in the department 10.000. of them 2500 were men 2500 women and Children.

They were at the following places.

At Newbern and vicinity 7.500   At Roanoke Island and posts adjacent 1.000. At Washington, Hatteras, Carolina and Beaufort 1.500.

In the four months that I had charge of them. the men built three first class earth work forts; Fort Totten at Newbern. a large work. Fort Burnside on the upper end of Roanok [Il –] & [Fort?] at Washington N.C. These three forts were our chief reliance for defence against the rebels. in case of an attack. have since been sucesfully used for that purpuse by our forces under Major Genl Foster.

The negroes loaded and discharged cargoes. for about three hunderd vessels. served regularly as crews on about forty steamers. and acted as permanent gangs of laborers in all the Quatermasters. Commissary and Ordnance offices of the department.

A number of the men were good carpenters. blacksmiths coopers &c. and did effective work in their [. . .] at bridge building ship joining &c   The large railroad bridge across the Trent was built chiefly by them. as was also the bridge across Bateholors & other creeks. & the docks at Roanoke Island & elsewhere   Upwards of fifty volunteers of the best & most courageous were kept constantly employed on the perilous. but most important duty of spies. scouts and guides.   In the work they were invaluable and almost indispensable.   They frequently went from thirty to three hundred miles within the enemy's lines; visiting his principle camps and most important posts and bringing us back important reliable information.

They visited Kingston Goldsboro. Trenton Onslow Swansboro, Tarboro of points on the Roanoke river; after these errands barely escaping with their lives.   They were pursued on several occasions by blood hounds   two or three of them were taken prisoners; one of these was shot; the fate of the others not known.   The pay they received for this work was small but satisfactory.   They seemed to think their lives were well spent, if necessary in giving rest, security, and success, to the Union troops, whom they regarded as their deliverers.   They usually knelt in solemn prayer before they left, & on their return, from that hazardous duty.

. . . .

The women and children supported themselves with but little aid from the government by washing, ironing. cooking, making pies, cakes &c. for the troops   The few women that were employed by the government in the hospitals received 4$ a month, clothes and one ration.

Those in the neighborhood of Newbern were ordered to report at my office as soon as they arrived within our lines.   They obtained quarters in the out-houses, kitcheons and poorer classes of dwellings, deserted by the citizens on the taking of Newbern.   They attended our free schools & churches regularly and with great earnestness.   They were peaceable, orderly, cleanly, &

industrious. There was seldom a quarrel known among them. They consider it a duty to work for the U.S. government & though they could in many cases have made more money at other conditions; there was a public opinion among them that tabooed any one that refuses to work for the Government. The churches & schools established for their benefit, with no cost to the government, were of great value in building up this public opinion among them.

As I have previously related, that the men frequently led foraging parties, to places where supplies necessary for the department were obtained. In this way boat-loads of prime and oak wood for the hospitals. Government officers. a steam boat load of cotton bales for the protection of the gunboats and with forage for the same, number of horses and mules for the Quarter Master Department. Small sheep were obtained at no other cost than the small wages of the men. Without doubt property far exceeding in value all that was ever paid to the blacks, was thus obtained for the Government. Under my appointment as Superintendent of the Poor, from Major Genl. Burnside. I had to attend to the suffering poor whites as well as blacks. There were 18.00 men, women, & children of the poor whites. who felt compelled to call for provisions at my office. To those 18.00 was distributed gratuitously during the three months as follows.

1.800.
To white people.

Flour	76 1/2 Barrels.		Meal	432	Lbs.
Beef	116	"	Fresh Beef	169	"
Hominy	4 1/2	"	Peas.	549	"
Coffee	20 1/2	"	Salt.	219	"
Sugar	24 1/2	"	Hard Bread	107	bxs
Pork	38	"	Molasses	43	gall.
Bacon	29 1/2	"	Vinegar	6	gall.
Rice	37	[bbl.]	Soap.	39.	lbs.
Tea	65	lbs.	Beans.	7 1/2	bbls.
Candles	379.	lbs.			

While to the 75.00 poor blacks over 4 times the number that were of the whites, there was called for and given in the same line as follows:

75.00
To colored people.

Flour	19	Blls.		Hominy	237	lbs.
Sugar	7	"	Beans	369	"
Coffee	5	"	Peas	308	"
Rice	8	"	Hard Bread	3262	"
Beef	4 1/2	"	Soap.	805	"
Pork	16 1/2	"	Salt.	44	"

Candles	27 1/2	lbs.	Fresh Beef.	19	"
Tea	4	"	Molasses	31	gall.
Meal	433	"	Vinegar	15	qts

On an avarage in most articles of *sixteen* times as much, was called for by the poor whites, as was wanted by the poor blacks. Work was offered to both. to the whites 12.$ month

   "   "   "   " "   "   " Blacks $8.   "

. . . .

HLcSr   Vincent Colyer

Excerpts from Vincent Colyer to Hon. Rob. Dale Owen, 25 May 1863, filed with O-328 1863, Letters Received, ser. 12, RG 94 [K-84]. Topical labels in the margin are omitted. Seven pages of a thirty-one-page letter; the omitted portions concerned the entry of fugitive slaves into federal lines, their role in providing military intelligence, religious and educational activities among them, and suggestions for their organization and treatment.

8: Provost Marshal of the Department of Virginia to the Commander of the Department

Fort Monroe [*Va.*], June 5 *1862*
General, I wish to call your attention to a great nuisance, fostered by Mr Wilder, – I refer to the erection of Booths at the head of the Wharf. For some days past I have counted, from Thirty to Forty able bodied negroes, who there congregate for the ostensible purpose of selling apples; and among them all, they probably do not have 1 Bbl. for sale. Yesterday my Guards found two Bottles of whiskey, in their Booths, which I have no doubt is retailed to Sailors. I have represented these facts to Mr Wilder, who excuses their idleness by saying they cannot get work, and must do that or starve.

In reply to that, I am informed by Capt. Thomas. A.Q.M. that he is ready and anxious to hire every black laborer at $10. pr month, and one ration pr day.

I respectfully suggest that Mr Wilder be ordered to have the Booths taken down, and report the men for work to the Qr Masters Dept.

I also wish to call your attention to the fact that the negroes in their quarters appear to be in possession of firearms. The officer of the Day, (Capt Bates) reported to me, that he saw frequent discharges of weapons, last evening, and that one ball came in dangerous proximity to his person.

An order to search their persons and premises, would soon abate the nuisance. I have the honor to be Very Respectfully Your Obt Servant

ALS

W^m P Jones.

Major Wm. P. Jones to Major Gen. John A. Dix, 5 June 1862, J-18 1862, Letters Received, ser. 5063, Dept. of VA & 7th Army Corps, RG 393 Pt. 1 [C-3002].

9: Superintendent of Contrabands in the Department of Virginia to the Commander of the Department

Fort Monroe [*Va.*] June 27 /62

Dr Sir. I have the honour to repeat to you what I have before mentioned, that the abuses practised upon the Col^d people in Hampton & the region above are Continued, & in many Cases since Gen. Wool left, with increased rigor, by Rebel Sympathisers, Straggling Soldiers & Governmental Officers, Stripping them of whatever is found in their possession, generrally of little or no value to any one else, tho it may be their little all, assuming that it was Stolen as I believe without evidence or investigation. Several new cases have come to my knowledge to day, & I believe all or nearly so, are Carried on out of hatred to the Col^d people, & generally in utter disregard of the letter & spirit of Gen. Wools Order No 36, & yours to Gen. Mansfield on the first or Second day of your arrival. Your Obt. Sevt.

ALS

C. B. Wilder

C. B. Wilder to Maj. Gen. Dix, 27 June 1862, W-152 1862, Letters Received, ser. 5063, Dept. of VA & 7th Army Corps, RG 393 Pt. 1 [C-3007]. General Order 36, issued on April 13, 1862, by General John E. Wool, the previous commander of the Department of Virginia, had authorized Wilder to permit black people to settle on abandoned land owned by "Rebels in Arms against the Government." (See above, doc. 5n.) The order said to have been given to General Joseph K. F. Mansfield, on the first or second day of the arrival of Wool's successor, General John A. Dix, has not been found in the letters-sent volumes or orders of the department; Mansfield was the commander at Newport News, Virginia. In response to Wilder's complaint of June 27, General Dix assured the superintendent of contrabands that violations of General Order 36 would be "properly redressed," but "unless they are pointed out to me, I cannot know where my action is required." (Maj. Genl. John A. Dix to C. B. Wilder, Esq., 27 June 1862, vol. -/3 VaNc, p. 243, Letters Sent, ser. 5046, Dept. of VA & 7th Army Corps, RG 393 Pt. 1 [C-3204].)

10: Testimony by a Virginia Freedman before the
Southern Claims Commission

[*Norfolk, Va.*] 31st day of July 1877
Claim of Edward Whitehurst (cold)
No 10817
My name is Edward Whitehurst. My age 47 years. my residence
near Hampton Elizabeth City County Virginia. where I have lived
since 1866. my occupation Farming now. I am the Claimant   I
was the slave of William Ivey at the beginning of war, who now
lives near Hampton now. (having been a slave questions 1″ to 43
were not asked).
To question^s 44, 45, 46, 47, 48, 49 & 50 He says *"No Sir."*
To question 51. He says. I was in the Union Army. I went into
Hospital service at Newport News on the peninsula 1861. on May
8th, assistant Steward, under Genl Phelps commanding, there till 5″
day of August 1861. then I went to Fortress Monroe V^a to the
Hygea Hospital. staid there a short time, then by permission of
Genl Butler, I went over near Hampton & in Hampton and started a
store and Bake House.   I never enlisted in the Army but volunteered
as a nurse, was never Sworn in to the service.
To question 66. He says. I was the sole owner of the property
when it was taken.   I became the owner by purchasing the same
with money I had saved before and during the war.   before the war I
hired My time of my master and saved all I could, and when I was
in Hospital service I managed to save a little all the time.   I had
over $500 – in gold and silver when the war broke out.   Kept it in
my trunk and with my wife.
To question 67 He says. from Parish'^{s} farm near Newport news
and Sinclair'^{s} farm near Hampton I cultivated between 18 and 20
acres   a great many colored people lived on these farms, by
permission of the officers in charge.   Capt Wilder was one of those
officers.   those that were able to pay had to,   I had to pay for what I
used.   I paid $2 – for per acre
To question 68 He says I dont know –
To question 70 He says, I was a slave at the beginning of the
war.   I was not free until President Lincoln^s proclamation in reality,
but I was free to all intents after the 27″ day of May 1861, when
my master went off and left me. – as I have said I farmed & Kept a
store & Bake shop.   I saved the money used in purchasing the
property before the war, as I hired my own time from my master.   I
bought the property in the store and Bake House, some from John
Moody in the Fort, he Kept a store there, some in Baltimore & the
property taken from the farms I raised.   My former master William

Ivey is not a witness for he was in Southern army until 1862, in october he came home. he knew nothing of the taking of the property. I dont work for him now, nor on his land. I live on my own land, that I bought from Frank H. Dennis. I donot owe my former master any thing. No person but myself has any interest in this claim but myself

To quest 72. He says. Yes sir. I saw part of it taken at different times. I saw corn Hogs. Fodder. Potatoes. Flour, Ginger Cakes, Butter & Green corn.

To question 73 He says. I dont know whether any was taken in the night time or not, nor secretly

To ques 74 He says. Complained to the Provost Guard Sergeant Martin, I complained. I dont know whether he belonged to 11 Wisconsin or 14 Massachusetts Regt., He told me, "you cant do anything", "if they come into my house to holler and he would come, but not to make any resistance, as the soldiers were hungry, and would get something to eat. No attempt was ever made by any officer to stop them until they had taken all they wanted and could get.

To Ques 75. He says. No vouchers or receipts were given or asked for or given. I did not think to ask for any.

" Ques 76 He says. No payment has ever been made for any property charged in this Claim, nor any ever taken from me. This is the only claim I ever made for the property

" Ques 77 He says. The property claimed was taken partly by troops encamped in the vicinity and partly by troops going through. some were out on scouting expeditions towards Yorktown, & other places. No battles near there, some small skirmishing.

To ques 78 He says. I saw Hogs, old corn, Fodder, Potatoes Flour, Ginger cakes Butter & Green Corn taken

To ques 79 He says. I saw a sow and ten Pigs taken. I Judge the sow would weigh 150 or 200 lbs and the pigs would average from 70 to 80 lbs. they were taken at different times. they were taken from the lot where I lived right by the Bake house. live hogs there then was high, and selling from ~~20 to 25~~ 18 to 20 cts per lb. they were taken during 1863 at different times I do not know to what command the troops belonged. they killed 3 or 4 right in the lot. and others right in front of the Bake house. put them in wagons and carried them away. I dont Know exactly where, sergeants & corporals were present they told their men to hurry up and put in the wagon. when I asked them for pay. was told the Government would pay me.

The Corn, Fodder, Potatoes Flour Cakes Butter and Green corn was all taken in just about the same manner. by different squads of troops

There was about 21 or 22 Bbls (5 Bus to Barrel) of old
corn. there was two army wagon loads in the car. Corn was then
worth 50 cts per peck then. $2— per bushel. The Fodder was taken
from stacks, there were 2 or 3 stacks & some under a shed   I can
only guess at the amount and Judge there was 1000, or 1500
lbs. Fodder was worth two dollars per hundred lbs
   The potatoes were taken from the Bakehouse in Hampton,   I
dont remember how many there and can only guess, and Judge there
was 20 or 30 Bushels.   they were worth at that time I suppose $2—
per bushel   The Flour was taken from the Bake house   There was
two Barrels taken. I paid $8. to $9. per Bbl. Two Bbls of Cakes
were taken from Bake house. there were worth then about 9 to 10
dollars per Bbl. The Butter taken from Bakehouse one tub about 40
pounds and was worth 30 cts per lb. The green corn was standing
in the field was large enough for roasting. on the Parrish
farm. there was also some taken from the Sinclair farm. there was
about 15 or 16 acres in corn on the Parrish farm and between 5 & 6
acres on the Sinclair farm. it would not be worth less than 20
dollars an acre. and I Judge there was at least 20 acres. They drove
into the field and cut and loaded their wagons and hauled into
Camp or I saw them going that way. No other officers were present
except those mentioned. I have seen 3 wagons in the field at one
time and a company of soldiers. cutting and loading   In taking the
other things from the Bake house. they just came and took them
and loaded their wagons and drove off. they cleaned out the
Bakehouse in one day. they were off and on taking my corn, a week
or two. I believe the soldiers had orders from their superior officers
to take the property, as they always came in charge of Sergeants &
Corporals & had wagons & horses. and always started directly back
to Camp. and further this deponent saith not.
HDS   Edward. Whitehurst

Testimony of Edward Whitehurst, 31 July 1877, claim of Edward Whitehurst, Elizabeth City Co. VA case files, Approved Claims, ser. 732, Southern
Claims Commission, 3rd Auditor, RG 217 [I-162]. Sworn before a special
commissioner of the Southern Claims Commission. The questions that correspond to the enumerated responses are in the file. According to other documents in the file, Whitehurst had submitted a claim for $722 as compensation
for the following property taken by Union soldiers in August 1862: 6 hogs, 50
bushels corn, 2,000 pounds fodder, 40 bushels potatoes, 2 barrels flour, 2
barrels ginger cakes, 40 pounds butter, and 20 acres of corn "cut and used as
forage." He was awarded only $115, the commissioners having judged that
the items taken from his bakeshop "must be charged to pillage" rather than
official military use and that the hogs were "chiefly pigs & not to be regarded
as an army supply."

11: Commander of the Department of Virginia to the Governor of Massachusetts

Fort Monroe [*Va.*], 5th Nov. 1862

Sir: In consequence of the detention of Major Bolles by indisposition I did not receive until yesterday, your letter to him of the 16th ult. in regard to the reception for a limited period of a portion of the contrabands at this Post and in its vicinity –

As the proposition was declined I should not have deemed it necessary to reply to your letter were it not that I desire to correct some misapprehensions, under which you labor in regard to this post and to the persons in whose behalf your friendly aid was invoked. I have never entertained or expressed the slightest apprehension in regard to the safety of this Fort. – I do not think it possible for the insurgents to reduce it by any force they can bring against it. – But in case of an investment the physical conformation of the narrow strip of land on which it stands, renders it impracticable to afford shelter outside of its walls to non-combatants, and within there is no room except for the garrison. Thus, though I have no fear whatever for the Fort, it is possible for a cavalry force by a sudden movement, like a recent one into Maryland, to seize and carry off to Richmond from some of our contraband camps the able-bodied males, as the insurgents are now doing in all directions outside of our lines. –

My object in seeking a temporary asylum for the contrabands here, especially the women and children, was two fold: 1st to remove them from the Seat of war where they ought not to be and 2nd to make a better provision for them than it is possible – with the best intentions, to afford here. –

When I asked permission of the Government to negociate with the Governors of the Northern States for their reception until some permanent asylum could be provided for them, there were here and in the vicinity about 7000 sick and wounded soldiers of whom about 1500 were in tents. – When I asked for the removal of the Contrabands I asked also for the removal of the sick, and a large number of the latter were sent to Northern Hospitals. – In the same district there were about 3100 negroes, of whom only 700 were males. Of these about 1300 were living in tents. They were very unhealthy and were dying at the rate of from four to six a day. They were decimated by desease in thirty days. They were as well provided for as our Soldiers: but they do not bear the same exposure. –

Under these privations and with this mortality thinning their ranks a considerable number of them asked permission to return to their masters and their former homes. All persons in the Military and Naval service, as you know, are prohibited by act of Congress from surrendering fugitive slaves to any one claiming their Service or labor.[1] This provision has been faithfully carried out. But where the fugitive himself has asked permission to return to his master, I have not considered myself as possessing any authority to prevent him, accordingly I have given the desired permission, in repeated instances: and the Superintendent of Contrabands, Mr. *Wilder*, from your State, between whom and myself there has always been a friendly understanding has given a much larger number of permits both under Gen[l] Wool's Administration and mine. The moving cause in most of these cases was probably a desire to escape from the perils and privations of a camp. Had these persons been in Massachusetts with proper shelter and in the enjoyment of the comforts, with which it was reasonable to suppose they would have been provided, none of these cases would have occurred.

It was under these circumstances that I deemed it my duty to appeal to your Excellency, to make temporary provision for a portion of them. – And to whom could I with more propriety apply in the first instance, than to the Governor of Massachusetts? Maj. Gen[l] *Butler* of your State was the first to inaugurate here the plan of receiving and providing for fugitives from service under the denomination of contrabands. Your two Senators in Congress have been pre-eminent in their labors in the cause of emancipation. Your own zeal has not been inferior to theirs. I did not doubt, therefore, that an appeal to your humanity to co-operate in relieving them from possible danger in the future and from the ravages of desease, which they were actually suffering, would have been favorably received. –

In declining to receive any portion of them, you advise me to arm them, and if I am attacked, to let them fight with the forces under my command. I trust no contingency will arise to render such a measure necessary in any quarter. – If the twenty millions of whites – in the loyal States cannot suppress the insurrection of the five millions in the States, which have passed resolutions of secession; if they have not the courage, the constancy, and the indifference to personal suffering and sacrifice, which are necessary to uphold their Government and to maintain their national existence, it will never be done by other hands. I shall not arm these people for the defence of my command. If I desired to do so, my purpose would be met by an insuperable obstacle. Their indisposition to take up arms is nearly universal. They say they are willing to work, but they do not wish to fight. – Of some 1700 at Hampton and Newport News the adult males were all questioned, and not more than five or six expressed a willingness to be armed. The same

reluctance has been manifested in other quarters. There are
exceptional cases. But a reliance on any considerable aid from the
slave population of the South by arming them to put down the
rebellion, even if we could reconcile ourselves to the policy or the
morality of employing them for the purpose, would prove utterly
fallacious. Not a sufficient number to constitute a single battalion
have volunteered their services from the commencement of the war
to the present day, for our support; nor although we have had several
hundred thousand men in arms in the insurgent States, has the
Slightest disposition been manifested on the part of the blacks to
avail themselves of so favorable an opportunity for asserting their
freedom. It is time for us to look the difficulties we have to
encounter Steadily in the face – to know the true elements of our
strength, and to discard all confidence in any other resources
excepting those, which our own firmness, energy and perseverance
supply.

I need not to suggest to you that the close contact of these people
with our camps is not calculated to improve the moral condition
of either: and while I give all credit to your Excellency's motives,
I am constrained to think that your view of the whole subject is
erroneous. If these women and children were sent to you
for a temporary asylum, I cannot believe that the people of
Massachusetts would permit them to become "a swarm of homeless
wanderers." And I may say almost in your own language, that it is
precisely because I desire to "save their wives and children from
perishing" by exposure and desease & "because I do not wish their
new freedom to become license, corruption and infamy," that I
would remove them temporarily from the perils and temptations of
the camp, to a community where the highest order reigns, and from
a region devastated and perpetually agitated by war, to one of peace
domestic quietude and abundance.

The Governor of Rhode Island obeying the generous impulses of
his character, said promptly in reply to my suggestion that the
public necessities might require for them a temporary asylum,
"Should you send them here, Rhode Island would take care of
them." I have nevertheless decided to retain them at present and do
all in my power to render their condition supportable during the
coming season, should they remain so long. I have ordered our sick
and wounded to be removed from the buildings at Newport News,
nine miles from this Post, the nearest point where the contrabands
can be placed under shelter. – They will occupy log-cabins with few
of the appliances by which the people of New England contrive to
make their dwellings far more comfortable during the rigors of
winter than the habitations in this latitude; but no effort on my part

will be spared to provide for their wants and secure them from the
ravages of desease. Should the exigencies of War demand the
removal of the women and children to a more secure Asylum for a
limited period, I shall not hesitate to send them to some Northern
State, and if a portion of them should find their way to
Massachusetts, I venture to hope, notwithstanding your Excellency's
strong disapprobation of my purpose, that they will be hospitably
received and generously provided for— I am, very respectfully Your
ob'd't Serv't

HLcS

John A. Dix

Maj. Genl. John A. Dix to His Excellency John A. Andrew, 5 Nov. 1862,
vol. -/3 VaNc, pp. 407–11, Letters Sent, ser. 5046, Dept. of VA & 7th
Army Corps, RG 393 Pt. 1 [C-3203]. On September 12, 1862, General Dix
had asked the Secretary of War for permission to make arrangements with the
governors of Massachusetts and other Northern states to forward about 2,000
black men, women, and children, who were then under the supervision of
Charles B. Wilder at Old Point Comfort. "The contraband negroes who have
been permitted to collect in great numbers at this fort," Dix had complained, " . . . have always been and are now a very great source of embar-
rassment to the troops in this garrison and in the camps hereabouts and to
the white population in this neighborhood. In case the fort should be invested or approached by the enemy's forces I should feel obliged to ship them
all to the North." Permission was granted one week later, whereupon Dix
immediately dispatched his aide-de-camp, Major John A. Bolles, to confer
with the governors of New York and each New England state and to urge
that they accept some of the "helpless and unhappy persons who are now cast
upon the care of the Government and for whom some asylum ought to be
provided remote from Camps and Armies until peace is restored or a permanent Colony be established for their reception." (*Official Records*, ser. 1, vol.
18, pp. 391, 395; Maj. Genl. John A. Dix to His Excellency E. D. Morgan,
23 Sept. 1862, vol. -/3 VaNc, pp. 335–36, Letters Sent, ser. 5046, Dept.
of VA & 7th Army Corps, RG 393 Pt. 1 [C-3235].) John A. Andrew, the
governor of Massachusetts, had refused to "concur in any way or to any
degree in the plan proposed." Instead, in his letter to Bolles of October 16,
he had argued that the former slaves should be retained in the South and
placed under arms. "Here Providence has given to them a chance to complete
their emancipation from Slavery by a victory over prejudice." "If you are
attacked," Andrew had advised, "let the blacks fight to preserve their freedom!" (*Freedom*, ser. 2: doc. 41.)

1 Both the additional article of war adopted in March 1862 and the Second
Confiscation Act of July 1862 contained such prohibitions. (*Statutes at Large*,
vol. 12, pp. 354, 589–92.)

12: Superintendent of Contrabands at Newport News, Virginia, to the Commander of the Department of Virginia

Newport News [*Va.*] Nov. 7th 1862.

Sir   In compliance with your order of the 5th inst I would submit the following statistics pertaining to the contrabands at this Post.   although slight errors may exist they are as nearly correct as could be procured from such materiel as they had to be obtained.

The whole Number of contrabands at the Post is 506

Whole Number of Males	255
" " Females	251
Whole Number of able bodied Males over fifteem years of age	150
Number of children under fifteen yr[s] of age	148

About one Hundred of the above have been employed in the Hospital and Quartermasters Departments   Of those employed in the Hospital Department the Males have not received any pay.   the Females have been paid five dollars each from the Hospital Fund.

Those employed in the Quartermaster's Department (about thirty) have been paid to October 1st

Besides those enumerated above (506) there are about one Hundred and fifty within three miles of the post.   these are squatters upon deserted farms and subsist upon what they have raised and by stealing — a large amount of their produce was taken from them by the soldiers — Many of these have arms which I am taking from them as fast as they can be found.

Of the number at the Post.   thirty eight are willing (or profess to be) to go to Washington to work for the Government.   They will take with them thirteen women and children

I think one Hundred more will be ready to leave in one or two weeks, or when they become satisfied that no more money can be earned about here.

The number now subsisted wholly or in part by the Government is one hundred and fifty.   This number is rapidly increasing on account of the discontinuance of the Hospital.   cuting off their communication with the country and the lateness of the season   Respectfuly submitted

ALS   O. Brown.

Contract Surgeon O. Brown to Major General Dix, 7 Nov. 1862, B-223 1862, Letters Received, ser. 5063, Dept. of VA & 7th Army Corps, RG 393 Pt. 1 [C-3001]. An order assigning Brown to "take charge of the contrabands now at Newports News or hereafter to be sent there" was issued the same day. (Special Orders No. 153, Head Quarters, Dept. of Virginia, Seventh Army Corps, 7 Nov. 1862, vol. -/5 VaNc, pp. 372–73, Special Orders Issued, ser. 5084, Dept. of VA & 7th Army Corps, RG 393 Pt. 1 [C-3395].)

13: Commander of the Department of Virginia
to the Secretary of War

[*Fortress Monroe, Va.*] 22. Nov. 1862.
Sir: I have received your order appointing Dr. *LeGrand Russell* "Special Commissioner to take charge of the colored refugees from the enemy at Fortress Monroe and its vicinity,"[1] and shall do all in my power to aid him in the proper discharge of his duties.

The peculiar phraseology of the order suggests the propriety of stating that all the negroes here are not refugees from the enemy. On the contrary, there are a number, who are fugitives from the service of Union men, who have been persecuted by the Secessionists for their fidelity to the Government of the U.S. and a few, who belong to persons residing in districts, which have never been in possession of the insurgents. Some Union families in this neighborhood have lost all their negroes, whom I have in obedience to the Act of Congress, refused to give up. –[2] It will be troublesome to separate one class from the other, and assuming that the order was not intended to make any distinction, I shall, unless otherwise directed, put Dr. *Russell* in charge of both.

I avail myself of the opportunity of stating, that under your authority, I opened negociations with the Governors of the States of Maine, Massachusetts and Rhode Island with a view to provide a temporary asylum for the Contrabands here, until the Government could make some permanent provision for them. The proposition was received with such marked disfavor by Governor Andrew of Mass. that I decided, notwithstanding a very prompt and kind response from Governor *Sprague* of Rhode Island, to retain them here and make suitable provision for them for the winter.[3] Accordingly I withdrew the sick from the Hospital at Newport News, and sent over a thousand of the colored fugitives there. But the very day they were removed from their encampment, where they were dying rapidly, I was advised that the Irish Legion under General *Corcoran* would arrive on the following day. Their tents had been so injured in New York by a storm on the eve of their departure, that they were obliged to be put under cover, and having no place for them but Newport News, I was compelled to remove the colored people again. — They were sent to Craney Island, and the Quartermaster is, under my instructions erecting barracks for them. They will all be covered in the course of the coming week. — I am, very respectfully Your ob'd't Serv't,

HLcS

John A. Dix

Maj. Genl. John A. Dix to Hon. E. M. Stanton, 22 Nov. 1862, vol. -/3 VaNc, pp. 423–24, Letters Sent, ser. 5046, Dept. of VA & 7th Army Corps, RG 393 Pt. 1 [C-3208]. Not all the former slaves displaced by General Michael Corcoran's "Irish Legion" had been sent to Craney Island at the time Dix reported the transfer to the Secretary of War; Corcoran's men took charge of removing those who remained. On November 26, Dix called Corcoran to account for complaints "that the colored people who are to go to Craney Island, have been forced to remain all night on the wharf without shelter and without food, that one has died and that others are suffering with disease, and that your men have turned them out of their houses which they have built themselves and have robbed some of them of their money and personal effects." "These people are in our care," Dix admonished Corcoran, "and we are bound by every principle of humanity to treat them with kindness and protect them from exposure and injury." Corcoran acknowledged that, in accordance with orders from Dix, "all colored people" except the families of quartermaster and commissary employees had, during the previous two days, been "removed from the buildings occupied by them," but he insisted "that the removal was conducted mildly and without any violence whatever, [and] that every effort was made to secure to them all alleged rights." "One per day is a small proportion of mortality among these people," he argued, "much smaller than at any previous day since our arrival here." (Maj. Genl. John A. Dix to Brig. Genl. M. Corcoran, 26 Nov. 1862, vol. -/3 VaNc, p. 428, Letters Sent, ser. 5046, Dept. of VA & 7th Army Corps, RG 393 Pt. 1 [C-3207]; Brig. Genl. Michael Corcoran to Major Genl. John A. Dix, 26 Nov. 1862, C-198 1862, Letters Received, ser. 5063, Dept of VA & 7th Army Corps, RG 393 Pt. 1 [C-3000].)

1 LeBaron (not LeGrand) Russell, secretary of the Boston Educational Commission, had been appointed "to examine the condition of the colored Refugees from the enemy" in the vicinity of Fortress Monroe, but the letter transmitting the Secretary of War's order had described Russell's mandate as "to take charge" of the refugees. (Brig. Gen. C. P. Buckingham to Major Gen. John A. Dix, 18 Nov. 1862, and order by Edwin M. Stanton, 18 Nov. 1862, vol. 1, p. 117, Records & Orders, RG 107 [L-319].)

2 The Second Confiscation Act of July 1862 had forbidden Union soldiers to surrender any fugitive slave to any claimant, or to "decide on the validity of the claim of any person to the service or labor of any other person." (*Statutes at Large*, vol. 12, pp. 589–92.)

3 For part of the department commander's correspondence with the New England governors, see *Freedom*, ser. 2: doc. 41, and above, doc. 11.

14: Commander of the Department of Virginia to the Secretary of War

Fort Monroe, Va. 13th Dec. *1862*

Sir: Complaints have been made by those who take a strong interest in the condition of fugitives from service here, usually denominated "Contrabands," that their labor since they have been employed by the U.S. has not been fully paid for. There are other grounds of complaint, also, and with a view to remove them I desire to make the following suggestions; viz.

1st The labor of these persons was not paid for until Nov. 1861. at which time a system of compensation was adopted under Maj. Genl Wool.[1] Before that time a large number of them had been employed and supplied with food and clothing. — If the payment of wages was right after Nov. 1st it would have been equally right before that time. The only difficulty is in ascertaining the exact amount of labor performed. Up to July 4th 1861, an accurate account was kept, and at the rate of $10. per month, per man, they were then entitled to $970. From July 4th to Nov. 1st 1861, no rolls were kept, and the amount of labor performed during that interval is uncertain. There are, however, some data for an estimate. The numbers employed July 4th and Nov. 1st are known, and by assuming a mean number an approximation to the truth may be reached. I do not put this mean higher than 200. At the above rate of compensation they would have earned $2000. per month, for the respective months of July, Aug. Sept. and Oct. deducting four days in the first named month and amounting in the aggregate to $7.741. 95/100. —

While Capt. Tallmadge, Qr. Master (recently deceased) was charged with the employment and compensation of these persons, some arrearages accumulated, which, for reasons that need not be ennumerated, remain unpaid. On the 1st of March 1862 there was due to them the sum of $1171. 75/100. Their earnings during the month of March amount to $2450. Both these sums should be paid. Many of the persons, who performed the labor on account of which these arrears accrued, are no longer here and many of them will not be found. It is, therefore, respectfully suggested that after waiting a reasonable time, say six months, for the claimants to present themselves, the balance unclaimed, shall become a fund for the relief and support of the poor, who are fugitives from service. —

There is admitted to be due from the Subsistence Department $152. —

There is also due from the Hospital Department the sum of $880. for the services of 220 colored nurses during the months of Nov. & Dec. 1861. and Jan. & Feby. 1862.

In these two cases there will be the same difficulty, in ascertaining the persons to whom the money is due; and the same disposition is recommended.

The payment of these amounts requiring the order of the Secretary of War, as do also the three bills forwarded with an explanatory letter by the Commanding General of this Department, Oct. 9. 1862, said three bills amounting in the aggregate to $1479.34. I respectfully ask for such an order. –

There are arrears now due for several months which, like those that have accrued in the Military Service, are unpaid. But they are within the authority of the Quartermaster and will be paid when he is in funds without any further order. The amount of these arrears Dec. 1st is about $16.590.91/100, making with the sums before mentioned an aggregate of $31,435.95 now due for contraband labor. –

2nd In order to remove the contraband women and children from contact with the Camps – a contact injurious to both – they have been transferred to Craney Island, where quarters are in preparation for them & where they will be required to furnish such labor as they are able to perform in picking oakum, fishing, &c. – It is respectfully asked that the needful authority be given to supply rooms for schools, & places of worship, at moderate expense for them. The Government having adopted the policy of receiving these fugitives and, by implication, promised them protection and security, it is respectfully submitted that some provision should be made for their intellectual and religious as well as for their physical wants. – I am very respectfully, Your obt. servt.

HLS

John A. Dix

Maj. Genl. John A. Dix to Hon. Edwin M. Stanton, 13 Dec. 1862, D-77 1862, Letters Received Irregular, RG 107 [L-99]. The three bills that General Dix had forwarded along with his "explanatory letter" of October 9 were for wages owed to former slaves who had been employed at Fortress Monroe and could not be paid without explicit authorization from the Secretary of War: one for "a party of Contrabands employed in police duties," the second for hospital employees, and the third for "waiters employed in the contraband quarters." "These quarters," Dix had explained with respect to the third bill, "are occupied by a large number of women and children who get no pay and draw no rations. The women make what they can by work, and as they are not provided for by Government, the persons for whose service compensation is claimed, were employed to keep the quarters in order and do the work required for their inmates." Almost three months later, the War Department informed Dix that the quartermaster general had reached a decision respecting the three categories of laborers (and, implicitly, other former slaves who were owed back wages): "the 'Contrabands' employed as nurses should be paid by the Medical Department; the rest by the

Quartermasters Department. Regular reports of persons should be made out by the Quartermaster and forwarded to the Quartermaster General, embracing the names of those to whom the Quartermaster Department should make payment." (Maj. Genl. John A. Dix to Hon. Edwin M. Stanton, 9 Oct. 1862, vol. -/3 VaNc, p. 364, Letters Sent, ser. 5046, Dept. of VA & 7th Army Corps, RG 393 Pt. 1 [C-3294]; Brig. Gen. C. P. Buckingham to Maj. Gen. J. A. Dix, 30 Dec. 1862, vol. 1, p. 104, Letters, Telegrams, & Orders Sent & Issued Relating to Union Army Volunteers, RG 107 [L-325].) Little was done under those instructions until late January 1863, when Charles B. Wilder, superintendent of contrabands in the Department of Virginia, was authorized by the Secretary of War to settle "the unpaid claims of contrabands for labor." (See doc. 15, immediately below.)

1 For the system instituted by General John E. Wool, then commander of the Department of Virginia, see above, doc. 2.

15: Order by the Secretary of War

Washington City January 28th 1863

ORDERED: —

1ST— That C. B. Wilder Assistant Quarter-Master, be specially detailed for duty as Superintendent of Colored persons at Fortress Monroe and within the command of Major General Dix.

2ND— That he be authorized to exercise the powers vested in him as Superintendent of Contrabands by the Orders No. 21 & 36 of Major General Wool.[1]

3RD— That he audit, settle and return to the Quarter-Master General the unpaid claims of contrabands for labor for the United States which are justly due and unpaid and pay the same under direction of the Quarter-Master General.

4TH— That under the orders and supervision of the Commanding General he take possession of all the vacant lands and plantations within the aforesaid command and put them in possession for the term of one year of such colored persons as will cultivate and manage the same in a proper manner upon such terms and regulations as he may deem proper and as shall be approved by the Commanding General.

5TH— That he return to the Quarter-Master General a schedule and description of the lands and plantations so taken and the persons in whose possession they are placed and on what terms and conditions.

6TH— That he shall exercise general supervision and police over the Contrabands upon the lands and plantations, and within the command aforesaid, prescribing and enforcing such sanitary and police regulations as he may deem proper, and shall be approved by the commanding general and make report to the Commanding General and the Quarter-Master General upon such matters as from time to time may require further order and regulations. By Order of the Secretary of War.

HDc

Order, In relation to Contrabands at Fortress Monroe, War Department, 28 Jan. 1863, vol. 1, p. 149, Orders Relating to Volunteers, RG 107 [L-318]. Copies of this order, along with instructions "to take such measures as may be necessary to enable Captain Wilder to perform the duties and exercise the powers vested in him," were sent to General John A. Dix, commander of the Department of Virginia, and to Montgomery C. Meigs, the quartermaster general. (Asst. Adjt. General Geo. D. Ruggles to Major Gen. John A. Dix, 28 Jan. 1863, and Asst. Adjt. Geo. D. Ruggles to Brig. Gen. M. C. Meigs, 28 Jan. 1863, vol. 1, p. 150, Orders Relating to Volunteers, RG 107 [L-318].) Armed with the Secretary of War's authorization, Wilder set about the work of settling the claims of former slaves who had worked for the government at and near Fortress Monroe. At the end of May, 1863, he reported that he had collected the names of more than 1,000 claimants, some of whom he had paid. There remained, however, many claims that he "could not liquidate for want of vouchers, or because their labor had been performed in the Quartermaster's, or some other, department, the officer in charge of which was authorized to pay the laborers, but for various reasons had failed to do so." (Capt. C. B. Wilder to Major General John A. Dix, 30 May 1863, enclosed in Maj. Genl. John A. Dix to Hon. E. M. Stanton, 1 June 1863, D-78 1863, Letters Received Irregular, RG 107 [L-99].) Six weeks later, Wilder complained that he had received conflicting documentation regarding labor performed between November 1861 and the end of February 1862, and "[n]o data of any kind" for the seven or eight months before that. "From such data," he despaired, "it is utterly impossible for me to audit and settle the claims of laborers contemplated in my instructions from the Secretary of War." (Capt. C. B. Wilder to Major General John A. Dix, 16 July 1863, enclosed in Brig. Genl. D. H. Rucker to Brig. Genl. M. C. Meigs, 8 Aug. 1863, "Negroes: Fortress Monroe," Consolidated Correspondence File, ser. 225, Central Records, RG 92 [Y-720].) At the end of the war, freedpeople who had labored at Fortress Monroe and vicinity during 1861 and 1862 were still trying to collect their wages. (See, for example, above, doc. 1.)

---

1 General Order 21, issued on March 15, 1862, by General John E. Wool, then commander of the Department of Virginia, had appointed Charles B. Wilder superintendent of contrabands in the department. (See above, doc. 4n.) General Order 36, issued on April 13, 1862, had authorized Wilder to permit "Colored persons" to settle on land abandoned by disloyal proprietors. (See above, doc. 5n.)

16: Testimony by the Superintendent of Contrabands in the Department of Virginia before the American Freedmen's Inquiry Commission

[*Fortress Monroe, Va. May 9, 1863*]
Testimony of Capt. C. B. Wilder.

Question How many of the people called contrabands, have come under your observation?

Answer Some 10,000 have come under our control, to be fed in part, and clothed in part, but I cannot speak accurately in regard to the number. This is the rendezvous. They come here from all about, from Richmond and 200 miles off in North Carolina There was one gang that started from Richmond 23 strong and only 3 got through.

Q. As a general thing do you find them disposed to work fair wages?

A. Yes Sir. If they could be reasonably paid. I would as lief have them as white laborers. White men are paid $1.00 pr day; the colored people two shillings The Quartermaster has sent off the colored people and sent to Boston for white men to do the work.

Q Do I understand you to say that they are not paid the same amount of money for the same amount of work?

A Not a quarter. The government officers will not pay a colored mechanic but $10.00. Gen Wool established the rule that a man should be paid according to the value of his labor,[1] but that has not been carried out since he left. The result is that the best men who can get good prices go away and the Government is left with the poorest men, for the reason that they will not pay but $10.00 pr month, and good men will not work for that, as they can go away and get more.

Q What were these men worth as a general thing to their masters? For instance, if the masters were to come back and go to cultivating their plantations to day what would they pay them?

A. Ten dollars a month. They come here now and say they can't do without them, that if they can't have them as slaves they must have them as freemen. A man by the name of Bartlett, whose slave has been at work in the Department came here within a week and said the man was worth $26.00 a month and that he was just as good as any white man

Q. Have you any knowledge of white men being brought here from Boston to work when there were colored men out of employment?

A They have brought down from 75 to 100 within a month from Boston.

Q What is the character of the colored people as laborers in comparison with white men?

A. Those who have employed them say that they are tougher and hardier and more easily managed. When you get a gang of Irishmen here they are crabbed and will work only so many hours a day; but these men are afraid and if they are decently paid they will work nights or any time and do any thing you want done. I am authorized to pay good men more than the $10. a month by a special order of Gen. Wool, but the authorities will not sustain it. He said if ordinary laborers were worth $10. a month, better men ought to be worth $15. and mechanics $20. I wrote out a regulation to this effect and Gen Wool signed it. I put in a provision that I and the employer should confer together and if he said a man was worth $20. or $30. a month, I should allow him at least $20. but they won't agree to pay over $10. and don't pay even that.

Q. Have any gone away in consequence of the nonpayment of their wages?

A I warrant if the truth was known that it would be found that 2000 have gone away.

Q. Is there any thing to prevent these men going away and seeking the best market for their labor?

A. They cannot get away. Up here in Hampton a black man is not allowed to keep a store to supply these people with stores, but some white man is allowed to come here and swindle them at the rate of 200 per cent. advance on the goods they buy. I can prove to you that they have sold clothing for $50 and $60. a suit when we could give them as good for $12.

Q The point I want to make out clearly is, whether restrictions are imposed upon their free movement, that are not imposed upon white men of the same class?

A Certainly by thousands. They are not allowed to go away unless you can make out a clear case to Gen Dix when he will give a pass, but he will not allow one of his aids to do it.

Q Is there any difference made between free black men and men made free by the proclammation?

A Yes Sir. If there is a man who carries free papers they will give him a pass, to go to Baltimore or any where; but there is not one in 500 who has free papers.

Q Gen Wool went upon the principle that the Black People should have the same rights as white people?

A Yes Sir, and Gen Dix endorses that principle, professedly, but he fails in carrying it out. He lets one thing and another push it one side

143

Q. Can you concieve any good reason why there should be any restriction put upon any man's going from our lines to the North? A No Sir Gen Wool charged me to let them go and said that if any body interfered in the matter he would have them arrested and sent to the Rip Raps (that is our prison). He was a very blunt right-up-and-down-man and in some respects was not as good as Gen. Dix; but he would have been if he had remained here because he had got authority from the Secretary of War to do any thing he thought best. But just then he was removed and Gen. Dix put in his place. He assurred me that he intended to carry out the plans of Gen Wool and wished me to carry them out. I told him I could not get along, because his subordinates would interfere with me "Well, he said, come to me" So I go to him.

. . . .

Q Did I understand you to say that when these stevedores were sent here from Boston, their expenses from Boston were paid? A Their expenses were paid and they recieved $25. a month and rations. When the subordinates found they could not control these contrabands for the Government, they threatened to drive them off and actually assailed and took possession of these buildings, and advertised for men in a Philadelphia paper. I happened to hear of it and wrote to the editor that we could supply the men for quarter the money. We have had gangs of white men at work here. Capt. Tallmadge told me that he had at one time twenty-five teamsters from Boston at a dollar and a half a day and kept them three months, but finding the negroes worked as well as they did, he finally paid them all off and put negroes in their places.

Q How many plantations has the Government taken possession of? A We are occupying twenty five or fifty plantations. The rebel owners have their agents on those plantations who send them letters and papers. They come down here through some colored man, and get papers and things and start off in the night, on horseback (and sometimes they steal our horses) and drive twenty five or thirty miles and perhaps go to Williamsburgh or Richmond or Yorktown Documents and papers in this way going to the rebels continually; and this is winked at because the Gen. does not order searching men and honest men to attend to this matter.

Q There are three principle things that you complain of, as I understand it, First that the contrabands have not been paid. A I don't make any complaint of that now, for I think now that I have the appointment of pay master, the money will be sent to me and they will be paid off. I don't know however that the difficulty is entirely remedied, because the Quartermaster refuses to give us payrolls by which to make up the accounts. Then there are half a dozen gangs in the Quartermasters employ whom he promises to pay but instead of paying them for ten, twelve or fifteen months he pays them for only one month and lets the rest run, and perhaps in three or four months he will pay them for another month and keep the other back.

Q The second thing is, that the Government employs white stevedores at $25. a month when black men could be hired at $10. a month.

A Yes, Sir, they come here begging for work; we have to drive them away.

Q And, third, that contrabands desiring to go North cannot get passage except under great difficulties? Those are the three principle difficulties?

A Yes, Sir.

Q Beyond these three what else do you consider a difficulty?

A If those three were remedied, it do wonders. I think we should see a great reform among the planters. As it is now the planters in the reserved counties of the state[2] will not allow a freedman having a wife or children in that reserved country to visit them.

Q In your opinion do the intelligent planters in this neighborhood have any desire for the introduction of Northern labor here?

A Sensible and intelligent men do. A great many have expressed that desire; and they say the whole state will run out unless they have it. Senator Bowden when he heard that we had taken possession of these plantations, told Major Bolles that he hoped they would put in Northern men to take charge of them. He urged the importance of bringing in Northern men, farmers and workmen, men industry and practical skill, with their improvements in tools &c to carry on these plantations. Another very essential thing is that these plantations may be put in such position that they can be sold for taxes as in Carolina.[3] We have hundreds of colored men who have saved some money. Let these plantations be bought up for a small sum and parcelled off into lots of ten acres and let every black man have a little homestead of his own where he can live and go out to work. We are introducing cotton and tobacco here which will become a great source of revenue if we can retain the colored people here. I know men who will invest a hundred thousand dollars in the purchase of these plantations and cut them up into small homesteads for these people. We have got our schools all over this part of the country and are teaching them to read. We try to inspire them with the idea that they are to be free and that this is one of the conditions of freedom; and we tell them that when the war is over they can buy a spot of land, and have a little hut to live in with their families like any body else. When those employed by the Government are paid off they will have quite a little sum of money; and we let out some of the plantations on shares and if the season is favorable when the crops come in, hundreds of them will have fifty or one hundred dollars, apeice. If the sale of these lands was opened every man who could spare twenty dollars would buy ten acres pay part of it down and the rest as he was able. There would be no risk run for the mortgage on the land would be good security, and it would please them and inspire them with the spirit of emulation.

Q Upon the whole comparing the state of things now with that which existed when you first came here, is there more or less disposition on the part of the whites to do justice to the blacks?

A Yes, Sir, a great deal more.

Q Then upon the whole have the negroes justified your hopes and expectations of their conduct and improvement?

A. More than that. I did not believe that we could make very much out of them. I did not think they had so much brain. They have got as many brains as you or I have, though they have an odd way of showing it, I have explained to them that if they expect freedom they must be worthy of it; that they must break up every evil habit and be industrious, virtuous, and economical. Heretofore, they have always been driven to work, now our chief men will say that they have never known men to work better.

HD

Excerpts from testimony of Capt. C. B. Wilder before the American Freedmen's Inquiry Commission, 9 May 1863, filed with O-328 1863, Letters Received, ser. 12, RG 94 [K-68]. Approximately seven pages of testimony totaling ten pages; for the omitted portion, see *Freedom*, ser. 1, vol. 1: doc. 12. Topical labels in the margin are omitted.

1 General John E. Wool, a previous commander of the Department of Virginia, had established the "rule" on March 18, 1862, in General Order 22. (See above, doc. 4n.)

2 The seven counties of Virginia exempted from the Emancipation Proclamation of January 1, 1863: York, Elizabeth City, Norfolk, and Princess Anne, which bordered Hampton Roads; Accomac and Northampton, on the eastern shore; and Berkeley, in the northern part of the state.

3 In March 1863, several plantations in the Sea Islands of South Carolina had been sold in accordance with the Direct Tax Act of June 1862, which provided for forfeiture to the U.S. government and subsequent sale of land in the seceded states whose owners failed to pay their portion of a direct tax levied upon each state in August 1861. Three direct-tax commissioners had been appointed for Virginia by the time of Captain Wilder's testimony, but no sales

had yet taken place. (*Statutes at Large*, vol. 12, pp. 422–26; U.S., Senate, "Letter of the Secretary of the Treasury . . . ," *Senate Executive Documents*, 38th Cong., 1st sess., No. 35.)

17: Testimony by the Superintendent of Contrabands at Norfolk, Virginia, before the American Freedmen's Inquiry Commission

[*Norfolk?, Va. May 10, 1863*]
Testimony of Dr Brown Supt. of Contrabands at Norfolk

Q. How long have you been engaged among the contrabands?

A. Six months.

Q About what number have come under your observation?

A Probably 20,000

Q What number are under your observation now?

A Between 12 and 1300

Q Have there been any considerable number of these men employed by Government?

A Last December when I made a report to Gen Dix, we had 1625 upon Craney Island. Of that number but 189, I think, were able-bodied men – or men between the ages of 16 and 50. There were upon the Island 653 women and minor children whose husbands and fathers were then in the employ of the Government.

Q If these men had been in the regular reciept of their pay by the Government, what proportion would have supported their families?

A I think that the 653 (if that was the exact number) might have been supported, had the pay which should have been recieved by the husbands and fathers been applied to their support.

Q They sent nothing that went to the support of their families?

A They sent nothing.

Q Do you know whether they recieved their pay from the Gov't or not?

A I am unable to say; but there had been 683 months of labor performed for the Government by the men on the Island and their average pay was 16 2/3 cts. a month. The women had performed labor for somewhere about the same number of months and their pay amounted to somewhere about 15 1/3 cents a month. They had been employed in the hospital at Newport news and they were the slaves of the hospital. All they were to recieve was $5.00 a month, out of the hospital fund. They were not paid because the regulations did not authorize the payment of such help. I should think that as early as December or January Gen. Dix proposed placing them upon the farms of the rebels. We had not the most

147

profitable material to be employed upon the farms – there were very few men mostly women and children; but we commenced taking farms and placing the negroes upon them. The Gen. said we could promise them one half what they raised, that we could support them until we got the crops and it would not take more than half the crops to pay the expenses of the Government. We have followed up that plan, and so far we have not been benefitted by any charitable institutions. The Government has furnished everything – Seed, ploughs &c. Much has been done from the savings in the rations and their clothing has been wholly supplied by the charity of the North. We shall probably have three thousand acres of land in cultivation – mostly in grain. We are going into cotton to some extent, tobacco more largely and we have gone quite extensively into truck; but owing to the lateness of the season we shall not reap so large a profit as we hoped. We have two grist mills and one saw mill and are putting them in order. We are giving employment to some in chopping wood and the General has authorized me to carry on wooding and lumbering. Gen Dix has afforded every facility in regard to taking possession of the farms of absentee disloyalists. My aim has been as far as possible to make the labor of the negroes support them. The negroes frequently bring in horses mules and carts which are taken possession of by the Quartermaster and they recieve no credit for them. I believe that what they earn with what they bring with them will fully pay all they cost the Government.

Q Do you furnish them with any clothing?

A The Government does not.

Q How do they work?

A They work well. Let me have the management of them and I can unload a ship twice as quick with them as I can with white men.

Q What will be the amount likely to come to these men when the crop is in?

A. I have not made the calculation. I have an account kept of what each man does every day   If he has done a day and an eighth, he is credited with that. If a woman has not done more than half a days work, that is credited to her; and every saturday night the amount of work they have done during the week is made known to them, so they know just what proportion of the work they have done. The only fair way will be when the crops are brought in, to divide their share among the men in proportion to what they have done.

Q Do you happen to know what their rations, on average cost the Government delivered here?

*A I do not sir.[1]

Q Where can we get that information?

A Of the Commissary General, Col. Taylor.

Q Do you suppose it would be about 20¢ a day?

A No Sir—less than that. The cost price of the ration only is given; the transportation is not reckoned.

Q How do you think it would work, if the Government were to pay these men a certain amount of wages each week, the money being put into the hands of the superintendent himself, who should organize a system of payment?

A The first thing that comes into my mind is the encouragement to labor that would be afforded by the immediate reciept of remuneration   They have not been looking for it immediately and they have not recieved it, either immediate or remote. It would be a great incentive to labor, but they would need to be paid as you would pay any man in proportion to what they did. I think it would be upon the whole a good thing for them. And I think it would encourage them more because they have no money to use now—not even to buy them tobacco. Then the next inquiry is would they save the money or waste it? I think they would take pretty good care of the dimes after they got them. I have some men at work chopping wood by the cord and I think they work better than those I hire by the month to work on the farm. They come to me and want their time on the Island in order to get pay for their work—and some of them worked well. I say "I have no means to pay you and dont know whether you will be paid or not. I told you so when you were on the Island" They were a community by themselves and helping themselves but it is very hard to make them realize that Craney Island was a pauper settlement.

It was made up of those who had nothing to do and were not able to support themselves. It is the universal testimony of the overseers on these farms—and I have some who were accustomed to work them as slaves—that they work well. I tried to get men as overseers from the North but they were not on the spot; and when I got a farm, I had to put an overseer on it at once.

Q You say that for certain reasons it would be better to pay them money instead of rations. Now how would it do, instead of paying them this uncertain half of crop to pay them once a month?

A Did you understand me to say that it would be better to give them money instead of rations? I did not mean that. The money would not buy them half enough. Provisions are terribly high in Norfolk.

Q On Craney Island, how did you find them—quarrelsome or otherwise

A With 1825 on the Island for several months—and these what might be called a pauper population—there were not exceeding six cases of disturbance calling for arrest.

Dr Brown stated that inasmuch as the rations allowed by law to the contrabands were considerably greater than was necessary for their actual support he had held back and saved sufficient out of them to give him a contingent fund of $1500. which he had employed in procuring seeds and in paying other necessary expenses upon the farms and otherwise in contingent expenses for the contrabands   (*Mem.* Such a system as this however justifiable in this emergency will never do as a general rule).

HD

Testimony of Dr. [Orlando] Brown before the American Freedmen's Inquiry Commission, [10 May 1863], filed with O-328 1863, Letters Received, ser. 12, RG 94 [K-68]. Topical labels in the margin are omitted.

1 At the bottom of the page appears the following footnote: "*We afterwards ascertained that they cost 14 1/2 cts a day."

18: Testimony by a Northern Teacher before the American Freedmen's Inquiry Commission

[*Portsmouth, Va.*] May 10*th* [*1863*]
Testimony of Miss Lucy Chase at Portsmouth Virginia May 10th.
I went to Craney Island with my sister on the first of January and have just left. There were at that time 1800 colored people on that Island – a desolate and exposed place. All but about 300 have now been taken away and put upon farms. The ablebodied men are supposed to be in the employ of the government and the disabled men with the women and children remain on Craney Island. That is a kind of Government poor house and it was designed that they should as far as practicable support themselves. Being an island all the wood that was used had to be brought from the main land every day. The island has communication with the main land by a ford and the wood was sometimes brought by mules across the ford, but generally by boats. The organization of the colored people was very fine. I think Dr Brown the contraband supt. at Norfolk has a wonderful gift at organizing. There was a squad of wood cutters and a squad of grave-diggers organized. After every storm there would be a most alarming mortality   The wind drove over the Island all day and it was very sharp. I think the East winds of Boston are luxuriously comfortable compared with the winds at Craney Island   The Rebels when they took possession of the Island built very comfortable quarters. We occupied the Colonels house,

which was rather elegant than otherwise; but being open to the winds, there always came in between the boards a sharp strong wind. But it was rather luxurious quarters after all. The rebels destroyed almost all their Barracks, so that the Dr was obliged to build Barracks for the negroes. Some were placed in tents and some in Barracks. Then there was a squad of oystermen. The design was to plant oysters and throw them into the market at the proper time, to enable the community to be as self supporting as possible; but the oysters were mostly stolen   I dont know whether the men on the Island took them at night or whether others stole them, but when we wanted to throw them into the market they were not to be found. Dr Brown was the originator of the idea of taking the farms of rebels and cultivating them by contraband labor. He visited Gov. Andrew and went to Washington over a year ago to see about it. Gen Dix, however, was slow to become interested in the matter and finally reccommended that the women should be set to work making army clothing. So the Dr built a large sewing room. They really becoming educated paupers; the greediest and most persistent beggars that could be imagined. One's moral courage was put to the severest test by going among them. I could not walk from the house to the office without being beset by a clamoring crowd. There were a good many boys on the Island—a large number of them orphans who were organized into a squad of sweepers and the island swept still every day. Then there were a number of disabled men and some men competent to labor, but who were needed for the interest of the island. Every ten had a squad-master and there was a squad-woman for every Barrack, each Barrack having a hundred people. It really was very masterly. The necessities of every hour almost would be met, there was no laying up for the morrow at all.

The Island was entirely a Government quarter, and the people were all sent there by the Department. There were people there from Tennessee, Kentucky and North and South Carolina—a great many from Virginia. Most of them had drifted into the army and moved along with it; and some times they would say "poor things when we asked them how they got along, "Well I have had a very good time since I have been travelling." We found how significant that word "travelling" was, for almost all of them were first taken to Newport News, then to Hampton then to Yorktown and then to Craney Island, where many of them died; and perhaps those who lived were sent back to Hampton and then back again to Craney Island, and so the poor things were shifted about continually. Dr Brown had said that the women should no longer work in the field, but he found that idleness was ruining them and they were called in to the office and he asked them how they would like to go out and work on a farm. "Oh Dr" they said – "that pleases us; that makes us of some account, we did'n't feel of no account doing nothing." Then he made the proposition that they should have half that they raised which appeared to satisfy them.

I have found them all very anxious to learn and full of ambition, without exception I never saw such greedy people for study. Then there is great ambition to be able to read the Bible for themselves. I have not seen an indifferent child nor an indolent one – dull ones, I have seen of course; they are all zealous. In teaching them to write I have invariably had them begin with making A's. Some of them write A so well that you can scarcely believe them when they tell you they never wrote before and others it takes a week to form it, but they are so imitative that there are very few that it takes so long as that.

We see a great deal to encourage us in the improvement that has taken place during the few months that we have been here

When we arrived on the Island the colored people had been there only about six weeks and 1800 were crowded into a few houses and tents and the mortality was very great. They were dying as they died at Hampton by hundreds and thousands. Every woman will say she lost three or more children. But the mortality decreased steadily as their quarters were enlarged and they were made more comfortable. The Dr. was working for the community as it stood, when we arrived, and for some time after with these projects in his head. We found when we arrived that very few had beds and as there was a quantity of sacking in waiting in the clothing room, at the Dr's suggestion, we set the women at work making them up into beds. They were clamorous for work and we come have had them nearly all if we had had enough for them to do. We were engaged on this work perhaps a week; and to give them all a chance we had different ones come each day. We were surprised to find them all good sewers – children and all. I had supposed that field hands would know nothing about it. They have a ravenous fondness for washing. I don't know whether it is natural or because they have nothing else to do; but they are always at the wash-tub.

Sometime after that, the Quartermaster Capt. Ludlow said he had five thousand grain bags, that had been rejected, that he would like very well to retain if they could be repaired at a slight expense, and they were brought down to the island for that purpose. My sister and myself were sick at the time so that we could not superintend the work and we employed a lady who had recently come from Philadelphia to teach the contrabands, to superintend it. The women sewed upon these bags also with great readiness and they were always anxious to find work to do. They managed the repairing of the bags very well; and it requires more skill to do such work than to make up clothing.

Gen Viele[1] has been a most persistent stumbling block in the way of Dr Brown all the time. He wanted to clean the island entirely except of the sick. Indeed the Surgeon General has told the Doctor that if there should be fighting at Suffolk the hospital would probably be stationed there. A large portion of the farms that the Dr, has taken, he has obtained by making appeals to Gen Dix and could obtain them only in that way. Gen Viele always throws obstacles in the way. He is a West Pointer, and is a very conciliatory and courteous person. There is always some such reason as in a case I will mention. We were to have gone upon a very fine place in Norfolk, in a diary district where there was a splendid conservatory. The Dr. took the place, but Gen Viele demurred and said the lady had been very kind to him and he did not like to have the place taken. So it was given up and the Dr took another farm, on the west branch of the Elizabeth River within a quarter of a mile of the ferry, a superb place. Mr Lovell who is the chief overseer says he has not seen a place in Virginia that compares with it. The Dr took this place by order of Gen Dix; but Gen Viele sent a Colonel down there with some orders and he saw Mr Lovell and said "What are you doing here?" "What are *you* doing here?" said Mr Lovell. They had a good deal of talk of that character and then Gen. Viele visited Mr Lovell and said that when the owner went away, he gave him the rent and he staid there six months and he did not feel exactly like having it taken and so the Dr had to leave that place. The owner of the place is a rebel and Gen Viele ought to have taken it.

I think it is very bad to have the colored people crowded together in large numbers

With regard to their willingness to be—soldiers—which is a subject that I suppose you feel an interest in—you know the race well enough to know that they do not care for change, that comes very much from slavery, of course and the uncertainty of their conditions but I suppose there was not a man on the island who would not have shrunk from the idea of fighting. I do not think one of them would have been willing to enlist. Hearing that Gov. Andrew was about visiting the island—as we did at one time though he did not come—the Dr. called in some men from the farms and asked them "How would you like to be soldiers my men"? "Well Dr" one of them said "I think I make the best soldier now, Give me an axe and I think I shall make the best soldier then" The rest grunted assent but no one spoke. We found them docile but they are great liars and great theives. As Dr Brown says, it would be too much to the credit of slavery if they were as good as some radical anti-slavery people represent them to be. They are so befogged that many of them do not know but that they are in slavery now. Gen Dix has been a most noble gentleman in his relations with this matter.

There are about seventy people on this plantation. My idea is to keep education alive on the twenty five farms and to look after the wants of the people in the way of clothing. A great many are unable to work in the fields because they have not clothing. There are teachers on three or four of the farms and my design is to spend a few hours on each farm, call the people together leave slates in their hands and books and take the most advanced pupils and put the others in their charge while I am away. We found our supply of slates giving out but we went to Pig Island one day and my sister climbed on the roof of one of the rebel buildings near the battery there and tore off some of the slates to be used in our schools.

I found but very little disposition to quarrel among the people on Craney Island   I should think it would be a very large estimate to say that there were a dozen quarrelsome persons out of the 1800 on that Island. They show great respect for age as is manifest from one custom of theirs. They always call an older person Aunt or Uncle. They use these terms to quite young people. We had two servants living with us. One a boy and the other a girl. The boy who was the younger always called the girl "Aunt."

HD

Testimony of Miss Lucy Chase before the American Freedmen's Inquiry Commission, 10 May [1863], filed with O-328 1863, Letters Received, ser. 12, RG 94 [K-68]. Topical labels in the margin are omitted.

1 General Egbert L. Viele, military governor of Norfolk, Virginia.

19: An Aide of the Chief Quartermaster, Army of the Potomac, to the Chief Quartermaster

Washington [D.C.], June. 15″ 1863

General,   In compliance with your instructions of the 4″ Inst. I have the honor to report that I proceeded on the 5″ Inst. with Steamers "Hero" and "Sylvan Shore" to Fortress Monroe, and Newbern. N.C. for the purpose of procuring negro laborers for service in the Army of the Potomac.

On my arrival at Fortress Monroe Colonel Thomas and myself had an interview with General Dix in reference to procuring these laborers, but we arrived at no conclusion save that I might have all that would willingly consent to go.

Col. Thomas urged upon Gen. Dix the necessity of impressing the "Contrabands" into the service of the Qr. Mrs. Dep't.; but the General would not consent to such a step, for any service outside of his own Military Department, at the same time he authorized Captain Ludlow, A.Q.M. at Norfolk, to impress from 500 to 1,000, for Gen. Getty, who had applied for this number for work on fortifications near Suffolk. This impressment he regarded as a military necessity. I endeavored to get the military necessity extended to my wants, but failed.

I then as my only resort proceeded to Norfolk, and caused it to be generally made known, that I wanted from 500 to 1,000 negroes. I had it announced in three of their churches on Sunday, the result was that I only procured from 50 to 60, these I started on the "Sylvan Shore" for Aquia Creek.

Col. Thomas and Captain Ludlow, extended me all the assistance in their power, but in the absence of authority to impress these laborers, they could render me but little service.

On the 9' Inst. I left Norfolk for Newbern. N.C., on my arrival there, I had an interview with General Foster, who informed me that he had orders from the War Dept. to enlist all the able bodied negroes in his Department, and could let none go out of his Dep't. as laborers. This ended my mission there.

I am informed that there are some 2000 idle negroes in Gen. Dix's Dep't., but the only way their services can be obtained is by *forcible persuasion.*

I returned to this point this morning, somewhat mortified at the result of my trip. I am Very Respectfully Your obt. Ser't.

ALS   Chas. B. Wagner

Capt. Chas. B. Wagner to Brig. Gen. Rufus Ingalls, 15 June 1863, "Contraband Fund," Consolidated Correspondence File, ser. 225, Central Records, RG 92 [Y-35]. The commanders at Fortress Monroe and at New Berne were, respectively, General John A. Dix, commander of the Department of Virginia, and General John G. Foster, commander of the Department of North Carolina. Plans for Wagner's trip to their departments had begun in mid-May 1863, when both the chief quartermaster of the Washington depot and the chief quartermaster of the Army of the Potomac were beseiging the quartermaster general, Montgomery C. Meigs, with requests for additional "negro laborers." On May 18, Meigs had written nearly identical letters to the chief quartermaster of the Department of North Carolina and to General Dix, informing them that he had authorized Rufus Ingalls, chief quartermaster of the Army of the Potomac, to send a steamer to obtain 300 black laborers "for service at the wharves & depots

& with the trains" of that army. The fugitive slaves, Meigs had declared, "live upon the U. States and are bound to render services therefor." (See below, doc. 62n.; Qr. Mr. Gen'l M. C. Meigs to Col. R. Ingalls, 18 May 1863, Qr. Mr. Gen'l. M. C. Meigs to Lt. Col. H. Biggs, 18 May 1863, and Qr. Mr. Gen. M. C. Meigs to Maj. Gen. John A. Dix, 18 May 1863, vol. 68, pp. 478–79, Letters Sent, ser. 9, Central Records, RG 92 [Y-714].) Obstacles to Wagner's mission had become evident even before he departed. On June 3, the day before Ingalls gave Wagner instructions for the trip (which have not been found), Meigs informed Ingalls that the chief quartermaster of the Department of North Carolina, responding to an earlier request for 150 black laborers for the Washington depot, had reported that "all the able bodied colored men in this Department are being enlisted by Brig. Gen. Wild, for the armed service of the United States." (Qr. Mr. Genl. M. C. Meigs to Brig. Gen. R. Ingalls, 3 June 1863, and Lt. Col. Herman Biggs to Brig. Gen. M. C. Meigs, 30 May 1863, vol. 69, pp. 160–61, Letters Sent, ser. 9, Central Records, RG 92 [Y-714].) On June 19, after Wagner returned to Washington nearly empty-handed, Ingalls referred Wagner's report to the quartermaster general, warning that although the Army of the Potomac had for the moment "sufficient force of negro labor," a larger number "will be required . . . when new Depots are established." According to an endorsement of June 24, Meigs consulted with Secretary of War Edwin M. Stanton, who "decided that when advised of the necessity of impressing these idle negros he would give the authority," but that until then, "the matter had better be deferred." It was a brief deferral. Only three days later, Meigs reported that the quartermaster of the Washington depot needed at least 400 additional teamsters and laborers, and asked that Stanton order General Dix to impress 1,000 able-bodied black men for labor in Washington, "where they will receive good wages and be well treated, and cared for." The women and children left behind in Virginia, Meigs added, "ought to be able to cultivate the soil, and produce enough for their own sustenance." Meigs drafted an order for Stanton's signature, and on July 1, in accordance with its provisions, Stanton instructed Dix to impress "as many able bodied colored laborers, not exceeding one thousand, as can be found among the colored refugees in the vicinity of Fort Monroe, and Norfolk." (Qr. Mr. Gen'l M. C. Meigs to Hon. Edwin M. Stanton, 27 June 1863, and draft of Secretary of War to Maj. Gen'l John A. Dix, June 1863, vol. 8, pp. 88–89, Press Copies of Reports & Letters Sent to the Secretary of War, ser. 16, Central Records, RG 92 [Y-550]; Asst. Adjt. General E. D. Townsend to Major General John A. Dix, 1 July 1863, filed as W-217 1863, Letters Received, ser. 5063, Dept. of VA & 7th Army Corps, RG 393 Pt. 1[C-3011].) General Dix promptly issued orders in compliance with Stanton's instructions; for a description of their enforcement, see doc. 20, immediately below.

20: Northern Minister to the Secretary of War

Washington D.C. July 11th /63

Dear Sir. In complyance with a suggestion just received at your Office I proceed to make the following statement of facts.

1st I am a missionary among the Contrabands at Fortress Monroe & vicinity. My present location is at Norfolk, Va.

2^{d} I have no intention of *interfering in the least* with any military order, but simply to state facts, & make a few requests.

3^{d} On Saturday July 4th an order was received at Norfolk, from the War Department, by way of Fortress Monroe, which was understood by the authorities at the two places to require them to *impress* all ablebodied colored men in the two places to the Number of 1000 or 1500 & send them to Washington to work in the Quartermaster's Department. The authorities commenced executing said order at the Fort & Hampton on the 4th, & at Norfolk on Sund. the 5th Inst. In executing said order the following events transpired.

(a) In the afternoon a large congregation of colored people were assembled at the Colored Methodist Church for divine worship. As the Minister closed his sermon, the soldiers entered the house, called out a large number of men, & marched them to the Dock & put them under guard.

Others were taken in the streets. Some of them were allowed to go home during the night & change their clothing; others say they had not such opportunity. Some were brought away without shoes, & some without coats; many without any change whatever.

(b) There were a large number of contrabands on Craney Island. Some of them had been at work on Government fortifications in the vicinity of Suffolk & Portsmouth, *but had not received their pay.* Soldiers went to the Island & told the men to go up to Norfolk in the Boat & get their pay. They went without bidding their families good bye, & without any extra clothing, & were not allowed to return. Their families do not know where they the men are gone

(c) I beg leave to call attention to a few individual cases. The men brought up are in two divisions called on the List of Trasportation "From Norfolk,' & "From Hampton." Among those from *Norfolk*, are the following.

John Jordan, has worked on Fortifications & otherwise *twelve months* & received but *86 cents.* Cannot he, & others in similar circumstances, have assurance from the War Department of pay *for past services,* as well as for the future. It will do much to quiet their apprehensions & render them contented.

Nelson Sprewell says he has a rupture & is unfit for Service.

Cornelius Smith says he has free papers, at home place.

Richard Stewart says he was born free & has free papers at some place.

Nelson Wiley is an old man, drove a carriage all his life.

Among the men "From Hampton" I mention the following: Philip Bright, Edward Bright Henry Tabb, Emanuel

Savage, Miles Hope, Willson Hope, Joseph Hope, Ned Whitehouse, Carl Holloway, Charles Smith, Thomas Needham, Jacob Sanders, Francis Garrar, & Anthony Armsted. Except the last two names, & these men have rented farms, purchased teams, seed corn & fencing, & have good crops well under way. They were taken away from their families & farms, & leave no one to care for them. To appearance they will loose every thing. *Their all is invested in their farms*.

Anthony Armstead is a shoemaker & left a sick family with none to care for them.

W^m R Johnson is an old man 62 years of age, conducted Gen Butler to *"Big Bethel,"* two years ago; Has served in the Hospital much of the time since, but has *received no pay*.

Henry Minor, is 63 years old, was free born & has free papers which he was obliged to leave in the vicinity of Whitehouse only the day previous to being taken up at Hampton.

George Parker, has a store & goods worth about $100. from which he was taken without notice, & left no one to care for them.

Thomas Risby is a School Teacher, was taken without notice

Lewis Roberson left a team & hogs worth $50. with none to care for them.

Merrit Morris is Ruptured & had been discharged by Lieut Sage as unfit for service.

In view of these facts I would respectfully inquire.

1st Cannot those men who came without proper clothing be supplied?

2^d Can the men whom I have specified by name all, or any part of them, be discharged & sent to their homes?

3^d Can arrangements be made by which the families of these men can draw a part of their wages, *at their request, each month*, at Fortress Monroe or Norfolk?

4th Would it be proper for you to give me an official statement for the benefit of their friends, specifying what wages these men will receive per month, about what time they will be allowed to return home, & what they will be required to perform while here?

5th If some of these men think best to send for their families, will they be allowed to come & make this their home?

6th Will you give me permission to visit these men before my return & tell them the results of my interview with you? I am Very Respectfully Yours,

ALS   Asa Prescott.

Asa Prescott to Hon. E. M. Stanton, 11 July 1863, enclosed in Brig. Genl. D. H. Rucker to Brig. Genl. M. C. Meigs, 8 Aug. 1863, "Negroes: Fortress

Monroe," Consolidated Correspondence File, ser. 225, Central Records, RG 92 [Y-720]. According to endorsements, the War Department immediately referred Prescott's letter to the commander of the Department of Virginia, requesting a report with respect to "the allegation that many contrabands have been employed on public works . . . and have not been paid for their services," but ignoring Prescott's charges of abuse in the impressment of black men. From the headquarters of the Department of Virginia, the letter was referred on July 17 to Captain Charles B. Wilder, superintendent of contrabands at Fortress Monroe, who reported, in a letter prepared the previous day, that incomplete, contradictory, or altogether missing records had made it impossible for him to settle the claims of hundreds of former slaves who were owed wages for military labor. (Capt. C. B. Wilder to Major General John A. Dix, 16 July 1863, in the same file.) Further endorsements referred Prescott's letter back to the War Department, where it eventually came to rest, along with additional documents, in the records of the quartermaster general. No reply to Prescott has been found in the records of the War Department. On the developments that prompted the impressment of black men in the Department of Virginia, see doc. 19, immediately above.

21: Superintendent of Contrabands in the District of Virginia to the Headquarters of the Department of Virginia and North Carolina

Fortress Monroe, Virginia, August 8th 1863.
Colonel, I have the honor to acknowledge the receipt of your Note of inquiry of the 6th inst. in regard to giving colored men passes to leave the Department. A temporary absence is my apology for not returning an answer sooner.

It was ordered by General Wool, and fully endorsed by Mr. Secretary Stanton in his Orders to me January 28, 1863 that my passes should pass all Colored persons, giving satisfactory reasons, to and from all places within the lines.[1]

In some cases this arrangement has been obstructed by Government subordinates; on reporting the same to General Dix, he informed me the next day, that he had instructed Capt. Blake, the Provost Marshal, to approve all my papers, except to Baltimore. There, he said, were different laws, and he did not think it advisable to encourage Colored people to go that way, unless as servants, or with those who would see them through and protect them, but he added, that in all such cases, if I would save him the trouble of investigating them, and give passes to such as ought to go, he would approve them.

To forcibly detain peaceable negroes, both Generals Wool and Dix decided, would amount almost to making the Government slaveholding, unless a military necessity required it.

It is very common for men to ask for passes, who are on their way to their Officers, or from them to their homes, it may be in Baltimore or Washington, or anywhere out of rebeldom. How unjust that they must stay here, after a long absence from home, and be impressed, or what is but a little better, forced to stay here among strangers and enemies, often without a cent for expenses, or but barely enough to get them home, not having been paid off.

I cannot beleive that it is the purpose of the Commanding General, to abridge the few rights granted them by the Government, while such large numbers are glad to enlist in the Army and Navy, or work in other Departments. I have the honor to be, Very Respectfully Your ob't. ser'vt

HLS   C. B. Wilder

[*Endorsement*] Hd Qrs Dept Va & N.C Aug 12 '63 ~~The orders will be carried out.~~ and capn Wilder will be informed that the extensive powers which he fancies he should possess to give passes to colored people, are curtailed to the ordinary rules of the service. The colored men are wanted either to enlist or work, & not to be allowed to be running about in idleness & expense to the General Government— J. G. Foster, Maj. Gen. Comd'g.

Capt. C. B. Wilder to Lt. Col. Louis H. Pelouze, 8 Aug. 1863, W-11 1863, Letters Received, ser. 5063, Dept. of VA & NC & 18th Army Corps, RG 393 Pt. 1 [C-3017]. The "Note of inquiry" of August 6 has not been found in the letters-sent volumes of the Department of Virginia and North Carolina. On August 18, an adjutant of General John G. Foster, the department commander, conveyed Foster's curt reply to Wilder: "[I]t is not desirable to have Passes given to Negroes in any number, the privilege is certain to be abused by them." (Asst. Adjt. General S. H. to Captn. C. B. Wilder, 18 Aug. 1863, vol. 49/69 VaNc, pp. 14–15, Letters Sent, ser. 5046, Dept. of VA & NC & 18th Army Corps, RG 393 Pt. 1 [C-3296].) Foster's predecessor, General John A. Dix, had also restricted Wilder's authority to issue military passes. In June 1863, Dix, who commanded the Department of Virginia before its merger with the Department of North Carolina, had prohibited Wilder from issuing passes to any "colored persons (Contrabands or otherwise) who are employed & paid by the Several Chiefs of the Staff departments" without first securing the permission of the employer. He had also forbidden Wilder to permit any "Contrabands or colored Vagrants," not so employed, "to come inside Fort Monroe, or any other Military Post, or to go on board public transports, from one place to another in this department, or to go out of the Department." (Asst. Adjt. Genl. to Capt. C. B. Wilder, 1 June 1863, vol. 56/57 VaNc, pp. 29–30, Letters Sent, ser. 5046, Dept. of VA & 7th Army Corps, RG 393 Pt. 1 [C-3017].)

1 For the order by General John E. Wool, issued on March 13, 1862, at which time he was commanding the Department of Virginia, see above, doc. 5n.; the order of January 28, 1863, by the Secretary of War is printed above, as doc. 15.

22: Superintendent of Blacks in the District of North Carolina to the Commander of the Department of Virginia and North Carolina

Roanoke Island [*N.C.*] Septr 5th 1863 – General, Learning from Gen. Peck that you had felt it necessary to delay your coming to N.C. I made haste to pay a brief visit to this island to assure myself that the colony should not suffer for the want of proper attention. I am gratified to find the eleven or twelve hundred negroes now here in a very comfortable condition, happy and contented, with the one exception that many of them have not been paid after having labored more than a year for the government. Let those of them who are laboring for the gov^t but receive their *pay*, and they would be able to buy clothing, *which they greatly need*, and make themselves very comfortable – Serjeant Sanderson, late of the 40th Mass, left here by Gen. Wild to locate families and superintend operations, has laid out streets, and lots 200 ft. square, along the northern and western part of the island between head quarters and Ft. Reno – This gives 40.000 sq. feet to a lot, an acre being 43,550 ft. But the decimal measurement is much easier, and we thus make square work – The streets have been run at right angles, the longer ones running in a direction nearly parallel with the shore, which may be called avenues, the others narrower and numbered 1st, 2^d, 3^d &c. beginning at the head of the island – The parallelograms between the streets will include six lots shaped thus. –

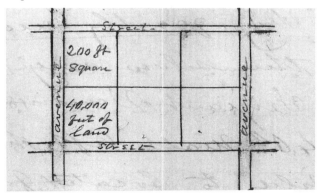

The serjeant has performed the work thus far in such a manner as pleases me, and will I trust gratify you. The negroes select their lots and commence making improvements with the greatest avidity, and are spending every moment of their time in getting up their first rude log houses. They must depend mostly upon these for *this* winter I suppose. There is at present *not a team nor an animal* for the whole colony. Our greatest want at present lies in this direction. If an order could be issued turning over to its use such broken down mules & horses and harnesses & waggons as might be picked up at New bern, they would be invaluable to us. We would turn the animals loose, and bring most of them up to servicable use —

We have intruded upon no persons cleared or enclosed land. But there is one house owned by three brothers Meekins, (one of whom is in the rebel army,) and now occupied by negroes, that I propose to take and fit up for *teachers*, & get them here at once — The island appears to be very healthy. On the whole the colony is doing *well* — Very faithfully and respectfully yours,

Horace James

P.S. I return to newbern this evening —

ALS

Horace James to Major Genl. J. G. Foster, 5 Sept. 1863, filed with J-34 1863, Letters Received, ser. 5063, Dept. of VA & NC & 18th Army Corps, RG 393 Pt. 1 [C-3010]. On September 10, 1863, General John J. Peck, commander of the Army and District of North Carolina, ordered Chaplain James, "superintendent of blacks for the District of North Carolina," to "assume charge of the colonization of Roanoke Island with negroes." James was to "take possession of all unoccupied lands on the island, and lay them out and assign them . . . to the families of colored soldiers, to invalids, and other blacks in the employ of the Government, giving them full possession of the same until annulled by the Government or by due process of United States law." By early October, following a personal inspection of the island, Peck had arranged to have draft animals and wagons turned over to the settlement, whose prospects he considered encouraging. "The success of the enterprise I regard as certain," he declared, "and believe that this African colony can be made self-supporting after the first year." (*Official Records*, ser. 1, vol. 29, pt. 2, pp. 166, 243–44.) Two weeks later, Chaplain James offered an equally optimistic assessment. "New accessions are made to the colony every week," he reported. "It is becoming increasingly popular among the negroes, and the drift of (black) sentiment is decidedly toward the enterprize. The negroes are happy and industrious, and work with a *will*, because they have a *motive* —" However, James complained, lack of a quartermaster meant that "no steps can be taken" toward paying those residents of the camp who were or had been employed by the government, "which is the first duty we owe *them*, and the best relief for the *government* —" "Nor," he added, "can I hire, or promise to pay, a gang of men to put up rude houses for the wives and children of colored soldiers, whom we have *pledged ourselves* to care for, and cover from the cold weather of the coming winter." The chief medical officer at New Berne, North Carolina, hoped to send some 800 or 1,000 more freedpeople to Roanoke Island within the next six weeks, and this number, James believed, could be "easily" accommodated if he were "empowered to employ and pay the men to do the work" of constructing shelter. (Horace James to Major Genl. J. G. Foster, 17 Oct. 1863, J-34 1863, Letters Received, ser. 5063, Dept. of VA & NC & 18th Army Corps, RG 393 Pt. 1 [C-3010].)

23: Superintendent of Contrabands in the District of Virginia to the Headquarters of the Department of Virginia and North Carolina

Fort Monroe Va   September 18, 1863

Colonel   Being desirous of making the occupancy of the Plantations, turn to the best account both for the Goverment, and the colored people, I have the honor to most respectfully submit a few suggestions which if they meet with your approval, will greatly facilitate in my judgement, both objects, and nearly if not quite enable us to remunerate the Goverment, for all expenses it may have to incur, for the support of Contrabands, the coming year upon the Plantations.

1st That all Plantations needed should be used for the above purpose, as contemplated by the Orders of the Secretary of War,[1] all others to be rented, if suitable persons offer reasonable inducements, On paying the rent quarterly in advance or giving satisfactory security

2nd That the families, all that can nearly take care of themselves, be furnished with a small spot of land, and assisted a little if absolutely necessary, in getting up a little Cabin for that purpose

3^{d} That the manure from the Goverment-Stables and yards instead of being carted out upon vacant lands, be carted upon the Plantations we may direct

4th That we be allowed the use of a number of the outside Goverment teams, when standing idle to haul manure Wood &^{c}, and break up the hardest lands, the first time, as may be deemed necessary. The best lands are generally the hardest to break up, and our Condemned horses being entirely unable to do such heavy work, They do as well as could be expected, for all the lighter work. Also that a few condemned carts and Wagons & Harness be allowed us, in which to use and employ the condemned horses

5th That a Steam Saw and Grist Mill would be of very great service,

There is an Old Grist Mill on one of the Plantations now rented which can be fitted up for that purpose after this year. Very Respectfully Your obt Servant

HLS   C. B. Wilder.

Capt. C. B. Wilder to Lt. Col. Southard Hoffman, 18 Sept. 1863, W-36 1863, Letters Received, ser. 5063, Dept. of VA & NC & 18th Army Corps, RG 393 Pt. 1 [C-3202]. Wilder signed as superintendent of contrabands in the Department of Virginia — a military jurisdiction that no longer existed, having been incorporated into the Department of Virginia and North Carolina in July 1863. No reply has been found in the letters-sent volumes of that department.

1 For the orders, issued on January 28, 1863, see above, doc. 15.

24: Superintendent of Contrabands in the District of Virginia to the Commander of the Department of Virginia and North Carolina

Fort. Monroe [*Va.*] Nov. 11 /63.

General I have the honor to report to you that in consequence of a recent decision of the Provost Judge allowing armed Rebels in the neighborhood of our plantations to threaten & drive off our men in the peaceful prosecution of our appropriate work, or run the risk of losing their lives — As this is contrary to the letter & spirit of all my instructions from the previous Commanding Generals and the Hon. Sec. of War, & in my judgment destructive of all our plantation operations, I respectfully ask your attention to the following facts. I had rented out a plantation (belonging to a Rebel) in York Co. Mr. W. H. Russell (a notorious secesh sympathizer & abuser of union men white or black, & the Govr not excepting yourself in the most profane manner) takes possession of, & rents an adjoining lot unfenced. When it came to our knowledge, we claimed of the occupant the same rate of rent, as for the rest of the place, to which he made no objection. When we came to send for what was agreed on in fodder, said Russell came over in great rage, directly from his house & ordered the men to unload, or take the consequences, like the highwayman with a double bb^l gun in hand cocked & cap^t thus threatening their lives if they refused. They gave up, being unarmed, & knowing the desperate character of the man.

We entered a complaint before the Provost Judge for assault & battery with intent to kill, & although the above was proved by three witnesses of undoubted character & loyalty as you will see by the accompanying testimonials. It was also proved by the same & other witnesses (Judge Bowden being one) that he was a notorious sesesh sympathiser. One stated that he recently had told him that he was sorry he did not go off with the Rebels, & that if he had he should now have been on Gen. Wise staff. There was no testimony to the contrary, but his own evasive version of the matter, & two of his employees or tenants, who were not present & knew nothing, except they said they saw Mr. Russell going toward our men from another diriction. Notwithstanding all this the verdict was in favor of the Rebel.

Judge Bowden though defending him as a personal friend, said that he & all such men ought to be arrested & punished or sent beyond the lines for their treasonable language & conduct.

I had supposed that if the man was wronged his remedy was in an appeal to the court or the General commanding, & not to the bowie knife & revolver, but be that as it may, I humbly submit that to acquit a rebel without an intimation that his conduct was not all satisfactory, & let him go at large while accepting mob law to vindicate the pretended rights of another rebel in arms against the Gov^t is an outrage against law justice & humanity –

Already it has gone out that, now there will be no more difficulty, rebels & squatters may hold or rent their places & defend them, & as 7/8th of all white inhabitants in this & York Co. are confessedly secesh what use is there I respectfully ask, of trying to do anything with any of the plantations, with such decisions.

The remedy that I think you once suggested, to let us & the colored people defend ourselves, is a merciless one, except as against midnight outrages & personal assaults, when compared with the true remedy adopted by Genl Wool in simelar cases, that all disturbers white or black should be arrested & visited with the severest penalties of military law, who interfered with or molested any loyal person in the quiet pursuit of his lawful business. If these facts are denied I respectfully ask the privilege of calling the witnesses before you, or giving you their written testimony, not that I care to have this decision altered, now that it is past, but to satisfy you that something ought to be done for the protection of loyal men, against the abuses of rebels this side the lines. I respectfully ask a general order to that effect. I have the honor to be gen^l very Respectfully your Obt. Sevt.

ALS   C. B. Wilder

Capt. C. B. Wilder to Maj. Genl. Butler, 11 Nov. 1863, W-140 1863, Letters Received, ser. 5063, Dept. of VA & NC & 18th Army Corps, RG 393

Pt. 1 [C-3200]. Endorsements. The testimonials said to have been enclosed are not in the file. Wilder's letter was addressed to General Benjamin F. Butler on the very day that Butler assumed command of the Department of Virginia and North Carolina, and the new commander wasted no time in acting upon its contents. On November 12, as Wilder had requested, Butler issued a general order reporting "[r]epresentations . . . that certain disloyally disposed persons within this department do occasionally by force interfere with, and by opprobrious and threatening language insult and annoy, loyal persons employed in the quiet discharge of their lawful occupations." "[A]ll such conduct and language," the order declared, "is hereafter strictly forbidden, and will be punished with military severity." (*Official Records*, ser. 1, vol. 29, pt. 2, pp. 447, 449.)

25: North Carolina Freedmen to the Commander of the Department of Virginia and North Carolina

Beaufort N. Carolina N^{ov} 20th 1863

the undersigned Colored Citizens of the town of Beaufort in behaf of the Colord population of this Commuinty in view of the manner in which their Brotheren on oppressed by the military authurities in this Vicenity Respeckfuley pitision you are at the Head of this military Department for a redress of grievunces

Your [politiness] disire to make known to you that they and there brothern to the President of the United States are undiscriminatly inpressed by the authorities to labor upon the Public woorks without compensation   that in Consequence of this System of fource labor they Have no means of paying Rents and otherwise Providing for ther families

Your pitisioners disire futher to Express ther Entire Willingness to Contribute to the Cause of the union in anyway consistant with there cause as Freemen and the Rights of their families

Anything that can Be don By You to relieve us from the Burden which wee are nou Labooring will Be Highly appriciated By Your Pitistior[ers]

And your pititioners Will Ever pray   Yours Respeckfully & Soforth

HDSr   [*17 signatures*]

Rober Henry et al. to Maj. Genl. B. F. Butler, 20 Nov. 1863, Miscellaneous Letters & Reports Received, ser. 5076, Dept. of VA & NC & 18th Army Corps, RG 393 Pt. 1 [C-3044]. The concurrence of "fifty outher" was noted below the signatures, which appear to be in two or three different handwritings. No response has been found in the letters-sent volumes of the Department of Virginia and North Carolina.

To Maj Genl B. F. Butler
Commanding Department of Virginia
& North Carolina.

The undersigned Colored Citizens of the town of Beaufort in behalf of the Colored population of this Community in view of the manner in which their Brethren are oppressed by the military authorities in this Vicinity Respectfully petition You are at the Head of this Military Department for a redress of grievances

Your politeness desire to make Known to You that they and their brothern to the President of the United States are undiscriminately impressed by the authorities to labor upon the Public works without Compensation that in Consequence of this System of fource labor they Have no means of paying Rents and otherwise Providing for their families

Your petitioners desire further to Express their entire Willingness to Contribute to the Cause of the union in anyway Consistant with their Cause as Freemen and the Rights of their families

Anything that Can Be don By You to relieve us from the Burden which wee are Now Labouring will Be Highly appreciated By Your Petitioners

Robert Henry And Your petitioners Will Ever pray
Charles Henry
Enoch McAfee
H W Henderson   Beaufort   N. Carolina
Ganon Gaskill   Nov 20th 1863
Levi Turner
Jacob Yours Respeckfully & Soforth
J. Anderson

Document 25

26: Order by the Commander of the Department of Virginia and North Carolina

Fort Monroe, Va., December 5th, 1863. General Orders, No. 46. The recruitment of colored troops has become the settled purpose of the Government. It is therefore the duty of every officer and soldier to aid in carrying out that purpose, by every proper means, irrespective of personal predilections. To do this effectually, the former condition of the blacks, their change of relation; the new rights acquired by them; the new obligations imposed upon them; the duty of the Government to them; the great stake they have in the War; and the claims their ignorance and the helplessness of their women and children, make upon each of us, who hold a higher grade in social and political life must all be carefully considered.

It will also be taken into account that the colored soldiers have none of the machinery of "State aid" for the support of their families while fighting our battles, so liberally provided for the white soldiers, nor the generous bounties given by the State and National Governments in the loyal States – although this last is far more than compensated to the black man by the great boon awarded to him, the result of the war – Freedom for himself and his race forever!

To deal with these several aspects of this subject, so that as few of the negroes as possible shall become chargeable either upon the bounty of Government or the charities of the benevolent, and at the same time to do justice to those who shall enlist, to encourage enlistments, and to cause all capable of working to employ themselves for their support, and that of their families – either in arms or other service – and that the rights of negroes and the Government may both be protected, it is ordered:

I. In this Department, after the 1st day of December, instant, and until otherwise ordered, every able bodied colored man who shall enlist and be mustered into the service of the United States for three years or during the war, shall be paid as bounty, to supply his immediate wants, the sum of ten (10) dollars. And it shall be the duty of each mustering officer to return to these Head Quarters duplicate rolls of recruits so enlisted and mustered into the service on the 10th, 20th and last days of each month, so that the bounty may be promptly paid and accounted for.

II. To the family of each colored soldier so enlisted and mustered so long as he shall remain in the service and behave well, shall be furnished suitable subsistence, under the direction of the Superintendent of Negro Affairs, or their Assistants; and each soldier shall be furnished with a certificate of subsistence for his family, as soon as he is mustered; and any soldier deserting, or whose pay and allowances are forfeited by Court-Martial, shall be reported by his Captain to the Superintendent of the District where his family lives, and the subsistence may be stopped, – provided that such subsistence shall be continued for at least six months to the family of any colored soldier who shall die in the service by disease, wound, or battle.

III. Every enlisted colored man shall have the same uniform, clothing, arms, equipments, camp equipage, rations, medical and hospital treatment as are furnished to the United States soldiers of a like arm of the service, unless, upon request, some modification thereof shall be granted from these Head Quarters.

IV. The pay of the colored soldiers shall be ten ($10.) dollars per month, three of which may be retained for clothing. But the non-commissioned officers, whether colored or white shall have the same addition to their pay as other non-commissioned officers. It is, however, hoped and believed by the Commanding General, that Congress, as an act of justice, will increase the pay of the colored troops to a uniform rate with other troops of the United States. He can see no reason why a colored soldier should be asked to fight upon less pay than any other. The colored man fills an equal space in ranks while he lives and an equal grave when he falls.

V. It appears by returns from the several recruiting officers that enlistments are discouraged, and the Government is competing against itself, because of the payment of sums larger than the pay of colored soldiers to the colored employees in the several Staff Departments, and that, too, while the charities of the Government and individuals are supporting the families of the laborer. It is further ordered: That no officer or other person on behalf of the Government, or to be paid by the Government, on land in this Department, shall employ or hire any colored man for a greater rate of wages than ten dollars per month, or the pay of a colored soldier and rations, or fifteen dollars per month without rations, except that mechanics and skilled laborers may be employed at other rates – regard being had, however, to the pay of the soldier in fixing such rates.

VI. The best use during the war for an able-bodied colored man, as well for himself as the country, is to be a soldier; it is therefore further ordered: That no colored man, between the ages of eighteen and forty-five, who can pass the Surgeon's examination for a soldier, shall be employed on land by any person in behalf of the Government (mechanics and skilled laborers alone excepted.) And it shall be the duty of each officer or other person employing colored labor in this Department to be paid by or on behalf of the Government, to cause each laborer to be examined by the Surgeons detailed to examine colored recruits, who shall furnish the laborer with a certificate of disability or ability, as the case may be, and after the first day of January next, no employment rolls of colored laborers will be certified or passed at these Head Quarters wherein this order has not been complied with, and are not vouched for by such certificates of disability of the employees. And whenever hereafter a colored employee of the Government shall not be paid within sixty days after his wages shall become due and payable, the officer or other person having the funds to make such payment shall be dismissed the service, subject to the approval of the President.

VII. Promptness of payment of labor, and the facilities furnished by the Government and the benevolent, will enable colored laborers in the service of the Government to be supported from the proceeds of their labor; Therefore no subsistence will be furnished to the families of those employed by the Government at labor, but the Superintendent of Negro Affairs may issue subsistence to those so employed, and charge the amount against their wages, and furnish the officer in charge of payment of such laborers with the amounts so issued, on the first day of each month, or be himself chargable with the amount so issued.

VIII. Political freedom rightly defined is liberty to work, and to be protected in the full enjoyment of the fruits of labor; and no one with ability to work shall enjoy the fruits of another's labor: Therefore, no subsistence will be permitted to any negro or his family with whom he lives, who is able to work and does not work. It is, therefore, the duty of the Superintendent of Negro Affairs to furnish employment to all the negroes able to labor, and see that their families are supplied with the necessaries of life. Any negro who refuses to work when able, and neglects his family, will be arrested and reported to these Head Quarters to be sent to labor on the fortifications, where he will be made to work. No negro will be required to labor on the Sabbath, unless upon the most urgent necessity.

IX. The Commanding General is informed that officers and soldiers in the Department have by impressment and force, compelled the labor of negroes, sometimes for private use, and often without any imperitive necessity.

Negroes have rights so long as they fulfil their duties: Therefore it is ordered, that no officer or soldier shall impress or force to labor for any private purpose whatever, any negro; and negro labor shall not be impressed or forced for any public purpose, unless under orders from these Head Quarters, or because of imperitive military necessity, and where the labor of white citizens would be compelled, if present. And any orders of any officer compelling any labor by negroes or white citizens shall be forthwith reported to these Head

Quarters, and the reasons which called for the necessity for such order be fully set forth.

In case of a necessity compelling negro or white labor for the purpose of building fortifications, bridges, roads, or aiding transportation or other military purpose, it shall be the duty of the Superintendent of negroes in that District, to cause employment rolls to be made of those so compelled to labor, and to present said rolls, as soon as the necessity ceases, to the Assistant Quartermaster of the District, that the laborers may be paid; and the Superintendent shall see that those that labor shall have proper subsistence, and may draw from the Commissary, of Subsistence rations therefor. Any officer offending willfully against the provisions of this order, will be dismissed the service, subject to the approval of the President.

And no negro shall be impressed into military service of the United States, except under orders from these Head Quarters – by a draft, which shall equally apply to the white and colored citizens.

X. The theory upon which negroes are received into the Union lines, and employed, either as laborers or soldiers, is that every negro able to work who leaves the rebel lines, diminishes by so much the producing power of the rebellion to supply itself with food and labor necessary to be done outside of military operations to sustain its armies; and the United States thereby gains either a soldier or a producer. Women and children are received, because it would be manifestly iniquitous and unjust to take the husband and father and leave the wife and child to ill-treatment and starvation. Women and children are also received when unaccompanied by the husband and father, because the negro has the domestic affections in as strong a degree as the white man, and however far south his master may drive him, he will sooner or later return to his family.

Therefore it is ordered: That every officer and soldier of this command shall aid by every means in his power, the coming of all colored people within the Union lines; that all officers commanding Expeditions and Raids shall bring in with them all the negroes possible, affording them transportation, aid, protection and encouragement. Any officer bringing or admitting negroes within his lines shall forthwith report the same to the Superintendent of Negro Affairs within his District, so they may be cared for and protected, enlisted or set to work. Any officer, soldier or citizen who shall dissuade, hinder, prevent, or endeavor to hinder or prevent any negro from coming within the Union lines; or shall dissuade, hinder, prevent, or endeavor to prevent or hinder any negro from enlisting; or who shall insult, abuse, ridicule or interfere with, for the purpose of casting ridicule or contempt upon colored troops or individual soldiers, because they are colored, shall be deemed to be, and held liable under the several acts of Congress applicable to this subject, and be punished with military severity for obstructing recruiting.

XI. In consideration of the ignorance and helplessness of the negroes, arising from the condition in which they have been heretofore held, it becomes necessary that the Government should exercise more and peculiar care and protection over them than over its white citizens, accustomed to self-control and self-support, so that their sustenance may be assured, their rights respected, their helplessness protected, and their wrongs redressed; and that there be one system of management of negro affairs.

It is ordered, that Lieutenant Colonel J. Burnham *Kinsman,* A.D.C., be detailed at these Head Quarters, as General Superintendent of Negro Affairs in this Department, to whom all reports and communications relating thereto, required to be sent to these Head Quarters, shall be addressed. He shall have a general superintendence over all the colored people of this Department; and all other Superintendents of Negro Affairs shall report to Lieutenant Colonel *Kinsman,* who is acting for the Commanding General in this behalf.

All the teritory of Virginia south of the James River shall be under the superintendence of Captain Orlando *Brown,* Assistant Quartermaster. All the territory north of James River shall be under the superintendence of Captain Charles B. *Wilder,* Assistant Quartermaster. The District of North Carolina shall be under the superintendence of the Reverand Horace *James,* Chaplain.

Each Superintendent shall have the power to select and appoint such Assistant Superintendents for such Sub-Districts in his District as may be necessary, to be approved by the Commanding General; such appointments to be confirmed by the Commanding General.

The pay of such assistant, if a civilian, shall in no case exceed the pay of a first class clerk in the Quartermaster's Department.

It shall be the duty of each Superintendent, under the direction of the General Superintendent, to take care of the colored inhabitants of his District, not slaves, under the actual control of a loyal master in his District; (and in all questions arising as to freedom or slavery of any colored person, the presumption shall be that the man, woman or child is free or has claimed protection of the military authorities of the United States, which entitles the claimant to freedom;) to cause an accurate census to be taken of colored inhabitants in his District, and their employment; to cause all to be provided with necessary shelter, clothing, food, and medicines. To see that all able to work shall have some employment, and that such employment shall be industriously pursued; to see that in all contracts for labor or other things made by the negroes with white persons, the negro is not defrauded, and to annul all contracts made by the negro which are unconscionable and injurious, and that such contracts as are fulfilled by the negro shall be paid; to take charge of all lands and all property alloted, turned over, or given to the use of the negroes, whether by Government or by charity; to keep accurate accounts of the same, and of all expenditure; to audit all accounts of the negroes against Government, and to have all proper allowances made as well to the negro as the Government; and to have all claims put in train for payment by the Government; to keep accurate accounts of all expenses of the negro to the Government, and of his earnings for the Government; to see that the negroes wrought on land furnished by the Government on shares, shall have their just portion, and to aid in disposing of the same for the best good of the negro and Government; to make quarterly returns and exhibits of all accounts of matters committed to them; and to hold all monies arising from the surplus earnings of the negro over the expenditures by the United States, for the use and benefit of the negroes, under orders from these Head Quarters.

XII. It appearing to the Commanding General that some of the labor done by the negroes in this Department remains unpaid—some for the space of more than two years, although contracts were duly made by the proper officers of the Government for the payment thereof—whereby the faith of the negro in the justice of the Government is impaired, and the trust in its protection is weakened, it is ordered, that each Superintendent shall be a Commissioner, to audit all such account procure evidence of their validity, make out accurate pay-rolls, and return the same, so that they may be presented for adjustment, to the proper Departments, Provided, however, that no sale of any such claim against the Government shall be valid, and no payment shall be made of any such claim, except in hand to the person actually earning it—if he is within this Department—or to his legal representative, if the person earning it be deceased.

XIII. Religious, benevolent and humane persons have come into this Department for the charitable purpose of giving to the negroes secular and religious instructions; and this, too, without any adequate pay or material reward. It is, therefore, ordered, that every officer and soldier shall treat all such persons with the utmost respect; shall aid them by all proper means, in their laudable avocations; and that transportation be furnished them, whenever it may be necessary in pursuit of their business.

XIV. As it is necessary to prevent [*preserve*] uniformity of system, and that information shall be had as to the needs and the supplies for the negro; and as certain authorizations are had to raise troops in the Department, a practice has grown up of corresponding directly with the War and other Departments of the Government, to the manifest injury of the service. — It is, therefore, ordered, that all correspondence in relation to the raising or recruiting of colored troops, and relating to the care and control of the negroes in this Department, with any official organized body or society, or any Department or Bureau, of the Government, must be transmitted through these Head Quarters, as by regulation all other military correspondence is required to be done.

XV. Courts Martial and Courts of Inquiry in relation to all offences committed by, or against any of the colored troops, or any person in the service of the United States connected with the care, or serving with the colored troops, shall have a majority of its members composed of officers of colored troops, when such can be detailed without manifest injury to the service.

All offences by citizens against the negroes, or by the negroes against citizens — except of a high and aggravated nature — shall be heard and tried before the Provost Court.

XVI. This order shall be published, and furnished to each regiment and detached post within the Department — a copy for every commanding officer thereof, — and every commander of a company, or detachment less than a company, shall cause the same to be read once, at least, to his company or detachment; and this order, shall be printed for the information of the citizens, once, at least, in each newspaper published in the Department.

By command of Major General Butler.

HD

General Orders, No. 46, Head Quarters Dept. of Va. and North Carolina, 5 Dec. 1863, vol. 52 VaNc, General Orders Issued, ser. 5078, Dept. of VA & NC & 18th Army Corps, RG 393 Pt. 1 [C-3062].

27: Engineer at Fortress Monroe, Virginia, to the Chief of Engineers

Fort Monroe Va. Decr 11$''$ 1863.

Sir, I have the honor to transmit herewith a copy of Genl Orders, No. 46, Head Quarters Eighteenth Army Corps, &c, &c, dated Fort Monroe Va Decr 5. 1863[1] — taken from a newspaper of the 8$''$ inst, to which my attention has been called by one of the Engineer employés — No copy of the order has been furnished me from any official source —

Information has been given me that Captain Charles B. Wilder, Ass'nt. Quartermaster referred to in paragraph XI of the order, has been advising one or more negroes employed on Fort Monroe or Fort Wool to enlist, stating that if it was not done, he or they would be drafted, leading to the supposition that *all* would be drafted or compelled to serve in the army, whether or no—

It has been with the utmost difficulty for the past two years that any force of laborers has been kept together on the works in this vicinity. Irish & German laborers of a very inferior class have from time to time at great trouble been procured from New York, been tried, found wanting & discharged— About a year since some of the worst laborers at this work at a critical moment in the operations for the year, combined, compelled the others to join them, and taking advantage of the well known difficulty in procuring labor, refused to work unless their demands were complied with— They were discharged and directions given to procure what negro laborers could be obtained, with the condition that this office was to have nothing to do with Capt. Wilder, who was in charge of those who could not take care of themselves— Wages less than those given to white laborers were offered; the negroes were to support themselves & be paid directly from this office as any other laborers— The wages were supposed to be sufficient to enable an industrious person to support himself & family & not enough to encourage one not accustomed to the use of much money to any wasteful expenditure, or to indulge in intervals of idleness— The plan has worked well— The negroes when paid directly for their labor, without the intervention of unnecessary agents, have proved in general, industrious, fair workmen, docile, more orderly & cleanly than the white laborers, and work has progressed far more satisfactorily to all concerned and with less cost to Government than heretofore—

If this order is to be enforced it will prove very detrimental to operations on these works— It is I believe wholly illegal, arbitrary and injudicious, so far as regards Engineer operations, which are not under the control of the Commanding General of the Department of Virginia & N. Carolina, but are carried on under the authority of the War Department through the instructions &c, received from the Engineer Bureau— I am not aware of any law which forbids any officer of the Government, in the legitimate exercise of his duties, from employing any well behaved citizen be he white, red, yellow or black, in the particular labor for which he is fitted, for fair compensation, agreed upon between the parties, or fixed by the War Department through its proper bureau; or which authorizes a General Commanding a Department to regulate the wages of employés in the different Departments without the permission of the heads of the different bureaux to which they belong— Nor do I believe it is the policy of the Government to prevent the free negroes from learning as rapidly as possible to take care of themselves & families and prevent emulation by fixing a certain rate of pay as the highest which they shall receive, whether they develop capabilities of earning twice that amount or not— Enlistment of negroes is not probably the highest stage to which the authorities would wish them to attain, and offering them fair wages no more discourages enlistment than it does in case of the white laborers, & if that plea is to regulate the employment of labor, it would require a cessation of work on all the fortifications in this vicinity— So long as laborers are allowed within the Department & behave themselves as good & loyal citizens, I have a right to employ them for the Government, when & where required unless ordered otherwise by my proper superiors.

As an Engineer officer in the exercise of his duty I protest against this assumption of authority by the General Commanding this Department, and unless otherwise ordered by the Engineer or War Department shall continue to employ free negro laborers as heretofore and without any regard to the provisions, on that point of the General Orders No. 46, referred to herein, and would respectfully urge, that the attention of the Secretary of War be called to that order and it be ascertained whether in issuing it the General Commanding the Department of Virginia & N. Carolina, is carrying out the views of the Government or not— I have the honor to be, Sir, Very Respectfully your obedt Servt

ALS   C. Seaforth Stewart—

Maj. of Engrs. C. Seaforth Stewart to Brigr. Genl. Joseph G. Totten, 11 Dec. 1863, Engineer 79, 1863, Letters Received from the President, Executive Departments, & War Department Bureaus, RG 107 [L-321]. Enclosure. On December 16, the chief of engineers referred the letter to Secretary of War Edwin M. Stanton, noting that Major Stewart's replacement of white laborers with black ones had been of "great advantage and economy to the public interest," and suggesting that the "restraint placed upon the operations of the Engineer Department" by General Order 46 "be abrogated by the War Department, so that operations may go on with the same liberty as they have heretofore, and as they now do at the other fortifications generally, which are under construction or repair by the Engineer Department." Three days later, General Benjamin F. Butler, who had issued General Order 46, was informed of Stanton's decision that the engineer officers at Fortress Monroe "are not to be interfered with, and that the workmen employed by [Major Stewart] are not to be withdrawn for any other service, nor his control over them in any way disturbed." (Brig. Genl. Ed. R. S. Canby to Major Genl. B. F. Butler, 19 Dec. 1863, vol. 53A, p. 315, Letters Sent, RG 107 [L-320].)

1 General Order 46, issued by General Benjamin F. Butler (who commanded both the 18th Army Corps and the Department of Virginia and North Carolina), is printed immediately above, as doc. 26.

28: Testimony by a Northern Abolitionist before the American Freedmen's Inquiry Commission

[*Washington, D.C.?   December 24, 1863*]
Testimony of Hon. F. W. Bird

Question   I understand Mr Bird that you have lately had an opportunity of observing the Freedmen in Eastern Virginia and I would like to know the result of your observations.

Answer   I have lately visited the Department of Virginia with a view to a particular examination of the condition of the Freedmen employed upon the Government Farms.   I first visited those near Hampton in charge of Capt. Chas. B. Wilder assistant superintendent of Freedmen.   These freedmen are fugitives partly from the peninsular in the vicinity of Richmond, but, mostly from the neighborhood of Norfolk and Suffolk and the adjacent portions of North Carolina.   They commenced their labors on the farm late in the season and under very great disadvantages.   A large portion of the ground was not ploughed at all until April Whereas the ploughing season in that section commences in January.   They experienced considerable loss also from the failure of the crops, owing to drought.   A large portion of the seed they were obliged to replant from the first planting being so late, and a large portion of the crop imperfectly ripened.   Some of these laborers were of the large number who were herded upon Craney Island in the winter and spring, where very many of them contracted disease unfitting them for active labor.

Q   Were these people men women and children?

A   Yes.   It is also to be borne in mind that very few able bodied men are now employed upon these farms, nearly all of that class having been drawn either into the army or employed in other labor for the Government.   Notwithstanding these drawbacks I think it is safe to say, that on all these farms the laborers have raised crops abundantly sufficient to support themselves and their families until the next harvest.

A portion of the farms are worked "to halves" as it is called, for the Government – the Government furnishing seed agricultural implements and horses and recieving one third or one half of the produce; another portion of the freedmen have managed entirely on their own account. I did not take accurate statistics of many of the Farms; and I was the less anxious to do this as the Superindents will very soon make reports in full of the results of the season. The facts in the cases of which I took notes are in entire accordance with the results upon the other farms, so far as I learned.

Here is the case of a farm carried on by Gibberty Davis – an old man 70 or 80 years of age. His wife is free. His master is a Captain in the rebel service. He is the only one remaining on the farm out of a gang of thirty slaves   He has cultivated with the assistance of two boys who are free thirty acres on which they have raised, besides supporting themselves 250 Bushels of corn and 150 pounds of cotton. They were obliged to replant nearly the whole of the corn. Mr Davis said he should have had four or five hundred pounds of cotton but for the early frost. The corn is worth 90 cts pr bushel and the cotton perhaps 60¢ pr pound; showing that he has now more than enough left to support himself and family until the next crop.

Another is the farm of Wm Jones consisting of 400 acres where seventy four slaves were formerly employed, of whom only ten are left. The master is in the Rebel Army. They have raised 1000 bushels of shelled corn and 145 Bbls. of Sweet Potatoes. They all have families and have raised enough to carry them all through the season; and they all said they had lived better than they ever did under their masters. This last was a Government Farm; the other was not. These two cases are fair specimens of all that I saw and are I believe fair specimens of the whole.

I found a very bad state of things at what is known as the tobacco drying house where several hundred of the Freedmen last taken from Craney Island were crowded together very closely with nothing to do – all infirm old men and women and children – with great liability to fire, which would almost inevitably prove particularly if occurring in the night, very destructive to life. They seem to be there from necessity, for the present as the Superintendent has found it impossible to provide huts for them rapidly enough to prevent this crowding. Capt Wilder is doing every thing in his power to provide huts and to encourage the freedmen in building huts for themselves, for separate livings. In some cases where the men are employed at a distance by the Government, they gather in villages in large numbers as at Hampton where the ruins of the houses of the First Families of Virginia are now covered with the cabins of their former Slaves, many of them built out of the same material as their masters houses. – Where it has been practicable they have been assisted in building cabins with a view to giving to each family a seperate allotment of ten acres for their own cultivation. Their collection in villages has been discouraged except in special cases.

Some five or six miles from Hampton, Capt Wilder has just started a Steam Saw Mill, which has been dumped down in the forest and is set at work in the open air turning out some five thousand feet of boards per day, which are furnished to the freedmen for their cabins.

With the exception of the state of things at the tobacco drying house, the condition of the freedmen of this district is as good as could be expected; wonderfully improved since my visit there a year and a half ago. This improvement is due to the change of policy in their treatment. Then they were treated as men who had no rights that white men were bound to respect; now they are beginning to comprehend that if they behave like men, they will be treated like men. Only one thing is needed and that they crave above all other boons; and that is the right to own the soil.

I also visited several of the farms in the vicinity of Norfolk under the charge of Capt. Orlando Brown, Assistant Superintendent of Freedmen. Most of these are carried on "to halves" for the Government.

The Poindexter Farm.

This farm is under a white overseer – a native of Norfolk. He has four men on the farm, all married. They have raised 730 bushels of shelled corn, forty bushells of sweet potatoes, and have sold about $300 worth of Milk. The Government furnished seed, utensils and teams.

The Baxter Farm.

I next visited the Baxter Farm, consisting of 3000 acres, which was formerly owned by Oscar F. Baxter, a surgeon in the Federal navy, now a surgeon in the Rebel army. He had as Jack Herring told us "jam by" (nearly) forty slaves. I give the results of the labor on this farm, as furnished by the assistant Superintendent. The place is known as Woodlawn. The whole number of freedmen on the farm is 70 of whom thirty eight are able bodied. Three hundred acres have been cultivated and there are now on hand 5090 bushels of corn

Jack Herring, one of Dr Baxter's late slaves, has cultivated, this last season, about thirty acres of this farm. He has done all the work himself, except what he hired. He had a little money of his own in the spring and his "boss" when he ran away left him corn enough for seed. He has raised 500 bushells of shelled corn. He has bought his team with his own money, and has one cow and twenty pigs. I was struck with the difference between the results of this poor freedmans labor and those of the Poindexter Farm. This latter as I have said was managed by a white native of Norfolk; and yet every thing about the place was slovenly and slip-shod. The overseer seemed hardly able to take care of himself and I have no doubt the men would have done better without him than with him. Certainly they would have done very much better, if they had had one intelligent negroe for their overseer instead of him.

The Wise Farm.

I also visited the place known as "Rolleston" which was occupied by Gen Wise for two years before the Rebellion. The results of the season on this farm are given from the figures furnished by the Assistant Superintendent. – The whole number of freed people on the farm of all ages, is 61. Of these the number of able bodied men is five stout boys and men over 15, four. Boys under fifteen, five. Able bodied women, fifteen. Girls under fifteen who work occasionally, seven. Leaving the number aged and young unfit to work, twenty five. – Two hundred and fifty acres of land were cultivated. The amount of produce sent off or on hand was, potatoes 100 Barrells, corn 2100 bushels.

It should be observed to the credit of the experiment, how small the proportion of able-bodied men is to the non-producers on these farms, to the infirm and the women and children, whom they have had to support. With the exception of Herrings place one half of the crops on these farms belongs to the Government; and in all cases so far as I could understand this half more than pays for all the materials furnished by the Government

Another fact must be borne in mind, that all the teams used on these farms, in both districts, are condemned horses. Capt. Brown is doing his best to furnish all the freedmen with huts and cabins of their own. He has been very much embarrassed by the want of land which was safe from Guerrillas, and by the want of houses for the freedmen. He has now several hundred built and is well prepared to commence operations early in the ensueing season. The same difficulty was experienced here as on the other side, in consequence of the late planting; but they are now already commencing their ploughing, and unless something extraordinary happens, will show much better results another year.

I was very much struck with the view from the mansion house on the Baxter Farm. Stretching around the outskirts of the farm for a mile or more are the huts of the freedmen at a distance of ten or twenty rods apart; the plan being for each family to have an allotment of its own of ten acres thus laying the foundation of an industrious and self supporting peasantry who at the same time will be able to work for the owner of the central farm. All that is needed to establish there a truly loyal and prosperous community is that the men and women who have watered the soil with their tears and blood, should be allowed to own it when they have earned it by their own labor. They regard it a great boon that they are allowed to own their share of the crops, the boon will be infinitely greater when they are allowed to own the soil.

The schools in both districts are represented to be in a very flourishing condition. I visited only those in Norfolk, and am entirely safe in saying from my own experience in the management of schools and from the testimony of teachers that they have made at least as great progress as white children could have made in the same condition of life and under simular discouraging circumstances.

Q How far do these people show a disposition to re-establish their old family relations?

A Their opinions of conjugal fidelity are very loose.

Q How is it in regard to parental instincts?

A The fathers I should think are indifferent – much more so than the mothers. I am not prepared to state very positively from my own enquiries except from those I made of the superintendents and teachers. They all say, that the men are very much inclined when they get tired of their wives to change them and think it is hard if they cannot.

Q How far do the Government Superintendents rely upon the intelligence of the negroes to direct their farming operations, in comparison with what they would if they were employing Irish or other laborers?

A I think quite as much, particularly where they find slaves on the farms where they have lived.

Q Do they trust them with the care of cattle, seeds, tools &c?

A I think so entirely. I heard no complaints of dishonesty or untrustworthiness.

Q How far do these men show any thrift or economy in the management of what they get – their rations, seeds, tools, and things of that kind?

A I dont think that question can be answered intelligently because the crops have not been sold yet and the proceeds have not been placed in the freedmen's hands. They have just had their living out of their farms and are waiting for the reports of the Assistant Supt. soon to be made up, when there will be a division of the produce.

Q From what you have seen of these people, how far do you think they would succeed in taking care of themselves if not placed under white supervision, but put on the land, and aided in the outset with seeds and tools?

A That is a hard question to answer. I don't see why a great many of them would not do as well as Gibberty Davis or Jack Herring has done.

Q Would they be inclined to try that experiment?

A A portion of them would have confidence enough to do it – perhaps as large a portion as would be the case among the poor whites but the majority, perhaps, would rather work under superintendence.

Q How far are they thrifty with what little money they do get?

A I only know from the testimony of the superintendents, that they are thrifty and economical, and save their money and deposit it.

Q Are they apt to spend money in drink?

A No.

Q Do you find any instances of quarrelling among them?

A No, they don't seem to need any police.

Q Are any of them trusted with arms?

A They have on the Baxter Farm a squad of men who drill an hour a day. It was found that the Government being short of troops, was unable to protect them from guerillas, and a few weeks ago, Capt Brown organized this squad and placed twenty five muskets in their hands. I saw them drill. They are very proud of a musket and will do better service in taking care of guerillas than white soldiers. Capt. Brown says he would altogether prefer for a scouting party to hunt for guerillas, black soldiers to white.

Q On the whole from what you saw what is the inference as to the capacity and disposition of these men to support themselves, and assume their places as citizens of the country?

. . . [1]

HDf

Testimony of Hon. F. W. Bird before the American Freedmen's Inquiry Commission, [24 Dec. 1863], filed with O-328 1863, Letters Received, ser. 12, RG 94 [K-68]. Topical labels in the margin are omitted.

1 Subsequent page or pages missing.

29: North Carolina Black Soldier to the Commander of the Department of Virginia and North Carolina, and Surgeon-in-Chief of Contrabands in the District of North Carolina to the Medical Director of the District

NewBern No C. [*January* 1864]

Dear Genl   I write to you this morning on buisness of importance   I write to know if theire cant be some protection for

the colerd people of newBern   the peopple of coler when they are
taken with the small pox they have to be draged across the river and
thire they have not half medical attendanc for them   it is said by
the folks that has got well that they do not get enough to eat and
when thy die thy have A hole dug and put them in without any
coffin and I think this is A most horible treatment and therefore thy
ought to have some person that will look after them in A better
manner then this   the is. A great distinction made betwen the
white an the col.d in Such cases as this   when the whites are taken
with this disseas thy taken care of and so you will please to look
into this matter

   Nothing More   awaiting and Ans   Youre Humble Servant
ALS   John. Williams

                           New Berne N.C.   February 8th 1864
Sir   Having read the communication of John Williams to Major
Genl. Butler, in reference to the harsh treatment of Contrabands
who have the small pox, I have the honor to make the following
statement; Williams says;

   1st That, "the people of color, when they are taken with the
small pox have to be dragged across the river"; he is mistaken; all
possible gentleness is shown towards these people when they are
removed from their homes to the small pox hospital; they are taken
in ambulances to the wharf, where they are made comfortable in a
small house near by, until the regular trip of the boat. This boat has
been arranged so that those who are too feeble to sit may lie, and in
it, both whites and blacks are conveyed across the river."

   2nd "They have not half medical attendance for them." A
medical officer has been detailed who gives his entire attention to
prescribing for the sick, and I am positive that he not only does his
duty, but that he takes great interest in the welfare of his patients;
he is amply provided with clerks, wardmasters, nurses &C. who are
not at all remiss in their duties.

   3rd "It is said by the folks that has got well, that they do not get
enough to eat." On Sunday the 7th instant, accompanied by Surgn
Cowgill U.S.V. Medical Inspector, I made a thorough inspection of
the small pox hospital and camp, and in each of the wards, the
question was asked, if there is any one here who does not get
enough to eat, let him say so. Out of the two hundred and fifty
patients, we found one convalescent man who said, that he thought
he should get strong faster if he could have fresh meat in place of
soup; and a man and wife, both quite well and very anxious to
return to town, who said that they did not have bread enough; the

reason of which so far as could be ascertained seemed to be, that they were too lazy to go up to the cook house and ask for more. In the "Exposed Camp" (it is here that all those who have been exposed to the disease are Kept, much against their will, for three weeks) we found quite a number who said that they did not have enough to eat. If perfectly well people are too lazy to cook the food *given* to them, I think they ought to go hungry. As far as the ration is concerned, they are as amply provided as any general hospital for white soldiers, with the exception of extra articles purchased with the hospital fund. Hospitals for blacks other than soldiers cannot make a fund.

4th "When they die they have a hole dug and put them in without any coffin." When the Hospital was moved across the river in December last, quite a number died within forty eight hours, some of these were put in the ground without coffins. The necessity of burying the corpse when death occurs from small pox, as quickly as possible, justified this course as at that time it was utterly impossible to procure coffins in time for the burial. It was with the greatest difficulty that we moved the patients and hospital effects to the present location. The Quarter master had to force his men to work, and in one instance a steamboat Captain refused to obey orders and was accordingly discharged. When it is remembered that most people fear the small pox more than they do bullets, the difficulties that we had to encounter and overcome at the outset in getting our new hospital into running order will be appreciated.

5th "A great distinction is made between the white and colored in such cases." We have now under treatment for small pox, some fifteen white patients (Soldiers and citizens); they are quartered in hospital tents, while all the acute cases among the blacks are in large and commodious wooden buildings constructed with special regard to comfort and ventilation. The same medical officer prescribes for each; there is no difference in the food, which is prepared by the same cooks and the hospital furniture is precisely alike throughout all the wards. From the tenor of John Williams complaints I should say that they we[re] made up from hearsay and not personal observation; he has probably given ear to those disaffected "Exposed," who generally return to town complaining bitterly of the restraint to which they have been subjected; a sanitary measure of the utmost importance. In conclusion I would remark that should Genl Butler, with the known interest which he takes in the welfare of the blacks, visit our Hospital I feel confident he would say, – well done   I am Sir Very Respectfully Your Obt Servt

HLS   E P. Morong

Orderly Sargt. John Williams to Genl., [Jan. 1864], filed with Surgn. E. P. Morong to Surgn. D. W. Hand, 8 Feb. 1864, M-53 1864, Letters Received, ser. 5063, Dept. of VA & NC & 18th Army Corps, RG 393 Pt. 1 [C-3019]. Williams signed as orderly sergeant, "3^d Regt Wilds Brigade." Having been instructed (by an endorsement of January 26) "to remedy the evil complained of," the medical director of the District of North Carolina added the following endorsement when he forwarded Morong's report on February 10: "The 'evil complained of' does not exist." Another endorsement.

30: Superintendent of an American Missionary Association School to the General Superintendent of Negro Affairs in the Department of Virginia and North Carolina

[Portsmouth, Va. February 16, 1864]

Sir: I beg leave respectfully to represent to you that in, & about Portsmouth, there are many cheap houses & sheds that can be rented at comparatively low prices. That hundreds of Colored families, unable to rent the more valuable buildings of Norfolk, have taken refuge in these, thus bringing before us, and within our reach, a large share of the poverty and consequent suffering, now experienced by this class of people. That while our Government furnishes them wood and rations to some extent, their other wants are only partially met by Benevolent Societies. That at this inclement season, with a virulent disease raging in our midst, we find these means insufficient, to save them from absolute suffering. There is great mortality among them, especially among children, which may be owing in a great measure to these causes—the want of sufficient *clothing* and *bedding*—the want of unslacked *Lime* for whitewashing their dingy dwellings, soap for cleaning floors etc.— Their only Benevolent Soc. in Portsmouth is largely indebted to the Undertaker for burying the dead—more than they can ever pay. Notwithstanding the Govr furnishes Coffins, it is very hard sometimes to secure the burial of the Poor, as I have known as many as four or five deaths among them in a day.

Another matter I wish to bring before you, which is, that rations are withheld from Boys and Girls attending school, on the ground that they ought to work—while work cannot be obtained for one in five of them. If they are withdrawn from school, rations are allowed them, and they hang about military Camps and the Streets of the City where the tendency is to demoralize and vitiate. Being daily conversant with these evils, among the Comfortless abodes of more than six thousand people, I respectfully, but earnestly solicit such relief as it may be in your power to give. I am, Sir With great respect Yours &c

ALS   H. S. Beals

H. S. Beals to Col. Kinsman, [16 Feb. 1864], Letters, Orders, & Telegrams Received by Lt. Col. J. B. Kinsman, ser. 4108, Ft. Monroe VA Dept. of Negro Affairs, RG 105 [A-7853]. Beals signed as "Sup. of Mission Sc." at Portsmouth, Virginia.

31: Chief Surgeon of the Contraband Hospital at Norfolk, Virginia, to the Surgeon-in-Chief for Norfolk and Portsmouth, Virginia

Norfolk Va. Feb. 19th 1864

Sir, In obediance to your orders, I have this day visited the Contraband School of orphan children at Ferry Point, & upon examination, find 51 cases of Scurvy, in a majority of whom the gums are more or less ulcerated, & bleed at the slightest toutch— In Several of the cases, their faces were Swollen, but no other Symptoms of Scurvy were present— There were 86 children in the School, who have been allowed only one barrel of potatoes per month, & no other vegetables— About 5 gals molasses have been allowed pr. month— The Superintendant informed me, that if all were Supplied, it would require about 1/2 bushel of potatoes, & one gal. molasses pr. day— I prescribed for the cases alluded to, & advised an immediate change of diet from salted meats to vegetable— Very Respectfully Your ob^t Sv^t

ALS—   C K S. Millard

A.A. Surg. C. K. S. Millard to Surg. Henry A. Martin, 19 Feb. 1864, M-24 1864, Letters Received, ser. 1628, U.S. Forces Norfolk & Portsmouth, RG 393 Pt. 2 No. 72 [C-3123]. Endorsement.

32: Superintendent of Negro Affairs in the 1st District of the Department of Virginia and North Carolina to the Commander of the Department, and the Latter's Reply

Fortress Monroe V^a February 24, 1864

General I have the honor to state such wants, as I deem essential to the successful prosecution of our plantation operations, and the comfortable support of the surplus population, on our hands, without any obstructions,

I. The liberty to take possession of all Rebel abandoned plantations in this District, about which there is no question, and to refer all doubtful ones to the General Superintendent or Provost Judges—the burden of proof to rest with the objector—all to be used for the Goverment, at the best possible advantage, and all to be reported to the General Superintendent as required in General Order No 46.¹ or oftener

II. The privilige of selecting such Assistants and laborers, and securing such tools and seeds as are necessary, also the use and control of a Wagon train, and the use of a hundred Condemned horses,

III The privilige of buying of the Goverment or elsewhere at cost or apprisal—all the Forage, Seeds, and Subsistance Stores, that are needful, also of purchasing such old Wagons, carts, Ambulances, harnesses, and tools as have become unserviceable, to loan or sell to those who work the farms, also to sell all the surplus productions of the farms, that are not necessary for consumption,

IV The privilige of locating the surplus Contrabands, where they can be most advantageously used and Cared for,

V. The privilige of keeping as heretofore, a small supply of such necessary Articles, as the colored people need and can pay for, at the time of purchasing or when the crops come in

All of which is respectfully submitted

HLcSr   (Signed) C B Wilder

[*Fortress Monroe, Va. February 24?, 1864*]

Capt Wilder

Your first proposition is granted

Your second except Wagon trains, that must be more definite

III All the Articles Condemned property will be turned over to you upon request and designation of what you need

and Forage oats and Corn for seed will be sold at cost

IV Is granted as you have always had it.

V I have Ordered a House to be put at the disposal of the Society of friends" the Massenburg House, for the purpose indicated   Yours respectfully

(Signed) Benj F Butler

Shew this to Lt Col Kinsman Supt &C   Signed BFB

HLcSr

Capt. C. B. Wilder to Major General B. F. Butler, 24 Feb. 1864, and Maj. Genl. Benj. F. Butler to Capt. Wilder, [24? Feb. 1864], Letters Received by the Superintendent, ser. 4109, Ft. Monroe VA Dept. of Negro Affairs, RG 105 [A-8313].) A notation dated February 27, [1864], identifies the first letter as "[a] true copy of the original in possession of Capt. C. B. Wilder."

1 For the order, issued on December 5, 1863, by General Benjamin F. Butler, commander of the Department of Virginia and North Carolina, see above, doc. 26.

33: Headquarters of a Virginia Black Regiment to the Superintendent of Negro Affairs in the 2nd District of the Department of Virginia and North Carolina

Camp Mix. Va. Apr. 3rd 1864

Sir— I am directed by the Col. Comd'g. this Regiment to call your attention to the following case. Private Decatur King of this Regt. complains that the Commissary will not furnish rations to his wife Mary King, unless she will leave her home and live on the "Government Farm". I would respectfully inquire if this is the invariable rule. I have the honor to be Very Respectfully Your Obedient Servant

HLcS   Fred. W. Smith

2d. Lt. Fred. W. Smith to Rev. Dr. Brown, 3 Apr. 1864, Letters Sent, 1st USCC, Regimental Books & Papers USCT, RG 94 [G-67]. Smith was a lieutenant in the 1st USCC, a regiment organized in tidewater Virginia. On April 9, the superintendent of Negro affairs, Captain Orlando Brown, responded as follows: "It is not the invariable rule to stop the rations unless the families will live on Govt Farms. as quarters are not yet provided for all. It is however the intention to make this the rule, as soon as sufficient quarters are provided, except in the few instances where the parties have houses of their own." (Summary of letter from Capt. O. Brown, 9 Apr. [1864], Letters Received, 1st USCC, Regimental Books & Papers USCT, RG 94 [G-67].) The new rule was in effect by mid-June, when Captain Brown informed a superior officer that he was stopping the issue of rations to the families of black soldiers in Norfolk and Portsmouth, Virginia, "unless they will remove to Gov' farms. The large number of Negros in these cities without employment is the reason for the Order." (Capt. O. Brown to Lt. Col. Kinsman, 15 June 1864, Letters Received by the Superintendent, ser. 4108, Ft. Monroe VA Dept. of Negro Affairs, RG 105 [A-7852].)

34: Commander of the Department of Virginia and North Carolina to the Superintendent of Negro Affairs in the 1st District of the Department

Fortress Monroe [*Va.*], April 13th 1864

Captain   Report to me at once the condition of the title and who the occupants are of Dr Woods house,   Also any reasons, if you know of any, why it cannot be occupied as an asylum for the orphan black children.

Report to me how many families, taking whole families, where at least one half of them shall be above the age of 10 years can be got ready to be sent to Philadelphia

I have the honor to remain very Respectfully Your Obediant Servant

HLS   Benj F Butler

[*Endorsement*] Fortress Monroe Va April 29 1864. Very respectfully returned.

In regard to sending families &c to Philadelphia, I have the honor to state, after careful investigation, I can scarcely find one willing to go, unless they can be made to feel satisfied in regard to thier situation after arrival.

A few have returned, who report among their associates, that they were not well used, which makes them hesitate about going. Very few whole families are now to be found, so numerous have been the applications for men, women, boys and girls during the last six months, or more.

I had hoped some plan would have been offered, by which large numbers of the families of soldiers and others would be induced to go North in companies, with some one in whom they have confidence, to look out for them. Thus, they could obtain employment and education together, and be where their husbands could find them when the war is over, or if they pefer to return with their small accumulations, they could purchase for themselves a homestead and become permanent citizens upon the soil that gave them birth. Respectfully submitted C. B. Wilder Capt & A.Q.M. & Supt N.A. 1st Dist Dept Va & No Ca.

[*Endorsement*] Head Qr's Dep't Va & N.C. May 1st 1864 Respectfully referred to Lt Col Kinsman with directions to confer with Capt Wilder and arrange upon some plan by which these people can be sent forward— By Command of Maj Genl Butler H C Clarke Capt & A.D.C.

Maj. Genl. Benj. F. Butler to Captain Wilder, 13 Apr. 1864, Letters, Orders, & Telegrams Received by Lt. Col. J. B. Kinsman, ser. 4108, Ft. Monroe VA Dept. of Negro Affairs, RG 105 [A-7847]. Former slaves elsewhere in tidewater Virginia showed no greater willingness to migrate to the North and rebuffed attempts by the superintendents of Negro affairs to persuade them to do so. In July 1864, when Colonel J. Burnham Kinsman, the general superintendent, asked Captain Orlando Brown, superintendent at Norfolk, to forward – "for the purpose of being sent North" – "one hundred of the Negro women not belonging to the families of soldiers [who were] without occupation and supported by the Government," Brown was unable to comply. "[T]here exists on the part of these persons strong objections to leaving," he explained. "I would therefore respectfully ask for permission to compel them to go – of course useing as little severity as possible towards them." (Capt. O. Brown to Lt. Col. Kinsman, 14 July 1864, Letters, Orders, & Telegrams Received by Lt. Col. J. B. Kinsman, ser. 4108, Fort Monroe VA Dept. of Negro Affairs, RG 105 [A-7847].) It is not known whether Brown received the authority he requested; neither the letters received by him during 1864, nor any letters-sent volumes of the general superintendent are extant.

35: Commander of the Department of Virginia and North Carolina to an Agent of a Massachusetts Manufacturing Company

Fort Monroe [*Va.*]   April 25th 1864.

Sir.   I have been informed from various sources that there is a great scarcity of female help in the mills at Lowell.   We have a great surplus of female help here – Women and children from 16 years upward.

Although darker skinned they are quite as intelligent as the green Irish help which you take into your mills.

If arrangements can be made to take care of the families I have no doubt we can furnish you quite a supply.   I wish you would put it before the mill agents and see if it is practicable to do anything.

Both sides would be benefitted in my belief by the transaction.   I have the honor to remain Very Respectfully Your Obt Servant,

HLcIr   B. F. B.

Maj. Gen. B. F. B[utler] to John Wright, 25 Apr. 1864, vol. 50 VaNc, pp. 350–51, Letters Sent, ser. 5046, Dept. of VA & NC & 18th Army Corps, RG 393 Pt. 1 [C-3221]. The addressee, John Wright, was an agent of the Suffolk Manufacturing Company of Lowell, Massachusetts. No reply from him has been found among the letters received by the Department of Virginia and North Carolina.

36: Superintendent of Negro Affairs in the 2nd District of the Department of Virginia and North Carolina to the General Superintendent of Negro Affairs in the Department

Norfolk Va May 12 1864

Colonel; I have the honor to report that about 6 A.M. Monday May 9th, I was applied to by a large number of colored women and children to release their husbands, fathers Etc, who were being taken by guards to the wharf to be transported up the James River to work for the Government — Upon inquiring I learned that the order for their impressment proceeded from Brig. Genl. Shepley, comdg. the Dist. of Norfolk & Portsmouth. I immediately called, with Capt. Plato A.Q.M., upon the General, who informed me that urgent military necessity compelled the impressment of Sixty laborers. I called his attention to par. 9 — Gen. O — No 46, which requires the impressment of "white laborers, in such cases, if present —"[1] He gave as a reason, for not doing so (what seemed to me a good one) that the white laborers in Norfolk, could not be trusted so near the front. He ordered Capt. Plato and myself to examine the cases and send those that we thought could best be spared. We found this a very difficult matter, as all had some good or some imaginary reason for remaining. Thinking it necessary to accompany them, to see that their Muster Rolls should be properly made out, I spoke to them of the urgency of the case, and under a pledge that I would go with them, the whole number was readily made up by Volunteers — We immediately embarked and proceeded to the landing at Bermuda Hundreds, arriving about dark the same evening. I reported at Hd. Qrs. and was informed that a much larger number of Laborers would be required. Having noticed several negroes on the banks of the river as we were passing up, I suggested that these might be employed, and received the following order —

Hd. Qrs. in the field.
May 9 1864

Capt. O. Brown A.Q.M and Supt. Negro Affairs, will collect all of the able bodied negroes that can be found on the banks of the James River, and turn them over to the Q.M. Dept — Quartermasters will furnish the necessary transportation —
By Order Maj. Genl. Butler
signed — J. H Shaffer Col & Chf of Staff

The next morning I was furnished with the steamer Portsmouth, and proceeded down the River, about twenty miles, stopping at all available points, and succeeded in taking up forty five (45) negroes, which I turned over as ordered — On reporting at Hd. Qrs. I received the order of which the following is a copy —

Hd Qrs. Dept. Va & NC. May 11 1864

Capt. O Brown AQM, will proceed to Ft. Monroe and Norfolk and procure without delay two hundred negroes and bring them to Bermuda Landing. Quartermasters will furnish the necessary transportation.

By Comd. Maj. Genl. Butler
J. H. Shaffer Col & Chf. Staff—

The steamer Portsmouth was procured about 12 O'clock, when we started down the river, stopping at the different military stations and removing from them to Norfolk one hundred & fifty women & Children, who were wholly without tents or shelter of any Kind. These persons are now comfortably provided for in Norfolk. We also found eight men, who will be taken to Bermuda Landing as a part of the two hundred I am greatly indebted to Mr. Reuben J. Todd who was the only person with me and who rendered most valuable assistance— I am engaged to day in procuring all the negroes I can find in Norfolk and vicinity and shall leave for Fort Monroe during the night, with about one hundred. I would respectfully ask to carry out the instructions from Maj. Genl. Butler, that Capt. C. B. Wilder be ordered to have at least one hundred men ready for me at 10 A.M. tomorrow. These men are to receive twenty dollars per month and rations. I am informed on good authority that hundreds can be procured in Hampton and vicinity.

I am happy to add that I find everything going on well in Norfolk— Very Respectfully Your Obt. Servt—

HLS   O Brown

Capt. O. Brown to Lt. Col. J. B. Kinsman, 12 May 1864, Letters, Orders, & Telegrams Received by Lt. Col. J. B. Kinsman, ser. 4108, Ft. Monroe VA Dept. of Negro Affairs, RG 105 [A-8308]. In the course of military operations at Bermuda Hundred, the Union army impressed hundreds of black laborers from tidewater Virginia and North Carolina, often under promises that were not fulfilled and with little thought about the fate of their families. "[S]ome dozens of colored teamsters" were sent from New Berne in early June 1864, reported Captain Horace James (superintendent of Negro affairs in Union-occupied North Carolina) about six weeks after their departure. "They left in great haste," James recalled, "some of them not bidding farewell to their families. They have not been paid for some time, have no money, and but few clothes, and are I judge in a poor way. They were promised that they should be sent back immediately. In the meantime we have to feed their families here." If the teamsters could be spared from the front, James asked that they be "permitted to rejoin and provide for their families." (Capt. Horace James to Major Genl. B. F. Butler, 19 July 1864, Letters, Orders, & Telegrams Received by Lt. Col. J. B. Kinsman, ser. 4108, Ft. Monroe VA Dept. of Negro Affairs, RG 105 [A-8312].)

1 The order is printed above, as doc. 26.

37: Maps of Government Farms in the 1st and 2nd Districts of the Department of Negro Affairs, Department of Virginia and North Carolina

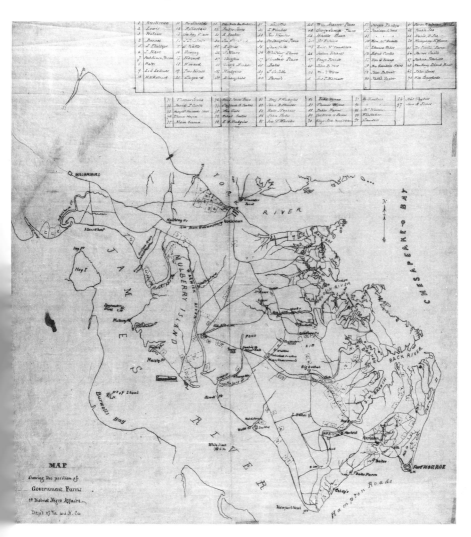

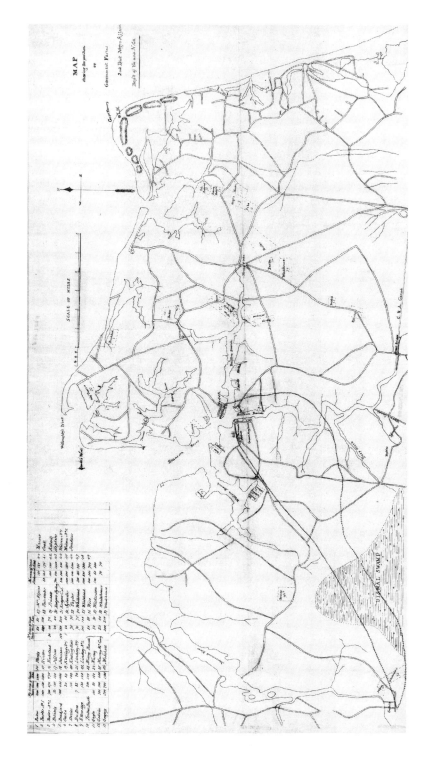

MAP
showing the position
of
Government Forces
in
Dep't of Va. and N. Ca.

"Map showing the position of Government Farms 1ˢᵗ District Negro Affairs — Dep't of Va and N. Ca," [May or June 1864], and "Map showing the position of Government Farms 2nd Dist Negro Affairs Dep't of Va and N. Ca," [May or June 1864], Maps of Government Farms for Freedmen in Southeastern Virginia, ser. 691, Audiovisual Records, RG 56 [X-999]. The two maps were evidently created at the instance of Hanson A. Risley, supervising agent of the Treasury Department's 2nd Special Agency, whose jurisdiction embraced Union-occupied Virginia. On May 6, 1864, Risley requested from Colonel J. Burnham Kinsman, general superintendent of Negro affairs in the Department of Virginia and North Carolina, a "detailed statement" of those abandoned plantations in tidewater Virginia (except the eastern shore) that were occupied by former slaves, as well as "a Map with the abandoned plantations marked thereon"; on June 18, Kinsman sent Risley "two District Maps, of abandoned farms in Virginia." (H. A. Risley to Lt. Col. J. B. Kinsman, 6 May 1864, Letters, Orders, & Telegrams Received by Lt. Col. J. B. Kinsman, ser. 4108, Ft. Monroe VA Dept. of Negro Affairs, RG 105 [A-7848]; Lt. Col. J. B. Kinsman to Hon. H. A. Risley, 18 June 1864, Correspondence Received by the Supervising Special Agent, 7th Agency, RG 366 [Q-301].)

38: Supervising Agent of the Treasury Department 3rd Special Agency to the Secretary of the Treasury

New Berne N.C. May 20ᵗʰ 1864

Sir: A narrative of the organization of this Agency and of its operations for the last year would be a statement of continued anxiety, and labor, crowned at last by a success which has made the Agency a recognized power and an acknowledged benefit to this community, — as well as a source of no small revenue to the U.S. Treasury.

For four months, I was without Assistants, and my labors were excessive and incessant. My first and most difficult and delicate duty, was to secure a friendly and cordial cooperation from the military and naval authorities; without this, even the intention of Congress and your excellent Regulations founded thereon, to a great extent, must have been inoperative.

Previous to my arrival in North Carolina, in May 1863, the military were much embarrassed in controlling matters of trade, and the disposition of all abandoned property. You will readily conceive that many obstacles could be interposed to the easy or successful prosecution of my duties, notwithstanding the comprehensive orders issued by the War Department

I am happy to state that by a firm, but it is believed, a respectful assertion and maintenance of our official rights and duties, prejudice has been almost without exception, overcome; and the Departments of War, the Navy and the Treasury work together effectively and harmoniously. I am especially grateful in this connection to acknowledge the willing and earnest co-operation and aid always rendered me by Maj. Gen. John J. Peck, until quite recently commanding this District. Brig. Gen. I. N. Palmer, the present commander, is now, also, giving me a most cordial support.

. . . .

ABANDONED PLANTATIONS

By the following order of the Secretary of War N° 331 issued on the 9th of October last, all abandoned and deserted Lands and Plantations within our military lines in this State passed under the control of this Agency.

"War Department

Adjutant General's Office

General Orders }

N° 331 }

Washington October 9th 1863

1. All houses, tenements, lands and plantations, except such as may be required for military purposes, which have been or may be deserted and abandoned by insurgents within the lines of the military occupation of the United States forces, in states declared by Proclamation of the President to be in insurrection will hereafter be under the supervision and control of the Supervising Special Agents of the Treasury Department.

2. All commanders of military departments, districts and posts, will upon receipt of this Order, surrender and turn over to the proper Supervising Special Agent such houses, tenements, lands, and plantations, not required for military uses, as may be in their possession or under their control; and all officers of the Army of the United States will at all times render to the Agents appointed by the Secretary of the Treasury, all such aid as may be necessary to enable them to obtain possession of such houses, tenements, lands and plantations and to maintain their authority over the same

By Order of the Secretary of War

(Signed) E. D. Townsend

Assistant Adjutant General"

This important order necessarily involved new duties, and the attention of this Office has been largely engrossed with this important charge, devolving upon it, for the past six months. In determining what precise course to adopt in relation to these plantations, two problems presented themselves as important for consideration and solution.

First,

How can these estates of rebellious subjects and insurgents be made to yield the largest revenue for the support of the National Treasury in suppressing the present Rebellion?

Second

Can the attainment of this end be made to consist with the relief and benefit not only of the colored freedmen, but of white Union Refugees thrown into new economic and moral relations with our government by the events of the war?

Major Gen[l] Peck commanding the District at that time was fully consulted and concurred in the importance of the latter consideration, in view, especially, of the thousands of colored refugees crowded into the Cities and their suburbs and dependent in a measure upon the Commissary for their daily bread. The plan finally adopted by me with your sanction? was to lease the lands for one year in large or small parcels to such applicants, white and black, as seemed trustworthy and competent, and whose character thus enabled them to give a proper Bond, for the faithful discharge of their obligations. The purposes thus had in view have been embodied in the following plain but specific conditions, which enter into the bond exacted in every case

(Conditions of Bond.)[1]

First. – That the parties to this Bond are loyal to the United States Government. All of the premises and property so leased, shall be cultivated and worked in a proper manner so as to produce the best result for the Government and lessee, and at the same time result in as little injury to the premises and property as possible.

Second. – That due care shall be exercised in giving employment, with proper compensation, to such colored persons living on the premises as are industrious and able to labor, and that in the absence of a sufficient number of laborers to be found on the premises, proper efforts shall be used to obtain laborers, white and colored, from the towns and cities within the Federal military lines. Any unnecessary acts of severity, or of manifest injustice toward laborers, or acts of expressions of disloyalty, will subject the lease to cancellation.

Third. – That an account of the expenditures incurred and the results realized in managing and cultivating said property shall be kept as correctly as circumstances will admit.

Fourth. – That one equal fourth part of the productions realized by the cultivation and working of said property shall be properly gathered, prepared and delivered, ready for transportation, in due season, in charge of the Supervising Special Agent, or Assistant Special Agent, of the Third Special Agency, Treasury Department, aforesaid, or such other persons as may be authorized by either of said officers. Upon such delivery of one fourth, the remaining three fourths of said productions shall vest in the lessee.

Under this arrangement, about *eighty leases* have been issued to over a hundred lessees, a majority of them colored persons.

The extent of premises or privileges thus leased has varied from a single acre to "a one horse farm" (to use the parlance of this people) or an entire plantation. I have not hesitated to divide an estate or even the distinct privileges upon an estate where I could make arrangements more advantageous to the Government and more favorable to a needy and deserving lessee. Of the *pecuniary* results of this system to the Government, it is perhaps premature at this date, to speak, although I confess to very sanguine expectations. In the case of turpentine lands, the rents have just *begun* to accrue, – while Cotton and Corn Crops cannot be realized until the coming Autumn. A number of lessees have expended large sums in the cultivation of their lands, and should their expectations and my own be realized, and no unforeseen interference from the enemy occur, it is believed a very handsome sum for the Treasury will be realized from this source.

Of the social and moral results already achieved, I can speak with greater confidence. On offering the Plantations, a demand was created for laborers; not less than twelve hundred able bodied men were withdrawn from the crowded Cities and Towns and removed from the position of beneficiaries to that of self-reliant and self-supporting workers. So decided was this effect, that it led in some instances to a practical remonstance from the Military Authorities, who before had been anxious for relief from the care of this class of residents. A General Order was issued forbidding the payment of higher wages to laborers: than the amount paid for laborers in Military employ, which had already been fixed by the Department Commander at the sum paid the Colored Soldier.[2] This control of the wages of laborers in Civil service was strongly justified upon the ground of positive Military necessity, as it had become impossible to obtain sufficient men to work in the Quartermaster, and Commissary Departments. The superabundance of able bodied blacks had suddenly given place to a dearth of laborers.

Again, a large proportion of these plantation hands have families, so that it is quite safe to say that not less than 5000 freedmen, women and children have been and are now supported by the free and compensated labor policy, inaugurated, it may be said without presumption, under the auspices of this Office. From such estimates as we are enabled to make at present, the amount that will be distributed by lessees among these colored persons during the year, for labor and rations, will not fall short of *Two Hundred Thousand Dollars* ($200.000.^{00}). The superiority of a system which thus teaches the liberated slave, self reliance, and invests him at once with the responsibility of the support of himself and family, over any eleemosynary scheme which seems to regard him as a child or a pauper, and is too apt to encourage in him the old habit of dependence begotten in Slavery, must commend itself without argument to any patriotic man and intelligent friend of the race. I only regret that the danger of guerilla raids has restricted the field in which this experiment could be tried, to a very limited area, within this Agency. I am satisfied however with the result so far as it has developed itself and am most hopeful for the future.

. . . .

HLS   D. Heaton

Excerpts from D. Heaton to Hon. S. P. Chase, 20 May 1864, enclosed in D. Heaton to The Secretary of the Treasury, 31 May 1864, H-64 1864, Letters Received by the Division, ser. 315, Divison of Captured Property, Claims, & Land, RG 56 [X-74]. Approximately eight pages of an eighteen-page letter. The omitted portions discussed the establishment of the 3rd Special Agency, the regulation of commerce, and the rental of abandoned houses in New Berne, Beaufort, and Washington, North Carolina.

1 The enumerated conditions are in the form of a printed clipping attached to the page.
2 Paragraph 5 of General Order 46, issued by the commander of the Department of Virginia and North Carolina on December 5, 1863, had directed that the pay of black soldiers, $10 per month, be used as the standard for that of black military laborers. (See above, doc. 26.)

39: Report by the Superintendent of Negro Affairs in the 3rd District of the Department of Virginia and North Carolina

[*New Berne, N.C. July* 1864]

A Statement of the Stations occupied, and duties performed, by Capt. Horace James, A.Q.M. during the time, he has served in the Quartermaster's Department, up to June 30th 1864.

My Office is in New Berne, N.C, and there is my post office address; but my duties lie in every part of the State of N. Carolina which is held by the Union army. Consequently it has been necessary for me to visit frequently Beaufort, Roanoke Island, Plymouth, and Washington.

From New-Berne to Beaufort is 38 miles, from Newberne to Roanoke 130, from Newberne to Plymouth (by water) 190 miles. The property for which I am responsible is scattered over this whole region. My duties, as Superintendent of Negro Affairs, require that I should have assistants in each of these places, and constantly supervise their labors. This circumstance has made my work more arduous than it would otherwise have been. Early in the month of February, 1864, the enemy appeared before Newberne in formidable force, under the Rebel Gen[l] Pickett; drove in our outposts and compelled all, both white and colored, to retire within our inner line of defences. They then retired. But two months later they made another attack, and summoned the city to surrender. The commanding Gen[l] declined the summons, and the Rebels again withdrew.

During these movements of the enemy, the negros came flocking into town for protection, and I was especially busy in feeding, sheltering, and caring for their comfort, as well as in arming and organizing some fifteen hundred of the men to aid in the defence of the city.

After these warlike movements were over, I was ordered to bring all the negros in the settlements outside the town within our line of fortifications, and lay out for them a stationary camp, which was done at once. A village of not less than one thousand houses, constructed in a neat and orderly manner, though very cheaply, now covers the sandy spot of perhaps 100 acres assigned to this camp, and shelters a refugee population of not less than (5000) five thousand souls. Not more than one fourth (1/4) of these, however, are supplied with rations from the government.

Towards the dependent negros and families of colored soldiers throughout the District, I am obliged to perform the duties of a Commissary of Subsistence, but I make no returns to the Commissary Department.

Immediately after the disturbances in New-Berne, which excited at the north serious apprehensions for the safety of this city, a still more determined attack was made on the town of Plymouth, (the Ram "Albemarle" being at the same time sent down the Roanoke river), which resulted in the capture of the town. No Quartermaster's property was lost there for which I am responsible. A portion of the negros escaped to Roanoke Island, New Berne, and Beaufort, some where cruelly murdered, others sent back to their former masters in the interior. This was on or about the 20th of April, 1864.

Ten days later it was thought prudent to evacuate Washington. This was done while I was absent at Norfolk whither I had gone by order of the Q.M. Gen[l] to report, as an A.Q.M, to Gen[l] Butler for duty. Being ordered by him to resume my former position and duties, I arrived in Newbern May 1st to find nearly the whole population of Washington, white and colored, landing upon its piers. I made immediate provision for the temporary shelter of (3000) three thousand negros, by drawing worn and condemned tents for them, which were duly issued and expended for their use.

I regret to say that in bringing the people away from Washington my assistant there was compelled to leave behind, to fall into rebel hands, the following list of property, nearly all of which had been inspected & condemned, and turned over to me as such for the use of the negros.

(16)	Sixteen Horses –	(condemned)
(6)	Six Mules	(")
(7)	Seven Oxen	
(6)	Collars	(")
(6)	Carts	(")
(5)	Cart Harnesses	(")
(10)	Lead Harnesses	(")
(10)	Wheel "	(")

The oxen above mentioned were captured from the enemy; and were being used in logging and lumbering, and making ready for the culture of a large tract of land in cotton and corn, all which had to be abandoned on the evacuation of the town.

The large Steam Saw mill on Roanoke Island, was nearly completed before the 30th June 1864, (now finished) and will be of great advantage to the troops that garrison the island, as well as to the contrabands. The funds for this were mostly contributed by private charity. The negro labor employed in erecting it was met by the Quartermaster's Department.

The amount and variety of my personal labors is very great. From the nature of my employment and the ignorance and helplessness of the people of whom I have charge, I am compelled to do many things that other officers can entrust to clerks. Permit me modestly to say that in addition to performing the secular duties of my office, which occupy my attention by day and until late at night without intermission, I have also performed the proper duties of a *chaplain*, preaching every sabbath before a large audience of Officers, soldiers and civilians, with not a little visitation of the sick, and service at funerals of my brother officers and fellow-soldiers. I have the honor to be Very respectfully, yours,

HDS   Horace James

"A Statement of the Stations occupied, and duties performed, by Capt. Horace James," [July 1864], Annual, Personal, & Special Reports of Quartermaster Officers, ser. 1105, Personnel, RG 92 [Y-503]. In April 1864, in the midst of the Confederate attack on Plymouth, David Heaton, supervising agent of the Treasury Department's 3rd Special Agency, had warned the Secretary of the Treasury that more effective military protection was needed for the plantations and farms under treasury control: "The free labor system has received special encouragement within the last few months, and it seems deplorable that the excellent results arising therefrom should be demolished for the want of a few thousand more troops." (D. Heaton to Hon. Salmon P. Chase, 19 Apr. 1864, H-35 1864, Letters Received by the Division, ser. 315, Division of Captured Property, Claims, & Land, RG 56 [X-52].)

40: North Carolina Freedmen to the Commander of the Department of Virginia and North Carolina

Bermuda Hundred's V.A. Septm 1864

Sir, you will pardon us for troubling you with this report, but knowing you to be a Gentleman of Justice and a friend to the Negro race in this country, we take the liberty to send you the following facts.

Forty five of us Colored people, worked for four months throughing up breast work's at Roanoke Island. Augt 31st we were told to report at head quarters to be paid. we went according to orders. when we got there, a guard of soldiers was put over us, and we marched on board a steamer, at the point of the bayonet. we were told the paymaster was on board the steamer, to pay us, then we was to go to Fortress Munroe. then told that we was going to Dutch Gap to be paid. true we was on the way to Dutch Gap to work on the canal.

guards were then sent over the Island to take up every man that could be found indiscriminately young and old sick and well. the soldiers broke into the coulored people's house's taken sick men out of bed. men that had sick wives, and men that had large family's of children and no wife or person to cut wood for them or take care of them, were taken, and not asked one question or word about going, had we been asked to go to dutch gap a large number would have gone without causeing the suffering that has been caused, we are willing to go where our labour is wanted and we are ready at any time to do all we can for the goverment at any place and feel it our duty to help the goverment all we can, but goverment dont know the treatment we receive from Sup^{t}s of contrabands.

we have not been paid for our work don at Roanoke, consequently our wives and family's are there suffering for clothes. Captn James has paid us for only two months work this year, the month's of Febuary and January. No one knows the injustice practiced on the negro's at Roanoke, our garden's are plundere'd by the white soldiers. what we raise to surport ourselves with is stolen from us, and if we say any thing about it we are sent to the guard house. rations that the goverment allows the contrabands are sold to

the white secech citizen's, and got out the way at night. its no
uncommon thing to see weman and children crying for something to
eat, Old clothes sent to the Island from the North for contraband's
are sold to the white secesh sitizen's, by the sss^{tn} Superintendant Mr
Sanderson,

Genl these thing's are not gesse'd at but things that can be
prove'd by those that saw them, and many more things that we can
prove, Captn James. does not look after things, so Mr Sanderson
has his own way   he now talk's of sending two hundred weman
from Roanoke, then our family's will be sent one way and we in
another direction, most of the weman there are soldiers wives sent
there by Genl Wild for protection, must they be sent away when
their husbands are in the army fighting. we humbley ask you to
look into these things, and do something for the negro's at Roanoke
Island   we remain your humble servants

    Ned Baxter
    Saml Owen's
    and forty three other contrabands from Roanoke Island *N.C.*

HLSr

[*Endorsement*]   Hd Qs 18th A.C.   Oct 6th 1864   I have the honor to
state that quite a number or contrabands were employed at Roanoke
Island to work on Fortifications, and that they have not been
paid. Gen. Weitzel has made repeated applications to the Chief
Engr for funds to make these payments but he has not succeeded in
obtaining them— About four weeks ago Capt. Martin came to
North Carolina to obtain laborers and, in order to obtain them in
the shortest poss[ible] time it was thought best to take the gang
which had been at work on fortifications. As these men had not
been paid and were very much in need of clothing &c. I took the
responsibility of giving them certificates of ind[eb]tedness which
enabled them to draw clothing and which will assist in identifying
them when the funds come to pay them. They were brought away
by force but I think no one was authorized to tell them they were to
be paid or practice any other deception complained of— Capt.
Martin can doubtless give any other information in regard to the
within petition— Respectfully submitted W. R. King 1st Lt US.
Engrs

Ned Baxter et al. to Major Genl. Butler, Sept. 1864, Miscellaneous Letters &
Reports Received, ser. 5076, Dept. of VA & NC & Army of the James, RG
393 Pt. 1 [C-3041]. Other endorsements. Both signatures are in the same
handwriting as the body of the document. Next to his name, Baxter indicated

that he was "working for Captn Walbridge A.A.Q.M, Bermuda 100's"; Owens, that he was "working for Captn Bayley 37 USC Troops 1ˢᵗ Brg 3 Dev 18 A. Core Wilsons landing." The impressment of black men from Roanoke Island in late August 1864 was part of a wider effort to obtain laborers in North Carolina for work in Virginia. At the instance of General Benjamin F. Butler, commander of the Department of Virginia and North Carolina, Lieutenant William R. King and Captain Frederick Martin (the latter an aide to Butler) had gone to Roanoke Island "for the purpose of procuring all the colored laborers it is possible to get together for duty" with Butler's army. On August 29, General Innis N. Palmer, commander of the District of North Carolina, had instructed the federal commander on the island that "every such man that can be spared should go," including those at work on the fortifications. Palmer had promised that the laborers would receive wages of $16 per month, plus rations, and that "their families would be provided for during their absence," but he had also insisted that "[i]f these men cannot be persuaded to go willingly they must go." On August 31, military officials had begun to impress black men at both Roanoke Island and New Berne. Writing to General Butler's headquarters on September 1 – and apparently responding to "the complaints of outsiders" – Palmer had justified his resort to force: "The matter has been fairly explained to the contrabands, and they have been treated with the utmost consideration, but they will not go willingly." "I am aware," he acknowledged, "that this may be considered a harsh measure, but at such a time we must not stop at trifles." (*Official Records*, ser. 1, vol. 42, pt. 2, pp. 411, 590, 610–11, 654.)

41: Secretary of the New York and Brooklyn Freedmen's Employment Bureau to the General Superintendent of Negro Affairs in the Department of Virginia and North Carolina

Brooklyn N.Y. Nov. 19, 1864.

Dear Sir— The Association which I represent has undertaken to look after the numerous Freedmen and Ex slaves who are, in various ways, making their way to this city and N. York—

Our plan of operations is simply this—

By advertising in the proper channels we seek out a class of humane and Christian families who express a sympathy for the blacks and a desire to employ them.

We record the names *only* of those who engage to board, clothe and instruct them in the useful offices of domestic life and to make provision for their being instructed to read, and of being taken to church, Sunday School & We have a very large number of families of this character, both in the city and country ready to receive them on these terms. We could easily place a thousand in a week—where they would be comfortably provided for, and, in many respects, would be greatly improved in all kinds of useful knowledge –

We have most favorable reports from those whom we have thus disposed of, and could point out some remarkable cases of improvement –

Of the fifty whom you brought on the 6th of August not *one*, so far as we know, has failed to find a good home through our Agency, and we are continually hearing most encouraging reports from them. If the opposers of our work could see the contrast these poor girls present in their present condition to the condition they were in when they came here, their objections would be greatly modified –

So of others whom we are continually rescuing from degradation as we find them in the streets or as they are sent to us by humane persons who gather them up from the low haunts where they are driven by want –

The arguments in favor of large numbers being sent up here are various

1st It releives the government of supporting them – I am sure 10,000 could easily find good places in this city and in the N. England States and earn their own living –

2^{d} It would save a vast amount of suffering – For with all the care of the government they cannot be made as comfortable in the unsettled state of things South at present, as they can be in the homes they would have here –

3^{d} It is a good educational idea – A residence of only a few months in our free states will be of very great service in lifting them up into a higher civilization than they have ever known – Some things they can learn better here, by direct contact with our best christian society, than could be taught them by instructors sent to them from here – Of course this can be done only to a fraction of the whole number, for the great work of teaching and civilizing them must, in the main, be done at the South – But a few thousand, brought to the North and then, after a year or two or three returned to the South, would be valuable teachers to their race –

All these arguments you have considered before – and I only mention them as being illustrated and confirmed by practical observation of what is now seen among large numbers now scattered about in some of the best families in this and other neighborhoods –

There are several prominent citizens of New York and Brooklyn who have taken great interest in our work and who are ready to endorse us – Among them are Mr. Horace Greely, The Mayor of Brooklyn, Postmaster Lincoln – Senator Strong – Mr. H. W. Beecher and others of like character.

If it is possible to convince the proper authorities of the *benefit* to the blacks, – of the present relief to the government – and of the advantage to the North of their labor, I suppose we might have some hundreds of them brought up here this fall. The *demand* is immense. We have had in five months, not less than 1500 applications for them – 1000 of which applications come from good families –

If you think favorably of our making another attempt to get up a few loads, or *one* load this Fall, please inform me what would be the best mode of proceedure to get the permission.

Our plan is briefly this – If a vessel leaves Norfolk let a telegraphic dispatch inform me immediately – I should then fill out blanks to send to the parties who are ready to take them. (A specimen of the blank I enclose.)

At the appointed time the parties will be supplied with tickets to go on board the boat (which would come directly to a Brooklyn wharf) and select and take home the freedwoman or boy wanted, immediately. In this way a vessel load of 200 could be disposed of in 3 or 4 hours.

I shall write to Mr. Woodbury and Capt. Wilder so as to reach as many of you gentlemen, who have influence, as possible –

Any suggestions you can give will be thankfully received –

Should you favor the project, do you think it would be of any advantage for me to come down myself? Very respectfully yours,

ALS   Oliver S. St. John –

Oliver S. St. John to Col. J. B. Kinsman, 19 Nov. 1864, Letters, Orders, & Telegrams Received by Lt. Col. J. B. Kinsman, ser. 4108, Ft. Monroe VA Dept. of Negro Affairs, RG 105 [A-7847]. The blank form said to have been enclosed is not in the file. Demand for black domestic servants of Southern origin ran high in northeastern cities throughout 1864. In July, William G. Hawkins, secretary of the executive committee of the New York-based National Freedman's Relief Association, ventured that if "a shipload of 500, or 800 females adult would be landed here or at New Haven or Boston . . . good homes could be procured for them all. The demand here is so great that they could in a short time make their own terms as to wages." In late August, an officer of the Pennsylvania Abolition Society, who had already hired one group of Virginia freedpeople to employers in Philadelphia, reported having "100 or more" requests for servants on file, with "fresh applications for them daily." "If a little care is used in selecting those sent forward," he predicted, "no trouble will be found in getting places for a large number." (Wm. G. Hawkins to Lt. Col. J. B. Kinsman, 2 July 1864, and Jos. M. Truman Jr. to Respected Friend, 11 June 1864, 31 Aug. 1864, Letters, Orders, & Telegrams Received by Lt. Col. J. B. Kinsman, ser. 4108, Ft. Monroe VA Dept. of Negro Affairs, RG 105 [A-7847].)

42: Superintendent of Negro Affairs in the 2nd District of the Department of Virginia and North Carolina to the General Superintendent of Negro Affairs in the Department

Norfolk Va. Dec. 9th 1864

Major. In obedience to orders received from Department Head Quarters, I have the honor to transmit herewith the Report of Negro Affairs for the Second District, for the year ending December 5th 1864

The following table will show the number of persons within the District at the beginning of the year; and the number received from beyond our lines since.

No. of persons in the District Dec. 5th 1863				
No. over 14 yrs. of age	No. under 14 yrs. of age	Males	Females	Total
11641	9564	10932	10273	21205

No. received from beyond our lines during the year				
No. over 14 yrs of age	No. under 14 yrs of age	Males	Females	Total.
2039	1606	2114	1531	3645
Total				24850

As nearly as can be ascertained, the number of births and deaths among the colored population in the District during the year is about equal.

In carrying out the policy indicated in Genl. Order, No. 46,[1] the entire colored population of the District, is naturally divided into three classes.

The first class, numbering twelve thousand four hundred and sixty nine, (12469) is composed of those who provide for themselves; choosing their own field of labor, and requiring no other aid or protection from Government, than that impartial execution of Military law, that secures the rights of property and labor to both white and black. This class is the main industrial force of the District; and is largely represented in every department of business. Among its members are found servants in private families and hotels; drivers of carriages and carts; hands on Steamboats and Sailing vessels; market men; farm laborers; lessees of small farms; oyster men and fishermen. They also perform a large amount of labor for Government, in the Engineer, Commissary, and Quartermasters Departments.

Many of them are skillful mechanics; and *all* are employed at good wages.

About one thousand acres of abandoned land have been rented to the Freedmen of this class, in lots of eight or ten acres each. For the cultivation of this land the necessary seeds, implements, and teams, have been provided by Government; the occupant paying one third of the crop for rent. Many of them have supported their families out of the proceeds of their labor for the farmers in their neighborhood, thus having their share of the crop raised on this land as the profit for their seasons work.

To prevent the making of "injurious and unconscionable contracts", as well as to provide the colored laborer and white employer with written evidence of thier terms of agreement, the accompanying blank form of contract, (marked L.) has been successfully used; one copy being furnished to each of the parties, and one filed in the office of the Superintendent.

Soldiers and thier families, numbering seven thousand six hundred and seventeen, (7617) constitute the second class. Over four thousand (4000) colored soldiers have been enlisted within the District; most of them under Genl. Order No. 46, which gave them a bounty of ten dollars ($10.) and ten dollars ($10) per month. By the provisions of this order subsistence is furnished to the families of enlisted men; the number of persons thus supplied with rations, is three thousand six hundred and seventeen; (3617) the cost to the Government for this subsistence, is one hundred and forty five thousand six hundred and eleven dollars and twenty six cents 145611,26. (Abs C.) Although Congress has increased the pay of the colored soldiers,[2] thier families still receive the subsistence promised in this Order. It has also been necessary to furnish many of this class with fuel, quarters, and clothing; they not having received any of the pay, for this purpose, from the soldiers who should support them. The Taylor farm on Little Bay, has been assigned to these families. One hundred and twenty six (126) houses have been built for them; to each house is attached one and one half acres of land, which the occupants are allowed to cultivate on thier own account. Efforts are now being made to provide suitable employment for these persons. As the cost to the Government for the support of the families of colored soldiers is a part of the bounty promised the recruit for enlistment, it cannot, in justice, be charged against the Negros of the District.

The third class numbering four thousand seven hundred and sixty four, (4764) includes all that remain; and comprises all, except soldiers families, that are dependent on the Government for labor or subsistence. It is made up mostly of disabled men, women, and children, and is continually recruited by refugees from beyond our lines, who come into the District without immediate means of support, and require temporary aid. An extensive Rope Walk has been fitted up as quarters for these persons, and will accommodate fifteen hundred. (1500). They are placed here until otherwise provided for. From these refugees, the able bodied and most industrious, are soon taken, either by the recruiting officer, or by offers of good wages; they with thier families passing into the first or second class, leaving only the women, children and disabled men behind.

As the ratio of this class to the whole colored population, shows the capacity of the freedmen for self support, it may not be out of place to state that, notwithstanding the great amount of property owned by *white* citizens, within the District; a larger percentage of thier number than of the colored population, receive aid from Government. In providing subsistence for this (third) class, all applications for aid are thoroughly investigated, and only such rations or parts of rations are furnished, as the applicants could not by thier own labor, provide for themselves. To prevent suffering for want of food, the teachers of colored schools act as a committee for thier respective School Districts, and report all cases of destitution that may occur.

The cost of the subsistence furnished by the Government to this class, during the year, is one hundred and six thousand one hundred and thirteen dollars and twenty five cents ($106113.25) (Abs. C.) or less than seven (7) cents a day for each person; being eighty six thousand nine hundred and six dollars and thirty two cents ($86906.32) (Abs. C.) less than the value of the full rations allowed by Genl. Order No. 30 of the War Department. Jany. 25th 1864.[3]

Beleiving the first and most important lesson to be taught the Freedmen; to be the providing for thier own physical necesities, without being dependent on Government or others, all available means have been used to provide for this class suitable employment; the proceeds of which should reimburse the Government for the subsistence furnished. The necessary military occupation of the District and the attendent uncertainty of the ordinary business operations of civil life, have made this exceedingly difficult. To overcome these obstacles, to avoid the demoralization of camp life, and to avail ourselves of the only source of labor within our reach, possession has been taken of all the abandoned farms within the District, and about eight thousand (8000) acres of land have been placed under cultivation. Comfortable houses have been erected, and such as were able to work, have, as far as possible been provided with employment.

As neither the character of the labor employed, or the tenure by which these lands were held, would warrent the expenditure for such fertilizers as were necessary for the successful cultivation of early vegetables, (the most profitable crop in this locality,) most of the land has been devoted to corn, as the crop best adapted to the soil and the help employed: but owing to the extreme drought during the summer, not more than half the average crop was produced.

Early in the occupation of these lands hostile demonstrations on the part of the inhabitants in their vicinity, made it necessary to procure arms for the protection of the property on the farms, and thier occupants.

This was done; and all the men and boys capable of bearing arms, were drilled in thier use, and have now become an efficient Militia force.

The superintendency of the labor on the farms, has been performed partly by disabled soldiers, and partly by civilians employed for that purpose. Much of the farm labor has been performed by women; the men being mostly engaged in manufacturing staves and lumber and chopping wood. The lumber and wood not required for Negro Affairs, have been turned over to the Q.M. Department. Two fisheries have also been worked. These have aided largely in the saving of rations, besides paying to Government over sixteen hundred dollars ($1600) in money. The necessary team work for carrying on the farming, wood and lumber operations, has been performed by condemned horses, turned over to Negro affairs by the Quartermasters Department. The bad condition of these animals occasioned much delay in preparing the ground for crops, and has proved the truth of the farmers maxim, that "cheap horses are dear"; large numbers have died, but careful management has increased the value of those remaining to more than that of the whole when first turned over to Negro Affairs.

The necessary forage has been drawn partly from the Quartermasters Department, and partly produced on the farms. The large amount of forage consumed in proportion to the work performed, has materially affected the pecuniary results of the business of the District. As shown in the accompanying Summary and Abstracts, the value of the property produced during the year by the Negros of this class, exceeds the amount expended for them, twenty two thousand nine hundred and seventy three dollars and sixty seven cents ($22973.67)

Beleiving it to be as essential to the freedom of the colored race, – to releace them from the ignorance, vice, and dependence, that necessarily belonged to thier former condition of servitude, as to release them from the servitude itself, the object of all efforts and regulations in the District have been to aid and encourage them to help themselves; to leave them as far as possible to thier own resources; to teach them that freedom from slavery is not freedom from labor; and that they cannot become really free, until thier dependence upon Government or upon charity for support shall cease.

For the successful prosecution of this work we are largely indebted to the various benevolent societies of the North; which have not only aided the Negros by a judicious distribution of such charities as they needed; but have afforded more important aid, by the sending of intelligent and sympathizing persons to labor among them as teachers and counselors.

These Societies have also sent a large amount of clothing into the District. As most of this has been sent to thier agents, and distributed by them, it has been impossible to ascertain its value. A system has recently been adopted, by which all clothing sent for gratuitous distribution is received into one storehouse, where it is appraised classified and numbered. The teachers of colored schools act as local committees of distribution, in thier respective School Districts, the whole being under the supervision of a General Committee. By this system the value of the clothing can be ascertained; an equal distribution to all parts of the District secured; and the evil of giving to those who can provide for themselves avoided: as each teacher can readily ascertain the necessities of all person, in his or her School District.

A store has been opened in Norfolk and one on the Dozier farm for the sale of goods at cost prices. The keepers of these stores are not allowed to sell to any persons but Negros; and to those only for thier own use. They are required to make a monthly exhibit of thier business, and to keep a correct record of the names of all persons to whom sales are made, and the prices at which the goods are sold.

Under the auspices of the Benevolent societies before named, schools for colored children had been established and were in successful operation; but no regular system of education embracing all the colored children within the District was organized until October 1st, 1864. At that time the whole territory was divided into School Districts; School houses were prepared; and a sufficient number of teachers were sent from the North by these Societies to furnish one to each school of fifty scholars. Schools are now opened in nearly all the Districts; and about four thousand (4000) children are attending them.

Besides day schools, several evening schools have been established for adults, and hundreds who one year ago did not know a letter of the alphabet can now read and write. Teachers have been furnished by Government with fuel, quarters, and rations. The concurrent testimony of *all* engaged in teaching the Negros, has established the fact, that they can learn to read and write as readily as white children.

The Marine Hospital at Ferry Point has been used as an Asylum for Orphan Children; of which one hundred and eighty six (186) have been received during the year; of this number sixty seven (67) have been sent North, where they have been provided with good homes.

Respectfully submitted with accompanying Abstracts. Very Respectfully Your obt. Servant,

HLS   O Brown

Capt. O. Brown to Maj. George J. Carney, 9 Dec. 1864, enclosed in Lt. Col. Horace Porter to Brevet Major Gen. John W. Turner, 24 Mar. 1865, filed as V-87 1865, Letters Received, ser. 12, RG 94 [K-118]. The blank contract ("L"), said to have been enclosed, is in the same file, as is "Abstract C," a month-by-month account of rations drawn and issued by Captain Brown during 1864.

1 For the order, issued by the commander of the Department of Virginia and North Carolina on December 5, 1863, see above, doc. 26.

2 On June 15, 1864, Congress had provided that black soldiers receive the same pay as white soldiers of equal rank, retroactive to January 1, 1864. Five days later, it had increased the pay of all Union soldiers, black and white, effective May 1, 1864. Under the two acts, the pay of a black private was $13 per month beginning January 1, and $16 per month beginning May 1. (See *Freedom*, ser. 2: p. 367.)

3 The order had established the amounts of various foodstuffs that would constitute the ration issued "to adult refugees and to adult colored persons, commonly called 'contrabands,' when they are not employed at labor by the Government, and who may have no means of subsisting themselves." The ration included ten ounces of pork or bacon, or one pound of fresh beef per day; one pound of corn meal five times a week, and one pound of flour or soft bread, or twelve ounces of hard bread, twice a week; plus smaller amounts of beans, peas, or hominy, salt, sugar, vinegar, and potatoes ("when practicable"); as well as soap and candles. Women and children were also to receive "roasted rye coffee" or tea. (*Official Records*, ser. 3, vol. 4, pp. 44–45.)

43: Superintendent of Negro Affairs in the 1st District of the Department of Virginia and North Carolina to the General Superintendent of Negro Affairs in the Department

Fort Monroe, Va. December 30th 1864.

Major, In obedience to your request, I have the honor to submit the following Report of operations in Department Negro Affairs, in the

First District Department Va and No. Ca., for the year ending December 4th, 1864.

This District, which in January last, had a colored population of Ten thousand five hundred and forty-nine persons; according to a census just completed, now has in it, Thirteen thousand three hundred and five such persons; distributed as follows; –

Census Colored Population in First District
Dept. Va & No. Ca. December 4th 1864.

Counties.	Males.		Females.		Total.
	Under 14 years.	Over 14 years.	Under 14 years.	Over 14 years.	
James City.	49	109	42	99	299
York.	877	1304	869	1577	4627
Warwick.	93	191	96	176	556
Elizabeth City.	1504	2018	1502	2799	7823
	2523	3622	2509	4651	13,305

This is a gain in ten months of Two thousand eight hundred and fifty-six persons, or eleven hundred twenty one males, and seventeen hundred thirty five females. This increase is made by the refugees who are constantly fleeing from their rebel masters, and seeking protection within our lines, as the drain on the male colored population from enlistments in the Army and Navy, added to the number of deaths has fully equalled the number of births.

Between the first day of March, and the fourth day of December, the number of refugees registered as arriving at Fort Monroe, was eighteen hundred and eleven. Five hundred have come in at Newport News, since the establishment there, of the Camp for Colored recruits – a space of about three months.

They also cross the lines in large numbers in the vicinity of Williamsburg. The number of able-bodied men, who have come into this District the past year, and not entered the service of the United States, is very small; as far as can be ascertained, not exceeding two hundred.

These new arrivals are women and children and old men; all needing the generous aid of Government, in the first few months of their freedom.

. . . .

Sixteen hundred and seventeen persons, or five hundred fourteen adults, and eleven hundred three children, – members of families dependent upon soldiers and sailors in the United States service, – are now receiving rations, as provided by General Orders No. 46 Head Quarters Dept. Va. & No. Ca. Series 1863.[1] The subsistence so provided being part of the soldiers pay, and not an expense incidental to the Department Negro Affairs, its cost is deducted from the total value of all the rations issued in this District for the year, leaving the sum of Ninety thousand four hundred fifty six dollars and seventeen cents – the expense to the Commissary Department for the support of this people for the year.

As far as possible to make the Negro self-supporting, and place him in a condition to remain so, has been the policy adopted and maintained in this District. That seventy-eight per cent of the adult colored population in it – all of whom less than four years ago were in slavery. – are now independent of assistance, fully shows its success.

Early in the year 1862, Major General Wool, then commanding this Department, was induced to authorize the colored people to locate upon, and cultivate the abandoned lands in and beyond Hampton. This course was fully sanctioned by the Secretary of War, and by Congress. That year, owing to the bitter hostility of subordinate Government officials, little was accomplished by it. The Spring of 1863 found hundreds of the negroes scattered about upon the plantations in extreme destitution, many of them being at the point of starvation. After a little assistance, with the promise of protection, and the stimulus of having a share of the crops raised, for their own benefit, they were encouraged to work. They were supplied with such stock, tools &c, as could possibly be got for them. Instead of issuing to them rations, they were furnished with such subsistence as they needed, and it was charged against their share of the crop. That year, they much more than supported themselves, and generally had enough to supply their wants until the following Spring. The plan proved successful. This year, with much more liberal means, notwithstanding the drougth, and another obstacle, now most fortunately removed, it has been pursued with far greater results.

Eighty-five plantations in the District have been thus cultivated, either wholly or in part. Many of those hireing farms preferring to pay their rent in money, forty of the farms have been so let, producing a rental of Four thousand three hundred sixty-two dollars and twenty one cents.

Of the others, thirteen have been rented to them at the halves, one at a third, thirty at a quarter, and one at a fifth of their crops; the terms varying according to the quality of the soil, the buildings upon the plantations, and the assistance in the way of tools, teams, seeds &c, furnished. These supplies are provided by special agreement, and a lien is had upon the crops, until all dues are paid.

A general but thorough supervision is had over all their operations; they are visited often, always with encouraging words and suggestions, when doing well, but with firm correction of all abuses.

Three hundred and eighty five horses, thirty two mules, one hundred sets of harnesses, and thirty wagons, — condemned property, furnished by the Quarter Master's Department — have been used on these plantations. No forage has been drawn from Government for these animals, nor have the negroes cultivating the lands received rations from it, for themselves or families. The stock on hand — corn and fodder, the result of operations in 1863 — has been issued to them and payment received, either in cash, or in kind, since their crops have been secured.

The end of the year finds them out of debt, a supply of corn on hand sufficient to meet all their wants for some time to come, and more than all, with a feeling of independence — a self reliant knowledge that they can take care of themselves — all gained by the year's experience.

Most of those assisted the present year, have already leased their land for the year coming, and generally at a cash rent. The aid extended to them heretofore, they are able to dispense with, in favor of new beginners, whose needs are greater.

In the Fall of 1863, it was found necessary to procure some place for an asylum, for the large number of the old and infirm of both sexes, who need assistance, and of whom, from their age and infirmities, it cannot reasonably be expected that they will ever be able to support themselves. The want of such accommodation being at that time pressing and immediate, the "Downey Plantation" — the depot for supplies for plantation operations in this District — offering the best advantages for such purposes, was taken for this use. The large tobacco warehouse upon it was renovated and repaired, and has since been occupied by this class of persons.

This year the farm on which it is located, has been cultivated in behalf of the United States, thereby furnishing employment for such ones gathered there, as are able to work. They have been paid for their labor, at a rate of wages, corresponding to the services respectively rendered. This has encouraged habits of industry among them, and taught them that even with infirmities, it was more honorable to work, than "to eat the bread of idleness." About six hundred acres on this farm have been cultivated by their labor, and have produced the following income, — to wit; —

5000 Bu. Shelled Corn,	@	1.50	7500.00
500 " Oats,		1.00	500.00
500 " Turnips,		.50	250.00
70 Tons Fodder,		20.00	1400.00
50 Bbls. Potatoes,		4.00	200.00
Broom Corn Seed,			250.00
Estimated value of Crop raised.			$ 10,100.00

Expenditures, –		
For Seeds and Tools	1681.55	
Labor (paid by Q.M. Dept.)	4654.99	6,336.54
Net Income		$3763.46

. . . .

Schools.

Increased facilities are being daily afforded for the education of the colored people. Since my semi-annual Report in June last, there have been established in this District, twelve schools, with an increase of twenty-two teachers, and eight hundred and twenty-three scholars. It has now eighteen Day Schools, and eleven Night Schools. The following statement presents some statistics in regard to them.

Report of Schools for Colored People, in the First District, Dept. Va & No. Ca. December 4th 1864.								
Location		No. of Day Schools.	Teachers.			Average No. of Scholars –	Night School	
			Male.	Female.	Total		No.	Scholars
Eliz. City County	Fort Monroe	1		2	2	67	1	112
	Hampton,	5	2	7	9	567	2	250
	Camp Hamilton.	1	1	4	5	225	1	150
	Newport News.	1	1	1	2	65		
	Downey Farm.	1	1	2	3	100	1	not giv
	Vaughn Farm,	1		3	3	65	1	80
	Whiting Farm,	1	1		1	30	1	50
York County.	Yorktown.	4		6	6	388	2	80
	Darlington Farm.	1	1	1	2	65		
	Bellefield Farm.	1	1		1	30	1	20
	Williamsburg.	1	1		1	50	1	60
Total.		18	9	26	35	1652	11	802

The Teachers in these schools are sent here and supported by Northern Benevolent Societies, the "American Missionary Association," and the "Friends Association for the Relief of Colored Freedmen," being largely represented in this work. The latter

Society has had especial charge of the schools at Yorktown, and has been very efficient in their management.

In Hampton, under the superintendence of Mr. Charles P. Day — whose pioneer labors in behalf of the educational interests of the colored people, there began, three years since — the schools have been graded, and with much benefit to both teacher and pupil. Commencing with the alphabetical school, after attaining there, a certain degree of proficiency, the child is transferred to the next higher, and thus on. This systematizes the labors of the teacher, and in the prospect of advancement furnished to the scholar, an incentive to study, and regularity of attendance. For the schools at this place, the services of a competent and successful teacher of Vocal Music have recently been secured, and already the progress of the children in this civilizing and refining branch of education, has been very rapid.

Throughout the District, the colored people have sought with alacrity, the advantages afforded them for improvement, and their progress in learning to read, spell and write, has been very gratifying. The children, for the most part, do not show that dullness, which so often characterizes the adults, but are smart, bright and quick to learn, and one can scarcely observe any difference in the rate of progress, between them, and so many white children.

The Management of the Freedmen.

The dogma of the "Lords of the Lash," that negroes are very valuable as slaves, but when free, worthless, and unable to take care of themselves, is now exploded. On the contrary, it makes all the difference, in the result of their labors, whether they are forced, or encouraged to work.

Anything resembling "overseeing," they dread, hence the policy of carrying on Plantation operations with them, substantially as farming is done at the North.

It is a very mistaken and unjust way, to use the negro as we do tools and cattle, — renting them out, or working them under task-masters, to see how much can be made out of them as in slavery; or giving them only an acre or two of land, to get a living upon, and forcing them to stay there, as is done in some districts, thus leaving them, a few years hence, not only discouraged and disheartened, but also about as poor as when they left their masters. This is cruel, and entirely needless, when there are thousands of acres of good unoccupied lands, near and safe for occupation, awaiting cultivation.

It is often stated, how much has been made in the employment of negroes by the Government, on plantations, and in other ways, with little or no evidence shown of how much they have drawn from the Government in the way of subsistence, clothing, etc.

If they are worked and fed by the Government, and not paid half enough to support their families, and are clothed by charity, what follows to them, but perpetual poverty, and to the benevolent, unending contributions, while the Government expends two dollars, and receives one.

I maintain that the paramount object of our labors, is the elevation of the colored race, and that it may be made to secure greater economy to the Government, than merely working them for a profit. Modes may vary, but the end sought, never.

This work of preparing an hitherto enslaved race for freedom, is second only to that of liberating it, and the elevation of the Negro depends upon the influences brought to bear upon him, as he throws off his shackles, and steps forth a freeman. Where friends inculcate the virtues essential to their elevation, by teaching, preaching, and living among them in the practice of all they teach and preach, there is steady progress daily perceptible. There the marriage relation is honored, the Sabbath kept, as never before, and vice and crime disappear. Hence the great difference in classes and camps, where these reformatory influences are unfelt and unknown.

In regard to their morals, remember the school in which they have been brought up. Yet no other people that I have ever seen, are so impressible to the teachings of the Gospel, and yield so readily to its restraining power.

Labor is money, and it is now generally conceded that the labor of one freeman, is worth that of two slaves. To wean the negro from all bad habits and practices, by presenting to him a good example, by showing him "a more excellent way," and impressing upon him the truth that "Knowledge is power," and that what is being done for him, by friends and the Government, is designed to reform and elevate him, and at the same time, make him prosperous and respectable, must be our first step.

The negro is a natural imitator, and will do almost anything he sees a white man do, and therefore the wonderful influence and inducement of example.

What is needed is, to have experienced business men, and practical farmers, fully in sympathy with the work, live and labor among them, introducing the modern improvements in labor, making industry respected in the sight of all classes, so that by precept and example, they may learn what is for their highest good, and thus become inspired with the true idea of liberty, and learn that if it is to be enjoyed by them, they must be fitted for it, and made worthy of it.

This with the excellent educational and religious privileges so liberally provided by Northern friends, will not only fully determine the status of the negro, but convince an unbelieving world that the colored race are capable of self-support and elevation to citizenship, with all its responsibilities, but also, that they are destined ere long to become a source of great power and wealth to the nation. I am Major, Very respectfully your ob'dt serv't,

HLcSr   (Signed) Chas. B. Wilder.

Excerpts from Capt. Chas. B. Wilder to Major Geo. J. Carney, 30 Dec. 1864, Annual, Personal, & Special Reports of Quartermaster Officers, ser. 1105, Personnel, RG 92 [Y-500]. Endorsement. Approximately fifteen pages of a twenty-four page report. The omitted passages included a month-by-month accounting of the number of men, women, and children issued rations and the cost of the rations issued; and ten tables pertaining to the operation of plantations in the district during 1864.

1 The order, issued on December 5, 1863, is printed above, as doc. 26.

44: Virginia Unionist to the Secretary of War

Eastville Northampton County State of Virginia Jany 16th 1865
Sir At the most Earnest request of maney of the Free men of Colour of this place I have the honor to address you this communication Stating the facts of their Grieviousencis, How they are treated by the Government Officers at this place Lt. Col. Frank J White who is in command here and who has none but the most Rabid Secessionist Rebels in his employee as Clerks, agents, and advisers, have been and are hiering out by force all the Free Coloured people of this District inclueding all who were born free, maney who have Families and Farms (all are included) and who have alway been good and respectible Citizens have to hier their Sons and Dauthers wives & husbands and a fee of two dollars and five cents is demanded and paid on each one so hiered Now Sir They appeal to you to say is Law is right that they should be thus placed in a worst Bondage then the Slaves ever was Sir they appeal to you for a redress of their Grievencis. As to the truth of the above They most Earnesly invite an Investacation of the facts by an officier of Government I have thus stated as brief as I am able in my humble way and requst your earlest attention to the matter You obedient Servent

ALS   B. L. Parrish

[*Endorsement*] Hdq^{rs} U.S. Forces. East^n Shore Va Eastville Feb^{ry} 15 /65

Resp^{ly} returned. The Statements of B. L. Parish are entirely false. My employees are more loyal than the party making the charges, and are entirely worthy of the trust placed in them.

The Statements made concerning the hiring of colored persons by force is also false. These Statements are based upon an order issued from my office requiring all colored persons to labor for a livelihood.[1] This order in all it's details has been approved by Major Carney Supt. of Negro affairs Dept: Va, by Brig: Genl Shepley Com^g the Dist: of East^n Va, by Major Genl Ord Com^g this Dept: and was approved by Major Genl Butler when in Command of the Dept of Va & N.C.

For a more complete answer to within letter I would resp^{ly} refer to my Communication of the 6th inst: addressed to the Major Genl: Com^g this Dept: forwarded through Hdq^{rs} Dist: East^n Va.[2] Frank J. White Lt Col Com^g U.S. Forces East^n Shore Va.

[*Endorsement*] H^d Qrs Dept of V^a Feby – 23^d 65 – I have inspected Col Whites District, heard the Complaints (and there were but one or two of each) from whites and colored citizens – found them the complaints not serious – or such as to do any thing but credit to Col White – the complaints of the colored citizens were to the effect that certain taxes were collected on oystering and that, in one instance a man was ordered to hire out his daughters – (the taxes were remitted; and the daughters – were allowed to "ply their vocation" not a very moral one – E. O. C. Ord Maj Genl Vols Comdg –

B. L. Parrish to the Honorable Mr. Stanton, 16 Jan. 1865, P-29 1865, Letters Received, ser. 360, Colored Troops Division, RG 94 [B-179]. According to other endorsements, the Adjutant General's Office referred Parrish's letter to General Ord "for report" on January 23, and Ord's subordinates forwarded it to Colonel White. Additional endorsements.

1 The order, issued on November 4, 1864, is quoted below, in doc. 46.

2 Colonel White's letter of February 6 had sought the approval of General Edward O. C. Ord, the new commander of the Department of Virginia, for "the policy adopted with reference to the Colored population of this [Eastern] Shore." The policy, embodied in his Special Order 81, was intended, White had explained, "to encourage industry, to prevent idleness, to show the adherents of slavery, the value of free labor, to teach the Contrabands the importance, of honest toil and the blessings attaching to it, and to vindicate Emancipation." "The order," he claimed, "has accomplished all of its objects." "All that are able to work are earning a subsistence," and the "bitter spirit" previously prevailing

between black and white people "is now subdued." Indeed, "a majority of the Citizens of this Shore would to day ratify an emancipation ordinance." (Lt. Col. Frank J. White to Major Ord, 6 Feb. 1865, vol. 246/614 VaNc, pp. 136–49, Letters Sent, ser. 923, U.S. Forces Eastern Shore of VA, RG 393 Pt. 2 No. 19 [C-3399].) Special Order 81 is quoted below, in doc. 46.

45: Superintendent of Negro Affairs in the 4th District of the Department of Virginia to the Headquarters of the District of Eastern Virginia

EASTVILLE [*Va.*], February 16th 1865.

Major   I have the honor to Submit, for the Consideration of the Brig Gen Comd'g the District of Eastern V[a], my action in the case of one Griffin Collins, a colored farmer of this Shore.

The demoralization of the Colored population of this District, rendered it necessary to issue an order, requiring that all colored persons should engage in some steady employment.[1] This order was approved by the Brig Gen Comdg the District, and the Maj Gen Comdg the Dep[t], and was accordingly enforced, the colored persons not employed, Choosing their employers, and making their own bargains. Under the present existing Statutes of the state of Virginia, no colored person can find Justice in a civil court. I therefore ordered that whenever a complaint should be brought by an employer against a colored employee, the complaint should be made before me, and that all bargains for labor should be made in writing and filed in my office, both for the protection of the employer and for the purpose of furnishing me with data, from which, to ascertain whether all of the laboring population were industrously employed?

Griffin Collins, refered to, has from the outset, made himself a leader of a small class of colored persons who have since their emancipation, refused to labor for a livelihood, and who have maintained themselves principally by theft. He, himself, was industrious and well to do, but stired up publicly, as much opposition as possible, among the colored people, advising them to refuse to obey the order referred to, and stating that he, himself, should not obey it.

During Maj Gen Ord's visit to this Dis[t], Collins waited upon him and found that the General, although willing to make some exceptions in his case, was disposed to enforced my orders, After the General left the Shore, Collins caused a letter to be written to the Secretary of War, filled with personal abuse of myself and making false Statements concerning the restrictions placed upon the colored population –[2]

Collins had rented a farm, and by the provisions of my order, was obliged to file in my office, in writing, the contracts made with laborers. As the laborers, on his farm were his own sons, I notified him personaly, that I would make an exception in his case and require, simply, that he should make an agreement to keep his sons industrously employed during the year, requiring no other contract. He refused to do anything, which, would, in any way recognise my authority to make him conform to the rules which are required to be followed by white or black farmers, and defied me to enforce my orders. Had he been a white citizen, I should have punished him, both, for the insolent language he used and for his refusal to obey the written orders received from me.

Under the circumstances I have simply notified him that he can only employ laborers upon the terms required by my orders, and submit the matter for further instructions. I have the honor to remain Very Respectfully Your Ob^r Servt,

HLS   Frank J White.

Lieut. Col. Frank J. White to Major, 16 Feb. 1865, W-36 1865, Letters Received, ser. 1628, Dist. of Eastern VA, RG 393 Pt. 2 No. 72 [C-3128]. White was also commander of U.S. forces on the eastern shore. General George H. Gordon, who had only recently assumed command of the District of Eastern Virginia, directed his adjutant to reply "that he is aware of no reason why a colored person should not be subject to military laws, or, if he violates those laws, be punished as a white man would be punished." Accordingly, Gordon instructed White to arrest Collins and forward him to Norfolk "with proper evidence," for trial by a military commission that was then in session. (A.A. General Wickham Hoffman to Lieut. Col. F. J. White, 21 Feb. 1865, vol. 87 VaNc, p. 516, Letters Sent, ser. 1622, Dist. of Eastern VA, RG 393 Pt. 2 No. 72 [C-3128].) No record of a trial has been found among the court-martial case files in the records of the judge advocate general.

1 The order, issued on November 4, 1864, is quoted below, in doc. 46.
2 The letter is printed immediately above, as doc. 44.

46: Superintendent of Negro Affairs in the 4th District of the Department of Virginia to the Headquarters of the Department

Eastville [*Va.*] Feby 28th 1865

Copy

Col   I have the honor to submit for the consideration of the Major Genl Comdg the Department, the following statement of the present condition and organization of the colored population of this District, in order that he may signify his approval or disapproval of the course hitherto adopted by me.

Upon the first of October last, I was appointed by Major Genl Butler Superintendent of Negro affairs for the 4th District, embracing the counties of Accomac and Northampton Va.

My duties were to take charge of, protect and assist the Contrabands of this District, to aid them in sickness or distress and to see that their rights as freemen were respected.

I then, as now, commanded the U.S. Forces on this Shore, my duties in that office being as I conceived in addition to the ordinary duties of a commanding officer, to see, that all loyal citizens were protected in such civil rights as they could properly exercise while residents of an insurrectionary District, and to make such regulations for the benefit of the Community, as in the absence of competent civil Legislation could only be made or enforced by military authority.

The duties of these two offices could not come in conflict, the Contrabands having acquired through emancipation all of the rights of Citizens, and being no more nor less than loyal or disloyal residents of the District.

Upon assuming charge of this District, I found a laborious task before me. A system for the support and protection of the freedmen had been established, but nothing had been done for their social or moral elevation. Notice had been given by the former Superintendent, that all freedmen should be obliged to work for their livelihood, but this notice not being enforced by Military Authority had but little result.

Six thousand men and women coming from the darkness of Slavery, into the broad day of freedom, could not while their wrongs were yet unforgotten and their new found rights exaggerated through past deprivation, know or obey the obligations of their changed condition; and hence, the women of the District were still as in days of Slavery wanting in chastity, and the men, living in comparative idleness and dishonesty. These poor creatures were only carrying out the lessons taught by Slavery, and obeying the instincts begotten by their past. Forced labor had taught them to look upon idleness as the greatest blessing freedom could bring. The denial of the rights of their own flesh and blood, or to the earnings of their daily toil, had made to them, honesty, a fiction, & the rights of property a farce.

A bed which had been outraged by bringing its fruits to the Slave-block, could not in a day, recover its lost sanctity; nor could marriage relations, for years trampled on by the law, become once more true and steadfast, until time had blotted out the memories and evil influences of the past.

Their past education taught them to have no care for the future, and from the present, they only asked the few necessaries that could be obtained by irregular labor, and time to indulge their strong social propensities. Continued idleness was not long in producing its results, dishonesty, suffering & disease

Upon the other hand, the citizens of this Shore, all of whom had taken the oath of allegiance were obliged to let their farms lay idle, their barns were plundered, incendiaries were not uncommon, and they suffered many personal indignities. A bitter spirit was springing up between the two classes, which years could not eradicate, and emancipation was charged with results for which it was not responsible. By this course the freedmen were not only working to themselves a present injury, but were ruining their future.

To organize a system which should change and elevate the moral condition of the Freedmen, a system to be carried out within the limited remaining period of the war, was a problem difficult of solution, and involved a careful consideration of the theories prevailing among those who had for years devoted heart and brain to the labor of elevating the African race.

Many claimed that this result could be obtained by living with and among them, teaching them by contact and example, admitting them to a social equality, and through miscegenation, gaining their confidence and rousing their pride.

It is possible that this scheme might be successful within the narrow limits of an asylum, but not if attempted on a larger scale, if for no other reason, from the impossibility of procuring the necessary number of Philanthopists prepared from pure and disinterested motives to act as co-laborers in such a work. Even if the necessary number could be introduced into this District, I would not feel inclined to try the experiment, having found as a general rule, that such enthusiasts, though abounding in benevolence and possessed of the noble attributes of human nature, lack the hard practical sense and habits of system essential in the proper and enlightened performance of the duties they would be called upon to assume.

An enthusiasts of this description, may influence many to espouse a just cause or may carry to a successful issue a principle or an idea; but in a larger field, where a social problem is to be solved, upon the true solution of which, the destinies of thousands depend; men of a sterner intellectual cast are required.

A second system proposed, was to establish upon the confiscated lands in the District, Government farms, to be given to the freedmen for cultivation.

I objected to this system, for the reason, that is [*if*] encouraged to form isolated communities, the freedmen would advance but slowly, and upon the close of the war, would be looked upon with distrust and hostility by the white citizens of the State.

No more certain scheme, than a communistic one of this kind could be devised for the purpose of dividing, instead of uniting the interests of the two classes and storing trouble in the future for the freedmen: trouble and persecution, which would come at a time, when they would be obliged mainly to depend on themselves for protection

Such a system would defeat the great desideratum of bringing at once together in their new relations, the emancipated Slave and his former owner, an experience from which the planter might learn the value of free labor, the freedman the value of a market for that labor, and both, to respect their mutual rights before the dawning of peace should leave this task to Legislative Enactment, based upon an experience of Emancipation, not followed by a wise guidance of those it benefitted. It is true, that many object to the restoration of relations of any kind between the Emancipated freedmen and their former owners. This objection is naturally caused by the desire to take them entirely from without their sphere or control; but this result can only be accomplished, if at all, through the slow process of years.

Where could a million of freedmen find a home within the life of this generation?

Not in New England. Her cities, fields and forests can only maintain men whose intellects are fitted for the learned professions or the enterprise of commerce, and sinewy sons of toil accustomed to unremitting labor and exposure.

Not in the Middle States, where upon the return of our armies the labor market will be supplied by men with whom the African could not compete; Nor in the free States of the West meeded for our inceasing Emigration.

Believing that the homes of a majority of the Freedmen must be for years to come, in the South, it seemed to me to be the wisest policy, to at once treat them as Citizens responsible to the community for their conduct equally with others; protecting and assisting them where needful, but requiring in return, industry and honesty. The following order, milder in its provisions than any Vagrant Act of a Northern State, was therefore issued, and entirely approved by Major General Butler then in command, and since approved by the Brig Genl Comdg the District, and the Major Genl Comdg the Department

Head Quarters
Provost Marshals Office
Eastern Shore of Virginia
Eastville Va Nov 4th 1864

Special Orders }
No 81 }

Complaints have been made at this Office that many of the Freed Slaves and coloured inhabitants of the Eastern Shore of Virginia are living in idleness, refusing to labor for their livelihood, and subsisting in great part by depredating upon the property of others

In order to correct the above evils and to provide a sufficiency of labor for the farmers of this District, it is ordered,

I That a census of all coloured persons over the age of fourteen, be at once made by the assistant Provost Marshals of the Eastern Shore of Virginia, and that the following facts be ascertained, viz: their conditions residence and occupation; in the case of women, the number of children depending on them for support.

This census will be used by Assistant Provost Marshals in providing labour for those Negroes not engaged in some steady employment. All citizens are requested to report any coloured persons living on their lands who may have been formerly owned or hired by them.

II All coloured persons able to work and not engaged in steady employment by which they can earn a full support, will be required to engage themselves under a written contract to some employer at a fair remuneration.

III Assistant Provost Marshals will appoint in their Districts a loyal responsible citizen as Superintendent of Labor, whose duty it shall be to carry out under the instructions of the Assistant Provost Marshal the provisions of this order. Such Superintendents shall be paid a monthly salary of seventy five dollars, the expenses of such Office to be provided for by a fee of fifty cents, to be paid by the employer for each laborer hired.

IV All persons desiring to procure field or house servants can do so, by making proper application at the Office of the Superintendent of Labour and filing in such Office a written contract.

V Labour by the day or week need not be contracted for at the Office of the Superintendent of Labor.

VI Assistant Provost Marshals will see that all coloured persons male or female able to work steadily, contract for labor, by the month, season or year.

VII Any violation of contract upon the part of the Employer or Employee shall be a matter of adjudication and punishment in the Provost Court of this District. Bad or cruel treatment upon the part of employers, and insolence insubordination or improper conduct upon the part of Employees shall be considered a violation of contract. Any charge which could properly be brought against a white laborer shall be held tenable as against a Negro laborer and upon the same principle, treatment improper in the case of a white laborer shall be equally unjustifiable in the case of a hired negro.

VIII All necessary forms and blanks will be furnished from this Office.

To all colored persons who shall in pursuance of above orders, lead a regular, honest and industrious life, assistance in sickness, destitution or distress, shall be given by the government.

It is hoped that a strict compliance with the above regulations will result to the benefit of all concerned, furnishing to the farmers and residents of this shore economical and regular labor, and to the colored population a lawful and profitable means of subsistence

(Signed) Frank J. White

Lieut Col & Provost Marshal

Head Qrs. Pro. Mar. Office

Eastern Shore of Virginia

Eastville Va. Dec. 23^d 1864

Circular

Superintendents of labor will hereafter carry out the following instructions in organizing the laboring population of the shore under special Order No 81.

1. On and after the 1$''$ day of January 1865, all colored persons remaining unemployed will be reported to this office.

2 All colored persons able to work must engage themselves at some steady labor, except those hereinafter enumerated.

3 No one person will be allowed to engage more laborers than he can furnish with steady employment,

4 Where either party to a contract for labor shall violate such contract, upon complaint being made to the superintendent of labor, he shall investigate carefully into the matter and forward to this office a full written statement of the facts.

5. If any colored persons shall have more children helpless from infancy or disease then they can support by their labor, the Superintendent of labor shall report to this office the necessary amount of assistance which in his judgment the Government should render to such persons. Any Colored person in like manner helpless from age or disease shall be reported.

6. Employers can rent to their Employees such houses or lands as they may desire.

7. Any person renting to a colored person a house and farm must, by a bond, bind himself to report to the superintendent of Labor, any continued idleness or improper conduct upon the part of the tenant. In no case must more persons able to labor be allowed to live in such house, than are provided with steady employment upon the farm or otherwise.

8. The conditions of a contract between Employer and Employee, must be entirely agreed upon between the parties concerned without any interference on the part of superintendents.

227

9. Contraband rations will be issued to those deserving of them by the Commanding officers of posts upon the Certificate of a superintendent of labor.

10. Two asylums for the old, infirm and diseased will be established; one in Accomac County and one in Northampton County, to which all such persons will be forwarded.

11. Assistant Superintendents will select one-tenth of the laboring population in each sub. district to remain as day laborers, such persons being furnished with a certificate from four responsible citizens that have hitherto born a good character for honesty and industry. The provisions of this order shall not in any way affect such day laborers. In addition to such persons, the following will be permitted to follow their usual avocations: Blacksmiths, Carpenters, Shoemakers and skilled hewers of wood. All persons above enumerated will be permitted to work at such times and places as they may desire during good conduct, and no persons, employers or otherwise will be held responsible for them.

12. Oystermen, during the oystering season, can continue their business, but on the expiration of the oystering season shall engage in other steady employment.

13. Persons renting land to colored persons on shares will not be obliged to give any bond for the good conduct of the tenant.

14. Employers will not be permitted to inflict corporeal punishment upon their colored employees.

15. No Contracts for labor, except for day labor, shall be made for a less period than *three months*, nor more than *one year*.

16. Upon the expiration of contracts employers must report the fact to the superintendent of Labor, in whose office such contracts have been made.

17. To create a fund for the support of those that would otherwise be thrown upon the community, for the payment of superintendents Labor, and for other contingent expenses, the following fees will be charged by the superintendents of Labor for each contract filed or certificate issued.

For each contract for three months or over, the sum of fifty cents.

For each contract for six months or over the sum of one dollar.

For each contract for one year the sum of two dollars. Such fees to be paid by employers,

No fee shall be charged to colored persons engaging laborers.

For each certificate given to those exempt from order No 81, the sum of fifty cents. The fund thus created will provide for the poor and infirm of this District, and will be repaid to those furnishing it, by a reliable and economical system of labor.

18. Superintendents of Labor will forward to this office on the 15" and 30." of each month full reports of all contracts made by them and funds received.

19. Blank forms for Bonds, Certificates and contracts will be furnished from this office.

Superintendents are required to use judgment and discretion in

the execution of this order. Their main duties are to see that labor is
furnished to all colored persons seeking it, that no idleness or the
demoralization inevitable upon it be permitted; that all contracts
filed by them are strictly enforced, and that colored persons be
protected in all of their rights and punished for any wrong doing.

sgd.   Frank. J. White
Lt. Col. & Pro. Mar.

A military order was necessary, because no other means would suffice
to Change the habits of two years and successfully inaugurate the
needed reforms

Advice or request would have been useless, steady labor was
required for the reason, that no person white or Colored, Could
otherwise, unless possessed of a Competency, obtain an honest or
sufficient support; nor Could farmers engage labor, which Could not
be depended on for a season

From this order were exempted, "Oystermen, skilled laborers,
mechanics, midwives, and one tenth of the total colored population,
that number being able to procure employment by the day,

Many special exceptions were also made, when Circumstances
justified them,

No scale of wages was established, for the reason, that the
demand for labor, being in excess of the supply, good compensation
Could be obtained, without military interference,

I also Conceived, that although I might have the right to require
industry, I had no right to force any man to labor for a less sum,
than the highest he could procure

All Complaints made by employers or employees of violation of
Contract were to be adjudicated in my office, because the Civil
authorities Could not, while acting under statutes as yet unrepealed,
do justice to the Freedmen who since the passage of those acts, had
obtained new rights not Contemplated by them,

This order Could not, as a rule, operate to seperate Husband from
Wife, or Mother from Children for the reason, that in a large
majority of Cases, whole families could be employed together and
generally by the owner of the land upon which they lived, The fees
required were Charged for the purpose of establishing a fund for the
support of the "aged and Helpless,"

These fees have been paid willingly and, by the fund thus
Created, over four hundred objects of Charity are enabled to live in
Comfort,

The order has accomplished its objects; the freedmen are all
furnished with homes and paid good wages,

Four thousand six hundred and thirty five men & women have
been furnished with homes and employment without Cost to the
government and are living Comfortably and industriously, Their

229

employers treat them kindly, and Comply strictly with the Conditions of their Contracts, I have not yet, after three months experience of this system, found a single Case of improper treatment on the part of an employer,

The wages given in addition to good food and lodging, average as follows,

House servants per month four dollars,
Farm laborers (Male) per month twelve dollars,
Farm laborers (female) per month five dollars,
Wood Cutters per month twenty five dollars,
Boys (between 12 & 16) per month six dollars.

The effect upon the well being of the Community has been very great, The suspension of farm Cultivation during the last three years had nearly ruined those who depended upon the yearly produce of their lands for support, but the present year promises to once more renew their former prosperity. Land is much increased in value and the Crops more than four fold exceed any made since the outbreak of the Rebellion,

The demand for labor is in excess of the supply, I can find good homes for five hundred additional laborers at the wages quoted above,

In carrying out this system I have encountered the prejudices and abuse of those who beleive the freedman to be worthless, and of a small Class found floating in every military Department who have a special mission to inaugurate impracticable theories, prompted by worthy zeal, but not warranted by Common sense; men who find in the freedman only an opportunity for the development of benvolent hobbies, and the exercise of curious experiments; who by making him dependent upon a bounty that can not last, would enevitably render him helpless in the future, To persons of this description labor Can only signify *bondage*, and the Common industrial restraints imposed in every Civilized Community – *oppression*. They teach the Freedmen that he has acquired great, imperishable rights; but forget to warn him of the practical obligations and responsibilities of the life before him. Too many such men have been entrusted with the labor of moulding for a future, pregnant with trial and vicissitude; a race, young in intellect, but old in the evil habits of slavery.

My earnest interest in the great cause of emancipation, must be my excuse for the length of this communication. Trusting that the Major General Commanding may approve of my course in th matter I have the honor to remain Col, Very Respectfully Your obt. Servt.

HLcSr   (sgd) Frank J White

Lieut. Col. Frank J. White to Col. E. W. Smith, 28 Feb. 1865, enclosed in Lt. Col. Horace Porter to Brevet Major Gen. John W. Turner, 24 Mar. 1865, filed as V-87 1865, Letters Received, ser. 12, RG 94 [K-118]. Appended is a copy of an endorsement, dated March 4, 1865, by General Edward O. C. Ord, commander of the Department of Virginia, approving White's policies. "[T]here probably have been some cases," Ord conceded, "when the general rules worked individual hardship—but such Cases were few." Moreover, special inspectors had been sent "to hunt up such caces and provide for them—" Ord pronounced White's "system . . . a good one," under which "white and black have learned that they are laboring in a Common Cause for their mutual benefit." Former slaves and free blacks on Virginia's eastern shore did not share Ord's assessment. In October 1865, long after Colonel White had departed the region, the military officer in command there reported "considerable dissatisfaction amongst them on account of the System of forced contracts which was adopted at the begining of this year." "[I]n many cases," he concluded, "the forcing them to make contracts was unjust and injurious but the System has no doubt prevented a considerable amount of vagrancy." (Capt. Edwin A. Evans to Lieut. Col. N. Church, 14 Oct. 1865, Weekly Operational Reports of Subordinate Commands, ser. 5102, Dept. of VA, RG 393 Pt. 1 [C-3047].)

47A: North Carolina Freedmen to the President and to the Secretary of War

Roanoke Island N.C march 9th 1865.
Mr President Dear Sir   We Colored men of this Island held a meeting to consult over the affairs of our present conditions and our rights and we find that our arms are so Short that we cant doe any thing with in our Selves So we Concluded the best thing we could do was to apply to you or Some of your cabinets   we are told and also we have read that you have declared all the Colored people free bothe men and woman that is in the Union lines and if that be so we want to know where our wrights is or are we to be Stamp down or troden under feet by our Superintendent which he is the very man that we look to for assistents,   in the first place his Proclamation was that no able boded man was to draw any rations except he was at work for the Government   we all agreed to that and was willing to doe as we had done for $10,00 per month and our rations though we Seldom ever get the mony

the next thing he said that he wanted us to work and get our living as White men and not apply to the Government and that is vry thing we want to doe, but after we do this we cant satisfie him   Soon as he Sees we are trying to Support our Selves without the aid of the Government he comes and make a Call for the men,

that is not working for the Government to Goe away and if we are
not willing to Goe he orders the Guards to take us by the point of
the bayonet, and we have no power to help it   we know it is
wright and are willing to doe any thing that the President or our
head Commanders want us to doe but we are not willing to be pull
and haul a bout so much by those head men as we have been for the
last two years and we may say Get nothing for it,   last fall a large
number of we men was Conscript and sent up to the front and all of
them has never return[1]   Some Got Kill Some died and When they
taken them they treated us mean and our owners ever did   they
taken us just like we had been dum beast

We Colored people on Roanok Island are willing to Submit to
any thing that we know the President or his cabinet Say because we
have Got since enough to believe it is our duty to doe every thing
we Can doe to aid Mr Lyncoln and the Government but we are not
willing to work as we have done for Chaplain James and be Troden
under foot and Get nothing for it   we have work faithful Since we
have been on the Island   we have built our log houses   we have
Cultivate our acre of Ground and have Tried to be less exspence to
the Government as we Possible Could be and we are yet Trying to
help the Government all we Can for our lives   those head men have
done every thing to us that our masters have done except by and Sell
us and now they are Trying to Starve the woman & children to death
cutting off they ration   they have Got so now that they wont Give
them no meat to eat, every ration day beef & a little fish and befor
the Ten days is out they are going from one to another Trying to
borrow a little meal to last until ration day   Mr Streeter will just
order one barrell of meet for his fish men and the others he Gives
nothing but beaf but we thank the Lord for that if we no it is the
President or the Secretarys orders   this is what want to know whoes
orders it is,   one of our minister children was fool to ration house
and Sent off and his father working three days in every week for his
ration

Roanoke Island N.C   march 9th 1865
   we have appeal to General Butler and Genl Butler wrote to Capt
James to do Better and Capt James has promies to do Better and
instead of doing better he has done worst and now we appeal to you
which is the last resort and only help we have got, feeling that we
are entily friendless,   on the Island there numrous of Soldiers wives
and they Can hardly get any rations and some of them are almost
starving
   we dont exspect to have the same wrights as white men doe   we
know that are in a millitary country and we exspect to obey the

rules and orders of our authories and doe as they say doe, any thing
in reason   we thank God and thank our President all of his aids for
what has been done for us but we are not satisfide with our
Supertendent nor the treatement we receives   now we want you to
send us answer what to depen upon   let it be good or bad and we
will be Satisfide   Respectifully yours

HL   Roanoke Island N.C.

Roanoke Island N.C   March 9th 1865
    we want to know from the Secretary of War has the Rev Chaplain
James which is our Superintendent of negros affairs has any wright
to take our boy Children from us and from the School and Send
them to newbern to work to pay for they ration without they parent
Consint   if he has we thinks it very hard indeed   he essued a
Proclamation that no boys Should have any rations at 14 years
old   well we thought was very hard that we had to find our boy
Children to Goe to School hard as times are, but rather then they
Should Goe without learning we thought we would try and doe it
and say no more a bout it and the first thing we knowed M^r
Stereeter the Gentlemen that ration the Contrabands had Gone a
round to all the White School-Teachers and told them to Give the
boys orders to goe and get they ration on a Cirtain day   so the
negros as we are Call are use to the Cesesh plots Suspicion the Game
they was Going to play and a Greate many never Sent they
Children. So Some twenty or twenty-five went and Mr Streeter Give
them they rations and the Guard march them down to the head
quarters and put them on board the boat and carried them to
newbern   here is woman here on the Island which their husbands
are in the army just had one little boy to help them to cut & lug
wood & to Goe arrand for them   Chaplain James has taken them
and sent them away   Some of these little ones he sent off wasen oer
12 years olds. the mothers of Some went to Chaplain and Grieved
and beg for the little boys but he would not let them have
them   we want to know if the Prisident done essued any ration for
School boys   if he dont then we are satisfide   we have men on the
Island that Can Support the boys to Goe to School but here are Poor
woman are not able to do it So the orphans must Goe without they
learning   that all we can say a bout the matter

    the next is Concerning of our White Soldiers   they Come to our
Church and we treat them with all the Politeness that we can and
Some of them treats us as though we were beast and we cant help
our Selves   Some of them brings Pop Crackers and Christmas devils
and throws a mong the woman and if we Say any thing to them
they will talk about mobin us. we report them to the Capt he will

Say you must find out Which ones it was and that we cant do but we think very hard it   they put the pistols to our ministers breast because he Spoke to them about they behavour in the Church,   the next is Capt James told us When he got the mill built he would let us have plank to buil our houses   we negroes went to work and cut and hewd the timber and built the mill under the northern men derection and now he Charges us 3 and 4 dollars a hundred for plank and if we Carry 3 logs to the mill he takes 2 and Gives us one.   that is he has the logs haul and takes one for hauling and one for Sawing and we thinks that is to much Without he paid us better then he does.   and the next thing is he wont allow a man any ration While he is trying to buil him Self a house. to live in and how are negroes to live at that rate   we Cant See no way to live under Such laws, Without Some Altiration

Roanoke Island N.C.   March 9th 1865

here is men here that has been working for the last three year and has not been paid for it.   they, work on the forts and Cut spiles and drove them and done any thing that they was told to do   Capt James Came on the Island Jan. 1864 and told they men that he had made all the matters wright a bout they back pay and now says he I want all of you men that has due bills to carry them to Mr Bonnell at head quarters and all them has not got no paper to show for they work I will make them Swear and kiss the Bibel   and the men done just as he told them and he told us that he had made out the rolls and sent them up to Washington City and now he says that money is all dead   So we are very well Satisfide just So we know that he has never received it for our head men has fool us so much just because they think that we are igorant we have lost all Confidince in them.   so all we wants is a Chance and we can Get a living like White men   we are praying to God every day for the war to Stop So we wont be beholding to the Government for Something to Eat   Yours Respectfully

HL   Roanoke Island.

Roanoke Island N.C. to Mr. President, 9 Mar. 1865, and Roanoke Island to [Secretary of War], 9 Mar. 1865, both filed as B-2 1865, Letters Received, ser. 15, Washington Hdqrs., RG 105 [A-2966]. The petitions (possibly, a single petition) are in several fragments whose intended arrangement is not self-evident. All the fragments are in the same handwriting, probably that of Richard Boyle, a black schoolteacher on Roanoke Island, who, according to a War Department memorandum (in the same file), presented them at the department on April 6, 1865. At an unspecified later date, they were forwarded to the headquarters of the Freedmen's Bureau; on May 30, 1865, that office referred them to Captain Horace James, the bureau superintendent in eastern North Carolina, who during the war had been superintendent of Negro affairs in the region. James's report is printed immediately below, as doc. 47B. The reduction of government rations issued to the freedpeople on Roanoke Island provoked still further protests that same spring. In early June 1865, Northern schoolteachers on the island reported that "the sweeping reduction of the rations brings hundreds suddenly face to face with starvation." "It is a daily occurrence to see scores of women and children crying for bread, whose husbands, Sons and fathers are in the army today." Meanwhile, several of those husbands, sons, and fathers, then stationed in Virginia, reminded the commissioner of the Freedmen's Bureau that the government had promised rations to their families as a condition of their enlistment, yet their wives and children were now receiving but half the regular ration. "Consequently," asserted the soldiers, "three or four days out of every ten days, [they] have nothing to eat." The soldiers denounced Holland Streeter, the assistant superintendent on the island, as a "Cooper head a man who says that he is no part of a Abolitionist . . . A man who kicks our wives and children out of the ration house . . . sells the rations . . . and our family's suffer for something to eat." (*Freedom*, ser. 2: docs. 315A–B.)

1 On the impressment of men from Roanoke Island in the fall of 1864, for labor at the front in Virginia, see above, doc. 40.

47B: Freedmen's Bureau Superintendent of the Eastern District of North Carolina to the Headquarters of the Freedmen's Bureau Commissioner

New Berne N.C. July 10, 1865
Dear Sir, A complaint of Richard Boyle, school teacher on Roanoke Island referred by you to me for investigation and report, and found here on my return from leave of absence, has been attentively considered and weighed. And it amounts just to this. The colored people who have been within our lines three years or more have been so long receiving aid from the government, as to count it their *right* to receive it, even when in many cases they might support themselves —
When boys fourteen years old and upwards are denied rations, and told to work for their own living, a howl of dissatisfaction is raised by the colored people. When beef and fish are given them instead of *bacon* they complain of having "no meat", and speak of starvation — The first instance of starvation upon Roanoke Island, or of real suffering for want of food has yet to occur, as will be evident when it is known that from 50,000 to 80,000 rations per mo. have been issued to a population of not more than 3,000 colored people — The truth is *they have had too much* given them, And the times of wholesome *retrenchment* are the times of letter-writing, petitioning, and professed abuse by their Superintendents — Give

them all they want of food, clothing and other things, and they find no fault— The *grand remedy* for Roanoke Island, now that the war is over and the thing is possible and safe, is to *put two thirds of its people upon plantations on the main land*, a result we mean to effect as soon as possible. Having just spent three days upon the island, and well knowing its whole history, I am compelled to pronounce Mr Boyle's statements of suffering gross exaggerations— Himself a respectable man, trying to do good to his people, he does great injustice to his superintendents through short-sightedness and ignorance. Worthy of pity rather than of blame, I look upon him, and others like him, as persons to be treated like children, who do not know when they are well used, and whose complaints should influence us but a little, while we do for them that which we know will promote their best good. Those who come most in contact with the negros in the work of doing them good, *seldom win their gratitude*— I have the honor to be very faithfully yours,

ALS   Horace James

Capt. Horace James to Col. J. S. Fullerton, 10 July 1865, filed with B-2 1865, Letters Received, ser. 15, Washington Hdqrs., RG 105 [A-2966]. The "complaint of Richard Boyle" that had been referred to James is the petition printed immediately above, as doc. 47A. Colonel Eliphalet Whittlesey, Freedmen's Bureau assistant commissioner for North Carolina, forwarded with James's report a letter of his own. Having made "careful inquiries on the ground" regarding the "troubles on Roanoke Island," Whittlesey had concluded "that the Govt. has done and is now doing *too much* for that Colony." Convinced that "[t]here are many able-bodied men & boys there, living in idleness, because they recive gratuitous support," Whittlesey had ordered that rations be reduced "as fast as possible"; "when this process begins," he warned the commissioner of the bureau, "another series of Complaints will come in." Whittlesey was confident that Captain James had "done all that could be done by any man for the comfort of the people." The charges against Streeter he believed to be "greatly exagerated," but he had ordered a special investigation. (Col. E. Whittlesey to General, 12 July 1865, in the same file.)

48: Assistant Superintendent of Negro Affairs at Yorktown, Virginia, to the Commander of the District of the Peninsula

Yorktown Va. April 21ˢᵗ 1865.

General   In compliance with your request I have the honor to submit the following report of the management of the Department of Negro Affairs under my command.

My District is comprised within the County of York, extending from Back River on the south, and bounded on the southwest, and West, by the counties of Warwick and James City, to Queens Creek on the North, with a colored population according to a Census just taken of 4283. – The county extends some distance to the North of Queen's Creek, but as that portion has not heretofore been within our lines, I have not taken charge of any property or negroes in it.

I have under my control 23 farms; 5 on York River and Queens Creek; 4 near Williamsburg; 8 near Yorktown; and 6 in the lower end of the county in the vicinity of the Half Way House: – 3603 acres are at this time under lease, almost exclusively to colored persons, although since I have taken charge. that has not been made a condition of leasing. – Whenever a white person has made application for land, I have given him equal privileges, having taken it for granted that the Government does not intend to benefit the negroes to the exclusion of the whites.

I have received no instructions in regard to the management of these people, and have been guided entirely by my own judgment; previous to my assuming control, they were under the management of a citizen, acting as the agent of Capt Wilder. A.Q.M. Fort Monroe:[1] I found them somewhat insubordinate, roberry and theft were of almost daily occurrence, and there appeared to be but little disposition to check the evil. – raids into Gloucester and Matthews counties were quite common: sometimes the negroes were accompanied or led by white Soldiers, and at other times they seemed to be acting on their own responsibility. – Since I have been here, but one affair of the kind has come to my knowlege, and the promt arrest of all concerned with it has had a most excellent effect, and I do not anticipate any further trouble of the kind.

By direction of Major General E. O. C. Ord I have organized a Police Force, consisting of thirty one men, who are at present on duty in the villages adjoining Yorktown, and have also appointed a few on each farm: the first named are to be paid, fed, and cloathed at the same rate as soldiers, and will of course have no other employment; the latter class receive nothing but their rations, will attend to their usual business of farming, and whenever their services are required to preserve order, or to make arrests they will be called upon.

The only trouble I anticipate in managing my District, is the fear of a collision with the Provost Marshal in the exercise of our respective duties. – When my predecessor (Mr Churchill) was in charge it was of frequent occurrence, but he being a citizen was of course almost powerless and had to yield; that in my opinion was one of the great causes of the disorder existing here. – the negroes knowing his inability to control or punish them, paid but little attention to his orders, and the consequence was they did very much as they pleased. In addition they had the bad example of many of the white soldiers at Fort Magruder and Yorktown to encourage them in their evil doings.

I think the position of Provost Marshal, and Superintendant of Negro Affairs should be held by the same Officer, giving him entire control of both Departments, and holding him to a strict accountability for the good order of his District: — the Superintendant of Negro Affairs cannot preserve order without assuming some of the duties of the Provost Marshal, and to do so is sure to produce ill feeling between the two Officers: — the work is not too great for one man and in my opinion it would be to the interest of Government to combine the two. — A large proportion of the Negroes are governed entirely by their fears, and not from any apparent sense of right and wrong: let them see that the Superintendant who has charge of them and who is laboring for their benefit has the power to have them punished without calling upon other officers to aid him, and they will at once see that lawlessness and disorder must cease. The Eastern Shore of Virginia has probably been better governed in this respect than any District in the Department, and I, in a great measure attribute the success of Lt Col White to the fact that he has held the two positions.[2]

All the able bodied men in this District are compelled to support themselves and families, in no case are rations knowingly issued to such: old and helpless men, women, and children are rationed, if they have no friends or relatives to take charge of them. We have a large number of girls perfectly able to work, and most of them willing to do so, for whom I can obtain no employment; I did hope to have partial work for them this summer upon a large farm I designed cultivating, but the failure to obtain a supply of horses will I fear prevent its accomplishment; should they arrive however within the next two weeks, I can partially carry out the project — I have attempted to hire out some of these girls to citizens in this vicinity, but so few of this class are able to employ them, that it has proved a failure — In localities where the citizens are willing and able to employ these people, on their farms or otherwise, I think they should be encouraged to take service with them, and if necessary forced to do so, or they will be thrown upon the Government for support. — A system can no doubt be adopted which will be perfectly just to employer and employee, which will keep these people at their homes, prevent their congregating in cities, or forming large settlements in the country, and living a life of idleness and crime; the sooner they are taught that liberty is not idleness and license the better; the lesson will have to be learned some time, and the quicker they comprehend it: the better it will be for themselves, and the people with whom in future years they will be compelled to mingle.

I find the Negroes are very much attached to their old homes, and from this fact I presume we might get rid of a portion of our surplus labor, which is composed almost exclusively of females – if the counties of Gloucester and Matthews were declared within our lines: A majority of the colored people here are from those two counties, and if they were assured they could return there in safety, many would doubtless go back and hire with their former masters: before they were permitted to do so however I would suggest that such regulations should be adopted, as would secure their full compensation for their labor, and good treatment from their employers.

I send you herewith a statement showing how the colored population of this District is made up; the number of able bodied men, their occupations, old persons, children &c &c: I also inclose a sketch of York County giving the location of the different farms, and the villages occupied by the colored people. I am General very respectfully Your obt servt

HLS   E. W. Coffin

Capt. E. W. Coffin to Bvt. Brigr. Genl. B. C. Ludlow, 21 Apr. 1865, Letters Received by Supt. of Negro Affairs, ser. 4301, Williamsburg VA Asst. Subasst. Comr., RG 105 [A-7905]. Neither of the items said to have been enclosed is in the file.

1 The civilian who had acted as agent in York County was Rodney Churchill; he had served under Captain Charles B. Wilder, the superintendent of Negro affairs for the peninsula between the York and James rivers.
2 For the policies of Colonel Frank J. White on the eastern shore, see above, docs. 44–46.

49: Free-Black Military Laborer to the Secretary of State

[*Warwick County, Va.*] May 3d 1865
Dear Sir   I take my pen to inform of my Case   I Came in the Lines on the last day of febury 64 and wife and Childrin and I hav bin working In a goverment saw mill in warwick County Virginia ever Since the 27 of December Up to this day and have not recevd a cent of money and my famley is aseffring for the sorport of my labor for i Can not by inney thing without money   I am a free man born of fre parants and I hope that theas Lines will not be an offence   it is the

first time that I venuder [*venture*] to be Right as far as wasnton and to So greater frend   nothing more at present But Remanes your cecier freind

Abraham Cannaday

Lutenint Davis at york town is one of the boses and the cortermaster at fortes monroe Is the other bost

ALS

Abraham Cannaday to Sir, 3 May 1865, filed as S-1537 1865, Letters Received, RG 107 [L-65]. By an unsigned endorsement of May 8, the State Department forwarded the letter to the Secretary of War.

CHAPTER 2

The District of Columbia

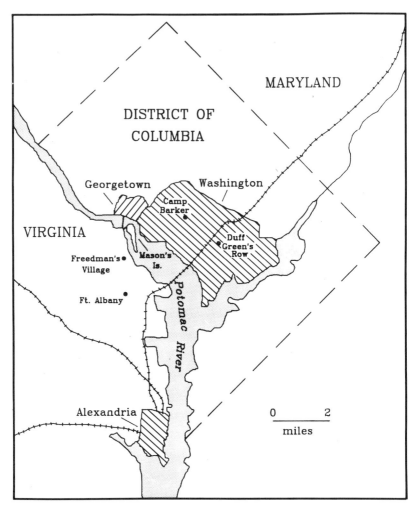

The District of Columbia

The District of Columbia

SLAVERY had been on the decline in the District of Columbia for several decades before the Civil War. At the time of Abraham Lincoln's election, slaves composed barely one-fifth of the 15,000 black people living in the District. Led by a coterie of literate and property-owning artisans and professionals, free people were both numerically preponderant and socially dominant in the local black population. A large majority of the District's black men and women supported themselves as free laborers, the men working chiefly as common laborers and the women as domestics.[1]

Events unleashed by the war delivered a death blow to slavery and sped the development of free labor. Slaves from the Maryland and Virginia countryside fled to the District of Columbia in quest of freedom. Antislavery Northerners, who had long denounced the presence of human bondage in the nation's capital, urged Congress to use its constitutional authority over the District to abolish slavery. In April 1862, within days of the war's first anniversary, the lawmakers did so. The early triumph of emancipation set the District apart from those areas of the Upper South—especially the border states and middle Tennessee—where the continuing legality of slavery obstructed the emergence of free labor.[2]

The federal government not only ended slavery in the District, but also became the largest employer of former slaves and free-black people.

[1] This chapter concerns the wartime evolution of free labor in the District of Columbia (which included the cities of Washington and Georgetown) and adjacent parts of northern Virginia. In this essay, quotations and statements of fact that appear without footnotes are drawn from the documents included in the chapter. Secondary accounts of wartime life and labor in the District of Columbia and its vicinity include Elaine Cutler Everly, "The Freedmen's Bureau in the National Capital" (Ph.D. diss., George Washington University, 1972), especially chaps. 2–4; Constance McLaughlin Green, *Washington: Village and Capital, 1800–1878* (Princeton, N.J., 1962), chaps. 10–11, and *The Secret City: A History of Race Relations in the Nation's Capital* (Princeton, N.J., 1967), chaps. 4–5; Allan John Johnston, "Surviving Freedom: The Black Community of Washington, D.C., 1860–1880" (Ph.D. diss., Duke University, 1980); Margaret Leech, *Reveille in Washington, 1860–1865* (New York, 1941), especially chap. 12; Joseph P. Reidy, " 'Coming from the Shadow of the Past': The Transition from Slavery to Freedom at Freedmen's Village, 1863–1900," *Virginia Magazine of History and Biography* 95 (Oct. 1987): 403–28.

[2] On emancipation in the District of Columbia, see *Freedom*, ser. 1, vol. 1: chap. 3.

As Washington and Alexandria, Virginia, just across the Potomac River, became the principal supply center for the eastern theater, the Union army and navy employed thousands of black men and hundreds of black women. Contractors dependent on government business hired hundreds more, as did individual officers. Private employers had to match or better the terms offered by military employers if they hoped to attract and retain black workers, especially able-bodied men. Military labor shaped the development of free labor in the District to a greater degree than in any other Union-occupied region.

At the same time, emancipation and warfare gave rise to a massive problem of relief. Destitute fugitive slaves and refugees uprooted by military operations swelled the District's population. Tens of thousands of former slaves received assistance from the government, generally only temporarily, but sometimes for long periods. The specter of poverty and dependency also loomed over most black men and women who supported themselves by their own labor. The booming economy generated jobs aplenty, but it also fueled inflation and created a scarcity of housing. In crowded wartime Washington, epidemic disease posed a grave threat to life and livelihood. Faced with large numbers of needy ex-slaves, most of whom were the relatives and friends of government workers, federal authorities assumed an unparalleled responsibility for their welfare. They issued rations and clothing and established contraband camps, employment depots, and hospitals. Agents of private benevolent societies also ministered to the newly freed slaves, sometimes working in accord with government officials, sometimes at cross-purposes.

In the distinctive setting of the national capital, amid the trying circumstances of war, black people struggled to gain the independence they believed to be freedom's birthright. They did so under close public scrutiny. Going about their daily business, congressmen and members of the Lincoln administration encountered fugitive slaves, black military laborers, and Northern ministers and teachers who worked with the freedpeople. Reporters assigned to chronicle the progress of the war investigated the government's treatment of its employees and the condition of its contraband camps. Black people in and around the District were acutely aware of their special relationship to the United States. Living in the seat of national authority and working for the government gave them a sense of personal connection to officials and institutions that seemed remote to their counterparts elsewhere in the South. That connection shaped their wartime experience with free labor.

The attack on Fort Sumter in April 1861 transformed Washington into a city at war. The secession of Virginia the following month brought the Confederacy within eyesight of the presidential mansion, and the wavering loyalty of Maryland raised fears that the capital might be enveloped by hostile territory. Rushing to strengthen the District's defenses, Union officials organized white men as soldiers and white and black men as laborers. Federal troops crossed the Potomac River to secure Alexandria and its strategic railroad facilities. Army engineers supervised the reinforcement of existing fortifications and the construction of new ones. In both the District of Columbia and northern Virginia, new rail lines, roads, and warehouses were built to facilitate the movement of men and supplies. Meanwhile, the army's medical department prepared for the inevitable tide of sick and wounded soldiers. Wartime mobilization assigned battalions of clerks to pen and paper and brigades of laborers to pick and shovel. Although no black people advanced beyond the rank of messenger in the swollen federal bureaucracy, they found abundant work as manual laborers, both skilled and unskilled.[3]

Amid the bustle of activity, thousands of slaves sought freedom. In the first months of the war, federal authorities and city police worked zealously to capture fugitive slaves, remanding them either to their masters or to the city jail. Before long, however, runaways from rebellious Virginia received a friendlier reception. In July 1861, General Joseph K. F. Mansfield, commander of the Department of Washington, designated Virginia slaves who had taken refuge in the District "contrabands" and suggested that they be employed "about the jail or for the improvement of public premises, in its neighbourhood." In deference to slaveholders in loyal Maryland, military authorities refused to accord contraband status to runaways from that state. But by claiming to be Virginians or finding Union soldiers willing to harbor them, many fugitive slaves from southern Maryland managed to gain practical if not legal freedom. Some women and children who escaped to Union camps in Maryland became free when General Joseph Hooker, who employed their husbands and fathers as military laborers, had them transported to Washington.[4]

General Mansfield forwarded many of the contrabands to the Old Capitol Prison, a facility that also held political prisoners and captured Confederates. William P. Wood, the prison's superintendent, tried to find them "situations" with military or private employers. By late February 1862, Wood had received several hundred contrabands, most of whom had been hired out and were reportedly "doing well." Yet the confinement of former slaves near white prisoners offended some observers, including an army surgeon who urged "as a sanitary measure" that the black inmates be "kept more apart from respectable white people."

[3] On the wartime mobilization, see Green, *Washington*, chaps. 9–10.
[4] On fugitive slaves in the District between the beginning of the war and April 1862, and federal policy concerning them, see *Freedom*, ser. 1, vol. 1: pp. 160–64, and docs. 41–51.

General James S. Wadsworth, who became military governor of the District of Columbia in March, evidently agreed. Soon after assuming office, he ordered the contrabands relocated to Duff Green's Row, a cluster of tenements just east of the Capitol. Wood remained in charge of them and continued to hire out those for whom he could find employment.[5]

Emancipation, enacted in April 1862, transformed the District of Columbia into a beacon of liberty for slaves from miles around.[6] The tide of fugitives from Virginia and Maryland surged in response to the new opportunity to gain freedom. A number of the District's free-black residents, however, doubted that emancipation would remove the legal and customary discrimination against which they had long contended. Some sought to avail themselves of a provision in the emancipation law that appropriated money for colonizing black people outside the United States. At least sixty men, among them Henry M. Turner, a minister of the African Methodist Episcopal Church, petitioned Congress for aid in emigrating where "they may seek and secure, by their own industry, that mental and physical development which will allow them an honorable position in the families of God's great world." Dismissing Liberia as "too distant from the land of our birth" and Haiti as dominated by a corrupt elite, they set their sights on Central America, a region "bearing spontaneously all that is suited to our race." In the end, plans to establish a Central American colony collapsed, and few black people emigrated elsewhere. The vast majority were optimistic about the possibilities created by emancipation and too preoccupied with earning a living even to consider removal.

A major military campaign in the spring of 1862 contributed to the District's swelling population of fugitive slaves. In March, General George B. McClellan's Army of the Potomac departed Washington for Fortress Monroe, in tidewater Virginia, aiming to capture the Confederate capital. Setting that juggernaut in motion required the services of thousands of laborers and teamsters, many of them black men from Washington and its vicinity. While McClellan's army inched its way toward Richmond, Union troops commanded by General Irwin McDowell maneuvered against General Thomas J. Jackson in the Virginia counties south and west of Washington. The movement of contending armies enabled hundreds of northern Virginia slaves to escape their owners, and the devastation of the countryside encouraged many of them to seek a livelihood in Alexandria or Washington. Some free-black landowners in northern Virginia, fearing for their safety and subsistence, joined the exodus.

Private relief organizations, both local and national, endeavored to

---

[5] In addition to the relevant documents in this chapter, see Leech, *Reveille in Washington*, p. 246.
[6] For the emancipation act, see *Statutes at Large*, vol. 12, pp. 376–78.

assist the former slaves. Closest to home were the National Freedman's Relief Association of the District of Columbia, formed in March 1862 by abolitionist civil servants and professionals, and the Contraband Relief Association, organized some months later by "well-to-do colored people," including Elizabeth Keckley, a seamstress whose clients included Mary Todd Lincoln. Both groups sought to relieve the "immediate bodily wants" of the former slaves, to educate them, and to "bring them under moral and religious influences." From points North, newly formed freedmen's aid societies sent agents to Washington and Alexandria to teach and preach among the contrabands, as did long-established antislavery societies and religious organizations such as the American Missionary Association and the American Tract Society.[7]

Pressed to provide for the growing number of fugitive slaves, General Wadsworth welcomed the reformers' assistance. In June 1862, he transferred control over the former slaves at Duff Green's Row to Danforth B. Nichols, a Methodist minister affiliated with both the National Freedman's Relief Association and the American Missionary Association who had once headed a reform school in Chicago. Nichols issued food and blankets from government stores and distributed clothing donated by Northern aid societies. He also continued to hire out able-bodied adults. Soon Wadsworth expanded Nichols's jurisdiction to include destitute freedpeople throughout the District of Columbia.[8]

In the close quarters of Duff Green's Row, sanitary conditions deteriorated and disease spread rapidly. An outbreak of smallpox in July prompted fears of an epidemic that might menace the entire city. In response, Nichols relocated his charges to a block of recently vacated army barracks and stables in a sparsely populated neighborhood. The new settlement, known as Camp Barker, became the center of the government's effort to provide relief and employment for former slaves in the District of Columbia. Incoming fugitives were registered, issued "free papers," and supplied with food, clothing, and shelter. The number of admissions grew rapidly in the months that followed, peaking in September 1862 after McClellan returned to northern Virginia and

---

[7] Everly, "Freedmen's Bureau in the National Capital," chap. 4; *First Annual Report of the National Freedman's Relief Association of the District of Columbia* (Washington, D.C., 1863); Green, *Washington*, pp. 280–81; Elizabeth Keckley, *Behind the Scenes. Or, Thirty Years a Slave, and Four Years in the White House* (1868; reprint ed., New York, 1968), pp. 111–16. In time, as the government increasingly provided basic necessities for many destitute ex-slaves, the National Freedman's Relief Association concentrated upon defending the legal rights of freedpeople and sponsoring schools, while the Contraband Relief Association (subsequently the Freedmen and Soldiers' Relief Association) worked especially on behalf of the families of black soldiers. (*Second Annual Report of the National Freedman's Relief Association of the District of Columbia* [Washington, D.C., 1864]; *Second Annual Report, of the Freedmen and Soldiers' Relief Association . . .* [Washington, 1864].)

[8] In addition to the relevant documents in this chapter, see Everly, "Freedmen's Bureau in the National Capital," pp. 34–36.

Confederate forces invaded Maryland. In that month alone, more than 1,400 former slaves entered the camp.[9]

Conditions at Camp Barker discouraged a lengthy stay. The barracks, averaging ten by twelve feet in size, routinely housed two or three families apiece; one cabin sheltered twenty-six people. Cramped even by the rude standards of life in slavery, such quarters afforded their inhabitants no privacy and virtually guaranteed the rapid spread of disease. Nichols did not encourage freedpeople to remain for long. His notion of their best interests, as well as the orders of his superiors, enjoined niggardly dispensation of relief, and that only to the deserving. In determining who was eligible for assistance, Nichols exercised his authority in ways that struck the former slaves and other observers as arbitrary and even tyrannical. His authoritarian bent—at times manifested in physical abuse—earned him the enmity of many of his charges. One of them judged his conduct "worse than the general treatment of slave owners."

A far cry from their expectations of freedom, life at Camp Barker reinforced the former slaves' determination "to do for themselves." Most able-bodied men stayed only briefly before hiring with military or private employers. Only a handful were retained for necessary work about the camp; they received $6 per month plus rations and quarters, considerably less than the going rate elsewhere. Healthy women with few or no children also had little trouble obtaining work as domestic servants, laundresses, or attendants in military hospitals.[10]

Because freedpeople capable of supporting themselves and their families left Camp Barker as fast as newcomers arrived, its population grew but little, generally ranging between 500 and 700. Of the 4,900 former slaves who entered the camp between its founding and April 1863, only 557 remained on hand at the end of the period. The long-term residents were mostly women with small children and elderly, sick, or disabled people. Casting about for ways to occupy those capable of some labor, Nichols proposed to employ the women in "a systematic laundry," but his plan came to naught. With few alternatives, women in the camp busied themselves with nonremunerative chores and child-rearing, while children and old and disabled men did odd jobs.

Military labor was an important road to free labor for former slaves throughout the Union-occupied South, but nowhere was the road more

<hr>

9 Everly, "Freedmen's Bureau in the National Capital," pp. 36–37; Leech, *Reveille in Washington*, pp. 246, 249; Register of Freedmen at Camp Barker, June 1862–Dec. 1863, vol. 101, ser. 570, Camp Barker DC, RG 105 [A-10092]. Data from this source are analyzed in Johnston, "Surviving Freedom," pp. 188–217.

10 In addition to the relevant documents in this chapter, see Register of Freedmen at Camp Barker, June 1862–Dec. 1863, vol. 101, ser. 570, Camp Barker DC, RG 105 [A-10092]; testimony of Wm. Slade before the American Freedmen's Inquiry Commission, [Apr.? 1863], filed with O-328 1863, Letters Received, ser. 12, RG 94 [K-67].

heavily traveled than in the District of Columbia and northern Virginia. Military employers found former slaves eager to work and willing to perform more grueling tasks, at lower pay and under stricter supervision, than even the most desperate white workers would tolerate. At army hospitals, freedmen were put to work "cleansing cesspools, scrubbing privies and policing the grounds . . . , whitewashing, and hauling wood and water." White civilians shunned these tasks, and soldiers found them "so repugnant . . . that they will not even imperfectly, perform them, except under the fear of punishment." Black laborers on fortifications often found themselves working in gangs of thirty or more under the command of an "overseer" or "boss." Although black men and women avoided such work when they could, they did not always have a choice.[11]

As free people, black military laborers both expected and needed to receive wages. But dollars often moved slowly from the U.S. Treasury to their pockets. Many military laborers drew pay only once every three months, and some experienced even longer delays. A large number were never paid at all, in some cases because government employers reasoned that "[s]ustenance & freedom" were compensation enough. Even when the laborers subsisted on government rations, they still required cash for rent and other necessities, as well as food for their families. Delays in wage payments forced workers to purchase supplies on credit from merchants who, one group of black military laborers charged, had "no interest in our people, except to make all they can out of them."

Civilian employers did no better by black workers than their military counterparts. Many householders engaged domestic servants for a month or so and then dismissed them without pay. By charging their employees exorbitant prices for quarters and supplies, some government contractors recouped their outlay for wages and then some. So common was such bilking of black workers by civilian employers that General Wadsworth ordered his provost marshal to investigate allegations and arrest wrongdoers. But in the absence of more systematic military supervision, former slaves in private employ remained vulnerable. Confidence men took advantage of the unsuspecting and the desperate. "From the moment the contraband lands within our lines and gets any money," observed Nichols, "he is the victim of fraud and robbery."

Initially unschooled in the ways of free labor, former slaves proved to be quick studies. They learned to negotiate favorable terms of employ-

[11] In addition to the relevant documents in this chapter, see Lt. Col. B. S. Alexander to Brig. Gen. J. G. Barnard, 3 Nov. 1862, enclosed in Brig. Genl. J. G. Barnard to Col. C. Mc-Keever, 3 Nov. 1862, B-132 1862, Letters Received, ser. 5382, Defenses of Washington, RG 393 Pt. 1 [C-4580]; Capt. John P. Sherburne to Brig. Gen. Whipple, 14 May 1862, vol. 98 DW, pp. 78–79, Letters Sent, ser. 642, Military Dist. of Washington, RG 393 Pt. 2 No. 12 [C-4719].

ment with private and military employers, often playing one against the other. And as former slaves tested their options regarding the varieties and conditions of employment, both military and private employers found themselves compelled to offer higher pay, improved working conditions, and other inducements in order to attract workers.

Wages rose in response to the mounting demand for labor and the freedpeople's awareness of the value of their services. By the fall of 1862, pay for black military laborers and teamsters ranged from $20 to $25 per month, "nearly double the wages paid to farm laborers at the North," according to General Wadsworth, and more than double the $10 stipulated in the Militia Act of July 1862. Quartermaster General Montgomery C. Meigs affirmed the necessity of paying the going rate; any reduction, he predicted, would "produce much dissatisfaction and suffering" among the laborers and "probably deprive the Government of the services of a large portion of them." The judge advocate general concurred, ruling that the Militia Act applied only to black workers formally enrolled under its provisions. But that distinction proved impossible to maintain. When ex-slave laborers employed with the Army of the Potomac, who had been rated at $10, "demanded equality" with better-paid co-workers who had been free before the war, the quartermasters in charge of them had little choice but to acquiesce. The pay restrictions of the Militia Act became a dead letter in the District of Columbia and northern Virginia. Military employers, like civilian ones, had to "pay wages such as the market price of labor requires."[12]

Unfortunately for black workers, prices rose at least as fast as wages. Men earning $20 per month found that "every thing is so high" their money would "not go any whare." Affordable shelter was all but unobtainable. Wartime immigration created an enormous demand for housing, and a construction boom inflated real estate values. The combination sent rents skyrocketing, making it difficult for freedpeople to find a place to live. Although some military employers provided quarters for their workers, none accommodated entire families. Many former slaves turned squatters, constructing crude dwellings in alleys and vacant lots. Although these makeshift hovels cost little to construct, they boasted few comforts, and their occupants might be evicted at any time.

The housing shortage was especially severe in Alexandria. By the fall of 1862, former slaves had appropriated virtually every unoccupied structure in the city, whatever its intended use. Julia A. Wilbur, an

[12] For the Militia Act, see *Statutes at Large*, vol. 12, pp. 597–600. On the wages paid black quartermaster employees in the Army of the Potomac, see Chf. Qr. Master Rufus Ingalls to Brg. Genl. M. C. Meigs, 18 Jan. 1863, enclosing Circular, Head Quarters Army of the Potomac, Office of Chief Quartermaster, 1 Nov. 1862, and Circular, Head Quarters Army of the Potomac, Office of Chief Quartermaster, 1 Jan. 1863, "Contraband Fund," Consolidated Correspondence File, ser. 225, Central Records, RG 92 [Y-33].

agent of the Ladies Anti-Slavery Society of Rochester, New York, found hundreds of freedpeople huddled in an old slave pen, an abandoned schoolhouse, and "several tenements that can hardly be called a shelter." She alternately petitioned, pleaded, and demanded that the government furnish housing for destitute fugitive slaves. General Samuel P. Heintzelman, commander of the defenses of Washington south of the Potomac, balked at doing so, lest freedpeople inundate the city "when they learn[ed] that the Government will feed & shelter them." Yet former slaves kept coming even without such encouragement, eventually forcing military authorities to construct several new barracks and permit freedpeople to reside in other government-controlled buildings.

In assuming the role of landlord, federal authorities in Alexandria pursued a course that alienated their tenants. Determined to reduce expenses and foster self-reliance, military officials ordered the black residents of government-controlled housing to pay rent if they could afford to do so. Former slaves accepted that policy in principle; indeed, reported a provost marshal, most met the obligation "cheerfully, feeling that it is honorable to do so." But many of them objected to the manner in which it was enforced by Albert Gladwin, a Northern minister who was assigned to collect the rents. Not only did Gladwin evict tenants who were temporarily unable to pay because of illness or nonpayment of wages, but he also charged rates that many residents deemed exorbitant. Julia Wilbur and other Northern missionaries, backed by a faction of army officers, also criticized Gladwin's overbearing manner and his practice of renting out structures "fit only for a hog pen or chicken coop." The controversy escalated when Gladwin emerged as the leading candidate for the position of superintendent of contrabands in Alexandria. Wilbur and her allies denounced him as "a brutal man," while his military supporters dismissed such criticism as the carping of "female 'busybodies' " and "would-be-philanthropists" who sought to make the former slaves dependent on charity instead of their own exertions. The conflict over Gladwin's appointment exposed complex rivalries among the freedpeople's self-proclaimed friends – rivalries fueled by ambition and personal animosity as well as differing conceptions of how best to advance the welfare of the former slaves.

In the fall of 1862, federal authorities moved to reduce expenditures for the relief of destitute ex-slaves. Assuming that all persons of African descent – free and ex-slave – constituted a single community responsible for all its members, they shifted responsibility for the support of dependent freedpeople to the shoulders of the able-bodied black men employed by the government. In early October, at the instance of General Wadsworth, the War Department began deducting $5 from the monthly earnings of black teamsters and laborers employed by quartermasters in the District of Columbia and Alexandria, creating from the proceeds a fund to support needy ex-slaves. Black workers hired by other military employers were not subject to the tax, an anomaly that led many quartermaster laborers to take jobs in other departments. One wily quartermaster resorted to "withholding the pay already due" his black employees to prevent them from defecting.[13] To end such competition, the War Department extended the $5 deduction to almost all black military laborers in the District of Columbia and northern Virginia. The department also assessed a "hospital tax" of 1 percent of wages to defray the cost of medical care, but this tax, unlike the $5 deduction, applied to white laborers as well.

Administrative problems plagued the so-called contraband fund. Guidelines governing the wage deductions were loose and their supervision looser. Lacking clear instructions, some military employers simply failed to impose the tax. Those who did often had no idea of how to dispose of the accumulated funds. A few evidently diverted the money to their own pockets. The chief quartermaster of the Army of the Potomac terminated "the stoppage system" in his jurisdiction because it "could not be executed in the field without many abuses on the part of Quartermasters, and much injustice to the colored employés."[14]

Black military laborers had their own reasons to criticize the contraband fund. The monthly deduction represented a de facto pay cut of 20 to 25 percent for all but the most highly skilled and best-paid. The proportion was even larger for workers who lost time through sickness or disability but still had the deduction taken from their short pay. All too often, the tax left black wage-earners with barely enough to make ends meet – if that much. Large numbers quit military labor to accept better terms from private employers. Beyond the widely shared dissatisfaction with the reduction of their wages, many black workers who had been free before the war disputed the rationale behind the tax, arguing that it discriminated against them and in favor of former slaves. One group in Alexandria complained that their newly freed co-workers enjoyed "all the attention," including government-supplied housing, "provission for them selves and families, and even wood a[nd] coal to cook with," whereas freeborn men "have to support our selves and families, and provide for them in every respect with the exceptions of our own rations." It was "nomore then wright," they argued, "that the contrabands em-

[13] Capt. C. B. Ferguson to Brig. Genl. L. Thomas, 5 Dec. 1862, F-486 1862, Letters Received, ser. 12, RG 94 [K-225].

[14] On difficulties in the administration of the contraband fund, see, in addition to the relevant documents in this chapter, Chf. Qr. Master Rufus Ingalls to Brg. Genl. M. C. Meigs, 18 Jan. 1863; Lieut. Col. Elias M. Greene to Brig. Gen. M. C. Meigs, 22 Feb. 1864; and Lt. Col. Elias M. Greene to Brevet Major Genl. M. C. Meigs, 11 Aug. 1864, all filed under "Contraband Fund," Consolidated Correspondence File, ser. 225, Central Records, RG 92 [Y-32, Y-33, Y-36]; Maj. Morris S. Miller to Genl. M. C. Meigs, 23 Mar. 1863, M-7 (Book 52) 1863; Maj. Morris S. Miller to General M. C. Meigs, 1 Apr. 1863, M-139 (Book 52) 1863; Maj. Morris S. Miller to Genl. M. C. Meigs, 16 Apr. 1863 (two letters), M-260 & M-264 (Book 52) 1863, Letters Received, ser. 20, Central Records, RG 92 [Y-615].

ployed in the government, service should be curtailed in wages for the surport of they fellow men." The freemen questioned, however, why they should be obligated "to pay a tax for the benefit of the contrabands any more then white labours of our class." Despite complaints about the wage deductions, self-supporting black people – both freeborn and newly liberated – were generally willing to assist the needy. They objected to the contraband fund not only because their contributions were compulsory and white military laborers were exempt, but also because they had no control over its disbursement.

Repeated protests by black military laborers eventually prompted a defense of the contraband fund by the officials who administered it. Colonel Elias M. Greene, chief quartermaster of the Department of Washington, insisted that the tax was neither burdensome nor discriminatory. Even after the deduction, he maintained, the workers earned enough to provide for their families. The contraband fund purchased food, blankets, and firewood for distribution to destitute freedpeople, especially the families of laborers absent in the field. Left unexamined was the premise that the burden for the relief of former slaves should be borne entirely by black military laborers instead of constituting part of the government's larger obligation to shelter and feed loyal civilians displaced by the war.

Military events in the spring and summer of 1863 increased both the fund's contributors and its beneficiaries. The advances and retreats of the Confederate and Union armies dislodged thousands of slaves, who took refuge in Washington and Alexandria. Government employers immediately claimed those fit for military labor. As of August, an estimated 4,700 black men were working at the quartermaster's depots in Washington and Alexandria, and 11,000 more were in the field with the Army of the Potomac.[15] Even those large numbers failed to meet the needs of quartermasters and engineers, who sought to remedy local shortages by importing black laborers from other jurisdictions.[16]

The enlistment of black men in the Union army, beginning in the spring of 1863, accounted for part of the shortfall. Once given the opportunity, many black men enthusiastically took up arms against the

---

[15] Qr. Mr. Gen'l M. C. Meigs to Hon. E. M. Stanton, 5 Aug. 1863, vol. 8, pp. 168–9, Letters, Endorsements, & Reports Sent to the Secretary of War & Heads of Depts., ser. 10, Central Records, RG 92 [Y-696].

[16] In their quest for black laborers, federal officials in the District turned first to tidewater Virginia and North Carolina. (Lt. Col. B. S. Alexander to Brig. Gen. J. G. Barnard, 4 Oct. 1862, filed as H-141 1862 [Book 50], Letters Received, ser. 20, Central Records, RG 92 [Y-642]; see above, doc. 19.) Before long, they were also looking to western Maryland, the Midwest, the South Carolina Sea Islands, and Louisiana. (Bvt. Col. E. S. Sibley to Capt. W. G. Pinckard, 4 Apr. 1863, vol. 67, p. 455; Cap't. Benj. C. Card to Cap't. A. C. Woolfolk, 1 Aug. 1863, vol. 70, p. 492; Col. J. J. Dana to Gen. D. H. Rucker, 6 Sept. 1864, vol. 79, pp. 343–44; Col. J. J. Dana to Brig. Genl. D. H. Rucker, 28 Oct. 1864, vol. 80, p. 498, Letters Sent, ser. 9, Central Records, RG 92 [Y-616, Y-717, Y-687].)

Confederacy. The Reverend Henry M. Turner, a champion of colonization just one year earlier, opened his church to federal recruiting officers and accepted a chaplaincy in one of the two black regiments raised in the District. But volunteering slackened when black men found that armed service, subject to the restrictions of the Militia Act, paid less than half as much as common labor. Recruiting depots continued to attract young, unmarried men, but men with families to support generally preferred military labor or private employment. As enlistments waned, recruiters resorted to impressment, dragooning freemen and former slaves in both town and country.[17]

The enlistment or employment of able-bodied black men did not guarantee food and shelter for the thousands of black women, children, and old and disabled men within federal lines. Their growing number impelled Colonel Greene to devise a comprehensive plan for short-term relief and long-term improvement. Greene's proposal centered on resettling the dependent freedpeople at Camp Barker and elsewhere in the District on abandoned farms in northern Virginia. There they could raise their own food and grow vegetables for Union troops and forage for the army's draft animals. Such arrangements, Greene argued, would at one stroke "conduce to the sanitary and moral improvement of the contrabands," relieve overcrowding in Washington, and "save the Gov^t an immense amount of money."

Greene's proposal won the approbation of his superiors. In May 1863, General Heintzelman (now commanding the Department of Washington) granted him authority over several abandoned estates on the Virginia side of the Potomac and jurisdiction over all former slaves in the department who were not employed by the government. The following month, Secretary of War Edwin M. Stanton gave him control over the contraband fund. In short order, Greene established five "government farms," which would eventually have nearly 1,300 acres under cultivation. He also began to construct a contraband camp, "Freedman's Village," at Arlington, the estate of Confederate General Robert E. Lee.[18] In contrast to the squalid conditions at Camp Barker, Freedman's Village boasted roomy dwellings and land for gardens, neatly arranged atop a hill overlooking Washington. Also featured were a hospital, a chapel, and workshops where young men were to learn skilled trades

[17] On the recruitment of black regiments in the District of Columbia, see *Freedom*, ser. 2: docs. 147A–B; J. D. Turner and Wm. G. Raymond to Maj. Vincent, 25 May 1863, filed with T-4 1863, Letters Received, ser. 360, Colored Troops Division, RG 94 [B-607]. On impressment, see, in addition to the relevant documents in this chapter, Catherine Johnson to Sir, 2 [July] 1863, enclosed in Major Elias Wright to Capt. C. W. Foster, 3 July 1863, W-37 1863, Letters Received, ser. 360, Colored Troops Division, RG 94 [B-45]; Brig. Genl. [John H. Martindale] to Major Raymond, 7 July 1863, vol. 99 DW, pp. 160–61, Letters Sent, ser. 642, Military Dist. of Washington, RG 393 Pt. 2 No. 12 [C-4726].

[18] On Freedman's Village, see, in addition to the relevant documents in this chapter, Reidy, " 'Coming from the Shadow of the Past.' "

and young women "the use of the needle & of the sewing machine." A company of soldiers provided security. With Greene's encouragement, the American Tract Society organized a school. Greene appointed Danforth Nichols superintendent of Freedman's Village and assigned experienced farmers to manage each of the government farms.

Greene and like-minded officials envisioned Freedman's Village as a sort of halfway house where former slaves would reside for a time, acquire useful skills, and develop habits of industry and independence before moving on to productive lives without further government assistance. In addition to quarters and rations, freedpeople employed in the village and on the government farms received wages of $10 per month for men and $6 for women, with boys and girls aged twelve to fourteen earning half those amounts. From their earnings, they were expected to purchase their own clothing and other necessities.[19] The modest level of compensation, Greene argued, provided an incentive to labor without creating "undue encouragement to remain" in the camp instead of seeking "more remunerative employment."

In reality, only a small proportion of the former slaves at Freedman's Village worked for wages. As of late September 1863, most of the 900 residents were women, children, and old or disabled people—"paupers" in the camp's system of classification. Only 150 were healthy men. Yet unlike Camp Barker, which was little more than a receiving depot for fugitive slaves and a refuge of last resort for the desperate, the new camp exhibited at least the potential of becoming self-sustaining. By the end of the year, the freedpeople on the government farms had harvested crops and manured fields for the next year's cultivation. At the same time, disbursements from the contraband fund and donations from benevolent societies provided for the material and educational needs of the "indigent and infirm" at Freedman's Village. A tireless promoter of both Freedman's Village and his own career, Colonel Greene paraded distinguished visitors through the camp, touting it as a showcase for transforming destitute former slaves into upstanding citizens.

Although most freedpeople in the District of Columbia and northern Virginia sustained themselves without government assistance, the rising cost of living challenged even the most industrious. Many private employers increased wages to offset inflation, but the federal government—the area's largest employer—held the line. Its intransigence sparked widespread protest during the fall of 1863, involving both white and black workers. Tradesmen and laborers at the Treasury building and bookbinders and typesetters at the Government Printing Office struck for higher wages and shorter hours of work. Employees at the navy yard and the arsenal petitioned for a ten-hour day. Work-

[19] Testimony of Dr. D. B. Nichols, [Jan.? 1864], Miscellaneous Records, ser. 5412, Dept. of Washington & 22nd Army Corps, RG 393 Pt. 1 [C-4757].

ers in the quartermaster's department also demanded higher wages. To the grievances of their white counterparts black military laborers added longstanding dissatisfaction with the contraband-fund deductions. Claiming "Some faint Conceptions. of the value of our Labor," a group of free-black quartermaster employees declared their compensation "unequal To the Services We Render and the Demands of the Times." They petitioned for "Removal of The . . . Contraband Tax." By late November, federal authorities were facing a tidal wave of discontent. Amid rumors of an impending strike "among the Mechanics, Teamsters, Hostlers, Stablemen & Laborers," quartermasters feared that the war effort would be thrown into "utter confusion."[20]

That prospect goaded military employers to increase wages. Beginning in December 1863, quartermaster employees received a 20 percent raise. Black laborers and teamsters who had earned gross wages of $25 per month now earned $30, minus, as before, the $5 levy for the contraband fund and the 1 percent hospital tax.[21] Other military departments followed suit. Federal officials later made minor concessions to opponents of the contraband tax. Defending the deduction in principle, Colonel Greene and others conceded its burden upon the small minority of military laborers who earned $20 per month or less and acknowledged the injustice of requiring workers to pay both the contraband tax and the hospital tax. Accordingly, Secretary of War Stanton exempted the lower-paid black laborers from the contraband-fund levy and excused the better-paid from the hospital tax. But federal authorities rejected a general repeal of the deductions.

As the government's commitment to Freedman's Village and the government farms increased, so did its disapproval of unsanctioned settlements of black people. Some of them consisted of former slaves who supported themselves on their home estates after they were abandoned by their owners.[22] Other settlements were established on vacant land by refugees from the Confederate interior. In northern Virginia, army officers systematically relocated such squatters to Freedman's Vil-

[20] On the grievances of government workers, see, in addition to the relevant documents in this chapter, Leech, *Reveille in Washington*, pp. 273–74; Robert Rocket et al. to Capt. Daniel G. Thomas, 23 Nov. 1863, "Wages," Consolidated Correspondence File, ser. 225, Central Records, RG 92 [Y-746]. On the rumor of a general strike, see Capt. Chas. H. Tompkins to Brig. Genl. D. H. Rucker, 24 Nov. 1863, enclosed in Brig. Genl. D. H. Rucker to Brig. Genl. M. C. Meigs, 24 Nov. 1863, "Wages," Consolidated Correspondence File, ser. 225, Central Records, RG 92 [Y-746]; Asst. Qr. Mr. General Chs. Thomas to Brig. Gen'l. M. C. Meigs, 22 Jan. 1864, vol. 74, pp. 158–60, Letters Sent, ser. 9, Central Records, RG 92 [Y-681].

[21] Asst. Qr. Mr. General Chs. Thomas to Brig. Gen'l. M. C. Meigs, 22 Jan. 1864, vol. 74, pp. 158–60, Letters Sent, ser. 9, Central Records, RG 92 [Y-681].

[22] *Freedom*, ser. 1, vol. 1: doc. 43; Prov. Mar. Genl. Jas. A. Tait to Major Genl. Heintzelman, 20 Jan. 1862 [1863], vol. 363 DW, pp. 39–40, Letters Sent by the Provost Marshal, ser. 1457, Defenses of Washington South of the Potomac, Provost Marshal Field Organizations, RG 393 Pt. 4 [C-4775]; Adjutant General L. Thomas to Colonel J. P. Taylor, 2 Jan. 1862, "Arlington Estate," Consolidated Correspondence File, ser. 225, Central Records, RG 92 [Y-125].

lage. One group of about sixteen families had constructed shanties in the shadow of Fort Albany, a federal installation near Arlington. There they had succeeded, observers agreed, in "supporting themselves, and families, after the manner of white laborers." Avowing that they "did not want to be of any expense to the government but desired to live on the produce of their own labor" without "any superintendent or overseer," they resisted efforts to uproot them. But federal officials would have it no other way. Late in 1863, while the men were absent performing military labor, Union soldiers routed the settlement, removing some of its residents to Freedman's Village and others to Washington. Outraged by their dispossession, some of the freedpeople swore "they [would] rather go back into slavery than to receive such treatment."

In late December 1863, the remaining residents of Camp Barker suffered a similar fate. They numbered about 685, the "cullings" of some 15,000 freedpeople who had entered the camp since its inception.[23] Colonel Greene ordered their transfer to Freedman's Village, citing the comfortable accommodations there and the necessity of containing the spread of smallpox, which had ravaged Camp Barker during the fall. The freedpeople, however, objected to being sent to the Virginia side of the Potomac River, away from friends and relatives in Washington. Rumors circulated that "they were going over to be under slave owners or slave drivers" and that they would be exposed to guerrilla attacks. The prospect of once again being under the authority of Danforth Nichols so distressed some of them that they preferred to "starve in Washington than go to Arlington." Even those who were willing to relocate had no desire to do so in the bone-chilling weather that had settled over the area. Captain James I. Ferree, Camp Barker's military superintendent, urged a postponement "for humanity's sake," but to no avail. When Union soldiers commenced the transfer, hundreds of freedpeople fled the scene, taking refuge wherever they could. In the end, the military escort succeeded in transporting only 180 inhabitants of Camp Barker to Freedman's Village. There the uprooted freedpeople found conditions little better than those they had left. Awaiting the construction of cabins, they slept in tents, shivering against the cold wind and damp ground. Exposure to the elements reduced resistance to disease, and smallpox reappeared. Disease and disorder frightened established residents of Freedman's Village, who shunned the sickly and demoralized newcomers.

Despite the brutal measures sometimes employed to transfer them to its quarters, many inhabitants of Freedman's Village found life there preferable to the harsh struggle for survival in Washington and Alexandria. Former slaves in Freedman's Village, unlike those in the city, were

---

[23] On the population of Camp Barker, see, in addition to the relevant documents in this chapter, the sources cited above, in note 9.

257

at least assured rations and shelter when unable to work because of ill-ness, infirmity, or age. Moreover, the officials in charge of Freedman's Village respected the freedpeople's desire to maintain the integrity of their families — a central concern to people whose kinship connections had, under slavery, been constantly at risk. Residents could share quar-ters with their spouses, children, and aged parents. Families whose chief wage-earners had enlisted in the Union army or were absent at military labor could be assured of finding each other when their duty ended. Children could attend school. For these reasons, and contrary to the hopes of Colonel Greene, many of the former slaves at Freedman's Village displayed little inclination to hire out for "service with private families or individuals." The heavy-handed methods of military recruit-ers made enlistment a similarly unappealing alternative for the few eligible men in the camp. Over time, some long-term residents came to regard Freedman's Village as home, developing a sense of proprietor-ship in their cabins and the gardens they worked. After the war, amid a controversy over the closing of the camp and the return of the estate to its antebellum owners, residents would remember that "the govern-ment fully impressed upon the people the idea that in some way they would come to possess a valid claim to a part of Arlington."[24]

The reluctance of some freedpeople to leave Freedman's Village com-plicated efforts by federal authorities to provide for new arrivals. In March 1864, more than 400 bedraggled survivors of a colony on Ile à Vache, Haiti, were assigned to Freedman's Village after being rescued from the ill-fated settlement. Hundreds of other newcomers hailed from contested territory in Virginia and from southern Maryland, where slavery tottered on its last legs. In July, Confederate General Jubal A. Early's raid through western Maryland to the outskirts of Washington prompted additional accessions, as black people fled ex-posed areas of the countryside for the security of garrisoned places. By the time Early retreated into Virginia, nearly 2,200 former slaves were living at Freedman's Village, with several hundred more on the govern-ment farms.[25]

Faced with an influx of needy freedpeople, Greene and his subordi-nates redoubled their efforts to induce residents of Freedman's Village to accept employment elsewhere. In June 1864, Greene took over a camp on Mason's (now Roosevelt) Island, in the Potomac River, that had previously served as a rendezvous for black soldiers, placing it

[24] John B. Syphax to the Honorable, Wm. C. Endicott, 18 Jan. 1888, "Freedman's Village," Consolidated Correspondence File, ser. 225, Central Records, RG 92 [Y-77].

[25] In addition to the relevant documents in this chapter, see Johnston, "Surviving Freedom," pp. 198–204. On the Ile à Vache colony, which had been sponsored by the Lincoln administration, see Willis D. Boyd, "Negro Colonization in the National Crisis, 1860–1870" (Ph.D. diss., University of California, Los Angeles, 1953), chap. 13.

under Nichols's supervision. "[S]ituated very conveniently for persons desiring to get Servants," the island was to be an employment depot for freedpeople prepared to support themselves, while Freedman's Village would continue to serve the needs of the unemployable. Accommodations at Mason's Island were deliberately spartan, lest "comfortable" facilities make its inmates "unwilling to go out to Service." A guard of soldiers and the currents of the Potomac isolated the freedpeople from friends and relatives at Freedman's Village, as well as from the temptations of Washington.

Notwithstanding the intentions of its founders, Mason's Island became home to a population virtually indistinguishable from that of Freedman's Village. Officials dumped former slaves on the island regardless of their prospects of employment. A month after its establishment, the camp housed nearly 1,200 freedpeople, more than half of them children. Residents of its cramped barracks complained that people of both sexes had to "[sleep] on the floor promiscuously." Determined to reduce the population of the camp, Nichols and his assistants welcomed prospective employers with little or no scrutiny. Nine-year-old Carter Holmes, apprenticed at Mason's Island to a Maryland farmer, was supposed to receive food, clothing, and schooling; instead, he endured three years of abuse and beatings before fleeing from his new master.[26]

The somber verdict from such evidence remained in the future; meanwhile, Colonel Greene extolled his regime in a bid to direct the national "Bureau of Emancipation" under consideration in Congress.[27] But not every government official accepted Greene's flattering assessment of his work. Majors Elisha H. Ludington and Charles E. Compton, who inspected Freedman's Village, Mason's Island, and the government farms in July 1864, raised serious questions. Although they found Freedman's Village well-tended and conceded that the government farms "compare favorably with others in the vicinity," they condemned the former as a costly "burden upon Government" and the latter as "expensive toys." Mason's Island they pronounced a disaster.

Ludington and Compton disputed Greene's contention that the freedpeople under his supervision were self-supporting, arguing instead that expenses for their sustenance, shelter, and protection far outstripped earnings. They enumerated "Errors in Theory [and] Defects in Practice," accusing Greene of reinforcing the former slaves' "erroneous idea that 'emancipation' signifies a claim upon Government for support

---

[26] In addition to the relevant documents in this chapter, see below, doc. 157.

[27] In addition to the relevant documents in this chapter, see Chf. Q.M. Elias M. Greene to the Hon. W. Whiting, 9 Jan. 1864, enclosed in Lieut. Col. Elias M. Greene to Brig. Genl. M. C. Meigs, 19 Jan. 1864, "Bureau of Emancipation," Consolidated Correspondence File, ser. 225, Central Records, RG 92 [Y-155].

in idleness." More tellingly, they faulted him for refusing to hire mothers out to service unless their children could accompany them. The inspectors' "[s]uggestions for improvement" would have sundered the freedpeople's families: Able-bodied men, they proposed, should enlist in the army or work as military laborers, and able-bodied women should be relocated with their youngest children "to those portions of our Country where labor is greatly demanded," while children aged four to fourteen should remain at Freedman's Village to be "supported and educated" by the government.

The inspectors' report caused a stir. Greene ordered a cleanup of Mason's Island. Quartermaster General Meigs defended his subordinate, reexamining the accounts of the government farms and finding their operations profitable. Looking beyond the narrow question of expenses, Meigs cited the benefits of providing former slaves with shelter and employment in a healthful setting and preventing the spread of smallpox from them to the white population of Washington. The black women and children supported by the government included dependents of men fighting in the army, and "the United States . . . must take care that they do not starve," Meigs insisted. In the end, the contraband camps and government farms established by Greene survived the inspectors' harsh critique. Greene himself did not. In September, he was transferred to the western theater. Most of his authority respecting former slaves devolved upon Captain Joseph M. Brown, an assistant quartermaster who became chief of the Department of Washington's new Bureau of Freedmen and Government Farms. [28]

Even more than his predecessor, Brown was determined to reduce the number of freedpeople supported by the government. He hired out adults and apprenticed minors to local farmers and householders. Intent upon "sending as many as possible of the Contrabands . . . to the North," he corresponded with philanthropic organizations to make the necessary arrangements. [29] Brown's objective, an army inspec-

---

[28] On Greene's reassignment, see commission file of Elias M. Greene, G-644 1864, Letters Received, ser. 297, Appointments, Commissions, & Personal Branch, RG 94 [K-227]. Some months after Greene's departure, George E. H. Day, a commissioner of the National Freedman's Relief Association, accused him of owing "thousands of dollars to laborers whose rolls are *marked* paid but were not in fact paid." The Quartermaster General's Office dismissed the charge as "altogether too general to warrant any definite action." (George E. H. Day to the Hon. E. M. Stanton, 14 Jan. 1865, "Lt. Col. Greene," Consolidated Correspondence File, ser. 225, Central Records, RG 92 [Y-693]; Bvt. Brig. General Chs. Thomas to Geo. E. H. Day Esq., 21 Jan. 1865, vol. 82, p. 337, Letters Sent, ser. 9, Central Records, RG 92 [Y-693].)

[29] In addition to the relevant documents in this chapter, see below, doc. 150; Capt. J. M. Brown to Mr. Geo. E. H. Day, 10 Oct. [1864], and Capt. J. M. Brown to the School teacher at Camp Wadsworth, 11 Oct. [1864], vol. 66, pp. 18–21, Press Copies of Letters Sent, Requisitions, & Receipts, ser. 528, Asst. Quartermaster & Disbursing Officer, DC Asst. Comr., RG 105 [A-10623, A-10624]. On efforts by freedmen's aid societies to transport freedpeople from the District of Columbia and its vicinity to the North, see Joshua Clendenon to Hon. E. M. Stanton, 18 Aug. 1864, and other correspondence filed with T-978 1864, Letters Received,

tor noted disapprovingly, "appears to be to get rid of these people in *any* way; often by throwing them upon the community at large." So conceived, the policy succeeded. Between July 1864 and March 1865, the population of Freedman's Village shrank from 2,200 to 1,400; that of Mason's Island, from 1,200 to 500. Brown displayed scant sympathy for the freedpeople's desire to control the conditions under which they worked and lived. When a superintendent complained of refractory behavior by laborers on one of the government farms, Brown assured him that "you, not they will decide when they are to work and when not." Further resistance would warrant a stint in "the guard house on bread & water until such time as they are willing to go to work and obey orders."[30] Brown's draconian regimen discouraged newly arrived fugitives from seeking even temporary refuge at Freedman's Village or Mason's Island.

In any case, freedpeople generally preferred living on their own. They found jobs in workshops and warehouses, hotels and restaurants, and private homes and offices. A few opened small shops, "clubbing together" to purchase property. But those who fended for themselves often had problems making ends meet. Intermittent unemployment, low wages, and high prices undermined their efforts. Housing remained scarce and expensive. The families of soldiers and laborers who were absent in the field experienced particular difficulties. Many lived on the verge of starvation. Aid societies opened soup kitchens and channeled other kinds of relief their way. During the winter of 1864–1865, one agent of the National Freedman's Relief Association, Josephine S. Griffing, distributed more than 1,000 cords of wood, 3,300 blankets, 300 bedsteads, and large amounts of clothing to freedpeople in the District of Columbia.[31]

Meanwhile, black men and women mobilized their modest resources for their own security and well-being. They organized benevolent societies, which collected dues "to provide for the care and comfort of such members as shall be sick, disabled or dependent . . . and also to provide for the decent interment" of members and their families. By early 1865, members of the Colored Union Benevolent Association of Washington City had accumulated "a small property in real estate," for which they sought the protection of a congressional charter. By the closing months of the war, some black Washingtonians – not all of

RG 107 [L-233]; Capt. J. M. Brown to Jos. M. Truman, Jr., 31 Dec. 1864, vol. 60, p. 39, Press Copies of Letters Sent, ser. 527, Asst. Quartermaster & Disbursing Officer, DC Asst. Comr., RG 105 [A-10639].

[30] E. A. Holman to Mr. O. G. Besley, 10 Dec. 1864, vol. 66, p. 88, Press Copies of Letters Sent, Requisitions, & Receipts, ser. 528, Asst. Quartermaster & Disbursing Officer, DC Asst. Comr., RG 105 [A-10629].

[31] In addition to the relevant documents in this chapter, see Josephine S. Griffing to Sir, 25 July 1865, Communications Received, Central Office, ser. 740, U.S. Christian Commission, RG 94 [RR-1].

them freeborn or longtime residents – had been able to put aside part of their wartime earnings for purposes other than mere subsistence.

In the spring of 1865, former slaves began to anticipate the return of peace in a world peopled by free men and women instead of slaveholders and slaves. On the basis of their wartime service, they pressed the federal government to meet its obligations to them. "Colored Citizens & Tax-payers" of Washington – depicting themselves as "intelligent enough to be industrious, to have accumulated property, and to build and sustain Churches" – had already petitioned Congress for the right to vote, declaring that "[t]heir loyalty has never been questioned, their patriotism is unbounded, for in all their Country's trials they have responded voluntarily and with alacrity, *pay or no pay, bounty or no bounty, promotion or no promotion.*" Surely, they argued, such devotion warranted favorable consideration.[32] A mass meeting of black people in Alexandria took a similar stand in demanding the repeal of local laws that discriminated against them in judicial proceedings, so "that justice and equal rights in respect to persons and property may be guaranteed to all."

The mass meetings and other political activity underscored the momentous changes wrought by emancipation and free labor in the District of Columbia and its Virginia suburbs. Initially loath to hire and provide for former slaves, by the end of the war the government was employing thousands of freedpeople and providing food, clothing, and shelter to thousands more. Of the approximately 40,000 black people who lived in the District during the war,[33] most worked for the government or availed themselves of federal relief measures. That shared experience drew together free people and freedpeople, longtime residents and recent immigrants. Their work on behalf of the Union in the national capital reinforced the claims of all black people to the rights of citizens.

[32] C. A. Steward et al. to the Honorable 38th Congress, Senate & House of Representatives, [Apr. 1864], 38A-J4, Senate Committee on Slavery, Petitions & Memorials Tabled, 38th Congress, RG 46 [E-80].

[33] For an accounting of the black people in the District and its vicinity during the war, see above, pp. 78–79n.

50: Federal Commissioner of Public Buildings to the Secretary of War

WASHINGTON CITY, Feby 13, 1862

Sir, Having partially under my charge the Civil Department of the "Old Capitol Prison," I am led by duty, to visit it often. I happened to meet Brigade Surgeon Stewart there this morning, & he called my particular attention to the negroes confined there as "contrabands." He says that he thinks it improper that so many should be there confined; that, as a sanitary measure, they should be removed to some place where they can be kept more apart from respectable white people, and where, if possible constant employment can be given to them. He told me that in every case of small pox that had come under his notice, there, it originated among negroes.

When there to day, I saw some twenty or more herded together, on the sunny side of the building, entirely idle, & having any thing but the appearance of cleanliness and order. Mr. Wood, the Superintendent, undoubtedly does all he can to make them comfortable, but, when it is considered that the prison is now absolutely crowded with white prisoners, the natural conclusion is that negroes by scores, can hardly be provided for with any comfort to themselves or to the whites.

I have thought it my duty to call your attention officially to this subject, that it may have your consideration. I am with high respect your Obt. Servt.

HLS

B. B. French

B. B. French to Hon. Edwin M. Stanton, 13 Feb. 1862, F-187 1862, Letters Received, RG 107 [L-12]. No reply has been found among the records of the commissioner of public buildings or those of the Secretary of War. Later in February, William P. Wood, superintendent of the prison, stated that some 200 to 300 contrabands had been placed in his charge since the fall of 1861. He had "obtained situations" for all of them and believed them to be, "as far as I know, doing well." (U.S., Senate, "Report . . . into the Condition and Management of the Jail in the City of Washington," *Senate Reports*, 37th Cong., 2nd sess., No. 60, pp. 24–27.)

51: Forty District of Columbia Black Men to the Congress

[*Washington, D.C. late April 1862*]

MEMORIAL.

To the Honorable the Senate and House of Representatives of the United States of America, in Congress assembled:

The undersigned, for themselves, their relatives, and friends, whom they represent; desire, by this memorial, most respectfully to show to the Congress and people of this great country – of which, too, they are natives, but humbly born – that they appreciate, to the fullest extent, the humane actions which are now inaugurated to give freedom to their so long oppressed colored race;[1] but they believe that this freedom will result injuriously, unless there shall be opened to colored people a region, to which they may immigrate – a country which is suited to their organization, and in which they may seek and secure, by their own industry, that mental and physical development which will allow them an honorable position in the families of God's great world.

That there is ignorance in the mass of the colored race, is not to be denied: this is caused by the peculiar condition in which they have been raised – without the advantages of general education so wisely and freely accorded to the white citizens. But there are those amongst them who have secured the blessings of knowledge, and who are capable of informing their brethren of what is for their ultimate good, as the leaders of the Pilgrim Fathers informed those who came with them to plant civil and religious liberty upon this continent.

To these we are indebted for the knowledge that Liberia is too distant from the land of our birth, and that however kindly and wisely the original plans of colonization may have been laid for that country, neither those plans, nor that region, are suited to our present condition, and that it will be impossible for us ever to move there in sufficient numbers to secure for us the full liberties of the human race, the elements of which we have learned here.

From them, too, we have learned the deep degradation and wretchedness in which our relatives were sunk, who were induced by heartless speculators to immigrate to Hayti.[2] Slavery, if it must be borne, is more endurable under a race we have long been taught to look up to and regard as superior, than under one originating in Africa, degraded by abject slavery under Spanish and French greed, and still further brutalized by unrestrained and licentious liberty, such as exists with those who hold the power to control the poor immigrant in Hayti, or either of the Africo-West India Islands.

Of our own will, we cannot go either to Liberia or these islands. We have, in the United States, been taught to venerate virtue, to strive to attain it, and we can, with humble pride, point to as wide spread examples of the benefit of these teachings, as can any similar number of men, with no greater advantages than ourselves. Therefore we wish to shun those countries where the opposite of virtue rules, where vice reigns supreme, where our very blood would be required if we opposed its indulgence.

Though colored, and debarred from rights of citizenship, our hearts, none the less, cling to the land of our birth. We do not wish to be driven beyond the Ocean, where old hands of kindness cannot reach us, where we cannot hear from those with whom we have grown up, with all the fond remembrances of childhood.

We now number as many souls as won the freedom of your sires from British rule. We may not *now* be as capable to govern ourselves as they were, but we will, with your aid, be as zealous, and with God's blessing, we will be as successful.

There is a land – part of this your own continent – to which we wish to go. It is that portion generally called Central America. There are lands there without inhabitants, yet bearing spontaneously all that is suited to our race.

Aid us to get there – protect us for a short while, and we will prove ourselves worthy and grateful. The labor which, in servitude, has raised cotton, sugar, and tobacco, will do the same, not in the blood of bondage, but in the free spirit of liberty, and with the exultant knowledge, that it is to be part of your commerce, and to be given in exchange for the productions of our old native land.

If we are regarded as an evil here, (and we may become so by our competing with your white labor while here for the necessities of existence,) send us where, instead of being an evil, we may be made a blessing, by increasing the value of that white labor, while at the same time we offer to it greater comforts in reducing the costs in producing, by our own labor, those articles in abundance which all require for health and sustenance.

Do not, we beseech you, recognize and build up foreign nations of the black race, who have no sympathy in thought or language with that race which has grown up with you, and who only seek by such recognition, shaped, as it is, by European diplomacy, to sow discord and trouble with us here, that you and ourselves may be involved in a common ruin.

Send us – our prayer is, *send us* – to that country we have indicated, that we may not be wholly excluded from you, that we may aid in bringing to you that great commerce of the Pacific, which will still further increase the wealth and power of your country: and your petitioners will every pray.

PDS   [40 *signatures*]

Joseph Enoch Williams et al. to the Honorable the Senate and House of Representatives, [Apr. 1862], 37A-G21.4, Select Committee on Emancipation, Petitions & Memorials, ser. 467, 37th Congress, RG 233 [D-83]. Received in the House of Representatives on April 21, 1862, the petition was referred to the Select Committee on Emancipation and Colonization. In the same file is another copy of the petition, received on April 23, which was signed by twenty black men, including the Reverend Henry M. Turner. The first signature on both petitions is that of Joseph E. Williams of Indiana, formerly an agent of the Haitian Emigration Bureau, who, in the summer of 1861, had joined a colony of black immigrants from the United States in Haiti. Initially "pleased with the Island," Williams had become disenchanted after discovering that the colonists "were to hold inferior positions, to become mere slaves, 'hewers of wood and drawers of water' for men of our own color, and no better than ourselves." He had therefore returned to the United States and become an outspoken opponent of emigration to Haiti. (New York *Weekly Anglo-African*, 20 Apr. 1861, 12 Apr. 1862; *Pine and Palm*, 10 Aug., 31 Aug. 1861, all in Black Abolitionist Papers, 1830–1865, microfilm, reel 13, fr. 470, 628, 714, reel 14, fr. 237; clipping from Washington *Star*, [3 May 1862], Letters Received & Other Records, ser. 376, Records Relating to the Suppression of the African Slave Trade & to Negro Colonization, RG 48 [LL-157].)

1 Congress had recently adopted two measures touching upon emancipation. The first, a joint resolution approved on April 10, 1862, offered monetary assistance to any state that undertook gradual emancipation. The second, a law adopted on April 16, 1862, abolished slavery in the District of Columbia, providing compensation to loyal slaveholders. The latter act also appropriated $100,000 "to aid in the colonization and settlement of such free persons of African descent now residing in said District, including those to be liberated by this act, as may desire to emigrate to the Republics of Hayti or Liberia, or such other country beyond the limits of the United States as the President may determine." (*Statutes at Large*, vol. 12, pp. 376–78, 617.)

2 A reference to the scheme promoted by James Redpath, a white abolitionist, whose Haitian Emigration Bureau sponsored the relocation of 2,000 free-black people from the United States to Haiti between 1860 and 1862. (John R. McKivigan, "James Redpath and Black Reaction to the Haitian Emigration Bureau," *Mid-America* 69 [Oct. 1987]: 139–53.)

52: Engineer in Charge of the Defenses of Washington to the Military Governor of the District of Columbia

[*Washington, D.C.*] June 7ᵗʰ 1862

General, I have the honor to request a detail of "Contrabands" for work on the Fortifications on the Maryland side of the Potomac. As the Government subsists them it would be advisable to get some return for the expense.

I could easily employ two hundred and fifty (250) discharge the hired laborers now working on these forts and thus very much diminish the expense of finishing the work. Several Roads connecting our System of Defenses need repair, and others must be built. There is also considerable sodding of earth slopes to be done which I consider very necessary, the expense of which would be trifling if use were made of negro labor. If you approve this, I request that the necessary orders be issued at once. I propose to have the negroes posted as follows —

At Forts Franklin, Alexander & Ripley	20 negroes
At Forts Gaines & Pennsylvania	20 negroes
" " De Russey, Massachusetts & Slocum	30 "
" " Totten & Slemmer	20 "
" " Bunker Hill & Saratoga	20 "
" " Thayer & Lincoln	20 "
" Fort Mahan	20 "
" Forts Meigs, Dupont, & Davis	20 "
" " Baker, Wagner & Ricketts	30 "
" " Stanton & Snyder	30 "
" " Carroll & Greble	20 "
Total	250

I would like orders issued detailing a non-Commissioned officer at each fort to "boss" the working parties who shall receive his instructions about the manner and place of working his force from myself and assistants— If this management is carried out at once, I propose to reduce my present force working on the forts, and only leave a few overseers and intelligent laborers to show the negroes the proper manner of doing the various kinds of work. I have the honor to be Very Respectfully Your Obedient Sevt

HLcSr   (signed) Wm E. Merrill

1st Lieut. Engrs. Wm. E. Merrill to Genl. Wadsworth, 7 June 1862, enclosed in Lt. Col. J. A. Haskin to Gen'l S. D. Sturgis, 7 Aug. 1862, H-698 1862, Letters Received, ser. 12, RG 94 [K-34]. Two months later, William C. Gunnell, an engineer whom Merrill had placed in charge of the defenses north of the Potomac, informed the commander of the defenses that, despite repeated applications, the military governor had not provided "Contrabands" to accomplish the necessary labor on the fortifications. "Instead of being improved and finished," Gunnell warned, "the works are deteriorating every day." "Contrabands" had been employed "the entire season" on the forts south of the Potomac, "but we have never been able to get any on this side." Gunnell requested "3 details of 100 negros each" to undertake "very essential & necessary improvements in the condition of the works and roads of communication," but if that number could not be obtained, "I should like to get whatever can be— Even two dozen would be of some assistance." (Wm. C. Gunnell to Lt. Col. Haskin, 6 Aug. 1862, in the same file.) In a letter covering those of both Gunnell and Merrill, the commander of the defenses north of the Potomac asked that Gunnell's application be approved, and, in a series of endorsements between August 7 and 13, high-ranking military officials—including the general-in-chief and an assistant secretary of war—also urged that black laborers be assigned to work on the forts. When, however, the letters were referred to General James S. Wadsworth, the military governor, his (undated) endorsement reported "only about one hundred contrabands under my direction" and "these are needed for policing hospitals & other duties." Accordingly, in an endorsement of August 15, the assistant secretary of war instructed the adjutant general to "inform the officer in charge of the Fortifications that there are no unemployed contrabands to be detailed."

53: Mayor of Alexandria, Virginia, to the Secretary of War

Alexandria [*Va.*] September 19th 1862

Sir   In view of the Fact of the large number of Contrabands that have come into Alexandria For Protection from the Rebels, and of which a large number is helpless women with their children, and as the Season is advancing, and many of them are without Shelter, I have to Request if consistent with your views of propriety to Request Capt. C B. Ferguson Qr Master here to have erected some Wooden Buildings to Protect them during the Fall and Winter.   I will be glad to aid in any way in this Matter and will furnish the Lots on which the Buildings can be erected.   Yr obt servt

Lewis M[c]Kenzie

Every house in the city is full, & there is in fact a great lack of houses from the large number occupied as hospitals & soldiers' quarters.   Many of those used for the latter purpose would, when cleansed of the filth accumulated in them, make excellent hospitals.   It seems to me that the soldiers would find much healthier quarters in tents on the outskirts.   When living in houses in closely built parts of the City, as they have been, they become a nuisance to themselves & the citizens, besides abusing the houses most shamefully.

ALS

Lewis McKenzie to Honl. E. M. Stanton, 19 Sept. 1862, enclosed in Brigdr. Genl. Jno. P. Slough to Hon. E. M. Stanton, 25 Sept. 1862, S-91 1862, Letters Received Irregular, RG 107 [L-179]. The postscript is in a handwriting different from that of the body of the letter and its signature. By an undated endorsement, the Secretary of War forwarded McKenzie's letter to General John P. Slough, military governor of Alexandria, for a report "upon the facts and reccommendation within expressed." Slough in turn referred it to Captain John C. Wyman, provost marshal of the city, who, in a report of September 25 (in the same file), informed Slough that he did "not find the existing state of things quite as deplorable as represented in the letter of Mayor M[c]Kenzie." Many of the former slaves who had come to Alexandria as refugees "during the recent advance of the Rebels upon Manassas have since returned [to their homes]," Wyman noted, "and at the present time I think there are none who are not housed." The shortage of housing, Wyman acknowledged, "requires the crowding of [the former slaves] to such a degree as must prove exceedingly dangerous to their own, and perhaps to the health of the city," but he assured Slough that he could "make such changes . . . as will provide against any serious consequences" and therefore suggested "that no immediate measures in reference to them be taken." General Slough returned McKenzie's letter and Wyman's report to the Secretary of War with a covering letter recommending only that a surgeon be detailed to attend to sick ex-slaves. "This being done the wants of this class of people will be as well supplied as the poor whites in cities." Less than four weeks later, however, Captain Wyman himself submitted plans for four "buildings to be erected for the accomodation of the Contrabands now living in this city." "The few buildings which are available for their use," he explained, "are already so crowded – that great danger exists of diseases which may prove contagious – and fatal." General Slough commended Wyman's proposal to the commander of the defenses of Washington, who asked Quartermaster General Montgomery C. Meigs "to expedite the matter as much as possible." On October 27, Meigs directed the chief quartermaster of the Washington depot to have the assistant quartermaster at Alexandria supervise construction of the buildings. (Capt. John C. Wyman to Brig. Genl. Jno. P. Slough, 21 Oct. 1862, and endorsements, enclosed in Qr. Mr. Gen'l M. C. Meigs to Hon. E. M. Stanton, 13 Dec. 1862, "Alexandria, Va.," Consolidated Correspondence File, ser. 225, Central Records, RG 92 [Y-226].) The barracks were not completed until February 1863. (See below, docs. 57n., 59A.)

54: Military Governor of the District of Columbia to the Secretary of War

[*Washington, D.C.*] Sep 25. 1862

Sir   I beg leave to ask your attention to the following statement of facts –

Several hundred coloured men are employed in the Qr Masters Depart^r of this District, as Teamsters & Laborers, the former at \$25 per month & a ration and the latter at \$20 per mo. and a ration – Most of these men are fugitives from slavery – & the wages they receive are nearly double the wages paid to farm laborers at the North.

While these men are receiving these very high wages, which many of them are incompetent to take care of, and waste in dissipation, the Goverment is supporting six or eight hundred women & children of the same class, who are unable to find employment.

I respectfully recommend that ~~three~~ five dollars per month be stopped against the pay of all the coloured laborers in the Qr Masters Department in this City & in the City of Alexandria & paid over to a commissioner to be designated by the War Department & to be expended by him in providing for the women & children referred to, and to provide a Hospital fund for the care of the sick from among the coloured laborers & teamsters from whom the fund is derived— I have the honor to be yr obt sert

ALS   Ja⁵ S. Wadsworth

Brig. Genl. Jas. S. Wadsworth to the Hon. the Secy. of War, 25 Sept. 1862, W-1068 1862, Letters Received, ser. 12, RG 94 [K-47]. An unsigned, undated endorsement referred Wadsworth's letter to the adjutant general of the army, who was to prepare an order. In a letter of September 27 (quoted in doc. 55, immediately below), the adjutant general instructed the quartermaster general to begin making the monthly deductions.

55: Quartermaster General to the Secretary of War

[*Washington, D.C.*] 4ᵗʰ October [186]2.
Copy

Sir: I have received, through the Adjutant General, the following order, in relation to a deduction of five dollars per month from the wages of colored teamsters and laborers in the District of Columbia and Alexandria, viz:

"War Department
Adjutant General's Office,
Washington, Sept' 27ᵗʰ 1862

Brigadier General Meigs,
          Quartermaster General,
                    U.S. Army.
Sir:
    The Secretary of War is informed that a large number of colored men are employed in this District and in Alexandria as teamsters and laborers at the rate of twenty five dollars per month and a ration to the former and twenty dollars and a ration to the latter. In view of the fact that the Government is supporting several hundred women and children of the same class, who are unable to find employment and also furnished medical care, support and attendance, to the sick and helpless, the Secretary directs that you cause five dollars per month to be deducted from the pay of the said colored teamsters and laborers in the Quarter Masters Department to be paid over to a Commissioner who will be appointed by the Secretary of War, and who will expend the fund thus accruing for the benefit of the women and children, and as a hospital fund for the sick among the men from whom it is derived. I am, Sir, very respectfully

Your obedt Serv'
(signed) L. Thomas
Adjutant General"

I have given the necessary directions to effect the object of the order, by letters addressed to Col. Rucker and Gen[l] Ingalls,[1] Chief Quartermasters dated Oct 1st 1862

In connection with this subject I respectfully call the attention of the Department to Sections 12, 13 & 15 of the Act of Congress approved July 17th 1862[2] page 599 of the pamphlet Laws, viz:

"Sec 12. That the President be and he is hereby, authorized to receive into the Service of the United States, for the purpose of constructing intrenchments, or performing camp service, or any other labor, or any military or naval service for which they may be found competent, persons of African descent, and such persons shall be enrolled and organized under such regulations, not inconsistent with the Constitution and laws as the President may be prescribe."

"Sec 13. That when any man or boy of African descent, who, by the Laws of any State shall owe Service or labor to any person who, during the present rebellion, has levied war or has borne arms against the United States, or adhered to their enemies by giving them aid and comfort, shall render any such service as is provided for in this Act, he, his mother and his wife and children shall forever thereafter be free, any law, usage or custom whatsoever to the contrary notwithstanding. Provided that the mother, wife, and children of such man or boy of African descent shall not be made free by the operation of this Act, except where such mother, wife or children owe service or labor to some person who, during the present rebellion, has borne arms against the United States, or adhered to their enemies by giving them aid and comfort."

"Sec. 15. That all persons who have been or shall be hereafter enrolled in the service of the United States under this Act shall receive the pay and rations now allowed by law to soldiers according to their respective grades: Provided, that persons of African descent, who under this law shall be employed, shall receive ten dollars per month and one ration, three dollars of which monthly may be in clothing."

It is important to the service that it should be decided by legal authority as soon as possible whether Section 15 of the Act quoted will affect the wages of persons of African descent employed by the Quarter Masters Department as teamsters, laborers, &c.

There were a large number so employed before the enactment of this law who have received wages such as were given to white teamsters and laborers. Teamsters generally receive in this neighborhood $25 per month and a ration. Some of them are freemen; some of them freed by the emancipation of the Slaves in the District of Columbia, many, doubtless, are fugitives from within the lines of rebellion and entitled to their freedom under Acts of Congress.[3]

They have not been employed, however, generally under the Act referred to. They have not been mustered or enrolled, or sworn into service as soldiers are for a long period of enlistment. They were hired by special agreement or contract in each case as white teamsters or other employés of the Quartermaster's Department upon such terms as were sufficient to secure their services.

The number is large, and the reduction of their wages is considerable, and it is important to them. At this place we find to this time no surplus of this sort of labor, and if it is decided that this law applies to them and requires this reduction of their pay to ten dollars a month, it will produce much dissatisfaction and suffering, and will probably deprive the Government of the services of a large portion of them. A forced service from them would not [tend] to the efficiency of the Quartermasters Department.

If it applies to these persons, it will probably apply to all persons of African descent employed by the United States throughout the loyal States and throughout the naval service. Free colored persons in Northern States cannot generally be hired at such rates.

In the Rebel States, within the sphere of active military operations there will probably be no difficulty in carrying out the law and it was, perhaps, to fugitives in such territory that the law was intended particularly to apply.

I respectfully ask that the question be decided by authority, whether the law requires all persons of African descent employed in the Quartermasters Department to be paid ten dollars a month and a ration, and no more, or whether the officers of the Department are at liberty to continue to pay wages such as the market price of labor requires to persons of African descent already employed or hereafter employed and not enrolled into service under special regulations of the President under the law of 17th July 1862. With great respect, Your obed^r Servt,

HLpSr   (signed) M. C Meigs,

[*Endorsement*] Endorsed. Referred to the Judge Advocate General for his opinion   (signed) Edwin M. Stanton, Sec of War.

[*Endorsement*] The 15th Sec. of Act of 17th July 1862 applies, so far as persons of African descent are concerned, *only to those employed under and by virtue of the Act itself*. These persons are required to be enrolled, and organized under regulations to be prescribed by the President and are thus made to occupy a quasi military position. Such is not the status of the teamsters & laborers in the service of the Quarter Mrs Department, who are not enrolled or subjected at all to the regulations contemplated by the Act. It was

well known to Congress that persons of African descent were thus employed before and at the passage of this law and also the rates at which they were compensated. This act was not intended to interfere with this system of hiring, but as its history shows, had reference to those who it was anticipated might enter the public Service under different circumstances, and for a different object   (signed) J. Holt   Judge Advocate General
To the Quarter Master General   October 11 1862.

Quartermaster General M. C. Meigs to Hon. Edwin M. Stanton, 4 Oct. 1862, and endorsements, vol. 20, pp. 149–56, Press Copies of "Miscellaneous" Letters Sent Relating to Such Matters as the Assignment of Personnel, Property & Supplies, Transportation, & the Organization & Administration of the Quartermaster Dept., ser. 14, Central Records, RG 92 [Y-549]. A third endorsement, dated November 7, 1862, indicated that the Secretary of War approved the judge advocate general's ruling. The letter and its endorsements are all in the form of press copies made from fair copies prepared by the Quartermaster General's Office for transmittal (on November 8, 1862) to General James S. Wadsworth, military governor of the District of Columbia.

1 Daniel H. Rucker, chief quartermaster of the Washington depot, and Rufus Ingalls, chief quartermaster of the Army of the Potomac.
2 The Militia Act. (*Statutes at Large*, vol. 12, pp. 597–600.)
3 The First Confiscation Act, adopted August 6, 1861, had nullified the owner's claim to any slave who had been employed on behalf of the Confederate war effort. The Second Confiscation Act, adopted July 17, 1862, had declared free those slaves who came under Union control (by flight to Union lines or by the advance of the federal armies) and whose owners had engaged in or aided the rebellion. (*Statutes at Large*, vol. 12, pp. 319, 589–92.)

56: Testimony by a Virginia Free Man of Color before the Southern Claims Commission

[*Alexandria, Va.*]   6th day of March 1878
Deposition of George W. Simms, Colored, a claimant who being duly sworn deposes and says:–
In ans to the 1st
My name is George W. Simms my age 65 years, my residence Alexandria Virginia. I have lived in Alexandria since the 25th day of December 1861. My occupation a blacksmith.
In ans. to the 2[d]
I am the claimant.
In ans to the 3[d]

I was born in Fairfax County Virginia

In ans to the 4th

I was residing at Pohick Church Fairfax County Virginia   I was blacksmything, and farming some   I remained there until December 1861 when I left and came to Alexandria, where I remained engaged in blacksmithing.   I worked for the United States about Eleven months in the time of the war.

In ans to the 5th

On the side of the Union from the beginning to the end. . . .

In ans. to the 8th

I have, I gave the Union troops information, I came over, and gave information to Mr. Wright a northern man who lived near Woodlawn, The union officers used to stop at his place. I gave information to Mr. Jonathan Roberts another northern man, I remember a party of union cavalry who came down there in 1861, Some rebels had been along there in the morning. I went to the Union troops and told them the rebels had been there and all I knew about them. . . .

In ans to the 10th

I was employed by the United States as a blacksmith about eleven months. I was under Capt. Ferguson, They reduced my wages five dollars or retained it and said they had a right to do it, to every colored man. I don't know why they retained the five dollars. I was only getting thirty five dollars a month. I left because I could not support myself and family on thirty dollars.

In ans. to the 11th

When I worked in the government shop, I Contributed twenty five cents a month for hospital purposes.

In ans. to the 12th.

I was always on the Union side. I said very little, A colored man was not allowed to say much.

. . . .

In ans. to the 23^d

They [*Confederates*] made me shoe their horses once. They came there early in the morning and forced me to go to the shop, and put one shoe on.

. . . .

In ans. to the 66th

I was, I owned the farm.

In ans. to the 67th

There was 162 acres, situated near Pohick Church Fairfax County Virginia   It is about 12 miles from Alexandria. There was some 12 or 15 acres, I was cultivating when the war commenced. There was some 60 acres in timber and the balance was "old fields". . . .

In ans to the 70th

I was a free man   I was born free. . . .
In ans to the 76th
No sir. I was not on my place when my property was taken   I
was in Alexandria. I heard the rebels were going to take me to
Manassas and I abandoned my home and everything and took my
family and Came to Alexandria—

                            . . . .

HDS   G. W. Simms

Excerpts from testimony of G. W. Simms, 6 Mar. 1878, claim of George W.
Simms, Alexandria Co. VA case files, Approved Claims, ser. 732, Southern
Claims Commission, 3rd Auditor, RG 217 [I-655]. Sworn before a special
commissioner of the Southern Claims Commission. A copy of the questions
that correspond to the enumerated responses is in the same file. According to
other documents in the file, Simms had submitted a claim for $835 as compen-
sation for the following property taken or destroyed by Union soldiers in
January 1862: sixty bushels of corn, sixty bushels of wheat, a house and
outbuildings, fencing, and a blacksmith shop and tools. He was awarded
$120. In other testimony in the same file, a former slave who had lived near
Simms's farm recalled that Simms had "assisted the slave people in getting
away [to freedom], and he had to leave, because the rebels did not think he was
a man to trust." At the time Union troops arrived at Simms's farm, the
"buildings were in good condition and he was mighty well fixed." (Testimony
of John T. Bushrod, 8 Mar. 1878.) The reduction in wages that caused Simms
to quit his blacksmith's work for the government (probably in November
1862) had resulted from orders issued on October 1, 1862, by the quartermaster general to the chief quartermasters in the Washington area. (See above,
doc. 55.)

57: Agent of the Ladies Anti-Slavery Society of Rochester,
New York, to the President; and Provost Marshal of
Alexandria, Virginia, to the Military Governor of Alexandria

                              Alexandria Va. Nov. 7 – 1862
    Will you permit me although a stranger to claim your attention
for a moment? Although addressing the chief Magistrate of the
nation, I know that I am appealing to a kind heart, & I come as a
child to its father to ask for help in behalf of the most wretched of
God's creatures.
    I have been sent here by & at the expense of a Ladies' Society
in Rochester N.Y. to see in what way we can help the
Contrabands. Of the 700 in Alexandria now, some are in the old
school house, some in the old slave pen & others in several

tenements that can hardly be called a shelter. Women & children are sick & dying, not for want of necessary food, but for want of suitable shelter from this cold storm. Could barracks be built for them at once so that we could have them move together & a physician & medical stores be provided for them, I think we can get supplies of clothing & bedding from the North, & they can be made comparatively comfortable for the winter. A few persons now are working night & day in caring for their sick, in burying their dead, & in relieving their most pressing wants, But, little can be accomplished until suitable buildings are provided for them. Gen. Banks & Gen. Wadsworth[1] have given me their sanction & approval to act as matron, visitor, adviser & instructor to these poor women & children. The Provost Marshal here is ready to help in any way he can. I understand that Gen. Slough[2] has turned the matter over to Capt. Wyman, the Pro. Marshal, & Sec. Stanton assured me some 10 days ago that "the wants of these contrabands should be attended to." But no help comes yet, & on this wintry morning I have presumed to appeal even to the President of the U.S. in behalf of suffering humanity. Could you assure me that what I ask, could be obtained soon, I could work with renewed courage, & in God's name I would forever bless that of *Abraham Lincoln*   Very Respectfully

ALS   Julia A. Wilbur

Alexandria [*Va.*] Nov 24. 1862

In answer to the communication Which I herewith Enclose, I would respectfully report

The condition of the Contrabands in this City is demanding the sympathy and deserving the assistance of the Government. I had the honour several weeks since of submitting to you, (with plans and estimates of cost) a Report in reference to what I thought was required to make suitable provision for them —[3] After waiting some weeks for a response to the proposition which I had submitted I addressed you again inquiring the result, and have since been advised by you that both the Report and inquiry were forwarded, but you had received no reply to either.[4]

The largely increased population of Alexandria, in consequence of the great number of men who are employed in the various Departments of the Government, together with other reasons connected with its being an important Military Post — makes it impossible to furnish suitable room or shelter for this class, who require both care and protection. Homes are not to be had, and in view of this fact, I asked for authority to build some cheap Barracks, in which they could be made Comfortable, and at the same time, by being kept together, subjected to the necessary supervision and Control— They are now scattered thoroughout the city, and as they are very migratory in disposition, there is great difficulty in keeping a very reliable record of them—

I am now with your consent and approval having a few buildings which were very much dilapidated and had been deserted prepared for the accomodation of a portion of them—but I would still respectfully urge, that a very careful consideration of the case does not suggest to my mind any plan so effective and economical, by which they can be suitably provided for as the one I have already submitted to you   I am yours very respectfully

ALS

John C. Wyman

Julia A. Wilbur to Abraham Lincoln, 7 Nov. 1862, and Capt. John C. Wyman to Brig. Genl. John P. Slough, 24 Nov. 1862, both filed with W-1263 1862, Letters Received, ser. 12, RG 94 [K-55]. Endorsements. The "communication" enclosed by Captain Wyman was Wilbur's letter of November 7. General John P. Slough, military governor of Alexandria, forwarded Wyman's report and Wilbur's letter to General Samuel P. Heintzelman, commander of the defenses of Washington south of the Potomac. Evidently unaware that the construction of barracks had already been approved (see above, doc. 53n.), Heintzelman requested "a tabular statement of the condition, number of men, women and children, and effective working men of the contrabands in Alexandria" before he took "such action as may be necessary." In the same file is the resulting tabulation, prepared by Wyman, which reported a total of 1,230 contrabands: 475 men (315 working for and subsisted by the commissary or quartermaster's department, 75 drawing rations from the government, 85 not drawing rations), 276 women (220 drawing rations, 56 not drawing rations), 439 children (399 drawing rations, 40 not drawing rations), and 40 individuals (sex and age not specified) in the "Pest House" or the "Small Pox room." "It is my purpose and effort," Wyman declared, "to make all who are able to do so earn their own living." Of the 75 men receiving government rations, only 40 or 50 "are in condition to render service—and they are constantly employed about the Hospitals, and offices and buildings in the use of the Govt." As to the general condition of the contrabands in Alexandria, Wyman concluded that the government had made "ample provision" for feeding them, but "many . . . [were] suffering for suitable room and shelter." By the adoption of his plan to construct barracks, he suggested, "the Contrabands of Alexandria can be made quite comfortable at small expense to the Govt." (Capt. John C. Wyman to Brig. General John P. Slough, 24 Nov. 1862.) In an endorsement of November 26, General Heintzelman approved the use of "deserted tenements" to house former slaves but objected to constructing new buildings: "If we build temporary barracks they will soon be filled. Now there are a number of 'Contrabands' in this vicinity, who are supporting themselves. When they learn that the Government will feed & shelter them, they will flock to Alexandria. The men who work will spend their wages & leave the women & children a tax on the Government." Heintzelman proposed no solution of his own: "What shall be done with these people, beyond temporary expedients, I have not the time to consider." About the same time, Secretary of War Edwin M. Stanton, learning that smallpox had broken out among the former slaves at Alexandria, directed General Slough to "report what measures have been taken to prevent its spreading." In response, Captain Wyman advised Slough that it was "impossible under present circumstances to control the disease and prevent its spreading for the reason that this class of persons are located all over the city." Wyman once again urged the construction of barracks where former slaves "could be collected, and subjected to such rules and regulations, as would preserve order and promote health." (Asst. Adjt. Genl. Chauncey McKeever to Brig. Genl. Slough, 28 Nov. 1862, filed with Capt. John C. Wyman to Brig. General John P. Slough, 29 Nov. 1862, W-1279 1862, Letters Received, ser. 12, RG 94 [K-232].) On December 9, Stanton asked the quartermaster general "why the buildings for the contrabands have not been completed," and the following day, the quartermaster at the Alexandria depot reported that "the work is now being pushed, with all the means, which we can command, and will very soon reach a state of completion." (Asst. Adjt. Genl. Chauncey McKeever to Brig. Gen. Meigs, 9 Dec. 1862, and Capt. C. B. Ferguson to Col. D. H. Rucker, 10 Dec. 1862, both enclosed in Qr. Mr. Gen'l M. C. Meigs to Hon. E. M. Stanton, 13 Dec. 1862, "Alexandria, Va.," Consolidated Correspondence File, ser. 225, Central Records, RG 92 [Y-226].)

1 Nathaniel P. Banks, who had commanded the defenses of Washington in September and October 1862, and James S. Wadsworth, military governor of the District of Columbia.
2 John P. Slough, military governor of Alexandria.
3 On October 21, 1862, the provost marshal, Captain John C. Wyman, had proposed that four wooden barracks be constructed in which to house the contrabands. (See above, doc. 53n.)
4 Apparently unbeknownst to Captain Wyman, the commander of the defenses of Washington and the quartermaster general had already approved his suggestion, and the quartermaster at Alexandria had been ordered to build the barracks. (See above, doc. 53n.)

58: Testimony by a Virginia Freedman before the Southern Claims Commission

[*Alexandria, Va.*] 22^d day of November 1873.
Deposition of George Shorter colored who being duly sworn deposes and says my name is George Shorter   My age 40 years   My residence Alexandria County Virginia   I am a farmer, work on the farm with Mr. Frazer.   I am not related to Levi Jones the claimant, and have no beneficial interest in this claim.   I was a slave man before the war   I belonged to Mr. Blanford of Prince George

County Md. I first got acquainted with Levi Jones the fall 1862, I went to him then to ask him to let me build a house on his place for myself and family, he let me do so and I lived on his place until after the close of the war. I had talk with Levi Jones about the war I was on the side of the Union, and wanted the rebels whipped, whenever Levi Jones would hear of the Union troops being beaten he would be down hearted and whenever he would hear of them beating the rebels he would cheer up. I am confident that Levi Jones was a Union man. Every one who knew Levi Jones regarded him as a Union man I Knew I was a slave man and had left my master and he was the only one who gave me any assistance

Item 1 picket fencing

When I came on to Levi Jones place there was a picket fence along the road on the north side and part of the west end, the south side of the place was brush fence, or what was called a wattleing fence and part of the west end was wattleing fence. I went on Levi Jones place in August and on Sunday just before Christmas following, Lieut. Johnson came to me and told me I had to move my house. I looked upon the hill and saw the whole hill was covered with soldiers and they came down and encamped all over his place and pitched their tents rigth in his door-yard. I went into my cabin and remained there. In the morning there was not a spect of fenceing on the farm, they kept up monstrous fires all night. They had their teams with them I think they had ten or twelve teams. Levi Jones had a stack of hay on his place I suppose about a ton and half in it. I saw them take the hay and use some of it for bedding Next morning the hay was all scattered all through camp

Item 3 barn

The same soldiers the next day commenced to pull the boards off the barn, it was a frame barn boarded up and down and covered with boards a flat roof, it was a small barn. It would hold three horses and three cows, it had a loft for hay and a floor to it. Monday morning following there was no barn left, they carried the boards to their camps and made bunks out of them, I saw the bunks made of the boards in their Sibley Tents. These troops remained there some couple or three weeks

Item 5 wood

When I first came to Levi Jones place I noticed a good deal of his timber was cut down and the trees lying on the ground I also saw soldiers afterwards cutting up this timber and hauling it to their forts they hauled it to Fort Bondey [*Barnard?*] and Fort Blenker. I saw them three or four different days hauling timber, and they had 2 two wagons each time

Item 7 Horse

I know Levi Jones had a big horse when I went on his place. I know some soldiers come one day and borrowed the horse to haul away some brush out of the Convalescent camp, I was at Levi Jones when they came for the horse, and I heard the soldiers ask for the horse I saw a soldier ride the towards the camp and I saw the horse afterwards working in the camp, the horse was never brought back to Levi Jones and I never saw the horse after that.

Item 9 Hay

This hay was taken the first night the soldiers came as I have stated I dont know of any other hay being taking besides that

Item 12 peach trees. –

When I came to the place Levi Jones had about 35 or 40 peach trees as near as I can come at it, after the troops left, which came there on Sunday as I have there was not a peach tree left. I did not see anyone cut them down as I remember and I dont know what became of them

And further this deponent saith not

HDSr

His
George X Shorter
mark

Testimony of George Shorter, 22 Nov. 1873, claim of Levi Jones, Alexandria Co. VA case files, Approved Claims, ser. 732, Southern Claims Commission, 3rd Auditor, RG 217 [I-653]. Sworn before a special commissioner of the Southern Claims Commission. According to other testimony in the same file, the claimant, Levi Jones, had been born free; his seventeen-acre farm was located about four miles south of Alexandria. At the time Union troops seized his property, he "was carrying on dairy and selling milk to the soldiers." (Testimony of Levi Jones, 14 Nov. 1873.) According to other documents in the file, Jones had submitted a claim for $2,580 as compensation for the use, seizure, or destruction of property by Union soldiers, including $800 for 400 rods of picket fence and another $800 as four years' rent for land "occupied as encampment, known as Fort Blenker." He was awarded only $183, including $80 for the fence and nothing in the way of rent.

59A: Agent of the Ladies Anti-Slavery Society of Rochester, New York, to the Secretary of War

Alexandria [Va.] Mar 24th '/63

I presume you have entirely forgotten the person who, at Gen. Wadsworth's suggestion, called at your office in Nov. last &

informed you of the condition & wants of the Contrabands in Alexandria. You very kindly assured me that "their wants should be attended to," & soon after a physician was appointed & medical stores provided for these people, And I shall never cease to feel grateful to yourself & President Lincoln for ordering comfortable habitations to be built for these people, & I am sure it was no fault of either of you that the buildings progressed so slowly, that it is only about three weeks since that they were ready to be occupied,

There are three buildings each 150 ft. in length, containing together 35 living rooms with the same number of sleeping rooms & one large school room, the whole intended to accommodate 500 persons. The former Pro. Mar.[1] took pleasure in carrying out your orders & through his kindness I obtained some little conveniences for the rooms. I watched the progress of these buildings with great interest & was allowed to plan some of the interior arrangements. I am here to aid these people in this their transition state, & have some plans for their improvement,

I supposed that these Barracks were intended for those who could not get comfortable shelter elsewhere & they were to be temporary homes for such persons; & that in these buildings the sick, the old, the widows & children would find a shelter & not be asked to pay for it. Among the 500 deaths from smallpox during the winter there was a large proportion of men & this has added materially to the number of widows & orphans. I have not thought for a moment that either yourself or the President intended to extort from the Contrabands in Alex. $17 00 a year as rent for these rude barracks, But such seems to be the present policy, but perhaps not exactly on the part of the present Pro. Mar, for he says "the poorest ones may live in them without paying rent." He has had but little experience here & there is a person at his elbow who gives him any thing but a correct impression of things. It is with extreme reluctance that I say this & no personal considerations would induce me to do it. But I think that what is done for these 1500 or 2000 contrabands in Alex. is something done for the entire race. I believe in their supporting themselves as fast & as far as possible, but I do not like to see advantage taken of these poor creatures.

Some of these people have taken care of themselves entirely since they came here; others wd. have done so had they been paid regularly for their work, But there is a large proportion of needy helpless ones who must be cared for at present. Their condition on the whole is very much improved, & I wish to add what is much to their credit that in this city where arrests are so frequent it is very seldom that a colored man is arrested. At one time rations were issued to about 1300, But some of these have not drawn rations lately, & others draw only half rations. There is a want of system &

order here that hinders the accomplishment of much good that might otherwise be done, & with all proper deference I would say that an efficient & capable superintendent is very much needed here. He should be in the first place a *humane* man; he should be large-minded & thoroughly conscientious; one who believes that these people can be elevated & improved; not one who habitually speaks of them as "thievish, deceitful, ungrateful dishonest"; a people "whom you cannot teach any more than you can horses." Mr. Gladwin who wants to be superintendent here has been active in various ways & has helped these people in some things & I do not wish to detract a particle from his merit. But I am not alone in the opinion that he is altogether unfit for Superintendent of these people,

The Freedmen's Association in Washington perhaps knows of some person who is suitable for such a position,

I wish to labor here among these people as I have done during the past five months, & I am willing to act *with* any reasonable, capable person, or even to act *under* a person who will be kind & give to these unfortunates.

I am not asking for any personal favors, although a month ago I did think of asking for the position of *Assistant Superintendent.* There is much that I do that does not come within a man's province, & perhaps it is quite as necessary & important as any work that is done, & I could do still more were I invested with a little more authority. Although a *woman* I would like an appointment with a fair salary attached to it, & I would expect to deserve a salary. But if there is anything in this wish that would operate against the appointment of a good & efficient superintendent I would not indulge it for a moment.

The government has in my humble opinion, done generously by the Contrabands in Alex. & I wish them to reap the benefit of this generosity & I trust they will not become the prey of selfish & designing men. With suitable instruction & proper protection I am sure they will not disappoint the hopes of their friends.

A thousands pardons for trespassing so far on your time, It has been done reluctantly. But you have treated these people with much consideration, & I feel that you are & will continue to be their friend & may God bless you for it; & when, if they ever do, get to living in these new buildings like civilved people I am sure it would give you pleasure to see our 'Freedman's Home' in Alex. Hoping devoutly for such a consummation & that I have not presumed too much on your time & patience I beg leave to subscribe myself Very gratefully & respectfully Yours

ALS   Julia A. Wilbur

282

Julia A. Wilbur to Hon. E. M. Stanton, 24 Mar. 1863, W-477 1863, Letters Received, RG 107 [L-23]. Although Wilbur's letter was received at the War Department on March 25, it was not filed until the end of April; in the intervening weeks, other letters reached the department concerning the former slaves at Alexandria, and it may have been considered in conjunction with them. On March 31, Anna Barnes, secretary of the society sponsoring Wilbur, complained to President Lincoln of an objectionable procedure reported by Wilbur: "At 'The Slave Pen' [in Alexandria] not only colored *men*, but colored *women* are stripped, and put in the shower bath by our *Union soldiers*." Seeking Lincoln's intervention ("not only for the sake of the women, who are degraded enough now but for the sake of the Soldiers who are already brutal enough!"), Barnes also took the occasion to warn the President about the Reverend Albert Gladwin, "a brutal man" who was seeking the position of superintendent of contrabands at Alexandria. "[S]moother than butter, to superiors," she alleged, "he is harder than iron to the defenceless." (Anna M. C. Barnes to Abraham Lincoln, 31 Mar. 1863, B-427 1863, Letters Received, RG 107 [L-23].) The Secretary of War, to whom Barnes's letter was referred, forwarded it to General John P. Slough, military governor of Alexandria, who in turn referred it to Colonel Henry H. Wells, provost marshal of the city, for a report. Meanwhile, on April 1, having received no reply to her letter of March 24, Wilbur renewed her protest about the rental charges, this time addressing the assistant secretary of war. She had supposed that in the newly constructed barracks, "the old, the disabled, the widows & orphans would find a home free of expense"; Colonel Wells, however, insisted "that the rooms must be rented, & this is now done at the rate of $4 to $5 a month." "The plan," Wilbur believed, "is to induce some family who *can* pay to take a room & then fill it up with those who are unable to pay, at the rate of twelve & sixteen persons in a room." Wilbur next trained her sights upon Gladwin, whom Wells had employed to collect the rent. He was, she charged, "fitted neither by nature, education nor habit" for the office of superintendent of contrabands. "He has excluded me from the schoolrooms entirely, using them for meetings & a school of his own," and he was attempting "to keep me from two other rooms" that the provost marshal had promised her "for the use of the orphans." In conjunction with Harriet Jacobs, a black woman who had been sent to Alexandria by a Quaker society in New York, Wilbur had devised a system to provide for black orphans, and they believed their work would be hindered if Gladwin became superintendent. "In our opinion," Wilbur concluded, "what is most needed is an *honest* & efficient Superintendent, who would be authorized to look after the interests of the Government while he protected the Contrabands, (men, women & children) from the rapacity & cruelty of Contractors, sutlers, disloyal citizens & others who are ever ready to take advantage of these people." Both she and Jacobs, Wilbur pointedly noted, were laboring without any compensation from the government. (Julia A. Wilbur to Hon. P. H. Watson, 1 Apr. 1863, W-394 1863, Letters Received, RG 107 [L-23].) Wilbur's letter, like Barnes's, was forwarded to General Slough and referred by him to Colonel Wells. For the latter officer's response, see document 59B, immediately below.

1 Captain John C. Wyman, whose efforts to obtain housing for the former slaves are discussed above, in docs. 53n., 57.

59B: Provost Marshal of Alexandria, Virginia, to the Military Governor of Alexandria

Alexandria Va. April, 12th 1863.

General. I have the honor to acknowledge the receipt of the letter of Julia A. Wilbur. dated April 1st 1863 – addressed to the assistant Sec'y of War.[1] and by him referred to you. on the 9th day of April 1863. and by your order. referred to me for investigation, and immediate report. on the 11th of April 1863.

In obedience to your orders I have to report, that on coming into this office. on the first day of February 1863. I was called upon by Miss Wilbur. who desired an interview with me on the subject of contrabands. She then exhibited to me a letter from an anti-slavery society. directing her to visit Alexandria, for the purpose of laboring for. and looking after the condition of contrabands She had also in her possession, reccommendations from distinguished persons. fully endorsing her. At that interview she expressed considerable interest on the subject of the control or influence, which she was to have in the management of the colored people. and complained that she had labored for some time in procuring the erection of quarters. and had not been consulted so much. as she deemed she had a right to be. I then informed her that it would give me great pleasure to see her at all times. and recieve her suggestions, at the same time informing her. that after hearing her. and the other friends of the colored people. I should be compelled to act for myself – as I only – was responsible for the proper discharge. of that duty. I invited the like advice and suggestions from Captain Wyman. my immediate predecessor.

As soon as the barracks were completed – I directed that they be occupied by precisely the number, (and no more, that they were originally intended for. but before this was done Miss Wilbur called upon me to know who were to go to these quarters, and I then. said to her. that my orders – were, that those who were poor and destitute were to be first accommodated. and then those who were able to pay. would have quarters furnished them. on the payment of from four to five dollars per month.

With this arrangement she expressed herself. as perfectly satisfied. and so much of her letter, as charges that I informed her that the rooms "must be rented", is entirely untrue. She also requested that I would allow her two rooms. in the quarters for the use of orphans, and young women. which I immediately did. but she has never chosen to occupy the same. and they are now, and always have been vacant. There is one very large. and commodious room. devoted to school purposes. and in which a school. with a regular attendance. of nearly one hundred. is kept by Mr. Gladwin. I am not aware. and do not believe. that Mr. Gladwin, or any other person has attempted to prevent the occupation of these rooms – by Miss Wilbur – and certainly no such complaint has been made to me. In addition to the quarters thus furnished I have furnished bunks. tables and benches. for all the rooms. and also have. from the first furnished these people with their fuel. (wood and coal) without any charge whatever. More than one half – and I should say three quarters – of these contrabands are employed, and now receiving much larger pay. as a general rule. than the soldiers of our army. and as far as I could do so. I have reduced the expenses. furnishing only such assistants as was necessary and calculated to benefit the colored people. and not render them more dependent and indolent than they now are.

The total amount received up to this time, for rent of these buildings. is seventy dollars. from the 23rd day of Feb. when the occupation of the barracks commenced. to the 6th day of April 1863.

On one occasion Miss. Wilbur complained, verbally that some persons, who in her judgment ought not to pay. rent, had been required to do so. I then desired her to put her complaint in writing, and notified her that all written charges – and complaints, would at once receive respectful and prompt attention – and every complaint so made to me. has at once been investigated, and where there was a fault. it has been corrected. and the statement contained in Miss. W's letter. that the reasonable complaint of those people are disregarded, is untrue. The charges of cruelty. and rapacity. so freely made by Miss Wilbur. against Mr. Gladwin. I believe are entirely without cause or foundation. carefully observing his acts. as I have, during my service here. and sustained as he is. by the unqualified endorsement. of Capt. Wyman. my immediate predecessor. (who in the very last conversation I had with him. urged that an effort should be made to procure the regular appointment of Mr. Gladwin. and spoke in the highest terms of commendation, of that gentleman.) I again cordially endorse him. I have from the first, been aware. that Miss. Wilbur was very bitterly opposed to Mr. Gladwin. but I could find no cause for it – except a desire on her part, to have the control, and management of the contrabands.

Miss Wilbur is entirely mistaken in the covert assumption which she makes. that I am not interested in these people. She very well knows, that such is not the fact. I *am* interested in them. and intend to do my duty towards them. but do not intend, (until so ordered) to be directed by her. nor to allow the expenditure of one dollar. which I think unnecessary, or improper. They are well, and tenderly cared for. and are not abused or ill-treated, as she states, and they cannot be made more happy by her meddlesome interference. I have the honor to remain, General, your obedient Servant,

HLS   H. H. Wells

Lt. Col. H. H. Wells to Brig. Gen'l J. P. Slough, 12 Apr. 1863, filed with W-394 1863, Letters Received, RG 107 [L-23]. On the previous day, while responding to a complaint by Anna Barnes, secretary of the society sponsoring Julia Wilbur (summarized above, in doc. 59An.), Colonel Wells had levied even sterner criticism against Wilbur. The practice objected to by Barnes, Wells explained, had been a solitary incident involving "a drunken, disorderly prostitute" who was sentenced by the provost judge "to receive a 'shower bath'" at the slave pen. What is more, Wells himself had already ordered that "the shower bath" not thereafter be employed as a punishment for women. Turning to Barnes's and Wilbur's criticism of Gladwin, Wells defended him as "a kind-hearted christian gentleman, [who] has labored most indefatigably since, October or November last, in ameliorating the condition of the colored people of Alexandria." Gladwin, Wells argued, "believes that as soon as possible, they should support themselves, instead of depending upon the charity of the Gov't." With Wells's approval, he furnished quarters without charge to contrabands who were unable to pay, but charged rent "to them who are able to pay." "I am happy to say, for the credit of the colored people," Wells added, "that they generally pay cheerfully, feeling that it is honorable to do so." Wilbur's "principal cause of complaint against Mr. Gladwin," Wells believed, lay "in the fact that he is so striving to make the people self sustaining." She, on the other hand, "seems to labor under the belief that the chief object is to make life easy, and obtain for them the largest possible grants from the Gov't." "I am compelled to say," he concluded, "that while respecting Miss. Wilbur's goodness of heart, and broad benevolence, I regard her as an interfering, and troublesome person." On April 12, when General John P. Slough, the military governor, returned Barnes's letter to the War Department with Wells's report, he added an endorsement suggesting that "[i]f the ladies referred to would make known to me their cause of complaint there would be no necessity on their part of troubling the President or War Department. It too often occurs that these ladies in a mistaken zeal act as if they would usurp the whole power of Military Governor. Such a disposition is manifested by Miss Wilbur. As auxiliary to a male superintendent her services are valuable – she has done much good and I gladly second her efforts but must be permitted to prevent her attempts at encroachment." Slough recommended that Gladwin be appointed superintendent of contrabands at Alexandria. (Lt. Col. H. H. Wells to Brig. Gen'l John P. Slough, 11 Apr. 1863, filed with B-427 1863, Letters Received, RG 107 [L-23].) Draft replies to Barnes and to Wilbur, filed with their respective letters, indicate that in each case the War Department simply forwarded a copy of Wells's report. Despite Wilbur's objections, but in accordance with the views of Wells and Slough, Gladwin received the appointment.

1 Wilbur's letter is summarized in the endnote of doc. 59A, immediately above.

60: Testimony by the Superintendent of Contrabands at Camp Barker before the American Freedmen's Inquiry Commission

[*Washington, D.C. April? 1863*]
Testimony of D. B. Nichols
Superintendent of Contrabands.

Q. What office has Capt Ferree?

A. – He is a Chaplain in the Volunteer service, and Chaplin Ferree was detailed as Military Commandant of the Camp; which I retained the office of Civil Superintendent

Q. – What number of colored freedmen have come under your supervision?

A. – We have had in the Camp the total number of 4.939.

Q. – How many are there in Camp at the present time, not on the Sick list.

A. – 557.

Q– How many able bodiedmen above the age of Sixteen, fit for service? &c

20.

Q. – How many able-bodied women over the age of fourteen – fit for service?

A. – 177.

Q. – How many infirm our sick women over fourteen unfit for service?

A. – 50.

Q. – How many boy,s under sixteen in good health?

Ans 145

Q. – How many sick under the age of sixteen not in Hospital.

A. – 6.

Q. – How many Girls under the age of fourteen, who are well?

A 108.

Q. – How many Girls under that age, who are sick?

8 [. . .]

Q. – Are any abled-bodied men Employed about the camps?

Ans Yes – 20. – at $6.00 per month and promptly

Q How these been regularly and promptly paid?

A. – Yes; those employed about the camps and Hospitals, have been promptly paid.

Q. – Do you know wither the men who have gon out from the camps, and are employed by Goverment as – Teamsters, &c, have been regularly paid, and at what intearvals?

A They have been paid Generally about once three months.

Q. – Do you know if they have worked in a satisfactory manner?

Ans. – I have not heard any complaints in regard to their working Col Beckwith, of the Commissary Depart., said he found them very industrious faithful and obedient, and that he preferred them to whites. Those who have superintended their work on the Entrenchments, say they dug better then whites, I think there are not [so] many Employed by Goverment, as hitherto; the custome of withholdin 5.00 per month from a black mans wages, having driven them away.

Q Was $5.00 per month then deducted from the wages of all colered men?

Answer – Not all; but from the wages of those who received $15. $20 per month $5 was and is invariable taken for this Camp fund – to support the sick and infirm contrabands. No matter wither the workman were originally free people or not. There is now a larg sum of money which has accumulated in the hands of the Custodians of the fund.

Q. – But in case a man had no relations in the camp, or in a condition to receive the benefits of the fund, would the same amount be deducted from the wages?

A. – Yes; it would no difference and worse then that; if he received at the rate of $25 a month, and was sick three-quarters of the time, getting but $6.00 the $5 would be deducted by the Government and $1, only paid to the laborer. It has been said, by those who had the oppertunity of knowing, that when the colored laborers at Harpers Ferry were paid off, the same sume was retained; though they were paid but 40 cents a day.[1] I have heard the colored people complain often of this policy on the part of the Government.

Q. – In your opinion, would contrabands Employed by Government or otherwise prefer to pay rent for their own cabins themselves, to being supported by in a Government Camp?

They undoubtedly would very-much prefer to pay rent for cabins. They feel that it is my duty to go and hunt them up a place. If there were avarleable Cabins., which they could rent, the Enterprise would be self-supporting and would thin out the camp rapidly.

Q. – Does Each family in camp have a sepearate Cabin?

A. – No Sir; it is impossible to do it   We have often been obliged to put two families in a cabin, and sometimes three, and, in some instances, single and married together. We are obliged to crowed them together in this way, in consequence of a want of room.

Q. – What is the greatest number you have put into any single cabin?

A. – I think we have had as many as 26 in one Cabin.

Q. – Of what dimensions are the Cabins.

A. – Generally about 10 feet × 12. and 7 feet high on an average.

Q. – What were the huts formerly used for?

A. – One portion of them was occupied as barracks for Capt Barker's Co of the McClel[elam's] Dragoons; and all those on the north were stables when we moved in there   the building occupied for our Kitchen was originally a stable.

Q. – In your opinion has this promiscuous herding of people been promotive of immorality?

A. – Yes sir. to a considerable degree. I think We could not guard them sufficiently against those conditions which every where produce immorality. We have tried to classify and separate them properly, but our opportunities were too limited.

Q. – What does the Goverment provide?

It provides the huts, and rations and the Wages of Superintendant, assistat Superintendant, and Surgeon   They provide no clothing and no bedding, Except for the Hospitals.

Q. – Has there been any systematic effort made to give occupation to all the people in the camps.

A Very little; I tried to establish a wash-house, and have washing brought in and taken out, but the Authorities did not favor it.

Q. – In your opinion, could the able bodied women in camp be usefully Employed in doing the washing for Govertment Hospitals?

A Under proper supervision, they could   There has been great difficulty, on account of a frequent loss of garments. If there was a systematic laundry Established, it would be a capital thing, and a profitable thing, for the labour of those women could be made very available for the use of Goverment.

Q. – In your opinion is the ventilation of the cabins sufficient?

A. – I am very sure it is not; there is no thorogh ventilation on the north at all, on account of the danger of slave holders from that direction. We have had a small guard, and were very much troubled with these individuals when we were all inside; and now that a part of us are outside we are still more troubled. We are more troubled now then ever.

Q. – Are there any Enclosed yards back of the cabins?

Ans. – No; Sir. –

Q. – Is there a sufficient number of privies?

A. – No, sir; and I consider that a very great want. I have twice drawn lumber for this very purpose, but the small pox patients in each case seemed to need our immediate attention, and I used the lumber for the flooring of their Hospitable tents. I tried to recover from the medical Dept the lumber which I had appropriated for their use, but faild to get the requisition through.

Q. – When men are taken off as teamsters. have they ever been taken with violence?

In one or two cases, there was violence used, I believe. In one instance when I was away. I have never seen any-thing of the kind till since they have had a guard and since Capt Ferrer came.

Q. – Are contrabands ever put in the guard house all night previous to being taken off as teamsters?

A – Never to My Knowledge – though they are sometimes taken against their own will.

Q. – To your Knowledge has any corporal punishment been inflicted upon any of them?

A. – Yes. sir. I have never seen it; but I understood that Capt Mackey did occasionally use that kind of punishment He was a man of violent temper; and once threatened to shoot me.

Q. – Do the freedman require severe discipline for their Government?

No, Sir; far less then whites so far as my experience goes. They are much more docile and submissive then whites; always more yielding to authority.

Q. – Do you consider camp life, such as they are obliged to lead, to be demoralising

A. – do, most decidedly, the longer they stay there the worse they become; the more vicious in their habits, and the less inclind to work.

Q. – When they come in to camp, do they seek to renew their old family ties? – or form new ones?

A. – As a general rule, I am sure they wish and seek to preserve family ties renewing again there relations as parents, children, husband and wife whenever they are able.

Q. – Do they generally have family names. handed down from father to son, or do they go by their christian name. and change their family names as they change their masters?

A. – They usually adopt the family names of their masters.

Q. – Are arangements being made for a new Hospital?

A. – Yessir, one is building. It is to be spacious and well

ventilated, after the most approved modern style of Hospitals, and promises to be quite an affair when completed. It is located near the present camp.

Q. – Have these people shown any vindictive feelings towards their masters?

A. – No. sir.

Q. – Have you Known of them carrying concealed weapons?

A. – I have known of two instance; it is not at all Common.

Q. – As compared with the poor class of whites people, what are their habits as respects Temperance.

A. – As a people, they are temperate, very; before the groceries were set up near, they were remarkably temperate. But the l[onge] they stay in that Camp, the more demoralised they become in every respect.

Q. – Do they manifest more or less religious disposition then poorer classes of white people?

A. – Vastly more then any class of whites. They are the most religious people I have ever had anything to do with, and are Exceedingly devoted and fervent, as compared with the poor classes of white people

Q. – How do they compare with regard to the parental and filial affection, with the poorer classes of whites?

A. – These people are peculiar in this respect. They have so trained themselves to believe that it is better to be dead then to be in Slavery, that they rarely ever cry when their relations die. Though 554 have died since I have been connected with the camp, I have not seen a dozen enclined to shed tears.

Q. – Does this arise from insensibility, or any lack of affection?

A. – No, sir, I am sure it does not They have greater family affection while living, but seem to have acquired this Stoical habit from the thought that death is better then slavery They make great manifestations of sorrow at separation here.

Another reason perhaps is their great faith in a future life. This is universal all believe in future reward and punishment and are Evangelical and Orthodox in the strictest sense

Q. – As compared with the poor classes of whites, are these people lazy or disinclined to work?

A. – No, sir, I think they are no more so then whites would be in similar circumstances, I can see no difference between the contrabands boy,s and the Reformed school boy,s of whom I was superintendent in Chicago, about that. The children of corresponding ages here, are much the more docile and obedient. The contrabands are the most Easily managed people I ever saw.

Q. – You think then, that they would work under an organised system of labor?

A. – Undoubtedly, and they would Earn their living well. They love to talk to me about it; and they would be delighted if they could to go out and work on a farm under employment.

Q. – Have any children been boarded out in Maryland?

A. – Some of the children have gon to servis there. [Q.] From whom did the authority come to send them there.

A. – Permission came from Gen Martindale, and also for Marylanders to come and apply for them and get them

Q. – Were the other colored people of the camp willing to have them go?

A. – No Sir; they were a good deal excited about it. They are much afraid of Maryland.

Q. – Has Capt Ferrer the control of that?

A. – He has ultimately. Genl. Martindale's instructions are that in every case where there is a conflict of authority I should yield to him.

Q. – Can a colored person be found [*bound*] out to [serve?] in M.d.?

A. – Not according to the laws of M.d. But three children were recently taken out, by a man who had recently lost a family of nine children slave-children, who had run a way. He had been to the camp several times hunting for them, and finally he was permitted to take off these three. The mistress is a Miss Hershy, or something like that, and the family are said to sympathise with the rebels.

Q. – Have you known of any contrabands here having been abducted from the camp in to Slavery?

A. – Not directly from the camp; but several who have gon out to work; or were absent from the Camp, have been caught up. and taken off there, have been of these about a dozen cases in all. Some we hav heard from in M.d. jail These have some of them taken place when they have been furnished with a military pass, signed in the proper manner; and after breaking out of jail, have brought with them these passes.

Q. – Have these contrabands been, or are they now, in fear of being returned to slavery?

A. – Terrible. An Episcopal minister, of the name of Scott, came up from Va, with a Slaveholder, professing to be loyal. They got a permit from Genl Wadsworth to visit the camp and see their fugitives slaves. They wanted to talk with the Contraband in private, but were not allowed to do so. So they talked with them in my private room. The Contraband who had been his slave watched me very closely, and did not want to talk with their master at

all. They thought he had a mittimus. one old colerd women came
to me and said "Mr Nichols, you have a mission." what is that I
asked. To take this butche Knife" she said, and let the wicked
blood out of that man who has come to take my daughters! He
argued with them and plead with them Saying Havent you had your
pig? and dident I let you go to meeting? and now will you let
your poor master go back alone?" He did not convince one of them;
through the minister had been to Duff Green,s row, when th camp
was there, and went home and told that there were a hunderd who
wanted to go back.

Q. – Are the contrabands who chop for contractors paid
regularly?

A. They get a promise of the highest price; but it is said that the
sub-contractors make more money bording them than by the
contract. The money is got away from them one way or another and
they generally bring none back   They work hard but their wages
are all taken for board, cooking utensils &c.

From the moment the contraband lands within our lines and gets
any money he is the victim of fraud and robbery; in overcharges
passing upon them bogus gold for greenbacks. We have discovered
several of these swindlers and put them in the guard-house.

Hack drivers also frequently charge three or four times the legal
price in carrying these persons. Many private families where they
are hired, have been in the habit of hiring them by the month; then
discharging them without any pay before the expiration of the
month. I reported some cases to headquarters & Gen. Wadsworth
helped me with an order that they should be paid.[2] Since that,
whenever I have written a letter to these parties, threatening them &
enclosing the order they have paid up.

Q. – Are the freedmen inclined to be forgot [*frugal*]?

A. – Many of them. They like to turn over their money to some
white friend and take a note for it. They are about as economical as
a similar class of poor whites.

Q. What do you think of the capacity and disposition of these
men for military service?

I believe they can learn military tactics more readily than white
people. As to courage and endurance I think that led by officers in
whom they had confidence they would go where they went & do
whatever commanded. With good leaders they will make excellent
soldiers.

Q. Would they help to defend Washington if it should be in
danger?

A. Undoubtedly. When Stonewall Jackson was said to be
crossing the Potomac above here and our soldiers were withdrawn

from the rear of Washington to the front We had an armed black guard out for two nights. They were vigilant and otherwise like other soldiers.

Q. – In your opinion would a colored guard be more or less efficient than a white one at the Contraband Camp.

A. – They would be more efficient as guards for they would follow the order whatever it was.

HD

Testimony of D. B. Nichols before the American Freedmen's Inquiry Commission, [Apr.? 1863], filed with O-328 1863, Letters Received, ser. 12, RG 94 [K-67]. Topical labels in the margin are omitted. Camp Barker, in northwest Washington, had been established in July 1862, when General James S. Wadsworth, then military governor of the District of Columbia, authorized Danforth B. Nichols, superintendent of contrabands at Duff Green's Row, "to take possession of one block of the McClellan Dragoons barracks for the use of the families of Contrabands employed by the Government." (A.D.C. John A. Kress to Mr. Nichols, 2 July 1862, vol. 98 DW, p. 155, Letters Sent, ser. 642, Military Dist. of Washington, RG 393 Pt. 2 No. 12 [C-4716].) In January 1863, General John H. Martindale, who succeeded Wadsworth, had assigned Chaplain James I. Ferree, a Methodist minister from Illinois, to take charge of the contrabands at Camp Barker. (James Inglish Ferree to Gen. Lorenzo Thomas, 15 July 1862, F-285 1862, and Hospital Chaplain James I. Ferree to Adjutant General L. Thomas, 30 June 1864, F-261 1864, Letters Received, ser. 12, RG 94 [K-229, K-228].)

1 The black laborers at Harper's Ferry had worked to improve the defenses of the upper Potomac after the Confederate invasion of Maryland in September 1862. They included men dispatched from Washington in response to the request of General George B. McClellan, commander of the Army of the Potomac, for 2,000 black laborers. (*Official Records*, ser. 1, vol. 19, pt. 2, pp. 360–63.)

2 In October 1862, General James S. Wadsworth, military governor of the District of Columbia and commander of the Military District of Washington, had ordered the superintendent of contrabands to report to the district provost marshal "any cases in which persons under his protection have been defrauded of their wages, or otherwise maltreated." After investigating such cases, the provost marshal was to report them to Wadsworth's headquarters "for further action." (Orders, Head Quarters Military District of Washington D.C., 17 Oct. 1862, vol. 98 DW, p. 339, Letters Sent, ser. 642, Military Dist. of Washington, RG 393 Pt. 2 No. 12 [C-4581].)

61: Testimony by a Former Maryland Slave

[Freedman's Village, Va.? January? 1864]
Lewis Johnson.

Q What is your age

A I am 31; & came to Camp Barker in May 1862.

Q Who had charge of the camp and what have you to say about the state of things.

A Well Sir, Mr Nichols had charge and Mr. Small was under him. I worked for Mr Nichols two months; I was night cook. Mr Nichols was not very kind to me; would not give us tea and coffee nor full rations and he would not allow me any better place than the horse stables to sleep in; asked him for a better place but he would not give me any, nor would he give me any blankets all the time I staid with him.

I was sick in camp, had been kicked by a mule; had had a fever and was suffering generally with the consumption.

About two weeks before Christmas I was in a tent with four other persons. Mr Nichols took our stove away; we had no bed; lay on a plank with no blankets and the tent was so old and good for nothing that every time it rained I got wet and cold because the tent would always let in the water by leaking or blowing down. I told Mr. Nichols about these things and he told me I was no use to him, nor to others and that all such ~~fellows~~ negroes and I too might as well be dead. The Medical Director ordered me sent to the Hospital or I never would have been there.

I could not get anything from Mr. Nichols unless I paid cash down. I had been to work for him but he would not pay me what he owed me and so I never had any money to pay cash down.

Mr. Nichols I know used to drink whiskey. There used to be a certain bottle in the Doctors office and it had liquor in it. Mr Nichols used to tell me to watch that closely and not let any one take it. I used to see Mr Nichols drink from it and he would take two and three parts of a glass full at a time. I seen his wife and daughter put him to bed one night when he was drunk. but I never see this but once.

Mr Nichols was not kind to the people under him in the camp; he used to knock them about and kick them right smart.

A woman in camp, had a little child; Nichols told her she must go to work and she told him she was not ready to go to work; he told her she was and that she must do so; the woman did not go to work, so Mr. Nichols put her child over the lines and then beat its mother off; and he beat the woman out the camp with one of the soldiers sword canes and his fist. I can not tell the number of persons he used to abuse, but there were a great many.

I was a slave for a long time; my masters name was Lukie Pierce and we lived on Carrolls manor in Maryland. My master was a first rate man and if he was living to day I would be under him. I rather be under him by ten degrees than be with Nichols. My good old master never whipped any of his slaves, and he would never allow any of his overseers to abuse any of his slaves. He set us all free one year before the war began. My owner was better than many masters but I speak from my heart before the Lord when I say that the conduct of Mr Nichols was worse than the general treatment of slave owners

Q Johnson have you any unkind feelings toward Mr. Nichols?

A "Deed sir not de least bit. I'm this minute suffering despertly on my sick bed, and as certain as I have a maker, everything I have said about Mr Nichols, and every thing else is true as de Lord in heaven. It is certainly so as I tell it. I have not even any hard feelings against Mr. Nichols, & I forgive him all he has done to me, & I hope de Lord will forgive him too. I must die & I know I have to stand before my maker and I speak de whole truth"

(This man is very sick with catarrh of the bladder in the Hospital at Contraband Camp. There is every evidence of sincrity and reliability about this man & his testimony)

HD

Testimony of Lewis Johnson, [Jan.? 1864], Miscellaneous Records, ser. 5412, Dept. of Washington, RG 393 Pt. 1 [C-4757]. Filed with the testimony of two other former slaves who had resided at Camp Barker and collectively labeled "Intemperance of Nichols and his treatment of the Inmates of Camp Barker in Washington." The three documents are in turn filed with testimony by more than fifty people regarding the treatment of freedpeople at Camp Barker and at Freedman's Village. The file provides no information about the composition or mandate of the investigating body; it may have been established by Colonel Elias M. Greene, chief quartermaster of the Department of Washington, as a result of complaints about Danforth B. Nichols. (See below, doc. 71.)

62: Assistant Quartermaster at the Washington Depot to the Chief Quartermaster of the Depot

Washington, D.C. 1ˢᵗ May 1863.

Colonel I have the honor to call your attention to the replacing of white laborers in my department, by Negroes, the former (principally Irish) being very negligent of their duties as a mass, and much inclined to dissipation. The negroes are much superior workers, more attentive to their duties, less inclined to dissipation, and readily controlled. About 150 Negroes would meet the wants of my Department at present.

I would also respectfully call the attention of Colonel Rucker to the fact, that much dissatisfaction exists among the colored employees, on account of the Tax imposed for Contraband support, many of my most excellent workmen in the government mills threaten to leave on this account. I would most respectfully suggest that some measures be taken that the colored laborers be allowed to receive the full amount of their monthly dues.

The colored laborers which have been furnished me from the Contraband Camp, have not come up to the standard of steady workers, Most of them after receiving a few weeks pay usually leave. I am Sir Very Respectfully Your obt Servant

HLcSr   (signed) Chas H. Tompkins.

Capt. Chas. H. Tompkins to Colonel D. H. Rucker, 1 May 1863, enclosed in Col. D. H. Rucker to Brig. Genl. M. C. Meigs, 1 May 1863, R-327 1863, Letters Received, ser. 20, Central Records, RG 92 [Y-617]. In his covering letter, which forwarded Tompkins's letter to the quartermaster general, the chief quartermaster of the Washington depot, Colonel Daniel H. Rucker, proposed that 150 "colored laborers" be sent from New Berne, North Carolina, or Fortress Monroe, Virginia, for service in Washington. With respect to the objections voiced by Tompkins's black employees to the "stoppage" on their wages, Rucker warned that "[t]here are some of these men engaged in the horse mills who are unusually good men and understand that particular business who, now, I learn, talk of leaving and seeking employment in mills in and about Georgetown, where they are offered $25 per month. These men," Rucker concluded, "are, in my opinion, worth that sum to the Government." By an endorsement of May 14, Montgomery C. Meigs, the quartermaster general, directed a subordinate to "advise" the chief quartermaster of the Department of North Carolina that 150 "able bodied colored men are wanted in the transportation dept of the Washington depot . . . if he has them to spare & willing to come." They would be employed "as $10 per month contrabands." Meigs did not address Tompkins's and Rucker's objection to the $5 per month tax on black workers. The request for laborers from North Carolina was unproductive; the chief quartermaster at New Berne replied that all the able-bodied black men were being enlisted in the Union army. (See above, doc. 19n.) For subsequent efforts by quartermaster officers to procure black workers in tidewater Virginia and North Carolina for service in and around Washington, see above, docs. 19–20.

63: Chief Quartermaster of the Department of Washington to the Commander of the Department

Washington, D.C., May 5th *1863.*

General: I have the honor to submit the following statements and suggestions in reference to the farm lands in this Department, South of the Potomac river, which have been abandoned by rebel owners, and are now lying idle.

On quite a number of these farms the houses are left standing – of these, there are enough to provide quarters for, from 500 to 750 field hands, with a very small outlay for additions and improvements.

The force of contrabands, males and females, now idle in this City, and a dead weight on the Government, can be employed to very great advantage in cultivating the above lands, raising corn and millet, cutting Hay (of which it is estimated more than One thousand tons may be cured) for this Department.

The families need not be separated as they can still be united, and may be fully as well provided for as at their present quarters in this City and at less expense.

Besides this, there is a decided advantage afforded to them of the salutary effects of good pure country air, and a return to their former healthy avocations, as "field hands" under much happier auspices than heretofore, which must prove beneficial to them, and will tend to prevent the increase of diseases now prevalent among them.

I also propose establishing a large vegetable garden, south of the Potomac, to be cultivated by the younger contrabands, and others of them who are unable to do heavy field work.

The proceeds of such labor would be considerable as regular stands for the sale of the produce (to be attended to by the old women) could be established in this City, or the vegetables might be distributed among the troops, as my be directed by the War Department.

The arrangement I propose will not only in my opinion conduce to the sanitary and moral improvement of the contrabands, but will save the Gov[t] an immense amount of money.

My proposition may be simply stated as a scheme to give employment to all of the Contrabands in this Department, and make such employment profitable both to them, and to the Government. Yourself and the Quarter Master General having verbally signified your approbation of the plans herein proposed, I have taken the preliminary steps towards carrying them out.

Before I can proceed further, it is necessary that I have control of all of the Contrabands in good health at present idle in the Camp in this City under direction of Brig Gen[l] Martindale.

The present Superintendent of the Contrabands approves of my plans and being a gentleman well qualified for the position he holds, I propose to retain him in it, if the force is transferred to me for the purposes hereinbefore mentioned. I respectfully suggest that the matter should be decided within the next 48 hours.

It will be absolutely necessary to commence any farming operations for the present season immediately, otherwise it will be too late to plant. I have the honor to be Very Respectfully Your Obed' Servant

HLcSr   (Signed)   Elias M Greene.

Lt. Col. Elias M. Greene to Maj. Genl. S. P. Heintzelman, 5 May 1863, "Arlington Va.," Consolidated Correspondence File, ser. 225, Central Records, RG 92 [Y-121]. General John H. Martindale was military governor of the District of Columbia. The superintendent of contrabands whose services Greene wished to retain was Danforth B. Nichols, the civilian superintendent at Camp Barker in Washington. The commander of the Department of Washington, General Samuel P. Heintzelman, approved Greene's proposal in an endorsement of the same day: "I fully concur in these suggestions & respectfully recommend them." General Montgomery C. Meigs, the quartermaster general, also concurred and recommended that Heintzelman be authorized to issue the appropriate orders. On May 14, the Secretary of War approved Meigs's recommendation. (Summary of endorsements, 7, 14 May 1863, vol. 3, p. 658, Register of Letters Received Irregular, RG 107 [L-180].) Accordingly, on May 22, Heintzelman ordered that "[a]ll 'Contrabands' now in the cities of Washington, D.C., and Alexandria, Va., dependent on the Government of the United States for support, (with the exception of those employed in the Quartermaster's Department, or other branches of the service,) will be immediately reported by Superintendents of Contrabands, Provost Marshals, or others in charge" to Colonel Greene, such reports to specify number, age, sex, and condition. The order also authorized Greene to "take possession of all rebel lands, farm houses and tenements thereon, at present abandoned by their owners, . . . situated south of the Potomac and within the lines of this command" and to "proceed to cultivate said lands by such Contrabands, and in such a manner as may be most beneficial to the Government." (General Orders No. 28, Headquarters, Dep't of Washington, 22 May 1863, vol. 55A DW, General Orders [Printed], ser. 5385, Dept. of Washington, RG 393 Pt. 1 [C-5500].)

64: Assistant Surgeon to the Surgeon in Charge of Contrabands at Alexandria

[Alexandria, Va.] June 14th 1863

Dear Sir   It is Sunday afternoon and my mind feels sad in view of the sickening rehearsals of the interview between the once enslaved.

but the now worse than enslaved negroes and their new Master, on Saturday evening I am told that Mr A. Gladwin the very man who last October started a mission under the auspices of the Free Mission Society and who actuated by pure love for the African race. was willing to wear out his life in their service and that without compensation has recently without asking for it as he avers been appointed Superintendant of Contrabands

Well what is he doing to benefit the poor downtrodden people. let them answer the question

Without going back to other deeds of darkness let us follow him through the quarters accompanied by an officer— Some are threatened with being put into the cars and sent to Richmond unless the rent is paid Monday morning   others are threatened with expulsion unless they respond to the call. Robert Foster is a grave digger for Government been employed 2 months has drawn no money and but fifteen days rations. must leave unless rent is paid Monday. Charles Johnson has been employed in Commisary Dept some three months has received $18. per month the first two months has been sick with dysentery, large family draws no rations unable to work, must leave Monday unless the money is forthcoming   Oscar Baltimore works at Contraband Commisary Dept had no pay for 10 months, wife has quarters in Barracks must leave unless rent is paid Monday

These are only a few of the many complaints made to me while visiting the sick this morning   I am also told that on last Sabbath Mr Gladwin sent the Guards to compel all at the Barracks to attend church with a threat that all who did not respond to the call should be put in the "Slave Pen"   These people are naturally inclined to be religious and are fond of attending church But I have yet to meet with the first Colored man or woman in the Barracks that does not sigh for the cruelties of Slavery rather than enjoy the tender mercies of A. Gladwin

It is a well known fact that the Barracks were built and designed for a home for the aged infirm and helpless of the Contraband   Mr Gladwin orriginated and carried out the plan for making them pay rent and in order to make every room contain as many as possible and pay rent one family was placed in each room supposed capable of paying rent and then filled up to the maximum number (14 to 16) in a room. The negro can read character and soon learn to appreciate and love their friends. How can such a missionary benefit them? can he gain their confidence so as to lead them Heavenward? If so the bayonet would not be needed to compel attendence on church to listen to the teachings of an ambasador of Christ.

You may think I am stepping aside from my legitimate duties as your Act Ast Surgeon, but Sir humanity alone would prompt the revelation. While I know that my province is the physical welfare of the contraband, yet I feel that some one should care for their moral and spiritual wellbeing hence this appeal to you not only as the Surgeon in charge but as a Philanthropist & Christian

I feel that this people are now in a transition state from Slavery to freedom, jealous of the white mans power over them and they should be taught by some one in whom they have confidence, not only how to care for themselves physically but morally & spiritually

Now sir can you not have an influence with the Superintendant to divert him from this course of tyrany and oppression and induce him to be governed by the pure motive of love   I forbear writing more now lest I may weary you although there are many issues connected with the subject upon which I would like to write   Your Act As Surgeon U.S.A.

ALS   Samuel Shaw.

Samuel Shaw to Dr. J. R. Bigelow, 14 June 1863, filed with G-43 1863, Letters Received, ser. 360, Colored Troops Division, RG 94 [B-29]. Shaw's letter, which is filed with a large number of other documents concerning the Reverend Albert Gladwin, superintendent of contrabands at Alexandria, came to the attention of the War Department in September 1863, when a committee of the National Freedman's Relief Association of Washington made formal charges against Gladwin to the Secretary of War. (Statement by G. Buckingham et al., [Sept. 1863], in the same file.) Among the other evidence presented by the committee was a letter to the association, dated July 30, 1863, from Shaw and two other physicians working among the former slaves at Alexandria, who announced that "we deem it criminal to remain longer silent." "We were utterly astonished at [Gladwin's] appointment . . . knowing as we did his entire unfitness and incompetency for the position." "We believe in inducing [the ex-slaves] to care for themselves," the doctors asserted, "and have found them capable, desirous, and even proud in so doing, but when poverty & sickness stare them in the face we feel that they need as much care and sympathy as other folks. We believe also that they can be better managed by the unchanging law of *love* than by threats of the 'Slave Pen' and 'Shower bath.'" The three physicians complained in particular about the rents Gladwin charged the freedpeople, reporting that "all who do not pay rent at the Barracks are to leave them; and all who receive rations must go to Arlington Flats or have their rations cut off. Many of the better class," they noted, "have submitted to the loss of their rations rather than their liberty." (A.A. Surgeon J. R. Bigelow et al. to the Freedman's Relief Association, 30 July 1863, in the same file.) For the slave pen and showerbath punishments, see above, docs. 59An., 59Bn. One of the physicians, Surgeon J. W. Graves, furnished further "particulars" in a later letter, citing rental charges for habitations other than the government barracks. He described an old grist mill, occupied by four or five families of ex-slaves, which lacked a chimney and whose roof was so defective that "it affords an excellent opportunity for its inmates to become astronomers." For this building, "worth only what the old bricks will sell for," Gladwin was charging $18 per month. In another building, "fit only for a hog pen or chicken coop," lived families with "no male members able to work and some neither male or female," all of whom should be entitled to rations, "but these have been sent off and they are compelled to obtain their own living and pay from $1. to $3. per month rent, the whole building renting for $27 per month." Graves emphasized that Gladwin had originally proposed to collect rent "only of those who were willing and able to pay," but "now he compells them to pay." "[S]ome he has even required to pay back rent unpaid by the previous occupant before being allowed possession." Finally, Graves complained that when "new comers" arrived from the military front, Gladwin forwarded them to Washington even if they had relatives in Alexandria. "[P]arents who have children here & children who have parents brothers & sisters relatives or friends in search of each other are given no time for making enquires." "[S]ometimes they meet," Graves wrote, "and those meetings are truly affecting but as of old . . . husbands and wives are rudely separated and all the family relations are respected but little if at all." (A.A. Surg. J. W. Graves to Mr. Buckingham, 12 Sept. [1863], in the same file.) The War Department called for an investigation, and on October 1, 1863, Captain W. McL. Gwynne, aide-de-camp to General John P. Slough (military governor of Alexandria), reported that he had inspected "all of the Contraband Quarters" in Alexandria. He dismissed the statements of the physicians as "very much exaggerated, if not *untrue.*" They had all been candidates for Gladwin's position, he believed, and "[t]wo women Mrs. Harriet Jacobs (colored) and Miss Julia Wilbur (White) have also been meddling . . . and endeavoring to sour the minds of the negroes against their Superintendant." Gwynne found the freedpeople in surprisingly "good order." "Their rooms, particularly in the Barracks on Prince street were clean, their clothes, and yard, in good condition and I was particularly pleased with the school. I found nearly all comfortable, not crowded in their rooms, and the rent moderate from two to five dollars per month for a house of two rooms sometimes three men, each earning 15 or 20 dollars and rations per month, in a house." "[I]n no case," he asserted, "has a person really unable to pay rent, been required to do so," although some freedmen had been imprisoned for refusal to pay "when it was known they were able." In Gwynne's view, Gladwin's "system" of rental charges "has resulted in learning them to be self reliant: the consequence is that near two hundred shanties have been built in the suburbs of the City: and the Government instead of issuing near twelve hundred rations per day, issue but little over three hundred, and the majority of persons receiving these are aged, and widows with families." Any feeling against Gladwin on the part of the freedpeople, Gwynne believed, had been "gotten up, no doubt, by female 'busybodies,' and urged by . . . the Medical Officers." In a letter forwarding Gwynne's report, General Slough pointed out that "under [Gladwin's] administration the expense of the support of [the ex-slaves] has been very materially reduced," while their condition was "better than that of the poor working *whites* of the North." "I commend the policy inaugurated by Mr Gladwin of as soon as possible making them self-dependent, rather than that policy which intermeddling, would-be-philanthropists would inaugurate, of depending upon others or the Government." (Capt. W. McL. Gwynne to Brig. Gen. J. P. Slough, 1 Oct. 1863, and Brig. Gen. Jno. P. Slough to Asst. Adjt.

General, 1 Oct. 1863, in the same file.) Endorsements at the War Department concluded that the charges against Gladwin were groundless and should be dismissed.

65A: Assistant Quartermaster at the Washington Depot to the Chief Quartermaster of the Depot

Washington, D.C., July 31" *1863*

General: I have the honor to report, that in accordance with your instructions of the 28" inst. I have examined into the manner in which the contrabands, reported by Lt. N. W. Carroll, are employed, and respectfully submit the following as the result of such investigation.

At Columbian Hospital there are Eleven (11) men. employed, as follows. (6). Six. Policeing ditching and draining (2) Carrying water & Cleaning floors (2) Two Sawing wood for Hospital Kitchens (1) Surgeon's Waiter & Ostler

At Carver Hospital Twenty nine men are employed, as follows. (22) Twenty two. Policeing. Ditching and Draining (2) Two. Sawing wood for Wash House & Laundry. (1) One. Washing Sinks (4) Four, Hauling water for Officers Mess, Stewards Mess & Cooking purposes, removing Slops from wards, Cook House &c,

At Harewood Hospital Forty nine (49) men are employed as follows. (2) Asst. Cooks. One for Contrabands and One for Clerks Mess, (3) Assistants to Hospital Bakers, (2) Taking Care of Ambulance Horses, (36) Policeing and improving grounds, (1) Grinding Coffee &c. at Hospt. Commissary (3) Sawing wood. Carrying water and hanging out Clothes at Laundry (2) Sawing wood for Wards and Bake House.

At Finley Hospital Thirty Seven (37) men are employed, as follows— (1) One, Assisting Mason (1) One Assisting Carpenter (1) One Assisting Gardner (8) Eight, Cleaning Spittoons, Sinks & Wards. (1) One, Ostler for Surgeon's and Ambulance Horses. (2) Two, Pumping Water for, and making fires in Laundry (20) Twenty, Policeing & improving grounds. (3) Three Sawing wood for Surgeon, Clerks, and Laundry.

At Emory Hospital Thirty eight (38) men are employed as follows (3) Chopping wood and making fires in Hospital and Laundry (1) Waiter at Surgeons Quarters, (1) Ostler (1) Waiter at Commissary building (1) Waiter at Dispensary (31) Policeing and improving grounds,

At Lincoln Hospital Fifty One (51) men are employed, as follows, (3) Pumping Water for Hospital. (5) Cleaning Sinks & Quarters (1) Teamster (2) Cooks (40) Policeing and improving grounds

At Armory Square Hospital Twenty Six 26. men are employed (1) One. As Teamster and (25) Twenty five in Policeing Grounds &c.

At Campbell Hospital Twelve (12) men are employed in Policeing and improving the grounds

At Camp Hayti, There are Fifty Six (56) men employed as follows (18) Scavengers (3) Cooks for Contraband messes (36) Laborers, burrying Horses, night soil &c.

I am informed by Lt. N. W. Carroll that no definite instructions have been given him in regard to the kinds of work for which these men should be employed at Hospitals. The Contrabands have, in most cases, been detailed by the Military Governor, and the Surgeons have considered themselves as having entire control of the men when so detailed and, as above stated, have used them as waiters, Ostlers, for hanging out clothes &c.

I would respectfully recommend that definite instructions be given to Lt. Carroll, with authority to enable him to carry out such instructions, he having been detailed by the Military Governor to take charge of these Contrabands.

The force at the Hospitals could be reduced at least one third, and in my opinion, might be wholly dispensed with, by having the work they now do, done by convalescents. All the scavenger work at the Hospitals is now done by the Camp Hayti Scavengers. I have the honor to be, General, Very Respectfly Your obd Servt,

HLS   E. E. Camp

Capt. E. E. Camp to Brig. Genl. D. H. Rucker, 31 July 1863, enclosed in Act. Surgeon General W. K. Barnes to Brig. General M. C. Meigs, 7 Sept. 1863, "Negroes Employed in Washington DC Hospitals," Consolidated Correspondence File, ser. 225, Central Records, RG 92 [Y-5]. On August 1, the chief quartermaster forwarded Camp's report to the quartermaster general, adding in a covering letter his own opinion "that the number of contrabands now employed at the Hospitals can be reduced without injury to the service." "There must necessarily be a large number of convalescents at all of these hospitals," he argued, "who . . . should be made to perform all the necessary policing and work of that description about the Hospitals, and the Government saved the expense of hiring laborers to perform it." On August 4, the quartermaster general forwarded both letters to the surgeon general, noting that the number of contrabands employed "seems large, and in many cases the duties appear to be such as could be performed by convalescents, while in others the men should be paid by the person employing them, instead of the payment being a charge to the public." Reminding the surgeon general that there was "great demand for laborers and teamsters at the depôt in this city," he asked whether some of the workers at the hospitals might be transferred to other employment. (Brig. Gen. D. H. Rucker to Brig. Gen. M. C. Meigs, 1 Aug. 1863, and Quartermaster General M. C. Meigs to Brigadier General W. A. Hammond, 4 Aug. 1863, in the same file.) An endorsement by the acting surgeon general referred the papers to the medical director of the Department of Washington, for whose reply see doc. 65B, immediately below.

65B: Medical Director of the Department of Washington to the Surgeon General

Washington, Sept. 4th *1863.*

Sir: – I have the honor to acknowledge the receipt of the papers from the Quartermaster General, relative to the employment of Contrabands in the General Hospitals of this Department, and in accordance with your endorsement, submit the following report.

In almost all the Hospitals of the Department, Contrabands are employed to perform such duties as it has been found impossible, or impracticable to have poroperly attended to by convalescents, or details from the Invalid Corps. These duties consist principally in cleansing cesspools, scrubbing privies and policing the grounds in their immediate vicinity, whitewashing, and hauling wood and water when the labor is arduous. Some of these duties require strong, vigorous men, and others are so repugnant to the soldiers, that they will not even imperfectly, perform them, except under the fear of punishment. These difficulties are overcome, and the administration of the Hospitals greatly facilitated, by the employment of contrabands.

At present, the contrabands are detailed for Hospital service, by the Military Governor, upon application through this Office. At each Hospital they are placed under an overseer, and the overseers are responsible to a General Superintendent. As the Superintendent claims exclusive control over the contrabands – though they are attached to, and reside within the limits of the Hospital – collision of authority occasionally occurs, which it would be well for the interest of the service to prevent.

I would therefore respectfully recommend that the contrabands be placed under the jurisdiction of the Surgeon in charge, and that the Senior Officer of the Invalid Corps attached to the Hospital, (Military Assistant) have the immediate charge of them. He should be required to make out the muster and Pay Rolls, and perform generally the functions that now devolve upon the Superintendent.

The number of contrabands to be assigned to each Hospital, and the duties they are to perform, should be strictly defined by order; and as these duties pertain especially to the Quartermaster's Department, they should be paid by that Department.

In my opinion, four (4) contrabands for every hundred beds in Hospital, would be a proper assignment. Very Respectfully Your Obdt. Servt.

HLS   R. O. Abbott

Surgeon R. O. Abbott to Brig. Genl. W. A. Hammond, 4 Sept. 1863, enclosed in Act. Surgeon General W. K. Barnes to Brig. General M. C. Meigs, 7 Sept. 1863, "Negroes Employed in Washington DC Hospitals," Consolidated Correspondence File, ser. 225, Central Records, RG 92 [Y-5]. In the covering letter, the acting surgeon general informed the quartermaster general that convalescent patients and members of the invalid corps were not available in numbers "equal to the outdoor labors constantly demanded, and the employment of contrabands for such work is found to be an urgent necessity . . . their services are considered indispensable to . . . the large General Hospitals" of Washington. He conceded, however, that the number of black workers at the hospitals could be reduced to the ratio proposed by Abbott, and he proposed that they be placed under the control of the surgeon in charge of each hospital, who would see that they worked at duties legitimately the responsibility of the quartermaster's department, "and not as servants or waiters to officers, or as laundrymen, cooks &c., who are properly hospital employees."

66: Free-Black Military Laborers to the Secretary of War

Alexandria [*Va.*] Aug 31st 1863
Dear Sir, we a potion of the free people of Alexandria Virginia, that has been imployed in Lieut Co¹ Bell Commissary in this place ever since the commencement of the war, and has laboured hard though all wheathers, night and day, sundies included, and we hope that you will pardon us for these liberties in writing to your honour for the purpose of asking you to add a little more to our wages as, L, Co¹, George Bell says it is with you to raise our wages or not, when we first went to the commissary to word, our pay was $30, per month, after one or two months they was curtailed to $25 per month with which we made out to get along with, since the first of December 1862 we has been curtailed to $20 per month so said to be for the benefit of the contrabands, and the men that is in the employment is provided for by the government, houses to live

in, provission for them selves and families, and even wood a coal to cook with; and has all the attention, and we the free men has to pay a tax of $5 per month for they benefit, and have to support our selves and families, and provide for them in every respect with the exceptions of our own rations, and we have tried to get along without saying any thing, but sir every thing is so high that you know your self sir that our $20 will not go any whare, it is true that the government, has agreat expence, and it is nomore then wright, that the contrabands employed in the government, service should be curtailed in wages for the surport of they fellow men, but we free people I dont think sir has any rite to pay a tax for the benefit of the contrabands any more then white labours of our class, which we have on our works, which they receive they 25 dollars and Co¹ Bell has some favourite men whom he pays 25 dollars to and others has to get along the best they can, and undergo deprivation, so we embraced this opportunity of laying the case before you and if you thinks [it] right, sir, then we made our selves satisfied, but we believe that you will do all for us you can in the case, as we believe sir that you is a gentlemen that works on the squar. we remain your obedient servants,

HD   Colord labours of Alexandria va Commissary Dept

Colord labours of Alexandria va Commissary Dept to Honorble Secretary Stanton, 31 Aug. 1863, "Alexandria Va.," Consolidated Correspondence File, ser. 225, Central Records, RG 92 [Y-120]. Earlier in the month, the free-black commissary workers at Alexandria had addressed two similarly worded appeals to Colonel George Bell, the officer by whom they were employed. In those petitions they had emphasized their status as "free born men" who had "been working hard for our selves from our youth up" and many of whom had "served severl years in the naval service." Arguing that they had "no friends on this Contraband list," they questioned why they should be obliged to support newly freed slaves, especially when "the contrabands has all the attention from evey private source," and the government "provides house room pervission and fuell for there wives and Children, and for the men themselves when out of emply." By contrast, the petitioners asserted, "we always as well as now, had to depend up on our own labour for the surport, of our selves and families." "We could just make out to get along" with wages of $25 per month, they claimed, "but now sir as high as every thing is, it is very hard to get along at all." The petitioners had therefore requested that Colonel Bell "add to our wages the five dollars that we have been curtailed of." (Unsigned petitions to Col. Bell, 3 Aug. 1863 and 16 Aug. 1863, in the same file.) Bell had forwarded the petitions to Secretary of War Edwin M. Stanton, noting in an endorsement that a large number of the men were stevedores who had been employed by the subsistence department since June 1861. On August 27, 1863, Stanton had disapproved the laborers' request for revocation of the $5 monthly tax. (A.A.G. J. A. H. to Lt. Col. G. Bell, 27 Aug. 1863, in the same file.)

307

67: Testimony by a Northern Woman

[*Washington, D.C.? January 14, 1864*]
The case of
Lucy Ellen Johnson.

Luisa Jane Barker (wife of Rev Stephen Barker Chaplain of 1st Mass. Heavy Artillery) testifies, I was living in the house of Lieut Chas H. Shepard, Provost Marshall of said Reg^t at Fort Albany on the 18th of November, when Lieut Shepard brought to my room Lucy Ellen Johnson in a state of great agitation, she was weeping violently and rubbing her hands and arms which she said were in great pain. Her thumbs were scarred across with welts showing the marks of cords by which she had been tied. Her wrists bore similar marks but larger Her bonnet was torn and one of her sleeves was torn in two— In reply to my enquiry she said she had just been released by the guards of the camp near Arlington—the colored village—who had tied her up to a tree and subjected her to gross abuse— I took down in writing what she said; but it required about two hours to soothe and collect the distracted mind of this outraged girl. I put her upon her conscience not to add to nor diminish one atom from the truth the substance of her account is as follows

"I came from Fredericksburg during the bombardment, Served two months as chambermaid on the Steamboat Zephyr, Capt Wheeler, Then came to Washington, found my mother and went with her to live on the Arlington estate. whilst there married Louis Johnson— soon after went to live in the service of Major Draper. 1st. Mass. Heavy Artillery at Fort Albany— my husband found employment with Lieut Hart of same Regiment. Remained in these places until taken sick: and after some time finding I could not work, we left our employers. My husband found work near the Long Bridge and hired a shanty on the riverbank where we lived peaceably until disturbed at night by soldiers. In consequence of these attacks my husband obtained work at the Gov't Corrale, and asked leave of Mr Nichols to place me under his protection in the camp whilst he continued his work at the Corrale— I was to earn my food and clothing like the other contrabands, it was on this understanding that I entered the contraband camp— I was sick at the time and for the first week was not able to work, when the day came for drawing rations I applied—and also asked for a bed tick, a blanket, a pair of shoes and a dress— Mr Nichols had been sick for the last two months and had not seen me until this time. He enquired what I had done— I told him I had been too sick to begin work, but hoped to do so next week.

Q Have you a husband?
A Yes.
Q How much does he earn a month?
A Twenty five Dollars.

The case of
Lucy Ellen Johnson.

Louisa Jane Parker (wife of Rev Stephen
Parker Chaplain of 1st Mass. Heavy Artillery)
testifies, I was living in the house of Lieut
Chas. N. Shepard, Provost Marshall of said Regt
at Fort Albany on the 18th of November, when Lieut
Shepard brought to my room Lucy Ellen Johnson in
a state of great agitation, she was weeping violently
and rubbing her hands and arms which she said were
in great pain. Her thumbs were scarred across with
welts showing the marks of cords by which she had
been tied. Her wrists bore similar marks but larger
Her bonnet was torn and one of her sleeves was torn
in two — In reply to my inquiry she said she had
just been released by the guards of the camp near
Arlington — the colored village — who had tied her up
to a tree and subjected her to gross abuse — I took
down in writing what she said; but it required
about two hours to soothe and collect the distracted
mind of this outraged girl. I put her upon her conscience
not to add to nor diminish one atom from the truth
the substance of her account is as follows "I came from
" Fredericksburg during the bombardment, Served two
" months as chambermaid on the Steamboat Zephyr, Capt
" Wheeler, Then came to Washington, found my mother
" and went with her to live on the Arlington estate.
" whilst there married Louis Johnson — Soon after went to
" live in the service of Major Draper, 1st Mass Heavy

Q What do you want anything of me for? You can't have anything, you must pay your board.

A I am here to *earn* my board and the same clothes that others have— If I have to *pay* my board I might as well pay it anywhere else as here But I need the articles and if they are to be paid for my husband will pay for them

A You cant buy them of me—you cant have anything.

At this I replied that "if this was the case Mr Nichols ought to have explained it to my husband when he asked to bring me into camp"— Mr. Nichols became angry and ordered me to come into the room— I was afraid of him and hesitated— He then siezed me by the shoulder and forced me along into a chair— I rose up, Mr Nichols forced me down a second time— I again rose up— He forced me down a third time with the order to "*sit there.*" This time I obeyed and remained until a guard entered— He siezed me by the shoulder and gave me a push saying—"G-d d--n you come out of here. I'll have you in the guard house bucked and gagged." At the door they were joined by a corporal, a sergeant and some soldiers who took me to the guard tent, on the way some pushed me and some kicked me and one siezed me by the throat till I was almost choked. They fastened a rope round my two thumbs and passing it over the limb of a tree raised me from the ground so that my weight was suspended by the thumbs— The Lieut walked into his tent— I eased the cord upon my thumbs— They then took it off and tied it on my wrist—again raising me as before with arms outstretched and without any power to relieve myself— In this position one kicked me—another choked my throat—another stuffed dirty wool in my mouth— After nearly half an hour they released me and the Lieut advised me to leave the camp— I said I had no other place to go. He then advised me to keep out of Nichols sight"

Witness (Mrs Barker) subsequently learned from Miss Draper that their family were so well satisfied with Lucy E. Johnson that they hired another woman to do her work whilst she was sick, still paying her wages in hope of securing her services after recovery from sickness— Her excellent disposition kindness to children and willingness to work were mentioned in terms of high recommendation.

HD

Testimony of Luisa Jane Barker, [14 Jan. 1864], Miscellaneous Records, ser. 5412, Dept. of Washington, RG 393 Pt. 1 [C-4757]. Filed with the testimony of nineteen other witnesses in a packet labeled "The case of Lucy Ellen Johnson who was tied up by the Thumbs November 18 1864 [1863] at Arlington Colord Camp." The same date (including the same erroneous year) is noted at the end of Barker's testimony. The testimony regarding Johnson is in turn filed with testimony by more than thirty other people, all regarding the treatment of freedpeople at Camp Barker and at Freedman's Village. The file provides no information about the composition or mandate of the investigating body; it may have been established by Colonel Elias M. Greene, chief quartermaster of the Department of Washington, in response to complaints about Danforth B. Nichols, superintendent of contrabands at Freedman's Village. (See below, doc. 71.) Among the other testimony about Lucy Ellen Johnson is that of her father, Fielding Lewis, also taken on January 14, 1864. By that date, he reported, her husband had died of smallpox. Lewis had witnessed his daughter's punishment in November 1863, when "she was treated very barberously indeed." Observing the guards dragging her to the tree, he had begged them to stop. "One of the soldiers took his sword and put it on the end of his gun and then told her if she did'nt go on he would run it into her. I just stepped up and told him 'I reckon not.'" When one of the guards asked Johnson what she had done, she replied, "I aint done any thing but ask Mr Nichols for some clothing," whereupon that soldier refused to participate further. Describing in detail the steps taken to tie up and gag his daughter, Lewis testified that the guards had next whipped and beaten her. "I stood down there until I cried about my child; she was hanging up by a limb — tied by her thumb and wrist. One of the guard took their foot and kicked her right under her clothes." "Lucy kept on begging them to let her alone as long as she could speak; she spoke as long as She could, and when they stuffed and crammed so many rags & things in her mouth that she couldn't speak — then she said ah, ah, ah." Questioned as to how long she had remained in that condition, Lewis replied, "She was hung up a right smart time and while they were beating her I could have walked a mile."

68: Testimony by a Northern Woman

[*Washington, D.C.? January? 1864*]

Mrs Louisa Jane Barker (wife of Chaplain Barker (1ˢᵗ Mass Heavy Artillery

I know the spot of ground which was assigned by Lieut Shepard to the colord people to build their cottages upon. A little village had collected there. I made frequent visits among them to ascertain their wants, plans occupations &c   Their freedom had been taken mostly under the Presidents proclamation of January 1ˢᵗ 1863   Since that time they had not only supported themselves, and their families, but saved money enough to build the little shanties they then occupied   They expressed great reluctance to enter the contraband camp, because they felt more independent in supporting themselves, and families, after the manner of white laborers.

I think they were proud of their past success —   The first help they required was education —   Every head of a family eagerly entered into my proposition to start a school for their children   They gave their names to be responsible for tuition at any rate I might decide upon to be paid monthly —   A well educated mulatto woman engaged to take the school as soon as a building could be procured   I interested some gentlemen of Boston in my plan, and had obtained the promise of a contribution of a part, if not the whole of a school house, when the whole project was thwarted by a sudden order for a second removal of this village outside of the Rifle pits or into the Contraband Camp. This order created great unhappiness amongst them —

I enquired of the most intelligent negro whether any complaint had been made to him as to the new settlement — He had not heard of any just ground of complaint from any one — several groundless complaints had been mad: there was no truth in them.

About ten days after this conversation a body of soldiers entered the village claiming to have been sent by Genl Augur with peremptory orders "to clear out this village." This order was executed so literally that even a dying child was ordered out of the house — The grandmother who had taken care of it since its mothers death begged leave to stay until the child died, but she was refused

The men who were absent at work, came home at night to find empty houses, and their families gone, they knew not whither! — Some of them came to Lieut Shepard to enquire for their lost wives and children —

In tears and indignation they protested against a tyranny worse than their past experiences of slavery — One man said "I am going back to my old master — I never saw hard times till since I called myself a freeman —

I have never seen any of the sixteen families composing this settlement since the conversation above alluded to; and I regret to find that I have lost the list of their names —

HD

Testimony of Mrs. Louisa Jane Barker, [Jan.? 1864], Miscellaneous Records, ser. 5412, Dept. of Washington, RG 393 Pt. 1 [C-4757]. Filed with testimony by Lieutenant Charles H. Shepard, an officer in the 1st Massachusetts Heavy Artillery, and by Danforth B. Nichols, superintendent of contrabands at Freedman's Village, all undated and collectively labeled "Destruction of a Contraband Village settled near the Colord Camp at Arlington." Those documents are in turn filed with the testimony of more than fifty people regarding the treatment of freedpeople at Camp Barker and at Freedman's Village. The file provides no information about the composition or mandate of the investigating body; it may have been established by Colonel Elias M. Greene, chief quartermaster of the Department of Washington. (See below, doc. 71.) The officer who ordered that the independent "village" of ex-slaves be "clear[ed] out" was General Christopher C. Augur, who had assumed command of the Department of Washington in October 1863. A copy of the eviction order was incorporated into Nichols's testimony, where it is dated November 31, 1863, a nonexistent date; the correct date is not known. In his testimony, Lieutenant Shepard explained that the uprooted freedpeople had originally built cabins "in the front of the Arlington House," but one of his superior officers had complained "that they injured the look of the Estate which the government intended to sell at the best advantage." Shepard had therefore relocated them to the back of the contraband camp at Freedman's Village, near Fort Albany. At the time they numbered between 60 and 100. Nichols testified that he had sanctioned the new settlement and offered its residents advice about constructing their houses "with regard to uniformity of size, shape, and location." "They were useing commendable efforts to support themselves," he recalled, "& while there successfully did so." According to both Shepard and Nichols, the commander of Fort Albany had repeatedly complained about the proximity of the settlement and charged that its residents were "stealing from fort to fort," but it was not until Augur assumed command that the complaints bore fruit. Augur had ordered "that the Contraband who have located themselves near Fort Albany, be removed at once." He instructed Nichols to receive into the contraband camp such of the evicted families "as are worthy & fit to be received . . . & the rest will be sent under guard to [Washington]." At sundown, as Nichols recalled the scene, soldiers surrounded the settlement, and "every human being, except the sick and those unable to move, were brought away," including 150 to 200 women and children. "[A] goodly number" chose to enter Freedman's Village; the rest, as Shepard described it, "were marched over to Washington that night, and were obliged to stay out in the cold." At least one of the evicted freedpeople died "in consequence of that removal." At the time of the eviction, Nichols noted, the men of the settlement were away at work, many of them at the government corral, some in the engineer corps at Balls River. "[O]ne man," Shepard reported, "said he thought it was mighty hard that, after they had laid out every dollar they had, they should be treated so; & some said they rather go back into slavery than to receive such treatment: they seemed to think they were imposed upon, & said they were as much slaves now & they ever had been: they said they would rather be independent; did not want to be of any expense to the government but desired to live on the produce of their own labor & did not want any superintendent or overseer."

69: Free-Black Quartermaster Employees to the Secretary of War

Washington November 27th 1863
Honored Sir. We the undersigned. (Colored Men) Employed In the Quartermasters Department And rated as Cooks. Most Respectfully beg leave to Present to Your Honor A few brief Items Relative To the Meagre Compensation We are now Receiving. Many of us have been Employed In the Quartermasters Department for two Years Past. And have Never Yet Received Wages Averaging More than twenty (20) Dollars Per Month. from Which have been Deducted a

Tax Of five (5) Dollars Per Month. for the Assistance of the Numerous Contrabands or (freed Men Women and Children) That have been and are now Stationed Within the Limits of the District of Columbia. We have also been Subjected to an additional Tax of one per ct for the Hospital fee. Leaving the Paltry Sum of fourteen (14) Dollars Eighty five (85) cts. As Monthly Pay. In view of the fact that. We are A Portion of that Class Of Colored Men (Termed free) And Pretending as We Do. To have Some faint Conceptions. of the value of our Labor. Regard this as being unequal To the Services We Render and the Demands of the Times. We Therefore

Humbly beg an Interference upon your Honors Part For the Removal of The Above Mentioned Contraband Tax   Respectfully Your Humble Servants

		Robert. A. Stanley
	Signed	James. C. Waters
		John. H. Slocum

on the Part of one Hundred Others. Employees Quartermasters Department Kindall Green and Railroad Parks

HLSr

Robert A. Stanley et al. to His Honor The Honourable Edwin M. Stanton, 27 Nov. 1863, "Contraband Fund," Consolidated Correspondence File, ser. 225, Central Records, RG 92 [Y-37]. According to endorsements and other documents in the same file, the acting quartermaster general, Charles Thomas, to whom the petition was referred, at first responded merely by noting that the deduction of $5 per month had been made in accordance with a War Department order of September 27, 1862. (Acting Qr. Mr. General Chs. Thomas to Hon. Edwin M. Stanton, 8 Dec. 1863; the order is quoted above, in doc. 55.) When Secretary of War Edwin M. Stanton returned the petition to Thomas, this time asking that he "express an opinion as to the expediency of remitting the tax, as prayed by the memorialists," Thomas referred the question to Colonel Elias M. Greene, chief quartermaster of the Department of Washington, who had been placed in charge of the money accumulated from the wage deductions; for his report, see doc. 70, immediately below. On December 28, Thomas forwarded Greene's report, along with his own judgment that the tax was "wise, prudent and just to the colored persons, who have been gathered in and around this City; that it has already accomplished much good, and should it be continued, will produce still more." (Actg. Qr. Mr. General Chs. Thomas to Hon. E. M. Stanton, 28 Dec. 1863.) In an endorsement of the following day, Stanton approved Greene's recommendations that the monthly tax of $5 be continued for black employees of the quartermaster and subsistence departments who earned more than $20 per month, while being remitted for those who earned $20 or less, and that the hospital tax (1 percent of wages) levied on both black and white workers be waived for black employees subject to the $5 deduction. In early January 1864, Thomas reported Stanton's ruling to the commissary general of subsistence and to each of the chief quartermasters in the Washington area, describing it as a rejection of the petition of Robert Stanley and his colleagues. (Acting Qr. Mr. General Chs. Thomas to Brig. Genl. J. P. Taylor, to Maj. Genl. D. H. Rucker, to Brig. Genl. R. Ingalls, and to Lt. Col. E. M. Greene, 5 Jan. [186]4, vol. 50, pp. 298–301, Press Copies of Miscellaneous Letters Sent, ser. 14, Central Records, RG 92 [Y-492].)

70: Chief Quartermaster of the Department of Washington to the Acting Quartermaster General

[*Washington, D.C.*] December 17ᵗʰ 1863

Colonel, In accordance with your request, I have the honor to submit the following expression of my views, as to the expediency of remitting the tax, of $5 per month, deducted from the pay of colored men, employed in the Quarter Masters, and Subsistence Departments; for the support of aged, indigent, and infirm, colored people.

After a full consideration of the subject, in all its bearings, I have come to the conclusion, that the deduction authorized by the Secretary of War, is a wise, and prudent measure, that it has accomplished great good, and that it should be continued, in the case of colored laborers, teamsters, & mechanics, who are rated at $25. or more per month, but prohibited, in the case of colored employès, who are rated at $20. or less, per month.

I will now proceed to state as briefly as possible, the reasons which prompt this opinion.

A vast majority of the colored men engaged in the public service, within the limits of the Department of Washington, are employed as teamsters, and laborers, and receive the same pay, as white men similarly employed. (I have never made any distinction on my rolls, but always paid white, & colored, at the same rate.)

Their pay previous to November the 27ᵗʰ, was $25. per month and a ration; increased by your order of that date, to $30 per month and a ration.¹

The teamsters lodge with their trains, and are furnished with mess kits to cook their food; and the laborers, are lodged in public quarters, and have their food prepared in public mess houses.

It will thus be seen, that these two classes of colored employès, actually receive, as wages after the authorized deduction of $5 is made, Twenty five dollars per month, with food and lodging: a higher rate of pay than is received by most of the colored, and white laborers, employed throughout the Country, or by our soldiers even.

A very intelligent class of colored people, employed as waiters in the hotels, consider themselves well paid, when they received $16 per month, and food; which is the rate allowed at "Willard's" in this City; and it is well known, that in most sections of our country, farm laborers receive only $10 to $15 per month, with board and lodging. – Barbers, Stevedores, hod-carriers, quarrymen, &c average from $20 to $30 per month, and board, and lodge themselves.

I am thus forced to the conclusion, that after the deduction is made, they are still amply remunerated, for their labor.

A small number of colored men are employed in the Quarter Masters Dept; as blacksmiths, wheelwrights, &c. These receive, from $35 to $60 per month, and can better afford the deduction, than the two classes already named.

The number of colored men employed in the public service, within the limits of this Department, who receive $20 per month, or less, is very small indeed. They are mostly cooks, and cart drivers, who seldom receive a higher rate of pay, from private individuals, who hire them. – The laborers on the Government farms, receive a low rate of wages, but I propose to notice this matter, more fully before I conclude.

Many of all the classes named, have their wives, children, aged parents, &c dependent upon the Government for shelter and rations. These are rid of such a responsibility very cheaply, at a cost of only one fifth, or less, of their monthly pay; and few white laborers are so favorably circumstanced. In concluding this branch of the subject, I will only state further, that after the deduction is made from the wages of those, receiving the higher rates of pay, I consider the amount which remains, amply sufficient for their wants; and I will now proceed to the consideration, of what good has already been done, and what remains to be, accomplished, by the fund accruing from these deductions. And first as to what has already been done.

In a communication to Major Gen Heintzelman, commanding the Department of Washington, dated on the 5th day of May last, I made certain statements, and suggestions, in reference to the farm lands in this Department, South of the Potomac, which had been abandoned by rebel owners, and were then lying uncultivated. –[2] I recommended the cultivation of these farms, by the force of Contrabands, male, and female, then idle in this City and dependent upon the Government for support; stating that on quite a number of said farms, houses were left standing to accomodate the laborers; that in carrying out this scheme the families need not be separated, as they Could still be united, and might be fully as well provided for as at their public quarters in this City, and at less expense; and that besides this, there was the decided advantage afforded them, of the salutary effect of good pure country air, and a return to their former healthy avocations, as "field hands" under much happier auspices than heretofore; which must prove beneficial to them, and would tend to prevent the increase of diseases, then prevalent among them.

I also proposed establishing a large vegetable garden, on the Arlington Estate, to be cultivated by the younger, and more infirm colored people; stating that the arrangements I proposed, would in my opinion, conduce to the sanitary, & moral improvement of the Contrabands, and save the Government an immense amount of money; and might be simply stated as a scheme, to give employment to all of the contrabands in this Department, and make such employment profitable, both to themselves, and to the Government.

My recommendations were approved by Major Gen. Heintzelman, and the Quarter Master Gen'l, and forwarded to the Secretary of War; who gave me authority to carry them out, by the removal of the unemployed Contrabands in Camp, in this City, to the South side of the Potomac, for the purpose named. The scheme was at once inaugurated, but I soon found, that a large proportion of the colored people, transferred to me, were aged, infirm, and children. I therefore on the 16th day of June, in a communication to the Quarter Master General, recommended, that the fund accruing from the deduction of $5 per month, from the pay of colored people, employed in the Qr. Mr. Department, should be transferred to me, to be applied in providing for the wants of those classes, for whose benefit it was raised. – This recommendation met the approval of the Quarter Master General, and of the Secretary of War, who ordered the transfer to me, of the fund accruing from such deductions.

My application made a few weeks afterwards, to have the same fund, in the hands of officers of the Subsistence Department, transferred to me, was approved by the same officer, and the transfer was ordered by the Secretary of War.

The amount received was considerable. – A small portion of it was applied to the immediate relief of the aged and infirm, by the purchase of clothing &c for them.

They were established on the Arlington Estate, and were for a time sheltered in old tents, which would have been no protection against the inclemency of the weather in winter. – The next thing to do, therefore, was to provide them with comfortable homes. – With the approval of the Quarter Master General I selected a suitable location, a fine plateau on the top of a hill on the Arlington Estate – airy and healthy – and a "Freedmans Village" was soon erected thereon. The site is a fine one, and commands a beautiful view of the Potomac in the foreground, and Washington and Georgetown in the distance. – The dwellings are constructed in

groups—four under each roof—each with two rooms, and access to a
yard of its own. Wells have been dug and there is an ample supply
of pure water. – Each dwelling is furnished with a cheap cooking
Stove. – Hospitals have been erected also, and workshops; where
the women, and children, may not only contribute somewhat to
their own support, and consequent relief of the Government, but be
taught such occupations, as will fit them for a career of
independence, and usefulness, when thrown upon their own
resources.

This system of workshops may be advantageously extended, to the
men employed upon the Government farms. – During the winter,
they may be employed in Carpenters, blacksmiths, wheelwrights,
work &c. and be thus taught Mechanical occupations, which will fit
them to become useful Citizens, instead of a burden on the
Community. – The tailors shop is now in full operation, and
women heretofore idle, are profitably employed, in the manufacture
of clothing for distribution, to the aged, and infirm; and for sale to
the laboring colored people; and are acquiring at the same time, the
use of the needle & of the sewing machine.

So much has already been accomplished by the "Contraband
fund," our enterprize may be so far considered a decided success, and
has attracted considerable attention; One result of which is, that
contributions for the indigent, are received from charitable persons,
almost daily; About 2000 articles of clothing, have been thus
received, for gratuitous distribution. While the physical comfort,
and well being of these people, is thus provided for by a proper use
of the funds raised for their benefit: their moral and mental
education is not neglected. – The American Tract Society have
taken this matter earnestly in hand, and with my consent, and
approval, have erected at the Freedmans Village, a comfortable, and
well furnished Schoolhouse, and Chapel, also a home for the infirm;
which buildings were constructed, and are managed, without
expense to the Government, or the "Contraband fund."

Other benevolent societies, are willing to lend their assistance,
and letters are daily received, tendering aid, from associations, and
individuals.

It may be necessary here to interpolate a few remarks by way of
Explanation. Although the Cultivation of the Govt. farms, and the
care of the aged, indigent and infirm colored people, are necessarily
two distinct matters, and require the rendition of separate accounts,
and returns; yet there are great advantages, in managing the two in
conjunction.

Thus supposing the arrival of a large number of contrabands,
men, women, & children; sick, and well, at Arlington; If we had
only the farm there, a few might be profitably employed, in its

cultivation, while those unable to work, would be a tax upon the Government; If we had only the home for the aged and infirm, we should have to take care of those, able to work, until they could obtain suitable employment, and they would thus, unjustly be a burden upon the "Contraband fund"; As it is now, all are properly disposed of. Those unable to work, are sent to the home provided for them; those best fitted for it, are sent to the workshops to be instructed; while even the humblest laborer, can be of public service, on the Govt. farms, and earn enough to support himself or herself at the same time. – As the cultivation of the Govt. farms, was originally intended, only to furnish employment to those colored people, who would otherwise be idle, the laborers are fed, lodged, and clothed, and paid a small amount in money; not exceeding in any case $10 per month. Thus they have no undue encouragement to remain, but are expected to give place to others, as soon as they are fitted for, and can obtain, more remunerative employment. (The same course will be pursued, in regard to those being instructed in mechanical occupations).

So far as the cultivation of these farms is concerned, I have every reason to be satisfied, with the result. Not only has employment been given, to a great number of persons, who would otherwise have been a tax upon the public; but notwithstanding the drawbacks encountered, which were, the commencement of operations very late in the season, and the abandonment of the outer farms for several weeks in the busy season (caused by the withdrawal of our troops from our front by Major Gen. Hooker), notwithstanding these, there was raised, and secured, during the season, more than 200 tons of hay, (worth more than $30 pr ton), 191 tons of corn fodder (worth $12 p ton), a great quantity of potatoes, and other vegetables, (distributed to hospitals,) while crops of beans, buckwheat, &c. still remain to be properly disposed of.

When we take into consideration the facts, that the large quantity of stock, and agricultural implements, necessary to commence this enterprize, are still on hand, in good condition; that the seed for the winter crops, (wheat &c) has been purchased; and that these crops are in the ground; it may be asserted with confidence, that the scheme has paid a profit to the Government, this year; and with the small outlay, necessary to be made, for purchases next season, will be very productive indeed.

I do not doubt that I can supply the hospitals, in this Department with vegetables, next season; and that at least, 2000 tons of hay can be cured besides the crops of wheat, beans, corn &c, which I propose to raise.

Having stated what good has been accomplished so far with the "Contraband fund," I will proceed to state briefly, what remains to be done; And propose to make such suggestions, and recommendations, based upon my experience, as it will be proper to mention in this connection. I desire however to premise this, by the statement, that in my opinion, the best proof of the wisdom of the course pursued by the Secretary of War, in authorizing the deduction, is the praise which all parties accord, to the results accomplished on the Arlington Estate, by the fund thus raised.

The best friends of the black race, are satisfied to find, the physical, & mental, Condition of the Colored people so well cared for; while their antagonists, who have blamed the Government, for supporting the contrabands in idleness; no longer have it in their power, to censure the authorities, for their humanity; as the paupers among the colored people, are supported by a not burdensome tax, upon the wages of that portion of them able to labor.

The number of those dependent upon the "Contraband fund" for support, is gradually increasing; but the Contributions to it, increase in about the same proportion. – Remit the $5 tax, and the old state of things is restored. – Instead of being gathered together in one place, where they can be economically provided for, and properly trained; the colored people who come within our lines, will be scattered in sickly camps, through the city, as has been the case heretofore; living a life of idleness at the public expense; subject to the most demoralizing influences; and in return for the moral contamination they receive, from contact with the worst class of citizens; spreading the small pox, and other infectious diseases, to which they are extremely liable, when living idly in crowded barracks in the close air of a city.

Continue the tax, and the little colony on Arlington Estate, will gradually increase; all capable of labor will be profitably employed; all the children will receive a common school education; men, women, and children, will be taught self reliance, and sent into the world with a sense of their duties, and obligations which they do not now possess; and all this, without expense to the Government.

I am so firmly convinced of the excellence of the plans adopted, in the Arlington Estate, that I earnestly desire, to see the same course pursued throughout the country. – In this connection I beg leave to refer to my communication to you of Sept 29th in response to Sec 5. of General Orders No 13. from your office, dated July 22nd 1863.[3] In that Communication the following passage occurs. "As the subject of the disposition to be made of the Contrabands is already one of some magnitude, and likely to become of great importance. – I beg leave to respectfully recommend, the establishment of a Bureau of the War Department, to have full control, under proper restrictions, of all matters pertaining to the Colored people, who have heretofore, or may hereafter, come within our lines. This will ensure a uniform system of management throughout the country; and relieve the several Commanding Officers of our Armies, in the rebellious States, from the consideration of this heretofore embarrassing question. – I would also respectfully recommend the adoption, of a plan of management, throughout the Country, based on that, I have adopted in this Department."

Such a Bureau under the direction of a Competent head, to be selected by the Secretary of War, might accomplish great good; and I respectfully, but earnestly request, that you will call his attention to the matter, if you think proper to do so.

In conclusion, I respectfully recommend that, if the Secretary of War directs a continuance of the deduction of $5 per month from the pay of colored employès, receiving the higher rates of pay; orders may be issued at the same time, forbidding the further reduction, of the pay of said Employès, by the deduction of the usual tax, of one per cent, levied alike on white, and black, employès, in the Quarter Masters Department, for hospital purposes. Very Respectfully, Your Obdt Serv't.

HLS   Elias M. Greene

Lt. Col. Elias M. Greene to Col. Chas. Thomas, 17 Dec. 1863, "Contraband Fund," Consolidated Correspondence File, ser. 225, Central Records, RG 92 [Y-38]. For the inquiry that prompted Greene's report, see doc. 69, immediately above. For the Secretary of War's decision regarding the monthly deduction and the hospital tax, see doc. 69n. In late September 1863, in a description of Freedman's Village submitted as part of his annual report, Greene had offered a more specific account of the freedpeople living there: Of 900 residents, he estimated, only 150 were able-bodied men, "the remainder being women, children and aged persons." He also mentioned that he had by that date received nearly $30,000 from the contraband fund, from which circumstance he concluded "that the fund will be amply sufficient to provide for the wants of the necessarily large number of paupers among these people at present in this Department." (Lt. Col. Elias M. Greene to Acting Qr. Mr. General Charles Thomas, 29 Sept. 1863, enclosed in Lt. Col. Elias M. Greene to Act'g Q. M. Gen'l Chas. Thomas, 29 Sept. 1863, Annual, Personal, & Special Reports of Quartermaster Officers, ser. 1105, Personnel, RG 92 [Y-138].)

1 On November 27, 1863, the acting quartermaster general had informed the chief quartermaster that the Secretary of War had approved a 20 percent increase in the pay of "mechanics, teamsters, and laborers"; the chief quartermaster was directed to "govern yourself accordingly." (Acting Qr. Mr. General Chs. Thomas to Lt. Col. E. M. Greene, 27 Nov. [186]3, and Act'g Qr. Mr. Gen'l Chs. Thomas to Hon. E. M. Stanton, 24 Nov. [186]3, vol. 47, pp. 219–20, Press Copies of Miscellaneous Letters Sent, ser. 14, Central Records, RG 92 [Y-229].)

2 The letter is printed above, as doc. 63.
3 General Order 13 had called for reports and accounts regarding the fiscal year ending June 30, 1863. In response to section five (a request for suggestions), the chief quartermaster had described his own solution, exemplified by Freedman's Village, to the question of "what should be done with, and for the contrabands flocking within our lines" and proposed its systematic extension to other parts of the Union-occupied South. (Lt. Col. Elias M. Greene to Act'g Q.M. Gen'l Chas. Thomas, 29 Sept. 1863, Annual, Personal, & Special Reports of Quartermaster Officers, ser. 1105, Personnel, RG 92 [Y-138].)

71: Chief Quartermaster of the Department of Washington to the Headquarters of the Department

Washington, D.C., January 30th *1863 [1864]*.
Colonel. I have the honor to enclose for information of Maj: Gen[1] Augur; Commanding Department of Washington, a list of all articles purchased for use of Freedmen, and paid for by me, out of the Contraband Fund in my hands to December 31st 1863 (see enclosure marked "A") amounting to $12661.80, including stoves &^c yet on hand.

Of these purchases there were remaining on hand December 24th 1863, clothing amounting to $6961.13 (See account of stock enclosed marked "B") It will thus be seen that the actual total expenditures for the Freedmen under my direction during a period of more than six months only amounts to $5700.67, and this embraces all the debts incurred on that account, except the amount due the Quarter Masters Department for building materials.

I beg leave to state that the settlement for Freedmen on the Arlington Estate is very prosperous; that the Government Farms are in good condition; fences having been built at each one, they not being enclosed heretofore; that in addition to the farms already under cultivation, two more, containing about One thousand Acres have been added and will be cultivated the coming season, that the land has been thoroughly manured for Summer Crops, and the Winter Crops are in the ground, that the able-bodied Contrabands, Male and female, are all employed profitably to themselves and the Government, on the farms, in the tailor shops &^c that the indigent and infirm are being properly cared for in comfortable buildings, well warmed, lighted and ventilated, that the children are all attending school, that the hospital accommodations are ample; that the religious and moral instruction of the colored people: in my charge has been undertaken by the American Tract Society, which Association is doing great good through the agency of the persons it has chosen for that work, and that new buildings are being erected, and measures taken to secure an ample supply of water for Sanitary and police purposes; new work-shops for conducting various mechanical operations being constructed, and other means taken to benefit the Freedmen, who are or may hereafter be entrusted to my charge.

So well satisfied are the colored people with their present condition at Arlington, that they can hardly be induced to accept service with private families or individuals in this City and vicinity, and generally endeavor to return to the public quarters provided for them.

A few weeks since the buildings at Camp Barker (the Contraband Camp in this City) were torn down by me under authority from the Secretary of War, to be removed to the Arlington Estate and erected there. Whilst the buildings were being removed and rebuilt it was necessary to provide some sort of shelter for the former inmates, either at Camp Barker or at Arlington. The best provision I could make was to remove the colored people in a body from Camp Barker to Arlington, and place them in tents, On their arrival at the latter point they were found by my Superintendents and Agents to be in a horribly filthy condition, bearing evidences upon their persons of gross neglect. (See enclosed copies of statements marked C. D. E. F & G. of the following Officers and Citizens, comprising all on duty at Freedmans Village at the time referred to, Viz: Capt: Robt E. Perry 111th N.Y. Vol^s Comd^g Det: guarding Gov^t Farms, Lieut S. M. Lattin, Co. "C" 111th N.Y. Vol^s Comd^g Guard at Freedmans Village, Rev: D. B. Nichols Sup^t at Greene Heights, E. A. Holman, Sup^t Gov^t Farms, W. A. Benedict, Agent of the American Tract Society and H. E. Simmons, Principal of school.)

Of course it took sometime to clean them and provide them with comfortable clothing and bedding. In this "transition" period there was no doubt some discomfort, the weather at that time setting in cold and stormy, but it continued only a few days.

The number of sick has been so small at Arlington (only averaging five or six) previous to the arrivals from Camp Barker that those needing medical attendance were sheltered in Hospital tents at the suggestion of the Surgeon in charge, the labor being used in fitting up the additional buildings for the accommodation of the new arrivals, thus deferring the finishing of the new hospital buildings at that point; But upon the removal of Camp Barker there was found to be a much larger proportion of sick than was expected and immediate steps were then taken to finish and fit up the new Hospital Buildings. At this date all the sick are in a cleanly condition, comfortably clothed, and well cared for in the new Hospital buildings, none being in tents.

A copy of the regulations established for government of the

Freedmans Village and the farms, is enclosed herewith marked "H." These would accomplish what I desire, but having to trust their execution to Citizen Employe's, there is not that promptness and exactness in the administration, which there ought to be.

Another difficulty in having a Superintendent for this work from civil life is, that while many good men and women are earnestly engaged in the work of ameliorating the condition of the Freedmen without hope of reward, there are some pretended philanthropists who are only anxious to obtain employment at remunerative wages, and these being envious and jealous of each other, indulge in charges and recriminations, intended to set themselves up and put their rivals down. Serious charges have been made against my present Superintendent of Contrabands Rev: D. B. Nichols, who had my entire confidence, and was continued as Sup^t by me for that reason and because he was originally appointed by the Secretary of War. I ordered a full investigation of these charges and an inquiry into the past and present condition of the Colored people: and when the result is known, some change of administration may be necessary. All these difficulties (and they are the source of great trouble) might be obviated by the Assignment of a Commissioned Officer to report to me for duty at Arlington

As he would have to be accountable for a great deal of property and for the disbursements, he should in my opinion be a bonded Officer of the Quarter Masters Department, and he should be an earnest sympathizer with the Administration in its emancipation policy.

As I knew of no such Officer in this Department, who can well be spared, I made the Quarter Master General acquainted some days since with my wish to have Lieut: E. E. White A.A.Q.M. 39th Mass: Vol^s (now with the Army of the Potomac) ordered to report to me for duty, believing him to be eminently qualified for the position. His application for appointment as Captain & Assistant Quarter Master of Vol^s is on file in the War Department, and it would add to his efficiency in the duty I have proposed if his application was granted.[1]

May I be excused from requesting that this report, with its enclosures may be forwarded to the Secretary of War, if not incompatible with the public interests. I am Colonel, Very Respectfully Your Obedient Servant

HLcSr

(Signed) Elias M. Greene

Lt. Col. Elias M. Greene to Lieut. Col. J. H. Taylor, 30 Jan. 1863 [1864], enclosed in Lt. Col. Elias M. Greene to Brig. Gen. M. C. Meigs, 8 Feb. 1864, "Contraband Fund," Consolidated Correspondence File, ser. 225, Central Records, RG 94 [Y-41]. Copies of all the enclosures except "H" are in the same file. The list of items purchased from the contraband fund for the use of the freedpeople (enclosure "A") included 1,600 blankets, 59 stoves, stovepipe material, 390 pairs of shoes, a wide variety and large quantity of clothing, thousands of yards of various fabrics, and equipment for sewing. The statements by military and civilian officials at Freedman's Village (enclosures "C" through "G") all emphasized the wretched condition of the freedpeople transferred from Camp Barker on December 21, 1863, and defended as efficient and humane the steps taken to provide for them. According to Danforth B. Nichols, the first arrivals from Camp Barker had numbered 120; two or three days later, 57 more joined them. They had been housed in tents, which lacked floors until lumber from Camp Barker was also moved across the river. "At present," Nichols wrote on January 23, 1864, more than a month after the transfer, "they are being removed into comfortable tenements which are being erected at a rapid rate and completed at a rate of 8 tenements a day. I hope by to-night to have these people most of them in houses, at least all who occupy worn tents." (D. B. Nichols to Lieut. Col. Elias M. Greene, 23 Jan. 1864.) The army officer in command of the guard at the government farms reported that the Camp Barker freedpeople had arrived "in a *shamefully wretched* and destitute condition. Sickness and neglect, had left their mark upon them. Many of these poor people had no blankets, – their clothing was insufficient, and in some cases (females) barely enough to preserve decency." Tents, fuel, blankets, and clothing had been provided, he claimed, "as fast as the supply in Mr Nichols' hands would permit." (Capt. R. C. Perry to Lieut. Col. E. M. Greene, 22 Jan. 1864.) The superintendent of the government farms asserted that the people from Camp Barker had been "in a most destitute and uncleanly Condition, so much so, that the inhabitants of the village were unwilling to admit them into their houses, or to associate with them, until they had been furnished with new clothing, and placed in a proper condition." "Much care was required in moving them into the Village, many of them being sick with the small pox, and other diseases, which will account for the seeming delay in getting them into the houses." (E. A. Holman to Lt. Col. E. M. Greene, 23 Jan. 1864.) For the principal of the school at Freedman's Village, the contrast between the freedpeople from Camp Barker and the residents of the village "fully Confirmed . . . the wisdom of the plan now being carried out here." "[H]ere, they are comparatively neat, tidy, and *very* comfortable while *there* they were dirty, discontented, and uncomfortable." (H. E. Simmons to Lt. Col. E. M. Greene, 23 Jan. 1864.)

1 No record of White's assignment to duty at Freedman's Village has been found in the records of the Department of Washington or in White's service record.

72: Testimony by the Former Superintendent of Camp Barker

[Washington, D.C.? January? 1864]

James I. Ferree. Superintendent of Camp Barker Washington

Q. State your condition of health for some time previous and up to the breaking up of the Contraband Camp?

A. From the 26th day of November until the breaking up of the Camp I was utterly unable to attend to any business, except to sign my name to official papers when they were brought to me; was confined to my bed nearly all the time, and exercised only to the extent of walking about a little for a few days.

Q. How many inmates in the Camp when it was broken up?

A. There were about six hundred & fifty, and had been about the same for six months previous, it was broken up on the 21st day of December 1863.

Q. State the condition of the Camp previous and at that time?

A October was a sickly month for the Camp, but in November and December the Matrons who had all the business of the Camp said that the sickness was much less than it had been in October. All the Surgeons' in the hospital whose duty it was to attend to the Camp became sick in October, I think it was, if not in September, and they were unable to give anything but occasional attention to the Camp through the entire month of October; and in fact they were unable to give full attention to the hospital from about the close of the month of September up to the 21st day of December the time of breaking up the Camp.

Q. State what you know as to the Smallpox when it was most prevalent in Camp, and also the condition of the Smallpox at the time it was broken up.

A. Well, according to the best of my reccollection the Small pox was most prevalent in December. We endeavored to have every body vaccinated when they came into Camp, but at times the Doctors would be out of vaccine matter and could not vaccinate them, yet as a general rule none of the cases of vaccination took during the months of November and December, and I dont know, but October also. It was a universal complaint that the cases of vaccination were not effective.

Q. What was the number of Small pox patients during the time?

A. I don't know.

Q. Give us an idea of the extent of it in numbers.

A It was a very uncommon thing for a half dozen cases to be in Camp, it would range from three to four, and as soon as discovered they were removed at once up to the time we began to send them to Kalorama, then we had to send for an ambulance, and it was no unusual thing for us to send for an ambulance today and receive it to-morrow, and that was one great occasion for the prevalence of the Small pox; think that was the main cause of so much Small pox being in Camp, although we thought it very light compared to what it might have been.

Q. Do you mean to say three or four cases would be discovered in a day?

A. Well, perhaps we would discover as many as that in some days, but seldom discovered more than one or two.

Q. What was the average number per day?

A. I do not know that I can form any correct estimate, though I am very sure there was enough to make one a day.

Q. What have you to say about the facts concerning the removal of the Camp?

A. The Camp was removed just at the commencement of that very cold weather during the latter part of December. I had sent word to Colonel Green not to break up the Camp for humanity's sake until that weather changed. I do not know however, positively that he got the report. I know I sent word to some of the Committees of the Freedmens Association, and it was reported to me that Judge Underwood would see to that matter the evening before the removal was ordered. I cannot say whether or not Col Green received the information. The day of the breaking up of the Camp I think was about the third day of this cold spell.

Q. State the condition of the people as to warmth and comforts before broken up?

A They were entirely comfortable.

Q Well supplied with beds?

A Well supplied; they were better than they had ever been.

Q Were they on beds or on the floor?

A Generally on beds, they rarely lay on the floor.

Q Had they sufficient clothing to keep them warm?

A Plenty.

Q Fires?

A All had fires and enough to keep them comfortable day and night.

Q Any other diseases reported than Small-pox?

A Some cases of chills and fevers, colds and Such things, and we had many cases of Chronic Invalids; it was a mass of Old folks – men, women and children constituted the population of the camp.

Q Do you recolect the proportion of men, women and children?

(Witness refers to written weekly written reports in his possession and reads the report of Dec 7th 1863)

A The last report I have on hand states the whole number in camp at that date to be 685.

Able bodied males fit for duty.	98
Infirm and Sick unfit for duty	71
Able bodied females over 14 fit for duty	132
Infirm and Sick females unfit for duty	119
Boys under 16 and well	93
Boys under 16 and sick	46
Girls under 14 and well	86
Girls under 14 and sick	40

Q You state that the camp was Chiefly of infirm? give the reason of this being so largely composed of such persons?

A Because all persons able to get places to go out and work did so, except those which it was necessary for us to retain in Camp, and those the government employed at $10 and a daily ration the month; they quartered and rationed at Camp.

Q How long had they been in Camp?

A The number of the inhabitants of the Camp at this time was the cullings of about 15,000, which had reported there from the beginning of the camp.

Q Cap^r what time in the day were they removed?

A They commenced early in the morning

Q How soon did they leave?

A Not until sometime in the afternoon, I cannot tell what time the first wagon started.

Q Did you go to the New Camp?

A The day the camp was broken up I went over to the Freedmen's Village; the next morning I called on Mr Holt for an official report of the number there who had come over; he gave it as 115. Two or three of them came to me and told me they would not go over and be under Mr Nichols.

Q Did they say any thing else before leaving Camp?

A They said if Mr Holt and I were to be there they would go and stay.

Q Why did Cap^r Holt make out the report?

A Prior to my going over I ordered Mr Holt to take a Census of the Camp and upon that a provision return was made out which I signed officially.

HD

Testimony of James I. Ferree, [Jan.? 1864], Miscellaneous Records, ser. 5412, Dept. of Washington, RG 393 Pt. 1 [C-4757]. In a file labeled "Condition of Camp Barker for the few weeks previous to its removal," which is in turn filed with testimony by more than fifty witnesses regarding the treatment of freed-people at Camp Barker and Freedman's Village. The file provides no informa-tion about the composition or mandate of the investigating body; it may have been established by Colonel Elias M. Greene, chief quartermaster of the Depart-ment of Washington, in response to complaints about Danforth B. Nichols, superintendent of contrabands at Freedman's Village and previously superinten-dent at Camp Barker. (See above, doc. 71.) In the same file is undated testimony by other officials at Camp Barker about the inclement weather on December 21, 1863, when freedpeople from the camp were transferred to Freedman's Village, and about the reluctance of most of them to go. J. B. Holt, Ferree's assistant, testified that on the evening of December 20, he had asked Judge John C. Underwood to see Colonel Greene about deferring the move until the weather improved. Late the following day, after 115 freedpeople—many of them very feeble—had been moved from Camp Barker, Holt had gone to Freedman's Village, where he witnessed a lack of preparation for them: floorless tents, no blankets, and "worthless" stoves. When questioned about the condition of the freedpeople before leaving Camp Barker, Holt admitted that an inadequate water supply had "produced great uncleanliness" and some residents had lacked beds, but he explained that "[n]early all that had beds & other necessary things here [at Camp Barker], refused to go over," so that "it was the needy more than those well supplied here, that went over, hence the destitution of those who arrived at the Arlington Camp." Holt claimed that he and other officials at Camp Barker had "used all the influence we had" to persuade the freedpeople to go to Freedman's Village "and in many instances we had to command them to go." Nevertheless, "not more than a third" had made the trip. "A report or word in some way got into Camp among them that they were going over to be under slave owners or those who had been slave drivers and others were afraid to go where they said they had heard the guerrillas came." The reluctance of still others stemmed from "unfavorable reports of Nichols"; indeed, "those that knew him refused to be under him." B. E. Messer, a clerk at Camp Barker, described its residents as having been "[v]ery much opposed to going." "By order of Mr Holt," he testified, "I took a paper to get the names of all who desired to go, went to every individual in camp & not one would go. They would generally remark, 'I aint going over dar'—Dont want to be under dat old Nichols' &c & finally those that did go went because we had to compel them to go."

73: Testimony by a Former Missionary at Camp Barker

[*Freedman's Village, Va.? January?* 1864]

Georgiana Willets

Has been engaged at Camp Barker since 1st of November until the breaking up of the camp, in visiting the cabins and distributing clothing of which I had charge— I also taught school occasionally— Reside in Jersey City—came to Washington for this purpose. For the last 4 or 5 weeks of the existence of the Camp it was my practice every day and sometimes twice a day to visit the cabins to see if there were any sick; and to attend to their necessities as far as I could do so. These visits were made in conjunction with Miss Nichols; and all the cabins were visited every day by one or other of us. The number of inmates were generally about 700—but fluctuated—by arrivals and departures— They generally arrived destitute of clothing—were chiefly women & children and arrived at all hours of the day & night— The people in the cabins were generally well supplied with bedding but they were occasionally deficient in clothing— Our supply of clothing was contributed gratuitously by people in the North—

During the month of November we found cases of small Pox

occasionally. – In many instances the people tried to conceal it, because they had great reluctance to go or have their children sent into the Hospital – They said they would surely die if they went there. They appeared to have no confidence in the Doctors in charge (cold) We found on one occasion seven cases of small Pox in the whole camp of 700 people Sometimes for several days we found none – At others 1 2 & 3 cases in a day We reported all cases to the office as soon as discoverd During the month of December until the camp was broken up the health of the people was much better; but little sickness; and the small pox in the camp almost ceased. There were but three cases that I remember in the last two weeks in that half of the camp which I visited – The Camp was broken up in cold weather – and stormy weather followed for several days –

The large proportion of the people remained in Washington – most of them refused to go to Arlington because they would not be under Nichols – There was no attempt on the part of any one that I know or heard of to dissuad them from going; but on the contrary, they were urged to go – I urged them because I thought they would suffer if they remained – Some replied that they would rather starve in Washington than go to Arlington to be under Nichols who was remembered as the former superintendent of Camp Barker – They seemed reluctant to give their reasons and appeared to have an instinctive dread of the place Many of them now live by days work & washing – There is now some suffering but it is chiefly amongst the women who have small children – These can barely obtain the necessaries of life I think the contraband hospital should be in charge of a white surgeon – There appears a deficiency of sympathy in the colord surgeons – It was with the greatest difficulty we could get them to attend to any cases of sickness in the camp outside of the hospital.

HD

Testimony of Georgiana Willets, [Jan.? 1864], Miscellaneous Records, ser. 5412, Dept. of Washington, RG 393 Pt. 1 [C-4757]. In a file labeled "Condition of Camp Barker for the few weeks previous to its removal," which in turn is filed with testimony by more than fifty witnesses regarding the treatment of freedpeople at Camp Barker and Freedman's Village. The file provides no information about the composition or mandate of the investigating body; it may have been established by Colonel Elias M. Greene, chief quartermaster of the Department of Washington, in response to complaints about Danforth B. Nichols, superintendent of contrabands at Freedman's Village and previously superintendent of Camp Barker. (See above, doc. 71.) In the same file is undated testimony by two other Northern women who had worked at Camp Barker and planned to accompany its residents to Freedman's Village. Emily

Howland had been at the camp since February 1863, teaching and distributing clothing supplied by Northern aid societies; she was "waiting with trunks packed" when Colonel Greene's order came that the white people at the camp must remain in Washington. Caroline Nichols of Ohio, who had been at Camp Barker since mid-October, testified that she and the other Northern women "all expected to go to Arlington with the people of the camp" and "were waiting with bonnets on." Upon learning of Greene's order, she recalled, "[t]he colord people were much disappointed and thought at first that we had deceived them. I am sure that not one half of those who went would have gone unless they had supposed that we would go also—"

74: Testimony by a District of Columbia Freedwoman

[*Washington, D.C.? January? 1864*]
Lucy Smith.

Q How old are you?

A I was 76 years last June.

Q How long have you lived at Camp Barker?

A I have been living here most two years; did not go over the River when the Camp was broken up, my brother did not want me to go; have a good many children in the city who are doing right smart and they wanted me to stay with them. I have many large and small children scattered about and could I get them together in a little house we would all be better off than we are now.

Q Have you anything to say about the state of things in Camp?

A Well, Mr Nichols had charge when I first got here; he was kind to me but a great many persons found a great deal of fault with him, and I think very often they had good reasons to think so. I used to see him when they or we went after rations toss it in their faces, I did not think such action as it looked very bright for a man.

Q Did you know Mr Nichols pretty well?

A Yes sir I was well acquainted with him.

Q Were his habits good and temperate?

A I never Saw Mr Nichols drink, though I have had people call on me to look at him when they said he was drunk, but I would never take pains to look at him; he used frequently to appear that way; but for all this I used to tell the people I thought him a temperate man, and I tried to make them think he was a good man. I have seen people play drunk, and perhaps *he* was fooling; he always used to talk to the people against drinking, and he used to preach the folks to be sober; my reasons for believing he would not drink, was not so much from his actions, as from his preaching. My own children used to call "Now Mamma just look at

Mr. Nichols and see him act just like he was drunk" and I would tell them not to think or talk of such things about him; and I believed my children would be better off to follow his preaching than his practice.

HD

Testimony of Lucy Smith, [Jan.? 1864], Miscellaneous Records, ser. 5412, Dept. of Washington, RG 393 Pt. 1 [C-4754]. In a file labeled "Intemperance of Nichols and his treatment of the Inmates of Camp Barker in Washington," which is in turn filed with testimony by more than fifty witnesses regarding the treatment of freedpeople at Camp Barker and Freedman's Village. The file provides no information about the composition or mandate of the investigating body; it may have been established by Colonel Elias M. Greene, chief quartermaster of the Department of Washington, in response to complaints about Danforth B. Nichols, the superintendent of contrabands at Freedman's Village, who had previously been superintendent at Camp Barker. (See above, doc. 71.)

75: Superintendent of Contrabands at Freedman's Village to the Chief Quartermaster of the Department of Washington, Enclosing a Map of Freedman's Village

Freedman's Village Greene Heights [Va.] April 2nd 1864.

(Copy)

Colonel: I have the honor to report, in relation to a complaint, made by Lt. Warren F. Ward of the 23rd U.S.C.T, that Private Henry Smith Co "F," of his Reg^t was arrested in the discharge of his duty, conducting a detatchment of recruits to the said quarters, by a sentry said to be acting under my direction, as Sup^t of "Freedman's Village." Smith being at the time without the line of my sentinels. He the said Smith, was soon after released, but the recruits were detained and have not since been returned to his charge. He further asserts that similar cases have occurred before.

I have the honor, to reply to the several allegations as follows: On the second day of March last, as I was engaged with two Clergymen, three privates, one wearing the dress of a sergeant of the Colored Reg^t, forming at Casey, applied for admission into this Camp to see their friends, which of course was readily granted and they went in: immediately after this I had occasion to go outside the Camp on business and was absent about an hour, and when I returned I was met by a crowd of the women in great distress, saying that colored men had been inside and taken away five or six persons by force, entirely against their will: that they had escaped between the posts of the guard and had taken off the men to the camp. Upon reaching my quarters, I immediately reported the affair to the Lieut in command of the guard and made out a despatch to Major Ball of the Colored Reg^t and sent it by an orderly, which communication and endorsement was transmitted to you in a report of the affair the next day (March 3^d). This affair had a most unfortunate influence upon the minds of the inhabitants of "Freedman's Village," so that many of them were kept from night Schools and meetings, for fear of being pressed into service against their will. I did all that I could to quiet the people, informing them that they would be protected and that I would immediately order renewed vigilance in keeping improper persons from the camp. Thus a written order was given to the guard by Capt. Perry, instructing them to admit no Colored soldier to the camp, unless upon a written order, except it was to attend church on the Sabbath; nor could any white person be admitted if it was thought that the object of the visit was to interfere with the order and regulations of the Camp. Thus things passed until the 22nd of March, when I received at the Camp 407 persons, recently returned from the Island of "A'Vache". These were disposed of, late in the afternoon and on the next morning (the 23rd,) quite early, a number of colored soldiers came down to my quarters and asked permission to enter the camp for the purpose of enlisting men from those recently from Hayti. I replied that I had been instructed to send all persons to the Head Quarters of the Chief Quarter Master of the Dep't of Washington, who might desire to enter the Camp for the purpose of recruiting: thus, I could not admit them into the Camp for that purpose; that I did not know as yet the intention of the Government in ordering these people here. The next day I was engaged the *entire day* in issuing clothing and other necessary supplies to the returned people from Hayti, but I had given *no additional* order in relation to the guard excepting the *old* order, as there was such an increase of people and this would require an increase of vigilance on the part of the guard. Some time during the day, Lt Hurd, the one who here complains, came to my storeroom, in the presence of my assistant Mr Johnson and Lt. Lattier, the one who commanded the guard, and while he condemned the first transaction and said all the men connected therewith had been properly punished, and while he acknowledged that I had a perfect right to keep his men out of the camp, yet he said, a transaction had just occurred which would subject the parties to censure, who allowed it; that he had sent a private, with a number of men, for the purpose of recruiting on the borders of our lines, which he regarded as outside of the beat of our Sentinels. That a number of recruits had been obtained from the number of returned Haytiens and that while in the act of marching the same away, there were forcibly taken possession of by our guard and brought inside the village. I told him that I knew nothing of the transaction, that the guard had only acted upon the general order that I had given some days before; that this case had not come to my ears. He next asked how far our lines extended; I remarked that we were shut in by natural boundaries, the boundaries being a ravine between our camp and the camp of the engineers; that our guard was not posted on the outside of the lines, but owing to the scarcity of men, we were obliged to place the guard inside of Hamlin circle. (see map of ground accompanying this paper.) I further remarked to him that it was my preference that these men should go into the U.S. Service; that I would do all in my power to further this end, but that I was under orders from the Chief Quarter Master Lt Col Greene, and that I could do nothing without his sanction and direct authority. I requested the Lieut who was commanding the guard to inquire into the affair, whose report is herewith transmitted, also the Capt of the Guard Detachment for the "Government Farms." If these people are permitted to come here without the Knowledge or sanction of the proper authorities and enlist men, by saying to them, "if you go quietly you will receive fifteen dollars bounty, but if you refuse, you will get no money and we shall draft you." This is the manner in which one of my teamsters was addressed, who has been in the employ of the Government for eleven months. It has filled these people with such fear that the communication is most entirely broken off between this Village and "Camp Todd" (another of our Camps bordered on the "Gov^t Farms" under this command) this Camp being situated beyond the barracks where the Colored Reg^t is situated. Some of the inmates of this Village have been stopped by colored Soldiers and threatened, if they would not enlist; and the only manner they saved themselves from being pressed, was because they possessed greater physical strength.

I would call attention to the evil of sending out squads of colored men, with a promise of a bounty for each recruit to go at will about the country to pick up men, some who are engaged in the service of the F   some in the Engineers Dep^t some who have come from the Army of the Potomac, as servants of Officers, to see their friends and others are employed on the Government Farms.

We felt that we were acting under instructions, for the protection of these people, to see that they were fairly dealt by. If they know what they are doing and then go into the service, or if they are drafted even against their will let it be by those who have authority, but let it not be by a squad of Black Soldiers, who have been promised so much bounty on the obtaining a certain number of Recruits. Yours Respectfully

(Signed) D. B. Nichols

334

[Enclosure]

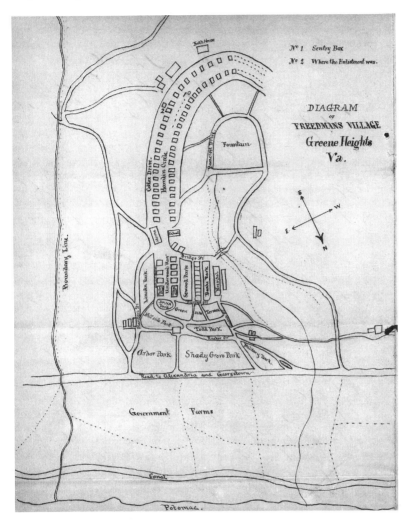

D. B. Nichols to Lt. Col. Greene, 2 Apr. 1864, enclosing Diagram of
Freedmans Village, both enclosed in Lt. Col. Elias M. Greene to Maj. C. H.
Raymond, 25 May 1864, filed with H-204 1864, Letters Received, ser.
360, Colored Troops Division, RG 94 [B-100]. In the same file is the
complaint by Lieutenant Warren H. Hurd (erroneously rendered as Warren F.
Ward in the opening sentence of Nichols's letter) that had been referred to
Nichols. Hurd had asked his regimental commander by what authority
Nichols, a civilian, could "prevent the able bodied men in Freedman's Vil-

lage from entering the military service of the United States if they freely choose to do so." (Lt. Warren H. Hurd to Lt. Col. Campbell, 24 Mar. 1864.) Hurd's letter had been transmitted through military channels to the War Department and thence to the commander of the Department of Washington, who on March 31 had forwarded it to Colonel Elias M. Greene, chief quartermaster of the department; Greene in turn referred it to Nichols. In the same file are copies of letters by Lieutenant J. M. Lattin and Captain Robert C. Perry, commanders of the guard at Freedman's Village and the government farms. Lattin gave an account of the recruiter's arrest similar to that of Nichols and asserted that "[t]he effort to recruit by Col'd Volunteers, in or about this Camp has . . . been exceedingly deleterious to the good order and quietude of this Village." Perry reported that he had for months been "exceedingly annoyed" by soldiers of the 23rd USCI, who, after entering Freedman's Village "under various pretences, such as visiting friends and relatives attending School and meeting . . . clandestinely attempt to get men away." In response to such "irregular and outrageous" tactics, he had ordered his sentries to deny admittance to black soldiers; thereafter, recruiters "would hover around and just outside the Camp, and had it not been for the vigilance of the Guard would have succeeded in enticing men with them." "My resistance, and the vigilance of the guard," Perry added, "has incensed and provoked these Recruiting-Officers, beyond measure. They have threatened to 'Clean out the Village' a threat which *fortunately* for the parties concerned, was never attempted to be enforced. There would have been some Colored Soldiers less." (1st Lt. J. M. Lattin to D. B. Nichols, 3 Apr. 1864; Capt. Robert C. Perry to Lieut. Col. E. M. Greene, 3 Apr. 1864.) On May 25, Greene submitted the reports of Nichols, Lattin, and Perry to the headquarters of the Department of Washington, together with his own conclusions. "Freedmans Village is necessarily under Military Government," he pointed out, and it was therefore entirely proper to refuse "indiscriminate entrance . . . of unauthorized persons, who would at their own discretion, seize, and carry off the inmates with or without their consent, and without the Knowledge of the Officers commanding the Camp." By regulating recruitment, he could ensure that enlistment bounties were paid to the recruits "and not go to enrich Agents and Speculators," and he could also make arrangements to have "a portion of their pay devoted to the support of their families." (Lt. Col. Elias M. Greene to Maj. C. H. Raymond, 25 May 1864, in the same file.) Endorsements returned all the documents to the War Department, which, on May 30, 1864, pronounced further action in the case "unnecessary."

76: Virginia Freedman to the Secretary of War

Alexandria [*Va.*] April 3rd 1864

Sir   My House that I Now Occupy Belongs to Mr Henry Dangerfeild and for the Last twelve Months Mr A H Gladwin Supt^d of Contrabands are Bin Chargeing me from fifteen down to thirteen

Dollars Per Month. Wilce thare are White Lady and Sevel other Persons Lives In One Posion of the House that doant Pay a cent and thay tell me that He Has No rite to Recive rent for Mr Dangerfields Property   this is And Old wether-borded House Situated On the out Skirts of the City Near Patrick St   Nowing that this is An UnJoust Proceeding of Mr Gladwin I obtained a pass from my Quarter Master to Come over and See you about it   the Lady that Lives In One Half of the House Hire Name is Mrs Grimes   I Remain your Umble and Obeadent Servent

ALS   Edward Smith   Cold

Edward Smith to Hon. E. M. Staunton, 3 Apr. 1864, S-400 1864, Letters Received, ser. 360, Colored Troops Division, RG 94 [B-576]. Endorsements. The War Department referred Smith's letter to General John P. Slough, military governor of Alexandria, "for investigation and report," and he in turn forwarded it to Albert Gladwin, superintendent of contrabands in the city. Gladwin explained that he had begun collecting rent for the house in question in July 1863, in compliance with an order from Slough "to take charge of such houses as were occupied by contrabands, and owned by disloyal persons and collect a reasonable rent for the same." Half of the house, consisting of four rooms, "had been previously occupied for a considerable time by said Edward Smith," who was renting out part of it to other parties. Gladwin had collected rents of between $3 and $5 per month from Smith and from the other black occupants. Meanwhile, he had charged no rent at all for "the other house under the same roof, occupied by a white family," because he "had no order to collect rents except from Contrabands." (A. Gladwin to Brig. Genl. John P. Slough, 7 May 1864, in the same file.) Slough returned Smith's letter and Gladwin's report to the War Department, where they were evidently filed without further action.

77: Two Army Inspectors to the Inspector General

Washington D.C.   July 30" 1864.
Sir: In obedience to your orders of the 20" instant,[1] we made a special inspection of "Freedman's Village" "Government Farms" and matters pertaining thereto, and have the honor to submit the following report: —

I. Of the theory in relation to, and organization of
    Freedman's Village and Government Farms.

The large number of destitute Freedmen coming into the Department of Washington led to the establishment, upon the Arlington estate, of Freedman's Village for their reception, in the summer of 1863. Its organization and management were placed in the hands of *Lt. Col. E. M. Greene*, Chief Quartermaster of the Department. As a provision for its support, it was ordered that five dollars per month be deducted from the pay of each colored man in the civil employ of Government in this Department. From the fund so accruing, a village was built, affording comfortable homes for two thousand persons, An ample supply of water was furnished from a reservoir, through pipes laid in all the streets; Stoves and cooking utensils provided for all families; a home for the infirm established; a school for children and adults opened by the American Tract Society; and, in short, every provision made for the comfort of the negroes, without requiring them to labor. No special effort has been made to economize, because it is in theory using the Freedmen's money for the benefit of the Freedmen; and despite of liberal expenditure the fund accumulates.

Such articles as could not be drawn from the Q.M. department were to be purchased out of the fund, but all rations were to be regularly issued by the Subsistence department, and medicine and medical attendance to be supplied by the Medical department.

It was assumed that the great demand for labor throughout the country would secure employment for the freedmen immediately after their reception, and that thus the Village would prove merely a "Rest" for them on their journey from slavery to freedom.

Lt. Col. Greene was also authorized to cultivate the abandoned farms of disloyal owners, it being supposed that with no rents to pay, and with ample supply of freedmen's labor at nominal wages, the crops would yield profitable returns. Accordingly five farms, comprising 1270 Acres, were fenced and manured late in season of 1863, and fully cultivated in 1864. The results will be set forth in another part of this report.

II Condition of Freedmans Village.

Upon the 26″ instant there were at the Village 411. Men, 658. women and 1097. Children, making a total of 2166 souls. All had comfortable homes, a bare sufficiency of clothing, plenty of food, and appeared healthy. The village is well located and kept clean. The School house was built by Am. Tract Society which supplies teachers and conducts the school. Some four hundred children were in attendance – their improvement is evident, and we take pleasure in pronouncing the school excellent.

At the *"Home for the infirm"* we found a number of decrepit and disabled persons, very comfortably cared for. No labor is required of the residents at the Village, beyond keeping themselves and their houses clean. This is tolerably well done, but might be improved. At the *"Tailor Shop"* a number of women are employed in manufacturing clothing. Fair wages are paid them, and as the clothing is sold just at cost, their labor benefits

338

themselves only. Necessary clothing is furnished gratis to the non-working population. Those who draw wages pay for their clothing. Children are each allowed one half of a ration.

The entire Village is a burden upon Government to the amount expended for rations, transportation, hospital expenses and payment of officers and guard. It is a burden upon the "contraband fund" for clothing, expenses of buildings and repairs and salaries to white employees. Computing the ration at 10$ per month (including use of stoves, fuel &c.) we estimate the expenses of the Village as follows:

Rations for 1069 Adults @ 10$ per month		$10.690
" " 1097 Children 5.		5.485
" " 9 Employees 10.		90
Pay of officer in charge. and 9 employees		690
Clothing for 2166 at 50¢ per month		1.083
Total		$18.038

Per month, exclusive of transportation, hospital, building. repairs, and support of one company of guards, numbering, 1. Officer and 55 men.

III. Condition of Mason's Island.

The village not being sufficient to accommodate the rapidly increasing numbers of Freedmen, this Island, with barracks &c., was assigned to use of Lt. Col. Greene about 15″ June. Upon the 26″ Instant there were upon the Island 149 Men, 418 Women and 615 Children, making a total of 1182 souls. At the time of our first visit (21″ Inst) we found dirt and disorder reigning supreme. The people were tumbled into barracks without classification, and this, too, in face of the theory that only those were kept upon the Island who were candidates to go out to service. We found infirm, disabled, sick and children here in numbers – just as they had arrived in fact. If we are to credit the statements of contrabands, men and women were thrust in the same barracks, and slept on the floor promiscuously. Our ears were assailed with all sorts of complaints – mostly about want of clothes; non-payment of wages for their time passed in utter idleness; their not being so well situated as those in the Village; the crowded condition of barracks; the want of a hospital; the refusal of Lt. Col. Greene to furnish them transportation to visit their friends in the village, and the like. We thought their only well-founded complaints those about the barracks and hospital. Lt. Col. Greene's excuses for this state of things are annexed marked "Exhibit A".[2]

A week later we found a material change in the condition of the Island. The barracks were clean – the infirm had been sent to the "Home" – a hospital had been established. – the people classified, and the sexes separated. There was no diminution of complaints, but most were without any reasonable foundation. There is no labor exacted from those upon the Island, beyond making themselves comfortable. Of course it is a burden upon the Government and the Contraband fund, just as is the "Village". Estimated as in case of the latter, the cost of mantaining the Island is $9.659. per month, exclusive of transportation, hospital, building, and repairs.

There are teachers at the Island, provided by the "Friends' Society" of Philadelphia, and schools will soon be opened. The present condition of the Island is as good as circumstances will admit. It strikes us as being a bad location for a hospital.

IV Government Farms.

The Government Farms are five in number, comprising 1270. Acres under cultivation, situated in vicinity of Arlington. The expenses incident to their cultivation are paid as follows: Wages of employees, building and repairs from funds of Q.M. Department. Subsistence is issued by Subsistence Department. and no re-imbursements made. Horses, wagons, farming implements &c are supplied by Q.M. Department. Guards, to the number of 1 officer and 85 men, are detailed from V.R. Corps. All crops, or the proceeds for their sale, are turned in to the Q.M. Department.

The land is the abandoned property of disloyal owners, and is of poor, thin soil, for the most part. When occupied it was without fences and overgrown with brush. It was necessary to clear and fence it, involving a heavy expenditure. Only two buildings were erected by Q.M. Department, one being for residence of Superintendent, and one barn. The employees have built themselves comfortable log-huts at very slight expense. Except Superintendents, all employees are Freedmen, who receive wages of from 2.$ to 10.$ each per month, and one ration. These Farms appear well, the crops are fair; the employees comfortably cared for, and in all respects the farms compare favorably with others in the vicinity. A detailed statement of the cost of labor on each farm and of the produce raised is given in "Schedule B" hereto annexed.[3]

As much success has been achieved this year as could be reasonably expected; but the result exhibits a loss to Government of an alarmingly large sum. As fairly estimated as practicable, from all data we could obtain, the account for this experimental farming, from 1 June '63 to 1" July '64 stands thus:

Dr.

For wages paid Employees; building & incidentals	
1" June 64 (from Lt. Col. Greenes Books)	$39.789.09
" Estimated wages June & July '64.	6.000.00
" Rations to 225 persons @ 9$ per month for 13.m.	26.325.00

" Use and forage of 80' horses	10$	"	"	10.400.00
" Support of 85 men (Guard)	30.	"	"	33.150.00
" " " 1 officer "	125.	"	"	1.625.00
	Total			$117.289.09

Cr

By value of crops raised in '63.	$ 8.294.50
" " " " " 64.	
partly sold, and balance estimated by Superintendents	$39.974.50
Total	$48.269.00
Loss on 13 Months' operations	$69.020.09

The expenses of the Guard alone amounts to three fourths of the whole receipts. For wages alone there is paid within 3000$ as much as all the farms yield. And yet the crop is put at the highest estimate in amount, and valued at present extraordinary prices. The number of employees is based on the rolls for this month, there having been little variation in the amount paid as wages in each month. We do not think it necessary to mention objectionable details in this system of farming, for the immense losses exhibited as a general result are certainly sufficient to condemn it. Only a very wealthy Government can afford such expensive toys.

V. Contraband Fund.

The amount expended prior to January 1" 1864 was $13.514.52 Amount received $63.799.83, leaving a balance on hand of

	$ 50.285.31
Receipts from 1" Jan to 1" July 1864	$ 94.304.17
	$144.589.48
Expenditures in same period, the ⎱ pay-rolls for June being unpaid ⎰	$ 91.936.76
Leaving on hand a balance of	$ 52.652.72

Vouchers were examined, and balance on hand verified – $42.903.68 being in 1" National Bank and $9.749.04 in Certificates of Indebtedness, deposited in U.S. Treasury.

Lt. Col. Greene estimates the amount accrued in hands of officers, and not yet paid over to him, at $40.000. No accounts of the expenses of sustaining these institutions are kept by Lt. Col. Greene beyond the payment of employees and incidentals, and of course his books exhibit only a small portion of the real cost, if we include rations, guards &c. Monthly accounts current are rendered to U.S. Treasurer and Q.M. General.

It is our opinion that the estimated balance of $92.000 should be turned over to the Subsistence department in payment for rations furnished to Freedmen at Village, Island and Farms.

VI Results obtained from these Establishments:
Errors in Theory: Defects in Practice.

The perceptible results obtained by the organization of these establishment are, briefly, these: — Freedmen to the [estimated]⁴ number of 6.000 have been received during the past thirteen months, and supplied with the necessaries of life. We have no means of determining the average duration of their stay. The number now on hand is 3.728. Out of the whole number received 239 have been provided employment other than that supplied by Government. About 900 children are enjoying the benefits of a well-conducted school; certainly a noble charity — worthy the fostering care, and if need be, the support of Government.

We fail to discover any improvement in the character or conduct of the Adults. Judging from what we saw, they are of the most ignorant class of slaves. Few have knowledge of any labor above field labor, and are but little skilled even in that. Their erroneous idea that "emancipation" signifies a claim upon Government for support in idleness, has been confirmed rather than corrected. They complain of everything, and deem themselves wronged in that they receive no wages. These results, and the possession of a village that accommodates two thousand people, are all that have been obtained by an expenditure of $105.451.28, exclusive of rations furnished.

In regard to the Farms, we see decided results. Taking this season alone, it being an ordinarily favorable one, the loss amounts to $22.757.50. Taking the two seasons together the loss is $69.120.09

We consider the following *theories of Lt. Col. Greene*, in relation to the organization and management of these establishments, erroneous:

1. That they are supported by the Freedmen.

We find that in fact the expenses paid from the Contraband Fund are only a small portion of the whole amount incurred. Besides, the Freedmen, as a rule, consider themselves well paid at the rate of $25 per month, and know little and care less what disposition is made of the remaining 5$ allowed them. And, again, it is the unanimous opinion of many Quartermasters and Superintendents who employ Freedmen and were consulted by us, that Contraband labor is not more than half as valuable as white labor. So that Government pay's the Contraband ten dollars per month more than the comparative value of his labor, and in addition contributes five dollars extra to this "Contraband Fund", The whole expense is really paid by Government.

2' That parents must not be permitted to go out to service unless all their Children are also taken.

This cannot be maintained on principles of humanity, for these people are seldom married — have little idea of training children, and

cannot hope to give them such advantages as are afforded by the
Schools at the "Village"   Moreover, the necessities of the times
compel separations.   It is hard to find an unbroken family circle
among our white people.   It is certainly bad economy.   For very few
are found willing to be burdened with a whole family of children, as
the price of employing the parents; and thus all remain a burden
upon the "Village".

Very few able-bodied men are found among the recent arrivals.   It
is safe to assume, in fact, that all are infirm men, women and
children.   These women being ignorant of housework, and there
being no demand for female field hands in our Northern States, the
number accumulated is quite large, with litte prospects of
diminution under the present management.   Nearly every women
being burdened with children lessens the chances of her
employment.

At Mason's Island we discovered the worst of faults – that
of general mismanagement, resulting from incapacity or
negligence.   The Superintendent here, *Dr. Nichols*, made upon us an
unfavorable impression as to capacity, and despite the excuses of Lt.
Col. Greene, we consider the condition in which the Island was first
found so disgraceful as to demand the removal of Dr Nichols.   Capt
Brown, A.Q.M. Vol., had recently assumed charge of the "Village"
and did not seem familiar with the duties of his position.   But we
think him earnest and competent, and that he will soon show
satisfactory management.   The fact that there is no labor to be
performed at these establishments unfits them for the residence of
adults.   Only steady employment will improve either the morals or
manners of these Contrabands.

VII. Suggestions for improvement.

Our orders require us not only to show the existing condition of
things, but also to suggest improvements.   Fully realizing the
difficulties surrounding the subject with which we have to deal – the
proper employment and management of "contrabands" whom our
Government not only makes free, but seeks, also, to educate to a
proper conception of the duties and rights of free men – we submit
with all deference, the following suggestions

1. It being impracticable, at any reasonable expense, to educate
the adult population thrown upon us, that the males be received
into the Military or Civil employment of Government at the true
value of their services.

2. That if they choose civil employment, a tax of sufficient
amount – say $2. per month – be levied upon each of them, for the
support of infirm freedmen and children.

3. That such adult females as are not required or may not be fit
for cooks &c. for male employees, be sent to those portions of our

Country where labor is greatly demanded, taking with them their children under 4 years of age.

4. That children from 4. to 14. years of age be supported and educated out of the Contraband Fund. We think the Home for infirm and schools for children at Freedmans Village a good basis, and recommend their continuance.

5. That Freedmans Village be only a home for infirm and children, and a "Rest" for adults for a very limited period after their arrival.

6. That all farming operations be discontinued as soon as the present crop is secured.

7. That as soon as practicable all Freedmen be removed from Mason's Island.

8. That an officer be detailed who shall be directly responsible for, and have full control of the management of Freedmen.

9. That, so far as practicable, rations issued to contrabands be paid for out of the "Fund."

All of which is very respectfully submitted, And we have the honor to be, Sir, Your most Ob'd't Servants

E. H. Ludington

C. E. Compton

HLS

Maj. E. H. Ludington and Maj. C. E. Compton to Col. James A. Hardie, 30 July 1864, L-25 1864, Letters Received, ser. 15, RG 159 [J-8]. Ludington signed as an assistant inspector general; Compton, as major of the 47th USCI and acting assistant inspector general. Endorsements indicate that the inspectors' report was forwarded by the inspector general to the Secretary of War, who on August 4 referred it to Quartermaster General Montgomery C. Meigs "for his perusal." In the same file is a letter of August 15 from Meigs to the secretary disputing the inspectors' conclusions. On the basis of information provided by Colonel Greene concerning expenditures and the value of produce, Meigs supported Greene's contention that the farms were profitable. For one thing, the cost of the guard was not "a proper charge" against the farms, because it "was hired for the purpose of police and restraint upon the troops camped in the vicinity, rather than of the Freedmen themselves." Besides, Meigs insisted, the value of Greene's system could not be ascertained by mere cost-accounting. The government farms had "provid[ed] healthful and useful employment for a considerable number of men and women not fit for the active and hard work of the army" who would otherwise have "spent their time in sloth and idleness" at government expense. Removing the freedpeople from Washington to Freedman's Village and the government farms had saved hundreds of them from "death by disease" and reduced the incidence of smallpox, which had "threatened to spread to the white population of the city." Furthermore, Meigs argued, the government had an obligation to the families of black men who were serving the country as soldiers and military laborers. "Their women and children come here, and the United States . . . must take care that they do not starve." Meigs next addressed the inspectors' concluding recommendations. "Any able-bodied black man" he noted, "is eagerly hired . . . by the Quartermaster or Commissary, or enlisted, and the demand and need are greater than the supply." As for the tax on the wages of black military laborers, the existing levy of $5 per month on men earning more than $20 per month "is not onerous, and does not produce too large a fund." With respect to the disposition of black women and children, the former were already being hired to private employers "as fast as proper persons apply for them," and the latter were already being provided for and educated out of the contraband fund. Addressing the suggestion that Freedman's Village be used only as a home for children and the infirm and a temporary refuge for other adults, Meigs declared that such had always been "the theory of Freedman's Village, and the practice will, I trust, be gradually brought into full conformity with the theory." Meigs disapproved the recommendation that the government farms be discontinued, although he suggested that only women and infirm freedpeople be employed thereon and that wages "be reduced . . . to a mere reward, enabling the laborer to procure tobacco or some such luxury." He likewise disapproved the inspectors' recommendation that the freedpeople at Mason's Island be transferred, noting that the camp there "is now clean and well-conducted" and the number hired out to employers had "very considerably increased." In response to the eighth recommendation, Meigs noted that Captain Joseph M. Brown had already been placed in charge of the former slaves (under Greene's supervision), but he added that to Greene himself belonged credit for "the improvement in the condition, treatment and health of these poor creatures, and the cessation of the criticisms and complaints of the press." Finally, Meigs rejected the inspectors' recommendation that the contraband fund be applied to the cost of rations. "On all our lines of active operations," he observed, "large quantities of subsistence are issued to the destitute refugees, white and black, and those negroes under Col. Greene's care are the only refugees not hired into the Quartermaster Department, Commissary Department, or enlisted, who, so far as I know, have made any return for their food." A subsequent endorsement by the inspector general referred Meigs's letter to Major Ludington and invited him to reconsider his inspection report. In response, Ludington revised his account of the revenues and expenses of the government farms, reducing, but not eliminating, the deficit. However, after addressing various other points made by Meigs, he concluded, "I see no reason to withdraw or modify any suggestion" in the original report. (Maj. E. H. Ludington to Col. Jas. A. Hardie, 22 Sept. 1864, in the same file.)

1 On July 20, 1864, the Secretary of War ordered Major Elisha H. Ludington and Major Charles E. Compton "to make a thorough Inspection of the Freedmans Village under charge of *Lt. Col. E. M. Greene,* and all matters pertaining to the organization and control of the Freedmen in the Dept of Washington." (Order, War Dept., 20 July 1864, vol. 1, p. 77, Letters Sent, ser. 12, RG 159 [J-8].)
2 Exhibit "A," a letter from Greene, explained that he had detailed men from

Freedman's Village to clean and repair the camp at Mason's Island but they had been reassigned to more pressing duties before the work was finished. (Lt. Col. Elias M. Greene to Maj. E. H. Ludington, 26 July 1864).
3 According to exhibit "B," an undated table, the farms employed a total of 241 black laborers (169 men, 53 women, 19 boys), who were growing corn, oats, hay, rye, and vegetables. The "cost of labor" for each farm was the sum of wages paid the laborers and their superintendents and the expense of maintaining draft horses; it ranged from $3,864 to $10,432, with a total for the five farms of $39,352. The estimated value of produce ranged from $2,250 to $13,945, totaling $39,974.50. Against the "Apparent" balance in favor of the farms of $622.50, the inspectors charged $23,380 in additional expenses – including the wages of a general superintendent, an assistant superintendent, and the officer and eighty-five soldiers serving as a guard – for a projected "Loss this Season" of $22,757.50.
4 Brackets in manuscript.

78: Maryland Black Apprentice to the Freedmen's Bureau Superintendent at Washington, D.C.

Washington D.C. April 22^d 1867

Colonel: I respectfully make the following statement and request that such action may be taken by you in the premises as shall be deemed just.

About three years ago while at Mason's Island I was indentured or bound out by the person in charge there – Dr Nicholls I think – to James Suit living in Prince George County Md about 4 miles from Bladensburgh – who promised me to clothe me, feed and educate me, in compensation for services rendered by me to him –

Mr Suit has been kind to me generally but neither clothed me decently nor sent me to school   Once – yes several times I have been whipped by Mr Suit without justification and by Mrs S. also –   one time I was struck by her with a shovel – injuring my head very much because I could not fix a pot on a cook stove as she desired.

I have been so tired of not receiving any compensation for my services – no clothing, no chance for school – nothing but *whippings* that I determined to leave Mr Suit and arrived in this city yesterday –

Please don't let Mr Suit take me back for I have a mother and father (named *Sylva* and *Abraham* Holmes) who would care for me if they knew where I was. I think they are in this city. Respectfully Yours

HLSr

his
Carter X Holmes
mark

346

Carter Holmes to Lieut. Col. Wm. M. Beebe, 22 Apr. 1867, #1716 1867, Letters Received, ser. 456, DC Asst. Comr., RG 105 [A-9836]. Witnessed. Beneath Holmes's mark are the words "freed-boy—aged 12 years." According to an endorsement, the Freedmen's Bureau superintendent sent Holmes to "the Orphan's Home" in Washington.

79: Superintendent of Contrabands in Alexandria, Virginia, to the Headquarters of the Military Governor of Alexandria

Alexandria, Va., Oct. 1st 1864

Captain: I have the honor to report that the month just closed has witnessed a decided improvement upon the month previous in the sanitary condition of the people, the mortality being less by more than 50 cases.

We have had much to do in the settlement of matters financial, and otherwise, which, as the people begin to accumulate property, seem to increase, especially where parties have died leaving some effects—the houses and other property not unfrequently having been created by clubbing together; and as the people have no means of keeping accounts for themselves, it is difficult to obtain the correct state of things. We have in several instances written wills for them, but these are not always satisfactory

Our attention has most frequently been called to cases of kidnapping under the pretence of arresting deserters, or of enlisting boys from fifteen to eighteen years of age. Several of these cases have been brought to Head Quarters as you are already aware, together with the evidence elicited by me. And I have been informed that guards have been dispatched to obtain their release; and I have been told that one man—Peter White—who was taken from his wife and family was released. But if that was the case, no doubt parties were in readiness to retake him, before he left the vicinity of Camp Casey, where he had been lawlessly taken, and to make game of the authorities by which he had been released. In every case which I have examined, these acts of violence have been clearly traceable to white parties in authority, and evidently with the base purpose of making money, and not of serving their country; as the persons thus kidnapped were not such as could be accepted as soldiers by an honest and intelligent examination. It has been as barefaced and ungodly a trafficking in human beings, as that which has brought this terrible curse of rebellion and war upon us; and while it may be done professedly in the interest of the country, and against rebellion, it is really adding burning coals to the fiery indignation of a justly incensed Jehovah. The contempt with which the efforts to suppress these aggressions were received, was manifested in sending back the men, who had been sent out of the city under guard, with foul mouthed imprecations upon those who should presume to interfere with their operations. And thus, over the heads of Military Governor and Provost Marshal, they authorize subordinates, without any discriptive list of the persons, to hurl them from under their jurisdiction, without a chance to say a word in their own defence, or an opportunity to make their case Known to them, from whom they have a right to look for protection; and it is evident that investigation and punishment should be pushed, to recover and secure the innocent, and restrain or prevent the wicked from repeating their criminal acts, to the extent which is necessary to secure that end.

Our general operations have been about as in months past. On the 24th inst. the time of Corp^l A. H. Denman, 1st DC V. who was detailed to this department in July 1863 – expired, and he received an honorable discharge, and he has left the service much to the regret of all associated with him.

The amount of money collected, and turned over to Capt. T. K. Church during the month is – for rents, $216.00, and for coffins $21.00.

The number of deaths reported to us for burial is 71, of which 13 were from the hospitals of the city. Very Respectfully Your Obt Servt

HLSr   A. Gladwin

A. Gladwin to Capt. Rolland C. Gale, 1 Oct. 1864, Letters Received, ser. 2053, Alexandria VA, Offices of Military Governors, RG 393 Pt. 4 [C-4705]. In mid-July 1864, Gladwin had estimated that between 7,000 and 8,000 freedpeople were living in Alexandria, compared with 2,000 to 3,000 in May 1863. Most of the able-bodied men were employed by the government at $20 to $25 per month, plus rations; only thirty-five former slaves, "embracing mainly the indigent, old and young," were receiving rations from the government without being in its employ (down from 1,200 in 1863). Gladwin also estimated that freedpeople in the city had constructed for themselves 700 or 800 houses, at a cost of $50 to $150 each. (A. Gladwin to Lt. W. W. Winship, 16 July 1864, Records of the Provost Marshal, ser. 1468, Defenses South of the Potomac, Provost Marshal Field Organizations, RG 393 Pt. 4 [C-4771].)

80: Army Inspector to the Inspector General

Washington Oct. 13th 1864.
Colonel: I have the honor to report that in accordance with your instructions of the 10' inst. I proceeded to Mason'[s] Island and made a thorough inspection of the condition and management of the contrabands located there.

Mason'[s] Island is very well adapted for a camp of this kind, being very easy of access from Washington and Georgetown.

The primary object for the establishment of this camp was to make it a general depot for hireing out Contrabands.

No Contrabands are received unless by an order from Col. Ellison, Chief Quarter-Master of the Dept. of Washington, or Capt. Brown, Ass't. Quarter-master, who has charge of all the Quarter-master'[s] property on the island. None are Sent out to Service without an order from the same Source.

The camp is in charge of Dr. Nichols, Sup't. of Contrabands. He is assisted by two employees of the Quartermasters Department, one of whom is employed as a Clerk, the other is acting as Commissary of Subsistence for the Camp.

Dr. Nichols seems to be a man very well Suited for the position he occupies, and I should judge had had a good deal of experience in the management of Camps of this Kind.

There are Seven buildings used as Barracks, Six of these are, each, one hundred feet long and twenty feet wide. The other is about one hundred and fifty feet long and thirty feet wide. The Hospital building is the Same Size. There is another building used as a Commissary Depot.

There are six smaller buildings used as Offices, guard rooms &c.

All these buildings were built as Barracks for the use of Colored troops. They are very comfortable and answer the purpose for which they are now being used, very well. Most of the buildings which are used for Barracks have very comfortable bunks in them. These barracks are kept in very good condition.

The supply of water for cooking, washing &c, is limited, there being only one well on the island and that is Situated at a great distance from the barracks.

They are now at work digging another and have it almost finished. I think when it is done the supply of water will be Sufficient for the use of the camp.

They are about to erect another building, which is to be used as a meeting house and School-room. All repairs &c. are made by money from the Contraband fund.

The Superintendent keeps an account of all Contrabands who are received, also of all who leave the island; in this way they can tell the number of rations to be drawn and issued. The Ration issued is the one directed to be issued to Contrabands and called the "Contraband Ration."[1] To all persons over fourteen years old, the full ration is issued; to all under that age, half rations are issued. No Savings are allowed to be made from these rations.

The Rations are all of a good quality with the exception of the indian meal which is musty and Sour.

The number of Contrabands on the Island is four hundred and ten (410) classified as follows, viz: forty one (41) men; one hundred an Sixty (160) women; one hundred and Six (106) boys and one hundred and three (103) Girls.

During the month of August there were eight hundred Contrabands on the island; during that month the number of deaths was one hundred and eighteen; and the number hired out during the same time was two hundred and twenty two. During the month of September there were between five and Seven hundred Contrabands in the Camp, and of this number there was sixty (60) deaths and one hundred and Seventy Seven (177) persons hired out to Service. During the present month there have been eleven (11) deaths and forty eight hired out to Service.

Good and Substantial clothing is issued to the Contrabands; this clothing is furnished by the government and a fixed price placed on each article by the Quarter-Master's Department. This Clothing is issued by the Superintendent, who keeps a regular "Clothing Receipt Roll" of all Clothing issued. He makes a regular monthly return of all Clothing issued by him, to Capt. Brown A.Q.M. The government is reimbursed for this Clothing from the Contraband fund.

Wood is also issued for cooking, washing &c.

The Hospital is under the charge of the Medical Director of the Department of Washington. The Hospital Building is large and very well ventilated, having a large number of hospital cots in it and in fact everything that is necessary to make the patients comfortable.

The Hospital savings for the month of August were one hundred and fourteen dollars and fifty seven cents ($114.57). Amount expended for necessaries for hospital purposes sixty two dollars and twenty cents ($62.20) leaving a balance on hand of fifty two dollars and thirty seven cents ($52.37). The savings for the month of September had not as yet been balanced.

There is a guard of twelve men under charge of a Sergeant Stationed on the island. I think this number is sufficient as there is but one way to get to or from the island.

I would most respectfully recommend that this camp be allowed to remain where it is, for the following reasons; viz:

In the first place Mason's Island is very well adapted for a camp of this kind, the contrabands not being able to get off of it without a pass are not Straying around the country at their leisure. It is also situated very conveniently for persons desiring to get Servants; and this seems to me to be a great object; for it is certainly to the interest of the government to hire out to Service as many of these people as possible. If these people, who are fit to go out to Service, were at the Freedmens village, it would be much harder to get them off to Service, as there they have comfortable houses to live in, and the most of these negroes are unwilling to go out to Service as long as they have a house to live in and are well clothed and fed. The Barracks on Mason'ˢ Island are comfortable and do very well for the purpose for which they are being used. Again I do not see that there is any additional expense entailed on the government by keeping this camp where it is; these people must be taken care of by the government and if they were removed to the freedmens village or any other camp the expense for their keeping would be equally as great as it is now. The Same number of persons would have to be employed to see after them that there are now. The government would be compelled to issue to them the same number of rations and the same amount of clothing and wood that they now do.

There is a fine, large Ice House on the Island which can be filled this winter by the Contrabands and the ice used by the government. Very Respectfully Submitted

HLS   *Kilburn Knox*

1st Lieut. Kilburn Knox to Col. James A. Hardie, 13 Oct. 1864, K-11 1864, Letters Received, ser. 15, RG 159 [J-6]. Topical labels in the margin are omitted. Knox signed as an officer in the 13th U.S. Infantry. A penciled notation on the wrapper, probably by an official of the Inspector General's Office, instructed Lieutenant Knox to report upon "the *police* of the Camp," and, following a second inspection, he revised the favorable conclusions of his first report. Although Danforth B. Nichols, the camp's superintendent, was well-intentioned, Knox now suggested, he "lacks energy and fitness for organizing, or compelling those under him to move with system." The hiring practices instituted by Nichols's superiors also came in for criticism. There was "scarcely an able bodied man" to be found among the 410 freedpeople at Mason's Island, "the greater part [of whom] could not expect to obtain employment very readily, being women with several small children, or men and women too old for usefulness." "In theory," Knox continued, "only those fit for hiring out are sent to the Island—in fact, they are of the same classes as those at Freedmen's village." Knox was especially critical of a practice permitted by Captain Joseph M. Brown, the assistant quartermaster in charge of Mason's Island, of "[letting] any of these people go whose friends may apply for them." Residents of the camp, Knox urged, "should not be allowed to leave the Island unless the Superintendant is satisfied, that they can take care of themselves or will be taken care of, & that they will not become a burden to the community to which they go." "The object of the present management," he declared, "appears to be to get rid of these people in *any* way; often by throwing them upon the community at large; the prevention of which was the object of the establishment of the Freedmen's Village." (1″ Lieut. Kilburn Knox to Col. James A. Hardie, 18 Oct. 1864, in the same file.)

1 For the composition of the contraband ration, as established by the War Department in January 1864, see above, doc. 42n.

81: Surgeon in Charge of an Army Hospital to the Provost Marshal General of the Defenses of Washington South of the Potomac; and an Assistant Provost Marshal to the Headquarters of the Provost Marshal General of the Defenses

Fairfax Seminary Va. November 1. /64

Col: – I have the honor to address you, to endeavor to have removed from the vicinity of this Hospital, a colony of Negroes whose depredations upon the Hospital Property have been carried on of late upon an enormous scale.

I have recently recovered from these Hovels, over one hundred (100) Army Hospital Blankets, together with other valuable articles As far as I know, these people have no claim to the property they have settled upon, and they are a source of constant anxiety to me. Very Respectfully Your Obt Servt,

HLS
H. Allen

Alexandria, Va, Nov 1ˢᵗ 1864.

Capt, I have the honor to report that the "colony of negroes" mentioned in the communication of Surg. Allen – Fairfax Sem. Hosptl are, so far as I can learn from white people – other than those at the Hosptl – an industrious community and almost all the males are at work, one place or another, for the Govt. Some of them have little garden spots with vegetables yet in the ground and it would be, in my opinion, rather hard to eject them from the premises at present, They seem clean, orderly and well disposed.

The Govt. blankets mentioned by the Surg. were, no doubt, purchased by them from soldiers in the Hospital & vicinity as all the white people in the neighborhood say that they have had blankets offered them, by soldiers, very often and frequently for a mere trifle – they refusing to take the blankets, however, knowing them to be Govt. property.

One lady who lives in a large house only a few steps from the negro quarters told me that she had frequently left clothing out doors on the clothesline all night and frequently left her doors unlocked but has never missed any thing and she thinks if the negroes would steal from any body they would from her.

Surg. Allen says he offered them work which they refused, probably because they could get better wages at Fort Ward and the block houses on the rail road which have been building all summer and wher most of them say they are at work. I am Capt Very respectfully your obt. sert.

ALS   Geo. R. Alvord

Asst. Surg. H. Allen to Lt. Col. H. H. Wells, 1 Nov. 1864, filed with 1st Lt. Geo. R. Alvord to Capt. W. W. Winship, 1 Nov. 1864, Records of the Provost Marshal, ser. 1468, Defenses South of the Potomac, Provost Marshal Field Organizations, RG 393 Pt. 4 [C-4771]. Endorsement. Alvord signed as a lieutenant in the 1st Michigan Cavalry. No reply to Allen has been found in the volumes of letters sent by the provost marshal general of the defenses south of the Potomac.

82: Black Military Laborers at Alexandria, Virginia, to the Secretary of War

Alexandria, Va, Nov. 28th 1864

From the undersigned and many others – Freedmen – laborers in the Quartermaster's Department of the U.S. Government – Greeting:

We would respectfully report to you through our representative, Serg[t] Edward Thomas, unanimously chosen at a large meeting assembled for the purposes hereinafter expressed – that we are, by our own pleasure, employees under the Government, and the most of us have been such in one capacity or another since 1862; that we are the sincere friends of this Government, by and under which it has pleased God to translate us from a condition of chattelhood to the estate of free men; and we intend cheerfully to submit to all the requirements of the Government – so far as we are permitted to understand them, believing that they are intended for our good.

But there are some things touching our relations and obligations to the Government, which we do not understand, and which have caused us much perplexity in our endeavor to ascertain the will of the Government; and it is on this account that we beg leave to trouble you for that light upon the subject which we have thus far failed to obtain from other sources.

353

For something like a year, in our monthly payment of wages, which usually takes place from twenty to twenty-eight days after the expiration of the time for which payment is made, we have been called upon to touch the pen for $30 — while we have received but $24.75. If the deduction is made as a necessary and just tax, and we can be made to see that it is subserving some good and useful purpose, and is made in pursuance of general orders, bearing alike on all persons similarly situated at the various military posts, it will, instead of being a source of perplexity, be submitted to with pleasure

But, if the Government does not require this unusual tax of over one-sixth of what we nominally receive as our wages, and have not ordered the deduction so made, then, the circumstances in which we find ourselves in our transition state, from a condition of utter destitution with regard to the possession of property — many of us with large families and paying exorbitant rents — demand that we should strive to secure to ourselves all the advantages which the Government has deemed necessary, and has so generously provided for us, that we may prepare ourselves as soon as may be, to reciprocate these favors, and help bear the burdens which this unrighteous rebellion has imposed upon it.

Whatever may be the intention with regard to the amount of our wages, we would beg leave to know to what purpose the very large fund created, and being created by these deductions, has been, is, and is to be applied; and also, whether the facilities are, or can be afforded by the Government, for the uniform payment of our wages as to time; since, an unexpected delay compels many who have families to obtain a credit for provisions and other necessaries, leaving them at the mercy of those with whom they deal — the most of them having no interest in our people, except to make all they can out of them, and which operates so unfavorably with many as to keep them in debt to such extent that their receipts will scarcely bring up arrearages.

We beg leave also to ask whether, since we cannot read for ourselves, it is not due to us to have all matters which we are required to sign, first read, and, if need be, explained to us, so that we may act understandingly.

Begging pardon for thus trespassing upon your patience, and trusting that you will set us right in all these matters — We are most respectfully your Obt Servts

Edwd Thomas

Hezekiah Agee   Albert Henderson

Wesley Simms

Jacob R. Harris   John Thomas

Jacob Banks

Tyler Bovey   Joe Ford
                    Jerry Smith
Frank Toliver   Sam Johnson
HLSr   And many others.

Sergt. Edwd. Thomas et al. to Hon. E. M. Stanton, 28 Nov 1864, T-18 1864, Letters Received, ser. 15, RG 159 [J-23]. The signatures are all in the same handwriting. At the War Department, an endorsement by the inspector general instructed an adjutant, Captain Murray Davis, "to investigate the subject of complaint." On December 3, Davis reported that the black laborers in question, numbering about 1,200, were employed by Captain James G. C. Lee, an assistant quartermaster at Alexandria, who had been withholding "two distinct items" from the monthly pay of each black employee: $5.00 for the contraband fund, deducted in compliance with an order from the Secretary of War of September 27, 1862 (quoted above, in doc. 55), and $.25 to maintain a hospital for black employees of the quartermaster's department. A tax of 1 percent per month for hospital purposes had formerly been authorized, Davis pointed out, and Captain Lee mistakenly believed it to be still in force. In fact, however, instructions of early January 1864 had promulgated a ruling by the Secretary of War that the hospital tax should no longer be charged against the wages of employees who were subject to deductions for the contraband fund. (See above, doc. 69n.) According to Lee, the "colored hospital" would have to close if the tax were disallowed, "and much suffering will ensue, as no monies for its support are received from the contraband fund or from any other source." The petitioners themselves, Davis reported, "spoke of this Hospital as the only source from which they could obtain treatment and medicine, and expressed themselves as willing to contribute this amount towards its mainte- nance if necessary." Nevertheless, Davis acknowleged, the hospital tax had been neither voluntary nor authorized, and the $4,000 it raised per year was "a large sum to be expended . . . without any accountability whatever." Davis's report did not address the petitioners' questions about whether the deduction for the contraband fund was assessed on all military laborers or about the uses to which the fund was put. He concluded by dismissing their complaint about delayed and irregular payment of wages, arguing that the men were usually paid about the 20th of each month, "and, as this payment is regular it seems to be as convenient for the employee's as an earlier date, there being only one month between any two payments." (Captain Murray Davis to Colonel James A. Hardie, 3 Dec. 1864, D-8 1864, Letters Received, ser. 15, RG 159 [J-2].) No response to the petitioners or correspondence with Captain Lee on the subjects they addressed has been found in the letters-sent volumes of the inspector general, the quartermaster general, the Secretary of War, or the Adjutant General's Office.

83: Agent of the National Freedman's Relief Association of Washington to the Secretary of War

Washington D.C. [*December 27?, 1864*]

Sir I have visited and carried wood to over one hundred families of the Freedpeople in this city within the last ten days, and have found several families of women and children without food of any description. The Mothers confined with infants with four, six, and seven children in their care—their Husbands either in Gov't-Service or dead. Several other cases of the same kind must occur soon unless some provision is made for them.

I find all these families are paying from five to eight dollars pr. month for Shantee Rent, and where they own the Shantee, twenty-five and thirty dollars per. year for Ground Rent. It is this exorbitant Rent, that is starving these Freedwomen and children to death. If it is not paid monthly, the family are liable to be put out on the Street. Cases of this kind have occured quite lately. Is there any way of regulating Rents? Can these families who have no Husbands, or Fathers and no means of getting food be furnished Rations from the Gov't, at the expense of the Contraband or Freedmens Fund? Respectfully

ALS   Josephine S. Griffing

Josephine S. Griffing to Hon. E. M. Staunton, [27? Dec. 1864], "Josephine Griffing," Consolidated Correspondence File, ser. 225, Central Records, RG 92 [Y-72]. Griffing's letter was referred to the Quartermaster General's Office, which replied that it had "no authority to interfere with rents Charged by private individuals," that inquiries about the issue of rations should be addressed to the commissary general of subsistence, and that needy families of black government employees could be cared for at Freedman's Village, in Arlington, Virginia. (Col. J. J. Dana to Mrs. Josephine S. Griffing, 29 Dec. 1864, vol. 82, p. 102, Letters Sent, ser. 9, Central Records, RG 92 [Y-72].) On December 30, George E. H. Day, James I. Ferree, and William Slade, commissioners of the National Freedman's Relief Association, also addressed the Secretary of War about the "great destitution & much suffering" reported by Griffing. Could the association use a room in a quartermaster or commissary building, they asked, as well as surplus cooking utensils, "to prepare & dispense *soup* to the families of the Freed-men who are in a starving Condition?" "Most of the heads of these families," they noted, "are in the army while many others are absent in the Q. Masters service." Their request was denied on the grounds that government appropriations for room rent and for the purchase of cooking utensils could be used only for the military service. The contraband fund, on the other hand, "was created for the express purpose of affording relief to this class of persons," and "[e]xtensive arrangements" had been made at Arlington "to provide for the necessities of the destitute wives and children of colored employés of the Government." (George E. H. Day et al. to the Hon. Secretary of War, 30 Dec. 1864, "Freedmen," Consolidated Correspondence File, ser. 225, Central Records, RG 92 [Y-45]; Col. J. J. Dana to Messrs. Geo. E. H. Day et al., 10 Jan. 1865, vol. 82, pp. 219–20, Letters Sent, ser. 9, Central Records, RG 92 [Y-45].) At the end of January 1865, Griffing informed the quartermaster general that she had "visited over one thousand families of the women and children of the Freedmen—and find most of their Shanties very open and damp and often very little or no fire. A large number of these children sleep on the floor on rags or with no bed at all." Although she had distributed 1,000 blankets (provided by the War Department from the contraband fund), "still hundreds each day, crowd in, and around my house, asking that I come and see their condition, or, if possible give them a Blanket, —as they brought no bedding with them, have no means of getting any—and they, and their children suffer this cold weather exceedingly." Griffing requested another thousand blankets "for these suffering women and children, most of whose Husbands & Fathers are in the employ of Government, and with whom these women have little or no communication." The War Department approved both her request for the blankets and an earlier application for 200 cords of wood, all to be paid for from the contraband fund. By early March, she had distributed some 3,000 blankets and was applying for 500 more. (Josephine S. Griffing to Quarter Master General Charles Thomas, 30 Jan. 1865, Bvt. Brig. Genl. Chs. Thomas to Capt. J. M. Brown, 30 Jan. 1865, Capt. J. M. Brown to Major Gen. M. C. Meigs, 12 Mar. 1865, all filed as "Josephine Griffing," Consolidated Correspondence File, ser. 225, Central Records, RG 92 [Y-119].)

84: Colored Union Benevolent Association of Washington to the Congress

[*Washington, D.C. February 1865*]
To the Honorable The Senate and House of Representatives of the United States in Congress assembled.

Your petititioners whose names are hereunto signed, respectfully state that they have associated themselves together under the name of the Colored Union Benevolent Association of Washington City, for the purpose of charity and mutual assistance in time of need; that they have been so associated for some time past and have acquired by contributions a small property in real estate.

They respectfully ask the passage of an act by which they and their successors may be constituted and declared a body corporate and politic by the name and title above given and by said name to have perpetual succession with power to sue and be sued, to plead and be impleaded in any Court of the United States or of the District of Columbia of competent jurisdiction, to receive subscriptions, gifts and benefits, and to make such rules and by-laws as shall be deemed necessary and expedient for the government of the society and to alter the same from time to time in such mode as shall be prescribed therein.

Provided always, that such rules and by-laws shall be in no wise inconsistent with the Constitution of the United States or with the objects of the Society.

The objects of the society are hereby declared to be to provide for the care and comfort of such members as shall be sick, disabled or dependent and of the families of such members, in cases where the proper Officers of the Society shall deem it expedient; and also to provide for the decent interment of such persons as may die in membership of this Society or belonging to the families of such members.

They respectfully ask further that they be empowered to hold real estate or personal and mixed estate, by purchase gift or devise for the purposes of this Society and no other, and to lease, sell or convey such real estate or mixed estate or personal property as may be donated or devised to such Society and the leasing or sale of which is deemed conducive to the interests of said Society

And your petitioners will ever pray.

Gurden Snowden	Charles Wilson
Charles H Brown	Henry Brooks
James. H. Wright	Jhon Shoter.
Sandy Alexander	Joseph Shorter
Henry Loggens	

HDS

Gurden Snowden et al. to the Honorable The Senate and the House of Representatives, [Feb. 1865], 38A-H4, Senate Committee on the District of Columbia, Petitions & Memorials, ser. 582, 39th Congress, RG 46 [E-3]. Each signature is in a different handwriting. On March 3, 1865, Congress approved a law incorporating the Colored Union Benevolent Association. (*Statutes at Large*, vol. 13, pp. 535–36.)

85: Officers of a Mass Meeting of Alexandria, Virginia, Freedpeople to the Military Governor of Alexandria

Alexandria, Va., April 28ᵗʰ 1865.

General: We would respectfully represent to you, that, at several duly notified Mass Meetings of recent date, largely attended by the colored people of Alexandria, Va., for the discussion of various matters of interest to them, the subject matter of the following preamble and resolutions was considered, and on the 28ᵗʰ inst. were unanimously adopted, to wit:

Whereas, the Military Governor of this city, Brig. Gen[l] John P. Slough, has recently addressed the municipal authorities of the same, in a communication which contemplates the turning over to them of certain matters which have hitherto been prosecuted by him, some of them deeply affecting us as a people, especially the following article, viz:

"As the colored population is nearly one half of that of the city, and has large property interests in the same, I request that if possible, they may be protected in their persons and property by the municipal authorities—that all local laws that draw a distinction between the white and black races upon the subjects of punishments and testimony be repealed, and that justice and equal rights in respect to persons and property may be guaranteed to all"— Therefore:

Resolved, that we extend our kind and grateful regards to our Military Governor, General John P. Slough, for the generally quiet and peaceful manner in we have, under his administration, been permitted to pursue our labors, and enjoy our religious, educational and social privileges, in the midst of these exciting and perilous; and we earnestly desire that he may be retained in this command; and we would most respectfully request, that he will continue to exercise his jurisdiction over us, until his just and humane request made as above to the municipal authorities of Alexandria concerning us, shall not only be fully acceded to by them; but furthermore, until, in according to the late emancipation act,[1] (not to make reference at present to other matters which we desire to see accomplished) the laws of this state shall be so revised as to extend to us the same just and liberal principles of dealing as contemplated by our worthy Military Governor; or, in default of such organization, until some special court shall be established in the place of that now held open by him, and recognizing our equal rights, to which any cases of transfer or appeal affecting us must be taken if removed at all: In short, that there be no change in the direction indicated, until there be a uniform adoption of these principles of dealing by each and every court before which we shall, under any circumstances be liable to be brought.

Resolved, that, in case there should be any military change by which our present Military Governor should leave this command, we would respectfully request, that he should make known our views and desires in these matters, to such persons or authorities as the governing of our persons and affairs should be transmitted to, and afford us the benefit of his influence in securing to us all rights and privileges which we are entitled to, since justice is the only legitimate guaranty of order, which we most devoutly desire to maintain. And for his kind consideration in these timely and necessary provisions made on our behalf, as in duty bound, we will ever pray that he may have a happy and prosperous future career.

Resolved, that our committee on resolutions be authorized and requested to wait upon General Slough at an early day with a copy of them as adopted, and report at a meeting which shall be called for that purpose.

Rev. Samson White — Chairman
" Geo W Parker Secretary

Committee

Rev. Geo. W. Parker   Mr. Lewis Williams
"   Samson White   "   Charles Watson
"   Thomas   "   Henry Marshall
HLSr   Richard H Lyles.

Rev. Samson White and [Rev.] Geo. W. Parker to Brig. Genl. John P. Slough, 28 Apr. 1865, Letters Received, ser. 2053, Alexandria VA, Offices of Military Governor, RG 393 Pt. 4 [C-4784].

1 Presumably Congress's approval, on January 31, 1865, of the Thirteenth Amendment, which, upon its ratification the following December, abolished slavery throughout the United States.

86: Quartermaster General to the Secretary of War

Washington, D.C— May 8th. 1865 —

Sir: I have the honor to transmit a Copy of the report of Capt. J. M. Brown A.Q.M., in charge of the Bureau of Freedmen, Department of Washington, dated March 9th. 1865, covering a census, taken under his direction, of the Colored Refugees (not including house servants) in the District of Columbia; also of a Copy of his report, dated March 18th 1865, submitting a Census of the Colored population, at Alexandria, Virginia.

District of Columbia.

Total Number of Colored Persons   7.754.
Number over 12 Years: 4.395.
Number under 12 Years: 3.359.
               7.754.

There are about Freedmans Village 1.400, and, at Mason's Island, 500 in addition.

This does not include Colored persons employed by the

Quartermaster's Department, and living in the Mess. Houses of the United States, but does include those living in their own, or hired houses.

Alexandria, Virginia.

Total number of Persons   7.653 –
    Number over 12 Years: 4.585.
    Number under 12 Years: 3.068.
                   7.653.

It was intended only to take a Census of the Colored Refugees in Alexandria, but, from a misapprehension of the order of Capt. Brown, the whole Colored population was taken. However, the number of Blacks other than refugees is quite small, probably not more than 1.215, the number residing in Alexandria, at the beginning of the War.

Recapitulation.

Total in Distr. Columbia, over 12. Yrs. 4.395.	Under 12 Yrs. 3.359	Total	7.754
Total in Alexandria. Va., over 12. Yrs. 4.585.	Under 12 Yrs. 3.068.	Total	7.653
Aggregate: – 8.980.	6.427.	Total	15.407.

Add to this the estimated Number
at Freedman's Village 1.400, and
at Mason's Island   500,   1.900,
And we have an Aggregate of   17.307,
    Deducting the estimated number of others
than refugees in Alexandria at the beginning of the War   1.215,
             Total Refugees: 16.092.

Three thousand blankets have been distributed through Mrs. Griffing, to the destitute Colored families.

The reports of Capt. Brown exhibit some interesting facts, and show the beneficent character of the measures adopted by the Government for the welfare of the Colored people. I am Very Respectfully, Your obedient Servant,

HLS

M. C. Meigs

Brevt. Major General M. C. Meigs to Hon. Edwin M. Stanton, 8 May 1865, filed as Q-4 1865, Letters Received, ser. 15, Washington Hdqrs., RG 105 [A-10603]. Enclosed are copies of the reports of March 9 and 18 by Captain Joseph M. Brown, who had charge of the Department of Washington's Bureau of Freedmen, and of a report of May 8 by James I. Ferree, superintendent of contrabands in Alexandria; Meigs's letter consolidated figures from the three documents. Brown's report of March 9 cited "[m]uch difficulty . . . in obtaining from refugees . . . a correct statement of their number and condition," because they did not understand the purpose of the census; consequently, "recourse was had to their neighbors to procure the necessary information." Of 976 families visited by the provost marshals who served as enumerators, "2860 persons were found to be more or less in need of assistance," and "263. persons were found destitute." Brown's report of March 18, transmitting the results of Ferree's census, noted 39 destitute freedpeople and 183 "needing assistance," chiefly clothing. "All destitute Colored Persons unable to earn a livelihood now within the Ancient limits of the District of Columbia can be accomodated at 'Freedmens Village' and 'Masons Island,'" Brown concluded. He added, however, that "[t]here is at this time an urgent, and increasing demand for Laborers, men, Women, and children, and many persons in the District, reported as needing assistance, could maintain themselves comfortably by their own exertions."

87: Freedmen's Bureau Superintendent at Alexandria, Virginia, to the District of Columbia Freedmen's Bureau Assistant Commissioner

Alexandria, Va., Dec'r. 15. *1865.*

General: — I have the honor to transmit herewith duplicate reports of persons employed in this city during the early part of the year 1863 by the Provost Marshal — i.e. under his orders.

Months ago it was represented to this office by prominent gentlemen residing here and by many of those immediately interested that there were in the city and vicinity a large number of colored persons, men and women, who had labored faithfully for the government in various capacities early in 1863, who had been promised remuneration but had never been paid for their services. An enlisted man named Birge, whose present whereabouts is unknown, was, under the Provost Marshal of this city, placed in general charge of these colored laborers and their interests and it seems to have been through his ignorance and neglect that they were not properly reported for payment by the Qr. Mr. Dep't.

When these representations were made, Corporal John G. Richardson, 116th Company 2nd Batt. Vet. Res. Corps was on duty at this office and as he was the person who had succeeded the man Birge in charge of "Contraband Gov't Employees" in this city and who had in his keeping all of Birge's books and papers, this non-com'd. officer was directed to thoroughly investigate the matter and to prepare a roll of the colored people who had labored faithfully under official promise of pay without receiving it. — with the time each labored and amount due each at the usual rates.

No Quarter Master or other proper person could be found who could certify absolutely to the facts as is required on Form 15. Q.M. Dep't. but for convenience that form was used in making the roll. After many weeks continual work Corp. Richardson completed the enclosed reports, he did the work very carefully and I have since verified the rolls with much labor, they having been kept in this office several months for that purpose.

No one can certify to these reports so as to make them accord with the regulations of the Qr. Mr. Dep't. and no one can *swear* to their correctness in every particular but they have as before stated been slowly prepared, with the greatest possible care, taking all possible evidence in every case, and where there was any doubt, the benefit was given to the government, so it is believed that the reports as they now stand are correct in every particular.

It is *certain*, proven beyond a doubt, that every one of these persons labored faithfully in the various capacities stated, under control of the military authorities, for the time stated, have received no pay therefor, and whether by regulations or not, the sums set opposite their names respectively are *in equity* due to them from the United States.

In many cases they *claim* more than is named as due, but only that has been reported which has been *proven* by good testimony.

Accompanying these reports are several papers bearing upon the case of these parties.

Many of them are now in *great* need and I earnestly request that some measures may immediately be taken to secure to these poor people payment for their services on rolls corresponding to these reports. Very respectfully, your ob't, serv't

ALS   *Henry E. Alvord.*

Henry E. Alvord to Bvt. Brig. Gen. John Eaton, Jr., 15 Dec. 1865, enclosed in Bvt. Major General M. C. Meigs to Major General O. O. Howard, 5 Apr. 1866, Unregistered Letters Received, ser. 3853, Alexandria VA Supt., RG 105 [A-10015]. Alvord signed as "late Major, 2ᵈ Mass. Cav'y." Enclosed is an undated copy of a "Report of Persons and Articles employed and hired at Alexandria, Va." between late 1862 and April 1863. It listed seventy-one men (fifty-five laborers, thirteen grave-diggers, two whitewashers, and one cook) and four women (three seamstresses and one nurse); most were owed amounts between $10 and $40. Also enclosed are statements by several officers familiar with the labor performed by the claimants. Corporal John G. Richardson, who had prepared the labor rolls, explained that the freedpeople had worked "in Policing around the different Military Hospitals . . . digging Sinks, drains, &c — digging Graves in the Contraband Cemeteries here & at the Claremont Small Pox Hospital — Policing the Streets of this city — Sawing wood at the Public Offices &c &c." (Statement of Corp'l. John G. Richardson, [mid-Dec. 1865].) A former quartermaster at Alexandria stated that had he been authorized to do so, he would have paid the laborers "long ago — but the men being connected with & for Hospital purposes, it was deemed entirely out of my province." (Late Capt. T. K. Church to Mr. Henry E. Alvord, 18 Dec. 1865.)

According to file notations and endorsements, Alvord's letter and its accompanying documents were not received at the headquarters of the District of Columbia Freedmen's Bureau until early February 1866; on February 16, by which time Alvord had been replaced as bureau superintendent, they were returned to his successor, who, by an endorsement of February 23, sent them back with a notation that he knew nothing about them except that "persons . . . on the rolls are constantly calling at this office pressing their claims and from conversation with them and others it is my belief that the money is due them." The documents eventually reached the national headquarters of the Freedmen's Bureau, which evidently forwarded them to Quartermaster General Montgomery C. Meigs. After referring the matter to Colonel James G. C. Lee, formerly quartermaster of the Alexandria depot, Meigs returned the file to the Freedmen's Bureau on April 5, indicating in a covering letter that he did "not feel authorized to direct the payment of these claims." "The service does not appear to have been rendered under the direction of any officer of this Department," Meigs contended, "and it is doubtful whether they are entitled to pay from any Department." Colonel Lee believed the claimants to have been among the many "contrabands" who received government rations in Alexandria during late 1862 and early 1863. "These persons being idle, and thus supported by the government, it was deemed proper to make them work for their subsistence . . . and it was understood that the service was to be without pay, and the men were not borne upon any rolls." "Sustenance & freedom given at great cost by the United States," Meigs concluded, "has fully compensated such services." Other endorsements.

CHAPTER 3
Middle and East Tennessee and Northern Alabama

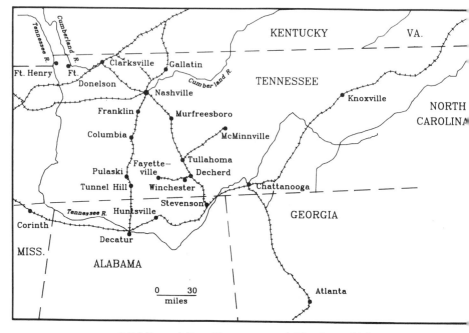

Middle and East Tennessee and Northern Alabama

3
Middle and East Tennessee and Northern Alabama

FREE LABOR developed in uneasy coexistence with slavery in middle and east Tennessee and in northern Alabama.[1] Beginning with the arrival of Northern troops in early 1862, slavery in middle Tennessee eroded under the pressure of military occupation and slave flight. The employment of thousands of black men as military laborers, both at the federal post of Nashville and with regiments in the field, hastened slavery's decline. By the fall of 1863, Union occupation of northern Alabama and east Tennessee had further expanded the domain of freedom. Widespread recruitment of black soldiers in the following months sealed the fate of the old order.

Until late in the war, however, federal authorities balked at inaugurating a system of free labor to replace chattel bondage. Loath to alienate slaveholding Tennesseans, many of whom were unionists, the Lincoln administration continued to recognize the legality of slavery long after it had ceased to function. The appointment of a prominent Tennessee unionist, Senator Andrew Johnson, as military governor reflected Lincoln's solicitude for loyal slave owners, as did the state's exemption from the Emancipation Proclamation. Union officers took pains to prevent the employment of black military laborers from precipitating an exodus of slaves who could not directly aid the war effort. They insisted that slave women and children, along with men unfit for military labor, be supported by their owners, not the government. In northern Alabama, by contrast, the Emancipation Proclamation de-

[1] This chapter concerns the wartime evolution of free labor in middle and east Tennessee and in the adjoining counties of northern Alabama, especially the Tennessee River Valley. Developments in west Tennessee and other parts of the Mississippi Valley are considered in *Freedom*, ser. 1, vol. 3: chap. 3. In the present essay, quotations and statements of fact that appear without footnotes are drawn from the documents included in the chapter. Pertinent secondary works include Stephen V. Ash, *Middle Tennessee Society Transformed, 1860–1870: War and Peace in the Upper South* (Baton Rouge, La., 1988), especially chaps. 4–7; John Cimprich, *Slavery's End in Tennessee, 1861–1865* (University, Ala., 1985), and "Slavery's End in East Tennessee," *East Tennessee Historical Society Publications* (1980–81): 78–88; Peter Maslowski, *Treason Must Be Made Odious: Military Occupation and Wartime Reconstruction in Nashville, Tennessee, 1862–65* (Millwood, N.Y., 1978), especially chap. 6; Armstead L. Robinson, " 'Worser dan Jeff Davis': The Coming of Free Labor during the Civil War, 1861–1865," in *Essays on the Postbellum Southern Economy*, ed. Thavolia Glymph and John J. Kushma (College Station, Tex., 1985), pp. 11–47.

clared slavery at an end, but there, too, military officials proved reluctant to take active steps to establish free labor. For many months after their counterparts elsewhere in the occupied Confederacy had established contraband camps and instituted plantation-leasing systems, authorities in middle and east Tennessee and in northern Alabama resisted such measures. Not until early 1864, with the enlistment of black soldiers in full swing, did they organize contraband camps and begin to supervise labor relations between former slaves and private employers.

In the absence of federal intervention, many former slaves negotiated free-labor arrangements on their own, sometimes with their former masters and mistresses, but often with other employers. Even after Union officers assumed some control over the transition to free labor, the particulars of working conditions and the amount of compensation usually resulted not from military decree but from bargaining between freedpeople and their hirers. A large proportion of the black people in middle and east Tennessee had entered the world of free labor well before February 1865, when the state's voters approved a constitutional amendment abolishing slavery.

Slavery was fundamental to the mixed agricultural economy of middle Tennessee and northern Alabama, which rested as much on grain and livestock production as on cotton and, in the northernmost counties, tobacco. The region's economic and political commitment to slavery had grown during the prosperous 1850s, as newly constructed railroads linked planters and farmers to markets North and South. A substantial proportion of white households owned slaves, generally in small numbers. Slave hiring – common in both countryside and town – gave many nonslaveholders a direct interest in slavery. Although a few estates with twenty or more slaves dotted the valleys of the Tennessee and Cumberland rivers, most slaves lived on farms, not plantations. In middle Tennessee and northern Alabama as a whole, slaves made up about two-fifths of the population, but in a few cotton-growing counties they outnumbered free people. By contrast, mountainous and thinly populated east Tennessee had few slaveholders, few slaves, and hardly any plantations. But even there, where slavery was least entrenched and unionist sentiment strongest, slaveholders wielded disproportionate political and social influence.[2]

Mindful of slavery's strength among Tennessee unionists, the Northern army entered the state committed to noninterference with the institution. General Don Carlos Buell's Army of the Ohio, which

[2] On slavery in middle and east Tennessee and in northern Alabama, see Ash, *Middle Tennessee Society Transformed*, chaps. 1–3; Chase C. Mooney, *Slavery in Tennessee* (Bloomington, Ind., 1957); James B. Sellers, *Slavery in Alabama* (University, Ala., 1950). Population figures are drawn from U.S., Census Office, 8th Census, *Population of the United States in 1860* (Washington, 1864), pp. 8, 466–67.

occupied Nashville in March 1862, marched under strict orders to exclude slaves from its lines unless they had worked for the Confederacy and were therefore entitled to freedom under the First Confiscation Act. As his troops secured substantial parts of middle Tennessee and northern Alabama during the spring and summer of 1862, Buell continued to insist that they refrain from harboring fugitive slaves and respect the property rights of slaveholders.[3]

Buell's policy notwithstanding, the Northern army posed a grave threat to slavery. Slaveholders met the threat by tightening discipline or removing their slaves from the war zone. The slaves, for their part, maneuvered to make the most of the possibilities opened by the invasion. Some bid for freedom by fleeing to the federals; others threatened to do so unless their owners reduced punishment and extended new privileges. A few slaves became free in fact, if not at law, when their owners simply abandoned efforts to maintain the old regime or offered new inducements to keep their laborers at work. After the Union occupation of Huntsville, Alabama, one former slave recalled, his owners "said they had nothing more to do with me, and for me to go to work for myself." Renting a tract of land, he farmed independently for the rest of the war. Another northern Alabama slaveholder directed his slaves "to go and gather the crops, – put so much in his crib, and so much in theirs," apportioning hogs and cattle in the same way.[4]

But for the majority of slaves, whose owners refused to concede the demise of slavery, flight to federal lines offered the best hope of sustenance, safety, and freedom. Accordingly, slaves in large numbers escaped to Union army camps. The runaways frequently brought valuable military information to the Yankees and nearly always evinced a willingness to work for their cause.[5] Many of the soldiers and officers welcomed the fugitive slaves. Because so many of the region's white men had either joined the Confederate army or fled at the invaders' approach, slaves were the chief – and often the only – source of labor in the occupied zone. Military employers put fugitive-slave men to work as teamsters, artisans, and laborers, and employed women as laundresses and hospital attendants. Officers engaged men and, occasionally, women as personal servants. Common soldiers gladly allowed "contrabands" to relieve them of camp chores and fatigue duty. Before long, hundreds of black people were working for the Union army and for individual officers and soldiers in middle Tennessee and northern Alabama. Declar-

---

[3] On the exclusion policy in middle Tennessee (and the Mississippi Valley generally), see *Freedom*, ser. 1, vol. 1: pp. 251–59, and docs. 83, 85, 200. For the First Confiscation Act, see *Statutes at Large*, vol. 12, p. 319.
[4] In addition to the relevant documents in this chapter, see testimony of B. P. McCrary, 7 Jan. 1878, claim of John Langford, Madison Co. AL case files, Approved Claims, ser. 732, Southern Claims Commission, 3rd Auditor, RG 217 [I-114].
[5] See, for example, *Freedom*, ser. 1, vol. 1: docs. 86, 91A–B, 99–100, 104.

ing that "[t]he negroes are our only friends," General Ormsby M. Mitchel, commander of a division of Buell's army in northern Alabama, maintained that without their assistance he could not have held his position.[6]

In time, authorities in Washington came to understand what the troops in the field already knew. In July 1862, the Second Confiscation Act and the Militia Act freed the slaves of disloyal owners, forbade the return of fugitive slaves to their claimants, authorized the widespread employment of black people as military laborers, and promised freedom to slaves so employed. In the wake of the new legislation, even commanders who had been devotees of exclusion felt bound to accept black men who could perform military labor.[7]

Military exigency sped their conversion. In August 1862, a Confederate invasion of Kentucky sent the Union army scrambling in pursuit. Forced to abandon northern Alabama and most of middle Tennessee, Buell left a small garrison at Nashville, charged with holding the city at all costs. He assigned his chief engineer, General James St. Clair Morton, to construct fortifications that could withstand attack by a superior force. Morton assembled an enormous labor force, detailing soldiers from the ranks, soliciting volunteers from the city's white residents, and gathering all the slave and free-black men he could find. Some of the black workers were inmates of the county jail, released by military order.[8] Others were refugees from the region evacuated by Buell's army. But most were impressed from the streets of Nashville and the fields of the surrounding countryside. Although Buell ordered that slaves belonging to loyal owners be taken only as a last resort, press gangs with quotas to fill were not fastidious.[9] By early September, some 1,300 black men were at work on the Nashville fortifications. After the military emergency subsided, most of the white laborers were released from service. However, work on the defenses continued for more than a year, with black men performing virtually all the unskilled labor.

The work was as arduous as it was unrelenting. The laborers were organized into large gangs, overseen by armed guards. They received meager issues of rations and clothing and often slept on bare ground. Such harsh conditions took their toll. About 800 workers died between September 1862 and November 1863. Of those who survived, few

---

[6] For Mitchel's statement, see *Freedom*, ser. 1, vol. 1: doc. 86n.

[7] For the laws, see *Statutes at Large*, vol. 12, pp. 589–92, 597–600. For an example of policy changes by field commanders, see *Freedom*, ser. 1, vol. 1: doc. 93.

[8] On the liberation and employment of the jailed black men, see James M. Hinton to His Excellency Hon. E. M. Stanton, 12 Jan. 1864, enclosing account of jail fees, [Aug. 1862?], H-112 1864, Letters Received, RG 107 [L-41].

[9] On Buell's impressment orders and their enforcement, see *Official Records*, ser. 1, vol. 16, pt. 2, pp. 222, 227–28, 255, 268–69, 287.

collected any pay. In December 1862, Morton reported that about 900 black men were employed upon the fortifications "at no wages," while only 50 – presumably men who had been free before the war – were receiving $7 per month.[10]

Nonpayment alienated the workers. Some remained for a time, especially slaves whose claim to freedom rested upon their labor for the army. But, as Morton discovered, even slaves needed "some inducement to prevent their being disgusted with such hard labour." He eventually promised that all who remained "faithfully" at work would receive $7 per month at the time of their discharge. But promises could not feed or clothe the workers' families. Months passed before Morton received funds with which to pay wages. Even then, he hesitated to compensate former slaves until his superiors decided "whether the money is due to them or to their owners."

In the meantime, the laborers and their dependents suffered. Disheartened by their treatment at the hands of Union authorities, a great number of men slipped the guard and "deserted." Some of them appropriated government tools as partial payment for their toil. After leaving Morton's service, they could easily find work with the quartermaster's department, with regiments in the field, or with private individuals in and near Nashville. Having learned a hard lesson about free labor, they refused to accept terms that did not explicitly acknowledge their right to compensation.

But free-labor employment with civilians, like that with the federal army, rested on a weak legal foundation. Slaveholding unionists, with Governor Johnson at their head, mobilized to keep emancipation at bay. President Lincoln gave them ample room to maneuver. In his preliminary Emancipation Proclamation of September 1862, he promised to exempt from the final proclamation any state that signified its loyalty by electing representatives to Congress before January 1, 1863. He dispatched a personal emissary to woo Tennesseans who wished "to avoid the unsatisfactory prospect" of emancipation and were willing "to have peace again upon the old terms, under the Constitution of the United States." Governor Johnson and Nashville-area unionists petitioned for special consideration, arguing that much as they wanted to hold elections, the proximity of Confederate forces made it unsafe to do so. Lincoln agreed, and Tennessee was spared the Emancipation Proclamation. The federal government remained obligated to uphold the property rights of loyal slaveholders in the state. As a result, many secessionist masters took false oaths of allegiance in order to retain their

---

[10] In addition to the relevant documents in this chapter, see "Return of Officers and Hired Men on Contingencies of Fortifications . . . for the Month of December, 1862," [Jan.? 1863], filed with M-4188, Letters Received, ser. 18, General Correspondence, Central Office, RG 77 [VV-1].

slaves, further entangling the question of emancipation with that of political loyalty.[11]

Important military developments, as well as political ones, marked the new year. Following a Union victory at the battle of Murfreesboro, General William S. Rosecrans's Army of the Cumberland reoccupied much of the territory in middle Tennessee that Buell had evacuated. After establishing a protective ring of posts around Nashville – including Fort Donelson, Murfreesboro, Franklin, Gallatin, and Clarksville – Rosecrans spent months methodically constructing fortifications, amassing supplies, and preparing his army to advance into rebel-controlled east Tennessee.

To perform his army's drudgery, Rosecrans wanted to substitute hired laborers – white or black – for soldiers. But he felt bound to respect the distinction between slaves who fled from secessionist owners (free by virtue of the confiscation acts) and those claimed by loyal owners (legally still slaves). In January 1863, he ordered his subordinates to employ, first, black men who were "free and roaming at large"; second, the slaves of disloyal owners; and finally, "when it becomes an absolute necessity," slaves whose owners were loyal. Free-black laborers and the slaves of disloyal owners were to receive wages, but payment for work performed by the slaves of loyal owners was to go to the owners.

Under Rosecrans's order, the Union army mobilized thousands of much-needed workers. Many ex-slave men volunteered to exchange military labor for freedom, including large numbers from east Tennessee, northern Alabama, and southern Kentucky, who evaded slave catchers and negotiated inhospitable terrain to reach Nashville and its outposts. Impressment parties dragooned hundreds more. Though the Army of the Cumberland controlled a relatively small amount of territory, its insatiable demand for laborers enabled physically vigorous black men far from the zone of occupation to find protection and work within its lines.

The wives, young children, and aged parents of such men had far more limited prospects. Hoping to steer clear of both logistical and political problems, Rosecrans sought to exclude slaves and former slaves who could not serve immediate military needs. Under a system of registration instituted in January 1863, all black people without proof of employment faced expulsion from Union camps. Most women were unwelcome. Rosecrans insisted upon "great caution in [their] employment . . . when it might lead to immorality"; only a few hospital attendants and laundresses managed to avoid ejection. In late March, as fugitive slaves of all ages and both sexes continued to seek refuge with

---

[11] For the preliminary and final emancipation proclamations, see *Statutes at Large*, vol. 12, pp. 1267–68. On the political maneuvering leading to Tennessee's exemption, see *Official Records*, ser. 3, vol. 2, pp. 675–76; Cimprich, *Slavery's End in Tennessee*, pp. 100–101. Johnson ordered elections in only two congressional districts, both in west Tennessee, and they were disrupted by Confederate raiders.

his army, Rosecrans further tightened restrictions by denying admission to any but able-bodied men.[12] Rather than return to their old homes, many of the women, children, and old people crowded into Nashville and the region's smaller towns, each of which soon housed a substantial population of black refugees.

Governor Johnson had authority to provide for the refugees, but he was no more inclined to do so than Rosecrans. In April 1863, Secretary of War Edwin M. Stanton empowered Johnson to seize property vacated by rebel owners, to lease out abandoned lands, and to "take in charge" all slaves of disloyal masters "and provide for their useful employment and subsistence." Stanton also directed Johnson to "take measures to secure employment and reasonable compensation" for former slaves who were not employed by the army. About the same time, President Lincoln urged Johnson to enlist black men as soldiers.[13] Had he been willing, the governor might have immediately established contraband camps and leased out plantations, much as Adjutant General Lorenzo Thomas was doing in the Mississippi Valley. But Johnson's reluctance to interfere with slavery made him averse to such measures, and months passed before he began to use the authority conferred upon him. In the meantime, the presence of the Union army in middle Tennessee disrupted slavery while opening only limited opportunities for free labor.

Such opportunities as appeared were shaped by the wartime devastation of the middle Tennessee countryside. Since early 1862, the contending armies had foraged liberally across the region, stripping plantations and farms of food and livestock. Civilian partisans of both belligerents waged a murderous guerrilla war. The upheaval in rural neighborhoods jeopardized the livelihood of all civilians—black and white, free and slave, loyal and rebel. Many planters and farmers abandoned their estates in despair, and others greatly reduced planting operations. Agriculturists, predicted one unionist in late 1862, would make "little or no effort at cultivating the lands in the spring, because they can count on nothing but robery by the one [army] & taking by force by the other." At times, the unsettled state of affairs benefited slaves and ex-slaves. Some landowners consigned their property to their slaves before departing for the Confederacy, promising the custodians a portion—in a few cases, the

---

[12]   In addition to the relevant documents in this chapter, see below, doc. 207A; Circular, Head Quars. Department of the Cumberland, 29 Mar. 1863, Letters & Reports Received by Headquarters, Staff Members, & Units, ser. 5700, 14th Army Corps, RG 393 Pt. 2 No. 371 [C-8769]; A.A.A.G. Henry Stone to Maj. Genl. Geo. H. Thomas, 10 Mar. 1863, Letters & Reports Received by Headquarters, Staff Members, & Units, ser. 5700, 14th Army Corps, RG 393 Pt. 2 No. 371 [C-8768].

[13]   *Official Records*, ser. 3, vol. 3, pp. 103, 122–23. Johnson's authority did not extend to west Tennessee. The recruitment and employment of former slaves in that region, along with those in adjoining parts of the Mississippi Valley, were administered by Adjutant General Lorenzo Thomas, whose instructions from the Secretary of War closely resembled those issued to Johnson. On Thomas's role in the Mississippi Valley, see *Freedom*, ser. 1, vol. 3: chap. 3.

entirety – of any crops raised in their absence. Other planters and farmers made unused land available to renters, including former slaves and free-black men and women. Landlords as well as tenants found such arrangements advantageous: Federal foraging parties were less likely to seize the property of black farmers – generally presumed to be adherents of the Union – than that of white farmers of dubious loyalty. As one white Tennessean recalled, a black tenant "could protect the place . . . better than a white man, and . . . a negro's crop would be left alone when a rich white man's would not."[14]

Black people who owned personal property were better positioned to become renters than their propertyless compatriots. Some of them had purchased livestock and farm implements before the war, and others – fortunate enough to be compensated for labor with the Union army or private employers – parlayed their earnings into the means with which to work for themselves. Possession of a mule and a few tools enabled many a former slave to farm on his own.

But wartime events could limit, as well as expand, opportunities for freedpeople to attain a measure of economic independence. Confederate raiders and foraging parties thought nothing of seizing the provisions, livestock, or crops of black farmers. And military circumstances sometimes required Union forces to make requisitions on the loyal as well as the disloyal. For black squatters and tenants, whose modest stock of productive property and small reserves of food were all that stood between them and starvation, such appropriations spelled disaster. Numerous black men and women gained property during the war only to lose it again, sometimes several times in succession.

Even in areas remote from Union lines, the exodus of slave men, often accompanied by their families, unsettled slavery and disrupted the agricultural economy. Tennessee slaves who did not flee to federal posts exploited their owners' fear that they might do so. They pressed for freedom on their home ground, demanding new working and living arrangements. Faced with the likelihood of losing their laborers, many slaveholders capitulated. They induced their nominal slaves to remain at home by exempting them from onerous tasks and punishments, increasing the size of their gardens and the time available to work them, or promising payments of cash or a share of the crop.

As informal free-labor agreements took form amid legal slavery, the options available to ex-slaves and free blacks increased. Many military laborers, especially those who were unable to support their families because of unpaid wages, quit the quartermasters and engineers and

---

[14] In addition to the relevant documents in this chapter, see W. B. Campbell to Hon. Horace Maynard, 25 Dec. 1862, filed as M-218 1862, Letters Received Irregular, RG 107 [L-333]; testimony of Minas L. Fletcher, 27 Aug. 1877, Claim of Edd Peters, Rutherford Co. TN case files, Approved Claims, ser. 732, Southern Claims Commission, 3rd Auditor, RG 217 [I-242]; *Freedom*, ser. 1, vol. 1: doc. 111; Ash, *Middle Tennessee Society Transformed*, chap. 5.

went to work for civilian employers who were ready to pay cash. People who possessed skills or property could prosper on their own, especially in Nashville, whose economy boomed under Union occupation. Artisans commanded premium wages, and virtually any man with a horse and wagon could establish himself as a drayman.

With prospects for independent enterprise or remunerative employment improving, black workers in Tennessee learned to play military and civilian employers against each other, threatening alternately to flee to or from the federal army in search of more desirable work arrangements. Large numbers of former slaves shunned military employment altogether. Before long, desertion by black laborers had slowed the progress of essential projects. In March 1863, when Lieutenant George Burroughs, principal engineer of the Nashville fortifications, called upon the city's chief of police to impress black men, the latter official hesitated lest he harm "the Interest of Persens engaged in Planting."[15] Military employers in middle Tennessee came to realize that they were losing the competition for the labor of black men, in part because of their record of harsh treatment and nonpayment. Hoping to reverse this trend, General Rosecrans implored the War Department to expedite payment of the still-unremunerated workers at Nashville, noting that, "from want, say, nine-tenths have deserted, and I think justly."

Rosecrans's solicitude reflected his reliance on black laborers – a reliance that deepened after June 1863, when his army commenced a campaign that would eventually lead it into east Tennessee. In August, a Union quartermaster estimated that more than 10,000 black people were performing military labor in the Department of the Cumberland: 800 at the quartermaster's depot in Nashville, 5,000 in the field as teamsters and laborers, 3,700 as cooks and servants, and 1,000 with the engineer's department. The numbers increased in the months that followed, as the Nashville depot became the chief supply center for the Northern armies operating in Tennessee, northern Alabama, and northern Georgia.[16] Hundreds more worked for private contractors, cutting cordwood and crossties for the railroads that conveyed troops and materiel to the front.

For both military and political reasons, Governor Johnson preferred that black men work for the Union rather than fight for it. Convinced by late 1863 that slavery's demise was inevitable, Johnson nevertheless declined to champion the enlistment of black men lest he alienate proslavery unionists and splinter his fragile political coalition. Freedmen, he contended, could best aid the war effort by driving teams and digging trenches. Moreover, wage-work, whether for the army or for

---

[15] *Freedom*, ser. 1, vol. 1: doc. 103.
[16] In early 1864, the Nashville depot employed a total of 15,700 people, only 1,300 fewer than the city's entire population in 1860. (*Official Records*, ser. 1, vol. 52, pt. 1, pp. 680–89; U.S., 8th Census, *Population of the United States in 1860*, p. 467.)

private individuals, would "give them an idea of contracts" and prepare them "to take care of themselves" after the war; by contrast, he argued, "a soldier's life is a lazy one." Only a few companies of black soldiers were recruited under Johnson's auspices. They consisted chiefly of engineer employees and other military laborers, who were mustered under instructions by General Rosecrans to enlist them in order to obtain payment for their labor.[17]

For former slaves physically unsuited to military labor, Johnson viewed private wage employment as the best road to freedom. He instructed such freedpeople to hire themselves to their former owners or other employers, who must "pay them for their work." Indeed, he was doing exactly that with his own former slaves. At the same time, he insisted that freedpeople who were unable to work should be supported by their titular owners, not by the government. Allowing ex-slave workers to hire themselves out while saddling owners with the support of nonworkers, Johnson believed, would cause slaveholders to see slavery as a burden that could be lifted by emancipation. He therefore discouraged the establishment of contraband camps or the settlement of freedpeople on abandoned plantations. Opposed in principle to using public resources for the relief of former slaves, Johnson also worried about the reaction of his political constituency if he permitted destitute black people to occupy government-controlled land while denying the same privilege to destitute white people.

By September 1863, when Union forces occupied Chattanooga and Knoxville, the War Department had grown impatient with the glacial pace of recruitment in Tennessee. Secretary of War Stanton dispatched Major George L. Stearns, a well-known abolitionist, to Nashville to take charge of enlisting black men. Stearns and his assistant, Captain Reuben D. Mussey, established recruitment rendezvous at Nashville, Clarksville, Gallatin, and Pulaski in middle Tennessee; Chattanooga and Knoxville in east Tennessee; and Stevenson in northern Alabama. In the final months of 1863, Union victories cleared east Tennessee of armed rebels, reestablished federal control in northern Alabama, and opened the way for full-scale recruitment. By the end of the war, about two-fifths of the black men of military age in Tennessee had joined the Union army. Enlistment probably claimed a similar proportion in northern Alabama.[18]

[17] In addition to the relevant documents in this chapter, see *Freedom*, ser. 2: doc. 63. On the black soldiers recruited under Johnson before the fall of 1863, see *Official Records*, ser. 3, vol. 4, pp. 762–74. On recruitment in middle and east Tennessee more generally, see *Freedom*, ser. 2: chap. 3, especially doc. 63.

[18] On Stearns and the expansion of black recruitment, see *Freedom*, ser 2: chap. 3, and doc. 35. Stearns remained in Tennessee only a few months; by the end of 1863, Mussey had been named acting commissioner of the organization of black troops in the Department of the Cumberland. In Tennessee as a whole, about 20,000 black soldiers enlisted. Although the roughly 5,000 soldiers credited to Alabama accounted for only 6 percent of the state's black men of military

Because each black man who enlisted diminished the number available to military and civilian employers, recruitment intensified the competition for black workers. To the chagrin of quartermasters and engineering officers, army recruiters enjoyed particular success among military laborers. Within a few months after recruitment commenced at Knoxville, the post commander was worried that there were "not negroes enough . . . to drive the teams and do the work about the city." About the same time, General Morton, now in charge of fortifications throughout the Department of the Cumberland, found himself unable to obtain more than a small fraction of the 5,000 laborers needed to complete necessary work. Only a "trifling" number of men were available, and they were unwilling to labor without assurance of compensation.[19]

Difficulties in attracting and retaining military laborers goaded officials in the field and in Washington to action. In November 1863, the War Department finally settled a long-mooted question by authorizing the engineer department to pay wages directly to ex-slave laborers instead of to their owners. Recognizing that "it is becoming day by day more difficult to procure labor" in middle and east Tennessee, Quartermaster General Montgomery C. Meigs authorized his subordinates to increase wages. By February 1864, black laborers employed by quartermasters in Nashville were receiving $25 per month, teamsters from $25 to $30, and woodcutters $30.[20]

Monetary inducements were not the only means by which military employers obtained laborers. They showed no hesitation in using force as a last resort—and often as a first resort. Any officer in need of black laborers, protested Major Stearns, "impresses on his own authority." During a typical episode, Union troops in Nashville dragged black men from their homes and workplaces, disregarding exemptions given to those who had voluntarily performed military labor and even hauling in a few soldiers. But despite the addition of impressed laborers, military employers remained chronically short-handed.[21]

The shortage was especially acute in Nashville. Unable to hire local civilians except at premium wages or to attract laborers from the North

age, they were drawn disproportionately from the Union-occupied northern counties. (*Freedom*, ser. 2: p. 12.)

[19] Major J. T. Anderson to Major Geo. L. Stearns, 17 Dec. 1863, vol. 6/4 DO, p. 59, Letters Sent, ser. 3504, Dept. of the OH, RG 393 Pt. 1 [C-4622]; Brig. Genl. J. St. C. Morton to Major J. C. Woodruff, 25 Nov. 1863, M-4499, Letters Received, ser. 18, Central Office, RG 77 [VV-69].

[20] On wage increases in the quartermaster's department, see *Official Records*, ser. 1, vol. 32, pt. 2, pp. 437–39; S. & S. Qr. Mr. J. L. Donaldson to Maj. Genl. G. H. Thomas, 26 Feb. 1864, enclosing General Orders, No. 6, Senior and Supervising Quartermaster's Office, Department of the Cumberland, 24 Jan. 1864, filed as A-286 1864, Letters Received from the Adjutant General, ser. 28, Central Records, RG 92 [Y-652].

[21] In addition to the relevant documents in this chapter, see *Freedom*, ser. 2: docs. 64–66.

on any terms, Colonel James L. Donaldson, the senior quartermaster at the post, put increasing numbers of black soldiers to work. Not only did they cost the government far less than civilian employees, but they were also subject to military discipline and therefore less likely to desert. Further blurring the line between soldiers and laborers, in February 1864 Adjutant General Lorenzo Thomas authorized the formation of "invalid regiments" at Nashville and Chattanooga, composed of men unfit for field service but capable of fatigue labor and garrison duty. If black soldiers routinely worked as military laborers, laborers sometimes served as "quasi soldiers." In early 1864, after a reduction of Nashville's garrison left government warehouses and shops vulnerable to Confederate attack, Colonel Donaldson armed and drilled several thousand civilian employees for local defense.[22]

Slaveholders and other civilian employers had to counter the attractions of military labor and armed service if they hoped to retain their workers. Many black men seized the opportunity to negotiate favorable terms of employment – or to renegotiate even better terms. Planters and farmers who depended on black laborers increasingly had to accept the "accomplished and immutable fact" of emancipation.[23] Slaveholders in middle Tennessee spoke openly of ways to "[secure] the services of there slaves – or in other words to conciliate & prevent them from running away." Unable to command workers by force, they offered compensation in money, a share of the crop, or access to land for independent cultivation. Farmers in the vicinity of Murfreesboro proffered various terms: subsistence plus 10 cents per pound of cotton produced, cash wages of $70 per year, vague promises that their laborers would be made "as well off as those employed by the Goverment. or others." Unionist masters who refused on principle to hire their slaves or whose offers fell short of the slaves' expectations might still salvage something from their investment in bondage by escorting the men to a recruitment office and applying for the $300 bounty promised to loyal owners of slave enlistees.[24]

Black enlistment and the spread of informal free-labor arrangements tipped the political balance in favor of emancipation. Shortly after beginning his work in middle Tennessee, Major Stearns discerned "a strong and defiant Anti-Slavery Sentiment" taking hold among prominent slaveholders who had concluded that abolition was not only unavoidable but desirable.[25] In December 1863, Governor Johnson ex-

---

[22] On the invalid regiments, see *Official Records*, ser. 3, vol. 4, p. 765. On the military organization of quartermaster employees, see *Official Records*, ser. 1, vol. 52, pt. 1, pp. 630–32.

[23] *Freedom*, ser. 2: doc. 65.

[24] On the bounty policy and owners applying to have their slaves enlisted under it, see, in addition to the relevant documents in this chapter, *Freedom*, ser. 1, vol. 1: doc. 117; *Freedom*, ser. 2: docs. 64n., 66.

[25] *Freedom*, ser. 2: docs. 63–64, 67.

pressed confidence that the question of "emancipating the negroes in Tennessee" was "already settled." President Lincoln encouraged him and other unionists to take the final step, legal abolition of slavery. Lincoln's Proclamation of Amnesty and Reconstruction, issued that same month, made emancipation a precondition for the readmission of seceded states into the Union.[26]

The enemies of emancipation fought a bitter rear-guard battle. Rather than bend with the winds of change, some masters inflicted harsh punishment upon slaves who attempted to enlist in the army or hire themselves out. Slaveholders in the Clarksville area instituted a "patrolling system" to drive would-be soldiers "back under the *lash and ball* to their homes." Near Knoxville, the owner of a slave who contracted frostbite in a failed attempt to escape had the man's feet amputated; the episode, a Union officer believed, was a ghastly object lesson intended "to terrify and intimidate the colored people."[27]

While the diehards battled with brutal desperation, lukewarm friends of freedom seemed reluctant to take the initiative. Even slaveholders who professed to accept emancipation, Stearns reported, cherished "a lingering hope that by some hocus-pocus things will get back to the old state." So believing, "the master has not made up his mind to hire his slave, & the slave finds that it is very difficult to work for anybody who will pay him." Because slavery still existed at law, free labor had no formal underpinning.

As a result, nascent free-labor arrangements were extremely volatile. Fundamental antagonism lay beneath any veneer of mutual accord, and changing circumstances might lead either party to renounce the original agreement. Slaves-turned-employees maneuvered to gain greater independence and better compensation from their masters-turned-employers, who sought to reclaim authority they had only reluctantly surrendered. Although at times new negotiations ensued and new terms were struck, the contradictory demands often proved irreconcilable. Then, former slaves might flee their employer as they had earlier fled the slave master; former owners might lash out with abuse reminiscent of the old regime or forcibly evict laborers and their families.

Struggling for advantage, former slaves and former owners selectively appropriated the usages of free labor, embracing those that suited them and rejecting those that did not. Many freedpeople continued to reside with their erstwhile masters, demanding customary provisions while working for their own benefit. Slaves in the Nashville area, noted a Union general, "leave their homes to work for themselves boarding and lodging with their Masters defiantly asserting their right to do so." Exasperated owners begged Union officers to take custody of slaves who

---

[26] For the proclamation, see *Statutes at Large*, vol. 13, pp. 737–39.

[27] Col. Wm. B. Gaw to Colonel A. A. Smith, 1 Feb. 1864, Letters Sent, 16th USCI, Regimental Books & Papers USCT, RG 94 [G-300]; *Freedom*, ser. 1, vol. 1: doc. 114.

would no longer do their bidding. For their part, onetime slaveholders were happy to jettison the old obligation to feed and clothe their workers, but reluctant to fulfill their new obligation to pay wages.[28]

Federal authorities occasionally intervened in disputes arising from the collapse of slavery and the emergence of free labor, but only on an ad hoc basis. General Rosecrans provided little guidance. In July 1863, he directed subordinate officers, when "justice and humanity" demanded, to "prevent injustice and disorders whether coming from Masters or their Servants; requiring each to perform their legal duties." Aside from the problems inherent in leaving such judgments to the discretion of individual officers, Rosecrans's instructions begged the question of just what the respective parties' "legal duties" were.

Rosecrans's subordinates interpreted his orders according to their own understanding of proper labor relations and the role of military authority. General Eleazer A. Paine, commander of the post of Gallatin, welcomed the chance to speed the development of wage labor. In the spring of 1863, when the trustees of one plantation requested that he compel its slaves to work, he agreed to do so – but not in the way they had in mind. Paine insisted that the slaves be paid wages and that the overseer be subject to military authority. Evidently satisfied with this arrangement, the laborers produced enough to feed themselves, pay their wages, and return a profit to the estate. Under General Grenville M. Dodge, commander of a wing of the 16th Army Corps, military supervision of labor included the establishment of contraband camps for unemployed freedpeople. When he set up headquarters at Pulaski, Tennessee, in late 1863, Dodge found the area crowded with fugitive slaves, principally women and children. Familiar with the administration of contraband camps by virtue of previous duty at Corinth, Mississippi, Dodge appropriated the abandoned estate of a Confederate planter, placed it under the control of a superintendent of contrabands, and put the freedpeople to work harvesting cotton and corn.

Not all Union commanders so eagerly assented to free-labor arrangements. One who did not was General Lovell H. Rousseau, a Kentuckian who commanded the District of Nashville. Rousseau lamented slavery's dissolution and recoiled at reports of former slaves who "stroll[ed] over the country uncontrolled" and of "wagon loads of Negro women and children" brought into Nashville by Union soldiers and thrown upon the charity of the federal government. He repeatedly remanded fugitive slaves to the custody of their owners, citing the supposed "willingness" of the fugitive to return. Rousseau's policies emboldened proslavery soldiers and officers. Pickets sometimes refused runaway slaves admittance into Nashville, and a few soldiers did unofficial duty as slave catchers.[29]

[28] In addition to the relevant documents in this chapter, see *Freedom*, ser. 1, vol. 1: doc. 113.
[29] In addition to the relevant documents in this chapter, see *Freedom*, ser. 1, vol. 1: docs. 116–17, 120; F. Copeland to Major Geo. L. Stearns, 5 Mar. 1864, and Charles Follen to Major

Rousseau's respect for slavery put him at odds with General Paine, who was his subordinate. Their conflict came to a head in January 1864, after Paine informed landowners near Gallatin that he expected them to hire black workers for wages, and began distributing printed contract forms for the purpose. Rejecting Paine's assumption "that there should be none but free labor," Rousseau complained to General George H. Thomas, who had succeeded Rosecrans as commander of the Department of the Cumberland. Agreeing with Rousseau that Paine had exceeded his authority, Thomas ordered Paine and other officers to "have as little to do with the negro as possible, it being considered best to let the Masters and Slaves settle their own affairs without Military interference."

By that time, however, the inadequacy of such instructions had become apparent to "masters," to "slaves," and to most federal officials. With the slave code unenforceable and no legal underpinnings for a free-labor economy, efforts to reestablish production on the war-torn plantations and farms of middle Tennessee were hampered by uncertainty. Fear of capture deterred many fugitive slaves from searching for more advantageous employment. Laws that prohibited hiring a slave without the owner's consent deterred would-be employers, including white smallholders, from bidding for the services of black workers. Prospective employers were "averse" to hiring black men and women, explained a Union officer, "first because [the laborers] are the former slaves of their neighbors and second because they have no assurance that they can retain them."

As the 1864 planting season neared, increasing numbers of former slaveholders welcomed military sponsorship of free labor. Many landowners, General Dodge noted, wanted the government to adopt some "settled plan" for "employing such negroes as the Government does not require." Anyone who sought the labor of black workers, he reasoned, would have no choice but to conform to the scheme, if only "for Self protection, – as negroes will go where they can get paid for their labor – and Government will protect them in doing it."

Political considerations also favored military intervention. To encourage latent unionism, Lincoln's amnesty proclamation allowed repentant Confederates to retain their property, cultivate their estates, and participate in the formation of loyal state governments – provided they accept emancipation. Army officers in middle and east Tennessee had a large role to play in advancing that policy. In addition to protecting occupied areas from rebel attack and aiding unionist political movements, they

Geo. L. Stearns, 4 Mar. 1864, both enclosed in George L. Stearns to Major General George H. Thomas, 6 Mar. 1864, S-883 1864, Letters Received, ser. 925, Dept. of the Cumberland, RG 393 Pt. 1 [C-20]; U.S., Senate, "Report of the Commissioners of Investigation of Colored Refugees in Kentucky, Tennessee, and Alabama," *Senate Executive Documents*, 38th Cong., 2nd sess., No. 28, pp. 15–18.

could also help farmers and planters obtain laborers and keep them at work through the agricultural year. But that could not be accomplished without guaranteeing freedom, compensation, and decent treatment to the former slaves.

Adjutant General Lorenzo Thomas understood as much. In February 1864, he extended to the Department of the Cumberland a more modest version of the system of recruitment, relief, and agricultural labor that he had instituted along the Mississippi River the previous year.[30] Thomas directed that a contraband camp be established at Nashville and sanctioned similar facilities that had developed informally since the previous fall. The camps, he emphasized, were to be temporary refuges, whose residents would be "required to perform such labor, as may be suited to their several conditions," either for the army or for civilian employers. Thomas ordered the appointment of a military superintendent for each camp, whose duties included hiring freedpeople to civilians under annual contracts, at wages of at least $7 per month for men and $5 for women. If private employers did not hire all the available ex-slaves, commanders could lease abandoned estates to loyal citizens who would employ them, or designate particular plantations "to be worked by the negroes" under military supervision.

Thomas's order put free-labor arrangements on a sounder basis. Although he acknowledged the legality of slavery in Tennessee, his policy sanctioned existing private contracts and promised to enforce them. It signaled that wage-labor relations were no longer anomalies but instead the standard. Military oversight of such arrangements, asserted a Union officer, marked a "starting point in the great labor question" by establishing the freedpeople's "right to deal, and be dealt with."

Federal authorities, both military and civilian, worked assiduously to convince former slaveholders and other prospective employers to accept the new dispensation. Army officers at every level promised protection to landowners who hired black workers, pledging to exempt their livestock and crops from seizure and their laborers from impressment. Agents of the Treasury Department, who entered middle Tennessee and northern Alabama during early 1864, permitted such employers to purchase plantation supplies and market their crops. Planters in northern Alabama, reported one treasury agent, began "to awaken to the necessity of *hireing their former slaves*."[31] Expediency, conviction, or a combination of the two pushed former slaveholders throughout the region to the same conclusion.

[30] On Thomas's system in the Mississippi Valley, see *Freedom*, ser. 1, vol. 3: chap. 3.
[31] For guarantees of military protection, see, for example, *Official Records*, ser. 1, vol. 32, pt. 2, pp. 470, 477. On the Treasury agents, see Z. S. Spaulding to Wm. P. Mellen Esq., 1 Apr. 1864, Letters Received from Assistant Special Agents, Records of the General Agent, RG 366 [Q-166].

With resident landowners eager to hire ex-slave laborers, military and treasury officials saw little need to institute other arrangements for employing them. Plantation leasing never assumed large proportions, in part because Northern investors bypassed middle Tennessee and northern Alabama for more lucrative prospects in the Mississippi Valley. By April 1864, the treasury agent for Giles County, Tennessee, and Limestone County, Alabama, had rented out only ten estates, and the agent for Rutherford County, Tennessee, just sixteen. All told, plantation leasing embraced a few dozen estates and perhaps 1,000 workers.[32]

By contrast, thousands of former slaves took refuge at the contraband camps. In addition to soldiers' families and refugees from slavery, growing numbers of people arrived at the camps as outcasts from the emerging free-labor order who had nowhere else to turn when former owners or other employers exercised their new freedom to discharge unwanted hands. Freedpeople who could do little or no work were typically the first to go, but as the 1864 harvest came to an end, farmers and planters also evicted able-bodied laborers to avoid paying them for their work or supporting them during the winter. Many employers broadened the range of offenses punishable by discharge to include any real or imagined challenge to their own authority. "[W]henever a negro shows a disposition to send his children to school or to favor the *Yankees* the Master will drive him off," reported the officer in charge of a contraband camp near Gallatin. Forced to fend for themselves with few resources but their capacity to work, such freedpeople had little choice but to hire on to another employer or head for the nearest contraband camp.

Taking their cue from Adjutant General Thomas, superintendents of the camps enlisted all the men suitable for armed service and hired out other able-bodied former slaves as fast as employers presented themselves. But they found few takers for elderly people, the sick and infirm, or women with young children. As a result, the contraband camps filled with those freedpeople least able to support themselves and most in need of assistance. As of September 1864, the camps in middle Tennessee and northern Alabama housed some 4,700 former slaves: 480

---

[32] Of the sixteen tracts of land leased out in Rutherford County, Tennessee, eight had 60 acres or less under cultivation; only one had more than 100 acres. Of the twelve parcels leased out by the Treasury Department's assistant special agent at Huntsville, Alabama, eight had 140 or fewer cultivated acres; the largest, 1,000. The Huntsville agent reported that 160 freedpeople were employed by the lessees and 292 (presumably the employees' dependents) were "subsisted" by them. ("List of Abandoned Plantations in Rutherford County, Tenn. rented by Brig. Gen. Van Cleve," [Feb.? 1864], #21677, and "Tabular Statement, showing the number of abandoned plantations, leased . . . ," 1 May 1864, enclosed in C. W. Hobart to Wm. P. Mellen Esqr., 1 May 1864, #21675, Case Files of Claims for Cotton & Captured & Abandoned Property, ser. 370, Miscellaneous Division, RG 56 [X-521].)

at Nashville, 1,100 at Clarksville, 270 at Gallatin, 225 at Huntsville, and 2,600 near Decatur, Alabama.[33]

Conditions in the contraband camps discouraged a lengthy stay. At the Nashville camp, the freedpeople lived in cast-off army tents unshaded from the summer sun. In June 1864, commissioners sent by the War Department to investigate the treatment of "colored refugees" in Tennessee and Alabama found the site "wholly destitute of anything tending to the reasonable comfort of its most unfortunate inmates." "[W]e have never," they declared, "witnessed an aggregate of wretchedness and misery equal to that we were here called to look upon." The officers in charge of the camp did nothing to ameliorate conditions; those not actively corrupt were incompetent, giving their work "mere eye-service." Although some of the offending officers were removed, the Nashville camp remained notorious. A visiting black soldier witnessed a grisly routine in which the corpses of as many as thirty people per day were "carried out by wagon loads, without coffins, & thrown promiscuously, like brutes, into a trench." Few former slaves willingly tarried in such surroundings.[34]

Nevertheless, access to even the most squalid contraband camp abetted the freedpeople in their struggle to secure favorable terms of labor. The threat of flight to a camp became a bargaining chip as they negotiated with old owners or new employers. An assessment by the War Department commissioners of the significance of the Clarksville camp held true for the others as well: "The master knows his slave has the power to leave him and to reach this camp . . . and consequently the tasks and punishments he has been accustomed to exact, or to inflict, are greatly reduced and ameliorated."[35]

The experience of freedpeople in the contraband camps at Pulaski and Tunnel Hill, Tennessee, demonstrated the vagaries of life within the settlements. The two camps, supervised by Lieutenant J. W. Harris, began the 1864 crop season with the goal of becoming self-sustaining. Residents cultivated cotton, corn, and vegetables and performed nonagricultural labor in a sawmill, grist mill, and blacksmith shop. The obstacles to self-support were considerable. Because Harris hired many of the able-bodied residents to private employers, the camps' own work force consisted chiefly of women, children, and old men. The only draft animals were worn-out horses and mules "condemned" by army quartermasters. Nonetheless, as the harvest approached Harris confidently pre-

---

[33] In addition to the relevant documents in this chapter, see Col. R. W. Barnard to Col. R. D. Mussey, 25 Sept. 1864, enclosed in Col. R. D. Mussey to Major C. W. Foster, 10 Oct. 1864, M-750 1864, Letters Received, ser. 360, Colored Troops Division, RG 94 [B-48].

[34] In addition to the relevant documents in this chapter, see "Report of the Commissioners of Investigation of Colored Refugees," pp. 3–5.

[35] In addition to the relevant documents in this chapter, see "Report of the Commissioners of Investigation of Colored Refugees," p. 10.

dicted that his charges would produce enough to feed themselves plus a profitable surplus for the government.[36]

By the end of the year, however, Confederate incursions had sabotaged the freedpeople's prospects for self-sufficiency. In late September, rebel cavalry overran and burned the camp at Tunnel Hill. In December, General John Bell Hood's advance on Nashville caused Union forces to evacuate the southern part of middle Tennessee, including Pulaski. The hapless residents of the two contraband camps had to abandon crops that would have seen them through the winter. Many of them scattered into the countryside, while others embarked on a grueling march to Nashville, where military authorities crowded them into a vermin-infested army barracks. Debilitated and neglected, dozens died.

Meanwhile, the Union troops who mobilized to repulse Hood impressed draft animals from freedpeople in Nashville and the nearby countryside. They also dragooned black men to shore up the fortifications — sometimes the very men whose horses and mules had been seized. In mid-December, at the battle of Nashville, Hood's desperate campaign reached a disastrous conclusion. The subsequent disintegration of his army as it retreated into Alabama wreaked further havoc upon the lives of black working people. Both the defeated rebels and the pursuing Yankees expropriated livestock and food from the black farmers they encountered along the way. Hood's campaign once again demonstrated the disruptive effects of military conflict upon free-labor arrangements, whether Union-sponsored or privately negotiated.

But if the war sometimes slowed the progress of free labor, it could never fully impede it. Former slaves had too much at stake in the new order to accept a return to the old, and, increasingly, so did former slaveholders and other employers of black workers. As free labor gained federal sanction in middle and east Tennessee, the antislavery cause won new adherents. Black people, especially in Nashville, lent their numbers and voices to the movement for emancipation, sometimes taking to the streets in its support. By the fall of 1864, the momentum had become irresistible. In September, Governor Johnson elevated all black Tennesseans to the status of antebellum free Negroes, whose freedom was compromised by numerous legal disabilities, including disfranchisement and exclusion from serving on juries or testifying against white defendants. In January 1865, a state convention approved a constitutional amendment abolishing slavery, which voters ratified the following month.[37]

---

[36] In addition to the relevant documents in this chapter, see Lt. J. W. Harris to Col. J. B. Weaver, 10 May 1864, filed with H-32 1864, Letters Received by Adjutant General L. Thomas, ser. 363, Colored Troops Division, RG 94 [V-80]; Col. R. D. Mussey to Capt. O. P. Brown, 31 Oct. 1864, M-1864, Letters Received, ser. 925, Dept. of Cumberland, RG 393 Pt. 1 [C-14].

[37] *Freedom*, ser. 1, vol. 1: pp. 267–68; *Freedom*, ser. 2: doc. 362; John Cimprich, "The Beginning of the Black Suffrage Movement in Tennessee, 1864–65," *Journal of Negro History* 45 (Summer 1980): 185–95.

With slavery formally ended in Tennessee, civil officials and courts, as well as Union military authorities, quickly became embroiled in questions concerning the transition from slavery to free labor. Among the most pressing were conflicts arising from informal labor arrangements entered into before legal emancipation. Disputes turned on knotty legal issues: When had particular slaves become free? Were erstwhile masters bound to fulfill verbal bargains made with individuals who, at the time, were still legally enslaved? Such cases often dragged on for months or years. Many were never resolved.

Free of the complications engendered by Tennessee's exemption from the Emancipation Proclamation, but lacking any support from state courts or local officials, free labor in northern Alabama also gained ground during the waning months of the war. "The sweets of freedom have been tasted by the slave," proclaimed an Alabama unionist in early 1865, "and his stay with his old master is relieved of the details of antecedent slave management." New working arrangements took shape, some sponsored by the Union army but most negotiated between former slaveholders and former slaves themselves. Even in areas of Alabama still under Confederate control, a number of slaveholders began to contemplate the reconstruction of labor relations. With the defeat of the Confederacy at hand and the specter of confiscation threatening obdurate rebels, they resigned themselves to emancipation and compensated labor, if only "to save their wealth from devastation and for their own use."[38]

By the spring of 1865, free labor had carried the day in middle and east Tennessee and made significant inroads in northern Alabama. Most black people were working on terms that acknowledged their liberty and offered at least the promise of compensation. A few had done a good deal better. They had accumulated property, rented land, or established themselves as independent artisans and tradesmen. With the end of the war, they struggled to retain hard-won advances as they entered the new era of freedom.

---

[38] In addition to the relevant documents in this chapter, see *Official Records*, ser. 1, vol. 49, pt. 1, pp. 590–92.

88: Headquarters of the 3rd Division of the Army of the Ohio to the Commander of a Brigade in the Division

Camp Taylor [*Huntsville, Ala.*] Aug 15th 1862

Sir   The General commanding directs me to call your attention to the fact, that many of the Slaves detailed to work upon the fortifications in the prcess of Construction at this place, have been relieved. and permitted to go home upon the plea of Sickness, which he has every assurance is false and the Negro's go home, and loaf about the plantations from which they were taken.

He desires that you will investigate this matter and prohibit the recurrence of such indulgences upon false representations. I am very Respectfully Your Ob^r Serv^r

HLcS

F J. Jones

A.A.A.G. F. J. Jones to Col. W. H. Lytle, 15 Aug. 1862, vol. 16/25 14AC, p. 10, Letters & Circulars Sent, ser. 5837, 3rd Division, Army of the OH, RG 393 Pt. 2 No. 384 [C-8050]. The general commanding the division was Lovell H. Rousseau.

89: Testimony by a Tennessee Freedman before the Southern Claims Commission

Fountain Head   Sumner Co. [*Tenn.*]   14th October 1874

Harvy Penticord claimant having been by me first duly sworn deposes and says

My name is Harvy Pendicord (col). I am 42 years of age. I reside near Fountain Head Sumner County Tennessee. I am the claimant;

Before the war I belonged to Columbus Pendicord, who married my young mistress Isabella Saver; She was a widow when Mr Pendicord married her;

When the war began I was a slave and was hired to a Mr Childs as a slave; In 1862 I was hired as a slave to Mr O. P. Butler, I then left Mr Butler's and again went to work for Mr Child's cutting wood for him on the Louisville R.R. and worked for him until the war closed when I became free;

During the whole war I was a slave and was hired out as a slave to the above parties by my mistress, who received the hire; During this time my wife belonged to and lived at Mr Butler's and I staid there also every night; When I became free I leased a small place near Fountain Head Sumner County Tenn where I now still live;

In 1862 when I was hired to Mr Butler he gave me a half Saturday at times to work for myself; and while there I leased a small tract of land from Mr Lewis Perdue, to work for myself; This land was new land and was to be cleared by me for the use of it for that year; Curran Butler (col) a slave of Mr Butler helped me to clear it, and we did so by working at night and on Saturday

387

afternoons; In the summer of 1862 we planted and raised upon the place some three or four acres of corn: I leased the land and employed Curran to help me raise the corn; and I was to give whatever part of it I saw fit to do, to him for helping me; By the fall of 1862 we had raised a fine crop of corn of some three or four acres; The land planted in corn was bottom land and raised fine corn, and after the summer was in fine condition; There were in each acre about ten barrells; I think that there are five bushels in a barrell; I allowed about ten barrells to an acre, and five bushels to the barrell, but I cannot now calculate the number of bushels in all that would make;

During the fall we raised this corn and while it was still on the stalk in the field, (and before it was injured by the weather) the United States army came by the place on the march back to Kentucky; Of this army a large number of soldiers encamped for the night near my field of corn; I do not remember the name of the officer in command near the place nor do I know the officers or regiments that encamped there for the night; All went away next morning; On the night the soldiers were encamped at the place the soldiers drove the stock and their horses into the corn field, and also gathered it in their arms and carried it to their horses near by; I went down where them were and talked with some of the soldiers and some officers (but I don't know their names) and told them that it was my corn and asked them not to take it, when they told me that it was some "butternut's" corn and that I had been sent to tell that tale to save it; and moreover I was arrested and kept under guard that whole night, since they said that I was a spy for Morgan; After they had left I went into the field and found that all the corn had been eaten, and that scarcely an ear was left; The next morning I was released and went with a soldier to see the General of the army (I don't know what his name was) and told him that the corn was mine and that I had made it by working at night and on Sundays; when the General stated that if he knew for certain that it was mine that he would pay me, but that he had been fooled that way before, and that if he paid me that I would take it and give it to some "butternut" who owned the corn; He did not give me the pay nor did he give me any paper of any kind; I placed this claim in the hands of some white man and a black man at Gallatin for collection some eight years ago; Hilary Kee was the colored man, I cannot remember the white man's name; I do not know what they did with it. I never got any money from them. I understand that these men were appointed commissioners or something of the kind to collect the money from the state;

I was to allow Curran Butler (col) a part of the corn for helping me, but I leased the land, Curran was then a boy. about 14 years old and was a nephew of mine; I have not since paid him for helping me; Curran has never said anything about this claim or laid any claim whatever to a share of it;

Corn was then worth per barrell I think at $4.50

HDSr

his

Harvy X Pendicord

mark

Testimony of Harvy Pendicord, 14 Oct. 1874, claim of Harvey Penticord, Sumner Co. TN case files, Approved Claims, ser. 732, Southern Claims Commission, 3rd Auditor, RG 217 [I-251]. Sworn before a special commissioner of the Southern Claims Commission. In the same file is testimony of the same date by Oliver P. Butler, to whom Pendicord had been hired in 1862. Butler testified that Pendicord was not the only resident of their neighborhood to have property taken by the Union soldiers (some 7,000 in number) who passed through in August 1862 en route to Kentucky. The troops, whom he identified as a division of the Army of the Ohio, had been "on a forced march . . . the Rail-Road was torn up, and [they] had little or no rations and were dependent upon the country for supplies." According to other documents in the file, Pendicord had submitted a claim for $100 for 125 bushels of corn. He was awarded $60.

90: Chief Engineer of the Army of the Ohio to the Chief of Engineers

Nashville Tenn. Sept. 5th '62

Sir   Having been suddenly charged with the duty of fortifying this city as well as practicable with fieldworks, and being enjoined to use every diligence towards that end, I have conceived it my duty to assume certain responsibilities, among which is that of employing men as foremen, wagon-masters &c, and fixing their wages, without first submitting the case to you, which in the state of our communications would have required considerable time.

It was my first idea to make use of enlisted men and of officers as assistants; but the continual movements of the regiments and changes of detail render such system impracticable. I find it necessary to hire competent and trustworthy men for the following situations, viz Foreman of Laborers, ditto of Carts, Wagon Master, Forage Master; at the rates respectively of $3.—, $1.50, $2.50, and $1.33 1/3 per day. Considering the number of negroes I keep at work, I trust you will regard these bargains as reasonable: I have over 1300 negroes, about 30 teams, and 30 carts constantly busy.

I have the honour to request, that in view of these circumstances, you will approve my course. I am, Sir, very respectfully your obed. servt.

ALS   J S^t C Morton

Capt. Engrs. J. St. C. Morton to Gen. Jos. G. Totten, 5 Sept. 1862, filed with M-4188, Letters Received, ser. 18, General Correspondence, Central Office, RG 77 [VV-1]. In an endorsement dated October 10, 1862, the chief of engineers approved Captain Morton's course. Another endorsement. On September 3, Morton had reported that he was employing a "rather large force" of white mechanics, augmented by impressed black laborers. Whenever necessary, he had explained, "I impress teams, carts, negroes and all the spades picks & chopping axes of the neighborhood. Some of the mechanics are appointed to oversee the negroes and lay out their work, and others work at their trades. I either impress provisions and cooking utensils &c, or make the Qm'r or Comm^s Dept. feed & clothe the negroes." (Capt. Engrs. Jas. St. C. Morton to Gen. Jos. G. Totten, 3 Sept. 1862, M-4187, Letters Received, ser. 18, General Correspondence, Central Office, RG 77 [VV-2].)

91: Order by the Commander of the Department of the Cumberland

Murfreesboro, Ten. Jany. 27th, 1863,

General Orders, N° 6. The General Commanding desiring to increase as far as possible the effective force of this Army, by returning to their regiments able-bodied men, now on detached service as teamsters, laborers, and hospital attendants, directs that their places be supplied as far as possible by the substitution of men hired for the purpose.

To accomplish this, the following directions are given:

I. Citizens residing within or without the limits of this Department may be employed and paid by Quartermasters, as teamsters, wagon-Masters and laborers, and by the Medical Department as hospital attendants.

II. Negroes may be employed and paid in conformity with the Act of Congress,[1] as follows:

1st— As teamsters, on Quartermasters trains, provided a sufficient number of white teamsters and wagon-Masters are retained to preserve order.

2nd. As laborers, in the Quartermaster and Engineer department.

3rd. As cooks, nurses and attendants in Hospitals.

4th. As company cooks, two to a Company.

5th. As officers servants, according to the number allowed by law.[2]

Commanders of Corps, Divisions, Brigades and independent Posts, are authorized to procure and employ negroes as above: –
1st. From those found free and roaming at large.
2nd. From those belonging to masters serving in the rebel army, or who have been employed, in any manner, in the rebel service.
3rd. From those belonging to persons who, though not now serving in the rebel cause, are disloyal, or have children or other near relatives in the rebel army, who are benefited or maintained by the labor of such slaves.

Lastly, when it becomes an absolute necessity, from among those belonging to loyal men. In this case a copy of the order directing their employment, and a descriptive list of persons so employed, shall be given to the owner, duly authenticated by the commanding officer of the troops in whose service they are employed.

The Commanding General enjoins great caution in the employment of women, in any case when it might lead to immorality.

III. All persons so employed in each regiment, except those employed as officers' servants, will be entered on Quartermasters Rolls as laborers or teamsters, stating their age, sex, name of master or claimant, date of employment, and the length of time employed; and in the column of "Remarks," will be noted on what duty and by whom employed. Those employed by the Engineer, Quartermaster or Medical departments will be entered on their appropriate rolls. They will be provided with clothing, to be deducted from their pay, the balance to be paid to the person employed, unless he belong to a loyal master, in which case payment will be made to the master.

Every negro thus employed will receive a certificate from his employer, setting forth the fact and nature of his employment, and no male or female negro will remain in camp, or be subsisted therein, without such certificate.

IV. Commanding Officers and Medical Directors of Corps, Divisions, Brigades and Posts, are directed to substitute hired labor as far as practicable for that of detailed men, and are ordered to return all soldiers now performing such duty to their regiments as fast as their places can be supplied. By command of Major General Rosecrans.

HD

General Orders, No. 6, Head Quarters Dept. of the Cumberland, 27 Jan. 1863, vol. 45A DC, pp. 8–10, General Orders, ser. 940, Dept. of the Cumberland, RG 393 Pt. 1 [C-403].

1 The Militia Act of July 1862, which had authorized the employment of "persons of African descent" in "constructing intrenchments, or performing camp service, or any other labor, or any military or naval service for which they may be found competent," and provided that persons so employed were to receive $10 per month (minus $3 for clothing) and one ration. (*Statutes at Large*, vol. 12, pp. 597–600.)

2 Army regulations allowed each commissioned officer, as part of his compensation, a specified number of servants, according to his rank: lieutenant and captain, one servant; major, lieutenant-colonel, and colonel, two; brigadier-general, three; major-general and lieutenant-general, four. (U.S., War Department, *Revised United States Army Regulations* [Washington, 1863], pp. 544–45.)

92: Chief Engineer of the Department of the Cumberland to the Chief of Engineers

[*Nashville, Tenn.*] March 2nd '63

Sir   I have the honour to acknowledge receipt of Dept. letter & Circular of Feb'y 13th & 4th.

I judge that some mistake in my office prevented the "Report of Estimates" (mentioned in the former as not enclosed in mine of the 14th Jan'y) from going to yours.

The following Estimate is respectfully submitted.

Due for Wages, on acct. App^n Field Works, July	'62	6. –
Aug.	"	333. –
Sept.	"	400. –
October	"	591. –
Nov'^{r}	"	3610.63
Dec'^{r}	"	5583.40
Jan'y	'63	4958.06
Feb'^{r}	"	(say,) 5000. –

Total due for Citizen Labour on Fortific'^{ns}, Dep^t of Cumb^d		20,482.09
For extra pay of Pioneers of same Dep'^{t} Dec'^{r} '62.	9,000. –	
Jan. '63.	9,000. –	
Feb'y "	9,000. –	

Total due for Soldiers Labour on Fortifications (about)	27,000
Aggregate due for Labour on Fortifications Dept. of Cumd.	47,482.09

The Dept. has no doubt observed that no wages have been paid to negroes working on the Fortifications. In the first place, it is very difficult to decide, in the majority of cases, whether the money is due to them or to their owners, or whether they have any owners: and secondly, they steal tools and provisions whenever they can, to an extent that they deserve the loss of their wages, in many cases:

and above all, they elude their guards and desert in such numbers that there is no keeping any accounts with them. For these reasons I was obliged to content myself with telling them that whoever should do his duty, and faithfully remain in the Engineer employ, should certainly receive seven dollars per month when discharged, for the whole period of his service. This whether slaves or free, for the slaves require, it would seem, some inducement to prevent their being disgusted with such hard labour, as well as free negroes: and whether their masters are ever paid or not, I think such slaves ought to get this pittance. To be able to keep my word I estimated for 50 negroes on my Return of Officers & Hired men, for every month, and continue to do so, still beleiving that estimate sufficient.

Had I the means of paying negroes wages, as the Q.M. and other Dep'^{ts} of this army do, I could secure many more, and would not lose them by desertion.

In the same way I can get better mechanics & more work done, if the means are granted by the Treasury to pay up promptly. I am, Sir, very respectfully your obed. Servt

ALS   J St C Morton

Capt. of Engineers J. St. C. Morton to Gen. Jos. G. Totten, 2 Mar. 1863, M-4256 Letters Received, ser. 18, General Correspondence, Central Office, RG 77 [VV-2]. Nearly two months later, Captain Morton had still not paid the black laborers. On April 29, 1863, he informed an assistant of General Joseph G. Totten, the chief of engineers, that General William S. Rosecrans, commander of the Department of the Cumberland, "has expressed his wish that the negroes employed upon the fortifications at Nashville be paid wages, and so enabled to support their families." Morton noted that he would "prepare and forward estimate to put this matter in definite shape." "The chief difficulties," he explained, "are, of course, the obtaining the money and the doubt as to propriety of paying slave negroes of loyal and of rebel owners not present, or free negroes who cannot prove their being free." General Rosecrans, in a blunt endorsement on Morton's letter, emphasized "[t]he necessity for paying [the black laborers]": "from want, say, nine-tenths have deserted, and I think justly." (*Official Records*, ser. 1, vol. 23, pt. 2, pp. 290–91.) On May 1, 1863, General Totten informed Morton that $27,000 had been forwarded for the labor completed by black workers, and he promised that the issue of whether to pay the slaves themselves or their owners would be submitted to the War Department. Later that same month, Morton turned the money over to Lieutenant George Burroughs, his successor as supervising engineer for the fortifications at Nashville. (Brg. Genl. Jos. G. Totten to Brig. Genl. J. St. C. Morton, 1 May 1863, vol. 35, p. 214, Letters Sent to Engineer Officers, ser. 6, General Correspondence, Central Office, RG 77 [VV-2]; see below, doc. 103.) But Burroughs would not disburse the money without instructions from his superiors, which were slow in coming. In a letter dated July 11 (filed with Morton's letter of March 2), Burroughs reiterated the unresolved questions: "Shall I pay owners; or the Negroes themselves? If I am to pay owners, shall I reserve a certain portion for the Negroes? If so, how much?" He noted the difficulty of evaluating the loyalty of slaveholders in middle Tennessee, many of whom "were *disloyal at first*, but have lately taken the 'Oath of Allegiance to avoid being sent beyond the lines." Burroughs declared himself "anxious to pay the Negroes," as "they have actually performed the labor and need encouragement," while their owners had been relieved of the expense of supporting them. An undated, penciled memorandum filed with Morton's and Burroughs's letters offers a clue to the delay in resolving the question of who should be paid: "Morton was told (May 1) the subject would be submitted to the S. of War. – This does not appear to have been done." The question had certainly not been settled by July 24, 1863, when General Rosecrans, noting that many workers on the Nashville fortifications were the slaves of "poor loyal citizens" and widows, asked General Totten whether there was "any legal bar" to his ordering the laborers' wages paid to such owners. Totten referred the question to Secretary of War Edwin M. Stanton, who indicated "that legal objections exist to such payments," but neither specified the objections nor set forth any larger principle under which his subordinates should proceed. About the same time, Morton met in person with Stanton, praised the contributions made by the black laborers at Nashville, and proposed that, "if the owners are to receive payment for the labour, some public test of loyalty should be prescribed, to be acted on without delay; in order that the Rolls (which are prepared, as well as the necessary funds provided for paying them) may be promptly settled, & to prevent evasion of the test on the part of citizens who secretly sympathize with the rebel cause but will present claims against the U.S., upon the close of the rebellion, as if they had remained loyal." (Maj. Gen'l W. S. Rosecrans to Gen. Totten, 24 July 1863, Asst. Adjt. Genl. Jas. A. Hardie to Brigadier General J. G. Totten, 25 July 1863, and Brg. Gen. J. St. C. Morton to Brig. Gen. Jos. G. Totten, 3 Aug. 1863, #4202, 4013, Letters Received Irregular, RG 107 [L-322]; see also below, doc. 103.) For Stanton's eventual decision respecting payment for the labor performed by black men on the Nashville fortifications, see below. doc. 99.

93: Commander of U.S. Forces at Fort Donelson, Tennessee, to the Headquarters of the Department of the Cumberland

Ft. Donelson. Tenn July 3rd 1863

I have the honor to acknowledge the receipt on the 1st inst of communication, herewith returned from Thos. J. Mumford. Clarkville Tenn relative to the loss of his negroes, and in obedience to the order thereon endorsed to submit the following report of the facts in the case so far, as I have any information upon the subject.

1st The negroes named in Mr. Mumfords letter are all at this Post. – and their present status is as follows.

Joshua, Blacksmith for 83 Ill. Col. Smith.

Oliver – son of Joshua – helper as striker for his father

Mary – wife of Joshua – housekeeper for husband & son
William – Wagoner 83rd Ill
Edmund   Do   "   "
Daniel – Sick in contraband Hospital
Abram – Ofcrs. svt in 13th Wis Vol
Spencer – working on fortifications
Geo. Jackson – Ofcrs servt. in 13th Wis Vol.
Ephraim – Wagoner in 83rd Ill. Vol
Henry – Nurse in Contraband Hospital
Prince – Employed in Post C.S. Dept.
Peter – Sent to Smithland to load transports per ordr from Hd Qrs

II Joshua. Oliver. William and another Jim (who died soon after at this place) found their way into our lines at Ft Henry in November or December last – and I took them into Gov – service giving. Mr M. a certificate of the fact, under orders from Col. Lowe – then in command

When the forces at Ft Henry were ordered to this Post in March last – we found here Edmund. Daniel & Abram,

Mary. George Jackson and Prince came into camp early in June – in company with or immediately after an expedition which I sent out under command of Major Bond of the 83rd Ill. to press horses for Goverment use. Spencer, Ephraim, Henry and Peter came in some days afterwards – without the presence of any military force in their neighborhood so far as I am informed

3rd – As to the circumstances under which these negroes came into our lines. There can be no doubt that eight of them got here soon after the return of the expedition under Gen Ransom, after the return from Kentucky, last fall – and that the presence of that force near Mr Munford farm was the occasion of their leaving him at that time. I accompanied that expedition, my regiment forming a part of it and it is proper for me to say that Gen Ransom made every exertion in his power – going to the uttermost limit of his power to prevent the negroes from following the troops. And in these exertions he was cordially supported. I think by all of his Ofcrs. My reccollection is that very few came in with us although I am satisfied that a large number followed or immediately preceeded us.

As to those who came in at or about the time Major Bond returned, I have the best of evidence. aside from the fact that the Major Bond is a high-minded, honorable gentleman and a most valuable Officer. – that they came without his consent – or knowledge or that of any responsible person in his command. The negroes probably skulked back with the train – keeping themselves out of view of the Officers. The three who went to Mr M^s house were

Joshua, Oliver and Edmund. Joshua states that no soldiers from Major Bonds command went with them or knew anything where they were going. He denies using violence – exhibiting weapons or making threats, He says that the 5th Iowa Cavalry were passing through the neighborhood at the time and some of the Soldiers of that Regiment, on being told that he was after his wife advised him to "wade in" I do not however place much confidence in the truth of his statements

The result of my investigations has been to convince me that no person belonging to the army has had anything to do with decoying. Mr Mumfords negroes from him, but that they have left in consequence of the deep and wide spread spirit of discontent which exists among these people – caused, or at least made apparent by the present war.

I beg leave to add, that I have the pleasure of a personal accquaintance with Mr Mumford, and beleive that he is a kind humane master – a most honorable gentleman and a loyal man. When he visited us at Ft Henry last Fall he made every possible effort to secure the welfare of his negroes – leaving with me a considerable sum of money to be distributed amongst them I have the Honor to be Your Respectfully

HLcSr   William P. Lyon

Col. William P. Lyon to Major Wm. W. Michael, 3 July 1863, vol. 172/214 DMT, pp. 82–84, Letters Sent, ser. 406, U.S. Forces Ft. Donelson TN, RG 393 Pt. 4 [C-2078]. No reply to Lyon's report has been found in the copies of letters sent by the Department of the Cumberland.

94: Order by the Commander of the Department of the Cumberland

Winchester, Tenn. July 23d 1863, General Orders, No 172. To avoid misapprehension and correct certain evils now existing in regard to colored persons coming within the lines of this army, it is hereby ordered –

I That all officers commanding troops in the field will conscript and employ such able-bodied negroes as are allowed by law[1] for teamsters, cooks, laundresses, Quartermaster's laborers, and servants to officers who by law, are permitted to employ soldiers,[2] taking the servants of loyal people only in cases of necesity, and always leaving such as may be absolutely requisite for the care of the family. Every cook or teamster shall be properly enrolled and mustered into service, according to law, without delay, Every other employee or

Servant must be enrolled by the Quartermaster of the command in which he is employed. Officers entitled to have a soldier for servant will be permitted to employ servants from such enrolled persons, for whom they will furnish requisitions, approved by the superior officer of the command, The Quartermaster will thereupon enter the name of the Officer on the rolls opposite the name of the servant, and will give the Servant a certificate of his assignment, giving the name of his officer, which certificate, the Servant must be directed to preserve, and have renewed if worn out or lost, No changes of Servants will be permitted without notifying the Quartermaster, that he may issue certificates, and note the changes in his rolls, The officer having such servants will drop the charge for Servants from his pay accounts, as in case of having Soldiers for Servants, and the servants will be paid by the Quartermaster as other employees.

For all negroes employed in pursuance of this order, the officer conscripting or employing shall, on application, furnish the owner or claimant a descriptive roll, certifying that the person described is employed in the service of the United States, and in what manner, Duplicate descriptive rolls of all negroes in camps and at the Posts in this Department will be made with out delay

II To prevent vagrancy demoralization, immoralities, and expense to the Government, all officers are forbidden to admit within their lines and harbor runaway Negroes, unless their servises are needed, or in cases where humanity demands it, In these cases lists of the persons admitted, and the reasons for their admittance, will be forwarded to the Provost Marshal General of this Department without delay

III To ensure protection and prompt payment to colored persons employed in the Engineer Department or as laborers, they will be organized and mustered into service by detachments or companies, as Infantry, and then assigned to duty. Applicants for commission in these organizations will be examined, and, if quallified, appointed and commissioned pursuant to instructions from the War Department

IV In the absence of civil law commanders of troops will exert their authority to prevent injustice and disorders whether coming from Masters or their Servants; requiring each to perform their legal duties, whenever intervention is practicable and demanded by justice and humanity. By Command of Major General Rosecrans

HDc

General Orders, No. 172, Head-Quarters Dept. of the Cumberland, 23 July 1863, vol. 45A DC, pp. 390–92, General Orders, ser. 940, Dept. of the Cumberland, RG 393 Pt. 1 [C-404].

1 The Militia Act, which authorized the employment of "persons of African descent" in "constructing intrenchments, or performing camp service, or any other labor, or any military or naval service for which they may be found competent." (*Statutes at Large*, vol. 12, pp. 597–600.)
2 For a summary of the army regulation governing the employment of servants by commissioned officers, see above, doc. 91n.

95: Quartermaster at the Nashville Depot to the Quartermaster General

Nashville [*Tenn.*] August 5 *1863*.
M C Meigs   In my estimation the number of colored men employed in the Dept of Cumberland as follows – Eight hundred in quarter masters Dept at this Depot   five thousand with all troops in field & at Posts as teamsters & laborers   one thousand with Engineer Dept Building forts & three thousand seven hundred (3700) as cooks & Servants with Army & officers   in all between ten & eleven thousand (11000)
HWSr   F S Winslow

Capt. F. S. Winslow to M. C. Meigs, 5 Aug. 1863, "Negroes: Employment," Consolidated Correspondence File, ser. 225, Central Records, RG 92 [Y-12].

96: Testimony by an Alabama Freedman before the Southern Claims Commission

[*Huntsville, Ala. September 26, 1874*]
Deposition of Jackson Daniel
In answer to the First General Interrogatory, the Deponent says:
My name is Jackson Daniel, *my age* 57 *or* 58 *years, my residence* near Maysville, *in the State of* Alabama, *and my occupation a* Farmer; *I am the claimant*, Jackson Daniel *and have a beneficial interest in the claim.*
To the 2nd Interrogatory, deponent Says: I resided in Jackson County Alabama from the beginning of the war up to the winter of 1862 and 1863, then I moved to Maysville Madison County Alabama, then I lived at Maysville until the close of the war, I lived with my old master up to the time I was freed. His name was Kibble T. Daniel. I was freed the year 1863, I was freed when I came to maysville, that was the first of my being free, Then I farmed from that out, only the soldiers would come and get me, and

I helped to a heap of work on the Block Houses at Brownsboro station on the Memphis and Charleston Rail Road, about a mile and a half from Maysville to my understanding – . . . .

To the 18th he says:

No sir, not a particle in no way shape, form or fashion, never did give the rebals any information – they never trusted us black folks for any thing of that kind.

. . . .

To the 25th he says:

I have had a heap taken by rebels, they taken all the meal and meat I had once, and one thing and another that I can't recollect at present, that was the year of the surrender, when all the federals were up at Nashville, when they taken the meat and meal, They made my wife cook it up and they carried it to the rest of them, they left me without anything, I did not have a thing to eat, no sir, they did not pay for it, my wife was cooking for them till morning till dinner time, and they put it in large sacks and carried it off

To the 26th he says:

Well, they have at times threatened me right smart but they never hurt me nor nothing – Just before the fight was at Nashville before the surrender, Well, I don't know sir what their names, was, it was when we objected to them taking all our meat and meal, They threatened to take me off with them and make me work for the government if I said any thing more to them about the meat or meat,

To the 27th he says:

Well I, when they, no sir, I was not, Well, my wife was a very fractious woman, and when she saw them taking her meal, she objected to it and they talked about slaying of her, see, I just told her to hush and say nothing and it would be best for us,

To the 28th he says:

No no, Did not have nothing to give, me and my wife could not do any thing but cook and was[h] for the Yankees.

To the 29th he says:

I hauled and worked on their Block Houses is the most I ever done for the Yankees, Hauled corn and fodder and meat you can put down, I was the first darkie who went with them from Daniel Plantation, I Hauled for them for three weeks, I furnished my own team, I went and borrowed the team in my own name, from one of the neighbors, I worked on Block House for three weeks, No sir they never paid me a particle of nothing for my work for them –

. . . .

To the 40th he says:

I sympathized with the Union cause of course, I thought I

desired to be free and wanted to be free and I was glad that the
Federal army was so lucky as to free me, I wanted the Federal army
to over come the others, that I might be free, my language was at
the beginning of the war I wanted to see the Yankees come— I had
no influence, but I just prayed with my whole heart that the
Yankees might come and over come my old masters, and whip them
out, I could not express to you the whole of my feelings, and hopes
and regard I had for the Federal army, as sure as you are born it
was a great thing, and as they first passed along—as long as I had
milk or any thing I carried it to them, and my wife sot up all night
a cooking for them and we never charged them nothing for it, and
when anything was about to come on dangerous to the Yankees and
I could not get to them, I stated it to my wife and she would take
it to the camps.

To the 41st he says:

I do solemnly declare that from the beginning of hostilities to the
end thereof my sympathies were constantly with the cause of the
United States; that I never of my own free will and accord, did any
thing, offered or sought or attempted to do any thing by word or
deed to injure said cause or retard its success, and that I was ready
and willing when called upon or if called upon to aid and assist the
cause of the Union and its supporters so far as my means and power
and the circumstances of the case permitted, And thank God I can
hold up my hand and kiss the Bibble in saying it,

I was one of the Darkies who did not go into the Federal Army,
but when the wife of a colored soldier came to my house although I
was some times hard pressed for some thing to eat I always divided
with them— I though as the soldiers were in the Army fighting for
me it was my duty to do all I could for their families—

To the 42nd he says:

I was a slave at the beginning of the war, I became free in 1863,
in the summer, when the yankees come by and said I could go to
work for myself— I was farming after that, I got the mule from
colonel Mittey. Well, if I mistake not he belonged to Wilders
Brigade, Don't Rember his Regiment, I bought him from the
Colonel, I waited on him and carried his men around a foraging,
where they knowed not I worked for him a long time, three weeks
or more, then I carried him potatoes and chickens. I carried them
so often I could not tell you how many I did furnish him I went
around through the country and bought them up and carried them
to him, He stayed there about two months, and all I got for it in
the world was the mule, I had to take all these things to him
before he would let me have the mule, The mule was not
branded, the colonel said it was no Government mule,

Me and my son carried marketing and things to the same Colonel and got the mare about the same way we did the mule, No, No, sir, she had no brands on her,

I bought the cattle, a large cow and bull, and paid evry dollar down for them, I bought them of a Man by the name of Austin, I paid forty dollars for them, I just worked night and day making shoes and got the money   see I am a shoe maker and I make Baskets and such things, I worked for any one who had the money to pay me,

I bought two sows and raised the shoats from them   I worked as sure as you are born and got the money for to pay for them.   I paid ten $ for one and Eleven $s for the other,

Kibble T. Daniel was my former master, He is dead now, he got killed in time of the war, no sir I have bought land of my own since the surrender and live on it, I bought it of Colonel Wortham.   I do not owe my old masters estate a thing in the world,   no, sir, no one has any interest in this claim but myself –

In answer to the Questions as to the taking or furnishing of the property – deponent to Question One says:

Yes sir, I was present when the hogs were taken. well, I was present when the mule was taken, I was not present when the mare and cattle were taken –   they were taken by the Forage master,

To the 2nd he says:

Yes sir, I saw the mule when she was taken, and the hogs taken – by the Yankees, My little girl was on the mare, she had went over to our old place where we had moved from to get some potatoes and things, and she came back walking and said the Yankees had tuk the mare, she came crying and said the yankees had taken the mare, I did not see the cattle taken,

To the 3rd he says:

Item 2,   Well, the mule was taken, and they said they wanted the mule, that they were obliged to have it, that they were out after stock to use about their wagons and were obliged to have her, and that we would get pay for her, I told them if she would do them any good to take her along and I would make out the best I could,   they just come and went to my stable and tuk her right out and came on to the house with her, and I asked them what in the world I would do now, and I told them I had bought her to take care of my family, but if she would do them any good to help them through to take her along as I wished to do anything I could to help the Union Army, they put a black man on her who I knowed well, Bill Bingham and they took her off –

Well, they just come and drove the hogs right off to camps, they drove them from right in front of my door, The men who took them never said a word but drove them on off— Other men, who belonged to the Brigade said if I would come down to the colonel, he would give me a receipt for them and I would get pay some time or another— I jus thought to my self I would not put my self to any on plush [*anguish?*] about it, and if they would do them any good they might have them,

We had an old man who lived on the place, and was there when they were taken by the forage master— He told them the cow and bull belonged to the black people, and they said they did not want to take Black peoples things, but they had them in the drove and could not get them out, this is what the old man told me, and if we would come to camps we could get pay for them, but we could not go, for if we had been caught in the wilderness going to their camps, the Bushwhackers were liable to kill us,

the mare was taken from my little girl when she was going after some things and I don't know much about it only as she told, she said the Yankees took her off the mare and said they wanted her and took her on, and she came home crying,

To the 4th he says:

They were taken from Daniel Plantation where I lived at that time, I cant tell you the year It was taken in I think it was in 1863, It was after we had commenced doing for ourselves, the mare and mule were taken by Ousterhous' men, I do not know any of the Regements, and the Beff cattle, and general Grangers men tooken the hogs, as they were going from the vacuation of Huntsville, at that time a black man did not know the days of the week he was pestered so, when it was day I would wish it was night, and at night I would wish it was day,

. . . .

his
Jackson X Daniel
mark

HDSr

Excerpts from testimony of Jackson Daniel, 26 Sept. 1874, claim of Jackson Daniel, Madison Co. AL case files, Approved Claims, ser. 732, Southern Claims Commission, 3rd Auditor, RG 217 [I-109]. Sworn before a special commissioner of the Southern Claims Commission. The response to the first interrogatory is in the form of handwritten insertions into a printed form. Marginal notations that repeat the question numbers have been omitted. The questions that correspond to the enumerated responses are not in the file. According to other documents in the file, Daniel had submitted a claim for $345 as compensation for the following property taken by Union soldiers: 1 mare, 1 mule, 600 pounds of beef, and 1,050 pounds of pork. He was awarded only $36.00, the commissioners having concluded that he held no title to the mare and mule and that the seizure of his hogs had been conducted in an irregular manner not encompassed by the law establishing the claims commission.

97: Testimony by a Tennessee Freedman before the Southern Claims Commission

[*Nashville, Tenn. February 9, 1872*]

Samuel Larkin Claimant
vs
The Government of the United States
   Samuel Larkin aged 31 years being duly sworn and examined by his Attorny A. W. Wills stated as follows:
   Am a colored man. I live in Davidson County. Ten miles from Nashville on the Lebanon Turnpike – have lived there, and about two miles from there since 1864 – Before the War I lived in Huntsville Ala. and came to Nashville Tenn. with Col. Chapins Regiment (Union) in 1862. and remained with the Regiment several months. I then settled in Nashville. and had with me about five hundred Dollars. that I had made by working. which money I invested in horses. I bought three horses one mule. and a blind horse. which animals I worked in teams hauling different stores &c. for merchants and others in Nashville Tenn. and did an express business. I kept my stock in a stable on Vine St. near Church. Sometime in the month of August 1863, my three horses, mule and blind horse – were working as usual. two of the horses in one wagon. two in another. and the mule in a dray. when a squad of Soldiers under charge of an Officer took them all. wagons and dray included. drove them to a Government Wagon yard on corner of Broad and Spruce Sts. Nashville Tenn. when one of my drivers came to me. (I was then working on Cedar St. Nashville) and told me the Government Troops had taken all my stock. I immediately went to the Wagon yard on corner of Broad & Spruce Sts. and found my wagons. and the Blind horse – they had taken the other three horses and the mule on toward the Camps on Franklin Turnpike. I followed on out, and met the Officer and Soldiers who had my stock with others. and I asked the Officer to return me my Stock. he asked if I could point them out. I said yes. and did so – He then said he could not return them. that he had orders to press all serviceable stock he could find. for the use of the Government, but that I would be paid in full for all my Stock. Upon finding that I could not get my Stock, I returned to the aforesaid Wagon Yard and

my blind horse. with the two Wagons was returned to me. but I never got back the three horses and mule. nor did I ever get pay for the same— I saw my three horses and mule. many times afterward. being driven in Government teams. and used by the Government. The stock was as follows.

One mule 6 yrs. old, worth $125.00
One Bay Horse " 95.00
One Sorrel " " 85.00
One " " " 95.00
$400.00

I make the prices thus low. because the Officer who took them said that this was the amount the Government would allow me for them. The drivers of the different teams, that were with them at the time they were taken have all settled in different parts of the Country. and I dont know where they are— I am a colored man, and have always been loyal to the United States Government. and worked for the Government—

Cross Examination by Special Commissioner

Ans. 1 I resided at Huntsville Alabama in April 1861 and was the slave of Geo. W. Drake. In 1862 I left there with Col Chapin Regimt, and came to Nashville Tennessee where I have resided ever since and have been at home in person farming part of the time and carrying on a Barber shop.

. . . .

The Horses and Mule were aged from 5 to 7 years old and good servicable farm and wagon stock. I bought the stock with mony I earned in Col. Chapins regiment and used the stock in wagons for about 12 months. Thy were taken from me while in Nashville. The stock was taken in day time publicly. Gen R S. Granger was then in command of the post of Nashville. I do not know how long he had been here or how long he stayed

I know thy were taken and used in the army and I have never got any pay for them or any other articles the army ever took from me.

HDSr

his
Samuel X Larkin
mark

Excerpts from testimony of Samuel Larkin, 9 Feb. 1872, claim of Samuel Larkin, Davidson Co. TN case files, Approved Claims, ser. 732, Southern Claims Commission, 3rd Auditor, RG 217 [I-202]. The questions that correspond to the enumerated responses are not in the file. According to other documents in the file, Larkin was awarded $350 as compensation for the mule and three horses.

98: Testimony by a Tennessee Free Man of Color before the Southern Claims Commission

Decherd, Tenn Aug 3rd 1877

Deposition of Frederick A. Starkey (col) who in answer to the questions deposes and says as follows, my name is Frederick A. Starkey I reside at Tullahoma Coffee County Tenn, am forty six years old. I am the claimant and am a barber by trade. I am the only man interested in this claim. I was born in Oglethorp County Georgia, but was removed into Alabama when about eight years old. When I arrived at the age of Twenty one years I was set free by my master Jesse Starkey who died in a few years after he set me free. I then came to Bellfonte Alabama, and learned the Barber's trade and have followed that business ever since. I lived at Stevenson Alabama from 1857 till the federal troops came there during the war and from that time to the close of the war I was most of the time with the federal army. During about one year of that time I was Post Barber at Gen'l George H. Thomas' Head Quarters I lived at Stevenson till 1871, when I removed with my family to Tullahoma and have lived there ever since.

Questions 5th 6th & 7th Claimant answers

My sympathies were on the union side from the first of the contest to the last and when General Mitchel Came into Stevenson Ala. in the Spring of 1862 and the most of the white people and many of the colored fled from Stevenson toward the South I staid at Stevenson and volunteered to give General Mitchel all the information I could and piloted him up to Boliver a little village towards Bridgport and then on to Running Water Bridge half way from Stevenson to Bridport. I remained with the federals the short time Mitchels Command remained at Stevenson, and when Buels Command came to Stevenson I gave him and his officers all the Information I could get, or find out, and I was Barber at Buels Head Quarters Col. Turchins Command of Buels army was up at Bridgport on the Tenn. river and Capt. Warner Commanding the Post Stevenson found out that the rebels were crossing the river below Stevenson to try to get between Bridgport and Stevenson and he sent me with this intelligence from Stevenson to Bridgport to Col. Turchin. Col. Turchin at once threw out his forces and had a fight with the rebels and drove them back to the South side of the river. –

I was at all times ready to do any thing I could to aid union men or the union army or cause. I was out early one morning with a foraging party near the Tennessee river and discovered the rebels crossing the river and coming into the woods & gave the officer in

command of the party the information   we hastened to Stevenson
and the troops were at once got ready and in a short time rebels
were in sight of Stevenson and skirmishing and fighting went on all
day. I was busy under the orders of the union officers all day till
the troops got in from Bridgport and all the rolling stock was run
from the track of the Memphis and Charleston Railroad to the
Nashville and Chattanooga R. Road and in the evening the trains
were loaded with white union refugees and everything that the
union forces could carry away and Stevenson was evacuated.

The union soldiers and officers gave me a good deal of provisions
and other things that they could not carry away because I had done
so much for them. When the rebel soldiers came in they plundered
me of all this property and cursed me a great deal for having been
among the Yankees. –

To the 8th Claimant continues – I managed to live at Stevenson
till General Rosecran's army again got possession of this part of the
country and from that time till the close of the war I was all the
time more or less doing something for the union officers soldiers or
union people.

To 9th Ques. Claimant ans, I had no kin that I knew of near me
and I do not know that I had any in the Union army.

Ques 10th & 11th Claimant ans.

That in 1864 a command of Rosecrans, or Sherman's army was
stationed at Bridgport and there were some colored troops there and
were recruiting and I enlisted and in a short time after enlisting I
was in a skirmish with the rebels on the river below Bridgport and
was wounded in the head with a shell and was brought back to
Bridgport & lay in the hospital about ten weeks, when I was able to
be sent to my home at Stevenson; but when I got up my head
would inflame whenever I did hard work and I got let off from duty
as a soldier then barbered for the officers.

I did not get any soldiers discharge. I did not ask for any
discharge for I was released from duty and did not know the
advantage of a discharge. I often assisted union men that were
distitute and had got to the union lines for there were always
persons needing help. I gave a good union man, old James Russell,
both provisions and money to help him along when he was in
distress   He now lives in Grasy Cove, about 14 miles from
Stevenson   I also brought old man Ance Marshall across the Tenn.
River when the rebels were after him to kill him for being a union
man   he had to desert his place and come across the river – and I
helped him across and he was so poor that I helped him in money
and other ways till he got employment on the R. Roads. I also
took care of Jo. Timberlake and kept him hid for a time out of the
way of the rebels – supported him and finally sent him back into the

federal lines. — I did a great many things that I suppose I need not
tire the Commissioners with.

But to the 12th 13th & 14th ques, he answers I adhered to the
union cause throughout the whole Contest — I recollect hearing Mr.
Ramsey — the present Special Commissioner make a union speech in
Stevenson in 1860. he was Douglas elector and my feelings never
changed.

To Ques 15th & 16th He ans,

I was always recognized as a union man & so treated by union
men and union soldiers I dont recollect taking any oathes, —

To Ques 17 & 18th He answers

I was frequently threatened by rebels and rebel soldiers after I had
been with the union armies of Mitchel and Buel. The rebels
threatened to hang me time & again.

To Ques 19 & 20th He ans,

Just after Gen'l Buel evacuated Stevenson the rebels arrested me
and kept me a prisoner about a half day & let me go home. they
did not ask me to give a bond or take any oath but they took as I
stated above all the property I had got from the federal troops.

To Ques 21, & 22nd He ans,

None of my property was confiscated. I never did anything to
aid the confederates, — for my principles were known and the rebels
would not let me associate with their slaves because I was free. I
will also state that, not only, was my life threatened but, — I was
badly beaten at Stevenson after Buels army retreated from the
place. A union soldier named John Bull was sick at my house &
could not get away & was forgotten by his comrades and after the
rebels got possession of the place they captured him and some of
their soldiers gave me a bad beating.
. . . .

To ques. 66 67 & 68 He answers

I was the sole owner of all the property. charged in this
account. I was the owner of two lots in Stevenson Alabama with
houses on them and the frame house that is charged for in my
account was in the way of building a fort by the union soldiers and
was torn down and used by them to build quarters, & for other uses
such as the army needed. I had been for years raising my own
Cattle & hogs. I had no land except my town lots — but could, &
did rent good land near Stevenson.

I never filed any petition in bankruptcy.

To ques. 70th He ans, I have stated when and how, I became
free I bought the Town lots after I came to Stevenson to live. I
bought both town lots from a white man named John Williams in
1859. I had made the money to pay for them by my business as a
barber and keeping and selling confectionaries My old master died

some years before the war   I have never seen any of my old master's people, or children since began except a son named David Starkey who was a soldier in the union army and I understand now lives in Miss. I have lost sight of all the rest of them, and none of them are witnesses – and no person except myself has any interest in this claim.

. . . .

HDS   Fred a Starky

Excerpts from testimony of Fred a. Starky, 3 Aug. 1877, claim of Frederick A. Starkey, Coffee Co. TN case files, Approved Claims, ser. 732, Southern Claims Commission, 3rd Auditor, RG 217 [I-205]. Sworn before John W. Ramsey, a special commissioner of the Southern Claims Commission. The questions that correspond to the enumerated responses are in the file. The final portion of Starky's testimony recounted the episodes in which his property was taken: In late August 1862, just before they evacuated Stevenson, Union soldiers had slaughtered four oxen, a cow and calf, and twenty-five hogs; about a year later, after the reoccupation of northern Alabama, they had taken a horse and seventy-five bushels of wheat (the latter of which Starky had raised on land rented from "a good union man") and dismantled a frame house. Starky had submitted a claim for $1,352.50; he was awarded $435.

99: Commander of U.S. Forces at Fort Donelson, Tennessee, to the Headquarters of the 3rd Division, Reserve Corps, Army of the Cumberland

Fort Donelson Tenn.   October 14th 1863.
There are at this Post about one hundred and twenty negroes who have been at work for the Government of the U.S. without pay since the first of June last.   In order to get paid they must be mustered into the service as Infantry soldiers and detailed in the Engineer Department.   Their services will be needed here for some time.   Can there not be an officer sent here to muster them at once?
HLcSr   (sgd)   E. C. Brott.

[*Endorsement*]   Hd. Qur[s] Com[r] Org. U.S.CT.   Nashville   Nov 5″ 1863.   Respectfully referred to Major Gen[l] Thomas Comdg Dep[t] of Cumberland, Chattanooga Tenn.   There is a large amount of money due negroes for work on the fortifications in the Department and I am informed by Lieut Burroughs (Eng. Corps) that there is money in his hands to pay them.   Many families are suffering for want of money earned from six to twelve months since.   The 1st Reg[t] U.S.

Col^d Vol^s of Tenn. earned by labor on the fortifications previous to Aug 15 Eighteen to twenty thousand dollars which is still due them. (sgd) Geo. L. Stearns Maj. & A.A.G. USV. Com^r Org^n U.S.C. Troops

[*Endorsement*] Hd. Qurs. Dep^t Cumb^d Chattanooga [*Tenn.*] Nov 11 /63 Respy referred to Brig Genl W F Smith. Chief Engineer. It was understood that Lt Burroughs had instructions to settle these arrears of pay By order of Maj Genl Thomas. (sgd). C. Goddard. A.A.G.

[*Endorsement*] Hd Qurs. Ch'f Eng^r DC Chattanooga Tenn Nov 12 /63 Respectfully forwarded If the troops have been employed in the Eng^r Dept^t I would recommend that Genl Morton be sent to settle with & pay them. If this cannot be done I would urge that a mustering Officer be detailed to go and muster them into the service. and that the Pay Dep^t be instructed to pay them. (sg'd). Wm F. Smith Brig Genl & Chf. Eng^r.

[*Endorsement*] Hd. Qur^s Dep^t Cumb^d Chattanooga [*Tenn.*] Nov. 12 /63 Respectfully referred to Brig Genl Morton. It was understood that arrangements had been made to pay all these negroes. By order of Maj. Genl Thomas (sg'd) C. Goddard A.A.G.

[*Endorsement*] Hd Qurs Pioneer Brigade Chattanooga [*Tenn.*] Nov. 13. /63 Resp'y returned with report that on May 19" 1863 I turned over to Lt Burroughs thirty thousand dollars. ($30.000. −) which I had estimated for on acc^t of wages of negroes, with orders to pay said wages whenever the War Dept or the Comdg Genl of this Dep^t should authorize the payment, and decide whether the slaves should be paid, or their masters in the differant cases which should arise. of the latter being loyal, disloyal, or of doubtful or unknown sentiments towards the Gov^t.

Such authority has not as yet, that I know of been given by said War Dep^t or Comdg Genl. In August I waited on the Sec'y of War by order of Gen. Rosecrans, and solicited his decision, but have not yet heard from him in regard to the matter. I believe Capt Merrill. Corps Eng^r, when Chief Eng^r of this Dep^t authorized Lt Burroughs to pay the negro payrolls but how he directed it to be done I do not now remember (if ever I knew) nor do I believe his authority was sufficient in the premises to do more than take the responsibility

from Lt Burroughs and place it upon himself   (sg'd) J. S. G.
Morton Brig Gen¹ Vols.

[*Endorsement*] Hd. Qurs Dep^t Cumb^d Chattanooga [*Tenn.*] Nov. 13
/63   Respectfully referred to the Adj^t Gen¹ of the Army for the
consideration of the Secretary of War. The negroes employed by the
Gov^t in Nashville were collected from all quarters and it is extremely
difficult & in most cases impossible to ascertain to whom they
belong or whether their owners are loyal or disloyal. Yet no
disbursing officer is willing to pay them when their owners may
hereafter appear and claim the wages. In view of these facts it is
respectfully requested that an order may be given authorizing the
Engineer Disbursing Officer to pay the negroes themselves the
amounts due them respectively. (sgd) Geo. H. Thomas Maj Gen¹
USV. Comgd

[*Endorsement*] War Department [*Washington, D.C.*] Nov. 25.
1863. Maj. Gen¹ Thomas' recommendation is approved and the
payment ordered. (sg'd). P. H. Watson Act. Sec. ^of War

Lt. Col. E. C. Brott to A.A. Genl., 14 Oct. 1863, filed as A-1937, Letters
Received, ser. 18, General Correspondence, Central Office, RG 77 [VV-3].
Other endorsements. This copy of Brott's letter (with its endorsements) was
furnished to the chief of engineers, along with a copy of a letter to General
Thomas, which reported the War Department's approval of his recommendation
that the disbursing officer pay the black laborers themselves and directed
Thomas to "give the necessary instructions." (Assist. Adjt. Genl. C. W. Foster
to Major General George H. Thomas, 25 Nov. 1863, in the same file.) The
decision was evidently considered a statement of general policy, applicable to
other military jurisdictions as well. (See, for example, Brig. Genl. Jos. G. Totten to Maj. J. H. Simpson, 1 Dec. 1863, vol. 36, p. 179, Letters Sent to Engineer Officers, ser. 6, General Correspondence, Central Office, RG 77 [VV-19].)

100: **Engineer at Nashville, Tennessee, to the Chief Engineer
of the Department of the Cumberland**

Nashville Tenn. –   October 24th 1863 –
General   I have the honor to state that when the first regiment of
colored troops for *this Dep^{mt}* was organized, about five hundred
negroes, employed by the Engineer Dep^{mt} at Nashville, were
mustered into the service and sent to that regiment at Elk River

Bridge, by order of the General Comdg the Dep^mt, General
Rosencrans informed me, about that time that it was a military
necessity to take them away; and that after being drilled and
organized they would be sent back; they have now been away over
two months— Laborers are greatly needed at this post, as well for
the effective maintainance of this Eng^r Depot as for pushing the
Fortifications, Dep^mt, Depot, Magazines &c; If it can be done I
would respectfully request that those men or an equal and if possible
greater number be ordered back, The work here is almost at a
stand, as far as regards the forts, the only labor on them being
convicts a few Negroes and mechanics on "Fort Houston," mechanics
& a few negroes on "Fort Negley", no work whatever on "Fort
Morton"—. The majority of negroes & mechanics are required in
the shops, at the Saw Mill—cutting & hauling logs &c and on the
Depot Magazines, on the last work we have now a temporary force
of volunteer negroes (pr one month) improvised for our benefit by
Maj Stearns A.A.G. for organization of colored troops—.
    This resource will soon fail, and we shall then have an additional
need of men, which as far as I can see. can only be met in the
manner proposed. I am General Very Respectfully Your Obedient
Servant
HLS   George Burroughs

Lieut. Engineers George Burroughs to Brig. Gen. Smith, 24 Oct. 1863, B-
1512 1863, Letters Received, ser. 925, Dept. of the Cumberland, RG 393 Pt.
1 [C-5]. By an endorsement dated October 31, 1863, the chief engineer
forwarded Burroughs's letter to the headquarters of the Department of the
Cumberland, "with a request that the troops of African descent may be returned to Nashville as soon as they can be spared." A penciled notation on the
wrapper suggests that the letter was merely filed at department headquarters.
Major George L. Stearns, who had "improvised" a force of laborers for the
engineer department, had arrived in Nashville in early September 1863, bearing a commission from the War Department to recruit black troops in middle
and east Tennessee. The regiment into which hundreds of former employees of
the engineer department had been enlisted became the 12th USCI.

101: **Testimony by the Military Governor of Tennessee before the
American Freedmen's Inquiry Commission**

NASHVILLE, Tenn., Nov. 23^d, 1863.
Testimony of Gov. Andrew Johnson.
Q Suppose the slaves emancipated throughout the South, do you
think they would be able to maintain their position, without any
interference on the part of the Federal Gov't, to make up to them

the disadvantages they have incurred in slavery, in the way of education & the capability of taking care of themselves?

A I dont think they will be in a condition to do it. There is a vast difference between the mass of the negroes in South Carolina, & the mass of negroes here. We have found that by undertaking to gather them into contraband camps, we got only the dross; and instead of doing that, we now tell the masters that they ought to begin at once to give them employment and pay them for their work; and the moment that begins, the whole question is settled. No longer ago than week before last, there was a gentleman here who wanted to go into the making of cotton quite extensively, with hired negro labor. Women & children come in here in great numbers, and say they need a house and something to eat, and some of them will say, "My husband is in the service"; and they expect the Gov't will support them. I tell them, "There are white women whose husbands are in the service, and they have to work. The idea of freedom is not to do nothing; you must go to work. We have not brought you away from your masters, but we are not going to send you back. You must go to work and depend upon yourselves, and live by your own industry. We will give you a few days rations, and you must go round and get work." And in most instances they have done so; and we find this plan works much better than getting them all together in that squallid, debased condition which we see in contraband camps. I have thought it was better to set the negroes to work, paying them wages, than to make soldiers of them, because a soldier's life is a lazy one; but by setting the negroes at work, we give them an idea of contracts, and when the rebellion is over, they will be in a better condition to take care of themselves than if they were put into camps. A good many will not go into the service, but will go to work, and so we are able to employ them in both capacities. The women are kept at work cooking & washing, so that all are employed. Our experience so far has proved that to be the best policy.

I think the negro population in this State can be better managed than in South Carolina or Georgia, if we can only go along and give them work. There are hundreds of thousands of negroes here who will stay here, and almost perish in the gutters, rather than colonize. They will stay, unless there is some compulsory process to drive them away.

Q Should you consider it necessary that Superintendents should be appointed to take care of the women and children, put them on plantations, pay them wages, and reimburse the Gov't from the proceeds of their labor?

A We have been talking about that here, too. There will be a good deal of property confiscated, but it has not been yet. So far as we can carry out the policy, in pursuance of law, I think it had better be done; but I have thought it not best to take property until the whole thing is settled. While there are hundreds of thousands of white families perfectly destitute, because the Gov't has not given them that protection in time, which they ought to have, I should not be disposed to cut up the plantations and put the negro women and children upon them. Such a course would create a good deal of feeling.

Q You think, then, they should be left alone?

A I think it is better to leave things as they are than to commence the other system, because many are making contracts now, and in many instances, their owners are paying them wages.

The idea that cotton cannot be made by white men is all a mistake. I was born and raised in a slave State, and I can remember when I went into the cotton field and picked out cotton, and I could do more than any negro boy I ever saw; and if all the Alabama country was taken, and cut up into reasonable sized farms, with a white population, and the negroes hired, at fair wages, they would make more cotton than they could with slave labor, and raise their own meat & bread. It is true, no one would raise so many bales as the large planters have raised, but the aggregate product would be as great. If the rebellion was all settled up, I think a large portion of the servants would go right back, if they were stimulated with the offer of fair wages for their work.

Q To what extent do you think the slaveholders of Tennessee fall into the plan of hiring negroes?

A I don't think I have sufficient data to approximate a conclusion. A good many, however, are looking to that, and some have made application and want to go into it. If we could have two or three instances that succeeded pretty well, a large proportion of the slave labor would be absorbed.

Q You think the best way is to let that thing work itself out as it is, without Gov't interference?

A I think so.

Q Previous to the war, when negroes were hired out, what was the average price paid for them?

A In the last few years, I think they would average from $100 to $120. The hands about the iron works & the cotton plantations were hired for more than the others, and women, of course, for less. The person who hires is generally required to pay the taxes & furnish clothing. Let me give you one single illustration. There has been a great mistake about the wealth of the South. Here is a man who has five whites in his family, and it is with difficulty that he makes one year's end meet the other. He is looked upon as a very poor man. Right over there is a man with fifty, sixty or a hundred negroes, and at the end of the year, it is with difficulty that he can pay his debts. Now, he is just about as poor as the other man. My idea is, that with proper management, free labor can be made more profitable than slavery in a very few years. This will place the negroes upon & within the great Democratic rule; it will unfetter industry, & if they have the talents and enterprise in them to rise, let them come. In adjusting this thing, the object is, to make them take the best and most beneficial relation to society. Now, here are the women and children, who are incapable of making contracts. Sometimes, the children have no parents at all, and have become a charge upon the community. Now, we have in the State statutes in reference to orphan children, and the question comes up if a large portion of this negro population might not be made to take a much better position in society through the means of orphan asylums & similar institutions. When everybody occupies the same position in reference to slavery, everybody will be in favor of that system which will make their condition advantageous to society. There will be no squabbling when that takes place. There must be vagrant laws for the negroes, as there are for whites, and laws to prevent their congregating in improper assemblies. So we should go on, & the time would come when black boys, as well as white, would be put to apprenticeships. I was a regular indentured apprentice myself, and I don't think it would hurt them at all. And these things are just as much needed for a great many of the whites as for the blacks.

Q. How is it about kidnapping in this State?

A. There is very little of it in this State. There have been a great many negroes run off further South. I think some of the rebels, notwithstanding they were great Southern men, have stolen negroes sometimes, sold them, and put the money in their pockets. When we came here, we just cleaned out the slave pens & the workhouses of all negroes that were not put in for crime, and I have no doubt that had some influence. Do not understand me as speaking against anything being done. I mean, let us see the practical condition of things, & conform our action to that.

Q What do you consider the legal status of the slaves in Tennessee?

A So far as emancipating the negroes in Tennessee is concerned, I don't think you need to trouble yourself much about that. I think that is already settled.

Q Have you any colored troops here?

A Oh, yes, we have three regiments here.

Q How have they acted?

A They have performed much better than I expected. I was very agreeably disappointed. The negro takes to discipline easier than white men, and there is more imitation about them than about white men. Then another thing: when the idea is in his mind, that the connection between him and his master is broken, and he has got white men to stand by him and give him encouragement, and a gov't which says, "There is freedom before you—put down the enemies of the country; and if you desert, there is death behind you," my impression is that, after a little while, he will fight. Of course, he must have some experience. The thing succeeded much better than I expected, and the recruiting is still going on.

I object to massing the colored people together, and think they should be scattered as much as possible among the whites, because the influence of the whites upon them is beneficial, whereas the influences that surround them when congregated together are not calculated to elevate or improve them.

HD

Testimony of Gov. Andrew Johnson before the American Freedmen's Inquiry Commission, 23 Nov. 1863, filed with O-328 1863, Letters Received, ser. 12, RG 94 [K-96]. Topical labels in the margin are omitted.

102: Testimony by the Commissioner for the Organization of Black Troops in Middle and East Tennessee before the American Freedmen's Inquiry Commission

[*Nashville, Tenn. November 23, 1863*]
Testimony of Maj. Geo. L. Stearns.

Q How do you find things here?

A Slavery is dead; that is the first thing. That is what we all begin with here, who know the state of affairs. The next most distinguishing feature in this country, in relation to slavery & the Gov't is, the manner in which these people are cowed by the force of the Gov't. Slaveholders of all classes,—the common farmer, the most aristocratic man and the most aristocratic lady—come into this room to talk with me about their slaves, and are the most polite people I ever saw. I should say the bulk of the people here are not yet exactly satisfied that the slaves are to be free. Many of them give it up, but there is a lingering hope that by some hocus-pocus things will get back to the old state. So long as that continues, the master has not made up his mind to hire his slave, & the slave finds that it is very difficult to work for anybody who will pay him. The great difficulty here has been the injustice of the U.S. Gov't to the slave. I do not mean to say that it was intentional on the part of anybody; on the contrary, the more I see of it, the more I see it was a political necessity

Q In what does the injustice consist?

A One case will suffice for all. Brig. Gen. Morton, now of the Engineer Corps, was ordered by Gen. Buell, a year ago last July, to superintend the fortifications of Nashville. It was a very important work; and, as he told me this morning, they collected by impressment and by voluntary offer of service, some three thousand negroes to work on the fortifications. They were obliged to give them poor food, because they had nothing better; they had no tents, and slept in the open air. These men lived upon inferior meat & bread, – the refuse, of course, of the army supplies, – & slept on the hill-side at night. He says they worked well, and through all that were cheerful, although in the fifteen months that they have been employed at that fort – Fort Negley – about 800 have died. He says he thinks it was necessary, because, by the building of that fort, at that time, the safety of Nashville was secured, and we were enabled to hold Nashville, instead of making a stand at Fort Donelson.

Q How were they paid?

A They never have been paid. Such examples are everywhere. I know from what I see in this department that they must be everywhere, and they exist from the same cause; and that is, the refusal of the Gov't, at the time, to decide whether the negro or his master should be paid. They blinked the question here, as they blinked it everywhere. I want you to understand, that this is all hearsay testimony, and I am not to be called upon to prove it. I will give you the names of parties familiar with the facts. [NOTE. See letter of Capt. Morton, at end of Nashville testimony.][1]

Q You say slavery is dead. Now, the practical question we are concerned in is, to what extent and in what way ought the gov't to interfere to aid the transition. Ought they to let the problem work out itself, or do something to relieve the suffering incidental to such a condition; and if so, what should they do?

A It is my impression, that the less gov't interference we can have, the better. But there seems to me to be two necessities; these complied with, Gov't may leave everything else alone. First, the necessity of the Gov't for troops. They must have them, and they can get them in the South cheaper, and with less disturbance to the country than they can anywhere else.

Q And as good troops?

A Better. I should be willing to risk all I have upon making, within six months, better troops in this department, than you can find in the United States army.

Q You will risk 10,000 of them, well officered, against 10,000 confederates?

A Confederates or Yankees either.

Q That is the first necessity. What is the other?

A. The other is, that in taking these men – the gov't say they want 20,000 – there will be a large number of women & their families left, who have attached themselves to these soldiers, and whom these soldiers recognize as their wives and children, whether they are their own children or not.

Q Before you pass from that, just tell us whether you suppose they would have any objection to being married?

A. On the contrary, there is nothing that would delight them so much as to have the marriage ceremony performed, and particularly in church. The negro, you know, is very religious. The value of the negro to us, at this moment, is in his enthusiasm, which far exceeds that of the white; in his cheerfulness, which is to be seen everywhere, North & South, especially under privation; in his capacity to bear hardships, and in his capacity for discipline. You can discipline colored troops in half the time that you can white. The negro gives his whole attention to the work, and takes a pride in it. They want to enlist. They do not feel themselves to be soldiers, until they get the muskets. They never feel sure of it, because they have been told so many times that they were enlisting for soldiers, and found themselves laborers.

Q Do you find that they prefer to be soldiers or laborers?

A I should say that two-thirds of them would prefer being soldiers to being laborers.

Q Are they unwilling as soldiers to labor, when labor is called for?

A Oh, no, they labor cheerfully.

Q Your opinion is, that in the course of six months, well-drilled, they will become, on the average, at least as good soldiers as whites?

A Yes; I do not think it admits of a question.

Q How many colored soldiers have you in this department?

A We have about the equivalent of three regiments – 3000 men.

Q Are they consolidated in regiments?

A Yes; they are not scattered any more than the white troops; perhaps not so much as many of the white regiments.

Q What is to be done with the women and children? Is it necessary for the gov't to interfere for their protection & comfort?

A At this time, there are a large number of them who are destitute, because the soldiers and laborers on the fortifications have never been paid. In view of this destitution of the families, which at one time was pressing upon us very severely, and is still, though I do not think it has been increasing for the last two or three weeks, I wrote a letter to the Governor, to induce him to interfere in the matter, as he has the power to do, but he cannot see the end of it,

417

and is very loath to enter upon it. I proposed to the Governor to take the Fairview estate, near Gallatin, which contains 1500 acres, probably 1000 arable land and 300 woodland, and lay off 200 lots of two acres each, and put a hut on each lot, – one hut to each family; the lots to be cultivated for their own use. There will then be a farm of 600 acres left, on which they will work six hours per day in summer and four in winter, leaving them the rest of the time to culvitate their own patches. They will have a Commissary and Quartermaster to supply their food & clothing, as far as the Gov't can supply them, a Chaplain to educate the children and enforce cleanliness in and about their farms, and a farmer to manage the farm. The negro is very anxious to know what will become of his family if he enlists, and would be very glad to allot his pay for their support. If the Gov't pays him $13,00 a month, he can spare $10.00;[2] but the money will never reach his family, if they are scattered round the country; but on the plan I propose, they could be reached readily. Thus we should have 200 families, each receiving $10.00 per month, or $2000 in all. The details of subsistence, & the supplying of clothing to each family could be adjusted in time.

Q About what proportion of Tenn. do we now hold?

A. Practically, it is less than half the State. That is, you are safe inside our picket lines, and are not safe anywhere else. The State is under our dominion, but you, going out through this State, and your business being known as a Gov't commission, or myself going out, being known as the Commissioner for enlisting colored troops, it would be a question whether your life or mine would be safe. The guerrillas are everywhere. I should provide, that the moment any of these families undertook to take care of themselves, they should be permitted to go. Interfere as little as possible. If they can make a bargain to work for any farmer on better terms than they can obtain on the plantation, let them do so. The moment the Gov't lets up the price of labor, by allowing their Quartermasters & their engineers & other officers to employ men at fair rates of wages, that moment you change the whole condition of labor in this department, at least. Every able-bodied man then brings his price. The only difficulty in this operation is, you see, that the laborer is transferred to the army, and under the ordinary state of affairs, there is no mode by which his wages can be paid to his family.

Q You say the Governor has power to provide for the families?

A Yes, I think so; but you shall judge for yourselves. [Maj. Stearns here presented extracts from the instructions to Gov. Johnson, which fully confirmed his statement.][3]

. . . .

Q In a general way, in Middle & Eastern Tennessee, do the negro women work on the plantations?

A Yes, Sir.

Q Do you think the reverse is true of Ky?

A I should think it cannot be true, from what I have heard.

Q You think, then, no further interference is needed on the part of the Gov't than you propose?

A No; I am certain that is enough. I think that would be an advantage to the whole country. The idea is this: that the moment you bring the supply of labor low, so that the whites will be glad to take any labor rather than work themselves, the question is settled. The black will then receive good treatment and good pay, because, if he don't, he will say, "I won't work for you." That will come, the moment peace is restored to the land. The moment this rebellion is quelled, and no hope of any other control than that of the United States, and no hope of the restoration of slavery, that moment, they will begin to cast about to see what they shall do; and there will come such a demand for labor, that from that moment the question is settled.

Q What wages do negroes receive here?

A They can readily get a dollar a day for ordinary work. It is, of the greatest importance that all these men, when employed by the Gov't, should be regularly paid. If payment is delayed, they have no faith in the ultimate intentions of the Gov't. The Gov't is losing, here in the immediate vicinity of Nashville, not less than a million of dollars, by the loss of necessary labor, which by paying promptly, they might have obtained. The principal officer of engineers, Brig. Genl Morton, said to me that he could profitably employ 10000 more negroes, if he had them, on the works from Fort Donelson to Murfreesboro'.

One feature in the slave system of Tennessee should be borne in mind, and that is, that the chief value of the negroes is in rearing young negroes for the Southern market.

The important element in the civilization of the negro is good wages, regularly paid. He knows well enough what he wants, and he knows how to get what he wants, if he has fair pay and his liberty He knows, too, what he should avoid, and has a very fair perception of self-interest, and considerable sagacity. I am speaking of the negroes of Tennessee.

It seems to me of great importance that in all the Federal courts, the evidence of the negro should be taken just as that of the white man is. [*Query* – Do the Federal Courts follow the State laws in this respect?][4]

It is a mistake to suppose that the reports which appear in the Northern papers of cruelties exercised towards the negroes in the extreme South are untrue. Those who have witnessed them testify to this fact. I have often been assured that the planters here in Tennessee have sometimes to watch their daughters to keep them from intercourse with the negroes. This, though of course exceptional, is yet common enough to be a source of uneasiness to parents.

Numerous applications have been made to me by planters in the vicinity of Nashville, especially during the last month, to take their slaves by force, as they say they have become a nuisance to them, and they want me to make soldiers of them. These applications have come from men & women from both farmers and mechanics. Many of them wished their slaves taken, whether they got compensation or not. About forty have been offered to me in the last month.

There are striking examples of ability occasionally met with among slaves. I know a slave at Mrs. Acklands, near Nashville, a slave who manages the hot-houses and green-houses there, and I have never seen any in the North managed with more judgment. I know another, who is a blacksmith, who has earned for his mistress an average of a thousand dollars a year for fifteen or twenty years. He continued to work for her after the insurrection, but having accidentally hurt himself, and wishing to have some medicine, he sent to his mistress and asked for it. She refused to give it to him, telling him he might buy it himself; upon which he resolved that instead of working for her, he would work for himself. He is now doing so, and in the regular receipt of five dollars a day. His mistress came to me recently and urged me to take this negro by force; but not desiring to take these men by force, I declined to do so.

I find that the prejudice of color fades away before negro recruiting, whereever it is tried. I believe the enlisting of the negro as a soldier will do more to elevate the negro character than any other influence—more, probably, than all other influences combined. I think that, in the end, the two races will harmonize, and my opinion is that the black man will elevate himself faster than the Southern white, especially that class called the poor whites of the South. Before the war, there were no negro schools here; but now there are ten or twelve such schools established in this city, and all of them supported by blacks. The average attendance in these schools is 800.

. . . .

HD

Excerpts from testimony of Maj. Geo. L. Stearns before the American Freedmen's Inquiry Commission, [23 Nov. 1863], filed with O-328 1863, Letters

Received, ser. 12, RG 94 [K-98]. Topical labels in the margin are omitted. Omitted portions concerned white officers for black troops, the recruitment of black soldiers, the intelligence of black people in Tennessee, and the degradation of white women under slavery.

1 Brackets in manuscript. For the letter in question, see doc. 103, immediately below.
2 At the time, black soldiers were in fact paid only $10 per month, minus $3 for clothing, whereas white privates received $13, plus clothing. (See *Freedom*, ser. 2: chap. 7.)
3 Brackets in manuscript. The instructions to Andrew Johnson, military governor of Tennessee, were presumably those issued by the Secretary of War in April 1863, which directed Johnson, among other things, to "take in charge" the slaves of disloyal owners "and provide for their useful employment and subsistence," to "take measures to secure employment and reasonable compensation for the labor of all others [slaves] of whatever age or sex," to take possession of abandoned property and use it "as you deem proper," and to lease out abandoned plantations. (*Official Records*, ser. 3, vol. 3, pp. 122–23.)
4 Brackets in manuscript. Federal courts did indeed follow state laws respecting the competency of witnesses, which meant, in all Southern states and many Northern ones, that black witnesses could not testify in cases to which white people were party. In July 1864, however, Congress forbade the exclusion of witnesses from federal courts on account of color. (*Statutes at Large*, vol. 12, pp. 588–89, and vol. 13, p. 351.)

103: Supervising Engineer of the Defenses of Nashville to the Acting Commissioner for the Organization of Black Troops in Middle and East Tennessee

Nashville, Tenn., Dec. 4, 1863.
Captain: I have the honor to acknowledge the receipt of your communication of 3^d inst., and to furnish the following replies to the interrogatories of the Secretary of the Commission of which Hon. Robt Dale Owen is President.[1]
I. The number of negroes employed on the defences of Nashville, from the time of breaking ground in August, 1862, to April 1st, 1863, as per the rolls in the Engineer Office, which are as nearly exact as circumstances have permitted, was twenty-seven hundred and sixty-eight (2,768) The average number constantly employed was fifteen hundred and twenty-three (1523). The number on the morning Reports from April 1st, 1863, to Dec. 1st, 1863, is twenty-one hundred and thirty-three (2133) The number constantly employed for the same period was, on an average, five hundred and twenty-four. (524)

II. The wages have been rated as follows: — For hands belonging to the Camp, and found in clothing, fuel, quarters, & medical attendance, *seven dollars ($7) per month.*

The "volunteer" negroes, who do not stay in Camp, and find their own clothing, *Ten ($10) dollars per month.*

III. Wages have been paid to "volunteer" negroes to the amount of twenty-two hundred and eighty dollars ($2.280), being the total amount earned by that class to December 1st, namely, for 228 volunteers, employed one month each. (N.B. This amount of labor is not included in the reply to the second interrogatory.) In a very few instances, the owner of the negro or negros has been paid the earnings of said negroes, upon special orders to that effect from Head quarters, Department of the Cumberland.

IV. The negroes have, as a general rule, been faithful and diligent — far more so than could reasonably have been expected, considering the circumstances of exposure & privation of proper clothing, blankets, &c., under which they were at first employed.

In many cases, dishonesty has been properly chargeable to them. On the other hand, when Nashville was, on one occasion, momentarily expected to be attacked, they cheerfully and zealously turned out, after a hard day's work, and labored all night, or nearly so, strengthening the defences; and even, with a certain degree of enthusiasm, pledged themselves to maintain a part of the line with their axes and other implements, against the anticipated rebel attack.

The principal difficulty in regard to the payment of wages for the labor of negroes in this Department arises from the uncertainty whether said earnings are properly due to the negroes or to their masters. The former Commanding General of this Department, Maj. Gen'l Rosecrans, ordered me to Washington, in July last, to wait upon the Hon. Sec^y of War, to lay before him a statement of the case, in order that a decision might be obtained from the proper authority in Washington in regard to it. I had previously, namely, in May last, turned over to Lieut. Burroughs, of the Engineer Corps, who had been in charge of the works of defence at Nashville since 1863, the sum of thirty thousand dollars, to be devoted to paying the wages of negroes, whenever said point should be decided. I am, Sir, Very respectfully, Your ob't servt,

HLcSr   (Signed) Ja^s St. C. Morton

Capt. Eng'rs. Jas. St. C. Morton to Capt. R. D. Mussey, 4 Dec. 1863, filed with O-328 1863, Letters Received, ser. 12, RG 94 [K-99]. For the efforts by Morton and General William S. Rosecrans, former commander of the Department of the Cumberland, to secure the payment of wages owed to black men

who had labored on the fortifications of Nashville, see above, doc. 92n.
Although Morton had evidently not yet learned of the decision, the Secretary
of War had, on November 25, approved a recommendation by General George
H. Thomas, Rosecrans's successor, that the wages be paid from engineer
department funds to the laborers themselves, and not to their owners. (See
above, doc. 99.)

1 The commission in question was the American Freedmen's Inquiry Commission, whose secretary had asked that the following questions be answered by
the supervising engineer of the defenses of Nashville: "1. How many negroes
have been employed on the public works in and near Nashville? 2. What has
been the stipulated price to be paid for such labor? 3. Have the wages, in
whole or in part, been paid; and if only in part, what part? 4. Have the blacks
labored industriously or otherwise?" (J. M. W. Yerrinton to My dear Muzzey,
28 Nov. 1863, Records of Capt. R. D. Mussey & of Maj. George L. Stearns,
ser. 1149, Organization of USCT, Dept. of the Cumberland, RG 393 Pt. 1
[C-407].)

104: Acting Commissioner for the Organization of Black Troops in Middle and East Tennessee to a Northern Friend

Nashville [*Tenn.*] Dec 19th *1863*

My dear Reid   I wish you would get your friend Lovejoy to
ventilate in the House the recent outrages in this city in the matter
of impressment of colored men.

Gen[l] Ward comd'g Brigade here under Genl. R. S. Granger was
ordered to furnish 150 of his men for fatigue duty to Capts Perkins
& Stubbs A.Q.Ms.   He obtained from Gen[l] Granger permission to
furnish negro men instead—   He thereupon set his officers to work
to impress negroes wherever they could find them—   The
impressment was without exception the most arbitrary unjust and
cruel thing of the sort I ever saw.

Men were taken from their shops, their houses, dragged off their
hacks and not allowed to put up their teams which were left
standing in the streets   men who had exemption papers—in
consideration of having voluntarily worked for the Government—
were taken with out regard to their papers, government employees
were taken and the work on the magazine here the next day was
stopped therefor—and the pressing parties went so far even as to
press some colored soldiers I had here.   Every one of these assertions
I can prove by undoubted testimony.   I complained of the matter
here and received several indorsements in reply which did not
controvert nor contradict one single assertion I made.

General Ward is from Kentucky and when not too drunk—which

is nearly all the time—to talk. talks the everlasting Negro— Dr— Bowen whom you know says. General Ward's idea is to bring the Government—and enlistments of colored men—into disrepute. He is certainly doing this whether he intends it or not. I am yours truly

ALS   R Delavan Mussey

Capt. R. Delavan Mussey to My dear Reid, 19 Dec. 1863, M-190 1863, Letters Received, ser. 360, Colored Troops Division, RG 94 [B-413]. Mussey signed as a captain in the 19th U.S. Infantry. The addressee (probably Whitelaw Reid, a Northern journalist) evidently referred Mussey's letter to Owen Lovejoy, a Republican congressman from Illinois, who, in an undated endorsement, wrote, "Capt. Mussey is of the Regular Army & his Statements are fully reliable." Other endorsements indicate that the letter reached the War Department on March 26, 1864, and was then forwarded to the Bureau of Colored Troops. On March 31, the chief of that bureau, without addressing the substance of the complaint, scolded Mussey for failing to report "through the prescribed military channels, in order that the facts may be properly investigated." (A.A. Genl. C. W. Foster to Capt. R. D. Mussey, 31 Mar. 1864, vol. 2, p. 470, Letters Sent, ser. 342, Colored Troops Division, RG 94 [B-413].) Neither Mussey's complaint to officers at Nashville respecting the impressment of black men, nor any of the "several indorsements" he received in reply has been found, but on December 19, 1863 (the date of Mussey's letter to Reid), an adjutant of the commander of the District of Nashville informed Mussey that his "communications" about impressment had been referred to General William T. Ward, who had been "directed to arrest the parties complained of . . . , release the negroes and not to impress any more until further orders." (A.A.A.G. to Capt. Mussey, 19 Dec. 1863, vol. 2 DMT, p. 46, Letters Sent, ser. 2915, Dist. of Nashville, RG 393 Pt. 2 No. 184 [C-406].)

105: Commander of the Left Wing of the 16th Army Corps to the Adjutant General of the Army

Pulaski Tenn. January 19th 1864

General   There are in this State a large number of planters who have decided to act upon the fact that Slaves are free and that they can no longer hold them to labor, and they are anxious to have some settled plan upon which they can act in employing such negroes as the Government does not require. I have always encouraged planters and farmers to hire their slaves— (such as I could not enlist—) and in most Cases they are anxious and willing; but to do it successfully the Commander of the troops or the General Government must lay down some policy upon which the farmer can act, and by which they can hold the Freedmen to live up to their part of the Contract. Those that come to my lines I generally put to work on abandoned plantations, or hire out to parties to pick cotton, &c. – But this is only a very small proportion of the slaves in the country who are not fit for the Army, and I desire your views as to fair wages. what would be a proper method for making the slaves (after having voluntarily contracted to work a year) live up to their contract? – A uniform price would be better, from the fact – that it will keep negroes from running about to obtain higher prices. –

I submit this matter as it is different, you see, from the method pursued on the Mississippi River, from the fact that most of the plantations are occupied by their owners – and many of the slaves are Still upon them. – The policy once inaugurated that all the slaves in the State are free – and must be hired and their labor paid for – it will force all to adopt the policy. – No matter whether those opposed to it – agree to it or not, they will have to do it for Self protection, – as negroes will go where they can get paid for their labor – and Government will protect them in doing it.

I may state that I have already recruited, under your old order,[1] two Regiments in North Alabama, known as 2^d and 3^d Alabama Infantry AD., and will soon have another under way. I find no difficulty in raising a few Regiments whenever I happen to Stop on any march, – and would like authority to appoint from my command a board of Officers to examine applicants from the command for positions in the Regiments.

I will soon forward list of Officers who have been appointed by me to the Regiments named – that they may receive proper appointments from you. I have the honor to remain – General Very Respectfully your. Obt. Servt

HLcSr

G. M. Dodge

Brig. Genl. G. M. Dodge to Brig. Genl. L. Thomas, 19 Jan. 1864, vol. 32 16AC, pp. 346–47, Letters Sent, ser. 6159, Left Wing, 16th Army Corps, RG 393 Pt. 2 No. 406 [C-2154]. A few days later, General Dodge outlined for a subordinate officer the labor policy he had adopted: "I encourage all Negroes (that the Government does not want) to Stay at home and seek Employment from their former owners; and, if permitted by the United States Government, will make such negroes as do this live up to their part of the Contract." Dodge also permitted private employers to hire former slaves who had come into the camps of his command and were "of no account to us." (Brig. Genl. G. M. Dodge to Col. H. R. Mizener, 23 Jan. 1864, vol. 32 16AC, pp. 348–50, Letters Sent, ser. 6159, Left Wing, 16th Army Corps, RG 393 Pt. 2 No. 406 [C-2155].) On February 4, 1864, Adjutant General Lorenzo Thomas issued a comprehensive order respecting the reception, recruitment, and employment of former slaves in middle and east Tennessee and northern Alabama, which addressed many of the issues raised by Dodge. Thomas's order authorized military officers to supervise annual contracts between freedpeople and civilian employers, to enforce contractual obligations upon both parties, and to lease "to loyal citizens" land that had been abandoned by disloyal owners. Under that order, General Dodge rented out at least eight plantations and farms, requiring that the lessees "treat the Negroes employed upon their farms *as free*," and pay them wages in cash or one-third of the crop. (See below, doc. 109; Z. S. Spaulding to Wm. P. Mellen, Esq., 1 Apr. 1864, enclosing "List of Farms leased by Brig. Genl. G. M. Dodge," Letters Received from Assistant Special Agents, Records of the General Agent, RG 366 [Q-166].)

1 Probably Special Order 45, issued by the adjutant general on August 18, 1863, which had directed Union commanders in the Mississippi Valley to promote the enlistment of "all able bodied male negroes . . . into the Military service of the United States." (*Freedom*, ser. 1, vol. 3: doc. 172.)

106A: Commander of U.S. Forces at Gallatin, Tennessee, to the Headquarters of the District of Nashville

Gallatin Tennessee January 26th 1864

Capt   I wish to report to you the direction given to the labor of the blacks in this vicinity to induce a change from slave to compensated labor. A year ago last month I hired out ten to assist in obtaining lumber for use of the Quartermaster at this Post— I hired out about three hundred to chop wood along the Rail Road at an average of about $12 per month—but the most important effort was upon the Franklin or so called Fairview Estate about three miles from this Post— Sometime in the month of March and before I was acquainted with either the Overseer or Trustees of said Estate, about sixty of the negroes old and young with wagons, horses. household furniture &c came to Gallatin, I immediately sent them back only three miles, and told them I could protect them there, as well as I could in Gallatin— They had comfortable Brick houses to live in and a large plantation, twenty three hundred acres to raise their own provisions and materials for clothing— At this time the Trustees— Albert Franklin and D[r] John W. Franklin and the Overseer M[r] Oliver were all violent, vindictive Rebels. determined that they would never again recognise the U.S. Government— There were on this Estate at that time one hundred and sixty seven negroes—old and young— Since the occupation of the Country by the Federal troops, these blacks had become more and more insurbordinate.

And a strong reason for it was the fact that the Franklins and Overseer continued their cowardly and malignant opposition to the Authorities— In the month of April last the Trustees and Overseer called on me requesting me to compel the blacks to work, saying that there was a thousand Acres of plow land to be worked, but as matters stood, there would not be produce enough raised to feed the slaves, to say nothing about, cattle horses &^{c}— I refused promptly to act the Overseer or Negro Whipper for them— Again they came in the month of April, again I refused. Early in the Month of May they came again and said that the slaves would become a charge on the Government then, next. now this winter, unless I took control of the Estate— I then told them I would do so, but that I should tell the slaves, that they should be paid for their labor. The Overseer and Trustees agreed to it at once and were glad of it— Two days afterwards I rode out to the Estate— the negroes were called together and I told them they would be required to work, to cultivate the farm lands well, to raise enough to support themselves, as the Government would not issue rations to them— "Now" said I. "although I require you to work faithfully and diligently, I will also see that you men are paid eight and you women five dollars per month for your labor" I told the Overseer to report to me every week, and if any of the hands were idle to report them— He had no trouble with them—and late in the Season as it was, more was produced on the Estate—than had for any one year, for ten years before— Besides enough to pay all of the laborers and Overseer, there is at least $1200 clear for the Estate— The corn was gathered and the Quarter master until within two weeks has been hauling it to this Post for the Government enough at least to pay the laborers— There are now vouchers in the Quarter masters hands, to pay about two thirds of the price of the labor— On the 14th inst I received an Order from Major General Rousseau,[1] preventing me from interfering with the Estate— This order was sent me without permitting me to make a statement of the facts but was based on a letter written by a fellow by the name of Edwin H Ewing, an unmitigated cowardly rebel—who assisted as much as Isham G. Harris to drive the State of Tennessee out of the Union—and who has recently taken the Amnesty Oath and published a letter in which he has the damnable impudence to criticise and instruct the President on the recent Proclamation—[2] Of course the Order of Major Gen Rousseau leaves to the Trustees a large amount of grain, which was raised under my authority and upon my promise to the slaves, in the presence of the Overseer and Trustees, and with their hearty Approval, that they the slaves should be paid for their labor. and a part of which grain should be taken by the Quarter Master at this Post and the money therefor paid to the slaves. The amount of money required to pay the blacks is $1600 of which about $300 has been paid them in clothing– There is now $1000 in the hands of the Quarter master for them and there is at least $2000 worth of produce on the Estate of which it requires only $300 more to pay for the labor. I respectfully ask permission to take that amount from the Estate to make my word good with the slaves– As a citizen the slaves would not have obeyed me, They did so because I was an officer and relied upon my keeping my promise– The faith of the Government is indirectly pledged to these ignorant people– I therefore respectfully protest against Maj Gen Rousseau's Order–Because he took the word of Dr John W Franklin a vile traitor, who stated a deliberate falsehood. Because Major Gen Rousseau denied me the privilege of making a report in the matter, a courtesy allowed every Officer of the Army. And because the Order works great injustice to the slaves who worked the Estate and worked well, under the promise that they should be paid

I respectfully ask permission to send a copy of this report to the Secretary of War through the Head Quarters of Major Gen. Rousseau and Major General Thomas   Respectfully Submitted

HLS   E. A. Paine

Brig. Gen. E. A. Paine to Capt. B. H. Polk, 26 Jan. 1864, enclosed in Maj. Genl. Lovell H. Rousseau to Brig. Genl. Wm. D. Whipple, 30 Jan. 1864, filed as N-20 1864, Letters Received, ser. 925, Dept. of the Cumberland, RG 393 Pt. 1 [C-18]. The final paragraph was added by General Paine in his own handwriting. General Lovell H. Rousseau, commander of the District of Nashville, forwarded Paine's report to the headquarters of General George H. Thomas, commander of the Department of the Cumberland, with a covering letter that denounced Paine's "administration of affairs at and about Gallatin," especially "his undertaking to hire out negroes to their owners and asserting that there should be none but free labor." Many slaveholders, Rousseau reported, "have entered into the Contract. . . . This action is against the Law, the Presidents [Emancipation] Proclamation and the policy heretofore and now existing in this Department." Rousseau also forwarded a report by the inspector general of the District of Nashville, who had investigated "matters pertaining to the Post of Gallatin, and the troops under command of General Paine." The inspector had spoken with the trustees of the Fairview estate, whose account conformed with that of Paine, "with the exception of their having understood that the Slaves were to be paid. They state that they *knew nothing* of such an arrangement until General Paine spoke of it to the negroes; but that they did *not* dissent at the time, nor do they *now* from paying the negroes." Indeed, one of the trustees had admitted "that they could have done nothing with the slaves, if it had not been for the interference of Gen'l Paine," to whom "he felt under great obligations." (Capt. G. M. L. Johnson to Capt. B. H. Polk, 27 Jan. 1864, in the same file.)

1 Lovell H. Rousseau, commander of the District of Nashville.
2 The Proclamation of Amnesty and Reconstruction, issued by President Abraham Lincoln on December 8, 1863. The edict offered "full pardon" – including restoration of all property rights "except as to slaves, and in property cases where rights of third parties shall have intervened" – to most persons who had engaged in the rebellion, once they had taken an oath of allegiance to the United States that required their adherence to congressional acts and presidential proclamations respecting slavery. The proclamation also outlined a procedure whereby the loyal residents of a seceded state might establish a new state government and seek readmission to the Union. (*Statutes at Large*, vol. 13, pp. 737–39.)

106B: Commander of the District of Nashville to the Headquarters of the Department of the Cumberland, Enclosing a Blank Contract Form

Nashville, Tennessee, January 30th 1864.
General   I think it proper I should report to you touching affairs in this District generally and I do so.

The troops are generally under good discipline and very well drilled far better than I expected to find. They are well equipped and in good condition excepting of course the 5th Tenn. Cavalry Col Stokes and a few others who are neither well drilled disciplined or equipped.

It is proper for me to remark here that two battalions of that regiment will never be of service together and I shall press upon Gov^{nr} Johnson the suggestion of the General Comdg the Dept. to separate them.

Generally matters go on pretty well between the Military and the people in the District but with some exceptions. They have not gone so well at and about Gallatin. At other posts in the District there has been no real cause for complaint The Post Commanders having been vigilant in suppressing the rebellion and just in their treatment of the people.

I call especial attention to the admirable administration of affairs in his command by Colonel Henry R. Mizner, 14th Mich Vol^{s} at Columbia. His troops (generally led by Major James C. Fitzgibbon, a very efficient and gallant officer) have captured I believe more armed rebels than he has men in his regiment.

The disposition of the people to return to their allegiance is general and apparent. I think that eight tenths of the people of this District desire the restoration of civil authority and the old Government and will say so when the proper occasion is offered.

I have conversed with most of the leading and influential men of the District and think I am not deceived The change is very marked and decided and the Genl Comd[g] himself would be surprised to see it. The disorders and confusion incident to the war have caused great suffering of which they are heartily tired and are desirous of peace on almost any terms.

The Negro population is giving much trouble to the Military as well as to the people. Slavery is virtually dead in Tennessee, although the State is excepted from the Emancipation Proclamation. Negroes leave their homes and stroll over the country uncontrolled. Hundreds of them are supported by the Government, who neither work nor are able to work. Many straggling negroes have arms obtained from soldiers and by their insolence and threats greatly alarm and intimidate white families who are not allowed to keep arms or who would generally be afraid to use if they had them.

The Military cannot look after these things through the country and there are no civil authorities to do it.

In many cases negroes leave their homes to work for themselves boarding and lodging with their Masters defiantly asserting their right to do so.

It is now and has been for some time the practice of soldiers to go to the country and bring in wagon loads of Negro women and children to this city and I suppose to other posts. Protections are granted to some slaves to remain with their owners exempt from labor as in case of Mrs Buchanan (relative to Secr.y E. H. East.) whose letter on that subject is forwarded with this. Genl Paine has adopted the policy of hiring slaves to their owners by printed contracts made in blank and filled up for the occasion, which though a flagrant usurpation I have not interfered with his action on that and many other subjects preferring to submit such matters to the consideration of the Gen[l] commanding the Dept. which I shall do in a separate communication forwarded at the same time this goes. Enclosed I send you blank contract used by Brig Gen Paine.

Officers in command of Colored troops are in constant habit of pressing all able bodied slaves into the Military service of the U.S. One communication from citizens near M[c]Minnville on that subject I have already forwarded you, many similar complaints have been made This State being excepted from the emancipation proclamation I suppose all things are against good faith and the policy of the Government, Forced enlistments, I have endeavored to stop but find it difficult if not impracticable to do so. In fact as District commander I am satisfied I am unable to correct the evils complained of, connected with the black population and besides I am not willing to take upon myself the fixing of any rules in these matters without orders or advice from Dept. Head Quarters. At best the remedy would be difficult to find and I suppose can only be furnished by the restoration of civil authorities. By proclamation Govr Johnson has ordered elections in March of Civil Officers.

I desire to call attention to another matter. From impressments legal and illegal and from thefts there are very few horses, mules or oxen left on the farms and the few that are left are almost worthless. At present there are many large farms without one servicable work beast on the place. The farmers are afraid to purchase because of repeated impressments. Every mounted regiment that goes through the country takes what it pleases of stock &c and pays what price or none at all it likes. Between the loyal and disloyal no discrimination is made. Unless an order be made preventing future impressments and protecting the farmers little or no crops will be produced.

When the Civil Authority shall be restored, assurances of protection from Dept. H. Qrs. to all persons who would take the oath of amnesty prescribed in the Presidents proclamation[1] in my opinion would induce the community almost in a body to voluntarily take that oath and seek the protection of Government. At present that proclamation is of little practical utility amongst the people as there is no person appointed by whom the oath should be administered. No place or time fixed for that purpose. It would seem that some importance should be attached to the administration of that oath to produce the effect designed, and should not be (as oaths heretofore) lightly administered.

. . . .

HLS   Lovell H. Rousseau

[Enclosure]

THIS AGREEMENT

MADE AT GALLATIN, SUMNER Co , TENN., this............day of ....
A. D., 1864, between..and........ ....

....

WITNESSETH : That the said..
hires and employs the said....................... ....as a laborer, for the term of ono year,
commencing on the............day of.............................and ending on the ....day
of........................... The said................................... agrees to pay the said
....for said services, at the rate of............................
dollars per month, for the entire term, ...dollars to be paid at the
end of half of the term. and the balance at the expiration thereof; to pay for necessary medical attendance, furnish a comfortable cabin or room to live or board in—also good and
wholesome provisions—and if the said................................... .... shall die, to decently
bury his remains—also to furnish the said.. ....two suits of good,
suitable summer clothes, one suit of good winter clothing, ono hat, and two pairs of good
shoes, suitable for his work.

And the said...... ....in consideration of the undertakings and
promises of the said.....................................herein made, hereby agrees to labor
faithfully and diligently for the said...as he may direct, for
said term of one year ; And the said...further agrees to
have deducted from his pay the amount which would be due for all time. lost during said
term.

IN WITNESS WHEREOF. the parties have subscribed this agreement.

Excerpt from Maj. General Lovell H. Rousseau to Brig. Gen. W. D. Whipple, 30 Jan. 1864, enclosing printed contract form, [Jan. 1864], filed as N-20 1864, Letters Received, ser. 925, Dept. of the Cumberland, RG 393 Pt. 1 [C-18]. In the remainder of the letter, General Rousseau complained about the seizure of private homes in Nashville for military purposes and reported on the construction and defense of the Nashville and Western Railroad. The letter from Mrs. Buchanan, said to have been enclosed, is not in the file. The petition from citizens near McMinnville has not been found in the files of letters received by the Department of the Cumberland. For Rousseau's "separate communication" regarding the administration of General Eleazer A. Paine, see doc. 106An., immediately above. In response to Rousseau's letters, the department commander, General George H. Thomas, ruled that "the Military authorities should have as little to do with the negro as possible, it being considered best to let the Masters and Slaves settle their own affairs without Military interference." Thomas instructed Rousseau to "give such orders as will prevent the bringing in of wagon loads of Colored Women and

Children, of whom no use can be made," and to order General Paine "to recall the papers requiring persons employing Negroes to pay them a certain amount of wages, and furnish them with a certain amount of Clothing, as that is a matter which he as the Military Commander of that Section, is not called upon to adjust." (Brig. Genl. Wm. D. Whipple to Maj. Genl. L. H. Rousseau, 3 Feb. 1864, Letters & Reports Received, ser. 2922, Dist. of Nashville, RG 393 Pt. 2 No. 184 [C-2034].) On February 11, 1864, General Thomas forwarded to Adjutant General Lorenzo Thomas several documents respecting Paine's administration, especially his labor policy, whereupon the adjutant general undertook his own investigation of the various complaints against Paine; his conclusions are printed immediately below, as doc. 106C.

1 The Proclamation of Amnesty and Reconstruction, issued by President Abraham Lincoln on December 8, 1863. For its provisions, see above, doc. 106An.

106C: **Adjutant General of the Army to the Commander of the Department of the Cumberland**

Louisville, Kentucky. February 27, 1864.
General: I have made a special visit to the town of Gallatin, in order to inquire into the condition of affairs in connection with the numerous papers you placed in my hands, making complaints by citizens against Brigadier General E. A. Paine.

I repaired to the estate of Fair-View, left in trust by the late Mr. Franklin, for educational purposes, and I find, from personal conversation with two of the trustees, that General Paine's arrangement with regard to making the negroes labor, and raise a crop, was in accordance with their wishes, and met their approval.

Without the payment of wages, I am satisfied, not even food for the negroes would have been raised. Now, after all payments are made, there will be a surplus. I have decided that the negroes shall be paid according to General Paine's arrangement, and have charged him to see that it is done. The complaints made by the trustees, arose more, they said, from fear that the plantation was to be taken for a Contraband Camp, which will not be done, and they are satisfied. I have stated to the Trustees that this property being under trust, it will not be interfered with, but, in order to secure the labor of the Negro, I have advised the lessees to make a distinct and fair bargain for their services, as otherwise they would, as is generally the case in this region of country, refuse to labor. I learn, of the crops of 1862, the Government took a quantity of corn and hay, equal to about Eleven hundred dollars, the claim for which has been presented to the Commissioner, at Nashville. The proceeds of the farm should not be seized even if the Trustees were at that time disloyal, and I have stated to them that these accounts shall be paid, which indeed is necessary, to pay for the maintainance of the negroes during last year, when making a crop. I will thank you to order the payment of these accounts.

The house occupied by General Paine, is necessary for himself and Staff. It was perfectly proper that he should take it, and Dr. Thompson ought not to complain, as he has been furnished with a suitable and comfortable residence without rent. Rent for his house is out of the question, and ought not to be paid.

Mrs. McGregor complains that General Paine took her furniture and was going to take her plantation, – she living five miles therefrom: Any officer in General Paine's position would have done the same thing, as the furniture was needed for the Provost Marshal. Her claim to the ownership of this place is utterly groundless. Her father, Pauldney Anderson, made the purchase of the estate from Captain Miller, now in the rebel service. Four thousand dollars was paid on it, and the balance of six thousand, remained unpaid, and no title has yet been given. Captain Miller will claim to return to this place, should he quit the rebel cause and take the oath of allegiance. Mrs McGregor's husband is now a Major in the rebel service. This is property which General Paine has clearly the right to take possession of, for the public interest.

In regard to the several complaints respecting negroes, I judge that General Paine's course has been entirely proper. He recognizes the institution of slavery in the State, and does not interfere with those negroes who choose to remain with their former masters. He does object to masters' bringing to his post, or receiving those who would be dependent upon the United States. If any such come, he will either send them back, or hire them out at wages, to such persons as are able to pay them. He encourages all such persons to remain at their former homes, where they are more comfortable than he can make them. I think General Paine's system a wise one, as he adopts the same principle I did towards those that came within our lines. Those that can work and won't work, shall not eat: in other words, they must make their own subsistence.

In the concentration of negroes in this region under my orders,[1] it may be impossible to hire all the contrabands sent from the front, where it is difficult to maintain them. If General Paine cannot do so, he will find it necessary to take possession of uncultivated plantations, or those belonging to rebels, for the purpose of putting the surplus at work, to earn their own living, and, if he does, the property to which Mrs. McGregor lays claim, should, I think, be the first place he should take possession of. I desire that he may receive full instructions to the above effect, as all these complaints went through Major General Rousseau–some of whose decisions are adverse to my own. I desire that he, as well as General Paine, may receive official copies of this communication.

I respectfully enclose all the papers referred to. I am, General, Very Respectfully, Your Obedient Servant,

HLc   [*Lorenzo Thomas*]

Adjutant General [Lorenzo Thomas] to Major General G. H. Thomas, 27 Feb. 1864, Letters & Telegrams Sent by L. Thomas, Adjutant General, ser. 9, RG 94 [V-106]. The enclosures, which were not copied into Thomas's letters-sent book, presumably included the letters printed immediately above as docs. 106A and 106B, as well as others filed with them.

1 For the adjutant general's order respecting former slaves in the Department of the Cumberland, see below, doc. 109.

107: Tennessee Unionist to the Adjutant General of the Army, Enclosing Two Memoranda

Murfresboro [*Tenn.*] Jany. 27. 1864

Dear Sir. A plan for the settlement employment & self support of Col^d refugees who have escaped from servitude & sought protection & support within the Federal lines, involves in some doubt, an enterprise. the practicability of which, experience alone can solve

The Freedman enters on a new theater of action, without any sagacious calculations that look beyond his release from the restrictions on his personal action while a Slave– His new condition must therfore (when he realises his dependence on the wisdom & humanity of others) greatly perplex him; and how ever desirious he may be to avail himself of his present liberty to promote his future welfare, he is made concious that the direction must be pointed out, by those who are supposed to sympathise with him, and hence the Gov^t through its Agents will have to assume a protectorate over this Class. to provide for their future welfare, as well, as to relieve itself from the burthen of their support & care

To this end. therfore we would respectfully propose that, the Gov^t shall take posession of all abandon'd lands, and lease the same for a stated period to responsible parties to cultivate the same on their own account–upon the agreement that they shall employ Col^d refugees at monthly wages to work said lands–said refugees being within the post lines of the Federal army, an as such subject to the authority of the Gov^t

The lessee in addition to the foregoing agreement, shall contract to house & support in a comfortable manner—as well as to cloath the Freedman so employ'd by him. The cost of the said cloathing to be deducted from the agreed value of his services.

The lessee shall also contract to receive & house & furnish with food & raiment the wife. children or parents who may be non producers—out of the wages of the producing members of the family—

In the selection of labouring hands it should be stipulated. that those who have wife—families or aged parents. shall not be disconnected from them—but go with them that they may be supported out of the proceeds of the labour of those of the family who are able to work.

The lessees of abandon'd lands shall provide comfortable quarters for the labourers employ'd by them

The lessees to give Bond & Security for the faithfull compliance with these obligation to employ—subsist—cloath, & pay quarterly the agreed value of services rendere'd

Should the wages of the Freedman, fall short of the cost of the support of himself or family—because of his or there disability. then such difiency on satisfactory proof shall be refunded by the Gov^t to the lessee— Or, an agreed rent per acre shall be fixed on. to be paid by the lessee, and appropriated—to the support of non producers—or those who. from disability are prevented from labour—

The above are presented as General views. the details to be hereafter filled up—if occasion should require

There are parties now here. to whom I have foreshadowed the above plans. who I think are anxious to arrange for the land & labour under them—

I leave this morning for Louisville for a short abscence— The Census is not finished though it will be to night & be enclosed with this— I regret I am not able to analize the census to report on the character effecency & value of the labouring part of those included in the return

If. Genl you should conclude to adopt some plan for the use of Lands & their cultivatn no time should be lost in arranging for its adoption—as the season for work is at hand & much labour will be required before the pitching of the Crops. Very Truly Your friend

W. Bosson

Enclosed—you have the terms on which Planters are proposing to retain & employ their servants

also

Schedule of Lands abandoned in this Vicinity.

ALS

[*Enclosure*]   [*Murfreesboro, Tenn. January 1864*]
    Planters in the County of Rutherford with the view of securing
the services of there slaves – or in other words to conciliate & prevent
them from running away – have promised to give them 10 cts p^r lb
for all the cotton they may produce & take care of & support them
as they have before done –
    Other planters are hiring their own Slaves. agreeing to give them
$70.00 p^r year and cloath & support them – requiring them to work
as they have usually done –
    Others. say to their slaves to go on as usual. and they will see
they are as well off as those employed by the Goverment. or others
    A common farm hand can easily cultivate – 8 acres of Land – 6 in
Cotton & 2 acers in Corn
    One Horse or mule can tend 20 Acres
    200^{lbs} of Ginn'd Cotton per Acre is a good average Crop –
    5 Bbls of Corn. or 25 Bushels is a fair average Crop –
HD

[*Enclosure*]   [*Murfreesboro, Tenn. January 1864*]
    Schedule of abandoned Lands. in the Vicinity of Murfresboro their
former owners & occupants having gone South

Frank Lytle	200 Acres	
Maj. John Childers	300	"
R B. Jetton	500	"
J. M. Avent	150	"
H. P. Keeble	150	"
D H. Spence	300	"
David Maney	400	"
John Bill Jr	150	"
Joseph Ewin	300	"

Note – It is thought there are 5000 Acres of good Cotton & Corn
land within 5 miles. that would require to cultivate them. 700
hands

Note. The above are situated within 3 miles of the
Town – Outside of this line there are other abandon'd Lands –
estimated to be equal in number of Acres to those reported.
HD

W. Bosson to Maj. Genl. Thomas, 27 Jan. 1864, enclosing terms of employ-
ment, [Jan. 1864], and schedule of abandoned lands, [Jan. 1864], B-2 1864,
Letters Received by Adjutant General L. Thomas, ser. 363, Colored Troops
Division, RG 94 [V-81]. The memoranda are in the same handwriting as the

letter. The census said to have been enclosed is not in the file. Bosson, who was born and raised in the North, had lived in Tennessee for more than two decades. In September 1863, in a petition to the Secretary of War, he and other "citizens of Tennessee, more or less interested in Negro Slavery," who now conceded emancipation to be "an accomplished and immutable fact," had denounced the impressment and abuse of black military laborers by the Union army and urged that "able bodied negro men be regularly inlisted into the service of the United States with the promise of pay and freedom, according to the laws of Congress." (Andrew Johnson, *The Papers of Andrew Johnson*, ed. LeRoy P. Graf, Ralph W. Haskins, and Paul H. Bergeron, 8 vols. to date [Knoxville, Tenn., 1967–], vol. 7, p. 432n.; John W. Bowen et al. to the Hon. Secretary of War, 26 Sept. 1863, B-242 1863, Letters Received, ser. 360, Colored Troops Division, RG 94 [B-26]; for the text of the petition, see *Freedom*, ser. 2: doc. 65.)

108: Acting Commissioner for the Organization of Black Troops in Middle and East Tennessee to the Headquarters of the Department of the Cumberland

Nashville [*Tenn.*] January 30" 1864

General, I have had considerable conversation with Mr. Spooner, Gov. Johnson and Capt Hunt relative to the establishment of Contraband Camps.

Gov. Johnson desires to segregate rather than congregate negroes. This policy he has steadily pursued. He thinks if the women and children compel their owners to subsist them the cup of rebellion which they drink will be more bitter– Such negroes as come within our lines he Endeavors to have set at seeking their own living hiring themselves out &c– He desires to make them self-reliant so far as he can. The Governor also favors such a disposition of the Negroes who are "loafing about" as shall compel them to work or fight for the Government that furnishes them rations & clothing. He expressed to me approval of Gen Butlers Gen. Ord. 46– 1863[1] a copy of which I forwarded some time ago.

Capt Hunt– has been ordered by General Granger to establish a contraband camp here. Capt. Hunt while admitting the necessity for some place here to receive the negroes who come into our lines foresees great evils in the establishment near this City of a large and permanent Camp of negroes; women of course there would be in large numbers and their proximity to our Camps of Soldiers here would be fruitful of Evil

Captain Hunt therefore suggests that a Plantation– or Plantations as the case may require– be selected somewhere near this City upon the line of the L.&N. R.R. near Gallatin– for instance– from lands abandoned by Rebels – Whereupon a Contraband Camp could be located under the charge of a Competent Superintendent I could order from the Regiments of Colored Troops organizing – from time to time – say Two Companies to act as a Guard These Troops should at once erect a Stockade of sufficient strength to protect the stores against any raid of cavalry or infantry. There might be posted here one or two pieces of artillery – old smooth bore six pounders – Huts for the contrabands should be erected. & hospital accommodations furnished – It should be the Endeavor of the Superintendent to hire out, under just restrictions as to wages, separation of families &c. such of these Contrabands as he could. With the others he should Endeavor to raise forage and vegetables Enough to make the Camp, Self-supporting or, if possible, remunerative – The Superintendent would require only "condemned" mules and wagons for teams – He should have however certain agricultural implements which if the plan be carried into operation should be procured at once

The Superintendent should keep a full Register of the names, ages, sex, personal descriptions, claimants' names, residences, where hired &c. &c. of the Negroes at the Camp or hired out from it

He should also keep an account of the Farm charging to it all articles and rations furnished by the Government and crediting it with the proceeds of all sales.

Governor Johnson as Military Governor has instructions that authorize such seizure and use of lands – and I think a fair inference from Par 2. Gen Ord A.G.O. 331 – /1863 confers such power on a Department Commander.[2]

If such a farm is to go into operation a beginning should be made at once. for ground should be broken by the middle of the next month

I enclose a copy of Treasury Regulations referring to this matter which really apply to this State – though so far they have been practically applied only upon the Mississippi I am General Very Respectfully Your Obt Servt

ALS   R D Mussey

Capt. R. D. Mussey to Brig. Genl. W. D. Whipple, 30 Jan. 1864, filed as C-86 1864, Letters Received, ser. 925, Dept. of the Cumberland, RG 393 Pt. 1 [C-8]. Enclosed is a copy of the Treasury Department regulations of January 7, 1864, regarding the leasing of plantations and employment of freedpeople, for which see *Freedom*, ser. 1, vol. 3: doc. 188. Several months later, Mussey recounted the circumstances that led to the establishment of a contraband camp near Nashville. When the recruitment of black soldiers began in earnest in September 1863, "there was no organized provision for contrabands," although "a crowd" of them could be found at "about every army depot"; indeed,

military policy "was to repress their coming into our lines." With the enlistment of black men, however, their families "required care, and contrabands
came upon our hands." As a "makeshift," Major George L. Stearns, then the
commissioner for the organization of colored troops, had housed some black
women and children in a deserted chapel outside Nashville, where "[r]ations
were drawn for them, and as fast as possible they were hired out." On December 19, 1863, the Secretary of War had directed General George H. Thomas,
commander of the Department of the Cumberland, "to receive destitute
women and children" at Stevenson, Alabama, and at Nashville, "and supply
their necessities." At Stevenson, the post commander initially made "[s]ome
rude provision," but then, on January 26, 1864, "about a hundred infirm men
and women and children were sent by rail" from that point to Nashville, where
"[t]hey were dumped at the Chattanooga depot and left for hours between the
tracks." Captain Mussey had reported the circumstances to General Ulysses S.
Grant, commander of the Military Division of the Mississippi, whereupon an
order had been issued directing General Robert S. Granger, commander of the
post of Nashville, to provide for the former slaves. (*Official Records*, ser. 3, vol.
4, pp. 762–74.)

1 For the order, issued by General Benjamin F. Butler as commander of the
Department of Virginia and North Carolina, see above, doc. 26.
2 For the instructions to Johnson, given by the Secretary of War in April
1863, see above, doc. 102n. Paragraph 2 of General Order 331 issued by the
War Department on October 9, 1863, directed "commanders of military
departments, districts, and posts" to turn over to the Treasury Department all
captured and abandoned "houses, tenements, lands, and plantations," except
those required for military purposes. (Quoted above, in doc. 38.)

109: Order by the Adjutant General of the Army

Nashville, Tennessee February 4th, 1864.
Orders. No. 2.
   I. A camp for the reception of contrabands will at once be
established in the vicinity of Nashville, Tennessee. The entire
control and supervision of the same will be under Captain Ralph
Hunt, 1st Regiment Kentucky Volunteers, subject to such orders as
he may receive from the commanding General of the Department of
the Cumberland. The Quartermaster's Department will furnish all
the materials and supplies necessary to shelter and protect the
negroes destined to be located in this camp. If practicable, the
contrabands will be quartered in log houses, to be constructed by
the negroes, themselves; but in the interim, tents will be furnished
for their accomodation. The several Staff Departments will issue all
supplies necessary for the wants of these people, on the requisition of

the Officer in charge of the Camp, – approved by the Officer commanding the nearest Post.

II. A detail of eight subalterns from Regiments of African Descent, will be ordered to report for duty to Captain Ralph Hunt, 1st Kentucky Volunteers, Commandant of the Camp, for the purpose of aiding him in the performance of his duties. It shall form a part of their duties to visit the plantations, farms, woodyards, and other places where negroes may be employed, for the purpose of enquiring into their condition, and to see that the engagements between them and their employers are properly and faithfully carried out on both sides. Any failure on the employer to carry out his engagements, will be immediately reported to the Commanding General of the nearest military district, who will at once take an action in the matter.

III. The following regulations for the government of freedmen in the Department of the Cumberland, are announced, for the information of all concerned.

1st. All male negroes coming within our lines, who, after examination, shall be found capable of bearing arms, will be mustered into companies and regiments of colored troops in process of organization. All others, including men incapable of bearing arms, women and children, instead of being permitted to remain in camp in idleness, will be required to perform such labor, as may be suited to their several conditions, in the respective Staff Departments of the army, on plantations or farms, leased or otherwise, within our lines, as woodchoppers, teamsters, or in any way that their labor can be made available.

2nd. All civilians of known loyalty, having possession of plantations, farms, woodyards, or otherwise engaged, may, upon application to the commandant of the Contraband Camp, hire such negroes, (including a fair proportion of children,) as they may desire, if disposable, for actual service. In all such cases the employers will enter into a written engagement to pay, feed and treat humanely all the negroes turned over to them; and none shall be hired for a less term than one year, commencing on the 1st day of January 1864. Should it be desirable, and the employer furnishing clothing to the hired hands, the same shall be deducted from their pay at the actual cost price.

3rd. When found impracticable to find persons of sufficient character and responsibility to give employment to all the negroes, liable to be employed, the respective Generals of Districts may designate such abandoned or confiscated plantations or farms as they may deem most suitable to be worked by the negroes, upon such terms as in their judgment shall be best adapted to the welfare of this class of people, – taking care that in all cases the negroes shall be self-sustaining, and not a burthen upon the Government. 4th. The wages to be paid for labor, shall be as follows: For all able bodied males over fifteen years of age, not less than seven dollars per month; for able bodied females over fifteen years of age, not less than five dollars per month; for children between the age of twelve and fifteen, half the above amounts; children under fourteen years of age shall not be used as field hands, and families must be kept together when so desired. The employer also must furnish such medicines and medical advice as may be required, at his own expense.

IV. In order the more fully to carry out the requirements of this order, the Commanders of Military Districts are authorized, when necessary, to lease abandoned plantations to loyal citizens, on such terms as may be equitable. By order of the Secretary of War.

HDcS   L. Thomas

Orders No. 2, 4 Feb. 1864, Records of Capt. R. D. Mussey & of Maj. George L. Stearns, ser. 1149, Organization of USCT, Dept. of the Cumberland, RG 393 Pt. 1 [C-32].

110: Commander of U.S. Forces at Clarksville, Tennessee, to the Superintendent of the Contraband Camp at Nashville, Tennessee

Clarksville Tenn, March 5th, 1864

Captain: I have recently completed a census of the Co'l'd. fugitives within and near my lines, and find their numbers, to be about as follows:

"Destitute" or those who will necessarily be a charge upon the government:

Men (49) Forty nine.
Women (151) one hundred and fifty one
Children (162) one hundred and sixty two.

"Moderate." or those who now have means of support within themselves:

Men (39) thirty nine
Women (143) one hundred and forty three.
Children (163) one hundred and sixty three.

Whose condition is "good" or who seem to be in condition to live without assistance:

Men (8) eight.
Women (14) fourteen.

Children (22) twenty two.
    Total:
Men (96.) ninety six.
Women (308) Three hundred and eight.
Children (347) Three hundred and forty seven
Grand Total (751) seven hundred and fifty one.

Among the women are about one hundred and thirty (130) who are wives of soldiers of the Colored regiment organizing here, and who are parents of a proportionate number of children enumerated.

During the time I have been in command here I have issued and taken every possible measure to enforce orders to exclude them from the lines but notwithstanding all this there have I presume at least two thirds 2/3 of the number. now here come in during the past five (5) months for with the insufficiency of my Guard lines, and the negro recruiting here it has been utterly impossible to exclude them. As yet I have issued no rations to any part of them, but I apprehend that it will soon be necessary to prevent absolute suffering among them. I would most respectfully suggest that if possible some measures be taken to colonize or put them in Camp upon the abandoned plantations within this vicinity (a report of which I have recently made to Genl *Rousseau* comd'g. Disc't, Nashville) or elsewhere in order that they may be placed in a condition to maintain themselves: or be properly hired out with assurances of protection, to both parties. Most people in this section who are in need of services of negroes the negroes are averse to employing them as it is now first because they are the former slaves of their neighbors and second because they have no assurance that they can retain them. All of which is most respectfully submitted   I am. Capt. Most Respectfully Your Ob'd't. Servant.

HLcS
                             A. A. Smith

Col. A. A. Smith to Captain Ralph Hunt, 5 Mar. 1864, vol. 170/205 DMT, pp. 17–19, Letters Sent, ser. 3023, U.S. Forces, Clarksville TN, RG 393 Pt. 2 No. 192 [C-2065]. Smith signed as colonel of the 83rd Illinois Infantry. In his report to General Lovell H. Rousseau, commander of the District of Nashville, Smith had acknowledged that "a large number of Negro women and children and a few disabled, or decrepid negro men" had assembled at Clarksville, despite efforts to exclude them. Deeming it "an act of inhumanity to put them out by force," he had warned that the fugitives would "be brought to extreme suffering" unless supplied with food and clothing. "Many of the women and children," Smith noted, "are the families of colored soldiers of the regiment recruiting here, and it would seem that they might be entitled to assistance from the Gov't. In my opinion there is not within the state of Tennessee a community which more greatly demands a system of home Colonization upon deserted farms, or some other system establish under the auspices of the General Gov't, to put them to work at something which shall in some way compensate for the aid and protection which they are likely to require." (Col. A. A. Smith to Captain B. H. Polk, 18 Feb. 1864, vol. 170/205 DMT, pp. 13–14, Letters Sent, ser. 3023, U.S. Forces, Clarksville TN, RG 393 Pt. 2 No. 192 [C-2064].)

111: Commander of a Tennessee Black Regiment to the Headquarters of the Chief of Artillery in the Department of the Ohio

Knoxville Tenn.   March 6" 1864.
I have the honor respectfully to request information in regard to providing for the families of those men who have enlisted or who may enlist in this Regiment.

Some fifty families are now here. and no adequate provision has either been made or authorized for them, in Consequence thereof the men so burdened are a Continual Source of annoyance, in making enquiry and asking permission to be absent for the purpose of providing for them, many absent themselves without permission; In addition a large number of those enlisted, Whose families are yet in the Country, Complain daily of their necessities and Show much dissatisfaction.

From their Statements it Would appear (and their is good reason for believing) that the Country in which they live is almost entirely destitute of Subsistence. Without providing for the families of these men, it will be apparent that nothing like Satisfaction Can exist

I will therefore most respectfully urge that some method be adopted for providing for the Wants of the families of those men belonging to this Regt Satisfied that it will result in inducing enlistments and be Conducive to the good of the organization. I am Sir Very Respectfully Your. Obt. Servt

HLcSr

Sg^d John A. Shannon

Maj. John A. Shannon to Lt. W. W. Deane, 6 Mar. 1864, Letters Sent, 1st USCHA, Regimental Books & Papers USCT, RG 94 [G-6]. Shannon, a major in an Ohio regiment, signed as "in charge" of the 1st USCHA. Ten days later, Shannon reiterated that the men of his regiment had become "a Constant annoyance to their officers, in asking what their Wives & Children shall do for Subsistence &C." He suggested that an order be issued requiring the surgeon in charge of military hospitals in Knoxville to employ black women as nurses, assistants, and laborers, giving "preference to the families of the men of this Regt." (Major John A. Shannon to Lt. W. W. Deane, 16 Mar. 1864, Letters Sent, 1st USCHA, Regimental Books & Papers USCT, RG 94 [G-6].) In response, the commander of the Department of the Ohio ruled that the wives of black soldiers were "entitled" to "preference" when hospital employees were being selected. (Endorsement by A.A.G. R. Morrow, 29 Mar. 1864, vol. 34 DO, p. 274, Endorsements Sent, ser. 3507, Dept. of the OH, RG 393 Pt. 1 [C-418].)

112: **Testimony by an Alabama Freedman before the Southern Claims Commission**

[*Huntsville, Ala. July 31, 1872*]
Deposition of Alfred Scruggs, Colored,
In answer to the First General Interrogatory, the Deponent says:
My name is Alfred Scruggs, *my age* 45 *years, my residence* Near Huntsville, *in the State of* Alabama, *and my occupation a* Farmer; *I am the claimant, and have a beneficial interest in the claim.*
To the 2nd he says:
Near Huntsville Alabama, In 1861 I came from Arkansas to Huntsville. In 1862 or until June I was hired by consent of my Master James H Scruggs to Col David Kelley. In June 1862 I was turned loose by my old master to make a living for my self— When I was turned loose I went to hauling wood to Huntsville. The team belonged to my old master, My old master gave me the use of the team if I would feed and take care of. I used the team until the Yankee soldiers took them from me in the latter part of the summer 1862. In 1863 I had my own team. I rented about forty acres of land from Mrs Patteson, near Huntsville and raised a crop of cotton and corn that year. I also hauled wood during the time I was not in my crop, During the year 1864 I farmed on Mr Ed Spotswoods place four miles of Huntsville. I had about twenty five acres in corn, I hauled wood and everything that I could get to do. I did not use my own team that year or all of that year, In the early part of the year 1865 I was preparing to farm on Mr Nash Malones place
. . . .
To the 28th he says.
Yes they took corn fodder meat and meal, I did not put it in my claim because I was willing to let that go to help the United States Government that much for what they done for me.
. . . .
To the 43rd he says:
I was a slave. I was free when we was declared free, but my master turned me loose in 1862 Hauling working and making money in any way I could in an honorable manner. I bought this property. I cant tell the exact date. I bought my property about

445

the end of 1862. or about 1863, I worked and made the money in 1862 by hauling and jobbing with my fingers: and my wife washing and ironing is the way I made the money which I paid for the property in my claim. James H Scruggs was my former master. I am not in his employment. I do not live on his land, Do not live on land purchased from him, I do not owe him, he owes me. No one saveing me has any interest in this claim.

To the Questions as to the taking or furnishing of property deponent,
To the 1st Question says:
yes.
To the 2nd he says
Yes, I saw them when they took bay mule roane horse, ox, & cow.
To the 3rd he says
When they took this item of one bay mule I was there. They said that Colonel Wilder sent them out to take all the mules and horses that was fit for service as they were going off the next morning. They came to my house and went to my stable and taken the mule. they led him away.
They came one evening and got this item of one rone horse. They just went to the stable and had it unlocke and they taken the horse out   That is all of it. They rode the horse off.
They just killed these itemes of one ox and one cow about one hundred yards from my house. The cows were there in pasture   they did not say a word just drove them up and killed them. Their camp was right there.
To the 4th he says
These articles were taken from Mr Scruggs' place where I was living that time. If I make no mistake it was in the year 1864, I cant remember exactly as we were all head over heels then, Mr Wilder took the two mules. dont know the names of the other officers, who took ox &c   more than one soldier was present and helped to take the property. seven or eight took the horse and mules – and a whole regiment was camped right there when they took the ox and cow. They were not more than fifteen or twenty minutes taking the mules, and the other property they just took right away
To the 5th he says
Harrison Dox, Jordan Hamlet, Randal Ragland, Calvin Scruggs, and a large number of woman were on the place,
To the 6th he says
Lieutents were there when the mules were taken, Don't

remember of any officer being present   when the roane horse was
taken when the ox & cow were taken plenty of officers were present
but I do not know their regiment or their names,   They ordered it
to be taken.   They said that they wante the mules for a force march
the next morning.   They did not say any thing took the horse cow
& ox

. . . .

his
HDSr   Alfred X Scruggs.
mark

Excerpts from testimony of Alfred Scruggs, [31 July 1872], Claim of Alfred
Scruggs, Madison Co. AL case files, Approved Claims, ser. 732, Southern
Claims Commission, 3rd Auditor, RG 217 [I-119]. Sworn before a special
commissioner of the Southern Claims Commission. The heading and the first
question and answer are in the form of handwritten insertions into a printed
form. Item labels in the margin are omitted. The questions that correspond to
the enumerated responses are not in the file. According to other documents in
the file, Scruggs had submitted a claim for $381 as compensation for the
livestock taken by Union soldiers. He was awarded $340.

113: Testimony by a Tennessee Freedman before the Southern
Claims Commission

Gallatin Tenn Jany 17th 1877
   Squire Newman (col) having been by me first duly sworn deposes
and says
   My name is Squire Newman (col)   I am 58 years of age,   I reside
in Gallatin Tenn, where I have lived for the last forty two years;   I
live in Gallatin, but I always rent land in the country and attend to
it and I also run a wagon hauling wood &c   Before the war I
belonged to Thomas Newman; But I was always hired out;   I was
hired out to Misses Ann and Mary Banks, and I staid with them
after the war began until the death of Miss Mary Banks who died on
the 22nd of May 1863, when I became free;   Gen Paine was then in
command at Gallatin;   I then went away from Miss Mary Banks and
went and lived with my wife, and after this I was free and took care
of myself and wife;
   In the Spring of 1864 I went to Gen Paine and got from him a
written permission and papers of protection to rent me some land
and to raise a crop;   I then went to Mr Levi Warner and rented from

him some land; I rented from him about twenty four acres; This land was east of Gallatin on the Huntsville pike and was distant from town about two miles; I was to give him one third of the crop raised for the rent; I never paid him since the crop was taken; I do not know where Mr Warner now is, after the war he sold his place and moved away;

I put all this land rented in corn;

I raised the crop that year and I myself and a hired hand did the work;

In December of this year just before Christmas and about the time of the fight at Nashville I was pressed with about one hundred other hands and taken to work on a fort at the tunnell not far from Gallatin; when I came back I found that my corn had been taken and upon inquiry found that the U.S. authorities at Gallatin had sent out and had it taken;

I had in corn twenty four acres so Mr Warner told me the field contained and in renting it was so understood; I put the whole of it in corn; I raised a very good crop since that was a good crop year; when I went away I had not gathered in the crop since for two or three weeks before I went away it was bad and rainy weather and I was waiting for good weather to gather it, when I was pressed and taken away;

Some of the drivers of the wagons among them Marshall Robb (col) told me that their wagons had taken the corn and he belonged to the wagon train of Capt Hunter Quarter master at Gallatin; When I came home and found the corn gone, I did not go to see the U.S. authorities since I did not think that it would do any good; nor did I ever get any papers or pay for it; I gave up it simply as lost;

The field would have produced between eight and nine barrells per acre; All in the field was taken; The wagons had gone into the field and loaded by pulling from the stalk

his
Squire X Newman
mark

HDSr

Testimony of Squire Newman, 17 Jan. 1877, claim of Squire Newman, Sumner Co. TN case files, Approved Claims, ser. 732, Southern Claims Commission, 3rd Auditor, RG 217 [I-249]. Sworn before a special commissioner of the Southern Claims Commission. According to other documents in the same file, Newman had submitted a claim for $400 as compensation for 500 bushels of corn seized by Union soldiers. He was awarded $250, the commissioners having reasoned that, because he would have paid one-third of the crop as rent, he was entitled to only two-thirds of its value.

114: Officer in an Indiana Regiment to the Secretary of War

Gallatin Tenn   Oct 13 1864

This is entirely unofficial

Sir   Asking your pardon for thus encroaching on your time I will briefly make my statement premising that it is entirely unofficial in order that you may have some knowledge of how matters are going— When the President issued his proclamation freeing the negros & authorizing their enlistment he did not intend to leave them unprotected. Yet in this section they are worse off than before. All the able bodied Males are in the army, working for Q.M. Dept or have gone off except some few that hired themselves & some that the Federal authorities hired out.   The women & children whose protectors have enlisted or gone off as stated some of them left their masters & are now in what is called the "contraband Camp" living in *tents* drawing rations from the U.S. Govt. & this winter will freeze & die   An officer who is engaged in recruiting a company or Regt has not time to attend to the outside ones   The citizens here now that their crops made & winter coming on are *driving* their negro's away in order to save taking care of them during the winter. & infact whenever a negro shows a disposition to send his children to school or to favor the *Yankees* the Master will drive him off.   There are many abuses that should be stopped but I am well aware that you have no time to look after them   But it does seem to me that if the Govt would appoint an energetic honest officer in each Military district in this Dept give him the rank & pay say of a Col of Cav at least in *fact he must* have rank enough for influence & pay *enough to Keep him honest*   Let him place all negros on deserted farms of which there is plenty   work the farms with horses run down in the service (most of whom in that way would be again fit for service)   allow each negro a certain price per month for his labor to be paid off the farm

Allow no negro to hire himself out but force the citizens to come to the Govt agent to hire them.   Then if the negro did not work according to contract make him & the party hiring him did not live up to his part *make him* (as I have done & am doing)   By picking the negros up Laborers would become scarce & the citizens would have to come & hire them— He should appoint an agent on each farm & should require Monthly (or oftener) reports of the number sex age condition whereabouts of every negro placed on the farm & if any were hired out to whom—

He should fix a price that should be paid those who worked on the farm & the price that citizens should pay   I would make the price that was paid by the farm less than that allowed by citizens   by that the negro's would be anxious to hire to citizens &

in a short time comparitivly the citizen & negro would learn to hire & be hired & the Govt by making them observe the marital relations would in a short time be clear of them. & in the meantime the farms would pay the expense with a handsome surplus after the first year or 18 months

This officer have a QM assigned him

I merely give you an outline of my idea & I have made it a study since I have been in the service & for the last 8 months with but few intervals having had the command of this Post have had an opportunity to know

Askg again your pardon & assuring you that it is for the future of my country that I am thus bold to address you I will close by referring you to Mess Judge Hood & General Bostwick your special commr⁵ to whom I gave my ideas in full & who will vouch that I do take a deep interest in this matter & that I am actuated by the best of motives

Trusting sir if I have erred in thus addressing you that you will attribute it to the head & not the heart I have the honor to be Your Most Obedient Servant

ALS   Ben S Nicklin

Capt. Ben S. Nicklin to Hon. E. M. Stanton, 13 Oct. 1864, N-568 1864, Letters Received, RG 107 [L-58]. Thomas Hood and S. W. Bostwick had, in June 1864, been appointed by the Secretary of War to investigate the treatment of "colored refugees" in Kentucky, Tennessee, and Alabama. According to their report of December 1864, Captain Nicklin had unofficially supervised the contraband camp at Gallatin from September 1863 until July 1864, when another officer was appointed superintendent. (U.S., Senate, "Report of the Commissioners of Investigation of Colored Refugees in Kentucky, Tennessee, and Alabama," *Senate Executive Documents*, 38th Cong., 2nd sess., No. 28, pp. 10–11.)

115: Woodyard Contractor to the Treasury Department Assistant Special Agent at Nashville, Tennessee

Nashville Tenn Oᶜᵗ 17ᵗʰ 1864

Sir   I am a Contractor for the furnishing of Sawed Lumber and wood to a large amount to the Government – on the Nashville and Northwestern Rail Road – 22 1/4 miles from this city. I have under that contract purchased and placed there a steam saw mill & purchased a large tract of timbered land at an Expence of about – ten thousand dollars,   I have employed a large number of persons with families. and to comply with my contract must Employ at least one hundred men to labor, most of whom are *contrabands or* negros with families in a most destitute condition, I also employ many white persons that have families, and I find that one man with a family is worth to me – two or three who has not a family. When I undertook these contracts it was with the distinct understanding – that I should have the privilege of taking to the work all articles necessary to supply the wants of all persons and their families in my employ on that work –

But under the late rule[1] – nothing is permitted but, Bread & meat and plain articles of food, It is just as necessary that men and their families should be clothed as fed, and it is of but little use that men have money, if deprived of the wants of life. and they cannot or nearly all cannot come to Nashville for the articles they must have and if they could do so – it would cause them a great loss of time and deprive me of their labor, I am therefore compeled – to Either have the prvilege of supplying – their wants or to abandon my contracts – at a great loss to myself – and to the Government *Moreove*, I can obtain labor – and provisions for men and forage for amamils – for necessary goods, of citizens which I can not obtain for money at any price, The people in that locality are not *disloyal* – but on the cont[rary] are generally. strongly attached to the Lawful Government of the United States – and with kind treatment may be made as much so as any people South of the Ohio River

As to myself, I can give you any Evidence you may require of persons – Civil or Military here in this City or in the State of Ohio – of my devotion to the cause of the Union – which I served in the a[rmey] until compeled from ill health to resign. I therefore as leave to take to the place mentioned – of – goods – of the value of – two thousand ($2000) per month consisting of such general varity as are necessary for the purpose before mentioned – with liberty to sell or Exchange. for labor or produce, with such Loyal citizens as may forward the purpose aforesaid All of which is most respectfully submitted With Esteem. I am Your Obt Sevt

ALS   John. M. Palmer

John M. Palmer to C. A. Fuller Esq., 17 Oct. 1864, Letters Received by Assistant Special Agents, 1st Agency, RG 366 [Q-202]. "Gould & Davenport," contractors who were furnishing wood, crossties, and timber to the military railroads in middle Tennessee, entered a similar complaint about restrictions on the shipment of supplies. "We employ almost exclusively the labor we find in the country – black and white," the contractors reported, and local shortages of food, clothing, and other necessities demanded that they make supplies available for sale to their workers. To that end, they had operated a "trade store" at Decherd, Tennessee, until permits for such trade were rescinded. Now they were allowed to purchase from army commissaries "such subsistance stores as are needed, and which cannot be obtained elsewhere," but they could not obtain permission to ship from Nashville "such articles of clothing &C as are absolutely necessary for [the laborers'] use." Military and civil authorities would authorize shipments only "as family supplies, for each individual person," a policy Gould and Davenport pronounced "almost entirely impracticable." "There are not far from 1,000 of these persons . . . scattered along the RR Line for more than ninety miles – mostly in the woods," they explained. "They are principally negroes and that class of people who are too unintelligent or inert to comprehend such matters, and act advisedly. And to bring them to Nashville or to points where their wants can be supplied involves great trouble and unnecessary expense" and disrupts "indispensable" work. (Gould & Davenport to Charles A. Fuller Esqr., 13 Oct. 1864, Letters Received by Assistant Special Agents, 1st Agency, RG 366 [Q-202].)

1 The rule in question has not been identified, but it probably represented local implementation of Treasury Department regulations of July 29, 1864, which, among other things, revoked existing trade permits in the Union-occupied South, required persons wishing to sell supplies to obtain the approval of local treasury agents and military commanders, and forbade the transportation of goods without permission. At authorized stores, loyal residents were to be allowed to purchase "such individual, family, or plantation supplies as may be necessary for their own use." (U.S., House of Representatives, "Report of the Secretary of the Treasury on the State of the Finances, for the Year 1864," *House Executive Documents*, 38th Cong., 2nd sess., No. 3, pp. 296–312; see also Robert Frank Futrell, "Federal Trade with the Confederate States, 1861–1865: A Study of Governmental Policy" [Ph.D. diss., Vanderbilt University, 1950], pp. 384–85, 405–8.)

116: Testimony by an Alabama Freedman before the Southern Claims Commission

[*Huntsville, Ala. May 14, 1875*]

Deposition of Benjamin Haynes, *cold*

My name is Benjamin Haynes, My age is about seventy five years, Residence, on Mr Willis Harris Jr place South of Huntsville, about half way between Huntsville and Whitesburg, in Madison County Alabama, I have been living there about five years, before that time I had been living on Mr Ogdens place, Hayns & Ogdens place, in Madison County, and about a mile and a half from where I now live.

Occupation farming,

I am the claimant in this case,

To the 70th he says:

At the beginning of the war I was a slave, I come to be free after General Mitchell, came in this country with the Northern Army, Well, I do not remember eactly what year that was, Mr Hayns and Ogden after General Mitchell came in here said they had nothing more to do with me, and for me to go to work for myself, Hayns and Odgen were my owners, I went to farming for my self—and I stayed right there on their place till after the surrender. they said I could have land to tend.

I raised the corn on my former owners place, I bought two hogs myself—and my white people gave me one, and that one I kept for a brood sow.

John Ogden and Stephen Haynes were my owners before I got free, Haynes is dead. Mr John Odgen is leving— He lives over in the cove about thirteen miles from Huntsville, and about the same distance from where I now live.

Mr John Ogden will be a witness for me if you want him to come, not in his service now, I worked some for him since the surrender at day work, but it was in time of Mr Hayne's life, Do not live on land purchased from either of them, I do not owe either of them any thing

This claim is all mine, no one has any interest in it.

I made the corn crop on Mr Haynes & Ogdens place the year before the war ended, to the best of my mind, They told me to raise the corn and do the best I could, as they could not farm as they had nothing to farm with, I had in corn that year about twenty acres, I had just one mule and an old mare to make the crop with, the mule was mine and the old mare belonged to them, Oh yes, I paid them corn for the rent of the land, I paid them till they were satisfied. I done that as soon as it was ready for gathering,

In answer to question 72nd he says

Yes sir, I was present right there when them northern ones got my corn and hogs, I looked right at 'em taking of it, My hogs and corn,

To the 73rd he says:

All taken in broad day time, Well I could not tell the time of the day, but they come down after morning with their wagons,

To the 74th he says:

I was talking to the wagonmaster about it and told me the government would pay me for it, I told him I did not want him to take it, then I told him not to take it all, for I wanted some corn to live on   I did not talk to no other officer but the wagon master, I do not remember his name, I do not know his Regiment, for I did not pay any attention to Regiments. I thought they were all the same, and it excited me, there was another officer there who was in the house talking to the white people but I did not have any thing to say to him at all, He was the one who sent them to get the corn then he went in to the white folks, to get som milk, or he asked for som, Mr and Mrs Haynes were in the house,

To the 75th he says:
No, sir, none at all, I told the wagon master to give me a showing for my corn, He told me I must make my complaint to Head Quarters in town here, and said I could go along back with his wagons, but I was afraid to go with him, I was afraid they would press me and carry me off—for I was too old for that business,

. . . .

his

Benjamin X Haynes,

mark

HDSr

Excerpt from testimony of Benjamin Haynes, 14 May 1875, claim of Benjamin Haynes, Madison Co. AL case files, Approved Claims, ser. 732, Southern Claims Commission, 3rd Auditor, RG 217 [I-110]. Sworn before a special commissioner of the Southern Claims Commission. The questions that correspond to the enumerated responses are in the file. In the omitted portion of his testimony, Haynes noted that the wagon master who supervised the seizure of his corn had not taken the whole crop, but had "told his boys . . . to leave me some to live on." According to other documents in the same file, Haynes had submitted a claim for $149 as compensation for 125 bushels of corn and two hogs seized by Union soldiers. He was awarded $90. Other testimony in the file includes that of a freedman who confirmed that the corn had belonged to Haynes ("Old Ben") and that "it was the understanding by all who lived around there that he was working for himself." John Ogden, one of Haynes's former owners, testified that after the federal army occupied northern Alabama in 1862, he and Stephen Haynes had no longer claimed him as a slave. Instead, they had furnished him land to tend for himself, and "he worked for us some during the time he was making his own crop." "He is the only boy who stayed with us after we gave them their freedom in 1864," Ogden noted. "He remained till after the war closed." (Testimony of David Crow, 14 May 1875; testimony of John Ogden, 14 May 1875.)

117: Testimony by a Tennessee Freedman before the Southern Claims Commission

[*Columbia, Tenn. May 12, 1873*]
Deposition of Charles Bunch Colored
In answer to the First General Interrogatory, the Deponent says:
My name is Charles Bunch, *my age* 34 *years, my residence* Maury County, *in the State of* Tennessee, *and my occupation a* Farmer; I am the Claimant *and have a beneficial interest in the claim.*
& deposes as follows. that he is a free man of Color. that in Slave times he belonged to Mr Sol. Bunch of Maury Co Tennessee. That

in the year 1863. his master Mr Bunch did not require his labor Considering him deponent to be free, and he was allowed to labor for himself, that he the deponent thereupon rented a piece of land from his late Mistress Containing 22 & 1/4 acres. that he commenced work on that piece of land. in the Spring of 1863, that he put in 15 acres of Corn & 6 acres of Cotton. that he bought on a Credit. (2), horses. 1 horse from. Sam. McKissick Colored for $100^{oo} and one Mare. from. Mr Wesley Lockridge. a white man for $100^{oo} to be paid when he made his Crop. & the Same was paid in the fall. of the Same year. that at the time he commenced to farm for him Self he purchased Some Hogs from Mr Albert Odell. and. from them he raised Sufficient pork to do his family. that during the year 1864 in consequence of the troublesome times throughout the Country he did not farm but went to Nashvill Tennessee and. worked for the Govrment in Q.M. dept, leaving his Family at the plantation of his late master. also his Horses   That in the month of November 1864. the rebel. Army under the Command. of General. Hood, Came in to the State of Tennessee the Federal. forces retreating on Nashville   that on or about the 29" day of November 1864 the federal. army were encamped. all around. the plantation of Mr Bunch. where deponent had his Horses. and provission. that they took from Said plantation Said Horses enumerated and described. in his application also the amount of Bacon described in the Same. that he was not at home. at the time. he being employed in the quarter masters department at Nashville, that after the Battle of Nashville fought. on the 15" & 16. Dec. 1864, the U.S. Troops being successfull the rebel. army retreated and the Federal forces advanced. then deponent returned home with the Army. and. learned or was told by his wife and. others that his property described in his Application was taken by the Federal. Troops on their retreat to Nashville Tennessee, and that no receipt or Voucher. was. given for the Same. that he then heard. what Command had taken his property. and went to Gen Hatch to See about it. & was told by him that he Could not be paid then but that he would be paid when the War was over. & that he has never been paid in whole or in part. for the property taken from him.

Ques^r 43rd where do you live now? at Dr Bunche's, who was my former master. I am now in his employment; I live on his land, I am not indebted to him, Simply hired to work for him by the month at fifteen dollars per month, No body has any interest in this claim besides myself, I have answered all, in my examination in chief, therefore deponent Sayeth no more,

his

Charles X Bunch col'd

mark

HDSr

Testimony of Charles Bunch, 12 May 1873, claim of Charles Bunch, Maury Co. TN case files, Approved Claims, ser. 732, Southern Claims Commission, 3rd Auditor, RG 217 [I-229]. Sworn before a special commissioner of the Southern Claims Commission. The heading and the first paragraph of Bunch's reply to the first interrogatory are in the form of handwritten insertions into a printed form. The questions that correspond to the enumerated responses are not in the file. According to other documents in the same file, Bunch had submitted a claim for $361.25 as compensation for two horses and 245 pounds of bacon taken by Union soldiers. He was awarded $240.

118: Testimony by a Tennessee Freedman before the Southern Claims Commission

[*Nashville, Tenn.*] April 10, 1873
Deposition of Richard Traynor
In answer to the First General Interrogatory, the Deponent says:
My name is Richard Traynor, *my age* 38 *years, my residence* Nashville, *in the State of* Tennessee, *and my occupation a* Brick mason; *I am the claimant, and have the beneficial interest in the claim.*

In answer to Revised questions to be answered by Claimants deponent says in answer to

No 2 On April 1. 1861 I was living in Cleveland Tennessee. In September 1862 I removed from Cleveland Tenn. to Nashville Tennessee. I remained in Nashville Tenn. from that date on up to June 1. 1865 and afterwards. I did not during any of the time included in the above dates live on my own land. My occupation during the most of that time was hauling freight. I did change my residence as above set out from Cleveland to Nashville Tenn. I did not change my occupation during that time.

                    . . . .

No 24 In the month of June 1862 I was arrested by the rebel military authorities at Cleveland Tenn. where I then lived and charged with aiding and assisting certain Union men in going across the mountains into the federal lines. I was kept under arrest two days and one night and then released by them. why I never knew. I took no oath of any kind for the purpose of securing my release. I was never arrested by the United States Government. Except that at the time of the battle of Nashville I was pressed into the service and compelled to help throw op entrenchments dig & shovel as many other citizens were.

No 25 No. I had no property when I was among the rebels I was then held as property myself.

No 26 I was threatened to be hung and everything else done to me when the rebels arrested me as above set out.

No 27 I was arrested and threatened as above stated.

No 28 I gave many things to the union soldiers. hats. clothes tobacco. food & small items.

No 29 When pressed into the service at the battle of Nashville I did. and I aided after the battle in removing the dead & wounded union soldiers from the battle field.

. . . .

No 40 At the beginning of the rebellion I sympathised with the union cause. My feelings of course were to get out bondage and my language was taking about the "Yankees" whom I looked upon as my deliverers and wanting to see them. I exerted my influence on the Union side. I had no vote. I adhered to the Union cause at all times.

. . . .

No 43 I was held as a slave. though I was free born. My mother & her seven children were set free by their master. and so I lived up to the time I was ten. then by some legal proceedings we were thrown back into slavery. From that slavery I became free by operation of the war. It was during the time my mother was free I was born. My business after I became free was hauling freight generally in Nashville. When I came to Nashville I had some two hundred dollars in gold and silver that I had saved while a slave. This I sold or exchanged for greenbacks. receiving about $2.64 in greenbacks for $1.00 in specie. that being the time when the premium was highest. With the money thus obtained I bought four mules and two drays and the necessary harness. Those were the mules I have claimed pay for. My former master was John D. Traynor of Cleveland Tennessee. He is dead now. He died in 1852. After that his widow owned me. I have not been in her employment since 1862. I do not live on his or her lands. nor on land purchased from them. I am indebted to neither of them for anything. No one but my self has any interest in this claim.

In answer to questions as to the taking or furnishing of property. . . . .

No 3 I kept two horses and four mules in a stable on Church street in Nashville. The four mules and gray horse were taken from the stable by cavalry soldiers in my absence as I was informed. A few moments after they were taken I came to the stable riding my bay horse. I was then informed by the stable keeper Edward Goff col. that my gray horse and mules had just been pressed by order of General Thomas, commanding the Army about Nashville. This was while the battle of Nashville was raging. I at once started on my bay horse to overtake and recover if possible the gray horse & mules I had gone but a little distance until I met with a captain and a detachment of soldiers all on horse back. They halted me and asked me where I was going. I told them I was hunting my horse & mules. They asked me then whose horse was that I was on. I told him mine. He then said I have orders to press all serviceable stock for the use of the army and ordered me to dismount. They ordered me to take my saddle off. They took my horse and away they went. This was taken by a Captain & men of the 2nd Tenn. Cavalry. U.S. Army. I never saw the bay horse afterwards. One day after this I saw the gray horse being rode by a non-Commissioned officer in the Regiment 4th Tenn. Cavalry. I saw him Crossing a pontoon bridge across the river Cumberland River at Nashville. I said "there's my horse now". The non-commissioned officer who was riding him said "He's Uncle Sam's horse now". That was the only answer I got.

. . . .

No 8 The horse was led off by a halter around the head.
No 9 They took him towards the carell in North Nashville. I followed them part way out there where I was met by a detachment of soldiers pressing *men* to work on the fortifications, and they then and there pressed me into the service and put me at work on the fortifications about Nashville.

. . . .

HDS   Ri[ch Y] Traynor

Excerpts from testimony of Ri[ch. Y.] Traynor, 10 Apr. 1873, claim of Richard Y. Traynor, Davidson Co. TN case files, Approved Claims, ser. 732, Southern Claims Commission, 3rd Auditor, RG 217 [I-258]. Sworn before a special commissioner of the Southern Claims Commission. The heading and the reply to the first interrogatory are in the form of handwritten insertions into a printed form. The questions that correspond to the enumerated responses are not in the file. According to other documents in the same file, Traynor had submitted a claim for $950 as compensation for two horses and four mules taken by Union soldiers. He was awarded $625.

119A: **Commander of a Barracks in Nashville, Tennessee, to the Military Governor of Tennessee**

Head Quarters Tennessee Barracks Nashville, Dec 20th 1864
Sir: I respectfully beg to inform you, which I believe to be my duty, that on inspection of that portion of the Barracks occupied by the "contrabands," I found six dead bodies, covered with vermin. Some having been dead two days and no effort made to bury them, unless they are doing so this morning.

I would not trouble Your Excellency with such reports but I think that humanity demands that some order should be issued that would force the officers in charge of those unfortunate people to bury their dead out of the way of the living.

The barracks they occupy are lined with vermin, and the condition of the negroes cannot be bettered so long as they remain in their present position. I have the honor to be, very resp'y your ob't serv't

HLS   R. H. Clinton

Capt. R. H. Clinton to His Excellency Brig. Gen'l Andrew Johnson, 20 Dec. 1864, Letters Received, ser. 867, Post of Nashville, RG 393 Pt. 4 [C-8939]. Beneath his signature, Clinton identified himself as captain of company F, 10th Tennessee Infantry. The former slaves at Tennessee Barracks were refugees uprooted from contraband camps near Pulaski and Tunnel Hill, Tennessee, when General John B. Hood's Confederate army advanced into southern Tennessee in late November 1864. For a description of their evacuation, see below, doc. 129. Endorsements indicate that Military Governor Andrew Johnson referred Clinton's letter to the commander of the post of Nashville, "with the hope that the matter will be looked into and investigated"; the post commander in turn started it on its way through the ranks of officers in charge of contrabands. According to other documents in the same file, the surgeon in charge of the contraband hospital dismissed Clinton's statement as "without foundation and a slander upon myself and those in charge of cont camp," and Lieutenant Lorenzo D. Barnes, the assistant superintendent at Sherman Barracks, who was in charge of the refugees at Tennessee Barracks, pronounced it "entirely untrue." "[E]very thing has been done that could be done under the present circumstances" for the contrabands, Barnes asserted; "every dead body has been buried as soon as coffins could be obtained." (Act. Asst. Surg. William Wands to Col. R. W. Banard, 22 Dec. 1864; Lieut. L. D. Barnes to Col. R. W. Barnard, 23 Dec. 1864.) Another series of endorsements referred the two exculpatory reports back through the chain of command to Governor Johnson, who, on December 28, returned the papers to the post commander, along with statements from other officers having knowledge of conditions at the barracks, for which see doc. 119B, immediately below.

119B: Statement by the Adjutant of the Commander of a Barracks in Nashville, Tennessee

Tennessee Barracks Nashville Dec. 28th., 1864

I certify, on honor, that during the occupation of Company & Officers Quarters No's 1 – 2 – 3 – 4 – & 5 at these Barracks by the contrabands, their condition was wretched in the extreme, that their officers evinced the most culpable neglect and carelessness in regard their comfort and health. The stench arising from the excrement & urine in and around their quarters was intolerable even in the coldest weather, and in my oppinion was the cause of many deaths among them. I am prepared to swear that their surgeon used scarcely any exertions sanitary or medicinal in their behalf. That I have seen them dying in the alleys & houses and on the steps of their quarters, with no one rendering them assistance.

I furthermore certify that I saw in Company quarters No. 5 upwards of 4 dead bodies, which to my certain knowledge had been there two or three days. Others to the number of 12 were reported dead at one time. I also certify that Capt. R. H. Clinton 10th Tenn. Inf comd'g Barracks used every exertion to have the nuisance abated but with little result.

The negroes reported to me on several occasions that the officers and other white men in charge of them selected mulatto women with whom they were in the habit of sleeping, thus demoralizing instead of bettering the condition of these truly unfortunate people.
ADS   S V Clevenger

Statement of 1st Lieut. S. V. Clevenger, 28 Dec. 1864, filed with Capt. R. H. Clinton to His Excellency Brig. Gen'l Andrew Johnson, 20 Dec. 1864, Letters Received, ser. 867, Post of Nashville, RG 393 Pt. 4 [C-8939]. In the same file is a statement made the same day by L. C. Fonts, a surgeon at Tennessee Barracks, who confirmed that dead bodies had lain unattended for days and reported that he had himself, upon entering a building occupied by the black refugees, "beheld with disgust the greatest amount of filth and uncleanliness of both person and apartment that I had ever witnessed anywhere else." On one occasion, Fonts recalled, Captain Robert H. Clinton, the commander of the barracks, had summoned Lieutenant Lorenzo D. Barnes, the officer in charge of the refugees, and "remonstrated against the general uncleanliness of their part of the Barracks, and especially to the accumulation of human feces," whereupon Barnes "agreed to have the thing attended to." "Still," Fonts added, "I think there was little or no change in the appearance of things while they remained there."

120: Commander of a Tennessee Black Regiment to the Headquarters of the Department of the Cumberland

Chattanooga, T[enn.], Jan 30 1865
Sir, Many of the men of this Command have wives and families in some Camp (either "refugee" or "contraband") at Nashville, The Stories that are brought me of the treatment these people receive,

have determined me to address you this communication, – One
man, just returned from furlough, informs me that the suffering
from hungar & cold is so great that those wretched people are dying
by scores – that sometimes thirty per day die & are carried out by
wagon loads, without coffins, & thrown promiscuously, like brutes,
into a trench – ,

A few weeks ago the family, – wife & six small children – of an
enlisted man of this regt, were sent from here to Nashville by order
of the Post Comd^r. – Today the children were brought back, – how
or by whom I cannot learn, They are nearly starved, their limbs are
frozen, – one of them is likely to loose both feet, – Their mother
died in the camp at Nashville, – Why these children were not kept
& taken care of instead of being sent back here I have no means of
Knowing,

The men of my command appeal to me for relief from such
treatment, – I cannot disregard their request,

I have therefore the honor most respy to lay this matter before the
Comdg General & to most earnestly request that measures may be
taken to relieve the condition of these most wretched people, Very
respy Your obt servt

ALS   Jos. R. Putnam

Lt. Col. Jos. R. Putnam to Brig. Gen. W. D. Whipple, 30 Jan. 1865, filed
among unentered letters 1865, Letters Received, ser. 925, Dept. of the Cumberland, RG 393 Pt. 1 [C-85]. Endorsement. Putnam commanded the 42nd
USCI.

121: **Commander of the Post of Columbia, Tennessee, to the
Commander of U.S. Forces at Pulaski, Tennessee**

Columbia, Tenn. *March 12" 1865.*

We have a large number of Negroes in and arround this Post who
will not work for themselves or hire to any one – Shall I gather
them up and send them to Contraband Camps, and if so will you
please designate what point I shall send them to –

They are stealing and committing all sorts of depradations and tis
impossible to arrest the proper ones – I have notified them by
an Order to procur for themselves situations where they can
work – some have done so still a number remains on hand
yet   please inform me what I shall do – I am Genl very
respectfully

ALS   Dan McCoy

[*Endorsement*] Head Quarters U.S. Forces. Pulaski Tenn Mar. 14 1865 Respectfully forwarded   I recommend that the vagrant negroes in the vicinity of Columbia be collected and sent to Nashville or vicinity There to be established in Contraband Camp,

This in view of the fact that the government must feed them wherever they may be collected, and the transportation of rations from Nashville South might be thus saved.

I also respectfully make the same recommendation as to The Contraband Camp near This place, R W Johnson Brig Genl Vols

Lt. Col. Dan. McCoy to Brig. Gen. R. W. Johnson, 12 Mar. 1865, M-353 1865, Letters Received, ser. 925, Dept. of the Cumberland, RG 393 Pt. 1 [C-17]. In the same file is an undated, penciled opinion by Colonel Robert W. Barnard, superintendent of contrabands in the Department of the Cumberland, which approved General Johnson's proposal to send the contrabands at Columbia to Nashville, but opposed moving those near Pulaski, who "are on a Plantation, and will raise enough this year to give them a fair start and [make?] them independent of Govt Support. They are industrous and work faithfully." However, no written reply to either Colonel McCoy or General Johnson has been found in the letters-sent volumes of the Department of the Cumberland.

122: Tennessee Brewer to the Governor of Tennessee

Nashville, Tenn., April 10th 1865.

Sir, I have the honor to make the following representation, and invoke your interference in behalf of justice.

At the inception of the rebellion Samuel Emery (colored) together with his wife, and four children, were slaves, resident in Wilson County Tenn,

During the progress of the war, this man Emery was pressed to labor upon the fortifications erecting for the defence of this city. soon after, his wife, the bearer of this, who with her children was owned by Mrs Eveline Blair, was likewise brought to this city by the federal Army, and subsequently joined her husband and under the operation of the emancipation proclamation began and continue the honest, industrious pursuit of a livelihood, The husband now being in my employ,

On several occasions, the last of which was but a day or two since, these parents presented themselves before the former Mistress of their Children who *now* retains them in bondage, and supplicated her for them, On each occasion she has indignantly spurned their united supplication uttering the most opprobrious epithets against

the federal government and declaring the children should never be granted their freedom thus evincing an utter disregard for the federal government and the earnest solicitations of these oppressed people. I therefore beg that you may take such action, if consistent with your official duty, as shall warrant the rendition of the children to their parents, who are fully competent to properly care for them, or if not within the sphere of your official province that you will ind[*icate the?*] process proper to s[*ecure the end?*] desired, In behalf [. . .]¹ I am, Governor, Very Resp[*ectfully*] Your ob'd[*t servant*]
ALS   Urbain [*Ozanne*]

Urbain [Ozanne] to his Excellency Wm. G. Brownlow, 10 Apr. 1865, Letters & Reports Received, ser. 2922, Dist. of Middle TN, RG 393 Pt. 2 No. 184 [C-410]. A portion of the second page, about two inches square, is missing, accounting for the missing and bracketed parts of the concluding paragraph and the signature. On letterhead of the "Nashville Union Brewery," operated by "U. Ozanne & Co., Manufacturers of Ale & Beer." Governor William G. Brownlow evidently forwarded Ozanne's letter to the headquarters of the District of Middle Tennessee, among whose records it is filed. No evidence of action upon its contents has been found in the records of that district.

1 Letter torn; two or three words missing.

123: Superintendent of Freedmen in the Department of the Cumberland to the Freedmen's Bureau Commissioner, Enclosing a List of Contraband Camps in the Department

Nashville Tenn. May. 30ᵗʰ 1865

General: In compliance with your circular letter of May 16ᵗʰ 1865¹ I have the honor to make the following report concerning the Freedmen in this Department.

On June 14ᵗʰ 1864 I was ordered by Major General George H. Thomas, Comdg. Department of the Cumberland, to Nashville to relieve Captain Ralph Hunt   Kentucky Vol. Infty. then in charge of Freedmen Department of the Cumberland,

I found at that time Seven (7) "Contraband Camps" with about Five thousand Five hundred (5,500) refugees in them, These camps were carried on without system, without shelter for the people, and apparently, without any definate plan as to their future condition. they were entirely dependent upon the U.S. for support.

At present matters are in a much better condition, the numbers in Camp have been reduced to less than Four thousand (4000) and that too notwithstanding the large accessions received during the past winter which amounted to more than are now in the various Camps.

At all these Camps except the one at Nashville, by judiciously working the inmates at farming Milling, or Mechanical work of some Kind, the Expense to the Government is but very small and the people are taught to rely on their own Exertions for a livelyhood. We have now upwards of Twenty five hundred (2500) Acres in cultivation, in Cotton, Corn, and tobacco with a good prospect of heavy Crops, as the work is thoroughly done under supervision of Officers who understand their duties.

In addition we have one Shoe factory working about twenty (20) hands. Two (2) Grist Mills and One Steam Saw mill all in good order and successful operation.

Last year three (3) of these camps clothed themselves with the proceeds of their own labor and this year all but two are expected to do the same.

We employ no Agents to do Either our selling or purchasing, my experience in business, and Knowledge of merchandize Enabling me with advantage and great saving in expense, to attend personally to such matters.

I have the honor to forward as an appendix to this report a list of the different camps under my charge, with the rank and name of the Officer in Command, number of inmates, number of Acres worked, and the general condition of each camp.

I take pleasure in stating here that each and Every Officer under my command is faithful, honest, and zealous in the discharge of their duties, without fanatical zeal, and doing justice alike to the Freedmen and their former owners.

In conclusion I would respectfully recommend to your favorable notice, as a man capable, worthy and honest in the highest degree, for the position of Commissioner for this State (Tennessee) Alfred. L. Hough Captain 19th Infantry U.S.A and Brevet Major. U.S.A. All I have said of him would be more than Endorsed at the Head. Quarters Department of the Cumberland where Major Hough, now on General Thomas' staff, is held in the highest Estimation,

In justice to Major Hough I beg leave to state that he has not applied for the position. I recommend him solely on account of his fitness and ability. As an Officer. he has but few superiors in the line. I have the honor to be, General, Very Respectfully, Your Ob^{t}. Servt,

HLS

R. W. Barnard

Camps of Freedmen
Superintended by Col. R. W. Barnard 101ˢᵗ Regt. U.S.C. Inf'y.

N°	Located at —	Officer in charge	N° of inmates	Acres of Ground worked	– Remarks –
1	Nashville Tenn.	Lt. F. W. Crawford 101ˢᵗ U.S.C.I	688	Twenty five (25)	This Camp has good barracks and single houses built by Q.M. Dept.
2	Gallatin Tenn.	Capt. S. H. Eno 101ˢᵗ U.S.C.I	354	Two Hundred (200)	This Camp now engaged in building Quarters.
3	Hendersonville Tenn.	Lt. J. B. Nesbitt 101ˢᵗ U.S.C.I	535	Four Hundred (400)	Good Quarters in this camp built by Lt. Nesbitt with Camp labor
4	Clarksville Tenn.	Capt. Wᵐ Brunt. 16ᵗʰ U.S.C.I	1259	Three Hundred & fifty (350)	Good barracks for inmates built by Camp labor
5	Near Pulaski, Giles Co. Tenn.	Lt. L. D. Barnes 111ᵗʰ U.S.C.I	328	Three Hundred (300)	Log houses put up by inmates of the Camp.
6	Decatur Junction Ala.	Lt. J. B. Harris	487	Nine Hundred & fifty (950)	Good Quarters put up by the inmates of the camp and found on the place
7	Huntsville Ala.	Chaplain Stokes	243	Three Hundred (300)	Quarters built by inmates of Camp.

HD

Col. R. W. Barnard to Major General O. O. Howard, 30 May 1865, enclosing "Camps of Freedmen Superintended by Col. R. W. Barnard," [30 May 1865], B-14 1865], Registered Letters Received, ser. 3379, TN Asst. Comr., RG 105 [A-6072]. Endorsement. Barnard signed as a captain in the 19th U.S. Infantry, as well as superintendent of freedmen. The blank space in Captain Hunt's regimental affiliation appears in the manuscript.

1 The circular, actually dated May 15, 1865, had asked "[a]ll Commissioners however appointed who have the charge of Freedmen" to report "the character and extent of their work." (Circular Letter, Commissioner Refugees, Freedmen and Abandoned Lands, 15 May 1865, vol. 139, p. 1, Circulars, ser. 24, Washington Hdqrs., RG 105 [A-10701].)

124: Statement of a Tennessee Freedwoman

[Chattanooga, Tenn. February 27, 1866]

Statement of Anna Irwin Washerwoman in Genl Field Hospital D.C *[Department of the Cumberland]* Commenced work at Rasacca Geo. in the month of April 1864 – remained there about two months – then went to Big Shanty Stopped there four days – went to Cartersvill stayed ther four days – then went to Marietta stayed there about three weeks – then went to Vining station stayed there about two Months then went to Atlanta & stayed there about two months. then came to Chattanooga Tenn All the time under the charge of surgeon Woodruff When we came to Chattanooga were turned over to surgeon E. L. Bissell. then went to Huntsvill AL. left there on Christmas day 1864 then went to Bulls Gap Tenn remained there one month then went to Nashvill where we remained untill we were mustered out. – was to recieve four dollars pr week. Anna acted as foreman and was to recieve $5.00 pr week. they have recieve but $44^{oo}. Stewart Johnson & John Hardenberg took the money and made away. The other claimants names are Laura Irwin Rhoda Willis and Milly Humphries

The above named persons were discharged at Nashvill Tenn June 16th 1865 by virtue of special orders No 3 Gen Field Hospital, by E. L. Bissell Surg 5 Conn. Vols in charge

HD

Statement of Anna Irwin, [27 Feb. 1866], enclosed in Lt. Col. F. E. Trotter to Surgeon Genl. U.S.A., 27 Feb. 1866, T-1 1866, Registered Letters Received, ser. 3448, Chattanooga TN Supt., RG 105 [A-6423]. In the same file is a copy of the special order of June 16, 1865, that discharged the four women from service at the general field hospital in Nashville and instructed them to report to an assistant quartermaster for transportation to Chattanooga. In October 1865, according to other documents in the file, Anna Irwin and her co-workers had presented a similar account of their wartime employment to the Freedmen's Bureau assistant superintendent at Chattanooga and solicited his aid in collecting their wages. The superintendent had reported the case to the medical director of the Department of Tennessee, who advised him to "request the Surgeon General US.A. to examine the Pay Rolls of Col'd employees of Gen'l Field Hospital Army of the Cumberland for the year 1864–5." (Capt. N. B. Lucas to Surgeon Cooper, 19 Oct. 1865, and endorsement of Surgeon Geo. E. Cooper, 23 Oct. 1865.) That bureau superintendent had apparently taken no further action on behalf of the freedwomen, but his successor, after taking Irwin's statement of February 27, 1866, promptly forwarded it to the surgeon general in Washington, noting in a covering letter that "[d]aily applications are made at this office for settlement of similar claims many of which bear evidence of fraud haveing been practiced on the Negro by persons connected with the army." On March 26, 1866, the surgeon general's office returned the papers to the bureau superintendent at Chattanooga, with the following endorsement: "There is no information on file in this Office, relative to the employment, or payment, of the women named within. After so long an interval and the discharge of many of the officers in charge, it is impossible to take any action in the absence of certified accounts, or certificates of service."

125: Affidavit of Two Tennessee Freedmen

Freedmen Camp Tunnel Hill Tenn. June 19" 1865
Joseph Abernathy & Hustin Abernathy (Colored) being Duly Sworn Deposeth and Says
I That on the 1ˢ day of April 1865 Thomas E. Abernathy proposed to me that if I would take the hands that foremaly belonged to Said Thomas E. Abernathy and make him a good crop that he would give us the half of all raised on Said Thomas E Abernathy farm   that each one of you Shall make an equal division of your half of all products raised
II We was to put in (40) Fourty acres of cotton and (50) Fifty acres of corn (6) Six acres of Sorgum and (2) two of potatoes also Some cabbage all of wich we complied within good faith on our Side
III At the time of making this contract with Said Thomas E. Abernathy he did not live on his place but had abandon it for the space of (6) Six months prior to Said contract   after he returned to Said farm he told me that he could not give us the half of all produce raised on Said farm as he had agreed to do but I will make a new contract with you   I will give one third instead of one half of all products raised on said farm to wich we upon our part agreed to take in good faith   One week after that time he Said he would not give the One third that we did not have in crop Sufficient to justify him in giving us any portion of Said crop raised on Said farm   he then said that he wanted ten (10) more acres of corn put in to wich proposition we agreed provided he would give us the third as in accordiance with his Second bargain to wich he replied that he would not give us any portion of the crop   he then Said that he was going to employ a new man to attend to his business as overseer who turned out to be Mr John Howard from Pennsylvania   Mr

Howard after taking charge of Said farm told us that Mr Abernathy told him that he had made a bargain with us and that we was to have One third of all the products raised upon Said farm but that he could not now comply with his bargain Then we asked him what he would give Mr Howard replied that Mr Thomas E Abernathy Says that he will hire you and pay you $15°° Fifteen Dollars per month but your clothing provision and Doctor Bill must come out of Said $15°° Fifteen Dollars per month

IV And if you will not hire on those terms you Shall all leave the place after we Studied the mater over we Came to the Conclusion on account of our wives & Children that we would make this our third bargain with Thomas E. Abernathy wich we d[id] in good faith upon our part One week after this last contract was made he told us that he would not give us $15°° Fifteen Dollars per month again we asked him what will you give us when the Said Thomas E Abernathy replied I will not tell you what I will give you I will gi[ve] you just what I please and no more

V In 1864 we bargained & agreed with Said Thomas E Abernathy to raise a crop on Said farm on the following terms he told us to go on and raise all the cotton that we wanted to raise that he did not want any cotton for hisself that if he had any raised the yankees would take it from him all that he wanted was (5) five acres of corn raised by us for him to wich we agreed Said Thomas E Abernathy after Came to the Conclusion that he wanted Some cotton raised for his own use and benefit we asked him how much cotton he wanted planted Thomas E. Abernathy Said plant me (4) Four acres of cotton Seperate from yours is all that I ask of you we planted him his (4) Four acres of cotton raised picked gined and baled Seperate & apart from that raised as our own after we had gined & baled our own he marked it in his own name he told us that he was obliged to do that as we was not allowed to Sell any cotton we had (5) Fife bales of cotton averaging (500) Five hundred pounds each wich Said Thomas E. Abernathy tuck to Nashville Tenn. and disposed of Said Thomas E Abernathy kept all the proceeds accruing from Said Sales of Said Cotton with the exception of $150 One hundred and Fifty Dollars wich we received in goods we also raised in 1864 about (800) Eight hundred bushels of Corn wich Said Thomas E. Abernathy did take possession of use and make way with for his own private use and benefit also would not allow us to use any of it unless we paid him for it

VI We farthers testify and Say that of our own free will and accord gathered and delivered to Said Thomas E. Abernathy in person at Mrs Mary Rivers Residence where Said Thomas E Abernathy went to after he had abandon his own plantation the (5)

Five acres of corn that we raised for Said Thomas E Abernathy in 1864

HD

Affidavit of Joseph Abernathy and Hustin Abernathy, 19 June 1865, A-3 1865, Registered Letters Received, ser. 3379, TN Asst. Comr., RG 105 [A-6067]. Sworn before Lieutenant Lorenzo D. Barnes, assistant superintendent of freedmen at Pulaski, Tennessee, who evidently forwarded the affidavit to Colonel Robert W. Barnard, superintendent of freedmen in the Department of the Cumberland, along with copies of two orders Barnes had recently received regarding the former slaves on Thomas Abernathy's farm. In one, dated June 8, 1865, the commander of a cavalry division at Pulaski, citing repeated (but unspecified) complaints about the freedpeople, had directed Lieutenant Barnes to "go over and remove such of them as Mr. or Mrs. Abernathey may designate to the Contraband Camp." "By this," he had added, "I think the remainder will do better." In the second order, dated six days later, the general in command at Pulaski had noted with disapproval that "the Abernathy negroes have been permitted to leave the corral and hunt themselves homes in the neighborhood." Believing "that it is best for all parties that they should [be] KEPT at the coral where they can be governed and compeled to work," the general had instructed Barnes to "send for them and take them to the corral & retain them there." (Bret. Maj. Genl. R. W. Johnson to Lt. L. D. Barnes, 8 June 1865; A.A.G. E. T. Wells to Lt. L. D. Barnes, 14 June 1865.) Endorsements indicate that Colonel Barnard referred the papers to General Clinton B. Fisk, the Freedmen's Bureau assistant commissioner for Tennessee, who, on July 18, 1865, ordered that Thomas Abernathy be summoned to "report in person at these Headquarters [in Nashville] without delay." On July 26, presumably after Fisk had interviewed Thomas Abernathy, an aide added a final endorsement that summarized the assistant commissioner's decision in the case. When the five bales of cotton raised in 1864 were sold, Fisk ordered, the proceeds "shall be deposited with an officer of this Bureau," who would then settle the freedpeople's claim. With respect to the 1865 crop season, Fisk ordered that Thomas Abernathy "enter into a written contract with the freedmen on his farm upon the terms agreed upon between said freedmen & said Abernethy through his Agt. one Howard and by the terms of which the freedmen shall receive one third of the crop raised during the present year—" In early August, the proceeds from the five bales raised in 1864 were paid over to the Freedmen's Bureau, and Captain John H. Hull, bureau agent for Giles County, reported that he had made a contract for 1865 between Thomas Abernathy and the laborers on his farm, the terms of which conformed to Fisk's decision. In late October 1865, Hull oversaw a settlement in which each of five "Abernethy freedmen" received $68.67 as his share of the proceeds from the cotton raised in 1864. (Capt. John H. Hull to A.A.A. Gen. John H. Cochran, 8 Aug. 1865, H-141 1865, and Capt. John H. Hull to Capt. W. T. Clark, 26 Oct. 1865, H-173 1865, Registered Letters Received, ser. 3379, TN Asst. Comr., RG 105 [A-6067].)

126: Freedmen's Bureau Assistant Superintendent at Columbia, Tennessee, to the Tennessee Freedmen's Bureau Assistant Commissioner

Columbia Tenn. Aug. 1ˢᵗ 1865.

Sir. Finding it impossible to get any reply to communications through the proper channel, I take the liberty of writing you personally, concerning an important matter.

During the year 1863, a negro worked for a man who gave the owner of the negro a note of hand for $150,00. The man who gave the note is now willing to pay it, and applies to this office to know whether to pay it to the negro or his former owner, who holds the note.

Does the negro's title to his labor date from the time of the President's Proclamation, or from the adoption of the Constitutional Amendment by the State of Tenn.?[1]

As there are doubtless other similar cases, an answer is earnestly requested. Very Respectfully Your Obᵗ Serᵛᵗ

HLSr
Wᵐ Davenport

Wm. Davenport to C. B. Fiske, 1 Aug. 1865, D-19 1865, Registered Letters Received, ser. 3379, TN Asst. Comr., RG 105 [A-6105]. Davenport signed as a provost marshal as well as an officer of the Freedmen's Bureau. In a penciled notation, the assistant commissioner instructed his adjutant: "write him that if the owner was *disloyal* in *act word* or *deed*—that the negro was free from July 17th 1862" (the date of the Second Confiscation Act). "If the owner was a *loyal* Unionist his negro was property until Feb 1865—"

1 The respective dates were January 1, 1863, the Emancipation Proclamation, and February 22, 1865, ratification of an amendment to the state constitution abolishing slavery.

127: Tennessee Unionist to the Tennessee Freedmen's Bureau Assistant Commissioner

[*Fayetteville, Tenn.*] (Augst 8ᵗʰ 1865)

Genˡ I am called upon by some very worthy and deserving Freedmen to make a statement of their grieveances to the end that your advise & directions may be obtained by which they can govern themselves and to plead that an agent may be sent for their protection at your earliest convenience

The grievances of which they complain are as follows, that their former master Dr Wm Bonner abandoned them with all his other property in this county in June 1863 by taking what he could transport and going South in advance of our Army commanded by Genl Rosecrans   they were left with just such means of support as could not be moved   there were a few hogs left on the farm which were subsequently taken from them thereby throwing them entirely upon their own resourses.   Since then they have worked and lived   his Dr Bonners Daughter Mrs Lamb in the mean time has been taking from time to time such of their products as she thought proper for her own use with out compensation untill last winter when he returned and reassumed his authority over his possessions

   When by the act of the Loyal people of the state they were made free he first ordered them off his land. they were preparing to comply when he proposed to them that if they would remain and go to work he would make such arrangements as would be satisfactory to them and to the mutual interest of both parties, since which time they have frequently called on him to have the terms definitly understood but have as often failed in getting a satisfactory answer,   from what they can learn from himself and their fellow Freedmen his object is to defraud them of the present crop and if they will not submit to the old slave policy to drive them off the land   he has told them and reiterates that if they do not submit that not one of them will be allowed to remain on his land all of which they have great cause to fear without the benign influence of your authority is thrown around them as a wall of defence and a sure refuge in this their time of trouble   for the past Three years they have furnished all the salt they used and the last two have supported themselves entirely and this present year they have stocked the farm with what horses that has been used in making the crop paid the smiths bill and every expence not costing him one cent expence and now to loose it all under the circumstances they cannot they will not believe you will allow

   The complainants of the foregoing represents three families numbering 14 souls   they have managed to procure by purchase and otherwise about 70 head of Hogs Large and small and now William Bonner Sr tells them that they will not be allowed to have or to raise hogs or stock of any kind on the farm that is all his   they have also about 55 acres of corn and also about 30 acres of cotton with a very flattering prospect of a fine yield and with the fear of loseing their labor before them they will be very unesy untill they can hear from you   your attention to the foregoing is earnestly solicited and will place them and myself under obligations to your kindness   there is one other matter to which they desire me to call your attention and it is to know whether they are entitled to any remuneration for their services for last year. they have had read in

their hearing your Circular[1] and it gives entire satisfaction   they
make but one expression and that is unanimously in its favor and
with an agent within reach they would be entirely Content   and
another matter they are anxious about the next year for homes   they
wish to know whether an oppertunity will be afforded within the
year to procure a home out of those abandoned lands   there are
enough of such lands to accommodate all the freedmen and some for
refugees   I think from my recollection there are over Twenty
thousand acres that are abandon,d under the Law[2]   I have the
Honor to be your Obt Serv't

William French

ALS

William French to Brig. Genl. Clinton B. Fisk, 8 Aug. 1865, F-55 1865,
Registered Letters Received, ser. 3379, TN Asst. Comr., RG 105 [A-6121].
No reply has been found in the letters-sent volumes of the assistant commissioner. One month later, after French had been appointed Freedmen's Bureau
agent for Lincoln County, he reported that he had "notified Wm Bonner Jr to
restore to the freedmen of one of his fathers platations stock that . . . has been
unjustly taken from them." The ex-slaves had raised and bred the cattle, hogs,
and sheep left behind when the senior Bonner "absconded" in June 1863;
therefore, French contended, they had as much "right to a support out of [the
livestock] as their former master." Since returning to his plantation in January
1865, the elder Bonner "has refused peremptorily to furnish them with a
single pound of meat upon which to subsist." Moreover, French reported, he
"has been trying to coerce the Freedmen to submit to the old slave policy and
upon their refusal he has notified them that they shall not remain on his land
after the crops are gathered." Meanwhile, Bonner, Jr., "has been constantly
allarming them with Bushwhackers if they fail or refuse to do his bidding";
"with the aid of soldiers and some neighbors," he recently "took one of the
freedmen out of his House at the dead Hour of night tied him to a tree and
then struck him four or five hundred lashes on his bare back." The entire
Bonner family, French claimed, had been "active and intence Rebels"; William
Bonner, Jr., had served in the Confederate army, and his father and sisters had
become refugees into the Confederacy. Their land, French argued, was therefore subject to seizure "under the act of Confiscation" and also as abandoned
land, "and if they are to be passed by there are no Homes for the Refugee or
Freedman in this county." (Wm. French to Genl. Clinton B. Fisk, 14 Sept.
1865, F-72 1865, Registered Letters Received, ser. 3379, TN Asst. Comr.,
RG 105 [A-6121].)

1 Circular 2, issued by the assistant commissioner on July 24, 1865, had
summarized the objectives of the Freedmen's Bureau in Tennessee: "promotion
of productive industry," settlement of ex-slaves "in homes of their own, with
the guarantee of their absolute freedom and their right to justice before the
law . . . [and] the dissemination of virtuous intelligence." The circular forbade "[c]ompulsory, unpaid labor," encouraged ex-slaves to work "for an interest in the crop," and pledged that "Special efforts" would be made to settle

them on confiscated or abandoned land. (Circular No. 2, Bureau Refugees, Freedmen, and Aband. Lands, Office of Asst. Comr. for Ky., Tenn., and Northn. Ala., 24 July 1865, Special Orders & Circulars Issued, ser. 3384, TN Asst. Comr., RG 105 [A-10740].)

2 The law of March 3, 1865, that created the Freedmen's Bureau had authorized its commissioner to "set apart, for the use of loyal refugees and freedmen, such tracts of land within the insurrectionary states as shall have been abandoned, or to which the United States shall have acquired title by confiscation or sale." (*Statutes at Large*, vol. 13, pp. 507–9.)

128: Freedmen's Bureau Assistant Superintendent at Murfreesboro, Tennessee, to the Headquarters of the Tennessee Freedmen's Bureau Assistant Commissioner

Murfreesboro Tenn Sept 1st 1865

Col   I most respectfully ask to be informed on the following point viz   Did Freedom to the blacks in this County embrace 1864 or did it only take place Feby 1865?   If it did not take place to embrace last year Then I am guilty of maladministrati[on] for I have from the begining of my acts here ordered the payment of claims on contracs to the Colored people last year but not going further back than Jan 1864

I am led to this enquiry by the following circumstance   "Ellen (Colored) worked for Mrs Hawkett last year (in Comp^y with others) for one third of the Crop of Cotton and Corn   M^{rs} H refused to pay"   I wrote to Mrs Hawkitt to Come to the office and Answer to the Complaint on Friday Augt 17th at 10 Oclock."   Such is my Docket   Now instead of Coming here Mrs Hawkitt in person or by proxy goes to Nashville & obtains the opinion of the Solicitor of Genl Fisk's Court that the Complainants "had no claims they being Slaves up to Feb 1865"   On The presentation of this paper endorsed on the back of my notice for M^{rs} H to appear I had of Course the "lock Jaw" & am tied—   please send me Your opinion & if Genl Fisk has returned I would like his "Ex Officio"   I am Colonel Your Most Obt Servt

John Seage

Colonel   has Major Hotchkiss any instruction to turn over his office as US Treasury Agent to this Office to be under my Control as Ab Lands? John Seage Asst Supt

ALS

John Seage to Lt. Col. R. W. Barnard, 1 Sept. 1865, S-58 1865, Registered Letters Received, ser. 3379, TN Asst. Comr., RG 105 [A-6052]. "Genl Fisk's court" was the tribunal established in late July 1865 by General Clinton B. Fisk, the Freedmen's Bureau assistant commissioner for Tennessee, to adjudicate "matters of difference between freedmen, or between freedmen and others"; its solicitor was an officer on Fisk's staff. (Circular No. 4, Bureau Refugees Freedmen and Aband. Lands, Head Quarters Dist. Ky., Tenn., and North Ala., 28 July 1865, vol. 23, p. 258, Special Orders & Circulars Issued, ser. 3384, TN Asst. Comr., RG 105 [A-10741].) No reply to Seage's query has been found among the letters-sent volumes of Fisk's office.

129: Superintendent of a Contraband Camp near Hendersonville, Tennessee, to the Tennessee Freedmen's Bureau Assistant Commissioner

Nashvill [*Tenn.*] Dec. 16th 1865

General: By request I will try to give a few statements in regard to the formation of the Contraband Camps, at Pulaski, Tunnel Hill, and Hendersonville Tenn, and Decatur Junction Ala.

In November /'63 Gen¹ G. M. Dodge Comd'g L. W. 16th A.C. procured permission to raise Colored troops in his Dist. The officers were selected from non com. officrs and privates recomend by Comd'g officers of the various Rgtˢ of the Command.

These men being generally ambitious, very little respect was paid to the negro's preference, for, or against, the service. Impressment, was the order of the day, and men of all ages and every state of physical condition, were brought in and enrolled. The closest scrutiny of examining Surgeons, failed to keep these zealous, advocates for commissions, from getting men into their Coˢ, that have since proven to be but a burden to the public Treaˢ. Of those rejected by the Surgeons, many were taken for cooks, and servants. To appease the black-men until they could be properly mustered every facility was offered them to bring their families into camp. When the men would leave home with their families, it was not strange the old and helpless, should wish to leave too, or that the master should extend to them means to go, when for them to remain was an expense to him. Hence every forage-train, country wagon, horse and mule that came into camp was loaded down with negros of all grades of the race. Soon the lines of every Post where troops were stationed was crowded with these fugetives, and it as soon became manifest that the presence of so many slave-degraded women was fast degrading our troops.

With the law of Congress binding upon him, the Comd'g Gen¹ could not place these people out-side his lines with military

474

force.[1] But something must bed done. J. W. Harris Lieut 57th Ills. Inft. was ordered to act as "Supt. of Contrabands" and devise some means of taking care of them.

The first Camp was organized Dec. 1st /'63 on the Jno. Phillips plantation 2 1/2 miles from Pulaski. The second Jan'y 15th on the Tho[s] Brown place, 8 miles from Pulaski and near Tunnel Hill. The third was organized March 14th /'65 [*1864*] on the Hobbs' place near Decatur Junction Ala. On these several plantations the women, children, – and men rejected from the army – were gathered; houses built to shelter them and as much work as circumstances would permit was provided them. Cotton that had been abandoned, was gathered during the winter and sold amounting to some $9000.[oo]. The money was deposited in Post Trea[s] Pulaski, and drawn out by Lieut Harris as need, and I believe honestly expended. Condemned animals, and old Harness, were procured from the Q.M. Dept. and preperations for farming were commenced early in the spring. Abut 1000 acres of cotton was planted and 400 of corn.

In months of March and April [*1864*] the planters manifested quite a disposition to commence work, The Sup[t] responded to this by urging upon the negros, to returne to their homes and go to work for wages; but the blacks seemed to distrust their former masters, and but few complied, he then suggest that they work for a share of the crop. The negros remaining at home eagerly accepted such contracts, wherever the planters would do so. But moral suasion failed to drive many out of camp whilst Gov[t] rations were plentifully issued.

Here the Sup[t] took a step in the right direction but failed to go far enough. I believe these contracts did much good. By these partnerships the master, that early, acknowledged the negro's equality to a certain extent, and right to deal, and be dealt with. How profitable it proved to the negro pecuniarily is another question; but it was a step in the right direction; it was the starting point in the great labor question, in that part of the country. For its consequences we have only to glance at Giles Co Tenn. and Limestone Co. Ala. and it will be found that more bales of cotton, and acres of corn, were raised than any other two Co[s] south of Nashville and north of the Tenn River, in the years '64 and '65.

The camps kept increasing: every negro that came in was housed and fed. In May /'64 Maj. _____ 7th Ills Inft. Mounted went into Lauderdale Co. Ala. took the negros from their homes, loaded them into the planters wagons and sent them to Pulaski. Between six hundred and eight hundred arrived at camp on one day: the greater number of them were sent to Tunnel Hill Camp.

475

On the 1st August [1864] the Pulaski Camp contained—in round numbers—1000 persons: the Tunnel Hill Camp 1400 and the Decatur Junction camp contained 600 persons.

Sept. 25th /'65 [1864] Genl Bedford Forrest burned down the Tunnel Hill camp, consisting of 240 houses 14 × 6 ft., a Gin House and Gin also a stable containing about $300^{00} worth of corn and fodder. Many of the people left camp before the rebels got there; those who remained stated that the soldiers did nothing to injure them, but ordered them to take their things out of the houses previous to burning the camp, and that the citizens following the army set fire to, and burned up the negros clothing and stuff saved from the houses.

When Hood made his move into Tenn. and our army was ordered to evacuate that section, I used my personal influence to have the negros remain behind, to scatter out amoung the people: a few complied and I am happy to state that they did well. Some 1500 fell in with the army on its retreat to Nashville; hundreds "joined the band" as they marched along until there must have been 2000 on reaching this place. Everything was done that could be, under the circumstances. Partially empty wagons of the supply trains were loaded and some 200 animals were secured from Q.M. droves upon which were placed many children and sick persons, yet many died of exposures and fatigue on the road and many more from the effect of such exposures after reaching Nashville

After the battle of Nashville the Donaldson farm was secured and Lt. Barnes moved some 900 people upon it. I was put in charge of that Camp, Feb. 1st /'65, and soon determined to reduce its numbers: by the 1st of April the camp contained only 450 and had I been properly supported I am certain that with judicious management the camp could have been reduced to nothing but a Hospital by the 1st of June.

The Hendersonville Camp I think was the only one in the Dept. on the decrease at the time of your arrival here. I don't wish to be understood as reflecting upon any of my superior officers, but I have had my own opinions about these matters; though never troubling myself to advertise them, yet always expressed them freely when asked. I always made it a point to act to the best of my judgement so far as existing orders would permit. So in regard to these Camps I thought it a bad system; expensive to the Government and demoralizing in the extreme to the negro. Certainly any one could see that emancipation would be as sure to reach the slave at home as a fugetive.

Avarice impled men to make wholesale conscription of the negro, and gave his family encouragement to leave good homes to appease the natural feeling to have them with him and *misjudgement* permitted it, and formed these camps, fostering instead of crushing a great wrong. I am Gen[l] Very respectfully Your obt servt

ALS   James B. Nesbitt

1st Lieut. James B. Nesbitt to Brvt. Maj. Genl. Fisk, 16 Dec. 1865, N-33 1865, Registered Letters Received, ser. 3379, TN Asst. Comr., RG 105 [A-6183]. Nesbitt, the superintendent of the contraband camp on the Donelson farm, near Hendersonville, signed as a lieutenant in the 101st USCI. The same day, General Clinton B. Fisk, Freedmen's Bureau assistant commissioner for Tennessee, recounted for the bureau's commissioner his efforts to close the camps at Hendersonville, Gallatin, and Tunnel Hill, Tennessee, and at Decatur Junction and Huntsville, Alabama. When he assumed his post in June 1865, the camps had been "largely in debt and the growing crops very poor." Accordingly, he had ordered a subordinate to "close them up as rapidly as duty to the infirm and sick would permit." Since that time, Fisk added, the Donelson farm had been restored to the widow of its owner, "greatly to the loss of the laborers." (Bvt. Maj. Genl. Clinton B. Fisk to Genl. Howard, 16 Dec. [186]5, vol. 15, pp. 121–23 1/2, Press Copies of Letter Sent to General Howard & Staff, ser. 3374, TN Asst. Comr., RG 105 [A-6183].)

1 Although neither the March 1862 article of war nor section 10 of the Second Confiscation Act of July 1862 expressly forbade the expulsion of fugitive slaves from Union camps, both laws prohibited Union officers from using military force to return an escaped slave to a claimant. (*Statutes at Large*, vol. 12, pp. 354, 589–92.)

130: **Two Tennessee Freedmen to the Freedmen's Bureau Agent for Robertson County, Tennessee**

Nashville Tenn   Jany 2nd 1866
Dear Sir: We are colord men residents of Edgefield, and formerly the slaves of Geo A Washington, In the year 1863 we made a crop of tobacco, two hundred pounds each and sold it to our master, who has never paid us for it   The wife of Clinton Washington worked for him all of the year 1864 up to last of March 1865, and he never paid her or even clothed her   Her name is Rachel Washington & lives in Edgefield,
    Our witnesses are Ford Washington of Nashville Tenn, John Washington of Nashville Tenn. and if you will be so Kind as to let us Know the time set for examination of the matter, we will bring up these witnesses and furnish many others who are now at

springfield, Our address is Edgefield Tennessee   We are esteemed
sir very Respectfully

his
Clinton X Washington
mark
his
HLSr   Ford X Washington
mark

Clinton Washington and Ford Washington to Mr. D. D. Holman, 2 Jan.
1866, H-233 1865, Registered Letters Received, ser. 3379, TN Asst. Comr.,
RG 105 [A-6151]. At the bottom of the letter are the names of two witnesses
to the freedmen's signatures. The Freedmen's Bureau agent forwarded the
letter to General Clinton B. Fisk, assistant commissioner of the bureau in
Tennessee, who, by an endorsement of January 6, returned it to the local agent
for adjudication, with the following advice: "The Courts of Tennessee hold a
master to a contract made with his slave. Numerous decisions of this kind are
on record." In fact, however, postwar judicial rulings regarding wartime labor
arrangements did not uniformly sustain the claims of former slaves. In April
1867, for example, a resident of Shelby County, in west Tennessee, reported
that a freedwoman in his employ was being sued by her former master for
wages she had received during the war, when she was still legally a slave.
Recently, he noted, several former slaveholders had sued for the recovery of
such payments and won judgments from civil courts. (*Freedom*, ser. 1, vol. 3:
doc. 232.)

CHAPTER 4
Maryland

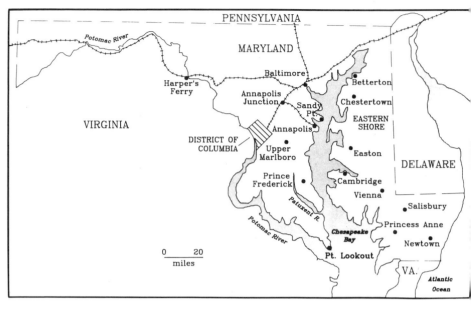

Maryland

4

Maryland

ON NOVEMBER 1, 1864, Maryland became the first of the border states to abolish slavery. In some respects, the new constitution proclaimed that day simply ratified the outcome of a process long under way. At the onset of the Civil War, nearly half of the black people in Maryland were already free, and wartime events greatly accelerated the deterioration of slavery. Still, the end did not come easily. Even with Confederate sympathizers excluded from the polls, the constitution received the approval of only a bare majority of the state's voters. Without special procedures allowing Union soldiers to vote in the field, emancipation would have gone down to defeat. The narrow margin of the victory could not, however, diminish its significance. Freedom had triumphed at last.[1]

Such an accomplishment seemed improbable in 1861. Slaveholders and their allies expected that Maryland's loyalty to the Union would safeguard slavery. But the introduction of federal troops into the state, especially into the counties where slaves were most numerous, almost immediately called the owners' control into question. The flight of slaves to Northern regiments and to the District of Columbia sapped the strength of slavery. In time, the enlistment of black men into the Union army dealt a fatal blow.[2]

The erosion of slavery invigorated advocates of emancipation. However, an absence of sustained military activity within the state, the brevity of large-scale occupation by Northern troops, the entrenched legal standing of slavery, and the reluctance of federal officials to interfere in the affairs of a loyal populace all obstructed the development of free labor. With only modest opportunities for military labor and hardly any federally sponsored agricultural operations or contraband camps, Maryland slaves generally had to flee the state in order to obtain

[1] In this essay, quotations and statements of fact that appear without footnotes are drawn from the documents included in the chapter. On the wartime politics of emancipation in Maryland, see Charles Lewis Wagandt, *The Mighty Revolution: Negro Emancipation in Maryland, 1862–1864* (Baltimore, 1964).

[2] On the destruction of slavery in Maryland during the Civil War, see *Freedom*, ser. 1, vol. 1: chap. 6; Barbara Jeanne Fields, *Slavery and Freedom on the Middle Ground: Maryland during the Nineteenth Century* (New Haven, Conn., 1985), chap. 5; Wagandt, *Mighty Revolution*. On the recruitment of black soldiers, see *Freedom*, ser. 2: chap. 4.

employment as free laborers. The debilitation of slavery could not by itself bring about free labor. Even after the constitution imposed emancipation, many former slaveholders manipulated state laws and local courts to retain control over people they once had owned. Wartime political and military circumstances limited the advance of free labor.

Slavery and free labor had long coexisted in Maryland.[3] Increasingly, however, they dominated different parts of the state. Slavery was most fully at home in southern Maryland, on the western shore of Chesapeake Bay. More than half of the state's 87,000 slaves lived and worked on the tobacco plantations and farms of the seven southern counties, in three of which they outnumbered white residents. Well over 40 percent of slaves in the region lived in units of twenty or more.[4] Slavery also had deep roots on the eastern shore of the Chesapeake. But there the institution had been in decline since the late eighteenth century, when landowners abandoned tobacco production for grains and manumission created a large class of black people who were free. In 1860, slaves still constituted one-sixth of the region's population, but free blacks outnumbered them. Eastern-shore slaveholders generally owned only a few slaves each, and both small-slaveholding and nonslaveholding white farmers depended upon the hired labor of free-black workers.[5]

In northern Maryland, an expansive free-labor economy pushed slavery to the margins. On the eve of the Civil War, slaves accounted for a mere 3 percent of the region's population, which, owing principally to large-scale European immigration, had grown rapidly in the antebellum decades. More than 60 percent of all Marylanders lived in the northern counties, with the city of Baltimore alone claiming almost one-third of the state's inhabitants. Thriving industry and commerce characterized the region, as did prosperous agriculture. Although slaves could be found in every sector of the economy, free laborers outnumbered them many times over. Even within the black population, freedom predominated; in Baltimore, there were nearly twelve free-black people for every slave.[6] Yet free labor, economic vitality, and increasing population did not translate into political power. As a result of inequita-

---

[3] On the intertwined histories of slavery and free labor, see Fields, *Slavery and Freedom*, chaps. 1–4.

[4] U.S., Census Office, 8th Census, *Population of the United States in 1860* (Washington, 1864), p. 214; U.S., Census Office, 8th Census, *Agriculture of the United States in 1860* (Washington, 1864), p. 231; Fields, *Slavery and Freedom*, pp. 70, 83. The 49,000 slaves in southern Maryland accounted for about 40 percent of the region's population. Throughout southern Maryland, slaves greatly outnumbered free-black people.

[5] U.S., 8th Census, *Population*, p. 214; Fields, *Slavery and Freedom*, pp. 70, 83. The population of the eastern shore included 25,000 slaves, 28,300 free-black people, and 91,900 white people.

[6] U.S., 8th Census, *Population*, p. 214; Fields, *Slavery and Freedom*, pp. 57, 62, 70, 83. Slaves in northern Maryland numbered 13,300 in a total population of 421,900. The median slaveholding was between one and two slaves.

ble legislative apportionment and other constitutional protections for slavery, northern Maryland remained politically subaltern to the slaveholders of southern Maryland and the eastern shore.[7]

Embedded in a polity that held such contradictory elements in uneasy tension, slavery in Maryland depended upon the maintenance of a delicate balance. The disturbance of any part threatened the stability of the whole. From its opening days, the Civil War unleashed forces that endangered that balance. Northern troops marched into Maryland to hold the state in the Union and protect the national capital. As they established defensive positions around Washington and along the Potomac River, slaves fled their owners and sought refuge in the Yankee camps. Angry slaveholders demanded the return of their fugitive property, and official policy required the army to honor their claims. Some commanders complied without hesitation. But many Northern soldiers and officers objected to playing slave catcher and resented the imperious manner of the masters and their agents. Others, especially those occupying southern Maryland (a "secession district," one officer declared), doubted the slaveholders' loyalty and saw no reason to assist Confederate sympathizers. Nearly all found the services of the runaways too valuable to forgo.[8]

Fugitive slaves quickly discovered that a readiness to assist Union soldiers in the labors of camp and field might secure protection from recapture. During the first year of the war, as officials in Washington struggled to evade the question of slavery, local commanders issued a steady stream of appeals for instructions regarding fugitives who reached their lines. While awaiting a response, they generally put the runaways to work, effectively contravening the intentions of superior authorities. In late November 1861, General Joseph Hooker, whose division was based in southern Maryland, asked what to do with sixty or seventy slaves then in his camp. Upon receiving orders to retain any of them who had previously been employed by the Confederate army but to expel the others, Hooker confessed that he had already sent the women to Washington and had placed the men at work "discharging the freight from the public transports."[9]

As Hooker's solution indicated, the Union army considered black women less suitable for military labor than black men. Since young men predominated in the ranks of fugitive slaves, the army could secure plenty of laborers without violating conventional notions of men's and

---

[7] Fields, *Slavery and Freedom*, pp. 20–21, 83. With more than twice the white population of southern Maryland and the eastern shore combined, northern Maryland had fewer than half the seats in the general assembly.

[8] *Freedom*, ser. 1, vol. 1: docs. 41, 44, 46, 51, 124–26, 129–32, 134–35. For the characterization of southern Maryland, see Brig. Gen'l. Joseph Hooker to Brig. Gen'l. S. Williams, 18 Mar. 1862, H-204 1862, Letters Received, ser. 12, RG 94 [K-33].

[9] *Freedom*, ser. 1, vol. 1: doc. 47n.

women's work. Officials also believed—not without reason—that army camps were improper, even dangerous, places for women, and that the proximity of women undermined the discipline of soldiers. Accordingly, Hooker and other commanders dispatched fugitive-slave women to the contraband camps of Washington, while retaining the men. If such arrangements separated families, soldiers far from their own wives and children were not likely to be particularly concerned.

The women forwarded by Hooker and other officers were not the only Maryland slaves who gained freedom in the District of Columbia. From the first days of the war, the District was a magnet for runaways from adjacent areas of Maryland. The attraction intensified after April 1862, when Congress abolished slavery in the national capital. What is more, in Washington freedom was associated with abundant opportunities for employment. The demand for workers soared as Washington became the chief supply depot in the eastern theater of the war. Virtually every able-bodied black man could quickly obtain employment. Women and children faced more limited prospects. Some of them worked in military hospitals or hired out as domestic servants. A large number became residents of the contraband camps established by federal authorities to provide for newly arrived fugitives and for those former slaves unable to earn a living. An enclave of freedom in the midst of slave territory, the District of Columbia promised free-labor employment and a means of support to Maryland slaves who could manage the journey.[10]

In Maryland itself, such opportunities were rare, because federal military operations were limited in both extent and duration. Only during the first year of the war was an army stationed within the borders of the state, and it was concentrated along the Potomac River and on the outskirts of the District of Columbia. The geography of military occupation made it difficult for slaves to escape their owners, circumscribed demand for military laborers, and relieved federal authorities of any need to provide for large numbers of ex-slaves.

On the western side of Chesapeake Bay, Annapolis and Baltimore were the only permanent military installations. Quartermasters, engineers, medical directors, and other military employers at the two posts hired numerous skilled and unskilled laborers, but they ordinarily managed to do so by drawing upon local free workers, black and white. When that supply proved insufficient or recalcitrant, they recruited in Northern seaboard cities or sent for former slaves from the Union-occupied Confederacy.[11] By passing as free, a few Maryland slaves ob-

---

[10] On the flight of Maryland slaves to the District of Columbia and emancipation there, see *Freedom*, ser. 1, vol. 1: chaps. 3, 6. On military labor and contraband camps in the District, see above, chap. 2.

[11] On the employment of mechanics and laborers from Northern cities, see Special Order No. 146, Head Quarters Coast Division, 26 Dec. 1861, and Capt. A. W. Putnam, memorandum,

tained military employment despite regulations. But vigilant masters pursued their fugitive property, demanding not only the slaves but also any wages credited to their account.

Aside from small bodies of troops along the Baltimore and Ohio Railroad and the Potomac River, the rural sections of northern Maryland escaped sustained military occupation. The corps of observation along the river offered little to would-be fugitive slaves, thanks to commanders like General Charles P. Stone, who instructed subordinates to return runaways to their owners and denounced soldiers who "so far [forgot] their duty as to excite and encourage insubordination among the colored servants in the neighbourhood of their camps."[12] Spurned by the troops nearest home, some slaves crossed the Potomac and found employment as teamsters with the federal armies in Virginia. Others joined the labor crews that constructed and reconstructed fortifications and pontoon bridges at Harper's Ferry.[13]

Few Union troops ever operated on Maryland's eastern shore. Virtually all of them were locally recruited regiments disinclined to interfere with their own and their neighbors' slaves. As a result, eastern-shore slaves had little chance to escape slavery, much less obtain free-labor employment. Military occupation posed a much greater danger to the security of slavery in southern Maryland. Not only were slaves most numerous in that part of the state, but so – for the first year of the war – were Northern soldiers. The proximity of federal forces encouraged slaves to escape, and the presence of fugitives within Union lines encouraged the army to put them to work. Employment was usually informal and small in scale. Most fugitive slaves simply helped out around camp, performing whatever services were asked of them, from unloading sup-

---

n.d., vol. 147/293 8AC, pp. 413, 416–17, Letters, Telegrams, & Orders Received, ser. 4881, Post Naval Academy, RG 393 Pt. 2 No. 315 [C-8940]; Quarter Master General M. C. Meigs to Col. Augustus Morse, 10 Mar. 1862, vol. 147/293 8AC, p. 460, Letters, Telegrams, & Orders Received, ser. 4881, Post of Annapolis, RG 393 Pt. 2 No. 315 [C-8940]. For a request for black laborers from the Union-occupied Confederacy (100 men from Fortress Monroe, Virginia), see Capt. Charles H. Tompkins to Brigadier General Montgomery C. Meigs, 7 Mar. 1862, T-111 (Book 48) 1862, Letters Received, ser. 20, Central Records, RG 92 [Y-635]; Q.M.G. M. C. Meigs to Maj. Genl. Wool, 8 Mar. 1862, vol. 58, p. 359, Letters Sent, ser. 9, Central Records, RG 92 [Y-635].

12 *Freedom*, ser. 1, vol. 1: docs. 127, 131A.

13 For an example of black men from Maryland working as teamsters and drovers with the Union army in Virginia, see Thos. E. Lloyd to Genl. M. C. Meigs, 17 Feb. 1863, enclosed in Capt. L. H. Peirce to Col. E. J. Sibley, 25 Feb. 1863, P-330 (Book 51) 1863, Letters Received, ser. 20, Central Records, RG 92 [Y-608]. On military labor at Harper's Ferry, see, for example, [Colonel Dixon S. Miles] to Capt. Rutherford, 15 June 1862, vol. 157/330 8AC, Letters Sent, ser. 4931, Railroad Brigade, Middle Dept., RG 393 Pt. 2 No. 320 [C-8897]. When particularly extensive work was necessary at Harper's Ferry, military authorities drew upon the much larger number of former slaves available in the District of Columbia; in late September 1862, General George McClellan requested 2,000 to reconstruct bridges and entrenchments that had been destroyed during the recent Confederate invasion. (*Official Records*, ser. 1, vol. 19, pt. 2, pp. 360–63, 366.)

plies or tending horses and mules to cooking and washing for individual officers and soldiers. Some served as spies and guides. Field hospitals claimed the labor of others.[14]

In return for their services, fugitive slaves generally gained protection from reenslavement. At first they received little else. An army ration could usually be had and sometimes cast-off or "irregular" clothing, but little or nothing in the way of wages. Not until the summer of 1862 did official policy encourage and regularize the employment of black military laborers.[15] By then, however, virtually all Northern troops had left Maryland and advanced into the Confederacy. With them went any likelihood that military employment would serve as an entering wedge for free labor.

Increased distance from military activity curtailed opportunities for Maryland slaves to escape, especially since slavery's legal standing undergirded the authority of owners and overseers. Except in the southern counties, where many masters had departed for the Confederacy, most slaveholders remained in residence, if no longer securely in control. Those most apprehensive about their slaves' intentions incarcerated them in public jails and private pens to forestall flight. State and local authorities enforced the slave code with vigor. Professional slave catchers did a booming business. With no refuge in their home state, fugitive slaves who somehow slipped the net generally directed their steps toward the District of Columbia to gain freedom and a means of supporting themselves.[16]

Although military circumstances in Maryland occasioned little sustained employment of black laborers by the Union army, both federal officials and local authorities were quick to commandeer black men whenever the enemy threatened. Every invasion by Confederate forces engendered massive mobilization, with impressment as likely as the muster of volunteers. As Robert E. Lee's army advanced into western Maryland in June 1863, on its way to Pennsylvania, some 4,000 free-black and slave men were hastily assembled to fortify Baltimore.[17] The following year, when Jubal A. Early's cavalry menaced the city, large numbers of black men wielded pick and shovel in its defense, some

---

[14] In addition to the relevant documents in this chapter, see *Freedom*, ser. 1, vol. 1: docs. 44, 47n., 53, 128–29, 141.

[15] The Militia Act of July 1862 authorized the employment of black military laborers, at wages of $10 per month. (*Statutes at Large*, vol. 12, pp. 597–600.)

[16] For examples of incarceration to forestall flight and of enforcement of the slave code, see *Freedom*, ser. 1, vol. 1: docs. 142–45; *Freedom*, ser. 2: docs. 70, 80B. In some areas slaveholders held meetings to devise means of preventing their slaves from escaping; see, for example, *Freedom*, ser. 1, vol. 1: doc. 138.

[17] Abraham Lincoln, *Collected Works*, ed. Roy P. Basler, Marion Dolores Pratt, and Lloyd A. Dunlap, 9 vols. (New Brunswick, N.J., 1953–55), vol. 6, p. 317n.; *Freedom*, ser. 2: doc. 69. White men believed to be rebel sympathizers were also impressed. (Wagandt, *Mighty Revolution*, p. 103.)

voluntarily, others under compulsion. But each emergency ended as quickly as it had begun, and both Confederate and Union troops once more withdrew from Maryland soil. The temporary crises engendered equally temporary reliance upon black military laborers.

Only at Point Lookout, an isolated outpost on the southern tip of the western shore, did military occupation inspire the steady arrival of fugitive slaves, their routine employment as military laborers, and the organization of a contraband camp. In mid-1862, as the peninsula campaign in tidewater Virginia ground to a halt and officials in Washington prepared to withdraw Union forces from that front, they established a large hospital at Point Lookout to receive the sick and wounded. Aside from the hospital, military operations in the vicinity were modest, but slaves nevertheless saw an opportunity to gain their freedom. Although a majority of the fugitives who reached Point Lookout hailed from secessionist Virginia, slaves from loyal Maryland also found their way into Union lines, confounding official efforts to distinguish between the two. Many of the men found employment with the quartermaster, and some of the women worked as laundresses. But the number of fugitives exceeded the need for military labor. As early as September 1862, the post commander was soliciting advice regarding "surplus contrabands."[18]

Informally at first and then with official sanction, runaway slaves formed a small contraband camp at Point Lookout. Drawing upon connections with Northern antislavery societies and benevolent associations, nurses at the military hospital obtained clothing and other supplies to meet some of the ex-slaves' needs. General Henry H. Lockwood, the district commander, authorized the issue of tents. But Lockwood's willingness to provide for fugitive slaves extended only to those who were entitled to freedom under the Emancipation Proclamation. Slaves from Virginia, he ordered in March 1863, would be "received and protected"; those from Maryland were not to be admitted and, if they entered "clandestinely," would be "placed without the lines." Lockwood also forbade military employers to hire black people from Maryland unless they had been free before the war.[19]

By pretending to be Virginians, by providing false names, and by gaining the sympathy and assistance of Northern nurses and convalescent soldiers, numerous slaves circumvented official restrictions to gain admission to the contraband camp and employment at military labor.

---

[18] Capt. H. J. VanKirk to Capt. R. W. Dawson, 8 Sept. 1862, filed as P-47 1862, Letters Received, ser. 5063, Dept. of VA & 7th Army Corps, RG 393 Pt. 1 [C-3005]; Sarah Hopper Emerson, *Life of Abby Hopper Gibbons, Told Chiefly through Her Correspondence*, 2 vols. (New York, 1897), chap. 22.

[19] In addition to the relevant document in this chapter, see *Freedom*, ser. 1, vol. 1: doc. 141, and the letters and diary of Abby Hopper Gibbons, a Quaker abolitionist who served as head nurse at the hospital (Emerson, *Life of Abby Hopper Gibbons*, chap. 22).

These strategies did not, however, ensure protection from pursuing masters or from sheriffs serving civil processes. Many of the fugitives were recaptured and returned to bondage. Increasingly convinced that no Maryland slave was safe at Point Lookout, sympathetic Yankees helped many of them depart for Washington and sent others to employment in the North.[20] By September 1863, only 175 black men, women, and children were still on hand; most of them had probably been slaves in Virginia, not Maryland.

Conditions at the Point Lookout contraband camp improved in the fall of 1863, when General Gilman Marston, the new district commander, ordered the construction of barracks to replace the tents that had served as shelter. Marston also revised Lockwood's policies with respect to slaves who escaped from Maryland owners, not only protecting them from recapture, but also removing them to the District of Columbia. Opportunities for military labor, however, expanded little, if at all. According to a census conducted in January 1864, fewer than 150 of the 6,700 black people in the county were employed by the government. Another 39 had enlisted in the Union army, and 240 were being "Helped by Gov't."[21]

For slaves throughout the state, enlistment in the Union army opened new doors to freedom and wage labor. The men who toiled on the fortifications of Baltimore during the Gettysburg campaign became the first recruits. As the emergency for which they had been assembled drew to a close, the military commander in Maryland urged authorities in Washington to seize the opportunity to raise one or more regiments of soldiers. By the end of July 1863, a recruiting officer sent by the War Department had enlisted not only men from the labor gangs but also the inmates of jails and pens where masters had confined their slaves.[22]

As in the other border states, federal authorities at first restricted recruitment to free-black men and the slaves of disloyal owners. President Lincoln himself intervened on behalf of slaveholders who complained that recruiting agents accepted volunteers without regard to their owners' standing. In other quarters, however, the official limitations were viewed less favorably. Nonslaveholders objected to the enlistment of free-black men—upon whose labor they depended—while the slaveholders' work force remained inviolate; they pressed for unrestricted enlistment of slaves. Slaves clamored to join the Union army and thereby gain their freedom. Officials struggling to fill depleted military ranks saw their readiness to enlist as a sign of untapped man-

[20] Emerson, *Life of Abby Hopper Gibbons*, chap. 22.
[21] In addition to the relevant document in this chapter, see Emerson, *Life of Abby Hopper Gibbons*, chap. 24; Census Return of Negro Population of Fourth District, State of Maryland, 1 Feb. 1864, Miscellaneous Records, ser. 4113, Ft. Monroe VA Dept. of Negro Affairs, RG 105 [A-7840].
[22] On the recruitment of black soldiers in Maryland, see *Freedom*, ser. 2: chap. 4.

power. Increasing numbers of white Marylanders saw it as a way to meet the state's draft quota. Under such pressure, the restrictions could not hold. Beginning in November 1863, official policy permitted the enlistment of any able-bodied black man, whatever his owner's politics.

Recruiting parties of armed black soldiers scoured the countryside, disrupting slavery as never before. Their activities were of particular consequence on the eastern shore, which had theretofore felt the effects of Union occupation less than the rest of the state. By the end of the war, more than 8,700 black soldiers had enlisted from Maryland, 28 percent of the black men of military age. At least 1,500 more served in the Union navy.[23]

In becoming soldiers and sailors, black men also became free laborers entitled to wages and subject to impersonal laws and regulations. However, their initiation into the practices of free labor seldom took place within their home state, for the War Department promptly dispatched new regiments to the front. No black troops remained in Maryland to hasten the advent of freedom or intervene in the development of free labor. Moreover, since army recruiters had no use for women, children, or men unsuited to military service, families and friends of black soldiers often remained in slavery. In Union-occupied parts of the Confederate states, the enlistment of black men required federal authorities to assume at least some responsibility for their families, usually by establishing contraband camps or government-supervised plantations. In the loyal border states, by contrast, the continued legality of slavery encouraged the federal government to withhold such measures. Slave owners, officials reasoned, were still obligated by law to support their slaves, including the wives and children of soldiers. With the soldiers themselves sent far from home, large-scale enlistment left black women and children to cope on their own with slavery's dissolution and the inauguration of free labor.[24]

If recruitment made manifest the slaveholders' declining power, it also exacerbated a labor shortage that had already attained significant proportions. Slave flight, especially in southern Maryland, had been depleting the work force since the beginning of the war. The enlistment of black men intensified competition for the remaining slave and free-black laborers. Nonslaveholders grew increasingly resentful of the slaveholders' privileged claim upon slave laborers. Resentment turned to anger when slaveholders encroached upon free-black workers whom nonslaveholders had customarily employed. At the same time, masters who had lost their adult slaves saw less and less advantage in a system that saddled them with responsibility for the children and old people.

[23] *Freedom*, ser. 2: pp. 12, 14n.
[24] For the out-of-state military service of black soldiers recruited in Maryland, see the regimental histories in Frederick H. Dyer, *A Compendium of the War of the Rebellion*, 3 vols. (Des Moines, Ia., 1908), vol. 3.

So severe was the drain of laborers from the countryside that in May 1864 the superintendent of black recruitment pronounced further enlistments "hurtful." "[A]ble bodied negroes between 20 & 45 have become exceedingly scarce," he explained, "and whenever the U.S. gets a soldier, sombody's plow stands still."[25]

The erosion of slavery and the growing labor shortage produced fresh converts to the cause of freedom. State elections in November 1863 registered their political strength. The new general assembly scheduled a referendum for early April 1864 on the question of holding a constitutional convention, with delegates to be elected at the same time. During the ensuing campaign, unconditional unionists found themselves at odds not only with supporters of slavery, but also with advocates of emancipation who could not countenance unqualified abolition. Conservative unionists demanded that slaveholders be compensated for the loss of their human property. Prominent citizens ventilated proposals for a system of apprenticeship to succeed slavery. Such divisions notwithstanding, emancipationists carried the day against overwhelming opposition from southern Maryland and much of the eastern shore. In late April, the constitutional convention set about the business of abolishing slavery. By the time the delegates adjourned in early September, they had also prohibited the use of state funds to compensate slaveholders, reduced the underrepresentation of northern Maryland in the general assembly, and adopted – then rescinded – an article regarding apprenticeship.[26]

During the spring and summer of 1864, while the convention rewrote the state's organic law, civilian and military employers scrambled to find and retain workers. Short of both mechanics and common laborers, Captain Garner S. Blodgett, the depot quartermaster at Annapolis, considered two strategies: improving the rewards of military labor and tapping new sources of men. In early March, he sought authority to increase wages by 20 percent. A few weeks later, he asked that 200 former slaves be sent to Annapolis from Washington. Spurned on both counts, he accepted the services of a private citizen who promised to furnish laborers. Soon, however, the contractor's recruitment of black men on the streets of Washington raised the specter of competition among military employers, offending Blodgett's superiors. "There is a great scarcity of such labor [in Washington], and at the front," telegraphed the quartermaster general. "It will not do for quartermasters to bid against each other."[27] Army engineers met with still less

---

[25] *Freedom*, ser. 2: doc. 82B.

[26] Wagandt, *Mighty Revolution*, chaps. 11–14. The apprenticeship article was discarded in the final days of the convention, after a proviso was added requiring would-be masters to take an oath of loyalty. (Wagandt, *Mighty Revolution*, p. 228.)

[27] Capt. G. S. Blodgett, 4 Mar. 1864 and 23 Mar. 1864, vol. 57, p. 369, and vol. 58, p. 93, Registers of Letters Received, ser. 19, Central Records, RG 92 [Y-745]; Capt. G. S. Blodgett

success. Neither in Baltimore nor elsewhere could men be found to construct defenses for the prisoner-of-war camp established at Point Lookout in 1863. Assistance from the mayor of Baltimore and his chief of police was unavailing; the latter's agents produced no one willing to sign on for $1.25 per day and rations. And not surprisingly, since black workers on the city's fortifications were receiving from $1.50 to $1.75 per day.

Military employers' access to black laborers increased in June 1864, when the War Department ordered recruiters in Maryland to accept all black men who volunteered, whether or not they were physically fit for armed service; those who failed to pass the medical examination were to be transferred to the chief quartermaster at Baltimore.[28] Slaves welcomed this extension of federal protection, because slaveholders – especially those on the eastern shore – had made concerted efforts to reclaim rejected recruits. Once assigned to the quartermaster, however, few black men remained in Maryland for long. Like their counterparts in the state's black regiments, they were forwarded to the front, where the summer's campaigns required a host of military laborers.

The expanded military dragnet intensified the labor shortage in the countryside. With freedom in the offing, some slaveholders looked reality in the face and moved toward free labor. The path was not entirely unfamiliar. Throughout Maryland, but especially on the eastern shore, slaveholding planters and farmers had routinely hired free-black workers to supplement the labor of their slaves. Now they extended similar arrangements to fugitive slaves from both within and without the state. Some landowners sought workers in the District of Columbia, often hiring them through superintendents of contrabands. In the Potomac River adjacent to Washington, Mason's Island served as an employment depot for the hiring of black men, women, and children.[29] Many slaves who had escaped from Maryland owners reentered their home state as free laborers under contracts negotiated at Mason's Island.

Although federal authorities indirectly encouraged the development of free labor in Maryland by permitting its citizens to hire freedpeople in Washington, more systematic programs to employ and provide for former slaves were scarcely considered. Confiscation of large amounts of rebel-owned land was never a serious possibility, partly because of the

to Brig. Genl. M. C. Meigs, 4 Apr. 1864, B-447 (Book 58) 1864, Letters Received, ser. 20, Central Records, RG 92 [Y-745]; Bvt. Col. E. S. Sibley to Capt. G. S. Blodgett, 12 Mar. 1864, Qr. Mr. Genl. M. C. Meigs to Capt. G. S. Blodgett, 1 Apr. 1864, A.Q.M. Genl. Chs. Thomas to Capt. Blodgett, 4 Apr. 1864, vol. 75, pp. 221, 457, 473, Letters Sent, ser. 9, Central Records, RG 92 [Y-745]. On the demand for military labor in Washington, see above, chap. 2.

[28] In addition to the relevant document in this chapter, see *Freedom*, ser. 1, vol. 1: doc. 146.
[29] On Mason's Island, see above, docs. 77–78, 80, and pp. 258–61.

Lincoln administration's fear of alienating proslavery unionists and partly because most landowners remained in residence. Nevertheless, Maryland became the site of the largest federally sponsored agricultural operation in the border states.

The "government farms" along the lower Patuxent River came into existence during the first half of 1864, when St. Mary's, the southernmost county of Maryland's western shore, was part of General Benjamin F. Butler's Department of Virginia and North Carolina. Having recently systematized relief and employment programs in the rest of his command, Butler appointed William G. Leonard, a Methodist minister from Massachusetts, to supervise the freedpeople of St. Mary's. Instructed to reduce the number of former slaves receiving government rations, Leonard searched out rebel-owned property on which his charges could support themselves. In February, he selected two farms whose owner, Joseph Forrest, had left for the Confederacy early in the war. They included some 1,500 acres and a sawmill. "The women & children could cultivate the farms," Leonard proposed, "& the men lumber." Successive commanders of St. Mary's District, eager to provide for the freedpeople "accumulating" at Point Lookout, also took an interest in estates abandoned by rebel owners. The most notorious such proprietor, John H. Sothoron, had fled in October 1863 after murdering a Northern recruiter of black soldiers. Sothoron's plantation consisted of about 1,100 acres. Authorized by General Butler to confiscate it and other abandoned estates, the commander of St. Mary's District seized more than 7,000 acres in the spring of 1864. He conveyed the Forrest and Sothoron properties to Leonard and his successor, Samuel M. Leathers, "to be worked by contraband labor."[30]

Expected to become self-supporting as quickly as possible, the freedpeople transferred to the government farms confronted numerous obstacles. Almost all of them were refugees from Virginia who had either escaped on their own or been spirited away by federal raiding parties. None had substantial material resources. Moreover, the estates themselves were extremely ill-equipped. Forrest had taken his slaves, livestock, and farming implements into the Confederacy. Sothoron's

---

[30] In addition to documents in this chapter, see Special Orders, No. 15, Head Quarters Dept. of Virginia and North Carolina, 15 Jan. 1864, Letters, Orders, & Telegrams Received by Lt. Col. J. B. Kinsman, ser. 4108, Ft. Monroe VA [A-8320]; pension file of William G. Leonard, SC 903033, Civil War Pension Files, RG 15 [P-18]; Wm. G. Leonard to Lt. Col. J. B. Kinsman, 12 Feb. 1864, Letters, Orders, & Telegrams Received by Lt. Col. J. B. Kinsman, ser. 4108, Ft. Monroe VA Dept. of Negro Affairs, RG 105 [A-8324]; testimony of Michael J. Stone, M.D., 18 Nov. 1865, in Report of Proceedings of a Board of Officers, 19 Dec. 1865, #197 1865, Letters Received, ser. 456, DC Asst. Comr., RG 105 [A-9794]. For the system of employment and relief established by Butler in the Department of Virginia and North Carolina, see above, chap. 1, especially doc. 26. Leathers replaced Leonard as assistant superintendent of "Negro Affairs" in May 1864, just after the former slaves were settled on the government farms.

family and friends had withdrawn much of his movable property, and Union soldiers seized what remained. By raiding across the Potomac, black soldiers at Point Lookout acquired some horses and equipment for the farms, but in early July, after St. Mary's was detached from Butler's domain, the new department commander barred further expeditions. Housing was also in short supply on the three estates, and crowding the result. Some of the freedpeople lived in one-time slave quarters or in log huts of their own construction, while others "huddled together in barns and outhouses."[31]

As of early October 1864, more than 600 former slaves were living and working on the three Patuxent River farms. Although only a few of them came from the immediate vicinity, the proportion of Marylanders increased thereafter, as emancipation loosed a flood of impoverished freedpeople cast out by erstwhile owners. Four months after the end of the Civil War, the farms still housed more than 500 people. Both during and after the war, most of the residents were women, children, and old and disabled people – those least able to support themselves and least desired by military and civilian employers.[32]

The government farms on the Patuxent constituted the only use of federally controlled land for purposes of relief anywhere in Maryland. Measures to enable former slaves to cultivate land on their own received still less official support. Even when it was granted, military sponsorship provided no assurance that labor would be rewarded. Patrick Scott, a black man in Prince George's County, discovered the limits of federal responsibility. Authorized by a local commander in late 1863 to occupy the estate and tend the livestock of an imprisoned rebel proprietor, Scott subsequently obtained permission to cultivate part of the land. He worked the farm during 1864 and, augmenting his own labor with that of hired hands, raised "quite a fine crop." But the return in November of the farm's owner – his property rights restored by President Lincoln – precipitated a struggle over the fruits of Scott's enter-

---

[31] In addition to the relevant document in this chapter, see testimony of Lieut. E. F. O'Brien, 18 Nov. 1865, in Report of Proceedings of a Board of Officers, 19 Dec. 1865, #197 1865, Letters Received, ser. 456, DC Asst. Comr., RG 105 [A-9794]; 1st Lieut. Edward F. OBrien to Brevet Brig. Genl. J. S. Fullerton, 30 Dec. 1865, #495 1865, Letters Received, ser. 456, DC Asst. Comr., RG 105 [A-9733]. For disapproval of an application to conduct raids into Virginia, see endorsement by Maj. Gen'l C. C. Augur, 2 July 1864, on Col. A. G. Draper, 30 June 1864, vol. 33 DW, p. 253, Endorsements Sent, ser. 5378, Dept. of Washington & 22nd Army Corps, RG 393 Pt. 1 [C-8909].

[32] In addition to the relevant document in this chapter, see Samuel M. Leathers to Hon. H. A. Risley Esq., 4 Oct. 1864, L-42 1864, Correspondence Received by H. A. Risley, 7th Agency, RG 366 [Q-132]; testimony of Lieut. E. F. O'Brien, 18 Nov. 1865, in Report of Proceedings of a Board of Officers, 19 Dec. 1865, #197 1865, Letters Received, ser. 456, DC Asst. Comr., RG 105 [A-9794]; Lieut. S. N. Clark to Col. John Eaton Jr., 24 Aug. 1865, Unregistered Letters Received, ser. 457, DC Asst. Comr., RG 105 [A-9862]. On the postwar history of the government farms, see Richard Paul Fuke, "A School for Freed Labor: The Maryland 'Government Farms,' 1864–1866," *Maryland Historian* 16 (Spring/Summer 1985): 11–23.

prise. Despite entreaties by federal officers and local white unionists, Scott lost much, if not all, of what he had produced.

General emancipation under the state constitution of November 1, 1864, inaugurated a new phase in the wartime development of free labor. By abolishing slavery, the constitution removed the major impediment. It failed, however, to extend to black people the legal rights necessary to protect their interests as free workers. Moreover, adoption of the constitution strengthened the claim of white Marylanders that, having ended slavery on their own, they were entitled to devise a new labor system without federal interference.

No sooner had emancipation taken effect than former slaveholders inaugurated a campaign to circumscribe the ex-slaves' liberty. Some diehard masters refused to relinquish custody of people they were no longer permitted to claim as property. Others – joined by white people who had never owned slaves – attempted to terrorize black men and women into obedience. Near Annapolis, mounted bands of toughs ran riot, "threatning to Shoot every Negroe that gives Back the first word after they Lacerate his flesh with the Whip." Throughout the state, many white Marylanders marked the first days of freedom with acts of "chicanery and violence" that "rendered [the new constitution] a nullity."[33]

Extralegal force was only one weapon in their arsenal. Apprenticeship became a favored device to regain control over newly freed slaves. The constitutional convention had failed to establish an apprenticeship system, but former slaveholders were not deterred. They simply pressed into service the antebellum statutes that had long been used to bind free-black children to white masters.[34] During the first weeks of November 1864, hundreds of former owners availed themselves of the old laws. In Dorchester County, on the eastern shore, they hauled newly freed chil-

---

[33] In addition to the relevant documents in this chapter, see *Freedom*, ser. 1, vol. 1: docs. 151–52.

[34] The statutes authorized the orphans courts of the state to "summon before them the child of any free negro" and, if the court judged "that it would be better for the habits and comfort of such child that it should be bound as an apprentice to some white person to learn to labor," the court should bind the child, to the age of twenty-one for boys and eighteen for girls. Such indentures, the law explicitly provided, need not require any provision for education. No child was to be bound if the parents "have the means and are willing to support such child, and keep the same employed so as to teach habits of industry." The law also required both that a parent be present at the binding and that the court give preference in the selection of a master to any suitable white person selected by the parents. Runaway apprentices were punished by extending their terms of service, and anyone convicted of enticing or persuading an apprentice to escape was subject to fine and imprisonment. ("Negro Apprentices," article 6, sections 31–40, *Maryland Code of Public General Laws, 1860* [Baltimore, 1860], pp. 38–39.) Secondary accounts of postemancipation apprenticeship in Maryland include Fields, *Slavery and Freedom*, pp. 139–42, 148–49, 151, 153–56; Richard Paul Fuke, "Planters, Apprenticeship, and Forced Labor: The Black Family under Pressure in Post-Emancipation Maryland," *Agricultural History* 62 (Fall 1988): 57–74, and "Black Marylanders, 1864–1868" (Ph.D. diss., University of Chicago, 1973), chaps. 9–10.

dren to the county courthouse "in ox Carts, waggons, and Carriages." Not far from Annapolis a single ferry boat carried more than 100 "young Neagroes . . . draged away forseble from there parents for the purpose of Haveing them Bound." After emancipation, as before, some apprentice-ships were arranged by parents who lacked the resources to support their children. But most were involuntary, instigated by would-be masters and expeditiously approved by the judges of the orphans courts. A few farsighted slaveholders preempted emancipation by manumitting chil-dren in order to have them bound as apprentices before the new constitu-tion went into effect.

Although former slaveholders apprenticed children of all ages, they generally preferred those who could be put to work at once. A large proportion of the children indentured just after emancipation were teenagers capable of supporting themselves or contributing to the liveli-hood of their families. In many instances, parents had already arranged wage employment for the children dragged into orphans court. Once the indentures were approved, some masters promptly hired their ap-prentices out and collected the wages. Inasmuch as the law authorized the binding of boys until the age of twenty-one and girls until the age of eighteen, masters could hope to reap several years' benefit from the labor of apprentices in their early or midteens.

Black youths of working age were not the sole targets of apprentice-ship. Many former slaveholders had young children and even infants bound to them, perhaps hoping thereby to ensure continued access to the services of their parents. Not only were the parents less likely to seek employment elsewhere when their sons and daughters were held hostage, but masters could also make visiting rights and other privi-leges contingent on the parents' remaining at hand and available for work.

Eager to accommodate would-be masters, the orphans courts ran roughshod over rights to which mothers and fathers were ostensibly entitled. Under the law, a parent was to be present at any apprentice-ship proceeding to offer evidence respecting his or her ability to provide for the child. But in many counties, judges bound out children without so much as notifying the parents, much less allowing them to address the court. Even when permitted to testify, they faced an uphill battle. If they could satisfy the judges that they possessed sufficient material resources to support their children, they might still be deemed incapa-ble of inculcating "habits of industry." Women whose husbands had left home to enlist in the Union army or to engage in military labor were especially likely to be found wanting, for the wages paid black women were so low that few of them could support large families without assistance. Before many judges, a father's absence constituted prima facie evidence that a child should be apprenticed. More was at work, however, than the calculation of wage rates. Logical consistency fell by the wayside as judges bound out teenaged children after finding their parents unable to support them, yet deemed the same parents responsible for dependent younger children. The orphans courts left black families with the burden of providing for nonworking children, while depriving them of the labor of their older brothers and sisters.

For former slaves, involuntary apprenticeship struck at the control over person and progeny that constituted the very essence of freedom. Freedpeople declared themselves entitled to the full benefits of custody of their children, their "society" as well as their labor. Parents had plans of their own for working-age offspring. The well-being of their households depended upon the labor of every able-bodied member – especially in the many families in which fathers were absent. Wages earned by older children could make the difference between sufficiency and want. Moreover, any hopes of improving their material circumstances or of working independently rested upon the economic contributions of the entire family. Many former slaves, reported one Union officer, had rented farms "expecting to have the labor of their childern." Instead, some of them were compelled to pay wages to masters in order to reclaim their own sons and daughters.

Freedpeople protested involuntary apprenticeship as a subversion of freedom. Yet they possessed only indirect means of redress. With civil authorities generally indisposed to hearing their objections, they sought out sympathetic white people, some of them natives of Maryland, others Northerners in the Union army. Not a day passed, noted a provost marshal at Chestertown in mid-November, "but what there are from three to six poor women making complaints to me."

Aggrieved parents and other black people were not the only Marylanders who objected to the wholesale apprenticing of freedchildren. Emancipationists regarded involuntary indentures as one facet of a larger campaign to make freedom a mockery. White smallholders, who had expected that emancipation would enable them to hire black workers, voiced disgust at developments in the early days of the new constitution. "[M]any poor tenants," explained one observer, "had made their arrangements to use this labor" and were "disappointed" when their plans were thwarted. "[T]he apprenticing works advantageously only for the rich slave holder – generally *disloyal* – and disadvantageously for the poor white tenant and colored man."

Even as many former masters of slaves rushed to become masters of apprentices, others disencumbered themselves of freedpeople they did not want. They evicted hundreds of women, children, and aged and disabled people from their homes. Severed from any means of support, such ex-slaves faced a bleak first winter in freedom. Castaways arrived in increasing numbers in Washington, in Baltimore, and at the government farms on the Patuxent River. In the cities, they joined a swelling tide of voluntary migrants, often equally destitute, who saw in urban life not only greater personal safety, but also opportunities for education and employment and access to established religious and social institutions.

The former slaveholders' response to emancipation took federal authorities by surprise. If their actions went unchecked, worried General Henry Lockwood (now commanding a division headquartered in Baltimore), black people in Maryland would "still be slaves in truth though free in name."[35] A flurry of complaints from army officers, white civilians, and freedpeople prompted intervention by General Lew Wallace, whose Middle Department and 8th Army Corps embraced most of the state. On November 9, barely a week after the legal end of slavery, Wallace issued General Order 112, which proclaimed his determination to thwart the "evil disposed parties" who were attempting to nullify emancipation by "availing themselves of certain laws, portions of the ancient slave code of Maryland, as yet unrepealed, to initiate . . . a system of forced apprenticeship." What legal rights the ex-slaves had were ineffective, Wallace argued, because civil officials were "so unfriendly to the newly made freedmen, and so hostile to the benignant measure that made them such, as to render appeals to the courts worse than folly." "[I]n order to carry out truly and effectively the grand purpose" of emancipation, it was imperative to establish "extraordinary" and "instantaneous" remedies for the grievances of the freedpeople. Wallace therefore placed them under "special military protection" until the state legislature "may, by its enactments, make such military protection unnecessary." He also established a departmental "Freedman's Bureau," whose superintendent was to investigate complaints and "make necessary arrests." As a temporary refuge for "the sick, helpless, and needy," General Order 112 created a "Freedman's Rest" in Baltimore, appropriating to its support all fines thereafter assessed by the department's provost marshal.

By asserting military power over the state's civil affairs, Wallace ventured onto treacherous political ground. The Lincoln administration, alive to the significance of Maryland's abolition of slavery, preferred to leave governance of the freedpeople to the civil authorities. With antislavery forces gaining ground in Missouri, Tennessee, and other Union-occupied parts of the Confederacy, officials in Washington were loath to undermine their efforts by presenting even the appearance of untoward federal interference.

Hoping to convince his superiors that military intervention was warranted, Wallace submitted extensive documentation of the abuse of former slaves, especially forcible apprenticeship. At the same time, he

---

[35] In addition to the relevant documents in this chapter, see *Freedom*, ser. 1, vol. 1: docs. 151–52.

promised not to enforce General Order 112 until he received instructions. Meanwhile, the order circulated throughout Maryland, and Wallace gave no public indication that it had not been fully sanctioned. Anticipating objections to its provisions regarding support for needy ex-slaves, Wallace appealed to private freedmen's aid societies; by mid-November, two groups – the Baltimore Association for the Moral Advancement of the Colored Race and the National Freedman's Relief Association – had agreed to support freedpeople who came under military jurisdiction through the order's operations. This arrangement, Wallace assured the War Department, would release the federal government from any financial burden.

At the beginning of December, Wallace sent General Lockwood to the eastern shore to "break up the practice now prevalent of apprenticing young negroes without the consent of their parents" and, if necessary, to arrest masters and hold them in custody until they agreed to liberate their apprentices. Children whose parents were unable to support them could be sent to Baltimore to be cared for by the Freedman's Bureau. By December 6, Lockwood had transferred his headquarters to Cambridge and was posting emphatic circulars that announced his mission. Within days, however, the Secretary of War directed Wallace to revoke the instructions given Lockwood. Astounded by the news, Lockwood reported "whole sale perversion" of the apprenticeship laws in the lower counties of the eastern shore and pleaded for restoration of his authority to intervene. Wallace endorsed Lockwood's protest and forwarded it to Washington, but to no avail.

Although apprenticeship continued to enjoy the sanction of state law, the publicity given General Order 112 caused some masters and mistresses to release indentured children and discouraged many others from applying to the orphans courts. Still, hundreds of black children remained in bondage. One mother, seeking the assistance of the Freedman's Bureau, described her apprenticed daughter as a "prisoner here in a free land." "We were delighted when we heard that the Constitution set us all free," she continued, "but God help us, our condition is bettered but little; free ourselves, but deprived of our children. . . . It was on their account we desired to be free."[36]

Hopes that state authorities would abolish apprenticeship and adopt laws to protect the freedpeople evaporated during the legislative session that began in January 1865. Although the legislators repealed the "black code" that had sustained slavery, they defeated a campaign to overturn apprenticeship and refused to grant the freedpeople any rights beyond emancipation itself. Meanwhile, the expiration of General Or-

---

[36] Lucy Lee to Lt. Col. W. E. W. Ross, 10 Jan. 1865, in "Communication from Major Gen'l Lew. Wallace, in Relation to the Freedman's Bureau, to the General Assembly of Maryland," *Maryland House Journal and Documents* (Annapolis, 1865), document J, pp. 68–69.

der 112 and General Wallace's abolition of the Freedman's Bureau removed the threat of military intervention.[37]
The closing months of the Civil War thus found black people in Maryland with limited resources and few allies. The apprenticeship of their children was only one aspect of the contest that had opened over the new labor system that would succeed slavery. Their right to contract, to travel, to testify in court – along with many other essential elements of their new status – were still at issue. As black Marylanders made arrangements for a new agricultural year, they faced the future with both hope and uncertainty. Freedom would no longer be constrained by slavery, but its precise content and meaning remained to be determined.

[37] For the order abolishing the Freedman's Bureau, see General Orders, No. 18, Head Quarters Middle Department, Eighth Army Corps, 30 Jan. 1865, vol. 62 8AC, General Orders (Printed), ser. 2352, Middle Dept. & 8th Army Corps, RG 393 Pt. 1 [C-4170].

131: Quartermaster General to the Surgeon in Charge of the Hospital for Hooker's Division

[*Washington, D.C.*] May 16th 1862.
Lieutenant, Your letter of the 11th inst, requesting instructions, with regard to the pay and clothing of negroes, employed at the Division Hospital at Budd's Ferry has been received.
The laborers you refer to, are employed in the Hospital Service. If the Medical Department has not made provision to pay for this service, I presume the only recourse will be to the appropriation for contingencies of the Army.
No more should be employed than are actually necessary, and their accounts should be supported by the certificates of the Surgeon in charge, and have the approval of the Medical Director.
The Quarter Master's Department has some irregular clothing in depot, for which issues may be made on requisition of the Surgeon appointed by the Surgeon General – The articles when issued to the laborers, should be charged to them at their value, as expressed in the invoices.
The Quarter Master General supposes, that no one will object, to an officer employing a negro servant – and paying him such wages as will satisfy him.
The negroes are, so far as the Army Officers are concerned, free to hire themselves out, and make their livelihood, as they best can – The sooner they find employment, the less expense to the United States.

HLcSr   (Sgd) M. C. Meigs.

499

Qr. Mr. Gen'l M. C. Meigs to Surgeon A. J. McKelways, 16 May 1862, vol.
60, pp. 48–49, Letters Sent, ser. 9, Central Records, RG 92 [Y-666]. The
surgeon's letter of May 11 has not been found, but a register entry indicates
that even before that date he had sought instructions "as to the wages to be
paid to 'Contrabands' in Service at the Hospital" of General Joseph Hooker's
division of the Army of the Potomac. (A. J. McKelway, 18 Apr. 1862, vol.
48, p. 519, Register of Letters Received, ser. 19, Central Records, RG 92 [Y-
666].) The division had occupied a sizable portion of southern Maryland from
late 1861 until April 1862, during which time fugitive slaves steadily made
their way into its camps – some of them finding employment as spies, guides,
servants, teamsters, and laborers; others being reclaimed by their owners.
When Hooker's troops embarked for Fortress Monroe, Virginia, in April, the
division hospital had remained behind at Budd's Ferry, in Charles County,
Maryland. (Ass't Adj't General Joseph Dickinson to Commanding Officer
Detachment 3d Indiana Cavalry, 3 Jan. 1862, Ass't Adj't General Joseph
Dickinson to Brig. Gen'l D. E. Sickles, 31 Jan. 1862, and Ass't Adjt. General
Joseph Dickinson to Brig. Gen'l D. E. Sickles, 24 Mar. 1862, vol. 2/4 1AC,
pp. 5, 51, 124–25, Letters Sent, ser. 3801, Hooker's Division, Army of the
Potomac, RG 393 Pt. 2 No. 241 [C-4576, C-4578]; Brig. Gen'l. Joseph
Hooker to Brig. Gen'l S. Williams, 18 Mar. 1862, H-204 1862, Letters
Received, ser. 12, RG 94 [K-33]; *Freedom*, ser. 1, vol. 1: docs. 47, 134–35.)

132: Depot Quartermaster at Annapolis, Maryland, to the
Quartermaster General, Enclosing a Bill
from a Maryland Slaveholder

Annapolis, Md., Feby 5ᵗʰ 1863.

General   I have the honor to transmit you the Enclosed
Copy. There has been employed at this Depot, as a Laborer, a
Negro named Richᵈ Thomas, who at the time of his employment
was supposed to be free. I find now that he is a Slave, owned by
William Stinchcomb, who has since taken him away. There is now
due him Forty Eight Dollars & Seventy Eight Cents ($48.78)   Will
you please inform me, whether it will be necessary for said negro
man to receipt, or make his mark, properly witnessed, or will it be
sufficient to have the receipt of his owner or authorized agent for the
amount due. I am General Very Respectfully Your Obt Srvt

G. S. Blodgett

ALS

[*Enclosure*]   [*Anne Arundel Co.? Md.*]   Feby 4″ 1863
                        Copy of Order
To Capt. Blodgett, U.S.A.   At sight please pay to the order of
James Revell the amount due for the services of my negro slave

Richd Thomas employed in the U.S. Hospital at Annapolis and hold this as my receipt for the same.

HDcSr   (Signed) William Stinchcomb

Capt. G. S. Blodgett to Brig. Gen. M. C. Meigs, 5 Feb. 1863, enclosing William Stinchcomb to Capt. Blodgett, 4 Feb. 1863, B-567 1863, Letters Received, ser. 20, Central Records, RG 92 [Y-605]. The copy of Stinchcomb's bill is in the handwriting of James Revell, a Maryland state's attorney. The quartermaster general's reply has not been located in the letters-sent volumes of his office, but a notation on the wrapper of Blodgett's letter indicates that he was instructed to "pay the man himself & take his receipt."

133: Quartermaster at Point Lookout, Maryland, to the Quartermaster General

Pt Lookout M^d September 15th 1863

General   I have the honor respectfully to represent that Brig. Genl. Marston Comdg. has ordered the construction of Barracks, for the contrabands, thus releiving the use of quite a number of Hospital Tents, the use of which, for them, was ordered by Genl Lockwood, formerly commanding. I respectfully request instructions in the matter

The number of men, women, and children now here are about 175, of whom only about 40 are effective laborers   I am General Your obedient servant

HLS   A Edwards

Capt. A. Edwards to Brig. Genl M. C. Meigs, 15 Sept. 1863, E-56 1863, Letters Received, ser. 20, Central Records, RG 92 [Y-626]. The Quartermaster General's Office authorized Captain Edwards to "[c]omply with the instructions of Gen. Marston, if there are no quarters that can be assigned them," but insisted that the barracks be "of the plainest description and of a temporary character." (Chs. Thomas to Captain A. Edwards, 26 Sept. 1863, vol. 72, p. 49, Letters Sent, ser. 9, Central Records, RG 92 [Y-626].) General Gilman Marston was the recently appointed commander of the District of St. Mary's, which had become an independent district at the end of July 1863 when a large prisoner-of-war camp was established at Point Lookout. During the first half of 1863, when Maryland's lower western shore had been under the jurisdiction of General Henry H. Lockwood (commander of the 1st Separate Brigade, 8th Army Corps), the former slaves at Point Lookout had numbered far more than the 175 reported by Edwards in September. In April, Lockwood had complained that "[q]uite a number of negroes" – including the slaves of Maryland owners – "had, prior to the assignment of this command to me, been permitted to come within the lines, and were employed in the Quartermasters Department at this Point, as day laborers." Believing it improper to harbor Maryland slaves, Lockwood had issued orders requiring quartermasters to employ only free-black people and fugitive slaves from Virginia. At the same time, he and his troops (themselves from the eastern shore of Maryland) had cooperated with Maryland masters and sheriffs who sought to reclaim runaway slaves. Fearing capture and reenslavement, many of the former slaves at Point Lookout (including military laborers) had escaped on their own in small boats, while convalescent Union soldiers and Northern nurses at the military hospital helped others take passage on steamers, sometimes for employment in the North. (*Freedom*, ser. 1, vol. 1: doc. 141; *Life of Abby Hopper Gibbons, Told Chiefly through Her Correspondence*, ed. Sarah Hopper Emerson, 2 vols. [New York, 1897], vol. 2, pp. 1–37.)

134: Commander of St. Mary's District to the Headquarters of the Department of Virginia and North Carolina, and an Endorsement by the Commander of the Department

Point Lookout [*Md.*] April 15th 1864

Major, It would be advantageous, for the interest of Government, undoubtedly, to posess itself of some one of the many estates in St. Mary's Co. abandoned by rebel owners, upon which to employ the negroes that are accumulating at this Point, but I have hesitated to take any steps in that direction without positive instructions from the Maj. Genl. Comdg. the Department.

The Thomas farm, on the Patuxent, can be made available for the purpose of employing some one hundred hands, but the mother of the three rebel Thomases resides in Baltimore, and has a life interest or right of dower in the estate.

To the Forrest estate there seems to be no pretended loyal owner, but there are no buildings thereon.

The Southern estate could be made available, but notwithstanding it is located within the limits of this District it is reported to be occupied by a portion of Gen. Birney's troops.

There are other like estates within the County, but before attempting to possess, occupy and enjoy them I request specific directions from the Maj. Gen. Comdg. as to what course to pursue in relation to part owners, whose souls have been sold to the Southern Confederacy, but whose bodies are entitled to the protection of our laws, and in relation to claims of creditors of similar or more loyal characters.

The season for farming operations will soon commence, and it is necessary that immediate action should be taken to secure the

profitable employment of accumulating contrabands. I am, Major,
Very respectfully Your Obt. Svt.
HLpS
Edwd. W. Hinks.

Hd Qrs Dept Va & N.C. [*Fortress Monroe, Va.*] April 16 1864
    In the case of an estate owned by parties in the rebel States there
can be no difficulty   The claims of creditors unless evidenced by
deed or judgement obtained before the war are not to be
allowed. Any persons claiming an estate must be loyal in fact before
their claims will be allowed. Under the light of these suggestions
you will have no difficulty in possessing, occupying and enjoying
such estates as may be proper in your district
HEcSr
Benj F Butler

Brig. Genl. Edwd. W. Hinks to Maj. R. S. Davis, 15 Apr. 1864, vol. 253
DW, pp. 32–34, Press Copies of Letters & Telegrams Sent, ser. 6844, Dist. of
St. Mary's, RG 393 Pt. 2 No. 468 [C-8905]; endorsement by Maj. Gen.
Benj. F. Butler, 16 Apr. 1864, on letter of Brig. Gen. Hinks, vol. 51 VaNc,
p. 113, Endorsements Sent, ser. 5053, Dept. of VA & NC & 18th Army
Corps, RG 393 Pt. 1 [C-8905]. The general whose troops were said to be
occupying the estate of John H. Sothoron was William Birney, superintendent
of black recruitment in Maryland. General Hinks was replaced as commander
of St. Mary's District before he could act upon General Butler's instructions,
but his successor wasted little time before seizing the property in question.
(See doc. 135, immediately below.) Hinks did order his provost marshal to
investigate reports that an overseer was abusing the slaves on the Thomas
farm, and, if warranted, to expel him from the district "and take possession of
the Farm in the name of the United States." (Cap't. H. Q. Sargent to Maj.
Weymouth, 21 Apr. 1864, vol. 255 DW, p. 87, Press Copies of Letters &
Telegrams Sent, ser. 6844, Dist. of St. Mary's, RG 393 Pt. 2 No. 468 [C-
8912].) St. Mary's County had become part of Butler's department in late
December 1863.

135: Commander of St. Mary's District to the Headquarters of
the Department of Virginia and North Carolina

Point Lookout [*Md.*] May 6th 1864.
Major: I have seized over 7,000 acres of land belonging to Rebels;—
have turned over two of the farms to the Dept. for Negro Affairs to
be worked by contraband labor.
    These farms are totally destitute of stock and tools, and I

therefore respectfully ask permission to make expeditions with about 350 men to the Western shore of the Potomac for the purpose of seizing stock and tools belonging to Rebels, and of capturing any contraband goods of which I may get information. I have the honor to be Very Respectfully Your Obt. Svt.

HLS   A. G. Draper

Col. A. G. Draper to Major R. S. Davis, 6 May 1864, D-134 1864, Letters Received, ser. 5063, Dept. of VA & NC & Army of the James, RG 393 Pt. 1 [C-3403]. Draper was also commander of the 36th USCI. By the middle of May the residents of the contraband camp at Point Lookout had been moved to the Patuxent River farms (the Forrest and Sothoron estates) that Draper turned over to the Department of Negro Affairs. The Forrest property included grist and saw mills and more than 200 acres of growing crops, chiefly corn, wheat, and oats. (C. S. Henry to Lt. Col. Kinsman, 16 May 1864, Letters, Orders, & Telegrams Received by Lt. Col. J. B. Kinsman, ser. 4108, Ft. Monroe VA Dept. of Negro Affairs, RG 105 [A-8322].) Meanwhile, Colonel Draper and black soldiers from his regiment conducted a highly successful raid into the northern neck of Virginia, and by the end of the month he was seeking permission not only to launch another such foray ("to procure horses and other property much needed in the Q.M. Dept., and on our Contraband Farms"), but also to undertake similar raids "whenever it appears to be necessary." General Benjamin F. Butler, commander of the Department of Virginia and North Carolina, authorized Draper "to make raids when he sees fit," and at. least one more expedition took place before the end of June, when St. Mary's County was removed from Butler's command. (Col. A. G. Draper to Maj. R. S. Davis, 28 May 1864, D-165 1864, Letters Received, ser. 5063, Dept. of VA & NC & Army of the James, RG 393 Pt. 1 [C-3403]; unsigned notation, 7 June 1864, on summary of letter from Col. A. G. Draper, 1 June 1864, vol. 46 VaNc, p. 140, Registers of Letters Received, ser. 5062, Dept. of VA & NC & Army of the James, RG 393 Pt. 1 [C-3403].)

136: Quartermaster General to the Commander of the Middle Department and 8th Army Corps

Washington, D.C., June 20th 1864

General: Information having been received at the War Department that there are in Maryland, particularly at the military posts on the Eastern Shore a considerable number of Slaves, who after being brought to the recruiting rendezvous are found to be unfit for military service, who yet desire military protection, this Department has been advised that the Secretary of War has directed the acceptance into the United States service of all colored recruits presenting themselves; – those fitted for the active duties of a soldier to be retained as soldiers; – the remainder to be turned over to the Quarter Master's Department as laborers. The Officers of the Quarter Master's Department within your command should be instructed to take charge of such persons when transferred to the Quarter Master's Department. They should be sent to the Chief Quarter Master of the Baltimore depot, who should report them to this office for instructions as to their destination, with a statement of their condition, and the service for which they are fitted. I am Very Respectfully Your ob^t Servt

HLS   M C Meigs

Quarter Master Genl. M. C. Meigs to Major Gen. Lew. Wallace, 20 June 1864, Q-16 1864, Letters Received, ser. 2343, Middle Dept. & 8th Army Corps, RG 393 Pt. 1 [C-4143]. On June 7, 1864, General Lew Wallace, commander of the Middle Department and 8th Army Corps, had forwarded the report of a subordinate regarding efforts by slaveholders on Maryland's eastern shore to reclaim slave men who, after running away to join the Union army, failed to pass the medical examination required for enlistment. The rejected slaves, the officer had written, "come to me for protection, and refuse to go back to their masters," but the masters claimed them, under state law, as runaway slaves. General Wallace had deemed the issue "a matter of such seriousness" that he sought instructions from the Secretary of War, who on June 15 directed that recruitment officers thereafter enlist all black men who volunteered: "Those fitted for the active duties of a soldier will be retained as soldiers, and the remainder will be turned over to the Quartermasters Department as laborers." (Maj. Gen. Lew. Wallace to Col. E. D. Townsend, 7 June 1864, enclosing Col. A. L. Brown to Captain, 4 June 1864, and endorsement by Col. Jas. A. Hardie, 15 June 1864, M-436 1864, Letters Received, ser. 360, Colored Troops Division, RG 94 [B-567].) On June 22, General Wallace instructed quartermasters in his department to take charge of the black men enlisted as laborers under the new policy. (General Orders. No. 47, Head-Quarters Middle Department, Eighth Army Corps, 22 June 1864, vol. 61 8AC, General Orders [Printed], ser. 2352, Middle Dept. & 8th Army Corps, RG 393 Pt. 1 [C-8920].)

137: **Head of the U.S. Engineer Office at Fortress Monroe, Virginia, to the Chief of Engineers**

Point Lookout, Md– July 24." 1864 –

Sir, I have the honor to report that Lieut. Mansfield returned yesterday from Baltimore – He had seen the Mayor of the City & the Chief of Police, the latter endeavored through his agents to procure laborers, but none would come for $1.25 and a ration, & they thought it impossible to get them at that rate – From other sources, as yet, none are procured— If I had money placed at my disposal and could state positively when they would be paid, I am informed by persons who have had laborers in their employment recently, that probably in the course of four or five days some fifty might be procured in the country, some miles from this, at rates varying from $1.25 to $1.50—that in the course of ten days very likely a larger number might come in.

Without funds at my command, nothing in the way of hiring men or purchasing material can be attempted.

While awaiting to hear the result of my application for funds, & while endeavoring to ascertain where labor may be procured, & how soon, the small details from the garrison, have been employed in accordance with Genl. Barnes'¹ wishes, in going on with the rough breastworks commenced before my arrival— Lieut. Jones has since his arrival been charged with the supervision of this work— The men composing the details are in part from the Veteran Reserve Corps & of course that corps does not number those capable of much work— This goes on very slowly, & several days will be required with the present details to put it in shape—

Lieut. Mansfield has important duties to attend to elsewhere requiring his attention, and his detention here, awaiting the time when the small details from the garrison will be available for the works referred to, in my letter of the 22nd inst., or until funds are to be had with which to procure labor & material, seems to me a waste of his time, to be avoided, I should recommend, by allowing him to return to his station—

To carry on the contemplated work, with the men who may presently be available, without hiring labor, will be an almost endless job— I therefore respectfully request, to enable me to do something, that definite instructions be given me as to how, when & where any laborers I may employ will receive their pay, so that they may understand what to expect, or that funds for that purpose be placed as soon as practicable to my credit in New. York— I have the honor to be, Sir, Very Respectfully Your obedt. Servt.

C. Seaforth Stewart—

ALS

Maj. of Engr. C. Seaforth Stewart to Brigr. Genl. Richard Delafield, 24 July 1864, S-9246, Letters Received, ser. 18, General Correspondence, Central Office, RG 77 [VV-68]. On July 12, 1864, in the midst of Confederate General Jubal Early's raid into Maryland, Stewart had been ordered by General Richard Delafield, chief of engineers, to suspend his duties at Fortress Monroe and go to Point Lookout, Maryland, to construct defenses against any attempt to liberate inmates of the prisoner-of-war camp there. The Engineer Department had also ordered Lieutenant Samuel M. Mansfield, ordinarily stationed at New Haven, Connecticut, to assist Stewart. Although the emergency had

subsided by the time the two engineers reached Point Lookout, the department decided that more secure defenses remained desirable. Obtaining a labor
force proved, however, to be nearly impossible. On July 22, while Mansfield
was in Baltimore trying to hire laborers, Stewart had reported to General
Delafield that it would be necessary to pay wages of at least $1.25 per day, plus
rations and housing; even that, he feared, might not be enough, since "*impressed* laborers in Baltimore are receiving from $1.50 to $1.75 per day." In
response, Delafield allocated $10,000, but Stewart continued to find it "very
difficult to get together and bring here a body of laborers for work, whether
from Baltimore, Fort Monroe, or this vicinity." He therefore proposed to
employ volunteers from among the Confederate prisoners, crediting each man
with "a small sum for each days work" – an arrangement that would not only
remedy the labor shortage, but save the government a great deal of money. On
July 30, the Commissary General of Prisoners endorsed Stewart's plan, "provided no more [prisoners] are employed at a time than can be securely
guarded." (Genl. Richd. Delafield to Maj. Chas. S. Stewart, 12 July 1864,
vol. 37, p. 131, Letters Sent to Engineer Officers, ser. 6, General Correspondence, Central Office, RG 77 [VV-68]; Maj. of Engr. C. Seaforth Stewart to
Brigr. Genl. Richard Delafield, 22 July 1864 [two letters], and Maj. of Engrs.
C. Seaforth Stewart to Brigr. Genl. Richard Delafield, 29 July 1864, S-9234,
S-9235, S-9241, Letters Received, ser. 18, General Correspondence, Central
Office, RG 77 [VV-68].)

1 James Barnes, commander of the District of St. Mary's.

138: Baltimore Black Men to the President

Baltimore [*Md.*] Aug 20 1864
Sir it is with Reverence we take this method to inform you of a
grevance which is growing to a fearful rate amoung the loyal free
colard people of Baltimore in the month of July thare was a
movement set on foot to organize the colard men of the wards into
milatary companeys under the title of melitia under which
circumstanc the colard men became allarmed called to gather some
fiew and appointed one rev. S. W. Chase to confer with the military
athorities upon the subgect[1] the procedes yor Exelancey will find in
print. this was followed by an ordor from General Wallace for the
organisation of all the able bodied men into melitia the matter was
subsequentley handed over to Col bowman[2] who isued ordors for the
wards of his choice to report to disignated halls som did but others
knowing the relation thay bore to the state and Government
declined to meet first we knew that the state of Maryland had her
mode for calling out her melitia which excludes us. that thay had
ben called out and the emergencey being over tha ware
disbanded during the emergencey however we volenteared our

THE WARTIME GENESIS OF FREE LABOR

service to handle the gun also the pick an shovel[3]   Secondley we
know that Congress has made us a part of the national force.[4]   we
now come to the trying part   Squads of colard soaldiers accompaned
som times by white men come to our houses demand admitance
under the authoritey of Col. Bowman. Surtches the house Curses our
wives our sisters or mothers or if the man be found he is made to
fall in and martch to the drilling room and thare give his
name   thare is one instance of a man being Shot at while trying to
escape   thare are others whare our white inemies go with thoas
Soaldiers for the purpos of Maltreating us. Our ocupation sometime
prohibits us from ariving home before those Squads do compel us to
fall in the rank and martch to the drilling room without supper   all
efforts of the people to come to gather in mass meting to protest
aganst it has ben defeated by threts.   The Congress of theas uninted
States has made us a part of the National force   then we hold that
we ar subject to the same regulation of the National force   We have
responded to the call by enlistment   We are allso subject to the
draft   the will of the Loyial Colard people of Baltimore citey is as a
part of the National force to be treated no wors then the lawes
Demand Governing the National force   And we are shore that the
Dignetey of this Government is too Loftey to Demand a man onley
by her Lawful Chanel   Your Exelencey will pleas Parden the maner
in which this Document is lade before you.   Yours with reverance
HD   Loyial Colard men of Baltimore Citey

Loyial Colard men of Baltimore Citey to His Exelencey The pesident of theas
uninted States of america, 20 Aug. 1864, B-2215 1864, Letters Received, RG
107 [L-49]. An endorsement from the War Department instructed General Lew
Wallace, commander of the Middle Department and 8th Army Corps, to "report
the facts" and questioned particularly "whether any part of the white population
are subjected to the same drill as is required from the men of color." Other
endorsements. In the same file is Wallace's report (dated August 30, 1864),
which recounted his efforts to organize a local militia for the defense of Baltimore. First, the white men of the city had been formed into three regiments.
However, Governor Augustus W. Bradford, who held constitutional authority
over the militia, "declined to recognize" the new units. "Shortly after the
organization of the whites was begun," Wallace continued, "that of the blacks
was attempted." Since the state constitution did not recognize black men as
"subject to militia service," Wallace believed that his authority over them was
unimpeded, and he had delegated responsibility for their enrollment to Colonel
Samuel M. Bowman, "who is quite popular with the class, and has proven
himself their devoted friend." Wallace admitted that "arbitrary" measures had
been used to enroll black men, but argued that "asking them to volunteer was
impossible, as many of them are the slaves or employees of secession citizens who
would of course prohibit such action." "That some instances of harshness have
ensued is not unlikely," he confessed, "but the sufferers had only to complain to

me to have their wrongs redressed." Affirming the military necessity of organizing a local militia, but acknowledging his inability to reach the white men
"[w]ithout an interference with the constitution of the state," Wallace pledged
to see that the black men "are not abused."

1 In late July 1864, alarmed by the danger to which Baltimore had been
exposed during a recent Confederate invasion, General Lew Wallace, commander of the Middle Department and 8th Army Corps, in conjunction with
the city's civil authorities, had undertaken the creation of a local militia
comprising both white and black men (in separate units). On July 28, he had
issued an order instructing officers of the municipal police, under the mayor's
direction, to "proceed immediately to organize the able-bodied negroes in
their respective wards into military companies for duty in this city." The
companies would elect their own noncommissioned officers, but the mayor
would appoint white men to the commissioned ranks. (*Official Records*, ser. 1,
vol. 37, pt. 2, pp. 489–90.) The following day, "the Free Colored Men of
Baltimore" had held a meeting at which they appointed the Reverend S. W.
Chase "to confer with the Military Authorities and the Mayor in reference to
the Military Organization of Colored Men," particularly with respect to
whether black men would receive the same pay and be subject to the same
regulations and duties as white men. (Col. S. M. Bowman and John Lee
Chapman to Rev. S. W. Chase, 1 Aug. 1864, filed with B-2215 1864, Letters
Received, RG 107 [L-49].)
2 Samuel M. Bowman, superintendent of black recruitment in Maryland.
3 The "emergency" during which the militia had been called out and the black
men of Baltimore had served under arms and worked on the city's fortifications
was the invasion of Maryland by Confederate General Jubal A. Early in the
first half of July.
4 Amendments of February 1864 to the Enrollment Act of March 1863 had
made all able-bodied black men between the ages of twenty and forty-five
"part of the national forces" and, as such, subject to enrollment and draft.
(*Statutes at Large*, vol. 13, pp. 6–11.)

139: Affidavit of a Former Slave from Virginia

[*St. Mary's County, Md.*] 17" Aug. 1865.
Henderson Fleet, of the U.S. Gov^t Farms, St. Mary^s Co. Md, but
formerly of Rappahannock Co, V^a being duly sworn says:
That he was a party to a certain agreement made and enterd into
in the month of August, 1864, with Mr. Joshua Jones of St. Marys
Co. Md, wherein he agreed, at the request of said Jones to cut hay
for, and at the rate of, 50 cents per 100 lbs and he performed work
and labor under said agreement for the space of six days, cutting
each day about 200 lb hay which under the terms agreed upon
would amount to six dollars,

2" That deponent after fulfilling his part of the agreement above stated, asked said Joshua Jones to fulfill his part, but that he refused, and tho. repeatedly requested, has utterly neglected to do so.

his

HDcSr   (Signed)   Henderson X Fleet

mark

Affidavit of Henderson Fleet, 17 Aug. 1865, enclosed in Col. John Eaton Jr. to Maj. Genl. O. O. Howard, 18 Sept. 1865, Unregistered Letters Received, ser. 16, Washington Hdqrs., RG 105 [A-9674]. Sworn before the Freedmen's Bureau agent at the government farms. Appended are two sworn statements corroborating Fleet's account: one by a freedman who had witnessed Fleet's agreement with Jones in August 1864; the other by a soldier on duty at the government farms, to whom Jones had recently acknowledged the validity of Fleet's claim. (Statement of Philip Holmes, 17 Aug. 1865; statement of Private Albert J. Farr, 17 Aug. 1865.)

140: Provost Marshal of the 1st District of Maryland to the Commander of the 3rd Separate Brigade, 8th Army Corps

Easton [*Md.*], November 4th 1864

General: — There is a persistant determination of the disloyal people of this County, to totally disregard the laws of Maryland, in regard to Slavery. Immediately after the Governer issued his Proclamation, declaring the New Constitution adopted, a rush was made to the Orphan's Court of this County, for the purpose of having all children under twenty one years of age, bound to their former owners, under the apprentice law of the State. In many instances, boys of 12 and 14 years are taken from their parents, under the pretence that they (the parents) are incapable of supporting them, while the younger children are left to be maintained by the parents. This is done without obtaining the parent's consent, and in direct violation of the provisions of the Act of Assembly, and almost in every instance by disloyal parties. Two of the members of the Orphan's Court being bitter enemies of the present organic law of the state, seem to be so prejudiced agains these poor creatures, that they do not regard their rights. The Court, as yet, has never taken any testimony relative to the capability of the parents to support their children, and where the parents are willing to bind them, they have been denied the choice of homes. In plain terms — the Rebels here are showing an evident determination to still hold this people in bondage, and call upon the Orphan's Court to give their proceeding the sanction of law.

510

My office is visited every day by numbers of these poor creatures, asking for redress, which I have not the power to give. They protest before the Court against binding their children to their former masters, who have dubtless treated them cruelly, and yet that same Court declares them vagrants, before they have enjoy liberty a single week. – in many instances before they have ever been permitted to leave their masters. The law in all instances requires the child or the parents' consent, but it is not done by Talbot County law. I am fearful there will be trouble here if measures are not taken to stop the proceeding. Loyalty is outraged, and justice has become a mockery.

I can furnish you with the names of the parties, – aggrieving and aggrieved – but am merly writing now, to inform you of the state of affairs existing here. Had I authority in the premises, I would stop the proceeding: Or did I occupy the position of a military command, I should lay an injunction on the Court until I could hear from you. But as it is, I can only warn you of impending danger.

Hoping you will receive this in kindness, and believe me actuated by patriotic motives in writing it, I remain Respectfully Your Obedient Servant

HLS   Andrew Stafford

Capt. Andrew Stafford to General H. H. Lockwood, 4 Nov. 1864, filed with M-1932 1864, Letters Received, ser. 12, RG 94 [K-4]. General Henry H. Lockwood, commander of the 3rd Separate Brigade, forwarded Stafford's letter to General Lew Wallace, commander of the Middle Department and 8th Army Corps, proposing "that immediate steps be taken to put a stop to these most outrageous and inhuman proceedings." In a previous letter, written the day after emancipation took effect in Maryland, Captain Stafford had already informed General Lockwood that citizens of Talbot County were ignoring the new constitution "so far as it relates to Slavery" and were "endeavoring to intimidate the colored, and compel them to bind their children to them, under the old apprenticeship law." Lockwood had also forwarded that letter to General Wallace, endorsing upon it his own belief that unless federal troops were stationed in "the lower counties" to enforce emancipation and protect the freedpeople, they "will still be slaves in truth though free in name." (*Freedom*, ser. 1, vol. 1: doc. 151.)

141: **Keeper of Sandy Point Lighthouse to a Baltimore Judge**

Sandy Point [*Md.*] Novr 6th 1864
Sir   i wish to impose A few moments on your Valuable time By Speaking to you after this maner   I Have bein Living or Rather

Staying on the Bay Shore about Seven miles N. East From annapolis
in the midts of a people Whose Hearts is Black in treason and a
more fearless peopel for Boldly Expressing it Lives not outside of the
Hosts that Bare Arms in upholding it

Since we the people have Proclaimed that Maryland Should Be
free the Most Bitter Hatred has bein Manifested againest the poor
Devils that Have Just Escaped from beneath there Lash there
actions Since Tusday Last[1] Indicates to me that there is all Ready
Orginized Bands Prowling apon Horse Back around the Country
armed with Revolvers and Horse Whips threatning to Shoot every
Negroe that gives Back the first word after they Lacerate his flesh
with the Whip i have bein told By Several Pearsons that a man By
the name of Nick Phips on Last Wesnsday the first Sun That Rose
apon the [wrech] in hes fredom after years of Bondage took in the
Seller of Tom Boons the Post Master of St Margrets a negroe Woman
stript her and with a Cow Hyde Lasarated her flesh untill the Blood
ozed from every cut and She with in a Month of giveing Burth to a
child She appeared Before Court with the Blood Still Streaming
from her To Cover his guilt he ivents a Charge She is thrown in
prson and he goes free the Same parties caught a Man By the name
of Foster Eight Miles from annapolis hand cuffed him and Drove
him before them and they on Horse With Such Rapidity that when
he got to Severen Ferry he fell apon the Beach Exausted Covered
with foam and this Man was Born free this mans offence was that
he nor no wife of his Should be Treated in that maner without
avenging it. What i have bein trying to get at is this Sam[1]
Richardson has taken to annapolis four Childern of one of his
Slaves apon the face of the Mothers Ojections in court he has had
them Bound to him after She stating that all the cloth they had on
were By her after Night there is a woman down heare By the name
Yewel She is allso Demanding of the wiman She has turned
without a stich of winters clothing all there childen to be bound to
her When she cannot get Bread for her Self On friday there was
upwards of hundred young Neagroes on the ferry with there old
Masters draged away forseble from there parents for the purpose of
Haveing them Bound

a number of other cases i could cite that i Will Not Bother you
with

In the Name of Humanity is there no Redress for those poor
ignorant down troden Wreches. Is this or is it not Involuntarey
Slavery you may juge what for peopels they are for ever cent worth
i purchase i have to get in Baltimore they will neather Lend give
nor Sell me any thing not even a ho[r]se to go for a Doctr if my
wife to be confined unfortunatly that acurs every Eleven or Twelve

Month'^{s} I would not stay heare if i could possible get away   unkel
Sam has got me stuck down heare on three hundred and fifty a
year   you may Juge how much i save out of that   there is five
Rooms in the house and each one you can pick up three or four
Children   I am the only union man within ten miles of my
Residence   you may guess the feelings of my neighbours towards
me   Some folks in Baltimoe to see this Letter would hint that it
was a fathers interest, manifested in young darkies but it not
so   every one of them are Jett Black and every knot of wool that
groes on there Heads Both ends groes in there Schull   therefore
there is no anglow Saxon in them   Yours $^{[\&c]}$

Thos B Davis

PS   please tender my kind Regards to Archabald Sterling Esqr
and Excuse my famieliarty   tell him i walked Seven miles to
annapolis and Back come to Baltimor and voted for him   cost six
dollars   could do him no good   he will be all Right nex
time   T B Davis

ALS

Thos. B. Davis to Hon. J. Lanox Bond, 6 Nov. 1864, filed with M-1932
1864, Letters Received, ser. 12, RG 94 [K-4]. The addressee, Hugh Lennox
Bond, was judge of the Baltimore Criminal Court and a prominent antislavery
unionist.

1 November 1, the day the state constitution abolishing slavery went into
effect.

**142: Order by the Commander of the Middle Department and
8th Army Corps**

Baltimore Md.   November 9th 1864.

General Orders. No. 112.

Official information having been furnished, making it clear that
evil disposed parties in certain counties of the State of Maryland,
within the limits of the Middle Department, intend obstructing the
operation, and nullifying, as far as they can, the emancipation
provision of the New Constitution: and that for this purpose they are
availing themselves of certain laws, portions of the ancient slave code
of Maryland, as yet unrepealed, to initiate as respects the persons
heretofore slaves, a system of forced apprenticeship; for this, and for

other reasons, among them that if they have any legal rights under existing laws, the persons spoken of are in ignorance of them; that in certain counties the law officers are so unfriendly to the newly made freedmen, and so hostile to the benignant measure that made them such, as to render appeals to the courts worse than folly, even if the victims had the money with which to hire lawyers; and that the necessities of the case make it essential, in order to carry out truly and effectively the grand purpose of the people of the State of Maryland – emancipation of every slave, man, woman and child, within her limits, from and after the 1st day of November of this present year – that there should be remedies extraordinary for all their grievances – remedies instantaneous without money or reward – and somebody to have care for them, to protect them, to show them the way to the freedom of which they have yet but vague and undefined ideas. *It is therefore ordered,*

I. That all persons within the limits of the Middle Department heretofore slaves, but now free, by operation of the New Constitution, shall be considered under special military protection, until the Legislature of Maryland may, by its enactments, make such military protection unnecessary.

II. A Freedman's Bureau for said Department, is hereby created, office in Baltimore, Major WM. M. ESTE, A.D.C. in charge.

III. Major ESTE is entrusted with the execution of this order; and to make it effective, he is authorized to institute investigations, to send for persons and papers, and to make necessary arrests.

IV. Provost Marshals in their several Districts, particularly those on the Eastern and Western Shores, are requested and directed to hear all complaints made to them by persons within the meaning of this order, to collect and forward information and proofs of wrongs done to such persons, and, generally, to render Major ESTE such assistance as he may require in the performance of his duty.

V. As it will be impossible to carry out this order without having a place in which the sick, helpless, and needy can be temporarily rested and provided for, Major Este is directed to take possession of the building known formerly as the Maryland Club House, but now named "Freedman's Rest," to select some excellent lady to take charge of the same as Matron, and to suitably prepare and furnish as many rooms as may be required for the purpose proposed. And that this may be speedily accomplished, donations are respectfully solicited from all philanthropic and christian persons wherever resident. All fines hereafter assessed and collected by the Provost Marshal of the Department will be appropriated to the support of the Freedman's Rest. To supply immediate wants, Major ESTE is further directed to draw on Col. WOOLLEY.

VI. Lest the moneys derived from donations, and from fines collected, should prove insufficient to support the institution in a manner corresponding to its importance, Major Este will proceed to make a list of all the avowed rebel sympathizers resident in the city of Baltimore, with a view to levying such contributions upon them in aid of the "Freedman's Rest," as may be from time to time required.

VII. Major Este will enter upon the execution of this order without delay.

By command of MAJOR GENL. WALLACE

PD

General Orders. No. 112, Head-Quarters Middle Department, Eighth Army Corps, 9 Nov. 1864, vol. 61 8AC, General Orders (Printed), ser. 2352, Middle Dept. & 8th Army Corps, RG 393 Pt. 1 [C-4170]. Colonel John Woolley, from whom Major Este was to draw funds, was provost marshal of the Middle Department and 8th Army Corps. On November 12, General Wallace submitted a copy of General Order 112 to the War Department, accompanied by a number of letters describing widespread obstruction of emancipation and abuse of freedpeople, which, he suggested, "make a basis for" the order. Wallace promised, however, that "no attempt [would] be made to execute" it until he received instructions from the Secretary of War. Three days later, he submitted a second, even larger packet. (Several of the letters and other documents forwarded by Wallace are printed above, as docs. 140, 141, and below, as docs. 143, 144, 145, 146, 149, 149n.) While General Order 112 was under consideration by his superiors, Wallace tried to improve its prospects by disposing of one possible objection. The Freedman's Society of Baltimore and the National Freedman's Relief Association of New York, he reported on November 19, would provide for any former slaves who were taken from their masters into military custody. This "arrangement," Wallace pointed out, "will relieve the Dep't and Gov't from the burthen of supporting negroes thus brought away." (Endorsements by Maj. Genl. Lew. Wallace, 12 Nov. 1864 and 15 Nov. 1864, on letters filed as M-1932 1864, and Maj. Gen. Lew. Wallace to Gen. E. D. Townsend, 19 Nov. 1864, filed with M-1932 1864, Letters Received, ser. 12, RG 94 [K-4].) While General Order 112 was under review by the War Department, Wallace neither suspended nor rescinded its publication; it received wide circulation in Maryland's newspapers and through military channels. No written instructions to Wallace regarding the order have been found in the copies of letters and telegrams sent by the War Department or in the files of letters and telegrams received by the Middle Department. However, in early December the Secretary of War evidently directed Wallace – perhaps verbally – to countermand instructions he had issued to enforce the order on Maryland's eastern shore. (See below, docs. 148n., 152.)

143: Maryland Quaker to His Mother

Betterton [*Md.*] 11/10. 1864

Dear Mother   Freedom is not established, notwithstanding our congratulations and celebrations and poetic effusions of rejoicing

The slaveholders with Judge Chambers[1] at their head are dragging the little children of Emancipated parents before proslavery magistrates and a proslavery Orphans Court, and are having them bound to their former masters without even a regard to the forms of Law.   The Orphan's Court announces publicly that it will give the preference to former owners and the poor blacks have not the choice of a master, which is allowed them by this iniquitous law, nor do they stop to ascertain if the parent can support the children which is the very foundation and excuse for the Law.   I wrote to Jno Graham to see eminent persons and write me what to do.   But since then as I have investigated the subject. I see no hope from Courts Lawyers judges or juries, – for all with us in a general sense are oppressors.   So to the many applications which have been made to me I have but one answer, "Suffer the oppression, or seek homes in other neighborhoods."   Many wish to leave here and my object is to solicit the aid of your Society in providing places of refuge in the City until homes in the Country can be had.   I have one family to look after now a mother and four children.   The oldest a boy can do good work

write at once

ALS   R T Turner

R. T. Turner to Mother, 10 Nov. 1864, enclosed in John Needlss and Saml. Townsend to Gen. Wallace, 14 Nov. 1864, both filed with M-1932 1864, Letters Received, ser. 12, RG 94 [K-4]. The covering letter, written by two Quaker abolitionists in Baltimore "on behalf of the Friends Association for the relief of Freedman," identified Turner as "a member of the Society of Friends in Kent Co Md" and asked the "immediate attention" of General Lew Wallace, commander of the Middle Department, to the "great oppression" he described. The deputy provost marshal at Chestertown, Maryland, drew a similar picture of the activities of the Kent County Orphans Court. By November 15, he reported, the court had apprenticed more than 100 "freed children" without their parents' consent; only one or two of the indentures were proper ones. "I do not think a greater injustice was ever committed," he declared. "There is not a day but what there are from three to six poor women making complaints to me." (Bartus Trew to Major Wm. M. Este, 15 Nov. 1864, T-320 1864, Letters Received, ser. 2343, Middle Dept. & 8th Army Corps, RG 393 Pt. 1 [C-4146].) A year and a half later, Turner recounted for the commissioner of the Freedmen's Bureau the events that had followed upon emancipation in Kent County: "In 1864 the Emancipation Constitution of the State was adopted. This measure so far from ending our troubles seemed to be almost the commencement of them. The liberated blacks flocked to us begging our aid to save their children. Clad in miserable garments too thin for the season, women with tears and distress told of their bereavements through the operation of the 'Negro Apprenticeship Laws,' which were put in full force . . . and in less than a week, the work was done of binding out all of the smaller Blacks that were desired by their former masters or others. Did the parents object, They were told that 'it was the Law', that 'their children had to be bound out', and knowing no better, an unwilling consent was in this way fraudulently obtained and thus in the moment of liberty, came the grief of separation." (R. T. Turner to Major Genl O. O. Howard, 30 Apr. 1866, T-168 1866, Letters Received, ser. 15, Washington Hdqrs., RG 105 [A-9661].)

1 Ezekiel F. Chambers, who had been a judge and a U.S. senator, was the Democratic candidate for governor of Maryland in the election of November 1864; he was defeated.

144: Black Minister to the Superintendent of the Middle Department Freedman's Bureau

Balt [*Md.*] N^{ov} 11th, 1864.
Dear Sir   You will please excuse me for troubling you but feeling much interest for my people, and being informed that you are to see that justice is to be done to them has prompted me to send this letter to you   I have been informed that a Mr Amos living on N. Charles st one door this side of Reed st has still several slaves which he still holds, I went there a few days ago and saw them there myself. Such has been his wife's System, that no one has ever been permited ever to see them   Mr Amos is a noted rebel sympathizer, and if his, and his friend – Dr. Doulan's houses Monument st were examined much rebel information would be obtained. praying that this communication may be strictly personal and that you will use all your influence in behalf of the oppressed. I have the honour to be Your's most Obedient
Justitia
Wm *A. Willyams*
PS. You will please use my signature *Justitia* if you may have occasion to use my information   *W^m A Willyams*
ALS

Wm. A. Willyams to Major Wm. M. Este, 11 Nov. 1864, filed with M-1932 1864, Letters Received, ser. 12, RG 94 [K-4].

Document 144

145: Statement of a Maryland Freedwoman

Bal^t [*Md.*] Novr 14" /64.
Statement Harriet Anne Maria Banks (negress)
My name is Harriet Anne Maria Banks & was the Slave of Dr.
S. S. Hughes of Vienna Maryland I left Dr. Hughes & came to

Baltimore. he treated me badly & this was my principal object in leaving   they informed me that Abraham Lincoln Could not free me that he had no right to do so.   there are Many coloured persons living in the Vicinity who desire to go into the Service of the United States but are prevented from So doing by their masters who disclaim the right of their being taken from them   I wish the privilege granted me of returning to my former home & getting possession of bed & clothing left there by me.

<table>
<tr><td>HDSr</td><td align="center">her
Harriet Anne X Maria Banks.
mark</td></tr>
</table>

Statement of Harriet Anne Maria Banks, 14 Nov. 1864, filed with M-1932 1864, Letters Received, ser. 12, RG 94 [K-4]. Given at the headquarters of the Middle Department and 8th Army Corps.

146: Statement of a Maryland Freedwoman

Bal^{to} [*Md.*]   Novr 14″/64
Statement of Jane Kamper
Slave of Wm Townsend of Talbot County Md.
I was the slave of Wm Townsend of Talbot county & told Mr. Townsend of my having become free & desired my master to give my children & my bedclothes   he told me that I was free but that my Children Should be bound to me [*him*].   he locked my Children up so that I could not find them   I afterwards got my children by stealth & brought them to Baltimore.   I desire to regain possession of my bed clothes & furniture.
My Master pursued me to the Boat to get possession of my children but I hid them on the boat

<table>
<tr><td>HDSr</td><td align="center">her
Jane X Kamper (fn)
mark</td></tr>
</table>

Statement of Jane Kamper, 14 Nov. 1864, filed with M-1932 1864, Letters Received, ser. 12, RG 94 [K-4]. Given at the headquarters of the Middle Department and 8th Army Corps.

147: Provost Marshal at Annapolis, Maryland, to the
Commander of the Post of Annapolis; Enclosing a Letter from
the Judges of the Orphans Court of Anne Arundel County
to the Provost Marshal

Annapolis. Md. Nov. 23ᵈ 1864.
Colonel: The accompanying papers explain themselves and it
remains for me to say that I am fully convinced of the fact that since
the adoption of the New Constitution by the State of Maryland that
the Judges of the Orphans Court in and for the county of Anne
Arundel. Md. have been binding out colored children to whoever
might apply for them (but giving their former owners the
prefference) against the express wish of their parents and in many
cases said parents were entirely ignorant of the fact that their
children were apprenticed untill they went to get them from their
former owners.

It is to reach all of the above cases that I aim. and most
respectfully ask for authority to annul indentures that have been
made since the adoption of the New Constitution that are illegal as
well as to stop further illegal proceedings of the court in this matter
and it will be but an act of justice to a class of persons whose
ignorance in regard to their rights is taken advantage of by men who
in almost every case have always been known as sympathizers with
(and to some extent) aiders of the rebels. I am Colonel: Very
Respectfully Your Obedient Servant
HLS   Geo. W. Curry

[Enclosure]   Court Room [Annapolis, Md.]. Nov. 22ⁿᵈ 1864
Dear Sir: In the recess of the court yours of the 18ᵗʰ was left with
the clerk of Register of Wills. to-day being our regular session, it
was opened & contents duly noted. we thoᵗ it due to simply state
the course we are pursuing in reference to minor children
particularly those under 14 years of age, & also to refer you to the
Law under which we are called upon to act— the recent convention
under which our new Constitution was framed in its deliberations
deemed the existing Statutes, amply sufficient for any provision that
might be required for negro children, leaving further Legislation,
if necessary, to a future Legislature   in the applications for
binding apprentices we have quite a numerous class above the age
of 14 soliciting the court to bind them to persons of their own
selection. such selections, when known to the court to be a proper
character, it has no hesitancy in granting— we would further state
there is a very large number of *Orphan* children whose ages ranging
from infancy to 10 or 12 yrˢ require some immediate action in their

behalf & when their previous owners are known to the court to be proper persons to care for & bring them up to habits of industry &^{c} we invariably bind to them— we have also applications from former masters to have negro children that they have raised. bound to them but when it is satisfactorily shown to the court that the parents of such children are in a condition to provide for them in NO INSTANCE does the court interfere— we think it very probable our course has been misrepresented by some mothers. who think they can support themselves & family, their previous antecedents being enquired into by the court it is made too apparent their utter inability to properly provide & teach habits of industry &^{c} in such cases the court regards it as an act of humanity when proper employers can be selected for them— we would further observe that our regular term of court is on Tuesdays & will be in session to-morrow (Wednesday) our proceedings are all open to the public & yourself or any one you may select can be present & take cogizance of our action— You will please inform us in writing from the frankness of the above wether you consider it necessary to suspend further proceedings in binding apprentices— the Law (which has invariably governed us in binding out of negro apprentices) we refer to, you will find on page 38 in the code of Public General Laws under the head of negro apprentices.[1] Respectfully Your Obt. Servts.

Philip Pettebone
Chas S. Welch
J. W. Hunter

HLcSr

Capt. Geo. W. Curry to Col. Adrian R. Root, 23 Nov. 1864, enclosing Philip Pettebone et al. to Geo. W. Curry, Esq., 22 Nov. 1864, C-643 1864, Letters Received, ser. 2343, Middle Dept. & 8th Army Corps, RG 393 Pt. 1 [C-4133]. Curry signed as a captain in the 4th Delaware Volunteers. Also enclosed is a copy of Curry's letter of November 18, in which he had informed the judges of complaints by "a large number" of freedpeople "that their children were being taken from them and apprenticed without their sanction and in direct opposition to their wishes." Curry had provided the judges with a copy of General Order 112, issued by the commander of the Middle Department on November 9, 1864, calling their attention to the paragraph that placed former slaves under "special military protection" until the state legislature enacted laws rendering such protection unnecessary. "I am confident," Curry had warned the judges, "that after you have been officially notified of . . . the above named Order that nothing will be done by your honorable body to counteract its provisions." (Capt. Geo. W. Curry to the Honorable Judges of the Orphans Court for Anne Arundel Co. Md., 18 Nov. 1864; General Order 112 is printed above, as doc. 142.) A series of endorsements indicates that on November 24, Colonel Adrian R. Root, commander of the post of Annapolis, forwarded the correspondence to

General Lew Wallace, commander of the Middle Department, who returned it with instructions to "inform the Judge of the Court that it will be for the interest of all parties, court, Masters, and apprentices, if the indenturing is delayed until further notification—" When Curry communicated that statement to the judges on November 29, their response ignored Wallace's request for indefinite suspension of their proceedings, but offered "not the slightest objection to suspend the apprenticing of Negro Children for a short period say until Tuesday next." Defending the indentures as humanitarian acts that were required of them by law, the judges advised Curry "that there are quite a large number of applicants to have children bound to them & that there are very many cases in which the children can be provided for only in the way the court is now pursueing—" (Philip Pettebone and Chas. S. Welch to Geo. W. Curry Esq., 30 Nov. 1864, in the same file.) Outmaneuvered by the judges and unsure of how to respond, Colonel Root on December 3 dispatched Curry to General Wallace's headquarters to "obtain definite instructions in regard to the subject of Indenturing Negro Children as Apprentices in Anne Arundel Co." It is not known what, if any, further action was taken by Wallace or his subordinates; no additional evidence has been found in the letters-sent volumes of the Middle Department, the post of Annapolis, or the provost marshal at Annapolis.

1 Article 6, sections 31–40, of the *Maryland Code of Public General Laws, 1860*, for which see above, p. 494n.

148: Headquarters of the Middle Department and 8th Army Corps to the Commander of the 3rd Separate Brigade, 8th Army Corps

[Baltimore, Md.] December 2nd [186]4

General, I am directed by the Major General Com'd'g to inform you that the situation in the Southern Counties of the Eastern Shore is such as to require the presence, for a time at least, of the General Com'd'g the District—

General *Lockwood* will therefore transfer his Head-Quarters, temporarily, to Cambridge, Dorchester County.

General *Lockwood* will give particular attention to the conduct of the disloyal inhabitants and take vigorous measures to protect loyal citizens and the colored people recently liberated

He will not hesitate to arrest persons who by threats or actions tend to disquiet or intimidate Union people and families—

He will give special attention to par. 1. of G.O. No 112, current series these Hd Qrs,[1] and break up the practice now prevalent of apprenticing young negroes without the consent of their parents, to their former masters. If necessary, he will not hesitate to arrest all masters who refuse liberty to such apprentices, or withold them from their parents, and keep them in custody until they consent to such liberation. In case the parents of apprentices are not able to support them, and they desire it, he will send them to Baltimore, to the care of Lieut. Colonel *W. E. W. Ross* 31st U.S.C.T., in charge of Freedman's Bureau. He will endeavor to keep families to-gether as far as possible: but at the same time use his influence to discourage emigration for the present, and only send to Baltimore those who cannot find homes, occupation and labor where they now are —

General *Lockwood* will arrest *Daniel Jones* and *Joseph Bratton*, of Somerset County, and *Levin D Waters* of Princess Anne, and send them as disaffected and dangerous men, by steamer to Fortress Monroe, to be sent across the lines, into Confederate jurisdiction — [2]

General *Lockwood* will resort to the most energetic and vigorous measures to quell the growing turbulence of secessionists in the counties along the Eastern Shore generally —

He will take with him to Cambridge one company of the U.S. regulars, and retain and use the mounted men now on the Eastern Shore under Lieut. *Mowbray*.

General *Lockwood* will leave an A.A.A.G., at his office in this city, to attend to the current business — I am General Very Respectfully Your Obedient Servant

HLpS

Saml B Lawrence

A.A.G. Saml. B. Lawrence to Brig. Genl. H. H. Lockwood, 2 Dec. 1864, vol. 35 8AC, pp. 169–71, Press Copies of Letters Sent, ser. 2328, Middle Dept. & 8th Army Corps, RG 393 Pt. 1 [C-4231]. A line was later drawn alongside the entire fifth paragraph—the one relating to General Order 112 and the apprenticing of black children—and a marginal notation by General Lew Wallace, commander of the Middle Department, instructed his adjutant to extract that paragraph and send it to General Henry H. Lockwood, commander of the 3rd Separate Brigade, "informing him not to proceed under it until further orders." A copy of that paragraph was forwarded to Lockwood on December 8, 1864, with an endorsement directing its suspension. (Extract filed as M-841 1864, Letters Received, ser. 4921, 3rd Separate Brigade, 8th Army Corps, RG 393 Pt. 2 No. 319 [C-4118].) On the same day, Wallace's adjutant forwarded to the War Department a copy of the full text of the December 2 instructions, with the fifth paragraph marked by a marginal line and an endorsement reporting that Lockwood had been told not to enforce it. (A.A.G. Saml. B. Lawrence to Brig. Genl. H. H. Lockwood, 2 Dec. 1864, filed with M-1932 1864, Letters Received, ser. 12, RG 94 [K-4].) No War Department directive has been found requiring Wallace to countermand his original instructions to Lockwood, but a letter written several months later by the latter's adjutant (to a black minister who was trying to reclaim his apprenticed children) identified the source of the decision: "I am directed by Gen. Lockwood to . . . say," the adjutant wrote, "that when he issued the orders on the Eastern Shore, in relation to the apprenticing of negro children, that it was his full intention to carry them out, but . . . [they] were revoked by the Secretary of War." (A.A.G. Wm. M. Boone to Jno. Dennis, 26 June 1865, vol. 94/178 8AC, p. 414, Letters Sent, ser. 4916, 3rd Separate Brigade 8th Army Corps, RG 393 Pt. 2 No. 319 [C-8895].) For Lockwood's response when he first learned that his authority to intervene in apprenticeship cases had been rescinded, see below, doc. 152.

1 The order, issued on November 9, 1864, is printed above, as doc. 142.
2 Jones and Bratton were judges of the Somerset County Orphans Court; Waters, a state senator-elect, was accused of having flown the Confederate flag from his office. General Lockwood arrested the three men, as instructed, but on December 13, President Abraham Lincoln ordered that they not be sent into Confederate lines, and soon thereafter the Secretary of War ordered the release of Jones and Bratton. Nor did Waters remain in custody for long; by late January 1865, following a trial by military commission, he had taken his seat in the state senate. (Abraham Lincoln, *Collected Works*, ed. Roy P. Basler, Marion D. Pratt, and Lloyd A. Dunlap, 9 vols. [New Brunswick, N.J., 1953–55], vol. 8, pp. 167, 172–73, 198, 229–30, 232, 251n.; Richard Paul Fuke, "Black Marylanders, 1864–1868" [Ph.D. diss., University of Chicago, 1973], p. 188.)

149: Postmaster at New Town, Maryland, to the Commander of the Middle Department and 8th Army Corps

New Town Md, December 5th 1864,

Dear Sir: After the interview which I had with you and after the publication of your order relating to the binding out of Coloured peoples Children,[1] I returned home and expected to have realized the Satisfaction of the faithful compliance upon the part of Citizens, and the Orphans Court, with that Order. But, To my great mortification I have found your Order to be contemtuously disregarded. The Citizens are laying hold, by violence, of Coloured peoples Children, carrying them to the Orphans Court and having them bound to themselves in Spite of all remonstrance upon the part of Parents, They are taking Boys and Girls as old as Sixteen years, Some of whom will hire out for Fifty and Sixty dollars a year, one case in particular, came under my own personal Knowledge, where the former owner laid hold of a boy Sixteen years old, The Mother refused to give up her Son, but was over powerd He threatend her with violence, The Mother came into the Post Office for Protection. The Man with a billet of wood came off his own premises crossed the Street and entered my door approached the Woman and Struck her on the Side of the head nearly Knocking her down, I Spoke to him in an instant not to do that, when he desisted, They are threatening Mothers with the severest punishment if they come on their premises, It is my opinion that the Orphans Court, The Register of Wills, and a certain Constable in this Community by the name of George Hargis is equally gilty with the Citizens in this matter The Mother who was Struck had her Son hired out for ten dollars pr month at the time he was taken from her, The parents of Children thus taken, are comeing to me daily and almost hourly for direction, is there no redress for Such high handed viliany with great respect I remain yours Truly,

ALS   James Murray

James Murray to Major General Lew. Wallace, 5 Dec. 1864, M-838 1864, Letters Received, ser. 2343, Middle Dept. & 8th Army Corps, RG 393 Pt. 1 [C-4141]. Wholesale apprenticing of black children prevailed throughout the southernmost counties of Maryland's eastern shore, and, concerned that the department commander fully understand "the deplorable condition of affairs" in that region, General Henry H. Lockwood, commander of the 3rd Separate Brigade, had in mid-November asked a recently discharged officer from an eastern-shore regiment to present eyewitness evidence at department headquarters. In Dorchester County, the former officer testified, he had seen black children "[c]arried from different portions of the County in ox Carts, waggons, and Carriages to the County town (Cambridge) to be Carried before the Court to be bound out as apprentices"; in some instances, "boys were bound out that would Command wages at sixty dollars per year." (*Official Records*, ser. 1, vol. 43, pt. 2, p. 632; John E. Graham to Major Genl. Lew Wallace, 15 Nov. 1864, filed with M-1932 1864, Letters Received, ser. 12, RG 94 [K-4].)

1 General Order 112, issued on November 9, 1864. (See above, doc. 142.)

150: Superintendent of the Bureau of Freedmen and Government Farms in the Department of Washington to the Headquarters of the Department

Washington D.C. Dec. 6.th 1864

Colonel, Lt. E. F. O'Brien V.R.C. Supt. "Goverment Farms" Pautuxent River Md. reports "that since the adoption of the new Constitution in Maryland, many colored people have applied (some of their own accord, others having been sent by their former masters) to be received upon the "Goverment farms" —
  Those now on these farms are principally refugees from Slavery, and are more than Suffcent in number to Cultivate the land —
  I would most respectfully ask for instructions — and if, the free

colored people of Maryland are to be received; authority to erect additional quarters and to provide clothing and other necessaries –
I would also suggest for your consideration – the plan of sending as many as possible of the Contrabands in this Department to the North, with a view to obtaining situations for them as servants and laborers, this could be effected by placing them in charge of private individuals and associations, provided, sufficient bonds were required to prevent the contrabands from again becoming a charge to the United States, the State, County, or town where they might be placed – Transportation to be furnished by the United States. I am Colonel, Very Respectfully Your obdt. Servant

ALS   J. M. Brown

[*Endorsement*] Hd Qrs Dept of Washington, 22^d A Corps, Dec 8" 1864. Respectfully forwarded to the Adjutant General, for instructions relative to the course to be pursued towards the Freedman of Maryland. I am informed that in many instances, the able bodied members of families, of many of them have gone away and left their dependent relatives behind. The Masters decline to care for them, and provision must be made, by some authority for their temporary care and support. I do not know that any better place could be selected for them, than these farms on the Patuxent. I approve of Capt Browns idea of sending such of these people, as can be provided with proper employers, to such points as they may be required – taking bonds for their good treatment and proper wages for such time as may be agreed upon.

The question has arisen, can these agreements be enforced, and the bonds collected in case of forfeiture? I am informed that it is very doubtful, unless Congress authorizes it, and prescribes the manner of doing it. Without the authority to enforce the agreements, it is idle to make them, as it places these helpless people, at the mercy of their employers. The whole question is respectfully submitted. C. C. Augur Major General Comd'g.

Capt. J. M. Brown to Lt. Col. J. H. Taylor, 6 Dec. 1864, B-3346 1864, Letters Received, RG 107 [L-57]. No reply to General Augur's endorsement has been found among the records of the Adjutant General's Office or the Secretary of War. Lieutenant Edward F. O'Brien had been assigned to the "government farms" in St. Mary's County, Maryland, in mid-November 1864, soon after the emancipation constitution became effective. In early October, O'Brien's prede-cessor had reported more than 600 ex-slaves on the three Patuxent River farms, all of them "in a destitute condition" and some "almost without any Clothing." (Samuel M. Leathers to Hon. H. A. Risley Esq., 4 Oct. 1864, L-42 1864, Correspondence Received by H. A. Risley, 7th Agency, RG 366 [Q-132].)

TO WHOM IT MAY CONCERN!

Warning is hereby given that the undersigned has arrived in these counties with orders to *BREAK UP* the practice now prevalent of

Apprenticing Negroes

without the consent of their parents, to their former masters or others. And if necessary to arrest all persons, who refuse liberty to such apprentices, or withold them from their parents, and keep them in custody until they consent to such liberation. Also to offer to all such parents as may not be able to maintain their children a free passage to the *"Freedman's Home"* in Baltimore if so desired.

The undersigned will be in the several Eastern Shore Counties for some time and may be addressed at Cambridge, Md., where for the present he has established his Head-quarters.

Dec. 6, 1864.

HENRY H. LOCKWOOD.

Brigadier General.

Circular by Brigadier General Henry H. Lockwood, 6 Dec. 1864, enclosed in Brigadier-General Henry H. Lockwood to Lieut: Col. S. B. Lawrence, 15 Dec. 1864, L-414 1864, Letters Received, ser. 2343, Middle Dept. & 8th Army Corps, RG 393 Pt. 1 [C-4139]. The circular was based directly upon instructions from the commander of the Middle Department. (See above, doc. 148.) On December 8, however, only two days after Lockwood announced his mission on the eastern shore, the department commander ordered him to suspend enforcement of the instructions. (See above, doc. 148n.) For Lockwood's response, see doc. 152, immediately below.

152: Commander of the Middle Department and 8th Army Corps to the Secretary of War

Baltimore Md Dec 11 1864.
Hon E M Stanton   On my return last evening I recd the following telegram from Gen Lockwood which explains itself. "Salisbury Md Dec 10 To Maj Gen Wallace. Just arrived here from below. Find a telegram from Lt Mulliken saying that orders have gone to me Cambridge countermanding my instructions so far as relates to the negroes.[1] Presuming that this refers to the subject of the recent apprenticeship in these counties I beg leave to submit a few remarks. It is impossible to convey to you by telegraph any idea of the hundreds of abuses that have come to my Knowledge of this system   I have Knowledge of cases where lads of sixteen (16) and eighteen (18) have been bound out and then hired to their fathers who are prosperous farmers for ten (10) & twelve (12) dollars a month.   both you & I are put in false position here by stopping short now.   I dont think that any one (1) can visit these counties as I have done without seeing the importance of stopping the whole sale perversion of what is designed to be a humane law   I will leave for Cambridge tomorrow & desire to hear from you by telegraph tonight   (signed) Gen Lockwood
HWSr   Lew Wallace

Maj. Gen. Lew Wallace to Hon. E. M. Stanton, 11 Dec. 1864, vol. 243, pp. 376–77, Telegrams Received by the Secretary of War, Telegrams Collected by the Office of the Secretary of War (Bound), RG 107 [L-328]. General Henry H. Lockwood, whose telegram Wallace quoted, was commander of the 3rd Separate Brigade of the 8th Army Corps. No reply to Wallace's telegram has been found among the copies of letters and telegrams sent by the Secretary of War or among the letters and telegrams received by the Middle Department.

1 For the countermanding orders, issued by the headquarters of the Middle Department on December 8, see above, doc. 148n.

153: Postmaster at New Town, Maryland, to the Commander of the Middle Department and 8th Army Corps

New Town Md,   December 14th 1864
Dear Sir: I am affraid I Shall weary you, and yet I must write. Humanity compells me to do so. While Gen[l] Lockwood was here adjusting the difficulties relative to the Coloured People, Some

of the Slave Owners, after the Profitable Boys and Girls were taken away from them, turned off the old women, the Mothers with their helpless Children, and they of course had to be provided for. Gen[l] Lockwood applied to me, to provide Quarters, and Provision for all such cases as come to my knowledge. I have Secured Houses for two or Three Families and am providing them with provisions. Yesterday I received a Telegraph dispatch from Gen[l] Lockwood at Salisbury, informing me that Indirect Information was received by him, that orders were at Cambridge awaiting him, Countermanding your, orders relative to apprentices, and that I need not provide for any more, than what I had on my hands at present and you of course would pay the Bill. Now Sir: I am apprehensive that, some persons have been trying to influence the Authorities at Washington to do this thing, and thereby through difficulties in the way of the coloured people, being self sustaining, and consequently bring the Emancipation cause into disrepute. What other object can they have. The course persud by you is one of Humanity, and Justice. And if the authorities at Washington think that there is any mistake in the Testimony before you, which has caused you to Isue your order, in this matter, I would here state if the taking of Children from Parents after they were Freed, when they had hired them out to other persons for 50 cts pr day and ten dollars pr month is Testimony needed, It can be furnished as clear as the beams of light that dart forth from the great orb of day. While the Orphans Court and the Register of Wills have authorized and incouraged this verry thing, The Register of Wills Doctr. Hubbell after he had an Interview (as I was informed) with you on this Subject, came home and cited (to appear before him or the orphans court) a Coloured woman and her son aged sixteen years, whom she had hired out for 50 cts pr day or ten dollars pr month, after the Mother remonstrated and was nearly Knocked down by the man claiming the Boy, the Orphans Court with the Register Bound this Boy to his former Master. The Orphans Court has said that they would not bind out any Coloured Boy or Girl to any one but a white person. The chief Judge of the Orphans Court told me that they would not take Security for the Maintenance of Coloured Children but that they must have homes with white persons, If I could have an interview with the President or Secretary of War, upon this Subject I think I could Set all doubt aside which might be in their minds, relative to the inhumanity of White people towards the Freed Coloured people. The facts which I have mentioned we can prove, and more than I have mentioned. Now My Dear Sir: What am I to do with these poor Creatures who come to me almost daily for assistance, Whose Husbands and Sons are in the Army or have fallen upon the battlefield, defending our rights. It is a hard

matter for me to turn them away empty, and yet in many instances I have it to do. I am poor myself and not able to assist them to any extent, and the Slave owner would rejoice could they see all the attempts to promote the down trodden Slave thwarted, and those who befriend them brought into disrepute. There are many cases of need, that ought to be assisted if it could be done without too much expence and trouble to the Goverment. If all such cases could be attended to here with as little or less expence than at the Freedmans Home in Baltimore, How would It do to let Them Stay with their Friends, which I am sure they would greatly prefer. I make this statement for your consideration, and if in your Judgement, you would approve of the plan, Government Stores could be dealt out to them, or they could be furnished here, at as low rates as any one can buy them for the cash. Will you be so kind as to let me hear from you soon in answer to this. with great respect I remain yours Truly
ALS   James Murray

[*Endorsement*] Head-Quarters, Middle Department, EIGHTH ARMY CORPS. *Baltimore, Md.,* Dec. 16th 1864. Respectfully referred to Brig. Genl. H. H. Lockwood, Comm'd'g 3[d] Sep. Brigade, for immediate report, of the number of persons and their age, sex and condition, now in charge of Mr. Murray, and whether it is understood that the expense of their maintenance is to be paid by the Government, if so, Genl. Lockwood will take immediate action to ascertain whether those people can be supported on the Eastern Shore, where they will be near their families and former homes, without expense to the Government. If they cannot be so supported, Genl. Lockwood will cause them to be brought to this City, and will give timely notice of their arrival to Lt. Col. W. E. W. Ross, in charge of Freedmans Bureau, so that he can arrange with the Secretary of the Freedmens Association for their reception, and direct Mr. Murray to send in his bill at once. This paper to be ret'd with report   By Command of Major Genl. Wallace Sam[l] B Lawrence A.A.G.

[*Endorsement*] Head Quarters 3rd Sep. Brig. 8th A.C. Baltimore Dec. 19th 1864   Respectfully returned to Dept. Hd. Qrs. with the information that there are now in Mr. Murrays care at Salisbury, three (3) old person, six (6) boys & two (2) girls. These people cannot be supported on the E.S. without expense to the Govmt. and I have consequently ordered them all to be sent to this city as soon as possible. The boat from Newtown is advertised to leave there to-morrow and I presume they will come up on it. Mr. Murray has been directed also to forward the bill of his expenses and to receive no more of these people. Henry H Lockwood Brig. Genl.

James Murray to Major Genl. Lew. Wallace, 14 Dec. 1864, M-866 1864, Letters Received, ser. 2343, Middle Dept. & 8th Army Corps, RG 393 Pt. 1 [C-8894]. On December 17, after receiving General Wallace's endorsement but before adding his own, General Lockwood wrote to Wallace's headquarters outlining the arrangement by which Murray had been authorized to receive and care for former slaves forwarded by Lockwood's officers, as well as other former slaves who, in Murray's judgment, were "proper objects." Upon learning that his authority to intervene in unjust apprenticeships had been rescinded, Lockwood had warned Murray "to be cautious in receiving other cases." Now Lockwood questioned what was to be done with the freedpeople already in Murray's hands. Murray himself "seemed to think that the method of providing for these people near home was to be preferred to bringing them to [Baltimore]." "[I]f they can be supported on the Army ration in Newton," Lockwood asked, "must they be sent to Baltimore? Or must they be sent only "if they cannot be supported without extra expense[?]" An endorsement on Lockwood's letter, also dated December 17, stated the intention of General Wallace more bluntly than before: "[I]t is not desired to keep these people, at all, at government expense, either by issuing rations or otherwise. . . . If the people cannot be kept on the Eastern Shore without expense, they must be brought here and turned over to the Freedmens Relief Association. – This only applies to those already cared for by Mr. Murray, none others will be received." (Brig. Genl. Henry H. Lockwood to Lt. Col. Lawrence, 17 Dec. 1864, Letters Received, ser. 4921, 3d Separate Brigade, 8th Army Corps, RG 393 Pt. 2 No. 319 [C-8878]; for Lockwood's orders and their revocation, see above, doc. 148.) Accordingly, on December 19, Lockwood instructed Murray to send all the freedpeople under his care to Baltimore. That telegram having failed to reach Murray, Lockwood's adjutant renewed the instructions on December 30, but still the former slaves were not dispatched – first because the steamer broke down, and then because winter weather closed all water-borne traffic into Baltimore. Not until early March 1865 was Murray able to send off the freedpeople and submit his bill for their subsistence and transportation. (Brig. Genl. H. H. Lockwood to Mr. James Murray, 19 Dec. 1864, and Lieut. James C. Mullikin to Mr. James Murray, 30 Dec. 1864, vol. 85/161 8AC, pp. 127, 138, Letters Sent, ser. 4915, 3d Separate Brigade, 8th Army Corps, RG 393 Pt. 2 No. 319 [C-4221, C-4223]; James Murray to Brig. Genl. H. H. Lockwood, 10 Jan. 1865, Letters Received, ser. 4921, 3d Separate Brigade, 8th Army Corps, RG 393 Pt. 2 No. 319 [C-8878]; Brig. Genl. Henry H. Lockwood to Col. S. B. Lawrence, 3 Mar. 1865, vol. 94/178 8AC, pp. 356–57, Letters Sent, ser. 4916, 3d Separate Brigade, 8th Army Corps, RG 393 Pt. 2 No. 319 [C-8894].)

THE WARTIME GENESIS OF FREE LABOR

154: Commander of the 3rd Separate Brigade, 8th Army Corps, to the Headquarters of the Middle Department and 8th Army Corps

Baltimore [*Md.*], December 15th. 1864.
Colonel: I have the honor to report, that in compliance with Your instructions of December 2[d] –[1] I proceeded to the lower counties of the Eastern Shore and put forth a circular, of which I enclose copy,[2] that I posted the same and in some cases executed it. – I found, that the binding-out had been very general and began as early as October last; masters having manumitted their slaves under 21 years of age for that purpose. I found, that the spirit of the apprentice law had been very generally disregarded, no attention being paid to whether parents could or could not support or to their wishes as to binding out. They were told, that they must select masters, willing or unwilling. In some cases the apprentices were at the time at hired service at good wages, – some 10– to 12$ per month. That many parents had rented small farms, expecting to have the labor of their childern; – that many poor tenants had made their arrangements to use this labor and are disappointed by the course pursued; That the apprenticing works advantageously only for the rich slave holder – generally *disloyal* – and disadvantageously for the poor white tenant and colored man. I could burden this report with cases, but deem it unnecessary, peticularly as I have not the names at hand. The feeling among our friends in Somerset and Worcester seemed to be, that the law, executed in its proper spirit is a good one, but that, as these gross abuses have attended it, something should be done.

Having on my arrival at Salisbury on Sunday last learned of Your Counter-instructions of the 8th inst.[3] – I came to this City. – Under General Orders No. 120. I will turn over such of Your instructions, as remain unchanged to General Kenly.[4]

I have not deemed it necessary to post any counter circulars. With Respect Your Obedt. Serv[t]
HLS   Henry H Lockwood

Brigadier-General Henry H. Lockwood to Lieut. Col. S. B. Lawrence, 15 Dec. 1864, L-414 1864, Letters Received, ser. 2343, Middle Dept. & 8th Army Corps, RG 393 Pt. 1 [C-4139]. Enclosure, endorsement.

1 The instructions are printed above, as doc. 148.
2 The circular is printed above, as doc. 150.
3 For the counterinstructions, see above, doc. 148n.
4 Issued on December 13, 1864, by the commander of the Middle Depart-

ment and 8th Army Corps, General Order 120 detached the eastern-shore counties of Maryland (Kent, Queen Anne, Talbot, Caroline, Dorchester, Somerset, and Worcester) from Lockwood's jurisdiction, designating them the District of the Eastern Shore of Maryland and placing General John R. Kenly in command. (*Official Records*, ser. 1, vol. 43, pt. 2, pp. 784–85.)

155A: **Black Military Laborer to the Superintendent of the Middle Department Freedman's Bureau**

Baltimore [*Md.*] Decem 20th 1864

Sir. I am an employee of the Commissary Department at Alexandria V[a] under Capt Brown or Lee; I have a wife and five children who lived with Somerset Parrin Prince Frederick Calvert Co. C.H. M[d] who, upon the issuing of the Emancipation Proclamation turned my wife and children out of doors, I rented a house from Henry Hutchins of the same County where my family resided untill last Thursday (15th inst), when Lum. Buckmarsh a Constable of the County went to the house my family occupied and by force carried them to the County Court, I was on my way to the house after my family had been taken away, when I was met by the said Buckmarsh who summoned me (verbally) to appear before the Court on Thursday, on being questioned by Nathaniel Dair P.M in the Court House as to whether I was able to support my family and whether I intended going into the employ of the Government again? to which I answered yes, immediately upon answering, I was struck and cut at by the Constable L. Buckmarsh and pursued some distance from the building, I was afraid to make any further attempt to procure my family and returned to Washington. My family were sent to Jail, where I suppose they are now. I am able to support them, and would wish to have them under my charge, please have this done for me. Very Respectfully

HLSr

his
John X Diggs
mark

John Diggs to Lt. Col. W. E. W. Ross, 20 Dec. 1864, D-320 1864, Letters Received, ser. 2343, Middle Dept. & 8th Army Corps, RG 393 Pt. 1 [C-4134]. Witnessed. Endorsements indicate that the Freedman's Bureau superintendent forwarded Diggs's letter to the headquarters of the Middle Department, whose commander, General Lew Wallace, in turn referred it to Augustus W. Bradford, governor of Maryland, asking, "Is there no civil remedy in such a case?" and adding, "If the Governor desires it, I will interfere to procure the release of the man's family." On January 5, 1865, Governor Bradford returned Diggs's statement, along with a letter from the former owner of Diggs's wife and children, which is printed immediately below, as doc. 155B.

155B: Maryland Former Slaveholder to the Governor of Maryland

Prince Frederick [*Md.*] Dec 30th 1864

Dear Sir   I have just read a communication from you to Jos A Wilson Esq our States atty, respecting a complaint made to Lt Col Ross in charge of Freedmans Bureau by a negro man named John Diggs the husband of a negro woman Eliza who belonged to me at the time of the adoption of the present Constitution   This negro man John Diggs in his complaint to Lt Col Ross states that "he had a wife & five children who lived with Somerset Parrin who upon the issuing of the Emancipation Proclamation turned his wife & children out of doors"   Instead of turning Eliza & her children out of doors she remained with her children in one of my negro quarters for about two weeks after she stopped working for me and during this time her family was fed by me

After she stopped work she went off in search of a place to live on & work during the year 1865. She returned in a few days and having informed me that she expected to rent a piece of land from Mr Henry Hutchins I offered no obstacle or objection to her leaving my farm and several days afterwards when she wanted a conveyance to remove her effects to the land which she had rented I offered my cart for her use & the offer was accepted.   Her husband John Diggs, who formerly belonged to a gentleman in Prince Georges Co, absconded I believe from his then owner and did not return to this neighbourhood until after Eliza & her children had left my farm nor have I seen him since his return

I have not had any of Elizas children bound to me, nor have I ever made any application to have them bound to me.   I did not want them nor would I have them as bound apprentices to me.   Although as a practising attorney I am often in Prince Frederick yet I have never heard of John Diggs children being in jail.   Eliza left my premises of her own free will and I have not seen either her or any of her children since she left.   Your obdnt servt

ALS   C. S. Parran

C. S. Parran to His Excellency A. W. Bradford, 30 Dec. 1864, filed with D-320 1864, Letters Received, ser. 2343, Middle Dept. & 8th Army Corps, RG

393 Pt. 1 [C-4134]. In the same file is a letter from Joseph A. Wilson, state's attorney for Calvert County, informing Governor Augustus W. Bradford that the keeper of the jail "has not now, nor has he ever had, the wife, or any child of John Diggs, committed to his custody for a single instant." Wilson reminded the governor that C. S. Parran had been a member of the state convention that drafted Maryland's emancipation constitution. (Jos. A. Wilson to His Excellency A. W. Bradford, 30 Dec. 1864.) In an endorsement of January 5, 1865, forwarding Wilson's and Parran's letters to the commander of the Middle Department and returning John Diggs's statement, Governor Bradford remarked pointedly that the state's attorney and the former master "make statements differing entirely from those made by Digges."

156A: Commander of the 3rd Separate Brigade, 8th Army Corps, to the Headquarters of the Middle Department and 8th Army Corps; Enclosing a Certificate by a War Department Provost Marshal and a Letter from the Commander of the Middle Department to a Maryland Freedman

Baltimore Md January 13th 1864 [*1865*].
Colonel, Having been appealed to in behalf of one Patrick Scott (col.), in a case in which the interference of the Military, is necessary to render justice to an individual, I, therefore, beg leave to present the facts of the case to the Major General Comd'g., to the end, that justice may be done this man, thro' the Military Authorities at Washington.

After the seizure of the estate of Col. J. Waring in Prince George's Co. Md., by the Military Authorities at Washington in 1863 & the removal of the furniture & stock to Washington, a certain colored man – Patrick Scott – was left in charge of the buildings & broken down stock (see paper "A.") Scott had a claim against Waring for certain Carpenter's work, and, besides, had married one of Waring's female servants. During the fall of 1863., I placed a company of Infantry on the farm, Scott still continuing in charge of the broken down Stock & farm.

During the winter of 1864., he applied to me to know if he could crop the land, & I wrote him the letter marked "B." During the Spring of 1864. the troops were removed; subsequently Col. Waring was released. It seems that Scott did crop the land, & produced quite a fine crop, & had some increase of the stock. On Col. Waring's arrival, he drove off Scott from the premises, seized the crop, & refused to allow him anything for his share on any portion of the same, or even to come on the premises to look after it; nor will any of the neighbours allow any of their teams to haul it away.

Scott is willing for Waring to have half, provided he can get the other half, as he wishes to sell it to the U.S.

The property is in the Department of Washington. Very respectfully Your obedt. Servt.

HLS   Henry H. Lockwood

[*Enclosure*]   *Washington City,* Nov 7 *1863*
To whom it may concern   Patrick Scott (a Colored) man has permission to take charge of and retain in his possession until futher orders the Sheep and Hoggs now on the farm of John H Waring

ADS   S. C. Williams

[*Enclosure*]   *Baltimore, Md.* Feb 13 *1864*
Patrick Scott   I rec^d your letter of the 10th Feb & reply. I am not aware of any purpose on the part of government to release Mr Waring, but presume that if released your crops will not be interfered with. Indeed I shall make it my business to see that you are not wronged. I think then that you may safely proceed to crop any portion of the land you see proper with the confidence of being able to secure the crop. Respectfully

ALS   Henry H Lockwood

Brig. Gen. Henry H. Lockwood to Lieut. Col. S. B. Lawrence, 13 Jan. 1864 [1865], enclosing Col. S. C. Williams to whom it may concern, 7 Nov. 1863, and Brigr. Genl. Henry H. Lockwood to Patrick Scott, 13 Feb. 1864, Adjutant General 183 1865, Letters Received from the President, Executive Departments, & War Department Bureaus, RG 107 [L-330]. The certificate of Colonel Williams (marked "A" on its wrapper) is on letterhead of the "Office, Provost Marshal, War Department, Washington City." General Lockwood's letter of February 13, 1864, to Patrick Scott (marked "B" on its wrapper) was written during the period, beginning in December 1863, that Lockwood served as commander of the Middle Department and 8th Army Corps; in late March 1864, when General Lew Wallace was assigned to that command, Lockwood resumed his subordinate position as a brigade commander. Patrick Scott's letter of February 10, 1864, to Lockwood has not been found among the records of the Middle Department. On January 21, 1865, General Wallace referred Lockwood's covering letter and its enclosures to the commander of the Department of Washington, who, claiming that "nothing is known at these Head Qurs of the circumstances attending the arrest and release of Colonel Waring," sought instructions from the War Department; whereupon the Secretary of War asked the judge advocate general "to report whether the case is one in which military tribunals, or military authority can properly do justice." In the same file is the opinion of Joseph Holt, the judge advocate general, written on February 9, 1865. Holt argued that the government, having taken possession of Waring's estate "in consequence of the traitorous practices of which Waring had been convicted," had a right to "work the same, or authorize the working thereof by others." The military commander "into whose custody the estate had been consigned" had granted Patrick Scott permission to cultivate the estate "under assurances that he should be allowed to gather the fruits of his labor," and Scott's right to his crop was, therefore, "such that the Government could not, without breach of faith, deprive him thereof." Holt enclosed a copy of President Lincoln's order, issued by the Adjutant General's Office on November 25, 1864, permitting John H. Waring "to re-occupy his premises in Maryland, with his family," but the judge advocate general maintained that "it is not to be supposed that while granting mercy and pardon to a criminal, it was designed to commit for [Waring's] benefit an act of bad faith and injustice." Holt therefore recommended "that the order of the President be so modified as to exclude from its operation the crop made by Scott under authority from General Lockwood, and that if it has been already appropriated by Waring, the military authorities be directed to compel its restoration." (J. Holt to the Secretary of War, 9 Feb. 1865, enclosing Special Orders No. 417, War Department, Adjutant General's Office, 25 Nov. 1864.) Evidently Holt's recommendation was not heeded–at any rate that was the conclusion of a War Department clerk who examined the file in late 1865 (when further correspondence reopened Scott's claim) and found nothing but an undated notation that the Secretary of War had directed the papers to be filed.

156B: White Unionist in Prince George's County, Maryland, to a White Unionist in Baltimore

[*Prince George's County, Md.*] January 24th 1865

My Dear Sir & Friend   I arived hom on satterday the 21st instant arfter a bad dayes travel   it raind & hailed & frosed as it fell all the way hom from Washington & I had to wride outside with the driver to Marlborough & had to walk hom through rain & snow & hale   I was very wet when I got hom & I took a very bad cole & hav felt bad ever cince but I found my famely all well,   I must say to you that I found when I got hom from what I can lern a grate dele of pregedus agance me groing out my renting my place to Partrick scoot   I fine that most every Bodey is agance the pore fellow it all groing out his being on Warrings place & I think that warring is the cose of it   he wonts all that Partrick made thare   he has taken from Partrick the kees of the corn houses & he is bringing up

charges agance him about taking things of the place & selling
them   Mr Warring & his friends are seeking & finding out every
thing thay can agance him & I dont know what will be the
result   I hav imployed him to work my place & I would like very
much for the leading athoretys to deside what intrust Partrick has
thare   if aney I think that Govement aught to proteck him in it
becose the govement put him thare to take care of the propety
& toled him to make what he could to pay himself for his
troble   Now Mr Warring wonts to know what has becom of his
poltrey & utentials & all of the little things left on the place   those
things was not put under Partrick charge but the farm & houses &
Fenceing was & you know that partrick took care of what was put
under his charge & toled him to pay himself of the place   from
what I can lern thay are trying to [reape] up all those charges agance
him   I beleave the fellow is truly honis & would state all of the
facts in the case   I wish you would asertane what he is entitel
to   he made a crop of corn last year at his on exspence & I think it
would be a hard case if Govement will not alow him apart of what
was rased as he rased it by his on laber & by hiering laber   I wish
you could so arange the mater so as partrick can get his writes & get
the govement to cend thare wagones down & buy his share of corn
& take it of & cend men with the wagons clothd with proper
athorety to settel the bisness betwen Partrick & Mr Warring &
ortherise those offercers to investergate the mater properly as
Partrick is a black man & you very well know that a bleck man has
no chance in this contrey & I think as Partrick has bin in the
Govement imploy & imployed by them I think it is thare dutey to
protect him   if he is entitel to aney thing he aught to have it &
thay aught to see he gets it   I hope you will make som inquire
about it & if he is entitel to a part of the corn & hay & other
provendor sell it to Govement & cend them down for the corn &
hay & cend men clothd with athorety to investegate the mater
& take it away & pay him for it   you are autherrise to sell his corn
& hay & other provendor such as shuckes & foder   Partrick thinkes
he made som 450 or 500 Barrels of corn & he has som 5 or 6 stacks
of good timethey hay & a grate maney shuckes & if Govement
thinkes he is entitel to aney thay can say how much & thay can cend
teames down to take all of it at once   if thinges are alowed to go on
as thay are at this time I think Partrick will be in a bad way & as
he has a letter from Generl Lockwood & athorety a wretin one two
from Govement thay aught to protect him & see that he getes his
writes   hoping you will attend to the mater for him & ceape me
out of the scrape as I am now very unpoperlor withe the peopel
W, N, B,

As I had not room to write you all I wonted to write you I am compeld to troble you with a few lines more now if you can get the Govement to cend you down with other offercers to investegate the mater I would be glad as you are acquanted with maney of the facts in the case & farther if shuch a investigation was to be made down in this contrey it mite alarm som of those hot headed Rebes & do som good it would be of benefit to the few that are loyal her & you know thare is few of them I am one & I hope I will not be her long as sune as you & T. B. Burch can get me a place I shall leave I dont hardly leave my home unless I leave it for a distance I hav no friends her but my famely & tharefor I cant fine aney consolation aney whare elce it seames to me that every thing is glume & despare with me I think it worst now than ever it has bin & it will continue to grow worst I think

Now my Dear Friend if you will put yourself to som troble to help me out in getting away from her & also in getting Partricks rights I will ever be under obligations to you & I am shure Partrick will feale the same towards you

when you com down you must be shure to call & see me as me & famely will be glad to see you give my best regardes to your famely & to T. B Burch if you meate with him & all inquiring friends

I hope you will write sune & cend the Papers of scoot & your opinion what he can do Partrick looks up to me as his only friend & I am looking up to you as my only friend to advise me about what aught to be dun Yours Respectfuly

ALS
Wm N. Burch

Wm. N. Burch to Cpt. Wm. H. Hogarth, 24 Jan. 1865, filed with Adjutant General 183 1865, Letters Received from the President, Executive Departments, & War Department Bureaus, RG 107 [L-330]. By an endorsement of January 28, General Henry H. Lockwood, commander of the 3rd Separate Brigade, 8th Army Corps, forwarded to the commander of the Middle Department and 8th Army Corps a copy of his own letter of January 13 (see doc. 156A, immediately above) and that of William Burch, "to the end that the same may be laid before the War Dept & justice done to this injured man." Other endorsements forwarded both letters to the Department of Washington, and thence to the War Department. As of April 1865, the War Department had taken no action in Scott's case, which, in the meantime, took a turn for the worse. On April 5, Lockwood informed General Christopher C. Augur, commander of the Department of Washington, "that [Waring] has possessed himself of all of Scott's crop, and refuses to allow him anything" – notwithstanding Waring's promise, made upon his release from arrest, to "deal liberally by" the black man. Scott had already appealed in person to General Augur, who considered the situation "a very hard one"; in response to Lockwood's letter, Augur once again called the attention of the War Department to Scott's case, hoping for "some plan . . . by which he may have justice rendered him." Augur's inquiry about the department's inaction elicited the explanation that the judge advocate general, to whom the case had been referred, had not returned the papers. (Brig. General Henry H. Lockwood to Maj. Gen. C. C. Augur, 5 Apr. 1865, filed with Adjutant General 183 1865, Letters Received from the President, Executive Departments, & War Department Bureaus, RG 107 [L-330]; Maj. Genl. C. C. Augur to Genl. Lockwood, 6 Apr. 186[5], Letters Received, ser. 4921, 3rd Separate Brigade, 8th Army Corps, RG 393 Pt. 2 No. 319 [C-1944].)

156C: Baltimore White Unionist to the Commander of the Department of Washington

Baltimore [*Md.*] Nov 14″ 1865

General Sometime in the arly part Last Spring I placed in the hands Brig General Henry S Lockwood some papers in connection with the case of Patrick Scott a Colored freedman against a traitor named Warring of Prince George County Md. General Lockwood went with me to Major General Wallace then commanding Mid Dept who forwarded the Papers to you Beeng in your Department since which time I have heard nothing of them

General this is an aggravated case   the Colored man was true to the goverment while warring was proven a traitor & sent to Fort Deleware   under the Promise of Protection from the goverment Scott worked hard raised a considerable crop   he has no protection but what the goverment may give him and it does not seem disposed to give him any   I may be wrong but it Looks like goverment in this case intends to Reward the traitor & punish the poor Loyal Negroe for it has released Warring & given him back his property allowing him to defraud the poor negroe out of one years Labor

will you be Kind enough to return me all the papers appertaining to scotts case so that I can place them in the hands of Major General Howard Comdg Freedmens Beureau   please answer   I am Sir your obdt Servt

ALS   William H Hogarth

William H. Hogarth to Major General Augur, 14 Nov. 1865, filed with Adjutant General 183 1865, Letters Received from the President, Executive Departments, & War Department Bureaus, RG 107 [L-330]. Beneath his signature Hogarth provided his address, 642 West Baltimore Street. Endorsements transmitted Hogarth's letter from the Department of Washington to the War Department, and thence to General Oliver O. Howard, commissioner of the Freedmen's Bureau. After linking it with earlier documents regarding Patrick Scott's case, Howard referred the file to the bureau's assistant commissioner for the District of Columbia (his jurisdiction included Prince George's County, Maryland), who, on December 20, 1865, appended the following endorsement: "The Military Authorities should be requested to compel Jno H. Waring to restore to Patrick Scott the crop raised by him and of which he was forcibly dispossessed, or to seize an amount of the crop raised this year by the said Waring sufficiently large to reimburse Scott for the loss he has sustained." Other endorsements: The final one returned the entire file to the Secretary of War; none of them provide any evidence regarding the ultimate disposition of Scott's claim.

157: Chaplain at Freedman's Hospital in Washington, D.C., to the District of Columbia Freedmen's Bureau Assistant Commissioner

[*Washington, D.C.*] June 13th, *1865*.
Sir. William Holland was a slave in Maryland also the wife— they have three children— Left Md. one year since— Was at Masons Island[1] from middle of June 1864 to September   The family were at this time engaged by Joseph Child of Millersville situated midway from Annapolis & Annapolis Junction 17 miles from the latter place   Mr. Child promised William $6 per month & his wife Jane $4— William left in February without settlement   Jane told him that Mr. C. said he was owing William $17— on his wages   William sent a letter to his wife on the third of April stating that he would come for her on the following Saturday   this letter was intercepted by Child who had watchers out and Child beat William badly with a club and after he had retreated from him a short distance fired at him the ball passing near his head   He was badly bruised and was taken to the Freedman's Hospital where he has been from May 1st for several weeks in consequence of the violent treatment received
   He is very anxious to recover his family   He believes there is due him $17—   He also states that there is due him for work done on Masons Island $20— about at $10— per month from middle of June to the first week of September following   William states that a hand on the place informed him that Child was active and virulent in opposition to the government   Very Respect^y Your most obed^t servant

Isaac Cross
P.S. William desires if practicable to accompany those who may be
sent for his family   I. C.

ALS

Chapn. Isaac Cross to Col. Jno. Eaton, 13 June 1865, Unregistered Letters
Received, ser. 457, DC Asst. Comr., RG 105 [A-9841]. Written on
Freedmen's Bureau letterhead. Neither a reply to the chaplain nor any order
respecting Holland's family has been found in the records of the assistant
commissioner.

1 Located in the Potomac River adjoining the District of Columbia, Mason's
Island had served in 1864 as a reception point for black refugees and a depot
from which both military and civilian employers hired black laborers. (See
above, doc. 77.)

158A: **Maryland White Unionist to the Freedmen's
Bureau Commissioner**

Prince Frederck Maryland   August 20" 1865
Major general Howard   Danuel Chase the barrer of this letter
requested me to say to you that he has five Children bound to therer
origeranal master. they ware set free by our state Constitution
which went in to effect on the first day of last november. he wants
the children himself. while I am writing about this matter I think I
will state to you how things is going on here in this County in
regard to the Condition of the darky who became free by the state
Constition. and as soon as they ware made free there former masters
Complaind to the orphans Court and had the Children bound by
said Court to themselves the masters, without regard to age sex or
Condition those that ware able to be of any service to there parrents.
without [even] there parrents Consent. when many of them Could
be of great service to there parrents. by helping to surport there
aged parrents. and so they have them so bound now. when there
parrents are entitled to ther severces. and there have been several
Cases where they have tried the Civil authorties to get them back
but in all of those Cases none have been lucky enough to have
Justice done them by such authority. for it is not Considerd popular
to do Justice here in this County where sesesh is rampant. no
Justice Could be meeted out to a darky because his skin is

black. that Commodity is reserved for there own seffesh
purposes. I have thought and still believe in order to have Justice
done to the Colord people of this County it would be well to have
established in this County a milatary Court and appoint some person
to see to there Condition and see that they are not Cheated out of
there labour as many of them will be under the pesant
Circumstances. this I write to you be cause I believe you have the
charge of there Condition. any information you may want I will
furnish you by addressing me at this office. Should you determin to
do anything in this Case please answer this letter and oblige your
humble servant.

ALS   Joseph Hall

Joseph Hall to Major General Howard, 20 Aug. 1865, Unregistered Letters
Received, ser. 457, DC Asst. Comr., RG 105 [A-9853]. For an affidavit by the
freedman, Daniel Chase, see document 158B, immediately below. In an earlier
letter to the Freedmen's Bureau commissioner, Hall had maintained that the
children bound out by the Calvert County Orphans Court immediately after
emancipation were "those that would hire for good wages," whereas the "young
and helpless" were left "to be taken care of by there parrents." Not only were the
parents thereby "Cheated of the servis of ther children," but they also lost "the
society of there Children, for in many Caces the Children have not the liberty to
go to see there parrents." Appeals to local civil authorities had been unavailing,
even when the parents could prove that, far from being unable to provide for
their children, they had already hired them out for wages before the binding
took place. What is more, parents who dared to protest the apprenticing of their
children had been arrested on charges of persuading apprentices to leave their
masters. (Joseph Hall to General Howard, 12 Aug. 1865, Unregistered Letters
Received, ser. 457, DC Asst. Comr., RG 105 [A-9853].)

158B: Affidavit of a Former Slave from Maryland

Washington, D.C. Aug. 24, 1865.
Danl. Chase of the City of Washington, being duty sworn states:
That he was formerly the slave of Virgil Gant, of Prince
Frederick, Calvert Co. Md., that when he left said Virgil Gant, in
1863, he left with him his five children, viz. Rachael Ann, aged 8,
Hanson, 7 – Sias & David (twins) 6 – & Caroline, 3 years, who,
about the time of the passage of the emancipation act, were bound
by the Orphans Court of Calvert Co. to the said Virgil Gant; &
further – that the said Gant has hired out to Mr. Danl. Bowen – the
boy Hanson, & "Sias," to Mr. Thos. Hutchins – he (Gant) to receive
their wages: that he went to Mr. Gants house in Prince Frederick,

the 19″ inst. and asked for his children, he wishing to bring them to Washington. He was refused possession of them: he further states that the children were bound without the Knowledge or consent of either himself or his wife—, the mother of the children: that his wife, Mina, the mother of the children went after them in Decembr 1864, as soon as she heard they were free, but was refused possession of them by Mr. Gant.

<table>
<tr><td>HDcSr</td><td></td><td>his</td></tr>
<tr><td></td><td>(Signed) Danl.</td><td>X Chase</td></tr>
<tr><td></td><td></td><td>mark</td></tr>
</table>

Affidavit of Danl. Chase, 24 Aug. 1865, enclosed in Col. John Eaton, Jr., to Maj. Genl. O. O. Howard, 18 Sept. 1865, Unregistered Letters Received, ser. 16, Washington Hdqrs., RG 105 [A-9674]. Sworn before an adjutant at the District of Columbia Freedmen's Bureau headquarters.

159A: **Maryland White Unionist to the District of Columbia Freedmen's Bureau Assistant Commissioner**

Prince Frederick [*Md.*] September 14′ 1865
General Howard or those having charge of freedmen. at Washington DC. I have been Called upon by Rindy M Allen the barrer of this. [she] [. . .] me to state to you her condition and situation in regard to her children. whis is as follows.

She has a boy which she had hired last Christmas for which she was drawing wages. besides the boy was Clothed and fed, but it seems some time after the boy was hired out by his mother. that Ira Young her former master complains to the orphans Court and the said Court bound the boy to him (young) the boy stayed with his employer about a month. Young then replevys the boy. and the Justice or something in shape of a human being called a Justice of the peace decided that the boy was the property of young, notwithstanding it was proved on trial that the boy was hired out by his mother and she geting wages for him. this man young treats the boy wors than a dog out to treated. he neither feeds or cloths the boy he does not get half enought to eat and no cloths but what his mother gives him.

Some time ago the boy left young and it was some weeks before he could find him but he found him at last. and on last Sunday young with two others found out where the boy was at and carred him home again and whiped him – the boy in an unhuman manner and still has him yet,. and I have stated in a former letter it is no use to appeal to the law here to have Justice done. in any Casese where a Colored person is to have or ought to have thre rights under the law. nor Can will it ever be any use as long as we have the officers of the that we now have. I sugusted in a former letter an establishment of a milatary court which is the only way that Justice can be done here now. as I before stated that the Colord people in this County. Can and would do very well if they Can have what they ought to have. that is to get there children un bound. or restored to them and have the privilege of hireing them or working them themselvs. in order that they can help now to surport there parrents in order that they may not be come a burthen opon the goverment. but if this state of thing is suffred to be Contued – some of them will be Compelled to leave ther native place for other quatrs and thus be come a burthen on the Goverment when they might home here in native place and be a use to themselves and to a great many white people whou will hire them and gave them good wages. and so all would be benefited. the Colord people ask of me to say that they ask the favor to interfare in ther behalf or appoint some person to do so. in order that they may be settled and know what to do. It may be that some person have or may state that what is stated here by me is not so. but all I ask is an examination and you will find what I have stated is not as bad as it is. it is to hoped that some thing will be done to have this matter investigated as I before stated any information wanted Concerning this affar Can be had by addressing Joseph Hall at this place

I forgot to state that this woman rindy is now. held to bail for court to be trid in about tow weeks for persuading this boy to leave young. which she never did but I would not be surprised if she will be Convicted be cause she probly may not be able to have justice done her. when she is not even gilty of any offence so you may know how justice is adminsterd here in this den of treason yours truly

Joseph Hall

Please ansur this

ALS

Joseph Hall to General Howard or those having charge of freedmen at Washington D.C., 14 Sept. 1865, #16 1865, Letters Received, ser. 456, DC Asst. Comr., RG 105 [A-9720]. Hall's rendition of the freedwoman's name was erroneous: Her son's surname was Allen, but hers was Smothers; and she evidently preferred Derinda to its diminutive form, Rindy. (See her affidavit, printed immediately below as doc. 159B.) On September 19, 1865, an adjutant at the headquarters of the District of Columbia Freedmen's Bureau assistant commissioner informed Hall that "[t]he woman sent here by you will have all possible under the circumstances done in her behalf" and suggested that her son might be released on a writ of habeas corpus. "It is to be hoped," concluded the adjutant, "that all will soon see the disadvantages of the policy, that [drives] labor elsewhere by its injustice." (Lieut. S. N. Clark to Joseph L. Hall, Esqre., 19 Sept. 1865, vol. 6, p. 79, Letters Sent, ser. 449, DC Asst. Comr., RG 105 [A-9720].)

159B: **Affidavit of a Maryland Freedwoman**

District of Columbia, City of Washington 18th day of Sept. 1865. Mrs. Derinda Smothers, being duly sworn, states, that shortly after the passage of the emancipation act, she hired her son Jas. M. Allen, aged about 14 years, to Mr. Frederick Greyson, but with the understanding that he was to remain with his former master Ira Young, until christmas. That Mr. Young told them that if they remained after that time, he would not pay them for their work. – That her son left the said Young, at the same time that the others of his slaves left. – That the boy went to Mr. Greyson,s to work, & that Deponent recd, from Mr. Greyson pay for his services. That Ira Young took possession of the boy, – claiming to have had him bound to him, though Deponent has never given her consent to anything of the Kind. That during the past spring the boy ran away from Mr. Young – on account of ill usage – but was afterward caught & taken back. That the said Young stripped him, tied him up & beat him in a most brutal manner. That Deponent was arrested at the instance of said Young & put in jail – because she would not tell where the boy was, which she failed to do – as she *did not* Know where he was. – That she was released on $500.00 bail – Mr. Gilbert Fowler going security for her appearance.

HDcSr

(Signed)   her
Derinda X Smothers
mark

Affidavit of Derinda Smothers, 18 Sept. 1865, enclosed in Col. John Eaton, Jr., to Maj. Genl. O. O. Howard, 18 Sept. 1865, Unregistered Letters Received, ser. 16, Washington Hdqrs., RG 105 [A-9674]. Sworn before an adjutant at the District of Columbia Freedmen's Bureau headquarters.

160: Register of Wills in Dorchester County, Maryland, to the
Headquarters of the Maryland Freedmen's Bureau
Assistant Commissioner; Enclosing a Table

Register's Office – Cambridge Md., Feby. 22nd. 1867 –
Sir, Yours of 18th. inst., requesting the number of negro
apprentices in this County &c., was duly received –
Annexed you will find a statement giving the desired
information, with the sex and the number bound in each year –
The whole number legally apprenticed is, you will observe, 274 –
but I will suggest that a very small part of them are in the service
and custody of their Masters – certainly not over one third – Some
of them are dead, some of the older ones entered the Army, some
have left the state, and very many of them have left their Masters
and either live with their parents or hire out to suit themselves, and
very few of the Masters will make any effort or go to any expence to
recover the service of any such apprentice – Nearly one half (111) of
the whole number were bound in the year 1864, just after the
adoption of the new Constitution, now I know that a very small
percentage of them ever went to their Masters, or were claimed after
such binding, as most of the Masters were well aware that there was
but little profit in attempting to hold them when they did not want
to remain – Respectfully &c –

ALS

E. W. LeCompte

[*Enclosure*] [*Cambridge, Md.*] Feby. 22nd, 1867 –
List of negro apprentices in Dorchester County Maryland, to
date –

	Male.	Female.
1852	3	1
1853	5	
1854	6	
1855	10	2
1856	4	
1857	18	12
1858	26	3
1859	11	4
1860	14	4
1861	8	2
1862	1	
1863	1	
1864	73	38
1865	6	5

$$
\begin{array}{rr}
1866 & 15 \quad 2 \\
\underline{1867} & \underline{0 \quad 0} \\
& 201 \;-\; 73 \\
& 201 \\
\text{Total} & \underline{274}
\end{array}
$$

HD

E. W. Lecompte to Lieut. E. C. Knower, 22 Feb. 1867, enclosing "List of negro apprentices in Dorchester County Maryland," 22 Feb. 1867, L-7 1867, Letters Received, ser. 1962, MD & DE Asst. Comr., RG 105 [A-9620]. In March 1867, in response to a similar request for the number of "colored Apprentices" in his jurisdiction, the register of wills for Queen Anne County, Maryland, claimed that it was impossible to provide the number "who *now* bear the relation of Apprentices." Since the registration of their indentures, many black apprentices had died, "absconded," or enlisted in the Union army. Moreover, an unknown number "were abandoned by their masters in consequence of the military orders of Gen. Wallace, a short time subsequently to the adoption of the present Constitution." Without revealing how many of the indentures dated from the weeks immediately following emancipation, he reported that a total of 149 black children had been apprenticed in the county since November 1, 1864–of which, he estimated, "the number that now sustain that relation is not . . . more than 75." (W. A. Johnson to Lieut. Ed. C. Knower, 6 Mar. 1867, J-15 1867, Letters Received, ser. 1962, MD & DE Asst. Comr., RG 105 [A-9620]; for Wallace's order, see above, doc. 142.)

CHAPTER 5
Missouri

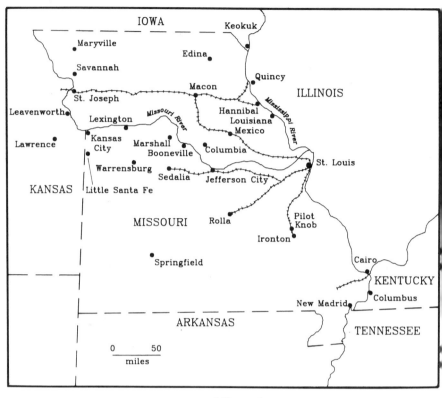

Missouri

5

Missouri

ALTHOUGH SLAVERY had been virtually destroyed in Missouri long before its formal abolition in January 1865, free labor replaced it neither swiftly nor surely. Instead, the new labor system advanced along a tortuous and violent path. With bondage legal until the closing months of the Civil War and federal authorities reluctant to alienate proslavery unionists, free labor rested on precarious footing.[1]

In Missouri, as elsewhere in the Union-occupied South, the employment of black men by the army advanced free labor. After the opening months of war, however, an absence of large-scale operations restricted demand for military laborers. A plentiful supply of white workers further reduced the role of military employment in transforming slaves into wage laborers. The army's use of black manpower increased dramatically once the recruitment of black soldiers began in 1863. But the new reliance on black men did not induce federal authorities to provide for the soldiers' families as they did in the occupied Confederacy. Commanders of the Department of the Missouri established no government farms or other federally sponsored agricultural operations. They organized only one contraband camp, at St. Louis, and it originated not to feed and shelter fugitive slaves from Missouri, but to care for refugees from Arkansas. Elsewhere in the state, military officials refused to assist destitute ex-slaves and sometimes collaborated with civil authorities to expel them from the garrisoned towns where they had taken refuge. Aside from a limited supervision of hiring arrangements in the St. Louis area, they rarely sponsored free labor. The only systematic effort to secure employment for black Missourians required their departure from the state.

If federal authorities did little to advance free labor, political circumstances also obstructed its development. Internecine political conflict engendered a local civil war within the national Civil War. White Missourians splintered into contentious factions of outright secessionists, rebel sympathizers, fence-sitters, and unionists of every stripe. Some unionists predicated their loyalty upon the preservation of slav-

---

[1] In this essay, quotations and statements of fact that appear without footnotes are drawn from the documents included in the chapter. On emancipation in Missouri, see *Freedom*, ser. 1, vol. 1: chap. 7. On the state's wartime politics, see William E. Parrish, *Turbulent Partnership: Missouri and the Union, 1861–1865* (Columbia, Mo., 1963).

ery; others favored gradual, compensated emancipation; still others advocated immediate and uncompensated abolition so as to hurry the state toward a free-labor future. A complex struggle raged in courthouse and statehouse, spilling over into demoralizing guerrilla warfare. Murderous attacks upon former slaves accompanied threats against employers who dared to hire them. In large stretches of the countryside, the *"rebellion in the brush"* made it impossible to reestablish agricultural production on any terms.

In Missouri as a whole, free labor greatly overshadowed slavery. On the eve of the Civil War, the state's 115,000 slaves accounted for less than 10 percent of the population, a smaller proportion than in every slave state but Delaware. Of the slave states that remained loyal to the Union, Missouri also had the smallest number of black people who were free. Nearly all black Missourians were enslaved. Only 3,600 free blacks were to be found in the entire state, more than half of them in St. Louis County.

However minor its place in most of the state, slavery dominated the rich agricultural economies of the Missouri River Valley and the Mississippi River counties north of St. Louis. Slaveholders in these regions owned three-quarters of the state's slaves. In the more recently settled western segment of the Missouri Valley, where hemp was the chief commercial crop, slavery expanded during the 1850s, gaining new adherents. The dramatic struggle between pro- and antislavery forces in neighboring Kansas galvanized slaveholders in western Missouri. Their counterparts in the tobacco-producing counties to the east, where slavery had deeper roots, remained equally committed to bound labor.

Even on slavery's firmest terrain, slaves constituted a minority of the population, exceeding one-third in only a single county. Most of the state was settled by small farmers, few of whom owned any slaves at all. In southeastern Missouri, slavery was important only in a few counties along the Mississippi River. It was insignificant throughout the sparsely populated southwest, except in the vicinity of Springfield. The same was true of the northernmost counties. Moreover, Missouri slaveholders generally owned just a handful of slaves. In the Missouri Valley, the region of largest slaveholdings, most slaves lived on farms, not plantations. In only one county were as many as half of them held in units of twenty or more.[2]

A marginal institution in much of the countryside, slavery had become entirely peripheral to the economy of St. Louis, whose spectacu-

---

[2] For population figures, the geographical distribution of slavery, and the size of slaveholdings, see Harrison Anthony Trexler, *Slavery in Missouri, 1804–1865* (Baltimore, 1914), pp. 10–18, 225–26; U.S., Census Office, 8th Census, *Population of the United States in 1860* (Washington, 1864), pp. 286–87; U.S., Census Office, 8th Census, *Agriculture of the United States in 1860* (Washington, 1864), pp. 233–34.

lar antebellum growth rested upon a heavy influx of European – chiefly German – immigrants. In 1860, fully 60 percent of the city's inhabitants were foreign-born, the highest proportion in the United States. A thriving center of commerce and industry, St. Louis boasted nearly 12,000 manufacturing workers. With free labor fueling expansion, the city's 1,500 slaves accounted for less than 1 percent of the population. Free-black people slightly outnumbered the slaves, but they were scarcely more important to the city's economy.[3]

A bastion of free labor in a slave state, St. Louis was home to the state's strongest antislavery sentiment. At the opening of the Civil War, the city's unionists played a crucial role in overpowering the pro-Southern state government and establishing a provisional government in its place. For several months, Missouri saw significant military activity within its borders. In February 1862, however, federal forces drove the Confederate army into Arkansas, sending the governor and his adherents into permanent exile. Thereafter Missouri's military significance shrank. Most of the Union army decamped for campaigns in the Confederacy. Although Southern cavalry periodically raided the state and guerrillas plagued much of the countryside, Missouri remained well behind Union lines for the remainder of the war.

With only a small federal force left to occupy the state, military commanders concentrated on defending St. Louis and its huge quartermaster's depot, guarding the railroads that radiated from the city, and protecting navigation along the Missouri and Mississippi rivers. Union military control seldom extended far beyond garrisoned points. What is more, most of the occupying troops were not volunteers from the free states, but regiments of the Missouri State Militia, a special force authorized by the federal government, or units of Enrolled Missouri Militia temporarily called into active service. Both organizations consisted entirely of Missourians, led by Missouri officers. Although their views on slavery varied as widely as those of unionists in the state at large, few members of either militia countenanced military interference with the institution. Many of them, especially in the Enrolled Militia, zealously defended slaveholders and their interests.[4]

As in the other border states, the Lincoln administration and its principal military commanders pledged support for local unionists, including slaveholders, and respect for civil authority, including the enforcement of slavery. Long after federal troops had been forbidden to

---

[3] Trexler, *Slavery in Missouri*, pp. 19, 226; Michael Fellman, *Inside War: The Guerrilla Conflict in Missouri during the American Civil War* (New York, 1989), p. 8.

[4] The Missouri State Militia was created for service solely within the state but was paid and equipped by the federal government. For a brief account of the establishment of the Missouri State Militia (M.S.M.) and the mobilization of the Enrolled Missouri Militia (E.M.M.), see *Official Records*, ser. 1, vol. 13, pp. 7–12. For an example of conflict between free-state volunteers and the militia, see *Freedom*, ser. 1, vol. 1: doc. 167.

return runaways to their owners and the government had committed itself to ending slavery in the Confederacy, Union officers in Missouri reiterated the themes. General Samuel R. Curtis, who assumed command of the Department of the Missouri in September 1862, had to accommodate his own antislavery convictions to the legality of bondage and the policy of his superiors. Citing the Second Confiscation Act, he instructed his provost marshals to issue "free papers" to slaves who escaped from disloyal owners, but fugitive slaves claimed by unionists were another matter. "*Bona fide* Union men must be treasured as friends," whatever their views on emancipation, ordered Curtis in March 1863. "While [slavery] exists we must tolerate it, and we must allow the civil authorities to dispose of the question." On another occasion, he insisted that the policy of military noninterference extended to permitting the forcible recapture of runaway slaves from army camps. "The state authorities must not be prevented from exercising force if they do not disturb the peace of Camp. Let alone is our duty. . . . It is a personal matter between the master & slave which we have nothing to do with."[5]

Far from solving the vexed question of slavery, the noninterference policy guaranteed continual confrontation. With civil officials zealously enforcing state laws, fugitive slaves stood in constant danger of reenslavement. Successful flight to Union lines did not guarantee safety. Sheriffs and other local officers entered federal camps in search of fugitives, sometimes even attempting to recapture men who had been hired for military labor. The attempts occasionally succeeded, and even when they failed they caused so much commotion that some military employers rid themselves of potential "annoyance" by dismissing ex-slave laborers.

Such decisions were feasible because the Union army in Missouri seldom needed black laborers. The quartermaster's depot at St. Louis, which required the largest force, drew principally upon the thousands of white workers who had done the bulk of the city's manual labor before the war. Military employers in St. Louis also hired white refugees who had been driven from the countryside by guerrilla warfare and Confederate raids. They never employed black men in large numbers. At smaller posts throughout the state, soldiers and white civilians performed most of the everyday tasks of the army, although former slaves sometimes toiled alongside them.[6]

At times, military authorities found it expedient to exploit the labor of slaves and ex-slaves. A quartermaster at Jefferson City reported in April 1864 that he had an "excelent set of contrabands" whom he considered "far more prefreble" than soldiers for work as teamsters – not only

[5] *Freedom*, ser. 1, vol. 1: docs. 172, 178n.; *Official Records*, ser. 1, vol. 22, pt. 2, pp. 134–35.
[6] On the St. Louis workers, see P. M. Gen'l Bernard G. Farrar et al. to Maj. General S. R. Curtis, 22 Aug. 1862, #3036, Letters Received, ser. 4676, Army of the Southwest, RG 393 Pt. 2 No. 299 [C-246].

more conscientious but also cheaper. The commander of the District of Southeast Missouri employed at least 220 black laborers on fortifications at Pilot Knob. When military necessity demanded, local commanders also called for the impressment of slaves, first taking "*Sesesh Negroes*" who belonged to rebel owners. But the availability of other workers – whose employment engendered no political opposition – usually made federal officials reluctant to mobilize black laborers on a large scale.[7]

Former slaves who worked as military laborers received both wages and rations in return. However, federal authorities in Missouri generally refused to feed or otherwise care for fugitive slaves not employed by the army. Because bondage remained legal, they reasoned, slaveholders were responsible for the support of their slaves. Questioned by a subordinate about appropriate relief measures for destitute fugitive slaves, General Egbert B. Brown, commander of the District of Central Missouri, directed that "[s]ubsistence will be issued only to persons in the service"; "we have nothing to do with feeding any other parties." Runaway slaves "can return to their homes and be provided for there," he advised another officer in September 1863; "there is no necessity for [government relief]."

Developments in neighboring states rendered these policies increasingly anomalous. With the North committed to emancipation in the seceded states, new practices respecting the labor and support of former slaves took shape in Union-occupied areas adjoining Missouri. In Arkansas, slaves liberated by the Second Confiscation Act and the Emancipation Proclamation gathered in a contraband camp at Helena. Federal authorities established similar camps at Cairo, Illinois, at Columbus, Kentucky, and at Island 10, Tennessee, all proximate to southeastern Missouri.[8] A provost marshal at Columbus went so far as to seize a rebel-owned plantation on the Missouri side of the river and settle eight freedpeople upon it "for the purpose of raising a crop."

By the spring of 1863, federal efforts to provide for former slaves in the occupied Confederacy were expanding into Missouri. In early March, the Union commander in eastern Arkansas, desperate to relieve overcrowding at Helena, shipped nearly 500 freedpeople to St. Louis. Supervised by Chaplain Samuel W. Sawyer, they arrived unannounced and unexpected. Overriding his own reservations and those of local unionists, who feared the refugees might be reenslaved, General Curtis

---

7 On the black laborers at Pilot Knob, see *Official Records*, ser. 1, vol. 22, pt. 2, pp. 567–68; ser. 1, vol. 34, pt. 2, pp. 434–35. On the impressment of slaves, see *Official Records*, ser. 1, vol. 8, pt. 1, pp. 463–64; Special Order No. 41, Head Quarters Dist. N.M. RR., 7 Mar. 1862, vol. 207/467 DMo, p. 28, General & Special Orders, Dist. of the North MO Railroad, RG 393 Pt. 3 [C-7700]; Major T. A. Switzler to Majr. L. J. Barnes, 6 Sept. 1862, General & Special Orders Received & Other Records, ser. 4687, Army of the Southwest, RG 393 Pt. 2 No. 299 [C-7568].

8 On the contraband camps at Helena, Cairo, Columbus, and Island 10, see below, docs. 205–6, 208; *Freedom*, ser. 1, vol. 3: docs. 152, 157–58, 160–61.

decided to permit the "shipping & unloading [of] contrabands" under military protection. He quartered them in an abandoned hotel – in effect, the first contraband camp in the state – and directed Sawyer to hire them to civilian employers. Within weeks, several hundred more former slaves arrived from Helena, and others followed. Sawyer had no difficulty finding work for most of them, either in St. Louis or in Iowa, Illinois, and Kansas. Indeed, applications from would-be employers outnumbered the refugees, leading Sawyer to envision St. Louis as "a 'contraband' Intelligence Office for the whole North West." Aided by successive superintendents and by the St. Louis Ladies' Contraband Relief Society, an estimated 2,500 freedpeople had been sent to the free states by midsummer. Although nearly all of them hailed from Arkansas and Mississippi, not Missouri, the appointment of a superintendent of contrabands, the provision of temporary housing and rations by military officials, and the transportation of former slaves to the free states established important precedents.[9]

If few Missouri slaves reached free territory under official auspices, a great many did so on their own initiative. Thousands fled to Kansas, continuing an exodus begun during the border wars of the 1850s. There they found work with farmers or in the towns of Lawrence and Leavenworth. Many of them became permanent residents. A few purchased plots of land. In similar fashion but much smaller numbers, slaves in northern Missouri passed into Iowa, while those along the Mississippi River crossed into Illinois.[10]

The recruitment of black soldiers in neighboring territory provided Missouri slaves with further inducements to leave the state. From as early as August 1862, men who reached Kansas could enlist in a black regiment forming (without War Department sanction) under the supervision of General James H. Lane. In July 1863, Colonel William A. Pile received authority to recruit black men in Missouri for regiments organizing in Arkansas, provided he restrict his efforts to freemen and the slaves of disloyal owners. The following month, General Thomas Ewing, commander of the District of the Border, began inducting men of the same classes into Kansas regiments (with War Department approval) and relocating their families to that state. The opening of recruitment rendezvous at Keokuk, Iowa, and Quincy, Illinois, precipitated an exodus of slave men from northeastern Missouri, often accompanied by their kin. By early 1864, some 400 black women and chil-

---

[9]   In addition to the relevant documents in this chapter, see *Freedom*, ser. 1, vol. 3: doc. 161.
[10] In addition to the relevant documents in this chapter, see testimony of Captain R. J. Hinton before the American Freedmen's Inquiry Commission, 14 Dec. 1863, filed with O-328 1863, Letters Received, ser. 12, RG 94 [K-213]; Richard B. Sheridan, "From Slavery in Missouri to Freedom in Kansas: The Influx of Black Fugitives and Contrabands into Kansas, 1854–1865," *Kansas History* 12 (Spring 1989): 28–47.

dren, the majority of them relatives of black soldiers, had taken up residence in Quincy.[11]

Such flight entailed grave risk. Antebellum laws forbidding common carriers to transport slaves without their owners' permission made it difficult for fugitives to secure passage on railroads or ferryboats. Slaves traveling overland without military protection were vulnerable to recapture by their masters or attack by guerrillas. "[T]hey dare not travel by land," noted General Ewing, "lest they be murdered on the road." Most of the state's slaves lived too far from free soil to attempt so dangerous an escape.[12]

Though restricted to a minority of Missouri's black men and confined to the margins of the state, the early efforts at recruitment sped the disintegration of slavery. Not only did significant numbers of slaves flee toward rendezvous along the borders, but a few recruiting parties visited farms in the interior. Some recruiters inevitably ignored instructions to refuse applicants whose owners were loyal to the Union. As a result, the enlistment of black men created labor shortages in certain areas. In one settlement, a slaveholder reported in June 1863, the grain crops stood "rotting in the Fields for want of Harvest hands" after recruiters "stripped" the neighborhood. Although desperate farmers were offering wages well above the going rate – sometimes as high as $3 per day – hired laborers "[could] not be got."[13]

Over the objections of conservative unionists, who lambasted enlistment as a "d-mb-d abolition Scheme to steal negroes," federal authorities in November 1863 extended military recruitment to all black men in Missouri, without regard to their owners' political standing. In the months that followed, they enlisted by the thousands. By the end of the war, more than 8,300 black Missourians – nearly two-fifths of the state's black men of military age – had joined the federal army.[14]

Although the soldiers were sent out of the state as soon as they could be organized into regiments, the repercussions of their enlistment spread through the countryside. Some farmers and planters who had lost laborers to the army increased the work loads of their remaining slaves, forcing women and children to undertake arduous tasks customarily reserved for men. Others ejected the families of black soldiers.

[11] On recruitment in Kansas in 1862, see *Freedom*, ser. 2: pp. 44–45, and docs. 12–15. On later recruitment in states adjoining Missouri, see, in addition to the relevant documents in this chapter, *Freedom*, ser. 2: pp. 187–88, and docs. 85–86; John Wood et al. to Hon. O. H. Browning, 5 Jan. 1864, Letters Received, 29th USCI, Regimental Books & Papers USCT, RG 94 [G-305].

[12] *Freedom*, ser. 1, vol. 1: doc. 183; *Freedom*, ser. 2: doc. 85.

[13] *Freedom*, ser. 2: docs. 84, 86.

[14] *Freedom*, ser. 1, vol. 1: doc. 188; *Freedom*, ser. 2: pp. 12, 188–90, and docs. 84–96; John W. Blassingame, "The Recruitment of Negro Troops in Missouri during the Civil War," *Missouri Historical Review* 58 (Apr. 1964): 326–38.

Now that "his men were all gone," one master reportedly informed his slaves, "he could not, and would not support the women." Eviction became a frequent occurrence during the winter of 1863–1864, as slaveholders relieved themselves of the responsibility and expense of supporting their slaves through the slack months of the agricultural year.[15]

Full-scale enlistment therefore increasingly brought into Union lines not only black soldiers but also their families and other black refugees. At first, military authorities dealt with the influx of women and children by reiterating the oft-stated policy that slaveholders should be made to support their slaves, sparing the government the burden of doing so. But against a backdrop of widespread eviction and abuse of the kin and friends of black volunteers, that policy seemed increasingly untenable, if not inhumane.

In St. Louis, the expansion of black recruitment formalized the involvement of the federal government in the welfare of former slaves. General John M. Schofield, who had replaced General Curtis as department commander, ordered the establishment of a new contraband camp at Benton Barracks, on the outskirts of the city, transferring to its quarters the freedpeople previously quartered at the Missouri Hotel. Fugitive slaves from the countryside were directed to Benton Barracks, where a superintendent oversaw their care and assisted them in finding employment, either locally or in the free states. Between the fall of 1863 and the end of the war thousands passed through the camp. Within its confines, disease and debility exacted a fearful toll. Appalling death rates plagued the installation. Survivors generally remained only briefly before leaving to search for work or being hired out by the superintendent. Of the 947 freedpeople who arrived at Benton Barracks between mid-January and late March 1864, 330 had by the end of March "taken the responsibility of seeking places for them selves," 234 had been hired out "to *loyal* responsible parties," and 101 had died. Only 268 remained on hand, 143 in quarters and 125 in hospital. Like its counterparts elsewhere in the Union-occupied South, the Benton Barracks contraband camp served as a long-term residence chiefly for the aged, sick, and infirm.

The relief and employment measures instituted at Benton Barracks suited the special circumstances of St. Louis, with its large local demand for free labor, easy access to the free states by river and rail, and security from guerrilla raids. Conditions elsewhere were far less advantageous. Whereas the economy of St. Louis boomed as a result of wartime trade and manufacturing, agricultural production languished in much of the countryside. Union foraging parties stripped farms and planta-

---

[15] On increased work loads, see, in addition to the relevant document in this chapter, *Freedom*, ser. 2: doc. 91. On eviction, see *Freedom*, ser. 1, vol. 1: docs. 191–92; *Freedom*, ser. 2: doc. 298.

tions of food, provender, and livestock. Rebel irregulars and civilian bushwhackers terrorized the populace. The charred remains of houses and outbuildings bore witness to the insecurity of life and property that made farmers afraid to put in crops. Frustrated in their efforts to suppress outlaws, federal officials forced the total evacuation of some localities whose inhabitants were suspected of harboring guerrillas. Along the Kansas-Missouri border, reported one officer in March 1864, it was "unsafe for a man, either Union or rebel, to live away from the immediate vicinity of the military stations." Because of guerrilla depredations, farmers in central Missouri complained, "[w]e have not been able to raise scarcely any crops for three years."[16]

Proslavery guerrillas particularly targeted former slaves working as wage laborers, as well as the farmers who employed them. Slaveholders joined or collaborated with bushwhackers to recapture fugitive slaves and dissuade would-be employers. In the hemp-growing region along the Missouri River, fugitive slaves who had gathered in the town of Lexington would "not hire out to the farmers here for fear of being taken by their masters." In the "bootheel" of southeastern Missouri, guerrillas vowed "that there shall not be any farms cultivated Or carried on by Contrabands labour," intimidating farmers who had planned to work land with hired freedpeople. Regulators in a northeastern county "[swore] that free negros shall not be permitted to stay in this Community." They paid nocturnal visits to "certain Citizens who had free negro's hired. and with force and threats drove off the negros."

In addition to extralegal coercion, slaveholders commanded legal means to obstruct the development of free labor. State and local laws prohibited the hiring of a slave without the owner's consent, and slaveholders threatened to prosecute anyone who violated them. The planting season of 1864 found farmers near Marshall "anxious to procure all the labor they can possibly get" from among the former slaves congregated in the town, but "deterred from hiring these negroes for fear of being Indicted by the Grand Jury." Masters and mistresses refused to reclaim the fugitive slaves "but object to any ones hiring them." Lawsuits brought by putative owners demonstrated that the threats were not idle. Fearful of legal action or vigilante attack, many short-handed farmers dared not employ black workers, however much they might have liked to.

Nevertheless, a number of former slaves overcame such obstacles and negotiated private free-labor arrangements. In some places, freedpeople who had fled their owners bargained openly with prospective employers. Slaveholders in Washington County sought the forcible enlistment of bondsmen who had "gone to work for them Selves." Ex-slave men in the town of Louisiana, grumbled a local unionist, refused either to enlist in the army or to "hire themselves out & their master cannot & dare not reclaim them." Because it was the "same with women & Boys," he added, "many of our Farmers have a good harvest & . . . no Hands to save it." The threat that the men might enlist if not induced to remain at home drove many slaveholders to negotiate with their own slaves. According to one report in the summer of 1864, owners had made "extraordinary efforts . . . to retain them in agricultural pursuits." Some offered shares of the crop; others, cash wages. One provost marshal explained the decline in black enlistments by noting that "[w]ages is high and demand for hands keep the negroes out of the Army." Yet such informal free-labor bargains were by no means universal. The legality of slavery and the terrors of guerrilla warfare limited their extent and significance. Moreover, few slaveholders who had lost their able-bodied male slaves showed much inclination to negotiate with the women, children, and old people who remained. For such unfortunates, eviction was a more likely prospect.[17]

With opportunities for free labor so limited, fugitive slaves continued to seek refuge in towns garrisoned by Union troops, especially those along the Missouri River and the railroad lines. Military authorities grappled with a growing problem of relief. Recruiting officers took their pick of the men, leaving the rest to be supported by the government. Destitute, frequently ill, and often unable to find work, they crowded into outbuildings, alleys, and hastily constructed shanties on the outskirts of town. Their presence raised a hue and cry from white residents, who demanded that federal authorities rid them of their unwanted neighbors.

Military officers stationed in the towns generally sympathized with the complaints of the white populace, but they disagreed about what should be done. Some restated the shopworn policy of turning fugitive slaves out of the lines and forcing their owners to support them. Others, more realistic about the extent of slavery's dissolution, proposed to deport them from the state. In March 1864, after civil authorities in Sedalia adopted an ordinance requiring the removal of all freedpeople, General Egbert B. Brown sought permission to transport them to the Kansas border. General William S. Rosecrans, who had assumed command of the Department of the Missouri in January, approved the transfer. Soon Brown urged a more general deportation of black people from towns and army posts in central Missouri, coupled with the expulsion of those who remained. Thus "distributed about the country," he suggested, "[they] will be able to make a subsistence by their labor which is much needed."

[17] In addition to the relevant document in this chapter, see 1st Liut. A. N. Grissom to Liut. Col. C. W. Marsh, 20 Mar. 1864, Letters Received, ser. 2786, Provost Marshal General, Dept. of the MO, RG 393 Pt. 1 [C-196]; *Freedom*, ser. 1, vol. 1: doc. 194; *Freedom*, ser. 2: doc. 96.

General William A. Pile, the superintendent of black recruitment in Missouri, denounced Brown's plan. The families of black soldiers deserved better, he believed, and the country had an obligation to them. Abandoning them to fend for themselves—whether in Missouri or Kansas—left them "the prey of bad men, with no redress for their wrongs or means of collecting their wages through either the civil or military authorities." Pile urged that unemployed freedpeople be forwarded to the contraband camp at Benton Barracks, where they could be housed and fed, their children could attend school, and, given the local demand for domestic servants, all the able-bodied could easily obtain work with "*loyal* and *humane* employers."[18]

Ignoring such objections, Rosecrans approved Brown's proposal, authorizing him to "make such removals as he may deem best for the interest of the public service." In late June 1864, Brown began by ordering the transfer from Warrensburg of "all *vagrant* and *unemployed Negroes.*" Implementation of the removal policy only worsened the exslaves' condition. Taken to Little Santa Fe, on the Kansas border, the deported freedpeople were not only barred by Kansas troops from entering that state but also prohibited from going elsewhere in Missouri. Several hundred refugees languished with scant food and clothing and no medical attention, amid an outbreak of smallpox. Nevertheless, General Brown continued to send additional people to the wretched settlement.

Even in the St. Louis area, where former slaves had the greatest opportunity for free-labor employment, superintendents of contrabands despaired of providing for all their charges. The high cost of food and housing made it difficult for able-bodied adults with few dependents to make ends meet; for those disabled by age or infirmity and those with large families to support, the obstacles were insurmountable. Drawing upon connections with churches, benevolent societies, and personal acquaintances throughout the Midwest, the superintendents found employment in Iowa, Illinois, and elsewhere for hundreds of Missouri slaves who had escaped to St. Louis. Only by leaving the state could they obtain both security from reenslavement and a means of self-support.

During the final months of 1864, an upsurge in the number of refugees from the countryside, most of whom were white, impelled military officials to assume a responsibility for relief that they had previously resisted. Intensified guerrilla warfare in the spring and summer set the stage for a Confederate raid, led by General Sterling Price, during September and October. The invaders were eventually driven back into Arkansas, but not before reaching the Missouri River and wreaking havoc in the southern half of the state. The guerrilla attacks

---

[18] In addition to the relevant documents in this chapter, see *Freedom*, ser. 1, vol. 1: doc. 191; *Freedom*, ser. 2: doc. 94.

and Price's raid uprooted thousands of rural Missourians, who sought shelter and protection at federal posts across the state.[19] At St. Louis, where the refugee population soared, superintendents of contrabands increasingly cared for destitute white as well as black people, and General Rosecrans ordered the construction of barracks for the new arrivals. Near the end of the year, his successor, General Grenville M. Dodge, established a "refugee bureau" to oversee the issue of rations throughout the state.

Government assistance, Dodge believed, should be extended only to "unfortunates" who "have been driven from their homes, and for the time being deprived of the means of making a support"; it should continue only "until by proper effort they can earn their own living." In view of the "existing demand for labor," he declared, no able-bodied man or woman "will be permitted to share the Government charity." He admonished superintendents of refugees to "scrutinize and examine all applicants for aid, . . . to see that the Government is not imposed upon by imposters, vagrants, idle loungers, and loafers."[20] Such strictures notwithstanding, the more systematic issue of rations that resulted from Dodge's order marked a significant expansion of military responsibility for civilians displaced by the war. Although it was the large increase of white refugees that spurred the new measures, former slaves occasionally shared the benefits. For all recipients, black and white, suspicion and niggardly levels of assistance characterized the army's provision of relief.

Events of early 1865 heartened those who foresaw a new era of free labor in Missouri. In January, a state constitutional convention abolished slavery, dislodging the most fundamental roadblock. Military authorities and officials of the Lincoln administration moved quickly to rescind martial law and restore the legitimacy of Missouri's civil government and courts. These developments, together with Union military successes on distant battlefields, seemed to portend peace and prosperity, as free labor rejuvenated a state blighted by slavery and devastated by internecine war.

But if emancipation cleared away the most formidable obstacle to free labor, others remained. In many parts of the state, particularly the Missouri River counties, guerrilla activity intensified. Former slaveholders unwilling to concede freedom mobilized outlaws to enforce both the obsolete slave code and breaches of customary practice. One bushwhacker had reportedly been "instigated by the late slave owners to hang or shoot every negro he can find absent from the old plantation." The "reign of terror" deterred landowners and laborers from entering into new working arrangements. "Many [farmers] are now

---

[19] On conditions among the refugees, see *Official Records*, ser. 1, vol. 41, pt. 4, p. 959.
[20] *Official Records*, ser. 1, vol. 41, pt. 4, pp. 944–45.

ready to hire men and women for wages" or shares of the crop, reported a resident of Columbia, and other landowners had arranged to rent their land to former slaves. But fear of guerrilla attacks kept the freedpeople crowded into towns and army posts. Despite the great need for ex-slaves as agricultural laborers, another observer noted, "many of their former masters refuse to give them employment and others who woul be wiling to employ them are afrade to do so."

With mounted troops in short supply, federal authorities seemed powerless to curb the violence. A white inhabitant of guerrilla-ravaged Boone County suggested that companies of black militia be organized to protect the freedpeople, but few of his fellow citizens looked favorably upon the presence of armed black men. A local military officer pronounced the proposal "entirely inexpedient." Acknowledging that the freedpeople "[would] not go to the country for fear of the bushwhackers," he saw no solution but their removal to other states "where they could be employed."

In response to "the wicked barbarity of the late Masters & Mistresses" and the resulting concentration of former slaves in garrisoned towns, General Clinton B. Fisk, commander of the District of North Missouri, sought new homes for the freedpeople of Boone and neighboring counties. Himself a Missourian, Fisk believed that "[w]e ought not to spare a single pound of our industrial element. We need to import rather than deport manuel labor." Nevertheless, by March 1865 he was transporting freedpeople to Kansas, Iowa, and Illinois. He also appointed an agent to encourage the migration of ex-slaves to Andrew and Nodaway counties, in the northwest corner of Missouri. Although many farmers in that region were reportedly ready to "avail themselves of Colored help," advocates warned that forming public committees to promote the scheme "would produce an unnecessary Excitement." Fisk's agent estimated that one-third of the citizens opposed the introduction of black laborers "very ambitiously." "[T]hey threatened to shoot me if I did not leave the country," he reported, "and otherwise to force away at the point of the Bayonett any *Immigration* I might make to that country."[21]

In other rural neighborhoods where slavery had never been important, guerrillas mobilized to expel the few resident black people and prevent others from settling. Farmers who introduced black laborers into previously all-white sections of the state became the targets of anonymous threats and direct assaults. Their new employees risked grievous harm. As a result, short-handed landowners who wanted to hire former slaves often feared to do so. If demand for workers was a necessary condition for the adoption of free labor, widespread objections to the presence of black people made it an insufficient one.

---

[21] In addition to the relevant documents in this chapter, see *Freedom*, ser. 1, vol. 1: doc. 196.

To make matters worse, there was little or no demand for many of the former slaves. The shortage of able-bodied black men caused by enlistment and out-of-state flight made some employers more willing to hire freedwomen, at least those with few or no dependents. But women with large families had difficulty finding work. Newly freed women and children, "being found rather unprofitable, and expensive – are turned loose upon the people to support," reported a provost marshal at Hannibal. "Their former owners make no provision for them, save hauling them to within a convenient distance of some military post, and set them out with orders to never return home – telling them they are free." Emancipation had severed the claim of such castaways to subsistence; hunger and want mingled with the joy of liberation. As the war drew to a close, slavery's "expiring agonies" left their mark on the state's emerging free-labor relations.[22]

[22] In addition to the relevant documents in this chapter, see *Freedom*, ser. 1, vol. 1: doc. 196.

161: Chaplain of a Kansas Regiment to the Commander of the Department of Kansas

Wyandott Kansas, Feb. 25th 1862

Sir, When Lane's Brigade left Springfield [*Missouri*] a large number of Slaves joined themselves to us – many of them bringing away considerable property from their masters – Of this property a fine Carriage, and a pair of mules not So fine was placed in my hands to trade for a piece of land for the benefit of the colored Family who brought the property a way – Upon reflection I doubt the propriety of my Selling or trading property that was taken in that way. I refer the Matter to you as the proper person and Shall await your orders. Yours truly

ALS   R. M. Fisk

Chapl'n R. M. Fisk to Maj. Gen. Hunter, 25 Feb. 1862, Unentered Letters Received, ser. 2096, Dept. of KS, RG 393 Pt. 1 [C-4420]. Fisk was chaplain of the 4th Kansas Infantry, part of the "Kansas Brigade" of General James H. Lane which, when it left Springfield and marched back into Kansas in November 1861, had reportedly "carried off 500 or 600 negroes, belonging to Union men as well as secessionists." (*Official Records*, ser. 1, vol. 3, pp. 742–43, 748.) A wrapper notation of March 8, 1862, on Fisk's letter indicates that it was set aside to be shown to General David Hunter, commander of the Department of Kansas, "on his return" (from a trip east). No reply to Fisk has been found in the appropriate letters-sent volume of the department, and no letters-sent volume survives for the District of Kansas, which replaced the Department of Kansas in mid-March.

162: Superintendent of Contrabands at Helena, Arkansas, to the Commander of the District of Eastern Arkansas

St. Louis Mo. March 16th 1863.

Dear Sir, I have delayed writing you purposely since my arrival here till the business in hand should be partially at least disposed of—

The evening we left Helena we came near having some trouble with the officers of the boat Jesse K. Bell— The acting Captain, the pilot, the Watchman, the Clerk & the bar-tender—all became intoxicated over the repulsive idea, of being required to take a load of contrabands—& they became quite turbulent & fractious. After various attempts to moderate them I tried a little authority— which succeeded admirably—& answered the purpose all the way to St Louis— The Capt. stopped to coal at Memphis—also at Cairo— Before we reached Cairo a child three years old died, but our number was kept complete by the birth of one, that was named from the boat *Jesse K. Bell*— The health of the crew was good—& in the main we had a pleasant trip—

Towards midnight Saturday we reached St. Louis & Sabbath handed our dispatches to Maj: Gen. Curtis— *Five hundred contrabands*! What in the world shall I do with them"! exclaimed the General— He sent for his Quarter Master of course to inquire about accommodations &c— While consulting on this matter some of the prominent citizens, called, & urged the General not to suffer the contrabands to land because Missouri being a slave state still their personal liberty might possibly be endangered again, but to ship them round to Cincinnati or on to Keokuk [*Iowa*]— Gen. Curtis listened to their statements & suggestions, but insisted, very wisely I thought, that a precedent of shipping & unloading contrabands by a quasi national authority should be established at some point where we had an armed force to prevent disturbance. So that with few words on my part, the end aimed at was reached. Monday evening the whole city nearly turned out to see the contrabands disembark & pack & load their baggage & strike a line for the Missouri Hotel— the place selected as their Head Quarters. The building is at the corner of Main & Morgan—near the river, has not been used as public house for several years, and is large enough to accommodate a thousand persons— Having executed your orders to the best of my ability I hoped the way was clear for me to visit my family for a few days (which I have not seen for over fifteen months), & then return to Helena— But the Gen. was peremptory & said I must remain here to organize a plan of distributing contrabands to applicants for them— This has been my special duty during the past week— I have a permanent guard, a Surgeon, & Quarter Master detailed—& things are moving on very harmoniously— Not a murmur has been heard from the press. We stand in a position to make a grand "fight", in case of any virulent attack—as the men here—& to follow from Helena—built the fort, loaded & unloaded govt. stores &c, & hold claims to a large amount against the government.[1]

I have disposed of one hundred & fifty & will send off one hundred & fifty more to-morrow— We are ready for another load— Gen. Curtis will not object to their coming—indeed from what I said to him he expects them— He told me the substance of his letter to you—[2] but he looks for you still to send the contrabands at your discretion.

We have had applications for over *two thousand* hands—a large per-centage of which came from Illinois— The calls from Iowa increase—

The contrabands are rather pleased with the idea of the negroes running a big Hotel in St Louis— We have an abundance of visitors—& many things pass before us worth remembering. If possible I will get relieved this week— There is quite a demand from Kansas for contraband—& five hundred might be sent to this point & shipped by rail to that state, under charge of Chaplain Fisher[3] or some other suitable man—

The General wishes the pay roll of hands employed at Office Public Works at Helena—completed & forwarded—& you will do me a favor to call the attention of Chaplain Forman[4] to the matter— I hope things are moving on pleasantly with him—

Should anything worthy of special note occur I will write again— Very respectfully—

Samuel Sawyer—

P.S. While conferring with Gen. Curtis a few moments since, I handed him the above to read—that I might not misinterpret his status about the contrabands arriving from Helena— He made no dissent, & you may feel at full liberty therefore to send all you wish to this point— This will be a "contraband" Intelligence Office for the whole North West—

Chaplain Fisher has arrived with his load of 227. Gen. Curtis referred him to me—& taking twenty seven of the lot who have relatives here, the two hundred will be sent to morrow on the steamer Magenta to Leavenworth for Kansas—[5]

An application from Wisconsin for 50 contrabands to be taken away Wednesday; came in to day— Thus the work progresses—

Since writing the above the papers bring the announcement that

you are added to the list of Maj: Generals— Please accept my
cordial congratulations— S. S.

ALS

Samuel Sawyer to Brig. Gen. Prentiss, 16 Mar. 1863, S-239 1863, Letters
Received, ser. 2593, Dept. of the MO, RG 393 Pt. 1 [C-138]. The letter is
headed "Head Quarters Contrabands." For a brief description of the circumstances that led to removing former slaves from Helena, see *Freedom*, ser. 1,
vol. 3: doc. 161. On March 3, General Benjamin M. Prentiss, commander of
the District of Eastern Arkansas, had ordered Chaplain Sawyer and several
assistants to accompany 450 contrabands to St. Louis on the steamer *Jesse K.
Bell*, turn them over to General Samuel R. Curtis, commander of the Department of the Missouri, and return "forthwith" to Helena. (Special Orders No.
19, Head Quarters Dist. Eastern Arkansas, 3 Mar. 1863, vol. 42/109 DArk,
pp. 249–50, Special Orders, ser. 4686, Dist. of Eastern AR, RG 393 Pt. 2
No. 299 [C-7546].) By March 20, more than three-quarters of the contrabands from Helena had been "disposed of," chiefly in the free states adjoining
Missouri, and Chaplain Sawyer believed that "under the system adopted, the
rest can be distributed with much less labor." (Chaplain Samuel Sawyer to
Maj. Gen. Curtis, 20 Mar. 1863, service record of Samuel W. Sawyer, 47th
IN Inf., Carded Records, Volunteer Organizations: Civil War, ser. 519, RG
94 [N-149].) The system was tested in the following weeks with the arrival of
still more former slaves from Helena, and General Curtis continued to detain
Sawyer to supervise arrangements for them. (See doc. 163, immediately below.) In mid-April Curtis formally assigned Sawyer to duty at Department of
the Missouri headquarters "in charge of contraband persons of African descent," retroactively dating the appointment from March 10. (Special Orders
No. 100, Head Quarters, Department of the Mo., 15 Apr. 1863, vol. 58
DMo, pp. 226–27, Special Orders, ser. 2625, Dept. of the MO, RG 393 Pt.
1 [C-7800].)

1 For examples of military labor performed at Helena, Arkansas, by former
slaves, see *Freedom*, ser. 1, vol. 3: docs. 150, 152.
2 General Samuel R. Curtis, commander of the Department of the Missouri,
had written in response to a letter of February 28, from General Benjamin M.
Prentiss, commander of the District of Eastern Arkansas, that arrived with the
contrabands. In that letter, Prentiss had explained that he was sending them to
St. Louis because it was impossible to provide quarters in Helena, and in
Missouri "something may be done with or for them that will better their
condition." "I do this," Prentiss had confessed, "with a full knowledge that
many complaints will be made concerning." Curtis had replied on March 9,
the day the contrabands disembarked. "The State of Missouri must not be
made the depot for the paupers of Arkansas," Curtis had scolded. Moreover, "it
is not a safe way of disposing of free negroes, because the laws of this State are
such as to endanger the freedom of persons of African descent. I know the
subject is troublesome and perplexing, but I respectfully suggest that you only
transfer it by sending the negroes to my command. . . . I will have to send

[them] back if you repeat the shipments." (Brig. Genl. B. M. Prentiss to Majr. Genl. Curtis, 28 Feb. 1863, filed as E-53 1863, Letters Received, ser. 2593, Dept. of the MO, RG 393 Pt. 1 [C-7811]; *Official Records*, ser. 1, vol. 22, pt. 2, p. 147.)

3 Hugh D. Fisher, assistant superintendent of contrabands at Helena, who was from Kansas. (Special Orders. No. 20, Head Quarters District of Eastern Arkansas, 4 Mar. 1863, service record of Hugh D. Fisher, 5th KS Cav., Carded Records, Volunteer Organizations: Civil War, ser. 519, RG 94 [N-150].)

4 Jacob G. Forman, post chaplain and superintendent of burials at Helena. (Special Orders No. 19, Head Quarters Dist. Eastern Arkansas, 3 Mar. 1863, vol. 42/109 DArk, pp. 249–50, Special Orders, ser. 4686, Dist. of Eastern AR, RG 393 Pt. 2 No. 299 [C-7546].)

5 On March 17, General Curtis ordered Chaplain Fisher to "proceed" to Leavenworth, Kansas, with 150 of the contrabands he had brought from Helena to St. Louis, and then return to Helena. By March 28, Fisher had found employment for 70 and had "a prospect of geting good places for all." (Special Orders No. 71, Head Quarters Dept. of the Missoura, 17 Mar. 1863, and Chaplain H. D. Fisher to Lieut. G. W. Decosta, 28 Mar. 1863, both in service record of Hugh D. Fisher, 5th KS Cav., Carded Records, Volunteer Organizations: Civil War, ser. 519, RG 94 [N-150].)

163: Superintendent of Contrabands at St. Louis, Missouri, to the Commander of the Department of the Missouri

St. Louis Mo. April 18th 1863 –

General – Having been detained here by your order, endorsed upon the order of Gen. Prentiss, to distribute the contrabands from these Head Quarters, I have the honor to report, that free papers have been made out for over eleven hundred persons, & a faithful record kept of their names – Most of this number have gone to comfortable homes in the free states – About eighteen per cent of the number have stopped temporarily in this city & state, – in places where their liberty & safety were properly guaranteed – House servants have generally been hired at five dollars per month, & field hands at ten dollars – Blank contracts have been made & signed at this office –

The evidence accumulates that there is a combination in this city, cooperating with a few in Evansville Ind. & many at Louisville Ky, to Kidnap colored people in this city & state, & to push them into Slavery in Kentucky – Two men from Barnum's Hotel on last Wednesday laid violent hand's on two persons of color sent with one of my guards to the Provost Marshal for a pass – & but for the resoluteness of the guard & the fear of the bayonet, they would have taken possession of the negroes & handed them over to the party for whom they were acting— Several of the city Hotels have been used as prisons to a number of colored people who were justly entitled to their liberty— In all such cases coming to the notice of the military authorities would it not be well to serve a notice upon the Proprietors that they would be held responsible for the value of the negroes, if they should leave without a judicial investigation? If more efficient measures have been adopted this suggestion will be pardoned—

Quite a number of the contrabands received & sent with free papers North-ward have claims against the Government for labor done on Fort Curtis & elsewhere— If the Commanding General at Helena Ark— would authorize some one to make out a full list of those who were employed by the Office of Public Works—with the amount due them,—to be forwarded to this city for payment—he would do a just & desirable thing— I think he will regard any wish you may express on the subject.

We have had applications for thousands of hands beyond our supply—& the demand instead of abating is on the increase. I have twenty letters before me from different points of the Compass still unanswered calling for hands, which I cannot supply— What may be done hereafter the future must determine—

My duty mainly done to the best of my ability here, I respectfully ask to be relieved, that I may return to my post at Helena— If I have managed with your approval, the business entrusted to me, you will do me a Kindness by so stating in a letter to Maj. Gen. Prentiss—as from his order & my long absence, he might feel that I had not used due diligence in carrying out my instructions— Very respectfully—

Samuel Sawyer

Any orders you may have for me at Helena I will execute with pleasure—

ALS

Samuel Sawyer to Maj. Gen. Curtis, 18 Apr. 1863, S-284 1863, Letters Received, ser. 2593, Dept. of the MO, RG 393 Pt. 1 [C-139]. On April 20, the department commander, General Samuel R. Curtis, commended Sawyer upon "the success of your efforts in finding homes & work for over 1100 Contrabands since you came within my Department." The former slaves, Curtis observed, "seem Contented & satisfied in the new field of labor where they have been placed," and their new employers "speak very favorably of [their] fidelity." In prescribing a form of contract and maintaining a record of employers and employees, his purpose, Curtis explained, had been to "make it very dangerous for the person hiring the Negro to consign him again to slavery." (Maj. Genl. S. R. Curtis to Rev. Samuel Sawyer, 20 Apr. 1863, vol. 13 DMo, p. 439, Letters Sent, ser. 2571, Dept. of the MO, RG 393 Pt. 1 [C-139].) On May 9, General Curtis relieved Sawyer as superintendent of contrabands in the Department of the Missouri, and he returned to Helena, Arkansas. (Special Orders No. 124, Head Quarters Department of the Missouri, 9 May 1863, vol. 58 DMo, pp. 246–47, Special Orders, ser. 2625, Dept. of the MO, RG 393 Pt. 1 [C-7800].)

164: Commander of the Camp of Instruction at Benton Barracks, Missouri, to the Headquarters of the St. Louis District

Benton Barracks, Mo., May 28th *1863.*
Captain, In compliance with the request of the Brigadier Genl. commanding the District, thro. Lt Clarkson, A.D.C., I have the honor to submit the following statement in regard to the disturbance respecting some negroes. –

Sometime yesterday two persons came to my office, – one of them claiming to be a civil officer – who presented a paper from Genl Davidson respecting some fugitive slaves said to be in the Barracks. – I told them I could do nothing in the case having made it a rule to avoid all interference in such matters or even their discussion

I am told that after I left the office the men accompanied with six or eight others went to the Corral saying that *they knew what to do,* and being referred by Lt Dickinson to Capt Wuerpel A.Q.M. the officer went to find him, while the citizens attempted to seize the negroes showing no written authority whatever. It is reported to me that the laborers at the Corral told these men that the negroes could go if willing but must not be maltreated. Nevertheless they caught hold of the negroes and knocked several of them down, when the laborers and the other negroes interfered and the melee ensued during which the citizens, struck the laborers, and drew a knife on them, and were themselves somewhat injured

The Officer Commanding the Provost Guard learning of the disturbance arrested the citizens but immediately afterwards released them. On my return from the city I ordered the arrest of all persons here, concerned in the matter.

I enclose herewith the statement of Lt Dickinson who was on duty at the Corral at the time.

All of which is respectfuly submitted. Very Respectfully Your ob't servt
HLS   B L E Bonneville

Col. B. L. E. Bonneville to Capt. H. C. Fillebrow[n], 28 May 1863, Unentered Letters Received, ser. 2594, Dept. of the MO, RG 393 Pt. 1 [C-113]. The commander of the St. Louis District was General John W. Davidson, the same officer whose "paper" had been presented at Benton Barracks by the civil officer. Enclosed in Colonel Bonneville's report is a statement by Lieutenant Edward S. Dickinson, who offered a similar account of events at the Benton Barracks corral. As to his own role, Dickinson claimed merely to have referred the civil officer and the citizens to Captain Wuerpel, the quartermaster who furnished laborers for the corral. He was not present when the citizens "seized upon some of the negroes, and a melee ensued between the citizens, the negroes & the laborers," nor were any other soldiers or officers in the corral. (Statement of 1st Lieut. Ed. S. Dickinson, 28 May 1863.) By late July 1863, following further appearances by civilians with warrants for fugitive slaves, Colonel Bonneville had decided to forestall such "annoyance" by sending away from Benton Barracks all "persons of color" employed by the quartermaster "and hereafter rigidly exclude them from the Post." (Col. B. L. E. Bonneville to Col. C. W. Marsh, 20 July 1863, B-664 1863, Letters Received, ser. 2593, Dept. of the MO, RG 393 Pt. 1 [C-115].)

165: St. Louis Attorney to the Commander of the Department of the Missouri

St. Louis [*Mo.*], May 30th 1863. Sir: In compliance with your request I present the following statement of the proceedings and policy of the military authorities in this part of the Department, so far as I have information, in relation to the blacks, whether "contrabands,"[1] or those freed by the Proclamation,[2] or by acts of Congress for the disloyalty of their particular owners.[3]

1. Contrabands. Since the date of the Proclamation these as a *class* have become unimportant, very few negroes from Missouri being employed by the rebels & captured by our forces. – They receive, however, on due evidence of the facts that they have been in the employ of rebel forces, certificates of freedom, from the Provost Marshal General, and the same protection as the following large class.

2. Freed men, under the Proclamation, This class have received from the Provost Marshal General a certificate that they are free, on simply showing their owner's residence in a state included in the Proclamation

3. Men entitled to freedom, (owned in Mo.) by virtue of the Confiscation & other acts for disloyalty of their owners. This class has been the most difficult to deal with, but on due proofs of disloyal ownership the Provost Marshal General & his

Division subordinates have issued certificates declaring such negroes emancipated— The form of these certificates differs from that of the other classes, but the language of either is not of essential importance— The same result is attained.

4. Negroes from Kentucky & Tennessee. These are not property [*properly*] entitled to certificates but are presumptively free, and are given passes to go out of the state in any direction unmolested. In many respects, indeed *practically*, this is hardly distinguishable from class number 3.

Systematic provision by the military authorities for the freed people of color began, I think, on the arrival of some 1500 sent here from Helena by Gen. Prentiss, under control of Rev. Samuel Sawyer, an Indiana Chaplain of Volunteers, and a very efficient man for the work. They arrived in February last, I believe.[4] At nearly the same time a "Ladies Contraband Relief Society" was formed here. One of their Circulars accompanies this paper.

Gen. Curtis immediately hired at Govt. expense the old Missouri Hotel, corner of Main & Morgan streets, detailed a guard of a few men from the 37th Iowa (Grey Beards), a quartermaster, – a surgeon – & some clerks from the ranks of a paroled regiment (91 Ill. Vols) and at once had the 1500 negroes quartered there & rations furnished. At the same time he provided the ladies of the above named society with a room, and a building for a hospital & assigned them an orderly.

This disposition of things was found to work admirably & has been continued to the present time–

There is a hospital at the hotel as well as the one above named, superintended by the ladies of the Contraband Relief Society.

At the Hotel a system of hiring out the negroes has been established, & few negroes remain there any considerable time. The 1500 were nearly all hired within two weeks & this was before any system had been established. Now these negroes come into the city from below & go at once to the hotel, from which they speedily go to good homes in the *free states*, or in this city & vicinity–

There has been an exceeding great & justifiable reluctance to allow them to hire–or remain–in this state, owing to the severity the barbarism–of our state laws, which favor & encourage reënslavement of these very classes, to whom the faith of the Govt. has been pledged by the Proclamation. Gen. Curtis therefore forbid any to be hired into this State beyond the limits of this county. And no applicant–from this county–for them can obtain any of them from the hotel except on written application, with sufficient vouchers for his loyalty & responsibility, to be approved by a Committee named by the Contraband Relief Society.

Govt. has been called upon to pay transportation of none to the

free states – Iowa, Wisconsin & Illinois – , but some hundreds have
been sent off at the expense of the Society. There is an eager
demand for this class of labor on either side of the Mississippi
northward, & for the Govt. it would be economy to send such as
gather at the hotel up the river *at once*, rather than to provide rations
here for a considerable time.

Just previous to being relieved from his command, Gen. Curtis
had arranged to bring here, and send to the free states, such negroes
as gathered at the various posts on railroad lines in the State, and
were owned by rebels, or unclaimed.[5] It is greatly for the interest of
the State that this plan be perfected. At Jefferson City, the Provost
Marshal has written that numbers, some hundreds, are gathered, the
"property of rebels who will not claim them," and that there is
suffering among them. He desired transportation for them to this
point. At other stations the same state of things exists.

Two alternatives present themselves. Either the government must
send these people to the states where they will be self-supporting, or
it must feed them here in idleness, disease & misery. The interests
of Missouri, and humanity point to the former course. –

I would respectfully suggest that some suitable person be directed
to visit the various prominent points in the state to investigate &
report the condition, numbers &c. &c. of the negroes there
gathered.

One matter further remains to be mentioned. Since slave
property has become so insecure in this state, rebels, speculators &
Kidnappers have been running negroes off to Kentucky. So much
villainy has been connected with this that by order of the Provost
Marshal General, no negro can be taken from the state by his owner
or claimant, without a special permit, granted on proof of loyalty,
ownership &c. –[6]

I think the foregoing sketch indicates the line of policy hitherto
pursued in this state. Any omissions, or further information I shall
be pleased to supply. Very Respectfully Your obt. servt,

ALS   Lucien Eaton

Lucien Eaton to Major Genl. Schofield, 30 May 1863, E-101 1863, Letters
Received, ser. 2593, Dept. of the MO, RG 393 Pt. 1 [C-122]. The circular
said to have been enclosed is not in the file. General John M. Schofield had
assumed command of the Department of the Missouri on May 24, only a few
days before Eaton's letter; he replaced General Samuel R. Curtis. The practice
of shipping former slaves from Helena, Arkansas, to St. Louis continued into
the summer of 1863, as did efforts to find employment for them in the St.
Louis area or outside the state; by mid-July, according to one estimate, 2,500
had been forwarded to the free states. (See below, doc. 171, and *Freedom*, ser.
1, vol. 3: doc. 167.)

1 Although the term "contrabands" ordinarily designated former slaves who had become free or were entitled to freedom by any avenue of law or circumstance, it refers in this letter exclusively to those entitled to freedom under the confiscation act of August 1861, which liberated slaves who had been employed at military labor on behalf of the Confederacy. (*Statutes at Large*, vol. 12, p. 319.)

2 The Emancipation Proclamation, issued by President Abraham Lincoln on January 1, 1863, which declared free all slaves in the Confederate states except those in Tennessee and in certain Union-occupied counties of Louisiana and Virginia. (*Statutes at Large*, vol. 12, pp. 1268–69.)

3 The Second Confiscation Act, approved on July 17, 1862, freed slaves whose owners had participated in, or aided, rebellion against the United States. The Militia Act, which became law the same day, granted freedom to slaves employed on behalf of the Union army or navy, and also freed the mothers, wives, and children of men so employed, provided their owner or owners were disloyal. (*Statutes at Large*, vol. 12, pp. 589–92, 597–600.)

4 The first group from Helena – forwarded by General Benjamin M. Prentiss, commander of the District of Eastern Arkansas – had arrived in early March 1863. (See above, doc. 162.)

5 On May 14, 1863, after being informed by Chaplain Samuel Sawyer that "many negroes who belonged to Rebels and Disloyal men and who are emancipated by the laws of the united States" were gathering at military camps and posts "in a destitute condition and without employment," General Samuel R. Curtis, then commander of the Department of the Missouri, had instructed Colonel Bernard G. Farrar, an assistant to the provost marshal general of the department, to visit the camps along the railroads of the state and "make such arangements for the employment or removal and transportation of such contrabands as may conduce to their being employed in a manner useful to the Goverment and beneficial to themselves." Curtis had, however, cautioned Farrar to "carefully avoid the removal of Slaves of loyal men or owners" and to "take only those, that are clearly, the property of Rebels." (Maj. Genl. [Samuel R. Curtis] to Col. Farrar, 14 May 1863, vol. 13 DMo, p. 457, Letters Sent, ser. 2571, Dept. of the MO, RG 393 Pt. 1 [C-7814].)

6 On April 23, 1863, Colonel Franklin A. Dick, provost marshal general of the Department of the Missouri during Curtis's command, had ordered that "[n]o negroes shall be allowed to be taken upon any Rail Road, Steam-Boat, Stage or other conveyance beyond the limits of this City [St. Louis], without a special permit describing such negro, issued by the District Provost Marshal or Provost Marshal General." The importance of slaves in the city's commerce had, however, complicated enforcement of the order, leading Colonel Dick to modify it on April 29. "The object of that order," he had announced, "is to prevent negroes who are free from being run off by Traders, to be illegally sold as slaves, and therefor it will not be construed to interfere with the ordinary use of slaves actually employed in this City or County – nor with negroes being taken upon Steamboats as hired servants or deck hands – nor will it prevent free negroes from voluntarily leaving the City." (Special Order No. 61, Head Quarters Department of the Missouri, Office of the Provost Marshal General, 23 Apr. 1863, and Special Order No. 66, Head Quarters Department of the Missouri, Office of the Provost Marshal General, 29 Apr. 1863, vol. 570

DMo, pp. 74–75, 78, Special Orders, ser. 2791, Provost Marshal General, Dept. of the MO, RG 393 Pt. 1 [C-7830].)

166: Provost Marshal of a Precinct in the District of Columbus, Kentucky, to the Provost Marshal of the District

Columbus Ky June 9th 1863

Major; In November last I ascertained that a large Plantation, lying in Mississippi Co., Missouri, opposite to, and contiguous to this Post, was the property of one Hunter, a Rebel, now in the Southern Army. I seized the property and placed it in charge of a Mrs. Sprouse, reporting the facts to Brigadier General Davies, then, in command of the District of Columbus; General Davies informed me verbally, only, to keep charge of the property, while he would make report to the General Commanding Department of Missouri, in whose Department, the property in question is situated. In January last, Major Eddie, then Commandant of the Post of Columbus, went to St. Louis and while there laid the matter before General Curtis, Comd'g Department of Missouri. General Curtis informed him verbally, only, that he desired the Military Authorities at Columbus to take charge of the property. So far I have been acting only in accordance with verbal orders; but, as an Officer of the United States Army, and desiring to further the interests of the Government of the United States, I have done the best I could with the plantation.

Last Winter Mr. Sprouse, the Agent, who I had placed in Charge of the Property was Assassinated, by a man of the name of Goldsmith, whom we have not succeeded in Capturing. Last Month I placed a man by the name of Floyd in Charge of the Estate, and sent Eight Contrabands to labor on the Farm for the purpose of raising a crop. They have planted One Hundred Acres of Corn, Several Acres of Oats, Potatoes &c; I pay the Contrabands Ten dollars per month, Clothe and feed them, all this, without any expense to the Government; for when the planting time is over, I set the Contrabands to Cutting Wood, of which there is an abundance on the bank of the River, the sale of which will more than pay the expenses of their Wages, Clothing &c. In the Fall, I shall be enabled to turn over to the Government, a few Thousand dollars worth of Corn, Oats, Potatoes, &c.

On last month I also ascertained that there was another farm lying Five miles up the River, on the Kentucky Shore, which had been in the possession of one B[unn]mell, who is now in the Southern Army. I took possession of the Farm, palaced a man by the name of Sams in Charge of it, as Agent of the Government; but as the season is so far advanced, and there being no Farming Utensils left on the Place, the Government can receive no benefit from Crops thereof this season. Respectfully Submitted,

HLS
J. H. Williams

Capt. J. H. Williams to Major W. R. Rowley, 9 June 1863, Letters Received, ser. 991, Dist. of Columbus, RG 393 Pt. 2 No. 24 [C-7219]. An endorsement referred Williams's letter to the commander of the District of Columbus, but no reply has been found in the letters-sent volumes of that district.

167: Commander of the District of Central Missouri to the Commander of the Department of the Missouri

Jeff City [*Mo.*] July 14 /63
General, This morning I recieved the telegraph of which the following is a copy.

"Two hundred and Seventy Negroes, arrived here last night mostly women and childern suffering for some thing to eat what shall I do with them dated Sedalia July 14 /63 and signed G. W. Murphy, Capt.

To which I sent the following —

"Capt G. W. Murphy, Sedalia, Subsistince will be issued only to persons in the service. we have nothing to do with feeding any other parties,

I am Truly Your Obdt Servt

HLc
[*Egbert B. Brown*]

[Egbert B. Brown] to Major Genl. J. M. Schofield, 14 July 1863, vol. 225/ 525 DMo, pp. 184–85, Letters Sent, ser. 3372, Dist. of Central MO, RG 393 Pt. 2 No. 217 [C-7129]. In a letter of the same date General Brown repeated his telegraphed instructions to issue no rations to the newly arrived fugitives and added the following admonition: "The Negroes have no business in the camps of troops and you will see that yours is cleared of all persons not in the service." To further ensure their expulsion, Brown also informed a higher-ranking subordinate that the "large number of idle and dissolute persons about the post of Sedalia, some of them Negroes and their families," should be "removed beyond your military posts." The "time and mode of their removal" he left to the officer's discretion. ([Egbert B. Brown] to Capt. G. W. Murphy, 14 July 1863, and [Egbert B. Brown] to Col. Geo. H. Hall, 15 July 1863, vol. 225/525 DMo, pp. 185–87, Letters Sent, ser. 3372, Dist. of Central MO, RG 393 Pt. 2 No. 217 [C-7129, C-7130].)

Missouri

168: Provost Marshal at Lexington, Missouri, to the Commander of the District of the Border

Lexington Mo Aug 14th 1863

General   The subject of this communication is one of peculiar interest and one that in this "City & County" is somewhat complicated. There are at the present time about two hundred and fifty or three hundred "negroes" men women & children in our camp. There are probably one hundred of them who have "Free Papers" given in accordance with Gen Order No 35 dated Head Quarters Department of the Mo St Louis Dec 24th 1862.[1]

Now such "Colored Men" are free, and have they not a right to go where, when, and in whose company they choose? Have they not the right to hire themselves, and sell their labor to a "Recruiting Officer" as well as to a farmer? I think they have – and if so is it necessary for them to first go to Kansas before they can make such a contract. Surely no one would argue that such business would be in violation of the orders prohibiting officers from other States to recruit in this State for they are not citizens, not men according to the laws of Mo and hense such orders would not apply to them. We have heard that you design getting authority to raise a "colored Regt" in this state. We have not learned whether you succeeded or not.[2] I hope you have but if not I believe that "Recruiting officers" from Kansas ought to be authorised to come here and recruit, from those who are clearly covered by the law and are legally entitled to freedom under the laws of Congress and the proclamation of the "President"   The Negro in this County is the all "inspiring theme" with many of the people. It is not the "Rebellion, the Bushwhackers or the Rebel Sympathisers in Mo. but the Negro is the source of all our trouble, and the great question that divides the people   Hundreds of men who were it not for the negro would be union men are now very doubtful. Many of them make the preservation of the institution of slavery a "condition precident" to the Union thereby effectually identifying their interests with the rebellion. I believe that some thing ought to be done about the "Negro Question" in this County, They are a perfect nuisance to our camp dirty, ragged, and demoralised, without any thing to do, or any thing to wear except what we give them. They will not hire out to the farmers here for fear of being taken by their masters. Men to who in sentiment are "bad Rebels" come and by Civil prosess get their Negroes who justice and equity would pronounce forever free

A short time since I passed through Kansas City and was much surprised to learn the feeling that existed there toward the 1st Regt all of which has grown out of a difference of policy upon the Negro question. I think that if there could be some change made in the troops stationed here or the troops here and at some other point change posts it would conduce to the benefit, and promote the interests of the service

While on a scout recently under the instructions of Col M'Ferran I ordered several familes to report here with their effects for the purpose of leaving the County   They were noted Rebels, Have harbored Bushwhackers continually without doubt, often they have been found at and chased from their houses. The Col seems to doubt our authority to require them to leave the County without your approval   We hope and the Union people of the County trust that you will approve of our action in this matter

Will there be a mustering officer at this place before next muster day   With Much Esteem I am very Respectfully Yr Obt Servant

ALS   H B Johnson

Capt. H. B. Johnson to General, 14 Aug. 1863, vol. 186 DMo, Letters Received, ser. 3107, Dist. of the Border, RG 393 Pt. 2 No. 200 [C-7507].

1 General Order 35, issued on December 24, 1862, by General Samuel R. Curtis, commander of the Department of the Missouri, had instructed provost marshals in the department to investigate the circumstances of fugitive slaves who sought protection at Union army posts and camps, and to issue certificates of freedom to those whose owners were disloyal. (*Freedom*, ser. 1, vol. 1: doc. 172.)

2 On August 3, 1863, General Thomas Ewing, Jr., whose District of the Border included western Missouri and eastern Kansas, had applied for authority to recruit free-black men into the Union army and organize them into companies for duty in Kansas or elsewhere. He had also proposed to increase the number of black men available for enlistment by offering military escort into Kansas to slaves in the western Missouri counties of Lafayette, Johnson, and St. Clair who were entitled to freedom because their owners were disloyal. The women and children so removed, Ewing assured the department commander, could readily find employment in Kansas, and the men would be enlisted. On August 14, instructions from Department of the Missouri headquarters authorized Ewing "to give practical freedom" to slaves clearly entitled to such under the confiscation acts, by escorting them to Kansas, but enjoined him to take "[s]pecial care" not to interfere with slaves whose owners were loyal. "Able-bodied men liberated under this authority," the instructions continued, "will be enlisted into the service of the United States. . . . Persons not enlisted as soldiers will . . . be provided with comfortable homes, where they can earn a livelihood without expense to the Government." (*Freedom*, ser. 2: doc. 85; *Official Records*, ser. 1, vol. 22, pt. 2, p. 450.)

169: Commander of the 4th Subdistrict of the District of Central Missouri to the Headquarters of the District, and Reply from the District Commander

Marshall [*Mo.*] Sept— 18th 1863

Major   There are so many run away slaves in the posts of Marshall and Miami in this sub-Dist—composed of women of all ages, children of all ages and sexes that unless something be done great suffering must ensue.   If these people could be sent to St Louis or to Kansas it would be an act of humanity.   The people in this country will not employ them.   They have nothing and have no shelter.   A large number came in to this place from Arrow Rock yesterday with Company B. 4th Cav M.S.M.   I sent them back to Arrow Rock this morning.   There is no shelter for them here.

Can these run away slaves be sent off?   If so where? and in what manner?   Your early consideration is respectfully requested   Respectfully Your Obt— Servant

ALS   George H. Hall

Jeff City [*Mo.*]   Sept 22 /63

Col   Your faver of the 18th Inst stating that there is a large number of slaves at the post of Miami and Marshall who will suffer if not provided with means of subsistence has been received—   The solution of the difficulty it seems to me is a simple one—prevent the soldiers from interfering with the Civil Officers in the discharge of their duty and the civil officers do theirs will soon correct it—   No subsistence can be issued to such persons as you name   As they can return to their homes and be provided for there is no necessity for it—   I can see no benefit to arise from sending them to Kansas or St Louis   if they are to starve which (they would in Kansas) they may as well be in reach of their former Homes which affords them a sure refuge as among strangers where they would surely die   I am Very Truly

HLcSr   E B Brown

Col. George H. Hall to Major James Rainsford, 18 Sept. 1863, Unentered Letters Received, ser. 2594, Dept. of the MO, RG 393 Pt. 1 [C-130]; E. B. Brown to Col. Geo. H. Hall, 22 Sept. 1863, vol. 225 DMo, p. 44, Letters Sent, ser. 3372, Dist. of Central MO, RG 393 Pt. 2 No. 217 [C-130]. Hall signed as colonel of the 4th Cavalry, Missouri State Militia.

170: Testimony by a Black Baptist Minister before the American Freedmen's Inquiry Commission

ST. LOUIS, TUESDAY, Dec. 1ˢᵗ, 1863.

Testimony of Rev. Edward L. Woodson.
Pastor of Colored Baptist church.

Q How many churches have the people in St. Louis?

A There are three Baptist churches and three Methodist churches.

Q Have you any idea how many members these churches have?

A The Baptists have about 1400, and the Methodists five or six hundred.

Q How many colored schools are there here?

A Four pay schools, and one free school.

Q How is that free school supported?

A By some friends East, I suppose.

Q What number of scholars do they have?

A There are about 160 children at the pay schools; I don't know the number at the free school. I suppose I am almost an example of the colored people of Missouri, from the fact that we were all slaves. I have fourteen children. I hired my own time, and bought myself, my wife and my children. We have one girl who can teach music.

Q Do you think there are many slaves here who hire their time?

A Very few, if any. That thing is played out.

Q Do you think there is much punishment of slaves now?

A Not so much as there was; and there never was much here. Back in the country, it was pretty bad, but that is pretty much at an end now. Most all of those who have got free have paid a good deal for themselves, and have done remarkably well. Most of them have bought property, more or less, and got along pretty fair.

Q What do you think of the views of the colored people in regard to enlisting?

A The colored people generally are not so much in favor of enlisting, but there are a good many who are in favor of it. The free people, who have bought themselves, are not much inclined to it, but the others are in favor of it. If you will only give the colored people a chance, you will find they will get along.

Q Have you any idea how many free colored people there are in the city?

A Before the war, there were from 2500 to 3000. A good many have emigrated here since the war, which would make it about 3500 —

Q Have you been instrumental in buying any other persons besides your own family?

A Yes, I have bought five or six

Q Did you furnish the means?

A They furnished the means, but not being free, they could not make any bargain, and I had to stand between them and their masters.

Q How is it in regard to the colored poor? Are they supported by public charity?

A No, Sir; the colored churches have each a poor fund, for the relief of needy persons, and when a man dies without leaving any property, we bury him. We have always done that, because we don't like to have the white people think we can't take care of ourselves.

Q When slaves become too old to work, are they ever set free, to shift for themselves?

A Oh, yes; it is a very common thing.

HD

Testimony of Rev. Edward L. Woodson before the American Freedmen's Inquiry Commission, 1 Dec. 1863, filed with O-328 1863, Letters Received, ser. 12, RG 94 [K-207]. Topical labels in the margin are omitted.

171: **Testimony by the St. Louis Ladies' Contraband Relief Society before the American Freedmen's Inquiry Commission**

[*St. Louis, Mo. December 2, 1863*]
The Ladies Contraband Society.

This (Wednesday) afternoon, the Commission met, by appointment, several of the leading members of the Ladies Contraband Relief Society, who made a statement of the operations of their Society, and expressed their opinions upon the several questions which the Commission have under consideration. The Society, they said, was organized on the 24th of January last, with the special object of relieving the physical wants of the contrabands, though they had not confined themselves to that, but had supplied books and papers wherever there had been opportunity and demand. A great many had been relieved in St. Louis, and at Columbus, Memphis, Island No. 10, Helena, and Bolivar, Miss. They gave $500 towards a church, school-house, and some sort of shelter for the contrabands on Island No. 10. Upwards of $5000 in money had been collected, besides a great many boxes of clothing and supplies from New York, Boston, & other places at the East, which were worth more than the money. Some of the boxes contained new clothing, blankets, shoes, etc. A great many urgent requests had come from below, and the need seemed to be greatest in and about Vicksburg. The probability was they would suffer more this winter than last. There were at least 100,000 on the river, between St. Louis and Vicksburg, who were in a suffering condition. These sufferers were mostly women and children, whose husbands and fathers had in many cases entered the Union army. Several thousand had been assisted at St. Louis. They came there, at one time, 500 on a boat. When Gen. Curtis was there, he took a building called the Missouri Hotel for them, but they had been removed from there to Benton Barracks.[1] There had often been as many as 1500 in the city at a time, and the Society did what they could to clothe them. Sometimes thirty or forty would be sent up at one time to be fitted out. Yesterday, a request was sent in to have forty clothed, and sent away. They were all destitute – wanting shoes and stockings and dresses and all kinds of garments, to fit them out to go to Iowa. These were women and children. At Keokuk, Iowa, there is a sort of Society, to whom these people go, and are distributed to different places. Four or five hundred have gone to Iowa and Wisconsin; 150 were fitted out with clothing and sent away at one time. That was before the men were taken into the army, and a great many were able-bodied men. No able-bodied men are now sent up the river, and many of those who went up have returned, and gone into the army. Some of the men are anxious to go into the army, & some seem to dread it; it is very much with them as it is with white men. The contrabands are more ready to go into the army than the free blacks. They very rarely decline, unless there is some influence brought to bear upon them.

Up to the middle of July, 2500 contrabands had been provided with homes in the free States, by this Society. Since then, only a few had been sent up at a time. The authorities put a stop to it, after a while, and would not allow any colored people to leave the State.[2] Perhaps the order had reference only to slaves, but it did not say so. A great many contraband who had come up the river were kidnapped and sent off there. It had been said that forty or fifty were sent down on the train almost every night. When Gen. Prentiss came here, he had officers to watch the trains, and prevent this.

Some of these contrabands are capable of taking care of themselves, but a great many have very little idea of taking care of themselves. [Another lady said – "I think, when they are put to the test, they can all take care of themselves. The poor people under our care cannot get anything to do, and we look upon them as idle and lazy; but all for whom I have succeeded in getting places have turned out to be good workers and very smart women. I have two, who have both learned to read. One was a man over fifty years old, and I have never seen so much anxiety to learn exhibited by any class of people.]³ The majority of those who come from the plantations have very little idea of taking care of themselves. The slaves from the South are much more helpless than the Missouri slaves. They have never been accustomed to household work. Many of them had never been in their mistress' house, and scarcely knew what a knife and fork were. That was the class the Society had the most of. Each one is for himself. A great many came here in a very low state of civilization – very degraded indeed. If they lost their children, they did not seem to mourn them at all – very few of them. One woman lost two children in one morning, and she didn't seem to mourn at all. Then there were others who mourned very deeply. They all show great resignation to the decrees of Providence. They think more of their children being sold South than of their death.

There is one free school here for the colored people, which was commenced last week. It commenced with twenty-four scholars, and has now about forty. There is also a school on the other side of the river, which has been established sometime, and is supported in part by this Society. The colored people in this city are proud. They say they can't see why we should establish a free school here. They say, "We are very glad to have you support those of us who are poor, but those of us who can pay are proud to do so." We never see a colored person begging here. Most of those who have applied to the Society for aid were contrabands. Perhaps one reason why the free colored people do not beg is because they are afraid to. They have had to get licenses to remain in the State, and if they had come upon the public, they would have been sent out of the State. The Managers of the Provident Association, which has been established here five or six years, have been surprised at having so few colored applicants for assistance.

Since July, we have received about 1000 contrabands. There is a Society in Switzerland, called the "Penny-a-week Society," (and we believe it extends to other countries of Europe) from whose agent here, (Mr Jacquard) we have received considerable money. He gave us fifty dollas a month while we, had charge of the contraband hospital, and whenever we are in need, he furnishes us with money. The original idea of the Society was, to assist in the purchase of slaves, but we have thought there was no occasion for that now in this State. We have no doubt of the necessity of some provision being made for the care and support of these people, especially the women and children. The condition of the country from which they come has been such, for two years, that when they arrive here, they are utterly destitute.

HD

Testimony of Ladies Contraband Society before the American Freedmen's Inquiry Commission, [2 Dec. 1863], filed with O-328 1863, Letters Received, ser. 12, RG 94 [K-209]. Topical labels in the margin are omitted.

1 On the arrival in St. Louis of former slaves from the lower Mississippi, and on the arrangements made for them by General Samuel R. Curtis, then commander of the Department of the Missouri, see above, docs. 162–63, 165. On September 1, 1863, General John M. Schofield, Curtis's successor, had ordered that the former slaves "now quartered in the building known as the old Missouri Hotel in St. Louis" be transferred to Benton Barracks, on the outskirts of the city. (Special Orders No. 238, Head Quarters, Dept. of the Mo., 1 Sept. 1863, vol. 59 DMo, pp. 33–36, Special Orders, ser. 2625, Dept. of the MO, RG 393 Pt. 1 [C-116].)

2 Orders issued in April 1863 to prevent the sale into slavery of black people entitled to freedom had provided that no black person could be transported from St. Louis out of the state without a permit from the provost marshal general of the Department of the Missouri or the provost marshal of the St. Louis District. (See above, doc. 165n.) The permit system created no impediment to the traffic in black people still legally held as slaves, and as slavery weakened in Missouri, owners transported or sold large numbers of them beyond the state's limits, chiefly to Kentucky. On November 10, 1863, after the inauguration of black recruitment in Missouri, General Schofield had ordered that thereafter no provost marshal could issue any pass that permitted the removal of slaves from the state. (Special Orders No. 307, Head Quarters, Dept. of the Mo., 10 Nov. 1863, vol. 59 DMo, pp. 180–81, Special Orders, ser. 2625, Dept. of the MO, RG 393 Pt. 1 [C-7831].)

3 Brackets in the original.

172: Account of Visits by the American Freedmen's Inquiry Commission to the Contraband Camp at Benton Barracks, Missouri, and to Two Schools in St. Louis

[*St. Louis, Mo. December 3, 1863*]
Contraband Camp and Hospital.

Thursday, the Commission visited the Contraband Camp and Hospital at Benton Barracks. The number now in camp is less than 100, though at times, as many as five or six hundred have been in together. The hospital arrangements and accommodations appeared to be excellent, but the contraband quarters were not in such good order nor so cleanly as they might and should be. Mr. Newell, the

Superintendent, stated that their rations consisted of fresh meat, corn meal, and some flour. The corn meal he regarded as much the best food for them. He said he had no trouble in finding places for them; on the contrary, he could have secured employment for a thousand more, if he had had them. Those now in were either too old to work, or had large families. One old woman was pointed out, who said her folks, when they found she could be of no further use to them, "just opened the door, & told her to go." An amusing instance of exclusiveness and State pride was exhibited here. The Superintendent pointed out a group of contrabands round one stove, who he said were from Mississippi, and another group round a second stove, from Missouri, and said the two parties would not fraternize at all. The Missouri negroes disdained to associate with those from Mississippi, considering themselves far above them.

Color'd Schools in St. Louis.

The Commission also visited two schools, one conducted under the auspices of the American Missionary Association, and the other supported by the colored people themselves. At the former, there were about 40 pupils, of ages varying probably from five to twenty. The school had been in operation but little over a week, yet very good order was observed, and the scholars seemed attentive and eager to learn. The other school had double the number of scholars, with even greater disparity in their ages, and the teacher had evidently not succeeded in establishing that degree of discipline which is essential to the attainment of the full advantages of the instruction furnished. The sum paid for tuition was said to be 25 cts. a week for each pupil.

HD

Account of visits to contraband camp and hospital and to color'd schools in St. Louis by the American Freedmen's Inquiry Commission, [3 Dec. 1863], filed with O-328, Letters Received, ser. 12, RG 94 [K-210]. Topical labels in the margin are omitted. Frederick R. Newell, chaplain of the 1st Infantry, Missouri State Militia, had been appointed superintendent of contrabands at St. Louis in June 1863. (Special Orders No. 166, Head Quarters, Dept. of the Mo., 20 June 1863, vol. 58 DMo, pp. 325–27, Special Orders, ser. 2625, Dept. of the MO, RG 393 Pt. 1 [C-7800].) The contraband camp at Benton Barracks, on the outskirts of the city, had been established in early September. (See doc. 171n., immediately above.)

173: Quartermaster at Quincy, Illinois, to the Secretary of War

Quincy Ills. Feb. 5. 1864
Sir: In reply to your letter of the 31ˢᵗ of Jany /64. in relation to fugitive Contrabands at this place; I have the honor to state, that on receipt of your telegraphic despatch of 14ᵗʰ Jany /64 I commenced issuing rations to such as were most needy and destitute. As the instructions confined me to those at the Camp of the 1ˢᵗ Regt. Colored Ills. Vols. I have only issued to 162 women and children, and only such parts of the regular ration as were absolutely necessary for support of life. I find, on enquiry, that there are now in this City, about 400, of this class, divided as follows, 80 women who are wives of Soldiers; about 150 children belonging to same, from 1 to 14 years of age, of both sexes; about 150 women and children not immediately connected with the Soldiers, but refugees from Missouri, and about 20 aged and infirm men not able to labor, and their number is daily increasing. These all arrive here in extreme want and destitution, most of them slaves just escaped from their masters. The men mostly enlist as Soldiers, leaving the women and children that come with them to be cared for by the citizens, whose charities have been heavily taxed since the war commenced in supporting the needy families of our white soldiers, and of white refugees from Missouri & Arkansas. $1500 in money, and large amounts of clothing have been contributed by our citizens within the last three months to the contrabands, among us – but this has been exhausted. What they need now, is, some comfortable shelter, where they can be got together, (as they are now scattered over the City. in miserable hovels and stables) fuel, food and clothing, and some proper person to have the care of them, and to find homes for them, where they can support themselves. In accordance with the suggestions received from you through the Hon: O. H. Browning, I have, as Quarter Master, employed Mr. J. K. Van Doorn to have the care of them. He has already spent much of his time and means in caring for them. If it is in the province of the Government to do so, I would respectfully suggest the propriety of collecting the children together in a school where they may be instructed, and thus prepared to take care of themselves. Efficient teachers can be obtained. Very Respectfully, Sir, Your Obedient Servant
HLS   Newton Flagg

Capt. Newton Flagg to Hon. Edwin M. Stanton, 5 Feb. 1864, F-131 1864, Letters Received, RG 107 [L-35]. In the same file is a copy of a letter from the Secretary of War to Captain Flagg, dated January 30, 1864, which had instructed Flagg to report the number, age, and sex of the "fugitive contrabands" at Quincy, Illinois, and to indicate "what provision should be made for the relief of these persons." The telegram of January 14 cited by Flagg had instructed him to issue rations to destitute black women and children at the camp of the 1st Illinois Colored Volunteers. (Brig. Genl. Ed. R. S. Canby to Capt. Flagg, 14 Jan. 1864, Telegrams Sent by the Secretary of War, Telegrams Collected by the Office of the Secretary of War [Bound], RG 107 [L-35].) Orville H. Browning, who lived in Quincy, was a U.S. senator. By early June, 1864, J. K. Van Doorn was issuing half-rations to about 300 black women and children "left destitute by the enlistment of their Husbands & Fathers," and fugitive slaves were continuing to arrive from Missouri. During the previous week alone, he informed Senator Browning, some 70 had crossed the river. The following August, Browning reported to the Secretary of War that between 1,200 and 1,500 "contrabands" were living in Quincy, including 400 women and children "in utterly destitute circumstances" who would be even worse off when winter came. By June 1865, partly as a result of lobbying by Browning and his wife, assistance had been rendered at Quincy to 5,000 black refugees, most of whom had fled the Missouri counties of Pike, Marion, and Lincoln. The government had contributed little beyond medical attendance and rations (the largest number of rations issued at any one time being 275, distributed among some 500 individuals), but contributions from local citizens, amounting to some $15,000, had been expended for housing, stoves, clothing, bedding, fuel, medicines, and burying the dead. Despite these efforts, death had claimed a great many of the former slaves, especially during the winter of 1864–1865, when between four and seven died each week. (J. K. Van Doorn to O. H. Browning, 7 June 1864, enclosed in O. H. Browning to Hon. E. M. Stanton, 15 July 1864, B-1891 1864, Letters Received, RG 107 [L-35]; O. H. Browning to Hon. E. M. Stanton, 12 Aug. 1864, B-2139 1864, Letters Received, RG 107 [L-35]; J. K. Van Doorn to Capt. Flagg, 26 June 1865, enclosed in Capt. Newton Flagg to Bvt. Maj. Genl. M. C. Meigs, 28 June 1865, "Negroes," Consolidated Correspondence File, ser. 225, Central Records, RG 92 [Y-24]; Chaplain A. Wright to Brig. Gen. J. W. Sprague, 9 Aug. 1865, W-150 1865, Letters Received, ser. 231, AR Asst. Comr., RG 105 [A-2298].)

174: **Provost Marshal of the 2nd Subdistrict of the District of North Missouri to the Commander of the District**

Hannibal [*Mo.*], Feby 26ᵗʰ 1864.

General   I have the honor to inform you that in my opinion. the negroes. now in the employ of Major E Wilmot, must be removed from this place, as they have been *educated* to *believe*, that they are a privileged Sett. formerly they were allowed to carry pistols, but now I believe there is not more than one or two, who have weapons. I have take two Pistols from the party, tis all I could anything about.

The reason they should be removed. from this place is that there are a set of *white men* here who are continually aging them, to commit disterbances, & riot.

on day before yesterday as I was passing to my office from dinner, I saw two negroes attack a white man on the street, (Constable who had in charge a woman as I undertand) and I immediately sent Sergt Fleming to the spot and arrested the negroes. I then had the Constable before me. and found that he had a writ. to arrest the negress and deliver her to his master from a magistrate in due form   I took his statement. of the affair which now have on file

When the Sergt arrested the negro men he brot them [to] the office, and as I understand the constable, kept the custody of the woman, and passed to Market Street. but when near a stone mill, on said street a large crowd of negroes compelld him & the owner of the negress, to take refuge in the mill. as soon as this was made Know to me I despatched Segt Fleming & others of the guard, to the locality, with a special verbal instruction not to interfere in any way. but if he found a mob there gathered. determined on mischief to warn them to *disperse immediately* whether composed of white or Black persons, and if they persisted in their violence to FIRE UPON untill they should disperse. The sergt performed the duty well and promptly, the negroes about (100) of them soon left the scene, after which the guard returned to qrs.

But these negroes talk defiantly, and their white aiders are continally at work with them, and I learn are determined to raise a *row*. I am informed that last night a band of negroes incited by 2 or more white men sought a negro whom they charge with giving information to the civil authorities

took him from the house and beat him most unmercifully, telling him they were ready to resist any process that might be had by reason of their conduct &c. I refered the negro to the civil authorities for redress. the case as I understand will come off before the Recorder, I recite these matters thus minutely in order to give you an idea of the State of affairs here   I believe these cowardly white "Devils" will suceed in getting up a general row & riot here if these negroes are suffered to remain here,

Therefore I would respectfuly suggest, that you should order Major Wilmot, to send them away from here. I cannot obtain the name of these white men or I would arrest them at once. they are very secret, in their Movements & should a riot occur, I would have not only the negroes but probably a hundred *white men* to contend with, and I sincerely desire. to avoid this Kind of trouble as my force would be inadiquate to cope with them   I am Genl Respectfuly

ALS   A B Cohen

Major A. B. Cohen to Brig. Gen. O. Guitar, 26 Feb. 1864, Unentered Letters Received, ser. 2594, Dept. of the MO, RG 393 Pt. 1 [C-179]. Three days later, General Odon Guitar, commander of the District of North Missouri, ordered Major Wilmot to remove all his black quartermaster employees from Hannibal, transferring them to Macon, the district headquarters. (Special Orders No. 12, Head Quarters Dist. North Mo., 29 Feb. 1864, vol. 290/676 DMo, p. 37, Special Orders, ser. 3545, Dist. of North MO, RG 393 Pt. 2 No. 226 [C-179].) The disarming of the black men employed by Major Wilmot had followed complaints in early December 1863 by the provost marshal that the quartermaster had "for a year past" employed "a considerable number of negroes" whom he allowed to carry revolvers and muskets. In November 1863, it was charged, after asking several white boys "if they did not think a *thousand negroes* could whip" the inhabitants of Hannibal and asserting that "he was going to kill somebody before he left the town," one of Wilmot's black employees had fired "at or in the direction of" two other white boys, killing one and wounding the other. Amid "considerable excitement," the local civil authorities had arrested the black man, proceeding thereafter to drag out their examination so as, the provost marshal believed, to enable "certain parties" to "rescue" the prisoner from official custody and dispense mob justice. Later, unknown parties had indeed "*released* [the prisoner] *from the calaboose.*" Of his fate once taken from the jail, the provost marshal made no mention. (Major A. B. Cohen to Brig. Genl. O. Guitar, 3 Dec. 1863 and 8 Dec. 1863, both in Letters Received, ser. 3537, Dist. of North MO, RG 393 Pt. 2 No. 226 [C-213].)

175: Commander of the Station at Independence, Missouri, to the Headquarters of the 4th Subdistrict of the District of Central Missouri

Independence Mo. March 15th 1864

Sir   I have the honor to call the attention of the Col. Comdg. 4th Sub. Dist, Dist. Central Mo to the fact that there are at this Station and in the vicinity of this Station from two hundred (200) to three hundred (300) refugees (black) consisting of old men, women and children, who are unable to get work, and thereby support themselves, consequently have to be supplied by Government with rations wood &c.

I would therefore most respectfully recommend that one or more of the deserted farms, in this vicinity, and belonging to rebels, be appropriated to their use, and they be required to move onto and till the same (with a sufficient number of overseers).   In my humble judgment it would not only keep them from eating the bread of idleness, and contracting habits of vice, but would be enabled, not only to support themselves (and thereby save a great expense to

Government) but would bring a revenue in *to Government*. Very Respectfully Your O.B.t. Servt.

ALS   J. Nelson Smith

Maj. J. Nelson Smith to 1st Lt. E. L. Burthoud, 15 Mar. 1864, Letters Received, ser. 3379, Dist. of Central MO, RG 393 Pt. 2 No. 217 [C-7149]. On March 21, the subdistrict commander forwarded Smith's letter to General Egbert B. Brown, commander of the District of Central Missouri, "for his decision"; on March 30, Brown in turn referred it to General William S. Rosecrans, commander of the Department of the Missouri. Neither an endorsement nor a letter from Rosecrans has been found among the records of the department, and it is not known when or under what circumstances Smith's letter was returned to the District of Central Missouri (among whose records it is filed).

176: Civil Official of Sedalia, Missouri, to the Commander of the District of Central Missouri

Sedalia [*Mo.*] 16ᵗʰ March 1864

Dʳ Sir   Our little village has bien incorporated, The board have passed an ordinance requiring all the negroes now quartered here to be moved, out of the place, Among them the Small Pox is, we have several cases also among the White population, This morning I called on Col Philips who informed me you had issued an order in relation to them requiring them to be moved West, and that the Post teams were also ordered to the West, Your idea to dispose of the Negroes as the Col informed me is I think the best that can be done with them. If the teams go West in a few days Will it not be best for you to order all the Negroes who are not employed to be transported with them not of course including those who are afflicted with Small pox, them we must provide for untill they can be [removed?]   The season of the year is now upon us when these negroes ought to be put in a position that they will not be a charge upon the Government   your idea as Col Philips informed me is I think the best arrangement that can be made with them, If the teams are ordered from here as he says they will be those who are well and not taking Care of themselves could no doubt be much better provided for under your plan than to remain here

Please let me hear from you at your earliest convenience as the Board have imposed upon me the task of having them removed out of the City limits or at least out of the white population, which really amounts to nothing except to prevent them from being

confined in large numbers in very small apartments where diseases
will be bred. I am sir very respectfully &C

ALS   G R Smith

[*Endorsement*] Head Q^{rs} Cent Dis^t Mo Warrensburg Mch 18 /64
Respectfully referred to Maj Gen Rosecrans Comdg Dept Mo   The
order for the removal of the families of negroes who had escaped to
Kansas or had joined the Service in that State to the *Line* of Missouri
was approved by Gen Schofield but no action was taken on it as the
weather was too cold and information was being obtained of the
number that had congregated about the Military Stations —[1] General
Order No 35 Dept Mo I understand would countermand previous
orders for the removal of the Negroes[2]   E B Brown Brig Gen
Vols Comg

[*Endorsement*] Hd Qrs Dept of the Mo St Louis Mch 22 1864.
Respectfully returned to Brig Gen E B Brown Comdg Central Dist
of Mo who will make a seperate report in each individual case, with
all the circumstances of the case to the Provost Marshal General of
the Dept who will be authorized to grant permits for the removal of
the negroes, with this exception General orders N° 35 is to be
rigidly enforced. By order of Maj Gen Rosecrans. Frank Eno Asst
Agt Genl

G. R. Smith to Genl. E. B. Brown, 16 Mar. 1864, Letters Received, ser.
3379, Dist. of Central MO, RG 393 Pt. 2 No. 217 [C-7150]. On March 18,
General Brown informed Smith that General John M. Schofield (Rosecrans's
predecessor) "had authorized me to remove the families of Negroes who had
fled to Kansas, to the Border," but that Rosecrans's General Order 35 "has
rendered it necessary that I should refer the question of the removal of those at
Sedalia to him." Promising to report Rosecrans's answer, Brown noted both
that "prompt action" should be taken to deal with "the disease that has broken
out among the Negroes" and that it would not be "practicable to move them to
Kansas until the weather is warm." (Brig. Genl. E. B. Brown to Genl. Geo.
R. Smith, 18 Mar. 1864, vol. 226 DMo, p. 46, Letters Sent, ser. 3372, Dist.
of Central MO, RG 393 Pt. 2 No. 217 [C-8761].) On March 21, the provost
marshal at Sedalia, who had "been informed that, there is a move on foot for
the benifit of the Destitute contrabands," reported to General William A.
Pile, who had charge of organizing black troops in Missouri, that many of the
black women and children in the town, having been driven away by their
owners after their husbands and fathers enlisted in the Union army, would "of
Nesesity, come to a state [of] suffering." "[H]umanity Demands that som-
thing should be done in their behalf," he declared. "[W]ith a little assistance

591

they will be able, to take care of themselves." On March 24, General Pile
forwarded the provost marshal's letter to General Rosecrans, asking that the
women and children at Sedalia be moved to the contraband camp at Benton
Barracks (in St. Louis). There, Pile proposed, "[a]ll the able bodied can be
provided with good homes at fair wages, and the helpless and infirm taken care
of and children sent to School." (*Freedom*, ser. 1, vol. 1: doc. 191.)

1 On January 27, 1864, a few days after complaining that black women and
children at posts in the District of Central Missouri were "a great annoyance"
and "everybody wants them removed," General Egbert B. Brown, commander
of the district, had sought permission from General John M. Schofield, commander of the Department of the Missouri, to transfer to the Missouri-Kansas
border the families of slaves who had escaped to Kansas. Four days later, an
endorsement from department headquarters had authorized Brown "to furnish
the transportation through his quarter master, provided it can be done without
injury to the public service." Although written over the name of General
William S. Rosecrans, who replaced Schofield as department commander on
January 30, the endorsement may have represented instructions from Schofield
and not Rosecrans; in any case, General Brown characterized the authorization
as having derived from Schofield. (Brig. Gen. E. B. Brown to Major O. D.
Greene, 22 Jan. 1864, filed as C-85 1864, Letters Received, ser. 2593, Dept.
of the MO, RG 393 Pt. 1 [C-8738]; summary of letter from Central Dist. of
Mo., 27 Jan. 1864, vol. 30 DMo, p. 121, Registers of Letters Received, ser.
2592, Dept. of the MO, RG 393 Pt. 1 [C-7828]; endorsement by A.A.G.
O. D. G., 31 Jan. 1863, vol. 41 DMo, p. 143, Endorsements Sent, ser.
2583, Dept. of the MO, RG 393 Pt. 1 [C-7828].) On February 8, General
Brown's adjutant had informed Colonel John F. Philips, the subdistrict commander at Sedalia, that authority had been received to "remove to some one or
more points on the Western Border, destitute negroes, (women and children)
who have been deserted alike by their men and masters," and he had directed
Philips to report the number of "destitute negroes of this class" at the posts in
his subdistrict. (A.A.G. James H. Steger to Colonel John F. Philips, 8 Feb.
1864, vol. 226 DMo, p. 4, Letters Sent, ser. 3372, Dist. of Central MO, RG
393 Pt. 2 No. 217 [C-8757].)
2 General Order 35, which General Brown believed to have nullified previous
permission to remove former slaves to the Kansas border, had been issued on
March 1, 1864, by General William S. Rosecrans. It prohibited "[t]he exporta-
tion of negroes from Missouri." "Missouri, for the coming year, needs all the
slave and other labor she has within her own border," Rosecrans had argued,
and "[h]umanity, as well as justice, forbids sending away to other States our
helpless slaves. Moreover, bad men have been engaged in stealing and carrying
negroes out of the State, and selling even those who were free." (*Official
Records*, ser. 1, vol. 34, pt. 2, p. 477.)

177: **Commander of the District of Central Missouri to the Headquarters of the Department of the Missouri, and Superintendent of the Organization of Black Troops in Missouri to the Headquarters of the Department**

Warrensburg [*Mo.*] March 19" 1864

Major   I have the honor to report in obedience to the orders of the Commanding General endorsed on the enclosed Communication from Lieut Swap A Pro Marshal to Brig Gen Pile[1] – That the situation of the these parties is similar to that of the same class of persons at numerous other places in this District and the same reasons for their removal from Tipton apply with equal force to the other points –   I estimate that this would take into S Louis about two thousand decrepid men, women, and children among whom the small pox and venereal prevails to a frightful extent –   As soon as those that are now congregated at the posts and towns were removed their places would be filled by a new emigration from the Country and the same necessity for their removal would follow   This would Continue as long as there were any slaves left in the Country –   The plea that these parties desire to follow their husbands who have entered the service has no force or truth in it, as in most Cases there are no binding Marital relations which they reccognise and they have new wives and husbands with every change of the seasons –   The reports of Capts B H Wilson at Marshal Capt R L. Ferguson at Sedalia and Hon Geo R Smith in behalf of the Municipal authorities of the latter place on this subject[2] which have been forwarded to Dept Head Quarters explains the situation of this class of persons at those points and are in their main features applicable to those at all others –   By the laws of this State the master is required to take care of his slaves and the statement that they are driven from their homes may be true in some cases though my investigations have not shown such a state of facts but in a few instances and they from the indolence and general worthlessness of the Slaves –   As soon as the weather becomes warm they may be ordered away from the posts and towns and when distributed about the country will be able to make a subsistence by their labor which is much needed –   Some of them may be sent to the Western Border where they can join their friends who have escaped into Kansas and by these means and by discouraging them from gathering about the villages and Military posts the evil will in a measure correct itself –   It would be a blessing to the country to move the negro families to St Louis as requested by Brig Gen Pile but it would be a serious evil to the city [and] would tend to [the] demoralisation disease and death of the negro   I am Very Truly Your ob^t Servant

ALS

E B Brown

Benton Bks Mo   March 29th 1864

Maj   I have the honor to report in relation to the subject matter refered to in the enclosed papers – that I have carefully read the communication of *Genl Brown* Comdg Disct of Central Mo, and not only fail to see any reasons for changing the request made in my endorsements of March 14th but additional reasons for urging the immediate removal of these persons to this place, that they may be cared for and protected.

The *"frightful"* prevalence of *"Small Pox and venereal"* among them shows most clearly that these persons have had no care or attention bestowed upon them,   Had they been properly vaccinated Small Pox would not have been *"Frightfully"* prevalent, and if the able bodied were hired out to labor as Servants in families where they would be stimulated to industry by the hope of reward (the great motive power prompting all men to labor except the Slave) and the infirm and aged furnished with Quarters, separated into family apartments: and the children sent to school – instead of being left to hang around military Posts to demoralize the soldiers and become demoralized and diseased themselves: they could be made useful to the State – preserved from the dangers that now threaten them – and the *disgrace* and *outrage* upon Humanity by their present condition avoided,

Enclosed you will find a report from Chaplain *Corkhill* Supt of Freed Persons giving the no under his care since Jany 12th 1864 and statistics in regard to diseases and deaths:

Attention is invited to the no of *Small Pox* and *venereal cases* and also to the number of deaths, taken in connection with the number recieved sick from the river and city, many of whom were in a dying condition when recieved, some to my own knowledge having died before they could be removed from the cars or waggons to hospital.

I submit that the danger apprehended by Genl Brown of the *"demoralization disease and death of the negros,"* by sending them here is purely immaginary.

The plainest dictates of common sense and *humanity* require that these *Homeless* and *friendless* people be taken charge of and provided for.

If a general System of superintendence and care could be provided, with authority to hire the able bodied out in localities where they congregate, to *loyal* and *humane* employers, and have the children, infirm, and aged cared for, this would perhaps be better than to have them all brought here –   but to order them "away from the Posts" to become the prey of bad men, with no redress for their wrongs or means of collecting their wages through either the civil or military authorities leaving "the evil" *thus* "to correct itself" would in my opinion be not only *cruel* but will result in the continuation of their present idle demoralized and diseased condition.

Unless some such general system of supervision and care can be provided I repeat most earnestly and respectfully the request that the women and children congregated around Military Posts and in want and suffering be sent to this place.

If this policy is adopted it would be better to have them sent in squads of twenty five to fifty in order to avoid crowding too large a number into quarters at once. Hundreds of applications for laborers both male and female are made per week that cannot be supplied. There is no difficulty in finding good homes for all who are able to work. I have the honor to be Very Respectfully Your Obt Servt

HLS

W^m. A. Pile

Brig. Gen. E. B. Brown to Major O. D. Greene, 19 Mar. 1864, and Brig. Genl. Wm. A. Pile to Maj. O. D. Greene, 29 Mar. 1864, both filed with S-264 1864, Letters Received, ser. 2593, Dept. of the MO, RG 393 Pt. 1 [C-163]. Enclosed in General Pile's letter is a report by W. H. Corkhill, the superintendent of contrabands at Benton Barracks (Hosp. Chap. W. H. Corkhill to Brig. Gen'l Pile, 29 Mar. 1864); it is nearly identical to one that is printed below, as doc. 179.

1 The letter from Lieutenant Franklin Swap, provost marshal at Tipton, Missouri, had been written on March 11 in response to an inquiry from General William A. Pile, superintendent of the organization of black troops in Missouri, about the condition of black soldiers' families who had been driven off by their owners. Swap had reported that none were suffering yet, "but from the number here who have left their masters or been driven off by them I am satisfied that many of them must suffer soon unless some measures are taken to prevent it." Many soldiers' relatives, he explained, followed their husbands, fathers, and brothers when they came to Tipton to enlist, "under the impression that they can go with them to St Louis." However, they were not permitted to travel on the railroad without a pass, which he was forbidden to give them. On March 14, General Pile had forwarded Swap's letter to the commander of the Department of the Missouri, with an endorsement proposing that Swap be directed to send the women and children to Benton Barracks (in St. Louis), "to be provided for in '*Contraband*' Department." From department headquarters, Swap's letter (and Pile's endorsement) had been forwarded to the commander of the District of Central Missouri "for investigation and report." (Lt. Franklin Swap to Brig. Genl. Wm. A. Pile, 11 Mar. 1864, S-264 1864, Letters Received, ser. 2593, Dept. of the MO, RG 393 Pt. 1 [C-163].)
2 The report of Captain Wilson has not been found among the records of the Department of the Missouri. Captain Ferguson's report, dated February 24, 1864, concerned "destitute refugees at Sedalia"; it had been forwarded to General William S. Rosecrans, the department commander, on March 15 with the following endorsement by General Egbert B. Brown, commander of the District of Central Missouri: "The men of These families have generally gone to Kansas and as soon as the weather becomes warm, I desire permission to

move their families after them." On March 18, by an endorsement that General Brown had not yet received, General Rosecrans had returned Ferguson's report and authorized Brown to remove "the families herein described." (Summary of letter from Capt. R. L. Ferguson, 24 Feb. 1864, vol. 30 DMo, p. 242, Registers of Letters Received, ser. 2592, Dept. of the MO, RG 393 Pt. 1 [C-7829]; endorsements by Col. John F. Philips, 24 Feb. 1864, Brig. Genl. E. B. Brown, 15 Mar. 1864, and Major Genl. Rosecrans, 18 Mar. 1864, vol. 41 DMo, pp. 398–400.) The letter from George R. Smith, on behalf of the municipal authorities of Sedalia, is printed above, as doc. 176.

178: Provost Marshal at New Madrid, Missouri, to the Commander of the St. Louis District

New Madrid Mo   March 24th /64

Sir. I have the honor to Submit a few facts for your Consideration. the Counties of New Madrid Pemiscott and Dunklin is in a deplorable condition. The out-laws Or Guerrillas has given Orders that there shall not be any farms cultivated Or carried on by Contrabands labour. And they are Enforceing their Orders. Mr″ Bushy of Pemiscott Co went to Memphis [*Tenn.*] and Employed about thirty Negros to work his farm and he has been compelled to take all his Contrabands back to Memphis. Also One Mr″ Weatherspoon had forty of those labourers and refused to comply with the above Orders and the Contrabands was Seized by the Guerrillas and taken to Arkansas. The Negros is all being Enrolled now and the prevailing Opinion is they will Soon be required to go in the Service. and they are being run off to Arkansas by those out-laws. And Refugees comeing in the neighborhood is being robed of all the Serviceable Horses & Mules on hand   Major Rabb Commanding this Post has only a Small Cavalry force at this Post, and it is useless to run after those roaming Bands when they are Operateing so far off. Caruthersville is on the Bank of the Miss. River forty miles below here in Pemiscott Co Mo. By the time a reporter gets up here and a Scout Started – they are in Arkansas. Now I would Suggest to you that if it is practicable in your Opinion to Establish a Small Post at Caruthersville it would protect the people in that Country in their farming and also protect transports on the River & would have a good Effect in controleing the Contraband trade that is being carried on in the border Counties, that is a good farming country   One hundred Cavalry would be of great importance and Easily subsisted. I would also say since restrictions has been removed in Mo. all kinds of Merchandise has been taken to Dunklin & Pemiscott Counties and it is about the

same as opening free trade with Arkansas. I am Very Respectfully
Your Ob^t^ Servt

ALS
O. P. Steele

Lt. O. P. Steele to Brig. Genl. C. B. Fisk, 24 Mar. 1864, Letters Received,
ser. 3285, St. Louis District, RG 393 Pt. 2 No. 211 [C-224]. No reply has
been found in the letters-sent volumes of the St. Louis District.

179: Superintendent of Contrabands at the Benton Barracks Contraband Camp to the Headquarters of the Superintendent of the Organization of Missouri Black Troops

Benton Barrack^s^ Mo March 28th 1864

Sir In obedience to your order of the 28th Inst I have the honor to
forward the following report. I entered upon my duties as
superintendent of Contrabands–Jany 12th 1864–Since which time
nine hundred and *forty Seven* (947) names have been entered upon my
books– Of these–*Two hundred* and *thirty four* (234) I have hired out
under contract to *loyal* responsible parties,– *Three hundred* and *thirty*
(330) have taken the responsibility of seeking places for them selves.
and have accordingly left for different parts of this and other
states– Ten (10) cases of small pox and Twenty (20) of Varioloid,
have occured A large propotion of these were from the City and
suburbs some comeing a distance of fourteen (14) miles with the
disease upon them, others have bee left upon the Levee by
steamboats in the advanced stages of the disease and forthwith have
been sent to these Quarters
   Five (5) cases of venereal disease have been under
treatment– *Three* (3) of these were contracted in the City and
reported here for medical treatment– The other *two* (2) were
contracted while on some kind of duty–perhaps as Laundress in the
Hospital–but no case has occured in or about these Quarters
   One hundred and *one* (101) have died *Eighteen* (18) of these were
small Children of the adults *thirty two* (32) were brought here sick
from other parts, many of them in a dying condition, when
arriveing at these Quarters presenting a terrible evidence of human
depravity on the part of those in whose employ they have been–
   We have now in Quarters *one hundred* and *forty three* (143), In
Hospital one hundred and twenty five (125) mostly Convalescents,
making a total in Camp of Two hundred and Sixty Eight (268) I
have no difficulty in procuring homes for all who are in a condition
to leave quarters as the demand is much greater than the supply

No arrests have been made in fact there has been no occasion. A more civil obedient people are not found in the State. – I have never heard an obsene expression and but few very few profane words – from any one of them.

Our quarters are daily visited by citizens and Soldiers prompted by business, or curiosity, and though trouble might very naturally be apprehended from this Service – still I am happy to be able to report that not a single case of disorder has ever occured – all visitors are ordered to leave the Quarters at roll Call and no one to my knowledge has in any instance refused to obey said Orders   I am General Very Respect Your obt Servt

HLcSr   Signed   W. H Corkhill

Hospital Chaplain W. H. Corkhill to A.A.A. Genl. J. H. Clendening, 28 Mar. 1864, Miscellaneous Letters & Reports Received, ser. 2595, Dept. of the MO, RG 393 Pt. 1 [C-172]. A month later, Corkhill reported that "the accumulation of Women and Children" at the contraband camp "and the number constantly arriving" demanded some arrangement for their support. High rents and food prices made it impossible for them to support themselves in the St. Louis area. Corkhill therefore proposed that he be authorized to travel to Mt. Pleasant, Iowa, "to confer with Friends of the Freedmen in that locality; In refference to this class, of persons, and make such provisions for them, as I may be able, to Effect." General William A. Pile, who was in charge of organizing black troops in Missouri, explained in an endorsement that the freedpeople in question were "women with Children who cannot be hired out to live in families as servants." "[T]heir removal to where rents are less and living Cheaper would enable them to support themselves." General Thomas Ewing, Jr., commander of the St. Louis District, also approved Corkhill's proposal, noting that the chaplain, formerly a resident of Mt. Pleasant, "feels confident he can arrange with farmers in that neighborhood to take these women and children and relieve the Government of all charge, except that of transporting them." On April 28, an order from the Department of the Missouri authorized the mission, which was evidently successful in establishing channels of employment; six months later, groups of freedpeople were still being transferred from St. Louis to Mt. Pleasant, under charge of Corkhill's successor. (Hospital Chap. W. H. Corkhill to A.A. General O. D. Greene, 27 Apr. 1864, C-415 1864, Letters Received, ser. 2593, Dept. of the MO, RG 393 Pt. 1 [C-153]; Special Orders No. 116, Head Quarters Dept. of the Mo., 28 Apr. 1864, vol. 59 DMo, pp. 555–57, Special Orders, ser. 2625, Dept. of the MO, RG 393 Pt. 1 [C-153]; Special Orders No. 292, Head Quarters Dept. of the Mo., 21 Oct. 1864, vol. 60 DMo, pp. 369–71, Special Orders, ser. 2625, Dept. of the MO, RG 393 Pt. 1 [C-153].)

180: Headquarters of the District of Central Missouri to the Commander of the 1st Subdistrict of the District of Central Missouri

Warrensburg [*Mo.*] March 29th 1864.

Colonel   I am directed by the General Commanding to state that information has been received at these Head Quarters to the effect that Negro Soldiers, on furlough from St Louis with the assistance of Squads of men belonging to the command stationed at Boonville, have repeatedly crossed into Howard County and Seizing upon wagons & Teams have loaded the same with Furniture, Tobacco and such other property as they desired and bringing with them their wives & children, recrossed to this side.

The Comd^g Officer at Boonville is said to rather encourage this unlawful proceeding as he is charged with leaving it optional with the men of his command whether they shall accompany the Negroes in their "Raids" or not.

Three such raids are said to have occurred during the first week of this Month

The General Commanding directs that you ascertain the facts and report with as little delay as possible   I have the honor to be Very Respectfully Your Ob^t Sev^t

HLcS   James H. Steger

Asst. Adjt. Genl. James H. Steger to Col. Geo. H. Hall, 29 Mar. 1864, vol. 226 DMo, pp. 58–59, Letters Sent, ser. 3372, Dist. of Central MO, RG 393 Pt. 2 No. 217 [C-8763]. No reply from the subdistrict commander has been found among the records of the District of Central Missouri. On April 12, the commander of the Department of the Missouri ordered the commander of the District of Central Missouri to "cause a restitution to be made of the value of the property taken or destroyed in Howard Co Mo. by certain colored soldiers on furlough in connection with some soldiers of Capt *Vansickle*'s Co 4" Cav MSM"; on the same day, his adjutant so informed the slaveholder whose property had been taken. (Asst. Adjt. Genl. Frank Eno to Brig. Genl. E. B. Brown, 12 Apr. 1864, and Asst. Adjt. Genl. Frank Eno to Mr. Thomas C. Boggs, 12 Apr. 1864, vol. 15 DMo, p. 217, Letters Sent, ser. 2571, Dept. of the MO, RG 393 Pt. 1 [C-181].)

181: Provost Marshal at Mexico, Missouri, to the Provost Marshal General of the Department of the Missouri

Mexico Mo Mar 31st 1864

Col. I am credibly informed that there are numerous bands of Bush whackers and Horse thieves prowling through the country. a number of Horses and considerable of money has been taken recently, mostly from Union Men. We have, and are still scouting through the country but our force in this Sub District is to small to do much, there being but one Co scattered through 4 counties when there should at least be four. in order to do much scouting, We have only about 25 or 30 men here, most of whom are Kept out much of the time, still we have been unable to capture any of these thieves.

There are some Negroe women here belonging to a widowed lady by the name of Harrison, their husbands enlisted some time since, and the mistress threatened to hire them out to different men to work out door, which they had never been in the habbit of doing, finding they were to be separated and made to work in the field they ran off and sought refuge here. the son of the mistress came the next day for the team they had taken and told the negroes they need never come back any more, that their mistress did not want them. the negroes consist of an old woman her two daughters, one having two children, what should be done with them.

I am informed that there are many cases where the negroe men enlist their wives are made to do the work formerly performed by the men. There is one other case I would lay before you, it is this, Some 9 months since a man by the name of   being a Rebel and not wishing to take the oath of alegiance to the government started for california and died on the way. he owned a negroe woman and two children   she supported herself and children for some nine months when a distant relative claims and takes her, puting one of her children in one part of the country, and taking her and the other to another part, Such cases seem unjust still I dont Know what course to pursue, therefore I respectfully submit the facts to you, Most Respectfully Your Obt Servt

ALS   A, A, Rice

[*Endorsement*] Head Qrs Dept of the Mo Off Provost Mar General Saint Louis Mo April 4 /64   Respectfully referred to the Gen[l] Com[dg] for his information, especially in regard to the want of troops in the counties referred to. The inquiry made in regard to negro women & children, how they are to be cared for, is but the repetition of such inquiry by every mail & from all parts of the

Dept. Some general policy will, of necessity, have to be adopted   J P Sanderson   Pro M[l] Gen[l]

Lt. A. A. Rice to Col., 31 Mar. 1864, Letters Received, ser. 2786, Provost Marshal General, Dept. of the MO, RG 393 Pt. 1 [C-7832]. The blank space in Rice's letter appears in the original.

182: Order by the Commander of the District of Central Missouri

Warrensburg Mo. April 5th 1864.
Special Orders N° 70   In accordance with directions from Head Quarters Department of the Missouri, the Negroes described in the reports herewith enclosed will be moved from *Sedalia* and *vicinity,* and from *Marshall* to *Little Santa Fe* Jackson County. Mo.

Col *John F. Philips,* Comdg 2[d] Sub District, will detail a competent officer and sufficient escort to protect them while being removed.

They will be furnished with *ten* days rations at *Sedalia* under the direction of Chaplain *R. A. Foster,* 7th Cav. M.S.M. who will be ordered by *Col Philips* to take charge of and remain with the Negroes at *Little Santa Fe,* until further orders.

On the arrival of the Negroes at *Little Santa Fe,* Chaplain *Foster* will supply them by requisition on the *A.C.S.* at *Kansas City* with *Sixty* days Rations, after which they will be expected to provide for themselves.

The Negroes referred to as being at *Marshall* will be moved direct to *Little Santa Fe.*

The Asst Quarter Master at *Sedalia* will furnish the necessary transportation for their removal.

Col Philips will see that this order is executed promptly and at the same time provision must be made for the health and comfort of the persons herein referred to.

. . . .

By order of Brig Genl Brown
HD

Excerpt from Special Orders No. 70, Head Quarters District of Central Mo., 5 Apr. 1864, vol. 248 DMo, pp. 48–49, Special Orders, ser. 3385, Dist. of Central MO, RG 393 Pt. 2 No. 217 [C-7818]. Little Santa Fe was on the western border of Missouri. The reports said to have been enclosed were not copied into the volume of special orders. The remainder of the order concerned several unrelated subjects. On May 21, a few weeks after the removal order was enforced, Colonel Philips pronounced the results in Sedalia "beneficial both to the negro and the citizens. With few exceptions," he declared, "women and children and men were sent off who were without any visible means of support, or what was needful to thin out the great excess of this vagrant population. Those who were left (and they were many), for fear they would likewise be sent off, diligently sought out employment and went industriously to work. There has been very little vagrancy here since, and I think those now here are behaving well and providing for themselves." (*Official Records*, ser. 1, vol. 34, pt. 3, p. 707.) For the condition of the people removed to Little Sante Fe, see below, doc. 190.

183: Provost Marshal of the 3rd Subdistrict of the District of Central Missouri to the Commander of the District

Warrensburg [*Mo.*] April 14th 1864

General   I have the honor to State that in accordance with your Order I have visited all of the Negro quarters at this Post, and find them in the following Condition   there are about thrity families of Negroes in this City. Occupying ten houses. generally but one room to the house.   Each family appear to have Six or Eight Children very poorly clad. and I think poorly fed. the most of them express a willingness to go any where in the Country. (that is.) if they Can be protected by the military.   the men are nearly all at work – Some for the Goverment. Some for the R.R. and others for the Citizens of the town.   their houses are generaly very filthy. and a good many of them are now Sick   as soon as the weather gets warmer they will Certainly Suffer from disease Caused by So many occupying a Small room.   I am General Very Respectfuly Your Obt Sevt

ALS   J H Smith

Lt. J. H. Smith to General E. B. Brown, 14 Apr. 1864, Unentered Letters Received, ser. 2594, Dept. of the MO, RG 393 Pt. 1 [C-185]. Endorsement.

184: Commander at Marshall, Missouri, to the Provost Marshal General of the Department of the Missouri

Marshall Mo April 15th 1864

Col.   We have quite a number of Negro men around here: who have left their masters.   The farmers about here are anxious to procure all the labor they can possibly get, but are deterred from hiring these negroes for fear of being Indicted by the Grand Jury. Their masters will not come & take them away. but object to any ones hiring them. Our county needs all the labor this year she can possibly get: Let the farmers procure all the labor possible and the crops this year will fall far short of any previous year; Please let me Know at your earliest convenience what can be done in the matter & oblige. Yours very Resptfly &c

ALS   B H Wilson

[*Endorsement*] Hd Qrs Dept of the Mo Off PM Genl St Louis Mo Apl 18 1864 Respectfully referred to the Genl Com^{dg} for his information. The time has arrived when, it seems to me, humanity imperatively demands the announcement of some definite policy or mode of action in these cases J P Sanderson PM Genl.

Captain B. H. Wilson to Col. J. P. Sanderson, 15 Apr. 1864, W-197 1864, Letters Received, ser. 2786, Provost Marshal General, Dept. of the MO, RG 393 Pt. 1 [C-199]. Wilson was an officer in the 7th Cavalry, Missouri State Militia. No response to Sanderson or to Wilson has been found in the letters-sent volumes of the Department of the Missouri.

185: Quartermaster of a Regiment of Missouri State Militia to the Chief Quartermaster of the Department of the Missouri

Jefferson City [*Mo.*] April 18th /64

Sir   your Order of April 15th /64 is Received ordering me to Discharge all citizens and contrabands teamsters employed under my direction in 4th Regt Cav M.S.M   permit me to state to you that I have an excelent set of contrabands employed as teamsters and they have always done their duty well and took excelent care of their teams and their mules are all looking well and I will further state that I have used all endevers to employ good contraband men that would do their duty and I have succeded well in doing so and further it is almost next to an impossability to get men detailed from the Ranks that will take an interest in taking care of their teams for as a general thing thy ar very carless in throwing down their Harness and not caring what becomes of the same and in fact I considder it with but a very few exceptions an injury to the service to detail men on extra duty as teamsters unless it is a case of actual necessity for I consider contrabands far more prefreble when they can be obtained and I would Request that they be retained in my

employ as teamsters if you Can possable do so   I am Cul very
Respectfuly your obedient Servant
ALS   D Bonham

[*Endorsement*] Head Q^{rs} Cent Dist Mo   Warrensburg Apl 21 /64
Respectfully referred to Maj^r Gen Rosecrans Comdg Dept Mo —   The
contraband teamsters are employed at a cost to the Governmt of $10
per month & Subsistence. The employment of Mounted Soldiers —
MSM costs — $28^{50} —   The employment of contrabands prevents their
families becoming a tax to the people or Governmt —   For these
reasons and that all the Soldiers used as teamsters reduces the
effective force I respectfuly reccommend that the order prohibiting
the employment of this class of persons for regimental teamsters be
countermanded   E B Brown   Brig Gen Vols   Comdg

Lt. D. Bonham to Col. Wm. Myres, 18 Apr. 1864, Letters Received, ser. 3379,
Dist. of Central MO, RG 393 Pt. 2 No. 217 [C-7146]. Other endorsements
referred Bonham's letter through military channels to the chief quartermaster,
whose own endorsement of April 26, 1864, informed General William S.
Rosecrans, the department commander, that the Quartermaster General's Office required regimental teamsters to be enlisted men. "Unless the Department
Commander authorizes the employment of Contrabands, those now in service
should be discharged." That same day Rosecrans ordered General Brown to
authorize the employment of contrabands as regimental teamsters in the District of Central Missouri. (Special Orders No. 114, Head Quarters Dept. of the
Mo., 26 Apr. 1864, vol. 59 DMo, pp. 548–51, Special Orders, ser. 2625,
Dept. of the MO, RG 393 Pt. 1 [C-7807].)

186: Officer in the Enrolled Missouri Militia to the Commander
of the District of North Missouri

Edina Knox. County Missou April 20th 1864
Dear Sir   Permit me to intrude upon your time for a few moments
to make some enquris in regard to certain matters that are
transpiring in this Community;   last night a number of men
Collected togethr and late in the night visited the houses of certain
Citizens who had free negro's hired. and with force and threats
drove off the negros from their employers with orders to leave the
Country,
    The negro's were men who had been servants to officrs in the 21
Reg Mo Vol. and who were recently home on furlough. and when
the returned permitted their servants to remain here. The negro's

were employed by loyal men, and the only charge I heard of that
was made against them was that they preferred loyal men as
employers rather than those of doubtful loyalty, The question then
is does the goverment intend to protect the free Negro? These men
swear that free negros shall not be permitted to stay in this
Community; and the [Com^y is? needing?] all the labor it Can
obtain. There is no hope to the negro from our Sheriff: [for?]
laboring under the *"Negro on the brain"*

I have been informed that for some weeks back there has been an
assemblage of men of doubtful loyalty, meeting once a week at
night, about Six or Seven miles from this place at the house of a
man who has been notoriously disloyal. Some of the loyal Citizens
of the neighborhood have been Somewhat uneasy on the
Subject. Our Union men watch with Jealous eye the movements of
the *late* rebels —

From the fact that in the troubles in 1862 I was in Command of
the Military Post at this Place as Col of the 50 Reg. E.M.M the
Union men come to me when any thing unusual occurs or [ther] fear
are arroused. We have no Pro Vost Marshall at this place. and I
have thought it proper that I Should Communcate thes facts to you
for your advice or action.

The loyal men of this County have the utmost Confidence in Your
action; which they had not in that of your predecessor — I have ben
requested to present these two case before you for your opinion   I
have the honor to be General Your Most Obt Svt

ALS

Samuel M Wirt

Col. Samuel M. Wirt to Brig. Genl. Clinton B. Fisk, 20 Apr. 1864, Letters
Received, ser. 3537, Dist. of North MO, RG 393 Pt. 2 No. 226 [C-217].
General Clinton B. Fisk (who had replaced General Odon Guitar as commander of the District of North Missouri in early April) replied with a request
for the names of the men who had driven off the freedmen, promising to "use
my authority against such dishonorable actions." (Brig. Genl. Clinton B. Fisk
to Col. Sam'l W. West, 30 Apr. 1864, vol. 284 DMo, p. 66, Letters Sent, ser.
3530, Dist. of North MO, RG 393 Pt. 2 No. 226 [C-217].)

187: Medical Director of the District of Central Missouri and
Quartermaster of the District to the Commander of the District

Warrensburg, Mo., May 18th *1864.*

General   We the undersigned a board of Officers appointed by
special orders No 106 Head-Quarters District of Central Missouri to
"examine into the condition of the contraband negroes at this station

and recommend the removal of all whose condition is such as to endanger the health of the people & themselves" have the honor to report as follows:

The board met at Nine oclock P.M. on Tuesday the 17" inst: present Surgeon R. P. Richardson Med Director & Capt T. S. Case Chief Q.M. and proceeded under the escort of Capt Chas Thurber, commanding Post, to visit twenty different old buildings occupied by negro families. In all instances we found these buildings very small, filthy and almost entirely without ventilation: & the occupants were crowded together in a manner calculated to ensure sickness among themselves & to spread it in the community. As an instance or evidence of the crowded condition of these huts we will state that in the twenty tenements visited by us, we found thirty three (33) men, fifty seven (57) women and ninety two children (92) being an average of over nine persons to each room, and that these rooms will not average over ten by twelve feet square.

Three deaths have already occurred in one of these buildings within the past few weeks and we are of the opinion that unless this condition of things is speedily amended by thinning out these negroes and compelling them to live in a more cleanly manner, epidemic disease of a violent & fatal character must result

We therefore respectfully recommend the removal of at least two thirds of these people to localities where they can have sufficient room to enable them to avoid the evil consequences of living as they now do   We have the honor General to be Your most obt Servants

Robt P. Richardson

HLS Theo. S. Case

[*Endorsement*] Head Q^{rs} Cent Dist Mo Warrensburg May 19 /64 Respectfully referred to Maj Gen Rosecrans Comdg Dept Mo with the request that I may be authorised to remove a part of the persons referred to in this report to the Border   E B Brown Brig Gen Vols Cmdg

[*Endorsement*] Hd Qrs Dept of the Mo Saint Louis June 7. 1864 Respectfully returned to Brig Genl E B Brown Comdg Central Dist of Missouri who is hereby authorized to make such removals as he may deem best for the interest of the public service. By order of Maj Genl Rosecrans Frank Eno, Asst Adjt Genl,

Surg. Robt. P. Richardson and Capt. Theo. S. Case to General, 18 May 1864, Letters Received, ser. 3379, Dist. of Central MO, RG 393 Pt. 2 No. 217 [C-

7147]. The report is written on the letterhead and in the handwriting of the quartermaster. The order appointing the board of officers had been issued by General Egbert B. Brown, commander of the district, on May 16, 1864. It had named as members of the board not only Surgeon Richardson and Captain Case, but also Colonel Theodore A. Switzler, provost marshal of the district. (Special Orders No. 106, Head Quarters District of Central Mo., 16 May 1864, vol. 248 DMo, p. 71, Special Orders, ser. 3385, Dist. of Central MO, RG 393 Pt. 2 No. 217 [C-7147].) On June 23, General Brown issued orders for removing from Warrensburg and its vicinity "all *vagrant* and *unemployed* Negroes . . . together with such as may wish to go." Supplied with twenty days' rations, they were to be taken to Little Santa Fe, Missouri, on the western border of the state, under the supervision of a chaplain who was empowered to draw rations for them "until otherwise directed." (Special Orders No. 133, Head Quarters District of Central Mo., 23 June 1864, vol. 248 DMo, pp. 91–92, Special Orders, ser. 3385, Dist. of Central MO, RG 393 Pt. 2 No. 217 [C-7818].) For a report on conditions in Little Santa Fe, see below, doc. 190.

188: Superintendent of the Organization of Missouri Black Troops to the Adjutant General of the Army

Benton Bks Mo May 21th 1864

Genl   I received your telegraph of 16th inst from Cairo Ills. and answered immediately,   since doing so I have learned of your proceeding to Washington, and deem it proper to report to you more in detail the State of the recruiting service for colored Regts in Mo.

There are from three to four thousand able bodied negros yet in the State but the time to enlist them has gone by.

Their masters have made contracts with them for the summer giving them part of the crop to be raised: and have succeeded in effectually over-coming their disposition to enlist; by filling their minds with the most terrible stories about the *"Fort Pillow"* massacre and getting them interested in the summer,s farming.

I am certain that the 72[d] is all that can be raised in the State during the Summer and doubtful about that being done.

All of these men might have been enlisted at the proper time – it is too late now.

Only two hundred recruits have been recieved at this rendezvous during the last thirty days.

I do not think that a change in the system of recruiting *now*; would materially increase the no of recruits until the Summer,s work is over.

I recommend that the organization of the Seventy second proceed under the charge of Lt Col Sears (in case I am sent to the field) and that no other Regts be commenced, but the surplus men if any be sent to fill up the Regts already raised. I have the honor to be Very Respectfully Your Obt Servt

W^m. A. Pile

HLS

Brig. Genl. Wm. A. Pile to Brig. Genl. L. Thomas, 21 May 1864, P-163 1864, Letters Received, ser. 360, Colored Troops Division, RG 94 [B-53]. Endorsement. The adjutant general recommended that Pile be reassigned to battlefield duty, and in July he was relieved by General Thomas Ewing, Jr., commander of the St. Louis District. (*Official Records*, ser. 3, vol. 4, pp. 433–34, 502.) Throughout the spring and summer of 1864, reports from various parts of the state complained that black men were deterred from enlisting by opportunities to earn wages or by incentives offered by their owners. In March, slaveholders in Washington County asked the local provost marshal to forcibly enlist their slaves, who had "left them and gone to work for themselves." In August, a resident of Callaway County who wanted slaves "draggooned" into the army to fill the county's draft quota complained that their owners had " 'out generaled' all attempts, to enlist them." "The majority, of these Negroes," he reported, "have been induced by their owners, to plant out large crops of tobacco, hoping to get them to Stay as long as possible." That same month, the provost marshal in Lafayette County reported the presence in Lexington of many black men who had left their masters and were "loafering about town or at work for themselves." Unless forced to do so, they would not enlist, because "[w]ages is high and demand for hands keep the negroes out of the Army." On August 5, following an inspection tour of the state, the judge advocate general of the army concluded that recruitment of black men in Missouri had "virtually closed." The remaining men, he estimated, would fill no more than a single regiment, "and from the very high price of labor and the extraordinary efforts made to retain them in agricultural pursuits, these, with limited exceptions, are not likely voluntarily to enter the military service." (*Freedom*, ser. 2: docs. 95n., 96; L. A. Thompson to Genl. C. B. Fisk, 4 Aug. 1864, Letters Received, ser. 3537, Dist. of North MO, RG 393 Pt. 2 No. 226 [C-7821]; *Official Records*, ser. 3, vol. 4, pp. 577–79.)

189: Commander of the District of North Missouri to the Commander of the Department of the Missouri

Saint Joseph [*Mo.*] May 31st 1864

General   I have the honor to submit in writing a statement of the case of which I made mention to you when I was last in St Louis, as having been temporarily suspended by my order from further prosecution in the Boone Court

The facts are as follows. Two Negro Men the property of James J Hickman of Boone County in the month of February 1863 ran away from their owner and sought refuge within our lines at Jefferson City, and were employed by the Quarter-Master   The Provost Marshal at Jefferson City after investigation issued to the said Negroes Henry and Henderson Bryant, certificates of freedom in pursuance of General Order No 35 Dept of Mo series of 1862.[1] Subsequently the Negroes were employed from the Quartermaster by one Pierce Buffington as laborers in his saw mill and remained with him as laborers and recieved wages regularly untill March 1864 — when they enlisted in the army of the Union; — joining one of the Regiment of A.D at Benton Barracks —   James J Hickman the former owner brought suit in the Boone Circuit Court — May term against Pierce Buffington claiming damages as follows   For their labor Six hundred and seventy six dollars and for their value — Three hundred dollars each six Hundred dollars —   Total damages twelve hundred and seventy six dollars.   The Grand Jury of Boone County in February last — found an indictment against the said Pierce Buffington for "Unlawfully dealing with slaves" and he Buffington was summoned for trial on said indictment at the May term.   Mr Buffingtons case was but one among many of the same kind — and the people who had employed Contrabands in that section being similarly involved petitioned the Millitary authorities to come to their relief —   After a thorough investigation of this case, I thought best to require the Boon Circuit Court to suspend the prosecutions against Mr Buffington untill all the facts could be placed before me

I therefore directed the Circuit Attorney of Boone County to suspend the prosecution both civil and criminal untill I could submit the cases to yourself —   I did this with reluctance as I desire to aid not to obstruct the civil law   But this was a point upon which there should be uniform action throughout the Department and one in which so many of our citizens are involved I thought it wise to arrest the proceeding.   Mr. Hickman was and is a secessionist beyond a doubt.   His slaves were free men by act of Congress and had a right to work for whom they desired and receive wages therefore   The Military authorities had given them papers of freedom and all Officers and men of the Dep't were commanded to respect them and their papers

Thousands of Citizens, Quartermasters, and others Goverment agents have employed these fugitives from slavery and paid them their wages —   All who have thus employed these fugitives from slavery are liable to prosecution both criminally and civilly under the statutes of Missouri   I have frequently myself compelled Negroes to go out from my camps and garrisons and go to work for farmers and others for wages. The articles of War prohibit me from returning them to their owners— My own judgement and the best interests of the Country, of the Service, and the Negroes themselves led me to remove them from idleness and crime to industry

I am even now enforcing that rule in St Joseph, Hannibal and Macon. I wish the blacks except such as can shoulder a Musket in the service of the Country would all stay at home with their masters, but they do not— I can not compel them to do so, but I can require them to work for somebody, and work they shall

It would look wrong for me to permit persons who employ them to be prosecuted for so doing

I have the honor to ask your early approval of my action in the case of Hickman vs Buffington and definite instructions as to other similar cases now pending in the rebel Counties I have the honor to be General Very Respectfully Your Obt Sev't

HLcSr   (signed) Clinton. B. Fisk

Brig. Genl. Clinton B. Fisk to Major Genl. W. S. Rosecrans, 31 May 1864, vol. 284 DMo, pp. 123–24, Letters Sent, ser. 3530, Dist. of North MO, RG 393 Pt. 2 No. 226 [C-7809]. In Macon, Fisk's "rule" had been announced only three days earlier, after the local military commander telegraphed that "Negroes of both sexes keep constantly coming in; they are crowding our camps. Think they ought not to be brought in so close contact with soldiers. Prostitution is worse than slavery." Fisk had immediately replied with instructions that "the negroes crowding into Macon must go to work on the farms where their labor is so much needed. We cannot permit them to remain in idleness and crime. We must not return them to masters nor encourage them to leave their homes, but we must insist upon industry, sobriety, and virtue; let them understand that work they must." (*Official Records*, ser. 1, vol. 34, pt. 4, pp. 92–93.) On June 3, the judge advocate of the Department of the Missouri, having considered the legal questions involved in the prosecution of Pierce Buffington, concluded that, because James Hickman "had aided and abetted" the rebellion, his slaves had become free when they entered Union military lines. Observing that Hickman's action against Buffington "is undoubtedly intended to oppose the Government and the emancipation of slaves," the judge advocate suggested that "[i]f General Fisk is authorized to check such proceedings now, it may save much trouble and annoyance in the future." (*Official Records*, ser. 1, vol. 34, pt. 4, pp. 191–92.)

1 General Order 35, issued by General Samuel R. Curtis, commander of the Department of the Missouri, in December 1862, had instructed provost marshals to investigate the circumstances of fugitive slaves who sought protection at Union military posts and camps, and to issue certificates of freedom to those whose owners were disloyal. (*Freedom*, ser. 1, vol. 1: doc. 172.)

Missouri

190: Provost Marshal of the 4th Subdistrict of the District of Central Missouri to the Provost Marshal of the District

Kansas City, Mo., July 1ˢᵗ *1864.*

Colonel, I have the honor to report that I have obtained information that there are several hundred Contrabands (Colored) consisting of women and children and old crippled men, a large number of whom were sent to Little Santa Fe Mo, by direction of General Brown, who are almost destitute of subsistance and clothing; also that the small Pox is raging among them to an alarming extent and that there is no Surgeon provided for them and none to be had in that vicinity—

The Kansas troops in that vicinity have established pickets to prevent them from going to Kansas and orders, I understand, have been issued, prohibiting them from going to Hickman Mils— This class of Contrabands are, consequently, in large numbers in the vicinity of Little Santa Fe Mo.

I would therefore most respectfully recommend that measures be at once taken, to provide them with medical assistance and subsistance— I am very respectfully Your obt Servt

ALS   J. C. W. Hall

Capt. J. C. W. Hall to Lt. Colonel T. A. Switzler, 1 July 1864, Letters Received, ser. 3379, Dist. of Central MO, RG 393 Pt. 2 No. 217 [C-8728]. By an endorsement of July 12, 1864, the district commander, General Egbert B. Brown, under whose authority the former slaves had been moved to the Missouri-Kansas border, referred Hall's letter to Colonel James H. Ford, commander of the 4th subdistrict, calling attention to a telegram of June 30 in which Brown had directed that Ford detail a noncommissioned officer "for this Service." Another endorsement. Conditions at Little Santa Fe did not deter General Brown from sending additional freedpeople there. On July 18, he instructed an officer escorting a forage train from Warrensburg to Hickman's Mill "to take charge of such Contraband and Refugee Negroes as desire to avail themselves of this opportunity of being removed to Little Santa Fe." (Special Orders No. 150, Head Quarters District of Central Mo., 18 July 1864, vol. 248 DMo, pp. 105–6, Special Orders, ser. 3385, Dist. of Central MO, RG 393 Pt. 2 No. 217 [C-7818].)

191: Daughter of a Missouri Employer to the Commander of the District of North Missouri

Kidder House [*Kidder, Mo.*] Aug 23 /64

Resp. Sir: My Mother has in her employ a black girl who formerly belonged to a rebel named Anderson Smith. The girl came here three weeks ago in company with her Mother (who is now in St Joe) saying Mr Smith had given them liberty to go & gave the girl money to help them through and went as far as to say that he did not want them to come back. He is here to-day trying to force the girl away. But on my Brother threatening him with a rebels portion of powder and lead he gave it up for the present and says he will aply to you for a permit to take her. Please inform me if she is his legal claim. He acknowledges the truth of thier assertions and wants to take her by force. Yours with respect

Hattie L Kies

P.S. Please answer at your earliest convienence   H. L. K.

ALS

Hattie L. Kies to Gen. Fisk, 23 Aug. 1864, Letters Received, ser. 3537, Dist. of North MO, RG 393 Pt. 2 No. 226 [C-7820]. Endorsement. The district commander's aide-de-camp assured Kies "that Mr. Anderson Smith will obtain no permit from this office to take back any slave. The black girl can live with your Mother in the enjoyment of the blessings of liberty as long as she may choose to do so." (1st Lt. W. T. Clarke to Miss Hattie L. Keis, 24 Aug. 1864, vol. 284 DMo, p. 33, Letters Sent, ser. 3530, Dist. of North MO, RG 393 Pt. 2 No. 226 [C-7820].)

192: Provost Marshal of the 2nd Subdistrict of North Missouri to the Provost Marshal General of the Department of the Missouri

Hannibal Mo   Jan. 12th 1865 —

Sir — I find that many of the Citizens of my Sub: Dist: especially the disloyal element — are anticipating the action of the state convention[1] and send their negroes adrift at such time as it suits them — and it is working very badly indeed up here —   The negro men have left their masters some time since — and those now on hand are principally women & children — and they being found rather unprofitable, and expensive — are turned loose upon the people to support —   Their former owners make no provision for them, save hauling them to within a convenient distance of some military post, and set them out with orders to never return home — telling them they are free.   There has one case come to my knowledge where the sons of an old man — drove the negroes off from the place — because the old man began to show signs of recognizing five of his servants as half brothers & sisters to his children lawfully begotten —   I have in two instances ordered that the former owners shall take care of these helpless negroes until some other provision is made for

612

them – and I think some action should be taken to let the rebels generally know that they shall not shirk in this manner. They, I think, fear the convention will resolve – that they shall take care of their helpless negroes on hand, until they get large enough to take care of themselves –

. . . .

ALS   John F. Tyler –

Excerpt from Col. John F. Tyler to Col. J. H. Baker, 12 Jan. 1865, N-66 1865, Letters Received, ser. 2786, Provost Marshal General, Dept. of the MO, RG 393 Pt. 1 [C-203]. The remainder of the letter reported the death of "[t]he notorious Childs," a bushwhacker, and threats against his captors. No reply has been found in the letters-sent volumes of the department's provost marshal general.

1 In the fall elections of 1864, Missouri voters had approved a call for, and elected delegates to, a state convention that would consider measures to abolish slavery. Assembling early in 1865, the convention on January 11 adopted a constitutional amendment providing for immediate and uncompensated emancipation, which, by proclamation of the governor, went into effect the same day.

193: Commander of the Post of Columbia, Missouri, to the Commander of the District of North Missouri

Columbia [*Mo.*] January 22nd 1865

General   There is one Subject here that is giving me much trouble. that is the collecting of large boddies of Negroes at this Place. I found a good many here when I assumed com'd on the 10th december 1864 and they have been Steadily increasing ever cince until they are ramed and Jamed in everry vacant house that they can get – it is true that they might get shelter for all with a reasonable amount of room if the citazens wer disposed to accomodate them – but in stead of making room for the blacks the citazens do every thing in their power to discomfeit them. here they are women and children many of their husbands in the federal army or have died there turned out of house and home without one meals victuals or one cent of money or even without wearing appearil suitable for winter or bedclothing to keep them from freezing this winter and unable to get employment – many of them are sick. I think the most of their sickness is caused from being crouded together and

613

they tell me that the Physicians of this place will not give them any attention unless they have the money to pay at the time the service is rendered

It is true that there is plenty of Room in the country but many of their former masters refuse to give them employment and others who woul be wiling to employ them are afrade to do so and further after a negro once comes to this Post it is considered unsafe for them to live in the country again Under the circumstances, General I think one of three things is necessary first to remove some of them from this Post Second to tax the citazens for the support of the negroes until some other arrangements can be made or they Will unquestionably have to Steal or Starve or freeze

you will confer a favor on me by giving Instructions on the Subject the citazens here are throwing every obstruction in my way that is posable and I have no doubt but they often make false representations in regard to what is going on here.

If It is in your power to have a provo marshal of the right kind sent here I think it would be a good thing for this country

The People here are wearing long faces cince the order for banishing some of the citazens of Boon came out.

You will doubtless receive petitions from so-called loyal men for the purpos of getting your orders revoked.

The shutting up of the whisky shops has caused you to get many a cursing here with such epithets as fool and coward.

If ever I saw a people who needed close watching and sever punishing it is the people of Boon county

I know of several citazens here who voted the radical ticket at the last Election and can out radical the original Radicals taking their words for it and at the same time they meet in secret with copperheads and plan your distruction for instance Col Frank Russel, who pretends to be our friend while with us and has been trying to get the Provo. Marshals office at this Place and at the same time he met our enemies in secret and wrote a piece calculated to injure you concerning your dilitariness in regard to sending troops (cav) here and had it published in the democrat signed Lincoln (it was published some weeks ago) I name this as one Instance only I could name others in regard to Col Russel and others

General I hope you will pardon. me for touching on somany subjects in the same communication I remain Gen'l your obe't Servt

ALS

Wm Colbert

Capt. Wm. Colbert to Brig. Gen'l C. B. Fisk, 22 Jan. 1865, C-30 1865, Letters Received, ser. 3537, Dist. of North MO, RG 393 Pt. 2 No. 226 [C-

218]. On January 25, the district commander referred Colbert's letter to General Grenville M. Dodge, commander of the Department of the Missouri, requesting "full instructions as to disposition to be made of the freed men in this and similar cases." An endorsement of the same date conveyed the orders of General Dodge: "They will be hired out to any person who needs them, and he will [be] protected in keeping them when rebels show disposition to drive them off: they will be quartered on them by orders and no person who owns slaves and has received their labor will be allowed to leave them out in cold. Put them on the abandoned plantations. Discretion must be used in this, but the Citizens must support them until they can take care of themselves." (Endorsement by Brig. General Clinton B. Fisk, 25 Jan. 1865, and endorsement by J. F. Bennett, 25 Jan. 1865, vol. 507 DMo, pp. 115–16, Endorsements Sent, ser. 2583, Dept. of the MO, RG 393 Pt. 2 No. 226 [C-218].)

194: **Superintendent of the Refugee Bureau in the Department of the Missouri to the Headquarters of the Department**

Saint Louis Mo Feb 13″ 1865

Dear Sir   I would like to go to Chicago & Milwaukee and try and make arrangements to send to those cities a number of Refugees white & black   Being extensively acquainted in those cities I believe I could subserve the Govt by such a trip–   I sent twenty families of colored people to Chicago late in the fall and I would like to ascertain how they are doing & if practicable send twenty or thirty more families off early in the spring   They are accumulating in considerable numbers just now and our new "Home" will soon be full   If this meets with the approbation of Gen Dodge and he will issue an order to that effect so I can get Transportation I will pay other expenses   I can leave for about ten days after my report is finished   I have the honor to be your most ob^t serv^t

ALS   A. Wright

Chaplain A. Wright to Major J. W. Barnes, 13 Feb. 1865, service record of Alpha Wright, 2nd U.S. Vol. Inf., Carded Records, Volunteer Organizations: Civil War, ser. 519, RG 94 [N-154]. A notation on the wrapper indicates that a special order was issued the same day sending Chaplain Wright to Chicago and Milwaukee. General Grenville M. Dodge, commander of the Department of the Missouri, had established the refugee bureau in late December 1864, by an order which also named Wright its superintendent. (*Official Records*, ser. 1, vol. 41, pt. 4, pp. 944–45.)

195: Resident of Columbia, Missouri, to the Commander of the
District of North Missouri

Columbia, Mo. Feb'y 21st 1865.
Gen'l. A negro man was hung, last night at Dr G. R. Jacob'^{s}, 6
miles from here, by Bushwhackers. This was in accordance with a
previous notice & order, from them, that all blacks were to leave in
10 Days, or be killed, by them. They alleged they had killed
another at Stephens, same day. Of course our blacks are in terrible
alarm.

I desire to tell you Gen'l, that we now have nearly about 4000,
colored people in this Co. & as many I expect in Callaway &
Howard Co^s.

What is to be done for their protection? Something surely. They
cannot get into our few garissoned places, there is *not* room for
them. & those already here are dyeing off at a fearful rate from their
Miserable condition. They cannot be removed, because they are too
numerous, & besides they are really needed in the country as
peasantry labourers. They want to stay too, & the home whites
need their assistance. They are free men, & ought not to be forced
off.

They, *at least* are loyal, & would fight if armed. Most of their
men, are off in the U.S. service, & those left are unarmed, &
helpless. So are all our white population, & unfortunately our
soldiers violently sieze nearly all arms they can find in the
country. Our Military are doubtless doing their best—as much as
could be expected— the fact is they have not horses enough, & may
be could not find them if they had.

I dare not offer suggestions, as to remedies, but it is my duty, &
privilege too, to call your attention to this sad state of these poor,
and innocent beings, & urge your better judg't to seek relief for
them.

Two colored Co^s of Militia, could be raised in the new Militia
organization, & if they are to be so treated, they might be armed.

I will gladly cooperate with you in taking any needed steps to
relieve this trouble.

Cap^n Bradley our Pro. Mar is Doing I think all in his
power   Respectfully
ALS   F. T. *Russell*

F. T. Russell to Gen'l, 21 Feb. 1865, Letters Received, ser. 3537, Dist. of
North MO, RG 393 Pt. 2 No. 226 [C-220]. On the following day Captain
H. N. Cook, 9th Cavalry, Missouri State Militia, who was stationed at Colum-
bia, also reported the hanging, and he enclosed the following note found on

the victim's body: "Killed for knot going into the federal arma by auder of Jim Jackson." Cook confessed that he could not explain "the object of this move, unless it is for the interest of the Substitute brokers, a great number of whom have made their appearance here since this occurance." As a result of the hanging, he added, "the negroes have been coming into town, in droves." (Capt. H. N. Cook to Lieut., 22 Feb. 1865, enclosing note, [20 Feb. 1865], Letters Received, ser. 3537, Dist. of North MO, RG 393 Pt. 2 No. 226 [C-220].) By an endorsement of February 24, General Clinton B. Fisk, commander of the District of North Missouri, referred Russell's letter to Captain Cook, asking his opinion "as to the expediency . . . of recruiting two companies of blacks for militia service in Boone Co." On February 28, in an endorsement that is no longer filed with Russell's letter, Cook responded that he thought it "entirely inexpedient" to organize a black militia and believed Russell to have made the proposal "solely for the purpose of getting control of affairs in this county." Although there were "quite a number" of black men of military age in Columbia, they were "not disposed to get into any kind of service" and "could as well be recruited for the U.S. service as for the militia." Some provision for freedpeople in the town was, Cook acknowledged, manifestly necessary. "There are something near 1,000 quartered in such a way as to make every kind of disease prevalent among them, and they are dying very rapidly." Although employment was available in the countryside, "they will not go to the country for fear of the bushwhackers." He therefore suggested "that arrangements be made to furnish them transportation to other States, where they could be employed." (*Official Records*, ser. 1, vol. 48, pt. 1, pp. 935–36.)

196: President of Columbia University to the Commander of the District of North Missouri

Columbia, Mo Mch 8 1865

Dear Sir, I shall be obliged to make brief reply to the communication with which you have honoured me, bearing date, Mch 4th inst. I propose to investigate the matter further, and report again.

The *main fact* touching the freedmen of Boone, is as you understand it. Those that remain in the County are, for the most part, congregated in Columbia; and in crowded quarters, with precarious support. *Measles* have been epidemic among them, and a good deal of fatality has occurred, from the force of the disease, and the exposure to which they have been subject. The picture has been overdrawn, by such as are disposed to disparage the ordinance of freedom. A coloured man, on whose judgment and truthfulness I rely, informs me that the deaths have been about *twenty five* in number; and he added that a like mortality, scattered over the county, would have passed without special remark. But that want and suffering have been aggravated by the congregating of these people in town, is undoubted.

When the army was first opened to the Africans, recruiting was out of favor *here*, and there was an exodus of the men of military age to Jefferson, Mexico, and other recruiting posts; and some women followed husbands and brothers. The result up to this time has been, that the county is depleted of its male coloured population, largely; and of negro *men*, the number here in Columbia is no greater now than before the rebellion. The crowd consists of women and children.

The farmers generally, throughout the county, would, I think, have preferred to provide these people work and support, on the farms; with or without special contracts for remuneration. Many are now ready to hire men and women for wages. – Many offer to let out their farms and farming stock to the freedmen on equal shares; – Others sell off their stock, and offer the *land* for cultivation – the tenant taking two thirds of the produce. There is a general disposition among former owners, to accept our altered social condition as a necessity; and, it is my belief, that arrangements would very readily be made for the absorption of the present surplus of black population in Columbia, throughout the County, were it not for the reign of terror, which makes the town less dangerous, for black and white, than the country. Within a few weeks, notices have been posted up in various places, warning black men and women that their lives were in peril, if found in the country, and several murders of colored people have followed in execution of the threat. This fact has caused the final influx of this people into town, and has broken up arrangements which were being made for the return of our previous surplus to the country. This brings us to the very pith of our trouble – to wit, the *rebellion in the brush*, which calls for military force in its suppression, just as distinctly as does the rebellion in Richmond. Civil power is just as inadequate a remedy, in this case, as in that. When *this case* shall have been successfully treated by the military power, so that no seed of rebellion be left to germinate in North Missouri I think we shall be able to dispose of the African, peaceably and successfully. Culture will bring out their moral as well as intellectual capabilities; – and their gentle and confiding nature will make them the *best peasantry in the world*; ill replaced by the sweepings of Europe. This is my theory; and if my cooperation were worth anything to you, I would very cheerfully offer it, in the work of developing, benefiting, and protecting this section of the human race. They are on our hands, & their best good is the problem we have to solve.

I have a favor to ask of the General.

Our University session will terminate in June. Three of our faculty are subject to military duty; and two of the three were drafted, and put in substitutes. Our young men are from various portions of Missouri, and from other states. My *petition* is, that the new military organization may be so managed, that we may be *practically* at ease, till the close of the present session. Please give this matter a favorable consideration.

You will, I hope, occasionally visit Columbia. We should be specially pleased to see you here at our Commencement, June 28th '65. Our graduating class is a good one, and the exercises not be uninteresting. I am, with great Respect, Yr. Obt. Serv.

ALS   J. H. Lathrop

J. H. Lathrop to Gen. Clinton B. Fisk, 8 Mar. 1865, Unentered Letters Received, ser. 2594, Dept. of the MO, RG 393 Pt. 1 [C-208]. The "communication" of March 4 from General Clinton B. Fisk, commander of the District of North Missouri, has not been found in the letters-sent volumes of that district. Fisk's response to Lathrop's letter merely thanked him for the information conveyed therein and accepted his invitation to attend commencement ceremonies. (Brig. Genl. Clinton B. Fisk to Rev. J. H. Lathrop, 13 Mar. 1865, vol. 284 DMo, p. 215, Letters Sent, ser. 3530, Dist. of North MO, RG 393 Pt. 2 No. 226 [C-208].)

197: Resident of Boone County, Missouri, to the Commander of the District of North Missouri, Enclosing a Letter from Two Residents of Nodaway County to the District Commander

Macon Mo. 22nd Mar" 1865.

Genl   I have the honor to report to you the result of my *Mission* into the *Platte Purchase* in behalf of the *Freedmen of Boone Cou Mo.* – Which was opposed by about one third of the inhabitants very ambitiously. in which they threatened to shoot me if I did not leave the country and otherwise to force away at the point of the Bayonett any *Immigration* I might make to that country.   In consequence of the inclemency of the weather high and impassible waters I was only able to embrace Andrew and Nodaway counties.

I was strenuously opposed by Messrs Russell & Philips of Savannah Thos Steele and McᶜCain's & Swinsford and [others of Nodaway county]. I assayed to form Aid Societies under the control of Committee's by which the first service of the freedmen were to be held for the aid rendered so as to render them self sustaining.   I had

an interview with a gentleman who resides at Omaha City who is to
have an interview with his Govenor and their R.R. Contractor &
make amicable arrangements for my objects & purposes & then
address me. I also wrote the Govenor of Mo. on the Subject. In
conclusion I can not omit reporting to you the Conductor of the
Savannah & St Joseph train who rejected my Passport Ticket with a
kind of triumph Mr. Tho'^{s} A. Massey who is not regarded in St
Joseph by loyalists as being loyal who should be displaced legally. I
herewith append accompanying letters of Messrs. Saunders Roseberry
& Alexander. Very affec^y

ALS   John W Jameson

[*Enclosure*]   Maryville [*Mo.*] March 14th 1865
Dr Sir   John W Jameson your agent on behalf of the Colored people
of Boon County and surrounding Country has visited our County
and used every Exertion, in the discharge of his duties as
such,   There is some opposition to the measure on the part of some
of our citizens, but we are satisfied that quited a number of Colored
persons can be introduced into this County by having an agent here
who may send for hands whenever they are desired, or, what is
better if the Government would send a number of hands, both male
& female here under the Care of an agent they would be imployed at
once at good wages, but we do not think it best to organize public
Committee for that purpose as it would produce an unnecessary
Excitement over the matter which Can be avoided in the manner
indicated   A large number of farmers are anxious to procure hands
for their farms and will as we believed as soon as an oppertunity is
offered avail themselves of Colored help.

We believe the Government could with safty send two hundred
hands to this County, say, 1/2 male & female and that every
one would be immediately employed, and that the person
hireing them would advance to the government the amount of
transportation.   Get them introduced once and all will be right, and
those now opposed will be as anxious to Employ them as any
one,   We remain Yours Respect

                                                    M. G. Roseberry
HLS   Joseph. E. Alexander

John W. Jameson to Majr. Genl. C. B. Fiske, 22 Mar. 1865, enclosing M. G.
Roseberry and Joseph E. Alexander to Genl. C. B. Fisk, 14 Mar. 1865,
Letters Received, ser. 3537, Dist. of North MO, RG 393 Pt. 2 No. 226 [C-
7817]. Also enclosed is a letter to the district commander from James

Saunders, a resident of Andrew County, where Jameson had also been trying to persuade farmers to import black laborers from Boone County. "Some foolish opposition has been made to their introduction here," Saunders reported; "but it was made in every instance that I can hear of, except one, by men and women who are but one remove above *dead matter*. . . . These modern savans or Solomons are either *Campbellites* or *Baptists*," the single exception being "an *Englishman*." "Many [black laborers] are wanted here nevertheless," but employers "are afraid to make advances in money in order to get the blacks here." (Ja. Saunders to Genl. Fisk, 20 Mar. 1865.) Jameson had undertaken his "mission" under the sponsorship of General Clinton B. Fisk, commander of the District of North Missouri. On March 3, 1865, in a letter introducing Jameson to Saunders, Fisk had reported that in Boone and neighboring counties along the Missouri River "many negroes with their families [are] seeking homes, fleeing from their old masters and from fear of assassination by guerrillas." Jameson, who was on his way to northwest Missouri, was "very kindly interesting himself in behalf of the refugee freedmen" and would "act as agent between the colored people and parties who desire their services." (*Official Records*, ser. 1, vol. 48, pt. 1, p. 1078.)

198: White Farmer or Farm Laborer to a White Farmer

[*southwest Missouri? spring? 1865*]
Mr. Campbell Sir   I am Ablede to go to town to day and I Cant help you   Mr Campbell Sir thare appears to be sum dissatisfaction about that niger setler on this side of the Creek   it appears that all the nabers is opposes to it   as we have had no nigers on this Sid of the Creek I think it would be beter for him to go back on his own Side   I am afraid it will Cass others to setel herere   that we had beter keep them out when we have them out

   Mr Campbell Sir I Send this to you not to rase any hard feeling
ALS   James Martin

James Martin to Mr. Campbell, [spring? 1865], Unentered Letters Received, ser. 2594, Dept. of the MO, RG 393 Pt. 1 [C-210]. Itself undated and lacking any covering letter or file notations, Martin's note is filed among documents dating chiefly from April and May, 1865, and addressed to the headquarters of the District of Southwest Missouri. There is other evidence from that district of opposition both to black settlers and to white farmers who employed them. In late March 1865, a militia officer reported that in the vicinity of Barclay's Mills, in Benton County, "rebels and rebel sympathizers" had "tried to prevent negroes from living in that vicinity, and have threatened to run them out of the county." They had also "made threats against all persons keeping negroes about them." (*Official Records*, ser. 1, vol. 48, pt. 1, p. 1273.)

199: Order by the Commander of the 4th Subdistrict of the
District of Central Missouri

Lexington Mo   April 25" 1865
General Orders No. 7   In as much as the Guerrillas have, in some
portions of this District, added to their hellish catalogue of crimes
the murder of unoffending negroes; and, as it has been frequently
reported at these Headquarters, that rebel families in Lafayette
County have threatened their former servants with the merciless
veangeance of the Bushwhacker, if they should presume to leave
them or exercise the simplest rights of freemen; and, as, in support
of this threat, the Bushwhackers have told the negroes that if they
could not produce certificates from their former masters, that they
were faithfully and uncomplainingly serving them as heretofore, that
the threat of their former masters would be carried out: therefore,
information of any family or persons having made such threats,
will be taken as sufficient evidence of their complicity with
Bushwhackers, upon which they will be arrested by any commander
of troops in this Sub District and forwarded to these Head Quarters
to be tried upon charges of consorting with Bushwhackers, and of
being accessories to murder   By order of B. K. Davis Maj. Comdg
4" Sub Dist Cent. Mo.
HDc

General Orders No. 7, Head Quarters 4" Sub. Dist., Cent. D, Mo., 25 Apr.
1865, vol. 383/942 DMo, General Orders, ser. 3367, 4th Subdist. of Central
MO, RG 393 Pt. 2 No. 216 [C-7105].

CHAPTER 6
Kentucky

Kentucky

6

Kentucky

THE LAST BORDER STATE to end slavery, Kentucky was also the most successful at obstructing free labor. Like their counterparts in Maryland and Missouri, slaveholders in Kentucky cited their loyalty to the Union to demand military protection of slavery and protest actions that threatened the institution. Although developments during the war converted some opponents of free labor into reluctant supporters, the process advanced more slowly than in the other border states. During the final months of the conflict, freedpeople in Maryland and Missouri – their emancipation accomplished by state action – could hire themselves as wage workers with comparative ease. In Kentucky, by contrast, slavery blocked the advance of free labor. Not only were many black people still held in bondage, but the legality of slavery also had a chilling effect on prospective employers. Although proslavery Kentuckians ultimately lost the fight to preserve the institution, their last-ditch struggle, which continued for months after the defeat of the Confederacy, imparted a distinctive cast to the evolution of new working arrangements.[1]

Slavery was both stronger and more widespread in Kentucky than in the other border states. Exceeding 225,000 in 1860, the state's slaves outnumbered those in Maryland and Missouri combined. They were also far less geographically concentrated. Except for the mountainous counties of eastern Kentucky, slaves could be found throughout the state. Most were owned in small units, but about one-fifth of them lived and worked on farms and plantations with twenty or more slaves, chiefly in the bluegrass region surrounding Lexington and in a few tobacco-raising counties bordering Tennessee. In the state as a whole, slaves accounted for 20 percent of the population.

Widespread ownership of slaves was supplemented by extensive hiring, giving many nonslaveholders an interest in slavery. In much of the

---

[1] In this essay, quotations and statements of fact that appear without footnotes are drawn from the documents included in the chapter. Accounts of the transition from slavery to freedom in Kentucky include *Freedom*, ser. 1, vol. 1: chap. 8; E. Merton Coulter, *The Civil War and Readjustment in Kentucky* (Chapel Hill, N.C., 1926); Victor B. Howard, *Black Liberation in Kentucky: Emancipation and Freedom, 1862–1884* (Lexington, Ky., 1983).

state, tobacco was the principal market crop, but the wealth of the bluegrass region rested on the production of hemp, grain, and livestock. Slaves worked in every sector of the economy. In Louisville, the state's metropolis, white workers, including European immigrants, greatly outnumbered slave laborers, but slavery had not been overwhelmed as it had in St. Louis and Baltimore. Nor did Kentucky have many black people who were free. Low rates of manumission and hostile legislation left fewer than 11,000 free blacks in the state on the eve of the Civil War.[2]

Once the war began, the character of federal occupation shaped the possibilities for free labor. After early 1862, when Union armies moved south to campaign in Tennessee and along the Mississippi River, Kentucky saw limited military activity. Save for a major Confederate counteroffensive in the fall of 1862, there was little sustained fighting within the state. Union forces occupied widely scattered posts along strategic rivers and railroad lines: Columbus and Paducah in western Kentucky; Louisville, Munfordville, Bowling Green, and Lebanon in the central part of the state. The bluegrass region, where the largest number of slaves was concentrated, had only small federal installations until 1863, when Camp Nelson, an important supply depot, was established not far from Lexington. Many Kentucky slaves were far removed from Union troops.

Throughout the war, the army pursued political as well as strategic goals. Besides defending the state from invasion and guarding the supply lines that sustained the troops operating further south, military authorities were charged with protecting the persons and property of loyal Kentuckians and maintaining the state's adherence to the Union. These tasks kept army officers in constant contact with state and local officials, who zealously enforced laws pertaining to slavery and insisted that Northern soldiers do the same. Mindful of Kentucky's strategic significance and its delicate political situation, the War Department deemed it best to garrison the state largely with Kentucky troops commanded by Kentucky officers.[3]

Sensitive to charges that the Union army fronted for abolitionism, federal commanders took pains to demonstrate their soundness on the slavery question. General Don Carlos Buell, who in November 1861 assumed command of the Department of the Ohio (including all of

[2]   On slavery in Kentucky, see *Freedom*, ser. 1. vol. 1: pp. 493–94; Ivan E. McDougle, *Slavery in Kentucky, 1792–1865* (1918; reprint ed., Westport, Conn., 1970); J. Winston Coleman, *Slavery Times in Kentucky* (Chapel Hill, N.C., 1940). For figures on population and slaveholding, see U.S., Census Office, 8th Census, *Population of the United States in 1860* (Washington, 1864), pp. 180–81; U.S., Census Office, 8th Census, *Agriculture of the United States in 1860* (Washington, 1864), pp. 228–29.

[3]   On military occupation and wartime politics in Kentucky, see *Freedom*, ser. 1, vol. 1: chap. 8.

Kentucky except the westernmost counties), took seriously the general-in-chief's injunction to give the state's "domestic institutions . . . every constitutional protection." When slaves began to seek refuge in federal encampments, Buell and other officers ruled that "constitutional protection" of slave property entailed denying the fugitives admittance and returning to their owners those who had already found shelter among the Yankees. If adherence to that policy meant turning away men who could contribute – or were already contributing – to the war effort, then so be it. Any gain to the Union army from mobilizing the labor of fugitive slaves was not worth alienating powerful and well-connected Kentuckians. Besides, with the civil law still in force, anyone who abetted a fugitive or employed a slave without the owner's consent was liable to both criminal prosecution and civil lawsuit. Thus one Northern general found the presence of runaway slaves in his camp "embarrassing," although he had put the men to work and found them "handy with teams, and generally useful." His superior officer, General William T. Sherman, displayed less ambivalence. "[M]y opinion," Sherman wrote, "is that the laws of the state of Kentucky are in full force and that negroes must be surrendered on application of their masters or agents or delivered over to the sheriff of the County."[4]

Even after Congress made it illegal for Union soldiers to remand fugitive slaves to owners or their agents, troops in Kentucky routinely expelled black people from their camps. The exiled freedpeople were often captured by civil authorities and either returned to their owners or jailed and sold. To avoid that fate, runaways cultivated personal relationships with Northern soldiers and officers, usually by serving as servants or company cooks. Sponsorship by individual Northerners, the slaves hoped, might provide both protection and freedom.

Denying themselves access to the labor of runaway slaves, federal commanders in Kentucky looked to others to perform the work of the army. Much of the burden fell upon soldiers detailed from the ranks. At times, shorthanded military employers also contracted with white civilians or hired slaves from their owners. At most posts, work gangs composed of soldiers, white laborers, and hired slaves ordinarily sufficed. When military necessity demanded a large number of laborers on short notice, impressment was the order of the day. Free-black men were especially attractive targets, since they generally lacked white patrons willing to intercede on their behalf, but their numbers were far too small to meet the army's needs. Impressment necessarily extended to white civilians and to slaves. In mid-1862, gangs of impressed slaves repaired the railroad leading southward from Columbus. During the Confederate invasion of Kentucky in August and September of that

---

[4] *Official Records*, ser. 1, vol. 4, p. 342; *Freedom*, ser. 1, vol. 1: pp. 495–98 and docs. 197, 199–201.

year, impressed slaves worked on the defenses of Louisville alongside free-black and white laborers.[5]

The impressment of slaves angered slaveholders, who opposed any military interference with their laborers. Yet however much it inconvenienced the masters, compulsory labor for the federal army offered no benefit to the slaves either. Forced to leave home and family, they often worked harder and longer for the Yankees than they had for their owners, receiving meager provisions and no wages at all. Upon completion of their tasks, they were simply returned to their owners. Forced labor for the Union meant neither freedom nor free labor.

By early 1863, slave and free-black Kentuckians were not the only black people working for the army within the state. The fortunes of war had brought into Kentucky large numbers of ex-slaves from Confederate territory to the south. Hailing from Tennessee, northern Alabama, and northern Mississippi, most of them could claim freedom under the confiscation acts or the Emancipation Proclamation. When General Buell's army returned to Kentucky in the fall of 1862 to counter the invasion of Confederate General Braxton Bragg, thousands of freedpeople accompanied the troops as laborers and refugees. In Kentucky, military authorities and civil officials labeled them "contrabands," employing that term to distinguish them from black people native to the state.[6]

The presence of contrabands from the Confederate states complicated the already problematic issues of slavery, military labor, and the relationship between military and civilian authority. Federal officials attempted to draw a bright line between contrabands from Confederate territory, who were presumed to be legally free, and the slaves of Kentuckians, who were presumed to be the rightful property of their owners. Able-bodied contrabands were assigned to military labor, whereas fugitive slaves from Kentucky were expelled from camp or even returned to their owners. Military employers became increasingly dependent upon the contrabands to do the army's labor. At Columbus, contraband workers replaced Irish laborers at one-third the wages, a considerable savings to the government. At Louisville, General Jeremiah T. Boyle, commander of the District of Western Kentucky, ordered that all able-bodied contraband men be put to work on the city's fortifications.[7]

---

[5] On Columbus, see Special Order No. 124, Hd. Qrs. Dist. of the Miss., 14 July 1862, vol. 101/248A DKy, pp. 67–68, Special Orders, ser. 995, Dist. of the MS, RG 393 Pt. 2 No. 24 [C-7242]; on Louisville, see *Official Records*, ser. 1, vol. 16, pt. 2, pp. 480–81, 542.

[6] In addition to the relevant documents in this chapter, see *Freedom*, ser. 1, vol. 1: p. 503, and docs. 209–11, 213–15.

[7] *Freedom*, ser. 1, vol. 1: docs. 210, 217An. Instead of working directly for military employers, some of the contrabands were hired to private contractors; see, for example, Col. M. Mundy to Lt. Col. Richmond, 6 May 1863, vol. 142/330 DKy, Letters Sent, ser. 729, Post of Louisville KY, RG 393 Pt. 4 [C-6001].

The distinction between contrabands – from the Confederacy – and fugitive slaves – from Kentucky – proved difficult to maintain. Civil officials commonly ignored it, arresting all black people found at large without passes, jailing them, and selling them to the highest bidder if no owner put in a claim. Thousands of freedpeople from Confederate territory were arrested in late 1862 and early 1863. Many of them had worked as the servants of Union officers and often carried passes from their employers. They were frequently taken into custody as they prepared to cross the Ohio River for employment in the North. At least 1,000 were eventually sold to Kentucky purchasers, the freedom conferred upon them by federal law nullified by civil officials in an ostensibly loyal state.[8] Under orders from President Lincoln, General Ambrose E. Burnside, commander of the Department of the Ohio, voided the sales and affirmed the contrabands' right to freedom. Yet, taking to heart instructions to "avoid . . . any forcible collision with State authority," Burnside also forbade Union soldiers and officers to "aid or abet" the escape of slaves who belonged to citizens of Kentucky, to employ them "against the consent of their owners," or to impede attempts by civil officials to recapture them.[9]

In enforcing Burnside's order, General Boyle directed that former slaves wrongfully jailed or sold should be set free, but not allowed to come and go as they pleased. Instead, they were considered "captives of war" and, as such, subject to military control. In May 1863, Boyle created a "contraband commission" at Louisville to enforce this policy, instructing its members to forward all contrabands to military employers. In the immediate vicinity of the city, the commission retrieved many freedpeople from bondage and took custody of former slaves from the Confederate states who had been intercepted by military authorities. The able-bodied men they assigned to labor on fortifications and railroads; the women, to military hospitals. Children were less easily disposed of. By November 1863, the commission had placed some fifty or sixty in the hands of private citizens who agreed "to take good care of them, feed and clothe them well, and hold them subject to our order."[10]

Reenslaved freedpeople distant from Louisville or other Union posts were less fortunate. Six months after its creation, the contraband commission complained that purchasers of former slaves in remote reaches of the countryside refused to relinquish them and civil authorities refused to cooperate in obtaining their release.[11]

---

[8] In addition to the relevant documents in this chapter, see *Freedom*, ser. 1, vol. 1: docs. 209–15, 216n., 223A.

[9] *Freedom*, ser. 1, vol. 1: docs. 215n., 216.

[10] For Boyle's instructions, see *Freedom*, ser. 1, vol. 1: doc. 217A. On the appointment of the contraband commission, see *Freedom*, ser. 1, vol. 1: doc. 217An. On its operations, see *Freedom*, ser. 1, vol. 1: doc. 223A. On the Louisville contrabands more generally, see *Freedom*, ser. 1, vol. 1: pp. 503–8, and docs. 209–217B, 223A–B.

[11] *Freedom*, ser. 1, vol. 1: doc. 223A.

The contrabands taken up by military authorities and assigned to military labor composed a large proportion of the army's work force in Kentucky. Contraband men "placed on the public works" received wages of $10.20 from the government. They labored not only on the fortifications at Louisville and other posts, but also at railroad construction and repair. In November 1863, the Louisville contraband commission reported that during the preceding month alone, it had sent 150 men to work on a railroad extension near the town of Lebanon. The availability of such laborers reduced the temptation to employ runaway Kentucky slaves. Elsewhere in the Union-occupied South, military labor offered free-labor employment to fugitive slaves, but in Kentucky such opportunities were severely limited.[12]

Aware of both the risk of recapture and the meager opportunities for free-labor employment in their home state, many Kentucky slaves fled beyond its borders. Thousands crossed the Ohio River to free territory in the Midwest. Communities of black refugees sprang up in towns and cities on the river's northern bank. Former slaves congregated at Jeffersonville and New Albany, Indiana, across from Louisville, and at Evansville, Indiana, near Henderson and Owensboro, Kentucky. As before the war, fugitive slaves from central and northern Kentucky headed for Cincinnati, Ohio, while runaways from the western part of the state sought their fortune in Cairo, Illinois. Once they reached the free states, able-bodied men had little trouble finding military or civilian employment, and women worked as nurses, laundresses, and domestic servants.[13]

Tennessee became another popular destination for Kentucky slaves, particularly in 1863 as the Union army prepared for the Chattanooga campaign. To support its advance into east Tennessee, the army needed thousands of teamsters, drovers, dockhands, railroad workers, and common laborers. Federal authorities in Tennessee, unlike those in Kentucky, asked few questions about the status and nativity of their black employees. Before long, military work gangs at Nashville, Clarksville, Fort Donelson, Gallatin, and other posts in middle Tennessee routinely included runaway slaves from Kentucky.[14]

The enlistment of black soldiers in the Midwest and in Tennessee created additional possibilities for Kentucky slaves. The War Department's authorization of black enlistment in the free states in 1863 led to the establishment of recruiting depots in Indiana and Ohio. Beginning that fall, hundreds of slaves from southern Kentucky also made their way to recruiting depots at Clarksville and Gallatin, in Tennessee. Their owners entered a vigorous protest, urging military authorities to

[12] In addition to the relevant documents in this chapter, see *Freedom*, ser. 1, vol. 1: doc. 223A.
[13] In addition to the relevant documents in this chapter, see *Freedom*, ser. 1, vol. 1: doc. 232; *Freedom*, ser. 2: doc. 98.
[14] In addition to the relevant documents in this chapter, see *Freedom*, ser. 1, vol. 1: doc. 224.

return the men or, failing that, at least send them back "long enough to enable them to prepare their crops for market." But the complaints were unavailing. In all, one well-placed Union official estimated, as many as 7,000 black people from Kentucky had fled the state by January 1864.[15]

Led by Governor Thomas E. Bramlette, slaveholders lobbied strenuously to prevent recruitment in Kentucky itself. For a time, they succeeded. Only in the westernmost counties of the state, administered by the Department of the Tennessee, did the army enlist black men during 1863. In theory, recruiters there were to confine their efforts to ex-slaves from Tennessee and other seceded states; no slaves from Kentucky were eligible unless their owners were rebels in arms or duly convicted of aiding the Confederates. In practice, however, some Kentucky slaves were accepted into the service, while others found work with quartermasters and engineers at Paducah and Columbus. As early as June 1863, slaveholders near Paducah were demanding military action to stem "the almost daily departure of slaves from their owners," which threatened "the most ruinous consequences . . . in the total loss of their crops, now in cultivation."[16]

No less disturbing to local slaveholders, Union authorities at Columbus established a contraband camp to house the women, children, and old people who accompanied prospective enlistees. To diminish the camp's unsettling effects upon slavery, however, many of its residents were relocated to Island 10, Tennessee, in the Mississippi River just south of the Kentucky border. Just as steadily, however, fugitive slaves continued to arrive at Columbus, once more swelling its black population.

Throughout 1863, except in the westernmost counties, federal military authorities in Kentucky undertook neither the recruitment of black soldiers nor the establishment of contraband camps. Indeed, rather than undermine slavery by mobilizing black labor, they attempted to put black men to military use by mobilizing slavery. In mid-August, General Boyle ordered the impressment of 6,000 slave men in central Kentucky; soon thereafter, he called for an additional 8,000.[17] The slaves were collected at Camp Nelson, on the southern edge of the bluegrass region. From there, they were sent to repair the wretched roads to East Tennessee, over which food, livestock, and materiel would be transported to supply the Union troops operating in that region. Other impressed slaves labored on a railroad under con-

---

[15] In addition to the relevant documents in this chapter, see *Freedom*, ser. 1, vol. 1: doc. 224; *Freedom*, ser. 2: docs. 97–98; *Official Records*, ser. 3, vol. 5, pp. 118–24.

[16] In addition to the relevant documents in this chapter, see *Freedom*, ser. 1, vol. 1: doc. 220; *Freedom*, ser. 2: p. 193, and doc. 99.

[17] In addition to the relevant documents in this chapter, see *Freedom*, ser. 1, vol. 1: docs. 221, 226.

struction from Lebanon, Kentucky, through Danville and toward East Tennessee. This massive military claim upon Kentucky's slave labor force figured prominently in the Lincoln administration's decision to postpone the enlistment of black soldiers within the state. Secretary of War Edwin M. Stanton deemed it less important that black men serve as soldiers than that they "be employed in labor for the supply of other troops."[18]

But implementation of Boyle's impressment orders demonstrated how thoroughly slavery hamstrung the mobilization of black laborers. Resistance from slaveholders slowed collection of the labor force, which never approached the hoped-for dimensions. As of late September 1863, only 2,300 slaves were working on the railroad, leading the War Department to doubt whether the project could be finished before the spring military campaign.[19] In the meantime, requests for laborers for other purposes went unfilled. Unable to obtain enough teamsters to move supplies to Knoxville, Tennessee, a frustrated General Boyle proposed to alter fundamentally the federal government's relationship with slave laborers in Kentucky. In November 1863, he sought permission to formally enlist as many as 3,000 slave men as teamsters, paying $300 to each of their owners. "The owners of negroes," Boyle assured the War Department, "prefer getting some compensation rather than loose the whole value of the slave." Secretary of War Stanton approved the proposal, stipulating that any slave so enlisted would become free and be paid $10 per month. But when Boyle tried to secure Governor Bramlette's cooperation, the governor identified an insuperable obstacle: Under the laws of Kentucky, manumitted slaves were required to leave the state immediately, and their owners were liable if they failed to do so. In the end, nothing came of Boyle's proposal. Still, facing the prospect of losing their investment in slaves who left Kentucky to enlist or perform military labor, a significant number of slaveholders saw advantage in hiring them to military employers within the state. Many owners, a Union officer in southern Kentucky reported, were "not only willing, but . . . exceedingly anxious" to make such arrangements.[20]

Yet if some Kentucky slaveholders were prepared to cede control of their slaves in exchange for monetary compensation, most were not. Large numbers hired slave men to military employers or private railroad companies, hoping at once to profit from the arrangement, safeguard their slaves from impressment, prevent them from running away, and retain the prerogatives of mastership. But their strategy sometimes backfired. Owners who hired slaves to work as teamsters under assurances that they would not be sent far beyond the nearby post of Lebanon

[18] *Freedom*, ser. 2: doc. 77.
[19] *Freedom*, ser. 1, vol. 1: doc. 221n.
[20] In addition to the relevant documents in this chapter, see *Freedom*, ser. 1, vol. 1: doc. 224; *Freedom*, ser. 2: doc. 97.

learned within weeks that they had been transferred to Nashville. There the quartermaster treated them as he did other black teamsters, paying wages to the men and not their owners. Military needs overrode the masters' property rights. When Governor Bramlette petitioned the War Department on the owners' behalf, the department's inaction attested to its growing impatience with interference in the mobilization of much-needed black workers.[21]

That mobilization entered a new phase beginning in the spring of 1864. With the recruitment of slave men well under way in the other border states, the War Department moved to end Kentucky's exemption. In February, recruiters in the western counties, previously forbidden to enlist slaves, received orders permitting such enlistment. Two months later, General Stephen G. Burbridge, who succeeded General Boyle as commander of the rest of the state, authorized the recruitment of free-black men and slaves whose owners consented to the enlistment. Finally, in early June, the War Department removed all restrictions on the enlistment of slaves, despite vocal opposition from slaveholders.[22] During the year that followed, black men from Kentucky joined the Union army by the thousands. Almost 60 percent of the state's black men of military age enlisted, the largest proportion of any Southern state. Recruitment received an additional boost in March 1865, when Congress freed the wives and children of black soldiers, wherever they resided and whoever claimed them as property. The enlistment of their husbands and fathers became a long-awaited means of liberation for slaves owned by unionist masters and mistresses.[23]

The wholesale recruitment of black men created problems for military employers as well as slaveholders. At Camp Nelson, where black men had been working on the fortifications, army engineers complained in the spring of 1864 that "[o]ur working force grows daily smaller" as their laborers enlisted.[24] Fortunately for the engineers, the camp's recruiting officers were so overwhelmed by the number of slaves arriving to join the army that they sent some 1,200 recruits to work for the engineers until arrangements could be made to organize them into regiments. At Camp Nelson and elsewhere in the state, quartermasters and commissary officers also pressed to have newly enlisted black soldiers assigned to them. Many military employers, in fact, preferred detailed black soldiers to hired black civilians. The former, governed by

---

[21] *Freedom*, ser. 1, vol. 1: docs. 225A–C.

[22] For a general discussion of the extension of recruitment to Kentucky and the other border states, see *Freedom*, ser. 2: chap. 4, especially pp. 192–94. On recruitment in western Kentucky, see *Freedom*, ser. 2: docs. 98–99. For a summary of recruitment elsewhere in state, see *Freedom*, ser. 2: doc. 100.

[23] For the joint resolution, see *Statutes at Large*, vol. 13, p. 571. For an accounting of black enlistments in Kentucky and elsewhere, see *Freedom*, ser. 2: p. 12.

[24] John R. Gilliss to Lt. Col. J. H. Simpson, 22 Apr. 1864, Letters & Reports Received, ser. 3541, Engineer, Dept. of the OH, RG 393 Pt. 1 [C-4650].

military regulations, were more easily disciplined than the latter. Not only were unenlisted freedmen subject in many instances to claims by putative owners, but, being "mere employées," they could "come and go at will."

The War Department agreed. In December, Adjutant General Thomas directed that black military laborers "should be enlisted," but he also stipulated that their places could be taken by "details made from Colored Troops" as well as by men unsuited for armed service. The organization of several "invalid" regiments, composed of men physically disqualified for field service but not for fatigue duty, eased the apprehension of military employers that recruitment would deplete the pool of available black laborers.

Increased employment of slave men as laborers and soldiers was not accompanied by any provision for their wives, children, and parents. In the Union-occupied Confederacy, military service carried with it a promise of support for dependents, but not in the border states. "[A]lthough the law prohibits the return of slaves to their owners by the military authorities," the Secretary of War ruled in July 1864, "yet it does not provide for their reception and support in idleness at military camps." Adjutant General Lorenzo Thomas ordered women, children, and other slaves not suitable for military duty "to remain at their respective homes, where, under the State laws, their masters are bound to take care of them." Moreover, Thomas averred, "all of this class of persons are required to assist in securing the crops, now suffering in many cases for the want of labor." A local recruiter pointedly advised the families of black recruits of their "error" in accompanying the men to Union camps and "promptly returned to thier Owners" any who refused to retrace their steps. Such measures aimed at sparing the government both the expense and the political complications that would follow the provision of relief to former slaves not employed by the army.[25]

Though legally obligated to support their slaves, many slaveholders spurned the responsibility. Owners whose men had left to enlist or perform military labor often expelled their families, either to punish them or to save the expense of their maintenance. Women with young children and the aged and disabled of both sexes were especially likely to be evicted. The mistress of Sarah Hill, a crippled slave, "refused her further support saying that the negroes would soon be free & she would have nothing more to do with them." Hill was taken in by a household of working-class white women, but many castaway slaves were less fortunate. Having no recourse to private charity, they journeyed to

---

[25] In addition to the relevant documents in this chapter, see *Freedom*, ser. 1, vol. 1: doc. 233; *Freedom*, ser. 2: docs. 102C, 105.

Union camps and recruitment rendezvous. Even as military authorities insisted that slaveholders provide for the families of black soldiers, many owners refused to do so.[26]

Despite the strictures of federal policy, settlements of black refugees sprang up near recruiting depots. The largest was at Camp Nelson, which was accessible to slaves in the bluegrass region. Living in makeshift huts constructed by their husbands and fathers, the women and children at Camp Nelson received no formal provision from military authorities. They eked out a livelihood by sharing the rations and wages of their men, augmented by whatever work they could find. In typical fashion, the wife of one black soldier "earned money by washing." She and her children received nary "a mouthfull off the Government."

Although some Union officers at Camp Nelson tolerated and even encouraged the refugee settlement, General Speed Smith Fry, a slaveholding Kentuckian who commanded the post, refused his sanction. Citing orders discouraging federal relief to Kentucky ex-slaves, he periodically expelled the refugees. But many of the evicted women and children made their way back into the camp, joined by newcomers from the countryside. In late 1864, after several cycles of eviction and reentry, about 400 refugees remained in residence.

On a frigid day that November, General Fry ordered the expulsion of all black women and children at Camp Nelson, irrespective of age or physical condition. The refugees watched in horror as soldiers tore down their quarters, sometimes before they could evacuate them. Driven from camp in government wagons and turned out into the bitter cold, they sought shelter at the nearby towns of Nicholasville and Lexington and in abandoned buildings along the road. Some died before they could find refuge. One desperate woman was "so pressed with hunger as to offer her child for sale . . . to obtain bread." Stunned and outraged, the black soldiers and laborers at Camp Nelson protested the inhumane treatment of their families. A number of Union officers and representatives of Northern benevolent societies echoed their sentiments, counterposing the men's service to the nation with the nation's abuse of their kin. The complaints – and the scathing publicity accorded the episode by the Northern press – precipitated a dramatic reversal of policy. Within a week of the expulsion, Fry's superiors ordered him to revoke his eviction order and assigned Captain Theron E. Hall, a quartermaster, to shelter and employ "every woman and child" who sought refuge at Camp Nelson.[27]

The "refugee home" established by Hall quickly filled to capacity. During the winter of 1864–1865, hundreds of ex-slave women, chil-

---

[26] In addition to the relevant documents in this chapter, see *Freedom*, ser. 1, vol. 1: docs. 231, 233; *Freedom*, ser. 2: docs. 107–8.

[27] In addition to the relevant documents in this chapter, see *Freedom*, ser. 2: docs. 107, 312A–B.

dren, and old people arrived at Camp Nelson, some of them accompanying would-be enlistees, others turned out of their quarters by vengeful masters.[28] Accessions continued throughout the spring and summer of 1865, as former slaves fled their homes in quest of freedom or were driven from them by their owners. Although federal authorities sponsored no other safe haven elsewhere in the state, soldiers' families and other black refugees also took up residence near military posts where black soldiers were stationed, sometimes receiving assistance from Northern freedmen's aid societies. Many others fled to Louisville or left Kentucky altogether.

The unrestricted enlistment of black men gave Kentucky slaves unprecedented leverage to negotiate labor arrangements with their owners. Many slaves demanded concessions in return for remaining at home. Although masters and mistresses usually rejected such demands outright, they sometimes came to terms. A slaveholder in western Kentucky agreed to give his slaves one-fifth of the tobacco they produced during 1864. Even that proved insufficient to keep the men out of the army – although one of them purportedly offered to return home in exchange for additional "priveliges and advantages." Explaining why enlistments had declined by the summer of 1864, a provost marshal noted that many a slaveholder had "adopted the plan of paying his negro wages to induce him to stay with him." Slave men enjoyed the broadest range of options, but some women also struck bargains. After one woman fled to claim the freedom due her by virtue of her husband's enlistment, her erstwhile owner convinced her to return by promising to "give her as much as was given to other colored persons."[29]

The continued legality of slavery, however, made private free-labor arrangements susceptible to abuse. Because they remained slaves in the eyes of the law, black people had no way to collect unpaid wages or bring suit against abusive employers. Slaveholders who promised wages or other compensation could renege with impunity. Under state laws that forbade hiring a slave without the owner's consent, they could also prosecute – or threaten to prosecute – anyone else who employed their "slaves." Some wily employers cited the same laws to avoid paying exslaves they had hired, on the grounds that the titular owner might yet enter a claim and they wished to "avoid the responsibility of paying both Owner and Slave." In addition to exploiting existing legal instruments, defenders of slavery crafted new ones. In March 1865, a state judge ruled that Congress had no authority to emancipate the wives and children of black soldiers in Kentucky. The decision threatened the

---

[28] On the origins and wartime history of the refugee home, see, in addition to the relevant documents in this chapter, *Freedom*, ser. 2: doc. 312B.

[29] In addition to the relevant documents in this chapter, see Capt. Wm. C. Grier to Maj. W. H. Sidell, 15 July 1864, Letters Received, ser. 3967, KY Actg. Asst. Pro. Mar. Gen., RG 110 [R-16].

livelihood of soldiers' families, whose employers "wish to keep them but cannot as they are liable to a heavy fine for doing so."[30]

The end of the war found slavery still in force in Kentucky. Through the remaining months of 1865, its legal standing hampered the efforts of military officials to protect former slaves who engaged in free-labor employment. Lacking authority to overturn state legislation, they could only induce – not compel – slaveholders to deal with their slaves as free workers. In June 1865, General John M. Palmer, commander of the Department of Kentucky, ordered that in all cases where owners pledged in writing to "regard [their slaves] as hired servants" and pay them wages, military authorities would enforce the agreements. Palmer "advised" black Kentuckians to make such pacts "whenever they can do so with just and humane masters." The desire to establish free labor in principle overshadowed attention to actual working conditions or amount of payment. The officer in charge of black recruitment in Kentucky instructed a subordinate to "[e]ncourage the negroes to hire out even at low wages, to parties who will recognize them as free agents." But relatively few slaveholders were prepared to contract with people they still claimed as property. What is more, the law was on their side. Months after the end of the war, an official of the Freedmen's Bureau deplored the total absence of "any law, Civil or Military, by which contracts could be enforced on the contracting parties." That circumstance, among others, drove General Clinton B. Fisk, the bureau's assistant commissioner in Tennessee and Kentucky, to decry the feasibility of administering a *"Freed*mens Bureau for *Slaves."*[31]

If some slaveholders struck formal or informal free-labor bargains with former slaves, others became increasingly determined to sustain the remnants of slavery. Despairing of obtaining freedom and remunerative employment on their home ground, slaves left the state by the thousands. Most of the emigrants journeyed only as far as southern Indiana and Ohio. "The Great Deep of Slavery in Kentucky is broken up," reported a resident of Evansville, Indiana, in late 1864, "and the fragments are rapidly drifting northward across the Ohio River." The fragments increased and the drift quickened in the months that followed. An order by General Palmer, issued in May 1865, accelerated the movement by authorizing the issue of military passes to all black people in Louisville who wished to travel in search of employment.

---

[30] On the state court decision and its effects, see *Freedom*, ser. 1, vol. 1: doc. 239; *Freedom*, ser. 2: doc. 112. On the use of state laws to obstruct the development of free labor, see, in addition to the relevant documents in this chapter, *Freedom*, ser. 1, vol. 1: docs. 247–49, 253.

[31] In addition to the relevant documents in this chapter, see Jas. P. Flint to Col. McCaleb, 8 Sept. 1865, enclosed in Lt. Col. H. A. McCaleb to Maj. Jno. H. Cochrane, 12 Sept. 1865, M-83 1865, Registered Letters Received, ser. 3379, TN Asst. Comr., RG 105 [A-6176]; *Freedom*, ser. 1, vol. 1: docs. 247–49, 254.

Later extended to the whole of Kentucky, the policy overrode state laws that forbade public conveyances to transport slaves without their owners' permission. In July, Palmer estimated that some 5,000 black people had crossed the Ohio River from Louisville alone. Farmers and planters near Lexington complained that, owing to the exodus, they could not "obtain help to save their Crop."[32]

Slaves who preferred to remain at home also took steps to liberate themselves. A few defiantly refused to work for their masters and mistresses while continuing to lodge in their accustomed quarters. One master sought the aid of federal authorities in ridding himself of a forty-nine-year-old "Boy" who would not "serve me any longer, and affirms that he is as free as I am."[33]

Enemies of free labor deployed naked force as well as legal niceties in attempting to thwart the emerging order. Slaveholders threatened not only slaves and former slaves who dared to hire themselves, but also white people who dared to hire them. The master of one black soldier's wife vowed to "kill any man that will take [her] in to a house to live with him." Often violence took collective form. During the summer and fall of 1865, guerrilla bands who had attacked white unionists during the war reconstituted themselves as regulators and turned their wrath against former slaves and their employers. Regulators and loosely organized groups of thugs ran rampant in areas beyond the reach of federal arms. Whether issued by individuals or groups, threats of violence led many former slaves to abandon free-labor employment for the sake of their lives. Some fifty freedpeople in one bluegrass county, who had rented a farm from their former owner and gathered a crop, lost it all shortly after the harvest, when they were "ordered to leave in a hurry" and their cabins were burned.[34]

Legal and extralegal intimidation obstructed the development of free labor in Kentucky, although not entirely. In the fall of 1865, one Freedmen's Bureau official noted that some slaveholders had contracted with their juridical slaves, "believing it to be more profitable to do so, than to hold them as formerly." But, by his own admission, such arrangements extended to only "[a] few" instances.[35] Not until ratification of the Thirteenth Amendment in December 1865 – eight months after the defeat of the Confederacy – could free labor take shape in Kentucky apart from the complications posed by slavery.

---

[32] On the northward migration, see, in addition to the relevant documents in this chapter, *Freedom*, ser. 2: doc. 303. For Palmer's pass order and its effects, see *Freedom*, ser. 1, vol. 1: docs. 240–41, 246.

[33] *Freedom*, ser. 1, vol. 1: doc. 238.

[34] In addition to the relevant documents in this chapter, see *Freedom*, ser. 2: doc. 304; E. P. Johnson to Mr. Frank Whiting, 14 Oct. 1865, enclosed in R. E. Farwell to Genl. Clinton B. Fisk, 14 Oct. 1865, F-89 1865, Registered Letters Received, ser. 3379, TN Asst. Comr., RG 105 [A-6117].

[35] Lt. Col. A. M. York to Brig. Gen'l C. B. Fisk, 2 Oct. 1865, Y-7 1865, Registered Letters Received, ser. 3379, TN Asst. Comr., RG 105 [A-6219].

Kentucky

200: Commander of the Department of the Ohio to the Commander of the District of Western Kentucky

Cincinnati Ohio Dec [*14?, 1862*]
General: Lieut *E. S. Richardson* 1ˢᵗ Tenn Vols AAQr. Master at Smithland in writing to Colon'l *Swords* AQ.M Gen'l, says he is much embarrassed by an order recently issued by Colonel *Foster*, directing that all "contrabands" be removed from the post, and as he is dependent upon negroes for the labor in his Dep't., he is at a loss where to obtain the ncessary force for the discharge of his duties.

Col *Foster's* order was based, I presume, upon one issued by you to prevent our garrison's becoming the asylum of worthess negroes who had no claims to Mil'y protection, and not to interfere with the employment of blacks or whites in any of the Depts, when hired or fatigue labor is necessary, and you will instruct Col *Foster* to modify or explain his order accordingly. Very Respectfully Your Obed't Servᵗ

HLcSr   (Signed) H G Wright

Maj. Gen'l H. G. Wright to Brig. Gen'l J. T. Boyle, [14?] Dec. [1862], vol. 4 DO, pp. 400–401, Letters Sent, ser. 3482, Dept. of the OH, RG 393 Pt. 1 [C-4619]. Colonel John W. Foster, whose order to expel contrabands had disrupted the quartermaster's labor force at Smithland, Kentucky, was himself headquartered at Henderson, Kentucky. On November 27, 1862, General Jeremiah T. Boyle, commander of the District of Western Kentucky, had ordered subordinate officers to permit no slaves to enter army camps and to "[place] beyond the guard lines" all who were then in camp. (*Freedom*, ser. 1, vol. 1: doc. 206.) There is no extant letters-sent volume in which to search for instructions that Boyle may have issued in compliance with General Wright's letter.

201: Ordnance Sergeant at Fort Anderson, Kentucky, to the Commander of the Post of Paducah, Kentucky

Fort Anderson   Paducah Ky   Feb. 1ˢᵗ 1863
Col   In Consequence of the late fire at the fort the place was in A Bad Condition walls Ready to fall at any moment   Col Nobl than Commanding Orderd A Board of Survey and it was Decided to pull the walls down and Save the Brick and Lead in the Old Building   at that time *Civel Law* Came in force[1] and it was almost impossible to keep the Contrabands civel officers Catching them Out On the Street and Returning them to thire Owners *or them that Claimed to Own them*   Capt G. A Pierce than Qʳ Master – Sent Some

eighty down to the fort But even than they where not Secure   the New Q^r Master – Lt Drake Sent me Orders to turn Some of them Out   I Reported the facts to you and you Orderd me to Keep them in the employ of the Ordnance Department But now find them turned Over to Lt Drake again and in consequence all my work must Stop for the present   I have but one Small magazene and that in Bad Condition   I have Some ten or twelve thousand [*bricks*] cleand and Lime slacked all Reddy to commence work   My amunition is piled up under platfors Some Only Covered with Tarpaulens to Shelter it from the weather – A great deal of it Stored in town in An unsafe place   if you Can let me have A Detael of Contrabands enugh to do my work I can take care of thire wives without any expene to the goverment   it would not only be the means of making the fort Secure for the parrepets by Constant Rains are washing away but it would be the means of Savng thousands of dollars to the Goverment   I am yours to Command

ALS   R. D. Cunningham

Ord. Srgt. R. D. Cunningham to Col. H. Dougherty, 1 Feb. 1863, Letters Received, ser. 991, Dist. of Columbus, RG 393 Pt. 2 No. 24 [C-7207]. Cunningham signed as commander of siege guns at Fort Anderson.

1 On December 7, 1862, General Ulysses S. Grant, commander of the 13th Army Corps and Department of the Tennessee, had issued an order reestablishing civil authority in the part of Kentucky that lay within his department (the counties west of the Tennessee River). It announced that at recent elections Kentucky had chosen Union men for all state offices, "both for enacting and executing her laws," and that, therefore, "the military authorities within this Department and in the State of Kentucky are prohibited from any interference in such execution." (Special Field Orders No. 16, Hd. Qrs. 13th Army Corps, Dept. of the Tennessee, 7 Dec. 1862, Orders & Circulars, ser. 44, RG 94 [DD-54].)

202: Chaplain in Charge of the Soldiers' Home at Columbus, Kentucky, to the President of the Western Sanitary Commission

Soldiers Home   Columbus [*Ky.*]   Feb 18. 1863.
Extract of a letter to the President of the Western Sanitary Commission.

x   x   x

The slave hunters have come down on us to day backed up with Sheriff & a civil process. They marched into our office four of them & asked permission to search the house for their [three] fugitives.   I

640

refused, They have gone to the Commander of Post for permission or order to me. The hunted ones have secreted themselves (I am told) & some fire arms are near them, There may be scenes in the Home.

I fear we must lose three of our best colored employees. One has been with the home over four months & given good satisfaction.

Other slaves were taken out of this town to day by consent of the Post commander *who also furnished transportation for the hunter & his victim,* This is hard to bear & the path of duty in my eyes is not exceeding clear.

Shall I pay wages to these "Chattels" for the certain benefit of their masters? Am I not bound to protect as far as in me lies these faithful servitors who claim my protection? They came early this morning asking if I would stand by them?

But perhaps Col Martin by an express order will relieve me from all responsibility in the matter – though not of unspeakable grief. As ever yours

HLcSr

E Nute Jr –

Extract from E. Nute Jr. to President of the Western Sanitary Commission, 18 Feb. 1863, enclosed in James E. Yeatman to Abraham Lincoln, 23 Feb. 1863, Y-2 1863, Letters Received Irregular, RG 107 [L-122]. A covering letter by James E. Yeatman, president of the Western Sanitary Commission, forwarded the extract to President Abraham Lincoln and warned him that "a condition of things, is arising, in regard to Contrabands, which is not provided for in your [Emancipation] proclamation and which is likely to give trouble, unless something is done." Yeatman identified Nute as chaplain of the 1st Kansas Infantry.

203: Daily Record of Events at the Headquarters of the Provost Marshal of the Post of Louisville

Louisville, Ky. April 27th 1863.

. . . .

A Negro sale advertised to come off today in which some contrabands were to be sold was stoped a few moments [ago] by Colonel Moore[1] with warnings or caution to the civil authorities not to sell and the parties not to buy certain negroes as he would hold them strictly accountable for their actions – Expect that it will make something of a fuss as the question is a tender one to Kentuckians.

. . . .

Louisville, Ky. May 1ˢᵗ 1863.

. . . .

The Colonel today issued an order relative to the Negro question which will evidently create some stir in the city tomorrow

" Hᵈ Qʳˢ Pro. Marˢˡ·

Louisville, Ky. May 1ˢᵗ 1863

Special Order, }
No. 12. }

Hereafter all unlawful interference with the authorized negro servants of officers of the United States Army and negroes legally entitled to their freedom, passing from Kentucky to Indiana, is prohibited and while the legal rights of the Citizens of Kentucky, *shall be strictly guarded,* Parties will be held responsible for such unlawful interference.

Signed

Orlando H. Moore.
Col. 25ᵗʰ Mich. Infy.
& Pro Marshal"

. . . .

Louisville, Ky. May 3ᵈ 1863.

Today has been very quiet indeed and has reminded us of a sabbath of old. As was expected the *negro question* referred to on the First caused considerable of a stir; the union people of the City are jubilant over the order then published and declare it just the thing it should be, but the Military Authorities look differently upon the subject and an order has been received asking the contramanding of it, it results entirely as we thought the commanders would look at it; the issue they dare not meet; this mornings paper contains the following —

Head Quarters Post Comdt.
Louisville, Ky. May 2ᵈ·

Col. O. H. Moore,
    Provost Marshal.
        Colonel: In compliance with orders from the Genˡ Commanding,[2] You will withdraw the order published in this morning's paperˢ.
    All contrabands coming to the city will be taken and placed in the Military Prison, to be put to work on the fortifications along the railroad.[3]

By order of
Col. M. Mundy, —
Comdg. Post.

(signed)
    C. C. Adams,
        Lieut. & A.A.A.G.

In compliance with the above instructions, the order referred to is withdrawn.

(Signed)   Orlando H. Moore,
Col. 25th Mich. Infy,
and Provost Marshal.

. . . .

Louisville, Ky. May 5th 1863.

There has been quiet in the extreem today but tonight has brought changes of moment.

Colonel Moores policy proving too strenious for the General Comdg. the Dist. and Colonel Comdg. the Post he was tonight relieived from duty as Provost Marshal and Maj. D. C. Fitch, 25th Mich. Infy. was appointed in his place; We trust that the change will better suit Kentucky orders and Kentucky policy.

. . . .

Louisville, Ky. May 9th, 1863.

Another day of quietness on all points save the Colored question which at the present time seems to make Kentucky tremble— the Contrabands are flocking to the Military Prison to be sent out on the fortifications as the all seem anxious to do something for the government.

. . . .

Louisville, Ky. May 13th, 1863.

. . . .

Col. Moore was today reinstated as Provost Marshal of the City of Louisville and will commence the duties of the office tomorrow.

. . . .

Louisville, Ky. May 14th, 1863

. . . .

A great many contrabands are coming in and they seem to furnish the only items of intrest—

. . . .

Louisville, Ky. May 15th, 63.

. . . .

Capt. C. C. Hare with his company left for Cloverport, Ky. under orders to bring in Some Contrabands said to be in jail there and offered for sale during the month.

. . . .

Louisville, May 21st, 1863.

Hea There has been no news of any kind today; the negro question still is in the ascendancy and will ever remain the subject of intrest while this war continues; those proclaimed free by the War measures of the Government will be entitled to that freedom.

. . . .

643

Louisville, Ky. June 7th 1863.
Today has been another Sunday and quiet in the extreem.
This evening orders were received removing Col. Moore as
Provost Marshal and ordering five companies of the 25th Mich. Infy.
to proceed to Rolling Fork Bridge and reinstating Maj. Fitch as
Provost Marshal of Louisville— thus *Kentucky* element has at last
predominated and *they* have full sway.

AD

Excerpts from daily record of events, 27 Apr.–7 June 1863, vol. 161/381
DKy, pp. 15–43, Miscellaneous Records, ser. 1644, Louisville KY, Provost
Marshal Field Organizations, RG 393 Pt. 4 [C-7002]. Topical labels in the
margin are omitted. The daily record is unsigned, but it was apparently
maintained by a clerk or other assistant at the headquarters of the provost
marshal, beginning on or about April 11, 1863. Its concluding entry, June 8,
1863, noted the supersession of Colonel Moore by Major Dewitt C. Fitch. For
a wider view of events chronicled in the daily record–including the jailing and
sale of "contrabands" entitled to freedom under the Emancipation Proclamation, conflicts between military officials in Louisville and officers who tried to
take or send their ex-slave servants across the Ohio River, and the decision to
consign all contrabands to the military prison and military labor–see *Freedom*,
ser. 1, vol. 1: docs. 209–19, 223A–B, and pp. 503–8.

1 Orlando H. Moore, provost marshal of the post of Louisville.
2 Jeremiah T. Boyle, commander of the District of Western Kentucky, whose
headquarters were at Louisville.
3 The following day, May 3, General Boyle's headquarters provided Colonel
Marcellus Mundy, commander of the post of Louisville, with additional instructions regarding the disposition of "contrabands." Boyle's instructions
asserted military custody and control over all former slaves who had come into
Kentucky from states subject to the Emancipation Proclamation, as well as any
black people who had been employed in Confederate service (whatever their
geographical origins), on the grounds that they were "captives of war." Mundy
and his subordinates were instructed to seize such contrabands and put them to
work "on the redoubts and fortifications in process of construction." Black
people being held in public or private jails were also to be taken into military
custody, "to be sent to the public works." (*Freedom*, ser. 1, vol. 1: doc. 217A.)
For an order issued by Mundy in accordance with Boyle's instructions, see doc.
204, immediately below.

204: Order by the Commander of the Post of Louisville

Louisville, Ky. May 4, 1863

Special Orders No. 100

. . . .

IV Captain Samuel L. Demorest 25 Mich. Vols. Inf. will immediately collect from the different jails and ~~poor~~ work houses in the Military District of Western Kentucky all negroes to be found therein, who have come or been brought into the state from states south of Tennessee, and all negroes who have been in employed in the rebel service coming within the lines, and turn them over to the Governor of the Military Prison in Louisville Ky, to be assigned to government work. You will be strictly governed in the execution of this order by the accompanying letter of instructions from District Head Quarters.[1] In all cases when you find such contrabands in the custody of Jailors you will give certificates that they are taken by the Military Authorities on government account so as to discharge the liability of the jailor. You will also take all contrabands found in private hands without receipt, and turn them over to the Military Prison. No officer has the right to appropriate negro slaves as servants, and all such will be taken and turned over upon Government works.

. . . .

By command of Col. M. Mundy

HD

Excerpt from Special Orders No. 100, Head Quartes Post Commandant, 4 May 1863, vol. 149/353 DKy, pp. 91–92, Special Orders Issued, ser. 739, Post of Louisville KY, RG 393 Pt. 4 [C-6002]. Omitted portions of the order dealt with several unrelated subjects.

1 For a description of the letter, see doc. 203n., immediately above.

205: Order by the Commander of the District of Columbus, Kentucky

Columbus, Ky., May 29, 1863.

GENERAL ORDERS, No. 34

I—Each Commander of a Post, within the District of Columbus, except Island No. 10, will, on the receipt of this order, detail a commissioned officer, as Superintendent of such persons of African descent, within the lines of the Post, who are now, or have been emancipated from slavery by the Treason of their former masters, and by the Proclamation of the President of the United States. Said Superintendent will cause to be detailed one enlisted man as a Clerk.

II – On a proper requisition from said Superintendent, each Post Quartermaster will provide suitable quarters, which shall be separate and apart from camps occupied by soldiers, and no communication between said quarters and camps will be permitted, except upon a written pass for each visit, from the Commander of the Post.

III – The said Superintendent shall enroll, and keep, or cause to be kept, a correct record of the name, trade, sex, age, heighth, fitness or unfitness for military duty, single or married, (if married, the number, age and sex of family,) of each and every such person of African descent, within the lines of his Post; and shall make a morning report to the Commander of the Post, which will show the number entitled to rations.

IV – When so collected, those who are unfitted or unwilling to avail themselves of the provisions contained in Section Nos. 2 and 8, of General Orders No. 32, current series, from these Headquarters,[1] will be sent, from time to time, to Colonies purposely provided for them within the District of Columbus, where every facility will be given for supporting themselves.

V – Able bodied males unwilling to enlist either as soldiers or laborers, and declining to earn their daily bread, will be forced into the military service and enrolled with the Volunteer recruits.

VI – The Books and Papers of the Post Superintendent must be, at all times, open to the inspection of Chaplain Benj. Thomas, who has been duly appointed "District Superintendent of Contrabands" for the District of Columbus; and any neglect, carelessness or violation of this, or any other order in relation thereto, should be promptly reported by him to these Headquarters for correction. ASBOTH, *Brig. Gen. Com'dg.*

PD

General Orders, No. 34, Headquarters District of Columbus, 29 May 1863, enclosed in Brig. G.C. Asboth to Lieut. Col. Henry Binmore, 8 June 1863, #5950 1863, Letters Received, ser. 391, 16th Army Corps, RG 393 Pt. 2 No. 7 [C-4894]. Island 10 was excepted from the first section because a superintendent of contrabands was already on duty there, namely Chaplain Benjamin Thomas, the district superintendent. In a covering letter to the headquarters of the 16th Army Corp, the commander of the District of Columbus, General Alexander S. Asboth, described the steps he had taken under orders of May 15 from General Stephen A. Hurlbut, the corps commander, authorizing him "to establish Colonies on the abandoned lands within my District, and raise a Colored force for their protection." In addition to General Order 34, Asboth enclosed two other orders he had issued in pursuance of Hurlbut's instructions.

The first, General Order 31, issued on May 18, had informed subordinates of Hurlbut's directive *"that no force must be shown towards any person within our lines to compel and return to servitude."* The second, General Order 32, issued on May 22, had established procedures for the recruitment of black men into the Union army to constitute "a force for garrison duty and the protection of such colonies of contrabands, on confiscated or abandoned lands, as are or may be established" in the district. "Men of family," Asboth had announced, "are especially to be informed that the force being intended as a guard to contraband colonies, they will, as soldiers, be guarding their own firesides, and their families will be allotted ground to occupy and cultivate." General Order 32 had further provided that volunteers rejected as unfit for military service would be employed by post quartermasters if their labor was needed; if not, they would be sent to the "contraband colonies" in the district "to work vacant lands." Black men already employed by quartermasters were not to leave their "working parties" to enlist until they were replaced by men unable or unwilling to serve as soldiers. Within days, Asboth's covering letter reported, 500 black men had indicated their readiness to enlist in the army "under above conditions"; 300 of them had already arrived in Columbus, accompanied by 150 women and children; the latter had been sent to Island 10 "pending the occupation of New Madrid Bend, which must be delayed at present, for want of sufficient force for its protection." Objecting to the efforts of an officer from the 1st Tennessee Heavy Artillery to claim the recruits for the garrison of Fort Pickering (at Memphis), General Asboth reported himself "confident of success" in organizing the 2nd Tennessee Heavy Artillery, which, he insisted, should be permitted to remain in his district, "partly for heavy Artillery service in the different Forts . . . and partly for the protection of Contraband Colonies."

1 General Order 32, issued on May 22, 1863, had inaugurated black recruitment in the District of Columbus. Section 2 provided for the voluntary enlistment of able-bodied men who had been freed by the Emancipation Proclamation. Section 8 provided that volunteers who were found unfit for military service could be employed as laborers by post quartermasters. (General Orders, No. 32, Headquarters District of Columbus, 22 May 1863, enclosed in Brig. G.C. Asboth to Lieut. Col. Henry Binmore, 8 June 1863, #5950 1863, Letters Received, ser. 391, 16th Army Corps, RG 393 Pt. 2 No. 7 [C-4894].)

206: Commander of the District of Columbus, Kentucky, to the Headquarters of the 16th Army Corps

Columbus Ky. June 22^d 1863

Colonel, I beg to enclose, for the notice of the Gen'l. Comdg. Corps, a copy of Sec IV, S.O. No. 150, issued by me yesterday, and a copy of Circular from Office of Chief Commissary of Subsistence,

St. Louis May 16. 1863, (See page 3, Sec. 5.) I respectfully submit that, in my opinion, under the very different State of affairs now existing, in regard to Colored Soldiers and laborers, as compared with the Status of "Contrabands" when G.O. No. 7, series of 1862 from Hdqrs. 13th. Army Corps,[1] was issued, the regulation in regard to Rations "for issue to Contrabands," "applies only to Contrabands not in the military service or employed as laborers by the Government" and as many of the least efficient Irish laborers in Q.M. employ at Columbus have been discharged, and their places filled by negroes at about one third of the wages paid white laborers, I consider it simply just and proper that negroes who work faithfully or volunteer to fight for our common cause, should have the same allowances as white men in the same vocations, and request the confirmation of my order by the General Commanding. – Respectfully Colonel, Your obdt. serv^r.

HLS   *Asboth*

Brig. G.C. Asboth to Lieut. Col. Henry Binmore, 22 June 1863, #6510 1863, Letters Received, ser. 391, 16th Army Corps, RG 393 Pt. 2 No. 7 [C-4895]. The command of General Alexander S. Asboth was designated 6th Division, 16th Army Corps, as well as District of Columbus. The order issued by Asboth on June 21 is enclosed, but the circular from the commissary of subsistence at St. Louis is not. Asboth's order announced his opinion that General Order 7 (1862) from the 13th Army Corps now applied "only to contrabands not in the Military Service or employed as laborers by the Govt.," and instructed the commissary at Columbus to issue to black soldiers and laborers the same ration as that furnished military laborers in the Department of the Missouri. (Special Orders, No. 150, Headquarters District of Columbus, 6th Division, 16th Army Corps, 21 June 1863.) In response to Asboth's letter, an endorsement of July 1 from the headquarters of the 16th Army Corps stated only that black troops "are entitled by law to the pay and allowances of volunteer forces." Consequently, by an endorsement of July 10, Asboth returned the letter to the 16th Army Corps, asking for orders from the corps commander "in regard to the rations of Colored *laborers*." No response to the latter inquiry has been found among the letters sent by the 16th Army Corps.

1 Issued on November 17, 1862, by General Ulysses S. Grant, General Order 7 had established a ration for contrabands both smaller than and somewhat different from a soldier's ration. For the standard soldier's ration and the contraband ration of General Order 7, see *Freedom*, ser. 1, vol. 3: doc. 160n.

207A: Commander of the Department of the Cumberland to the Commander of the Post of Fort Donelson, Tennessee

Clarksville, Tenn. June 17th 1863.
"By, Telegraph from Murfreesboro. June 17th 1863.
To Col Lyon.
You will immediately enter upon your rolls all negroes who come within your lines and set them to work. Give certificates to all loyal masters of the fact that their negroes have come into your camp as fugitives and are employed at labor.
You will not return any fugitives whether of loyal or disloyal Masters. Negroes must not be allowed to run off on boats
G. A. Garfield
Brig Genl. & Chief of Staff
The meaning and this order is that when a Comdg. Officer requires negroes for public service. he will receive fugitives. when he has no use for them. he will exclude all cases except when humanity manifestly demands it   When a fugitive gets within and is claimed – the Comdg. Officer is to give a certificate statement that such fugitive is there describing him or her and give a copy of said certificate to claimant.
HWcSr
W^{m}. S. Rosecrans

Maj. Genl. Wm. S. Rosecrans to Col. Lyon, 17 June 1863, vol. 172/214 DMT, p. 95, Letters Sent, ser. 406, Post of Fort Donelson TN, RG 393 Pt. 4 [C-2078]. General James A. Garfield (whose first initial was miscopied) was General Rosecrans's chief of staff. Copied into the same volume are several certificates issued by Colonel William P. Lyon, commander of the post of Fort Donelson, to Kentucky and Tennessee slaveholders, in compliance with Rosecrans's instructions. They include, for example, a certificate issued to Isaac Greencastle of Trigg County, Kentucky, on July 24, 1863, regarding a black man (employed as an officer's servant) and two black women ("unemployed") who had been within the lines of the post since April and June, respectively; and a certificate of July 27 "that Cupid a negro man claimed by S. L. Woolridge Esq of Christian C° Ky. has been within our lines and at work for the Government on our fortifications since July 6th 1863." (Vol. 172/214 DMT, pp. 94–95, Letters Sent, ser. 406, Post of Fort Donelson, RG 393 Pt. 4 [C-2078].)

207B: Kentucky Slaveholder to the Commander of the District of Kentucky

Empire City Iron Works. Trigg Co Ky June 29th 1863

Dr. Sir— I have intended to have written you for the last two weeks upon the subject I called to see you some time ago. As I told you Gen Rosecrans promised to make the negro order and gave me a paper while at Murfreesboro saying that the army and soldiers should protect my person and property. a kind of protection paper. I showed it to Col Bruce and he advised me to see Col. Lowe at Fort Donelson at once and said if it was him he would put the negroes outside of the lines at once so I could get them upon that paper. I saw Col. Lowe Comdt. at Fort Donelson at once and showed him my paper. He said he did not feel authorized to act in any way upon that paper—said he was ordered off to the front at Hd Qrs and would see Genl Rosecrans—in regard to the matter and for me to return in 10 days. On my return I found Col. Lowe had left—and not to return (Col Lyon in command who said he had no instructions from Lowe or Genl. Rosecrans Lowe having promised to enroll the negroes and give me a government voucher. (all of which I do not beleive he ever intended to do. I found 14 of my negroes— working in the Fort— several had left or were Kept out of my way. Two that were at Ft Heiman. I learn from Col. Henry (one of your officers now in command at that [*place*] were sent off a short time before his arrival there—after being swore in the service for 3 years or during the war and. that order there direct as twenty accumulate. that [are] to be sent off by an officer regularly commissioned & I have now between 20 or 30 off and large number of these have only been Kept by every way I can use to induce them it is best to stay for their own welfare— but sir I shall soon loose all my negroes in this way. I stopped making iron for over 18 months owing to the uncertain tenure of my hands—planted a good deal of wheat. Tobacco & and I do assure you I doubt whether I shall be able to Save my Crop. as they are constantly leaving

I wrote Genl. Rosecrans—on 11st from the Fort saying in the absence of the order which I hoped he would have made immediately after my interview with him I had not been able to get my negroes—or a voucher for them or them turned out of his lines. He wrote me on the 17th inst Saying he has ordered Coll Lyon to enroll loyal men negroes and to give vouchers and hoped this would reach the case. Now Genl. I have taken the liberty to trouble you with this long letter but you must excuse me for I Know of no one else to apply to and I consider my self one of your constituents and ask of you redress and protection—as you see from the facts I have detailed that I am only put off and trifled with and my negroes will all be taken away from me. I have the assessor at my elbow – to take my list of income tax to support the Govmt all of which by word and example I have encouraged to be paid and for the last two years my business has been a loosing one to large amts. It seems that this state of things will test the loyalty of any one and will I am certain damage the government materially in this section

You will find all men complaining of the acts and doings of the Fort Donelson Post in regard to negroes. hundreds of Ky. negroes have and will continue to go there and they are taken off in any way on Boats by private citizens from the free states and sent on Boats constantly

I hope you will write me at once and if nothing can be done I shall sell my stock and prepare to close up and stop expenses as far as I can. With high regard I am Yours

HLcSr
                                                    Daniel Hillman

Daniel Hillman to Brig. Gen. Boyle, 29 June 1863, vol. 172/214 DMT, pp. 90–91, Letters Sent, ser. 406, Post of Fort Donelson TN, RG 393 Pt. 4 [C-2078]. Hillman was a prominent iron master. General William S. Rosecrans commanded the Department of the Cumberland. Colonel Sanders D. Bruce was a brigade commander at Clarksville, Tennessee. For Rosecrans's instructions of June 17, 1863, to Colonel William P. Lyon, commander of the post of Ft. Donelson, see doc. 207A, immediately above. On July 4, 1863, Lyon certified that thirteen black men "claimed as the property of Daniel Hillman. Esq of Trigg C°. Ky" were working at Fort Donelson. Twelve were laborers on the fortifications; the thirteenth was a wagoner. Most of them had been employed at the fort since April. (Certificate by Col. Wm. P. Lyon, 4 July 1863, vol. 172/214 DMT, p. 82, Letters Sent, ser. 406, Post of Fort Donelson TN, RG 393 Pt. 4 [C-2078].) Meanwhile, General Jeremiah T. Boyle, commander of the District of Kentucky, forwarded Hillman's letter to General Rosecrans's headquarters, whence it was transmitted to Colonel Lyon. Lyon's reply, dated July 22, 1863, reported that on June 1, when he assumed command at Fort Donelson, twelve of Hillman's former slaves had been at work on the fortifications, and two more had afterward come into the lines, "one of whom returned voluntarily to his master." As required by department orders, Lyon had provided Hillman with a "voucher for his negroes"; Hillman had not been "put off and trifled with." Moreover, Lyon insisted, "Negroes are not encouraged to come into our lines for we have more than we Know what to do with. . . . [T]hey are always allowed to return to their masters when they desire to do so. They are *not* allowed to run off on boats – and 'all men' *do not* complain of the acts & doings of the Fort Donelson post in regard to negroes.' " (Col. W. P. Lyon to Major Wm. McMichael, 22 July 1863, vol. 172/214 DMT, pp. 91–92, Letters Sent, ser. 406, Post of Fort Donelson TN, RG 393 Pt. 4 [C-2078].) On August 1, General Rosecrans forwarded Lyon's report to General Boyle. (Vol. 35 DC, p. 73, Endorsements Sent, ser. 9111, Dept. of the Cumberland, RG 393 Pt. 1 [C-2078].)

207C: Commander of the Post of Fort Donelson, Tennessee, to the Headquarters of the Department of the Cumberland

Ft. Donelson [*Tenn.*] July 13th 1863

I have the honor to ask instructions upon the following questions which arise by reason of the presence of fugitive slaves in my lines

I   Where the master claims payment for the services of his slaves under Paragraph III Gen Orders No 6. – Series of 1863.[1] in what manner are the ownership of the slave and the loyalty of the claimant to be determined?

II   Where the slave of a loyal owner is employed as an Office[r']s servant. what course should be pursued to secure the payment to the master for the services of his slaves?

III. I find it difficult to execute the order received by Telegraph June 17th ult,[2] (a copy of which I enclose for convenience of reference) for the reason that large numbers of women and children. most of whom have husbands and fathers employed on our fortifications. have founed their way inside our lines. and we have nothing for them to do. Thus far I have neither registered, given certificates for, or subsisted women and children, I have protected them from being taken out of our lines against their will, but have allowed them to leave at their pleasure. Should their number increase materially I think they must be subsisted by the Government or suffer for food. I respectfully request instruction as to what shall be done with them

I beg leave to add that all ablebodied male negroes at this Post are profitably employed in the various departments of the Goverments service – ("wherein their Employment is authorized by Order No 6".) and upon the fortifications but an increase of the numbers. even of this class. does not seem to be required by the exigencies of the services, at this Post   I have the honor to be Col Very Respectfully Your Obdt Serv[t]

W P. Lyon

HLcSr

Col. W. P. Lyon to Col. C. Goddard, 13 July 1863, vol. 172/214 DMT, p. 88, Letters Sent, ser. 406, Post of Fort Donelson TN, RG 393 Pt. 4 [C-2078]. Lyon was colonel of the 13th Wisconsin Infantry and commander of U.S. forces at Fort Donelson. No reply has been found in the records of the Department of the Cumberland, and questions about paying for the services of black military laborers at Fort Donelson remained unresolved for several more months. In mid-October 1863, the commander of the post reported that 120 black laborers had been working there without pay since June 1. (See above, doc. 99.)

1 The order is printed above, as doc. 91.
2 See above, doc. 207A.

208: Superintendent of Contrabands in the District of Columbus, Kentucky, to the Headquarters of the District

Island No 10   Tenn   June 30th 1863
Dear sir   I have the honor to report to you that the men sent to
New-Madrid [*Missouri*] at the request of the commander of this Post
have returned.

I asked instructions in regard to the order calling them to
Columbus to work in the quarter masters Department.   While at
N. Madrid nine of them Enlisted.   Several of them were here on a
visit and volunteered to aid, in what was represented as an
emergency, for four days.   Shall I force all that were at Madrid to
Columbus?   They will not go unless they are compelled to go by
military power.

The men are generally old, or crippled or feeble and have
families.   I have taken every single able bodied man in our colony
and sent them to the Qr. Master at Columbus by the bearer of this,
Sarg't Welty.   Will you please give the instruction requested

My colony is crippled in our pursuits by the removal of all who
are now able to do a days work.   Many of our men are down with
measels: To take all these men, that have been to Madrid, is to take
our teamsters, blacksmiths, carpenters, & shoe makers, from us.   I
have the honor to be your ob't servant
ALS   B. Thomas

Chaplain B. Thomas to A.A. General T. H. Harris, 30 June 1863, Letters
Received, ser. 991, Dist. of Columbus, RG 393 Pt. 2 No. 24 [C-8649]. On
June 24, General Alexander S. Asboth, commander of the District of Columbus, had ordered Chaplain Thomas "to send the fifty contrabands now temporarily employed at New Madrid . . . to Columbus, to report to Capt. J. H.
McKay A.Q.M. as Quartermasters Department here is in great want of laborers." (Special Orders No. 153, Headquarters Dist. of Columbus, 6th Division
16th Army Corps, 24 June 1863, vol. 101/248A DKy, pp. 236–38, Special
Orders, ser. 995, Dist. of Columbus, RG 393 Pt. 2 No. 24 [C-8672].) No
reply to Thomas has been found among the letters-sent or telegrams-sent
volumes of the District of Columbus.

209: Superintendent of Contrabands at Columbus, Kentucky, to the Superintendent of Contrabands in the District of Columbus

Head Qrs. Contraband Camp Columbus Ky July 24" 1863
Duplicate
Sir   Herewith below I hand you Statistic report of Contrabands at this Post.

	In Government Employ				Employed by Individuals			Facilities for Education				State of Health			Mortality			Aggregate
	Soldiers	with Provost Marshall	with Qr. Master	In Hospitals	By Soldiers Home	By Army officers	By Citizens	No of Schools	No of Teachers	Whole No of Pupils	No that have learned to read	No Sick in Hospital	No sick in Quarters	No Convalescent	No of Births between Feb 1st & June 1st 1863	No of Deaths between Feb 1st & June 1st 1863	In camp not otherwise accounted for – wives of soldiers & so	Aggregate
Men	253	05	130	18	4	17	18	one	one	00	00	26	4	10	00	14	10	492
Women	00	00	00	14	6	32	43			3	1	8	9	8	00	13	87	241
Children	10	00	00	00	00	00	0			27	8	7	14	16	23	27	108	230
Total	253	5	130	32	10	49	61	1	1	30	9	41	27	34	23	54	205	963

In view of the colored people being scattered not only *co*extensive with the City but also with the sevral camps, no regular system of Policeing has been adopted. very Respectfully
ALcS   Joseph Cadwalader

Capt. Joseph Cadwalader to Chaplain B. Thomas, 24 July 1863, Letters Received, ser. 991, Dist. of Columbus, RG 393 Pt. 2 No. 24 [C-8654]. Cadwalader was an officer in the 32nd Iowa Infantry. [For the sake of readability, the editors have slightly altered the physical arrangement of the table.]

210: Testimony by a Former Kentucky Slave in the Court-Martial of the Former Superintendent of Black Military Laborers at Cairo, Illinois

[*Washington, D.C. December 31, 1863*]
*Morris M*ᶜ*Comb*, a witness for the prosecution was then called and being duly sworn by the Judge Advocate testified as follows:
Direct Examination.
Q by the J.A.   Where did you live before you came to Washington?
A. In Cairo, Illinois.

Q by the J.A. Do you know the accused, William Yokum?

A. Yes.

Q by the J.A. Were you a slave or free before you went to Cairo?

A. I was a slave of Jesse M'Comb or his son, of Kentucky

Q by the J.A. When did you leave your master and go to Cairo?

A. I think I left him sometime last May. I then went to Fort Donelson [*Tenn.*]. I worked then on the fortifications in the government employ. I ran away from my master. About the middle of the Summer I was sent to Cairo, – remained in Cairo till Mr. Gant took me away in the steamboat, which was in the summer. I worked in Cairo, in government employ under Mr. Yokum. He put my name down in a book when I first went there. He had charge of the colored men at Cairo.

Q by the J.A. State all the circumstances of your leaving Cairo, and what connection the accused had with your leaving?

A. Mr. Yocum came out to the barracks and called me. Then he says – "that is M'Comb is it," I says 'Yes' – Then he said 'get into the waggon with Jim, and then I got in the waggon and rode to Mr. Yocums house. That was outside the camp. He then told me to get on a mule. I got on. Then he got on his horse, then told me, "Come, go with me, and hunt for some sesesh cows." Then he says "A man at Mound City gave him a couple of sesesh cows and wanted I should drive them in, in the evening. By and by when we rid on and I saw a lot of cows, and I says "Mr Yocum, "mebbe thems your cows," then he says "No, we'll ride on further, and if we dont find them, then, we'll come back to them cows." Then we rid on all through the woods and high weeds every which way, and then come on out to the river, and Mr. Gant was on the river bank. We found him there, and when I saw him he was pretty nigh to me. He had a pistol drawn on me, and told me if I run he would shoot me, and then Mr. Gant catches hold of me and pulls me off the mule and handed Mr. Yocum something in a white paper over the horses neck, and then Mr. Gant takes me down on the river bank and ties my hands behind me. Mr. Yocum saw Mr. Gant pull me off the horse. He did not see him tie me. He saw him draw a pistol. Mr. Gant said "This is my boy" and said he would report Mr. Yocum at Washington City. I said, and Mr. Yocum heard me, "Mr. Yocum you have just brought me up here for Mr. Gant to catch me, and he said "No, he didnt," and then when Mr. Gant took me down to the river bank and tied me, he took off my hat and waved it. I had on a white hat and he had a black hat. He waved it as a signal for the boat to come ashore. It was a steamboat, and then the boat came ashore and run out a plank and he (Mr Gant) pushed me on board, cut the rope loose behind me and ran off towards the cabin, and the boat went up the river. I dont think Mr. Yocum was gone then. Mr. Yocum went away after Mr. Gant gave him the peice of paper. I was taken away against my will. Then after that the deck hands got around me and commenced talking to me, and before I could say any thing Mr. Gant called me up on deck into the cabin and put me in the cabin. Mr. Gant was in there, and Mr. McCombs, one or the other all of the time. They took me on to Paducah [Ky.], and the Provost guard took me off. Mr. McComb was my former master.

Q by the J.A. Did you get any cows?

A. No sir.

Cross examination.

Q by the Acc. Did I not plead with Mr. Gant not to treat you harshly?

A. No sir, I dont remember it.

Q by the Acc. Do you not recollect of my saying any thing?

A. No sir, not any thing more than I have stated to these gentlemen.

Q. by the Acc. How many days were you under my charge?

A. I think four weeks, lacking one day. One day I was sick.

Q by the Acc. How did you come to leave Fort Donelson?

A. We boys heard that they was going to send us up to Clarksville [Tenn.] so that our masters could get us. Then I went to the Provost Marshal and got a pass, and went down to Cairo. The Cook sergeant said I had better go down there.

Q by the Acc. How many days before you left Fort Donelson did you see your master there?

A. I dont know how many days. I saw my master there and talked with him.

Q by the Acc. Did he take any of his servants away from Fort Donelson?

A. He did some of them. They went with him.

Q. by the Acc. How many did he take from there?

A. I think five or six.

Q by the Acc. Did he say any thing to you about going with him?

A. Yes sir. He tried to get me to go home with him, but I wouldnt go.

Q by the Acc. How many days do you think this was before you left Fort Donelson?

A. I dont know, I dont recollect.

Q by the Court. How far did your master live from Fort Donelson, and where did he live?

A. I dont know how far he lived. We started on Saturday night

656

and got there Sunday night about 2 o'clock. It was on the other side of the river from Fort Donelson. He lives six miles this side of Hopkinsville, Kentucky. That is the nearest town I know of.

HD

Testimony of Morris McComb, 31 Dec. 1863, proceedings of general court-martial in the case of William Yokum, MM-1217, Court-Martial Case Files, ser. 15, RG 153 [H-65]. Yokum, a civilian who had supervised black quarter-master employees at Cairo, was charged with kidnapping and with violation of duty. The specifications alleged that on August 14, 1863, he had "induce[d] one Morris McComb, a contraband under his charge . . . to accompany him under a false pretence, to a point on the Ohio River near said Cairo, and did there deliver him to one Joseph K. Gant, who . . . seized and confined with ropes the said McComb, . . . in pursuance of a previous agreement between the said Gant and the said Yokum, and with the view of having the said McComb conveyed to the state of Kentucky and reduced to slavery." It was further charged that Gant had paid Yokum $50. According to other testimony and documents before the court, Morris McComb had been rescued (and Joseph Gant and Jesse McComb arrested) through the intervention of an army officer from Illinois who happened to be on board the steamer that picked up the former slave and his captor. Depositions from Jesse McComb and Joseph Gant acknowledged that they had arranged to pay Yokum to deliver up Morris McComb; Yokum himself denied having cooperated for pay, but defended delivering the former slave to "his lawful owner" on the grounds that he had known Jesse McComb to be loyal to the federal government and believed that loyal citizens were legally entitled "to recover their slave property." The pro-vost marshal at Cairo testified that orders from the post commander permitted loyal owners to reclaim fugitive slaves if the slave "was willing to go with him" but forbade the use of force "if the negro was not willing." Both Joseph Gant and Jesse McComb had quickly been released from arrest, but Yokum was dismissed from employment in the quartermaster's department and prose-cuted. On January 2, 1864, the court-martial found him guilty of all charges and specifications and sentenced him to imprisonment at hard labor for five years. Within weeks, however, President Abraham Lincoln, first upon his own initiative and then at the urging of several Kentucky congressmen, was propos-ing to pardon Yokum, on the grounds that only a short time earlier it had been lawful "to return a slave to a loyal owner" and Yokum had believed it still to be so. But Secretary of War Edwin M. Stanton, arguing "on behalf of the colored people to whom the President has promised protection and emancipation," strongly objected to a pardon. "[T]he President," he warned, "could commit no greater mistake, and in no way do . . . the sense of public justice & his own reputation so much harm." Lincoln thereupon dropped the matter until November 1864, when he arranged to have Yokum released from prison on condition of good behavior. (Abraham Lincoln, *Collected Works*, ed. Roy P. Basler, Marion D. Pratt, and Lloyd A. Dunlap, 9 vols. [New Brunswick, N.J., 1953–55], vol. 7, pp. 144, 167, 187, 254–57, 256n.; vol. 8, p. 119.)

657

211: Medical Inspector at Louisville, Kentucky,
to the Surgeon General

Louisville Ky: August 28th 1863
"Copy"

General, I have the honor to acknowledge the receipt of the accompanying letter of A.A. Surgeon W[m] W. Goldsmith, Surgeon in charge of U.S. Gen'l Hospital N[o] 7 at this place (asking that sundry improvements in and about said hospital be made) with references and comments thereon, and which has been referred to me for investigation and report. I would most respectfully report that the "Contrabands" referred to are employed at this Hospital, as laundresses, and in the performance of such duties as are absolutely necessary to the welfare and comfort of the sick in hospital, and are therefore in my opinion entitled to quarters, the same as if such duties were performed by employee's of another class or color.

At present these "contrabands" occupy tents of (cotton fabric) which will not afford them as comfortable protection from the inclemency of the approaching winter weather—[n]or are tents as *economical*, as board pavilions or huts.

. . . .

(signed) L Humphreys

HLcSr

Excerpt from Asst. Surgeon L. Humphreys to Brig: Gen'l Hammond, 28 Aug. 1863, "Louisville: Report on Government Buildings," Consolidated Correspondence File, ser. 225, Central Records, RG 92 [Y-218]. The remainder of the letter discussed the permanence or impermanence of Hospital No. 7. In the same file is the letter from Surgeon William W. Goldsmith that had launched Humphreys's investigation; it asked "that the Quarter Master be directed, to erect a suitable Building for Contraband Negro quarters." Endorsements upon it by the chief quartermaster of the District of Kentucky and by the assistant quartermaster general at Cincinnati, had questioned, respectively, the "propriety of erecting negro quarters" and the "authority for the erection of quarters for contrabands." (Act. Asst. Surg. William W. Goldsmith to Surg. G. G. Shumard, 20 July 1863.) On September 26, 1863, after the acting surgeon general had forwarded Humphreys's report to the quartermaster general, the latter's office instructed the assistant quartermaster general at Cincinnati to "cause comfortable huts to be erected for the shelter of these employes . . . the whole expenditure to be as economical as possible." (Acting Q.M. Gen'l Chs. Thomas to Col. Thomas Swords, 26 Sept. 1863, vol. 72, pp. 56–57, Letters Sent, ser. 9, Central Records, RG 92 [Y-676].)

212: Chief Engineer of the Department of the Ohio to the Commander of the Department

Cincinnati, 0. October 21st 186[3]

Gen Field Orders N° 1 directs that "certified vouchers shall be issued for value of labor" performed by negroes pressed into the service.

Will you please state at what rate the labor shall be valued. The L & N R.R. Co thought that $12 would be a fair compensation per month to those negroes they have hired from the Government, & from all I can understand, as labor is valued now, this rate is far from being high.

Would it not be a good thing to give certified vouchers at the rate of ten dollars per month to the masters and to the slaves, two dollars, to be paid to them monthly by the Quartermaster Department, if they *deserve* it.

Some such stimulus as this is necessary to bring out the full & persistent energies of the negro. If you agree with me please authorize the Asst. Adjt Genl here to issue an order to this effect. I am Very Respy Your Obt. Servt.

HLS

J. H. Simpson

Maj. Engr. J. H. Simpson to Maj. Genl. A. E. Burnside, 21 Oct. 186[3], A. E. Burnside Papers, Generals' Papers & Books, ser. 159, RG 94 [V-169]. General Field Order 1, issued by the commander of the Army of the Ohio on August 13, 1863, had placed General Jeremiah T. Boyle, commander of the District of Kentucky, in charge of slave men "impressed for service on the public works" in Kentucky, ordering that they be subsisted by quartermasters and commissaries in the same fashion as "other" (i.e., free) military laborers and that owners of the slaves be issued vouchers for the value of their labor. (*Official Records*, ser. 1, vol. 30, pt. 3, p. 23.) The company hiring black laborers from the government was the Louisville and Nashville Railroad. Large-scale impressment had been initiated on August 10, 1863, by an order calling for 6,000 slave men to construct military roads; a second order, issued on August 20, had authorized the impressment of as many as 8,000 slaves to build a railroad to east Tennessee. (See *Freedom*, ser. 1, vol. 1: doc. 221.)

213A: Commander of the District of Kentucky to the Secretary of War, and the Latter's Reply

Louisville, [Ky.] Nov. 14 1863
(Copy)

Hon. E. M. Stanton   It is almost impossible to procure teamsters for line of transportation to Knoxville. Can I enlist with consent of Gov. Bramlette from two to three thousand negroes as teamsters for three years. The owneres of negroes to be paid three hundred at the time and the negroes to be free men subject to their enlistment. They make the best teamsters. I can get them.
HWcSr
J. T. Boyle

Washington City, November 18ᵗʰ 1863
Copy
Telegram
   Your proposition to enlist from two to three thousand colored teamsters into the service of the United States during the war, paying to loyal owners three hundred dollars for the release of their interest or property in slaves, and the persons enlisted to be free at the end of their enlistment, has been considered by this Department, and is approved.
   You are authorized to take immediate measures to carry it into effect. The proposition, as understood by this Department, is on the following conditions:
   First. – Payment of three hundred dollars to loyal owners for the release of all right or claim to their slaves, or their service – the owners to execute a deed of release or manumission at the time of the enlistment.
   Second. – Monthly compensation to persons enlisted for this service at the rate authorized by the act of Congress of 17ᵗʰ July, 1862¹ – ten dollars per month.
   Third. – Slaves so enlisted to be forever free at the expiration of their term of enlistment.
HWcSr
(signed) Edwin M. Stanton

B.G. J. T. Boyle to Hon. E. M. Stanton, 14 Nov. 1863, and Edwin M. Stanton to Brigadier General Boyle, 18 Nov. 1863, both filed as B-352 1863, Letters Received, ser. 360, Colored Troops Division, RG 94 [B-41]. In the same file is a copy of a telegram from Montgomery C. Meigs, the quartermaster general, containing suggestions about the organization, supervision, and equipment of thirty companies of 100 black teamsters each, should General Boyle's plan be effected. Meigs proposed that in order "to make [the teamsters] efficient in the defence of their trains against small marauding parties, I think it would be well to put them through the drill of the school of the soldier, and of the company. They should be armed with smooth bore muskets carrying buckshot cartridges." (M. C. Meigs to Hon. E. M. Stanton, 21 Nov. 1863.) At the end of November, when Secretary of War Stanton inquired of Boyle what steps he had taken toward enlisting black teamsters, Boyle replied that he had not yet obtained the consent of the governor, and he asked whether Stanton's restriction of payment to loyal owners necessarily excluded Southern sympathizers who had been law-abiding and had not acted overtly in support of the Confederacy. (*Official Records*, ser. 3, vol. 3, pp. 1104–5.) Two weeks later, after consulting with the governor and others, Boyle made a full report to Stanton, for which see doc. 213B, immediately below.

1 The Milita Act. (*Statutes at Large*, vol. 12, pp. 597–600.)

213B: Commander of the District of Kentucky to the Secretary of War, Enclosing a Letter from the Governor of Kentucky to the District Commander

Louisville [Ky.], December 16ᵗʰ *1863.*

Sir, In reply to your despatches in regard to enlistment of negro teamsters I beg leave respectfully to state that this communication was delayed by my absence on the Big South Fork of the Cumberland River in execution of the orders of the General Commanding, and by sudden temporary sickness, and I have now the honor to submit for your consideration the following report.

I experienced great difficulty in procuring teamsters on the line of transportation to Knoxville, and found, only a very worthless class, who marauded and neglected every duty, offering their services— I was compelled to impress a few free negroes and some few slaves— The necessity for subsistence for the army increasing, I ordered the impressment of more, and I am fully satisfied that the negroes are the best teamsters, marauding very little, if any, and attending to their stock, watering and feeding, and obeying orders— I beleive it will be great saving to the government to have negro teamsters.

I was led to believe when I first communicated with you on the subject that I could readily obtain requisite number of negro teamsters— I am not so sanguine of success as I was then, though Brig Genˡ Fry and the Quarter Master of Camp Nelson, and others, feel quite confident that the requisite number can be enlisted, with consent of the owners, as proposed – No doubt a considerable number can be obtained.

One of the difficulties grows out of the restriction implied by the term "loyal owners", and as indicated in my despatch to you I submit for your consideration, whether the negroes of all peacable and quiet citizens, whatever may be their political opinions and sympathies, if they have been guilty of no overt act of treason and have not rendered, voluntarily, aid and comfort to the enemy, may be enlisted with their consent and paid for.

The time and manner of payment is important to the success of it – If the *money* is paid or *certicates* given, it will facilitate the business.

The large number of negro soldiers recruited at Gallatin, Clarksville and Nashville, from the slaves in the Southern Counties bordering on Tennessee, and the impressment of negroes on the military roads, and the escaping of many as servants in the regiments, have contributed to produce a willingness or readiness on the part of the owners to have their negroes enlist as teamsters on the terms proposed – Many men, heretofore, Known to me as pro-slavery men, have signified a readiness to dispose of their negroes in the manner proposed – This feeling is expressed by many who are most violent in opposition to their negroes enlisting as soldiers. Their opposition to have them enlist as soldiers, arises from their unwillingness to have them placed in position of danger and death, when their ignorance, growing out of their condition of slavery, does not qualify them to make an intelligent volunteer enlistment, or fit them to take care of themselves in places of danger.

I herewith enclose you copy of Governor Bramlette's letter on the subject by which it will be seen he consents and will make no opposition to enlistment, with consent of the owner, of negro teamsters as proposed – You will perceive that he interposes a constitutional difficulty growing out of an inhumane provision of our constitution – The fact that the constitution and laws devolve a responsibility upon the owner, will prevent many from entering into the arrangement – If the transfer of ownership could be made to the government or to some officer of the Government, with orders to execute deeds of release and emancipation, the difficulty in a measure might be obviated – I am satisfied that quite a number can be had notwithstanding the obstacles in the way. The owners of negroes prefer getting some compensation rather than loose the whole value of the slave.

It is proper to say that some of the friends of the Government and warm friends of Emancipation, seem not to favor the carrying the plan in execution now, apprehending it may effect a system of gradual emancipation in the State, which it is hoped the present legislature may adopt — There are some constitutional difficulties interposed to this however, and I do not see that the other would prejudice it.

I advocated emancipation in 1849 and I am still for it, and would not willingly do anything that would prejudice it. If the enlistment of teamsters would defeat or delay the adoption of Emancipation, I would gladly see it postponed, to give time for action of the legislature at its present session on the subject.

A large number of negroes have been impressed as laborers on the military roads, and some of them used as teamsters, but no attempt has been made to Enlist any of them as teamsters as yet, as I felt it necessary to receive further orders before action on the subject — It will require a number of forms of printed blanks, and I shall await further orders, and authority to have the blanks printed —, and for such other instructions as may be deemed necessary. I am Very Respectfully Your Ob^t Servt

HLS

J. T. Boyle

[*Enclosure*]   Frankfort [*Ky.*] Dec 3^d 1863.
                              "Copy"
Dear Sir: Your letter asking my consent as Executive of the State, to employ, with the consent of the owners, Slaves as teamsters; and to accept in such cases as owners may desire or prefer a relinquishment of title to the Government for the Slave, upon payment of $300, to be employed in conveying supplies to our army at Knoxville has been duly received and considered.

The owners of slaves have the undoubted legal right, to hire their slaves; or dispose of them to the Government upon the terms and for the purposes set forth in your letter; and as the Executive of the State, I have no right or power, — whatever may be my individual opinions as to policy, — to object to such arrangements. In all cases where title to the slave is relinquished by the owner with a view to his freedom at the expiration of the service — the owner and the slave should be advised that the Constitution of Kentucky and the laws made persuant thereto, forbid that he shall remain in Ky after his discharge.

Many will refuse to accept freedom upon the only terms admisable under our laws. Where no other provision is made for the removal and settlement of emancipated slaves, our laws require that the slave shall be hired out until a sufficient fund for his removal and settlement is raised, and then be removed and settled beyond the limits of the state, Whatever may be the views of others

663

as to the policy or humanity of this law, as Chief Executive of the State I shall enforce it without the slightest scruple or relaxation. Having no right whatever to interpose objection to the employment of slaves with the consent of owners, as proposed by you, I make none. Respectfully

HLcSr   (Signed) Thomas E. Bramlette

Brig. Genl. J. T. Boyle to Hon. E. M. Stanton, 16 Dec. 1863, enclosing Thomas E. Bramlette to Brig. Genl. J. T. Boyle, 3 Dec. 1863, B-1777 1863, Letters Received, RG 107 [L-317]. Endorsement. General Speed Smith Fry, who was said to be optimistic about the prospect of obtaining black teamsters, was in charge of the large-scale impressment of slave laborers that had begun in August 1863. (See *Freedom*, ser. 1, vol. 1: doc. 221.) In the end, thwarted by the state laws cited by Governor Bramlette, Boyle's proposal came to naught.

214: Quartermaster of the Engineer Department at Camp Nelson, Kentucky, to the Chief Engineer of the Department of the Ohio

Camp Nelson Ky. Jan. 8th. 1864.
Col. In accordance with an Order transmitted from your office, and directions from yourself, I have receipted to Lt. Wallace for all of the property which was in his hands; also to you, through Mr. Gillis, for such of the property, as you had furnished, according to his statements.

Lt. Wallace turned over to me of Surplus Commissary Stores, Rice, Bacon, Pilot Bread, Coffee &c. the amount of $171,31 cts. at government prices; also $85,98 cts. in cash, alias "Green Backs." I would prefer not retaining this money in my hands; and if—as according to directions on Page 36, verse 205, of Revised Regulations, it is *ever* to be disposed of for the benefit of those men, from whose rations it accrued, *now* is the time and, *these* are the men who should receive its benefits. Mittens and some trifling articles not furnished by Q.M. or Commissary, would add very much to comfort.

Pardon me for thus much, also for desiring that some measures be devised for furnishing the blacks with necessary clothing. It is hard to see men working out doors all day, such weather as this, when I know there are great holes in their shoes, and that they have no drawers, under-shirts or mittens; and then to see them lie down in front of the fire, to sleep on the floor, getting up occasionaly to build a fire to keep them warm during the night, and this because they have but a single blanket, and some none at all.

I need not add that men thus situated, soon become unfitted for work, and that if their labors are to be beneficial, the men must be made tolerably comfortable.

I shall be glad to hear of some means devised for their relief, also to assist in whatever way you think advisable.

Mr. Gillis says, there has been talk of purchasing clothing for the blacks, and deducting the amount furnished them, from their wages.

Now is the time. It is indeed hard to hear their complaints, and then to require them to work. I am Very respectfully Your Ob't. Serv't.

ALS

A. W. Slayton

Lt. A. W. Slayton to Lt. Col. J. H. Simpson, 8 Jan. 1864, Letters & Reports Received, ser. 3541, Engineer, Dept. of the OH, RG 393 Pt. 1 [C-4650]. Slayton signed as an officer in the 25th Michigan Infantry and as an acting assistant quartermaster; his letter is headed "Engineers Department." John R. Gilliss, a civil engineer, was in charge of the construction of fortifications at Camp Nelson. Former slaves assigned by military authorities to railroad construction were often similarly ill-equipped with respect to clothing and blankets. In November 1863, a quartermaster at Lebanon, Kentucky, reported that "the Contrabands, so called, employed upon the RR" were "in a filthy condition and destitute of clothing, so much so, that they are in a suffering condition." Seeking authority to furnish them with clothing and blankets "in advance of their earnings," he noted that the impressed slaves also at work on the railroad were "so provided by special agreement." (Capt. E. B. Whitman to Maj. J. H. Simpson, 14 Nov. 1863, Letters & Reports Received, ser. 3541, Engineer, Dept. of the OH, RG 393 Pt. 1 [C-4648].)

215: Officer in Charge of Fortifications at Bowling Green, Kentucky, to the Chief Engineer of the Department of the Ohio

Bowling Green Ky Feby. 6th 1864

Col. Owing to the Extreme Cold weather, during the past month, but little has been done upon the Fortifications at this Post, Nothing has been done to College Hill Fort. since my last Report, The Ditches of Battery Lytle have been opened to the depth of five (5) feet and full width, on all sides. The cistern (twenty (20) feet in diameter); is being advanced as rapidly as possible, I have but fifty (50) men left for duty. and the number is being daily reduced, by the Commander of the Post's releasing them, & unless more are impressed or details made from Soldiers, the work will hang on, there are between. six & Seven hundred men at the Post, not on daily duty, The former. & Present Commanders of the Post, object strenuously. to paying the men, (negroes), stating they do not come under the head of *Contrabands.* but are slaves belonging to *Rebel Sympathizers.* in this District, & if anyone is paid, it should be the masters, they in fact, hold themselves in a measure, responsible for the impressment of the Negroes, thinking they may be held accountable to the owners in damages after the war is over, by the *Kentucky Civil Courts* for this reason no Rolls have been made out. in fact I have not the means of making them out, farther back than the first of January, of this year, for the reason that I had nothing to do with the negroes previous to that time, they having been placed by the Commander of the Post. under the special charge of one of his Commissiond officers. I will forward you the Rolls for January. & if you say pay the *men*, it will be done   Very Respectfully Your Obd^r Servt,

ALS   N. S. Andrews

Lieut. N. S. Andrews to Lieut. Col. J. H. Simpson, 6 Feb. 1864, Letters & Reports Received, ser. 3541, Engineer, Dept. of the OH, RG 393 Pt. 1 [C-4652]. Andrews was an officer in the 6th Michigan Battery. A reply from Colonel James H. Simpson, the chief engineer, expressed disappointment that the small size of the available black labor force should have slowed progress on the fortifications, when fatigue parties could have been detailed from the large garrison of soldiers. "Be pleased to say to the Comd'g Officer that the fortifications in the Department have been mainly erected by the soldiers, and to them does the Government chiefly look for the completion of the works." With respect to the question of paying the impressed black laborers, Simpson maintained that his previous declaration to the effect that *"Contrabands"* were entitled to pay "of course meant, such negroes as had run away from disloyal masters, and not such as belonging to disloyal masters had been pressed into the service." (Lieut. Col. J. H. Simpson to Lieut. N. S. Andrews, 16 Feb. 1864, Press Copies of Letters Sent, ser. 3539, Engineer, Dept. of the OH, RG 393 Pt. 1 [C-4652].)

216: Chief Quartermaster of the 1st Division, 11th Army Corps, to the Chief Quartermaster of the Corps; and Quartermaster General to the Chief Quartermaster of the Department of the Cumberland

[*Chattanooga, Tenn.*] March 13th— *1864.*

Dr Sir, I have in my employ some 30 Negroes, said to belong to loyal men in Kentucky.

They were turned over to me by C H Gaubert, Capt & AQM, Leabanon Ky, as teamsters at 30 Dollars pr month, and nothing was said about any contract made with masters, except, in the Transfer under the head of, "By whom owned & where", the masters mames are mentioned. On the 1ˢᵗ of February last I referred the matter to Lt Col Donaldson[1] at Nashville who said, "pay the negro", which I did, the full amount due them up to Feby 1ˢᵗ, Since which time I have recᵈ letters from masters claiming the pay due said slaves, and giving references in regard to their loyalty. What am I to do? Shall I continue to pay the Slaves, or if the masters are loyal—am I to pay the masters. I am Very Respectfully Yr Obᵗ Svᵗ

ALS   B. F. Coolidge

[*Washington, D.C.*] April 1, 1864
Colonel: The letter of Lt. Coolidge relating to the payment of certain negroes employed as teamsters, for whose services their masters claim compensation, referred by you to this office on the 16ᵗʰ ult. for instructions has been received.

Please inform this office whether these negroes were or were not hired from their masters. If a contract was made with their masters, they are entitled to the wages.

If the negroes claim to be free, however, I do not see how under the laws of Congress they can be restored to the control of their masters.

No officer of the Army under the laws of 13ᵗʰ of March 1862 chap XL and July 17. 1862 Chap CXC Sections 9 and 10 can force the return of a fugitive.[2]

Hence if the negro within the lines of the Army denies the Masters claim and should be discharged from service by an officer, he has but to remain within the lines and hire himself to another officer to place himself within these laws protection.

Unless a written contract with the master exists and is of record, I think that the only practical result will be payment to the man who earned the money.

The case is delicate, however, and until I have full information I do not feel prepared to make a decision or refer it to the Secretary for action.

Extracts from the laws referred to are enclosed.

HLcSr   (Sgd) M. C. Meigs

Lt. B. F. Coolidge to Lt. Col. Hays, 13 Mar. 1864, filed as E-100 1864, Letters Received, ser. 20, Central Records, RG 92 [Y-645]; Qr. Mr. Genl.

M. C. Meigs to Lt. Col. L. C. Easton, 1 Apr. 1864, vol. 75, p. 467, Letters Sent, ser. 9, Central Records, RG 92 [Y-645]. The extracts said to have been enclosed were not copied into the letters-sent volume. Endorsements on Coolidge's letter transmitted it from the chief quartermaster of the 11th Army Corps to the chief quartermaster of the Department of the Cumberland, and from him to Quartermaster General Meigs. No subsequent report by the chief quartermaster of the Department of the Cumberland has been found among the files of letters received by the Quartermaster General's Office. For additional documents regarding Kentucky slaves who gained de facto freedom when they were transferred to Tennessee by military employers who had hired them from their owners, see *Freedom*, ser. 1, vol. 1: docs. 225A–C.

1 James L. Donaldson was supervising quartermaster of the Department of the Cumberland.
2 The law of March 13, 1862, had created an additional article of war prohibiting military and naval officers from using any of the forces under their command to return fugitive slaves to their owners. Section 9 of the confiscation act of July 17, 1862, had declared "forever free of their servitude" the slaves of disloyal owners whenever such slaves came into Union lines or under Union occupation; section 10 of the same act had forbidden anyone in the Union military service "under any pretence whatever" to rule upon the validity of a putative owner's claim to a slave or to "surrender up any such person to the claimant." (*Statutes at Large*, vol. 12, pp. 354, 591.)

217: Engineer at Camp Nelson, Kentucky, to the Chief Engineer of the Department of the Ohio

Camp Nelson [*Ky.*] May 20th [*1864*]

. . . .

On Tuesday over $3,000 was paid Brent of Bourbon County on powers of attorney.[1] This morning the contrabands here were paid off. $581,40 was this afternoon paid Pond taking his mem. receipt as part payment of the amount due him for clothing furnished the negroes—[2] His whole bill is $812.65 As Some of the negroes had overdrawn on clothing I made them sign a pay roll for the present month while signing the previous ones—so that if any left after payment their accounts could be settled when they had overdrawn.

. . . .

It has been a painful duty to pay off owners whose loyalty I cannot believe in in spite of the oath they have taken—and to tell the men who have worked faithfully for us for nearly a year that there was nothing for them.

Among others Sam, belonging to Mrs Preston (who has taken the oath and received the money) has for six months had the keys of our commissary. tool house, and stable – always steady, intelligent and reliable – For this he has not had a cent from the Govt.

As the time for which they have been pressed has expired I would suggest that since they are now only laborers whose pay you can fix yourself, that you allow me to put these men on the same roll as the contrabands – pay them half the amount and retain the balance for their masters – The negroes would receipt for the whole amount themselves –

No one can deny your right to fix the terms on which you *hire* laborers yourself.

I do not think the masters will call for them as they are almost sure to run away if they do. And I would rather that they should go home than be ashamed to look a negro in the face as sometimes happens now. Only five or six will be included in this arrangement. and the negro would be expected to clothe himself out of his half the money. Very Respy, Your Obedt. Servt

ALS   John R. Gilliss

Excerpts from John R. Gilliss to Lt. Col. J. H. Simpson, 20 May [1864], Letters & Reports Received, ser. 3541, Engineer, Dept. of the OH, RG 393 Pt. 1 [C-4653]. Gilliss's plan to assemble a new force of hired black laborers was thwarted by the advent of black enlistment at Camp Nelson. "Fourteen of our contrabands enlisted today in a negro regiment recruiting in camp," he reported on May 24. "I expect nearly all the negroes we have will leave us to enlist." (John R. Gilliss to Lt. Col. J. H. Simpson, 24 May 1864, Letters & Reports Received, ser. 3541, Engineer, Dept. of the Ohio, RG 393 Pt. 1 [C-4653].)

1 Hugh T. Brent was an agent of Bourbon County slaveholders whose slaves had been impressed for military labor.
2 Pond was a sutler from whom both impressed slave laborers and "contraband" laborers had received clothing; the cost of the clothing was deducted from the wages owed to the "contraband" laborers and to the owners of the slaves.

218: Engineer at Camp Nelson, Kentucky, to the Chief Engineer of the Department of the Ohio

Camp Nelson [*Ky.*] June 17th 1864

Col. On the evening of the 14th the remaining enlisted negroes in the camp were turned over to me by Capt Hall.

Camp & garrison equipage and subsistence have been drawn by Lt McFadden.

Last evening they were drawn into line and 1058 effective working men counted. Stragglers still to be collected will make the number 1200.

I have hired overseers and made overseers of all the detailed soldiers I can get so as to have one for each 50 men.

The previous arrangement of having the squads report from the camp of distribution was very unsatisfactory. they never got to work before 9 o'clock—and lost much time waiting for their dinner. to be sent— Sometimes it did not arrive and was never the full ration—

This has all been corrected and now I have them all well organized—

After inspection last evening Capt Hall massed the men together and made them a speech informing them that Gen Thomas was in Louisville on his way here to organize them— they would be armed, clothed and drilled in this Camp—and their muster be dated back to time of entry into the service—so that they will be paid for the time they are now working on Fortifications—

After that 300 of them under Folger and other overseers marched to [Fort] Bramlette tools & rations having been sent there in the morning—

Tomorrow 125 will commence on the road to Pollys Bend—

Next week French with 200 men is to commence the Fort on the neck.

The entire infantry line from the Ky to Hickman has been finished— Magazines all covered— Fort Nelson & Jackson sodded— Putnam commenced sodding— Taylor do— Jones 2/3 done—

Battery near Boones Knob on Turnpike finished 2 12 pdrs mounted 75 ft rifle pit protecting ford in Ky R. completed— Battery in mule corral back of Gen Frys. finished 2 mountain howitz mounted 200 ft rifle pit near do completed—

Battery between mule corrall & Fort Jones commenced— Timber cut across Hickman

I can work 1500 to advantage if they come in as is probable— Very Respy Your Obdt Servt

John R Gilliss

P.S. I wrote several days ago stating progress etc—and suggesting that you come down if convenient.

ALS

John R. Gilliss to Lt. Col. J. H. Simpson, 17 June 1864, Letters & Reports Received, ser. 3541, Engineer, Dept. of the Ohio, RG 393 Pt. 1 [C-4654]. The officer who had turned over the newly recruited black soldiers to Gilliss for temporary labor on the fortifications was Captain Theron E. Hall, chief quartermaster of the District of Central Kentucky. The official reportedly on his way to Camp Nelson to organize them into regiments was General Lorenzo Thomas, adjutant general of the army. By June 20 Gilliss was reporting an "effective negro working force" of 1,400. An officer who had just arrived to take charge of the recruits was satisfied with the arrangement whereby they were to work on the fortifications while awaiting organization. "I would therefore suggest taking advantage of this opportunity to strengthen these works in every possible manner," Gilliss proposed. "The only expense is that of overseers." (John R. Gilliss to Lt. Col. J. H. Simpson, 20 June 1864, Letters & Reports Received, ser. 3541, Engineer, Dept. of the OH, RG 393 Pt. 1 [C-4654].)

219: **Commander of the Post of Camp Nelson, Kentucky, to the Commander of the District of Kentucky; Circular by the Commander of the Post of Camp Nelson; and Telegram from the Headquarters of the Post of Camp Nelson to the Headquarters of the District**

Camp Nelson Ky   July 5" 1864

General— I have the honor to state that I have examined into the condition of the negro women, children and old men at this Post and find them very destitute, a burden to themselves as well as ourselves. If some means are not soon devised to return them to their homes we shall not only have war in the land but pestilence and famine in camp   I respectfully request that you will please give me some definite instructions how to act   Many cases of disease are already making their appearance among both sexes and of such a nature as to demand their removal beyond the limits of camp at once   I am General with much respect Your obt servt

HLcSr   (Sg'd) Speed S. Fry

[*Endorsement*] H'd Qrs Dist of K'y Lexington Ky July 5/64 Respy referred to Brig Genl L. Thomas Adjt Genl U.S.A. (Sgd) S. G. Burbridge Brvt Maj. Genl Comd'g

[*Endorsement*] Lexington K'y July 6. 1864 Major General Burbridge is desired to fix an early day when the class of negroes referred to within shall be placed beyond the camp that they may proceed to their respective homes where their masters under the law of Kentucky are bound to support them. Rations should be issued to the destitute to enable them to reach their homes— It would be well also to give notice of the day as many of the

owners of the slaves might desire to go to Camp Nelson to receive
them (Sgd) L. Thomas Adjt. Genl.

Camp Nelson Jessamine C° Ky July 6" 1864.
Circular
I In pursuance with instructions from Brig Gen. L. Thomas,
Adjutant General U.S.A. owners of slaves are hereby notified that on
and after Monday July 10" 1864, all colored men in camp unfit for
service in the Army and all women and children will be delivered up
to their owners upon application to these Head Quarters.
II All officers or other persons, having in their employ negro
men fit for service in the Army are hereby directed to report them
forthwith to Col Thos D. Sedgewick comdg U.S. Colored Troops at
this Post. All men fit for service, as above, who have come into
Camp since the issue of War Department Orders must be reported,
no matter at what engaged.
A prompt compliance with this circular is expected. By
command of Brig. Genl S. S. Fry
HD

[*Camp Nelson, Ky.*] July 6ᵗʰ [186]4
Telegram
General Fry went to Louisville to-day and before leaving,
instructed me to have all colered women & children brot here, and
to give passes to all that desired to return home. There is not one
among two hundred (200) that want to go. A great many are
willing to go outside the lines. There to shift for themselves. Shall
I keep them in camp, or not. They are laboring under the
impression that they will be Killed by their masters if they return,
and can not be assured to the contrary. Pleas reply giving me
definite instructions Respectfully
HWcSr   Geo A. Hanaford

Brig. Genl. Speed S. Fry to Brig. Genl. S. G. Burbridge, 5 July 1864, F-15
1864, Letters Received by Adjutant General L. Thomas, ser. 363, Colored
Troops Division, RG 94 [V-36]; Circular, Head Quarters Camp Nelson, 6
July 1864, vol. 111/256 DKy, p. 52, General Orders, ser. 905, Post of Camp
Nelson KY, RG 393 Pt. 4 [C-7318]; Lieut. Geo. A. Hanaford to Capt.
J. Bates Dickson, 6 July [186]4, vol. 107 DKy, p. 370, Press Copies of
Letters Sent, ser. 902, Post of Camp Nelson KY, RG 393 Pt. 4 [C-7317]. On

July 6, Adjutant General Lorenzo Thomas ordered that thenceforward "none but able-bodied men" would be received at Camp Nelson and the other depots for organizing black soldiers. "All others will be encouraged to remain at their respective homes, where, under the State laws, their masters are bound to take care of them." Those women, children, and old or infirm men already at Camp Nelson, he further ordered, "will be sent to their homes." Not only, he explained, had diseases appeared among them "of such a nature as to require their removal beyond the limits of the camp," but "all of this class of persons are required to assist in securing the crops, now suffering in many cases for the want of labor." Five days later, an adjutant at the headquarters of the District of Kentucky conveyed the substance of Thomas's order to General Fry, commander of the post of Camp Nelson, adding that it was not necessary for masters to take the oath of allegiance in order to have their fugitive slaves returned to them. (*Official Records*, ser. 3, vol. 4, p. 474; Capt. J. Bates Dickson to Brig. General S. S. Fry, 11 July [1864], vol. 62/119 DKy, p. 112, Telegrams Sent, ser. 2168, Dist. of KY, RG 393 Pt. 1 [C-7317].) Preventing further accessions of black women, children, and old or disabled men proved far easier to require than to accomplish, however, and determination to expel those who found their way into the camp did not necessarily produce results. Repeated orders by General Fry testified to both the determination and the lack of success. On July 5, he instructed the pickets to refuse admission to all but able-bodied men. On July 12, he ordered officers and military employers to turn over any black women, children, and infirm men "in their charge," retaining only those women hired as cooks and laundresses. On August 9, he ordered "that all negro women and children, old and infirm, negro men unfit for any military duty . . . be at once sent beyond the lines with instructions not to return." On August 23, he ordered that "[a]ll negro women in this Camp except those from Tennessee and other states south of Kentucky will at once be expelled," and instructed officers employing black women to "deliver them up to the Patrol." On August 24, he threatened stern punishment of guards who accepted bribes from black women seeking admission into the camp. And on September 3, he posted guards at "all the inlets to the Camp" and "all the openings in the fortifications," with instructions not to allow black women and children or "lewd white women" to enter. (Order, Head Quarters Camp Nelson Ky., 5 July 1864, vol. 107 DKy, p. 354, Press Copies of Letters Sent, ser. 902, Post of Camp Nelson KY, RG 393 Pt. 4 [C-7316]; General Orders No. 4, Hd. Qrs. Camp Nelson Ky, 12 July 1864, General Orders No. 14, Head Qrs. Camp Nelson, 9 Aug. 1864, General Orders No. 19, Head Quarters Camp Nelson, Ky., 23 Aug. 1864, Orders, Head Qrs., Camp Nelson, Ky., 24 Aug. 1864, and Orders, Head Quarters Camp Nelson Ky., 3 Sept. 1864, vol. 111/256 DKy, pp. 54, 73, 78–79, 84, General Orders, ser. 905, Post of Camp Nelson KY, RG 393 Pt. 4 [C-7318].) For a later and still more drastic expulsion of black women and children from Camp Nelson, see below, docs. 225A–D.

220: Quartermaster of the 3rd Division of the 23rd Army Corps to the Commander of the Post of Lexington, Kentucky

Lexington Ky. Aug. 29" 1864

Colonel: I would respectfully represent that I am ordered by Major Genl. Schofield[1] to take Mules to the front for the use of the Army. That Eighty four (84) men hired to take charge of this stock, who have made one trip to Georgia, and were relieved there & returned here for the purpose of taking charge of other stock to be forwarded at once, arrived here on Friday, and that yesterday one of said men, John Bryant (colored) was taken by J. C. McAlister, and is now forcibly detained from my camp—and further that the said McAlister in company with three soldiers *not* under Arms (except Revolvers) went to my Camp yesterday with the avowed purpose of taking away another of my men who had been regularly hired as Teamsters in Govt. Service, and is now on duty as such.

I would respectfully ask whether these men are to be discharged on the application of their masters, or substitute Brokers, or whether they are entitled to protection while in Government Service, and if so, would further ask for the release from custody of John Bryant and his return to my Camp. I am Colonel Very Respectfully Your obt. Servt

HLS

D. W. H. Day

Capt. D. W. H. Day to Col. Ratliffe, 29 Aug. 1864, Letters Received, ser. 1030, 1st Division, Dist. of KY, RG 393 Pt. 2 No. 25 [C-9025]. Endorsements indicate that the post commander, Colonel Robert W. Ratliff, referred Day's letter to the commander of the 1st Division of the District of Kentucky, who on August 31 instructed Ratliff to arrest both McAlister and Bryant and send them to division headquarters. That same day, Ratliff asked Day about the whereabouts of the two men, but, according to Day's response, the question had become moot: McAlister had appeared at Day's office "with an order for Bryant's pay" and a notation that the erstwhile drover had been enlisted as a soldier. By October 1864, efforts by former masters to reclaim fugitive slaves from Captain Day and other military employers, for forcible enlistment into the army, were widespread; what is more, high-ranking military authorities were increasingly lending their support. (See below, doc. 223.)

1 John M. Schofield commanded the 23rd Army Corps (Army of the Ohio), which was engaged in the Atlanta campaign.

221: Affidavit of a Kentucky White Woman; and Freedmen's Bureau Assistant Superintendent of the Subdistrict of Louisville to the Superintendent of the Subdistrict, Enclosing the Affidavit of a Kentucky Freedwoman

Louisville, Ky., November 20th *1866*

Mrs Mary DeForest, of Louisville Ky. (on Green St 3rd Door below Hancock), states that Mrs Hughes living on Jacob St, (at Henry Hughes) Louisville Ky. turned out of doors in August '64, a negro woman Sarah Hughes (her slave) crippled and unable to walk and refused her further support saying that the negroes would soon be free & she would have nothing more to do with them

That Mrs DeForest took her in & has Kept her ever since out of charity & has received no compensation whatever she deems under the Circumstances that Mrs Hughes should be compelled to pay for her Maintenance during that time, That she (Mrs DeForest) is a widow & unable to care for her any longer & desire the Bureau to take some action in the case

her

HDSr   Mary X DeForest

mark

Louisville, Ky., December 21st *1866.*

Gen[l] I have the honor to report in Compliance with Special Order No 24 Par I Extract dated Dec 10th 1866. from Hd Qrs Lou Sub Dist Lou Ky. the Case of Sarah Hill col[d] formerly the Slave of Mrs Mary Hughes who is now and has been Supported for 3. years by a person named Mrs Mary Defourester – out of Charity Said Mrs Defourester is the Mother of 7 children all living with her in this City. and who is a widow and bearing a very good Character in the Neighbourhood in which she lives – Said Mrs Hughes [*Defourester*] is not able to take care of Sarah Hill col[d] as she can barly support herself – I would therefor under the Circumstances of this Case think that Mrs Defourester is entittled to Some Compensation for the Keeping of the Said Sarah Hill Col[d] who is a Cripple and have been for a long time unable to be of any Service to the Said Mrs Defourester but only a bill of expense, Mrs Mary Hughes (white) the former Owner of Sarah Hill Col[d] is a widow and has been for Some Years. Efforts have been made to find her and her place of Residence but have failed Sarah Hill Col[d] has been placed in the Hospital at Crittenden Barracks and receiving Medical Treatment which releives Mrs Defourester from any further expense – I inclose with my Report Statement of *Sarah Hill* Mrs Ellen Vinecourt

Josephine Defourester which Statements I have taken at the Residence of Mrs Defourester under Oath Seperate and apart and believe them to be true in every particular   I am Sir very Resp^ct Your Obt Servt

ALS   R W Roberts

[*Enclosure*]   *Louisville, Ky.,* December 13th *1866.*
   Sarah Hill. Col^d being duly sworn says she was the slave of Mrs Susan Hughes from a girl untill about two years ago. when her Husband – Mr Hughes – Died, and she went to Boarding –   She told me to find a place and go to work wherever I could find anything to do and she would help me as she could not keep me in a Boarding House and would give me what she could spare   I lived with a Col^d woman one month when I fell down Stairs with a pail of water and injured my foot so as to have my large toe amputated was crippled to such an extent as not to be able to walk for three months   Mrs Hughes had up to this time only gave me one Dollar,   I then went to Fanny Kennedys a Col^d woman living on Main St between 1st & 2nd Sts   Staid there 3 months –   Said Fanny Kennedy told Mrs Hughs she did not want anything from her for my keep.   After leaving Mrs Kennedys I came here to Mrs Defourester   Mrs Hughes has not given Mrs Defourester any money for my support or given me any clothes Since I have been here

                                                                                      her
HDSr   Sarah X Hill
                                                                                     mark

Affidavit of Mary DeForest, 20 Nov. 1866, and Bvt. Maj. R. W. Roberts to Bvt. Brig. Genl. C. H. Frederick, 21 Dec. 1866, enclosing affidavit of Sarah Hill, 13 Dec. 1866, D-165 1866, Letters Received, ser. 1068, KY Asst. Comr., RG 105 [A-4229]. Endorsements. DeForest's affidavit sworn before an officer at the headquarters of the Freedmen's Bureau assistant commissioner for the state of Kentucky; Hill's affidavit sworn before Major Roberts. Also enclosed in Roberts's report are affidavits sworn on December 13, 1866, by Ellen Vinecore and Josephine Defourester, the widowed mother and fifteen-year-old daughter, respectively, of Mary DeForest (variously spelled as DeForester or Defourester), both of whom lived in the same household. Vinecore reported that when Mary Hughes "quit keeping House," she "let [Sarah Hill] work about wherever She Could earn 50 cents but since She has become entirely dependent upon others Mrs Hughs pays no attention to her   She comes once in about 6 months to see her but brings her nothing but a few old cast off clothes of her own." Mrs. Hughes, she insisted, "is fully able to Keep this woman Sally Hill, her Son Henry Hughes being a merchant on Main St and in the dry goods business."

222: Affidavit of a Kentucky Freedwoman

Louisville, Ky. August 23ᵈ *1866.*
Priscilla Dawson (colored) being Sworn says that she was formerly
the slave of Jackson Bell who lives five miles from New Hope
Station on the Louisville and Lebanon Rail Road in Marion
County   That in May 1864 her husband Sylvester Dawson enlisted
in the Union army.   That some two months after her husband
enlisted she heard from some white persons that there was a law
which freed the wives and children of enlisted colored soldiers and
she determined to profit by it.   That in some three weeks after that
she took her children and went to New Haven in Nelson County
and the next day after arriving at New Haven Bell came to her and
said to her if she would return and live with him and his family he
would give her as much as was given to other colored persons.   she
returned and lived with him until a few days in January 1866 when
she again left and went to New Haven and remained there until her
husband was discharged in March and came to her and they then
came to Louisville and are still here
    That during all the time spoken of Mʳ Bell gave her one Linsey
dress and one calico dress and the children one summer suit each
and this was all either clothing or money that she received   Mʳ Bell
told her twice that her husband was dead and she could only hear
from him thro others   she claims that Mʳ Bell should be made to
pay her reasonable wages for the time she was with him that for a
portion of the time she done all the cooking for the family and
assisted in housework and the balance of the time she had assistance

her
Priscilla X Dawson
mark

HDSr

[*Endorsement*] Bureau R.F&A.L.   Office Sub Dist. Marion &c.
Lebanon Ky. Sep 6 .66   Respy returned to Bvt Maj Gen *Davis*
A.C. BR.F&AL for Ky with information that *Jackson Bell* denies
emphatically that he owes the petitioner *Piscilla Dawson*. He alleges
that prior to Jany 1ˢᵗ 1866 he paid her all that he promised. That
on or about the 1ˢᵗ of Jany '66 he contracted with her for a years
labor which contract she refused to comply with & left him in Jany
1866. He further alleges that he at no time knew that the husband
of the petitioner was in the army of U.S.
    Attention is called to the fact that the act of Congress freeing the
wives of colored persons enlisting in the army was passed &
approved in March 1865 – ¹
    Until *Priscilla* makes out *her own account for services* I can do nome

[*no more*] with the case. Mr. Bell is reliable & responsible. Very
Respy Jams M Fidler Sup &c

Affidavit of Priscilla Dawson, 23 Aug. 1866, #178 1866, Letters Received,
ser. 1208, Louisville KY Supt., RG 105 [A-4493]. Sworn before a Freedmen's
Bureau officer at the headquarters of the Louisville subdistrict. Other endorsements transmitted Dawson's affidavit through Freedmen's Bureau channels to
James M. Fidler, and then returned the papers to the Louisville subdistrict. In
the same file and in the same handwriting as the affidavit is a bill calling upon
Jackson Bell to pay Sylvester Dawson for the services of Priscilla Dawson in
1864 and 1865; both the amount per month and the total owed are blank.

1 By a joint resolution approved on March 3, 1865, Congress provided that
the wife and children "of any person that has been, or may be, mustered into
the military or naval service of the United States, shall . . . be forever free."
(*Statutes at Large*, vol. 13, p. 571.)

223: Assistant Provost Marshal General for Kentucky to the Headquarters of the District of Kentucky

Louisville, Ky., 8″ October *1864*
Captain   Frequent just complaints are made at this office that many
slaves leave their masters and are employed by U.S. officers without
having been enlisted.   The severest complaints refer to Captain Day
of the Qʳ Mast. or Commy. Deptᵐᵗ who is said to have over four
hundred of such employed near Lancaster in Garrard Co. and intends
to send them south still unenlisted with cattle for Genl Sherman's
army   Other complaints state that there are from fifty to a hundred
at & about Camp Nelson still unenlisted.
   A great part of all belong to Garrard & Lincoln counties & their
masters are willing and anxious that they should enlist for the
counties to which they belong by which their proper credits may be
secured.
   There is no authority for this practice from any existing law or
regulation and there is no justification for it.   It might be tolerated
when an urgent military necessity requires that all services both of
whites & blacks shall be temporarily impressed but there is no such
necessity now.   & the fact that a large number of slaves, not able
bodied, but "capable of any military service in the Qʳ Masters
Commissaries or Engʳ Departments," have been enlisted and can be
applied to the work expected to be done by these unenlisted men is
a good reason that those enlisted men and not the unenlisted should
be so employed.

The evil may be corrected in only one way and that is a military order from competent authority forbidding the employment of runaway slaves who are not enlisted and by detailing a sufficient force of such as are enlisted to do the desired work—also *requiring* such officers as wish to employ these slaves to procure their enlistment & muster-in and further that any officers who employ them for their private purposes as servants &^{c} shall be held amenable to U.S. regulations as well as to state laws.

I respectfully request the issue of such an order from your H^d Quarters addressed to all whom it may concern Commanding officers as well as such officers as are pursuing the objectionable practice   I am Capt Respy Yr Obt Servt

ALS   W H Sidell

Major W. H. Sidell to Capt. J. Bates Dickson, 8 Oct. 1864, Letters Received, ser. 734, Post of Louisville KY, RG 393 Pt. 4 [C-6050]. A notation on the letter reads "file." For examples of the complaints received by Sidell, see *Freedom*, ser. 1, vol. 1: doc. 230. Meanwhile, Captain Deming W. H. Day, the quartermaster complained of in particular, was himself protesting against forcible seizure of his black teamsters and drovers by military recruiters, former masters, and substitute brokers intent upon enlisting them in the army. (See above, doc. 220; and Capt. D. W. H. Day to Lt. Col. W. S. Babcock, 22 Sept. 1864, Letters Received, 12th USCHA, Regimental Books & Papers USCT, RG 94 [G-38].) Not until November 13 did the headquarters of the District of Kentucky reply to Sidell's letter, informing him that, in accordance with an order of the previous June by General William T. Sherman (commander of the Military Division of the Mississippi), recruiting officers were forbidden to enlist black men who were employed in the quartermaster, commissary, and other staff departments. Convinced that Sherman's order was "unquestionably founded on wrong principles," Sidell immediately placed the issue before the provost marshal general, suggesting that he submit it "to the highest necessary authority." Slave men who left their owners and instead of enlisting "[took] service as hired men in the staff departments," Sidell complained, thereby deprived their masters of the compensation promised to loyal owners of slaves who enlisted and also deprived the state of credit against its draft quota. Moreover, former slaves hired as "mere employées" could "come and go at will." Although not officially made free (as they would be if they enlisted), they "yet ramble about as vagabonds when not employed"; because military labor provided no formal title to freedom, their masters continued to "have a lien on them" and "no U.S. law protects them." Sidell proposed that military employers be forbidden to hire fugitive slaves and that all military labor instead be accomplished by details of black soldiers. After consideration at the Provost Marshal General's Bureau and the Bureau of Colored Troops, the question was eventually referred to Adjutant General Lorenzo Thomas, who, in an endorsement of December 14, 1864, recommended that Sherman's order be declared "inoperative" in Kentucky. "All these negroes, whereever employed," Thomas insisted, "should be enlisted, and their places supplied by

those who are not able bodied . . . or by details made from Colored Troops."
(Lt. Col. W. H. Sidell to Brig. Genl. J. B. Fry, 15 Nov. 1864, enclosing Maj.
W. H. Sidell to Capt. J. Bates Dickson, 8 Oct. 1864, Capt. J. Bates Dickson
to Maj. W. H. Sidell, 13 Nov. 1864, and General Orders, No. 17, Headquarters, Military Division of the Mississippi, 21 June 1864, with endorsements,
all filed as S-1365 1864, Letters Received, ser. 18, Central Office, RG 110
[R-24].)

224: Surveyor of Customs at Evansville, Indiana, to the Secretary of the Treasury

Evansville Ind, Oct. 10, 1864
Sir, Permit me through you respectfully to direct the attention of
the proper Department of our Government to the condition of affairs
at this Port and all along this Ohio Border
    The Great Deep of Slavery in Kentucky is broken up and the
fragments are rapidly drifting northward across the Ohio River, The
Men are entering the Union Army by hundreds and
thousands— their *wives and children*, following their husbands,
without homes or even the necessaries of life are suffering *now* and
unless they shall be cared for by the Government, many of them
will no doubt *perish* during the winter which is fast
approaching, The task is too great for private charity, Please lay
this before the proper officer and greatly oblige   very truly yrs
ALS   A. L. Robinson

A. L. Robinson to Hon. W. P. Fessenden, 10 Oct. 1864, enclosed in J. F.
Hartley to Wm. P. Mellen, Esq., 17 Oct. 1864, Letters Received from the
Secretary of the Treasury, Records of the General Agent, RG 366 [Q-145].
The covering letter forwarded Robinson's letter to William P. Mellen, general
agent of the special agencies of the Treasury Department, with instructions to
"give it the proper reference."

225A: Superintendent of the Colored Refugee Home at Camp Nelson, Kentucky, to the Chief Quartermaster at Camp Nelson

Camp Nelson Ky. Dec 16" 1864.
Captain   In response to your communication of this date requesting
that I furnish you, without delay with any information which may
be in my possession relating to the late expulsion of colored women

and children from this camp, I have the honor to reply that the importance of the subject seems to demand from me a report which must of necessity be voluminous and detailed. On the morning of the 23" of November last while in Lexington I was informed by Lieut. G. A. Hanaford 47" Ky. Inft. and Assistant Superintendant for the organization of Colored troops, that Brig. Genl. Fry Commanding at Camp Nelson had given orders for the expulsion of all colored women and children in Camp, and that the order was being executed. As I had taken a very active part in the enlistment of colored troops here, knowing that such a course would operate most unfavorably upon such enlistments, remembering that these people had followed their husbands and fathers to Camp who were then in the Army fighting for that freedom of which it was by this act proposed to deprive their families and firmly believing that the wife and children of the colored soldier were entitled to protection from that government for the perpetuation of which he was imperiling his life, I felt it my duty to interfere, and if possible prevent the accomplishment of the contemplated outrage. The weather at the time was intensely cold, summarily expulsion, and exposure to the inclement atmosphere would occasion untold suffering: and knowing this, my efforts were prompted by the instincts of that common humanity to which every heart, not already hardened by familiarity with acts of cruelty, lays claim. I came to Camp on the evening of the 25" and found that the order had been executed indiscriminately   I found that large numbers were congregated at Nicholasville; some had found their way to Lexington, some were sitting by the road-side and all were suffering from cold and hunger. I addressed, at once, to Capt J. Bates Dickson A.A.G.[1] a telegram as follows

Camp Nelson Ky Nov 26" 1864

Capt J. Bates Dickson A.A.G.
                    Lexington
                              Can nothing be done for the poor women and children sent from this Camp by order of Genl. Fry? They are literally starving to death. I have the affidavit of one soldier whose family was sent out of Camp last Wednesday, that one of his children was frozen to death after being put out of the lines.[2]
(Signed) T. E. Hall Capt and A.Q.M

To which I received the following reply —

By Telegraph from Lexington Nov 27
To Capt T. E. Hall A.Q.M.
                    I have referred the matter of the colored women and children to the Genl,[3] by Telegraph
(Signed) J. Bates Dickson Capt.

In the meantime I made such investigations as I could, causing the affidavit of Joseph Miller referred to in your communication from the Quartermaster's Department, to be taken in your presence. As further evidence of the cruelty inflicted upon these poor people, I caused the affidavits of Privates Higgins and Burnside, Messrs Sears, Linen and Larter quartermaster's clerks, and the reverend messrs Schofield and Vetter, subsequently to be taken[4] While waiting for a reply from General Burbridge, the sufferers were enduring great privations, as will be seen by reference to the aforementioned affidavits copies of which I have the honor to enclose marked A. B. C. D. and E., hence before receiving any further advices I despatched the following to District Head-Quarters.

Camp Nelson Ky. Nov. 26" 1864

Capt J. Bates Dickson A.A.G.
Lexington
The colored women and children are still being put out of the Camp. It is done by the order of Genl Fry. Many of them are lying about the Depot in Lexington and are in a suffering condition. It is reported that one child was frozen to death the day they were sent out.

(Signed) T. E. Hall
Capt and A.Q.M.

On the 27" finding that the helpless outcasts were actually starving, I purchased of the Commissary 200 rations of meat, bread, coffee and sugar which I caused to be distributed among them, and on the same day I sent the following to the General Commanding the District of Kentucky, who was then absent with his troops in the field.

Camp Nelson Ky Nov. 27" 1864

Col. J. S. Brisbin Chief of Staff
Cumberland Gap.
More than four hundred poor women and children families of Colored soldiers have been sent from Camp the past week. Some have died and all are in a starving condition. They are sitting by the roadside and wandering about the fields. Can you not induce the General to interfere on their behalf. No more potent weapon could be placed in the hands of the rebels to prevent enlistments than this. The whole community are loud in denouncing the outrage. Please answer

(Signed) T. E. Hall Capt. and A.Q.M.

To which the General replied as follows

By Telegraph from Cumberland Gap Nov. 27" 18[64]
To Capt T. E. Hall A.Q.M.
The General Commanding has given orders to give quarters to every woman and child and, if need, be to erect

buildings for them. Have them all gathered into
Camp. Communicate with Capt Dickson
(Signed)   Chas. M. Keyser
Capt and A.A.A.G.

In conformity with the instructions thus received I communicated
with Capt Dickson by sending him a copy of the above telegram to
which he replied as follows.

By Telegraph from Lexington Nov. 28″ 1864
To Capt T. E. Hall A.Q.M.
While awaiting other orders at Camp Nelson
the General commanding directs that you superintend the
arrangements for the care of colored women and children at Camp
Nelson. If other shelter cannot be provided. have buildings erected
for them in a suitable place and have them profitably employed, See
that none are turned out until the General returns. General Fry has
been notified of these instructions and directed to afford you every
facility for carrying them out
(Signed) J. Bates Dickson Capt and A.A.G.

On the reception of this despatch I enclosed a copy thereof together
with that received from the General, in the following
communication to Genl Fry.

Camp Nelson Nov. 29″ [28″] 1864
Brig Genl. Fry
Commanding Camp Nelson
General
I have the honor to transmit copies of telegrams received from
Cumberland Gap also from Capt Dickson A.A.G. Capt Restieaux
informed me that the barracks on the east side of the Pike can be
used temporarily for thes people until others can be erected. I have
the honor to request that you will give such orders as shall enable me
to carry out the instructions of the General Commanding.
I have the honor to be
Very Respectfully
Your Obedient Servant

To this Genl Fry replied.

Hd Qrts Camp Nelson Ky
Nov 28″ 1864
Capt T. E. Hall A.Q.M.
Capt
I will confer with Capt Restieaux in regard to
Barracks and will then issue such orders as may be necessary
Yours Respty
(Signed) Speed S. Fry
Brig. Genl.

683

And

Head Quarters Camp Nelson
Nov 28" 1864
Capt T. E. Hall A.Q.M.
Capt.
I have my instructions from Capt Dickson in
regard to negro women and children and all orders on that subject
will eminate from these Head Quarters.
Respty Yours
(Signed) Speed S. Fry
Brig Genl

Finding that the poor people were still excluded from Camp as you
will perceive by referring to the affidavits of Messrs Sears, Linen,
Larter, Schofield and Vetter, I sent the following despatch to Capt
Dickson A.A.G.

Camp Nelson Ky Nov 29" 1864
Capt Dickson A.A.G.
Lexington
I have furnished Genl. Fry with copies of my
orders. He does not seem desposed to recognize me at all except to
notify me that all orders will eminate from his Head Quarters. He
has ordered Capt Restieaux to furnish quarters for such women with
their children as are employed by the Government. He says further
that he has telegraphed General Burbridge concerning the others. I
can do nothing unless Genl Fry is directed not to interfere with
me — Answer.
(Signed) T. E. Hall Capt and A.Q.M.

In response thereto Capt Dickson sent the following, to Genl. Fry
and furnished me with a copy

Lexington Nov. 29" 1864
Brig Genl S. S. Fry
Camp Nelson Ky.
Capt T. E. Hall A.Q.M. has been ordered
temporarily to take charge of, and superintend matters connected
with the colored women and children seeking refuge at Camp
Nelson. Those in Camp as well as those who have been turned out
and may return there are to be cared for in such manner as Capt Hall
may see best. You will afford him every facility in carrying out his
plans on this subject.
By Command of Brvt. Maj Genl. Burbridge
(Signed) J. Bates Dickson. A.A.G.

Learning that Adjutant General Thomas was in Lexington I went
there to present the case to him and while there I received the
following from Lt. Col. Whitfield 123" Regt U.S.C.T.

684

By telegraph from Camp Nelson
Nov 29" 1864

To Capt T. E. Hall
"The guards have positive orders not to admit the
colored women into Camp. They are turned back at all points along
the fortifications".[5]

I then had the honor of a personal interview with General Thomas
who at once sent a despatch to Genl. Fry ordering him in the most
peremptory manner to revoke his order turning the poor people from
Camp and directing, that all who sought refuge there should be
received and cared for. Since that time none have been turned
out to my knowledge but many who were sent away have
returned. Some alas! have gone where the cruelty to which they
were subjected here and which disgraces manhood, cannot reach
them. One who wandered from place to place until driven by
starvation to her former master, was, if the statement of her
husband is to be believed so cruelly beaten that she *died* in
consequence. Some four hundred are now in Camp and owing to
the fact that their former humble homes were ruthlesly destroyed by
the military authorities they are now sheltered in Barracks built by
the government. In accordance with orders from the Major General
Commanding buildings are in process of erection for them where it
is proposed to care for them in a more systematic manner than can
be done in their present condition. Their present condition
however loudly calls for immediate action on the part of the
Government. Many of them are destitute of shoes and all are
indifferently clad. Sincerely thanking you for your hearty
cooperation and sympathy in my efforts to ameliorate the condition
of these poor people and your politeness in receiving the affidavits
when other officers had refused, I have the honor to remain Very
Respectfully Your Obedient Servant

HLS   T. E. Hall

T. E. Hall to Captain E. B. W. Restieaux, 16 Dec. 1864, enclosed in Capt.
E. B. W. Restieaux to Maj. Genl. M. C. Meigs, 16 Dec. 1864, "Camp
Nelson, Ky.," Consolidated Correspondence File, ser. 225, Central Records,
RG 92 [Y-209]. Enclosures. Hall's report was written at the instance of
Captain Edward B. W. Restieaux, chief quartermaster at Camp Nelson, after
Restieaux was instructed by the Inspection Division of the Quartermaster
General's Office to "inquire into" the expulsion of the wives and children of
black soldiers and to "ascertain whether the officers of the Qr. Mrs. Dept. are
to any degree at fault." The episode had come to the attention of the quartermaster general by way of an item in the *New-York Daily Tribune*, a communication from Camp Nelson dated November 28, 1864, that included the affidavit
of Joseph Miller (taken before Restieaux); from that communication, wrote an

officer in the Inspection Division, "it appears that almost unparalleled atrocities have been committed in that locality – that the helpless women, wives and children of colored troops have been most inhumanly dealt with." (Colonel Geo. V. Rutherford to Capt. E. B. W. Restieaux, 7 Dec. 1864, vol. 81, p. 431, Letters Sent, ser. 9, Central Records, RG 92 [Y-209].) In a covering letter, which forwarded Hall's report and the numerous affidavits cited therein, Restieaux explained that the provost marshal of Camp Nelson had expelled the black women and children under verbal orders from General Speed Smith Fry, commander of the post, and that officers of the quartermaster's department were in no way responsible. To the contrary, it was a quartermaster officer, Captain Theron E. Hall, who "on being apprized of the condition to which the women and children were reduced promptly interposed in their behalf, procured them temporary sustenance, and relief at his own expense, and by the directions of Brvt Major General Burbridge, superintended their return to Camp." Restieaux also reported that he had recently received orders from the Secretary of War to provide shelter and food at Camp Nelson for the wives and children of black soldiers. For a shorter account by Hall of the freedpeople's expulsion and the subsequent establishment of the Colored Refugee Home, see *Freedom*, ser. 2: doc. 312B. For earlier efforts by General Fry to rid Camp Nelson of black women and children, see above, doc. 219.

1 Dickson was an adjutant to General Stephen G. Burbridge, commander of the District of Kentucky.
2 The affidavit, sworn by Private Joseph Miller, is enclosed. Another copy of it is printed as *Freedom*, ser. 2: doc. 107.
3 Stephen G. Burbridge, commander of the District of Kentucky. At the time, he was away from Lexington, the district headquarters, on a military expedition.
4 All the affidavits are enclosed. Those of Private John Higgins, Private John Burnside, and the Reverend John Vetter are printed immediately below, as docs. 225B–D; that of William A. Sears is described in doc. 225Dn. For the affidavits of Private Joseph Miller and the Reverend Abisha Scofield, see *Freedom*, ser. 2: docs. 107, 312A.
5 In the manuscript letter, the text that follows this quoted telegram is run in rather than begun on a new line; the editors have intervened to make it consistent with the writer's own arrangement in similar preceding passages.

225B: Affidavit of a Kentucky Black Soldier

Camp Nelson Ky.   November 28" 1864
Personally appeared before me Edward B. W. Restieaux Captain and Assistant Quartermaster, John Higgins, a man of color who being duly sworn, upon oath says.
I am a soldier in the service of the United States,   I belong to

Company "I" 124" Regt. U.S.C. Infty. When I [*came*] to Camp for the purpose of enlisting, my wife and two children came with me. This was in the latter part of October 1864. My family had been driven out of doors by their master Moses Robbins of Lincoln County Kentucky. I was told by the officer who enlisted me that my family would be provided for in some way within the Camp. In company with another man I built a small hut wher I resided with my family.

We were never notified to move until the evening of Thursday Nov 24" when the provost guard told my wife that she and her children must move out of the Camp on the following morning. On Friday afternoon, Nov 25" 1864, the guard came with a wagon into which they ordered my family. My wife was sick and begged that she might not be driven out into the cold, when the guard told her "that be damned, if you do not get out we will burn the house over your heads" or words to that effect.

Thus threatened, my family went into the wagon and were driven outside the lines.

On sunday, Nov. 27" I went in search of my family, I found them in Nicholasville, about six miles from Camp. They were in an old building through which the rain fell. It had rained hard while they were there. My wife, in consequence, of the exposure was very sick. While my family were in Camp they never eat a mouthfull off the Government. My wife earned money by washing. And further this deponent saith not

his

(Signed) John **X** Higgins

mark

HDcSr

Affidavit of John Higgins, 28 Nov. 1864, enclosed in Capt. E. B. W. Restieaux to Maj. Genl. M. C. Meigs, 16 Dec. 1864, "Camp Nelson, Ky.," Consolidated Correspondence File, ser. 225, Central Records, RG 92 [Y-209].

225C: Affidavit of a Kentucky Black Soldier

Camp Nelson Ky. Dec. [*15,*] 1864.

Personally appeared before me. E. B W. Restieaux Capt and A.Q.M. John Burnside—a man of color who being sworn upon oath says— I am a soldier in Company K. 124 Regt. U.S.C.T. I am a married man. My wife and children belonged to William Royster of Garrard County Ky. Royster had a son John who was with Morgan during his raid into Kentucky in June 1863. He got separated from Morgan's command and went home. The Provost Marshal instituted a search for him at two different times   He was not found. My family were charged with giving the information which led to the measures of the Provost Marshal. William Royster told me that my wife had been trying to ruin him for the last two years and if he found that this—meaning the information went out through the black family—meaning my family—he would scatter them to the four winds of heaven. This was said about the last of September 1864. In consequence of this threat my family were in constant dread, and desired to find protection and employment from the Government. At that time I had been employed at Camp Nelson and was not enlisted. A few days afterward I was sick at my mothers. I sent my sister to see Col. Sedgwick[1] and inquire if my family might come to Camp, and if they might, would they be protected: She returned the same night and informed me that Col. Sedgwick said tell him (me) to bring them in and I, Col Sedgwick, will protect them. Before, I was unwilling that they should come but on receiving the promised protection of Col. Sedgwick. I told them to come. While my wife and family were in Camp they never received any money or provision from the government but earned their living with hard work

On Friday afternoon Nov. 28. [25] 1864 the Provost guard ordered my wife and family out of Camp. The guard had a wagon into which my wife and family were forced to go and were then driven out the lines

They were driven to a wood belonging to Mr. Simpson about seven miles from Camp and there thrown out without any protection or any home. While they were in the wood it rained hard and my family were exposed to the storm. My eldest daughter had been sick for some time and was then slowly recovering. and further this deponent saith not.

HDcSr

John Burnside

Affidavit of John Burnside, 15 Dec. 1864, enclosed in Capt. E. B. W. Restieaux to Maj. Genl. M. C. Meigs, 16 Dec. 1864, "Camp Nelson, Ky.," Consolidated Correspondence File, ser. 225, Central Records, RG 92 [Y-209].

1 Thomas D. Sedgwick, colonel of the 114th USCI, was in charge of the organization of black troops at Camp Nelson.

Kentucky

225D: Affidavit of an Agent of the American Missionary Association

Camp Nelson Ky. Dec. 16. 1864.
Personally appeared before me E. B. W. Restieaux. Capt. and
A.Q.M. John Vetter who being duly sworn upon oath says— I am a
clergy man of the congregational church and have been laboring
among the Freedmen at Camp Nelson Ky. under the auspices of the
American Missionary Association since the 1st day of August
1864. I have heard and read the testimony of Rev. Abisha Schofield
regarding the huts Cabins &c. in which the wives and children of
the colored soldiers lived also, regarding their means of living, and I
fully corroborate said testimony in every particular.[1] I was in Camp
Nelson on the 22 day of last Nov. It was a bitter cold day   the
wind was blowing quite hard, and many of the women and children
were driven from the Camp. I counted six or eight wagon loads of
these women & children being driven away on Thursday or
Friday. When they were expelled their huts were destroyed and in
some instance before the inmates got out, the work of destruction
commenced. On Saturday Nov. 26. I went to Nicholasville to
inquire into the condition of the outcasts. I found that one hundred
or more had taken shelter in the woods having been driven from a
meeting house in which they had taken refuge. I saw some in the
town in a very destitute condition and the Provost Marshal of that
place Capt. Randolph told me that those in the woods were entirely
destitute of shelter or food. I returned to Camp on that night and
stated the facts to Capt. T. E. Hall who on the following morning
supplied Rev. Mr Schofield and myself with rations for distribution
among the sufferers. On reaching Nicholasville on Sunday Nov. 27
I found that those who had gone to the woods had been scattered by
the storm of the previous night and those we found were without
food. I helped to distribute the rations and saw that they were
entirely destitute. some were sick. I learned that several had
died. On Saturday Dec. 3rd I went to Lexington to ascertain the
condition of some of the women and children who having been
driven from this Camp had taken refuge there   I found fourteen in
an old shed doorless & floorless sitting around a stick of burning
wood with no food or bedding. One woman was apparently
overcome by exposure, and another had given birth to a child in
that place. Among those around the fire was a boy evidently near
death whom on the following morning I found dead. I believe he
died through exposure and want. In another old building I found
about half a dozen sick without even the necessaries of life. And
upon evidince which I believe I was assured that one woman had

been so pressed with hunger as to offer her child for sale in the city to obtain bread. I brought a number of the sick with me to Camp in an Ambulance. As a clergyman I believe the tendancy of the measure was very demoralizing and highly prejudicial to the interest of enlistments of colored troops. And further, this deponent saith not.

HDcSr   (Signed) John Vetter

Affidavit of John Vetter, 16 Dec. 1864, enclosed in Capt. E. B. W. Restieaux to Maj. Genl. M. C. Meigs, 16 Dec. 1864, "Camp Nelson, Ky.," Consolidated Correspondence File, ser. 225, Central Records, RG 92 [Y-209]. At the time of the expulsion of black women and children from Camp Nelson, Captain Theron E. Hall, who had been a quartermaster at the post, was still in the area, awaiting orders. In the same file is an affidavit by William A. Sears, a quartermaster's clerk who lived about two miles from the camp. On the afternoon of November 29, 1864, while on his way home, he had encountered a dozen black women and children who had unsuccessfully tried to gain readmission to Camp Nelson. One woman, babe in arms, informed Sears "that they had walked from Nicholasville and on applying for admission they were driven away by the guards who told them that if they did not go away they would be put in the 'Bull Pen', meaning thereby the Camp Prison." "When I left them," Sears concluded, "they were in the condition of poor houseless wanderers." (Affidavit of Wm. A. Sears, 16 Dec. 1864.)

1 For the testimony of the Reverend Abisha Schofield, also an agent of the American Missionary Association, see *Freedom*, ser. 2: doc. 312A.

226: Quartermaster at Camp Nelson, Kentucky, to the Headquarters of the Military District of Kentucky, Enclosing a Diagram of a Proposed Refuge for Black Soldiers' Families

Camp Nelson Ky. December 3^d 1864

Captain   I have the honor to inform you that there are several hundred women and children of colored soldiers, besides others dependent upon said soldiers now in this Camp, whose peculiar position require that some immediate steps be taken for their present and permanent relief— These persons have been compelled to leave their homes on account of the Masters indignation at the enlistment of the able-bodied men. Some have actually been driven away, and all have looked to the government for some protection. This has been usually accorded to them, and the interests of the government, as well as those of the proteges demand, that the protection should be regulated by some system. To this end I would respectfully recommend that a suitable structure with necessary appurtenances be erected in some locality, within the limits of this camp— In this building all such persons might be collected, placed under suitable restraints, and engaged in profitable employment. Here they would be prepared for freedom through a systematized process of educational and industrial discipline. They would be taught to form correct habits, and thoroughly instructed in the principals of pure morality. In the capacity of laundresses, in mending grain sacks, tents, Wagon Covers &c and by hiring out to such as required their services, the inmates would soon render the institution self sustaining, while the impetus it would give to enlistments would more than repay the government for the original outlay, The recruit has no desire to bring miseries upon his family which might be averted by his remaining in slavery, and his services can be of no avail to the government, if by joining the service. he subjects his wife and children to indignity and destitution. Indeed I have the authority of distinguished officers for saying, that in some instances soldiers have actually laid down their arms. when their families were driven from their sight without protection and a home. I need not further dwell upon the feasibility and expediency of the plan which I suggest, nor need I argue its legality. since it has already been in successful. operation at Arlington Heights [*Va.*], Portsmouth [*Va.*], Hilton Head [*S.C.*], and other points, and I am confident its merits will be sufficiently obvious to you to render further recommendation of establishment entirely superfluous. The accompanying plan may serve to convey some idea of the building which is recommended. The site could be selected in proximity to a spring whence the water necessary for the establishment could be collected in a reservoir situated in such a manner that while it could be approached from the open yard, it could also be reached from the laundry and the kitchen.

The proposed purposes of the several buildings are indicated on the plan, and the whole could be enclosed by a fence having but one entrance, The rules necessary for the regulation of the institution could be adopted by the authorities, and the establishment rendered profitable as regards present and prospective purposes. I have the honor to remain Your Obedient Servant

HLS

T. E. Hall

School Room 100 X 30

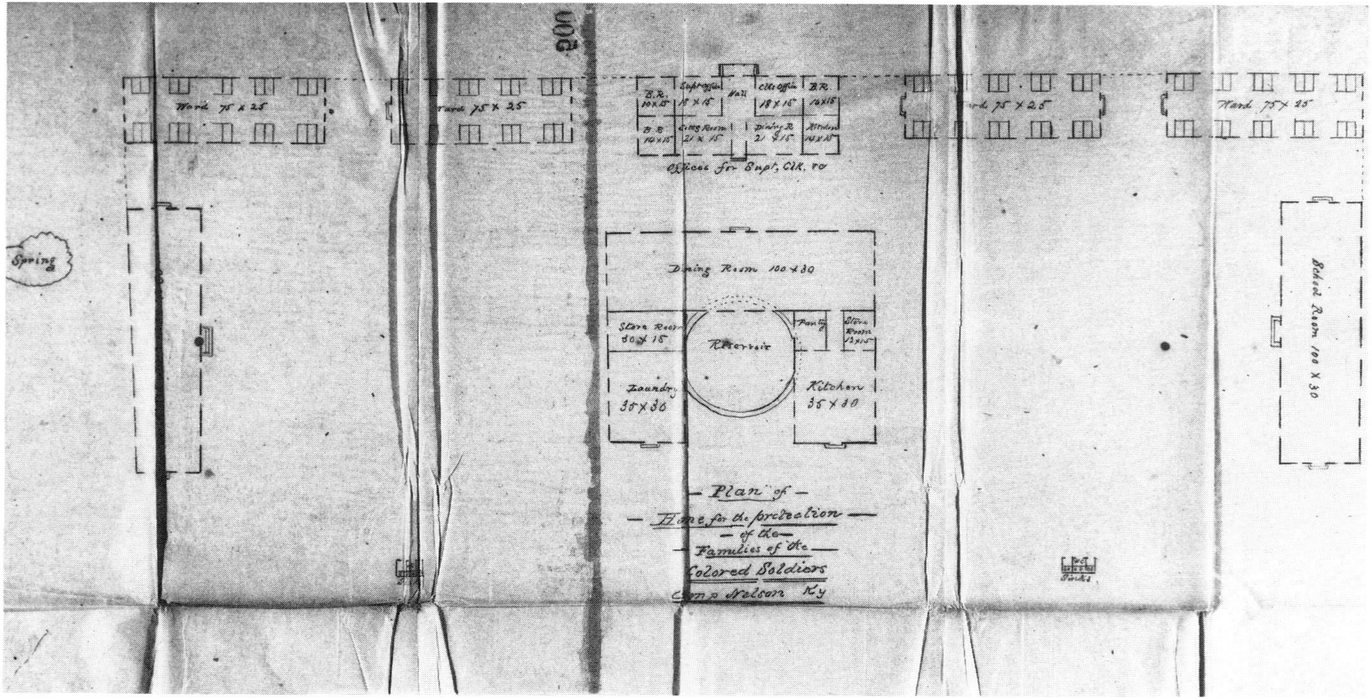

Dining Room 100 x 30

Kitchen 35 x 20

Store Room 100 x 15

Laundry 35 x 36

Officers For Boys, Clk. &c

— Plan of —
— Hare to Architecton —
— of the —
Families of the
Colored Soldiers
Camp Nelson Ky

$500

Spring

Capt. T. E. Hall to A.A. General J. Bates Dickson, 3 Dec. 1864, enclosing "Plan of Home for the protection of the Families of the Colored Soldiers Camp Nelson Ky," Letters Received, ser. 734, Post of Louisville KY, RG 393 Pt. 4 [C-6060]. File notations indicate that Hall's proposal was received not only at the headquarters of the Military District of Kentucky (date not indicated), but also by Adjutant General Lorenzo Thomas (on December 24, 1864). By an endorsement of January 2, 1865, Thomas referred it to General Stephen G. Burbridge, commander of the military district, "for such action as may seem to him advisable in connection with the late order of the Adjutant General in this matter." A telegram of November 29, 1864, from Burbridge to the Secretary of War had elicited the "late order." In the telegram, Burbridge had warned that unless shelter and rations were provided, there would be great suffering among the large number of black women and children who had "accumulated" at Camp Nelson. "For the sake of humanity," he had asked, "I hope you will issue the proper order in this case as soon as possible." By an endorsement of November 30, the assistant secretary of war had instructed the Adjutant General's Office to order the quartermaster general and the commissary general of subsistence "to supply the wants of these persons," and letters so ordering had been written on December 2. (Bv't. Maj. Gen'l S. G. Burbridge to Hon. Edwin M. Stanton, 29 Nov. 1864, with endorsement, W-2033 1864, Letters Received, ser. 12, RG 94 [K-758]; Asst. Adjt. Genl. E. D. Townsend to The Qr. Mr. General, 2 Dec. 1864, and Asst. Adjt. Genl. E. D. Townsend to The Commissary General, 2 Dec. 1864, vol. 38, pp. 325–26, Letters Sent, ser. 1, RG 94 [K-758].) For a description of the Colored Refugee Home subsequently established at Camp Nelson, see below, doc. 230.

227: Kentucky Physician to the President

Danville Ky. *Jany* 10. '65.

Mr President, As president of the United States & Commander in Chief of its armies &C — I appeal to you in behalf of suffering humanity. And I do so the more unreservedly because I have no pecuniary interest in the matter.

At Camp Nelson Ky. the authorities have been receiving & lately housing, clothing, & feeding all the negro women & children who will flock there. Many hundreds, perhaps a thousand are there now. Hundreds crowded together in one room. Some ragged, all dirty, filthy & debauched. Many pregnant since they went there — one half or more labouring under venerial diseases — contracted from the soldiers. Nothing to do, improvident, obscene. This is no exageration — it has to be seen to be appreciated in all its horrors.

And all this too in the name of humanity! It is a shame Sir on this Nation & to all in Authority. There are perhaps fifty or one hundred—who are employed as cooks & washerwomen—who are comparatively decent & comfortable.

Sir, there is no respectable General who would allow white women of such habits to remain in their camps for one day.

Gen Fry, as a man of humanity would long since have checked the evil, but for the interferance of Ajt Gen Thomas, & such like.

By force of necessity the instution of Slavery will soon cease in our State. And so long as the Masters will care for & provide for the women & children in their families—for the sake of the negroes—they should be allowed to do so.

In so far as those who are already in Camp I see no remedy. No decent family would receive them back again, after Sojourning for a time in the Camp. But the evil can be abated by peremtorily forbidding any more entering.

I sir, am no friend of Slavery— I voted for emancipation many years since. I have been a strictly loyal man—& by conversation & votes have sustained the administration. As a free & good Citizen I claim therefore to be *heard & heeded* by you in this matter. Yours &C

Joseph Smith M.D.

If you wish to known anything farther about me I refer you to my kinsman Hon. H. Grider or to Dr. R. J. Breckenridge of this place

ALS   *J.S.*

Joseph Smith M.D. to Mr. President, 10 Jan. 1865, S-187 1865, Letters Received, RG 107 [L-61]. General Speed Smith Fry, a Kentuckian, was the commander at Camp Nelson. Beginning in July, 1864, he had tried to exclude and evict black women and children from the camp, and in late November he had ordered their wholesale expulsion; the resultant suffering had led to orders from the War Department that they be readmitted and provided with shelter and rations. (See above, docs. 219, 225A–D, 226n.) For his part, Adjutant General Lorenzo Thomas, far from encouraging the reception of black women and children at Camp Nelson, had long labored to exclude them. (See above, doc. 219n.) However, in mid-December 1864, in an order ostensibly issued upon his own initiative, but probably resulting from recent changes in War Department policy, Thomas had instructed General Stephen G. Burbridge, commander of the Military District of Kentucky, to appoint "suitable officers" to take charge of the women and children at Camp Nelson, to "cause the erection of suitable buildings" for them, "and otherwise provide for their comfort." (Adjutant General [Lorenzo Thomas], Orders No. 29, 15 Dec. 1864, L. Thomas Letters & Orders, Generals' Papers & Books, ser. 159, RG 94 [V-49].)

Kentucky

228: Testimony in the Court-Martial of a Recruiting Officer

[Louisville, Ky. June 16, 1865]

P. B. McGoodwin, a witness for the prosecution being duly sworn deposed:

ques. State your name residence and occupation

Ans. P. B. McGoodwin Physician Princeton Ky —

ques. Do you recognize the Accused?

Ans. Yes sir, Capt Bunch, I recognize him

ques. State to the court all the circumstances relating to the enlistment of three negro boys that belonged to you, by Capt Bunch

Ans. He enlisted them in the town of Princton but as to the particular day when it was done I do not remember

ques. Well, state about the time?

Ans. It was about the latter part of February I think

ques. What were the names of these men

Ans. Bill, Isham and Frank.

. . . .

ques. Now state the conversation you had with Capt Bunch in full?

Ans. He told me at that interview that he was satisfied that the negros were reluctant to go; that they would go home and were satisfied to stay there, and that, if I would give him a certain compensation that he would release them — The understanding that Capt Bunch proposed himself was that the negros should not only express a willingness to go home, but a desire to be released — I told him I did not want to interfere with his duties as a recruiting officer unless the negros desired positively to be released; and if upon an interview with the negros by him self and I, they persisted in expressing a desire to be released, that I would give him what he required — Well I went home and examined the negroes separate and apart, and two of them expressed themselves as very decidedly wishing to be releived, the other was rather hesitating about it and intimated that he would like to make some arrangement; if he was released; that I was to give him some priveliges and advantages. I told him positively that if he was released he had to return to the old order of things, and that I had no conditions to make with him in any way. and without he felt disposed to do that I would turn over his papers then in my possession to Capt Bunch, and I started to do so. He called me back and told me that he was anxious to remain; that he did not want to go into the army under no considerations. Having settled the matter among them as I thought positively that they were unwilling and reluctant to go, I had an interview with Capt Bunch, paid him the money and started

695

off. The next morning I found the "niggers" in charge of Capt Bunch again. He came to me very politely and in a very gentlemanly manner told me that the niggers had changed their mind again, and had concluded to go, and that he felt as a gentleman he ought to refund the money, but said he had spent it and could not just exactly get hold of it at that time. That was the last of the niggers or money.

Ques. For what amount of money did Capt Bunch agree to release these negroes from the service?

Ans. For $100, which I paid him. He said that amount would about cover the amount he would make in making soldiers of them.

. . . .

ques. Was the $100^{oo} paid to Capt Bunch paid him for the benefit of these negros for their work for the year 1864?

Ans. By no manner of means; no such allusion

ques. Did you not state that to Capt Bunch on that occasion?

Ans. No sir

ques. For tobacco raised in 1864

Ans. No sir

. . . .

Louisville Ky June 20th 1865

. . . .

Lieut J. S. Harkness 2^d Lieut of Company   Acting, 5th U.S.C Cavalry was duly sworn as a witness for defence

ques. State whether or not you were present at Princeton Ky when an interview was held between Dr. McGoodwin and Capt Bunch, the Accused? If so state what occurred about the 1st day of March 1865

Ans. I was in my own office, and Capt Bunch was using my office as a recruiting office— I was present at the time Dr. McGoodwin paid to Capt Bunch some money said to be for tobacco

ques. State how much it was?

Ans. I could not swear— I did not see the amount—

ques. State what was said at that time?

Ans. That is nearly all I know of being said— He paid Capt Bunch the money said to be for tobacco belonging to boys whom Capt Bunch had recruited from said Dr. McGoodwin—

ques. What did you hear McGoodwin say?

Ans. I heard him say—I disremember exactly the words— Something, that this was the money for the tobacco that he had in his possession belonging to the negros

. . . .

Bill McGoodwin a witness for defence being duly sworn deposed:

ques. State your name rank Company and regiment?

696

Ans. William McGoodwin Private Co "C" 124th U.S.C. Inf.
ques. State at what time you were enlisted
Ans. I enlisted on the 28th of February agreeably to my recollection
ques. To whom did you belong before you were enlisted?
Ans. Dr. McGoodwin
ques. State whether or not you had any tobacco on the plantation of McGoodwin when you left him?
Ans. Well—yes sir I suppose I had some from the proposition he had made to me which was year before last: that he would give us the 1/5th of all we three men made when the tobacco was stripped cleaned and sold— I do not know what it amounted to but he paid us 65$ last year and promised us the same this last year and after we had enlisted we went to him for our pay, told him we had enlisted and were compelled to go away in a short time and wanted him to pay us for our tobacco— He said we had not made as much as we did the year before—It was because of the drouth. and he said he did not feel disposed to divide it but if we were a mind to strip it out he would pay for it.
ques. Were you ever paid your portion?
Ans. After we left Princeton and got to Louisville Capt Bunch paid me some $38 or $39 I do not remember the amount— I was staying Harmon house here— The boys reported that he paid the same amount to them

. . . .

—By the Court—
ques. When Capt Bunch paid you this money, did he tell you or not that this was the money he got from McGoodwin as for your share of the tobacco
Ans. He handed me the money on the street me and another man were standing together and told me says he "here William is this much of your money which I got out of the old Doctor for your tobacco

. . . .

HD

Excerpts from testimony of P. B. McGoodwin, 16 June 1865, Lt. J. S. Harkness, 20 June 1865, and William McGoodwin, 20 June 1865, proceedings of general court-martial in the case of Capt. Thomas H. Bunch, 5th USCC, MM-2547, Court-Martial Case Files, ser. 15, RG 153 [H-13]. Captain Thomas H. Bunch, an officer in the 5th U.S. Colored Cavalry, had been charged with "conduct unbecoming an officer and a gentleman." He was found not guilty of the charge and all its specifications, including the allegation that he had accepted $100 from P. B. McGoodwin in return for a promise to release the latter's slaves from their military enlistment. Enlistment papers filed as "Exhibit A" indicate that Bunch had enlisted "William McGooden" on February 20, 1865, but had temporarily left him in the custody of his master because he was ill.

229: Affidavit of a Kentucky Freedwoman

Camp Nelson Ky   March 26 [24] 1865

Personally appeared before me J M Kelley Notary Public in and for the County of Jessamine state of Ky Martha Cooley a woman of color who being duly sworn according to law doth depose and say.

I am a widow woman, my husband Simon Cooley was a Soldier in the 5th U.S.C. Cavalry and was killed at the Salt Works during Genl Burbridge's last raid. My master's name is John Nave and lives in Garrard County Ky. I have four children who belong to said Nave. About three weeks ago I told my master that I wanted to go to Camp Nelson. He said. "I will give you Camp" and immediately took a large hickory stick with which he commenced beating me. He gave me more than thirty blows striking me on my head and shoulders and breaking one of the bones of my left arm. I have not the right use of it now. I told him I wanted my children, He said I could neither have my children nor my clothes, My master beat me for this request. I watched my chance and ran away. I had to leave my children with my master. I have been in Camp about two weeks and am very anxious to get my children, and further deponent saith not

HDcSr   Signed   Martha Cooley

Affidavit of Martha Cooley, 26 [24] Mar. 1865, filed with H-8 1865, Registered Letters Received, ser. 3379, TN Asst. Comr., RG 105 [A-6148]. A notation at the bottom indicates that Cooley's affidavit was sworn on March 24; the accuracy of that date rather than the one that heads the affidavit is corroborated by an affidavit jointly sworn on March 24 by a Northern minister and by the superintendent of the Colored Refugee Home at Camp Nelson, in which they attested to their examination of Cooley's arm, which they found to have been broken. "The muscle of the arm," they added, "is much bruised displaying every evidence of recent and severe injury from the consequence of which the arm is at present powerless." (Affidavit of John G. Fee and T. E. Hall, 24 Mar. 1865, in the same file.)

Kentucky

230: War Department Inspector to the Inspector General

Washington, D.C. May 13. 1865.
I have the honor to submit the following report of an Inspection
made pursuant to Special Orders, No 173, War Department,
Adjutant General's Office April 17th 1865
1 *Camp Nelson, Kentucky,*
This camp is located on the Kentucky River, 6 miles from
Nicholasville, the terminous of the Ky. Central R.R. 100 miles
Northwest from Cumberland Gap, and 112 from Cincinnati. As a
defensible position it has probably no equal in the state, surrounded
as it is upon two sides (South and West) by the Ky: River whose
banks are high and precipitous and inaccessible by Artillery; and
upon the East bounded by Hickman Creek, a tributary of the last
named river, with almost equally formidable natural defences upon
the Western bank.

. . . .

The troops at this Camp consist of one Company, 2nd Battalion
V.R.C. (on duty at Gen. Hosp.) Detachment of 123rd & 124th U.S.
Col'd Inf., Battery "E" 1st Ky. Lt. Artillery, and a number of recruits
now being organized into the 119th US.C.I., in all, 894 officers and
men present. Of this number, but 180 are armed. The 124th
US.C.I. is an "Invalid Regiment," enlisted for duty in the Q.M. &
Engineer Depts. They present a very creditable appearance— The
expediency of enlisting men for this kind of service, without arms
has been, it is presumed, fully discussed and favorably determined &
is not now open to suggestions. About 300 of this Regiment are
detailed as teamsters and employees of the Q.M. Dept.

. . . .

Under authority from *Maj. Gen. Palmer*, a Camp has been
established for Contraband women and children, the families of
soldiers enlisting in the Army— About 1,700, of these people are
now provided for—furnished with quarters, rations and fuel. They
are coming into Camp very rapidly. 907 were received during the
month of April, and the Q.M.D. is taxed to the utmost to erect
barracks with sufficient despatch to provide for them. *Mr T. E.
Hall*, formerly A.Q.M. at this post, is the Superintendent, He was
absent at the time of my visit—is represented as an energetic &
efficient man; when A.Q.M. he was deemed an honest and
active Officer, but somewhat extravagant & injudicious in his
expenditures. The buildings erected, consist of the superintendent's
house (75 × 30 feet, and two stories in height) rather a munificent
provision for this officer and his assistants)—a Dining room and
Kitchen, (100 × 30 feet with two wings each 50 × 30 feet)—a

work Shop of about the same dimensions and of two stories which is now occupied by women and children as barracks—four buildings also used as barracks—25 × 75 each, and containing 120 refugees. and (30) thirty "Cottages" 32 × 16 feet, divided into two compartments and intended to contain 20 or 30 inmates— As many more are in process of erection. The cost of these "Cottages" is $400. each— I could get no accurate estimate of the cost of the larger buildings— The lumber is sawed almost entirely by the Machinery in charge of the Post Qr Master and the doors shingles &c. are made here. The cottages are to be paid for (theoretically) by the soldiers whose families occupy them, at the rate of $25 each, as a gross rental during the whole time occupied, but no contracts are made, and there is no practical system established for carrying out this design. 200 acres of arable land have been plowed and are to be devoted to gardening and raising broom corn this summer—from which brooms will be manufactured by the women during the Winter. This experiment is just being initiated and no data as to its economy or practical workings can be furnished.

The establishment is in excellent condition, the barracks clean, the general health of the people good, and the drainage and police of the grounds fair. This bids fair to become a large and expensive experiment, and without careful supervision by the Department Commander, extravagant outlays are to be apprehended— There are a number of buildings now unused, or not needed in Camp Nelson, the material of which is good and perfectly available for the erection of barracks for these people. I would suggest that the erection of New buildings be suspended until at least, this surplus material is used.

A "soldier's home" is among the needless appurtenances of Camp Nelson— The buildings belong to the Government and should be at once used for contrabands— The "Convalescent Camp" (of which I shall have occasion to speak further) has in use (8) eight buildings which are not needed. The reduction which it is presumed will soon take place in the business of the Q.M. Dept. will vacate many more, and I believe it will not be necessary to erect any more barracks from *new* materials for the purposes of this Refugee Home. The laws of Kentucky provide, I think, that the master shall care for the aged, infirm and helpless among his servants. It is not clear that the emancipation of slaves relieves him from this duty. Even if it does have this effect, he is still legally responsible for the care of women and children *not* freed by the enlistment of the head of the family, and many of those at Camp Nelson are of this class, and have been driven from home, oftentimes with the most malicious cruelty, because no longer useful. In view of the burdens of the General Government present and prospective, and the requirements of simple justice, the Masters of Kentucky should be compelled to provide for these people, or if cared for by the Government, the expenses should be assessed upon the owner. The charitable societies of the North have supplied a great deal of clothing for these people. What is most needed is some systematic and organized effort throughout the North West whose object shall be to secure for these people *labor* and *wages* and thus relieve the Government as soon as may be of their support, and at the same time constitute the most practical and needed charity to the refugees themselves.

The Nelson U.S. General Hospital under charge of Surgeon *H. L. W. Burritt*, U.S. Vols. is a well conducted and highly creditable establishment. Seven Acting Assistant Surgeons are Employed.

No. of Wards,	10.
No. of Beds.	700.
No of Sick.	517.
No of Attendants	50.

Since January 1st 1865. 1590 cases have been treated, of whom, 229 have died. This large proportion of deaths is owing in great measure to the large number of Colored inmates, among whom diseases are said to be more generally fatal, and to the lack of regimental Surgeons with the Colored Regiments to treat and arrest disease in its early stages. Many are past recovery before being sent to Genl. Hospitals.

. . . .

The Qr. Master's Department is in charge of Capt. *E. B. W. Restieaux*, who appears to be an accurate business man—active and competent.

Learning that Colonel J. D. *Bingham*, Inspector Q.M. Dept., had completed, a few days previous to my visit, a minute Inspection of Capt. *Restieaux's* accounts and vouchers, I deemed it unnecessary to examine them critically. To give a general idea of the extent of the business of this depot a list of public buildings and machinery is appended, to-gether with a list of employees. Of the latter, 1218 appear upon the rolls, and this number does not include nearly 300 enlisted men detailed as teamsters, woodchoppers &c from the 124th U.S.C. Inf. So long as the present amount of transportation and machinery is maintained at this depot, this formidable roll of employees may be necessary— a recruiting depot for worn out horses is a part of the establishment, requiring a large number of men— 437 are teamsters, and a large proportion of the remainder— are employed in repairing wagons and harness, and in the Steam Saw Mill and Machine Shops which have been established.

The present wants of the service it is presumed will not require the maintenance of so extensive a depot, and its immediate reduction is advisable. The recent orders from the Q.M.G.O. will lead to such a result. A charge was preferred by Lieut. *Charles Harkins*, 124 U.S.C.I. that a number of the detailed men from his reg't in the Q.M. Dept. performed no duty except menial service for clerks employed by Capt. R. He failed however to point out the men or to produce any evidence of the fact. The charge is denied by Capt. R. and it was not practicable to muster the men, many being absent in charge of supplies sent to Cumberland Gap, woodchopping etc. This is however an abuse likely to occur where so many unarmed colored soldiers are detailed, where no reports are made of the duty performed, and there is no accountability for a proper use of enlisted labor. I suggest that the attention of the Major General Commanding the Department be called to this subject.

. . . .

HLS   Murray Davis

Excerpts from Major Murray Davis to Bvt. Brig. Gen. Jas. A. Hardie, 13 May 1865, D-17 1865, Letters Received, ser. 15, RG 159 [J-26]. Enclosures, endorsements. Omitted portions described the defenses of Camp Nelson and operations of the quartermaster, provost marshal, and subsistence departments at the post. Topical labels in the margin are omitted. Davis had inspected Camp Nelson on April 26, 1865. General John M. Palmer, under whose authority the Colored Refugee Home was said to have been established, commanded the Department of Kentucky. In fact, establishment of the home antedated Palmer's arrival in the state. (On the origins of the home, see above, docs. 225A, 226n.) Once in command, however, Palmer not only approved its continuance, but also authorized subordinates to forward to Camp Nelson any slaves and former slaves who were turned out or abused by their owners and former owners. (See below, doc. 234.)

231: Order by the Commander of the Department of Kentucky

Louisville, Ky., June 18th *1865.*

GENERAL ORDERS, No. 43.

Application having been made at these Headquarters by the owners of slaves, that the freedom of their slaves be granted by military authority, to the end that the labor of such liberated slaves may be made available at home as hired laborers, their persons protected, and the wages agreed to be given be assured to them, it is hereby announced that, in all cases where the owners of slaves shall declare in writing to their slaves that they will in all things

702

regard them as hired servants, and in and by said writing agree to pay them wages for their labor, the arrangement will be protected in all its parts by military authority, provided said declaration in writing is made by the master before some military officer commanding a post or special detachment, or before some Provost Marshal, and assented to by said slave. The officer before whom such declaration is made, will furnish a copy thereof to the said owner, and any slave or party thereto.

Parents may accept similar declaration for their minor children.

The military authorities will regard the parties to such agreements as if free, and will enforce the payments of wages.

Colored persons are advised to enter into the agreements contemplated in this order whenever they can do so with just and humane masters. BY COMMAND OF MAJOR GENERAL J. M. PALMER:

PD

General Orders, No. 43, Head Quarters, Department of Kentucky, 18 June 1865, Orders & Circulars, ser. 44, RG 94 [DD-24].

232: Superintendent of the Organization of Kentucky Black Troops to the Commander of the Camp of Rendezvous at Bowling Green, Kentucky

[Lexington, Ky.] June 20th [*1865*]

Information having been received at this office to the effect, that a large number of negro men, women and children have congregated around your camp and that they are leading an idle and immoral life, your serious attention is directed to this matter.

A proper regard for the morals of your command and the health and convenience of the community around you renders it necessary that the black people who have gathered about your camp should be dispersed.

1. So far as you can induce the white people to hire them on written contracts made with the parties, a copy of which you will file in your office. –

2. Encourage the negroes to hire out even at low wages, to parties who will recognize them as free agents, entitled to pay for labor rendered.

3. As many of them as cannot be hired out and who desire to go North, furnish with transportation.

4. Every black person sent North should be furnished with a military pass in addition to transportation.

In dealing with this matter General Palmers Orders N° 32, dated Head Quarters, Dept. Ky. Louisville Ky. May 11th 1865 may be taken as a rule of your conduct.[1] Very Respectfully Your Obdt. Servt.

HLpS

Ja^s S. Brisbin

Brig. Genl. Jas. S. Brisbin to Commandg. Officer, Camp of Rendezvous, 20 June [1865], vol. 57 DKy, pp. 302–3, Press Copies of Letters Sent, ser. 2247, Organization of U.S. Colored Troops, Dept. of KY, RG 393 Pt. 1 [C-4342].

1 General Order 32, issued on May 11, 1865, by General John M. Palmer, commander of the Department of Kentucky, authorized the provost marshal of the post of Louisville to issue to "any colored person who may report him or herself as unable to find sufficient employment in the city of Louisville" a pass permitting both the applicant and his or her family to travel to any other point "to engage in or in search of employment." (*Freedom*, ser. 1, vol. 1: doc. 240.) Under the guise of solving an unemployment problem, the order overrode state laws impeding the free movement of black people; the thousands of passes issued under its provisions to people who were legally still slaves became, in effect, free papers. Palmer's order also required railroads, steamboats, ferryboats, and other public conveyances to honor the military passes, overriding state laws that made it a crime to transport slaves without the permission of their owners. On July 10, 1865, in General Order 49, Palmer extended the pass system to the entire state, especially urging "colored persons congregated about posts" to obtain passes to travel freely in search of employment. (*Freedom*, ser. 1, vol. 1: pp. 516–17.)

233: Three Officers at Bowling Green, Kentucky, to the Headquarters of the Post of Bowling Green

Bowling Green Ky, July 3, 1865

Lieutenant   In compliance with Special Orders N° 102, Paragraph II. from Hd. Qrs. Post Commandant Bowling Green Ky, we have the honor to report as follows concerning the number of wives and children of colored Soldiers of the U.S. Army;–the number of colored persons not, wives or children of U.S. soldiers; together with the means of subsistence and the sanitary condition of both classes.

We found forty four (44) women and eighty seven (87) children who claim to be Soldier's families, part of whom are doing well; living in comfortable houses for which they pay rent, The larger portion however are in destitute condition, having no means of subsistence except the small ration allowed them by Government, living in the building known as "the old school house", or in sheds, or deserted out buildings within the corporation limits, without beds or bedding, or any utensils for cooking.

We also found twenty (20) women and thirty (30) children, not families of U.S. Soldiers, who have left their masters and are living here in most destitute, and miserable condition. Many of this class are sick at this time, and a great many have already died.

We have been informed that a number of Soldiers wives are living in private families in the city, where they receive wages and are properly treated. We did not attempt to ascertain the number of this class, as the order evidently, did not refer to them.

By reference to the books of the Provost Marshal, we find that in the month of June eighty seven (87) families of colored Soldiers were supplied with rations,

L B Power
Paul R. Baldy
HLS   E. C. Stevens

Surgeon L. B. Power et al. to Lieut. D. S. Bosworth, 3 July 1865, Letters Received & Retained Reports, ser. 145, Post of Bowling Green KY, RG 393 Pt. 4 [C-7351]. Power was surgeon of the 12th USCHA and of the 1st brigade in the 2nd division of the Department of Kentucky; Baldy and Stevens, both lieutenants, were quartermaster and provost marshal, respectively, of the brigade.

234: Tennessee and Kentucky Freedmen's Bureau Assistant Commissioner to the Freedmen's Bureau Commissioner

Nashville, Tenn., July 20" 1865.

General   I have the honor to acknowledge receipt of your communication of the 14th inst and to State that I have just returned from a personal inspection of the "Colored Refugee Home" at Camp Nelson Ky.

Of Camp Nelson it may be truthfully and emphatically said *"Magna res est"* – [1] The Government's money has been most lavishly expended in the erection of buildings – construction of water works roads &c – &c – It does seem to me that hundreds of thousands of dollars might have been *saved*. and then furnished us with more and better accommodations for the Home than we now have.

I found the Home full – to overflowing – of colored women and children. and the numbers increasing daily – There has *not* been proper effort to find homes and employment for these refugees. The Supt— teachers & others have I conclude rather been inclined to keep up a *big* establishment— I at once inaugurated radical changes in the conduct of the entire institution and shall diligently labor to keep the family small. although it *will be* quite large in spite of all we can do to keep the number reduced—

Kentucky is just now stirred to its bitter depths on the slavery question— a hotly contested political canvass is agitating the entire state The only issue before the people is the ratification of the constitutional amendment forever prohibiting slavery in this Country.[2] The devotees of the barbarism cling to its putrid carcass with astonishing tenacity— Kentucky I fear will refuse to become one of the twenty seven (27) pall bearers required to bear the remains of the great abomination to its final resting place[3] Maj Genl Palmer Comdg the Dept of Kentucky has by General Order stricken the shackles from all slaves who will leave the State—[4] His Post Commandants throughout the State are granting a pass to each colored person making application   Rail Roads, Steamboats and Ferryboats are required to transport all who present the Military pass—and pay their fare. This order was issued on the 10th ins[t] and the result has been that thousands have crossed the Ohio and are now crowding the towns and cities of the States lying opposite. I am daily looking for a breeze from Indianapolis or other Northern City that may lift up its voice against the continuance of the *black vomit*— The Emancipation and deportation by Genl order and the agitation caused by the political canvass has aroused every colored individual in Kentucky to the importance of *striking for freedom*, and *now*— The consequence is that the negro population men women and Children. are generally on the move for some place beyond the reach of master. In many localities the most cruel & fiendish atrocities are being visited upon the Slaves by their maddened and despairing masters— especially is this true. as relates to the wives and children of the Colored men who have enlisted in our army from Kentucky and the latter class push for military posts— Genl Palmer has directed his Post Commandants to forward all such to Camp Nelson— "Receive all that come" is the General's order— Five hundred (500) of this class were sent to Camp Nelson during last week alone. – I give you these facts that you that you may fully understand the difficulties in the way of an early breaking up of the Refugee Home at Camp Nelson—

I have relieved Capt T. E. Hall from the Superintendency of the Home— I thought it best— He is not the man for the place— He is a good friend to the colored man: of this there is no doubt—but he loves Captain Hall also— I have not as yet appointed a permanent successor from the fact that I can not easily find the proper man— My chief difficulty throughout the District is the scarcity of the right kind of officers & men for duty in this Bureau— I have ordered that homes and employment be found for every man woman and youth who has ability to labor   It is almost impossible to procure employment for a woman who has five or more Children depending immediately upon her for care.   I have therefore directed that the surplus children—she can take one or two—be for the present retained in the cottages at the Home—in charge of the aged and infirm women—and be Kept in the schools—   The farm and gardens attached to the Home can be worked by the larger boys—   I assure you that every thing. that can be done.—consistent with our duty to the freedmen—shall *be done* to reduce the numbers at Camp Nelson but the Home there or elsewhere in Kentucky will be a *necessity* for some time to come—

Very many of the good union anti-slavery men of Kentucky have become prejudiced against the institution—because of a want of confidence in Capt Hall—   His removal will stop much of the just Clamor that has been raised against the Home—

The schools at Camp Nelson are in excellent hands—   I made many changes during my stay there. and trust my visit will result in good

I am pushing my District to organization as rapidly as possible—   I find much to do—but am daily overcoming difficulties. and bringing the people to a better understanding of their duties—   Very Respectfully Your Ob^r Servt

ALS   Clinton B. Fisk

Brig. Genl. Clinton B. Fisk to Maj. Genl. Howard, 20 July 1865, F-94 1/2 1865, Letters Received, ser. 15, Washington Hdqrs., RG 105 [A-6005]. The letter of July 14 from General Oliver O. Howard, commissioner of the Freedmen's Bureau, had informed Fisk that Howard was receiving many letters about Camp Nelson. "Can you not institute some method of gradually breaking up that camp[?]" Howard had asked. "It is hardly good to have a permanent institution of that kind. By careful distribution I think the people might be cared for & protected." (Maj. Gen. O. O. Howard to Brig. Gen. C. B. Fisk, 14 July 1865, H-50 1865, Registered Letters Received, ser. 3379, TN Asst. Comr., RG 105 [A-6005].)

1 Loosely translated as "A huge enterprise it is."
2 On August 7, 1865, the voters of Kentucky would elect U.S. representatives, a new state legislature, and other state officers. The chief issue of the campaign was whether Kentucky should ratify the constitutional amendment abolishing slavery that Congress had proposed in January 1865 and submitted to the states. It had been rejected in February by the previous state legislature.
3 A reference to the proposed constitutional amendment, whose ratification by

twenty-seven states was required before it would become part of the U.S. Constitution.

4 General Order 49, issued by General John M. Palmer on July 10, 1865, had extended to the entire state of Kentucky a pass system earlier instituted solely in Louisville. (See above, doc. 232n.) Under Palmer's order, provost marshals were issuing passes to slaves to cross the Ohio River into the Northern states.

235: Kentucky Slaveholder to the Commander of the Military Division of the Tennessee

Lexington Ky   July 26 /65

Dear Sir   The provost Marsal at this place Is giving the servants of Loyal Men. Passes to leave the state. Contrary to the wishes of their Masters and it is producing a bad state of things here   farmers cannot obtain help to save their Crop.   Will you be so Kind as to investigate the Matter And Inform me by whose authority the Marshals are acting   two of my servants got Passes on Saturday. and if the servants had come to me I would gladly give them passes to go out of the state.   I address you at the instigation of several Loyal Citizens   Very Respectfully Your most Obj't Servant,

John M Lee

ALS   (Formerly your Baker at Camp Dick Robinson Ky)

John M. Lee to Major Genl. G. H. Thomas, 26 July 1865, Letters Received, ser. 2173, Dept. of KY, RG 393 Pt. 1 [C-4330]. Mistakenly filed under the name "Gee." An adjutant to the commander of the Military Division of the Tennessee referred Lee's letter to the commander of the Department of Kentucky without comment. For the orders under which the provost marshal at Lexington, Kentucky, was issuing passes to slaves, see above, doc. 232n.

236: Provost Marshal of the 4th District of Kentucky to the Headquarters of the Department of Kentucky, and Assistant Provost Marshal General for Kentucky to the Provost Marshal of the 4th District

Lebanon [Ky.]   August 10" 1865

Captain: A large number of negroes from Central Kentucky have gone to Camp Nelson and procured the passes issued there under Gen Ords. No 32 & 49 C.S Dep' Ky.[1] for the purpose of going to Cincinnati. With these passes they have returned to their homes. While many of them Labor, a large number do nothing   The consequence is a considerable disturbance has been kept up by their former owners.   I desire to know whether these passes are to protect the holder from legal seizure by the (former) master?

My office is crowded daily by slave desiring passes to remain at their immediate homes [and labor for themselves.   Under instructions I have]² thought it best not to issue passes to Such persons.   Hence many of them have been reclaimed by their masters —   You will at once see that to decide that the passes issued at Camp Nelson to men who simply send or go after them protect the holders authorizes me to issue passes to all applicants provided they *ask* to be permitted to go to points outside of the state.

While I shall have no hesitancy in issuing passes required, for I thoroughly detest slavery, I desire to have instructions so explicit that I may not do wrong. —   I may say that from my reading of the Gen orders referred to I cannot see that I am authorized to issue passes to those who have simply left home for freedom.

ALpS   Jams. M Fidler

Louisville Ky. August 22 1865.

Captain; Your letter asking about the effect of the papers given at Camp Nelson, or elsewhere, to slaves to seek work at specified points, and their returning to Lebanon &c. and claiming that it exempted them from further obligation to serve their masters, was referred to *General Palmer* but has not been returned yet, he having been absent from Louisville until now.

I talked with him this morning; He says the main purpose was to compel public carriers to take them as passengers in the prescribed direction when they tendered their fare.   Those papers made for Cincinnati and exhibited at Lebanon are *null*, and all of that nature, and does not interfere with the relation between master and slave.   I am Respectfully Yours

HLcS   W H Sidell

Capt. Jams M. Fidler to Capt. E. B. Harlan, 10 Aug. 1865, vol. 6, pp. 175– 76, Press Copies of Letters Sent, ser. 4057, KY 4th Dist., RG 110 [R-40]; Bvt. Col. W. H. Sidell to Capt. James M. Fidler, 22 Aug. 1865, vol. 4, p. 515, Letters Sent, ser. 3962, KY Actg. Asst. Pro. Mar. Gen., RG 110 [R-40]. Although addressed to the headquarters of the Department of Kentucky, Fidler's letter was transmitted through Sidell's office, which forwarded it to General John M. Palmer, commander of the Department of Kentucky, on August 11, 1865. Palmer returned the letter to Fidler on August 22 with the following endorsement, which was far less conclusive than Sidell's rendering of the general's views: "Genl. Orders 32 and 49 enclosed are simply to be construed and complied with." (Endorsement by Maj. Genl. J. M. Palmer, 22 Aug. 1865, on F-77 1865, Register of Letters Received & Endorsements Sent, ser. 4060, KY 4th Dist., RG 110 [R-40].)

1 For a description of General Orders 32 and 49, see above, doc. 232n.
2 The bracketed passage was incompletely impressed on the press copy; it has been supplied from a paraphrase of the letter in a register of letters received. (Summary of letter from Capt. James M. Fidler, 10 Aug. 1865, F-191, vol. 3, Registers of Letters Received, ser. 3966, KY Actg. Asst. Pro. Mar. Gen., RG 110 [R-40].)

237: Affidavit of a Kentucky Freedwoman

Louisville Ky April 12th 1867

Fanny Nelson colored being sworn says that she was married to Moses Nelson a colored man near twenty years since

That they lived together as man and wife until June 1866 when he started to New Orleans as a deck hand on the steamer Louisiana, since which time he has not been heard from and she supposes he is dead

That she was the slave of George W Elder of this City up to the time that she was said to be free and had been so for about five years

That her husband was among the first of the colored men who enlisted in the army

That it was several months after her husband enlisted before she ascertained the fact that by orders of General Palmer she was free, she being the wife of a soldier[1]

That after she heard the report as above she told a Grand child of M[r] Elder that she would have to be paid wages now, as she was free by Gen[l] Palmers order. M[rs] Elder said upon this, that it was time enough to talk about this when Abe Lincoln said so.

That she continued to live at the house of M[r] Elder until M[rs] Elder commenced locking her up of nights to keep her from leaving. She ran from the house the first good chance she got

That when she did leave (it was in the early part of the night) it was impossible to take her clothes with her except a very few.

That she left a large lot of clothing & bedding and other articles, some of which she had bought herself, some were given her by her husband but the larger portion was given her by her former mistress and owner M[rs] D. P. Faulds of this city.

The following is a list of what she left with value attached

One feather bed	value	$ 20.00
one bedstead	"	10.00
4 sheets		6.00
5 white Blankets		6.00
1 comfort		2.00
4 feather pillows		6.00
1 large blue counterpaine		6.00
2 pair canton flannel drawers		2.50
2 flannel skirts		6.00
1 new quilt		6.00
14 or 15 calico, gingham, and Lawn dresses		45.00
2 shawls		24 00
8 white cotton skirts		16.00
8 new chemise		16.00
8 pillow cases		6.00
3 quilted skirts		9.00
4 pair woollen stockings		2 00
3 pair cotton stockings		1.50
		$190.00
Amt Brot over		$190.00
1 pair shoes		3.00
4 aprons		1.50
4 madrass Hkfs. (imitation)		3.00
2 parasols		8.00
1 Bureau		12.00
6 chairs		6.00
1 Rocking chair		2.50
5 smoothing irons		2.50
1 Ironing board		2.00
		$230.50

That it was several months after she left Mr Elder's house that she learned Mrs Elder had ascertained where she was and Mrs Elder came to the house where she was and took from her 1 comfort $3 – and two calico dresses $2.00 – value

That the last transaction happened only a few days before she was told that the colored people were freed.

That during the first part of the year 1866 her husband made application to this Bureau then having an office on Main street to have Mr Elder summoned before it to shew cause why he should not deliver to her her goods named above and in obedience to said summons Mrs Elder made her appearance and promised the attendance of her husband when he got home (Mr Elder is a steam Boat Pilot and is much from home) but said promise so far as she knows has not been fulfilled; and that this circumstance and the

absence of her husband she presumes is the cause why the case has
not been fully investigated

That she has waited until now for the return of her husband and
failing to hear from him and beleiving him dead she now comes in
her own person and asks to have the matters set forth fully
investigated and such releif meted out to her as Justice and right
may seem to demand

her

Fany X Nelson

mark

Fanny Nelson lives on ally bet 6 & 7 and Broadway & chestnut
George W Elder lives sou. side Green bet 14 & 15th streets

HDSr

Affidavit of Fany Nelson, 12 Apr. 1867, Affidavits & Records Relating to
Complaints, ser. 1218, Louisville KY Supt., RG 105 [A-4548]. Sworn before
the assistant Freedmen's Bureau superintendent of the Louisville subdistrict.
In the same file is an affidavit by George W. Elder, who had purchased Fanny
Nelson in 1860, when she was about forty-five years old. Insisting that Nelson
had possessed only "a small bundle" of clothing when he bought her, Elder
denied that she had owned the property listed in her affidavit and maintained
that when she left his house, she had taken with her all the clothing and
bedding that his family had given her. He also asserted that Nelson had never
to his knowledge claimed any man as her husband, nor had any man been seen
at the house claiming to be her husband. (Affidavit of G. W. Elder, 13 May
1867.) Elder dated Nelson's departure from his household as August 6, 1864,
but the year may be erroneous; General John M. Palmer issued his order
regarding the freedom of black soldiers' families in March 1865, and Nelson
described her escape as having followed that event. A record of court proceedings conducted by the bureau superintendent includes entries regarding the
case, but no indication of its outcome. (Vol. 153, pp. 37–38, 49–50, Proceedings of Freedmen's Court, ser. 1217, Louisville KY Supt., RG 105 [A-4548].)

1 General Order 10, issued on March 12, 1865, by General John M. Palmer,
commander of the Department of Kentucky, had announced "to the colored
men of Kentucky that by an act of Congress passed on the 3d day of March,
1865, the wives and children of all colored men who have heretofore enlisted,
or who may hereafter enlist, in the military service of the Government, are
made free." (*Freedom*, ser. 2: doc. 110.)

238: Former Superintendent of Black Enlistment at Camp Nelson, Kentucky, to the Freedmen's Bureau Commissioner

Nicholasville Ky. Sept 11th 1865

General: — I doubtless should ask pardon for offering suggestions upon the state of affairs which shall Constitute the subject of this letter viz: — the Condition of the Black Race and the prospects before them and us in Ky. Having been born and raised in Ky. having acted as Marshal for the County of Jessamine during the Rebellion — and as Superintendent of Colored Enlistment at Camp Nelson during the whole time that Colored men were enlisted there (some 9,000 or 10,000) much of their actual condition is thrown under my observation — They Come to me from far and near with their wants and their troubles.

Allow me then to state to you a plain unvarnished tale, from which flow some simple, but potent, and to us here in Ky. I think, some fearful deductions.

Near, perhaps quite, one half of the former Slaves in Ky. have left their homes and are wandering about the Country. Not a few of these have been driven off by their masters — A still larger number have left their masters and resolutely refuse ever to return — These two Classes Comprehend perhaps one half of the slaves in Kentucky. In the one case and in the other the owner forbids any one to hire the negro thus at large — tho' they are by no means able to keep them at work for them —

The one refusing to let them remain — the other utterly unable to keep them with him. This is the actual state of things here.

Now for the workings of this state of affairs which are already fearfully manifesting themselves.

The master, as before stated, forbids any one to hire his fugitive slave — threatning instant prosecution under State Statute upon that subject. — And not only threatens, but actually does prosecute and have fined those who hire them — This I have seen more than once within the last ten days.

The negro, as a general thing, is not only willing but anxious to obtain work provided he can receive the compensation for his labor. But he absolutely refuses to labor and allow his would-be master receive the proceeds — This I state of the above named classes of Colored persons —

The inevitable result of this is, that they pillage the Country for something to eat and live upon. Roberies are frequent and Continually increasing. If this is seen in the green tree, what will it be in the dry? If this is so apparent now when the earth is loaded with her spontaneous fruits; what will it be when winter shall find them unprovided with the necessaries of life? Starvation on the one hand, and robery and murder on the other—

It may be said that Kentucky deserves her fate in this respect, for not freeing herself at once from this horrible Curse, and thus meeting and averting this terrible Calamity.

Perhaps she does. May God then avert from her this portion of her just deserts! She certainly has acted with infinite folly in rejecting the Amendment.[1] But yet it must not be forgotten that *forty thousand* of her sons, showed by their ballots at the last Election that they were with the great heart of the Nation on this Subject. But we were beaten—a little. But the guilty do not alone suffer— The innocent suffer more perhaps in these throes than the guilty. For the poor man (who is generally with us on this subject) suffers more from the loss of his *few shoats* and his *one Cow* and his *few bushels* of Corn—than the rich man (who is generally against us) would suffer from the loss of thousands of dollars worth of produce and Stock. Nor is the one so able or likely to protect himself as the other.

Thus it happens that the very men who have most zealously favored and most ardently labored for our Cause are the men who have suffered and are likely to suffer most from these upheavals. These are the actual facts, in the case—

Will you tolerate a suggestion, just here? Colored persons laboring for the Government, whether free or Slave, are, by a Special Order, allowed to receive their own wages—[2] Could that Order be so extended as to allow them to do the same when Contracting with Citizens? This is all that is needed here. Let this be done, and some agent appointed in each County to attend to their rights and see that they are not imposed upon and all will be well with them and us— But if this cannot be done—the worst Consequences are to be apprehended, the Coming winter, for them and us.

We cannot so much blame the negro for *stealing Bread*, if he is not allowed to draw the proceeds of his own labor. These are facts— *all too true*

I have waited and insisted upon others wiser than myself, to lay these matters before you—but have been constrained at length to do so myself— Your wide reputation for sympathy with these poor oppressed people encourages me to lay these facts before you in this homely way.

My whole heart is with you in the great work before you. Your ob^dt Sevt

ALS   J. C. Randolph

J. C. Randolph to Maj. Gen. O. Howard, 11 Sept. 1865, R-25 1865, Registered Letters Received, ser. 3379, TN Asst. Comr., RG 105 [A-6190]. An endorsement referred Randolph's letter to General Clinton B. Fisk, assistant commissioner of the Freedmen's Bureau for Tennessee and Kentucky, but no reply has been found in the surviving records of his office. (The volume containing copies of letters sent between September 9 and October 2, 1865, is not extant, and no reply appears in the subsequent volume.)

1 The constitutional amendment abolishing slavery that had been proposed by Congress in January 1865 and submitted to the states for ratification. The Kentucky state legislature had rejected the amendment in February, and opponents of its ratification had also prevailed in the August 1865 elections for U.S. representatives, state senators and representatives, and other state officers. 2 For the War Department ruling to this effect, see above, doc. 99.

239: Freedmen's Bureau Superintendent of the Subdistrict of Louisville, Kentucky, to the Proprietors of the Louisville Hotel; and Reply by the Proprietors

Louisville Ky Sept 11th 1865

Gentlemen   Wilson Hail—a colored refugee. being duly sworn. states that he contracted with your steward to work for you at Twenty-five ($25^{00}) Dollars per month, that under this contract he worked for you from the 10th day of July 1865 until the present time. He states further that you paid him for July and that his former master has notified you not to pay him for August. The boy is a "refugee" and as such is entitled to his wages. You will pay the boy Wilson for his labor and refer parties claiming his earnings to this office. Very Respectfully

HLS   H A McCaleb

Louisville Ky September 11th 1865

Dear Sir   The colored man "Wilson" referred to in your order of this date makes a true statement that he was hired by the Stewart of the Hotel and that he was paid the amount of his earnings in the month of July. — He should also have stated to *You*, as he has to us, that he is a *slave man*—The *property* of H Hale of *Simpson Co. Kentucky*; that said Hale has heretofore allowed him a portion of his wages—That he Wilson is not now willing to divide his wages with Hale, and claims the whole amount. —

We would respectfully represent that about the first of the present month we received a verbal message from Hale, notifying us that

Wilson is his slave, and that he will hold us liable to him for the wages of Wilson

Under the Laws of the State of Kentucky, *now in force* there seems to be no doubt of our liability to owners of the hire of their slaves. – We desire to pay the money to the proper person, and avoid the responsibility of paying both Owner and Slave – and therefore request that the subject be referred to Maj. Gen[l.] O. O. Howard, Chief of Freedman's Bureau Washington City – and that Your order be suspended until his decission be had,

Please submit to the General Your order and this letter   Yours very truly

ALS   Kean, Steele & Co

[*Endorsement*]   Bureau Refugees Freedmen &c   Sub Dist Louisville   Louisville Ky   Sept 12 /65   Respectfully forwarded through Brig. Gen. C B Fisk Asst Com[r] Bureau R.F. and A.L. Nashville Tenn, with the remark that, this case involves a point of great importance to the people of Kentucky both white and black.

Gen. Orders No. 129, A.G.O. C.S. says: that "Neither *Whites* nor *Blacks* will be restrained from seeking employment elsewhere when they cannot obtain it at a just compensation at their homes and when not bound by voluntary agreement, nor will they be hindered from traveling from place to place on proper and legitimate business".[1]   Under this Order and Gen'l Order No. 32, Dept of Ky[2] slaves have left their homes by thousands.   Consequently Slavery in the State of Kentucky, under State law is merely a nominal institution   The slave after leaving his master becomes a "Refugee" and as such comes within the Jurisdiction of this Bureau.

Unless payment for their labor can be enforced to this class of refugees they will certainly be thrown upon the Government for support, A decision on this point from the Commissioner is respectfully solicited. H. A. M[c]Caleb Lieut Col and Supt

Lieut. Col. H. A. McCaleb to Messrs. Steel, Kane and Judd, 11 Sept. 1865, and Kean, Steele & Co. to Lt. Col. H. A. McCalebs, 11 Sept. 1865, K-17 1865, Registered Letters Received, ser. 3379, TN Asst. Comr., RG 105 [A-6157]. On September 16, General Fisk, the Freedmen's Bureau assistant commissioner for Tennessee and Kentucky, commended McCaleb's judgment and ordered him to enforce all contracts made by the hotel proprietors with any "persons who are under the jurisdiction of this Bureau," in this instance seeing that Wilson Hail received the money due him. If the owner of a slave objected, he would have to bring suit against the Freedmen's Bureau for recovery of the wages. (Bg. Gen. Clinton B. Fisk to Lt. Col. H. A. McCaleb, 16 Sept. 1865, Unregistered Letters Received, ser. 1209, Louisville KY Supt., RG 105 [A-6157].)

1 General Order 129 was issued by the Adjutant General's Office on July 25, 1865. (General Orders No. 129, War Department, Adjutant General's Office, 25 July 1865, Orders & Circulars, ser. 44, RG 94 [DD-31].)
2 For a description of General Order 32, issued by General John M. Palmer on May 11, 1865, see above, doc. 232n.

240: **Provost Marshal of the 4th District of Kentucky to the Commander of the Department of Kentucky**

Lebanon Ky Oct. 25 /65

General: The presence of troops is absolutely necessary at this place to prevent masters from reclaiming to slavery many of the wives and children of Colored soldiers. Eight slaves, who have been laboring for themselves for sometime have been re-enslaved, – four of whom have been incarcerated in jail. Masters threaten to return *all* slaves absent from their homes to slavery.

Two colored children, the children of freed-women and colored soldiers, were reclaimed yesterday. I have attempted to stop these arrests, but can do nothing. In one or two instances Intended masters refuse to give up children freed under the act of Congress.[1] Resp[t]

ALS   Jams M. Fidler

Capt. Jams. M. Fidler to Brig. Gen. Palmer, 25 Oct. 1865, F-275 1865, Letters Received, ser. 2173, Dept. of KY, RG 393 Pt. 1 [C-4334]. An endorsement from the headquarters of the Department of Kentucky referred Fidler's letter to General Jefferson C. Davis, commander of the department's 1st division, for "necessary action." By an endorsement of November 6, 1865, Davis returned the letter to department headquarters "with information that by the time all orders for the muster out of Troops & the sending of others to Missouri are Complied with – requisitions of this Kind cannot be filled –" Another endorsement. Meanwhile, on October 27 Fidler wrote a second letter to department headquarters urging the necessity of troops. Because Lebanon had been a provost marshal's headquarters for nearly two years, he reported, "a large number of negroes have congregated here – a majority of whom have been laboring for a time, – because they have been protected. To leave them unprotected now is not only to return them to Slavery, but to take from them their earnings. A *slave* can have no property; to be returned, then, to slavery is to deprive him of what he has." (Capt. Jams. M. Fidler to Capt. E. B. Harlan,

27 Oct. 1865, F-276 1865, Letters Received, ser. 2173, Dept. of KY, RG
393 Pt. 1 [C-4334].)

1 The joint resolution of Congress, adopted on March 3, 1865, that freed the
wives and children of black soldiers. (See above, doc. 222n.)

241: Freedmen's Bureau Superintendent at Henderson, Kentucky, to the Tennessee and Kentucky Freedmen's Bureau Assistant Commissioner; and Reply from the Latter's Headquarters

Henderson Ky Jany 27th /65 [1866]

Gen— The following is cop of the record of a case which I have
adjudicated upon which will explain itself, I wish to know your
opinion on the Subject, Mr Adams made no defence, all he asks is
to be protected against the note which Jordon yet holds against
him, I wish to know what sort of protection I can give Mr A, as it
is More than probable that suit will be brought on the note in the
circuit court of this county, it is also very probable Jordon will
recover a Judgement against Adams for the full amount of the note,

Baswel Jordon (Coloured)

vs   [S]ct, Debt $233^{33}

Joseph Adams

It appearing that Joseph Adams hired of W^m O Jordon a boy
named Baswel on the first day of January 1865 for one year, at the
price of four hundred dollars, and it further appearing that said boy
become free by his Father enlisting in the United States Military
Service, on the 26th day of May 1865, and has been duly discharged,

It is now ordered that said Joseph Adams pay to the said Baswel,
one hundred & forty one dollars & 73 cents, the balance due on the
price aforesaid, the said Baswel admtting in open Court the payment
of $91^{66} & said Jordon being in open court, this Judgement against
Adams is rendered under his protest   Adams is to have credit for
the amount he is ordered to pay, on his note to said Jordon, The
boy Baswel was proven to be twenty one years of age

T. F. Cheaney
Sup^r Refugees & Freedmen

This case, is the first of kind that has come before me, and is
creating a great deal of excitement, as it probable there will be
many mor just like it, an early answer from you will me much   I
am very Respectfuly your obt sevt

ALS   T. F. Cheaney

[*Nashville, Tenn.*] Feb 2nd [186]6

Sir— Yours of Jan 27th containing copy of the [result in?] the case of *Boswell Jordan* vs *Jos Adams* has been received.

1. You are right in rendering a judgment in favor of Jordan for all of the time he worked for Mr Adams after he became free by his father's enlistment in the Federal army. That decision is supported by both law and equity, and you need never to hesitate in rendering a similar judgment in a like case.

2. But with the question between Mr Jos. Adams and Mr. W. O. Jordan the Bureau has nothing to do. They are both white men and must submit to the verdict of the civil courts. What the Courts of Ky. will decide remains to be seen. Suppose Mr Adams had *bought* Boswell Jordan of Mr W[m] O. Jordan, and had given his notes for him, would he have the notes to pay? That is a similar question for the civil courts. Now as there is no law which would deprive Boswell of his *liberty* because Mr Jordan had sold him and Mr Adams had bought him on the eve of his emancipation, so there is no law which could deprive him of his *wages* because he was hired out just before his emancipation. I am sir very respfly Yr obed: Serv't—

ALpS   J E Jacobs

T. F. Cheaney to Bt. Maj. Gen. C. B. Fisk, 27 Jan. 1865 [1866], C-19 1866, Registered Letters Received, ser. 3379, TN Asst. Comr., RG 105 [A-6231]; Bt. Lt. Col. J. E. Jacobs to T. F. Cheaney, 2 Feb. [186]6, vol. 9, pp. 245–46, Press Copies of Letters Sent, ser. 3373, TN Asst. Comr., RG 105 [A-6231]. A few days later, the Freedmen's Bureau superintendent at Paris, Tennessee, reported a similar dispute, which involved the hiring of a Kentucky slave by a white Tennessean in January 1865. In early 1866, under orders from the bureau superintendent, the hirer had paid the year's wages to the former slave instead of to the former owner, whereupon the owner sued the hirer in a Kentucky court, claiming a right to the full amount of hire because "his negro was not free last year." The assistant commissioner's office decided that although the black man was a slave in Kentucky, he was working in Tennessee while hired out and had therefore become free on February 22, 1865, when that state abolished slavery. The bureau superintendent was, accordingly, correct in ordering payment of wages to the black man himself. As to the suit between the former owner and the hirer, the superintendent was instructed to leave the question to the civil courts "because it is a question *between white men*." (Jesse A. Brown to Gen. Clinton B. Fisk, 8 Feb. 1866, B-102 1866, Registered Letters Received, ser. 3379, TN Asst. Comr., RG 105 [A-6231]; Capt. H. S. Brown to Jesse A. Brown, 15 Mar. [186]6, vol. 10, p. 366, Press Copies of Letters Sent, ser. 3373, TN Asst. Comr., RG 105 [A-6231].)

242: Freedmen's Bureau Superintendent at Maysville, Kentucky, to a Former Slaveholder, Enclosing a Freedman's Bill; and Reply from the Former Slaveholder to the Superintendent

Maysville, Ky. Nov 21st *1866.*

Madam, I have the honor to call your attention to the enclosed bill of Henry Coleman (Freedman) amounting to $215^{00}, for the hire of his children after he enlisted in the U.S. Army. I suppose that you are aware, that the fact of his having enlisted in the U.S. Service freed his children, and that he was entitled to their hire from the date of his enlistment. You will please give the matter your immediate attention or I will be compelled to commence proceedings against you. I have no desire to litigate this matter, and to save you trouble and expense, I would advise you to meet Coleman at my office and settle the matter without a suit

Please favor me with an early reply   Very Respectfully,
(Duplicate)   C J True

HLcS

[*Enclosure*]   [*Maysville, Ky. November 21, 1866*]
Mrs Lucretia Cleaney
                                              To Henry Coleman   D^r
To 1 years hire of son Ralph, received from Mr Galbreath $ 85.00
 "   "   "   "   "   "   50.00
 " 1 years hire of Rachel from Burgoyne   30.00
 "   "   "   "   "   "   " Dr Sharpe   40.00
 "   "   "   "   "   Catherine " Griffith   10.00
                                                                              $215.00

(Duplicate)
HDc

Washington, Ky. 22^d Novr: 66.
Sir— Send no more your bills to Miss Clereny.

Her negroes were not freed, but *stolen* by a set of Yankee robbers. Yourself and that rascal Campbell, will make nothing by pothering Mrs Clereny.

Begin suit soon as convenient.
                                                                   R. P. Henry,
                                                              for Miss Clereny.

P.S. Suppose you and that [. . .] of honesty, Campbell, present that bill in person.

ALS

C. J. True to Mrs. Lucretia Cleaney, 21 Nov. 1866, enclosing bill of Henry Coleman, and R. P. Henry to J. C. True, 22 Nov. 1866, all enclosed in C. J. True to Bvt. Brig. Gen. Jno. Ely, 23 Nov. 1866, Letters Received, ser. 1228, Maysville KY Supt., RG 105 [A-4475]. The envelope containing R. P. Henry's note is addressed to "J. C. True of the Nigger Bureau." In the covering letter, True explained that Lucretia Cleaney (Clereny) had held Coleman's children as slaves while their father was away in the army (presumably during 1865), hiring them out to various parties and receiving a total of $215.00 for their labor. "There can be no doubt that Coleman is clearly entitled under the law to the amount claimed," observed True, who reported himself powerless to enforce the claim without the assistance of a squad of soldiers. "The visible power of the Govt. as exemplified in person of her Soldiers, is the only thing respected by the Rebels," and "neglect to collect the just claims of the Freedmen, brings the office which I hold into contempt." True noted that the Mr. Campbell referred to in Henry's letter was a lawyer in Maysville known for his "*unconditional Unionism*" who in fact had no connection with Coleman's claim. Endorsements passed the documents through the bureau's chain of command, returning them to True on November 28 with instructions to prosecute the case in the U.S. District Court under the Civil Rights Act.

Index

Department of the Ohio, Chief Engineer: letter from, 659; letters to, 664–66, 668–70; policy on military labor, 666n.

Department of the Ohio, Chief of Artillery: letter to, 444

Department of the South, Military Governor, 37, 54, 56–57, 66; land policy of, 59; policy on agricultural labor, 47

Department of the Tennessee, 28, 631; commander of, reinstates civil authority in western Kentucky, 640n.

Department of the Tennessee, Superintendent of Contrabands, 31, 37

Department of Virginia, 28–29, 159n.; endorsement by, 220; land policy of, 24, 90, 95, 121n., 127n., 147–48; letters from, 131–34, 136–39; letters to, 120–21, 126–27, 135, 222–30; order by, 111–12; policy on agricultural labor, 108, 147–48; policy on black soldiers' families, 109; policy on contraband camps, 132; policy on fugitive slaves, 121n., 134n.; policy on military labor, 13, 86–93, 111–12, 119–20n., 142–43, 155; policy on mobility of former slaves, 93, 143–44, 159–60; relief policy of, 13, 15–16, 86–92, 95, 109, 111–12, 120n.

Department of Virginia, investigative commission: report by, 114–19

Department of Virginia, Provost Marshal: letter from, 126–27

Department of Virginia, Superintendent of Contrabands, 54; land policy of, 24, 39, 90; letters from, 120–21, 127; policy on agricultural labor, 39; policy on military labor, 90; policy on mobility of former slaves, 132; relief policy of, 90; testimony by, 142–46

Department of Virginia, 2nd District, Superintendent of Negro Affairs: policy on agricultural labor, 109–10; relief policy of, 110

Department of Virginia, 4th District, Superintendent of Negro Affairs: circular by, 227–29; letters from, 221–30; order by, 226–27; policy on agricultural labor, 221–31; policy on tenancy, 227–28; relief policy of, 227–30

Department of Virginia and North Carolina, 166n.; endorsements by, 160, 189, 503; land policy of, 101, 103n., 187, 214, 503; leasing policy of, 173; letters from, 187, 189–90; letters to, 159–66, 182–83, 186–87, 202–3, 502–4; orders by, 168–74, 191–92; policy on agricultural labor, 172–73; policy on black soldiers' families, 101, 168–69, 208; policy on enlisting black soldiers, 100–101, 168–70, 173–74, 208; policy on families of military laborers, 170; policy on fugitive slaves, 171–72; policy on military labor, 100–101, 104, 170–71, 174–76, 191–92, 199n.; policy on mobility of former slaves, 99, 160; policy on personal property, 504n.; policy on relocating former slaves, 189–90; relief policy of, 172–73

Department of Virginia and North Carolina, General Superintendent of Negro Affairs, 101, 172; letters to, 185–86, 191–92, 204–19

Department of Virginia and North Carolina, 1st District, Department of Negro Affairs: map of government farms in, 193

Department of Virginia and North Carolina, 1st District, Superintendent of Negro Affairs, 101; endorsement by, 189; land policy of, 101–2; leasing policy of, 102, 214–15, 217–18; letters from, 186–87, 212–19; letters to, 187, 189; policy on agricultural labor, 102

Department of Virginia and North Carolina, 2nd District, Department of Negro Affairs: map of government farms in, 194

Department of Virginia and North Carolina, 2nd District, Superintendent of Negro Affairs, 101; land policy of, 101–2; leasing policy of, 102; letters from, 191–92, 207–12; letter to, 188; policy on agricultural labor, 102; policy on black soldiers' families, 188; relief policy of, 210–11

Department of Virginia and North Carolina, 3rd District, Superintendent of Negro Affairs, 101, 103; report by, 199–201

Index

INDEX

INDEX

Land (cont.)
36, 75; Fortress Monroe VA area,
140–41; Gallatin TN area, 418;
Georgia, 75; government-controlled,
35–36, 39, 144, 153, 163–64,
193–98, 201–2n., 254, 322, 337–
38, 340, 344–45n., 476, 555, 575–
76; Independence MO area, 589; independent occupation of, by former
slaves, 9, 16–17, 23–25, 43, 87,
90, 127, 135, 178, 214, 257, 311–
13, 352–53, 470–72, 493–94,
535–41; Kansas, 556, 564; Louisiana, 37–38, 43; Madison County
AL, 401; Maryland, 491–92; military policy on, 24, 36–39, 59, 75–
76, 90, 95–96, 101–3, 109, 120–
21, 127n., 140–41, 147–48,
162n., 187, 196, 214, 299n., 373,
412–13, 421n., 435, 440n., 441–
42, 492, 503, 535–41; Mississippi
County MO, 575; Mississippi Valley,
9, 37–38, 57–58; Missouri, 555;
Murfreesboro TN area, 435, 437;
North Carolina, 102, 108, 196–98,
201–2n.; Northerners' views on, 14–
15, 37, 56–57, 81, 100, 145–46,
180–81; ownership of, by former
slaves, 43, 59–60, 69–70, 401, 556;
ownership of, by free blacks, 246,
274–75, 280n., 407; ownership of,
by mutual-aid society, 261; presidential policy on, 35–36, 57, 59–60,
76, 101, 108–9, 493–94, 537n.;
Prince George's County MD, 493–
94, 535–41; Roanoke Island NC,
162; St. Mary's County MD, 502–4;
seized by Union army, 503n., 503–
4, 575; significance of, to former
slaves, 58–59; South Carolina, 9, 12,
16–17, 36–37, 43, 59–60, 69, 75;
Stevenson AL, 407; Tennessee, 441,
476; treasury policy on, 103; Virginia, 24, 39, 76, 101–2, 108–9,
120–21, 144, 153, 163–64, 177–
81, 187, 193–95, 208–10, 298–99,
316. See also Confiscation acts; Direct
Tax Act (1862); Leasing
(government-supervised); Tenancy
Lane, James H., 564n.; enlists black soldiers in Kansas, 556
Larkin, Samuel: testimony by, 403–4
Larter, John A., 682, 684
Lathrop, J. H.: letter from, 617–19

Lauderdale County AL: relocation of
former slaves from, 475
Lawrence, Samuel B.: endorsement by,
530; letter from, 522–23; letters to,
532, 535–36
Lawrence KS: former slaves from Missouri at, 556
Leasing (government-supervised): Alabama, 65, 368, 383, 426n.; assessments of federal policy on, 53–56;
black lessees, 43, 56, 65, 69–70,
102–4, 128, 157–58, 164, 177–78,
193–95, 197–99, 208, 210, 214–
15, 383; disrupted by Confederate
raids, 199 (see also Agricultural laborers: attacked by Confederate soldiers;
Agricultural laborers: attacked by
guerrillas); Fortress Monroe VA area,
140–41; Giles County TN, 383;
Hampton VA area, 128, 157–58,
177–78; Helena AR area, 69–70;
Huntsville AL area, 383n.; James
City County VA, 237; Limestone
County AL, 383; Louisiana, 37–39;
military policy on, 37–40, 102–3,
173, 214–15, 217–18, 237, 442;
Mississippi Valley, 38–39, 43, 54–
56, 65, 69–70, 383; Newport News
VA area, 128; North Carolina, 70–
71, 103, 173, 197–99; Northern lessees, 37–39; Rutherford County TN,
383; South Carolina, 54; Tennessee,
65, 368, 383, 442; treasury policy
on, 56, 101, 197–99; Vicksburg MS
area, 69–70; Virginia, 65, 70–71,
102–4, 128, 164, 173, 177–78,
193–95, 208, 210, 214–15; Warwick County VA, 237; York County
VA, 237. See also Land; Planters
(Lower South): Northern; Tenancy
Leathers, Samuel M.: takes charge of government farms in St. Mary's County
MD, 492
Leavenworth KS: former slaves from Missouri at, 556
Lebanon KY, 626; black soldiers' families at, 717; fugitive slaves in, recaptured by owners, 709; military labor
near, 630, 632; military laborers at,
665n.; slaveholders near, lose slaves
hired out as teamsters, 632–33;
slaves at, seek passes from provost
marshal, 709
LeCompte, E. W.: letter from, 547–48

INDEX

Index

36–38, 46, 48–49, 51, 54–55, 65–69, 425; agricultural laborers in, attacked by Confederate soldiers, 52–53, 68; black population of, 65, 77; black soldiers' families in, 62; contraband camps in, 40n., 373; enlistment of black soldiers in, 38, 426n.; government-supervised leasing in, 38–39, 43, 54–56, 65, 69–70, 383; land in, 37–38, 58; land in, occupied by former slaves, 9; military labor in, 20; reconstruction politics in, 53; relief in, 41–42; relocation of former slaves from, 28; tenancy in, 43. *See also name of particular state or place*

Missouri, 77n., 78–79; agricultural labor in, 558–60, 607–8; agricultural labor in, disrupted by black enlistment, 557; agricultural labor in, disrupted by guerrillas, 552, 559, 562–63; agricultural laborers in, attacked by guerrillas, 64, 562–63; black population of, 552; black soldiers from, 557; black soldiers in, 599; black soldiers' families in, 63, 557–58, 600–601, 616; courts of, 603, 608–10; elections in, 613n., 614; emancipation certificates in, 571–72, 577–78, 609–10; emancipation in, by state constitutional convention, 73, 562, 612–13; emancipation politics in, 551–52, 613n.; Emancipation Proclamation in, 571–72; employers in, hire former slaves at Memphis TN, 596; enlistment of black soldiers in, 62, 551, 557, 607–8, 618; eviction of slaves in, 560; extent of military activity in, 553; family life of slaves in, 593; former slaves in, hired by midwestern employers, 561; former slaves in, kidnapped for reenslavement in Kentucky, 573; former slaves in, removed by guerrillas to Arkansas, 596; free blacks in, 552–53; free labor in, obstructed by law of slavery, 551, 559, 572, 602–3, 609–10; fugitive slaves from, 586–87, 590–92; fugitive slaves in, 11, 62, 554, 557, 560, 572, 574n., 585, 593–96; land in, seized by Union army, 555; laws of, 557, 593, 609; migration of former slaves from, 72, 551, 556, 564; mili-

tary labor in, 551, 554–55, 603–4, 609; relief in, 555, 560–62; relocation of former slaves from, 63, 72–73, 560–61, 563; relocation of former slaves within, 563; slaveholder in, attempts to reclaim evicted slaves, 611–12; slaveholders in, 9–11, 552, 557–60; slaveholders in, abuse black soldiers' families, 557; slaveholders in, evict black soldiers' families, 557–58; slaveholders in, evict former slaves, 564; slaveholders in, evict slaves, 74, 560, 585, 611–12; slaveholders in, negotiate free-labor arrangements with slaves, 559–60, 607; slaveholders in, obstruct emancipation, 562–63; slaveholders in, prosecute employers of slaves, 559, 609–10; slaveholders in, recapture fugitive slaves, 559; slaveholders in, remove slaves to Kentucky, 573, 584n.; slaveholders in, remove slaves to neighboring states, 592n.; slaveholders in, seek forcible enlistment of slaves, 559; slavery in, 552–53, 580–81, 592n.; slaves in, 552; slaves in, impressed for military labor, 555; smallholders in, object to settlement by former slaves, 621; state constitutional convention in, 613n.; tenancy in, 563; unionists in, oppose black enlistment, 557. *See also name of particular county, town, or city*

Missouri Hotel (St. Louis MO): former slaves quartered at, 556, 558, 572–73, 582, 584n.

Missouri State Militia, 553; 4th Cavalry, 579, 599n., 603; 7th Cavalry, 601, 603n.; 9th Cavalry, 616n.; 1st Infantry, 585

Mitchel, Ormsby M., 370, 405, 407, 452

Mittey (Col.), 400–401

Mizner, Henry R., 429

Mobility of former slaves: agricultural laborers, 49–50; District of Columbia, 248, 297; Kentucky, 706, 708n., 708–9, 713; military laborers, 61, 297, 466; military policy on, 52, 71–72, 93, 99, 132, 143–45, 159–60, 572, 574n., 584n., 637–38, 704n., 706, 708n., 708–9, 716; restrictions on, 50, 52, 67, 71–72, 93–94, 143–45, 159–60, 611 (*see*

INDEX

North Carolina (*cont.*)
ers in, 70–71, 100, 103–4, 106–7;
attempts to recruit military laborers
from, 98–99, 154–56, 253n.,
297n.; black population of, 78; black
soldiers' families in, 97–99, 105; contraband camps in, 62; education in,
99–100; emancipation politics in,
93; enlistment of black soldiers in,
96–97, 156n., 168–70, 173–74,
297n.; families of military laborers
in, 99, 170; fishermen in, 103; free
blacks in, 86; free blacks in, impressed for military labor, 98; fugitive slaves from, 92, 142, 151, 177;
fugitive slaves in, 91, 97–98;
government-supervised leasing in,
70–71, 103, 173, 197–99; health
in, 106; impressment of military laborers in, 61–62, 98–99, 104–5;
land in, 102, 108, 196–98, 201–
2n.; military labor in, 85, 91, 122–
26, 161, 170–71, 173, 198; military laborers from, 61; military laborers in, 20, 81, 91, 123–25; mutual-
aid societies in, 99–100;
nonagricultural labor in, 86, 103,
124; Northern missionaries in, 173;
refugeeing from, 110; relief in, 85,
91, 97–100, 105–7, 122, 125–26;
religion in, 99–100; relocation of
former slaves from, 106; relocation of
former slaves within, 104; self-
support among former slaves in,
106–7, 124–26; slaveholders in, 86,
93; slavery in, 86; slavery in, undermined by Union occupation, 91;
Union occupation of, 90–91; wood-
cutters in, 103. *See also* Beaufort NC;
New Berne NC; Plymouth NC; Roanoke Island NC; Washington NC
North Carolina, Military Governor, 93
North Missouri, 2nd Subdistrict, Provost Marshal: letters from, 612–13
Northern states: antebellum social relations in, 2–6; demand for ex-slave
laborers in, 566, 569; enlistment of
black soldiers in, 33–34, 630; free
blacks in, 34; free-labor ideology in,
3–6, 14–16, 36–37, 80–81, 88–
89, 115–17, 217–19; freedmen's aid
societies in, 14, 29, 31–32, 69–70,
76, 96, 99–100, 106, 108, 211,
247 (*see also* American Missionary As-

sociation; American Tract Society;
Boston Educational Commission;
Free Mission Society; Freedmen's Relief Association [Baltimore MD];
Friends' Association for the Relief of
Freedmen [Maryland]; Ladies Anti-
Slavery Society [Rochester NY]; Ladies Contraband Relief Society [St.
Louis MO]; Missionaries [Northern];
National Freedman's Relief Association [New York]; National Freedman's Relief Association [Washing-
ton DC]; Pennsylvania Abolition Society; Western Sanitary Commission
[St. Louis MO]); Kentucky slaves escape to, 630–31; migration of former
slaves to, 72, 77, 143–45, 488,
502n., 629, 637–38, 706, 708n.,
708; military laborers from, 13, 93,
142–45, 175, 377–78; relief in, 5–
6; relocation of former slaves to, 28–
29, 38, 72–73, 77, 106, 189–90,
566–70, 703–4. *See also name of particular state or place*
Nute, Ephraim, Jr.: letter from, 640–41

O'Brien, Edward F.: and government
farms in St. Mary's County MD, 525
Odell, Albert, 455
Ogden, John: relinquishes claim to
slave, 452–54
Ohio: Kentucky slaves enlist in, 630; migration of former slaves to, 637
Old Capitol Prison (Washington DC):
contrabands held in, 245, 262–63
Oliver (former slave), 394–96
Oliver (Mr.) (overseer), 426–27
Ord, Edward O. C., 221, 237; contests
Charles B. Wilder's land purchases,
109; endorsement by, 220; policy on
agricultural labor, 108; policy on
black soldiers' families, 109; relief
policy of, 109
Overseers, 96, 149; and agricultural laborers, 46, 217, 426–27, 467–68;
and slaves, 296
Owen, Robert Dale, 421; letter to, 123–
26
Owens, Samuel, 204n.; letter from,
202–3
Ozanne, Urbain: letter from, 462–63

Paducah KY, 626; agricultural labor near,
631; enlistment of black soldiers near,

760

Index

litical allegiance of, 9–10, 93, 367–68, 371–72, 378–79, 386, 394n., 662; prosecute employers of slaves, 64–65, 559, 603, 609–10, 636–38, 713; pursue fugitive slaves, 292–93, 394–96, 483, 650–51, 656; recapture fugitive slaves, 500, 559, 577, 600–601, 655–56; reenslave former slaves, 717; refuse to employ former slaves, 614; relinquish claim to slaves, 369, 445–46, 452–55; retain property of former slaves, 519, 711, 712n.; Sedalia MO, 591n.; seek federal sponsorship of free labor, 424, 702–3; seek forcible enlistment of slaves, 378, 420, 559, 608n.; seek to reclaim evicted slaves, 611–12; and slaves, 695–97, 702–3; support proposal to enlist slaves as teamsters, 662; Tennessee, 9–10, 367–68, 371–72, 378–79, 381–82, 394n., 415, 424, 437–38, 462–63; threaten employers of former slaves, 638; threaten former slaves, 622, 638; threaten slaves, 688; Tipton MO, 593, 595n.; and Union soldiers, 94, 483; Virginia, 86, 93–94, 96–97, 292–93; Washington County KY, 720. *See also* Planters (Lower South); Slavery

Slavery, 7–9, 72; Alabama, 368; Baltimore MD, 482, 517; Caldwell County KY, 695; Columbia TN area, 470; congressional policy on, 11–12; continues in Kentucky after Civil War, 625, 637–38, 706, 708–9, 713–14, 716; discipline, 296, 580; District of Columbia, 243; Dorchester County MD, 518–19; Huntsville AL, 403, 445; Kentucky, 625–26, 702–3; Louisiana, 18–19; Louisville KY, 626, 675–76; maintained after emancipation, 462–63, 517–19, 622, 710; Maryland, 296, 482–83; Mexico MO area, 600; military policy on, 12, 18, 63, 367, 380–82, 428n., 432–34, 438, 553–54, 592n., 626–27; Missouri, 552–53, 580–81, 592n.; North Carolina, 86; organization of work in, 7–9; presidential policy on, 11–12, 553; St. Louis MO, 552–53; Sumner County TN, 387–88; Tennessee, 368, 413–14, 419–20; undermined by Union

occupation, 10, 12, 18, 23–25, 80, 91, 96, 367, 373–74, 430, 452–53; Virginia, 86, 128. *See also* Nonslaveholders; Overseers; Slaveholders; Slaves

Slaves, 6–9; Alabama, 12n.; attacked by slaveholders, 698, 706; Baltimore MD, 507–9; and Confederate soldiers, 456–57; District of Columbia, 243; evicted by owners, 74, 449, 560, 585, 611–13, 634–35, 675–76, 687, 700, 702n., 713; forcibly enlisted by owners, 674; Gallatin TN, 447; hired out by owners, 368, 387, 413, 445, 447, 470, 632–33, 715–16, 718–20, 721n.; impressment of, as teamsters, 661; impressment of, for military labor, 486, 555, 627–28, 631–32, 665n., 666, 668–69; impressment of, into militia, 507–9; jailed by owners, 507; Kentucky, 627–28, 631–32, 636; Missouri, 552, 555; negotiate free-labor arrangements with owners, 23–24, 64–65, 96–97, 369, 373–75, 378–80, 382, 386, 437, 467–69, 559–60, 607, 636, 677; and overseers, 296; political allegiance of, 399–400, 449, 457; self-hire by, 128, 580; skilled, 420; and slaveholders, 695–97, 702–3; threatened by owners, 688; and Union soldiers, 12n., 388. *See also* Family life of slaves and former slaves; Fugitive slaves; Property (personal): ownership of, by slaves; Slavery

Slayton, A. W.: letter from, 664–65
Slocum, John H.: letter from, 313–14
Slough, John P., 268–69n., 276, 277–78n., 283n., 286n., 302n.; advocates legal equality for former slaves, 359; housing policy of, 337n.; letters to, 276–77, 284–86, 358–60
Smith (Sgt.), 110, 113, 119n.
Smith, A. A.: letter from, 442–43; policy on fugitive slaves, 443
Smith, Abram D.: land policy of, 59
Smith, Anderson: attempts to reclaim former slave, 611–12
Smith, Charles, 158
Smith, Cornelius, 157
Smith, Edward: letter from, 336–37
Smith, Edward W.: letter to, 222–30
Smith, Frederick W.: letter from, 188

INDEX

INDEX